ENTERTAINMENT LAW

Aspen Select Series

Entertainment Law

Cases, Documents, and Materials

Attorney Ricky Anderson
Walt Champion

Wolters Kluwer

Published by Wolters Kluwer in New York.

Wolters Kluwer serves customers worldwide with CCH, Aspen Publishers, and Kluwer Law International products. (www.wolterskluwerlb.com)

To contact Customer Service, e-mail customer.service@wolterskluwer.com, call 1-800-234-1660, fax 1-800-901-9075, or mail correspondence to:

Wolters Kluwer
Attn: Order Department
PO Box 990
Frederick, MD 21705

Printed in the United States of America.

1 2 3 4 5 6 7 8 9 0

ISBN 978-1-4548-6987-0

About Wolters Kluwer Law & Business

Wolters Kluwer Law & Business is a leading global provider of intelligent information and digital solutions for legal and business professionals in key specialty areas, and respected educational resources for professors and law students. Wolters Kluwer Law & Business connects legal and business professionals as well as those in the education market with timely, specialized authoritative content and information-enabled solutions to support success through productivity, accuracy and mobility.

Serving customers worldwide, Wolters Kluwer Law & Business products include those under the Aspen Publishers, CCH, Kluwer Law International, Loislaw, ftwilliam.com and MediRegs family of products.

CCH products have been a trusted resource since 1913, and are highly regarded resources for legal, securities, antitrust and trade regulation, government contracting, banking, pension, payroll, employment and labor, and healthcare reimbursement and compliance professionals.

Aspen Publishers products provide essential information to attorneys, business professionals and law students. Written by preeminent authorities, the product line offers analytical and practical information in a range of specialty practice areas from securities law and intellectual property to mergers and acquisitions and pension/benefits. Aspen's trusted legal education resources provide professors and students with high-quality, up-to-date and effective resources for successful instruction and study in all areas of the law.

Kluwer Law International products provide the global business community with reliable international legal information in English. Legal practitioners, corporate counsel and business executives around the world rely on Kluwer Law journals, looseleafs, books, and electronic products for comprehensive information in many areas of international legal practice.

Loislaw is a comprehensive online legal research product providing legal content to law firm practitioners of various specializations. Loislaw provides attorneys with the ability to quickly and efficiently find the necessary legal information they need, when and where they need it, by facilitating access to primary law as well as state-specific law, records, forms and treatises.

ftwilliam.com offers employee benefits professionals the highest quality plan documents (retirement, welfare and non-qualified) and government forms (5500/PBGC, 1099 and IRS) software at highly competitive prices.

MediRegs products provide integrated health care compliance content and software solutions for professionals in healthcare, higher education and life sciences, including professionals in accounting, law and consulting.

Wolters Kluwer Law & Business, a division of Wolters Kluwer, is headquartered in New York. Wolters Kluwer is a market-leading global information services company focused on professionals.

This book is dedicated to my mother and father,
Ms. Cherry Anderson and the late Robert Anderson, Jr.
They both taught me well. Thank you Mom, for the continuous church experiences; and thank you Dad, for the inspiration and discipline.

Summary of Contents

TABLE OF CONTENTS

ACKNOWLEDGEMENTS

First, I must thank GOD, for Your guidance and allowing me to do Your work daily.

Thank you to my wife Toi, our daughter Alysia, and our son Ricky II for all of your love and support. That's right, Team Anderson always working!!!

Thank you to Prairie View A&M University and Thurgood Marshall School of Law for the exceptional education that these two great HBCUs, have provided me. You both are right: **"Knowledge Is Power**."

Thank you Steve Harvey, Rushion McDonald, Yolanda Adams, Mo'Nique Hicks, Sidney Hicks, Adele Givens, Judge Greg Mathis, Isaiah Washington, Cassi Davis, Earthquake, Rickey Smiley, Sinbad, Mary Mary, Bishop Hezekiah Walker, Dwayne Wiggins (and the "Tony Toni Tone" Team), and Mali Music; and I know that I am missing some names (so please, forgive me) that I will include in my music law book, next year. Also, the publisher asked me to limit the character count.

Thank you Attorney Wendle Van Smith. It's been a joy working with you for the past 28 years, my Omega Psi Phi fraternity brother.

David Villarreal (my paralegal), you are one of a kind and the best in the business. Thank you for your tireless efforts and sacrifices. Keep making your sons proud.

Professor Walter Champion, thank you for your friendship (since my law school days) and your support with this book.

To my many, many family members, Omega Psi Phi fraternity brothers, and friends, who are too many to include or the publisher will terminate my publishing agreement, please know that you are loved and appreciated.

Attorney Ricky Anderson
July 2015
www.AttorneyRickyAnderson.com

FOREWORD

It was a little over ten years ago and about my 15th year in the entertainment industry that I was, for the first time, analyzing the efforts of the representation around me, i.e., agent, management, legal, etc. A pivotal moment in my life was when Sidney (my husband) and I were in a meeting with managers and legal counsel, and it was stated to us that "Talent comes and goes, but the big businesses are here to stay, and it would behoove them (management, legal counsel) to maintain those relationships so when the 'Artist' is gone, the business relationships would still remain." At that moment my husband looked at me and said, when a person tells you how they operate, it is important that you believe them, and he asked me had I ever had an interaction with an attorney in this business, that I had a great experience with, but for whatever reason was not using them now? After giving it a little thought, I said, "Yes, with a brother named Ricky Anderson," and Sidney said, "Why aren't you still using him?" I said for no reason; I just went in the direction the agents sent me—he actually set me up with a great deal with literally no heavy lifting on my part. The light bulb went off in both of our minds, and we realized the best attorney to deal with Hollywood lives in Houston, Texas and his name is Ricky Anderson—and the rest is history, but still in the making.

It is a pleasure and honor to share my experiences about an individual who is writing a book for you aspiring lawyers to be, who are looking to make a big impact in the "Business," and are learning the creative and necessary language to make the best deals for your future clients. However, the best deal you can ever make for your client is the deal Ricky Anderson made with himself, and this is not something that he said to Sidney and me, but on the contrary is what he shows us daily, and that is to be honest, relentless, unafraid of the proverbial "Big Boys," and to hold your family dear. Also, despite all of the clients you may have in the future—and I'm sure you will have many if you paid attention to Attorney Anderson—most importantly you must make them feel like each client is your only client. You achieve that, you will be replicating the actions of the man who authored this book. Attorney Anderson is proof positive that the best things in Hollywood are so far from Hollywood, which is why aside from my husband in terms of representation, Ricky Anderson is the only representative I've ever written into my speech and that I ever thanked when I received an award for my performances, as he is the only one aside from my husband who, through their efforts and actions daily, have inspired me to do so. If you get nothing else from this commentary I hope you get this: It is better to be a great person than it is to be a great entertainment attorney; however, if you mirror what Attorney Anderson has done in his career, and who he is, you will find out that it is even far better to be both a great attorney and a great person!

Good luck to all who read this book, and we'll see you at the top!

Mo'Nique
Actress/Comedian

P.S. We love you Ricky Anderson, and thank you for everything!

CHAPTER 1
ENTERTAINMENT LAW GENERALLY

Entertainment law (or media law), as defined by the encyclopedia, is "legal services to the entertainment industry." Entertainment law overlaps with intellectual property law (especially trademarks, copyright, and the so-called "right of publicity"), but the practice of entertainment law often involves questions of employment law, contract law, torts, labor law, bankruptcy law, immigration, securities law, security interests, agency, right of privacy, defamation, advertising, criminal law, tax law, international law (especially private international law), and insurance law.

Much of the work of an entertainment law practice is transaction based (i.e., drafting contracts, negotiation and mediation). Some situations may lead to litigation or arbitration.

Entertainment law covers an area of law which involves media of all types (e.g., TV, film, music, publishing, advertising, Internet and news media, etc.), and stretches over various legal fields, including but not limited to corporate, finance, intellectual property, publicity and privacy, and First Amendment. For film, entertainment attorneys work with the actor's agent to finalize his or her contracts for projects. After an agent lines up work for a star, the entertainment attorney negotiates with the agent and buyer of the actor's talent for compensation and profit participation. Entertainment attorneys are under strict confidentiality so the specifics of their job are kept secret. But some entertainment attorney's job descriptions have become comparable to those of a star's agent, manager, or publicist. They are not limited to legal paperwork, rather assisting in building a client's career.

There have been early cases like Lumley v. Wagner, 1 De G.M. & G. 604, 42 Eng. Rep. 687 (1852), and Wood v. Lucy, Lady Duff Gordon, 222 N.Y. 88, 118 N.E. 214 (1917), that were clearly "entertainment law" cases. That is, one of the parties involved was an "entertainer." So, does the "law" follow the participants? If so, then must we also include "celebrities," like Lucy Lady Duff Gordon, maybe the first "reality" star? See Walter T. Champion, "Oh, What a Tangled Web We Weave: Reality TV Shines a False Light on Lady Duff-Gordan," 15 Seton Hall J. of Sports & Ent. L. 27 (2005). If that's the case, then should we also include the celebrated writer/"celebrity" Oscar Wilde and his trial of the (19th) century for sodomy, which is comparable to O.J. Simpson (athlete, actor, pitchman) and his "trial of the [20th] century" for the alleged murder of his wife and her friend.

Lumley v. Wagner is the famous case of a renowned opera singer who was enjoined from providing services as a singer for any other party. This concept of negative injunction was signed into sports, where it was discovered that athletes are also entertainers and their services are unique and can be enjoined upon breach of the threat to do so, because of their "fan appeal." Baseball Superstar Napoleon Lajoie's contract prohibited him from playing professional baseball with any other club. This ability to enjoin him from performing for anyone else was a part of the consideration for his employer's agreement to pay his salary. The injunction was issued since his services were unique, which rendered them of a peculiar value to the club. In other words, Napoleon Lajoie, like Johanna Wagner, was a unique entertainer and his services could not be duplicated. Consider Frank Sinatra, Michael Jordan, Bob Marley, Angelina Jolie, Steve Harvey, Maggie Smith, etc. (See Philadelphia Bell Club v. Lajoie, 51 a. 973 (Pa. 1902); and Walter T. Champion, Jr., Sports Law: Cases, Documents, and Materials 8-10 (NYC: Aspen, 2005)).

Entertainment law involves "talent" in the various mediums (e.g., TV, radio, film, music), including writers in the various mediums and the technicians, location people, studio musicians, editors, etc. We will loosely call these associated people and entities "handlers" (or enablers, associates, and in some cases staff, maybe even hangers-on or, collectively, posse). Sometimes, there is not much difference between the talent and their handlers; that is, both are creative.

So, in the entertainment business or industry, we have talent and those who are associated with that talent. We will loosely define talent as a person possessing a particular and unique skill based on popularity, acumen, or skill set. What marque name assures a standing room only crowd at the Bellagio in Las Vegas? What above title actor guarantees financial backing and box office success? Can box office success ever be truly guaranteed? Today, globalization and foreign box office receipts must be included in bottom line prognostications and results. What ties this all together? The answer is "entertainment law."

Our working definition of entertainment law can be grossly summarized as those contracts that connect talent to their associated handlers in an effort to bring a creative product to the public so as to generate profits. Entertainment is a multi-, multi-billion dollar business. Remember Cuba Gooding, Jr.'s line in *Jerry Maguire*: "Show Me the Money!" How does the talent get paid? They get paid through the nuances of copyright law, which is a legal field that also includes patents, trademarks, trade dress, etc. Copyright law generates the royalties and percentages that pay the talent. Copyright law also protects original works of authorship (or creative "genius") in a tangible medium of expression. A work must be within the constitutional and statutory definition of a work of authorship, it must be in a tangible form of expression, and it must be original. The copyright concerns in the entertainment business seem endless; they include TV, film, radio, video, music, and Internet productions and performances, not to mention screenplays, literary property, theatrical plays, syndication, broadcasts, rebroadcasts, etc. (See Champion, Fundamentals of Sports Law 643). One huge difference between sports law and entertainment law is that in sports law, you cannot seek specific performance when there is a breach of contract; that is, good luck on "forcing" our temperamental star shortstop to play. (That dog won't hunt.) However, it is certainly possible for a court to order a producer to give above title billing to a temperamental movie star.

Joseph Burstyn, Inc. v. Wilson, 343 U.S. 495 (1952), which follows, asks: What is sacrilegious? This case highlights the First's Amendment's ability to "shape" entertainment law. Is the N.Y. statute an unconstitutional abridgement of free speech and free press? Why is entertainment law important?

> It cannot be doubted that motion pictures are a significant medium for the communication of ideas. They may affect public attitudes and behavior in a variety of ways, ranging from direct espousal or a political or social doctrine to the subtle shaping of thought which characterizes all artistic expression that importance of motion pictures as an organ of public is not lessened by the fact that they are designed to entertain as well as to inform. Even though the production, distribution, and exhibition of motion pictures are a large-scale business conducted for private profit they are still a form of expression whose liberty is safeguarded by the First Amendment.

(Burstyn at 501.)

Copyright is not the only form of intellectual property that shapes entertainment law. Trademarks, branding, marketing, ambush marketing, and product placement are also important, as well as the right of publicity. We can envision entertainment law as a constant struggle to either support or disavow our First Amendment freedoms of free speech and free press. Zacchini v. Scripps-Howard Broadcasting Co., 433 U.S. 562 (1977), involves Hugo Zacchini, the "human cannonball," and what was to him a family business. It was all he had, packaged in a 10-second act. Hugo brought an action against a TV station to recover damages that he allegedly suffered when the station videotaped and broadcasted his entire performance. The First Amendment does not privilege the press (and their First Amendment protections) so as to give them the right to broadcast Zacchini's act in violation of his state-protected right of publicity.

JOSEPH BURSTYN, INC. v. WILSON
No. 522
343 U.S. 495
Decided May 26, 1952

Mr. Justice CLARK delivered the opinion of the Court.

The issue here is the constitutionality, under the First and Fourteenth Amendments, of a New York statute which permits the banning of motion picture films on the ground that they are 'sacrilegious.' That statute makes it unlawful 'to exhibit, or to sell, lease or lend for exhibition at any place of amusement for pay or in connection with any business in the state of New York, any motion picture film or reel (with specified exceptions not relevant here), unless there is at the time in full force and effect a valid license or permit therefor of the education department * * *.' The statute further provides:

> 'The director of the (motion picture) division (of the education department) or, when authorized by the regents, the officers of a local office or bureau shall cause to be promptly examined every motion picture film submitted to them as herein required, and unless such film or a part thereof is obscene, indecent, immoral, inhuman, sacrilegious, or is of such a character that its exhibition would tend to corrupt morals or incite to crime, shall issue a license therefor. If such director or, when so authorized, such officer shall not license any film submitted, he shall furnish to the applicant therefor a written report of the reasons for his refusal and a description of each rejected part of a film not rejected in toto.'

Appellant is a corporation engaged in the business of distributing motion pictures. It owns the exclusive rights to distribute throughout the United States a film produced in Italy entitled 'The Miracle.' On November 30, 1950, after having examined the picture, the motion picture division of the New York education department, acting under the statute quoted above, issued to appellant a license authorizing exhibition of 'The Miracle,' with English subtitles, as one part of a trilogy called 'Ways of Love.' Thereafter, for a period of approximately eight weeks, 'Ways of Love' was exhibited publicly in a motion picture theater in New York City under an agreement between appellant and the owner of the theater whereby appellant received a stated percentage of the admission price.

During this period, the New York State Board of Regents, which by statute is made the head of the education department, received 'hundreds of letters, telegrams, post cards, affidavits and other communications' both protesting against and defending the public exhibition of 'The Miracle.' The

Chancellor of the Board or Regents requested three members of the Board to view the picture and to make a report to the entire Board. After viewing the film, this committee reported to the Board that in its opinion there was basis for the claim that the picture was 'sacrilegious.' Thereafter, on January 19, 1951, the Regents directed appellant to show cause, at a hearing to be held on January 30, why its license to show 'The Miracle' should not be rescinded on that ground. Appellant appeared at this hearing, which was conducted by the same three-member committee of the Regents which had previously viewed the picture, and challenged the jurisdiction of the committee and of the Regents to proceed with the case. With the consent of the committee, various interested persons and organizations submitted to it briefs and exhibits bearing upon the merits of the picture and upon the constitutional and statutory questions involved. On February 16, 1951, the Regents, after viewing 'The Miracle,' determined that it was 'sacrilegious' and for that reason ordered the Commissioner of Education to rescind appellant's license to exhibit the picture. The Commissioner did so.

Appellant brought the present action in the New York courts to review the determination of the Regents. Among the claims advanced by appellant were (1) that the statute violates the Fourteenth Amendment as a prior restraint upon freedom of speech and of the press; (2) that it is invalid under the same Amendment as a violation of the guaranty of separate church and state and as a prohibition of the free exercise of religion; and, (3) that the term 'sacrilegious' is so vague and indefinite as to offend due process. The Appellate Division rejected all of appellant's contentions and upheld the Regents' determination. 278 App.Div. 253, 104 N.Y.S.2d 740. On appeal the New York Court of Appeals, two judges dissenting, affirmed the order of the Appellate Division. 303 N.Y. 242, 101 N.E.2d 665. The case is here on appeal. 28 U.S.C. § 1257(2), 28 U.S.C.A. § 1257(2).

As we view the case, we need consider only appellant's contention that the New York statute is an unconstitutional abridgment of free speech and a free press. In Mutual Film Corp. v. Industrial Comm. of Ohio, 1915, 236 U.S. 230, 35 S.Ct. 387, 59 L.Ed. 552, a distributor of motion pictures sought to enjoin the enforcement of an Ohio statute which required the prior approval of a board of censors before any motion picture could be publicly exhibited in the state, and which directed the board to approve only such films as it adjudged to be 'of a moral, educational, or amusing and harmless character.' The statute was assailed in part as an unconstitutional abridgment of the freedom of the press guaranteed by the First and Fourteenth Amendments. The District Court rejected this contention, stating that the first eight Amendments were not a restriction on state action. D.C.N.D.Ohio 1914, 215 F. 138, 141. On appeal to this Court, plaintiff in its brief abandoned this claim and contended merely that the statute in question violated the freedom of speech and publication guaranteed by the Constitution of Ohio....

In a series of decisions beginning with Gitlow v. People of State of New York, 1925, 268 U.S. 652, 45 S.Ct. 625, 69 L.Ed. 1138, this Court held that the liberty of speech and of the press which the First Amendment guarantees against abridgment by the federal government is within the liberty safeguarded by the Due Process Clause of the Fourteenth Amendment from invasion by state action. That principle has been followed and reaffirmed to the present day. Since this series of decisions came after the Mutual decision, the present case is the first to present squarely to us the question whether motion pictures are within the ambit of protection which the First Amendment, through the Fourteenth, secures to any form of 'speech' or 'the press.'

It cannot be doubted that motion pictures are a significant medium for the communication of ideas. They may affect public attitudes and behavior in a variety of ways, ranging from direct espousal of a political or social doctrine to the subtle shaping of thought which characterizes all artistic expression. The importance of motion pictures as an organ of public opinion is not lessened by the fact that they are designed to entertain as well as to inform....

It is urged that motion pictures do not fall within the First Amendment's aegis because their production, distribution, and exhibition is a large-scale business conducted for private profit. We cannot agree. That books, newspapers, and magazines are published and sold for profit does not prevent them from being a form of expression whose liberty is safeguarded by the First Amendment. We fail to see why operation for profit should have any different effect in the case of motion pictures.

It is further urged that motion pictures possess a greater capacity for evil, particularly among the youth of a community, than other modes of expression. Even if one were to accept this hypothesis, it does not follow that motion pictures should be disqualified from First Amendment protection. If there be capacity for evil it may be relevant in determining the permissible scope of community control, but it does not authorize substantially unbridled censorship such as we have here.

For the foregoing reasons, we conclude that expression by means of motion pictures is included within the free speech and free press guaranty of the First and Fourteenth Amendments. To the extent that language in the opinion in Mutual Film Corp. v. Industrial Comm., supra, is out of harmony with the views here set forth, we no longer adhere to it.

To hold that liberty of expression by means of motion pictures is guaranteed by the First and Fourteenth Amendments, however, is not the end of our problem. It does not follow that the Constitution requires absolute freedom to exhibit every motion picture of every kind at all times and all places. That much is evident from the series of decisions of this Court with respect to other media of communication of ideas. Nor does it follow that motion pictures are necessarily subject to the precise rules governing any other particular method of expression. Each method tends to present its own peculiar problems. But the basic principles of freedom of speech and the press, like the First Amendment's command, do not vary. Those principles, as they have frequently been enunciated by this Court, make freedom of expression the rule. There is no justification in this case for making an exception to that rule.

The statute involved here does not seek to punish, as a past offense, speech or writing falling within the permissible scope of subsequent punishment. On the contrary, New York requires that permission to communicate ideas be obtained in advance from state officials who judge the content of the words and pictures sought to be communicated. This Court recognized many years ago that such a previous restraint is a form of infringement upon freedom of expression to be especially condemned. Near v. State of Minnesota ex rel. Olson, 1931, 283 U.S. 697, 51 S.Ct. 625, 75 L.Ed. 1357. The Court there recounted the history which indicates that a major purpose of the First Amendment guaranty of a free press was to prevent prior restraints upon publication, although it was carefully pointed out that the liberty of the press is not limited to that protection. It was further stated that 'the protection even as to previous restraint is not absolutely unlimited. But the limitation has been recognized only in exceptional cases.' Id., 283 U.S. at page 716, 51 S.Ct. at page 631. In the light of the First Amendment's history and of the Near decision, the State has a heavy burden to demonstrate that the limitation challenged here presents such an exceptional case.

New York's highest court says there is 'nothing mysterious' about the statutory provision applied in this case: 'It is simply this: that no religion, as that word is understood by the ordinary, reasonable person, shall be treated with contempt, mockery, scorn and ridicule.' This is far from the kind of narrow exception to freedom of expression which a state may carve out to satisfy the adverse demands of other interests of society. In seeking to apply the broad and all-inclusive definition of 'sacrilegious' given by the New York courts, the censor is set adrift upon a boundless sea amid a myraid of conflicting currents of religious views, with no charts but those provided by the most vocal and powerful orthodoxies, New York cannot vest such unlimited restraining control over motion pictures in a censor. Cf. Kunz v. People of State of New York, 1951, 340 U.S. 290, 71 S.Ct. 312, 328, 95 L.Ed. 267, 280. Under such a standard the most careful and tolerant censor would find it virtually impossible to avoid favoring one religion over another, and he would be subject to an inevitable tendency to ban the expression of unpopular sentiments sacred to a religious minority. Application of the 'sacrilegious' test, in these or other respects, might raise substantial questions under the First Amendment's guaranty of separate church and state with freedom of worship for all. However, from the standpoint of freedom of speech and the press, it is enough to point out that the state has no legitimate interest in protecting any or all religions from views distasteful to them which is sufficient to justify prior restraints upon the expression of those views. It is not the business of government in our nation to suppress real or imagined attacks upon a particular religious doctrine, whether they appear in publications, speeches, or motion pictures.

Since the term 'sacrilegious' is the sole standard under attack here, it is not necessary for us to decide, for example, whether a state may censor motion pictures under a clearly drawn statute designed and applied to prevent the showing of obscene films. That is a very different question from the one now before us. We hold only that under the First and Fourteenth Amendments a state may not ban a film on the basis of a censor's conclusion that it is 'sacrilegious.'

Reversed.

Mr. Justice REED, concurring in the judgment of the Court.

Mr. Justice FRANKFURTER, whom Mr. Justice JACKSON joins, concurring in the judgment of the Court; Mr. Justice BURTON, having concurred in the opinion of the Court, also joins this opinion.

BENJAMIN R. WARD v. ROCK AGAINST RACISM
No. 88-226
Decided June 22, 1989
Rehearing Denied Aug. 30, 1989
491 U.S. 781, 105 L.Ed.2d 661
[See 492 U.S. 937, 110 S.Ct. 23]

Justice KENNEDY delivered the opinion of the Court.

In the southeast portion of New York City's Central Park, about 10 blocks upward from the park's beginning point at 59th Street, there is an amphitheater and stage structure known as the Naumberg Acoustic Bandshell. The bandshell faces west across the remaining width of the park. In close proximity to the bandshell, and lying within the directional path of its sound, is a grassy open area called the Sheep Meadow. The city has designated the Sheep Meadow as a quiet area for passive recreations like reclining, walking, and reading. Just beyond the park, and also within the potential sound range of the bandshell, are the apartments and residences of Central Park West.

This case arises from the city's attempt to regulate the volume of amplified music at the bandshell so the performances are satisfactory to the audience without intruding upon those who use the Sheep Meadow or live on Central Park West and in its vicinity.

The city's regulation requires bandshell performers to use sound-amplification equipment and a sound technician provided by the city. The challenge to this volume control technique comes from the sponsor of a rock concert. The trial court sustained the noise control measures, but the Court of Appeals for the Second Circuit reversed. We granted certiorari to resolve the important First Amendment issues presented by the case.

I

Rock Against Racism, respondent in this case, is an unincorporated association which, in its own words, is "dedicated to the espousal and promotion of antiracist views." App. to Pet. for Cert. 3. Each year from 1979 through 1986, RAR has sponsored a program of speeches and rock music at the bandshell. RAR has furnished the sound equipment and sound technician used by the various performing groups at these annual events.

Over the years, the city received numerous complaints about excessive sound amplification at respondent's concerts from park users and residents of areas adjacent to the park. On some occasions RAR was less than cooperative when city officials asked that the volume be reduced; at one concert, police felt compelled to cut off the power to the sound system, an action that caused the audience to become unruly and hostile. App. 127-131, 140-141, 212-214, 345-347.

Before the 1984 concert, city officials met with RAR representatives to discuss the problem of excessive noise. It was decided that the city would monitor sound levels at the edge of the concert ground, and would revoke respondent's event permit if specific volume limits were exceeded. Sound levels at the concert did exceed acceptable levels for sustained periods of time, despite repeated warnings and requests that the volume be lowered. Two citations for excessive volume were issued to respondent during the concert. When the power was eventually shut off, the audience became abusive and disruptive.

The following year, when respondent sought permission to hold its upcoming concert at the bandshell, the city declined to grant an event permit, citing its problems with noise and crowd control at RAR's previous concerts. The city suggested some other city-owned facilities as alternative sites for the concert. RAR declined the invitation and filed suit in United States District Court against the city, its mayor, and various police and parks department officials, seeking an injunction directing issuance of an event permit. After respondent agreed to abide by all applicable regulations, the parties reached agreement and a permit was issued.

The city then undertook to develop comprehensive New York City Parks Department Use Guidelines for the Naumberg Bandshell. A principal problem to be addressed by the guidelines was controlling the volume of amplified sound at bandshell events. A major concern was that at some bandshell performances the event sponsors had been unable to "provide the amplification levels required and 'crowds unhappy with the sound became disappointed or unruly.'" Brief for Petitioners 9. The city found that this problem had several causes, including inadequate sound equipment, sound technicians who were either unskilled at mixing sound outdoors or unfamiliar with the acoustics of the bandshell and its surroundings, and the like. Because some performers compensated for poor sound mix by raising volume, these factors tended to exacerbate the problem of excess noise. App. 30, 189, 218-219.

The city considered various solutions to the sound-amplification problem. The idea of a fixed decibel limit for all performers using the bandshell was rejected because the impact on listeners of a single decibel level is not constant, but varies in response to changes in air temperature, foliage, audience size, and like factors. Id., at 31, 220, 285-286. The city also rejected the possibility of employing a sound technician to operate the equipment provided by the various sponsors of bandshell events, because the city's technician might have had difficulty satisfying the needs of sponsors while operating unfamiliar, and perhaps inadequate, sound equipment. Id., at 220. Instead, the city concluded that the most effective way to achieve adequate but not excessive sound amplification would be for the city to furnish high quality sound equipment and retain an independent, experienced sound technician for all performances at the bandshell. After an extensive search the city hired a private sound company capable of meeting the needs of all the varied users of the bandshell.

The Use Guidelines were promulgated on March 21, 1986. After learning that it would be expected to comply with the guidelines at its upcoming annual concert in May 1986, respondent returned to the District Court and filed a motion for an injunction against the enforcement of certain aspects of the guidelines. The District Court preliminarily enjoined enforcement of the sound-amplification rule on May 1, 1986. See 636 F.Supp. 178 (S.D.N.Y.1986). Under the protection of the injunction, and alone among users of the bandshell in the 1986 season, RAR was permitted to use its own sound equipment and technician, just as it had done in prior years. RAR's 1986 concert again generated complaints about excessive noise from park users and nearby residents. App. 127, 138.

After the concert, respondent amended its complaint to seek damages and a declaratory judgment striking down the guidelines as facially invalid. After hearing five days of testimony about various aspects of the guidelines, the District Court issued its decision upholding the sound-amplification guideline. The court found that the city had been "motivated by a desire to obtain top-flight sound equipment and experienced operators" in selecting an independent contractor to provide the equipment and technician for bandshell events, and that the performers who did use the city's sound system in the 1986 season, in performances "which ran the full cultural gamut from grand opera to salsa to reggae," were uniformly pleased with the quality of the sound provided. 658 F.Supp. 1346, 1352 (S.D.N.Y.1987).

Although the city's sound technician controlled both sound volume and sound mix by virtue of his position at the mixing board, the court found that "[t]he City's practice for events at the Bandshell is to give the sponsor autonomy with respect to the sound mix: balancing treble with bass, highlighting a particular instrument or voice, and the like," and that the city's sound technician "does all he can to accommodate the sponsor's desires in those regards." Ibid. Even with respect to volume control, the city's practice was to confer with the sponsor before making any decision to turn the volume down. Ibid. In some instances, as with a New York Grand Opera performance, the sound technician accommodated the performers' unique needs by integrating special microphones with the city's equipment. The court specifically found that "[t]he City's implementation of the Bandshell guidelines provides for a sound amplification system capable of meeting RAR's technical needs and leaves control of the sound 'mix' in the hands of RAR." Id., at 1353. Applying this

Court's three-part test for judging the constitutionality of government regulation of the time, place, or manner of protected speech, the court found the city's regulation valid.

The Court of Appeals reversed. 848 F.2d 367 (C.A.2 1988). After recognizing that "[c]ontent neutral time, place and manner regulations are permissible so long as they are narrowly tailored to serve a substantial government interest and do not unreasonably limit alternative avenues of expression," the court added the proviso that "the method and extent of such regulation must be reasonable, that is, it must be the least intrusive upon the freedom of expression as is reasonably necessary to achieve a legitimate purpose of the regulation." Id., at 370 (citing United States v. O'Brien, 391 U.S. 367, 377, 88 S.Ct. 1673, 1679, 20 L.Ed.2d 672 (1968)). Applying this test, the court determined that the city's guideline was valid only to the extent necessary to achieve the city's legitimate interest in controlling excessive volume, but found there were various alternative means of controlling volume without also intruding on respondent's ability to control the sound mix. For example, the city could have directed respondent's sound technician to keep the volume below specified levels. Alternatively, a volume-limiting device could have been installed; and as a "last resort," the court suggested, "the plug can be pulled on the sound to enforce the volume limit." 848 F.2d, at 372, n. 6. In view of the potential availability of these seemingly less restrictive alternatives, the Court of Appeals concluded that the sound-amplification guideline was invalid because the city had failed to prove that its regulation "was the least intrusive means of regulating the volume." Id., at 371.

We granted certiorari, 488 U.S. 816, 109 S.Ct. 53, 102 L.Ed.2d 31 (1988), to clarify the legal standard applicable to governmental regulation of the time, place, or manner of protected speech. Because the Court of Appeals erred in requiring the city to prove that its regulation was the least intrusive means of furthering its legitimate governmental interests, and because the ordinance is valid on its face, we now reverse.

II

Music is one of the oldest forms of human expression. From Plato's discourse in the Republic to the totalitarian state in our own times, rulers have known its capacity to appeal to the intellect and to the emotions, and have censored musical compositions to serve the needs of the state... The Constitution prohibits any like attempts in our own legal order. Music, as a form of expression and communication, is protected under the First Amendment. In the case before us the performances apparently consisted of remarks by speakers, as well as rock music, but the case has been presented as one in which the constitutional challenge is to the city's regulation of the musical aspects of the concert; and, based on the principle we have stated, the city's guideline must meet the demands of the First Amendment. The parties do not appear to dispute that proposition.

We need not here discuss whether a municipality which owns a bandstand or stage facility may exercise, in some circumstances, a proprietary right to select performances and control their quality...

A

The principal inquiry in determining content neutrality, in speech cases generally and in time, place, or manner cases in particular, is whether the government has adopted a regulation of speech because of disagreement with the message it conveys. Community for Creative Non-Violence, supra, 468 U.S., at 295, 104 S.Ct., at 3070. The government's purpose is the controlling consideration. A regulation that serves purposes unrelated to the content of expression is deemed neutral, even if it has an incidental effect on some speakers or messages but not others. See Renton v. Playtime Theatres, Inc., 475 U.S. 41, 47-48, 106 S.Ct. 925, 929-930, 89 L.Ed.2d 29 (1986). Government regulation of expressive activity is content neutral so long as it is "justified without reference to the content of the regulated speech." Community for Creative Non-Violence, supra, 468 U.S., at 293, 104 S.Ct., at 3069 (emphasis added); Heffron, supra, 452 U.S., at 648, 101 S.Ct., at 2564 (quoting *792 Virginia Pharmacy Bd., supra, 425 U.S., at 771, 96 S.Ct., at 1830); see Boos v. Barry, 485 U.S. 312, 320-321, 108 S.Ct. 1157, 1163-1164, 99 L.Ed.2d 333 (1988) (opinion of O'CONNOR, J.).

The principal justification for the sound-amplification guideline is the city's desire to control noise levels at bandshell events, in order to retain the character of the Sheep Meadow and its more sedate activities, and to avoid undue intrusion into residential areas and other areas of the park. This justification for the guideline "ha[s] nothing to do with content," Boos v. Barry, supra, at 320, 108 S.Ct., at 1163, and it satisfies the requirement that time, place, or manner regulations be content neutral.

The only other justification offered below was the city's interest in "ensur [ing] the quality of sound at Bandshell events." 658 F.Supp., at 1352; see 848 F.2d, at 370, n. 3. Respondent urges that this justification is not content neutral because it is based upon the quality, and thus the content, of the speech being regulated. In respondent's view, the city is seeking to assert artistic control over performers at the bandshell by enforcing a bureaucratically determined, value-laden conception of good sound. That all performers who have used the city's sound equipment have been completely satisfied is of no moment, respondent argues, because "[t]he First Amendment does not permit and cannot tolerate state control of artistic expression merely because the State claims that [its] efforts will lead to 'top-quality' results." Brief for Respondent 19.

While respondent's arguments that the government may not interfere with artistic judgment may have much force in other contexts, they are inapplicable to the facts of this case. The city has disclaimed in express terms any interest in imposing its own view of appropriate sound mix on performers. To the contrary, as the District Court found, the city requires its sound technician to defer to the wishes of event sponsors concerning sound mix. 658 F.Supp., at 1352-1353. On this record, the city's concern with sound quality extends only to the clearly content-neutral goals of ensuring adequate sound amplification and avoiding the volume problems associated with inadequate sound mix. Any governmental attempt to serve purely esthetic goals by imposing subjective standards of acceptable sound mix on performers would raise serious First Amendment concerns, but this case provides us with no opportunity to address those questions. As related above, the District Court found that the city's equipment and its sound technician could meet all of the standards requested by the performers, including RAR.

Respondent argues further that the guideline, even if not content based in explicit terms, is nonetheless invalid on its face because it places unbridled discretion in the hands of city officials charged with enforcing it."

As a threshold matter, it is far from clear that respondent should be permitted to bring a facial challenge to this aspect of the regulation. Our cases permitting facial challenges to regulations that allegedly grant officials unconstrained authority to regulate speech have generally involved licensing schemes that "ves[t] unbridled discretion in a government official over whether to permit or deny expressive activity." Plain Dealer, supra, 486 U.S., at 755, 108 S.Ct., at 2143. The grant of discretion that respondent seeks to challenge here is of an entirely different, and lesser, order of magnitude, because respondent does not suggest that city officials enjoy unfettered discretion to deny bandshell permits altogether. Rather, respondent contends only that the city, by exercising what is concededly its right to regulate amplified sound, could choose to provide inadequate sound for performers based on the content of their speech. Since respondent does not claim that city officials enjoy unguided discretion to deny the right to speak altogether, it is open to question whether respondent's claim falls within the narrow class of permissible facial challenges to allegedly unconstrained grants of regulatory authority...

We need not decide, however, whether the "extraordinary doctrine" that permits facial challenges to some regulations of expression, see id., at 772, 108 S.Ct., at 2152 (WHITE, J., dissenting), should be extended to the circumstances of this case, for respondent's facial challenge fails on its merits. The city's guideline states that its goals are to "provide the best sound for all events" and to "insure appropriate sound quality balanced with respect for nearby residential neighbors and the mayorally decreed quiet zone of [the] Sheep Meadow." App. 375. While these standards are undoubtedly flexible, and the officials implementing them will exercise considerable discretion, perfect clarity and precise guidance have never been required even of regulations that restrict expressive activity... By its own terms the city's sound-amplification guideline must be interpreted to forbid city officials purposely to select inadequate sound systems or to vary the sound quality or volume based on the message being delivered by performers. The guideline is not vulnerable to respondent's facial challenge.

Even if the language of the guideline were not sufficient on its face to withstand challenge, our ultimate conclusion would be the same, for the city has interpreted the guideline in such a manner as to provide additional guidance to the officials charged with its enforcement. The District Court expressly found that the city's policy is to defer to the sponsor's desires concerning sound quality...

We think it also apparent that the city's interest in ensuring the sufficiency of sound amplification at bandshell events is a substantial one. The record indicates that inadequate sound amplification has had an adverse affect on the ability of some audiences to hear and enjoy performances at the bandshell. The city enjoys a substantial interest in ensuring the ability of its citizens to enjoy whatever benefits the city parks have to offer, from amplified music to silent meditation. See Community for Creative Non-Violence, supra, at 296, 104 S.Ct. at 3070.

The Court of Appeals recognized the city's substantial interest in limiting the sound emanating from the bandshell... See 848 F.2d, at 370. In the court's judgment, there were several alternative methods of achieving the desired end that would have been less restrictive of respondent's First Amendment rights.

The Court of Appeals erred in sifting through all the available or imagined alternative means of regulating sound volume in order to determine whether the city's solution was "the least intrusive means" of achieving the desired end. This "less-restrictive-alternative analysis ... has never been a part of the inquiry into the validity of a time, place, and manner regulation." Regan v. Time, Inc., 468 U.S. 641, 657, 104 S.Ct. 3262, 3271, 82 L.Ed.2d 487 (1984) (opinion of WHITE, J.). Instead, our cases quite clearly hold that restrictions on the time, place, or manner of protected speech are not invalid "simply because there is some imaginable alternative that might be less burdensome on speech." United States v. Albertini, 472 U.S. 675, 689, 105 S.Ct. 2897, 2906, 86 L.Ed.2d 536 (1985).

The Court of Appeals apparently drew its least-intrusive-means requirement from United States v. O'Brien, 391 U.S., at 377, 88 S.Ct., at 1679, the case in which we established the standard for judging the validity of restrictions on expressive conduct. See 848 F.2d, at 370. The court's reliance was misplaced, however, for we have held that the O'Brien test "in the last analysis is little, if any, different from the standard applied to time, place, or manner restrictions..."

Lest any confusion on the point remain, we reaffirm today that a regulation of the time, place, or manner of protected speech must be narrowly tailored to serve the government's legitimate, content-neutral interests but that it need not be the least restrictive or least intrusive means of doing so. Rather, the requirement of narrow tailoring is satisfied "so long as the ... regulation promotes a substantial government interest that would be achieved less effectively absent the regulation." United States v. Albertini, 472 U.S. 675, 689, 105 S.Ct. 2897, 2906, 86 L.Ed.2d 536 (1985); see also Community for Creative Non-Violence, supra, 468 U.S., at 297, 104 S.Ct., at 3071. To be sure, this standard does not mean that a time, place, or manner regulation may burden substantially more speech than is necessary to further the government's legitimate interests. Government may not regulate expression in such a manner that a substantial portion of the burden on speech does not serve to advance its goals. See Frisby v. Schultz, 487 U.S., at 485, 108 S.Ct., at 2502 ("A complete ban can be narrowly tailored but only if each activity within the proscription's scope is an appropriately targeted evil"). So long as the means chosen are not substantially broader than necessary to achieve the government's interest, however, the regulation will not be invalid simply because a court concludes that the government's interest could be adequately served by some less-speech-restrictive alternative. "The validity of [time, place, or manner] regulations does not turn on a judge's agreement with the responsible decisionmaker concerning the most appropriate method for promoting significant government interests" or the degree to which those interests should be promoted. United States v. Albertini, 472 U.S., at 689, 105 S.Ct., at 2906; see Community for Creative Non-Violence, supra, 468 U.S., at 299, 104 S.Ct., at 3072.

It is undeniable that the city's substantial interest in limiting sound volume is served in a direct and effective way by the requirement that the city's sound technician control the mixing board during performances. Absent this requirement, the city's interest would have been served less well, as is evidenced by the complaints about excessive volume generated by respondent's past concerts. The alternative regulatory methods hypothesized by the Court of Appeals reflect nothing more than a disagreement with the city over how much control of volume is appropriate or how that level of control is to be achieved. See Community for Creative Non-Violence, supra, at 299, 104 S.Ct., at 3072. The Court of Appeals erred in failing to defer to the city's reasonable determination that its interest in controlling volume would be best served by requiring bandshell performers to utilize the city's sound technician.

The city's second content-neutral justification for the guideline, that of ensuring "that the sound amplification [is] sufficient to reach all listeners within the defined concertground," 658 F.Supp., at 1352, also supports the city's choice of regulatory methods. By providing competent sound technicians and adequate amplification equipment, the city eliminated the problems of inexperienced technicians and insufficient sound volume that had plagued some bandshell performers in the past. No doubt this concern is not applicable to respondent's concerts, which apparently were characterized by more-than-adequate sound amplification. But that fact is beside the point, for the validity of the regulation depends on the relation it bears to the overall problem the government seeks to correct, not on the extent to which it furthers the government's interests in an individual case. Here, the regulation's effectiveness must be judged by considering all the varied groups that use the bandshell, and it is valid so long as the city could reasonably have determined that its interests overall would be served less effectively without the sound-amplification guideline than with it. United States v. Albertini, supra, 472 U.S., at 688-689, 105 S.Ct., at 2906-2907; Community for Creative Non-Violence, 468 U.S., at 296-297, 104 S.Ct., at 3070-3071. Considering these proffered justifications together, therefore, it is apparent that the guideline directly furthers the city's legitimate governmental interests and that those interests would have been less well served in the absence of the sound-amplification guideline.

Respondent nonetheless argues that the sound-amplification guideline is not narrowly tailored because, by placing control of sound mix in the hands of the city's technician, the guideline sweeps far more broadly than is necessary to further the city's legitimate concern with sound volume...

If the city's regulatory scheme had a substantial deleterious effect on the ability of bandshell performers to achieve the quality of sound they desired, respondent's concerns would have considerable force. The District Court found, however, that pursuant to city policy, the city's sound technician "give[s] the sponsor autonomy with respect to the sound mix ... [and] does all that he can to accommodate the sponsor's desires in those regards." 658 F.Supp., at 1352...

C

The final requirement, that the guideline leave open ample alternative channels of communication, is easily met. Indeed, in this respect the guideline is far less restrictive than regulations we have upheld in other cases, for it does not attempt to ban any particular manner or type of expression at a given place or time. Cf. Frisby, supra, 487 U.S., at 482-484, 108 S.Ct., at 2501-2502; Community for Creative Non-Violence, supra, 468 U.S., at 295, 104 S.Ct., at 3070; Renton v. Playtime Theatres, Inc., 475 U.S., at 53-54, 106 S.Ct., at 931-932. Rather, the guideline continues to permit expressive activity in the bandshell, and has no effect on the quantity or content of that expression beyond regulating the extent of amplification. That the city's limitations on volume may reduce to some degree the potential audience for respondent's speech is of no consequence, for there has been no showing that the remaining avenues of communication are inadequate....

III

The city's sound-amplification guideline is narrowly tailored to serve the substantial and content-neutral governmental interests of avoiding excessive sound volume and providing sufficient amplification within the bandshell concert ground, and the guideline leaves open ample channels of communication. Accordingly, it is valid under the First Amendment as a reasonable regulation of the place and manner of expression. The judgment of the Court of Appeals is Reversed.

Justice BLACKMUN concurs in the result.

Justice MARSHALL, with whom Justice BRENNAN and Justice STEVENS join, dissenting... From here, we move on from the First Amendment, which is we say, shapes the scope and reach of "Entertainment Law" to the more mundane pursuits of who gets and what, and how are these people billed? Because billing and credit for work performed is money. The next case, Buchwald v. Superior Court, 254 Cal.App.2d 347, 62 Cal.Rptr. 364 (1967), discusses California's Artists' Managers Act (Lab. Code, §§1700-1700.46), which has to regulate and prevent unqualified people from acting as managers for (creative) artists. The contract between an unlicensed artists' manager and an artist is void.

MARTYN BUCHWALD
v.
THE SUPERIOR COURT OF THE CITY OF SAN FRANCISCO
Civ. No. 24382
Court of Appeal, First District, Division 1, California
254 Cal.App.2d 347, 62 Cal.Rptr. 364
Sept. 15, 1967

ELKINGTON, J.

By their "Petition for Writ of Review (and/or, in the Alternative, a Writ of Prohibition or Mandamus)" petitioners seek review of orders of the superior court in an action commenced by them against Matthew Katz, hereinafter referred to as Katz, who is here the real party in interest. Concerned is the Artists' Managers Act which we shall hereafter refer to as the Act.

The Act comprises sections 1700-1700.46 of the Labor Code. It is found in division 2, part 6 of that code, relating to "Employment Agencies." It requires licensing, and regulates the business, of artists' managers.

The Act is a remedial statute. Statutes such as the Act are designed to correct abuses that have long been recognized and which have been the subject of both legislative action and judicial decision...

Since the clear object of the Act is to prevent improper persons from becoming artists' managers and to regulate such activity for the protection of the public, a contract between an unlicensed artists' manager and an artist is void...

Section 1700.44 of the Act, as pertinent here, provides: "In all cases of controversy arising under this chapter the parties involved shall refer the matters in dispute to the Labor Commissioner, who shall hear and determine the same, subject to an appeal within 10 days after determination, to the superior court where the same shall be heard de novo."

Petitioners constitute a professional musical group known as the "Jefferson Airplane." They are "artists" as defined by section 1700.4 of the Act. Each petitioner entered into a separate and identical contract with Katz, who for a percentage of each petitioner's earnings undertook, among other things, to act as "exclusive personal representative, advisor and manager in the entertainment field." The contract contained a provision reading: "It is clearly understood that you [Katz] are not an employment agent or theatrical agent, that you have not offered or attempted or promised to obtain employment or engagements for me, and you are not obligated, authorized or expected to do so." It also provided for arbitration of any dispute thereunder in accordance with the rules of the American Arbitration Association.

A dispute arose between the petitioners and Katz in relation to the subject matter of the contract. Katz thereupon, on September 21, 1966, commenced proceedings with the arbitration association seeking to compel arbitration of the dispute.

On October 18, 1966, petitioners filed with the Labor Commissioner a "Petition to Determine Controversy," alleging among other things: "Complainants complain that in September of 1965, defendant [Matthew Katz] acting as an artists-manager and through false and fraudulent statements and by duress, caused complainants to sign with defendant as an artists-manager; that defendant, prior to the time of signing said contracts, promised the complainants and each of them that he would procure bookings for them; that defendant thereafter procured bookings for the complainants and insisted that the complainants perform the bookings procured by him; that complainants sought to procure their own bookings, and that defendant refused them the right to procure their own bookings; that at the time that said contracts were negotiated, defendant Matthew Katz was not licensed as an artists-manager pursuant to the provisions of the California Labor Code, Section 1700.5; that the contract presented to each complainant was not submitted to the Labor Commissioner, State of California, as required under Section 1700.23; that Matthew Katz has not performed in accordance with Sections 1700.24, 1700.25, 1700.26, 1700.27, 1700.28, 1700.31, 1700.32, 1700.36 and 1700.40 of the Labor Code and other provisions of the Labor Code; that Matthew Katz never rendered an accounting to the complainants for thousands of dollars received by Mr. Katz for their services; that Matthew Katz has not allowed complainants to inspect the books and records maintained by Matthew Katz with respect to fees earned by the complainants; that Matthew Katz has and continues to obtain payments intended for one or more of the above complainants and has cashed checks intended for one or more of the above complainants for his own use and benefit."

Katz appeared and filed his answer to the petition, in which he objected to the jurisdiction of the Labor Commissioner and denied that he had agreed to act, or that he was or had been acting, as an artists' manager.

On October 21, 1966 while the Labor Commissioner proceedings were pending, petitioners filed an action against Katz in the superior court, seeking relief, among other things, that Katz be restrained from proceeding before the arbitration association.

In the superior court action Katz appeared and moved the court to order petitioners to arbitrate as provided by the contracts, and to restrain the proceedings before the Labor Commissioner. Petitioners opposed Katz' motion contending that a bona fide controversy existed before the Labor Commissioner as to whether Katz had agreed to act, and had been acting as their artists' manager, and as to the legality and validity of the contracts. They contended that the language of the contracts "you have not offered, or attempted or promised to obtain employment or engagements for me, etc." was but a subterfuge to conceal the fact that Katz did act, and had agreed to act, as an artists' manager. Evidence was introduced by petitioners in support of their contentions. Katz offered evidence to the contrary.

The court thereafter on January 17, 1967 made its orders denying petitioners' motion to restrain arbitration; restraining petitioners from proceeding further before the Labor Commissioner; and ordering them to arbitrate their dispute before the arbitration association. These orders are the subject of the instant proceedings.

Real party in interest Katz has rather clearly stated the issues to be determined in this proceeding. Our discussion will follow the contentions as presented by him.

First Contention: *Neither certiorari, prohibition nor mandamus is a proper remedy.*

It appears that the superior court's orders constitute completed judicial acts. If the orders were in excess of the court's jurisdiction and if there is available neither appeal nor other plain speedy and adequate remedy, certiorari is proper. (See 3 Witkin, Cal. Procedure (1954) Extraordinary Writs, pp. 2490-2493.)

An appeal does not lie from an order compelling arbitration (*Corbett v. Petroleum Maintenance Co.,* 119 Cal.App.2d 21 [258 P.2d 1077]); nor is any other plain, speedy or adequate remedy apparent. We consider certiorari to be the proper remedy.

Second Contention: *The Artists' Managers Act does not give the Labor Commissioner jurisdiction over an artists' manager who is not licensed as such by the commissioner.*

Admittedly Katz was not licensed as an artists' manager.

The Act, section 1700.3, defines "licensee" as an "artists' manager which holds a valid, unrevoked, and unforfeited license. ..." Section 1700.4 defines "artists' manager" (see fn. 2, *ante*).

Certain sections, i.e., 1700.17, 1700.19, 1700.21, 1700.42, 1700.43, refer to licensee in such context that the word can reasonably apply only to a licensed artists' manager. Other sections, including those which are the subject of the Petition to Determine Controversy, refer to artists' manager in such manner that they apply reasonably to both licensed and unlicensed artists' managers. The Act thus refers to and covers two classes of persons, "licensees" who are artists' managers with valid licenses, and "artists' managers" who may or may not be so licensed.

" 'It is well settled that a legislative body has the power within reasonable limitations to prescribe legal definitions of its own language, and when an act passed by it embodies a definition it is binding on the courts.' "

(*Application of Monrovia Evening Post,* 199 Cal. 263, 269-270 [248 P. 1017]; see also *People v. Western Air Lines, Inc.,* 42 Cal.2d 621, 638 [268 P.2d 723]; *In re Miller,* 31 Cal.2d 191, 198 [187 P.2d 722].) ([4]) If possible, significance should be given to every word and phrase of an act in pursuance of the legislative purpose. (*Select Base Materials v. Board of Equalization,* 51 Cal.2d 640, 645 [335 P.2d 672]; *People v. Hampton,* 236 Cal.App.2d 795, 801 [46 Cal.Rptr. 338]; *Brown v. Cranston,* 214 Cal.App.2d 660, 672-673 [29 Cal.Rptr. 725].)

Remedial statutes should be liberally construed to effect their objects and suppress the mischief at which they are directed It would be unreasonable to construe the Act as applying only to licensed artists' managers, thus allowing an artists' manager, by nonsubmission to the licensing provisions of the Act, to exclude himself from its restrictions and regulations enacted in the public interest.

We conclude that artists' managers (as defined by the Act), whether they be licensed or unlicensed, are bound and regulated by the Artists' Managers Act.

Third Contention: *By virtue of his written contract, Katz as a matter of law is not an artists' manager and therefore is not subject to the Artists' Managers Act.*

The Act gives the Labor Commissioner jurisdiction over those who are artists' managers in fact. The petition filed with the Labor Commissioner alleges facts which if true indicate that the written contracts were but subterfuges and that Katz had agreed to, and did, act as an artists' manager. Clearly the Act may not be circumvented by allowing language of the written contract to control—if Katz had in fact agreed to, and had acted as an artists' manager. The form of the transaction, rather than its substance would control...

The court, or as here, the Labor Commissioner, is free to search out illegality lying behind the form in which a transaction has been cast for the purpose of concealing such illegality...

In support of his position that as a matter of law he is not an artists' manager Katz cites *Raden v. Laurie,* 120 Cal.App.2d 778 [262 P.2d 61]. That case, decided in 1953, concerned the Private Employment Agencies Act, sections 1550-1650 (also found in part 2, div. 6 relating to "Employment Agencies") which at that time regulated persons doing business as artists' managers.

Raden was employed by Laurie, an actress, as a counselor and advisor under a written contract which specified he was to receive 10 percent of Laurie's professional earnings. Among other things the contract provided: " 'It is expressly agreed that ... nothing herein contained shall be deemed to require you or authorize you to seek or obtain employment for the undersigned [Laurie].' " (120 Cal.App.2d at p. 779.) Raden was not paid his 10 percent so he sued in the superior court. As to the subject matter of the complaint the superior court clearly had jurisdiction. Laurie moved for summary judgment, alleging the suit to be without merit. (Code Civ. Proc., § 437c.) She contended the contract was invalid because it was a subterfuge used by an artists' manager who had not complied with the Private Employment Agencies Act. The motion for summary judgment was granted by the superior court.

The appellate court reversed, stating as follows (at p. 782): "It would seem clear that his [Raden's] duties were intentionally limited to the rendition of services which would not require his being licensed as an artists' manager. Respondent says: 'It is the act of seeking employment, not the contract provision, which brings the legislation into play.' This might be true if the contract were a mere sham and pretext designed by plaintiff to misrepresent and conceal the true agreement of the parties and to evade the law. But there was no evidence which would have justified the court in reaching that conclusion. There was no evidence of misrepresentation, fraud or mistake as to the terms of the contract nor as to plaintiff's obligations thereunder, nor evidence that defendants did not understand and willingly accept the limitation of plaintiff's duties. ... *In the absence of any evidence that the July 30th agreement was a mere subterfuge or otherwise invalid the court was required to give effect to its clear and positive provisions.* ... Since plaintiff was employed only to counsel and advise [Laurie] and to act as her business manager in matters not related to obtaining engagements for her, he was not acting as an 'Employment Agency' as defined by section 1551, Labor Code." (Italics added; pp. 782-783.)

The inapplicability of *Raden v. Laurie* to the instant controversy is obvious. There, on a motion for summary judgment, no showing, prima facie or otherwise, was made (as regards the contract sued upon or its subject matter) that Raden had agreed to act, or had acted as an artists' manager (or employment agency)... a conclusion that the contract was a sham or pretext designed to conceal the true agreement or to evade the law. On the uncontroverted facts the court had jurisdiction over the controversy and the Labor Commissioner did not. In the proceedings before us a prima facia showing was made to the Labor Commissioner as to matters over which he had jurisdiction.

Fourth Contention: *The superior court had jurisdiction over the controversy referred to the Labor Commissioner by petitioners.*

The Artists' Managers Act (enacted in 1959) so far as we can determine, has never been mentioned in the reported decisions of the courts of this state. However, an earlier, similar and in many respects identical, statute has been frequently interpreted. This statute is the previously referred to Private Employment Agencies Law (§§ 1550-1650). Both statutes are, as previously stated, contained in part 6 (entitled "Employment Agencies") of division 2 of the Labor Code. Each is an outgrowth of a 1913 statute relating to employment agencies. (See Stats. 1913, ch. 282, p. 515, and amendments thereto.) Indeed, section 1700.44, previously quoted and on which the instant dispute is focused was taken word for word from section 1647 of the Private Employment Agencies Law, which language in turn was taken in its entirety from an amendment to the 1913 statute. (See Stats. 1923, ch. 412, p. 936)...

Applying to the Act the construction given to its sister and parent statutes the following appears: The Act is broad and comprehensive. The Labor Commissioner is empowered to hear and determine disputes under it, *including the validity of the artists' manager-artist contract* and the liability, if any, of the parties thereunder... In the settlement of disputes the jurisdiction of the Labor Commissioner is similar to, but broader, than the power of an arbitrator under Code of Civil Procedure sections 1280-1294.2

Section 1700.44 of the Act is mandatory. It provides that the parties involved, artists and artists' manager, in any controversy arising under the Act, *shall* refer the matters in dispute to the commissioner...

Since the instant controversy was pending before, and was properly within the jurisdiction of, the Labor Commissioner, the doctrine of "exhaustion of administrative remedies" applies...

We hold as to cases of controversies arising under the Artists' Managers Act that the Labor Commissioner has original jurisdiction to hear and determine the same to the exclusion of the superior court, subject to an appeal within 10 days after determination, to the superior court where the same shall be heard de novo. (See § 1700.44.)

Fifth Contention: *The petitioners waived any right they may have had to proceed before the Labor Commissioner by filing their action in the superior court...*

Sixth Contention: *Private arbitration being permissible under the Act* (§ *1700.45*) *and the parties having agreed to arbitrate before the American Arbitration Association, the orders of the superior court were proper.*

This argument overlooks the basic contention of petitioners that their agreement with Katz is wholly invalid because of his noncompliance with the Act. If the agreement is void no rights, including the claimed right to private arbitration, can be derived from it...

We conclude that petitioners are entitled, by way of certiorari, to the relief sought by them. The orders of the superior court dated January 17, 1967 are annulled.

Molinari, P. J., and Brown (H. C.), J., concurred.

A petition for a rehearing was denied September 29, 1967, and the petition of the real party in interest for a hearing by the Supreme Court was denied November 8, 1967...

RADEN v. LAURIE
Civ. 19600
District Court of Appeal, Second District, Division 3, California
Oct. 23, 1953
120 Cal.App.2d 778

SHINN, P. J.

Plaintiff appeals from a summary judgment entered in favor of defendant Charlotte Jacobs. Rosetta Jacobs, also a defendant, was not served. Defendant's motion for summary judgment was heard upon the complaint, the answer of defendant, and affidavits of Charlotte Jacobs and plaintiff. The ground of the motion was that the action has no merit.

In January, 1948, by an undated writing signed by plaintiff, by Rosetta Jacobs and Charlotte Jacobs, plaintiff was employed as a nonexclusive manager of Rosetta Jacobs with the duty of "the securing of engagements for me in the motion picture, theatrical, radio, television and allied fields with and upon the consent of myself and my legal guardian, Mrs. Charlotte Jacobs, and in accordance with our wishes," for a consideration of 10 per cent of all moneys received from engagements obtained directly or indirectly by plaintiff. No time was specified for duration of the agreement. On July 30, 1948, a second agreement was entered into.

"July 30, 1948

Mr. Ted Raden

1177 N. Ardmore Ave.

Los Angeles 27, Calif.

"Dear Mr. Raden:

Plaintiff sued on the second agreement alleging that Rosetta Jacobs, who it seems uses the name of Piper Laurie, had earned a considerable sum of money for professional services and had paid none of it to plaintiff; $3,100 was demanded as plaintiff's share of the earnings. It appeared from the affidavit of Charlotte Jacobs, the mother of Rosetta, that the latter was a minor, born January 22, 1932, and that on October 12, 1949, Rosetta by means of a communication addressed to plaintiff and signed by one Benj. T. Weinstein, terminated and disaffirmed the agreement of July 30, 1948. The affidavit also asserted that when the January, 1948, agreement was executed plaintiff stated to Rosetta and Charlotte that he would obtain employment in the entertainment field for the former, and that the same was the understanding between the parties until the notice of disaffirmance; that during 1948 and 1949, plaintiff attempted unsuccessfully to obtain such employment and several times took Rosetta to places where entertainers might find employment. It was also alleged that plaintiff presented the July writing saying merely that it was "a better form." It was further alleged, and is conceded to be a fact, that plaintiff was not licensed as an employment agent or artists' manager, and that the agreement was not approved by the Labor Commissioner of the State of California. While it was alleged that plaintiff did not handle any money for Rosetta or any records or books for her, it was not alleged that he did not keep and perform his obligations under the July 30th agreement. Plaintiff filed an affidavit setting forth that he counseled and advised both defendants respecting Rosetta's career, and in his affidavit he detailed the services which he rendered in transforming her from a "reticent, bashful, introverted, unassuming personality, without appeal, conversational ability, poise, or any social equilibrium" into a mature, interesting, and attractive personality with poise and aplomb which brought forth her ability and possibilities. The affidavit admitted that plaintiff had taken Rosetta to places where entertainers might have found employment, but denied that it was for the purpose of obtaining employment, and alleged that it was for the general development and education of the young woman. It was denied in the affidavit that plaintiff stated to either of the defendants that he could or would obtain employment for Rosetta. It was alleged that the agreement of January, 1948, was merged in and superseded by the agreement of July 30, 1948. It was also alleged that defendant Charlotte contributed a sum of money which affiant used to pay a part of the costs of a short motion picture which plaintiff caused to be written, directed and produced, starring Rosetta, and in which she made her professional debut. These services, it was alleged, continued over a period of more than a year and until Rosetta obtained a contract with Universal International Studio, at which time plaintiff was cast aside.

Plaintiff was not licensed as an artists' manager, theatrical manager or employment agent. It is said by respondent that her motion was granted upon the ground that plaintiff was either an unlicensed artists' manager or employment agent. The definition of artists' manager is contained in section 1650 of the Labor Code. One is not an artists' manager unless he both advises, counsels and directs artists in the development or advancement of their professional careers, and also procures, offers, promises or attempts to procure employment or engagements for an artist "only in connection with and as a part of the duties and obligations of such person under a contract with such artist by which such person contracts to render services of the nature above mentioned to such artist." Such is the clear wording of the statute.

We have experienced some difficulty in understanding defendant's construction of the section. It appears to be contended that one who is employed to advise, counsel and direct an artist, thereby promises to procure or attempt to procure employment for his principal; therefore, despite the language of the agreement, plaintiff was bound to seek employment for Rosetta; his efforts to do so were a part of his duties of counseling and advising and he was therefore an artists' manager.

The July agreement is explicit and unambiguous. It specifically provides that plaintiff has no authority and no duty to seek or obtain employment for Rosetta Jacobs. He is required only to give counsel and advice and to assist generally in her training for a professional career and the selection and employment of agents. Although it was alleged in the affidavit of Charlotte that plaintiff endeavored, unsuccessfully, to obtain employment for Rosetta, there was no showing that he procured, offered, promised or attempted to procure employment or engagements for Rosetta "only in connection with and as a part of the duties and obligations of such person under a contract with such artist." It would seem clear that his duties were intentionally limited to the rendition of services which would not require his being licensed as an artists' manager.

Respondent says: "It is the act of seeking employment, not the contract provision, which brings the legislation into play." This might be true if the contract were a mere sham and pretext designed by plaintiff to misrepresent and conceal the true agreement of the parties and to evade the law. But there was no evidence which would have justified the court in reaching that conclusion. There was no evidence of misrepresentation, fraud or mistake as to the terms of the contract nor as to plaintiff's obligations thereunder, nor evidence that defendants did not understand and willingly accept the limitation of plaintiff's duties. The assertions in defendant's affidavit that in January, 1948, plaintiff represented that he could and would obtain employment for Rosetta, while immaterial, were denied in plaintiff's affidavit. By the former agreement plaintiff undertook to seek engagements for Rosetta and to act as her manager, but not so under the July agreement.

In the absence of any evidence that the July 30th agreement was a mere subterfuge or otherwise invalid the court was required to give effect to its clear and positive provisions. It was to be presumed that the parties acted in good faith. If there was a doubt whether the later agreement was entered into in good faith, as a substitute for the earlier one, and that it expressed the real intentions of the parties, it should have been resolved in favor of plaintiff. These were not questions to be decided on a motion for summary judgment...

In plaintiff's affidavit it was also denied that plaintiff had promised, or that he attempted to obtain engagements or employment for Rosetta.

On the motion for summary judgment the averments of plaintiff's affidavit should have been taken as true... Therefore, plaintiff's denial that he agreed or endeavored to obtain engagement or employment for Rosetta was a sufficient answer to the motion for summary judgment.

Since plaintiff was employed only to counsel and advise Rosetta and to act as her business manager in matters not related to obtaining engagements for her, he was not acting as an "Employment Agency" as defined by section 1551, Labor Code.

The Labor Commissioner has filed an amicus brief in which he contends that the later agreement was a sham and subterfuge designed to conceal the fact that plaintiff was acting as an artists' manager. Upon the evidence that was before the court this contention, of itself, presents an issue for regular trial procedure.

We find no merit in the claim that the disaffirmance of the agreement by the minor operated to terminate the obligation of Charlotte Jacobs who, presumably, was entitled to receive the earnings of her daughter, and was one of plaintiff's employers.

The judgment is reversed.

WOOD (Parker), J., and VALLEE, J., concurred.

Respondent's petition for a hearing by the Supreme Court was denied December 17, 1953. EDMONDS, J., and TRAYNOR, J., were of the opinion that the petition should be granted.

KELSEY GRAMMER
v.
THE ARTISTS AGENCY WILLIAM MORRIS AGENCY, INC.
v.
THE ARTISTS AGENCY
United States Court of Appeals, Ninth Circuit.
Argued and Submitted Feb. 14, 2002
287 F.3d 880

TASHIMA, Circuit Judge.

Plaintiffs Kelsey Grammer and Grammnet, Inc. (collectively, "Grammer"), and William Morris Agency, Inc., appeal a district court order confirming a Screen Actors Guild ("SAG") labor arbitration award, totaling over $2 million in unpaid commissions. Grammer argues that the arbitrators made factual findings unsupported by the record and that they exceeded their jurisdiction. We have jurisdiction under 28 U.S.C. § 1291, and we affirm the district court.

I. FACTUAL BACKGROUND

The Artists Agency ("Artists Agency") began representing Grammer in the 1980s, representation that included both Grammer's television and motion picture projects. Grammer became increasingly dissatisfied with Artists Agency in the early 1990s, as its representation had secured no motion picture projects for him and Grammer's two most significant television projects ("Cheers" and "Frasier") were not obtained through Artists Agency.

Grammer sought modification of his Artists Agency contract so that he could seek alternative representation for potential theatrical motion picture projects. After some negotiation, Grammer and Artists Agency agreed in January 1995 that, in exchange for Grammer's extending for two years his television and commercial obligations to Artists Agency (the "renewal contracts"), Artists Agency would substantially release Grammer from his theatrical motion picture obligations (the "settlement agreement") (collectively, the "1995 agreements"). The settlement agreement was executed on January 11, 1995. The renewal contracts were executed on January 17, 1995, were post-dated to commence on May 20, 1996, and expired May 20, 1998.

Artists Agency filed the renewal contracts with SAG in May 1995, but they were originally rejected. Counsel for Artists Agency contacted Joan Meyer ("Meyer"), SAG's Executive Administrator, explained the arrangement forged between Grammer and Artists Agency, and forwarded to her the settlement agreement as evidence of that arrangement. Satisfied that the renewal contracts were in the best interests of Grammer, and that both sides had been competently represented by counsel, Meyer accepted the renewal contracts for filing with SAG.

In August 1996, Grammer terminated his relationship altogether with Artists Agency and, in August 1998, Grammer stopped paying commissions to Artists Agency. Grammer denied any obligations to Artists Agency, arguing that the 1995 agreements violated Rule 16(g) of the collective bargaining agreement ("CBA") among SAG, the Association of Talent Agents ("ATA"), and the National Association of Talent Representatives. Grammer alleged that the 1995 agreements: (1) were post-dated so that the execution date and the commencement date did not correspond, in violation of Rule 16(g) § IV(C)(4)(a); (2) effectively spanned longer than three years as a result of this post-dating, in violation of Rule 16(g) § IV(C)(4)(a); (3) were executed prior to the last third of the term of the previous contract between Grammer and Artists Agency, in violation of Rule 16(g) § IV(D)(3); and (4) were filed more than 15 days after their execution, in violation of Rule 16(g) § IV(C)(1). Any one of these violations arguably voids the renewal contracts. When Artists Agency filed a statement of claim with SAG, seeking payment of the commissions allegedly due, Grammer counterclaimed, alleging that Artists Agency owed him commissions already paid pursuant to those purportedly void contracts.

A three-member arbitration panel held hearings over the course of 18 days, at which witnesses were examined and cross-examined, and documentary evidence was introduced. The panel determined that the 1995 agreements were valid, that Artists Agency had enforceable rights pursuant to those 1995 agreements, that those rights entitled Artists Agency to more than $2 million in back commissions, and that Grammer's counterclaim was without merit. Specifically, the panel found that, while "[i]t is not disputed that the Settlement Agreement effected a transaction that was at variance from Rule 16(g)," Meyer had *de facto* granted a waiver of that variance after reviewing the settlement agreement, determining that Grammer's interests were both furthered and protected by legal counsel, and accepting the renewal contracts and settlement agreement for filing with SAG.

Grammer then filed this action for a declaration vacating the labor arbitration award. Grammer alleged that: (1) the arbitration panel did not apply the plain language of Rule 16(g), which would have rendered the 1995 agreements void and unenforceable; (2) there was no evidence in the record to support a finding that SAG had granted Artists Agency a waiver for its Rule 16(g) violations; (3) even if the 1995 agreements were valid, their execution in January 1995 voided the pre-existing agency agreement between Grammer and Artists Agency, meaning that Grammer owed Artists Agency no commissions for income derived between January 1995 and November 1996; and (4) the arbitration panel lacked jurisdiction to award Artists Agency a $36,000 commission on "consulting fees" paid to Grammer while working on the television show "Frasier." The district court rejected these arguments, confirmed the arbitration award, and denied Grammer's counterclaim.

II. STANDARD OF REVIEW

We review de novo the confirmation of an arbitration award. *First Options, Inc. v. Kaplan,* 514 U.S. 938, 947-48, 115 S.Ct. 1920, 131 L.Ed.2d 985 (1995); *Haw. Teamsters Union, Local 996 v. United Parcel Serv.,* 241 F.3d 1177, 1180 (9th Cir.2001). Although we apply "ordinary, not special standards" when reviewing a trial court's confirmation of an arbitration award, *First Options,* 514 U.S. at 948, 115 S.Ct. 1920, we nonetheless afford labor arbitration awards "nearly unparalleled ... deference."

We presume that factual findings underlying a labor arbitration award are correct, rebuttable only by a clear preponderance of the evidence...

III. DISCUSSION

All parties agree that the 1995 agreements violate the terms of Rule 16(g). We must decide whether the arbitration panel erred in concluding that the 1995 agreements were nevertheless enforceable. We hold that the arbitration panel's decision to enforce the 1995 agreements was a reasonable interpretation of the CBA; we therefore affirm the district court.

A. Waiver of Rule 16(g) Violations

At the very least, it is clear that the 1995 agreements were: (1) executed and set to commence on different dates, in violation of Rule 16(g) § IV(C)(4)(a); (2) executed prior to the last third of the term on the previous contract between Grammer and Artists Agency, in violation of Rule 16(g) § IV(D)(3); and (3) filed more than 15 days after their execution, in violation of Rule 16(g) § IV(C)(1). In light of these Rule 16(g) violations, the arbitration panel observed that "[i]t is not disputed that the Settlement Agreement effected a transaction that was at variance from Rule 16(g)," and the district court found that "the parties do not dispute that the various agreements at issue in the arbitration deviated from the standard regulations set forth in Rule 16(g)."

These Rule 16(g) violations, however, do not necessarily void the 1995 agreements. Grammer correctly observes that neither he nor Artists Agency ever requested a formal, written waiver from SAG. Citing Rule 16(g) § IV(J), Grammer argues that the absence of such a formal, written waiver renders the arbitration panel's determination patently inconsistent with the plain language of Rule 16(g), and it therefore should be vacated. However, although Rule 16(g) instructs that such violations void applicable contracts and that waivers of violations must be issued by SAG in writing, these ostensibly "plain" provisions must be construed in the larger context of Rule 16(g) specifically and industry practice generally. When Rule 16(g) is considered in its entirety, its text is not as "plain" as Grammer suggests. The arbitration panel characterized Rule 16(g) as "sometimes contradictory"; ample evidence supports this conclusion. Initially, Rule 16(g) is facially inconsistent when it comes to prescribing how waivers ought to be granted. For example, while § IV(J) suggests that waivers cannot be offered without SAG's written consent, § IV(C)(1) provides that "inadvertent error or oversight ... shall be deemed waived unless the objection of invalidity is raised by the actor or SAG within 60 days."

Contradictions such as these led Karen Stuart ("Stuart"), the executive director of the ATA, to testify that Rule 16(g) "is riddled with inconsistencies and that is why custom and practice become important and SAG and ATA speak almost daily because there are problems in interpreting this agreement."

Additionally, while arbitrators cannot ignore the plain wording of collectively bargained contracts, they also are "not confined to the express terms of the contract ... [They] may also consider the industrial common law which is equally a part of the collective bargaining agreement although not expressed in it." *Haw. Teamsters,* 241 F.3d at 1181 (citation and internal quotation marks omitted); *see also Transp.-Communication Employees Union v. Union Pac. R.R.,* 385 U.S. 157, 160-61, 87 S.Ct. 369, 17 L.Ed.2d 264 (1966) (holding that a CBA is not a private contract between two private parties but, rather, is a generalized code to govern a myriad of cases and parties, which cannot be interpreted without considering the practice, usage and custom pertaining to all such agreements); *Cannery Warehousemen, Local Union No. 748 v. Haig Berberian, Inc.,* 623 F.2d 77, 82 (9th Cir.1980) (noting that arbitrators may employ "industrial common law" to interpret a CBA).

There was sufficient evidence to sustain the arbitration panel's finding that SAG waived the variances between Rule 16(g) and the 1995 agreements. Meyer testified that SAG generally will accept agreements that do not strictly comport with the requirements of Rule 16(g) when there are side agreements protecting the actor and the agent. Furthermore, both Meyer and Stuart testified that SAG occasionally overlooks Rule 16(g) violations of the exact type asserted by Grammer, without the use of formal waivers. In light of this testimony, which explains the course and practice of SAG's Rule 16(g) interpretation, the arbitration panel's finding that SAG had granted a waiver by filing the renewal contracts easily meets the deferential standard of review that this court must apply.

B. Contractual Obligations Between January 1995 and May 1996

Grammer argues that even if the arbitration panel correctly held that SAG had granted waivers for the 1995 agreements' Rule 16(g) violations, when those agreements were executed in January 1995, the pre-existing agency contract between Grammer and Artists Agency was automatically terminated. Because the 1995 renewal contracts did not go into effect until May 1996, Grammer argues that there was no agency contract in effect between January 1995 and May 1996, and that Artists Agency is not entitled to commissions stemming from that period. The arbitration panel rejected this argument, finding that an agency agreement was in effect between January 1995 and May 1996. The district court affirmed this conclusion as a reasonable interpretation of Rule 16(g), and we affirm this district court holding.

The thrust of Meyer's and Stuart's testimony was that Rule 16(g) merely provides a default framework to protect the interests of actors and agents and that these rules can be waived when the parties are represented by counsel and (particularly) when the agreement in question benefits the SAG member. Here, Grammer was seeking to get out of contractual obligations to Artists Agency so that he could seek theatrical motion picture representation with United Talent Agency. The 1995 agreements permitted him to do exactly that, so long as he extended his television representation obligations to Artists Agency for an additional two years.

Grammer now tries to use a technicality found in Rule 16(g) § IV(D)(3) to assert that the 1995 agreements left him altogether uncommitted to Artists Agency from January 1995 to March 1996. This purported "lapse" in Grammer's and Artist Agency's contract, however, was an eventuality clearly not contemplated by the parties when forming the 1995 agreements. In fact, Grammer's interpretation of the 1995 agreements is belied by the fact that Artists Agency represented Grammer in November 1995 during negotiations with Paramount Studios. Obviously, Artists Agency would not have represented Grammer in these negotiations had it not believed that the 1993 agency agreement was still in effect. And, by permitting Artists Agency actively to represent him and to pursue his interests during this period, Grammar clearly intended that the representation continue uninterrupted.

Given that Rule 16(g) violations can be waived by SAG when the parties are represented by counsel, when the waiver is consistent with the parties' assent, and when the waiver benefits the SAG member, it was reasonable for the arbitration panel to find that a valid agency contract existed between Grammer and Artists Agency from January 1995 to May 1996.

C. Consulting Fees

The arbitration panel awarded Artists Agency $36,000 in commissions on Grammer's consulting fees. Pointing to the absence of a "consulting" category in the CBA, Grammer argues that SAG (and by implication, the SAG arbitration panel) did not have jurisdiction to award consulting fee commissions.

The arbitration panel rejected this argument, finding that payment for consulting fees is within the scope of the renewal contracts and Rule 16(g)...

We likewise conclude that the arbitration panel's determination was reasonable. Rule 16(g)'s language of "in connection with" is sufficiently vague to support the arbitration panel's interpretation and there is no contradictory provision that expressly precludes commissions on consulting fees. Thus, we defer to the arbitration panel and affirm its consulting fee award.

IV. CONCLUSION

For the foregoing reasons, we hold that the labor arbitration panel acted reasonably in concluding that SAG waived violations of Rule 16(g), that a representation contract existed between Grammer and Artists Agency from January 1995 to March 1996, and that an award of commissions on consulting fees was permitted under the CBA. The district court's order confirming the arbitration award is, therefore,

AFFIRMED.

H.A. ARTISTS & ASSOCIATES, INC.
v.
ACTORS' EQUITY ASSOCIATION
No. 80-348
Argued March 23, 1981
Decided May 26, 1981
451 U.S. 704, 68 L.Ed.2d 558

Justice STEWART delivered the opinion of the Court.

The respondent Actors' Equity Association (Equity) is a union representing the vast majority of stage actors and actresses in the United States. It enters into collective-bargaining agreements with theatrical producers that specify minimum wages and other terms and conditions of employment for those whom it represents. The petitioners are independent theatrical agents who place actors and actresses in jobs with producers. The Court of Appeals for the Second Circuit held that the respondents' system of regulation of theatrical agents is immune from antitrust liability by reason of the statutory labor exemption from the antitrust laws, 622 F.2d 647. We granted certiorari to consider the availability of that exemption in the circumstances presented by this case. 449 U.S. 991, 101 S.Ct. 526, 66 L.Ed.2d 288.

A

Equity is a national union that has represented stage actors and actresses since early in this century. Currently representing approximately 23,000 actors and actresses, it has collective-bargaining agreements with virtually all major theatrical producers in New York City, on and off Broadway, and with most other theatrical producers throughout the United States. The terms negotiated with producers are the minimum conditions of employment (called "scale"); an actor or actress is free to negotiate wages or terms more favorable than the collectively bargained minimum.

Theatrical agents are independent contractors who negotiate contracts and solicit employment for their clients. The agents do not participate in the negotiation of collective-bargaining agreements between Equity and the theatrical producers. If an agent succeeds in obtaining employment for a client, he receives a commission based on a percentage of the client's earnings. Agents who operate in New York City must be licensed as employment agencies and are regulated by the New York City Department of Consumer Affairs pursuant to New York law, which provides that the maximum commission a theatrical agent may charge his client is 10% of the client's compensation.

In 1928, concerned with the high unemployment rates in the legitimate theater and the vulnerability of actors and actresses to abuses by theatrical agents, including the extraction of high commissions that tended to undermine collectively bargained rates of compensation, Equity unilaterally established a licensing system for the regulation of agents. The regulations permitted Equity members to deal only with those agents who obtained Equity licenses and thereby agreed to meet the conditions of representation prescribed by Equity. Those members who dealt with nonlicensed agents were subject to union discipline.

The system established by the Equity regulations was immediately challenged. In *Edelstein v. Gillmore*, 35 F.2d 723, the Court of Appeals for the Second Circuit concluded that the regulations were a lawful effort to improve the employment conditions of Equity members.

The essential elements of Equity's regulation of theatrical agents have remained unchanged since 1928. A member of Equity is prohibited, on pain of union discipline, from using an agent who has not, through the mechanism of obtaining an Equity license (called a "franchise"), agreed to comply with the regulations. The most important of the regulations requires that a licensed agent must renounce any right to take a commission on an employment contract under which an actor or actress receives scale wages. To the extent a contract includes provisions under which an actor or actress will sometimes receive scale pay—for rehearsals or "chorus" employment, for example—and sometimes more, the regulations deny the agent any commission on the scale portions of the contract. Licensed agents are also precluded from taking commissions on out-of-town expense money paid to their clients. Moreover, commissions are limited on wages within 10% of scale pay, and an agent must allow his client to terminate a representation contract if the agent is not successful in procuring employment within a specified period. Finally, agents are required to pay franchise fees to Equity. The fee is $200 for the initial franchise, $60 a year thereafter for each agent, and $40 for any sub-agent working in the office of another. These fees are deposited by Equity in its general treasury and are not segregated from other union funds.

In 1977, after a dispute between Equity and Theatrical Artists Representatives Associates (TARA)—a trade association representing theatrical agents, see n. 7, *supra*—a group of agents, including the petitioners, resigned from TARA because of TARA's decision to abide by Equity's regulations. These agents also informed Equity that they would not accept Equity's regulations, or apply for franchises. The petitioners instituted this lawsuit in May 1978, contending that Equity's regulations of theatrical agents violated §§ 1 and 2 of the Sherman Act, 26 Stat. 209, as amended, 15 U.S.C. §§ 1 and 2.

The District Court found, after a bench trial, that Equity's creation and maintenance of the agency franchise system were fully protected by the statutory labor exemptions from the antitrust laws, and accordingly dismissed the petitioners' complaint. 478 F.Supp. 496 (SDNY). Among its factual conclusions, the trial court found that in the theatrical industry, agents play a critical role in securing employment for actors and actresses: . . .

The court also found "no evidence to suggest the existence of any conspiracy or illegal combination between Actors' Equity and TARA or between Actors' Equity and producers," and concluded that "[t]he Actors Equity franchising system was employed by Actors' Equity for the purpose of protecting the wages and working conditions of its members." *Id.*, at 499.

The Court of Appeals unanimously affirmed the judgment of the District Court. It determined that the threshold issue was, under *United States v. Hutcheson*, 312 U.S. 219, 232, 61 S.Ct. 463, 466, 85 L.Ed. 788, whether Equity's franchising system involved any combination between Equity and any "non-labor groups" or persons who are not "parties to a labor dispute." 622 F.2d, at 648–649. If it did, the court reasoned, the protection of the statutory labor exemption would not apply.

First, the Court of Appeals held that the District Court had not been clearly erroneous in finding no agreement, explicit or tacit, between Equity and the producers to establish or police the franchising system. *Ibid.* Next, the court turned to the relationship between the union and those agents who had agreed to become franchised, in order to determine whether those agreements would divest Equity's system of agency regulation of the statutory exemption. Relying on *Musicians v. Carroll*, 391 U.S. 99, 88 S.Ct. 1562, 20 L.Ed.2d 460, the court concluded that the agents were themselves a "labor group," because of their substantial "economic inter-relationship" with Equity, under which "the union [could] not eliminate wage competition among its members without regulation of the fees of the agents." 622 F.2d, at 650, 651. Accordingly, since the elimination of wage competition is plainly within the area of a union's legitimate self-interest, the court concluded that the exemption was applicable.

After deciding that the central feature of Equity's franchising system—the union's exaction of an agreement by agents not to charge commissions on certain types of work—was immune from antitrust challenge, the Court of Appeals turned to the petitioners' challenge of the franchise fees exacted from agents. Equity had argued that the fees were necessary to meet its expenses in administering the franchise system, but no evidence was presented at trial to show that the costs justified the fees actually levied. The Court of Appeals suggested that if the exactions exceeded the true costs, they could not legally be collected, as such exactions would be unconnected with any of the goals of national labor policy that justify the labor antitrust exemption. Despite the lack of any cost evidence at trial, however, the appellate court reasoned that the fees were sufficiently low that a remand to the District Court on this point "would not serve any useful purpose." *Id.*, at 651.

II

A

Labor unions are lawful combinations that serve the collective interests of workers, but they also possess the power to control the character of competition in an industry. Accordingly, there is an inherent tension between national antitrust policy, which seeks to maximize competition, and national labor policy, which encourages cooperation among workers to improve the conditions of employment. In the years immediately following passage of the Sherman Act, courts enjoined strikes as unlawful restraints of trade when a union's conduct or objectives were deemed "socially or economically harmful." *Duplex Printing Press Co. v. Deering*, 254 U.S. 443, 485, 41 S.Ct. 172, 183, 65 L.Ed. 349 (Brandeis, J., dissenting). In response to these practices, Congress acted, first in the Clayton Act, 38 Stat. 731, and later in the Norris-LaGuardia Act, 47 Stat. 70, to immunize labor unions and labor disputes from challenge under the Sherman Act.

Section 6 of the Clayton Act, 15 U.S.C. § 17, declares that human labor "is not a commodity or article of commerce," and immunizes from antitrust liability labor organizations and their members "lawfully carrying out" their "legitimate object[ives]." Section 20 of the Act prohibits injunctions against specified employee activities, such as strikes and boycotts, that are undertaken in the employees' self-interest and that occur in the course of disputes "concerning terms or conditions of employment," and states that none of the specified acts can be "held to be [a] violatio[n] of any law of the United States." 29 U.S.C. § 52. This protection is re-emphasized and expanded in the Norris-LaGuardia Act, which prohibits federal-court injunctions against single or organized employees engaged in enumerated activities, and specifically forbids such injunctions notwithstanding the claim of an unlawful combination or conspiracy. While the Norris-LaGuardia Act's bar of federal-court labor injunctions is not explicitly phrased as an exemption from the antitrust laws, it has been interpreted broadly as a statement of congressional policy that the courts must not use the antitrust laws as a vehicle to interfere in labor disputes.

In *United States v. Hutcheson*, 312 U.S. 219, 61 S.Ct. 463, 85 L.Ed. 788, the Court held that labor unions acting in their self-interest and not in combination with nonlabor groups enjoy a statutory exemption from Sherman Act liability...

The Court explained that this exemption derives not only from the Clayton Act, but also from the Norris-LaGuardia Act, particularly its definition of a "labor dispute," see n. 14, *supra*, in which Congress "reasserted the original purpose of the Clayton Act by infusing into it the immunized trade union activities as redefined by the later Act." 312 U.S., at 236, 61 S.Ct., at 468. Thus under *Hutcheson*, no federal injunction may issue over a "labor dispute," and

"§ 20 [of the Clayton Act] removes all such allowable conduct from the taint of being a 'violation of any law of the United States,' including the Sherman [Act]." *Ibid.*

The statutory exemption does not apply when a union combines with a "non-labor group." *Hutcheson, supra,* at 232, 61 S.Ct., at 466. Accordingly, antitrust immunity is forfeited when a union combines with one or more employers in an effort to restrain trade. In *Allen Bradley Co. v. Electrical Workers,* 325 U.S. 797, 65 S.Ct. 1533, 89 L.Ed. 1939, for example, the Court held that a union had violated the Sherman Act when it combined with manufacturers and contractors to erect a sheltered local business market in order "to bar all other business men from [the market], and to charge the public prices above a competitive level." *Id.,* at 809, 65 S.Ct., at 1539. The Court indicated that the union efforts would, standing alone, be exempt from antitrust liability, *ibid.,* but because the union had not acted unilaterally, the exemption was denied. Congress "intended to outlaw business monopolies. A business monopoly is no less such because a union participates, and such participation is a violation of the Act." *Id.,* at 811, 65 S.Ct., at 1540.

B

The Court of Appeals properly recognized that the threshold issue was to determine whether or not Equity's franchising of agents involved any combination between Equity and any "non-labor groups," or persons who are not "parties to a labor dispute." 622 F.2d, at 649 (quoting *Hutcheson,* 312 U.S., at 232, 61 S.Ct., at 466). And the court's conclusion that the trial court had not been clearly erroneous in its finding that there was no combination between Equity and the theatrical producers to create or maintain the franchise system is amply supported by the record.

The more difficult problem is whether the combination between Equity and the agents who agreed to become franchised was a combination with a "nonlabor group." The answer to this question is best understood in light of *Musicians v. Carroll,* 391 U.S. 99, 88 S.Ct. 1562, 20 L.Ed.2d 460. There, four orchestra leaders, members of the American Federation of Musicians, brought an action based on the Sherman Act challenging the union's unilateral system of regulating "club dates," or one-time musical engagements. These regulations, *inter alia,* enforced a closed shop; required orchestra leaders to engage a minimum number of "sidemen," or instrumentalists; prescribed minimum prices for local engagements; prescribed higher minimum prices for traveling orchestras; and permitted leaders to deal only with booking agents licensed by the union.

Without disturbing the finding of the Court of Appeals that the orchestra leaders were employers and independent contractors, the Court concluded that they were nonetheless a "labor group" and parties to a "labor dispute" within the meaning of the Norris-LaGuardia Act, and thus that their involvement in the union regulatory scheme was not an unlawful combination between "labor" and "nonlabor" groups. The Court agreed with the trial court that the applicable test was whether there was "job or wage competition or some other economic interrelationship affecting legitimate union interests between the union members and the independent contractors." *Id.*, at 106, 88 S.Ct., at 1567.

The Court also upheld the restrictions on booking agents, who were *not* involved in job or wage competition with union members. Accordingly, these restrictions had to meet the "other economic interrelationship" branch of the disjunctive test quoted above. And the test was met because those restrictions were " 'at least as intimately bound up with the subject of wages' ... as the price floors." *Id.*, at 113, 88 S.Ct., at 1570 (quoting *Teamsters v. Oliver*, 362 U.S. 605, 606, 80 S.Ct. 923, 926, 4 L.Ed.2d 1740). The Court noted that the booking agent restrictions had been adopted, in part, because agents had "charged exorbitant fees, and booked engagements for musicians at wages ... below union scale."

C

The restrictions challenged by the petitioners in this case are very similar to the agent restrictions upheld in the *Carroll* case. The essential features of the regulatory scheme are identical: members are permitted to deal only with agents who have agreed (1) to honor their fiduciary obligations by avoiding conflicts of interest, (2) not to charge excessive commissions, and (3) not to book members for jobs paying less than the union minimum. And as in *Carroll*, Equity's regulation of agents developed in response to abuses by employment agents who occupy a critical role in the relevant labor market. The agent stands directly between union members and jobs, and is in a powerful position to evade the union's negotiated wage structure.

The peculiar structure of the legitimate theater industry, where work is intermittent, where it is customary if not essential for union members to secure employment through agents, and where agents' fees are calculated as a percentage of a member's wage, makes it impossible for the union to defend even the integrity of the minimum wages it has negotiated without regulation of agency fees. The regulations are "brought within the labor exemption [because they are] necessary to assure that scale wages will be paid...." *Carroll*, 391 U.S., at 112, 88 S.Ct., at 1570. They "embody ... a direct frontal attack upon a problem thought to threaten the maintenance of the basic wage structure." *Teamsters v. Oliver*, 358 U.S. 283, 294, 79 S.Ct. 297, 303, 3 L.Ed.2d 312. Agents must, therefore, be considered a "labor group," and their controversy with Equity is plainly a "labor dispute" as defined in the Norris-LaGuardia Act:

"representation of persons in negotiating, fixing, maintaining, changing, or seeking to arrange terms or conditions of employment, regardless of whether or not the disputants stand in the proximate relation of employer and employee." 29 U.S.C. § 113(c).

Agents perform a function—the representation of union members in the sale of their labor—that in most nonentertainment industries is performed exclusively by unions. In effect, Equity's franchise system operates as a substitute for maintaining a hiring hall as the representative of its members seeking employment.

Finally, Equity's regulations are clearly designed to promote the union's legitimate self-interest. *Hutcheson*, 312 U.S., at 232, 61 S.Ct., at 466. In a case such as this, where there is no direct wage or job competition between the union and the group it regulates, the *Carroll* formulation to determine the presence of a nonlabor group—whether there is " 'some ... economic interrelationship affecting legitimate union interests ...,' " 391 U.S., at 106, 88 S.Ct., at 1567 (quoting District Court opinion)—necessarily resolves this issue.

D

The question remains whether the fees that Equity levies upon the agents who apply for franchises are a permissible component of the exempt regulatory system. We have concluded that Equity's justification for these fees is inadequate. Conceding that *Carroll* did not sanction union extraction of franchise fees from agents, Equity suggests, only in the most general terms, that the fees are somehow related to the basic purposes of its regulations: elimination of wage competition, upholding of the union wage scale, and promotion of fair access to jobs. But even assuming that the fees no more than cover the costs of administering the regulatory system, this is simply another way of saying that without the fees, the union's regulatory efforts would not be subsidized—and that the dues of Equity's members would perhaps have to be increased to offset the loss of a general revenue source. If Equity did not impose these franchise fees upon the agents, there is no reason to believe that any of its legitimate interests would be affected.

III

For the reasons stated, the judgment of the Court of Appeals is affirmed in part and reversed in part, and the case is remanded for proceedings consistent with this opinion.

It is so ordered.

Justice BRENNAN, with whom THE CHIEF JUSTICE and Justice MARSHALL join, concurring in part and dissenting in part.

RICHARD LANE v. MERCURY RECORD CORPORATION, APPELLANT
Court of Appeals of New York
Nov. 22, 1966
18 N.Y.2d 889

Appeal, by permission of the Appellate Division of the Supreme Court in the First Judicial Department, from an order of said court, entered October 13, 1964, which, without prejudice to defendant's moving for summary judgment, unanimously affirmed an order of the Supreme Court at Special Term (Thomas Dickens, J.), entered in New York County, denying a motion to dismiss the complaint for failure to state a cause of action. The original plaintiff, Dinah Washington, died while the appeal was pending in the Appellate Division and, by order of Special Term, Richard Lane, the administrator of her estate, was substituted as party plaintiff and the title of the action was amended accordingly. Dinah Washington, a vocalist and recording artist, sought to compel defendant, a record company, to account for all sales and moneys from the sales of phonograph records made by her and to pay her all moneys shown by said account to be due to her. In her complaint she alleged that, in 1951, 1954 and 1957, she and defendant had entered into agreements whereby defendant retained her services for the recording of phonograph records: that she had performed her part of said agreements; that, pursuant to them, defendant had agreed to account to her, semiannually, for all moneys received by it on account of the sales of the phonograph records and to pay her royalties thereon; that, from 1951 to the date of the complaint, defendant had sold large quantities of said records and, upon information and belief, had received substantial sums from the sales, of which a large portion had not been accounted for or paid; that she was completely lacking knowledge of the number of sales made and the true amount of royalties due thereon, and that, notwithstanding her demand therefor, defendant had refused to account to her. In denying the motion to dismiss for insufficiency, Special Term found that the complaint stated a cause of action for equitable relief. The Appellate Division stated that it was not necessary to pass upon the issue of whether the complaint was sufficient to maintain an action for equitable relief since the adoption of CPLR had eliminated the distinctions which had previously impeded the effective merger of equity and law actions and which were a result of fear that a complaint seeking only equitable relief would deprive a defendant of the right to a jury trial if it developed a plaintiff was only entitled to money damages; that this element of possible prejudice was eliminated by CPLR 4103 which gave to a defendant in such a situation the opportunity to demand a jury trial; that the present complaint clearly gave notice of the transactions intended to be proved and contained the material elements of a cause of action for royalties under a contract to make recordings for defendant, and that, accordingly, it was sufficient under the provisions of CPLR 3013 and 3026. In the Court of Appeals defendant argued that the complaint was insufficient under the law which controlled prior to CPLR; that, since the action had been commenced and defendant's motion to dismiss had been determined by Special Term prior to September 1, 1963, the effective date of CPLR, the Appellate Division erred in applying its liberalizing provisions to sustain the complaint, and that such a retroactive application was prejudicial to defendant's rights. The following question was certified by the Appellate Division: "Was the order of this Court filed October 13, 1964, properly made?"...

Order affirmed, with costs. Question certified answered in the affirmative. No opinion.

Concur: Chief Judge DESMOND and Judges FULD, VAN VOORHIS, BURKE, SCILEPPI, BERGAN and KEATING.

BRAD WAISBREN v. PEPPERCORN PRODUCTIONS, INC.
Court of Appeal, Second District, Division I, California
Dec. 20, 1995
41 Cal.App.4th 246, 48 Cal.Rptr.2d 437

In the entertainment industry, talent agents and personal managers perform valuable services for their clients. Talent agents, who seek to procure employment for artists, must be licensed under the Talent Agencies Act (Lab. Code, §§ 1700-1700.47). In contrast, personal managers, who advise and direct artists in the development of their careers, are not subject to any licensing requirements.

This appeal presents the question of whether a personal manager must be licensed under the Talent Agencies Act if he devotes an incidental portion of his business to the function of a talent agent-procuring employment for an artist. We conclude that he must be so licensed.

Background

Defendant Peppercorn Productions, Inc. (Peppercorn) is a California corporation specializing in the design and creation of puppets for use in the entertainment industry and advertising media. Peppercorn has also been involved in producing various television projects. Defendants David Pavelonis and Terrie Pavelonis are officers of Peppercorn.

In 1982, plaintiff Brad Waisbren agreed to promote Peppercorn. From 1982 through 1988, he performed numerous services for the company pursuant to an oral agreement. Among other things, Waisbren assisted in project development, managed certain business affairs, supervised client relations and publicity, performed casting duties, advised Peppercorn regarding the selection of artistic talent, coordinated production, and handled office functions, such as the hiring and firing of personnel. Occasionally, Waisbren procured employment for Peppercorn, but his efforts in that regard were incidental to his other responsibilities. For his services, Waisbren was to receive 15 percent of Peppercorn's profits.

In 1988, Peppercorn terminated its relationship with Waisbren. In 1990, he filed suit against defendants, alleging that they had not paid him in accordance with the parties' agreement. By way of a second amended complaint filed in 1991, Waisbren alleged six causes of action, all of which sought relief based on an alleged breach of the agreement.

In March 1994, defendants moved for summary judgment on the ground that the parties' agreement was void because Waisbren had performed the duties of a talent agent—by procuring employment for Peppercorn—without first obtaining the necessary license under the Talent Agencies Act. In opposing summary judgment, Waisbren admitted that he had no such license. However, he argued that a license was unnecessary since his procurement activities were minimal and merely incidental to his other responsibilities. In May 1994, the trial court granted defendants' summary judgment motion. Waisbren filed a timely appeal from the judgment.

Discussion

Summary judgment is appropriate if all the papers submitted show that there is no triable issue as to any material fact and that the moving party is entitled to judgment as a matter of law. (Code Civ. Proc., § 437c, subd. (c).)...

With these principles in mind, we turn first to the question of whether Waisbren had to be licensed as a talent agent, even though his efforts to procure employment for Peppercorn were minimal or incidental in relation to his other activities. Finding that a license was necessary, we then examine whether the trial court applied the proper remedy for Waisbren's unlicensed conduct (i.e., declaring the parties' agreement void and precluding Waisbren from seeking any recovery under it).

A. *The Licensing Scheme*

The Talent Agencies Act (the Act) provides that "[n]o person shall engage in or carry on the occupation of a talent agency without first procuring a license therefor from the Labor Commissioner." (Lab. Code, § 1700.5.) A "talent agency" is "a person or corporation who engages in the occupation of procuring, offering, promising, or attempting to procure employment or engagements for an artist or artists." (*Id.* § 1700.4, subd. (a).) An "artist," in turn, includes a broad spectrum of persons and entities working in the entertainment field.

Unlike a talent agent, a "personal manager" is not covered by the Act or any other statutory licensing scheme

1. *The Plain Meaning of the Act*

In construing the provisions of the Act, our goal is to ascertain and effectuate legislative intent. (*Burden v. Snowden* (1992) 2 Cal.4th 556, 562 [7 Cal.Rptr.2d 531, 828 P.2d 672].) In determining that intent, we look first to the language of the statute, giving effect to its plain meaning. (*Ibid.*)

The Act applies only if a person engages in the "occupation" of procuring employment for an artist. (Lab. Code, §§ 1700.4, subd. (a), 1700.5.) Waisbren contends that because "occupation" is defined as "the *principal* business of one's life" (see Webster's Third New Internat. Dict. (1981) p. 1560, col. 3, italics added), a license is not needed unless a person's principal responsibilities involve procuring employment for an artist. We disagree.

By limiting the concept of "occupation" to one's "principal" business endeavor, Waisbren ignores the possibility that a person can have more than one job. Plainly, an individual can be engaged in an "occupation" even if he does not spend most of his time in that pursuit. Moreover, Waisbren's argument rests on only one definition of "occupation." That term also means "a craft, trade, profession or other means of earning a living." (Webster's Third New Internat. Dict., *supra*, p. 1560, col. 3.) Further, "occupation" is synonymous with "employment" (*ibid.*), which includes "temporary or occasional work or service for pay" (*id.* at p. 743, col. 3). As these additional definitions make clear, a person can hold a particular "occupation" even if it is not his principal line of work. Thus, the Act is entirely consistent with the concept of dual occupations-for example, being a personal manager *and* a talent agent.

2. *The Remedial Purpose of the Act*

"The Act is a remedial statute. Statutes such as the Act are designed to correct abuses that have long been recognized and which have been the subject of both legislative action and judicial decision.... Such statutes are enacted for the protection of those seeking employment [i.e., the artists]." (*Buchwald v. Superior Court* (1967) 254 Cal.App.2d 347, 350-351 [62 Cal.Rptr. 364], citation omitted.)[7] Consequently, the Act should be liberally construed to promote the general object sought to be accomplished; it should "not [be] construed within narrow limits of the letter of the law."... To ensure the personal, professional, and financial welfare of artists, the Act strictly regulates a talent agent's conduct.

The statutory goal of protecting artists would be defeated if the Act applied only where a personal manager spends a significant part of his workday pursuing employment for artists. The fact that an unlicensed manager may devote an "incidental" portion of his time to procurement activities would be of little consolation to the client who falls victim to a violation of the Act. As a result, the licensing scheme contemplates that the "occasional talent agent," like the full-time agent, is subject to regulatory control.

We refuse to believe that the Legislature intended to exempt a personal manager from the Act-thereby allowing violations to go unremedied-unless his procurement efforts cross some nebulous threshold from "incidental" to "principal." Such a standard is so vague as to be unworkable and would undermine the purpose of the Act.

3. *The Labor Commissioner's Interpretation of the Act*

The Labor Commissioner, who is statutorily charged with enforcing the Act (Lab. Code, § 1700.44, subd. (a)), has long taken the position that a license is required for incidental procurement activities.

4. *Recent Legislative Action: The California Entertainment Commission*

Significantly, the Legislature has adopted the view that a license is required for incidental procurement activities...

Although the Commission concluded that the Act should remain unchanged with respect to requiring a license for any procurement activities (incidental or otherwise), the Commission did recommend statutory changes on other matters. (See Report at pp. 22-34.) In response, the Legislature adopted all of the Commission's recommendations, and the Governor signed them into law. (See Stats. 1986, ch. 488, §§ 1-19, pp. 1804-1808; 3d reading of Assem. Bill No. 3649 as amended Apr. 15, 1986 (1985-1986 Reg. Sess.) p. 3 ["This Bill is the result of a one and one-half year study conducted by the California Entertainment Commission"]; *Regulation of Attorneys, op. cit. supra,* 80 Cal.L.Rev. at p. 495 [the Legislature and Governor adopted the Commission's recommendations with some minor alterations in language]; *The Regulation of Artist Representation, op. cit. supra,* 8 Loy. Ent. L.J. at p. 66 [the Legislature codified the Commission's Report in the Act].) In accordance with the Commission's advice, the Legislature did not alter the requirement of a license for persons who occasionally procure employment for artists.

By creating the Commission, accepting the Report, and codifying the Commission's recommendations in the Act, the Legislature approved the Commission's view that "[e]xceptions in the nature of incidental, occasional or infrequent activities relating in any way to procuring employment for an artist cannot be permitted: one either is, or is not, licensed as a talent agent ...." (Report at p. 11.) This legislative approval extends to the Commission's finding that the Act imposes a *total* prohibition on the procurement efforts of unlicensed persons. (*Ibid.*) Given the Legislature's wholesale endorsement of the Report, we conclude, as did the Commission, that the Act requires a license to engage in *any* procurement activities. (Cf. *Harris v. Capital Growth Investors XIV* (1991) 52 Cal.3d 1142, 1155-1156 [278 Cal.Rptr. 614, 805 P.2d 873] [in amending statute without altering portion previously construed by the courts, Legislature acquiesces in previous judicial construction].)

5. *The Act's Limited Exception for Unlicensed Persons*

The Act specifically provides that an unlicensed person may nevertheless participate in negotiating an employment contract for an artist, provided he does so "in conjunction with, and at the request of, a licensed talent agency." (Lab. Code, § 1700.44, subd. (d).)...

6. *Prior Judicial Construction of the Act*

In *Buchwald v. Superior Court, supra,* 254 Cal.App.2d 347, a dispute arose between the members of a musical group (known as the "Jefferson Airplane") and their personal manager. The parties' written agreement stated that the manager had not agreed to obtain employment for the group and that he was not authorized to do so. (*Id.* at p. 351.) The group alleged that, despite the contractual language, the manager had in fact procured bookings for them. In seeking to avoid the licensing requirement, the manager argued that the written agreement established, as a matter of law, that he was not subject to statutory regulation.

Given *Wachs's* recognition of the limited nature of the issue before it, we regard as dicta the court's interpretation of the term "occupation" and its statement that the Act does not apply unless a person's procurement function is significant. Because the *Wachs* dicta is contrary to the Act's language and purpose, we decline to follow it. In that regard, we note that *Wachs* applied an overly narrow concept of "occupation" and did not consider the remedial purpose of the Act, the decisions of the Labor Commissioner, or the Legislature's adoption of the view (as expressed in the California Entertainment Commission's Report) that a license is necessary for incidental procurement activities. Thus, we conclude that the *Wachs* dicta is incorrect to the extent it indicates that a license is required only where a person's procurement efforts are "significant."

B. *The Sanction for Unlicensed Work...*

Waisbren nevertheless contends that declaring the parties' agreement to be void is too severe a penalty, especially in light of the fact that the Act does not contain criminal penalties for licensing violations. We disagree. Nothing in the case law requires the existence of criminal penalties as a prerequisite to declaring an illegal contract to be void. Moreover, the legislative history of the Act directly contradicts Waisbren's contention. In examining the licensing issue, the California Entertainment Commission specifically addressed the question of whether criminal sanctions should be imposed for violations of the Act. (Report at pp. 15-18.) It recommended that the Legislature not enact criminal penalties, in part because "the most effective weapon for assuring compliance with the Act is the power ... to ... declare any contract entered into between the parties void from the inception." (*Id.* at p. 17.) By following the Commission's advice and not enacting criminal penalties, the Legislature approved the remedy of declaring agreements void if they violate the Act. Thus, an agreement that violates the licensing requirement is illegal and unenforceable despite the lack of criminal sanctions...

Because all of Waisbren's causes of action are based on his illegal agreement or business arrangement with Peppercorn, he cannot establish his case against defendants "otherwise than through the medium of an illegal transaction to which [he] [was] a party." (*Wong v. Tenneco, Inc., supra,* 39 Cal.3d at p. 135, italics omitted.) Accordingly, the trial court properly disposed of the complaint in its entirety.

C. *The Propriety of Summary Judgment*

Waisbren argues that summary judgment was improper because there were disputed issues of fact as to whether he was a partner and coproducer with Peppercorn. According to Waisbren, the Act does not apply to an artist's "partner" or "co-producer." Regardless of the merits of Waisbren's interpretation of the Act-on which we express no opinion-he did not properly raise this argument in opposing summary judgment. His opposition papers did not make any such legal argument, and his separate statement (see Code Civ. Proc., § 437c, subd. (b)) did not set forth facts in support of that argument. Consequently, he waived this basis for opposing summary judgment...

Finally, Waisbren contends that the trial court should have continued the hearing on the summary judgment motion to allow him time to engage in additional discovery. This contention is without merit... The next case, Doe v. Capital Cities, 50 Cal.App.4th 1038, 58 Cal.Rptr. 2d 122 (1996), seques from the allegedly sleazy artists' manager to the definitionally sleazy "casting couch." The court held that the casting director's actions of drugging, raping, and gang raping an actor were sufficiently work-related so as to render the casting director's employer, and the movie director also liable under theories of respondeat superior and vicarious liability. Is there a difference between the actions of an artists' manager and this casting director. Should both have a fiduciary (trust) relationship to the artist?

JOHN DOE v. CAPITAL CITIES
No. B091857
Court of Appeal, Second District, Division 4, California
Nov. 8, 1996
50 Cal.App.4th 1038, 58 Cal.Rptr.2d 122

An aspiring actor is first drugged and then gang-raped by a casting director and four other men one Sunday at the casting director's home. Can the actor successfully allege causes of action for sexual harassment and negligent hiring against the casting director's employers? The trial court ruled against the actor, sustaining a demurrer without leave to amend. On this appeal, we analyze the allegations in the actor's second amended complaint in light of pertinent statutory and decisional law and conclude that he has adequately pled a cause of action for sexual harassment but that the allegations for negligent hiring are insufficient as a matter of law.

Factual Background

The Facts

The operative pleading is the second amended complaint. In reviewing the sufficiency of that pleading, we treat the demurrer as " 'admitting all material facts properly pleaded.' " (*Blank v. Kirwan* (1985) 39 Cal.3d 311, 318 [216 Cal.Rptr. 718, 703 P.2d 58].) Those core facts are as follows. Plaintiff is an aspiring actor. Defendant Jerry Marshall (Marshall) is an associate director of casting and talent of defendant ABC Entertainment, a division of American Broadcasting Companies, Inc., which, in turn, is a subsidiary of defendant Capital Cities. The business defendants will collectively be referred to as ABC.

Plaintiff met Marshall at a movie screening at the Directors Guild in July 1993. Marshall told plaintiff he worked as a casting director at ABC and gave plaintiff his business card. Marshall told plaintiff that he " 'had a great look' " and that ABC was developing programs that could be suitable for plaintiff. Marshall invited plaintiff to an interview at his office. The next day, plaintiff went to Marshall's office at the ABC Entertainment Center in Century City and read for him. Marshall responded positively to plaintiff's audition and introduced plaintiff to Marshall's supervisor who was likewise impressed.

In the following weeks, Marshall "spent several hours a day on most days ... working with [plaintiff], [efforts] which ... Marshall said[] would lead to an employment contract between ... ABC and [plaintiff]." These efforts included auditions, a taping, meetings with other entertainment industry executives, and attempts to find an agent and a publicist for plaintiff. When instructing plaintiff to perform particular tasks, Marshall "repeatedly told [him]: 'I'm your Manager at ABC.' " On several occasions, Marshall told plaintiff that he would be introduced as a new ABC star at an annual event held at the Page Museum on September 18, 1993. Based on all of these circumstances, plaintiff "fully believed that ... Marshall would hire him for an acting position in an ABC Entertainment production ...."

On Saturday, August 14, 1993, plaintiff spent the day at Marshall's office preparing for his final auditions. When they finished working, Marshall told plaintiff that "they would be meeting ABC executives for dinner that evening." "After dinner on August 14, 1993, ... Marshall advised [plaintiff] that he 'had a brunch to go to in the morning,' and to be at ... Marshall's home at 8:00 a.m. [the next morning]."

During the morning of Sunday, August 15, 1993, plaintiff went to Marshall's home. He did so "expecting to attend a meeting where he would meet entertainment industry executives representing ABC shows and/or for the purposes [of promoting his acting career]." Marshall gave plaintiff a glass of tea. Plaintiff drank the tea which, unknown to him, contained a drug. When plaintiff awoke, he was bound and tied. He was given multiple injections of an unknown drug and was beaten and gang-raped by Marshall and four named codefendants, none of whom is alleged to have any connection with ABC. At one point when plaintiff was untied, he attempted to escape but Marshall and a codefendant forcibly took him back into the house and again injected him with a drug. Marshall ultimately drove plaintiff in plaintiff's car to Beverly Hills where he abandoned him. Plaintiff was subsequently discovered by the police.

The ordeal caused plaintiff severe emotional distress as well as a temporary memory loss for several months.

In late October 1993, Marshall and others grabbed plaintiff outside of his home and stabbed him. Plaintiff reported the stabbing to the police and to ABC. In the following six months, the "defendants" physically harassed plaintiff, threatened him by phone and by writing, and poisoned his dogs.

In July 1994, plaintiff filed a complaint with the California Department of Fair Employment and Housing, alleging unlawful employment practices, including sexual harassment. (Plaintiff's brief asserts that Marshall and the other four assailants are being criminally prosecuted.)

The Causes of Action

Based upon the above allegations, plaintiff filed a complaint alleging 10 causes of action. Against Marshall and ABC, he alleged causes of action for statutory and common law sexual harassment, retaliation for opposing sexual harassment, and failure to prevent sexual harassment and retaliation. Against Marshall, ABC, and the other named individual defendants (see fn. 2, *ante*), he alleged causes of action for assault, battery, conspiracy to commit sexual assault, false imprisonment, and intentional infliction of emotional distress. Against ABC, he alleged a cause of action for negligent hiring, training, and supervision. Lastly, against Marshall and the other named individual defendants, he alleged a cause of action for defamation based upon the claim that they falsely told others that he had consented to the sexual assault.

The Trial Court's Ruling

This appeal only involves the claims against ABC. After ABC successfully demurred to all causes of action alleged against it, ABC was dismissed from the case. This appeal by plaintiff, in which he is joined by four amici curiae, follows.

Discussion

A

We begin our discussion by noting the theory of liability this case does *not* expressly involve-vicarious liability or respondeat superior. Plaintiff's second amended complaint had alleged that ABC was vicariously liable for the common law intentional torts (assault, battery, false imprisonment, and intentional infliction of emotional distress) committed by Marshall. ABC demurred on the basis that the torts were not committed in the course and scope of Marshall's employment. The trial court agreed. During the pendency of this case, our Supreme Court clarified the law governing an employer's vicarious liability for sexual assaults. (*Farmers Ins. Group v. County of Santa Clara* (1995) 11 Cal.4th 992 [47 Cal.Rptr.2d 478, 906 P.2d 440] and *Lisa M. v. Henry Mayo Newhall Memorial Hospital* (1995) 12 Cal.4th 291 [48 Cal.Rptr.2d 510, 907 P.2d 358].) As a result of those holdings, which will be analyzed later, plaintiff has abandoned his claims based upon vicarious liability.

Insofar as ABC is concerned, the primary thrust of plaintiff's action is that Marshall sexually harassed him in violation of state law and that pursuant to that statutory scheme, ABC is liable for those actions. Before we analyze the merits of that theory, we set forth the pertinent law.

The California Fair Employment and Housing Act (Gov. Code, § 12900 et seq., hereafter the Act) states that it is an unlawful employment practice for an employer to sexually harass an employee *or an applicant*. (Gov. Code, § 12940, subd. (h).) An applicant is "any individual who otherwise indicates a specific desire to an employer ... to be considered for employment." (Cal. Code Regs., tit. 2, § 7286.5, subd. (h).) ([2]) The Act applies to same gender sexual harassment. (*Matthews v. Superior Court* (1995) 34 Cal.App.4th 598 [40 Cal.Rptr.2d 350]; *Mogilefsky v. Superior Court* (1993) 20 Cal.App.4th 1409 [26 Cal.Rptr.2d 116].)

"California case law recognizes two theories upon which sexual harassment may be alleged. The first is quid pro quo harassment, where a term of employment is conditioned upon submission to unwelcome sexual advances. The second is hostile work environment, where the harassment is sufficiently pervasive so as to alter the conditions of employment and create an abusive work environment. [Citation.]" (*Mogilefsky v. Superior Court, supra,* 20 Cal.App.4th at p. 1414.)

In this case, plaintiff is proceeding upon the second theory. And contrary to what ABC seems to suggest, a violent sexual assault, such as that alleged by plaintiff, can be the basis of such a claim. "Harassment is defined to include physical harassment, such as an assault. (Cal. Code Regs., tit. 2, § 7287.6, subd. (b)(1)(B).)" (*Capitol City Foods, Inc. v. Superior Court* (1992) 5 Cal.App.4th 1042, 1047 [7 Cal.Rptr.2d 418].) Indeed, it is of no legal significance that the extreme and aggravated assault alleged here is criminal because other forms of sexual assault are also criminal and subject to prosecution. In none of the civil actions for sexual discrimination of which we are aware has it been contended that groping and grabbing of another's body is not both a civil and a criminal assault and we cannot fathom why the two claims should be mutually exclusive. "Conduct constituting sexual harassment may violate other laws as well, such as civil laws against slander and defamation criminal and tort laws against battery and rape." (Sexual Harassment in the Workplace (Cont.Ed.Bar 1995) ch. 2, p. 4; see also Lindemann & Kadue, Sexual Harassment in Employment Law (1992) Criminal Law, ch. 16, p. 371 et seq.) The fact that the sexual harassment may also be criminal in no way undermines the potential actionable culpability of an employer.

The crux of the matter is whether under the particular facts of this case, plaintiff can allege that ABC is liable for Marshall's actions. Government Code section 12940, subdivision (h)(1) provides, in pertinent part: "Harassment of an employee or applicant *by an employee other than an agent or supervisor* shall be unlawful if the entity, or its agents or supervisors, knows or should have known of this conduct and fails to take immediate and appropriate corrective action." (Italics added.) This section has been interpreted to mean that the employer is strictly liable for the harassing actions of its supervisors and agents (*Kelly-Zurian v. Wohl Shoe Co.* (1994) 22 Cal.App.4th 397, 415 & 416 [27 Cal.Rptr.2d 457]; *Fisher v. San Pedro Peninsula Hospital* (1989) 214 Cal.App.3d 590, 608, fn. 6 [262 Cal.Rptr. 842]), but that the employer is only liable for harassment by a coworker if the employer knew or should have known of the conduct and failed to take immediate corrective action. Thus, characterizing the employment status of the harasser is very significant. This then takes us to the issue of Marshall's status vis-a-vis ABC.

ABC contends that because plaintiff never explicitly alleged that Marshall was a supervisor or agent, it cannot be strictly liable for Marshall's actions, assuming the other predicates of the claim are present. ABC seems to suggest that Marshall was plaintiff's coworker so that ABC can only be liable if it knew of his conduct and failed to take immediate corrective action. We disagree. Liberally and reasonably construing plaintiff's allegations—as we must do (*Dale v. City of Mountain View* (1976) 55 Cal.App.3d 101, 105 [127 Cal.Rptr. 520])—we find they are sufficient to plead Marshall's status as an agent.

Plaintiff's complaint alleges that Marshall was an associate director of casting at ABC; that ABC was developing television shows that could be suitable for plaintiff; that pursuant to Marshall's request, plaintiff interviewed with him for an acting position; that Marshall introduced him to his supervisor; that Marshall told him that he was his manager; and that Marshall gave plaintiff many directions in preparation for auditions.

These allegations demonstrate that Marshall was an agent of ABC in regard to his relationship with plaintiff...

However, a conclusion that plaintiff has sufficiently pled Marshall's status as an agent so as to trigger ABC's potential strict liability for Marshall's actions does not dispose of the matter. A significant issue is presented by the fact that the sexual assault occurred on a Sunday at Marshall's home.

The relationship between the location of the act of sexual harassment and the employer's liability is addressed in a regulation promulgated under the Act. It states: "In view of the common law theory of respondeat superior and its codification in California Civil Code Section 2338, an employer ... shall be liable for the discriminatory actions of its supervisors, managers or agents committed within the scope of their employment or relationship with the covered entity ...." (Cal. Code Regs., tit. 2, § 7286.6, subd. (b).)

Turning to plaintiff's allegations, we find them adequate as a matter of law to hold ABC liable for Marshall's actions. Simply stated, Marshall's alleged conduct was sufficiently work-related so as to render ABC liable. It is not significant that plaintiff never alleged that Marshall told him that the Sunday brunch was an ABC-sponsored event or even a work-related event. Plaintiff alleged that Marshall regularly spent several hours a day with him, arranged auditions and meetings with agents and publicists, and invited him to dine with him to meet with entertainment executives for the purpose of enhancing plaintiff's opportunities. Plaintiff's allegations reveal a pattern of conduct by which plaintiff was essentially at Marshall's beck and call. Indeed, it is alleged that Marshall declared he was plaintiff's "Manager at ABC."

When Marshall advised plaintiff that Marshall had a brunch engagement the next morning and to be at his home at 8 a.m., it is hardly surprising that plaintiff would accede to this request. Because the relationship was driven by Marshall's demonstrable positive interest in furthering plaintiff's career, it is not farfetched that plaintiff believed his attendance had something to do with advancing his ambition to obtain employment as an actor. After all, the request that plaintiff attend the brunch was made at a dinner that was supposedly arranged by Marshall for the purpose of having plaintiff meet ABC executives.

Additionally, it is not significant that plaintiff is not an ABC employee. The Act's expansion of protection to applicants demonstrates an intent to protect those who could be subject to sexual harassment in the course of seeking work. Presumably such conduct generally occurs in the workplace, but not necessarily. Two of the amici curiae-the Screen Actors Guild, Inc., and the American Federation of Television and Radio Artists, AFL-CIO-make the cogent point that the hiring process for actors and actresses does not conform to the limited and traditional application process common place for most job applicants. As pleaded here, casting directors not only identify talent, but also develop and promote prospective applicants. Consequently, the circumstances germane to this case are not necessarily limited to a fixed site. Here, as plaintiff has alleged, the application process is far from static. All that is required is a showing of a legally sufficient nexus between the employment relationship and the act of harassment. That is, as long as the harassment occurs in a work-related context, the employer is liable. (*Capitol City Foods, Inc. v. Superior Court, supra*, 5 Cal.App.4th at p. 1045.) Plaintiff's presence at Marshall's home on August 15th was, at least for pleading purposes, a sufficient nexus to show that the assault and rape occurred in a work-related context.

Our conclusion is not inconsistent with the only published case which has addressed the issue of the employer's liability for a supervisor's sexual harassment conducted while off duty and not at the workplace. In *Capitol City Foods, Inc. v. Superior Court, supra*, 5 Cal.App.4th 1042, the case reached the Court of Appeal via a writ petition after the trial court had denied the employer's summary judgment motion. The evidence established that the plaintiff was an employee at a Burger King where Vernon Johnson was her supervisor. On January 29, the plaintiff and a coworker asked Johnson to go out with them after work. Johnson was unable to do so that evening so he and plaintiff made plans to go out January 31. Both believed the coworker would join them. On January 31, Johnson picked plaintiff up at a grocery store. Plaintiff was wearing her Burger King uniform because, unbeknownst to Johnson, Dan Singh had changed her schedule and she was now assigned to work later that evening. Johnson telephoned Burger King and told Singh that he should not have changed plaintiff's schedule without his (Johnson's) approval "and that if [plaintiff] wanted to work she would come in late." (*Id.* at p. 1044.) Later that evening, Johnson and plaintiff had sexual intercourse. Plaintiff claimed Johnson raped her; Johnson asserted it was consensual. The next day, plaintiff quit after she told her manager what had happened. Plaintiff sued, inter alia, for sexual harassment, asserting that Johnson compelled her to accompany him on January 31 and that he thereafter raped her. Based upon this record, the trial court ruled in the employer's favor on all the causes of action except the statutory claim for sexual harassment. The employer petitioned the Court of Appeal to overturn that ruling.

The issue in the writ petition was whether the evidence established a triable issue of fact of a sufficient nexus between the supervisor's conduct and his employment to hold the employer liable for the sexual harassment. The Court of Appeal answered the question in the negative. It wrote: "Plaintiff contends the nexus between Johnson's conduct and employment is 'overwhelming.' She argues 'but for' his position as her supervisor, the rape would not have occurred. Even assuming this speculative assertion were true, plaintiff must establish Johnson was acting within the scope of his employment or as defendant's agent. To show a sufficient nexus plaintiff points to the following: the 'date' was arranged in Johnson's office; when he picked her up she was in her Burger King uniform; and he exercised his authority to excuse her from work so she could be with him, facilitating the rape. This argument overlooks the fact that defendant conclusively refuted the allegation that Johnson forced plaintiff to accompany him or coerced her in any way prior to entering his bedroom. In light of this refutation Johnson's phone call to Burger King to excuse [the plaintiff] from work is insufficient to support an inference that Johnson was acting within the scope of his employment or as the agent of defendant." (5 Cal.App.4th at pp. 1049-1050.)

The facts in *Capitol City Foods, Inc. v. Superior Court*, *supra*, are not analogous to those alleged here. In the former matter, there was no evidence that the supervisor exercised his authority to compel the plaintiff to accompany him to the place in which the assault occurred. In fact, that case involved a non-work-related date, the impetus for which came from the plaintiff and a coworker who asked the supervisor (Johnson) to join them for a drink after closing. Because Johnson could not join the two, he and plaintiff arranged to meet on a different day, with each believing the coworker would also join them. Although the plaintiff was a trainee under Johnson's supervision, her place of employment was a fast-food restaurant and there was nothing about her date with Johnson to suggest that it took place in a work-related context. In short, *Capitol City Foods, Inc.*, *supra*, does not involve anything like the pattern of conduct alleged here where the applicant's admission to employment requires continuous participation in a variety of activities at various locations in pursuit of his acting career.

We therefore conclude that plaintiff's allegations in the first cause of action, pled pursuant to Government Code section 12940, subdivision (h), are adequate to establish a statutory claim for sexual harassment. It therefore follows that his fifth cause of action, labeled "Sexual Harassment in Violation of Public Policy," is legally sufficient because one of the alleged sources of public policy is Government Code section 12940.

In summary, plaintiff is an "applicant," casting director Marshall is an "agent" of ABC, and Marshall's conduct did subject plaintiff to sexual harassment in a work-related context pursuant to Government Code section 12940, subdivision (h). Our reading of the Act strictly imposes liability on ABC without regard to what ABC knew or should have known about Marshall's propensities if plaintiff can prove what he has alleged in his first and fifth causes of action. Plaintiff's other causes of action are inadequate as a matter of law for the reasons stated in the remainder of this opinion.

B

The second cause of action is labeled "Retaliation for Opposition to Sexual Harassment in Violation of" Government Code section 12940, subdivision (f)...

The third cause of action is labeled "Failure to Prevent Sexual Harassment and Retaliation" in violation of Government Code section 12940, subdivision (i). That section makes it unlawful for "an employer ... to fail to take all reasonable steps necessary to prevent discrimination and harassment from occurring." The allegations are insufficient because, as we shall now explain, plaintiff has failed to allege sufficient facts to show ABC's prior knowledge of Marshall's propensity to engage in this particular form of sexual harassment.

The eighth cause of action is labeled "Negligent Hiring, Training and/or Supervision." In essence, plaintiff asserts that ABC's negligence in either hiring or supervising Marshall resulted in the sexual assault and on that basis ABC can be held liable. ([8]) California case law recognizes the theory that an employer can be liable to a third person for negligently hiring, supervising, or retaining an unfit employee. (*Evan F. v. Hughson United Methodist Church* (1992) 8 Cal.App.4th 828, 836 [10 Cal.Rptr.2d 748].) Liability is based upon the facts that the employer knew or should have known that hiring the employee created a particular risk or hazard and that particular harm materializes. (*Id.* at pp. 836-837.) This is where plaintiff's complaint flounders.

Plaintiff alleged that ABC knew or should have known that "Marshall engaged in the purchase and use of serious, mind-altering illegal drugs, that defendant Marshall used his position at ABC to gain sexual favors, and that use of a 'casting couch' is common within the entertainment industry." Given the harm that plaintiff suffered-a brutal sexual assault after having been surreptitiously drugged-the pleading allegations are insufficient to allege a cause of action. ABC's knowledge that Marshall personally used "serious mind-altering drugs" does not equate with knowledge that he would surreptitiously use drugs to place a prospective employee into a situation of helplessness before violently assaulting him. Nor does ABC's knowledge that Marshall used his position "to gain sexual favors" have material relevance to this matter. Use of the word "gain" is consistent with the quid pro quo form of sexual harassment but that is not the basis of plaintiff's claim. The "casting couch" allegation suffers from a similar infirmity. That is, knowledge that Marshall used his position of authority to extract or to coerce sexual favors is not knowledge that he would first drug and then attack a potential employee. In the context of negligent hiring, those are qualitatively different situations. In sum, the cornerstone of a negligent hiring theory is the risk that the employee will act in a certain way and the employee does act in that way. Plaintiff has failed to allege those necessary facts.

Disposition

The judgment is reversed to the extent that the trial court sustained without leave to amend the demurrer to the first and fifth causes of action alleged against respondents in the second amended complaint and dismissed those causes of action. In all other respects, the judgment is affirmed. Appellant to recover his costs on appeal.

BARON, J., and ARANDA, J., concurred.

Respondents' petition for review by the Supreme Court was denied February 26, 1997.

QUESTIONS AND DISCUSSION

1. Is entertainment law drastically different than the law of other professions? Are there "similar" casting couches in other industries?

Entertainment has long been viewed as important to the American psyche and sense of well-being. It was the entertainment community that "saved" America from bantruptcy during World War II through war bond drives. Less than ten years later, however, many of these same entertainers were accused of being communists in the McCarthy "Red Scare" Senate hearings of the early 1950s and then blacklisted.

Entertainers are certainly treated differently. The media's coverage, particularly by the paparazzi, makes a personal life difficult if not impossible. Although some entertainers get paid well, their income-generating potential is directly tied to their popularity and media coverage. (As they say, there is no such thing as bad publicity.) But, it's a fact that many athletes are broke after six years.

Should the federal government step in and acknowledge that there is a fiduciary relationship between entertainers and the perception of well-being in the populace? Who are our heroes? Is the answer actors, athletes, pop stars, divas— "celebrities"—and should that be the answer? The acting industry does take care of their own to some extent with their assisted living centers for retired actors. Should this noble endeavor receive federal matching funds? (You certainly won't find nursing homes for retired boxers.)

Burstyn v. Wilson, Ward v. Rock Against Racism, Lacchini v. Scripps-Howard Broadcasting, and H.A. Artists & Associates, Inc. v. Actor's Equity Ass'n, are all U.S. Supreme Court Cases, which is unusual for any industry. And, we will see that there are many more U.S. Supreme Court cases in later chapters, especially in the copyright sections. Most of these cases, which have been edited to save trees, contain lively debate, although history only cares about the winners.

Most entertainment law questions that come to the Supreme Court, usually by certiorari (i.e., the case contains an important federal question and/or the circuits are split), concern federal law—that is, antitrust, copyright, and trademark issues covered by the Constitution or federal statutes. It is no secret that Los Angeles and, to a lesser extent, New York are hubs for where "entertainment law" cases are filed. Should there be an extraordinary particularized court for entertainment concerns? As in drug courts or the Court of Arbitration for Sports (CAS), you could be sure that judges will have a complete knowledge of the industry. But can they be elected? A great majority of entertainment-related corporations are based in Delaware because of their corporation-friendly laws. Many select California as their state of choice for litigation if a conflict arises, mostly because of the level of expertise, friendly laws, and cultural understanding of the entertainment industry there. Should this be made mandatory?

CHAPTER 2
ENTERTAINMENT LAW PRACTICE GENERALLY

The practice of entertainment law is somewhat different from entertainment law in theory. Entertainment law is nearly split between contracts and copyrights, whereas, the *practice* of entertainment law is more contracts and transactional law than any other legal discipline.

Again, we start out with two U.S. Supreme Court cases, Fred Fisher Music Co., Inc. v. M. Witmark & Sons, 318 U.S. 643 (1943) and Stewart v. Abend, 495 U.S. 207 (1990). Both cases look to copyright renewal interests and derivative copyrights. Who gets to drink from the money river? Recently, Bob Marley's heirs sold the Bob Marley brand of legal marijuana for seven figures to the leading legal marijuana purveyor. Genius. (Who wouldn't trust the "I Shot the Sheriff Panama Red Hashish?")

We will later discuss the so-called "Hollywood Handshake" contract. (See the movie *Argo*, Ben Affleck's Academy Award winning film about the C.I.A.'s actual use of a fake science fiction movie that was to be produced in Iran as a means of secretly extracting U.S. Embassy employees cloistered in Canadian Embassy.) The Hollywood Handshake contract is an implied-in fact contract that relies on standards and customs of the movie industry. It is based on reputation, custom, and shared experience.

The United States does not recognize the moral right of artists and creators. The French certainly do. It is all about artistic integrity—or as they say, "Art for art's sake, money for God's sake." In practice, many of the contracts will also deal with copyright and trademarks. Who ever expected that "Dr. Seuss," a.k.a., struggling artist Theodore Seuss Giesel (Geisel v. Poynter Products, Inc. 295 F.Supp. 331 (S.D. N.Y. 1968)), would go viral with *Cat in the Hat*. Note that many of these cases that deal with the practice of entertainment law also deal with celebrities and icons, such as the aforementioned Dr. Seuss, James Stewart (Stewart v. Abend), George Harrison (Abkeo Music Inc. v. Harrisongs Music, Ltd.), Monty Python (Gilliam v. ABC, Inc.), and Matthew McConaughey and Renee Zellweger (Grigson v. Creative Artists, LLC).

FRED FISHER MUSIC CO., INC., ET AL. v. WITMARK & SONS
No. 327
Argued Jan. 14, 15, 1943
Decided April 5, 1943
318 U.S. 643

Mr. Justice FRANKFURTER delivered the opinion of the Court.

This case presents a question never settled before, even though it concerns legislation having a history of more than two hundred years. The question itself can be stated very simply. Under § 23 of the Copyright Act of 1909, 35 Stat. 1075, as amended, 17 U.S.C.A. § 23 a copyright in a musical composition lasts for twenty-eight years from the date of its first publication, and the author can renew the copyright, if he is still living, for a further term of twenty-eight years by filing an application for renewal within a year before the expiration of the first twenty-eight year period. Section 42 of the Act provides that a copyright 'may be assigned by an instrument in writing signed by the proprietor of the copyright.' Concededly, the author can assign the original copyright and, after he has secured it, the renewal copyright as well. The question is—does the Act prevent the author from assigning his interest in the renewal copyright before he has secured it?

This litigation arises from a controversy over the renewal rights in the popular song 'When Irish Eyes Are Smiling'. It was written in 1912 by Ernest R. Ball, Chauncey Olcott, and George Graff, Jr., each of whom was under contract to a firm of music publishers, M. Witmark & Sons. Pursuant to the contracts Witmark on August 12, 1912, applied for and obtained the copyright in the song. On May 19, 1917, Graff and Witmark made a further agreement under which, for the sum of $1600, Graff assigned to Witmark 'all rights, title and interest' in a number of songs, including 'When Irish Eyes Are Smiling'. The contract provided for the conveyance of 'all copyrights and renewals of copyrights and the right to secure all copyrights and renewals of copyrights in the (songs), and any and all rights therein that I (Graff) or my heirs, executors, administrators or next of kin may at any time be entitled to'. To that end Witmark was given an irrevocable power of attorney to execute in Graff's name all documents 'necessary to secure to (Witmark) the renewals and extensions of the copyrights in said compositions and all rights therein for the terms of such renewals and extensions'. In addition, Graff agreed that, 'upon the expiration of the first term of any copyright', he would execute and deliver to Witmark 'all papers necessary in order to secure to it the renewals and extensions of all copyrights in said compositions and all rights therein for the terms of such renewals and extensions'. This agreement was duly recorded in the Copyright Office.

On August 12, 1939, the first day of the twenty-eighth year of the copyright in 'When Irish Eyes Are Smiling', Witmark applied for and registered the renewal copyright in Graff's name. On the same day, exercising its power of attorney under the agreement of May 19, 1917, Witmark also assigned to itself Graff's interest in the renewal. Eleven days later Graff himself applied for and registered the renewal copyright in his own name, and on October 24, 1939, he assigned his renewal interest to another music publishing firm, Fred Fisher Music Co., Inc. Both Graff and Fisher knew of the prior registration of the renewal by Witmark and of the latter's assignment to itself. Relying upon the validity of the assignment made to it on October 24, 1939, and without obtaining permission from Witmark, Fisher published and sold copies of 'When Irish Eyes Are Smiling', representing to the trade that it owned the renewal rights in the song. Witmark thereupon brought this suit to enjoin these activities. The District Court granted a preliminary injunction pendente lite solely upon the ground that there was no statutory bar against an author's assignment of his interest in the renewal before it was secured. 38 F.Supp. 72. The court considered no evidence and made no findings upon the question whether equitable relief should be denied on other grounds, such as inadequacy of consideration and the like. Upon appeal to the Circuit Court of Appeals for the Second Circuit under § 129 of the Judicial Code, 28 U.S.C. § 227, 28 U.S.C.A. § 227, permitting appeals from interlocutory decrees, the order was affirmed. 125 F.2d 949. The Circuit Court of Appeals limited itself, as did the parties before it, to the question of statutory construction, wholly apart from the particular circumstances of the case. The court expressly left open 'other contentions which the parties may wish and be entitled to raise on the merits, including possibly claims of inadequacy of consideration'. 125 F.2d at page 954. The petition for certiorari in this Court stated that the 'sole question is whether * * * an agreement to assign his renewal, made by an author in advance of the twenty-eighth year of the original term of copyright, is valid and enforceable'. Because of the obvious importance of this question of the proper construction of the Copyright Act, we brought the case here. 317 U.S. 611, 63 S.Ct. 63, 87 L.Ed. 496.

Plainly, there is only one question before us—does the Copyright Act nullify an agreement by an author, made during the original copyright term, to assign his renewal? The explicit words of the statute give the author an unqualified right to renew the copyright. No limitations are placed upon the assignability of his interest in the renewal. If we look only to what the Act says, there can be no doubt as to the answer. But each of the parties finds support for its conclusion in the historical background of copyright legislation, and to that we must turn to discover whether Congress meant more than it said.

Anglo-American copyright legislation begins in 1709 with the Statute of 8 Anne, c. 19. That act gave the author and his assigns the exclusive copyright for fourteen years from publication, and after the expiration of such term, if the author was still living, the copyright could be renewed for another fourteen years. The statute did not expressly provide that the author could assign his renewal interest during the original copyright term. But the English courts held that the author's right of renewal, although contingent upon his surviving the original fourteen-year period, could be assigned, and that if he did survive the original term he was bound by the assignment... In this country the copyright laws enacted by the original thirteen states prior to 1789 were based largely upon the Statute of Anne. In 1783 the Continental Congress passed a resolution calling upon the states to adopt copyright legislation for the protection of authors and publishers. The resolution recommended that copyright be given to authors and publishers 'for a certain time, not less than fourteen years from the first publication; and to secure to the said authors, if they shall survive the term first mentioned, and to their executors, administrators and assigns, the copyright of such books for another term of time not less than fourteen years'... In response to the resolution of the Congress, nine of the ten other states enacted copyright legislation. Only Delaware did not adopt a copyright statute. Five states accepted the recommendation of the Congress and followed the Statute of Anne: two copyright terms of fourteen years, the second term contingent upon the author's surviving the first. New Jersey, Acts of the General Assembly (Collins, 1783) c. 21; Pennsylvania, Laws (Bradford, 1784) c. 125; South Carolina, Acts, Ordinances and Resolves (Miller, 1784) 49-51; Candler, Colonial Records of Georgia (1911), vol. XIX, part 2, pp. 485-89; Laws of New York, 1786, c. 54. Four of these, like the earlier Connecticut statute, explicitly provided that the right of renewal could be exercised by the author's heirs and assigns, namely, New Jersey, Pennsylvania, Georgia, and New York. The four remaining states enacted statutes providing for single terms of varying lengths, ranging from fourteen to twenty-one years. New Hampshire Laws (Melcher, 1789) 161-62; Rhode Island, Acts and Resolves (Carter, 1783) 6-7; Virginia, Acts (Dunlap & Hayes, 1785) 8-9; North Carolina, Laws 1785, c. 24.

Exercising the power granted by Article 1, § 8 of the Constitution—'To promote the Progress of Science and useful Arts, by securing for limited Times to Authors and Inventors the exclusive Right to their respective Writings and Discoveries'—the first Congress enacted a copyright statute, the Act of May 31, 1790, 1 Stat. 124. As might have been expected, this Act reflected its historical antecedents. The author was given the copyright for fourteen years and 'if, at the expiration of the said term, the author or authors, or any of them, be living, and a citizen or citizens of these United States, or resident therein, the same exclusive right shall be continued to him or them, his or their executors, administrators or assigns, for the further term of fourteen years'. 1 Stat. 124. In view of the language and history of this provision, there can be no doubt that if the present case had arisen under the Act of 1790, there would be no statutory restriction upon the assignability of the author's renewal interest. The petitioners contend, however, that such a limitation was introduced by subsequent legislation, particularly the Copyright Acts of 1831 and 1909.

The Act of February 3, 1831, 4 Stat. 436, amended the 1790 Act in two important respects: the original term was increased from fourteen to twenty-eight years, and the renewal term, although still only fourteen years long, could pass to the author's widow or children if he did not survive the original term. The renewal provision, like the Statute of Anne, did not refer to the author's 'assigns'. The purpose of these changes, as stated in the report of the Committee on the Judiciary of the House of Representatives was 'chiefly to enlarge the period for the enjoyment of copy-right, and thereby to place authors in this country more nearly upon an equality with authors in other countries. In the United States, by the existing laws, a copy-right is secured to the author, in the first instance, for fourteen years; and if, at the end of that period, he be living, then for fourteen years more; but, if he be not then living, the copy-right is determined, although, by the very event of the death of the author, his family stand in more need of the only means of subsistence ordinarily left to them.' Register of Debates, vol. 7, appendix CXIX.

Plainly, therefore, the Copyright Act of 1831 merely enlarged the benefits of the copyright; it extended the length of the original term and gave the author's widow and children that which theretofore they did not possess, namely, the right of renewal to which the author would have been entitled if he had survived the original term. The petitioners attach much significance to a sentence appearing in the report of the committee: 'The question is, whether the author or the bookseller should receive the reward.' Ibid. The meaning of this sentence, read in its context is quite clear. By providing that, if the author should not survive the original term, his renewal interest should, instead of falling into the public domain, pass to his widow and children, Congress was of course preferring the author to the bookseller. But neither expressly nor impliedly did the Act of 1831 impose any restraints upon the right of the author himself to assign his contingent interest in the renewal. That the Act contained no such limitation was accepted without question both by the courts,...

We come, finally, to the Copyright Act of March 4, 1909, 35 Stat. 1075, 17 U.S.C.A. § 1 et seq. which, except for some minor amendments not relevant here, is the statute in effect at the present time. In December, 1905, President Theodore Roosevelt urged the Congress to undertake a revision of the copyright laws. H.Doc. 1, 59th Cong., 1st Sess., p. LII. In response to this message the Librarian of Congress, under whose authority the Copyright Office functions, invited persons interested in copyright legislation to attend a conference for the purpose of devising a satisfactory measure. Several conferences were held in

1905 and 1906, resulting in a bill which was introduced in the House and Senate by the chairman of the Committee on Patents in each body. This bill (H.R. 19853 and S. 6330, 59th Cong., 1st Sess.) provided, in the case of books and musical compositions, for a single copyright term lasting for the life of the author and for fifty years thereafter. Joint hearings by the House and Senate Committees were held on this bill, but no action was taken by the Fifty-ninth Congress. At the next session of Congress this and other bills to revise the copyright laws were again introduced. Extensive pulic hearings were held. The result of this elaborate legislative consideration of the problem of copyright was a bill (H.R. 28192; S. 9440) which became the Copyright Act of 1909. As stated in the report of the House committee, this bill 'differs in many respects from any of the bills previously introduced...

By providing for two copyright terms, each of relatively short duration, Congress enabled the author to sell his 'copyright' without losing his renewal interest...

We agree with the court below, therefore, that neither the language nor the history of the Copyright Act of 1909 lend support to the conclusion that the 'existing law' prior to 1909, under which authors were free to assign their renewal interests if they were so disposed, was intended to be altered. We agree, also, that there are no compelling considerations of policy which could justify reading into the Act a construction so at variance with its history. The policy of the copyright law, we are told, is to protect the author—if need be, from himself—and a construction under which the author is powerless to assign his renewal interest furthers this policy. We are asked to recognize that authors are congenitally irresponsible, that frequently they are so sorely pressed for funds that they are willing to sell their work for a mere pittance, and therefore assignments made by them should not be upheld. It is important that we distinguish between two problems implied in these situations: whether, despite the contrary direction given to this legislation by the momentum of history, we are to impute to Congress the enactment of an absolute statutory bar against assignments of authors' renewal interests, and secondly, whether, although there be no such statutory bar, a particular assignment should be denied enforcement by the courts because it was made under oppressive circumstances. The first question alone is presented here, and we make no intimations upon the other. It is one thing to hold that the courts should not make themselves instruments of injustice by lending their aid to the enforcement of an agreement where the author was under such coercion of circumstances that enforcement would be unconscionable. It is quite another matter to hold, as we are asked in this case, that regardless of the circumstances surrounding a particular assignment, no agreements by authors to assign their renewal interests are binding.

It is not for courts to judge whether the interests of authors clearly lie upon one side of this question rather than the other. If an author cannot make an effective assignment of his renewal, it may be worthless to him when he is most in need. Nobody would pay an author for something he cannot sell. We cannot draw a principle of law from the familiar stories of garret-poverty of some men of literary genius. Even if we could do so, we cannot say that such men would regard with favor a rule of law preventing them from realizing on their assets when they are most in need of funds. Nor can we be unmindful of the fact that authors have themselves devised means of safeguarding their interests. We do not have such assured knowledge about authorship, and particularly about song writing, or the psychology of gifted writers and composers, as to justify us as judges in importing into Congressional legislation a denial to authors of the freedom to dispose of their property possessed by others. While authors may have habits making for intermittent want, they may have no less a spirit of independence which would resent treatment of them as wards under guardianship of the law.

We conclude, therefore, that the Copyright Act of 1909 does not nullify agreements by authors to assign their renewal interests. We are fortified in this conclusion by reference to the actual practices of authors and publishers with respect to assignments of renewals, as disclosed by the records of the Copyright Office. Since the enactment of the Copyright Act of 1870, 16 Stat. 198, 213, assignments of copyrights must be recorded in the office of the Register of Copyrights. The records of the Copyright Office, we are advised, show that during the period from July, 1870, to July, 1871, the first period in which assignments were recorded in the Office, 223 assignments were registered. Of these 14 were assignments of renewal interests. Similarly, during the first six months of 1909, immediately preceding the enactment of the Copyright Act of that year, 304 assignments were recorded, and of these 62 were assignments of renewal interests. In the six-month period following the enactment of the Copyright Act of 1909, there was no significant change: 404 assignments, of which 68 were transfers of renewals. And, to round out the picture, in the most recent complete volume of records (covering the period from January 27, 1943, to February 12, 1943), 135 assignments were recorded, and of these 29 were assignments of renewals. Many assignments have thus been entered into a good faith upon the assumption that they were valid and enforceable.

In addition to all other books and pamphlets relevant to our problem, we have consulted all of the twenty treatises on the American law of copyright available at the Library of Congress. Eight of these state, without qualification, that an author can effectively agree to assign his renewal interest before it has been secured; two state the rule with some reservations; ten are either silent or ambiguous. And the forms of assignment of copyright in treatises and standard form-books generally contain a provision designed to transfer the renewal interest.

The available evidence indicates, therefore, that renewal interests of authors have been regarded as assignable both before and after the Copyright Act of 1909. To hold at this late date that, as a matter of law, such interests are not assignable would be to reject all relevant aids to construction.

Affirmed.

Mr. Justice RUTLEDGE took no part in the consideration or decision of this case.

Mr. Justice BLACK, Mr. Justice DOUGLAS, and Mr. Justice MURPHY conclude that the analysis of the language and history of the copyright law in the dissenting opinion of Judge Frank in the court below, 125 F.2d 949, 954, demonstrates a Congressional purpose to reserve the renewal privilege for the personal benefit of authors and their families. They believe the judgment below should be reversed.

STEWART v. ABEND
No. 88-2102
Argued Jan. 9, 1990
Decided April 24, 1990
495 U.S. 207, 109 L.Ed.2d 184

Justice O'CONNOR delivered the opinion of the Court.

The author of a pre-existing work may assign to another the right to use it in a derivative work. In this case the author of a pre-existing work agreed to assign the rights in his renewal copyright term to the owner of a derivative work, but died before the commencement of the renewal period. The question presented is whether the owner of the derivative work infringed the rights of the successor owner of the pre-existing work by continued distribution and publication of the derivative work during the renewal term of the pre-existing work.

I

Cornell Woolrich authored the story "It Had to Be Murder," which was first published in February 1942 in Dime Detective Magazine. The magazine's publisher, Popular Publications, Inc., obtained the rights to magazine publication of the story and Woolrich retained all other rights. Popular Publications obtained a blanket copyright for the issue of Dime Detective Magazine in which "It Had to Be Murder" was published.

The Copyright Act of 1909, 35 Stat. 1075, 17 U.S.C. § 1 *et seq.* (1976 ed.) (1909 Act), provided authors a 28-year initial term of copyright protection plus a 28-year renewal term. See 17 U.S.C. § 24 (1976 ed.). In 1945, Woolrich agreed to assign the rights to make motion picture versions of six of his stories, including "It Had to Be Murder," to B.G. De Sylva Productions for $9,250. He also agreed to renew the copyrights in the stories at the appropriate time and to assign the same motion picture rights to De Sylva Productions for the 28-year renewal term. In 1953, actor Jimmy Stewart and director Alfred Hitchcock formed a production company, Patron, Inc., which obtained the motion picture rights in "It Had to Be Murder" from De Sylva's successors in interest for $10,000.

In 1954, Patron, Inc., along with Paramount Pictures, produced and distributed "Rear Window," the motion picture version of Woolrich's story "It Had to Be Murder." Woolrich died in 1968 before he could obtain the rights in the renewal term for petitioners as promised and without a surviving spouse or child. He left his property to a trust administered by his executor, Chase

Manhattan Bank, for the benefit of Columbia University. On December 29, 1969, Chase Manhattan Bank renewed the copyright in the "It Had to Be Murder" story pursuant to 17 U.S.C. § 24 (1976 ed.). Chase Manhattan assigned the renewal rights to respondent Abend for $650 plus 10% of all proceeds from exploitation of the story.

"Rear Window" was broadcast on the ABC television network in 1971. Respondent then notified petitioners Hitchcock (now represented by cotrustees of his will), Stewart, and MCA Inc., the owners of the "Rear Window" motion picture and renewal rights in the motion picture, that he owned the renewal rights in the copyright and that their distribution of the motion picture without his permission infringed his copyright in the story. Hitchcock, Stewart, and MCA nonetheless entered into a second license with ABC to rebroadcast the motion picture. In 1974, respondent filed suit against these same petitioners, and others, in the United States District Court for the Southern District of New York, alleging copyright infringement. Respondent dismissed his complaint in return for $25,000.

Three years later, the United States Court of Appeals for the Second Circuit decided *Rohauer v. Killiam Shows, Inc.,* 551 F.2d 484, cert. denied, 431 U.S. 949, 97 S.Ct. 2666, 53 L.Ed.2d 266 (1977), in which it held that the owner of the copyright in a derivative work may continue to use the existing derivative work according to the original grant from the author of the pre-existing work even if the grant of rights in the pre-existing work lapsed. 551 F.2d, at 494. Several years later, apparently in reliance on *Rohauer,* petitioners re-released the motion picture in a variety of media, including new 35 and 16 millimeter prints for theatrical exhibition in the United States, videocassettes, and videodiscs. They also publicly exhibited the motion picture in theaters, over cable television, and through videodisc and videocassette rentals and sales.

Respondent then brought the instant suit in the United States District Court for the Central District of California against Hitchcock, Stewart, MCA, and Universal Film Exchanges, a subsidiary of MCA and the distributor of the motion picture. Respondent's complaint alleges that the re-release of the motion picture infringes his copyright in the story because petitioners' right to use the story during the renewal term lapsed when Woolrich died before he could register for the renewal term and transfer his renewal rights to them. Respondent also contends that petitioners have interfered with his rights in the renewal term of the story in other ways. He alleges that he sought to contract with Home Box Office (HBO) to produce a play and television version of the story, but that petitioners wrote to him and HBO stating that neither he nor HBO could use either the title, "Rear Window" or "It Had to Be Murder." Respondent also alleges that petitioners further interfered with the renewal copyright in the story by attempting to sell the right to make a television sequel and that the re-release of the original motion picture itself interfered with his ability to produce other derivative works.

Petitioners filed motions for summary judgment, one based on the decision in *Rohauer, supra,* and the other based on alleged defects in the story's copyright. Respondent moved for summary judgment on the ground that petitioners' use of the motion picture constituted copyright infringement. Petitioners responded with a third motion for summary judgment based on a "fair use" defense. The District Court granted petitioners' motions for summary judgment based on *Rohauer* and the fair use defense and denied respondent's motion for summary judgment, as well as petitioners' motion for summary judgment alleging defects in the story's copyright. Respondent appealed to the United States Court of Appeals for the Ninth Circuit and petitioners cross-appealed.

The Court of Appeals reversed, holding that respondent's copyright in the renewal term of the story was not defective, *Abend v. MCA, Inc.,* 863 F.2d 1465, 1472 (1988). The issue before the court, therefore, was whether petitioners were entitled to distribute and exhibit the motion picture without respondent's permission despite respondent's valid copyright in the pre-existing story. Relying on the renewal provision of the 1909 Act, 17 U.S.C. § 24 (1976 ed.), respondent argued before the Court of Appeals that because he obtained from Chase Manhattan Bank, the statutory successor, the renewal right free and clear of any purported assignments of any interest in the renewal copyright, petitioners' distribution and publication of "Rear Window" without authorization infringed his renewal copyright. Petitioners responded that they had the right to continue to exploit "Rear Window" during the 28-year renewal period because Woolrich had agreed to assign to petitioners' predecessor in interest the motion picture rights in the story for the renewal period.

Petitioners also relied, as did the District Court, on the decision in *Rohauer v. Killiam Shows, Inc., supra.* In *Rohauer,* the Court of Appeals for the Second Circuit held that statutory successors to the renewal copyright in a pre-existing work under § 24 could not "depriv[e] the proprietor of the derivative copyright of a right ... to use so much of the underlying copyrighted work as already has been embodied in the copyrighted derivative work, as a matter of copyright law." *Id.,* at 492. The Court of Appeals in the instant case rejected this reasoning, concluding that even if the pre-existing work had been incorporated into a derivative work, use of the pre-existing work was infringing unless the owner of the derivative work held a valid grant of rights in the renewal term.
The court relied on *Miller Music Corp. v. Charles N. Daniels, Inc.,* 362 U.S. 373, 80 S.Ct. 792, 4 L.Ed.2d 804 (1960), in which we held that assignment of renewal rights by an author before the time for renewal arrives cannot defeat the right of the author's statutory successor to the renewal rights if the author dies before the right to renewal accrues. An assignee of the renewal rights takes only

an expectancy: "Until [the time for registration of renewal rights] arrives, assignees of renewal rights take the risk that the rights acquired may never vest in their assignors. A purchaser of such an interest is deprived of nothing. Like all purchasers of contingent interests, he takes subject to the possibility that the contingency may not occur." *Id.,* at 378, 80 S.Ct., at 796. The Court of Appeals reasoned that "[i]f *Miller Music* makes assignment of the full renewal rights in the underlying copyright unenforceable when the author dies before effecting renewal of the copyright, then, *a fortiori,* an assignment of part of the rights in the underlying work, the right to produce a movie version, must also be unenforceable if the author dies before effecting renewal of the underlying copyright." 863 F.2d, at 1476. Finding further support in the legislative history of the 1909 Act and rejecting the *Rohauer* court's reliance on the equities and the termination provisions of the 1976 Act, 17 U.S.C. §§ 203(b)(1), 304(c)(6)(A) the Court of Appeals concluded that petitioners received from Woolrich only an expectancy in the renewal rights that never matured; upon Woolrich's death, Woolrich's statutory successor, Chase Manhattan Bank, became "entitled to a renewal and extension of the copyright," which Chase Manhattan secured "within one year prior to the expiration of the original term of copyright." 17 U.S.C. § 24 (1976 ed.). Chase Manhattan then assigned the existing rights in the copyright to respondent.

The Court of Appeals also addressed at length the proper remedy, an issue not relevant to the issue on which we granted certiorari. We granted certiorari to resolve the conflict between the decision in *Rohauer, supra,* and the decision below. 493 U.S. 807, 110 S.Ct. 47, 107 L.Ed.2d 16 (1989). Petitioners do not challenge the Court of Appeals' determination that respondent's copyright in the renewal term is valid, and we express no opinion regarding the Court of Appeals' decision on this point.

II

A

Petitioners would have us read into the Copyright Act a limitation on the statutorily created rights of the owner of an underlying work. They argue in essence that the rights of the owner of the copyright in the derivative use of the pre-existing work are extinguished once it is incorporated into the derivative work, assuming the author of the pre-existing work has agreed to assign his renewal rights. Because we find no support for such a curtailment of rights in either the 1909 Act or the 1976 Act, or in the legislative history of either, we affirm the judgment of the Court of Appeals.

Petitioners and *amicus* Register of Copyrights assert, as the Court of Appeals assumed, that § 23 of the 1909 Act, and the case law interpreting that provision, directly control the disposition of this case. Respondent counters that the provisions of the 1976 Act control, but that the 1976 Act reenacted § 24 in § 304 and, therefore, the language and judicial interpretation of § 24 are relevant to our consideration of this case. Under either theory, we must look to the language of and case law interpreting § 24.

The right of renewal found in § 24 provides authors a second opportunity to obtain remuneration for their works. Section 24 provides:

> Since the earliest copyright statute in this country, the copyright term of ownership has been split between an original term and a renewal term. Originally, the renewal was intended merely to serve as an extension of the original term; at the end of the original term, the renewal could be effected and claimed by the author, if living, or by the author's executors, administrators, or assigns.

See Copyright Act of May 31, 1790, ch. XV, § 1, 1 Stat. 124. In 1831, Congress altered the provision so that the author could assign his contingent interest in the renewal term, but could not, through his assignment, divest the rights of his widow or children in the renewal term. See Copyright Act of February 3, 1831, ch. XVI, 4 Stat. 436; see also G. Curtis, Law of Copyright 235 1847). The 1831 renewal provisions created "an entirely new policy, completely dissevering the title, breaking up the continuance ... and vesting an absolutely new title eo nomine in the persons designated." *White–Smith Music Publishing Co. v. Goff,* 187 F. 247, 250 (CA1 1911). In this way, Congress attempted to give the author a second chance to control and benefit from his work. Congress also intended to secure to the author's family the opportunity to exploit the work if the author died before he could register for the renewal term. See Bricker, Renewal and Extension of Copyright, 29 S.Cal.L.Rev. 23, 27 (1955) ("The renewal term of copyright is the law's second chance to the author and his family to profit from his mental labors"). "The evident purpose of [the renewal provision] is to provide for the family of the author after his death. Since the author cannot assign his family's renewal rights, [it] takes the form of a compulsory bequest of the copyright to the designated persons."...

In its debates leading up to the Copyright Act of 1909, Congress elaborated upon the policy underlying a system comprised of an original term and a completely separate renewal term... The renewal term permits the author, originally in a poor bargaining position, to renegotiate the terms of the grant once the value of the work has been tested. With these purposes in mind, Congress enacted the renewal provision of the Copyright Act of 1909, 17 U.S.C. § 24 (1976 ed.). With respect to works in their original or renewal term as of January 1, 1978, Congress retained the two-term system of copyright protection in the 1976 Act.

Applying these principles in *Miller Music Corp. v. Charles N. Daniels, Inc.,* 362 U.S. 373, 80 S.Ct. 792, 4 L.Ed.2d 804 (1960), this Court held that when an author dies before the renewal period arrives, his executor is entitled to the renewal rights, even though the author previously assigned his renewal rights to another party. If the author dies before that time, the "next of kin obtain the renewal copyright free of any claim founded upon an assignment made by the author in his lifetime. These results follow not because the author's assignment is invalid but because he had only an expectancy to assign; and his death, prior to the renewal period, terminates his interest in the renewal which by § 24 vests in the named classes." *Ibid.* The legislative history of the 1909 Act echoes this view: "The right of renewal is contingent. It does not vest until the end [of the original term]. If [the author] is alive at the time of renewal, then the original contract may pass it, but his widow or children or other persons entitled would not be bound by that contract." Thus, the renewal provisions were intended to give the author a second chance to obtain fair remuneration for his creative efforts and to provide the author's family a "new estate" if the author died before the renewal period arrived.

An author holds a bundle of exclusive rights in the copyrighted work, among them the right to copy and the right to incorporate the work into derivative works. By assigning the renewal copyright in the work without limitation, as in *Miller Music,* the author assigns all of these rights. After *Miller Music,* if the author dies before the commencement of the renewal period, the assignee holds nothing. If the assignee of all of the renewal rights holds nothing upon the death of the assignor before arrival of the renewal period, then, *a fortiori,* the assignee of a portion of the renewal rights, *e.g.,* the right to produce a derivative work, must also hold nothing... Therefore, if the author dies before the renewal period, then the assignee may continue to use the original work only if the author's successor transfers the renewal rights to the assignee. This is the rule adopted by the Court of Appeals below and advocated by the Register of Copyrights... Application of this rule to this case should end the inquiry. Woolrich died before the commencement of the renewal period in the story, and, therefore, petitioners hold only an unfulfilled expectancy. Petitioners have been "deprived of nothing. Like all purchasers of contingent interests, [they took] subject to the possibility that the contingency may not occur." *Miller Music, supra,* 362 U.S., at 378, 80 S.Ct., at 796.

B

The reason that our inquiry does not end here, and that we granted certiorari, is that the Court of Appeals for the Second Circuit reached a contrary result in *Rohauer v. Killiam Shows, Inc.,* 551 F.2d 484 (1977). Petitioners' theory is drawn largely from *Rohauer.* The Court of Appeals in *Rohauer* attempted to craft a "proper reconciliation" between the owner of the pre-existing work, who held the right to the work pursuant to *Miller Music,* and the owner of the derivative work, who had a great deal to lose if the work could not be published or distributed. 551 F.2d, at 490. Addressing a case factually similar to this case, the court concluded that even if the death of the author caused the renewal rights in the pre-existing work to revert to the statutory successor, the owner of the derivative work could continue to exploit that work. The court reasoned that the 1976 Act and the relevant precedents did not preclude such a result and that it was necessitated by a balancing of the equities...

The Court of Appeals for the Second Circuit thereby shifted the focus from the right to use the pre-existing work in a derivative work to a right inhering in the created derivative work itself. By rendering the renewal right to use the original work irrelevant, the court created an exception to our ruling in *Miller Music* and, as petitioners concede, created an "intrusion" on the statutorily created rights of the owner of the pre-existing work in the renewal term. Brief for Petitioners 33.

Though petitioners do not, indeed could not, argue that its language expressly supports the theory they draw from *Rohauer,* they implicitly rely on § 6 of the 1909 Act, 17 U.S.C. § 7 (1976 ed.), which states that "dramatizations ... of copyrighted works when produced with the consent of the proprietor of the copyright in such works ... shall be regarded as new works subject to copyright under the provisions of this title." Petitioners maintain that the creation of the "new," *i.e.,* derivative, work extinguishes any right the owner of rights in the pre-existing work might have had to sue for infringement that occurs during the renewal term.

We think, as stated in Nimmer, that "[t]his conclusion is neither warranted by any express provision of the Copyright Act, nor by the rationale as to the scope of protection achieved in a derivative work. It is moreover contrary to the axiomatic copyright principle that a person may exploit only such copyrighted literary material as he either owns or is licensed to use." 1 Nimmer § 3.07[A], pp. 3–23 to 3–24 (footnotes omitted). The aspects of a derivative work added by the derivative author are that author's property, but the element drawn from the pre-existing work remains on grant from the owner of the pre-existing work. See *Russell v. Price,* 612 F.2d 1123, 1128 (CA9 1979) (reaffirming "well-established doctrine that a derivative copyright protects only the new material contained in the derivative work, not the matter derived from the underlying work"), cert. denied, 446 U.S. 952, 100 S.Ct. 2919, 64 L.Ed.2d 809 (1980); see also *Harper & Row, Publishers, Inc. v. Nation Enterprises,* 471 U.S. 539, 547, 105 S.Ct. 2218, 2223, 85 L.Ed.2d 588 (1985) So long as the pre-existing work remains out of the public domain, its use is infringing if one who employs the work does not have a valid license or assignment for use of the pre-existing work. It is irrelevant whether the pre-existing work is inseparably intertwined with the derivative work. ("[C]opyright in the underlying script survives intact despite the incorporation of that work into a derivative work"). Indeed, the plain language of § 7 supports the view that the full force of the copyright in the pre-existing work is preserved despite incorporation into the derivative work.

Properly conceding there is no explicit support for their theory in the 1909 Act, its legislative history, or the case law, petitioners contend, as did the court in *Rohauer,* that the termination provisions of the 1976 Act, while not controlling, support their theory of the case. For works existing in their original or renewal terms as of January 1, 1978, the 1976 Act added 19 years to the 1909 Act's provision of 28 years of initial copyright protection and 28 years of renewal protection. See 17 U.S.C. §§ 304(a) and (b). For those works, the author has the power to terminate the grant of rights at the end of the renewal term and, therefore, to gain the benefit of that additional 19 years of protection. See § 304(c). In effect, the 1976 Act provides a third opportunity for the author to benefit from a work in its original or renewal term as of January 1, 1978. Congress, however, created one exception to the author's right to terminate: The author may not, at the end of the renewal term, terminate the right to use a derivative work for which the owner of the derivative work has held valid rights in the original and renewal terms. See § 304(c)(6)(A). The author, however, may terminate the right to create new derivative works. *Ibid.* For example, if petitioners held a valid copyright in the story throughout the original and renewal terms, and the renewal term in "Rear Window" were about to expire, petitioners could continue to distribute the motion picture even if respondent terminated the grant of rights, but could not create a new motion picture version of the story. Both the court in *Rohauer* and petitioners infer from this exception to the right to terminate an intent by Congress to prevent authors of pre-existing works from blocking distribution of derivative works. In other words, because Congress decided not to permit authors to exercise a third opportunity to benefit from a work incorporated into a derivative work, the Act expresses a general policy of undermining the author's second opportunity. We disagree.

The process of compromise between competing special interests leading to the enactment of the 1976 Act undermines any such attempt to draw an overarching policy out of § 304(c)(6)(A), which only prevents termination with respect to works in their original or renewal copyright terms as of January 1, 1978, and only at the end of the renewal period... "was part of a compromise package involving the controversial and intertwined issues of initial ownership, duration of copyright, and reversion of rights. The Register, convinced that the opposition ... would scuttle the proposed legislation, drafted a number of alternative proposals...."

In fact, if the 1976 Act's termination provisions provide any guidance at all in this case, they tilt against petitioners' theory. The plain language of the termination provision itself indicates that Congress assumed that the owner of the pre-existing work possessed the right to sue for infringement even after incorporation of the pre-existing work in the derivative work...

Congress would not have stated explicitly in § 304(c)(6)(A) that, at the end of the renewal term, the owner of the rights in the pre-existing work may not terminate use rights in existing derivative works unless Congress had assumed that the owner continued to hold the right to sue for infringement even after incorporation of the pre-existing work into the derivative work...

Accordingly, we conclude that neither the 1909 Act nor the 1976 Act provides support for the theory set forth in *Rohauer.* And even if the theory found some support in the statute or the legislative history, the approach set forth in *Rohauer* is problematic. Petitioners characterize the result in *Rohauer* as a bright-line "rule." The Court of Appeals in *Rohauer,* however, expressly implemented policy considerations as a means of reconciling what it viewed as the competing interests in that case. See 551 F.2d, at 493–494. While the result in *Rohauer* might make some sense in some contexts, it makes no sense in others. In the case of a condensed book, for example, the contribution by the derivative author may be little, while the contribution by the original author is great. Yet, under the *Rohauer* "rule," publication of the condensed book would not infringe the pre-existing work even though the derivative author has no license or valid grant of rights in the pre-existing work... Thus, even if the *Rohauer* "rule" made sense in terms of policy in that case, it makes little sense when it is applied across the derivative works spectrum. Indeed, in the view of the commentators, *Rohauer* did not announce a "rule," but rather an "interest-balancing approach." ...

Finally, petitioners urge us to consider the policies underlying the Copyright Act. They argue that the rule announced by the Court of Appeals will undermine one of the policies of the Act—the dissemination of creative works—by leading to many fewer works reaching the public... These arguments are better addressed by Congress than the courts.

In any event, the complaint that respondent's monetary request in this case is so high as to preclude agreement fails to acknowledge that an initially high asking price does not preclude bargaining. Presumably, respondent is asking for a share in the proceeds because he wants to profit from the distribution of the work, not because he seeks suppression of it.

Moreover, although dissemination of creative works is a goal of the Copyright Act, the Act creates a balance between the artist's right to control the work during the term of the copyright protection and the public's need for access to creative works. The copyright term is limited so that the public will not be permanently deprived of the fruits of an artist's labors. But nothing in the copyright statutes would prevent an author from hoarding all of his works during the term of the copyright. In fact, this Court has held that a copyright owner has the capacity arbitrarily to refuse to license one who seeks to exploit the work. See *Fox Film Corp. v. Doyal,* 286 U.S. 123, 127, 52 S.Ct. 546, 547, 76 L.Ed. 1010 (1932).

The limited monopoly granted to the artist is intended to provide the necessary bargaining capital to garner a fair price for the value of the works passing into public use.

With the Copyright Act of 1790, Congress provided an initial term of protection plus a renewal term that did not survive the author. In the Copyright Act of 1831, Congress devised a completely separate renewal term that survived the death of the author so as to create a "new estate" and to benefit the author's family, and, with the passage of the 1909 Act, his executors. See *supra,* at 1758–1759. The 1976 Copyright Act provides a single, fixed term, but provides an inalienable termination right. See 17 U.S.C. §§ 203, 302. This evolution of the duration of copyright protection tellingly illustrates the difficulties Congress faces in attempting to "secur[e] for limited Times to Authors ... the exclusive Right to their respective Writings." U.S. Const., Art. I, § 8, cl. 8. Absent an explicit statement of congressional intent that the rights in the renewal term of an owner of a pre-existing work are extinguished upon incorporation of his work into another work, it is not our role to alter the delicate balance Congress has labored to achieve.

C

In a creative, though ultimately indefensible, exposition of the 1909 Act, the dissent attempts to breathe life into petitioners' suggestion that the derivative work is somehow independent of the pre-existing work. Although no Court of Appeals in the 81 years since enactment of the 1909 Act has held as much, and although the petitioners have not argued the point, the dissent contends that "§ 7 was intended to ... give the original author the power to sell the right to make a derivative work that upon creation and copyright would be completely independent of the original work." *Post,* at 1772; see also *post,* at 1774. This assertion, far removed from the more modest holding of *Rohauer,* is derived from three erroneous premises.

The provision consists of one sentence with two clauses divided by a semicolon. The first clause lists the types of works that may be derivative works, explains that one may incorporate either copyrighted or public domain works into a derivative work, and further explains that the derivative work itself is copyrightable. The clause also expressly limits incorporation of copyrighted works to instances where the owner of the pre-existing work "consents."

The second clause explains what publication of the new work does *not* portend: Publication of the derivative work does not "*affect the force or validity of any subsisting copyright upon the matter employed* " (emphasis added); publication of the derivative work does not mean that use of the original work in other works is precluded; and publication does not mean that a copyright in the original work shall be secured, *e.g.,* if the work was in the public domain, or extended, as where the original work was copyrighted before the date that the derivative work is copyrighted. The plain meaning of the italicized sentence is that the copyright in the "matter employed"—the pre-existing work when it is incorporated into the derivative work—is not abrogated by publication of the new work. The succeeding phrases preserve the copyright status of the original work: Publication does not operate to prohibit other uses of the original work or to "secure or extend copyright in such original works." Cf. *post,* at 1775...

More important, however, is that under the express language of § 3, one obtains a copyright on the entire work, but the parts previously copyrighted get copyright protection only according to the "duration or scope" of the already existing copyright. Thus, if an author attempts to obtain copyright in a book derived from a short story, he can obtain copyright on the book for the full copyright term, but will receive protection of the story parts only for the duration and scope of the rights previously obtained. Correlatively, if an author attempts to copyright a novel, *e.g.,* about Cinderella, and the story elements are already in the public domain, the author holds a copyright in the novel, but may receive protection only for his original additions to the Cinderella story. See *McCaleb v. Fox Film Corp.,* 299 F. 48 (CA5 1924); *American Code Co. v. Bensinger,* 282 F. 829 (CA2 1922).

The plain language of the first clause of § 7 ensures that this scheme is carried out with respect to "[c]ompilations or abridgments, adaptations, arrangements, dramatizations, translations, or other versions of works in the public domain or of copyrighted works ... or works republished with new matter," *i.e.,* derivative works. The second clause of § 7 clarifies what might have been otherwise unclear—that the principle in § 3 of preservation of the duration or scope of the subsisting copyright applies to derivative works, and that neither the scope of the copyright in the matter employed nor the duration of the copyright in the original work is undermined by publication of the derivative work.

If one reads the plain language of § 7 and § 3 together, one must conclude that they were enacted in no small part to ensure that the copyright in the pre-existing work would not be abrogated by the derivative work. Section 7 requires consent by the author of the pre-existing work before the derivative work may be produced, and both provisions explicitly require that the copyright in the "subsisting work" will not be abrogated by incorporation of the work into another work...

In this case, the grant of rights in the pre-existing work lapsed and, therefore, the derivative work owners' rights to use those portions of the pre-existing work incorporated into the derivative work expired. Thus, continued use would be infringing; whether the derivative work may continue to be published is a matter of remedy, an issue which is not before us. To say otherwise is to say that the derivative work nullifies the "force" of the copyright in the "matter employed." Whether or not we believe that this is good policy, this is the system Congress has provided, as evidenced by the language of the 1909 Act and the cases decided under the 1909 Act. Although the dissent's theory may have been a plausible option for a legislature to have chosen, Congress did not so provide.

III

Petitioners assert that even if their use of "It Had to Be Murder" is unauthorized, it is a fair use and, therefore, not infringing. At common law, "the property of the author ... in his intellectual creation [was] absolute until he voluntarily part[ed] with the same." *American Tobacco Co. v. Werckmeister,* 207 U.S. 284, 299, 28 S.Ct. 72, 77, 52 L.Ed. 208 (1907). The fair use doctrine, which is incorporated into the 1976 Act, evolved in response to this absolute rule. See *Harper & Row,* 471 U.S., at 549–551, 105 S.Ct., at 2224–2226. The doctrine is an " 'equitable rule of reason,' " *Sony Corp. of America v. Universal City Studios, Inc.,* 464 U.S., at 448, 104 S.Ct., at 792, which "permits courts to avoid rigid application of the copyright statute when, on occasion, it would stifle the very creativity which that law is designed to foster." *Iowa State University Research Foundation, Inc. v. American Broadcasting Cos.,* 621 F.2d 57, 60 (CA2 1980). Petitioners contend that the fair use doctrine should be employed in this case to "avoid [a] rigid applicatio[n] of the Copyright Act." Brief for Petitioners 42.

In 17 U.S.C. § 107, Congress provided examples of fair use, *e.g.,* copying "for purposes such as criticism, comment, news reporting, teaching (including multiple copies for classroom use), scholarship, or research," and listed four nonexclusive factors that a court must consider in determining whether an unauthorized use is not infringing:

"(1) the purpose and character of the use, including whether such use is of a commercial nature or is for nonprofit educational purposes;

"(2) the nature of the copyrighted work;

"(3) the amount and substantiality of the portion used in relation to the copyrighted work as a whole; and

"(4) the effect of the use upon the potential market for or value of the copyrighted work."

The Court of Appeals determined that the use of Woolrich's story in petitioners' motion picture was not fair use. We agree. The motion picture neither falls into any of the categories enumerated in § 107 nor meets the four criteria set forth in § 107... Petitioners asserted before the Court of Appeals that their use was educational rather than commercial. The Court of Appeals found nothing in the record to support this assertion, nor do we.

Applying the second factor, the Court of Appeals pointed out that "[a] use is less likely to be deemed fair when the copyrighted work is a creative product." 863 F.2d, at 1481 (citing *Brewer v. Hustler Magazine, Inc.,* 749 F.2d 527, 529 (CA9 1984)). In general, fair use is more likely to be found in factual works than in fictional works. ... A motion picture based on a fictional short story obviously falls into the latter category.

Examining the third factor, the Court of Appeals determined that the story was a substantial portion of the motion picture... The motion picture expressly uses the story's unique setting, characters, plot, and sequence of events. Petitioners argue that the story constituted only 20% of the motion picture's story line, Brief for Petitioners 40, n. 69, but that does not mean that a substantial portion of the story was not used in the motion picture...

The fourth factor is the "most important, and indeed, central fair use factor." 3 Nimmer § 13.05[A], p. 13–81. The record supports the Court of Appeals' conclusion that re-release of the film impinged on the ability to market new versions of the story. Common sense would yield the same conclusion. Thus, all four factors point to unfair use. "This case presents a classic example of an unfair use: a commercial use of a fictional story that adversely affects the story owner's adaptation rights." 863 F.2d, at 1482.

For the foregoing reasons, the judgment of the Court of Appeals is affirmed, and the case is remanded for further proceedings consistent with this opinion.

It is so ordered.

Justice WHITE, concurring in the judgment...

Justice STEVENS, with whom THE CHIEF JUSTICE and Justice SCALIA join, dissenting...

JUDITH ROSSNER v. CBS, INC.
No. 83 Civ. 7543 (LFM)
United States District Court, S.D. New York
July 1, 1985
612 F.Supp. 334

MacMAHON, District Judge.

This is an action for injunctive relief and damages brought by Judith Rossner (Rossner) and Miriam Gibbon (Gibbon), as trustee of trusts for the benefit of Jean Rossner and Daniel Rossner, against CBS, Inc. (CBS), Grosso-Jacobson Productions, Inc. (Grosso-Jacobson), and Paramount Pictures Corporation (Paramount). The action was tried before us, without a jury, on March 25, 26, 27 and 28, 1985.

Plaintiffs seek to enjoin defendants permanently from using the word "Goodbar" as part of a title for a made-for-television movie entitled *Trackdown: Finding the Goodbar Killer (Trackdown).* Alleging that defendants' use of the word "Goodbar" constitutes a false designation of origin, plaintiffs claim violation of Lanham Act § 43(a), 15 U.S.C. § 1125(a) (1946), unfair competition and violation of N.Y.General Business Law § 368–d (McKinney 1984). Alternatively, asserting that *Trackdown* is a sequel to the movie *Looking for Mr. Goodbar* (*Goodbar* movie), plaintiffs seek $75,000 in damages from Paramount for alleged breach of a contract which required Paramount to pay Rossner that sum upon the production of any sequel to the *Goodbar* movie.

Plaintiffs also seek a permanent injunction directing defendants to broadcast a consent-ordered disclaimer with the credits of *Trackdown* during any future showing of the movie. Finally, plaintiffs seek compensatory damages, punitive damages, and attorneys' fees against all defendants.

JURISDICTION

We have subject matter jurisdiction of the federal claims pursuant to 15 U.S.C. § 1121 and 28 U.S.C. § 1338(a) and (b) and pendent jurisdiction of the state claims.

THE PARTIES

Plaintiff Rossner, a celebrated novelist, is a resident of New York. Defendant Grosso-Jacobson, a Delaware corporation with its principal place of business in New York, is an independent producer of movies primarily for broadcast on network television. Defendant CBS, a New York corporation with its principal place of business in New York, operates the CBS television broadcasting network. Defendant Paramount, a Delaware corporation with its principal place of business in California, is a major motion picture studio.

FACTS

After carefully considering the exhibits, hearing and observing the witnesses, and weighing all the evidence and the arguments of counsel, we find the following facts:

Roseann Quinn (Quinn), a twenty-eight year old school teacher, was brutally murdered in her apartment on the upper west side of Manhattan on January 1, 1973. The police apprehended and charged John Wayne Wilson (Wilson), a man whom Quinn had picked up in a singles' bar, with the murder. Both the murder and the ensuing investigation were extensively reported in the local newspapers.

Rossner read the reports and, sometime later, commenced writing a novel about a school teacher who is murdered by a man she meets in a singles' bar. The novel is not a factual account of the Quinn murder, but the characters and the events depicted are loosely based on the actual murder.

Rossner entitled her novel *Looking for Mr. Goodbar* (*Goodbar* novel). It was published by Simon & Schuster, Inc. in June 1975 and generated wide critical acclaim and popular success, selling approximately 133,000 copies in hardcover editions and 3,609,059 in paperback and appearing on best-seller lists for twenty-seven weeks.

On July 1, 1975, Rossner and Gibbon, along with another trustee, entered into an agreement with Paramount (Paramount Agreement), whereby Rossner granted and assigned to Paramount "the sole and exclusive rights" to use the *Goodbar* novel, its title, and any similar title "in the making of motion picture photoplays" based upon the novel (Paragraph Second, Paramount Agreement). Pursuant to the agreement, in 1977, Paramount released a movie entitled *Looking for Mr. Goodbar,* which was based on the *Goodbar* novel.

Two years earlier, in October 1975, Lacey Fosburgh (Fosburgh), the reporter who covered the Quinn murder for *The New York Times,* wrote an article about the murder entitled *Finding Mr. Goodbar,* which was published in *New Times* magazine. A similar Fosburgh article entitled *Finding the Real Mr. Goodbar* was published in *Cosmopolitan* magazine in June 1976. The *New Times* issue had a circulation of approximately 214,269 and the *Cosmopolitan* issue 2,221,623. Subsequently, Fosburgh wrote a novel based on the Quinn murder entitled *Closing Time: The True Story of the "Goodbar" Murder,* which was published by Dellacorte Press in 1977. Over 118,116 copies of the novel were sold.

At trial, Rossner testified that she was aware of these publications and of Fosburgh's continued use of the word "Goodbar" in their titles. Nevertheless, she decided not to take any legal action against Fosburgh because she found Fosburgh's titles to be sufficiently distinguishable from her own work.

As a result of the extensive awareness of Rossner's novel, its reviews, the Fosburgh publications, and the Paramount movie, the media has referred to the Quinn murder as "the Goodbar murder" and to Wilson as "the Goodbar killer." There is also some evidence that the word "Goodbar" has entered the vernacular as a word describing "the singles' scene" or a dangerous "pick-up."

In April 1981, Grosso-Jacobson agreed to produce a two-hour made-for-television movie for CBS based on the Quinn murder investigation. It hired John Lafferty, the detective primarily responsible for the actual investigation, as a consultant. Although aware of Rossner's prior use of the word "Goodbar," executives at CBS insisted that the word "Goodbar" be part of the movie's title because they believed that it identified an actual murder known to the public and, therefore, would be an exploitable title. The movie, ultimately titled *Trackdown: Finding the Goodbar Killer,* was broadcast on CBS at 9:00 P.M. on October 15, 1983.

Upon learning that *Trackdown* was in production, Rossner directed her agent to advise Paramount to protect its movie rights in the title "Looking for Mr. Goodbar." Paramount then wrote to CBS and Grosso-Jacobson claiming infringement of its rights to use of the word "Goodbar." They countered that the term "Goodbar Killer" was in the public domain as a result of the media's and Fosburgh's use of the term to identify Wilson.

After negotiations, Paramount, CBS, and Grosso-Jacobson and its umbrella insurance company, Centerpoint Productions, Inc., entered into an agreement dated March 15, 1983 (March 15 Agreement). Under the agreement, Paramount waived its right to object to the use of the word "Goodbar" in the *Trackdown* title provided that (1) the word would not be emphasized in the title, (2) the movie would be a factual account of the Quinn murder, and (3) the advertising would not refer to the movie as a sequel or as otherwise derived from the *Goodbar* novel or the *Goodbar* movie.

On October 14, 1983, plaintiffs moved, by order to show cause, for a preliminary injunction preventing the exhibition of *Trackdown,* alleging, *inter alia,* unfair competition and false designation of origin. After a hearing, this court (Edelstein, J.) issued a consent order which provided: "that the defendants' broadcast of the movie 'Trackdown: Finding the Goodbar Killer,' will contain at its beginning and at its end for three-four seconds the attached disclaimer displayed in written form on the screen."

The language of the disclaimer agreed to by the parties was as follows: "The following broadcast is based on fact. It is not related to the Judith

Rossner novel 'Looking For Mr. Goodbar,' and Miss Rossner has no connection with it."

The consent order implicitly incorporated the parties' agreement that the disclaimer would appear with the beginning and closing credits of *Trackdown*. The following evening, however, when CBS broadcast *Trackdown,* the disclaimer did not appear with the movie's credits but among commercials at the beginning and closing of the program hour.

DISCUSSION

We emphasize, at the outset, that plaintiffs are not bringing an action in copyright. Nor are they claiming that the characters, plot, themes or events portrayed in *Trackdown* infringe on the *Goodbar* novel. Their claim is simply that defendants, through their use of the word "Goodbar" in the title of *Trackdown,* are trading on Rossner's reputation and good will generated from the success of her novel. The claim arises from the fact that it was Rossner who, by virtue of her creative ability, first conceived of and used the word "Goodbar" to identify a fictionalized character in her novel.

Standing

Defendants' first contention is that Rossner lacks standing to claim misappropriation of title because she assigned all of her right to use of the title *Looking for Mr. Goodbar* in motion pictures to Paramount....

It appears that what Paramount essentially acquired from Rossner is the right to use her title in the making of motion pictures derived, to some degree, from her novel. Consequently, Rossner argues, and we agree, that from the bundle of literary property rights, she has retained that fraction of a right which allows her to use the title in movies not derived from her novel. This concept of fractional ownership is elusive. Nevertheless, after a careful reading of the Paramount Agreement, in light of the parties' intentions, we are convinced that Rossner has retained a small, but protectable interest which is at stake in this litigation. Specifically, she holds a right to protect against the unauthorized use of the title in motion pictures not based on her novel, and defendants themselves assert that Trackdown is not based on the *Goodbar* novel. We therefore conclude that she has standing to bring the instant action.

Lanham Act

Plaintiffs' initial claim is that defendants' use of the title *Trackdown: Finding the Goodbar Killer* for their movie constitutes a false designation of origin, in violation of the Lanham Act, 15 U.S.C. § 1125(a) (1946). Section 1125(a) provides, in pertinent part...

The Act has been construed to protect the title of a creative work when (1) the title has acquired "secondary meaning," *i.e.,* the public identifies the title with Rossner and her work, and (2) there is a "likelihood of public confusion," *i.e.,* the public will be mislead into believing that defendants' work originated or is sponsored by Rossner because both works bear similar titles.

The test of secondary meaning for literary titles is essentially one of establishing whether, in the minds of a significant number of the public, the title is associated with a single source of the literary work. Since defendants have not used Rossner's entire title, but only the word "Goodbar," plaintiffs must demonstrate secondary meaning in the word itself. The question for us then becomes whether the public associates the word "Goodbar" with a single, though possibly, anonymous source.

The advertisements, reviews and other press clippings relating to the *Goodbar* novel indicate that the word "Goodbar" was associated with Rossner when her novel first came into the public eye. The "strength" of the word as a trademark, however, has been diminished by the subsequent use of the mark to identify other sources.

First, Rossner sold her rights to the *Goodbar* title for use in motion pictures to Paramount. Paramount then produced the *Goodbar* movie and the word "Goodbar" became associated with Paramount and its movie. Second, Fosburgh wrote two articles and a book which prominently used the word "Goodbar" in their titles and identified Wilson as the "Goodbar Killer." Several newspaper articles reinforced this association in the minds of the public by referring to the Quinn murder as the "Goodbar murder" and to Wilson as the "Goodbar Killer." Finally, the word itself has been used in the vernacular, specifically, in other movies, television programs and news articles, to identify the "singles' scene," "a dangerous pick-up" or "Mr. Right."

"The strength or distinctiveness of a mark determines both the ease with which it may be established as a valid trademark and the degree of protection it will be accorded." The strength of the "Goodbar" mark refers to its ability to identify a work sold under the mark as emanating from a particular source, namely, Rossner. Although Rossner is "not required to act immediately against every possibly infringing use [of her mark] to avoid a holding of abandonment," her failure to police the mark has inevitably caused the mark to lose its primary significance as a source-denoting mark. The frequent and disparate uses of the word "Goodbar" in association with Paramount, Fosburgh and the Quinn murder, prevent Rossner from demonstrating secondary meaning in her mark.

Moreover, plaintiffs have presented no evidence that the public was mislead into believing that Rossner sponsored or was in any way involved in the production of *Trackdown.* Plaintiffs suggest that the various newspapers' "association" of *Trackdown* with the *Goodbar* novel is equivalent to confusion. More "association," however, is not sufficient to demonstrate a likelihood of confusion. The advertising of CBS and Grosso-Jacobson frequently explained that *Trackdown* was based on the event that inspired Rossner's novel. Such statements are a means of accurately distinguishing Rossner's work to avoid confusion.

To the extent that the viewers of *Trackdown* may have mistakenly believed that Rossner was associated with that film, the disclaimer, if it had been appropriately placed with the credits, is an adequate means of alleviating the viewers' confusion. "Disclaimers are a favored way of minimizing confusion as to source or sponsorship," and "[a]bsolute prohibitions of speech as provided for in [injunctive relief] are improper where there is any possibility that ... [a] disclaimer will suffice."

The problem with the disclaimer here is that it was buried within the commercials shown before and after the movie. The record is somewhat confusing, but it was clearly the intent of the court to grant an order, on consent of all counsel, incorporating the agreement reached between the parties concerning the placement and form of the disclaimer. Plaintiffs' counsel described the agreement as follows:

"If your honor please, we believe that we have an agreement, and I want to state what I understand to be clearly the agreement and what there may still be some question about it.

We have agreed that there be a disclaimer accompanying this program whenever it appears, not only tomorrow night but thereafter, and *that disclaimer will appear with the credits in the same size as the credits...*

We have insisted that the disclaimer appear with the credits at the beginning of the program saying, 'The following broadcast,' and at the end of the program saying, 'The preceding broadcast.' (emphasis added)."

Defendants' counsel at no time objected to placing the disclaimer within the credits. We are compelled to conclude that defendants failed, in good faith, to comply with the intent of the order and agreement, and undermined the impact and the intent of the disclaimer...

Unfair Competition and Anti-Dilution Statute

Plaintiffs' claims under the New York common law of unfair competition and the anti-dilution statute are premised, as is their claim under the Lanham Act, on the contention that the public was deceived as to the origin of *Trackdown.* We recognize the breadth of New York's common law tort of unfair competition but emphasize that, in each instance, the tort results from the deception of the public as to the origin of a work. As stated earlier, we find that plaintiffs have failed to establish such deception or confusion...

Sequel

Plaintiffs' alternative claim is that *Trackdown* is a sequel to the *Goodbar* movie and, thus, that Paramount owes Rossner $75,000 pursuant to the Paramount Agreement. Paramount contends that it did not license its sequel rights to Grosso-Jacobson or to CBS for the production of *Trackdown,* and, furthermore, that *Trackdown* is not a sequel to the *Goodbar* movie.

In the March 15 Agreement, Paramount agreed not to object to the use of the title *Trackdown: Finding the Goodbar Killer* for a movie which was a factual account of the Quinn murder investigation. Although defendants argue that this agreement is merely "a waiver of objection," it is, in essence, a covenant not to sue CBS or Grosso-Jacobson for their use of the word "Goodbar." Such a covenant has the practical effect of a license because it permits and induces the use of the word "Goodbar" in the title of *Trackdown* free from allegations of misappropriation.

Once we find that Paramount licensed its sequel rights, the question for us is whether *Trackdown* is a sequel to the *Goodbar* movie. Paragraph Seventeen of the Paramount Agreement provides that upon the commencement of the principal photography of any "sequel" to the *Goodbar* movie, which is longer than one and one-half hours, Paramount shall pay Rossner $75,000.

Since the language of the agreement is clear and unambiguous, we must interpret its terms exactly as written. By definition, then, whether a movie is a "sequel" under the Paramount Agreement depends on its content, not its title.

The *Goodbar* movie recounts the story of a lonely schoolteacher who frequents singles' bars in search of companionship. The last scene in the movie is a violent depiction of her murder by a man she met in one such bar. *Trackdown* begins where the *Goodbar* movie leaves off, with the murder of a young woman, and goes on to tell the "entirely new and different story" of the police investigation which leads to the final apprehension of her killer.

The "principal characters" in the *Goodbar* movie are Theresa Dunn, the schoolteacher; her father, her sister; James, her caring boyfriend; and Tony. Two other characters who appear in the movie, but only for a short duration, are the killer and the killer's homosexual lover. The only characters who are also found in *Trackdown* are the schoolteacher, the killer and his homosexual lover. Based on these three characters and the fact that the events in *Trackdown* logically follow those in the *Goodbar* movie, plaintiffs contend that *Trackdown* is a sequel to the *Goodbar* movie.

Initially, we note that the schoolteacher, the killer and his homosexual lover play relatively minor roles in *Trackdown*. Although the teacher's murder is the catalyst for the movie, the movie's primary focus is on the story of the detective, his investigation and his personal life. More importantly, even if these three characters were considered "principal characters," they are not taken from Rossner's fictionalized characters but from people involved in the Quinn murder.

Rossner may not have intended to model her characters in the *Goodbar* novel on actual persons. Nevertheless, her characters of Theresa Dunn, the victim, and Gary Cooper White, the killer, bear strong similarities to their real-life counterparts, Quinn and Wilson. Dunn, like Quinn, was Irish Catholic, taught deaf children, walked with a slight limp, and lived a fairly quiet and reserved life except for her attraction to singles' bars. White, like Wilson, was a young drifter with a pregnant wife in Florida and a homosexual lover in New York, had been in and out of jails, and had confessed to the brutal murder of a young schoolteacher whom he had picked up in a singles' bar.

We find that any similarities between the characters in *Trackdown* and those from Rossner's novel depicted in the *Goodbar* movie exist because Rossner drew fictional inspiration from an actual event and not because *Trackdown* is a sequel to the *Goodbar* movie.

Rossner cannot build a story and characters around an historical incident and then claim the exclusive right to use of the incident. Defendants have the right to avail themselves of the facts contained in Rossner's novel which relate to the Quinn murder and use such information in their movie.
We conclude that *Trackdown* was essentially a factual depiction of the Quinn murder investigation and, thus, is not a sequel to the *Goodbar* movie, as that term is defined in the Paramount Agreement.

Accordingly, defendants CBS, Inc. and Grosso-Jacobson Productions, Inc. are permanently enjoined from broadcasting the movie *Trackdown: Finding the Goodbar Killer* without simultaneously broadcasting the consent-ordered disclaimer with the opening and closing credits of the movie. Plaintiffs' action is dismissed in all other respects. The parties are directed to settle a judgment and order containing a form of permanent injunction consistent with this opinion within twenty (20) days.

In the following case, *Cardtoons, L.C. v. MLBPA*, 95 F.3d 1959 (10th Cir. 1996), the court looks at the conflict between Right of Publicity versus the First Amendment. These cards were gentle parodies, much like the brilliant Mel Brooks Young Frankenstein and High Anxiety, which, by the way, Alfred Hitchcock loved even though it "mocked" Hitch's Vertigo and the Classic Shower

Scene in Psycho. This is not unlike Weird Al Yankovic's musical parodies of rock songs. But, you can take your 10-year-old son to one of his shows.

CARDTOONS, L.C. v. MAJOR LEAGUE BASEBALL PLAYERS ASSOCIATION

United States Court of Appeals, Tenth Circuit
No. 95-5006
95 F.3d 959

TACHA, Circuit Judge.

Cardtoons, L.C., ("Cardtoons") brought this action to obtain a declaratory judgment that its parody trading cards featuring active major league baseball players do not infringe on the publicity rights of members of the Major League Baseball Players Association ("MLBPA"). The district court held that the trading cards constitute expression protected by the First Amendment and therefore read a parody exception into Oklahoma's statutory right of publicity. MLBPA appeals, arguing that (1) the district court lacked jurisdiction to issue a declaratory judgment and (2) Cardtoons does not have a First Amendment right to market its trading cards. We exercise jurisdiction pursuant to 28 U.S.C. § 1291. Because Cardtoons' First Amendment right to free expression outweighs MLBPA's proprietary right of publicity, we affirm.

I. Background

Cardtoons formed in late 1992 to produce parody trading cards featuring caricatures of major league baseball players. Cardtoons contracted with a political cartoonist, a sports artist, and a sports author and journalist, who designed a set of 130 cards. The majority of the cards, 71, have caricatures of active major league baseball players on the front and humorous commentary about their careers on the back. The balance of the set is comprised of 20 "Big Bang Bucks" cards (cartoon drawings of currency with caricatures of the most highly paid players on the front, yearly salary statistics on the back), 10 "Spectra" cards (caricatures of active players on the front, nothing on the back), 10 retired player cards (caricatures of retired players on the front, humorous commentary about their careers on the back), 11 "Politics in Baseball" cards (cartoons featuring caricatures of political and sports figures on the front, humorous text on the back), 7 standing cards (caricatures of team logos on the front, humorous text on the back), and 1 checklist card. Except for the Spectra cards, the back of each card bears the Cardtoons logo and the following statement: "Cardtoons baseball is a parody and is NOT licensed by Major League Baseball Properties or Major League Baseball Players Association."

A person reasonably familiar with baseball can readily identify the players lampooned on the parody trading cards. The cards use similar names, recognizable caricatures, distinctive team colors, and commentary about individual players. For example, the card parodying San Francisco Giants' outfielder Barry Bonds calls him "Treasury Bonds," and features a recognizable caricature of Bonds, complete with earring, tipping a bat boy for a 24 carat gold "Fort Knoxville Slugger." The back of the card has a team logo (the "Gents"), and the following text:

> Redemption qualities and why Treasury Bonds is the league's most valuable player:
>
> 1. Having Bonds on your team is like having money in the bank.
> 2. He plays so hard he gives 110 percent, compounded daily.
> 3. He turned down the chance to play other sports because he has a high interest rate in baseball.
> 4. He deposits the ball in the bleachers.
> 5. He is into male bonding.
> 6. He is a money player.
> 7. He has a 24-karat Gold Glove.
> 8. He always cashes in on the payoff pitch.

NOTICE: Bonds is not tax-free in all states but is double exempt. At the end of the 1992 season, Barry Bonds was a two-time winner of the National League's Most Valuable Player award, a three-time winner of a Gold Glove award, and had just signed a six-year contract for $43.75 million, making him the highest-paid player in baseball. Richard Hoffer, *The Importance of Being Barry: The Giants' Barry Bonds Is the Best Player in the Game Today—Just Ask Him,* Sports Illustrated, May 24, 1993, at 13. No one the least bit familiar with the game of baseball would mistake Cardtoons' "Treasury Bonds" for anyone other than the Giants' Barry Bonds. Other caricatures, such as "Ken Spiffy, Jr." of the "Mari–Nerds" (Ken Griffey, Jr., of the Seattle Mariners), are equally identifiable.

The trading cards ridicule the players using a variety of themes. A number of the cards, including the "Treasury Bonds" card and all of the Big Bang Bucks cards, humorously criticize players for their substantial salaries. (The irony of MLBPA's counterclaim for profits from the cards is not lost on this panel.) Other trading cards mock the players' narcissism, as exemplified by the card featuring "Egotisticky Henderson" of the "Pathetics," parodying Ricky Henderson, then of the Oakland Athletics. The card features a caricature of Henderson raising his finger in a "number one" sign while patting himself on the back, with the following text:

> Egotisticky Henderson, accepting the "Me–Me Award" from himself at the annual "Egotisticky Henderson Fan Club" banquet, sponsored by Egotisticky Henderson:
>
> "I would just like to thank myself for all I have done. (Pause for cheers.) I am the greatest of all time. (Raise arms triumphantly.) I love myself.

(Pause for more cheers.) I am honored to know me. (Pause for louder cheers.) I wish there were two of me so I could spend more time with myself. (Wipe tears from eyes.) I couldn't have done it without me. (Remove cap and hold it aloft.) It's friends like me that keep me going. (Wave to crowd and acknowledge standing ovation.)

The remainder of the cards poke fun at things such as the players' names ("Chili Dog Davis" who "plays the game with relish," a parody of designated hitter Chili Davis), physical characteristics ("Cloud Johnson," a parody of six-foot-ten-inch pitcher Randy Johnson), and onfield behavior (a backflipping "Ozzie Myth," a parody of shortstop Ozzie Smith).

The format of the parody trading cards is similar to that of traditional baseball cards. The cards, printed on cardboard stock measuring 2 ½ by 3 ½ inches, have images of players on the front and player information on the back. Like traditional cards, the parody cards use a variety of special effects, including foil embossing, stamping, spectra etching, and U–V coating. Cardtoons also takes advantage of a number of trading card industry techniques to enhance the value of its cards, such as limiting production, serially numbering cases of the cards, and randomly inserting subsets and "chase cards" (special trading cards) into the sets.

After designing its trading cards, Cardtoons contracted with a printer (Champs Marketing, Inc.) and distributor (TCM Associates) and implemented a marketing plan. As part of that plan, Cardtoons placed an advertisement in the May 14, 1993, issue of Sports Collectors Digest. That advertisement tipped off MLBPA, the defendant in this action, and prompted its attorney to write cease and desist letters to both Cardtoons and Champs.

MLBPA is the exclusive collective bargaining agent for all active major league baseball players, and operates a group licensing program in which it acts as the assignee of the individual publicity rights of all active players. Since 1966, MLBPA has entered into group licensing arrangements for a variety of products, such as candy bars, cookies, cereals, and, most importantly, baseball trading cards, which generate over seventy percent of its licensing revenue. MLBPA receives royalties from these sales and distributes the money to individual players.

After receiving the cease and desist letter from MLBPA, Champs advised Cardtoons that it would not print the parody cards until a court of competent jurisdiction had determined that the cards did not violate MLBPA' rights. Cardtoons then filed this suit seeking a declaratory judgment that its cards do not violate the publicity or other property rights of MLBPA or its members. Cardtoons also sought damages for tortious interference with its contractual relationship with Champs, as well as an injunction to prevent MLBPA from threatening legal action against Champs or other third parties with whom Cardtoons had contracted concerning the cards. MLBPA moved to dismiss for lack of subject matter jurisdiction, and counterclaimed for a declaratory judgment, injunction, and damages for violation of its members' rights of publicity under Oklahoma law.

The district court referred the case to a magistrate, who issued his Report and Recommendation in favor of MLBPA. The magistrate stated that the parody cards infringed on MLBPA's right of publicity and that, under either a trademark balancing test or a copyright fair use test, Cardtoons did not have a First Amendment right to market its cards without a license from MLBPA. The district court initially adopted the magistrate's Report and Recommendation, *Cardtoons, L.C. v. Major League Baseball Players Association,* 838 F.Supp. 1501 (N.D.Okla.1993), but subsequently vacated that decision and issued *Cardtoons, L.C. v. Major League Baseball Players Association,* 868 F.Supp. 1266 (N.D.Okla.1994). In its second opinion, the court wholly rejected application of a trademark balancing test to the right of publicity, and instead applied a copyright fair use analysis. Unlike the magistrate, however, the court held that a fair use analysis requires recognition of a parody exception to the Oklahoma publicity rights statute, and issued a declaratory judgment in favor of Cardtoons. This appeal followed.

II. Jurisdiction

MLBPA contends that the district court lacked jurisdiction over this case because there is no federal question, and because the suit does not involve a case or controversy. Whether this lawsuit involves a federal question, and whether a case or controversy exists, are separate inquiries. We turn to these questions below.

A. Federal Question Jurisdiction

MLBPA first contends that the district court lacked federal subject matter jurisdiction over this case...

District courts have original federal question jurisdiction over complaints that contain a claim that arises under federal law. 28 U.S.C. § 1331...

Accordingly, federal question jurisdiction in this case turns on whether there would be federal question jurisdiction over the well-pleaded complaint that MLBPA may bring against Cardtoons. The federal cause of action at issue here is a claim under section 43(a)(1) of the Lanham Act, which provides civil liability for any person who uses any "word, term, name, symbol, or device" in connection with goods or services that is likely to cause confusion "as to the affiliation, connection, or association of such person with another person, or as to the origin, sponsorship, or approval of his or her goods, services, or commercial activities by another person." 15 U.S.C. § 1125(a)(1). We evaluate the adequacy of the MLBPA's federal claim by the same standard that we would use to evaluate federal question jurisdiction if that claim were actually before us. *See Janakes v. United States Postal Serv.,* 768 F.2d 1091, 1093–95 (9th Cir.1985). Dismissal of a complaint for lack of subject matter jurisdiction would only be justified if "that claim were 'so attenuated and unsubstantial as to be absolutely devoid of merit' or 'frivolous.' " *Baker v. Carr,* 369 U.S. 186, 199, 82 S.Ct. 691, 701, 7 L.Ed.2d 663 (1962) (citations omitted). This case clearly survives that test: MLBPA could have brought a nonfrivolous Lanham Act claim against Cardtoons alleging that Cardtoons' use of the names and likenesses of major league baseball players on its cards was likely to cause confusion as to the association of MLBPA with Cardtoons or as to MLBPA's approval of the cards. Because MLBPA could have brought a federal Lanham Act claim as part of a well-pleaded complaint against Cardtoons, the district court had federal question jurisdiction over this declaratory judgment action.

Cardtoons maintains, and the district court agreed, that the court also had jurisdiction over this action because it involves substantial First Amendment questions. This assertion is incorrect. It is well settled that we look to the nature of the anticipated claims of the declaratory judgment defendant, not the anticipated defenses by the declaratory judgment plaintiff, to determine the presence of a federal question. *Wycoff,* 344 U.S. at 248, 73 S.Ct. at 242–43. " '[I]f, but for the availability of the declaratory judgment procedure, the federal claim would arise only as a defense to a state created action, jurisdiction is lacking.' " *Franchise Tax Bd.,* 463 U.S. at 16, 103 S.Ct. at 2850 (quoting 10A Charles A. Wright, Arthur R. Miller & Mary Kay Kane, *Federal Practice and Procedure* § 2767, at 744–45 (2d ed. 1983)). In this case, the First Amendment arises only as a potential *defense* to MLBPA's claimed right: MLBPA could neither bring an action based on the First Amendment nor assert a well-pleaded state claim that necessarily involved a First Amendment question. Thus, we cannot ground our jurisdiction on this basis because "the First Amendment as a defense does not constitute a basis for federal jurisdiction, for it is fundamental that anticipation of a defense cannot confer jurisdiction." *Monks v. Hetherington,* 573 F.2d 1164, 1166 (10th Cir.1978).

B. The Controversy Requirement

MLBPA further contends that this suit does not involve a case or controversy. We review this issue de novo...

In order to satisfy this threshold requirement, there must be "a real and substantial controversy admitting of specific relief through a decree of a conclusive character, as distinguished from an opinion advising what the law would be upon a hypothetical state of facts." *Aetna Life Ins. Co. v. Haworth,* 300 U.S. 227, 241, 57 S.Ct. 461, 464, 81 L.Ed. 617 (1937). In an intellectual property case, an actual controversy exists when (1) the declaratory plaintiff has produced or is prepared to produce the product in question and (2) the declaratory defendant's conduct has created a reasonable apprehension on the part of the declaratory plaintiff that it will face suit if it commences or continues the activity at issue...

Cardtoons has carried its burden by establishing both elements of the case or controversy test. The first element is satisfied because Cardtoons had completed all work in preparation for production of the cards when it filed its declaratory judgment complaint. The second element is satisfied by MLBPA's cease and desist letter in which it threatened to pursue its "full legal remedies" if Cardtoons did not immediately stop production and sale of the cards. That letter, along with MLBPA's history of suing other card companies in similar situations, *e.g., Major League Baseball Players Ass'n v. Dad's Kid Corp.,* 806 F.Supp. 458 (S.D.N.Y.1992), created a reasonable apprehension on the part of Cardtoons of impending litigation.

MLBPA argues that Cardtoons could not have reasonably feared a *federal* claim because MLBPA never explicitly threatened to bring a Lanham Act claim. As discussed above, whether MLBPA's potential suit could contain a federal claim is pivotal to our federal question jurisdiction. Whether MLBPA threatened to bring a federal claim, however, is immaterial to the controversy requirement, which is satisfied so long as MLBPA's conduct created a reasonable apprehension on the part of Cardtoons of the imminence of suit, with state or federal claims, upon publication. In any event, Cardtoons was reasonably apprehensive of a suit containing a federal claim given MLBPA's threat of pursuing its "*full* legal remedies" and its previous use of the Lanham Act in similar cases. Thus, the dispute between Cardtoons and MLBPA satisfies the case or controversy requirement.

III. The Merits

Cardtoons asks for a declaration that it can distribute its parody trading cards without the consent of MLBPA. There are three steps to our analysis of this issue. First, we determine whether the cards infringe upon MLBPA's property rights as established by either the Lanham Act or Oklahoma's right of publicity statute. If so, we then ascertain whether the cards are protected by the First Amendment. Finally, if both parties have cognizable rights at stake, we proceed to a final determination of the relative importance of those rights in the context of this case.

A. MLBPA's Property Rights
1. The Lanham Act

We begin by determining whether the cards violate MLBPA's property rights under the Lanham Act. Section 43(a)(1) of the Lanham Act, 15 U.S.C. § 1125(a)(1), creates a federal remedy for false representations or false designations of origin used in connection with the sale of a product...

Likelihood of confusion is a question of fact that we review for clear error. *Jordache,* 828 F.2d at 1484. The district court found that Cardtoons' parody cards created no likelihood of confusion. We agree that no one would mistake MLBPA and its members as anything other than the targets of the parody cards. Most of the cards have a Cardtoons logo and a statement that they are not licensed by MLBPA. In addition, as with all successful parodies, the effect of the cards is to amuse rather than confuse. "A parody relies upon a *difference* from the original mark, presumably a humorous difference, in order to produce its desired effect." *Id.* at 1486 (emphasis added). Cardtoons' success depends upon the humorous association of its parody cards with traditional, licensed baseball cards, not upon public confusion as to the source of the cards. The district court's decision that the parody cards do not create a likelihood of confusion is not clearly erroneous, and thus the cards do not infringe upon MLBPA's property rights under the Lanham Act.

2. The Right of Publicity

The right of publicity is the right of a person to control the commercial use of his or her identity. 1 J. Thomas McCarthy, *The Rights of Publicity and Privacy* § 1.1[A][1] (1996); *see Restatement (Third) of Unfair Competition* § 46 (1995). While the right was originally intertwined with the right of privacy, courts soon came to recognize a distinction between the personal right to be left alone and the business right to control use of one's identity in commerce. *McCarthy, supra,* §§ 1.1–1.6; Michael Madow, *Private Ownership of Public Image: Popular Culture and Publicity Rights,* 81 Cal.L.Rev. 127, 167–78 (1993). The latter was first acknowledged as a distinct privilege and termed the "right of publicity" in *Haelan Laboratories, Inc. v. Topps Chewing Gum, Inc.,* 202 F.2d 866 (2d Cir.), *cert. denied,* 346 U.S. 816, 74 S.Ct. 26, 98 L.Ed. 343 (1953). *Haelan Laboratories,* appropriately enough, involved two rival chewing gum manufacturers who were arguing over exclusive rights to use the image of a professional baseball player to promote their product. In resolving the dispute, the court concluded that "a man has a right in the publicity value of his photograph." *Id.* at 868.

The development of this new intellectual property right was further cultivated by Melville Nimmer in his seminal article *The Right of Publicity,* 19

Law & Contemp. Probs. 203 (1954). Nimmer, who was counsel for Paramount Pictures at the time, Madow, *supra,* at 174 n. 238, referred to "the needs of Broadway and Hollywood" in describing the foundations and parameters of the right, Nimmer, *supra,* at 203. The right of publicity is now recognized by common law or statute in twenty-five states. McCarthy, *supra,* § 6.1[B].

Like trademark and copyright, the right of publicity involves a cognizable property interest. *Zacchini v. Scripps–Howard Broadcasting Co.,* 433 U.S. 562, 573, 97 S.Ct. 2849, 2856, 53 L.Ed.2d 965 (1977); *Restatement (Third) of Unfair Competition* § 46 cmt. g. Most formulations of the right protect against the unauthorized use of certain features of a person's identity—such as name, likeness, or voice—for commercial purposes. *See* McCarthy, *supra,* §§ 4.9–4.15. Although publicity rights are related to laws preventing false endorsement, they offer substantially broader protection. Suppose, for example, that a company, Mitchell Fruit, wanted to use pop singer Madonna in an advertising campaign to sell bananas, but Madonna never ate its fruit and would not agree to endorse its products. If Mitchell Fruit posted a billboard featuring a picture of Madonna and the phrase, "Madonna may have ten platinum albums, but she's never had a Mitchell banana," Madonna would not have a claim for false endorsement. She would, however, have a publicity rights claim, because Mitchell Fruit misappropriated her name and likeness for commercial purposes. Publicity rights, then, are a form of property protection that allows people to profit from the full commercial value of their identities.

Oklahoma first recognized the right of publicity as early as 1965, but expanded the right in a 1985 statute that is virtually identical to California's right of publicity statute, Cal.Civ.Code §§ 990 and 3344.

Thus, a civil suit for infringement of MLBPA's publicity right under § 1449(A) requires proof of three elements: (1) knowing use of player names or likenesses (2) on products, merchandise, or goods (3) without MLBPA's prior consent. If MLBPA proves these three elements, then the burden shifts to Cardtoons to raise a valid defense.

There is little question that Cardtoons knowingly uses the names and likenesses of major league baseball players. This is evident from an examination of the cards and the testimony of the president of Cardtoons, who conceded that the cards borrow the likenesses of active players. Indeed, the caricatures are only humorous because they, along with the parodied name, team, and commentary, are accurate enough to allow identification of the players being parodied. The second and third elements of the statute are also satisfied. The cards are clearly a product, designed to be widely marketed and sold for profit. In addition, the parties have stipulated that MLBPA has not consented to Cardtoons' use of player likenesses. Cardtoons' parody cards, then, do infringe upon MLBPA's publicity right as defined in § 1449(A).

The Oklahoma publicity statute contains two exceptions designed to accommodate the First Amendment. The first, a "news" exception, exempts use of a person's identity in connection with any news, public affairs, or sports broadcast or account, or any political campaign, from the dictates of the statute. Okla. stat. tit. 12, § 1449(D). The second exception, roughly analogous to the First Amendment concept of "incidental use," exempts use in a commercial medium that is not directly connected with commercial sponsorship or paid advertising. Okla. stat. tit. 12, § 1449(F). The news and incidental use exceptions, however, provide no haven for Cardtoons. Cardtoons' commercial venture is not in connection with any news account. Moreover, the company's use of player likenesses is directly connected with a proposed commercial endeavor; indeed, the players were specifically selected for their wide market appeal. Thus, notwithstanding any First Amendment defense, Cardtoons' use of player likenesses on its cards violates the Oklahoma statute and infringes upon the property rights of MLBPA.

B. Cardtoons' First Amendment Right

Because the parody trading cards infringe upon MLBPA's property rights, we must consider whether Cardtoons has a countervailing First Amendment right to publish the cards. The First Amendment only protects speech from regulation by the government. Although this is a civil action between private parties, it involves application of a state statute that Cardtoons claims imposes restrictions on its right of free expression. Application of that statute thus satisfies the state action requirement of Cardtoons' First Amendment claim. *See New York Times Co. v. Sullivan,* 376 U.S. 254, 265, 84 S.Ct. 710, 718, 11 L.Ed.2d 686 (1964).

Cardtoons' parody trading cards receive full protection under the First Amendment. The cards provide social commentary on public figures, major league baseball players, who are involved in a significant commercial enterprise, major league baseball. While not core political speech (the cards do not, for example, adopt a position on the Ken Griffey, Jr., for President campaign), this type of commentary on an important social institution constitutes protected expression.

The cards are no less protected because they provide humorous rather than serious commentary. Speech that entertains, like speech that informs, is protected by the First Amendment because "[t]he line between the informing and the entertaining is too elusive for the protection of that basic right." *Winters v. New York,* 333 U.S. 507, 510, 68 S.Ct. 665, 667, 92 L.Ed. 840 (1948); *see Zacchini,* 433 U.S. 562, 578, 97 S.Ct. 2849, 2859, 53 L.Ed.2d 965. Moreover, Cardtoons makes use of artistic and literary devices with distinguished traditions. Parody, for example, is a humorous form of social commentary that dates to Greek antiquity, and has since made regular appearances in English literature. *See L.L. Bean, Inc. v. Drake Publishers, Inc.,* 811 F.2d 26, 28 (1st Cir.), *appeal dismissed and cert. denied,* 483 U.S. 1013, 107 S.Ct. 3254, 97 L.Ed.2d 753 (1987). In addition, cartoons and caricatures, such as those in the trading cards, have played a prominent role in public and political debate throughout our nation's history. *See Hustler Magazine v. Falwell,* 485 U.S. 46, 53–55, 108 S.Ct. 876, 880–82, 99 L.Ed.2d 41 (1988). Thus, the trading cards' commentary on these public figures and the major commercial enterprise in which they work receives no less protection because the cards are amusing.

MLBPA contends that Cardtoons' speech receives less protection because it fails to use a traditional medium of expression. The protections afforded by the First Amendment, however, have never been limited to newspapers and books. The Supreme Court has relied on the First Amendment to strike down ordinances that ban the distribution of pamphlets,… Thus, even if the trading cards are not a traditional medium of expression, they nonetheless contain protected speech.

Moreover, even if less common mediums of expression were to receive less First Amendment protection (perhaps out of concern for whether they contain any expression at all), trading cards do not fall into that category. Baseball cards have been an important means of informing the public about baseball players for over a century. "Trading, collecting and learning about players are the most common reasons for children to purchase baseball cards.… They are, in other words, an education in baseball." *Fleer Corp. v. Topps Chewing Gum, Inc.,* 501 F.Supp. 485, 495–96 (E.D.Pa.1980), *rev'd on other grounds,* 658 F.2d 139 (3d Cir.1981), *cert. denied,* 455 U.S. 1019, 102 S.Ct. 1715, 72 L.Ed.2d 137 (1982). In addition, non-sports trading cards have also been an important medium for disseminating information. Some recent examples feature topics such as saints, Norman Rockwell paintings, presidential candidates, the rise and fall of the Soviet Union, local police officers, and Rodney King. All of these trading cards, regardless of their topic, convey information about their subject and therefore constitute an important means of expression that deserves First Amendment protection.

MLBPA also maintains that the parody trading cards are commercial merchandise rather than protected speech. However, we see no principled distinction between speech and merchandise that informs our First Amendment analysis. The fact that expressive materials are sold neither renders the speech unprotected,… nor alters the level of protection under the First Amendment, Cardtoons need not give away its trading cards in order to bring them within the ambit of the First Amendment.

MLBPA further argues that the parody cards are commercial speech and should therefore receive less protection under the First Amendment. The Supreme Court has defined commercial speech as "expression related solely to the economic interests of the speaker and its audience." *Central Hudson Gas & Elec. Corp. v. Public Serv. Comm'n,* 447 U.S. 557, 561, 100 S.Ct. 2343, 2349, 65 L.Ed.2d 341 (1980). Speech that does no more than propose a commercial transaction, for example, is commercial speech. *See Virginia State Bd. of Pharmacy,* 425 U.S. at 762, 96 S.Ct. at 1825. Thus, commercial speech is best understood as speech that merely advertises a product or service for business purposes, *see 44 Liquormart, Inc. v. Rhode Island,* 517 U.S. 484, ——, 116 S.Ct. 1495, 1504, 134 L.Ed.2d 711 (1996) (plurality opinion) (outlining a brief history of commercial speech that is, essentially, a history of advertising). As such, commercial speech may receive something less than the strict review afforded other types of speech. *Id.* at ——, 116 S.Ct. at 1507.

Cardtoons' trading cards, however, are not commercial speech—they do not merely advertise another unrelated product. Although the cards are sold in the marketplace, they are not transformed into commercial speech merely because they are sold for profit. *Virginia State Bd. of Pharmacy,* 425 U.S. at 761, 96 S.Ct. at 1825. Contrary to MLBPA's argument, therefore, the cards are unlike the parody in the only other circuit court decision addressing the constitutional tensions inherent in a celebrity parody, *White v. Samsung Electronics America, Inc.,* 971 F.2d 1395 (9th Cir.), *cert. denied,* 508 U.S. 951, 113 S.Ct. 2443, 124 L.Ed.2d 660 (1993). In that case, defendant Samsung published an advertisement featuring a costumed robot that parodied Vanna White, the letter-turner on television's Wheel of Fortune, and White sued for violation of her right of publicity. The court noted that in cases of noncommercial parodies, "the first amendment hurdle will bar most right of publicity actions against those activities." *Id.* at 1401 n. 3. However, without engaging in a methodical commercial speech analysis of Samsung's First Amendment defense, the court ruled that White's claim was sufficient to withstand Samsung's motion for summary judgment. We disagree with the result in that case for reasons discussed in the two dissents that it engendered. *Id.* at 1407–08 (Alarcón, J., concurring in part and dissenting in part); *White v. Samsung Elecs. Am., Inc.,* 989 F.2d 1512, 1512–23 (9th Cir.1993) (denial of rehearing en banc) (Kozinski, J., dissenting). Moreover, our case is distinguished by the fact that the speech involved is not commercial, but rather speech subject to full First Amendment protection. *White,* therefore, is inapposite, and we must directly confront the central problem in this case: whether Cardtoons' First Amendment right trumps MLBPA's property right.

C. Balancing Free Speech Rights with Property Rights

In resolving the tension between the First Amendment and publicity rights in this case, we find little guidance in cases involving parodies of other forms of intellectual property. Trademark and copyright, for example, have built-in mechanisms that serve to avoid First Amendment concerns of this kind. As discussed above, proof of trademark infringement under the Lanham Act requires proof of a likelihood of confusion, but, in the case of a good trademark parody, there is little likelihood of confusion, since the humor lies in the difference between the original and the parody. The Copyright Act of 1976 contains a similar mechanism, the fair use exception, which permits the use of copyrighted materials for purposes such as criticism and comment. 17 U.S.C. § 107; *see Campbell v. Acuff–Rose Music, Inc.,* 510 U.S. 569, 114 S.Ct. 1164, 127 L.Ed.2d 500 (1994) (applying the fair use exception to parody). Oklahoma's right of publicity statute, however, does not provide a similar accommodation for parody, and we must therefore confront the First Amendment issue directly.

MLBPA urges us to adopt the framework established in *Lloyd Corp. v. Tanner,* 407 U.S. 551, 92 S.Ct. 2219, 33 L.Ed.2d 131 (1972), in order to reconcile the free speech and property rights at stake in this case. The issue in *Lloyd* was whether a private shopping center could prevent the distribution of handbills on its premises...

The Court held that the First Amendment did not require the shopping center to allow distribution of the handbills because the public sidewalks and streets surrounding the center provided an adequate alternative avenue of communication. *Id.* at 567–68, 92 S.Ct. at 2228–29. This type of analysis, usually applied to time, place, and manner restrictions, has also been applied in several cases where intellectual property rights have conflicted with the right to free expression.

MLBPA argues that application of the *Lloyd* analysis requires protection of its proprietary right of publicity. First, MLBPA maintains that there are many ways that Cardtoons could parody the institution of baseball that would not require use of player names and likenesses. Cardtoons could, for example, use generic images of baseball players to poke fun at the game. Second, MLBPA contends that Cardtoons could use recognizable players in a format other than trading cards, such as a newspaper or magazine, without infringing on its right of publicity. MLBPA argues that these alternative means of communication are adequate and, therefore, that we may uphold its property rights without seriously infringing upon Cardtoons' right to free expression.

We find, however, that in the context of intellectual property, *Lloyd's* "no adequate alternative avenues" test does not sufficiently accommodate the public's interest in free expression. *See Rogers v. Grimaldi,* 875 F.2d 994, 999 (2d Cir.1989); *Mutual of Omaha Ins. Co.,* 836 F.2d at 405–06 (Heaney, J., dissenting). Intellectual property, unlike real estate, includes the words, images, and sounds that we use to communicate, and "we cannot indulge in the facile assumption that one can forbid particular words without also running a substantial risk of suppressing ideas in the process," *Cohen,* 403 U.S. at 26, 91 S.Ct. at 1788; *see San Francisco Arts & Athletics,* 483 U.S. at 569–70, 107 S.Ct. at 2998–99

(Brennan, J., dissenting). Restrictions on the words or images that may be used by a speaker, therefore, are quite different than restrictions on the time, place, or manner of speech.

In this case, Cardtoons' expression requires use of player identities because, in addition to parodying the institution of baseball, the cards also lampoon individual players. Further, Cardtoons' use of the trading card format is an essential component of the parody because baseball cards have traditionally been used to celebrate baseball players and their accomplishments. Cardtoons expresses ideas through the use of major league baseball player identities, and MLBPA's attempts to enjoin the parody thus goes to the content of the speech, not merely to its time, place, or manner. For that reason, the *Lloyd* test is inapplicable in this case.

This case instead requires us to directly balance the magnitude of the speech restriction against the asserted governmental interest in protecting the intellectual property right. We thus begin our analysis by examining the importance of Cardtoons' right to free expression and the consequences of limiting that right. We then weigh those consequences against the effect of infringing on MLBPA's right of publicity.

1. The Effect of Infringing Upon Cardtoons' Right to Free Speech

Cardtoons' interest in publishing its parody trading cards implicates some of the core concerns of the First Amendment. "Parodies and caricatures," noted Aldous Huxley, "are the most penetrating of criticisms." *Point Counter Point,* ch. 13 (1928); *see Hustler Magazine,* 485 U.S. at 53–55, 108 S.Ct. at 880–82. A parodist can, with deft and wit, readily expose the foolish and absurd in society. Parody is also a valuable form of self-expression that allows artists to shed light on earlier works and, at the same time, create new ones. Thus, parody, both as social criticism and a means of self-expression, is a vital commodity in the marketplace of ideas.

Parodies of celebrities are an especially valuable means of expression because of the role celebrities play in modern society. As one commentator explained, celebrities are "common points of reference for millions of individuals who may never interact with one another, but who share, by virtue of their participation in a mediated culture, a common experience and a collective memory." John B. Thompson, *Ideology and Modern Culture: Critical Social Theory in the Era of Mass Communication* 163 (1990). Through their pervasive presence in the media, sports and entertainment celebrities come to symbolize certain ideas and values.

Because celebrities are an important part of our public vocabulary, a parody of a celebrity does not merely lampoon the celebrity, but exposes the weakness of the idea or value that the celebrity symbolizes in society.

Cardtoons' trading cards, for example, comment on the state of major league baseball by turning images of our sports heroes into modern-day personifications of avarice. In order to effectively criticize society, parodists need access to images that mean something to people, and thus celebrity parodies are a valuable communicative resource. Restricting the use of celebrity identities restricts the communication of ideas.

Without First Amendment protection, Cardtoons' trading cards and their irreverent commentary on the national pastime cannot be freely distributed to the public. Instead, as required by Oklahoma law, the production and distribution of the cards would be subject to MLBPA's consent. The problem with this scheme, as the Supreme Court noted in the context of copyright parody, is that "the unlikelihood that creators of imaginative works will license critical reviews or lampoons of their own productions removes such uses from the very notion of a potential licensing market." *Campbell,* 510 U.S. at ——, 114 S.Ct. at 1178. The potential for suppression is even greater in the context of publicity rights because the product involved is the celebrity's own persona. Indeed, the director of licensing for MLBPA testified that MLBPA would never license a parody which poked fun at the players. Thus, elevating the right of publicity above the right to free expression would likely prevent distribution of the parody trading cards. This would not only allow MLBPA to censor criticism of its members, but would also have a chilling effect upon future celebrity parodies. Such a result is clearly undesirable, for "[t]he last thing we need, the last thing the First Amendment will tolerate, is a law that lets public figures keep people from mocking them." *White,* 989 F.2d at 1519 (Kozinski, J., dissenting).

2. The Effect of Infringing Upon MLBPA's Right of Publicity

We now turn to an evaluation of society's interest in protecting MLBPA's publicity right. The justifications offered for the right of publicity fall into two categories, economic and noneconomic. The right is thought to further economic goals such as stimulating athletic and artistic achievement, promoting the efficient allocation of resources, and protecting consumers. In addition, the right of publicity is said to protect various noneconomic interests, such as safeguarding natural rights, securing the fruits of celebrity labors, preventing unjust enrichment, and averting emotional harm. We examine the applicability of each of these justifications to the facts of this case.

The principal economic argument made in support of the right of publicity is that it provides an incentive for creativity and achievement. *See, e.g., Zacchini,* 433 U.S. at 576–77, 97 S.Ct. at 2857–58; *Carson v. Here's Johnny Portable Toilets, Inc.,* 698 F.2d 831, 837 (6th Cir.1983). Under this view, publicity rights induce people to expend the time, effort, and resources to develop the talents prerequisite to public recognition. While those talents provide immediate benefit to those with commercially valuable identities, the products of their enterprise—such as movies, songs, and sporting events—ultimately benefit society as a whole. Thus, it is argued, society has an interest in a right of publicity that is closely analogous to its interest in other intellectual property protections such as copyright and patent law. *Zacchini,* 433 U.S. at 576, 97 S.Ct. at 2857.

This incentives argument is certainly a compelling justification for other forms of intellectual property. Copyright law, for example, protects the primary, if not only, source of a writer's income, and thus provides a significant incentive for creativity and achievement. The incentive effect of publicity rights, however, has been overstated. Most sports and entertainment celebrities with commercially valuable identities engage in activities that themselves generate a significant amount of income; the commercial value of their identities is merely a by-product of their performance values. *See Restatement (Third) of Unfair Competition* § 46 cmt. c. Although no one pays to watch Cormac McCarthy write a novel, many people pay a lot of money to watch Demi Moore "act" and Michael Jordan play basketball. Thus, the analogy to the incentive effect of other intellectual property protections is strained because "[a]bolition of the right of publicity would leave entirely unimpaired a celebrity's ability to earn a living from the activities that have generated his commercially marketable fame." Madow, *supra,* at 209.

This distinction between the value of a person's identity and the value of his performance explains why *Zacchini v. Scripps–Howard Broadcasting Co.,* 433 U.S. 562, 97 S.Ct. 2849, 53 L.Ed.2d 965 (1977), the Supreme Court's sole case involving a right of publicity claim, is a red herring. Hugo Zacchini, a performer in a human cannonball act, brought an action against a television station to recover damages he suffered when the station videotaped and broadcast his entire performance. The Supreme Court held that the First Amendment did not give the station the right to broadcast Zacchini's entire act in contravention of his state protected right of publicity. *Id.* at 574–75, 97 S.Ct. at 2856–57. Zacchini, however, complained of the appropriation of the economic value of his *performance,* not the economic value of his *identity.* The Court's incentive rationale is obviously more compelling in a right of performance case than in a more typical right of publicity case involving the appropriation of a celebrity's identity. *See Restatement (Third) of Unfair Competition* § 46 reporters' note cmt. c.

Moreover, the additional inducement for achievement produced by publicity rights are often inconsequential because most celebrities with valuable commercial identities are already handsomely compensated. Actor Jim Carrey, for example, received twenty million dollars for starring in the movie *The Cable Guy, see* Bernard Weinraub, *How a Sure Summer Hit Missed,* N.Y. Times, June 27, 1996, at C11, and major league baseball players' salaries currently average over one million dollars per year, *see* Bill Brashler, *Boooooooooooooooo! Let's Hear It for Pampered, Preening, Overpaid Whiners: The Jocks,* Chi.Trib., July 28, 1996, (Magazine), at 12. Such figures suggest that "even without the right of publicity the rate of return to stardom in the entertainment and sports fields is probably high enough to bring forth a more than 'adequate' supply of creative effort and achievement." Madow, *supra,* at 210. In addition, even in the absence of publicity rights, celebrities would still be able to reap financial reward from authorized appearances and endorsements. The extra income generated by licensing one's identity does not provide a necessary inducement to enter and achieve in the realm of sports and entertainment. Thus, while publicity rights may provide some incentive for creativity and achievement, the magnitude and importance of that incentive has been exaggerated.

The argument that publicity rights provide valuable incentives is even less compelling in the context of celebrity parodies. Since celebrities will seldom give permission for their identities to be parodied, granting them control over the parodic use of their identities would not directly provide them with any additional income. It would, instead, only allow them to shield themselves from ridicule and criticism. The only economic incentive gained by having control over the use of one's identity in parody is control over the potential effect the parody would have on the market for nonparodic use of one's identity. MLBPA claims, for example, that publication of the parody cards will decrease demand for traditional baseball cards because Cardtoons and other makers of parody trading cards would compete with manufacturers of licensed cards in the same limited trading card market. Parody, however, rarely acts as a market substitute for the original, *Campbell,* 510 U.S. 569 (1994), 114 S.Ct. at 1177–78, and there is no evidence in this record that convinces us otherwise. Even if there is some substitutive effect, and card collectors with limited resources decide to buy parody cards instead of traditional, licensed cards, the small amount of additional income generated by suppressing parody cards will have little, if any, effect on the incentive to become a major league baseball player.

The incentives argument would be even more tenuous, indeed perverse, if good-humored celebrities were to license use of their identities for parody. The right of publicity would then provide an incentive to engage in the socially undesirable behavior that might give rise to a reason to parody. Although part of any parody's market appeal depends upon the prominence of the celebrity, the critical element of the parody's value hinges on the accuracy of the caricature or criticism. Society does not have a significant interest in allowing a celebrity to protect the type of reputation that gives rise to parody.

We recognize that publicity rights do provide some incentive to achieve in the fields of sports and entertainment. However, the inducements generated by publicity rights are not nearly as important as those created by copyright and patent law, and the small incentive effect of publicity rights is reduced or eliminated in the context of celebrity parodies. In sum, it is unlikely that little leaguers will stop dreaming of the big leagues or major leaguers will start "dogging it" to first base if MLBPA is denied the right to control the use of its members' identities in parody.

The second economic justification for the right of publicity is that it promotes the efficient allocation of resources, a version of the familiar tragedy of the commons argument used to prove the superiority of private property over common property. *See, e.g., Matthews v. Wozencraft,* 15 F.3d 432, 437–38 (5th Cir.1994). Without the artificial scarcity created by publicity rights, identities would be commercially exploited until the marginal value of each use is zero. *Id.* "Creating artificial scarcity preserves the value to [the celebrity], to advertisers who contract for the use of his likeness, and in the end, to consumers, who receive information from the knowledge that he is being paid to endorse the product." *Id.* at 438. Giving people control of the commercial use of their identities, according to this analysis, maximizes the economic and informational value of those identities.

This efficiency argument is most persuasive in the context of advertising, where repeated use of a celebrity's likeness to sell products may eventually diminish its commercial value. The argument is not as persuasive, however, when applied to nonadvertising uses. It is not clear, for example, that the frequent appearance of a celebrity's likeness on t-shirts and coffee mugs will reduce its value; indeed, the value of the likeness may increase precisely because "everybody's got one." Madow, *supra,* at 222. Further, celebrities with control over the parodic use of their identities would not use the power to "ration the use of their names in order to maximize their value over time," *Matthews,* 15 F.3d at 438 n. 2. They would instead use that power to suppress criticism, and thus permanently remove a valuable source of information about their identity from the marketplace.

The final economic argument offered for rights of publicity is that they protect against consumer deception...

There are also several noneconomic reasons advanced for the right of publicity. First, some believe that publicity rights stem from some notion of natural rights...

The second noneconomic justification is that publicity rights allow celebrities to enjoy the fruits of their labors...

Celebrities, however, are often not fully responsible for their fame. Indeed, in the entertainment industry, a celebrity's fame may largely be the creation of the media or the audience. *See* Madow, *supra* at 184–96 (discussing the role of factors beyond a celebrity's control in developing a commercially marketable persona). As one actor put it, "Only that audience out there makes a star. It's up to them. You can't do anything about it.... Stars would all be Louis B. Mayer's cousins if you could make 'em up." Jack Nicholson, *quoted in* Jib Fowles,

Starstruck: Celebrity Performers and the American Public 84 (1992). Professional athletes may be more responsible for their celebrity status, however, because athletic success is fairly straightforwardly the result of an athlete's natural talent and dedication. Thus, baseball players may deserve to profit from the commercial value of their identities more than movie stars. Once again, however, the force of this justification is diminished in the case of parody, because there is little right to enjoy the fruits of socially undesirable behavior.

The third, related justification for publicity rights is the prevention of unjust enrichment. *See, e.g., Zacchini,* 433 U.S. at 576, 97 S.Ct. at 2857–58; *Ali,* 447 F.Supp. at 728–29. In this view, whether the commercial value of an identity is the result of a celebrity's hard work, media creation, or just pure dumb luck, no social purpose is served by allowing others to freely appropriate it. Cardtoons, however, is not merely hitching its wagon to a star. As in all celebrity parodies, Cardtoons added a significant creative component of its own to the celebrity identity and created an entirely new product. Indeed, allowing MLBPA to control or profit from the parody trading cards would actually sanction the theft of Cardtoons' creative enterprise.

A final justification offered for the right of publicity is that it prevents emotional injuries. For example, commercial misappropriation may greatly distress a celebrity who finds all commercial exploitation to be offensive. *Lugosi v. Universal Pictures,* 25 Cal.3d 813, 160 Cal.Rptr. 323, 337 n. 11, 603 P.2d 425, 439 n. 11 (1979) (Bird, C.J., dissenting). Even celebrities who crave public attention might find particular uses of their identities to be distressing. *See, e.g., O'Brien v. Pabst Sales Co.,* 124 F.2d 167, 170 (5th Cir.1942) (professional football player, active in an organization devoted to discouraging alcohol use among young people, sued to stop the use of his image in a Pabst Blue Ribbon beer advertising calendar). The right of publicity allows celebrities to avoid the emotional distress caused by unwanted commercial use of their identities. Publicity rights, however, are meant to protect against the loss of financial gain, not mental anguish. *Zacchini,* 433 U.S. at 573, 97 S.Ct. at 2856; *Lugosi,* 603 P.2d at 438–39 (Bird, C.J., dissenting). Laws preventing unfair competition, such as the Lanham Act, and laws prohibiting the intentional infliction of emotional distress adequately cover that ground. Moreover, fame is a double-edged sword—the law cannot allow those who enjoy the public limelight to so easily avoid the ridicule and criticism that sometimes accompany public prominence.

Thus, the noneconomic justifications for the right of publicity are no more compelling than the economic arguments. Those justifications further break down in the context of parody, where the right to profit from one's persona is reduced to the power to suppress criticism. In sum, the effect of limiting MLBPA's right of publicity in this case is negligible.

IV. Conclusion

One of the primary goals of intellectual property law is to maximize creative expression. The law attempts to achieve this goal by striking a proper balance between the right of a creator to the fruits of his labor and the right of future creators to free expression. Underprotection of intellectual property reduces the incentive to create; overprotection creates a monopoly over the raw material of creative expression. The application of the Oklahoma publicity rights statute to Cardtoons' trading cards presents a classic case of overprotection. Little is to be gained, and much lost, by protecting MLBPA's right to control the use of its members' identities in parody trading cards. The justifications for the right of publicity are not nearly as compelling as those offered for other forms of intellectual property, and are particularly unpersuasive in the case of celebrity parodies. The cards, on the other hand, are an important form of entertainment and social commentary that deserve First Amendment protection. Accordingly, we AFFIRM.

We GRANT the motion by First Amendment Publishing, Inc. for leave to file an amicus curiae brief, DENY the motion by appellee to strike, and GRANT the motion by appellee to file a supplemental appendix and brief in support.

In the following case, Abkco Music, Inc. v. Harrisongs Music, Ltd., 722 F.2d 986 (2d Cir. 1982), the court found that George Harrison's song, "My Sweet Lord" infringed on "He's So Fine." The court also stated that infringement can be found if it is based on subconscious copying.

ABKCO MUSIC, INC.,
v.
HARRISONGS MUSIC, LTD.,
v.
ABKCO INDUSTRIES, INC.
United States Court of Appeals, Second Circuit.
Nos. 505, 600, Dockets 82-7421, 82-7461
Argued Nov. 24, 1982
Decided Nov. 3, 1983
722 F.2d 988

PIERCE, Circuit Judge:

I. BACKGROUND

A. Events Leading to Liability Trial

On February 10, 1971, Bright Tunes Music Corporation (Bright Tunes), then copyright holder of the song "He's So Fine," composed by Ronald Mack, brought this copyright infringement action in the United States District Court for the Southern District of New York against former member of the musical group "The Beatles" George Harrison, and also against related entities (hereinafter referred to collectively as "Harrison Interests"), alleging that the Harrison composition, "My Sweet Lord," (hereinafter referred to alternatively as "MSL") infringed the Ronald Mack composition, "He's So Fine," (hereinafter referred to alternatively as "HSF").

When this action was commenced, the business affairs of The Beatles, including Harrison Interests, were handled by ABKCO Music, Inc. (ABKCO) and Allen B. Klein, its President and "moving spirit." *ABKCO Music, Inc. v. Harrisongs Music, Ltd.,* 508 F.Supp. 798, 799 (S.D.N.Y.1981). ABKCO was Harrison's business manager during the initial stages of the copyright liability action herein, at which time the litigation was handled for Harrison by ABKCO's General Counsel.

The following events preceded the instant appeal. Shortly after this action was commenced in February, 1971, Klein (representing Harrisongs Music, Inc. and George Harrison) met with Seymour Barash (President and major stockholder of Bright Tunes) to discuss possible settlement of this lawsuit. Although Klein, at trial, denied having specific knowledge of the details of this discussion, he testified that he had suggested to Barash, around February of 1971, a purchase of the entire stock of Bright Tunes as a way to dispose of this lawsuit. Thus, in 1971, Klein was acting on behalf of Harrison Interests in an effort to settle this copyright infringement claim brought by Bright Tunes, although no settlement resulted.

Subsequent to the Klein-Barash meeting, Bright Tunes went into "judicial dissolution proceedings." This infringement action was placed on the district court's suspense calendar on March 3, 1972, and was resumed by Bright Tunes (in receivership) in early 1973. Also in early 1973 (March 31), ABKCO's management contract with The Beatles expired. Bitter and protracted litigation ensued between The Beatles and ABKCO over the winding down of management affairs-a dispute that ended in 1977 with The Beatles paying ABKCO $4.2 million in settlement.

There is some disagreement as to whether further settlement negotiations took place between Harrison Interests and Bright Tunes between 1973 and mid-1975. It appears undisputed, however, that Harrison Interests' attorney at least initiated settlement talks in the late summer of 1975; that in the period October 1975 through February 1976, settlement discussions took place between Bright Tunes' counsel and counsel for Harrison Interests regarding settlement of this infringement action (an offer by Harrison Interests based on United States royalties); and that those discussions were in the 50%/50% or 60%/40% range. These discussions culminated in a $148,000 offer by Harrison Interests in January of 1976 (representing 40% of the United States royalties).

At about the same time (1975), apparently unknown to George Harrison, Klein had been negotiating with Bright Tunes to purchase all of Bright Tunes' stock. That such negotiations were taking place was confirmed as early as October 30, 1975, in a letter from Seymour Barash (Bright Tunes' former President) to Howard Sheldon (Bright Tunes' Receiver), in which Barash reported that there had been an offer from Klein for a substantial sum of money. The same letter observed that "[Klein] would not be interested in purchasing all of the stock of Bright Tunes ... if there was any doubt as to the outcome of this litigation."

In late November 1975, Klein (on behalf of ABKCO) offered to pay Bright Tunes $100,000 for a call on all Bright Tunes' stock, exercisable for an additional $160,000 upon a judicial determination as to copyright infringement. In connection with this offer, Klein furnished to Bright Tunes three schedules summarizing the following financial information concerning "My Sweet Lord:" (1) domestic royalty income of Harrisongs Music, Inc. on MSL; (2) an updated version of that first schedule; and (3) Klein's own estimated value of the copyright, including an estimate of foreign royalties (performance and mechanical) and his assessment of the total worldwide future earnings.

Barash considered the Klein offer only a starting point. He thought that a value of $600,000 was more accurate and recommended a $200,000 call, based on a $600,000 gross sales price. Also in December 1975, Barash noted, in a letter to counsel for the Peter Maurice Co., that Harrison Interests' counsel had never furnished a certified statement of worldwide royalties of MSL, but that from conversations between Stephen Tenenbaum (accountant for several Bright Tunes stockholders) and Klein, Bright Tunes had been given that information by Klein.

Shortly thereafter, on January 19, 1976, Barash informed Howard Sheldon (Bright Tunes' Receiver) of the Klein offer and of the Bright Tunes stockholders' unanimous decision to reject it. Barash noted that "[s]ince Mr. Klein is in a position to know the true earnings of 'My Sweet Lord', his offer should give all of us an indication of the true value of this copyright and litigation." Sheldon responded in a letter dated January 21, 1976, noting, *inter alia,* that Harrison's attorneys were informed that no settlement would be considered by Bright Tunes until total sales of MSL were determined after appropriate figures were checked.

On January 30, 1976, the eve of the liability trial, a meeting was held by Bright Tunes' attorney for all of Bright Tunes' stockholders (or their counsel) and representatives of Ronald Mack. The purpose of the meeting was to present Bright Tunes with an offer by Harrison Interests of $148,000, representing 40% of the writers' and publishers' royalties earned in the United States (but without relinquishment by Harrison of the MSL copyright). At the time, Bright Tunes' attorney regarded the offer as "a good one." 508 F.Supp. at 802. The Harrison offer was not accepted, however. Bright Tunes raised its demand from 50% of the United States royalties, to 75% worldwide, plus surrender of the MSL copyright. The parties were unable to reach agreement and the matter proceeded to trial.

B. Liability Trial and Events Thereafter

A three-day bench trial on liability was held before Judge Owen on February 23-25, 1976. On August 31, 1976 (amended September 1, 1976), the district judge rendered a decision for the plaintiff as to liability, based on his finding that "My Sweet Lord" was substantially similar to "He's So Fine" and that Harrison had had access to the latter. *Bright Tunes Music Corp. v. Harrisongs Music, Ltd.,* 420 F.Supp. 177 (S.D.N.Y.1976). The issue of damages and other relief was scheduled for trial at a later date.

Following the liability trial, Klein, still acting for ABKCO, continued to discuss with Bright Tunes the purchase of the rights to HSF. During 1977, no serious settlement discussions were held between Bright Tunes and Harrison Interests. Indeed, the record indicates that throughout 1977 Bright Tunes did not authorize its attorneys to give Harrison a specific settlement figure. By November 30, 1977, Bright Tunes' counsel noted that Klein had made an offer on behalf of ABKCO that "far exceeds any proposal that has been made by the defendants."

On February 8, 1978, another settlement meeting took place, but no agreement was reached at that meeting. Although it appears that everyone present felt that the case should be settled, it also appears that there were no further settlement discussions between Harrison Interests and Bright Tunes subsequent to that date. The Bright Tunes negotiations with ABKCO, however, culminated on April 13, 1978, in a purchase by ABKCO of the HSF copyright, the United States infringement claim herein, and the worldwide rights to HSF, for $587,000, an amount more than twice the original Klein (ABKCO) offer. This purchase was made known to George Harrison by Klein himself in April or May of 1978. Harrison "was a bit amazed to find out" about the purchase.

C. Damages Proceedings and Foreign Settlements

On July 17, 1978, ABKCO adopted Bright Tunes' complaint and was substituted as the sole party plaintiff in this action. In May 1979, Harrison Interests obtained leave to assert affirmative defenses and counterclaims against Klein and ABKCO for alleged breaches of fiduciary duty relating to the negotiation for and purchase of the Bright Tunes properties. An eight-day bench trial was held on damages and counterclaims between August 27 and October 15, 1979.

While the matter was still *sub judice,* Harrison Interests, on April 3, 1980, entered into an agreement with Essex Music International, Ltd. (Essex), authorizing Essex to negotiate and enter into settlement agreements, on a 60%/40% basis, on behalf of Harrison Interests throughout the world (except the United Kingdom, the United States and Canada) with any party owning an interest in HSF. These terms were consistent with those of the Maurice-Harrison settlement of the United Kingdom claim, whereby the parties were to use "best endeavours" to obtain 60%/40% settlements throughout the world. ABKCO then settled foreign claims with Essex, also on April 3, 1980.

The damages decision was filed on February 19, 1981. *ABKCO Music, Inc. v. Harrisongs Music, Ltd.,* 508 F.Supp. 798 (S.D.N.Y.1981). Having determined that the damages amounted to $1,599,987, the district judge held that ABKCO's conduct over the 1975-78 period limited its recovery, substantially because of the manner in which ABKCO had become a plaintiff in this case. Particularly "troublesome" to the court was "Klein's covert intrusion into the settlement negotiation picture in late 1975 and early 1976 immediately preceding the trial on the merits." *Id.* at 802. He found, *inter alia,* that Klein's status as Harrison's former business manager gave special credence to ABKCO's offers to Bright Tunes and made Bright Tunes less willing to settle with Harrison Interests either before or after the liability trial. Moreover, the court found that in the course of negotiating with Bright Tunes in 1975-76, Klein "covertly furnished" Bright Tunes with certain financial information about MSL which he obtained while in Harrison's employ as business manager. The foregoing conduct, in the court's view, amounted to a breach of ABKCO's fiduciary duty to Harrison. The court held that although it was not clear that "but for" ABKCO's conduct Harrison Interests and Bright Tunes would have settled, he found that good faith negotiations had been in progress between the parties and Klein's intrusion made their success less likely, since ABKCO's offer in January 1976 was viewed by Bright Tunes as an "insider's disclosure of the value of the case." *Id.* at 803. Consequently, the district judge directed that ABKCO hold the "fruits of its acquisition" from Bright Tunes in trust for Harrison Interests, to be transferred to Harrison Interests by ABKCO upon payment by Harrison Interests of $587,000 plus interest from the date of acquisition.

II. ABKCO'S ARGUMENTS ON APPEAL

ABKCO presents two principal arguments on appeal. First, it is argued that ABKCO did not breach its fiduciary duty to Harrison because (a) no confidential information was improperly passed from ABKCO to Bright Tunes during the negotiations to purchase HSF, and (b) there was no causal relationship between ABKCO's actions and Harrison Interests' failure to obtain settlement. Second, appellant argues that the scope of the constructive trust imposed by Judge Owen is too broad because it covers foreign rights. ABKCO contends that the remedy thus jeopardizes the post-liability-trial settlements of the foreign infringement claims between ABKCO and Harrison Interests (through Essex). As to the first contention, we reject appellant's arguments and affirm the decision of the district judge. With respect to appellant's objection to the scope of the remedy, however, we modify the judgment and remand the case for further consideration in light of this opinion.

A. Breach of Fiduciary Duty

There is no doubt but that the relationship between Harrison and ABKCO prior to the termination of the management agreement in 1973 was that of principal and agent, and that the relationship was fiduciary in nature. *See Meese v. Miller,* 79 A.D.2d 237, 241, 436 N.Y.S.2d 496, 499 (4th Dep't 1981). The rule applicable to our present inquiry is that an agent has a duty "not to use confidential knowledge acquired in his employment in competition with his principal." *Byrne v. Barrett,* 268 N.Y. 199, 206, 197 N.E. 217, 218 (1935). This duty "exists as well after the employment is terminated as during its continuance." *Id.; see also Restatement (Second) of Agency* § 396 (1958). On the other hand, use of information based on general business knowledge or gleaned from general business experience is not covered by the rule, and the former agent is permitted to compete with his former principal in reliance on such general publicly available information. *Byrne v. Barrett,* 268 N.Y. at 206, 197 N.E. at 218; *Restatement (Second) of Agency* § 395 comment b (1958). The principal issue before us in the instant case, then, is whether the district court committed clear error in concluding that Klein (hence, ABKCO) improperly used confidential information, gained as Harrison's former agent, in negotiating for the purchase of Bright Tunes' stock (including HSF) in 1975-76.

One aspect of this inquiry concerns the nature of three documents-schedules of MSL earnings-which Klein furnished to Bright Tunes in connection with the 1975-76 negotiations. Although the district judge did not make a specific finding as to whether each of these schedules was confidential, he determined that Bright Tunes at that time was not entitled to the information. 508 F.Supp. at 803. It appears that the first of the three schedules may have been previously turned over to Bright Tunes by Harrison. The two additional schedules which Klein gave to Bright Tunes (the detailed updating of royalty information and Klein's personal estimate of the value of MSL and future earnings) appear not to have been made available to Bright Tunes by Harrison. Moreover, it appears that at least some of the past royalty information was confidential. The evidence presented herein is not at all convincing that the information imparted to Bright Tunes by Klein was publicly available. *Cf. Franke v. Wiltschek,* 209 F.2d 493, 495 (2d Cir.1953) (former fiduciary precluded from using confidential information in competition with former principal even if the information is readily available from third parties or by other means). Furthermore, the district judge was in a better position to assess the credibility aspects of evidence bearing on this question than we are.

Another aspect of the breach of duty issue concerns the timing and nature of Klein's entry into the negotiation picture and the manner in which he became a plaintiff in this action. In our view, the record supports the position that Bright Tunes very likely gave special credence to Klein's position as an offeror because of his status as Harrison's former business manager and prior coordinator of the defense of this lawsuit. *See, e.g.,* letter from Barash to Sheldon, dated January 19, 1976 ("Since Mr. Klein is in a position to know the true earnings of My Sweet Lord, his offer should give all of us an indication of the true value of this copyright and litigation."). To a significant extent, that favorable bargaining position necessarily was achieved because Klein, as business manager, had intimate knowledge of the financial affairs of his client. Klein himself acknowledged at trial that his offers to Bright Tunes were based, at least in part, on knowledge he had acquired as Harrison's business manager.

Under the circumstances of this case, where there was sufficient evidence to support the district judge's finding that confidential information passed hands, or, at least, was utilized in a manner inconsistent with the duty of a former fiduciary at a time when this litigation was still pending, we conclude that the district judge did not err in holding that ABKCO had breached its duty to Harrison.

We find this case analogous to those "where an employee, with the use of information acquired through his former employment relationship, completes, for his own benefit, a transaction originally undertaken on the former employer's behalf." *Group Association Plans, Inc. v. Colquhoun,* 466 F.2d 469, 474 (D.C.Cir.1972); *cf. Renz v. Beeman,* 589 F.2d 735, 746 (2d Cir.1978) (opportunity for purchase that comes to [trustee] while in fiduciary capacity compels trustee to give right of first refusal to trust estate), *cert. denied,* 444 U.S. 834, 100 S.Ct. 65, 62 L.Ed.2d 43 (1979); *Meinhard v. Salmon,* 249 N.Y. 458, 467, 164 N.E. 545, 548 (1928) ("[T]here may be no abuse of special opportunities growing out of a special trust as manager or agent."). In this case, Klein had commenced a purchase transaction with Bright Tunes in 1971 on behalf of Harrison, which he pursued on his own account after the termination of his fiduciary relationship with Harrison. While the initial attempt to purchase Bright Tunes' catalogue was several years removed from the eventual purchase on ABKCO's own account, we are not of the view that such a fact rendered ABKCO unfettered in the later negotiations. Indeed, Klein pursued the later discussions armed with the intimate knowledge not only of Harrison's business affairs, but of the value of this lawsuit-and at a time when this action was still pending. Taking all of these circumstances together, we agree that appellant's conduct during the period 1975-78 did not meet the standard required of him as a former fiduciary.

In so concluding, we do not purport to establish a general "appearance of impropriety" rule with respect to the artist/manager relationship. That strict standard-reserved principally for the legal profession-would probably not suit the realities of the business world. The facts of this case otherwise permit the conclusion reached herein. Indeed, as Judge Owen noted in his Memorandum and Order of May 7, 1979 (permitting Harrison Interests to assert counterclaims), "The fact situation presented is novel in the extreme. Restated in simplest form, it amounts to the purchase by a business manager of a known claim against his former client where, the right to the claim having been established, all that remains to be done is to assess the monetary award." We find these facts not only novel, but unique. Indeed, the purchase, which rendered Harrison and ABKCO adversaries, occurred in the context of a lawsuit in which ABKCO had been the prior protector of Harrison's interests. Thus, although not wholly analogous to the side-switching cases involving attorneys and their former clients, this fact situation creates clear questions of impropriety. On the unique facts presented herein, we certainly cannot say that Judge Owen's findings and conclusions were clearly erroneous or not in accord with applicable law.

Appellant ABKCO also contends that even if there was a breach of duty, such breach should not limit ABKCO's recovery for copyright infringement because ABKCO's conduct did not cause the Bright Tunes/Harrison settlement negotiations to fail. *See* 508 F.Supp. at 803 & n. 15. Appellant urges, in essence, that a finding of breach of fiduciary duty by an agent, to be actionable, must be found to have been the proximate cause of injury to the principal. We do not accept appellant's proffered causation standard. An action for breach of fiduciary duty is a prophylactic rule intended to remove all incentive to breach-not simply to compensate for damages in the event of a breach. *See Diamond v. Oreamuno,* 24 N.Y.2d 494, 498, 248 N.E.2d 910, 912, 301 N.Y.S.2d 78, 81 (1969) ("[T]he function of [an action founded on breach of fiduciary duty] ... is not merely to compensate the plaintiff for wrongs committed by the defendant but ... 'to *prevent* them, by removing from agents and trustees all inducement to attempt dealing for their own benefit in matters which they have undertaken for others, or to which their agency or trust relates.' ") (emphasis in original). Having found that ABKCO's conduct constituted a breach of fiduciary duty, the district judge was not required to find a "but for" relationship between ABKCO's conduct and lack of success of Harrison Interests' settlement efforts.

ABKCO argues further that the offer to sell substantially what had been gained in the purchase from Bright Tunes to Harrison for $700,000, and Harrison's rejection of that offer, *see supra* note 7, bars Harrison Interests from obtaining a constructive trust in this action, *per Turner v. American Metal Co.,* 268 A.D. 239, 50 N.Y.S.2d 800 (1st Dep't 1944) (where former fiduciary offers former employer what he obtained in violation of fiduciary duty at price equivalent to his cost of acquisition and former employer refuses offer, fiduciary not held liable for breach of duty), *appeal dismissed,* 295 N.Y. 822, 66 N.E.2d 591 (1946). We find this argument unpersuasive. First, in *Turner,* unlike the case at bar, there was no finding of breach of fiduciary duty. Moreover, we find somewhat disingenuous ABKCO's claim that a $700,000 offer was a "price equivalent to his cost of acquisition," which had been $587,000. In any event, it is unclear whether that which ABKCO offered Harrison Interests was equivalent to that which ABKCO had brought from Bright Tunes.

Finally, on the facts herein, we agree that a constructive trust on the "fruits" of ABKCO's acquisition was a proper remedy...

B. Scope of Constructive Trust: Foreign Settlements

Finally, appellant asserts that if this court is to affirm the district judge's finding of breach and its imposition of a constructive trust, the scope of that constructive trust should be limited to the American infringement claim. Appellant's argument is two-fold. First, appellant contends that because Harrison insisted on settling only the American infringement claim throughout the negotiations, and because the complaint in this case related only to the American claim, the remedy should be limited to that claim. Second, appellant argues that because the constructive trust encompasses foreign rights, the remedy serves to disturb settlement agreements that have already been achieved as to the foreign infringement claims against Harrison. As to appellant's first contention, in our view the district judge was not constrained by the scope of the settlement negotiations in fashioning this equitable relief. Moreover, it was within the discretion of the district court to provide a remedy not simply as to appellant's claims, but also as to appellee's counterclaims. *See Alexander v. Hillman,* 296 U.S. 222, 242, 56 S.Ct. 204, 211, 80 L.Ed. 192 (1935) ("[C]ourts of equity ... will decide all matters in dispute and decree complete relief.").

The second point raised by appellant, however, in our view, warrants modification of the judgment and remand to the district court for reassessment of the scope of the constructive trust. On April 3, 1980, after the damages trial, but before Judge Owen rendered his opinion, Harrison Interests, through its agent, Essex Music International, with full knowledge that its counterclaim was pending before Judge Owen, voluntarily entered into agreements with ABKCO, settling MSL infringement claims in various foreign territories as between HSF subpublishers and MSL subpublishers. As a general matter, we note first that courts favor the policy of encouraging voluntary settlement of disputesBearing this principle in mind, we conclude that, since the parties or their agents entered into settlement agreements as to certain foreign infringement claims while the damages issues were *sub judice,* the trust should not include that portion of ABKCO's acquisition constituting a purchase of the foreign rights involved in those settlements. We remand the case to the district court to determine what portion of the $587,000 paid by ABKCO to Bright Tunes is attributable to the foreign rights involved in the April 3, 1980 settlement. That sum should be subtracted from the $587,000 to determine the amount the Harrison Interests must pay to acquire only the rights not affected by the April 3, 1980 settlement.

III. CROSS-APPEAL: COPYRIGHT INFRINGEMENT

"[I]t is well settled that copying may be inferred where a plaintiff establishes that the defendant had access to the copyrighted work and that the two works are substantially similar." *Warner Brothers v. American Broadcasting Companies,* 654 F.2d 204, 207 (2d Cir.1981). In this case, Judge Owen determined that "My Sweet Lord is the very same song as He's So Fine with different words, and Harrison had access to He's So Fine." *Bright Tunes Music Corp. v. Harrisongs Music, Ltd.,* 420 F.Supp. at 180-81. He concluded that the substantial similarity coupled with access constituted copyright infringement, even though subconsciously accomplished. *See id.* at 180, 181 (citing *Sheldon v. Metro-Goldwyn Pictures Corp.,* 81 F.2d 49, 54 (2d Cir.1936); *Northern Music Corp. v. Pacemaker Music Co.,* 147 U.S.P.Q. 358, 359 (S.D.N.Y.1965)).

Appellees argue on cross-appeal that the instant case differs significantly from those cases relied upon by the district court to support its conclusion of subconscious infringement, and from the only other case in this circuit which held that subconscious copying can constitute infringement, *i.e., Fred Fisher, Inc. v. Dillingham,* 298 F. 145 (S.D.N.Y.1924). In addition, they urge upon this court the position that it is unsound policy to permit a finding of copyright infringement on the basis of subconscious copying. We reject both arguments and affirm the decision of the district judge.

First, we do not find dispositive appellees' distinction between the instant case and *Sheldon* and *Fisher* cases. Appellees point out that in those two cases, the infringing work was created very shortly after the infringer had had access to the infringed work. Here, in contrast, appellees note, Harrison's access to HSF occurred in 1963, some six years before he composed MSL. We disagree with appellees' position that such temporal remoteness precludes a finding of access. First, Harrison himself admitted at trial that he remembered hearing HSF in the early sixties when it was popular. Moreover, even if there had not been such direct evidence of access, access still may have been found because of the wide dissemination of HSF at that time. *See Arnstein v. Porter,* 154 F.2d 464, 469 (2d Cir.1946); 3 M. Nimmer, *Nimmer on Copyright* § 13.02[A] (1983). Indeed, in 1963, the year of Harrison's admitted access to HSF, the song was "Number One on the *Billboard* charts" in the United States for five weeks, and it was one of the "Top Thirty Hits" in England for seven weeks that same year. Thus, even if the evidence, standing alone, "by no means compels the conclusion that there was access ... it does not compel the conclusion that there was not." *Heim v. Universal Pictures Co.,* 154 F.2d 480, 487 (2d Cir.1946).

As to the requisite finding of substantial similarity, we affirm the determinations of the district judge, since we do not find them to be clearly erroneous, *Bright Tunes Music Corp. v. Harrisongs Music, Ltd.,* 420 F.Supp. at 178-80. Even Harrison conceded at trial that the two songs were "strikingly similar" as played by a pianist during the liability trial.

This case in unlike *Darrell v. Joe Morris Music Co.,* 113 F.2d 80 (2d Cir.1940), cited by appellees. In *Darrell,* the Court of Appeals affirmed the district court's finding of no plagiarism, when there had been "substantial identity" between the songs at issue. The *Darrell* court found of particular significance that the songs' themes were trite and access had occurred some seven and a half years before the defendant's song was composed...

Appellees argue next that it is unsound policy to permit a finding of infringement for subconscious copying, particularly on the facts of this case. They assert that allowing for subconscious infringement brings the law of copyright improperly close to patent law, which imposes a requirement of novelty...

It is not new law in this circuit that when a defendant's work is copied from the plaintiff's, but the defendant in good faith has forgotten that the plaintiff's work was the source of his own, such "innocent copying" can nevertheless constitute an infringement. *See Sheldon v. Metro-Goldwyn Pictures Corp.*, 81 F.2d at 54; *see also* 3 M. Nimmer, *Nimmer on Copyright* § 13.08 (1983). We do not find this stance in conflict with the rule permitting independent creation of copyrighted material. Moreover, as a practical matter, the problems of proof inherent in a rule that would permit innocent intent as a defense to copyright infringement could substantially undermine the protections Congress intended to afford to copyright holders. We therefore see no reason to retreat from this circuit's prior position that copyright infringement can be subconscious.

Because there was sufficient evidence of record to support the district judge's findings of substantial similarity and access, we affirm the finding of copyright infringement.

IV. CONCLUSION

Having considered all of the parties' arguments on appeal and cross-appeal, we affirm, with modification, the decisions of the district court and remand to the district judge for reassessment of the scope of the remedy, consistent with this opinion. Each party is to bear its own fees and costs.

GEISEL v. POYNTER PRODUCTS, INC.
United States District Court
S.D. New York
No. 68 Civ. 997
Dec. 10, 1968
As Amended Dec. 23, 1968
295 F.Supp. 331

HERLANDS, District Judge:

Can an artist who sells his signed cartoon to a magazine validly object to the magazine's making and selling a doll which is truthfully advertised as based upon the cartoon? This capsulated, poses the critical issue herein.

The Complaint

Plaintiff, Theodor Seuss Geisel, is the world-famous artist and author, whose nom de plume is 'Dr. Seuss.' In a complaint against the four defendants, filed March 8, 1968, plaintiff charged that the defendants manufacture and were advertising and selling dolls 'derived from' (Complaint, P21) certain material which plaintiff 'prepared for publication' (Complaint, P17) for the now defunct Liberty Magazine in 1932 and which was published in that magazine from June to December 1932; that, although plaintiff had nothing to do with the design or manufacture of the dolls, they were being advertised and sold as 'Dr. Seuss' creations; and that the dolls are 'tasteless, unattractive and of an inferior qualify' (Complaint, P41; 23).

On the basis of these and other allegations, plaintiff requested compensatory and punitive damages as well as an injunction enjoining defendants from using the name 'Dr. Seuss' in any manner without plaintiff's consent, or in connection with any product not designed or approved by plaintiff.

In support of this prayer for relief plaintiff pleaded five causes of action: (1) violation of Section 43(a) of the Lanham Act, 15 U.S.C. § 1125(a) (1964); (2) unfair competition, including violation of Section 368-d of the New York General Business Law, McKinney's Consol.Laws, c. 20; (3) violation of plaintiff's right of privacy as provided by the New York Civil Rights Law, McKinney's Consol.Laws, §§ c. 50, 51; (4) defamation; and (5) conspiracy with intent to injure plaintiff (prima facie tort).

The Preliminary Injunction

An order to show cause for a preliminary injunction was signed on March 8, 1968. On March 12, this Court heard argument on that motion, issued a temporary restraining order (which, in substance, restrained defendants from using the name 'Dr. Seuss' in any manner in connection with any doll, toy or other product), and granted the parties leave to conduct discovery and to submit further papers.

On April 9, 1968, this Court concluded that there was a reasonable probability of plaintiff's success upon the trial of the Lanham Act (first) cause of action and issued a preliminary injunction restraining defendants ...

Defendants' Basic Contentions

It would be useful to summarize defendants' basic contentions, as formulated in the pre-trial order. Defendants claim that they have the right to manufacture and sell the dolls in question for the reason that either (1) defendant Liberty Library Corporation— as successor-assignee of Liberty Magazine— owns complete rights, including copyright, in the cartoons published in 1932, and 'the owner of copyright in cartoons has the exclusive right to make three-dimensional figures therefrom,' or (2) the cartoons are in the public domain and, therefore, 'anyone may use such cartoons as the basis for the three-dimensional figures.' Defendants contend that the dolls are specifically 'based on' Plaintiff's Exhibits 14A, 14B and 14C.

In addition, defendants argue that they have the right to state truthfully the relationship between plaintiff-cartoonist and the dolls, including the circumstance that the dolls were 'based on, adapted from or inspired by' the plaintiff's Liberty Magazine cartoons. Finally, defendants have urged a variety of other defenses to the causes of action set forth in the complaint (P.T.O. 4 (pp. 13-14)).

This opinion contains the findings of fact and conclusions of law required by Rule 52(a), Fed.R.Civ.P.

Certain Undisputed Facts

Certain facts relating to the parties to this suit have been stipulated as not in dispute or are undisputed:

1. Plaintiff, Theodor Seuss Geisel (hereafter Geisel or plaintiff), is a well-known author and illustrator and a resident of La Jolla, California.

2. Defendant, Poynter Products Inc. (hereafter Poynter), is an Ohio corporation having its principal place of business at 7 Arcadia Place, Cincinnati,

Ohio; it is engaged in the business of producing and selling toys and novelties. Its president and sole stockholder is Donald B. Poynter.

3. Defendant, Alabe Crafts, Inc. (hereafter Alabe), is an Ohio corporation having its principal place of business at 1632 Gest Street in Cincinnati, Ohio; it distributes, among other things, the products of Poynter Products Inc.

4. Defendant, Liberty Library Corporation (hereafter Liberty), is a New York corporation with its principal place of business at 353 West 57th Street, New York, New York. Its president is Miss Lorraine Lester (Mrs. George Lessner). Its vice-president and treasurer is George Lessner. Its executive administrator is Robert Whiteman. The stock of Liberty is completely owned by Mr. and Mrs. Lessner.

5. Defendant, Linder, Nathan & Heide, Inc. (hereafter Linder), is a New York corporation having its principal place of business at 200 Fifth Avenue, New York, New York. It is engaged in selling toys and novelties to retailers; it acts as manufacturers' representative in New York City for defendant Alabe and others. There is diversity of citizenship between the parties. The matter in controversy, exclusive of interest and costs, exceeds the sum of $10,000. It is not, therefore, necessary to decide whether there is an independent basis of jurisdiction.

The 1932 Agreement

At the trial, a substantial amount of the evidence concerned the nature of the 1932 agreement between plaintiff and Liberty Publishing Corporation (hereafter Liberty Magazine). Plaintiff contends that the evidence proves that plaintiff assigned to Liberty Magazine the title to the cartoons with their accompanying text

> '* * * with the understanding that Liberty would copyright this work as part of the entire issue of the magazines in which they appeared. It was understood, however, that while Liberty had the complete rights to publish these works in one issue of Liberty Magazine, Liberty held all other rights to this work (including the right to renew the copyright and the right to make other uses of the work) in trust of plaintiff.' (P.T.O. 3 (p. 12)).

Plaintiff presents this contention as an additional reason why he is entitled to the relief prayed for in the complaint.

On the other hand, defendants contend that the 1932 agreement provided for the transfer to Liberty Magazine of all or complete rights in the cartoons and accompanying text without reservation of any rights in plaintiff. Certain facts relating to the 1932 transaction have been stipulated as not in dispute. The parties agree that, in 1932, plaintiff '* * * prepared and sold to Liberty Magazine material which was published in weekly issues of Liberty Magazine during the months of June through December 1932' (P.T.O.Stip. 22);

that the material consisted of a series of twenty-three 'cartoon essays' and that 'each work (consisted of a page which) contained at least three cartoons and each cartoon contained several animal creations'...

There is also no dispute that the issues of Liberty Magazine in which the cartoons appeared were copyrighted by Liberty Magazine as entire issues (P.T.O.Stip. 23). Each issue contained the required notice of copyright; and Certificates of Copyright Registration were secured by Liberty Magazine... It is also agreed that 'no separate copyright was obtained * * *' by the plaintiff upon the cartoons.

The only evidence describing the negotiations and consummation of the agreement between plaintiff and Liberty Magazine in 1932 was the testimony of plaintiff himself and of Leland Hayward. Hayward, presently a theatrical producer, was a literary agent from about 1929 to 1943 (Hayward, 484-485). According to plaintiff's and Hayward's testimony, one Ben Wasson approached plaintiff and asked whether he could represent him in seeking to place his work in magazines. Plaintiff agreed... Ben Wasson, who did not appear as a witness, represented plaintiff in the negotiations with Liberty Magazine (Geisel, 1464; Hayward, 501). In so doing, Wasson acted as an employee of the Leland Hayward Agency. (Geisel, 942-943, 995; Hayward, 501). Although Hayward did not personally handle the transaction, he recalls that he had one conversation with Fulton Oursler, then editor-in-chief of Liberty Magazine. Oursler stated that plaintiff was 'popular' and that his work was 'very suitable' for Liberty Magazine (Hayward, 507). Hayward could not remember anything else said at that or any other time relating to the negotiations (494-495; 507). To the best of his recollection, there was no formal written contract executed in connection with this transaction (490).

Plaintiff's only contract in 1932 with Liberty Magazine was a meeting of about fifteen minutes' duration with Fulton Oursler (Geisel, 1463). However, all that plaintiff recalls of that occasion is that Oursler said '* * * 'Glad to have you aboard,' or something like that' (1463). Prior to that meeting, Wasson had told plaintiff of a 'firm commitment' for plaintiff '* * * to do a number of pages, a small number of pages, because everything was sort of on a try-out basis * * * to see if they worked. I don't know how many pages they said they would buy, but they were $300 a piece' (Geisel, 1464-1465). From this and other evidence (Geisel, 1466), the Court infers that the works which plaintiff sold to Liberty Magazine were not in existence at the time the contract was entered into; instead, they were created at Liberty Magazine's request.

The $300 payments were made by check to the Leland Hayward Agency, which deducted its commission as agent and then remitted the balance to plaintiff (Geisel, 1001; Hayward, 497-501).

Nothing was expressly said by either side during the negotiations regarding the scope of rights that Liberty Magazine obtained by the purchase of the material (Geisel, 1062). Plaintiff denies that the words 'all rights' or 'complete rights' were used by either side during the negotiations (1039-1040).

This evidence demonstrates that plaintiff agreed to prepare cartoons for publication in Liberty Magazine; that the cartoons were published; that plaintiff received $300 a page; that the only copyright upon this material was in the name of Liberty Publishing Company; and that plaintiff did not expressly reserve any rights in the cartoons.

There is evidence, and the Court so finds, that, with certain exceptions which do not apply in this case, the custom and usage in 1932 in the magazine trade were that an agreement for the sale of a work between authors or their agents and magazines was oral and not a formal written contract (Hayward, 486, 515-516; Geisel, 1028, 1036; Norton, 1357-1358; Wasserstrom, 1315). The agreement was usually reached after only monetary terms were discussed (Hayward, 486, 515-516). This contrasts with the custom in the book publishing field in which similar contracts were written (Geisel, 1028; Hayward, 531; Cerf, 569, 588).

If, arguendo, all rights in the cartoons were not assigned to Liberty Magazine in 1932, Liberty's copyright upon the entire issues of the magazine does not cover the cartoons. Mail & Express Co. v. Life Pub. Co., 192 F. 899, 900 (2nd Cir. 1912); Goodis v. United Artists Television, Inc., 278 F.Supp. 122, 125 (S.D.N.Y.1968) (novel published in magazine pursuant to agreement for one-time serialization rights before it was separately copyrighted and published in book form); Kaplan v. Fox Film Corporation, 19 F.Supp. 780, 781 (S.D.N.Y.1937). It would then follow that the cartoons would be in the public domain because admittedly they were published in 1932 without a separate copyright. Goodis v. United Artists Television, Inc., supra. This result would transpire for the reason that a work can be copyrighted only by its 'author or proprietor' (17 U.S.C. § 9); the 'proprietor' can be the assignee but not the licensee of the right to use the work; and to be the assignee of the work, one must have been assigned all rights in the work...

Consequently, if the cartoons are not to be deemed in the public domain, it must be shown that all rights in the cartoons were assigned to Liberty Magazine in 1932. To escape from this logical dilemma plaintiff argues that, although legal title to the copyright was in Liberty Magazine's name as assignee-' proprietor', the copyright was held in trust for the cartoon's true or equitable owner, plaintiff... Plaintiff, therefore, asks for judgment declaring that the defendants hold the copyright in trust for plaintiff and ordering that the copyright be assigned to plaintiff.

Whether this trust relationship exists is primarily a question of fact dependent upon the circumstances of the case. See Bisel v. Ladner, supra; Brennan v. Paramount Pictures Corporation, supra.

In this case, there was no express agreement that Liberty Magazine would hold the copyright in trust for plaintiff or that plaintiff reserved any rights in the cartoons. However, much evidence was offered by both sides with respect to the issue whether there was any settled and established custom and usage in the magazine publishing trade in 1932 by which any terms of conditions were implied in fact or understood to be part of a contract between an author or his agent and a weekly magazine; and if so, what were those implied-in-fact terms.

Evidence was also offered with respect to the issue whether there was any settled and established custom and usage concerning what the magazine was impliedly agreeing to in fact with respect to the extent of the magazine's use of the purchased material; and concerning the alleged practice of a magazine to hold its copyright in trust for the author and to reassign its copyright upon the request of the author...

Plaintiff offered the testimony of three witnesses with respect to the above-mentioned customs and usages in 1932 in the magazine publishing trade: Bennett Cerf, Leland, Hayward and plaintiff himself.

Mr. Cerf has been a book publisher since 1925 and has himself written books as well as articles for periodicals (Cerf, 275-276, 606). Plaintiff's books are published by the firm of which Cerf is chairman of the board (Cerf, 275; P.T.O. Stip. 33); and, in fact, plaintiff is the president of a division of that firm (Geisel, 920; P.T.O. Stip. 34). Mr. Cerf is an eminent personality in the field of book publishing. However, his testimony with respect to customs and usages in the magazine trade is found by the Court to be tenuous and unpersuasive. He repeatedly admitted his unfamiliarity with magazine customs (Cerf, 291, 295, 304) and with contracts between magazines and authors or their agents (Cerf, 588). Furthermore, some of his testimony presents internal inconsistencies and self-contradictions (see Cerf, 282, 297, 303 and 570; 296, 306 and 282, 283; 317 and 586).

Three witnesses called by defendants testified about the relevant customs and usages: Meyer Dworkin, Alfred Wasserstrom and Alden Norton. Mr. Dworkin, a retired attorney and accountant, was an adviser or 'righthand man' to the head of Macfadden Publications, a magazine publisher, which purchased Liberty Magazine in 1931. Dworkin was associated with Macfadden Publications from 1919 until 1961 (Dworkin, 405-407, 412, 417).

Alfred Wasserstrom, an attorney specializing in copyright and trademark law, is connected with the Hearst Corporation Legal Department. He has been with the Hearst Corporation since December 1933, when he was admitted to the bar. He has guest-lectured at law schools; is a member of the board of trustees of the Copyright Society of the U.S.A.; and is a member and chairman of the Copyright Committee of the Magazine Publishers Association (Wasserstrom, 1306-1308).

Alden Norton, advisory editor of Argosy Magazine, is in charge of its foreign sales and rights and subsidiary rights. In 1932, he began working as an editor for Frank A. Munsey Company, a magazine publisher, and remained there until 1935, when he left to join Popular Publications, publisher of Argosy (Norton, 1355-1356, 1369-1370). While an editor in the 1930's, Norton dealt with authors and their agents with respect to literary purchases (1357, 1370). He has also sold numerous stories and novels of his own to magazines since 1929 (1355, 1357).

On the basis of the great weight of the credible evidence, the Court finds that during the relevant period it was the custom and usage in the magazine trade for the magazine to obtain a copyright upon the entire contents of the magazine (Hayward, 487, 492; Dworkin, 475; Wasserstrom, 1389). However, the author or artist could also obtain a separate copyright upon his particular work, as plaintiff did with respect to a 'Quick, Henry the Flit' cartoon-advertisement which appeared in Liberty Magazine in 1931 (Deft.Ex. 21; P.T.O.Stip. 26; Geisel, 940-942, 945).

Virtually all the testimony was in agreement on the proposition, which the Court finds established, that there was a settled custom and usage in the magazine publishing trade in the early 1930's by which a term or condition defining the scope of rights was implied in fact or understood to be part of the agreement between the author or his agent and the magazine (Hayward, 488; Geisel, 915-917; Dworkin, 476-477; Norton, 1062, 1063-1064). What that term or condition provided is a subject, however, about which the testimony is sharply conflicting.

Mr. Cerf testified that, if nothing was said with respect to the scope of rights purchased, the term 'always' implied in the agreement provided for the sale of 'one-shot publication'— publication in one issue of the magazine— and return of the copyright thereafter upon the request of the author (Cerf, 299-300, 578, 619). He stated that the term 'all rights' meant this understanding (316).

Mr. Cerf indicated that the basis of his knowledge of this custom or understanding was the 'minimal' amount paid to plaintiff for the cartoons (Cerf, 300, 307). He also testified that, if an author-artist received anything less than $1,000 a page in 1932 for his work, it meant that only one-time magazine rights were sold (Cerf, 310-311).

Although the price paid may be a circumstance probative of the scope of rights purchased by Liberty Magazine in 1932 (see Norton, 1362-1363), the clear preponderance of the credible evidence demonstrates that the price of $300 per page in 1932 was a '* * * reasonable price for that particular year' in view of the near 'panic' caused by the depression (Hayward, 517; Norton, 1368).

Mr. Hayward testified that the 'standard practice' or usage in the magazine trade in 1932 '* * * was (for the material) to appear in one issue of the magazine or, in the case of a serialization, in several issues * * *' (486-487, 488). The magazine was limited in its use of the material to single or serial publication '* * * and those rights are called 'complete rights'— or were' (Hayward, 508, 509-509a). He, and other witnesses, stated that the expressions 'all rights' and 'complete rights' had the same meaning (Hayward, 530, 546; Norton, 1363; Wasserstrom, 1374-1375). But, Mr. Hayward repeatedly stated that 'all rights' did not mean 'all' and that 'complete rights' did not mean 'complete' (546); rather, that these terms had a limited meaning (510). According to Mr. Hayward, 'complete rights' in the magazine trade meant '* * * the complete right to publish that particular piece of material in a single issue * * * or, in the case of serial rights, to publish parts of the material in several or more issues * * *' (533-534). Mr. Hayward also testified that, although the term 'all rights' was not expressly used in negotiations, it was 'implicit' in the agreement (510).

Mr. Hayward further asserted that, after publication, the custom provided that the magazine '* * * would always assign the copyright to anyone the author requested'. The magazine was thus the 'custodian of the copyright' (492). He added that he had never heard of a magazine sharing the revenues gained on the material after the assignment back (547-548).

Plaintiff also testified that, in 1932, custom or usage implied in fact in the agreement a condition that the magazine would use the purchased material only in a single insertion in the United States and Canada (Geisel, 915, 917, 1035, 1037-1039).

If believed in its entirety, the evidence adduced in behalf of plaintiff would prove that in 1932 custom or usage in the magazine trade implied in fact in the Geisel-Liberty Magazine agreement that (a) each cartoon could be used only in a single insertion in the magazine; that (b) thereafter the copyright was held in trust for plaintiff and would be reassigned to him at his request; and that (c) the term 'all rights' or 'complete rights,' which was understood to mean (a) and/or (b), was 'implicit' in the agreement.

Meyer Dworkin, called as a witness for defendants, testified that he did not recall, and, in fact, there 'categorically' never was, any custom or understanding in 1932 whereby an author '* * * would reserve impliedly all rights except the right to have the magazine publish in that issue the particular work of art' (Dworkin, 449-450, 451). On the contrary, the custom was that 'where the author said nothing and sold the manuscript to the company, the company would receive all rights * * *' (Dworkin, 452). He stated that this custom was understood by Liberty Magazine, Mcfadden Publications and by the authors who dealt with them (476-477). Mr. Dworkin defined 'complete rights' as 'all rights, full rights' (445) with no residual rights in anyone else (446).

Although Mr. Dworkin admitted that Liberty Magazine (or Macfadden Publications) occasionally would reassign its rights to an author without charge, he stated that at other times the reassignment would be for a fee or for a share of the author's profits after the assignment back. Whether reassignment would be made and whether it would be made without payment depended upon who the author was and the purpose for which the assignment back was sought (Dworkin, 465, 468-469). Mr. Dworkin explained that sometimes reassignment would be made to retain the author's friendship and goodwill (451, 464).

Alden Norton convincingly testified that, although every story purchased by a magazine was individually bargained for, '* * * if you sold me a story and you didn't ask for anything, you sold me all rights and it would say so on the check' (1362). He also testified that, if there were no written or oral agreement and no legend on the check and the author or artist simply delivered the work to a magazine and was paid $300 a page, the custom and usage in 1932 provided that 'unless otherwise specified, (the author granted) all rights' (1363-1364, 1368). Mr. Norton rejected the assertion that, if nothing was said, only first publication rights were acquired by the magazine (1367-1368). He testified that, if all rights were not acquired, there were specific negotiations—i.e., something was said (1368)—and a lower price would be paid for the material (1362-1363).

Mr. Norton's testimony indicates that the words 'all rights' were a recognized term in the magazine trade in 1932. But he rejected plaintiff's contention that custom or usage gave these words a specialized meaning (1360-1362). As he said, 'all rights' meant literally all rights (1361)—i.e., '* * * dramatic, movie, television, skywriting on Mars, anything you want to say * * * everything' (1360, 1361-1362). He also said that where 'all rights' were purchased, the author '* * * retained absolutely nothing' (1362).

Alfred Wasserstrom also testified persuasively that he knew of no custom or usage which gave the words 'all rights' a specialized meaning in the magazine trade in 1935 (1327-1328, 1372). He agreed that the words 'all rights' had a plain, colloquial English meaning (1372-1374, 1375). Likewise, he testified that he knew of no custom or usage giving the words 'complete rights' '* * * any meaning different from their ordinary, accepted English meaning' (1375).

Mr. Wasserstrom stated that there was no implied in fact term or condition, according to the custom or usage in 1935 in the magazine trade, that a magazine could use material (such as Pltf.Ex. 14A-B-C) only for one insertion in the magazine (1376-1377).

Finally, he testified as to the alleged custom which implied a term in agreements between authors and magazines relating to reassignment of the copyright at the request of the author. He stated that such a custom existed in 1935 'if only limited rights were acquired * * *' (1382). Thus, it was customary that, where the magazine purchased limited or restricted rights, such as serial rights, the copyright taken out by the magazine would be reconveyed to the author at his request (Wasserstrom, 1382-1383). When such a reassignment of the copyright was made, the custom recognized that the magazine retained the limited rights (i.e. serial rights) originally acquired by the magazine (1384-1385, 1386, 1392-1393; Deft. Ex. 79-80). However, Mr. Wasserstrom stressed the fact that no such custom, whereby the magazine impliedly agreed to reassign the copyright at the author's request, existed where all or complete rights were purchased by the magazine; or where nothing was said as to rights (1383, 1394). He agreed, on cross examination, that where limited rights were acquired, the author impliedly gave authority to the magazine to secure a copyright on the material as part of the copyright on the entire issue which '* * * would then be held for the benefit of both parties to the extent of their respective interests' (1389).

On the basis of the clear preponderance of the credible evidence, the Court finds that the custom and usage in 1932 in the magazine trade implied in fact in the Geisel-Liberty Magazine agreement a provision whereby all rights or complete rights were assigned to Liberty Magazine (Hayward, 510; Dworkin, 452; Norton, 1363-1364, 1368; Wasserstrom, 1383).

In ordinary acceptance, the expressions 'all rights' or 'complete rights' have a nontechnical and literal meaning. Plaintiff has failed to sustain the burden of proof which is upon him when he seeks to impart to these words a connotation that is diametrically opposite to their plain, colloquial sense... The Court finds the testimonial assertions of plaintiff's witnesses, in this respect, to be incredible and factitious. The terms 'all rights' and 'complete rights,' when understood according to their plain meaning, signify a totality of rights, including the right of reproduction or common law copyright and the right to secure statutory copyright without qualification.

Stated otherwise, the Court finds, on the basis of the overwhelming preponderance of the credible evidence, that there was no custom or usage which implied in fact in the agreement in issue that Liberty Magazine was restricted, in any way, as to the uses to which the cartoons might be put. The Court rejects the simplistic and unconvincing testimony of plaintiff's witnesses concerning a custom whereby the copyright in this case was being held in trust for plaintiff. Instead, the Court adopts the testimony of defendants' two disinterested expert witnesses, Alden Norton and Alfred Wasserstrom, as to the custom and usage in the magazine trade during the period in question. The Court finds both Norton and Wasserstrom, and their testimony, to be credible, reliable and persuasive.

Although corroboration for defendants' position— that all or complete rights were purchased by Liberty Magazine in 1932— is not necessary, corroboration is provided by Liberty's 'permanent purchase record cards.' Some of these cards were introduced into evidence by defendants (e.g. Deft.Ex. 39-47). Each card specifies, among other things, the author's name, the title, the price paid, the date of purchase and date of publication, the 'character' of the material (e.g. article, cartoon, etc.) and the rights purchased. There is a separate card corresponding to each page of plaintiff's cartoons which appeared in Liberty Magazine (Deft.Ex. 46). Each of these cards relating to the Geisel-Liberty transaction expressly states that 'complete' rights were purchased.

The Court finds and concludes that these cards are admissible under the Federal Business Records Act, 28 U.S.C. § 1732 (1964) because manifestly they were made in regular course of Liberty Magazine's business and it was the regular course of such business to make such cards and the entries thereon. Meyer Dworkin testified extensively as to the regularity of these business practices at Liberty Magazine. The Court finds his detailed testimony regarding Liberty's practices to be credible and reliable (see, e.g., Dworkin, 408-411, 414-416, 425, 429, 434-435, 477-478). It may be, in fact, that these cards are a customary form of record utilized by magazines in 1932. Alden Norton testified that the same type of records was maintained and used by Frank A. Munsey Company, a magazine publisher, in 1932 (Norton, 1365-1368; Deft.Ex. 87-90 are examples of such cards).

Dworkin also testified that the same recital of rights which appeared on Liberty Magazine's cards was rubberstamped as a legend on the check sent to the author or his agent (Dworkin, 479-482). Although no cancelled check relating to this transaction was introduced into evidence, other checks of Liberty Magazine were (e.g. Deft.Ex. 48-50); and the legends on those checks correspond to the description of the cards of the rights purchased (Deft.Ex. 42-44).

Although oral agreements between authors or their agents and magazines were customary, the Court finds that it was also a custom or usage in 1932 that the scope of rights purchased by the magazine would be set forth in a legend on the check sent to the author or his agent . . .

Although plaintiff (Geisel, 1067-1068) and his agent in 1932, Leland Hayward (512), stated they were unfamiliar with this practice, Norton testified that Frank A. Munsey and Popular Publications and, in fact, other magazine publishers to which he sold articles as an author, had such an established practice (1358-1359). Wasserstrom testified that Hearst Corporation, which published several magazines, as well as other magazine publishers with which he was familiar, had such a practice (1318-1321); and Dworkin testified extensively to the same practice at Macfadden Publications, publisher of Liberty Magazine (446, 478-479).

The permanent purchase record cards also circumstantially support defendants' position that complete rights or all rights had their literal meaning. Defendants have also introduced other circumstantial evidence (e.g. Whiteman, 1411-1412; Deft.Ex. 1, 51) which tends to negate the testimonial assertions of plaintiff's witnesses that magazines 'never' asked for, received or used rights to material for other than one-shot or serial publication in the magazine.

The ineluctable conclusion is that, when Liberty Magazine bought the cartoons in question from plaintiff, it purchased all rights, including the common law copyright and the right to secure statutory copyright without reservation of any rights in plaintiff.

Absent a reservation of the common law copyright or other rights, the copyright and all other rights pass with an absolute and unconditional sale...

The parties formulate differently the rule of law deducible from the foregoing decisions,—the difference revolving around the point whether an implied reservation of rights may be as effective as an express reservation in precluding the transfer of all of the artist's rights. Regardless of the formulation, the evidence in the present case convincingly establishes only one conclusion: all rights (including the common law copyright) in the cartoons were transferred to Liberty without any equitable or other rights reserved to plaintiff. Liberty's statutory copyright likewise is not subject to any equitable or other rights in plaintiff.

Although there is evidence in the record that plaintiff prepared the cartoons for Liberty after an agreement had been reached between his agent and the magazine, the Court does not rely on the cases relating to commissioned works of art...

The Dolls

Having decided that Liberty Magazine acquired all rights to the cartoons published in 1932, the Court now considers and determines what rights defendants have to make the dolls (Pltf.Ex. 20A-B, 21A-B, 22A-B, 23A-B, 24A-B, 25A-B) and to what extent, if any, defendants may use the name 'Dr. Seuss' in connection therewith.

Plaintiff's basic contentions are that defendants '* * * may not use plaintiff's name in any way in connection with the toy dolls because the toy dolls do not bear a sufficient relationship to the original work and differ in material respects from it'; and that 'the toy dolls destroy the artistic integrity of plaintiff's original work and are so inferior in quality that the use of plaintiff's name in connection with them is disparaging and damaging to him.' (P.T.O. 3 (p. 12)).

Additional details of the factual background of this litigation must be mobilized in order to consider the respective rights of the parties in proper context.

On September 1, 1949, Lorraine Lester entered into an option agreement with Liberty Magazine, Inc. (Pltf.Ex. 1) which, as amended on March 13, 1950 (Pltf.Ex. 2), permitted her, upon certain conditions to exploit short story material which had appeared in Liberty Magazine during the period 1924 to 1949 for use in connection with radio, television and motion pictures.

Thereafter, on September 8, 1950 Lester-Fields and Liberty Magazine, Inc. entered into an agreement (Pltf.Ex. 9) terminating the 1949 option agreement with Miss Lester and providing in part as follows:

> "3. Liberty hereby sells, assigns and transfers to Lester any and all right, title or interest it may have in or to any and all of the stories and articles which have been published in Liberty Magazine from May 1924 to July 1950 inclusive, provided, however, that Liberty makes no representation as to the extent of its right, title or interest in and to such stories and articles..."

In August 1964 Mr. Robert Whiteman called on Miss Lester in connection with film production. In the course of their conversation, he saw the 90 bound volumes of Liberty Magazine on her shelves; and, after discussion, suggested that he could help her make money by exploiting the literary properties contained in those magazines. (Lester, 1087). Thereafter, Whiteman entered into an agreement with Liberty Library, whereby Whiteman represented Liberty 'on an exclusive basis' in exploiting the material from defendant Liberty Magazine (Pltf.Ex. 13; Lester, 1086-1088).

Commencing in 1964, defendant Liberty embarked on a program of actively exploiting the material which had appeared in Liberty Magazine from 1924 to 1950. In the course of selecting material for sale or licensing, Whiteman came upon plaintiff's cartoons in the 1932 issues of Liberty Magazine (Lester, 1090; P.T.O.Stip. 19). Whiteman checked the Liberty record cards and secured a copyright search on that material (Deft.Ex. 62). After receiving expressions of interest in the cartoons, 'as a matter of courtesy,' Whiteman contacted Random House which referred him to plaintiff's agent, Mrs. Phyllis Jackson of Ashley Famous Agency. Whiteman showed her copies of the cartoons and of the copyright search and offered plaintiff the opportunity either to join with Liberty in exploiting the material or to repurchase the rights in the works (P.T.O.Stip. 20). Whiteman agreed to keep her informed regarding any offers which he received with respect to the material (Deft.Ex. 24; Whiteman, 1406-1410; Jackson, 1166-1169). Subsequently, Whiteman informed her by letter of December 15, 1964, that he had received an offer for reprint rights to the material (Deft.Ex. 20; Jackson, 1172).

Prior to the letter of December 15th, Mrs. Jackson contacted plaintiff who rejected defendant Liberty's offer (Jackson, 1169, 1171). After the December 15th letter, Mrs. Jackson wrote to plaintiff advising him to have his attorney write to defendant Liberty in an effort to prevent exploitation of the cartoon material (Deft.Ex. 19; 63). Thereafter, plaintiff's California attorney, Frank Kockritz, Esq., sent a telegram to defendant Liberty (Pltf.Ex. 39) advising it that plaintiff did not recognize Liberty's rights in the cartoons and reserving the right to institute a lawsuit.

After receiving the telegram, Whiteman consulted his attorneys and, on May 14, 1965, completed a transaction with Universal Publishing and Distributing Corporation (Whiteman, 1421-1433). The agreement provided for licensing Universal to publish a paperback book of the Liberty 'Dr. Seuss' cartoons (Pltf.Ex. 42; P.T.O.Stip. 21). Universal subsequently wrote to plaintiff on June 6, 1966 asking plaintiff to retitle and revise his cartoons (Jackson, 1185). Plaintiff rejected the proposal (Geisel, 1014-1015, 1017); Mrs. Jackson informed Universal; and plaintiff's attorney, Mr. Kockritz, sent a protest letter to Universal (Pltf.Ex. 43). However, Universal went ahead and published a paperback entitled 'Dr. Seuss' Lost World Revisited' (Deft.Ex. 56).

After publication, defendant Liberty again offered to sell its rights in the cartoons back to plaintiff (Geisel, 1018-1019); Abelman, 1443-1444). This final offer of defendant Liberty to sell its rights in the cartoons back to plaintiff was suggested by Arthur , F. Abelman, Esq., who had previously discussed the matter with plaintiff's agent, Mrs. Jackson (Abelman, 1443).

Finally, in 1967, Whiteman undertook to sell merchandising rights to the cartoons (Jackson, 1187). Whiteman, who was experienced in licensing and merchandising items, including toys (Whiteman, 1425-1427), decided to grant a license to manufacture dolls based on the cartoons (Whiteman, 1425). Whiteman licensed defendant Poynter Products, Inc. because he had had successful dealings with Donald B. Poynter in the past and he considered Poynter to be '* * * a man of tremendous capabilities in the field of molding, sculpture, art, taste * * *' (Whiteman, 1427-1428). The licensing agreement (Pltf.Ex. 18) was executed (on September 8, 1967), after Poynter had been shown the cartoons and informed of plaintiff's objection to the publication of the paperback book (Poynter, 664-667).

Donald B. Poynter was and is an experienced designer and manufacturer of toys, novelties and gift items, including items made for children (Poynter, 640-648). He had previously designed a variety of items based upon works of well known artists (Poynter, 642-643, 649-651; Deft.Ex. 52-54). He had also produced puppets (Poynter, 785); 'premiums,' such as T-shirts and tags, given away by sponsors of children's radio and television shows (Poynter, 788); theatrical sets (Poynter, 790); and advertising artistic layouts for a large toy manufacturer (Poynter, 791).

In view of the protest telegram from plaintiff's attorney in 1964, Whiteman decided to submit everything done with respect to the dolls to Mr. Abelman. In fact, all meetings between Whiteman and Poynter took place in Mr. Abelman's office (Whiteman, 1430-1431). In November 1967, Whiteman and Poynter came to Mr. Abelman's office to discuss design of the dolls (Abelman, 1446). Poynter brought with him a hand sculptured styrofoam and papier-mache model (Deft.Ex. 55) of one of the cartoon 'characters' (from Pltf.Ex. 14B) which he had prepared from 'rough' sketches (Poynter, 812). Mr. Abelman found the prototype doll to be 'reasonable acceptable and a faithful reproduction' (Abelman, 1446) and Whiteman agreed (Poynter, 813).

At the meeting in November, 1967, Mr. Abelman also advised Poynter '* * * that under no circumstances should he consult any book written by Dr. Seuss, watch any television program by Dr. Seuss or use any material of Dr. Seuss outside the Liberty drawings in preparing the drawings for his dolls, and I told him that when he watched those drawings he should look at them very carefully, reproduce them as close as he possibly could, taking into account the fact that you are moving from a two-dimensional medium of paper and publishing into the three-dimensional medium of dolls' (Abelman, 1446-1447). In fact, the Court finds that Poynter used the cartoons only as they appeared in Liberty Magazine or in the paperback book (Poynter, 685, 810-811) in the preparation and design of the dolls.

After the meeting, Poynter prepared additional models and then went to Japan for six weeks to work on the dolls and choose a manufacturer (Poynter, 814). By letter dated January 12, 1968 (Pltf.Ex. 19), Poynter authorized the manufacture in Japan of a set of twelve small vinyl toy dolls designed from some of the creatures which appeared in the 1932 cartoons.

While in Japan and later when back in the United States, Poynter sculpted wax models of the dolls (Poynter, 815-819). These wax models became the basis of the molds in which the dolls were manufactured (Poynter, 819). During the design and manufacture of the dolls, minor changes were made so that the dolls which eventually were manufactured and sold were not precise copies of the original cartoons or of Poynter's initial transformation of the cartoons (Poynter, 688, 821). These modifications reflected manufacturing techniques, cost and sales requirements, the availability and choice of plastics, aesthetic considerations (Poynter, 806, 807, 820-821), and deviations representing Poynter's three-dimensional interpretative transmutation of the two-dimensional cartoons (Poynter, 688, 705).

The dolls which were ultimately manufactured and sold (Pltf.Ex. 20-25A and B) consist of six different vinyl figures, each of which comes in two different colors. At an earlier stage, Poynter made and rejected a stuffed doll version of the figures (Poynter, 712-714, 716; Deft.Ex. 36).

At a meeting in February 1968, Abelman, Whiteman and Poynter carefully examined each doll and compared it with the cartoons. Abelman expressed the opinion that Poynter '* * * had done a very fine job of faithfully reproducing the cartoons in the doll medium, the three-dimensional medium' (Abelman, 1448, 1449). Previously, Poynter had submitted to Abelman, by letter of December 30, 1967, prototypes of the 'hang tag' (Pltf.Ex. 26) which was originally used with the dolls (Pltf.Ex. 45). Abelman approved the tag and suggested that a copyright notice also be permanently imprinted in the base of each doll (Abelman, 1449-1450). By letter dated February 16, 1968, Whiteman approved the dolls and the advertising material which he had viewed at the meeting (Pltf.Ex. 45).

Prior to March 12, 1968 (when the Court entered a temporary restraining order in this matter), defendants offered and sold the dolls using the name 'Dr. Seuss' in the following ways:

1. It was engraved in very small letters on the vinyl bottom of each doll (Pltf.Ex. 20A and B) with the statement: 'From Original Illustrations of Dr. Seuss 1932 Liberty Library Corporation Copyright Renewed 1966 Poynter Products Inc., Cincinnati, Ohio Made in Japan.' This was done pursuant to the suggestion of defendants' counsel (Abelman, 1449-1450).

2. A round hang tag (Pltf.Ex. 26) tied around the neck of each doll stated, on one side: 'From the Wonderful World of Dr. Seuss— an original Merry Menagerie'; and, on the other side: 'This is my ——— (you name it) from Dr. Seuss' Merry Menagerie.' Mr. Abelman approved this tag (1455, 1460).

The following are reproductions of both sides of this hang tag:

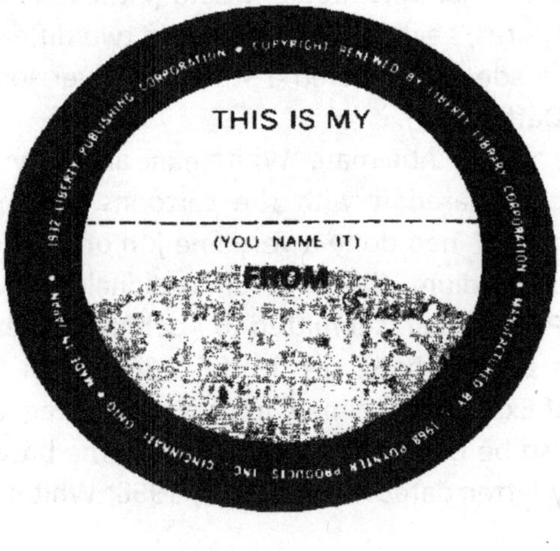

It is to be noted that the format of the name 'Dr. Seuss' copies exactly the characteristic style of plaintiff's nom de plume as it appears in all his works.

As will be pointed out shortly, defendants discontinued the above wording and format after March 12, 1968.

3. The dolls were sold in a display carton (Pltf.Ex. 27). On the base of this carton was the statement: 'Dr. Seuss' Merry Menagerie' and the words 'Lovable * * * Huggable'; on the backboard attached to the base of the carton was the statement: 'From the Wonderful World of Dr. Seuss * * * Everybody Loves 'em * * * From Original Illustrations by Dr. Seuss.' This carton, as well as the hang tag, also contained Liberty Library and Poyntor Products copyright notices. The carton contained a statement that defendant Alabe is the exclusive U.S.A. distributor. Although Abelman did not recall whether he approved the display box, he did approve the title 'From the Wonderful World of Dr. Seuss' and the remainder of the text used (Abelman, 1456-1457, 1460).

4. The dolls were advertised on a handbill (Pltf.Ex. 28) which stated: 'Dr. Seuss' Merry Menagerie' and 'From the Wonderful World of Dr. Seuss * * * Everybody Loves 'em.'

5. This handbill also contained the following statement on its reverse side: 'The Newest, Hottest Character Toy Line of 1968 * * * Dr. Seuss' (Pltf.Ex. 29).

6. The dolls were advertised or referred to in the Official Directory of the 65th Annual American Toy Fair (March 1968) held in New York (Pltf.Ex. 30) as 'Dr. Seuss' toys.

7. The dolls were referred to on invoices of defendants Alabe and Linder (Pltf.Ex. 32-33) as 'Dr. Seuss' Merry Menagerie.' Defendant Alabe's personnel and Poynter referred to the dolls as 'Dr. Seuss dolls' (Poynter, 767).

From March 12, 1968, when a temporary restraining order was entered in this action, until April 9, 1968, when a preliminary injunction was entered, defendants did not ship any of the dolls for sale (Poynter, 832). After the preliminary injunction was entered, defendants again began to offer the dolls for sale accompanied by revised labels and sales materials using the name 'Dr. Seuss' in the following manner:

a. The hang tag tied around the neck of each doll (Pltf.Ex. 46) stated, on one side: 'Wacky Merry Menagerie Everybody loves 'em'; and, on the other side: 'Toys Created, Designed & Produced Exclusively by Don Poynter MERRY MENAGERIE Based on Liberty Magazine Illustrations by Dr. Seuss';

The following are reproductions of both sides of this revised hang tag:

It is to be noted that, subsequent to April 9, 1968, defendants discontinued using plaintiff's characteristic style of printing 'Dr. Seuss'.

b. The backboard of the display cartoon (Deft.Ex. 58) stated:

"Merry Menagerie Toys Created, Designed Based On Liberty & Produced Exclusively Magazine Illustrations By Don Poynter By Dr. Seuss"

The name 'Dr. Seuss' and the name 'Don Poynter' were in the same size and style of type. The base section of the carton (Deft.Ex. 57) contained no mention of Dr. Seuss.

Extent of Defendants' Rights to Make the Dolls and to Use the Name 'Dr. Seuss'

As the owner of a copyright on the two-dimensional cartoons, defendant Liberty Library has the right to make three-dimensional figures or dolls therefrom or to license another (e.g., defendant Poynter Products) to do so. See King Features Syndicate v. Fleischer, 299 F. 533, 535 (2nd Cir. 1924) (owner of copyright upon cartoon sued manufacturer of toy horse '* * * fashioned after, labelled, and sold as * * *' 'Sparky', the cartoon character; held: there is a claim for copyright infringement because a three-dimensional toy figure can be a copy of a two-dimensional cartoon); Nutt v. National Institute Inc., 31 F.2d 236 (2nd Cir. 1929) (lecture notes); Fleischer Studios, Inc. v. Ralph A. Freundlich, Inc., 5 F.Supp. 808 (S.D.N.Y.1934) (owner of copyright upon cartoon sued manufacturer of 'Betty Boop' doll; held: there is a claim for infringement because an exact copy is not required).

A copyright upon a work in one medium may be asserted affirmatively by the copyright owner to obtain protection against infringement accomplished in a different medium...

A corollary of the rule just stated is that a copyright upon a work in one medium empowers the copyright owner to transform or copy the work into a different medium. More specifically, in this case the owner of the copyrighted two-dimensional cartoons has the right to make three-dimensional figures from the cartoons.

The manifest logic of the foregoing conclusion is demonstrated by assuming arguendo that the cartoons are in the public domain. In that suppositious situation, clearly defendants could copy the cartoons at will. In the present case, defendants, as owners of the copyrighted cartoons, cannot be in a less advantageous position.

Based upon a variety of legal theories set forth in the complaint, plaintiff's primary argument is that defendants' use of plaintiff's trade and pen name 'Dr. Seuss' is wrongful.

1. The Lanham Act and Unfair Competition Claims

Plaintiff charges that defendants have violated Section 43(a) of the Lanham Act, 15 U.S.C. § 1125(a), and are guilty of unfair competition and of violating Section 368-d of the New York General Business Law. The counterargument advanced by defendants is that a series of federal cases involving trademark infringement and unfair competition establishes the defendants' indisputable right to use the name 'Dr. Seuss' to describe truthfully the nature and origin of their product, the dolls.

In this area of federal trademark law, the governing principle was expounded by the Court of Appeals for this Circuit when it declared in Societe Comptoir De L'Industrie Cotonniere Etablissements Boussac v. Alexander's Department Stores, Inc., 299 F.2d 33, 36 (2nd Cir. 1962), aff'g, 190 F.Supp. 594 (S.D.N.Y.1961), that registration of a mark:

'* * * bestows upon the owner of the mark the limited right to protect his good will from possible harm by those uses of another as may engender a belief in the mind of the public that the product identified by the infringing mark is made or sponsored by the owner of the mark. Champion Spark Plug Co. v. Sanders, 331 U.S. 125, 67 S.Ct. 1136, 91 L.Ed. 1386 (1947) citing with approval, Prestonettes, Inc. v. Coty, 264 U.S. 359, 44 S.Ct. 350, 68 L.Ed. 731 (1924). The Lanham Act does not prohibit a commercial rival's truthfully denominating his goods a copy of a design in the public domain, though he uses the name of the designer to do so. Indeed it is difficult to see any other means that might be employed to inform the consuming public of the true origin of the design...."

In Prestonettes, Coty, the owner of a registered trade-mark, sought to enjoin another from selling Coty's genuine products in smaller bottles and packages with Coty's name on it. The District Court issued a limited injunction which allowed the defendant to affix a label truthfully describing the relationship between defendant's product and Coty's product. The Court of Appeals issued a broad, absolute injunction restraining defendant from using Coty's marks in any way (as plaintiff requests in the case at bar). The Supreme Court reversed, holding that defendant could state the nature of the component parts of its product and the source from which it was derived. In doing so, defendant could use Coty's mark because '* * * when the mark is used in a way that does not deceive the public we see no * * * sanctity in the words as to prevent its (the mark) being used to tell the truth' (264 U.S. at 368, 44 S.Ct. at 351).

In Champion Spark Plug, defendant repaired and reconditioned Champion's used sparkplugs and sold them using the name 'Champion'..

The doctrine of Prestonettes and Champion Spark Plug—that a trade name may be used by another as long as there is full and meticulously truthful disclosure communicating the actual character of the product—has been followed in a long line of decisions... Another case that illuminates the problem before the Court is Chamberlain v. Columbia Pictures Corp., 186 F.2d 923 (9th Cir. 1951). There the Court affirmed the dismissal of a complaint by the heirs of Samuel Clemens against the defendant which had released a motion picture advertised as 'A Story Only Mark Twain Could Tell,' 'Mark Twain's Tale of a Gamble in Hearts,' and 'Mark Twain's Favorite Story' and, therefore, assertedly conveyed the impression that Clemens had authored the picture. In fact, alleged plaintiff, the picture was of inferior quality; had only slight resemblance to Clemens' story; and was merely a 'corny love story.' The Court held that, because Clemens' story and, therefore, his name, were in the public domain, plaintiff had no monopoly in it and there could be no violation of plaintiff's rights; and that nothing in the advertisements could lead anyone to believe that the movie was plaintiff's business or that plaintiff was in any way connected with it (186 F.2d at 925). In the case at bar, plaintiff likewise has, to the extent that defendant Liberty Library owns all rights in the cartoons which appeared with the name 'Dr. Seuss,' no absolute monopoly in the name 'Dr. Seuss.'

With these guidelines as to the scope of the permissible use of the trade name 'Dr. Seuss' in mind, the Court reaffirms, on the merits, that defendants violated Section 43(a) of the Lanham Act by their 'use' of the name 'Dr. Seuss' 'in connection with' the advertising and sale of the dolls prior to March 12, 1968 (when this Court issued a temporary restraining order). See Geisel v. Poynter Products, Inc., 283 F.Supp. 261 (S.D.N.Y.1968) (opinion on preliminary injunction). In the exercise of the Court's discretion, see Parkway Baking Company v. Freihofer Baking Company, 255 F.2d 641, 649 (3rd Cir. 1958), the Court will make permanent that preliminary injunction.

On the present record, there is no showing of measurable damages because there is no proof of injury to plaintiff or of actual deception of a portion of the buying public. See Parkway Baking Company v. Freihofer Baking Company, supra, 255 F.2d at 648, and cases cited therein. However, if plaintiff has reason to believe that these deficiencies can be remedied without substantial delay, the Court will, upon appropriate motion and showing, appoint a master to ascertain the amount of any measurable damages.

The critical question for decision is whether defendants' 'use' of the name 'Dr. Seuss' after April 9, 1968 (when this Court issued a preliminary injunction) violates Section 43(a) of the Lanham Act. The Court holds that defendants' activities after April 9th do not constitute 'a false designation of origin, or any false description or representation' within the meaning of Section 43(a). Societe Comptoir De L'Industrie Cotonniere Etablissements Boussac v. Alexander's Department Stores, Inc., supra; Parkway Baking Company v. Freihofer Baking Company, supra. See also Smith v. Chanel, Inc., 402 F.2d 562 (9th Cir. 1968).

While defendants' prior activities created a false impression that the dolls were designed, manufactured or authorized by plaintiff, no such impression was intended to be, is, or can be, created by defendants' 'use' of the name 'Dr. Seuss' after April 9th.

No actual deception or confusion of, or tendency to deceive, the public is possible. Defendants have, in fact, satisfied the criteria of full and meticulously truthful disclosure. The phrase 'based on' or the word 'based,' as used by defendants after April 9th, like the phrases 'derived from,' 'suggested by,' or 'inspired by,' accurately characterizes the genetic link between the cartoons and the dolls. Differences between the two are readily discerned...The dolls are not exact reproductions or replicas of the cartoons. But these morphological differences are within the accepted limits in the licensed toy trade...

A comparison of other cartoon characters with the dolls or toys based on or derived from them discloses that some deviations between them, as between the cartoons and the dolls herein, are the inevitable result of the transmutation from two-dimensional drawings or cartoons to three-dimensional figures, manufacturing difficulties (including choice of material or medium), cost considerations, and aesthetic objectives (such as making the toy doll figures more 'doll-like' or 'huggable').

Plaintiff's experts, Charles M. Jones (of Metro-Goldwyn-Mayer's art department), Louis Lispi (art director of Walt Disney Productions), and Neil Estern (a noted sculptor) stated or implied that it is not possible to 'base' a three-dimensional doll on a single two-dimensional cartoon drawing. This testimony is rejected by the Court as unsound and, indeed, belied by the demonstrated facts of this very case: the defendants have 'based' their dolls on the plaintiff's cartoon characters. Despite the fantastic and imaginary character of plaintiff's cartoon animals (Geisel, 924-925), some of their 'component parts' exist in nature (Geisel, 1020; Poynter, 688) or did in prehistoric times (Poynter, 688). Consequently, Poynter was not working in primordial darkness when he had but one cartoon drawing upon which to base each doll.

To paraphrase the testimony of one of plaintiff's witnesses, the dolls are based on the cartoons in the same sense that a musical comedy may be based on a book despite obvious differences in the art forms and deviations in detail (Cerf, 328-329).

The Court does not adopt plaintiff's view that 'based on' is a misrepresentation because it allegedly implies that plaintiff approved the dolls (Geisel, 1052-1053, 1055). Section 43(a) of the Lanham Act cannot be read as permitting such an inference as to defendants' actions after April 9th without deleting the word 'false' from that statute. No such application of Section 43(a) is justified.

As to the claims of unfair competition, plaintiff cannot recover for the 'appropriation' of the cartoons themselves because defendant Liberty Library owns the copyright and plaintiff has no rights in them. See Cable Vision, inc. v. KUTV, Inc., 335 F.2d 348, 351 (9th Cir. 1964), cert. denied, 379 U.S. 989, 85 S.Ct. 700, 13 L.Ed.2d 609 (1965).

Plaintiff argues that he is entitled to recover under New York law for the unauthorized use and appropriation of the name 'Dr. Seuss' because of the false impression created that plaintiff sponsored or authorized defendants' dolls... Indubitably, one cannot attribute to an artist or author a work which the artist or author did not create or which substantially departs from his original work. Indeed, the New York courts have sometimes enjoined truthful references to another's trade or business name where there was a tendency to deceive the public.

A salient fact in this case is that defendants own all rights, including the copyright, in the cartoons. That ownership must include some right to use the name 'Dr. Seuss' because that name appeared on each of the pages of cartoons in Liberty Magazine. Although plaintiff did not design, manufacture or authorize the dolls, defendants have not, after April 9th, stated or implied that he did. In fact, defendants have truthfully stated plaintiff's relationship to the dolls. The Court reiterates that there is no tendency to deceive, or actual deception of, the public by virtue of defendants' use of the name 'Dr. Seuss' after April 9th.

Plaintiff also claims that he is entitled to an injunction under Section 368-d of the New York General Business Law. That statute requires a showing of some measure of customer confusion. Cue Publishing Co. v. Colgate-Palmolive Company, 45 Misc.2d 161, 256 N.Y.S.2d 239, 245-246 (Sup.Ct.N.Y.), aff'd, 23 A.D.2d 829, 259 N.Y.S.2d 377 (1965) (per curiam). That showing has not been made herein with respect to defendants' post-April 9th conduct. In the ordinary case of 'dilution' of a trade name, the parties are not in any contractual relationship involving the subject matter of the claim of dilution. See e.g., Cue Publishing Co. v. Colgate-Palmolive Company, supra; Triangle Publications v. Rohrlich, supra.

In this case, however, the applicability of the concept of dilution is precluded by the contractual relationship between the parties. Plaintiff's rights in the trade name 'Dr. Seuss' are monopolistic as to all the world except as to defendant Liberty Library, who acquired all rights in the cartoons from plaintiff in 1932. Consequently, defendants cannot be considered to be diluting plaintiff's trade name.

Finally, the Court finds that there has been no showing of a 'likelihood of injury to (plaintiff's) business reputation.' The Court, therefore, concludes that the claim under Section 368-d of the New York Business Law must be dismissed.

2. The Right of Privacy Claim

Plaintiff also seeks relief pursuant to article 5 of the New York Civil Rights Law, §§ 50, 51, which creates a 'right of privacy.'

Plaintiff consented neither to the manufacture and sale of the dolls nor to the use of the name 'Dr. Seuss' therewith... In addition, it cannot be doubted that the name 'Dr. Seuss' was '* * * used * * * for advertising purposes or for the purposes of trade * * *' within the meaning of Section 51.

However, plaintiff cannot succeed under the right of privacy statute because that statute does not protect an assumed or trade name.

In the case at bar, plaintiff's actual name is 'Theodor Seuss Geisel.' He began using the name 'Seuss' in 1925 and added the 'Dr.' to create the name 'Dr. Seuss' in 1927 (Geisel, 909-910). In fact, plaintiff stipulated that "Dr. Seuss' has been plaintiff's pen name and trade name since 1927 or 1928' (P.T.O.Stip. 35). The Court holds that the name 'Dr. Seuss' is an assumed name or pseudonym rather than a surname and is, therefore, not a protectible 'name' within the meaning of Section 51 of the New York Civil Rights Law.

Defendants also argue that plaintiff cannot recover under the privacy statute because of the express statutory exception to Section 51...

Clearly, the second and third conditions are met. Plaintiff 'sold' the cartoons and the name 'Dr. Seuss' appeared on each of them. Neyland v. Home pattern Co., Inc., supra (signed painting).

Plaintiff, however, contends that defendants have not satisfied the first condition for the reason that plaintiff 'sold or disposed of' cartoons—not dolls—and the dolls are not substantially related to the cartoons. There is some superficial merit to this argument. However, the Court finds that the dolls are substantially related to the cartoons. Thus, the evident statutory purpose of the exception encompasses the circumstances of this case.

Decisions interpreting the statute have long held that, if a work is in the public domain, a concomitant of the right to copy that work is the right to use the name of the creator of the work in connection therewith, or, in other words, to state truthfully the creator's association with the product.

The case at bar presents an a fortiori situation: the copyright and all rights in the cartoons are held by defendants...

The Court, therefore, holds that all the conditions of the exception to Section 51 of the New York Civil Rights Law are met. That exception, as well as the trade name exception, requires dismissal of the right of privacy claim.

3. The Defamation Claim

Plaintiff argues that the dolls are 'tasteless, unattractive and of an inferior quality' (Complaint, P41) and therefore, sale of them with his trade or pen name holds him up to ridicule and contempt in his profession as a distinguished artist and author...

That plaintiff is a distinguished artist and author is not disputed (P.T.O.Stip. 6, 28-33). The Court, however, rejects as unpersuasive and contrary to the preponderance of the credible evidence the testimony adduced in behalf of plaintiff that the dolls are 'repellant' and of 'inferior quality' (see, e.g., Cerf, 327, 602). The Court finds that the execution of defendants' dolls was done with great care, skill and judgment by a qualified designer and manufacturer. In addition, the Court, on the basis of the entire record (see, e.g., Lispi, 194, 218-219; Poynter, 835) and of its own close examination of the dolls, finds that they are attractive and of good quality. There is, therefore, no defamation.

This claim must also fail because defendants' activities after April 9th do not imply that plaintiff created, designed or approved of the dolls. Cf. Shostakovich v. Twentieth Century-Fox Film Corp., 196 Misc. 67, 80 N.Y.S.2d at 578 (no libel because no implication of approval exists where work is in public domain).

4. Conspiracy to Injure (Prima facie Tort)

Plaintiff alleges for his fifth and final cause of action essentially that defendants have conspired to commit all the other acts alleged with an intent to injure plaintiff. This claim has not been established.

The Court finds, on the basis of the great preponderance of the credible evidence, that with respect to the exploitation of plaintiff's cartoons by Liberty Library, Liberty's dealings with plaintiff's agent, Mrs. Jackson, reflect the good faith of defendant Liberty; and that all of the actions of defendant Liberty and of its licensee Poynter Products were under bona fide advice of experienced and competent counsel who had been specifically requested to remain in the role of advising defendants by plaintiff's agent (Abelman, 1446-1449). The Court reiterates that the designs and manufacture of the dolls were executed with great care and skill by persons with extensive experience.

Far from there being an intention to injure, the Court finds that defendants, at all stages of exploiting the Liberty Magazine cartoons, conducted themselves carefully and conservatively. There was no malice or intention to inflict injury on plaintiff. See Shostakovich v. Twentieth Century-Fox Film Corp., 196 Misc. 67, 80 N.Y.S.2d 575, 579 (wilful injury required).

It is important to note that plaintiff has not pleaded and proved special damages.

The prima facie tort claim must, therefore, be dismissed on the merits. The same showing of good faith and reliance upon counsel which requires dismissal of the prima facie tort claim also requires dismissal, as a matter of discretion, of all claims for punitive damages...

Finally, plaintiff has offered no evidence of such participation by Alabe Crafts, Inc. and Linder, Nathan & Heide, Inc. in the accused acts as to make either of those defendants liable.

The Court denies costs to either party.

If any of the parties desire additional or supplemental findings of fact and conclusions of law, such additional or supplemental findings and conclusions shall be submitted to the Court and opposing counsel within five days from the date of the filing of this opinion.

Settle a judgment in accordance with the views expressed in this opinion.

GILLIAM v. AMERICAN BROADCASTING COMPANIES, INC.
United States Court of Appeals, Second Circuit
Nos. 913, 1058, Dockets 75-7693, 76-7023
Argued April 13, 1976
Decided June 30, 1976
583 F.2d 14

LUMBARD, Circuit Judge:

Plaintiffs, a group of British writers and performers known as "Monty Python," appeal from a denial by Judge Lasker in the Southern District of a preliminary injunction to restrain the American Broadcasting Company (ABC) from broadcasting edited versions of three separate programs originally written and performed by Monty Python for broadcast by the British Broadcasting Corporation (BBC). We agree with Judge Lasker that the appellants have demonstrated that the excising done for ABC impairs the integrity of the original work. We further find that the countervailing injuries that Judge Lasker found might have accrued to ABC as a result of an injunction at a prior date no longer exist. We therefore direct the issuance of a preliminary injunction by the district court.

Since its formation in 1969, the Monty Python group has gained popularity primarily through its thirty-minute television programs created for BBC as part of a comedy series entitled "Monty Python's Flying Circus." In accordance with an agreement between Monty Python and BBC, the group writes and delivers to BBC scripts for use in the television series. This scriptwriters' agreement recites in great detail the procedure to be followed when any alterations are to be made in the script prior to recording of the program. The essence of this section of the agreement is that, while BBC retains final authority to make changes, appellants or their representatives exercise optimum control over the scripts consistent with BBC's authority and only minor changes may be made without prior consultation with the writers. Nothing in the scriptwriters' agreement entitles BBC to alter a program once it has been recorded. The agreement further provides that, subject to the terms therein, the group retains all rights in the script.

Under the agreement, BBC may license the transmission of recordings of the television programs in any overseas territory. The series has been broadcast in this country primarily on non-commercial public broadcasting television stations, although several of the programs have been broadcast on commercial stations in Texas and Nevada. In each instance, the thirty-minute programs have been broadcast as originally recorded and broadcast in England in their entirety and without commercial interruption.

In October 1973, Time-Life Films acquired the right to distribute in the United States certain BBC television programs, including the Monty Python series. Time-Life was permitted to edit the programs only "for insertion of commercials, applicable censorship or governmental . . . rules and regulations, and National Association of Broadcasters and time segment requirements." No similar clause was included in the scriptwriters' agreement between appellants and BBC. Prior to this time, ABC had sought to acquire the right to broadcast excerpts from various Monty Python programs in the spring of 1975, but the group rejected the proposal for such a disjoined format. Thereafter, in July 1975, ABC agreed with Time-Life to broadcast two ninety-minute specials each comprising three thirty-minute Monty Python programs that had not previously been shown in this country.

Correspondence between representatives of BBC and Monty Python reveals that these parties assumed that ABC would broadcast each of the Monty Python programs "in its entirety." On September 5, 1975, however, the group's British representative inquired of BBC how ABC planned to show the programs in their entirety if approximately 24 minutes of each 90 minute program were to be devoted to commercials. BBC replied on September 12, "we can only reassure you that ABC have decided to run the programmes 'back to back,' and that there is a firm undertaking not to segment them."

ABC broadcast the first of the specials on October 3, 1975. Appellants did not see a tape of the program until late November and were allegedly "appalled" at the discontinuity and "mutilation" that had resulted from the editing done by Time-Life for ABC. Twenty-four minutes of the original 90 minutes of recording had been omitted. Some of the editing had been done in order to make time for commercials; other material had been edited, according to ABC, because the original programs contained offensive or obscene matter.

In early December, Monty Python learned that ABC planned to broadcast the second special on December 26, 1975. The parties began negotiations concerning editing of that program and a delay of the broadcast until Monty Python could view it. These negotiations were futile, however, and on December 15 the group filed this action to enjoin the broadcast and for damages. Following an evidentiary hearing, Judge Lasker found that "the plaintiffs have established an impairment of the integrity of their work" which "caused the film or program . . . to lose its iconoclastic verve." According to Judge Lasker, "the damage that has been caused to the plaintiffs is irreparable by its nature." Nevertheless, the judge denied the motion for the preliminary injunction on the grounds that it was unclear who owned the copyright in the programs produced by BBC from the scripts written by Monty Python; that there was a question of whether Time-Life and BBC were indispensable parties to the litigation; that ABC would suffer significant financial loss if it were enjoined a week before the scheduled broadcast; and that Monty Python had displayed a "somewhat disturbing casualness" in their pursuance of the matter.

Judge Lasker granted Monty Python's request for more limited relief by requiring ABC to broadcast a disclaimer during the December 26 special to the effect that the group dissociated itself from the program because of the editing. A panel of this court, however, granted a stay of that order until this appeal could be heard and permitted ABC to broadcast, at the beginning of the special, only the legend that the program had been edited by ABC. We heard argument on April 13 and, at that time, enjoined ABC from any further broadcast of edited Monty Python programs pending the decision of the court.

I

In determining the availability of injunctive relief at this early stage of the proceedings, Judge Lasker properly considered the harm that would inure to the plaintiffs if the injunction were denied, the harm that defendant would suffer if the injunction were granted, and the likelihood that plaintiffs would ultimately succeed on the merits. See Hamilton Watch Co. v. Benrus Watch Co., 206 F.2d 738 (2d Cir. 1953). We direct the issuance of a preliminary injunction because we find that all these factors weigh in favor of appellants.

There is nothing clearly erroneous in Judge Lasker's conclusion that any injury suffered by appellants as a result of the broadcast of edited versions of their programs was irreparable by its nature. ABC presented the appellants with their first opportunity for broadcast to a nationwide network audience in this country. If ABC adversely misrepresented the quality of Monty Python's work, it is likely that many members of the audience, many of whom, by defendant's admission, were previously unfamiliar with appellants, would not become loyal followers of Monty Python productions. The subsequent injury to appellants' theatrical reputation would imperil their ability to attract the large audience necessary to the success of their venture. Such an injury to professional reputation cannot be measured in monetary terms or recompensed by other relief. See Coca-Cola Co. v. Gemini Rising, Inc., 346 F.Supp. 1183, 1189 (E.D.N.Y.1972); Estee Lauder, Inc. v. Watsky, 323 F.Supp. 1064, 1067 (S.D.N.Y.1970).

In contrast to the harm that Monty Python would suffer by a denial of the preliminary injunction, Judge Lasker found that ABC's relationship with its affiliates would be impaired by a grant of an injunction within a week of the scheduled December 26 broadcast. The court also found that ABC and its affiliates had advertised the program and had included it in listings of forthcoming television programs that were distributed to the public. Thus a last minute cancellation of the December 26 program, Judge Lasker concluded, would injure defendant financially and in its reputation with the public and its advertisers.

However valid these considerations may have been when the issue before the court was whether a preliminary injunction should immediately precede the broadcast, any injury to ABC is presently more speculative. No rebroadcast of the edited specials has been scheduled and no advertising costs have been incurred for the immediate future. Thus there is no danger that defendant's relations with affiliates or the public will suffer irreparably if subsequent broadcasts of the programs are enjoined pending a disposition of the issues.

We then reach the question whether there is a likelihood that appellants will succeed on the merits. In concluding that there is a likelihood of infringement here, we rely especially on the fact that the editing was substantial, i.e., approximately 27 per cent of the original program was omitted, and the editing contravened contractual provisions that limited the right to edit Monty Python material. It should be emphasized that our discussion of these matters refers only to such facts as have been developed upon the hearing for a preliminary injunction. Modified or contrary findings may become appropriate after a plenary trial.

Judge Lasker denied the preliminary injunction in part because he was unsure of the ownership of the copyright in the recorded program. Appellants first contend that the question of ownership is irrelevant because the recorded program was merely a derivative work taken from the script in which they hold the uncontested copyright. Thus, even if BBC owned the copyright in the recorded program, its use of that work would be limited by the license granted to BBC by Monty Python for use of the underlying script. We agree.

Section 7 of the Copyright Law, 17 U.S.C. § 7, provides in part that "adaptations, arrangements, dramatizations . . . or other versions of . . . copyrighted works when produced with the consent of the proprietor of the copyright in such works . . . shall be regarded as new works subject to copyright . . . ." Manifestly, the recorded program falls into this category as a dramatization of the script, and thus the program was itself entitled to copyright protection. However, section 7 limits the copyright protection of the derivative work, as works adapted from previously existing scripts have become known, to the novel additions made to the underlying work, Reyher v. Children's Television Workshop, 533 F.2d 87 (2d Cir. 1976), and the derivative work does not affect the "force or validity" of the copyright in the matter from which it is derived. See Grove Press, Inc. v. Greenleaf Publishing Co., 247 F.Supp. 518 (S.D.N.Y.1965). Thus, any ownership by BBC of the copyright in the recorded program would not affect the scope or ownership of the copyright in the underlying script.

Since the copyright in the underlying script survives intact despite the incorporation of that work into a derivative work, one who uses the script, even with the permission of the proprietor of the derivative work, may infringe the underlying copyright...

If the proprietor of the derivative work is licensed by the proprietor of the copyright in the underlying work to vend or distribute the derivative work to third parties, those parties will, of course, suffer no liability for their use of the underlying work consistent with the license to the proprietor of the derivative work. Obviously, it was just this type of arrangement that was contemplated in this instance. The scriptwriters' agreement between Monty Python and BBC specifically permitted the latter to license the transmission of the recordings made by BBC to distributors such as Time-Life for broadcast in overseas territories.

One who obtains permission to use a copyrighted script in the production of a derivative work, however, may not exceed the specific purpose for which permission was granted. Most of the decisions that have reached this conclusion have dealt with the improper extension of the underlying work into media or time, i. e., duration of the license, not covered by the grant of permission to the derivative work proprietor. Appellants herein do not claim that the broadcast by ABC violated media or time restrictions contained in the license of the script to BBC. Rather, they claim that revisions in the script, and ultimately in the program, could be made only after consultation with Monty Python, and that ABC's broadcast of a program edited after recording and without consultation with Monty Python exceeded the scope of any license that BBC was entitled to grant.

The rationale for finding infringement when a licensee exceeds time or media restrictions on his license the need to allow the proprietor of the underlying copyright to control the method in which his work is presented to the public applies equally to the situation in which a licensee makes an unauthorized use of the underlying work by publishing it in a truncated version. Whether intended to allow greater economic exploitation of the work, as in the media and time cases, or to ensure that the copyright proprietor retains a veto power over revisions desired for the derivative work, the ability of the copyright holder to control his work remains paramount in our copyright law. We find, therefore, that unauthorized editing of the underlying work, if proven, would constitute an infringement of the copyright in that work similar to any other use of a work that exceeded the license granted by the proprietor of the copyright.

If the broadcast of an edited version of the Monty Python program infringed the group's copyright in the script, ABC may obtain no solace from the fact that editing was permitted in the agreements between BBC and Time-Life or Time-Life and ABC. BBC was not entitled to make unilateral changes in the script and was not specifically empowered to alter the recordings once made;

Monty Python, moreover, had reserved to itself any rights not granted to BBC. Since a grantor may not convey greater rights than it owns, BBC's permission to allow Time-Life, and hence ABC, to edit appears to have been a nullity.

ABC answers appellants' infringement argument with a series of contentions, none of which seems meritorious at this stage of the litigation. The network asserts that Monty Python's British representative, Jill Foster, knew that ABC planned to exclude much of the original BBC program in the October 3 broadcast. ABC thus contends that by not previously objecting to this procedure, Monty Python ratified BBC's authority to license others to edit the underlying script.

Although the case of Ilyin v. Avon Publications, Inc., 144 F.Supp. 368, 373 (S.D.N.Y.1956), may be broadly read for the proposition that a holder of a derivative copyright may obtain rights in the underlying work through ratification, the conduct necessary to that conclusion has yet to be demonstrated in this case. It is undisputed that appellants did not have actual notice of the cuts in the October 3 broadcast until late November. Even if they are chargeable with the knowledge of their British representative, it is not clear that she had prior notice of the cuts or ratified the omissions, nor did Judge Lasker make any finding on the question. While Foster, on September 5, did question how ABC was to broadcast the entire program if it was going to interpose 24 minutes of commercials, she received assurances from BBC that the programs would not be "segmented." The fact that she knew precisely the length of material that would have to be omitted to allow for commercials does not prove that she ratified the deletions. This is especially true in light of previous assurances that the program would contain the original shows in their entirety. On the present record, it cannot be said that there was any ratification of BBC's grant of editing rights. ABC, of course, is entitled to attempt to prove otherwise during the trial on the merits.

ABC next argues that under the "joint work" theory adopted in Shapiro, Bernstein & Co. v. Jerry Vogel Music, Inc., 221 F.2d 569 (2d Cir. 1955), the script produced by Monty Python and the program recorded by BBC are symbiotic elements of a single production. Therefore, according to ABC, each contributor possesses an undivided ownership of all copyrightable elements in the final work and BBC could thus have licensed use of the script, including editing, written by appellants.

The joint work theory as extended in Shapiro has been criticized as inequitable unless "at the time of creation by the first author, the second author's contribution (is envisaged) as an integrated part of a single work," and the first author intends that the final product be a joint work. See 1 M. Nimmer, Copyright ss 67-73. Furthermore, this court appears to have receded from a broad application of the joint work doctrine where the contract which leads to collaboration between authors indicates that one will retain a superior interest.

See Szekely v. Eagle Lion Films, Inc., 242 F.2d 266 (2d Cir.), cert. denied, 354 U.S. 922, 77 S.Ct. 1382, 1 L.Ed.2d 1437 (1957). In the present case, the screenwriters' agreement between Monty Python and BBC provides that the group is to retain all rights in the script not granted in the agreement and that at some future point the group may license the scripts for use on television to parties other than BBC. These provisions suggest that the parties did not consider themselves joint authors of a single work. This matter is subject to further exploration at the trial, but in the present state of the record, it presents no bar to issuance of a preliminary injunction.

Aside from the question of who owns the relevant copyrights, ABC asserts that the contracts between appellants and BBC permit editing of the programs for commercial television in the United States. ABC argues that the scriptwriters' agreement allows appellants the right to participate in revisions of the script only prior to the recording of the programs, and thus infers that BBC had unrestricted authority to revise after that point. This argument, however, proves too much. A reading of the contract seems to indicate that Monty Python obtained control over editing the script only to ensure control over the program recorded from that script. Since the scriptwriters' agreement explicitly retains for the group all rights not granted by the contract, omission of any terms concerning alterations in the program after recording must be read as reserving to appellants exclusive authority for such revisions.

Finally, ABC contends that appellants must have expected that deletions would be made in the recordings to conform them for use on commercial television in the United States. ABC argues that licensing in the United States implicitly grants a license to insert commercials in a program and to remove offensive or obscene material prior to broadcast. According to the network, appellants should have anticipated that most of the excised material contained scatological references inappropriate for American television and that these scenes would be replaced with commercials, which presumably are more palatable to the American public.

The proof adduced up to this point, however, provides no basis for finding any implied consent to edit. Prior to the ABC broadcasts, Monty Python programs had been broadcast on a regular basis by both commercial and public television stations in this country without interruption or deletion. Indeed, there is no evidence of any prior broadcast of edited Monty Python material in the United States. These facts, combined with the persistent requests for assurances by the group and its representatives that the programs would be shown intact belie the argument that the group knew or should have known that deletions and commercial interruptions were inevitable.

Several of the deletions made for ABC, such as elimination of the words "hell" and "damn," seem inexplicable given today's standard television fare. If, however, ABC honestly determined that the programs were obscene in substantial part, it could have decided not to broadcast the specials at all, or it could have attempted to reconcile its differences with appellants. The network could not, however, free from a claim of infringement, broadcast in a substantially altered form a program incorporating the script over which the group had retained control.

Our resolution of these technical arguments serves to reinforce our initial inclination that the copyright law should be used to recognize the important role of the artist in our society and the need to encourage production and dissemination of artistic works by providing adequate legal protection for one who submits his work to the public. See Mazer v. Stein, 347 U.S. 201, 74 S.Ct. 460, 98 L.Ed. 630 (1954). We therefore conclude that there is a substantial likelihood that, after a full trial, appellants will succeed in proving infringement of their copyright by ABC's broadcast of edited versions of Monty Python programs. In reaching this conclusion, however, we need not accept appellants' assertion that any editing whatsoever would constitute infringement. Courts have recognized that licensees are entitled to some small degree of latitude in arranging the licensed work for presentation to the public in a manner consistent with the licensee's style or standards... That privilege, however, does not extend to the degree of editing that occurred here especially in light of contractual provisions that limited the right to edit Monty Python material.

II

It also seems likely that appellants will succeed on the theory that, regardless of the right ABC had to broadcast an edited program, the cuts made constituted an actionable mutilation of Monty Python's work. This cause of action, which seeks redress for deformation of an artist's work, finds its roots in the continental concept of droit moral, or moral right, which may generally be summarized as including the right of the artist to have his work attributed to him in the form in which he created it. See 1 M. Nimmer, supra, at § 110.1.

American copyright law, as presently written, does not recognize moral rights or provide a cause of action for their violation, since the law seeks to vindicate the economic, rather than the personal, rights of authors. Nevertheless, the economic incentive for artistic and intellectual creation that serves as the foundation for American copyright law, Goldstein v. California, 412 U.S. 546, 93 S.Ct. 2303, 37 L.Ed.2d 163 (1973); Mazer v. Stein, 347 U.S. 201, 74 S.Ct. 460, 98 L.Ed. 630 (1954), cannot be reconciled with the inability of artists to obtain relief for mutilation or misrepresentation of their work to the public on which the artists are financially dependent. Thus courts have long granted relief for misrepresentation of an artist's work by relying on theories outside the statutory law of copyright, such as contract law,... Although such decisions are clothed in terms of proprietary right in one's creation, they also properly vindicate the author's personal right to prevent the presentation of his work to the public in a distorted form.

Here, the appellants claim that the editing done for ABC mutilated the original work and that consequently the broadcast of those programs as the creation of Monty Python violated the Lanham Act § 43(a), 15 U.S.C. § 1125(a). This statute, the federal counterpart to state unfair competition laws, has been invoked to prevent misrepresentations that may injure plaintiff's business or personal reputation, even where no registered trademark is concerned. See Mortellito v. Nina of California, 335 F.Supp. 1288, 1294 (S.D.N.Y.1972). It is sufficient to violate the Act that a representation of a product, although technically true, creates a false impression of the product's origin. See Rich v. RCA Corp., 390 F.Supp. 530 (S.D.N.Y.1975) (recent picture of plaintiff on cover of album containing songs recorded in distant past held to be a false representation that the songs were new); Geisel v. Poynter Products, Inc., 283 F.Supp. 261, 267 (S.D.N.Y.1968).

These cases cannot be distinguished from the situation in which a television network broadcasts a program properly designated as having been written and performed by a group, but which has been edited, without the writer's consent, into a form that departs substantially from the original work. "To deform his work is to present him to the public as the creator of a work not his own, and thus makes him subject to criticism for work he has not done." Roeder, supra, at 569. In such a case, it is the writer or performer, rather than the network, who suffers the consequences of the mutilation, for the public will have only the final product by which to evaluate the work. Thus, an allegation that a defendant has presented to the public a " garbled," Granz v. Harris, supra (Frank, J., concurring), distorted version of plaintiff's work seeks to redress the very rights sought to be protected by the Lanham Act, 15 U.S.C. § 1125(a), and should be recognized as stating a cause of action under that statute. See Autry v. Republic Productions, Inc., 213 F.2d 667 (9th Cir. 1954); Jaeger v. American Intn'l Pictures, Inc., 330 F.Supp. 274 (S.D.N.Y.1971), which suggest the violation of such a right if mutilation could be proven.

During the hearing on the preliminary injunction, Judge Lasker viewed the edited version of the Monty Python program broadcast on December 26 and the original, unedited version. After hearing argument of this appeal, this panel also viewed and compared the two versions. We find that the truncated version at times omitted the climax of the skits to which appellants' rare brand of humor was leading and at other times deleted essential elements in the schematic development of a story line. We therefore agree with Judge Lasker's conclusion that the edited version broadcast by ABC impaired the integrity of appellants' work and represented to the public as the product of appellants what was actually a mere caricature of their talents. We believe that a valid cause of action for such distortion exists and that therefore a preliminary injunction may issue to prevent repetition of the broadcast prior to final determination of the issues.

III

We do not share Judge Lasker's concern about the procedures by which the appellants have pursued this action. The district court indicated agreement with ABC that appellants were guilty of laches in not requesting a preliminary injunction until 11 days prior to the broadcast. Our discussion above, however, suggests that the group did not know and had no reason to believe until late November that editing would take place. Several letters between BBC and Monty Python's representative indicate that appellants believed that the programs would be shown in their entirety. Furthermore, the group did act to prevent offensive editing of the second program immediately after viewing the tape of the first edited program. Thus we find no undue delay in the group's failure to institute this action until they were sufficiently advised regarding the facts necessary to support the action. In any event, ABC has not demonstrated how it was prejudiced by any delay. See Emle Industries, Inc. v. Patentex, Inc., 478 F.2d 562, 574 (2d Cir. 1973).

Finally, Judge Lasker denied a preliminary injunction because Monty Python had failed to join BBC and Time-Life as indispensable parties. We do not believe that either is an indispensable party. ABC argues that joinder of both was required because it acted in good faith pursuant to its contractual rights with Time-Life in broadcasting edited versions of the programs, and Time-Life, in turn, relied upon its contract with BBC. Furthermore, ABC argues, BBC must be joined since it owns the copyright in the recorded programs.

Even if BBC owns a copyright relevant to determination of the issues in this case, the formalistic rule that once required all owners of a copyright to be parties to an action for its infringement has given way to equitable considerations... Monty Python is relying solely on its copyright in the script and on its rights as an author. No claim is being made that Monty Python has rights derived from the copyright held by another. Compare First Financial Marketing Services Group, Inc. v. Field Promotions, Inc., 286 F.Supp. 295 (S.D.N.Y.1968). One of the parties is an English corporation, and any action that appellants, a group of English writers and performers, might have against that potential defendant would be better considered under English law in an English court.

Complete relief for the alleged infringement and mutilation complained of may be accorded between Monty Python and ABC, which alone broadcast the programs in dispute. If ABC is ultimately found liable to appellants, a permanent injunction against future broadcasts and a damage award would satisfy all of appellants' claims. ABC's assertion that failure to join BBC and Time-Life may leave it subject to inconsistent verdicts in a later action against its licensors may be resolved through the process of impleader, which ABC has thus far avoided despite a suggestion from the district court to use that procedure. Finally, neither of the parties considered by ABC to be indispensable has claimed any interest in the subject matter of this litigation. See Fed.R.Civ.P. 19(a)(2).

For these reasons we direct that the district court issue the preliminary injunction sought by the appellants.

The following case Grigson v. Creative Artists Agency, LLC., concerns the Academy award movie (NOT!), The Return of the Texas Chain Saw Massacre, starring the then obscure actors Matthew McConaughey and Renee Zellweger. The production company alleges that McConaughey tortiously interfered with the distribution agreement by pressuring the distributor to limit the release of the movie.

GRIGSON v. CREATIVE ARTISTS AGENCY, L.L.C.
United States Court of Appeals, Fifth Circuit
No. 98-51016
April 24, 2000
210 F.3d 524

RHESA HAWKINS BARKSDALE, Circuit Judge:

Solely at issue is whether the district court abused its discretion by applying equitable estoppel to compel arbitration for an action centered on tortious interference with a contract with an arbitration clause, brought by signatories to the contract against non-signatories, the court holding that, because this action is intertwined with, and dependent upon, that contract, its arbitration agreement should be given effect. We AFFIRM.

I.

"Return of the Texas Chain Saw Massacre" (the movie) was filmed in 1993–94; then "obscure actors" Matthew McConaughey and Renee Zellweger acted in it. The movie was produced by Ultra Muchos, Inc., and River City Films, Inc. The trustee for the movie's owners is Charles Grigson.

In October 1995, Ultra Muchos and River City entered into a distribution agreement with Columbia TriStar Home Video, Inc. It was given exclusive distribution rights and complete discretion on how to exercise them; the producers were to receive a percentage of the movie's gross revenue. And, by separate, earlier agreement, the owners were to receive a portion of the producers' percentage.

In the period post-acting in the movie and prior to the fall of 1996, McConaughey signed an agency contract with Creative Artists Agency, L.L.C. The movie's distribution was delayed by TriStar to take advantage of Zellweger and McConaughey's success in subsequent movies. Subsequently, however, TriStar gave the movie only a limited distribution.

In district court in mid-1997, Grigson, as trustee, sued Ultra Muchos, River City, and TriStar for breach of the distribution agreement. But, Grigson quickly and voluntarily had the action dismissed that fall, when TriStar sought to enforce the distribution agreement's arbitration clause, which contains a forum selection provision (Los Angeles County, California).

In late 1997, a few months after the voluntary dismissal of the first action, Grigson, *now joined by Ultra Muchos and River City,* filed this action in state court against McConaughey and Creative Artists (Defendants) for, *inter alia,* tortious interference with the distribution agreement, claiming that such interference occurred between McConaughey's signing with Creative Artists and the movie's limited distribution. In this regard, Defendants allegedly pressured TriStar to limit the release because they viewed it as an improper exploitation of McConaughey's success post-acting in the movie.

After the action was removed to federal court on the basis of diversity of citizenship, Defendants, although non-signatories to the distribution agreement, moved to compel arbitration under the agreement. The same district court that had permitted the voluntary dismissal of Grigson's first action ruled that Grigson, Ultra Muchos, and River City (Appellants) were equitably estopped from relying upon Defendants' being non-signatories. This was based upon holding that, because the claims are so intertwined with, and dependent upon, the distribution agreement, its arbitration clause should be given effect. Accordingly, in the light of the forum selection provision in the arbitration clause, the court dismissed the action so that the parties could proceed in the mandated forum (Los Angeles County, California).

II.

Arbitration is favored in the law... Accordingly, parties to such agreements cannot avoid them by casting their claims in tort, rather than in contract. Likewise, proceedings against parties and non-parties to the arbitration agreement are stayed pending the outcome of arbitration, when the action against the non-party is dependent upon interpretation of the underlying contract. Similarly, as discussed *infra,* in certain limited instances, pursuant to an equitable estoppel doctrine, a non-signatory-to-an-arbitration-agreement-defendant can nevertheless compel arbitration against a signatory-plaintiff.

In the distribution agreement, Ultra Muchos, River City, and TriStar agreed

> that any dispute or controversy relating to any of the matters referred to in clauses (d)(i),(ii), or (iii), above, shall be decided by a Rent-A-Judge, mutually selected by the parties (or, if they cannot agree, by the Presiding Judge of the Los Angeles Superior Court) appointed in accordance with California Code of Civil Procedure Section 638, sitting without a jury, in Los Angeles County California, and the Parties hereby submit to the jurisdiction of such court.

The parties to this action agree that this procedure is the equivalent of arbitration, which would be subject to the Federal Arbitration Act, 9 U.S.C. § 1 *et seq...*

Because the owners seek compensation through the distribution agreement, Grigson admits that he is a third party beneficiary of that agreement; and that, therefore, he is required, as are the signatory-producers, to arbitrate with TriStar all disputes concerning that agreement. Appellants contend, however, that they are *not* required to arbitrate with Defendants, because they are *not* parties to the distribution agreement; and because, in the alternative, Defendants do not fall within what Appellants view as the quite limited bases for application of equitable estoppel to compel arbitration: either a special relationship to the distribution agreement signatories, or a role in carrying out the agreement's obligations. Creative Artists and McConaughey counter that, because the charged tortious interference is intertwined with the distribution agreement, they are entitled, through application of equitable estoppel, to compel arbitration.

This is an issue of first impression for our circuit. Other circuits have, in a few instances, allowed a non-signatory to a contract with an arbitration clause to compel arbitration under an equitable estoppel theory, including when the action is intertwined with, and dependent upon, that contract...

The Eleventh Circuit has taken the lead in applying equitable estoppel under the intertwined-claims basis...

We agree with the intertwined-claims test formulated by the Eleventh Circuit. Each case, of course, turns on its facts. Such equitable estoppel is much more readily applicable when the case presents both independent bases advanced by the Eleventh Circuit for applying the intertwined-claims doctrine. That is the situation here. The linchpin for equitable estoppel is equity—fairness. For the case at hand, to not apply this intertwined-claims basis to compel arbitration would fly in the face of fairness.

For the above-quoted statement from *MS Dealer Serv. Corp.* that equitable estoppel is applied in order to fulfill federal pro-arbitration policy, the Eleventh Circuit quoted from our court's decision in *Sam Reisfeld & Son Import Co. v. S.A. Eteco*, 530 F.2d 679, 681 (5th Cir.1976), which used an intertwined-claims rationale for staying judicial proceedings against two defendants, with links to a third, pending arbitration with plaintiff. Unlike third-defendant, the other two were *not* signatories to the arbitration agreement with plaintiff... Accordingly, our court concluded that the district court had *not* abused its discretion.

Although *Reisfeld* does *not* apply equitable estoppel *per se*, its *ratio decidendi* comports with that for application of that doctrine to allow a defendant non-signatory to an arbitration agreement to compel arbitration with a plaintiff-signatory. In short, although arbitration is a matter of contract and cannot, in general, be required for a matter involving an arbitration agreement non-signatory, a signatory to that agreement *cannot*, in those instances described in *MS Dealer Serv. Corp.*, "have it both ways": it cannot, on the one hand, seek to hold the non-signatory liable pursuant to duties imposed by the agreement, which contains an arbitration provision, but, on the other hand, deny arbitration's applicability because the defendant is a non-signatory. *MS Dealer Serv. Corp.*, 177 F.3d at 947; *Hughes Masonry Co.*, 659 F.2d at 838–39.

Again, to allow such inconsistent positions would be inequitable, to say the least.

Moreover, as noted, it would be especially inequitable where, as here, a signatory non-defendant is charged with interdependent and concerted misconduct with a non-signatory defendant. In such instances, that signatory, in essence, becomes a party, with resulting loss, *inter alia,* of time and money because of its required participation in the proceeding. Concomitantly, detrimental reliance by that signatory *cannot* be denied: it and the signatory-plaintiff had agreed to arbitration in lieu of litigation (generally far more costly in terms of time and expense); but, the plaintiff is seeking to avoid that agreement by bringing the action against a non-signatory charged with acting in concert with that non-defendant signatory. Of course, detrimental reliance is one of the elements for the usual application of equitable estoppel...

Accordingly, whether to utilize equitable estoppel in this fashion is within the district court's discretion; we review to determine only whether it has been abusedTo constitute an abuse of discretion, the district court's decision must be either premised on an application of the law that is erroneous, or on an assessment of the evidence that is clearly erroneous.

The district court did *not* abuse its discretion by concluding "that Plaintiffs' claims are so intertwined with and dependent upon the Distribution Agreement that the arbitration agreement within the Distribution Agreement should be given effect". This conclusion is compelled by comparing the complaint (the operative facts for purposes of the motion to compel arbitration) with the distribution agreement (an exhibit to the complaint). This is quickly and amply demonstrated with but a few examples.

The distribution agreement is *not* the only contract for which tortious interference is claimed. Creative Artists is also charged with such interference with McConaughey's actor's contract for the movie (another exhibit to the complaint); he is charged with breach of that contract. Among other things, he was required by that actor's contract to allow use of "his name and photographs ... for commercial and advertising purposes".

The complaint uses that specific requirement in the actor's contract in describing how, for the theatrical release (as defined in the distribution agreement) mandated by the distribution agreement, TriStar

> had planned to distribute Chainsaw movie posters prominently featuring the likeness and name of McConaughey and, in fact, had printed posters reflecting this plan. Creative Artists, acting for McConaughey, contacted Columbia Tristar and successfully pressured it to retreat from its plan for the posters on the grounds that McConaughey's fame should not be exploited in such a manner in connection with the Chainsaw movie.

This is but part of the charged interference. In addition, the complaint alleges that the theatrical release was delayed initially to take advantage of Zellweger's post-movie success in another movie, *also released by TriStar;* that the plan changed to take advantage of both actors' success; that Creative Artists, on behalf of McConaughey, "pressured" TriStar to *not* make a major release of the movie and, instead, to make only a limited one, to Appellants' great financial detriment; and that, because of Defendants' actions, *"TriStar failed to exercise its good faith judgment in promoting, exploiting, and distributing" the movie.* (Emphasis added.)

As is obvious from the foregoing, and as the district court concluded, these allegations and claims are intertwined with, and dependent upon, the distribution agreement. In addition to Appellants relying on the terms of the agreement in asserting their claims, TriStar and Defendants are charged with interdependent and concerted misconduct.

The distribution agreement, in describing the movie, lists Zellweger and two others as "starring" in it; *McConaughey is not so listed.* All rights to the movie are given to TriStar; and, subject to it making a required minimum expenditure in connection with the theatrical release, TriStar has *"absolute discretion* concerning the exploitation of the [movie] in any and all media". (Emphasis added.)

In that provision, which obviously lies at the heart of this action, Appellants

> agree[d] that the *good faith judgment* of [TriStar] regarding any matter affecting the exploitation of the [movie] shall be binding and conclusive upon [Appellants] ([TriStar] shall make the determination, *within its sole discretion,* whether or not to release the [movie] in a given media and/or in a given territory).

(Emphasis added.) "Territory" includes, with some exceptions, "[t]he entire universe", while "media" includes, but is *not* limited to, movie theaters.

And, as noted, the distribution agreement's arbitration clause pertains, *inter alia,* to the "interpretation of [the distribution] agreement, ... the performance by the Parties of their respective obligations [there]under, and ... all other causes of action (whether sounding in contract *or in tort*) arising out of *or relating to* this Agreement". (Emphasis added.)

In short, the scope of the distribution, the "discretion", both "absolute" and "sole", vested in TriStar, and its "good faith judgment" are at the center of this dispute. Among other things, TriStar is charged with, as a result of the claimed interference ("pressure"), *not* using its "good faith judgment". Although *not* sued (an obvious attempt to make an end-run around the arbitration clause, as discussed *infra*), TriStar nevertheless will be involved extensively—and, no doubt, quite expensively—in this dispute, including whether it performed properly under the distribution agreement.

As stated, the foregoing are but a few examples of the intertwining of the claims with the distribution agreement, including the claimed concerted actions by Defendants (non-signatories), with TriStar, a signatory. How possible damages might be computed, in the light of the detailed "accounting" provisions of the agreement, is but another example.

This action is quite similar to Grigson's first action—against TriStar, discussed below. After quickly instituting a voluntary dismissal of that action, when TriStar moved to compel arbitration, Appellants brought this one against McConaughey and Creative Artists, non-signatories to the distribution agreement, for, *inter alia,* interfering with that agreement. As noted, this is a quite obvious, if not blatant, attempt to bypass the agreement's arbitration clause.

In Grigson's first action, against the two producers (who joined Grigson in this second action) and TriStar, Grigson charged TriStar, as it is also alleged to have done in the action at hand, with "breach[ing] the 'good faith judgment' clause ... of the distribution agreement". In the alternative, TriStar was charged with fraud. And, the producers, charged with failing to exploit the movie in breach of their contract with the owners, cross-claimed against TriStar. One of the exhibits to the complaint is a 7 January 1997 letter to TriStar from one of the persons owning rights to the movie, in which he stated that he and another similarly-situated person (who had also directed the movie) were "very eager to know what [was] being done by [TriStar] to fully explore the financial possibilities of [the movie]", and then advised: "It goes without saying that [TriStar] has *absolute discretion* in making those determinations but this does not change my obligation to my investors to see that those decisions are based on what is best for this film". (Emphasis added.) When TriStar moved promptly to compel arbitration, the owners and cross-claim producers quickly folded their tents. The action, filed in district court on 9 June 1997, was dismissed without prejudice on 10 September 1997.

The action at hand was filed two and one-half months later, on 22 December 1997. This time, it was filed in state court. *TriStar was no longer a defendant.* Its earlier-charged failure to use its contractually required "good faith judgment" was now alleged to have been caused by "pressure" from the new defendants, Creative Artists and McConaughey. In reality, the two actions are the same. *In essence, TriStar is a defendant.* Each action turns on the meaning of the distribution agreement's numerous—often intricate—provisions, which are unique to the film industry, and on TriStar's conduct in relation to that agreement.

Arguably, the inconsistent positions by Grigson and the two producers in the first and second actions bump up on, if indeed do not satisfy, the prerequisites for judicial estoppel.

In any event, comparison of the two actions demonstrates, quite vividly, why the district court, *which presided over both actions,* did *not* abuse its discretion in compelling arbitration in the second, by applying the equitable estoppel doctrine crafted for such situations. The claims are intertwined with, and dependent upon, the distribution agreement, including, but *not* limited to, Defendants (non-signatories) and TriStar (non-defendant signatory) being charged with interdependent and concerted misconduct. Indeed, this action is the quintessential situation for when the doctrine should be applied.

III.

For the foregoing reasons, the judgment is *AFFIRMED.*

DENNIS, Circuit Judge, dissenting...

QUESTIONS AND DISCUSSION

1. Fred Fisher Music Co., Inc. v. M. Witmark & Sons, 318 U.S. 643 (1943) asks: Who can assign your renewal interest? The answer is that the Copyright Act of 1909 does not nullify any agreement made by the original author, if it is made during the original copyright term, to assign his or her renewal right. In Roger Miller Music, Inc. v. Sony/ATV Publ'g, LLc, 2012 WL 555485 (6th Cir. 2012), the widowed bride of the legendary composer Roger Miller lost her lucrative copyright renewal interests to giant Sony. Is this fair?

2. James Stewart and Alfred Hitchcock were sued in Stewart v. Abend, 495 U.S. 207 (1909) by Cornell Woolrich, the author of a print article entitled, "It Had to Be Murder," which used it as the basis for the move *Vertigo*. Stewart and Hitchcock were holders of a derivative copyright. Woolrich died before his copyright renewal period arose. As owners of a derivative right, Stewart and Hitchcock did not retain the right to exploit that work when Woolrich's death caused the renewal rights in the preexisting article to revert to the statutory successors. Stewart and Hitchcock claimed that *Rear Window* was protected by the fair use doctrine, 17 U.S.C. §107. (Examples of fair use include criticism, comment, reporting, teacher, and scholarship.) Stewart and Hitchcock lost. Is that fair? Does it matter that the movie runs away from the story and is obviously, in many ways, a theatrical adventure? It is more Hitchcockian than anything else, complete with McGuffins, beautiful blondes, and unlikely heroes. Would this decision stop a Hitchcock from being Hitchcockian?

3. In Rosner v. CBS, Inc., 612 F.Supp. 334 (S.D.N.Y. 1985), the court held that a novelist retained a small but protectable interest against the unauthorized use of "Goodbar" in a motion picture title not based on her novel. The TV movie was a factual depiction of an actual murder investigation and not a sequel to the film based on her novel. That is, *Goodbar Killer* is in the public domain. The court placed a great deal of emphasis on the fact that the novelist failed to police the trademark; "Goodbar" inevitably caused the mark to lose its primary, source-denoting significance. Should the creative artist be forced to police his or her intellectual property, like Coca-Cola or Marlboro?

4. In Cardtoons L.C. v. MLBPA 95 F.3d 959 (10th Cir. 1996), parody baseball card producers' First Amendment rights outweighed the rights of the players depicted. But, in O'Bannon v. NCAA, 2014 WL 3899815 (N.D. Cal.), the court unusually found that former collegiate players had a publicity right in the commercial exploitation of their likenesses in video games, and that NCAA rules banning payments to collegiate players violated antitrust laws. Is there a difference between a parody and a video game?

5. There is much discussion of the artist's "moral rights," which is not a part of American law. In Geisel, Dr. Seuss lost his copyright interests in the manufacture, promotion, and sale of dolls based on plaintiff's drawings, but

defendant could not use the "Dr. Seuss" trademark with the sale of the dolls; rather, they can say, "based on" his drawings. Should the trademark be sufficient to thwart defendant's dolls based on Dr. Seuss drawings?

6. As Monty Python said, "No one expects the Spanish Inquisition." Here, there were unauthorized rebroadcasts of (sloppily) edited, classic BBC Monty Python episodes. The alleged "defamation" of an artist's work finds its roots in droit moral (moral rights), which includes the right of an artist to have his or her work attributed to in the form in which he or she created it. (Sounds like artistic integrity.) The edits were done for commercials and the court found for the Pythons in that it allowed their injunction prior to the final determination of issues. Can editing for commercials conceivably pigeonhole a fair use defense?

CHAPTER 3
THE MUSIC INDUSTRY

Contracts are at the heart of the music industry and its talent agencies, management agreements, record production agreements, booking agent agreeements, live performance agreements, etc. In Weatherly v. Universal Music Publishing Co., 125 Cal.App.4th 913, 23 Cal. Rptr.3d 157 (2004), plaintiff songwriter sued a publisher for rescission of their contract, an open book account, breach of fiduciary duty, constructive fraud, violation of Cal. Bus. & Prof. Code §17200 et seq., breach of contract, and breach of the implied covenant of good faith and fair dealing. The songwriter received royalty payments and statements twice a year, but hired an auditor who discovered that the publisher only reported 75 percent of the songwriter's income. The songwriter prevailed in that the summary judgment was reversed; the songwriter could continue his suit based on the breach of implied covenant of good faith and fair dealing.

Music producers have been known to try to exploit their artists. One method is to offer unconscionable contracts to unsophisticated artists. Another method is to pay a substantial sum (let's say $1 million), but then demand that the artist produce five albums in one year, which is impossible. In Weatherly, the publisher was guilty of skullduggery in his manipulations of the columns that allegedly reflected the publisher's ownership percentage for each song. In Evans v. Famous Music Corp., which follows, talent sues publisher for royalties.

EVANS v. FAMOUS MUSIC CORP.
Supreme Court of New York, Appellate Division, First Department
February 6, 2003, Decided
February 6, 2003, Entered
302 A.D.2d 216,
754 N.Y.S.2d 259

Order, Supreme Court, New York County (Richard Lowe, III, J.), entered August 14, 2002, which, insofar as appealed from as limited by the briefs, denied defendant's motion for summary judgment dismissing the breach of contract cause of action and granted plaintiffs' cross motion for partial summary judgment as to liability on their breach of contract claim, unanimously reversed, on the law, without costs, plaintiffs' cross motion for partial summary judgment denied and summary judgment dismissing the breach of contract cause of action granted.

Plaintiffs Ray Evans, Ginny Mancini, John L. Mercer, Amanda Mercer Neder, The Johnny Mercer Foundation, Margaret Whiting and Barbara Whiting Smith are composers, songwriters and musicians, or their heirs, assigns and successors in interest. Defendant Famous Music Corporation (Famous), a wholly owned subsidiary of Viacom, Inc., is a music publishing company which has entered into various contracts with plaintiffs and/or their predecessors in interest, inter alia, for the payment of royalties.

At issue are six contracts each containing a standard provision that the artist is to receive an amount equal to 50% of "all net sums actually received" by Famous, less all expenses and charges and less all deductions for taxes. Pursuant to these contracts, Famous licensed the use of the plaintiffs' compositions in various forms throughout the world through its subpublishers. In exchange for a fee, these foreign subpublishers administer Famous's catalog of songs and collect royalties for uses in their respective countries. After deducting their fees and the taxes imposed by the foreign jurisdictions, the foreign subpublishers remit to Famous the balance, generally on a semi-annual basis. It is undisputed that Famous had paid the plaintiffs 50% of the amount it had received from its foreign subpublishers. However, plaintiffs contend, inter alia, that Famous regularly received a foreign tax credit for such payments on its United States income tax and that Famous breached its contractual obligation to reimburse them for their proportional share of monies recouped from credits Famous received against the payment of foreign taxes.

Plaintiffs commenced the instant action, alleging breach of contract, unjust enrichment and "money had and received" by Famous. Famous interposed an answer asserting affirmative defenses based on a failure to state a cause of action, statute of limitations and the doctrine of laches, estoppel and waiver. Subsequently, Famous moved for summary judgment and plaintiffs cross-moved for partial summary judgment on their breach of contract claim.

In granting partial summary judgment to plaintiffs, the motion court found, inter alia, that the subject contracts clearly and unambiguously required Famous to share with plaintiffs the benefit of any foreign tax credit that may have been received by virtue of the payment of foreign taxes on the royalty income generated by plaintiffs' compositions. In particular, the motion court found that the contractual term "all net sums actually received" encompassed all monies and other value received by Famous, including the benefit of all credits for foreign tax payments. The motion court further determined that it was the intention of the parties that the artist would receive half the net profit realized by Famous after the deduction of amounts disbursed to cover the taxes Famous was to pay on the gross receipts. Since Famous deducted the foreign tax payments from the gross receipts when calculating the "net sums" upon which plaintiffs' royalty payments are based, the motion court concluded that plaintiffs were underpaid and that such underpayment constituted a breach of the contracts' payment clauses. We reverse.

It is well settled that a court may not, under the guise of interpretation, fashion a new contract for the parties by adding or excising terms and conditions if to do so would contradict the clearly expressed language of the contract. In the instant matter, the motion court's findings contradict the clearly expressed language of the subject contracts inasmuch as the benefit of any foreign tax credit was not contemplated by the parties. Although it is argued that the contractual language entitles plaintiffs to half the value of any benefit of a foreign tax credit, the specific language of these contracts specifically identifies and delineates all of the royalties in which plaintiffs are entitled to share. Under fundamental principles of contract interpretation, the failure to identify the foreign tax credit benefit indicates that such benefit was not envisioned by the parties to be an intended term in any of the subject contracts (*see Uribe v Merchants Bank of N.Y.,* 91 NY2d 336; *Surge Licensing v Copyright Promotions,* 258 AD2d 257).

Concur—Nardelli, J.P., Andrias, Saxe, Ellerin and Lerner, JJ.

WEATHERLY v. UNIVERSAL MUSIC PUBLISHING GROUP
Court of Appeal of California, Second Appellate District, Division Eight
December 13, 2004, Filed
B170395
123 Cal.App.4th 913, 23 Cal.Rptr.3d 157

COOPER, P.J.

In this appeal, we reject the argument that an unexercised contractual right to conduct an audit necessarily demonstrates a lack of diligence for purposes of the delayed discovery doctrine. We reverse the award of summary judgment, which the trial court based on a contractual limitations period. We also reverse an order of the trial court sustaining, without leave to amend, a demurrer to Weatherly's cause of action for breach of the implied covenant of good faith and fair dealing.

FACTUAL BACKGROUND

The Parties

Universal–PolyGram International Publishing, Inc. (UPIP) describes itself as a worldwide music publishing company. Universal Music Publishing Group (UMPG), the named defendant and respondent, describes itself as "a fictitious 'umbrella' name for a group of affiliated companies engaged in the business of music publishing, including Universal–PolyGram International Publishing, Inc."

Plaintiff and appellant, James Weatherly is a songwriter, who continues to reap the financial benefits of his songs through royalties paid by either UPIP or UMPG. The royalty checks are sent to Gursey, Schneider & Co., where Weatherly's accountant, Stanley Schneider, is employed and is responsible for depositing and handling monies received on Weatherly's behalf. As part of his responsibilities, Schneider cursorily reviewed Weatherly's royalty statements.

The Royalty Agreement

In 1974, Weatherly entered into an Exclusive Songwriter's and Composer's Agreement with KECA MUSIC, INC. (Agreement). In the Agreement, KECA MUSIC, INC. (KECA) is referred to as the Publisher and Weatherly is referred to as the Writer. UMPG or UPIP eventually acquired KECA's rights under the Agreement. The parties dispute whether UPIP or UMPG is now the Publisher. That issue was not included in the motion for summary judgment or demurrer, and therefore, we assume only for purposes of this appeal, that UMPG is the Publisher.

The provisions of the Agreement relevant to this appeal are as follows:

(1) Writer is entitled to "[f]ifty per cent [*sic*] (50%) of any and all net sums, after deduction of foreign taxes, actually received (less any costs for collection) by Publisher from sales and uses directly related to subject musical compositions in countries outside of the United States (other than public performance royalties....)"

(2) "Writer shall have the right, upon the giving of at least ten (10) days written notice to Publisher, to inspect the books and records of Publisher, insofar as the same concerns Writer, at the expense of Writer, at reasonable times during normal business hours for the purpose of verifying the accuracy of any transaction or entry relating to the accounting of all sums to which Writer may have the right to object ... but no more than once in any one (1) year period during the term hereof."

(3) "All royalty statements and other accounts rendered by Publisher shall be binding upon Writer and not subject to any objection for any reason, unless such objection is specific and is made in writing, stating the basis thereof, and delivered to Publisher within one (1) year from the date of such statement or account, and Writer shall be barred from maintaining or instituting any suit based on such objection unless such suit is commenced within one (1) year after the date on which Publisher notifies Writer that it denies the validity of the objection."

Royalty Statements

Weatherly receives a royalty payment and statement twice a year. The royalty statements are in the same format and contain the following information followed by columns of numbers: "Typ[e]," "Catalogue Number," "Units," "Period," "% Rcvd," "Amount received," "Your share," and "Amount due." Most but not all of the entries in the "% Rcvd" column contain the number "100.00."

The meaning of the information in the "% Rcvd" column is disputed by the parties and not explained in the royalty statements or the Agreement. Weatherly interpreted the meaning of "% Rcvd" as the monies received for his songs. Based on the royalty statements he understood UMPG "reported that my share of all income (including foreign income) was being calculated at 100% of all monies received for the songs I wrote." According to Weatherly, "I had no reason to believe there were any problems with UMPG's accountings and never saw anything on the statements that caused me concern." Weatherly's advisors, Schneider and Ali Adawiya, interpreted the royalty statements in the same manner as Weatherly.

According to a statement in UMPG's appellate brief, "The '% Rcvd' column had nothing to do with the existence or amount of any subpublishing fees. Rather, it reflected UPIP's ownership percentage of each individual song, based on whether Weatherly wrote alone or with co-writers."

The Audit

In 2001, Weatherly hired Adawiya to audit UMPG's books. Adawiya previously had audited UMPG records on behalf of other clients, and he recommended the audit to Weatherly. In the process of conducting the audit, Adawiya asked Anthony Saragueta, vice-president of royalties for UMPG, "whether they were reporting to Mr. Weatherly 100 percent of the amount received by the foreign companies at the source" and Saragueta responded that it reported "75 percent." According to Adawiya, Saragueta refused to give Adawiya the source documents but told Adawiya that foreign affiliates were taking 25 percent off the top.

Adawiya wrote UMPG, criticizing its accounting practices for the following reason: "local foreign overseas offices reported 100% of the receipts to a ("UM[P]G") main office, called the "HUB," located in the United Kingdom. [*sic*] where then ("UM[P]G") main office in the UK "HUB" kept 25% of the gross income and reported 75% of the income to their offices in the USA. Our contention is that ("UM[P]G") should report the income due to Mr. Weatherly based on the amount actually received by their local foreign offices as stated in the agreement...."

UMPG responded to Adawiya's letter as follows: "[s]ince KECA MUSIC, INC. was a United States corporation and since KECA MUSIC, INC. is defined as Publisher, UMPG is correct in applying a 50% royalty rate to amounts received in the United States. Therefore, there is no basis for this claim."

PROCEDURAL BACKGROUND

Weatherly filed suit on October 4, 2002. Weatherly claims that UMPG improperly calculated his royalty payments and sued UMPG for rescission, an accounting, open book account, breach of fiduciary duty, constructive fraud, violation of Business and Professions Code section 17200 et seq., breach of contract, and breach of the implied covenant of good faith and fair dealing. The complaint alleges numerous breaches, which concern the collection of royalties, calculation of the amount of the royalties, accounting of royalties, and the failure to provide requested documentation concerning the royalties.

The trial court dismissed the cause of action for breach of the implied covenant of good faith and fair dealing following UMPG's demurrer. The court denied Weatherly's request for leave to amend.

The court granted summary judgment on the remaining causes of action. It found "that there are no triable issues of material fact as to the contractual limitations period set forth in Paragraph 7.2 of the agreement. Plaintiff and Defendant agreed to the shortened limitations period. Planitiff [*sic*] had the right to audit the books at any time but chose to wait until 2001 to do so. The delayed discovery rule does not apply under these circumstances. All causes of action arise from the alleged failure by Defendant to pay royalties to Plaintiff. Thus, the 1-year contractual limitations period bars all causes of action."

Weatherly timely appealed.

DISCUSSION

*I. The Trial Court Erred in Granting Summary Judgment****

B. Failure to Conduct an Audit Does Not Automatically Show a Lack of Diligence

UMPG's principal legal argument is as follows: "California case law fully supports the principle that one with the right to monitor another's performance under a contract is charged with the knowledge he would have obtained if he had done so." According to UMPG "[t]he trial court correctly found that Weatherly's decision not to audit precluded him from demonstrating the *blameless* ignorance that is necessary to invoke the 'delayed discovery' doctrine." (Original italics.)

Weatherly argues, among other things, that the statute of limitations and contractual limitations period should be tolled because he provided evidence that UMPG's royalty statements were misleading in indicating that his "50% share was being calculated on 100% of all monies UPMG [*sic*] received...." According to Weatherly, "[i]n addition to improperly keeping 25% to 40% of the amounts due to Weatherly on the royalties collected, UMPG refused to provide requested source documentation from foreign performing rights societies and foreign suspense reports which would show the actual amount of royalties received for the exploitation of Weatherly's work abroad."

"The discovery rule protects those who are ignorant of their cause of action through no fault of their own. It permits delayed accrual until a plaintiff knew or should have known of the wrongful conduct at issue. [Citation.]" (*April Enterprises, Inc. v. KTTV* (1983) 147 Cal.App.3d 805, 832, 195 Cal.Rptr. 421 (*April Enterprises, Inc.*).) A plaintiff, prevented from discovery, should not suffer and a defendant should not "knowingly profit" from the plaintiff's ignorance. (*Id.* at p. 831, 195 Cal.Rptr. 421.) The same policies apply in the context of a contractual limitations provision. (*Moreno v. Sanchez* (2003) 106 Cal.App.4th 1415, 1429, 131 Cal.Rptr.2d 684.) "[N]o authority exists which sanctions a contractual provision permitting parties to opt out of the benefits of the discovery rule in situations where the discovery rule would otherwise apply." (*Id.* at p. 1433, 131 Cal.Rptr.2d 684.)

There is some authority in support of UMPG's argument that the discovery rule does not apply to a plaintiff who had the means to discover the wrongdoing. (*McKelvey v. Boeing North American, Inc.* (1999) 74 Cal.App.4th 151, 160 fn. 11, 86 Cal.Rptr.2d 645; *Atlantic Richfield Co. v. Lujan* (N.D.Okla.1992) 811 F.Supp. 1520, 1525.) Other cases reject the conclusion that the means of inquiry is automatically tantamount to a duty of inquiry. " 'Where no duty is imposed by law to make inquiry, and where, under the circumstances, a prudent man would not be put on inquiry, the mere fact that means of knowledge are open and not availed of does not operate to give constructive notice of the facts.' " (*Baker v. Beech Aircraft Corp.* (1974) 39 Cal.App.3d 315, 322, 114 Cal.Rptr. 171; see also *Prudential Home Mortgage Co. v. Superior Court* (1998) 66 Cal.App.4th 1236, 1248, 78 Cal.Rptr.2d 566 [rejecting argument that delayed discovery did not apply because information available in public records]; *Enterprise–Laredo v. Hachar's* (Tex.Ct.App.1992) 839 S.W.2d 822, 838 [rejecting an argument that delayed discovery did not apply because the lease in question gave the plaintiff the right to conduct an annual audit].)

In this case, Weatherly's argument goes beyond the claim that a prudent person would not have been put on inquiry notice prior to the audit; he argues that he was misled by the royalty statements, specifically the entries of 100% in the (% Rcvd) column. Applying the discovery rule in the context of a claim of a misrepresentation, the Ninth Circuit held, under California law, a defendant cannot hinder the plaintiff's discovery through misrepresentations and then fault the plaintiff for failing to investigate. (*El Pollo Loco, Inc. v. Hashim* (9th Cir.2003) 316 F.3d 1032, 1039 (*El Pollo Loco, Inc.*) [applying California law].) " 'The recipient of a fraudulent misrepresentation of fact is justified in relying upon its truth, although he might have ascertained the falsity of the representation had he undertaken an investigation.' " (*Id.* at p. 1040, quoting *Storage Servs. v. Oosterbaan* (1989) 214 Cal.App.3d 498, 508, 262 Cal.Rptr. 689.) The court found the limitations period was tolled under the discovery rule where the defendant applied for an El Pollo Loco franchise and provided fraudulent evidence indicating that he was not a franchisee of a competitor. (*Id.* at p. 1035.)

The reasoning of *El Pollo Loco, Inc.* is consistent with the purpose of the delayed discovery doctrine: a plaintiff, prevented from discovery, should not suffer and a defendant should not profit from the plaintiff's ignorance. Applied here, the right to conduct an audit is not dispositive of diligence where there is evidence that the plaintiff was "hindered" from discovering the breach by the defendant's misrepresentations. (*El Pollo Loco, Inc., supra,* 316 F.3d at p. 1040.)

C. Triable Issues of Material Fact Preclude Summary Judgment

II. The Trial Court Erred in Denying Weatherly Leave to Amend His Cause of Action for Breach of the Implied Covenant of Good Faith and Fair Dealing

DISPOSITION

The judgment is reversed. The order sustaining without leave to amend UMPG's demurrer to the cause of action for breach of the implied covenant of good faith and fair dealing is reversed. The case is remanded to the trial court. Weatherly is entitled to his costs on appeal.

We concur: FLIER and BOLAND, JJ.

AHERN V. SCHOLZ
United States Court of Appeals for the First Circuit
June 4, 1996, Decided
Nos. 95-1146, 95-1203, Nos. 95-1147, 95-1204
85 F.3d 774

TORRUELLA, Chief Judge.

The parties in this breach of contract case, a successful musician and his former manager, dispute whether royalties from record albums have been accounted for and paid to each other. The appeal is from a final judgment by the district court after a jury trial, disposing of all claims in respect to all parties.

BACKGROUND: A BAND OUT OF BOSTON

In this case, the parties dispute many of the facts and the inferences to be drawn from them. Thus we start with a sketch of the basic facts, and address the individual issues in more detail below. Appellant and cross-appellee Donald Thomas Scholz ("Scholz") is a musician, composer, and record producer who was, and is, a member of the musical group BOSTON ("BOSTON"). In late 1975, Scholz entered into three agreements with appellee and cross-appellant Paul F. Ahern ("Ahern"), who was engaged in the business of promoting and managing music groups, and his then partner, Charles McKenzie ("McKenzie") (collectively, the "1975 Agreements"). First, Scholz made a recording agreement (the "Recording Agreement") with Ahern and McKenzie d/b/a P.C. Productions, to which Bradley Delp, the lead singer of BOSTON, was also a party. Second was a management agreement (the "Management Agreement"), also between Scholz and P.C. Productions, under which Ahern and McKenzie were appointed Scholz' exclusive personal managers worldwide. The third agreement was a songwriter agreement made between Scholz and Ahern, under which Scholz was obligated to furnish Ahern his exclusive songwriting services for a period of five years.

In early 1976, CBS Records ("CBS") and Ahern Associates, a business name of Ahern and McKenzie, entered into a recording agreement for the exclusive recording services of BOSTON. The group's first album (the "first album") was released in 1976, and sold approximately 11 million copies—one of the highest-selling debut albums ever. Its second album (the "second album") was released in August 1978, and sold approximately 6 million copies.

In 1978, Scholz and the other members of BOSTON entered into a modification agreement with Ahern and P.C. Productions, dated April 24, 1978. Among other things, the First Modification Agreement modified the 1975 Agreements and changed the financial relationship between Scholz and his managers. Ahern and McKenzie dissolved their partnership. A few years later, in May of 1981, Ahern and Scholz, individually and under various business names, entered into a further modification agreement (the "Further Modification Agreement" or "FMA"), which is at the heart of this dispute. Ahern ceased to be Scholz' manager.

In 1982, with the third album not yet released, CBS cut off the payment of royalties generated from the first and second albums. In 1983, CBS brought suit against Scholz, Ahern, and the members of BOSTON for failure to timely deliver record albums. Scholz' counsel in that action was Donald S. Engel ("Engel"); Ahern had his own counsel. While that litigation was pending, the third album was released by MCA Records ("MCA") in 1986 and sold well over 4 million copies. At the close of trial—seven years after the CBS litigation began—the jury found that Scholz was not in breach of contract. Scholz incurred legal fees of about $3.4 million dollars.

In February 1991, Ahern commenced this action against Scholz for breach of the FMA claiming a failure to pay royalties due under the third album. Scholz asserted various affirmative defenses and counterclaims against Ahern, including breach of the FMA. During trial, Engel, Scholz' lead trial counsel, was twice called as a witness. At the close of the evidence, the court granted Scholz' directed verdict dismissing Ahern's Count III for fraud and IV for breach of implied covenant of good faith and fair dealing. The court also granted Ahern's motion for directed verdict dismissing Scholz' First, Second, and Third Counterclaims and his, Third, Fourth, and Fifth affirmative defenses. Only the parties' respective breach of contract claims went to the jury. The jury found that Scholz breached section 5.2.1 of the FMA to pay Ahern royalties from the third album, and found that Ahern had not breached the FMA to account for and pay Scholz royalties due from the first and second albums. It awarded Ahern $547,007 in damages.

The trial court sitting without a jury also found Scholz had breached the FMA, and heard Ahern's Count II for declaratory relief and Count V for violation of Mass. Gen. L. ch. 93A and Scholz' Fifth Counterclaim for recision of contract for failure to obtain a license. The court denied the declaratory relief Ahern sought in Count I, and awarded him costs, interest and attorney's fees pursuant to Count V for violation of Mass. Gen. L. ch. 93A §§ 2 & 11. The court denied the relief sought by Scholz in his Fifth Counterclaim and held that he waived his Counts VI and VII at oral argument. After a hearing on Ahern's bill of costs and application for reasonable attorney's fees and interest, the court awarded Ahern $265,000 in attorney's fees and $135,000 in costs.

The district court denied, without a hearing, Scholz' motion for a new trial, motion to amend the court's memorandum and order and judgment entered thereon, motion to admit new evidence, and motion to amend the court's memorandum and order and the judgment entered thereon regarding Scholz' Sixth Counterclaim. This appeal followed.

MOTION FOR A NEW TRIAL

Appellant first argues that the district court erred in denying his motion for a new trial, made pursuant to Fed.R.Civ.P. 59(a). We therefore review the record below to determine whether the evidence required that the district court grant the motion for a new trial. *See de Pérez v. Hospital del Maestro,* 910 F.2d 1004, 1006 (1st Cir.1990). In reviewing the record of the 16-day trial, we note that both parties presented extensive evidence. The jury heard testimony regarding a history that spans two decades, involves at least seven contracts, includes detailed numerical accounting, and references more than half a dozen other legal battles. The parties called a total of fifteen witnesses, seven of whom, including Ahern, Scholz, and Engel, Scholz' counsel, testified twice. In short, the jury faced a complex and sometimes conflicting set of facts in making its decision as to whether either, neither, or both parties breached the 1981 Further Modification Agreement. Ultimately, we find that the jury's verdict was not against the clear weight of the evidence, and the district court did not abuse its discretion in so finding.

A. *Standard of Review*

"A verdict may be set aside and new trial ordered 'when the verdict is against the clear weight of the evidence, or is based upon evidence which is false, or will result in a clear miscarriage of justice.' " In reaching its decision, "the district court has broad legal authority to determine whether or not a jury's verdict is against the 'clear weight of the evidence.' " *de Pérez,* 910 F.2d at 1006. Nonetheless, "the trial judge's discretion, although great, must be exercised with due regard to the rights of both parties to have questions which are fairly open resolved finally by the jury at a single trial." Thus, the district court judge "cannot displace a jury's verdict merely because he disagrees with it or would have found otherwise in a bench trial." "The mere fact that a contrary verdict may have been equally—or even more easily—supportable furnishes no cognizable ground for granting a new trial." *Freeman v. Package Mach. Co.,* 865 F.2d 1331, 1333–34 (1st Cir.1988).

Our review is circumscribed: we will disturb the district court's ruling on appellant's motion for a new trial only where there has been a clear abuse of discretion...

With our standard of review established, we turn to Scholz' argument and the record below. We address each of the two breach of contract claims the jury decided in turn.

B. *Did Ahern Breach the FMA?*

Scholz argues that Ahern breached his obligations under the 1981 FMA to both account for and pay to Scholz, every six months, his share of the royalties from the compositions on the first and second albums: indeed, Ahern admitted at trial that he had failed to make some payments he owed Scholz under the FMA. The jury and the trial court disagreed with Scholz, however, and found that Ahern's breach of the FMA was not material. The question facing us, then, is whether the district court abused its discretion in finding that the jury's decision was not against the weight of the evidence. After careful review of the record, we find no abuse of discretion in the lower court's decision not to disturb the jury's finding.

Scholz argues at some length on appeal that Ahern's breach was by definition material, both for his failure to account and his failure to pay. As for the first contention, we note that while Scholz' reading of the FMA as requiring that Ahern render Scholz direct accountings every six months is a convincing one, it is not the only plausible one. Indeed, Ahern contends that the FMA only required him to send irrevocable letters of direction to various entities involved directing them to send Scholz his share of the royalties when collected. In the end, it would not be against the clear weight of the evidence to find that letters of directions would satisfy Ahern's accounting obligations under the FMA, and that such letters were sent. Therefore, Ahern's failure to account every six months was not a material breach.

As for the second contention, Scholz supports his position that Ahern's failure to pay constitutes a separate, material breach by drawing on both New York and Massachusetts case law. He points to the Second Circuit's refusal to overturn summary judgment in *ARP Films, Inc. v. Marvel Entertainment Group, Inc.*, 952 F.2d 643, 649 (2d Cir.1991).

Scholz also points to a New York case holding that a licensee's failure to pay franchise fees totalling $40,129 over four months constituted a breach of contract, *McDonald's Corp. v. Robert Makin, Inc.*, 653 F.Supp. 401, 402–04 (W.D.N.Y.1986), as well as Massachusetts language indicating that "[a] material breach of an agreement occurs when there is a breach of 'an essential and inducing feature of the contract.' " *Lease-it, Inc. v. Massachusetts Port Auth.*, 33 Mass.App.Ct. 391, 600 N.E.2d 599, 602 (1992) (holding that six-month refusal to pay concession and rental fees was a material breach) (quoting *Buchholz v. Green Bros. Co.*, 272 Mass. 49, 172 N.E. 101 (1930)). Scholz argues that Ahern's breach, spanning thirteen years, is more egregious than these cases of a six-month failure to pay concession and rental fees, four-month failure to pay license and lease fees, and seven-month failure to pay (and five-month failure to account). Therefore, Scholz concludes, Ahern's failure to pay Scholz at least $459,000 is clearly a substantial breach.

We are not convinced. We remind appellant that under our standard of review, we do not sit as a juror, evaluating credibility and weighing evidence, as he seems to ask us to do. Rather, we simply weigh whether the district court committed a clear abuse of its discretion in determining that the jury verdict was not against the clear weight of the evidence. *Newell Puerto Rico,* 20 F.3d at 22; *Kearns,* 863 F.2d at 179. Our review of the record reveals that Ahern's counsel presented testimony questioning, to varying degrees, nine of the thirteen items of the estimate Scholz' accounting expert made of how much Ahern owed Scholz. Phillip Ames ("Ames"), a certified public accountant who served as business manager for both Ahern and BOSTON from 1976 through sometime in 1981 or 1982, made several estimates of how much Ahern owed Scholz, which he labelled "ball park figures." While we note that Ames' final estimate was $277,000, for a total of $459,000 with interest, we cannot assume that the jury accepted this figure as gospel. Given that Ahern sought over a million dollars in principal and interest from Scholz, the jury may reasonably have found that the Ames figure was not a substantial breach in the particular context of this case. It may have determined that the amount of money Ahern owed, taken in the perspective of the contract, Ahern's obligations, and the total amounts of money concerned, was not so significant a breach as to violate "an essential and inducing feature of the contract." *Lease-It,* 600 N.E.2d at 602. Finally, addressing the case law Scholz relies on for support, we note that here, unlike in those cases, the amount of money owed was in question.

Ultimately, examining the record in full, the evidence clearly provides the jury and trial court with a basis for finding that Ahern did not substantially breach the FMA. As this Circuit stated on another occasion,

> We can understand how a jury might have decided for [defendant] on the basis of this evidence. But the jury did not do this; it decided for [plaintiff]. We do not see how one could say that the jury clearly made a mistake. We do not see how one could say that the evidence overwhelmingly favored the [defendant]. Rather, the evidence simply was mixed and contradictory.

de Pérez, 910 F.2d at 1008. Therefore we cannot say that the district court committed a clear breach of its discretion on this point.

C. *Did Scholz Breach the FMA?*

Ahern claimed below that Scholz breached his obligation under section 5.2.1 of the FMA to pay Ahern his share of the royalties due from the third album. The evidence presented at trial centered on a document entitled "Artist Royalty Statement" ("the Scholz Statement"), which Scholz presented to Ahern. That statement listed over $6 million in gross royalties reported by MCA prior to December 31, 1993, but reduced that figure by deducting, among other things, a producer share and artist costs, so that the net artist royalties fell to below zero—and Ahern was not entitled to any money. Scholz argued at trial that he did not breach the FMA, but the jury and the trial court disagreed.

On appeal, Scholz contends that their finding is against the weight of the evidence, because Ahern's prior material breaches excused Scholz' performance under the Further Modification Agreement. Scholz points out that paragraph 2 of the FMA states that

> Scholz wishes to guarantee that Ahern shall receive at a minimum certain amounts of monies in connection with future recordings embodying the performances of the group "BOSTON" ... in exchange for the agreement of Ahern as set forth herein.

Scholz shapes his argument on appeal as follows: Since Ahern's only agreement of substance was his agreement to account for and pay royalties to Scholz for prior BOSTON albums, Ahern's breach of his commitment excused Scholz' performance. Indeed, Scholz notes, the parties' mutual commitments to account to and pay each other are expressly stated to be in consideration of each other. In such "bilateral contracts for an agreed exchange of performances, even though the promises are in form absolute, the law regards them as constructively conditioned in order to avoid an unjust result." *Industrial Mercantile Fac. Co. v. Daisy Sportswear,* 56 Misc.2d 104, 288 N.Y.S.2d 209, 211 (N.Y.Civ.Ct.1967), *order aff'd,* 56 Misc.2d 584, 289 N.Y.S.2d 332 (N.Y.Sup.Ct.1968); *see* Restatement (Second) of Contracts, § 237 cmt. a (1979). Moreover, Scholz continues, the non-occurrence of a condition of a party's duty excuses the non-breaching party's obligation to perform even though that party does not know of its non-occurrence, *id.,* § 237 cmt. c, and the intention or scienter of a breaching party are not considered in the elements of breach of contract. *See Agron v. The Trustees of Columbia Univ.,* 1993 WL 118495 (S.D.N.Y., April 12, 1993).

Considering this, Scholz points out that his first royalty statement regarding the third album was rendered by MCA on April 1, 1987. Thus the earliest he could have owed money to Ahern under the FMA was August 15, 1987—and by that date, he argues, Ahern had already failed to account to Scholz or pay him royalties with respect to the first two albums for over five years. Therefore, Scholz maintains he was excused, at least until Ahern tendered payment, from rendering an accounting or paying royalties to Ahern from the third album. At the very least, Scholz argues, he could have withheld payment of the $459,000 admittedly owed him as a set-off against any amount he owed Ahern.

In so arguing, Scholz does not contend that he did not in fact breach the FMA: he simply maintains that Ahern did so first. Since Scholz does not revisit the merits of the evidence presented at trial regarding his breach, we will not do so here. However, since we have already found that the verdict that Ahern did not substantially breach the FMA was not against the clear weight of the evidence, Scholz' argument here must fail. Clearly, it would be inconsistent with our acceptance of the verdict that Ahern did not substantially breach the FMA to find that Scholz' performance was excused by Ahern's material breach. Accordingly, we affirm the district court's decision to refuse the motion for a new trial on this issue.

D. *Sufficiency of the Evidence*

In a footnote, Scholz adds that he is appealing the verdict not only in terms of the denial of his motion for a new trial, as discussed above, but also that he appeals each of the jury's findings—i.e. that Scholz breached the FMA, that Ahern did not breach the Agreement, and that Ahern was entitled to damages—on the grounds of insufficiency of the evidence. Scholz relies on *Engine Specialties, Inc. v. Bombardier Ltd.,* 605 F.2d 1, 9 (1st Cir.1979), *cert. denied sub nom. Durham Distribs., Inc. v. Bombardier Ltd.,* 449 U.S. 890, 101 S.Ct. 248, 66 L.Ed.2d 116 (1980), to claim that our review of his alternative argument is limited to asking whether there is sufficient support in the record for the jury's finding...

We note that, in fact, this is the standard of review applicable to motions for judgment as a matter of law under Federal Rule of Civil Procedure 50. While it is a circumscribed review, it is nonetheless not as limited as our review of the district court's disposition of the motion for new trial. *See Sánchez,* 37 F.3d at 716–17 (comparing the two standards of review). We find nothing in the record to establish that appellant Scholz made a motion for judgment as a matter of law, so that he would be entitled to this less deferential standard of review. Rather, he argues sufficiency of the evidence in his motion for a new trial. Our review of the record, therefore, must be under the abuse of discretion standard outlined above. *See MacQuarrie v. Howard Johnson Co.,* 877 F.2d 126, 131 (1st Cir.1989) (noting that the strict "abuse of discretion" standard "is especially appropriate if the motion for a new trial is based on a claim that the verdict is against the weight of the evidence"); *Freeman,* 865 F.2d at 1341–43 (evaluating the weight of the evidence as part of a motion for a new trial, separately from its review of the denial of the motion for judgment notwithstanding the verdict).

Irrespective of which standard of review we apply, however, Scholz' alternative argument fails. First, the evidence was overwhelming that he breached the FMA by failing to pay Ahern his share of the royalties from the third album; indeed, Scholz does not attempt to argue otherwise. Second, although the issue of the materiality of Ahern's breach is fairly close, as discussed above, there was sufficient evidence in the record for the jury to determine that Ahern did not materially breach the Further Modification

Agreement. Finally, having made these two determinations, the award of damages was appropriate. Therefore, given the scope of the evidence as described, we find that the district court's denial of appellant's motion for a new trial was amply supported and not an abuse of discretion.

E. *The Length of the Jury Deliberations*

Scholz next contends that the jury failed to follow its instructions. The district court instructed the jury that damages could only be awarded if it found one party breached the FMA and the other did not. If it found that both parties were in breach, no damages could be awarded. In making his contention, Scholz reiterates his argument that the evidence was insufficient, emphasizing that Ahern admitted he did not perform his obligations under the FMA, and maintaining that Ahern's accountant admitted that he both failed to pay at least $459,000 to Scholz and mischaracterized an advance from a foreign sub-publisher as a loan. Under the jury instructions, Scholz argues, these factors preclude the jury from finding that Scholz breached the FMA, or at least from awarding Ahern any royalties. These contentions have been dismissed in our discussion above.

However, Scholz raises a new factor: he argues that the jury's verdict and the extremely short period of deliberations—one and a half hours following fifteen days of testimony—reveal that the jury ignored the court's instructions and rendered an erroneous and inconsistent verdict. He cites the fact that one of the jurors planned to go on a cruise two days after the date of the verdict as proof that the jury was in a hurry to finish its deliberations. The jury's questions, Scholz adds, demonstrates that it was determined to award Ahern $547,000 regardless of who was in breach. Between the insufficient evidence and the perfunctory deliberations, Scholz concludes, the district court had an affirmative duty to grant a new trial. He seeks support for his argument in *Kearns v. Keystone Shipping Co.,* 863 F.2d 177 (1st Cir.1988), where this Circuit held that a brief jury deliberation—one hour and eighteen minutes, following a three-day trial—coupled with a verdict contrary to the great weight of the evidence created a situation where the district court had an affirmative duty to set aside the verdict. *Id.* at 182.

We remain unswayed. Scholz' reliance on *Kearns* is misplaced. There, the court explicitly required that the brief deliberation be paired with a verdict contrary to the weight of the evidence, noting that " '[i]f the evidence is sufficient to support the verdict, the length of time the jury deliberates is immaterial.' " *Kearns,* 863 F.2d at 182 (quoting *Marx v. Hartford Accident and Indemnity Co.,* 321 F.2d 70, 71 (5th Cir.1963)). We have already determined that, here, there was evidence sufficient to support the verdict. Therefore, Scholz is merely left with a complaint that the jury should have deliberated longer. His complaint is easily defeated, as "no rule requires a jury to deliberate for any set length of time." *United States v. Peñagarícano–Soler,* 911 F.2d 833, 846 n. 15 (1st Cir.1990); *see United States v. Brotherton,* 427 F.2d 1286, 1289 (8th Cir.1970). Indeed, we have previously upheld a verdict on thirty-two counts which was reached in four hours, following a trial that lasted five weeks, incorporating more than fifty witnesses and hundreds of exhibits.

We also refuse to read a determination to award Ahern a set amount of money from the jury's questions, which simply clarified where it could award damages, and whose evidence it should consider. *Cf. Clark v. Moran,* 942 F.2d 24, 32 (1st Cir.1991) (refusing to impute reasonable doubt of guilt or of witnesses' credibility from fact that jury deliberation was lengthy or from questions asked). Finally, we note that the jury's task was relatively simple. Although it heard complex testimony and was asked to weigh detailed evidence, the district court had already dismissed as a matter of law all the claims except for the respective contract claims, and the sums at issue had been clearly defined in the evidence and closing arguments.

ENGEL'S TESTIMONY AT TRIAL

As noted above, Engel, Scholz' lead counsel, was called by both parties as a witness. Maintaining that Ahern called Engel as an expert witness, instead of a percipient witness, Scholz now argues that the district court committed prejudicial error by, first, permitting Ahern to do so, and second, by refusing to allow follow-up questioning by Engel's co-counsel, Passin.

Our examination of each of Scholz' contentions follows the same legal framework. In each analysis, two questions face us: first, whether the district court erred in admitting or refusing the testimony or motion; and second, whether that error was harmful. *See Doty v. Sewall,* 908 F.2d 1053, 1057 (1st Cir.1990). Only if we answer both questions in the positive will Scholz' argument on appeal prevail.

A trial court's error in an evidentiary ruling only rises to the level of harmful error if a party's substantial right is affected. *See* 28 U.S.C. § 2111; Fed.R.Evid. 103(a); *Lubanski v. Coleco Indus., Inc.,* 929 F.2d 42, 46 (1st Cir.1991). "In determining whether an error affected a party's substantial right, '[t]he central question is whether this court can say with fair assurance ... that the judgment was not substantially swayed by the error.' " *Espeaignnette v. Gene Tierney Co.,* 43 F.3d 1, 9 (1st Cir.1994) (quoting *Lubanski,* 929 F.2d at 46 (internal quotations omitted)). Factors we must consider in determining whether substantial rights are implicated include both the centrality of the evidence and the prejudicial effect of its exclusion or inclusion. *Lubanski,* 929 F.2d at 46. We weigh these factors in " 'the context of the case as gleaned from the record as a whole.' " *Id.* (quoting *Vincent v. Louis Marx & Co.,* 874 F.2d 36,

41 (1st Cir.1989)). We have repeatedly noted that "no substantial right of the party is affected where the evidence omitted was cumulative as to other admitted evidence." *Doty,* 908 F.2d at 1057. Should a reviewing court be in "grave doubt" as to the likely effect an error had on the verdict, the error must be treated as if it had in fact affected the verdict. *O'Neal v. McAninch,* 513 U.S. 432, ——, 115 S.Ct. 992, 994, 130 L.Ed.2d 947 (1995) (noting that "by 'grave doubt' we mean that, in the judge's mind, the matter is so evenly balanced as he feels himself in virtual equipoise as to the harmlessness of the error.").

We note that under Federal Rule of Evidence 103(a), we review the decision not only to determine whether a substantial right of the party is affected, but also to see whether a timely objection "appears of record, stating the specific ground of objection, if the specific ground was not apparent from the context." Fed.R.Evid. 103(a)(1); *see Bonilla v. Yamaha Motors Corp.,* 955 F.2d 150, 153 (1st Cir.1992). Here, Scholz' counsel objected at the time of the challenged rulings. Therefore, this element of our analysis is not at issue.

Having established the legal framework, we examine each of Scholz' contentions in turn.

A. *The Contested Testimony*

Phillips, Ahern's counsel, put Engel on the stand on the seventh day of trial. The objected-to portion of his questioning sought testimony regarding the Scholz Statement, which purported to account to Ahern for the royalties from the third album. In the Statement, Scholz deducted $1.7 million for legal fees charged by Engel's law firm, which the Statement listed as equivalent to half of the fees charged in relation to the negotiation of the agreement with MCA and the CBS litigation. The immediate issue at trial was whether this deduction was permissible as a "commercially reasonable recording expense" deductible from the royalties under section 5.2.1 of the FMA. Because the record is determinative of this issue, we quote it at length:

> Q. Now, as far as legal fees as recording costs are concerned, you've had some experience over the years, have you not, in reviewing the contracts of performing artists and groups in the musical field; is that right?
>
> A. Yes.
>
> Q. And could you give the Court and the jury some estimate of the number of contracts that you believe is an estimate that you reviewed over the period of time that you've been doing such matters in the entertainment field?
>
> A. Hundreds and hundreds and hundreds and more.
>
> Q. Okay...Have you ever seen legal fees as a recording cost in any of those hundreds and hundreds of contracts?

MR. PASSIN: Your Honor, I object. He hasn't been called as an expert witness.
THE COURT: Overruled.
Do you mean, are you saying that he can't answer that question?
THE WITNESS: No, your Honor, I would—
THE COURT: Overruled. If you can't answer it, say you can't answer it.
THE WITNESS: I can answer it, but it's a little awkward to call me as a witness, as an expert in my client's case.
THE COURT: Overruled. You were advised that you were going to be called, and you said that you wished to stay in this case and your client was so advised. The objection has been made. Overruled.
MR. ENGEL: At one point we said we wished to be out of the case. I think it should be clear. At one point we said out.
THE COURT: Overruled.
BY MR. PHILLIPS:
Q. Do you have the question in mind, Mr. Engel? In the hundreds and hundreds of contracts that you've reviewed for performing artists such as Mr. Scholz and other groups in the music field, have you ever seen legal fees as a recording cost or expense?
A. I have never seen legal fees—You mean designated in a contract?
Q. Yes, as a recording cost or expense.
A. No, I have never seen legal fees designated in a contract as anything, and certainly not as recording costs.
(Day 7, pages 71–73).

Scholz claims the district court erred in admitting the testimony over his counsel's objection, because Ahern's counsel was using Engel as an expert witness against his own client. First, he points out that Engel was not designated as an expert under Federal Rule of Civil Procedure 26. *See Prentiss & Carlisle Co. v. Koehring–Waterous Div. of Timberjack, Inc.,* 972 F.2d 6 (1st Cir.1992) (upholding trial court's refusal to hear expert testimony from witness not designated as an expert). Next, he maintains that under the applicable Rules of Professional Conduct, Engel should not have been required to testify against his client on an important and disputed point. *See* Model Code of Professional Responsibility DR 5–102(B). In turn, Ahern contends that the questions asked were not seeking Engel's expert opinion under Federal Rule of Evidence 701, or, in the alternative, that the district court acted within its discretion in admitting the testimony. *See Espeaignnette,* 43 F.3d at 10–11 ("Determinations of whether a witness is sufficiently qualified to testify as an expert on a given subject and whether such expert testimony would be helpful to the trier of fact are committed to the sound discretion of the trial court."); *United States v. Sepúlveda,* 15 F.3d 1161, 1183 (1st Cir.1993) (stating that manifest error standard applies to trial judge's rulings regarding expert testimony), *cert.*

denied, 512 U.S. 1223, 114 S.Ct. 2714, 129 L.Ed.2d 840 (1994). His final contention is that Scholz' complaint should be deemed waived because Scholz first injected Engel's opinion testimony into the case through his affidavits.

We need not consider these arguments, however, for we find that, even assuming the trial court erred in admitting the challenged section of Engel's testimony, it was not harmful error. Essentially, the challenged evidence was that in the "hundreds and hundreds and hundreds and more" contracts that he has reviewed, Engel never saw "legal fees designated in a contract as anything, and certainly not as recording costs." (Day 7, page 73). Having examined the record as a whole to determine if admitting this evidence affected Scholz' substantial rights, in accordance with our legal framework, we find that any court error did not amount to harmful error.

First, although the issue of whether Scholz breached the FMA was certainly a major focus of the case, and Engel's testimony related to the single largest deduction taken from the royalties on the Scholz Statement, we disagree with Scholz' contention that it was probably determinative for the jury, for several reasons. Ames and Stewart L. Levy ("Levy"), who has served as Ahern's counsel in the past and who was designated an expert on the subject of the reasonableness of the attorney's fees, both testified that attorney's fees are not recording expenses or recording costs. Ahern testified that they are not artist costs or expenses for recording purposes. We found no testimony, besides Engel's, contesting this point. Levy challenged the fees' inclusion on the Scholz Statement on another front as well, stating that Ahern was asked to pay for services that at times were working against his best interests, including time billed on motions to preclude a stipulation which would have had Sony or CBS dropping Ahern from the lawsuit. In short, he stated,

> We start off with the proposition that here is Mr. Ahern who is not directing Mr. Scholz to jump labels, not instructing Mr. Engel to do anything. Because Mr. Scholz decides to do what he is doing, not only does Mr. Ahern get sued by CBS, not only is Mr. Ahern's income from CBS cut off, now Mr. Scholz and his attorney, Mr. Engel, expect Mr. Ahern not only to accept that but to defray part of the cost of Mr. Engel doing this. I find that outrageous.

(Day 7, page 95). Engel testified that the attempt to keep Ahern in the case was not directed solely at him, but was part of an attempt to keep CBS from making deals with potential witnesses.

The fees were not disputed solely on the basis of the appropriateness of their deduction. Levy testified at length that the fees themselves were unreasonable. He testified that he felt that Engel's firm

> did the work without any regard to any kind of budget, without any cap on their work. Then they turned around and said, he said we had carte blanche.... Suddenly when the case is over in 1990, we are told it is $3

> million.... There were no parameters. Mr. Engel did what he wanted to do. No one was checking what he did to say it was too expensive, don't do it.

(Day 7, pages 104–05). In turn, Engel testified that the fees were higher than originally estimated because the head of CBS personally pursued the litigation to the "bitter end," despite repeated attempts to settle. Ultimately, he maintained, Scholz prevailed and won moneys for the entire band—and Ahern.

In fact, the attorney's fees were not the only challenged deduction on the Scholz Statement. There was lengthy testimony questioning and defending many of the other deductions, most notably the producer's fee and the more than 11,000 hours of studio time Scholz charged for. Therefore, even if the jury felt the deduction of the attorney's fees—or of some of them—was appropriate, they could still have reasonably found that Scholz materially breached the FMA. Between the additional evidence, on both sides, as to whether the legal fees could be commercially reasonable recording expenses, whether the amount of fees charged were reasonable, and whether other deductions on the Statement were reasonable, we find that Engel's challenged testimony was not central to the case.

Second, the evidence admitted did not have an unduly prejudicial effect. When called to the stand by his co-counsel, Engel was able to clarify that, while he felt he was asked about "recording costs," the FMA actually addresses "recording expenses":

> Q. Does the—The first question, does the further modification use the term "recording costs"?
>
> A. My recollection is, the [F]irst Modification Agreement uses the term "recording expenses." I was asked about recording costs.
>
> * * *
>
> Q. Do recording contracts use the term "recording expenses" or "recording costs"?
>
> A. I, in all the recording contracts I've seen, in many of them, I don't remember the term "recording expenses" ever used, it's always "recording costs" that I've seen in the clause.

(Day 13, pages 110–112). He followed up on this in his closing argument, stating that "[q]uestions were asked about recording costs, but recording costs is not the word used [in the FMA]." (Day 15, page 18). We find that this additional testimony by Engel counters the potential prejudicial effect of his challenged statement. Scholz argues on appeal that the prejudicial effect of the testimony was compounded by the statement of Ahern's counsel in his closing argument that

> there is no testimony before you, ladies and gentlemen, that legal costs in litigation that Mr. Scholz was in is a recording cost. In fact, to the

> contrary, the only testimony here has been that legal costs—legal fees and legal costs are not recording costs.
>
> You may recall Mr. Engel uncomfortably on the witness stand, after I qualified him on his expertise in matters of this sort, acknowledging that this was the case.

(Day 15, page 45). However, between the totality of the evidence at trial and the additional statements Engel himself made, both as witness and as counsel, we do not feel that this reference to Engel in the hour spent in closing argument by Ahern's counsel could be found to sway the jury's decision, prompting harmful error. *See Espeaignnette,* 43 F.3d at 9.

B. *The Omitted Testimony*

Scholz contends that the district court made a separate harmful error in upholding the objections made by Ahern's trial counsel when Engel's co-counsel called Engel to the stand on the thirteenth day of trial and tried to have him address his earlier testimony. After stating that the FMA used the term "recording expenses," not "recording costs," and reading out the pertinent section of the FMA, Engel's testimony continued as follows:

> Q. Have you seen contracts using only [the] words "recording costs" where artists were paid for legal fees?

On appeal, Scholz argues that the court "apparently believed that it would be too prejudicial to Ahern to permit Engel to explain his apparently adverse expert testimony but that it was not too prejudicial to Scholz to permit Engel to testify adversely to Scholz in the first place, a horrendous conclusion." (Appellant's Brief, page 34). We disagree. The first time Engel testified, he was asked about "contracts of performing artists and groups in the musical field." (Day 7, page 71). He stated in the disputed testimony that he had "never seen legal fees designated in a contract *as anything,* and certainly not as recording costs." (Day 7, page 73 (emphasis added)). When next called to the stand, Engel agreed that he *had* seen "contracts using only [the] words 'recording costs' where artists were paid for legal fees." (Day 13, page 112). The court's decision to sustain the objection made by Ahern's counsel in the ensuing dialogue was not a refusal to allow Engel to explain his evidence on the basis of its prejudicial effect against Ahern: it was evidently a reaction to the apparent inconsistency between these statements.

Essentially, on appeal Scholz maintains that Engel's co-counsel was not allowed to "cross-examine" him on the subject of his direct testimony for Ahern, thereby precluding him from presenting clarifying evidence or diminishing the "sting" of an attorney testifying against his own client. This error compounded the error of admitting Engel's expert testimony, Scholz contends. He complains that because of the court's ruling, the jury never got to hear Engel's testimony regarding other types of contracts, such as agreements between performers and managers, or the difference between "recording costs" and "recording expenses." Nor did they hear his explanation that his answer might differ if asked about "commercially reasonable recording expenses," not "recording costs," he notes. We view this final protest with some skepticism, however, in light of Engel's testimony on the stand that he had never seen legal fees designated "as anything," which would, presumably, include commercially reasonable recording expenses.

Assuming, *arguendo,* that Engel would have made the above testimony and that the district court erred in excluding the line of questioning, any resulting error was harmless. First, for the same reasons outlined above, the testimony, while related to a central issue, was not central in and of itself. Ames and Levy stated that they saw no difference between "recording costs" and "recording expenses." Additional testimony debated the total amount of fees charged as well as many other aspects of the Scholz Statement. As for the potential prejudicial effect, the testimony Engel was able to give, quoted above, made it clear that his earlier statement was directed to "recording costs," not "recording expenses," an argument he reiterated in his closing, mitigating the potential effect of the apparent inconsistency. Additionally, during his first day on the stand Engel stated, in response to questioning about the actual charging of recording costs or expenses by a group or a performing artist, that although he reviews accountings after the fact, he has never reviewed an accounting like that provided in the Scholz Statement. He testified that "[t]his is a special case. I don't remember any accounting that really falls into this category. This is not a standard contract." (Day 7, page 81). While this testimony does not go directly to his prior statements, it does emphasize that the FMA is not a standard contract, implying that his and others' statements about other contracts may not be pertinent. Weighing the above in the light of the record as a whole, *see Doty,* 908 F.2d at 1057, we cannot say that the court's evidentiary ruling excluded evidence that was either central or prejudicial in its effect such that it could have swayed the factfinders' decision. Thus, even if the court erred, it did not rise to the level of harmful error. *See Lubanski,* 929 F.2d at 46.

C. *The Overall Impact of Engel's Testimony*

Of course, it is not just the impact of the information elicited from Engel that we must evaluate under the harmless error standard. We must also address the potential prejudicial effect on the jury of seeing Engel, Scholz' counsel, take the stand, dispute with the court and opposing counsel over his testimony, and finally make a statement, apparently unwillingly, against his client's interest—a statement against which, he argues, he had to take an apparently inconsistent position in his closing argument. There is no doubt in our mind that this had some prejudicial effect on the jury. Nonetheless, we cannot say with " 'fair assurance ... that the judgment was [ ] substantially swayed by the error.' " *Espeaignnette,* 43 F.3d at 9 (quoting *Lubanski,* 929 F.2d at 46). The jury sat through fifteen days of trial, received substantial and often cumulative testimony on all points, and heard an hour of closing argument from each party's counsel. We find it highly unlikely that the verdict could have been the result of Engel's questioning and the attendant commentary. *Cf. United States v. Rosales,* 19 F.3d 763, 768 (1st Cir.1994) (holding that prosecutor's inappropriate argument in closing did not warrant new trial under harmless error standard).

There are significant reasons why trial counsel should not be able to testify at trial, no matter for which party counsel testifies...

The principal ethical considerations to a lawyer testifying on behalf of his client regarding contested issues are that the client's case will "be presented through the testimony of an obviously interested witness who is subject to impeachment on that account; and that the advocate is, in effect, put in the unseemly position of arguing his own credibility."

When the attorney is called to the stand by his client's opponent, the concerns are just as substantial, if not more. *See Siguel,* 141 F.R.D. at 396 ("Although there are degrees of adverse testimony, there are few, if any, situations that justify acceptance or continued employment in this circumstance."). Accordingly, Model Rule of Professional Conduct 3.7 states that a lawyer shall not act as advocate at a trial where he or she is likely to be a necessary witness, except, among other things, where the testimony relates to an uncontested issue or disqualification of the attorney would work substantial hardship on the client. Finally, there is also the danger that the performance of the dual roles of counsel and witness will create confusion on the jury's part as to when the attorney is speaking as a witness, "raising the possibility of the trier according testimonial credit to the prosecutor's closing argument," or, conversely, weighing the testimony as if it were argument...

All these concerns clearly come into play at a more heightened level when trial counsel acts as an expert. However, when counsel is asked to play that role for the length of one question in a fifteen-day trial, even acknowledging the impact of the attendant discussion with the court, attempts to examine him on the testimony and references to it in the closing arguments, we cannot hold that it rises to the level of harmful error affecting a party's substantial right where the testimony is cumulative and not a central part of the case. Any prejudice that resulted from the objected-to portions of Engel's testimony did not rise to the level of harmful error.

D. *Denial of Pre-Trial Motion for Continuance*

Prior to trial, Ahern filed two motions seeking to disqualify Engel as Scholz' counsel on the grounds that Engel was a percipient witness who ought to testify on Scholz' behalf. Scholz opposed, and the district court refused, both motions. When the parties presented their lists of witnesses, Engel appeared on both parties' lists. Approximately six weeks before trial was scheduled to begin, Ahern filed a third motion to disqualify. This time Scholz agreed to withdraw his counsel provided that he was given time to find new lead counsel. In his memorandum in support of his motion, Scholz stated that he "now [felt] he must retain new trial counsel in this matter, to avoid the risk of a disqualification of his counsel just prior to the trial, and for other reasons." (Scholz' Memorandum in Support of His Motion to Continue Trial, page 3). The district court, however, denied both Ahern's Renewed Motion to Disqualify and Scholz' Motion to Continue Trial.

As discussed above, Scholz maintains in his brief on appeal that the trial court erred by allowing Ahern to use Engel as his own expert against Scholz. One of the four contentions he uses to support this position is that

> the trial court itself placed Scholz in his precarious predicament when it refused to grant the last motion by Ahern to disqualify Engel.... The failure to grant the continuance under these circumstances, which resulted in severe prejudice to Scholz, is, itself, reversible error.

(Appellant's Brief, page 34). In support of his statement, Scholz cites several cases weighing district court decisions on motions for continuances. *See Lowe v. City of East Chicago,* 897 F.2d 272, 274–75 (7th Cir.1990) (concluding that it was an abuse of discretion to deny motion for continuance where plaintiff was faced with choice between voluntary dismissal and going to trial although his attorney was not ready for trial); *United States v. Flynt,* 756 F.2d 1352, 1358–59 (9th Cir.) (finding that district court abused its discretion in denying motion for continuance where doing so effectively foreclosed defendant from presenting a defense), *amended,* 764 F.2d 675 (9th Cir.1985). We need not prolong our discussion. Simply put, we do not feel the district court abused its discretion in denying the motion for a continuance. Even if it did, the error was harmless.

Finally, we note that while we ultimately hold that the court did not commit harmful error in making its evidentiary ruling, we find it very disturbing that trial counsel testified in this case. In making his appeal, Scholz directs us to a series of cases, several of which are referenced above, which lay out the real and serious concerns implicated by allowing counsel to testify at trial. *See, e.g., United States v. Dack,* 747 F.2d 1172, 1172 n. 5 (7th Cir.1984) ("Where evidence is easily available from other sources and absent 'extraordinary circumstances' or 'compelling reasons,' an attorney who participates in the case should not be called as a witness."). We ask whether Scholz and his counsel read these cases before opposing Ahern's first two motions to disqualify. The concerns the cases voice are implicated whether counsel testifies for his or her own client or for the opposing party. What is more, even if Engel testified solely as to ministerial matters, we still doubt the wisdom of allowing him on the stand, as the matter of his firm's legal fees—not only whether, as a whole, they were commercially reasonable recording expenses but also whether they were reasonable at all—was a matter of testimony. The jury heard deposition testimony from Ahern's expert Levy that the legal fees from the CBS litigation were, among other things, "excessive and totally inappropriate" (Day 7, page 86); whether Engel was called to the stand by Scholz or Ahern, indeed, even had he never testified, his integrity and judgment could have been questioned by the factfinders.

COUNTERCLAIM FOR FRAUD AND DECEIT AND AFFIRMATIVE DEFENSES

The Further Modification Agreement provided that Ahern was entitled to a share of the royalties of any album completed before October 24, 1984. Had the parties adhered to this provision, Ahern would not be entitled to any moneys from the third album, as it was completed after that date. Instead, Scholz waived the deadline, conveying his waiver through communications between the parties' attorneys in May of 1984. In this action, Scholz drew on his waiver of the deadline in his third counterclaim and several of his affirmative defenses to argue for rescission of the waiver agreement on the grounds of fraud and deceit and, alternatively, its invalidation. On appeal before us, he appeals the district court's directed verdict against him on these claims.

Our standard of review is a familiar one. A motion for judgment as a matter of law "should be granted only when the evidence, and the inferences to be drawn therefrom, viewed in the light most favorable to the nonmovant ... could lead reasonable persons to but one conclusion."

A. *Rescission*

In his Third Affirmative Defense and Third Counterclaim, Scholz sought recision of the waiver agreement on the grounds that Ahern fraudulently induced him to enter into the agreement by not disclosing that he had neither accounted for nor paid, since at least 1981, the royalties he owed Scholz under the FMA. Under New York law, applied here pursuant to the FMA choice of law provision, a party seeking to prove common law fraud must show that:

> (1) the [cross-]defendant made a material false representation, (2) the [cross-] defendant intended to defraud the [cross-] plaintiff thereby, (3) the [cross-] plaintiff reasonably relied upon the representation, and (4) the [cross-]plaintiff suffered damage as a result of such reliance...

The first element may be met by demonstrating not only a misrepresentation, but also a concealment or nondisclosure of a material fact.

In addition, the party claiming fraudulent concealment must demonstrate that the opposing party had a duty to disclose the material information in question and demonstrate each element of the claim by clear and convincing evidence. *See Banque Arabe et Internationale D'Investissement,* 57 F.3d at 153. We begin our analysis by weighing what duty Ahern owed Scholz, and then turn to the elements listed above, ultimately concluding that the district court erred in directing a verdict.

In the instant case, Scholz argues that Ahern owed Scholz a duty to disclose because he was a fiduciary. *See Brass v. American Film Techs.,* 987 F.2d 142, 150 (2d Cir.1993). Ahern contests that at the time the waiver was given in May 1984, the Management Agreement had terminated and so there was no fiduciary duty and, thus, no duty to disclose. "Under New York law, a fiduciary relationship includes 'both technical fiduciary relations and those informal relations which exist whenever one [person] trusts in, and relies upon, another.' " "New York courts typically focus on whether one person has reposed trust or confidence in another who thereby gains a resulting superiority or influence over the first." *Litton Inds., Inc. v. Lehman Bros. Kuhn Loeb Inc.,* 767 F.Supp. 1220, 1231 (S.D.N.Y.1991), *rev'd on other grounds,* 967 F.2d 742 (2d Cir.1992).

Scholz points us to the decision in *Apple Records, Inc. v. Capitol Records, Inc.,* where the court found that plaintiffs, the New York corporation of the Beatles, stated a claim that a fiduciary relationship existed...

Like the parties in *Apple Records,* at the time of the waiver in 1984 Ahern and Scholz had a long history of business dealings, marked by a series of agreements and modification agreements. Also as in that case, the relationship between the parties here was a profitable one for Ahern. However, unlike that case, Ahern no longer, as of several years previously, was Scholz' manager. Indeed, Scholz testified that in 1978, when he first started the process that culminated in the FMA, he was no longer on speaking terms with Ahern. While we do not doubt—and Ahern admitted at trial—that Ahern had a fiduciary duty to Scholz until 1981, the question remains whether there was such a special relationship of trust and confidence between the parties at the time of the waiver that a fiduciary relationship, at least as regards Ahern's duty to pay Scholz' share of the royalties from the first and second albums, remained. Since a reasonable juror could find that it did, however, a directed verdict is inappropriate on the question of whether Ahern owed Scholz a fiduciary duty. Therefore, we continue our analysis and turn to the evidence presented on the elements listed above.

First, as for the material false misrepresentation or nondisclosure, it is undisputed that Ahern did not disclose his failure to pay, a fact which a reasonable juror could easily find material. On the other hand, both Ahern and Barbara Sherry ("Sherry"), who provided business management services for

Ahern and BOSTON while Ames served as their business manager and served as Ahern's business manager from 1982 up through the time of trial, testified that they were not aware money was owed until after the waiver was made, and Scholz points to no evidence of concealment. Second, Scholz would have us read an intent to deceive into Sherry's testimony agreeing with Engel's statement that today, looking at a royalty statement from the company charged with administrating the publishing, "it's immediately plain to anyone who knows this business, that [the administration company] was not paying" the proper percentage to Scholz. (Day 6, pages 61–62). Scholz cannot rely on this as an admission that Sherry knew Scholz was not receiving all his moneys, however, since her actual testimony was that she did not know of the failure at the time. Instead, he seeks to build on her admission that one could have known from the face of the royalty statements that there was an error, as well as the fact that there was no evidence that letters of direction were prepared for the foreign sub-publishers, to support his contention that Ahern "had to have known" he was not making all his payments. Ahern presented no evidence indicating that he could not have known of the error, just that he did not. In essence, therefore, determining whether Ahern intended to deceive Scholz becomes an issue of credibility, one which of necessity is a question for the jury.

As for whether Scholz reasonably relied on Ahern's nondisclosure, his case is damaged by the fact that the evidence is undisputed that Ahern did not actually solicit the waiver. Scholz' attorney contacted his counsel and offered it to him. Scholz explained his motivation at trial:

> A. Well, I figured if I, if I finished the record six months later and I missed that date that Paul Ahern was entitled to his 12 percent of the royalties, you know, I missed that date and then six months later delivered the record, I was sure he would be upset about that and, and want his 12 percent anyway, and I didn't want to fight with him.
>
> Q. And was it your intention at that time—
>
> A. I had enough trouble at that point.
>
> Q. And did you ask for anything in return for that waiver?
>
> A. No.

(Day 10, pages 38–39). However, Scholz points to his testimony at trial that he "obviously" would not have agreed to the waiver had he known of Ahern's failure to pay him publishing royalties as evidence of his reliance. Giving Scholz the benefit of all the inferences, a reasonable juror could find under these circumstances that Ahern sought to induce Scholz into a fraudulent agreement, once it had been offered to him, through nondisclosure of his failure to pay. The presence of the fourth element, damages, Scholz contends, is witnessed by the fact that he now owes Ahern money: had he not waived the deadline, Ahern would not have been entitled to royalties from the third album. Given all of the above, we find that Scholz has mustered sufficient evidence for the issue to go to the jury.

B. *Invalidation of the Waiver*

In his Fourth and Fifth Affirmative Defenses, Scholz argues that the waiver should be invalidated because he did not knowingly give his consent. He maintains here that in order to prevail, all he must prove is that he would not have agreed to the waiver if he had known of Ahern's failure to account to and pay him royalties. Since he testified to that effect, he argues, the district court erred in granting a directed verdict. We disagree. First, we note that none of the cases Scholz looks to for support discuss invalidation as an affirmative defense under Federal Rule of Civil Procedure 8(c). Although the case law indicates that there is precedent for such an affirmative defense, *see, e.g., United States v. Krieger,* 773 F.Supp. 580, 583 (S.D.N.Y.1991) (denying summary judgment on, *inter alia,* claim for invalidity of guarantees despite failure to claim it as an affirmative defense), we have found, and the parties present, no comprehensive discussion of its nature. *See* 2A James Wm. Moore et al., *Moore's Federal Practice* ¶ 8.27[4] n.6 (2d ed.1995) (listing most common affirmative defenses, excluding invalidity).

We find no other support for Scholz' position in the cases he cites. *Allen,* which he looks to for the proposition that all he has to prove is that he would not have agreed to the waiver, does not address invalidity of a waiver or release. Rather, it notes that a court may *rescind* a release " 'where it finds either mutual mistake or one party's unilateral mistake coupled with some fraud ... of the other party.' Scholz did not plead mutual mistake, and his rescission claim based on fraud is addressed above.

Scholz states that he does not have to show Ahern owed him a fiduciary duty in order to state a claim for invalidation. Indeed, the court in *Allen* notes that where one party has superior knowledge not available to the other party, a duty to disclose may arise, apparently exclusive of a fiduciary duty, *id.* at 45, but Scholz does not point to any evidence that he could not have discovered that Ahern had not been paying him. His reliance on *Gishen v. Dura Corp.,* 362 Mass. 177, 285 N.E.2d 117 (1972), apparently for the proposition that "[a] party cannot waive information with respect to an error in calculation whose existence is unknown to him, particularly where his ignorance is caused by the very lack of disclosure in question and where the parties are not fully at arm's length," *id.* 285 N.E.2d at 122, is misplaced. First and most importantly, under the choice-of-law provision of the FMA, the parties here are applying New York, not Massachusetts, law. Second, the *Gishen* opinion addressed a request for a jury instruction on waiver, which was denied because the party had not previously presented the argument; it does not involve an affirmative defense.

Id. at 121. The quoted language is dicta—and seems to undercut Scholz' proposition that a fiduciary relationship is not necessary.

Scholz' citation to *Werking v. Amity Estates, Inc.,* 2 N.Y.2d 43, 155 N.Y.S.2d 633, 137 N.E.2d 321 (1956), also proves unfruitful. There, the court defines a waiver as " 'the intentional relinquishment of a known right with both knowledge of its existence and an intention to relinquish it.' " *Id.* 155 N.Y.S.2d at 639, 137 N.E.2d at 327 (quoting Whitney on Contracts 273 (4th ed.1946)). The court found the waiver in question, of jurisdictional defects in a tax sale of plaintiff's farm, invalid because plaintiff "had no knowledge of the right he is charged with having knowingly and intentionally relinquished." *Id.* Here, however, Scholz knew exactly what right he was relinquishing: the right not to pay Ahern 12 percent of the royalties from the third album.

MASSACHUSETTS LAW CLAIMS

We next turn to Ahern's claim against Scholz under Massachusetts General Law Chapter 93A, sections 2 and 11 ("Chapter 93A"). The district court found that Scholz' failure to pay royalties as provided in the FMA violated Chapter 93A. More specifically, it held that the Scholz Statement regarding the royalties on the third album constituted an unfair and deceptive business practice, and that it was a "deliberate and blatant attempt to deprive Plaintiff Ahern of moneys rightfully due and owing to him." (District Court Memorandum and Order, page 3). The court awarded Ahern $547,000 as well as costs, interest, and reasonable attorney's fees.

Scholz now contends that his actions do not rise to the level of unfair or deceptive trade practices within the meaning of Chapter 93A.

We begin with our standard of review; once it is established, we address Scholz' attack on the sufficiency of the district court's findings, and his contention that his acts did not rise to the level of "rascality" courts require of Chapter 93A violations. *See Quaker State Oil Ref. Corp. v. Garrity Oil Co.,* 884 F.2d 1510, 1513 (1st Cir.1989). Because we ultimately find that the district court erred as a matter of law in finding that Scholz violated Chapter 93A, we need not address the defenses Scholz raises to the application of that Chapter.

A. *Standard of Review*

We review the district court's findings of law *de novo,* and only set aside its findings of fact if "clearly erroneous."

"A finding of fact is ' "clearly erroneous" when although there is evidence to support it, the reviewing court on the entire evidence is left with the definite and firm conviction that a mistake has been committed.' " *Industrial Gen.,* 44 F.3d at 43 (quoting *Anderson v. City of Bessemer City,* 470 U.S. 564,

573, 105 S.Ct. 1504, 1511, 84 L.Ed.2d 518 (1985) (citation omitted)). "Although whether a particular set of acts, in their factual setting, is unfair or deceptive is a question of fact, the boundaries of what may qualify for consideration as a [Chapter] 93A violation is a question of law."

B. *The District Court's Findings*

The district court determined that Scholz had violated sections 2 and 11 through his failure to pay Ahern royalties from the third album, and made the following findings in its Memorandum and Order. First, it found that Scholz agreed to pay Ahern royalties after deduction of only a producer's royalty and all commercially reasonable recording expenses. Second, the court held that the Scholz Statement constituted an unfair and deceptive business practice. More specifically, it found that the deductions taken for legal fees, payment to Jeff Dorenfeld, time spent in the studio, and the resulting recording costs were all not commercially reasonable recording expenses. Rather, the court stated, $500,000 in recording expenses would be commercially reasonable. It next found that Scholz' Statement was

> a deliberate and blatant attempt to deprive the Plaintiff Ahern of monies rightfully due and owing to him as royalties from the sales of the third BOSTON album. Such egregious conduct ... is patently an unfair and deceptive practice. The submission of [the Scholz Statement] as an accounting by Scholz to Ahern is a shocking display of arrogant disdain for Ahern's contractual rights and was rendered in obvious bad faith.

(District Court Memorandum and Order, page 3).

Scholz challenges the sufficiency of these findings. Federal Rule of Civil Procedure 52(a) mandates that courts "find the facts specially and state separately [their] conclusions of law thereon" when trying facts without a jury. *See, e.g., Montañez v. Bagg,* 24 Mass.App.Ct. 954, 510 N.E.2d 298, 300 (1987) (noting that judge did not make detailed findings of fact regarding Chapter 93A claims under Mass. R. Civ. P. 52(a)). Scholz notes that the court did not state that the deductions were actually deceptive, and reminds us that the Scholz Statement set forth in some detail what each of the deductions were. Since the court did not make more specific findings as to unfair or deceptive practices, he maintains, we should reverse the Chapter 93A finding against him. *See Schwanbeck,* 578 N.E.2d at 803 (holding that district court finding of Chapter 93A violation lacked foundation in the court's subsidiary findings).

However, we remind Scholz that under Rule 52(a) "the judge need only make brief, definite pertinent findings and conclusions on the contested matters." *Makuc v. American Honda Motor Co.,* 835 F.2d 389, 394 (1st Cir.1987). Here, the district court found that Scholz breached the FMA, that four of his deductions were commercially unreasonable, while a figure of $0.5 million would be reasonable; and that the Scholz Statement was "a deliberate and blatant attempt to deprive" Ahern of moneys owed him. It is a question of law whether this attempt to deprive Ahern rises to the level of a violation of Chapter 93A, as the lower court held, and we believe the decision includes enough of a basis for the Chapter 93A finding to save the decision from remand. The district court has provided us with more than mere conclusions. *See Sidney Binder, Inc.*, 552 N.E.2d at 572 (holding that explanatory findings were necessary where court merely recited the evidence without making findings and concluded that "neither party ha[d] sustained its burden of proof" that Chapter 93A had been violated). We note, however, that our task would have been much simpler in this and other issues had the district court seen fit to explicate more of its decision-making on paper. There is a gap between finding that deductions are commercially unreasonable and finding that the Scholz Statement as a whole is an attempt to deprive Ahern deserving of the modifiers "unfair" and "deceptive": while we are willing to follow the lower court across the distance between them, a bridge would have been more than welcome.

C. *Scholz' Challenge to the Chapter 93A Findings*

Having set forth our standard of review and the findings of the district court, we turn to the heart of Scholz' challenge to the Chapter 93A award. As noted above, whether an act was unfair and/or deceptive is a question of fact. Based on our review of the evidence, we do not hesitate to find that the district court's findings of fact are not clearly erroneous, and we will not disturb them. *See United Truck Leasing Corp. v. Geltman,* 26 Mass.App.Ct. 847, 533 N.E.2d 647, 653 (1989), *aff'd,* 406 Mass. 811, 551 N.E.2d 20 (1990). Thus, we assess the lower court's award under Chapter 93A in the light of its finding that four deductions—which totalled \$4.2 million—were not reasonable, but \$0.5 million would be commercially reasonable recording costs, and that the Scholz Statement was a deliberate attempt to deprive Ahern of his percentage of the royalties from the third album. We ask now whether these facts rise to the level of a violation of Chapter 93A, section 11.

There is no clear definition of what conduct constitutes an "unfair or deceptive" act. Mass. Gen. L. ch. 93A, § 11. The Massachusetts courts "have noted, however, that '[t]he statute "does not contemplate an overly precise standard of ethical or moral behavior. It is the standard of the commercial marketplace." ' " *Shepard's Pharmacy, Inc. v. Stop & Shop Cos.,* 37 Mass.App.Ct. 516, 640 N.E.2d 1112, 1115 (1994) (quoting *USM Corp. v. Arthur D. Little Sys., Inc.,* 28 Mass.App.Ct. 108, 546 N.E.2d 888 (1989)), *review granted,* 419 Mass. 1102, 644 N.E.2d 226 (1994). In the extensive case law on Chapter 93A, "a common refrain has developed. 'The objectionable conduct must attain a level of rascality that would raise an eyebrow of someone inured to the rough and tumble of the world of commerce.' " *Id.* (quoting *PMP Assocs., Inc. v. Globe Newspaper Co.,* 366 Mass. 593, 321 N.E.2d 915, 917 (1975)). In evaluating whether an act or practice is unfair, we assess "the equities between the parties," including what both parties knew or should have known. *Swanson v. Bankers Life Co.,* 389 Mass. 345, 450 N.E.2d 577, 580 (1983).

It is well established that breach of a contract can lead to a violation of Chapter 93A. *See, e.g., Anthony's Pier Four, Inc. v. HBC Assocs.,* 411 Mass. 451, 583 N.E.2d 806, 821 (1991). The simple fact that a party knowingly breached a contract does not raise the breach to the level of a Chapter 93A violation, however. *Cf. Pepsi–Cola Metro. Bottling Co.,* 754 F.2d at 18 (stating that "mere breaches of contract, without more, do not violate [C]hapter 93A."). In the breach of contract context, the Massachusetts Supreme Judicial Court has "said that conduct 'in disregard of known contractual arrangements' and intended to secure benefits for the breaching party constitutes an unfair act or practice for [Chapter] 93A purposes." *Anthony's Pier Four,* 583 N.E.2d at 821; *see Wang Labs., Inc. v. Business Incentives, Inc.,* 398 Mass. 854, 501 N.E.2d 1163, 1165 (1986). Relying on the Appeals Court of Massachusetts' decision in *Atkinson v. Rosenthal,* 33 Mass.App.Ct. 219, 598 N.E.2d 666 (1992), Scholz seeks to limit this test. *Id.,* 598 N.E.2d at 670–71 (citation omitted). We have not addressed, and find no Massachusetts case law addressing, whether this language from *Atkinson* extends beyond its immediate context to limit award of Chapter 93A damages in breach of contract cases to cases with an "extortionate quality." *See NASCO, Inc. v. Public Storage, Inc.,* 29 F.3d 28, 33 (1st Cir.1994) (quoting *Atkinson* and accepting, *arguendo,* that "in a breach of contract situation, liability does not attach under [Chapter] 93A, section 11 unless a defendant knowingly breached a contact in order to secure additional benefits to itself to the detriment of a plaintiff.").

We need not do so today, however. First, if we accept the test for Chapter 93A violation Scholz claims *Atkinson* frames, the district court's award here will not stand because there has not been an extortionate element to the breach: Scholz tried to hold on to Ahern's money, but he was not using the breach "to force [Ahern] to do what otherwise [he] would not be legally required to do." *Pepsi–Cola Metro. Bottling Co.,* 754 F.2d at 18 (affirming Chapter 93A award where defendant withheld payment as a "wedge" to force plaintiff to supply more products); *see, e.g., Anthony's Pier Four,* 583 N.E.2d at 822 (holding that withholding approval as a pretext to force party into changing price of underlying contract violated Chapter 93A).

Second, if we were to find that *Atkinson* does not limit Chapter 93A liability to cases with an extortionate element, but rather address Scholz' acts under the test as stated in *Anthony's Pier Four,* we still find that Chapter 93A has not been violated. That test asks whether there has been conduct " 'in disregard of known contractual arrangements' and intended to secure benefits for the breaching party." *Anthony's Pier Four,* 583 N.E.2d at 821; *see Wang Labs.,* 501 N.E.2d at 1165 (finding liability under Chapter 93A where interference with contract "constituted a willful act calculated to obtain the benefits of [the] contract ... without cost and in disregard of known contractual arrangements"). Here, the court found that Scholz knowingly breached the contract in order to gain a benefit—Ahern's share of the royalties. But that would be true of any knowing breach of a contract. The question, then, is whether the level of "rascality" is sufficient to rise to the level of a violation of Chapter 93A. We find it is not. First, while the deductions that the court deemed commercially unreasonable ate up more than half of the royalties reported, we note that Scholz did not seek to conceal the nature of the deductions: he laid them out on the Scholz Statement in varying levels of detail. Next, while Scholz has an extensive degree of control over the moneys from the third album, there has been no allegation that he did not report all of the royalties from MCA on the Scholz Statement. Evidence was presented that the number of hours spent on the album was reconstructed after the fact, but the district court did not find that the figures given were inaccurate, just that they were not deductible. Scholz' breach amounted to more than a dispute over the commercial reasonableness of certain deductions, as he would have us believe. Nonetheless, his acts did not rise to the level of rascality required for Chapter 93A liability. Ultimately, therefore, we conclude that the district court erred as a matter of law in finding Scholz violated Chapter 93A, and reverse that holding.

PREJUDGMENT INTEREST AND ATTORNEY'S FEES

As we have found that Scholz did not violate Chapter 93A, we need not address the parties' arguments regarding the award of attorney's fees under that statute. Nor do we weigh Ahern's cross-appeal of the district court's refusal to award prejudgment interest, since that is based on his Chapter 93A contention. *See* Mass. Gen. L. ch. 231 § 6C ("interest shall be added ... to the amount of damages, at the contract rate, if established, or at the rate of twelve percent per annum from the date of the breach or demand."). It does not apply to his breach of contract claim, as that was brought under New York law...
No costs on appeal to either party.

CONCLUSION

For the reasons stated above, we *reverse* the lower court's decision regarding Chapter 93A violations, *affirm* its other holdings except on rescission, and *remand* for trial on the issue of rescission.

WIL-HELM AGENCY v. LYNN
Court of Appeals of Tennessee, Western Section
March 11, 1981
618 S.W.2d 748

MATHERNE, Judge.

The Wil-Helm Agency sues for damages due to the breach of a theatrical agency contract entered into between the agency and Loretta Lynn, an artist. Loretta Lynn filed a counterclaim wherein she avers that the agency breached the contract and, therefore, owes her damages and she further alleges that the agency released her from the contract. The chancellor found that the agency had breached the contract and, in addition, had released Loretta Lynn from the contract. The chancellor further held that the amounts due each party offset each other and allowed no monetary award to either party.

The agency appeals insisting that the chancellor erred in finding: (1) that the agency breached the contract; (2) that the agency released Loretta Lynn from the contract; and (3) that the damages due the parties offset each other.

I. Court Proceedings to Date

This lawsuit was originally heard by Chancellor Ned Lentz, who by Judgment entered on December 1, 1971, held that certain written communications between the attorneys for the parties constituted a release of the contract by the agency as of May 8, 1971. The agency appealed that decision, and this court reversed the chancellor and remanded for a trial. The Supreme Court of Tennessee granted certiorari and by Memorandum and Order, filed October 19, 1973, set aside the Judgments of both lower courts, and remanded the lawsuit to the trial court for "a hearing on all of the issues raised in the pleadings." The basis for the remand was that under the record complete justice could not be done the parties, and it appeared that more satisfactory evidence was available upon the primary issues raised, which when presented, would enable a court to reach the proper conclusion.

On remand the lawsuit was tried by Chancellor Ben H. Cantrell, who held that the agency had released Loretta Lynn from the contract and that the agency had breached the contract. The matter was referred to the clerk and master "for a hearing as to damages and as to accounting." The clerk and master reported that, after the filing of numerous depositions, he could not ascertain the amount of damages due either party without a ruling on the law applicable to the measure of damages. The chancellor, thereupon, proceeded to consider the entire matter of damages and ruled that the damages due each party was offset by the damages each party owed the other. This appeal is from Chancellor Cantrell's rulings in the lawsuit.

II. The Contract and Facts Surrounding the Alleged Breach Thereof

Loretta Lynn was born in the area of Van Leer, Kentucky, and at the age of fourteen years married O. V. Lynn of that same area. A few months after the marriage, O. V. Lynn went to the state of Washington and obtained employment as an agricultural laborer. Later Loretta joined him at Custer, Washington. Loretta began singing at local gatherings and formed a band which soon became fully booked in the area at various local places of entertainment. She appeared on the Buck Owens show and entered into a recording contract under the Zero label. Loretta wrote and recorded the song "I'm a Honky Tonk Girl," appeared on various radio shows, appeared as a guest performer on the Grand Ole Opry, and was becoming recognized as a budding young artist.

In 1961 she and her husband moved to Nashville, Tennessee. In that year she entered into her first two-year contract with the Wil-Helm Agency. Thereafter, she entered into another five-year contract with that agency. On April 12, 1966, she and the agency entered into the contract now under consideration. This contract provides in pertinent part as follows:

> **WITNESSETH**
>
> 1. The Artist hereby engages the Agent as his sole and exclusive personal representative and adviser in the radio, television, recording and personal appearances field of entertainment throughout the world and in outer space for a period of Twenty years (20 years)
> 2. The Agent's duties hereunder shall be as follows: To us all reasonable efforts to procure employment for the artist in any branch of the field of entertainment in which the Artist notifies the Agent that his services are or will be available. In addition, at the Artist's request to:
>
> (a) Assist the Artist in negotiating with respect to all forms of advertising and commercial tie-ups in all fields, wherever the Artist's name, business likeness or voice may be used, including but not limited to the radio, television, recording and personal appearances field of entertainment.
>
> (b) Counsel and advise the Artist in matters which concern his professional interest in the radio, television, recording and personal appearances field of entertainment.
>
> 3. The Agent hereby accepts this engagement and agrees to perform the services specified herein. The Agent shall have the right to render his services to other persons, either in a capacity in which he is hereby

> engaged or otherwise. However, the Artist agrees not to engage any other person to act for him in the capacity for which the Agent has been engaged. The Artist hereby represents and warrants that he is wholly free to enter into this agreement and has no contract or obligations which will conflict with it.

An Amendment of the same date was attached to the contract which provides in part as follows:

> (3) This Amendment and the Agreement shall be null and void in the event there is a change of ownership in the Agency. It being the Artist (demands) that she be associated only with current management.

The contract and the amendment were signed by Smiley Wilson for the agency and by Loretta Lynn.

The Wil-Helm Agency apparently was a partnership composed of the four Wilburn brothers: Doyle, Teddy, Leslie and Lester. As we view the lawsuit, it is immaterial whether there was a change in the ownership of the agency, and the amendment to the contract will not be further considered.

The parties enjoyed several years of successful association. Loretta's popularity grew, and she is now recognized as an outstanding star in the field of country music. From 1961 through the latter part of the 1960's, the agency assisted Loretta and played an important part in her rise to stardom. Teddy Wilburn worked closely with Loretta. When the 1966 contract was signed, he was spending several hours almost daily with Loretta. He assisted her in rewriting her songs and advised her on costumes, mannerisms, and lines. Loretta was very fond of Teddy Wilburn; she sought his counsel and followed his advice. She appeared as the only female artist on the Wilburn Brothers Show. The agency obtained a recording contract for Loretta with Decca Records. She made appearances on national television and followed a hard-working road show schedule.

In about 1967, Doyle Wilburn began to drink alcohol in excessive amounts. When drinking or drunk, he was extremely abusive and boorish. This conduct by Doyle resulted in Teddy Wilburn leaving the show in 1968. Teddy moved to California and returned to Nashville only to do certain television work. It appears that Smiley Wilson then became the member of the agency upon whom Loretta depended. Wilson did his job and aided the artist; however, she missed the expertise and experience of Teddy Wilburn. It seems that Teddy did relent and return to the show, only to leave again in 1971 for the same reason as previously stated.

With Teddy gone, it appears that Doyle Wilburn took it upon himself to be more closely identified with Loretta and her work. The record is replete with instances which reveal almost constant misconduct on the part of Doyle Wilburn acting as the agent of Loretta. Some of the more glaring instances of misconduct are: (1) insulting the producer of the Johnny Carson Show while there to close a deal for Loretta to appear on that show; (2) drunkenness on the part of Doyle Wilburn while on the stage acting as master of ceremonies; (3) actually disturbing Loretta during performances; (4) the telling of sacriligious jokes on Loretta's show in Boston, Massachusetts; (5) drunken vomiting on the dinner table at a post-performance party given for patrons, promoters, disc jockeys and their wives; (6) drunkenness throughout most of a tour in England; (7) drunkenness during the time Loretta was preparing jingles for the Coca Cola ads; (8) getting drunk and passing out during the signing of the Glo-coat contract; (9) being so drunk while emceeing Loretta's performance at a rodeo that he fell off the stage; (10) drunkenness when taping Loretta on the Ed Sullivan Show; (11) insulting the black musicians while on the David Frost Show; (12) being drunk on practically every road trip, interfering with Loretta's need for rest on the bus, ignoring instructions of airline personnel while on flights, and generally being an obnoxious drunk in the presence of people upon whom the success of the artist depended. This conduct was carried on while Doyle Wilburn was acting as the representative of the agency with whom Loretta had contracted. This conduct was known to all members of the agency; some effort was made to reason with Doyle, but to no avail.

In about October 1970 Smiley Wilson left the agency. He was replaced by Mr. Brumley who was then replaced by Leslie Hart. Hart advised Loretta that she was being woefully mismanaged and recommended that she see an attorney. Up to this time Loretta had not received independent advice on anything. The agency kept her books, handled her financing, and referred her to the agency's lawyer for any personal legal advice. Upon the advice of Hart, Loretta employed an attorney. Upon investigating the situation, the attorney wrote a letter dated April 1, 1971, to the agency saying the agency had breached the contract, and Loretta would not further abide by it. Further negotiations between the lawyers resulted in certain letters which the chancellor found constitute a release of the contract by the agency. As we view the situation, it is of no import whether the agency released Loretta from the contract; we hold that the contract was breached by the agency.

We agree with the chancellor that the conduct of Doyle Wilburn as the representative of the agency was entirely inconsistent with the duty owed the artist under the contract. The agreement is a bilateral contract wherein each party was obligated to the other to render certain performances, the carrying out of which by each party was essential to the realization of benefits under the contract. Each party to the contract was under an implied obligation to restrain from doing any act that would delay or prevent the other party's performance of the contract. Fritz-Rumer-Cooke Co. v. United States, 279 F.2d 200 (6th Cir. 1960). Each party had the right to proceed free of hinderance by the other party, and if such other party interfered, hindered, or prevented the performance to such an extent as to render the performance difficult and diminish the benefits to be received, the first party could treat the contract as broken and was not bound to proceed under the added burdens. See: Anvil Mining Co. v. Humble, 153 U.S. 540, 14 S.Ct. 876, 38 L.Ed. 814 (1894). See also: 1 Restatement, Contracts, § 315 (1932); 4 Corbin on Contracts, § 947 (1951).

There is ample material evidence that the agency, by the conduct of its representative, committed a substantial breach of its contract with Loretta Lynn. The chancellor is affirmed in this respect.

III. Damages

The chancellor referred the question of damages to the clerk and master, but, after the taking of considerable proof, that official passed the issue back to the chancellor without making a finding of any kind. Thereupon, the chancellor found as follows:

After sifting through the proof and after reviewing the previous Memorandum and the orders based on it, the Court concludes that the claims of the parties off-set each other and should be dismissed. The plaintiff Agency claims $178,556.72 due on the contract up until the date of termination with allowances for dates already booked to November of 1971. The defendant counter-claimed for damages for breach of the management agreement. The proof shows that the defendant was being booked at a fee of $2,500.00 to $4,000.00 per appearance up until the date of termination of the agreement while an artist of her stature should have commanded a much higher figure. A simple calculation based on the number of dates she worked in a few years prior to 1971 shows how much of a loss that was. In addition, the failure to expose her to national television and the stress of the conditions under which she worked result in damages that are reasonably certain and should off-set the plaintiff's claim.

The Court declines to speculate on the amount of damages the plaintiff would be entitled to if the decision had been otherwise.

We accept the figure of $178,556.72 as the amount due the agency under the contract up until the date of termination with allowances for dates already booked to November 1971. The artist claims that this amount can not be awarded to the plaintiff agency because the plaintiff breached the contract and is not entitled to any amount thereunder. We disagree with the artist in this respect.

The record reveals that the plaintiff agency committed a substantial breach of the contract. The defendant artist did not commit any breach of the contract. Therefore, if the plaintiff is to recover at all, it must do so upon the theory that it has rendered a part performance of value, that it has done more good than harm to the artist, and that the artist will be unjustly enriched and the plaintiff unjustly penalized if the artist is allowed to retain the beneficial part performance without paying anything in return. 5A Corbin on Contracts § 1124 (1964). By the same token, the plaintiff is the wrongdoer, and it must not be allowed to profit from its own wrong. Therefore, allowance must be made to the defendant artist in damages for the full extent of the injury that the plaintiff's breach has caused her. Corbin, supra. Under the facts of this bilateral contract, whereby each party agreed to carry out certain performances in return for performances by the other party, we conclude that the plaintiff agency is entitled to its commissions based upon its part performance less the amount of the injury to the artist caused by the breach. Having accepted the figure of $178,556.72 as the amount due the agency for its part performance, it must now be determined in what amount, if any, the artist was damaged by the breach.

The defendant artist averred by counterclaim that due to the conduct of Doyle Wilburn, she had been deprived of engagements as an artist, that she had suffered physical and emotional distress and had been rendered unable to perform to her capacity, and that subsequent to the breach and the termination of the contract, the agency had held itself out as the sole and exclusive agent of the artist thereby depriving her of engagements and the resulting revenues therefrom. By amendment to the counterclaim, the artist averred that over the years the agency had booked her for engagements at a price below that to which she was entitled and had entered into a recording contract for her at a rate substantially less than her professional ability demanded, all to her financial detriment and in breach of the agency's duties under the contract.

As noted, the chancellor found (1) that the artist was booked at a fee below that which an artist of her stature should have commanded, and (2) that the stress of the conditions under which she was forced to work resulted in damages that are reasonably certain.

There is competent and material evidence that Loretta Lynn won more awards, had a larger following, and was more sought after than any other artist in her field of entertainment. There is competent and material evidence that artists of less ability, following, and demand were drawing from $5,000 to $7,500 for a performance during the late 1960's and up to 1971. There is ample proof that Loretta Lynn should have been drawing those amounts instead of the $2,500 to $4,000 range in which she was booked. The plaintiff agency presented proof (Exhibit 53) which purported to list every performance of Loretta Lynn for which the agency claimed a commission. From a review of the number of those performances and an application of a reasonable average fee at which the artist should have been booked, the chancellor concluded that the damage she suffered from having been "underbooked" for several years more than offset the amount proved by the agency as owing to it.

The chancellor properly held that strain and stress unnecessarily suffered by the actress due to the conduct of the agency representatives resulted in damages for which the artist could recover. There is ample material evidence to sustain the finding that the conditions under which she had to work, rendered the artist nervous, uncertain, dismayed, and embarrassed, all to her professional detriment through no fault of her own.

Although not ruled on by the chancellor, we find another element of damage to the artist based upon the recording contract it entered into for the artist with Decca Records. It seems that in the early years of the recording industry a recording company suffered substantial losses due to records being broken while in transit to the buyers. As a result, a custom built up that when contracting with an artist the recording company would deduct 10% from the sales figures to take care of this breakage, and the artist was paid a royalty based upon 90% of the sales figure. Later records were made of plastic or some other material not subject to the breakage previously sustained. The proof establishes that as of 1966, when Decca contracted to record Loretta, all recording contracts being renewed and all new contracts being entered into provided for a royalty based upon the 100% figure. This was done at the mere request of the artist or agent. However, the plaintiff agency booked Loretta at a royalty based upon the 90% figure. In 1972, after the parties had gone their separate ways, Decca voluntarily changed the contract so as to pay royalties on the 100% figure. There is material evidence that the loss suffered by the artist because of this breach of duty on the part of the agency amounted to approximately $200,000 during the period from 1966 to 1971.

We, therefore, agree with the chancellor that the damages suffered by the artist more than offset those amounts claimed by the agency for its part performance of the contract. Admittedly, neither the chancellor nor this court fix the actual amount of damages to which the artist is entitled due to the breach of the contract by the agency. We have, however, fully satisfied ourselves that the damages thus suffered exceed the amount due the plaintiff agency. The artist did not appeal. We conclude that under all the circumstances of this lawsuit, the chancellor's decree is supported by a preponderance of the evidence, and that decree is affirmed.

The cost in this court is adjudged against the appellant, Wil-Helm Agency, for which execution may issue, if necessary.

SUMMERS, J., concurs.

West's Ann.Cal.Labor Code § 1700.4
§ 1700.4. Talent agency and artists defined

(a) "Talent agency" means a person or corporation who engages in the occupation of procuring, offering, promising, or attempting to procure employment or engagements for an artist or artists, except that the activities of procuring, offering, or promising to procure recording contracts for an artist or artists shall not of itself subject a person or corporation to regulation and licensing under this chapter. Talent agencies may, in addition, counsel or direct artists in the development of their professional careers.

(b) "Artists" means actors and actresses rendering services on the legitimate stage and in the production of motion pictures, radio artists, musical artists, musical organizations, directors of legitimate stage, motion picture and radio productions, musical directors, writers, cinematographers, composers, lyricists, arrangers, models, and other artists and persons rendering professional services in motion picture, theatrical, radio, television and other entertainment enterprises.

In the following case, Isley v. Motown Record Corp., the Isleys sued their former production company. The issue at trial was the date on which "It's Your Thing" was first recorded. But, as it turns out, the Isleys (allegedly) lied and the judge withdrew the favorable verdict concerning their right to income from their hit song.

ISLEY V. MOTOWN RECORD CORP.
United States District Court for the Southern District of New York
November 18, 1975
No. 69 Civ. 2556
60 F.R.D. 12

OWEN, District Judge.

Plaintiffs, three brothers, are 'pop' singers and recording artists. A jury found facts in their favor establishing their right to the income from a 'hit' song they recorded with instruments and voices called 'It's Your Thing'. This favorable verdict was based solely upon their own testimony in the course of which they repudiated their own earlier sworn testimony which clearly supported a contrary conclusion, characterizing such earlier conflicting testimony variously as a lie and false. Given this basis for the verdict, and there being persuasive documentary and testimonial evidence to the contrary, the plaintiffs' favorable verdict cannot stand. It is set aside and a new trial is ordered.

In the mercurial field of popular music, the plaintiffs, brothers Ronald, Rudolph and O'Kelly Isley, singers and recording artists under the name Isley Brothers, had had their ups and downs. In 1968 they had been under contract to defendant Motown Record Corporation for several years and were not doing well. Under that contract from time-to-time they would record new songs, sometimes composed by themselves, sometimes by others. The tapes of those recording sessions were then delivered to Motown to press into records and distribute and the Isleys were paid royalties thereon. In December 1968, the Isleys applied for and obtained a release from the Motown contract. Thereafter, using two wholly-owned companies, Triple Three for the sheet music and T-Neck for the records, the Isleys published and pressed records of 'It's Your Thing' using defendant Buddah Records, an independent firm, merely as a distributor. There is no question that the Isleys' income was greatly enhanced by marketing 'It's Your Thing' under their own label rather than on the Motown label, for 'It's Your Thing' was a hit and sold 1,750,000 copies.

The basic issue on the trial was the date on which 'It's Your Thing' was first recorded.

Motown offered substantial documentary and testimonial proof to the effect that 'It's Your Thing' was first recorded at the A & R Studios in New York on November 6, 1968 at a session for which Motown had advanced the money on condition the Isleys record original tunes; that at that time the Isleys were under contract to it, and that it was therefore entitled to the income from 'It's Your Thing' less the Isleys' royalties. The Isleys, to the contrary, testified that 'It's Your Thing' was composed in late December 1968, shortly after they got the release from their Motown contract, was first recorded on January 3, 1969, and that Motown had no rights in it at all.

The jury answered three written questions as follows:

1. Have Motown and Jobete proved by a preponderance of the evidence that O'Kelly Isley on behalf of the Isley Brothers agreed on or about November 1, 1968 with Ralph Seltzer of Motown to obtain and furnish him with songwriter agreements on the forthcoming recording session as part of Seltzer's agreement to advance the money for the session?

'No'

2. Do you find that Motown and Jobete had proved by a preponderance[5] of the evidence that 'It's Your Thing' and 'Turn On, Tune In, Drop Out' were recorded on November 6, 1968 at the A & R Studios in New York?

'No'

3. Do you find that the Isleys have proved by a preponderance of the evidence that 'It's Your Thing' and 'Turn On, Tune In, Drop Out' were recorded for the first time on January 3, 1969 at the Town Sound Studios in Englewood, New Jersey?

'Yes'

The infirmity in the Isleys' collective testimony, which was the sole support for the jury's several conclusions, is clearly demonstrated by a comparison of their 1969–70 testimony in depositions or before Judge Lasker with their 1975 testimony given on the trial.

The 1969–70 testimony was to the effect that after actually having auditioned another band, they engaged a band called the Midnight Movers as a second choice to do a couple of 'ideas' they (the Isleys) had; that they thereafter wrote Motown on November 1 that they were going to do a session with the Midnight Movers and asked for money for the session and agreed to deliver the tape after the session; that they received from Motown songwriters agreements to be executed for original tunes; that in preparation for the recording session they had a 3–4 hour rehearsal on the night of November 5; that Ronald and O'Kelly Isley composed the music the Midnight Movers rehearsed; that O'Kelly Isley arranged for the recording studio for November 6, and told A & R how to set it up; that the Midnight Movers were paid $850 for the recording session; that although the Isleys were supposed to send the tape of the session to Motown, they did not, and the tape was still [as of 1969–70] somewhere at O'Kelly's home.

Thus, in 1969–70, while the Isleys maintained that they had not recorded 'It's Your Thing' at the November 6 session, they clearly acknowledged that on that date they had made the various customary arrangements for a substantial recording session of *music of their own*, and absent the production of the tape, a trier of the fact could well conclude, given other evidence, that what they recorded was in fact 'It's Your Thing'.

However, on the trial in 1975 they presented a new story as follows: In the fall of 1968, they were broke and needed money for household expenses and Christmas presents; in order to get Motown to advance them some money, they decided to make up a story about doing a session; they told Motown of this stratagem to which Motown agreed, and wrote the November 1 letter to Motown about the 'session' at Motown's suggestion so that there would be a basis for sending the money; that the name of the Midnight Movers was inserted in the letter just to have the name of a band, not having any real awareness of whether that band was available or not; that they had but a 45–60 minutes rehearsal; that they did no 'ideas' of the Isleys, and no music composed by the Isleys was performed at either the rehearsal or the session at A & R the next night and in fact there was no vocal music at all; that the Midnight Movers were only paid $400 or $450 and the Isleys, pursuant to plan, pocketed the balance of the $850 they got from Motown for the band; and finally, that the tape from the session was thrown out by the Isleys' mother in cleaning O'Kelly's basement in December 1968, the month following the session.

Motown's proof consisted first of contemporaneous writings of both parties which were strong circumstantial if not direct evidence that the Isleys intended to and did record new vocal music in the November 6 session. These writings included 1) the Isleys' letter of November 1, written five days before the session, 2) the records of the A & R Studios for the studio on November 6, showing two things, first that the studio had been set up for a solo vocal with a group vocal to be 'overdubbed', (see n. 21 *infra*) and second, that during the recording session itself, a change was made as to which microphone was assigned to the 'vocal'; 3) the Motown letter sent prior to the session after discussion with the Isleys enclosing songwriters agreements to be executed for the original tunes to be recorded, and 4) the letters exchanged a few weeks later when the Isleys demanded releases, at which time Motown wrote insisting on repayment of the entire cost of the session since the Isleys had sent no tapes, to which the Isleys agreed, and repayment was made.

Motown's second area of proof was the testimony of one of the Midnight Movers, George Chillious, a trombone player who played at the November 6, 1968 but not at the January 3, 1969 session. He testified that he played the music for 'It's Your Thing' in the November 6 session from a written trombone part bearing the title 'It's Your Thing', and after the end of the instrumental session heard Ronald Isley record the vocal part.

While I would not on this record, permit this verdict to stand in any event, this is an especially appropriate case for the granting of a new trial since much direct proof is available on a new trial that was not heretofore presented. Frequently, in directing a new trial, a court is faced with the fact that a second jury can do no more than reappraise the same evidence heard on the first trial. Here, however, there are perhaps as many as ten other 'Midnight Movers' available who could give testimony as to what was recorded on November 6, 1968, as could the sound engineer of the A & R Studio that night.

On such disinterested testimony, a second jury could obviously *better* determine the issues.

The law is well established that it is the duty of the trial judge to set aside a verdict and grant a new trial if, in his opinion, the verdict is based upon evidence which is false or the verdict results in a miscarriage of justice. The trial court is empowered to do this even though there may be substantial evidence which would prevent the direction of a verdict. *Aetna Cas. & Surety Co. v. Yeatts*, 122 F.2d 350 (4th Cir. 1941); *Reyes v. Grace Line, Inc.*, 334 F.Supp. 1104 (S.D.N.Y.1971). In my judgment, this verdict, on this record, results in a miscarriage of justice and was in part, if not in whole, based upon evidence which was false. I deem it fundamental that a party may not do a testimonial about-face, concede prior testimony to be false or a lie and then prevail solely upon the basis of that altered self-serving testimony.

For the foregoing reasons and pursuant to Rule 59 Fed.R.Civ.P., the conclusions of the jury as to all issues raised by the three questions submitted to it are set aside and a new trial is ordered. The action is placed on the calendar for trial on January 19, 1976.

POLYGRAM RECORDS, INC. v. BUDDY BUIE PRODUCTIONS, INC.
United States District Court for the Southern District of New York
August 21, 1981
No. 81 Civ. 4781
520 F.Supp. 248

OPINION
FINDINGS OF FACT AND CONCLUSIONS OF LAW

EDWARD WEINFELD, District Judge.

Plaintiff, Polygram Records Inc. ("Polygram") is in the business of exploiting, marketing and selling phonograph records. Buddy Buie Productions Inc. ("BBP") is a production company which produces and furnishes the recording services of the five individual defendants, a rock and roll music band, professionally known as The Atlanta Rhythm Section ("ARS"). Perry C. Buie, "Buddy" Buie ("Buie") has been the President of BBP since its formation. BBP, under an agreement with the individual defendants, is entitled to their exclusive services in the recording of phonograph records. Polygram, BBP and the individual defendants had a contractual relationship commencing in 1973 under which Polygram became the exclusive recording company for all ARS records.

The 1973 agreement was superseded by another on October 1, 1977 (the "1977 agreement") under which the defendants again granted plaintiff Polygram the exclusive right to all ARS recordings during the existence of the agreement. Under its terms BBP was obligated to produce and deliver four albums of ARS master recordings to plaintiff for its exclusive exploitation, manufacture and distribution.

Plaintiff commenced this action upon a claim that the defendants breached their exclusive service agreement by entering into an agreement in May 1981 with CBS Records Inc., a competing record company. Plaintiff seeks to enjoin the defendants from producing or recording any records for CBS or any other recording company, and money damages. Plaintiff can prevail only if the 1977 agreement was in effect at the time of the alleged breach. The parties are in agreement that the resolution of this issue depends upon whether plaintiff timely and properly exercised an option to extend the agreement for a further period so that it was in effect when defendants entered into their agreement to record for CBS.

The initial period of the 1977 agreement was for a term beginning October 1, 1977 and ending 180 days subsequent to the delivery by BBP to Polygram of master recordings for the fourth and final ARS album. Polygram had an option to extend the agreement for a further term covering four additional albums by sending a written notice to BBP at least 30 days prior to the date that the contract otherwise would expire. Since the agreement by its terms expired 180 days after the delivery of the fourth album, the date of delivery is crucial on the issue of whether the option was timely exercised so that plaintiff was entitled to ARS' exclusive services at the time of the alleged breach.

Delivery under the agreement required BBP to "deliver completed, edited and fully mixed master tapes in accordance with the Company's reasonable instructions" comprising a two-track stereo and a discrete quadraphonic master tape for each Master recorded hereunder together with a "reference lacquer" therefor, which tape shall be fully edited, mixed and leadered prior to delivery to Company (Polygram) so that they are in proper form for the production of parts necessary for the manufacture of commercial Phonograph Records.

The defendants contend that they made delivery of the last and fourth album in accordance with the foregoing contract provisions by delivery on June 11, 1981 of a reference lacquer to plaintiff at its offices where it was played in the presence of various Polygram executives who approved and accepted it and on that day mailed a check for $150,000 to BBP as the final payment.

The plaintiff, contrariwise, contends that the reference disc played and delivered on June 11, 1980 was an "unapproved" disc and that the final approved reference disc was not delivered and accepted by it until June 17, 1980. Accordingly, plaintiff claims that its notice of exercise of the option mailed on November 14, 1980, was sent on the 150th day after delivery, within the required time for the exercise of the option and hence the contract was renewed for a further term and was in effect in May 1981, the date of the alleged breach by the defendants. The defendants not only dispute that June 17, 1980 was the date of delivery but they challenge that in fact the notice was mailed on November 14, 1980. The envelope in which the exercise of option letter was mailed bears a November 16 postmark and was received by BBP on November 18. Two days later, on November 20, defendants' counsel notified Polygram orally and in writing that plaintiff had not timely exercised its option and that the defendants deemed the agreement terminated. Plaintiff made no response to defendants' disavowal until two months later when, on January 19, 1981, it notified all recording companies that a contract existed between plaintiff and the defendants. Thus a threshold question is on what day, June 11 or June 17, 1980, delivery was made by BBP to plaintiff of a completed master tape and reference lacquer as required by the provisions of the contract.

Masterdisk Corporation is a disc-cutting studio where the final artistic changes are made in a recording. The artist's product is originally recorded on many different tracks and subsequently "mixed down" that is, reduced to a two-track tape which is then taken to a mastering facility, such as Masterdisk, where final sound adjustments are made. A reference disc and a master disc are produced. The reference disc is used so that it may be heard by those interested in the product either for approval or suggested changes or modifications. The master disc is retained by the studio and upon approval is sent to a plating plant where it is used to manufacture the record that is sold to the public. Masterdisk was the studio used for the mastering of the ARS recordings. The parties' practice with respect to the first three albums was that the final two-track tape, after mastering, was left at Masterdisk and, upon final approval, Polygram would contact Masterdisk and order "the parts" necessary for the production of the album. This was the procedure followed with respect to the fourth album, the subject matter of this action.

Plaintiff, to support its claim that June 17, 1980 is the effective delivery date, relies in the main upon the testimony of two witnesses, Stuart Fine, then its East Coast Director of Artists and Repertoire, and James Del Balzo, then its Assistant National Album Promotion Manager. Fine testified in substance that on June 11, 1980, Buddy Buie, who mastered the recordings of the artists, came to his office together with Ronnie Hammond, lead singer of the ARS artists, and their respective wives, and played, in his presence and at times in the presence of other executives, a reference disc which Buie said he had been working on the previous two days; that before other Polygram people joined the meeting Buie told him that there were still some changes to be made; that he had "to roll off the bottom end"; that he would be working with Bob Ludwig, Masterdisk's chief engineer, later that day at Masterdisk to effect the changes, and that what they would be listening to was an unapproved reference disc. Fine acknowledged that everybody who heard the record liked it. Finally, he testified that after Buie and Hammond left the office, he wrote upon the cover of the reference record "not approved." However, he did not inform any superior or anybody else that it was not approved.

Fine also testified that later that day Arnold Geller, co-manager of ARS, telephoned and advised him that Buie and Ludwig would make the final changes and Polygram was not to place the order for final parts until it received from Buie another reference disc or Fine heard from defendants. Fine stated that he did nothing further until Geller called him on June 17 and gave BBP's approval, whereupon Fine voluntarily waived further Polygram approval and sent the "reference" approval form to the production department so they would "order parts" and commence commercial production of the album.

Del Balzo testified that on June 11 he was present when Buie played the reference record and asked Buie for cassettes of the record, to which Buie responded, "no, it was not an approved record." Finally, in addition to the reference approval form, plaintiff offered other internal documents to support its claim that Polygram regarded June 17, 1980 as the delivery date. Based in large part upon the foregoing testimony and related events, plaintiff contends that the date of delivery was June 17.

Defendants' evidence is in sharp contradiction to that of plaintiff. Buie testified that on June 9 and 10 he and Bob Ludwig, the engineer at Masterdisk, worked there in producing a reference lacquer and two-track tape which were completed and in final and satisfactory form on June 10; that on June 11, accompanied by Hammond and their respective wives, he went to the Polygram offices for the purpose of delivering the reference lacquer to Polygram, to share his excitement about the record with company officials, and to obtain final payment of $150,000. He delivered the record to Fine in his office, where it was played for Fine and other Polygram executives, including Freddie Haayan, its President; that all who heard it were enthusiastic and ecstatic about the record; they, as well as he, approved the record, and Haayan was so enthusiastic that he asked for a cassette that Buie had in his hand. Buie categorically denied the testimony of Fine and Del Balzo that he said the reference disc was "unapproved" or that he had to "roll off some bass." Buie testified that nothing further was to be done on the record and that he did not return to Masterdisk at any time thereafter for the purpose of making any changes. He expected to receive payment of $150,000 of the balance due under the contract, then and there, but Ms. Barbara Patralites, contract administrator, said there had been a foul up and she would express mail the check to Atlanta. The next day, June 12, he received plaintiff's check for $150,000 accompanied by a letter dated June 11, which reads:

> Pursuant to paragraph 9(a)(ii) of the above-cited Agreement enclosed please find Polydor's check No. 219756 in the amount of $150,000.00 representing the balance due upon delivery of the 4th LP entitled "The Boys From Doraville."

The letter was signed by Ms. Patralites, who testified the check was drawn by her pursuant to instructions from Dr. Ekke Schnable, Senior Vice President, Legal & Business Affairs. The check stub contains the legend "ADVANCE DUE UPON DELIVERY OF THE 4TH LP BY THE ATLANTA RHYTHM SECTION PURSUANT TO PARAGRAPH 9(a)(ii) OF THE OCTOBER 1, 1977 AGREEMENT." In sum, Buie testified that the reference lacquer left with Fine and the master two-track tape left at Masterdisk were fully edited, mixed and leadered and were in proper form for the production of the parts necessary to make commercial phonograph records and that there was no further work to be done.

Hammond also testified and denied that he heard any discussion on June 11 as to the reference lacquer being either unapproved or unsatisfactory; that all those who listened to the album were "very excited" about it. He acknowledged he did not hear any conversation Buie may have had with Fine or Del Balzo.

Arnold Geller, co-manager of ARS, also testified and flatly denied that he told Fine that further work was required on the reference disc or that he called him to give BBP approval on June 17, 1980. Geller stated that he had acknowledgment from several senior officers of Polydor; that they had received the album, loved the album and accepted it.

The General Manager and Vice President of Masterdisk, Douglas Levine, whose duties included overseeing all work performed there, testified, based on company records and his own knowledge, that no work was done by Masterdisk on the records between June 11 and June 17, 1980 except on June 12 when, in response to Buie's request, a duplicate reference disc was made to replace the one Buie had lost on a plane trip on his way home to Atlanta, Georgia on June 11th. According to the company records, all work was completed on the records on June 10 and there was no further work to be done on them.

The plaintiff has the burden of proof to establish by a fair preponderance of the credible evidence the existence of the contract under which it claims to be entitled to injunctive relief and damages. Based upon an appraisal of the demeanor of the witnesses, notes made during the trial, a word-by-word re-reading of the trial transcript, analysis of the exhibits and consideration of all surrounding circumstances, the Court concludes that at best the credible evidence is in balance, in which circumstance, as juries are instructed, the party who has the burden of proof on an issue has failed to sustain it. But the Court further finds that the credible evidence preponderates in favor of the defendants and against the plaintiff a finding buttressed by circumstances that are not in dispute.

First, the reference record left with Fine on June 11 and retained by him was exactly similar to the master two-track disc produced by Masterdisk and used for the commercial production of the record upon plaintiff's order. In sum, no changes were made in the record as produced for distribution, a circumstance that in some measure challenges the testimony that the reference delivered to plaintiff on June 11 was "unapproved." Further, contrary to Fine's testimony that Buie said further work was to be done on the record and that he planned to return to Masterdisk for that purpose, the evidence establishes that Buie never returned there for that purpose.

Second, the mailing on June 11, after delivery of the reference disc to plaintiff, of the balance of $150,000 accompanied by a letter specifically stating it represented "the balance due upon delivery of the 4th LP" and a similar legend on the check stub. Although Fine knew that the final payment was to be made upon delivery, he did not inform anyone that the reference disc was "not approved" and did nothing to hold up the check.

Third, the plaintiff's failure to call as a witness at the trial Dr. Ekke Schnabel, to testify as to the circumstances attendant upon his direction for the issuance of the final payment check or to offer any explanation for his failure to testify at the trial.

Fourth, the plaintiff's failure to call as a witness Freddie Haayan, plaintiff's President, who, it was testified, was one of those who expressed approval of the record on June 11th, or to offer any explanation for his nonappearance as a witness.

Fifth, the failure over a period of almost two months to respond to defendants' letter of November 20, 1980 which rejected plaintiff's option notice of November 14 on the ground that plaintiff had "not timely exercised its option to extend the term of the agreement" and that defendants regarded the agreement as terminated. Significantly, this letter was addressed to the attention of David Braun, plaintiff's President at that time, a lawyer, with a copy to Eileen Garrish, also a lawyer and who, at the time, was Director of Legal and Business Affairs of Polygram and had drafted the option notice. Surely the significance of the defendants' denial that the contract had been extended could not have been lost upon Braun and Garrish. Common experience suggests that these plaintiff's executives, also lawyers, would have responded immediately and on the record rejected defendants' claim and would affirmatively have asserted plaintiff's position that the option notice had been timely and by reason thereof that the contract had been extended for another term. David Braun was not called as a witness nor any explanation offered for his nonappearance. Eileen Garrish did testify principally with respect to the mailing of the notice on November 14. However, with respect to defendants' November 20 letter, when asked why no response was made thereto she testified that she had been instructed by her superiors "not to do anything." It is rather singular that when defendants denied the effectiveness of the option notice and the renewal of the contract, two lawyers who were directly involved in the matter on behalf of plaintiff failed to assert plaintiff's basic position over a two-month period.

Upon the totality of all the credible evidence, the Court finds that the defendants made delivery to plaintiff on June 11, 1980 of the fourth and final album in accordance with the terms of the 1977 agreement and that plaintiff accepted such delivery on that day. The complaint is dismissed upon the merits and judgment may be entered accordingly.

The foregoing constitutes the Court's Findings of Fact and Conclusions of Law.

§ **3423**. Injunction; circumstances requiring denial

Currentness

An injunction may not be granted:

(a) To stay a judicial proceeding pending at the commencement of the action in which the injunction is demanded, unless this restraint is necessary to prevent a multiplicity of proceedings.

(b) To stay proceedings in a court of the United States.

(c) To stay proceedings in another state upon a judgment of a court of that state.

(d) To prevent the execution of a public statute, by officers of the law, for the public benefit.

(e) To prevent the breach of a contract the performance of which would not be specifically enforced, other than a contract in writing for the rendition of personal services from one to another where the promised service is of a special, unique, unusual, extraordinary, or intellectual character, which gives it peculiar value, the loss of which cannot be reasonably or adequately compensated in damages in an action at law, and where the compensation for the personal services is as follows:

(1) As to contracts entered into on or before December 31, 1993, the minimum compensation provided in the contract for the personal services shall be at the rate of six thousand dollars ($6,000) per annum.

(2) As to contracts entered into on or after January 1, 1994, the criteria of subparagraph (A) or (B), as follows, are satisfied:

(A) The compensation is as follows:

(i) The minimum compensation provided in the contract shall be at the rate of nine thousand dollars ($9,000) per annum for the first year of the contract, twelve thousand dollars ($12,000) per annum for the second year of the contract, and fifteen thousand dollars ($15,000) per annum for the third to seventh years, inclusive, of the contract.

(ii) In addition, after the third year of the contract, there shall actually have been paid for the services through and including the contract year during which the injunctive relief is sought, over and above the minimum contractual compensation specified in clause (i), the amount of fifteen thousand dollars ($15,000) per annum during the fourth and fifth years of the contract, and thirty thousand dollars ($30,000) per annum during the sixth and seventh years of the contract. As a condition to petitioning for an injunction, amounts payable under this clause may be paid at any time prior to seeking injunctive relief.

(B) The aggregate compensation actually received for the services provided under a contract that does not meet the criteria of subparagraph (A), is at least 10 times the applicable aggregate minimum amount specified in clauses (i) and (ii) of subparagraph (A) through and including the contract year during which the injunctive relief is sought. As a condition to petitioning for an injunction, amounts payable under this subparagraph may be paid at any time prior to seeking injunctive relief.

(3) Compensation paid in any contract year in excess of the minimums specified in subparagraphs (A) and (B) of paragraph (2) shall apply to reduce the compensation otherwise required to be paid under those provisions in any subsequent contract years.

However, an injunction may be granted to prevent the breach of a contract entered into between any nonprofit cooperative corporation or association and a member or stockholder thereof in respect to any provision regarding the sale or delivery to the corporation or association of the products produced or acquired by the member or stockholder.

(f) To prevent the exercise of a public or private office, in a lawful manner, by the person in possession.

(g) To prevent a legislative act by a municipal corporation.

KASS v. YOUNG
Court of Appeal of California, First Appellate District, Division Three
February 14, 1977
Civ. No. 38186
67 Cal.App.3d 100, 136 Cal.Rptr.469

DEVINE, J.

Plaintiff Kass appeals from an order vacating a default judgment in a class action and vacating the default of defendant Neil Young insofar as it relates to a class action, but allowing the default to remain against appellant Young to the extent that defendant as an individual is concerned (judgment to be subject to proof of damages as to plaintiff's individual rights). Appellant Young cross-appeals from the order allowing the limited default to remain. Both sides agree that the case appears to be one of first impression as to the effect of default in an alleged class action.

The complaint alleges that Kass was one of about 14,000 patrons at a "rock" concert on March 31, 1973, at the Oakland Coliseum. Defendant Young was the star performer. He terminated the concert by abruptly walking off the stage. The purchasers of tickets "did not receive the consideration of a full concert performance for which they had paid." Damages are alleged to be about $98,000, including ticket prices, transportation and parking expenses. It is alleged that the entire class of patrons is affected exactly as is plaintiff.
Summons and complaint were served personally on Young on September 30, 1973. His default was entered on November 12, 1973.

At the hearing, Kass testified that about 14,000 were present; that Young walked out in the middle of a song; that everyone stood for a long time clapping and yelling, but Young did not return. Counsel for Kass presented three ticket stubs, one of which was Kass's; he proposed $91,000 as the amount of damages, calculated by multiplying 14,000 by the median price of $6.50 (tickets were $7.50, $6.50 and $5.50, but there was no evidence of the number sold of each category); he waived (for the whole class presumably) the parking fee item; by silence, he waived (for the class) punitive damages which had been prayed for, based on alleged malice. Read into the record were newspaper accounts which reported that the "jarring" walkoff, a "rip off," a "temper tantrum" occurred about an hour after the concert started, and reported that Young had said he couldn't go on because of repressive action of the security guards. Although at the hearing nothing was made definite about the subject of proof of membership in the class, there was a suggestion by counsel that refunds would be made to those who had retained ticket stubs.

The judge (not the judge from whose order the present appeals are taken) rendered judgment on June 26, 1974, awarding to plaintiff Kass, on behalf of himself and of all others who purchased tickets for the concert, the sum of $91,000; 40 percent of the recovery was awarded to plaintiff's attorney; the whole amount collected was to be deposited in the attorney's trust account; payment was to be made to those who proved to the satisfaction of *counsel* that they were members of the class (no method of determining the amount to be paid to each is stated; presumably each would be reimbursed his or her actual outlay); the balance unclaimed, after a reasonable time (which was not defined), would be disposed of by the court. There was no provision for notice even by publication.

On October 10, 1974, Young moved to vacate the default and the default judgment. One of the grounds was that the default and the judgment were jurisdictionally defective in that no notice had been given to the alleged class and that no class had been certified. On this ground the vacating order was made and the proposed answer of Young was permitted to be filed. (The answer alleges that Young had substantially completed his performance when he was forced to leave the stage by unnerving disturbance among the audience.)

I. *Vacating of the Default Judgment*

It was proper to set aside the default judgment because of a jurisdictional deficiency, namely, that there had been no certification of the asserted class and no provision for notice to the asserted class. A default judgment which is in excess of jurisdiction may be set aside at any time either by motion or an independent action in equity. (*Sullivan v. Sullivan*, 256 Cal.App.2d 301 [64 Cal.Rptr. 82].) Although, as was said at the outset, a case involving default judgment in a class action has not been found, it is to be inferred from the cases relating to the necessity for certification and for notice in class actions that the procedures which have been decreed to be mandatory establish these procedures as jurisdictional; wherefore, default judgment rendered without compliance with them is subject to vacation. In *Home Sav. & Loan Assn. v. Superior Court*, 42 Cal.App.3d 1006 [117 Cal.Rptr. 485], a peremptory writ of prohibition was issued restraining the trial court from proceeding to trial on the substantive merits of the cause without prior adjudication of the suitability of the lawsuit as a class action, determination of the composition of the class, and appropriate notification to its members. Although the court in that case did not refer to the failure to meet the prescribed procedures as a jurisdictional defect in so many words, nevertheless the facts that it issued a writ which normally at least is employed only to restrain a lower tribunal from exceeding its jurisdiction (*Abelleira v. District Court of Appeal*, 17 Cal.2d 280 [109 P.2d 942, 132 A.L.R. 715]; 5 Witkin, Cal.

Procedure (2d ed. 1971) Extraordinary Writs, § 39, p. 3813), and that the court in *Home Sav. & Loan Assn.* based its decision in part on the constitutional requirement of due process of law (at pp. 1012, 1014) give evidence that the court did not regard the trial court's failure as mere procedural error.

But if *Home Sav. & Loan Assn.* be not authority for the proposition that the mandatory procedures are truly jurisdictional, we do not hesitate to declare them so. The strong language about the necessity of these procedures and the careful explanations of the reasons for that necessity appearing not only in *Home Sav. & Loan Assn.* but also in the *City of San Jose v. Superior Court,* 12 Cal.3d 447 [115 Cal.Rptr. 797, 525 P.2d 701]; *Vasquez v. Superior Court,* 4 Cal.3d 800, 820, 821 [94 Cal.Rptr. 796, 484 P.2d 964, 53 A.L.R.3d 513]; *Blue Chip Stamps v. Superior Court,* 18 Cal.3d 381, 385, 386 [134 Cal.Rptr. 393, 556 P.2d 755], are persuasive of the jurisdictional nature of prejudgment adjudication of the suitability of the action as a class action, determination of the composition, and appropriate notification. The elaborate and scholarly reasoning exhibited in those decisions need not be repeated here, but a few words may be said about the application of the principles established by those authorities to the present case. First, as to the parties: without determination of the proper class and of appropriate notice, the defendant would be subject not only to judgment in the purported class action but also to suits by individuals acting alone or in other asserted classes. (*Home Sav. & Loan Assn. v. Superior Court, supra,* at p. 1012.) To be sure, defendant Young chose not to answer the complaint; but a party in default is not made subject to unlimited effects of his default. Relief may not be given beyond that prayed for (Code Civ. Proc., § 580); damages except when fixed by contract must be proved (Code Civ. Proc., § 585; *Liberty Loan Corp. of North Park* v. *Petersen,* 24 Cal.App.3d 915 [101 Cal.Rptr. 395]); substantial amendment to the pleading after default is not permitted without second service of process (*Leo v. Dunlap,* 260 Cal.App.2d 24 [66 Cal.Rptr. 888]). In a purported class action, the defaulting defendant should be entitled to have the court either on motion of plaintiff's counsel or on its own motion decide the appropriateness of the class action so that if it truly be suitable and if the necessary notice be given to potential plaintiffs, there will be but a single binding judgment against him. As to potential plaintiffs, the prejudgment procedures are so connected with due process as to be jurisdictional. These persons are entitled to the best practical notice under the circumstances, advising them that they may be excluded from the class if they so request and that they will be bound by the judgment, whether favorable or not, if they do not request exclusion. (*Home Sav. & Loan Assn.* v. *Superior Court, supra,* at pp. 1012, 1013; *American Pipe & Construction Co. v. Utah,* 414 U.S. 538, 545-549 [38 L.Ed.2d 713, 722-724, 94 S.Ct. 756].)

Then there is a consideration of damages in this particular case relating to the potential plaintiffs which is rather unique. The representative plaintiff has simply assumed that all 14,000 patrons of the concert were equally damaged and that their damages amounted to the price of the average ticket.[3] It may be that many of the patrons or "fans" of the performer who had entertained them for an hour did not regard themselves cheated or that some may have sympathized with his antagonism toward a number of the security guards. In the absence of notice, the single plaintiff has been able to enlist 14,000 persons, willing or not, and wherever they may be, to join his cause. In *Weaver* v. *Pasadena Tournament of Roses*, 32 Cal.2d 833, 835 [198 P.2d 514], four appellants "'on behalf of themselves and all others similarly situated"' brought an action for damages, seeking $100 for each person (it was estimated there were 1,850) who had been promised that upon standing in line at the box office, he could purchase two tickets to the Rose Bowl. The box office was closed early and tickets were withdrawn from sale and distributed to favored parties. The trial court held that this was not a proper representative action; there was but a large number of individuals, each of whom may or may not have, or care to assert, a claim against defendants. Appellants' complaint, said the court, as we do now, can be regarded as no more than an invitation to such persons as may be interested in joining with them in their action.

Nor are the interests of the litigants the only ones to be considered in the prejudgment determination. The representative plaintiff must show that substantial benefit will result both to the litigants and *to the court*. (*Blue Chip Stamp v. Superior Court, supra*, 18 Cal.3d at p. 385; *City of San Jose* v. *Superior Court, supra*, 12 Cal.3d at pp. 458-460; *Collins* v. *Rocha*, 7 Cal.3d 232, 238 [102 Cal.Rptr. 1, 497 P.2d 225]; *Vasquez v. Superior Court, supra*, 4 Cal.3d at p. 811.) The resources of the judicial system may be called upon by one or more persons, under Code of Civil Procedure, section 382, when the parties are numerous and it is impracticable to bring them all before the court, for the *benefit of all*.

Plaintiff-appellant contends that, although ordinarily class action issues should be resolved before trial, the defendant has admitted the allegations relating to class by failing to answer. In support of this proposition, plaintiff cites *Hypolite v. Carleson, supra*, 52 Cal.App.3d 566. *Hypolite* was described by its author as "not a typical case." (At p. 582.) The defendant expressly admitted the pertinent class action allegations in his answer. (At p. 583.) Although the class action issues of the case were not decided until after trial, appeal, reversal and remand, the facts were such that by reason of uncomplicated identification of the parties from existing records, the class action issues were as readily resolved as they could have been at the earlier and proper time. (At p. 582.) Plaintiff-appellant also argues that notice to the class was provided by the judgment itself by the mandate "that any unclaimed monies remaining in the trust account of counsel is to be disposed of by proper application to this Court for further orders." This is by no means provision for notice. Besides, there was no certification of the class. Certification is essential and in this case it is completely lacking.

Finally, there is the matter of necessary showing that the jurisdictional amount required for suit in the superior court be made (*Home Sav. & Loan Assn.* v. *Superior Court, supra,* at p. 1014) if the action be not sustained in its representative grade.

The order setting aside the default judgment must be affirmed.

II. *Vacating the Default*

Plaintiff-appellant contends that it was error to set aside the default, which is a ministerial act, simply because this is a class action and that the plaintiff asserting his representative status need not give the defaulting defendant additional time to answer by withholding default until a class is ascertained. Defendant-appellant Young contends that the default as to the class was properly vacated but it was error to allow the default to stand as to the individual plaintiff because there can be but one judgment, and that if plaintiff were to proceed as an individual, his claim would fall within the jurisdiction of the municipal court. We agree with plaintiff-appellant that the default should not have been set aside at all. Although service of summons was the subject of controversy, the judge, after hearing the motion to vacate, concluded that defendant had flouted the process of the court. (There was evidence that Young tore up the summons and complaint.) The default, in our opinion, is an indivisible thing. The defendant has chosen not to reply. To set the default aside would, as plaintiff-appellant says, give to the defendant time in addition to that specified in the summons. Courts, out of respect to their own dignity, cannot permit parties to choose, without peril to themselves, to ignore the court's own process. It has been held that an action which is described in the pleadings as a class action remains such an action unless and until the court decides that it is one which is unsuitable for prosecution as a class action. (*Kahan v. Rosensteil,* 424 F.2d 161, 169; *Gaddis v. Wyman,* 304 F.Supp. 713, 715.)

Ordinarily, if a default were allowed to remain, the vacating of a default judgment would be meaningless, because the plaintiff would be entitled at once to a renewed judgment. (*Cumberpatch v. Nolan,* 125 Cal.App.2d 205 [270 P.2d 540, 271 P.2d 519].) But in the case of an asserted class action, there still must be decided, following default, as a jurisdictional matter, the suitability of the lawsuit as a class action as set forth under heading I. This is so because the rights of other persons, potential plaintiffs, must be canvassed, which is not so in the ordinary action; because the defendant, although deprived of his right to respond on the merits to the cause of action as stated in the complaint, is entitled to protection against two or more judgments of which but one would be rendered in the instant case; and because the courts must, for the benefit of all litigants, protect themselves from the unnecessary multiplication of lawsuits on the one hand and from being used almost purposelessly save for the compensation of counsel. The order vacating the default is reversed. The default will remain. The order allowing the filing of the purported answer by defendant is reversed.

III. *Further Proceedings*

So far as the individual plaintiff is concerned, his case may proceed following determination of the propriety of the class action. Perhaps it will have to be removed to the municipal court. If the cause proceeds as a class action, there will, of course, be but one judgment.

As was said at the outset, case law on the subject of defaults in class actions seems to be nonexistent. In our opinion, the defendant has lost his rights to defend on the merits of the action if the condition for class action be fulfilled. But the trial court, by reason of its authorities cited under heading I, must decide upon the suitability of the cause as a class action: whether it is manageable as such, whether the true purpose of a class action will be served, who the members of the class shall be, and if a class be certified, what notice shall be given. To be sure, in making inquiry into these matters, the court's scrutiny necessarily will come close into taking into account the merits of the case itself. But the court will observe a distinction, narrow though it may be, between the two subjects. The court will be concerned with such questions as: potential recovery to the individuals making up the asserted class; whether this recovery would be small in comparison with the time and expense consumed in distribution (*Blue Chip Stamp* v. *Superior Court, supra,* 18 Cal.3d at p. 386); whether the court's resources would really be employed for the benefit of the 14,000 or mainly for the class action attorney (at p. 386; *City of San Jose v. Superior Court, supra,* 12 Cal.3d at p. 462); whether the action would have a beneficial deterrent effect; what likelihood there is that individual patrons would be able to prove or would care to assert their participation at the concert and any resulting damages. These and other questions the court must answer in order to decide whether the lawsuit is to proceed as a class action.

The order vacating the default judgment is affirmed. The order setting aside the default and permitting the filing of defendant's answer is reversed. The cause is remanded for further proceedings in accordance with the views expressed herein. Costs on appeal to be borne one-half by each party.

Scott, Acting P. J., and Good, J., concurred.

QUESTIONS AND DISCUSSION

1. The term "occupation of procuring employment," Labor Code §1700.4, is not unconstitutionally vague. Of course, it was devised to create some flexibility within section §1700.4 and is a part of the Talent Agencies Act, Labor Code §§1700 et seq. This definitional looseness is a part of the "handshake" culture. Is it a good thing? See, Wachs v. Curry, 13 Cal.App.4th 616, 16 Cal.Rptr.2d 496 (1993).

2. An artist's manager must advise, counsel, and direct artists in their career development. They also attempt to procure employment.

3. Artist managers, (Labor Code §§1700-1700.46), whether licensed or not, are bound and regulated by the decision in Buchwald v. Superior Court, 254 Cal. App.2d 347, 62 Cal.Rptr. 364 (1967), which states that the Act is remedial in nature and was designed to correct longstanding abuses. Therefore, it should be read in a way that is proactive. Should it be read that way?

4. The doctrine of severability of contracts allows a manager the possibility of recovering an unpaid TV series commission, because the actress did not prove that the procurement of the gig was due to any alleged illegality on the part of the unlicensed agent. Should the fact that he was unlicensed be a sort of strict liability?

5. Under the arbitration provision, a lawyer vests exclusive original jurisdiction in the Labor Commissioner. See Ferrer v. Preston, 145 Cal.App.4th 440, 51 Cal.Rptr.3d 628 (2006), rev'd on other grounds, (2008). In Ferrer, there was a dispute over fees for a contract involving a TV judge. So, the Labor Commissioner trumps arbitration, which is somewhat unusual, isn't it? There was also the question of whether a lawyer was a talent agent. Is this a problem for the State Bar?

CHAPTER 4
THE MOVIE BUSINESS

In Desny v. Wilder, 46 Cal.2d 715, 299 P.2d 257 (Cal. 1956), an idea pitched to producers that allegedly led to a copyrighted film was discussed. Merely disclosing an idea is not actionable under copyright laws; neither common law nor statutory copyright extends protection to an idea as such. There must be something more. Moreover, a contract implied in fact requires a meeting of the minds. Here, it was the idea of a photoplay. "Generally speaking, ideas are as free as the air and as speech and the senses, and as potent or weak, interesting or drab as experiences, philosophies, vocabularies, and other variables of speaker and listener may combine to produce, to portray, or to comprehend. But there can be circumstances when neither air nor ideas may be acquired without cost." 299 P.2d 257, 264.

Another question is who prepared the contract because it will be construed against the preparer if there are ambiguities. The question of credit is always important.

In Zorich v. Petroff, 152 Cal.App.2d 806, 313 P.2d 118 (2d Dist., 1957), the associate producer did not receive screen credit, but he suffered no damage because the film was a failure.

In Welch v. Metro-Golden-Mayer Film Co., 254 Cal.Rptr. 645 (Cal.App.2d 1988), Raquel Welch was fired from the starring role in the movie *Cannery Row*. Defendant claimed she was in substantial breach of contract because she failed to report to the studio for makeup. Is that just an excuse? Jury found for Welch on the counts of breach of contract, conspiracy to induce breach of contract, slander, and breach of the implied covenant of good faith and fair dealing (bad faith). She received $2 million in compensating damages and over $8 million in punitive damages.

In Blaustein v. Burton, 9 Cal.App.3d 161, 88 Cal.Rptr. 319 (2d Dist. 1970), a motion picture producer sued to recover from movie stars. It was an informal contract, an implied-in-fact "Hollywood Handshake" contract. The functions of a producer of a motion picture company vary. He or she is the point guard. He is responsible for generating enthusiasm, searching for ideal locations, controlling the budget, seeking foreign government arrangements, supervising the script, editing, and publicity, as well as engaging the interests of stars and securing the services of the right director. Here, there was an idea to film a version of Shakespeare's "Taming of the Shrew" with Elizabeth Taylor and Richard Burton but the "idea man" received no screen or advertising credit. Plaintiff Julian Blaustein was an experienced producer of such films as the *Day the Earth Stood Still* (the original) ("Klaatu verada nicto"). But this idea is hardly unique; nor is it property. Abstract ideas must be obtained with an express promise to pay. But was there an implied-in-fact contract?

Judgment was for the plaintiff since there were triable issues as to whether his idea was made in confidence, and that the movie would not be made without his consent. Hollywood contracts seem to be an endless string of meetings. ("He does good meetings.") Blaustein's idea was implied by an implied contract, mostly because all of the parties were reputable Hollywood insiders.

DESNEY v. WILDER
Supreme Court of California
June 28, 1956
I.A. No. 23892
46 Cal.2d 715,
299 P.2d 257

SCHAUER, J.

Plaintiff appeals from a summary judgment rendered against him in this action to recover the reasonable value of a literary composition, or of an idea for a photoplay, a synopsis of which composition, embodying the idea, he asserts he submitted to defendants for sale, and which synopsis and idea, plaintiff alleges, were accepted and used by defendants in producing a photoplay.

The case as presented to us is perplexed by manifold problems, some of which appear only upon a composite view of the pleadings, the evidence, and the briefs on appeal. Among the questions are these: Is the plaintiff seeking to recover for (a) the conveyance of an abstract idea or (b) the sale of a literary property? Or (c) is he clutching at both theories? (d) Does plaintiff's evidence tend to show an express or implied contract or (e) facts from which the law might impose a so-called quasi-contractual obligation, as to either the idea or the synopsis? The ultimate question is (f), Does the record permit the conclusion that there is no triable issue of material fact pertinent to any tenable theory available to plaintiff?

To answer the above listed questions with any substantial degree of confidence requires statement of the factual substance of the record, explanation of the nature of the judgment appealed from and the rules governing our consideration of it, together also with some discussion of the law of ideas, the law of literary property, and the law of contracts as it relates to transactions concerning ideas and literary property, with definitive recognition of the somewhat differing situations to which, as descriptive of the "contract" or obligation, some authorities apply the terms "express," "inferred," "implied in fact," "implied-in-law" or "quasi- contractual," and the significance of the subjective and objective tests in determining contractual existence under the several possibly pertinent theories.

After threading the maze, we have concluded, for reasons hereinafter stated, that the summary judgment in favor of defendants was erroneously granted and should be reversed.

The Pleadings. The complaint alleges (Count I) that "Plaintiff conceived, originated and completed a certain untitled literary and dramatic composition (hereinafter called 'Plaintiff's Property') based upon the life of Floyd Collins. Plaintiff has, at all times ... been, and now is, the sole ... owner of Plaintiff's Property, ... Plaintiff submitted Plaintiff's Property to the Defendants ... In making said submission, Plaintiff stated ... that it was made for the purpose of sale of Plaintiff's Property to Defendants to be used ... only if Defendants paid to Plaintiff the reasonable value thereof. Defendants accepted submission of Plaintiff's Property ... [Shortly after accepting submission of plaintiff's property defendants] commenced the preparation of and ... actually photographed a motion picture photoplay entitled 'Ace In The Hole,' [and have exhibited the same] ... At all times [concerned] ... the Defendants knew ... that the Plaintiff expected them to pay him the reasonable value of Plaintiff's Property if used by them. With such knowledge ... the Defendants did copy and use Plaintiff's Property in and in connection with said motion picture photoplay." That the reasonable value of plaintiff's property at the time of use was $150,000, "no part ... of which has been paid." We do not consider Counts II and III, as plaintiff concedes that as to them the judgment should be affirmed.

The material allegations of the complaint were denied by defendants in their answer. Thereafter defendants filed notice of motion for summary judgment. The motion was heard upon affidavits filed by defendants and upon plaintiff's deposition, which is treated as an affidavit in opposition to the motion. The judgment entered upon the granting of such motion is the subject of this appeal.

Inasmuch as the contentions of the parties are largely related, directly or indirectly, to the significance and sufficiency of the evidence, and as all evidential contentions must be resolved in the light of the rules governing summary judgment proceedings it is desirable, before undertaking discussion of the principal problems, to indicate the pertinent rules concerning summary judgments.

The Law of Summary Judgments. Motions for summary judgment are provided for in section 437c of the Code of Civil Procedure. The principles to be observed in proceeding under that section are stated as follows in *Eagle Oil & Ref. Co. v. Prentice* (1942), 19 Cal.2d 553, 555-556 [122 P.2d 264]: The issue to be determined by the trial court in ruling upon a motion for summary judgment is whether or not the party opposing the motion "has presented any facts which give rise to a triable issue or defense, and not to pass upon or determine the issue itself, that is, the true facts in the case. [Citations.] ... [T]he better rule is that the facts alleged in the affidavits of the party against whom the motion is made must be accepted as true, and that such affidavits to be sufficient need not necessarily be composed wholly of strictly evidentiary factsA summary judgment is proper only if the affidavits in support of the moving party "would be sufficient to sustain judgment in his favor, and ... [his opponent] does not 'by affidavit or affidavits ... show such facts as may be deemed by the judge hearing the motion sufficient to present a triable issue of fact.' [Citations.]" (*Coyne v. Krempels* (1950), 36 Cal.2d 257, 261 [223 P.2d 244].) In other words, the affidavits are to be construed with all intendments in favor of the party opposing the motion-here, plaintiff.

The Facts upon Which the Claim of Contract Is Based. Construed agreeably to the rules above stated, it appears from the present record that defendant Wilder at the times here involved was employed by defendant Paramount Pictures Corporation (sometimes hereinafter referred to as Paramount) either as a writer, producer or director, or a combination of the three. In November, 1949, plaintiff telephoned Wilder's office. Wilder's secretary, who was also employed by Paramount, answered, and plaintiff stated that he wished to see Wilder. At the secretary's insistence that plaintiff explain his purpose, plaintiff "told her about this fantastic unusual story. ... I described to her the story in a few words. ... I told her that it was the life story of Floyd Collins who was trapped and made sensational news for two weeks ... and I told her the plot. ... I described to her the entrapment and the death, in ten minutes, probably. She seemed very much interested and she liked it. ... The main emphasis was the central idea, which was the entrapment, this boy who was trapped in a cave eighty- some feet deep. I also told her the picture had never been made with a cave background before." Plaintiff sought to send Wilder a copy of the story but when the secretary learned of its length of some 65 pages she stated that Wilder would not read it, that he wanted stories in synopsis form, that the story would first be sent to the script department, and "in case they think it is fantastic and wonderful, they will abbreviate it and condense it in about three or four pages, and the producers and directors get to see it." Plaintiff protested that he preferred to do the abbreviating of the story himself, and the secretary suggested that he do so. Two days later plaintiff, after preparing a three or four page outline of the story, telephoned Wilder's office a second time and told the secretary the synopsis was ready. The secretary requested plaintiff to read the synopsis to her over the telephone so that she could take it down in shorthand, and plaintiff did so. During the conversation the secretary told plaintiff that the story seemed interesting and that she liked it. "She said that she would talk it over with Billy Wilder and she would let me know." Plaintiff on his part told the secretary that defendants could use the story only if they paid him "the reasonable value of it ... I made it clear to her that I wrote the story and that I wanted to sell it. ... I naturally mentioned again that this story was my story which has taken me so much effort and research and time, and therefore if anybody used it they will have to pay for it ... She said that if Billy Wilder of Paramount uses the story, 'naturally we will pay you for it.' " Plaintiff did not remember whether in his first telephone conversation with the secretary anything was said concerning his purpose of selling the story to defendants. He did not at any time speak with defendant Wilder. It seems clear, however, that one of the authorized functions of the secretary was to receive and deliver messages to Wilder and hence, as is developed *infra,* that on this record her knowledge would be his knowledge. Plaintiff's only subsequent contact with the secretary was a telephone call to her in July, 1950, to protest the alleged use of his composition and idea in a photoplay produced and exhibited by defendants. The photoplay, as hereinafter shown in some detail, closely parallels both plaintiff's synopsis and the historical material concerning the life and death of Floyd Collins. It also includes a fictional incident which appears in plaintiff's synopsis and which he claims is his creation, presumably in the sense of being both original and novel in its combination with the facts from the public commons or public domain.

The Contentions of the Parties and Amici Curiae. In his opening brief plaintiff states "It is conceded *for purposes of argument* [italics added] that the synopsis submitted by plaintiff to defendants was not sufficiently unique or original to be the basis for recovery under the law of plagiarism or infringement. It is conceded that the plaintiff first obtained the central idea or theme of his story, which involves the entrapment of a man in an underground cave and the national interest promoted by the attempt to rescue him, from the Floyd Collins incident which occurred in the 1920's.

"It is appellant's [plaintiff's] contention, however, that in spite of this, the lower court committed reversible error in granting a summary judgment in this case for the reason that the summary judgment had the effect of denying the plaintiff the right to prove that his idea or synopsis was the subject of a contract wherein the defendants promised to pay him for it if they used it. It is clear that 'ideas,' as such, may still be the subject of a contract in California and may be protected, as such, even though not protectible under the laws of plagiarism."

Plaintiff also asserts that he "is not suing defendants for plagiarizing his idea but is suing defendants because they agreed to pay him the reasonable value of the use of his idea and story synopsis if they used his idea" and that "defendants so used plaintiff's idea and synopsis but refused to pay him as they agreed." But the complaint, as already shown, alleges that "Plaintiff conceived, originated and completed [and offered for sale to and defendants accepted submission of and thereafter used] a certain untitled literary and dramatic composition (hereinafter called 'Plaintiff's Property') based upon the life of Floyd Collins."

If plaintiff is seeking to recover for a mere abstract, unprotectible idea, he must meet certain rules; if he seeks recovery for a literary composition in which he conceivably had a property right, the rules are quite different, as will subsequently be shown.

It may be that plaintiff's concessions and arguments, in the light of the pleadings and evidence, are intended to suggest that there is some nebulous middle area between an abstract idea and a literary composition, wherein the idea has been cast in "concrete" form but not "concrete" enough to constitute a literary property. However, for the purposes of this case at least, we find it unnecessary and undesirable to recognize any such hybrid, although we are aware that the Supreme Court of the United States has spoken of a "quasi property" right in news gathered and disseminated by a news service agency The plaintiff here, we conclude, must stand or fall, and this case will be resolved, on rules applicable to ideas on the one hand or literary property on the other.

This court, of course, is not bound to accept concessions of parties as establishing the law applicable to a case. It is also to be noted that plaintiff's concession is qualified by the words "for purposes of argument." Hence, although plaintiff makes it clear that he is not suing for "plagiarism or infringement," we feel constrained to the view that in the light of the entire record we cannot disregard a possible property right interest in the literary composition *as a subject of contract,* express or implied, which could afford a basis for recovery.

Defendants concede, as they must, that "the act of disclosing an unprotectible idea, if that act is in fact the bargained-for exchange for a promise, may be consideration to support the promise." They then add, "But once the idea is disclosed without the protection of a contract, the law says that anyone is free to use it. Therefore, subsequent use of the idea cannot constitute consideration so as to support a promise to pay for such use." And as to the effect of the evidence defendants argue that plaintiff "disclosed his material before ... [defendants] did or could do anything to indicate their willingness or unwillingness to pay for the disclosure. The act of using the idea, from which appellant attempts to imply a promise to pay, came long after the disclosure ... Accordingly, even if a promise to pay could be found ... it came after the disclosure had been made and is therefore unenforceable." The conclusion of law asserted in the last sentence, insofar as it might be applicable to an express (whether proved by direct or by circumstantial evidence) promise to pay for the service (the conveyance of the idea) previously rendered from which a profit has been derived, for reasons which hereinafter appear *(infra,* pp. 803-804), is not tenable.

Relative to the subject of inferred or implied contractual liability, amici curiae Association of Motion Picture Producers, Inc., National Broadcasting Company, Inc., and Four Star Films, Inc., are concerned with the state of the law. They fear that what they conceive to be quasi contractual situations, wherein the law equitably but fictionally presumes of one the making of a promise which he not only did not make but never intended to make, will be confused with circumstances which evidence actual meeting-of-the-minds but unspoken contracts; i.e., what they appear to consider to be properly termed implied-in-fact contracts. They caution us that in a situation such as this, "One party cannot, by unilateral words or deeds, thrust upon another a contractual relationship unless the latter has, *by his own words or deeds,* consented thereto" and that "In the absence of manifest assent to the same thing upon the same terms *by both parties,* there is no contract." With the first of these cautionary propositions we unqualifiedly agree. Our agreement with the second, as will hereinafter appear, must depend on what it meant by "manifest assent." We do not agree with the further proposition, asserted or implied by defendants and their related amici, that an idea which before conveyance has sufficient value to constitute consideration for a promise to pay its reasonable value necessarily and *ipso facto* upon disclosure becomes devoid of value so that as a matter of law it cannot support a promise then—and only then—made to pay its reasonable value. A promise, made in advance of disclosure, to pay for the act of conveyance or disclosure of an idea which may or may not have value is one thing. A promise, made after conveyance of the idea to the promisor, to pay reasonable value for an idea which does have value to the promisor and which has been conveyed to, and has been used by, him is another contract, the possible enforceability of which is discussed *infra* at pages 803-804.

From what has been indicated above it appears necessary for us in the proper disposition of this case, having in mind the problems which apparently will confront the trial court at a trial on the merits and the duty imposed on us by section 53 of the Code of Civil Procedure, to consider not only (1) the rules for recovery pertaining to the conveyance of ideas, as such, but also (2) the question whether the synopsis of plaintiff's untitled composition could on any view of the evidence be deemed entitled to the status of a literary property, and (3) the rules defining rights of recovery, so far as pertinent on this record, if plaintiff has a literary property in his composition.

The Law Pertaining to Ideas. Generally speaking, ideas are as free as the air and as speech and the senses, and as potent or weak, interesting or drab, as the experiences, philosophies, vocabularies, and other variables of speaker and listener may combine to produce, to portray, or to comprehend. But there can be circumstances when neither air nor ideas may be acquired without cost. The diver who goes deep in the sea, even as the pilot who ascends high in the troposphere, knows full well that for life itself he, or someone on his behalf, must arrange for air (or its respiration-essential element, oxygen) to be specially provided at the time and place of need. The theatrical producer likewise may be dependent for his business life on the procurement of ideas from other persons as well as the dressing up and portrayal of his self-conceptions; he may not find his own sufficient for survival. As counsel for the Writers Guild aptly say, ideas "are not freely usable by the entertainment media until the latter are made aware of them." The producer may think up the idea himself, dress it and portray it; or he may purchase either the conveyance of the idea alone or a manuscript embodying the idea in the author's concept of a literary vehicle giving it form, adaptation and expression. It cannot be doubted that some ideas are of value to a producer.

An idea is usually not regarded as property, because all sentient beings may conceive and evolve ideas throughout the gamut of their powers of cerebration and because our concept of property implies something which may be owned and possessed to the exclusion of all other persons. We quote as an accurate statement of the law in this respect the following language of Mr. Justice Brandeis, dissenting in *International News Service v. Associated Press* (1918), *supra,* 248 U. S. 215, 250 [39 S.Ct. 68, 76, 63 L.Ed. 211, 225]: "An essential element of individual property is the legal right to exclude others from enjoying it. If the property is private, the right of exclusion may be absolute; if the property is affected with a public interest, the right of exclusion is qualified. But the fact that a product of the mind has cost its producer money and labor, and has a value for which others are willing to pay, is not sufficient to ensure to it this legal attribute of property. The general rule of law is, that the noblest of human productions-knowledge, truths ascertained, conceptions, and ideas-become, after voluntary communication to others, free as the air to common use." Of similar import, but stated negatively: "The doctrine that an author has a property right in his ideas and is entitled to demand for them the same protection which the law accords to the proprietor of personal property generally finds no recognition either in the common law or in the statutes of any civilized country." Whether the theory upon which this court sustained recovery in the Golding case may properly be classed as a property rights theory is not clear (see pp. 694-695 of 35 Cal.2d and pp. 831, 836-837 of 40 Cal.2d) but it is clear that California does not now accord individual property type protection to abstract ideas. (*Weitzenkorn v. Lesser* (1953), 40 Cal.2d 778, 788-789 [256 P.2d 947].) This accords with the general weight of authority. "There may be literary property in a particular combination of ideas [and this must presuppose an expression thereof] or in the form in which ideas are embodied. There can be none in the ideas." (*Fendler v. Morosco* (1930), 253 N. Y. 281, 287 [171 N.E. 56, 58].) Neither common law nor statutory copyright extends protection to an idea as such. "[O]nly in the 'expression' of a copyrighted work does any monopoly inhere; the 'theme,' the 'plot,' the 'ideas' may always be freely borrowed." (*Dellar v. Samuel Goldwyn, Inc.* (1945, 2d C.C.A.), 150 F.2d 612.)

The principles above stated do not, however, lead to the conclusion that ideas cannot be a subject of contract. As Mr. Justice Traynor stated in his dissenting opinion in *Stanley v. Columbia Broadcasting System* (1950), *supra,* 35 Cal.2d 653, 674: "The policy that precludes protection of an abstract idea by copyright does not prevent its protection by contract. Even though an idea is not property subject to exclusive ownership, its disclosure may be of substantial benefit to the person to whom it is disclosed. That disclosure may therefore be consideration for a promise to pay ... Even though the idea disclosed may be 'widely known and generally understood' [citation], it may be protected by an express contract providing that it will be paid for regardless of its lack of novelty Amici supporting plaintiff add, "If a studio wishes to have an idea disclosed to it and finds that idea of sufficient value to make use of it, it is difficult to see how any hardship is involved in requiring payment of the reasonable value of the material submitted." The principles enunciated in the above quotation from Justice Traynor's dissent are accepted as the law of California (*Weitzenkorn v. Lesser* (1953), *supra,* 40 Cal.2d 778, 791-792) and we have no quarrel with amici's postulation. This case, however, remains to be resolved.

The lawyer or doctor who applies specialized knowledge to a state of facts and gives advice for a fee is selling and conveying an idea. In doing that he is rendering a service. The lawyer and doctor have no property rights in their ideas, as such, but they do not ordinarily convey them without solicitation by client or patient. Usually the parties will expressly contract for the performance of and payment for such services, but, in the absence of an express contract, when the service is requested and rendered the law does not hesitate to infer or imply a promise to compensate for it. In other words the recovery may be based on contract either express or implied. The person who can and does convey a valuable idea to a producer who commercially solicits the service or who voluntarily accepts it knowing that it is tendered for a price should likewise be entitled to recover. In so holding we do not fail to recognize that free-lance writers are not necessarily members of a learned profession and as such bound to the exalted standards to which doctors and lawyers are dedicated. So too we are not oblivious of the hazards with which producers of the class represented here by defendants and their related amici are confronted through the unsolicited submission of numerous scripts on public domain materials in which public materials the producers through their own initiative may well find nuclei for legitimately developing the "stupendous and colossal." The law, however, is dedicated to the proposition that for every wrong there is a remedy (Civ. Code, § 3523) and for the sake of protecting one party it must not close the forum to the other. It will hear both and seek to judge the cause by standards fair to both. To that end the law of implied contracts assumes particular importance in literary idea and property controversies.

The Law Pertaining to Contracts, Express, Implied-in-Fact and Implied by Law, and Quasi Contractual Obligations, as Related to Ideas and Literary Property. The parties and amici, from their several viewpoints, discuss the law of contracts and caution us not to confuse the rules insofar as such rules may differentiate respectively among contracts which are express or implied-in-fact or implied-in-law, meaning by the latter expression to denote a quasi-contractual oblilation imposed by law. We agree that whether a contract be properly identified as express or as implied-in-fact or inferred from circumstances; or whether the bargain meets the subjective test of a meeting of minds or is held to reside in the objective evidence of words and acts with or without a meeting of minds; or whether the obligation be recognized as implied by law from acts having consensual aspects (and therefore often termed implied-in-fact); or whether the obligation be imposed by law because of acts and intents which, although tortious rather than consensual, should in justice give rise to an obligation resembling that created by contract and, hence, should be termed quasi- contractual, is important here to the extent that we recognize the situations and discriminate appropriately in the governing rules.

An eminent writer says that "The elements requisite for an informal contract ... are identical whether they are expressly stated or implied in fact," citing e. g., *Lombard v. Rahilly* (1914), 127 Minn. 449 [149 N.W. 950], holding "A 'contract implied in fact' requires a meeting of the minds, an agreement, just as much as an 'express contract'; the difference between the two being largely in the character of the evidence by which they are established"; see also *Silva v. Providence Hospital of Oakland* (1939), 14 Cal.2d 762, 773 [97 P.2d 798]. (Williston on Contracts, rev. ed., vol. 1, p. 8.) The same author describes quasi contracts by declaring that "as quasi contractual obligations are imposed by the law for the purpose of bringing about justice without reference to the intention of the parties, the only apparent restriction upon the power of the law to create such obligations is that they must be of such a sort as would have been appropriately enforced under common-law procedure by a contractual action. Indeed even this limitation is too narrow, for a bill in equity or a libel in admiralty might be the appropriate means of enforcing some quasi contractual obligations. As the law may impose any obligations that justice requires, the only limit in the last analysis to the category of quasi contracts is that the obligation in question more closely resembles those created by contract than those created by tort. On the other hand, a true contract cannot exist, however desirable it might be to have one, unless there is a manifestation of assent to the making of a promise. Furthermore, the measure of damages appropriate to contractual obligations differs from that applicable to quasi contracts ... It is also true that quasi contractual obligations are not so universally based on unjust enrichment or benefit as is sometimes supposed.[8] There are many cases where the law enforces in a contractual action a duty to restore the plaintiff to a former status-not merely to surrender the benefit which the defendant has received."

If it were not for precedent we should hesitate to speak of an implied-in-fact contract. In truth, contracts are either made in fact or the obligation is implied in law. If made in fact, contracts may be established by direct evidence or they may be inferred from circumstantial evidence. The only difference is in the method of proof. In either case they would appear to be express contracts. Otherwise, it would seem that they, or the presumed contractual obligation, must be implied at law. A so-called "implied-in-fact" contract, however, as the term is used by some writers, may be found although there has been no meeting of the mindsEven an express contract may be found where there has been no meeting of minds. The classic example of this situation is set up by the parol evidence rule. The law accepts the objective evidence of the written contract as constituting the contract and, subject, of course, to certain exceptions, precludes oral evidence to show that the minds of the parties did not meet in the writing. But that same reason has led us to the further conclusion that there are genuine implied-in-fact contracts of both the meeting-of-the-minds and the no-meeting-of-the-minds varieties."

Whether the resulting "contract" in the cases discussed by the learned professors is classified as express (as may be fictionized by the law's objective test) or as implied-in-fact (as also may be fictionized by the law) or whether in the same or slightly differing circumstances an obligation shall be "implied" and denominated "quasi contractual" because it is strong- armed by the law from nonconsensual acts and intents, is probably important in California-and for the purposes of resolving the problems now before us-principally as an aid to understanding the significance of rulings and discussions in authorities from other jurisdictions. Here, our terminology and the situations for application of the pertinent rules are simplified by codification.

Our Civil Code declares that (§ 1619) "A contract is either express or implied"; (§ 1620) "An express contract is one, the terms of which are stated in words" and (§ 1621) "An implied contract is one, the existence and terms of which are manifested by conduct." The same code further provides that (§ 1584) "[T]he acceptance of the consideration offered with a proposal, is an acceptance of the proposal"; (§ 1589) "A voluntary acceptance of the benefit of a transaction is equivalent to a consent to all the obligations arising from it, so far as the facts are known, or ought to be known, to the persons accepting"; (§ 1605) "Any benefit conferred ... upon the promisor, by any other person, to which the promisor is not lawfully entitled ... is a good consideration for a promise"; and (§ 1606) "[A] moral obligation originating in some benefit conferred upon the promisor ... is also a good consideration for a promise, to an extent corresponding with the extent of the obligation, but no further or otherwise."

From what has been shown respecting the law of ideas and of contracts we conclude that conveyance of an idea can constitute valuable consideration and can be bargained for before it is disclosed to the proposed purchaser, but once it is conveyed, i. e., disclosed to him and he has grasped it, it is henceforth his own and he may work with it and use it as he sees fit. In the field of entertainment the producer may properly and validly agree that he will pay for the service of conveying to him ideas which are valuable and which he can put to profitable use. Furthermore, where an idea has been conveyed with the expectation by the purveyor that compensation will be paid if the idea is used, there is no reason why the producer who has been the beneficiary of the conveyance of such an idea, and who finds it valuable and is profiting by it, may not then for the first time, although he is not at that time under any legal obligation so to do, promise to pay a reasonable compensation for that idea—that is, for the past service of furnishing it to him—and thus create a valid obligation. As said in 12 American Jurisprudence 603, section 110, "there is considerable authority which supports the view that the moral obligation arising from a benefit of a material or pecuniary kind conferred upon the promisor by past services, rendered in the expectation that they were to be paid for-or, at least, if rendered upon the assumption by the person rendering them, though mistaken, that they would create a real liability-and, otherwise, in circumstances creating a moral obligation on the part of the promisor to pay for the same, will support an executory promise to do so, although there was, previous to such promise, no legal liability or promise, perfect or imperfect." *Credit Bureau of San Diego v. Johnson* (1943), 61 Cal.App.2d Supp. 834, 839 But, assuming legality of consideration, the idea purveyor cannot prevail in an action to recover compensation for an abstract idea unless (a) before or after disclosure he has obtained an express promise to pay, or (b) the circumstances preceding and attending disclosure, together with the conduct of the offeree acting with knowledge of the circumstances, show a promise of the type usually referred to as "implied" or "implied-in-fact." That is, if the idea purveyor has clearly conditioned his offer to convey the idea upon an obligation to pay for it if it is used by the offeree and the offeree, knowing the condition before he knows the idea, voluntarily accepts its disclosure (necessarily on the specified basis) and finds it valuable and uses it, the law will either apply the objective test (discussed, *supra,* pp. 801-802) and hold that the parties have made an express (sometimes called implied-in-fact) contract, or under those circumstances, as some writers view it, the law itself, to prevent fraud and unjust enrichment, will imply a promise to compensate.

Such inferred or implied promise, if it is to be found at all, must be based on circumstances which were known to the producer at and preceding the time of disclosure of the idea to him and he must voluntarily accept the disclosure, knowing the conditions on which it is tendered... The idea man who blurts out his idea without having first made his bargain has no one but himself to blame for the loss of his bargaining power. The law will not in any event, from demands stated subsequent to the unconditioned disclosure of an abstract idea, imply a promise to pay for the idea, for its use, or for its previous disclosure. The law will not imply a promise to pay for an idea from the mere facts that the idea has been conveyed, is valuable, and has been used for profit; this is true even though the conveyance has been made with the hope or expectation that some obligation will ensue. So, if the plaintiff here is claiming only for the conveyance of the idea of making a dramatic production out of the life of Floyd Collins he must fail unless in conformity with the above stated rules he can establish a contract to pay.

From plaintiff's testimony, as epitomized above (pp. 791-793), it does not appear that a contract to pay for conveyance of the abstract photoplay idea had been made, or that the basis for inferring such a contract from subsequent related acts of the defendants had been established, at the time plaintiff disclosed his basic idea to the secretary. Defendants, consequently, were at that time and from then on free to use the abstract idea if they saw fit to engage in the necessary research and develop it to the point of a usable script. Whether defendants did that, or whether they actually accepted and used plaintiff's synopsis, is another question. And whether by accepting plaintiff's synopsis and using it, if they did accept and use it, they may be found to have implicitly-by the rules discussed *supra,* pages 798-802-agreed to pay for whatever value the synopsis possessed as a composition embodying, adapting and implementing the idea, is also a question which, upon the present summary judgment record, is pertinent for consideration in reaching our ultimate conclusion. That is, if the evidence suggests that defendants accepted plaintiff's synopsis, did they not necessarily accept it upon the terms on which he had offered it? Certainly the mere fact that the idea had been disclosed under the circumstances shown here would not preclude the finding of an implied (inferred in fact) contract to pay for the synopsis embodying, implementing and adapting the idea for photoplay production.

The Law Pertaining to Literary Property. "Literary property" is a general term which is used either to describe the interest of an author (or those who claim under him) in his works (whether before or after publication or before or after copyright has been secured) or to denote the corporeal property in which an intellectual production is embodied. (Bouvier's Law Dict. (1940), p. 731; 34 Am.Jur. 400, § 2; 18 C.J.S. 139, § 3.) Literary property in an intellectual production is afforded protection by the common law....

The basic distinction between the rights in and to literary productions as they may exist at common law and as they are granted by statutory copyright is that the common law protects only a property right while the copyright statute grants a limited monopolistic privilege. (34 Am.Jur. 401, § 2.) Plaintiff here has no statutory copyright. His claim as to the synopsis, therefore, necessarily must rest in a common law property right or in contract. He has chosen to rest it in contract. If plaintiff has a literary composition it may be the subject of a property right and its use by defendants, if established, could entitle him to remedies, notwithstanding the concessions he has made, which would be unavailable if he had only an idea to be appropriated or to be the subject of contract.

Literary property which is protectible may be created out of unprotectible material such as historical events. It has been said (and does not appear to have been successfully challenged) that "There are only thirty-six fundamental dramatic situations, various facets of which form the basis of all human drama." (Georges Polti, "The Thirty-Six Dramatic Situations"; see also Henry Albert Phillips. "The Universal Plot Catalog"; Eric Heath, "Story Plotting Simplified.") It is manifest that authors must work with and from ideas or themes which basically are in the public domain. History both in broadly significant and in very personal aspects has furnished a wealth of material for photoplays. The Crusades, The French Revolution, The War Between the States, the lives, or events from the lives, of rulers, ministers, doctors, lawyers, politicians, and military men, among others, all have contributed. Events from the life of the late General William Mitchell are even now the basic theme of a current showing. Events from the life of Floyd Collins were avowedly the basic theme of plaintiff's story. Certainly, it must be recognized that a literary composition does not depend upon novelty of plot or theme for the status of "property," if it is entitled to that status at all. The terms "originality" and "novelty" have often been confused, or used without differentiation, or with meanings which vary with different authorities. We therefore suggest the sense in which we use them. A literary composition may be original at least in a subjective sense, without being novel. To be original it must be a creation or construction of the author, not a mere copy of another's work. The author, of course, must almost inevitably work from old materials, from known themes or plots or historical events, because, except as knowledge unfolds and history takes place, there is nothing new with which to work. But "Creation, in its technical sense, is not essential to vest one with ownership of rights in intellectual property. Thus, a compiler who merely gathers and arranges, in some concrete form, materials which are open and accessible to all who have the mind to work with like diligence is as much the owner of the result of his labors as if his work were a creation rather than a construction."...

Writing - portraying characters and events and emotions with words, no less than with brush and oils-may be an art which expresses personality. Accordingly, the language of Mr. Justice Holmes, speaking for the Supreme Court in a copyright case relating to circus posters is apropos: "Others are free to copy the original. They are not free to copy the copy ... The copy is the personal reaction of an individual upon nature. Personality always contains something unique. It expresses singularity even in handwriting, and a very modest grade of art has in it something irreducible, which is one man's alone. That something he may copyright unless there is a restriction in the words of the act." (*Bleistein v. Donaldson Lithographing Co.* (1903), 188 U.S. 239, 249-250 [23 S.Ct. 298, 47 L.Ed. 460].) As indicated, the theme of a writer must almost inevitably be neither novel nor original. The finished work probably will not be novel because it deals only with the public domain or public commons facts. But the completed composition may well be the original product of the researcher who compiles or constructs it. He gives it genesis, and genesis in this sense requires only origin of the composition, not of the theme. The composition will be the property of the author. Whether it possesses substantial value, and to what extent, if any, it may be entitled to copyright protectibility, may be quite another matter.

The time of the author; his resourcefulness in, opportunity for and extent of, research; his penetration in perception and interpretation of source materials; the acumen of his axiological appraisals of the dramatic; and his skill and style of composition, including the art of so portraying accurate narration of events long past as to arouse vivid emotions of the present, are all elements which may contribute to the value of his product. Some of those elements in varying quanta and proportions must exist in any literary composition; thereby the composition reflects the personality of the author. And any literary composition, conceivably, may possess value in someone's estimation and be the subject of contract, or, conversely, it may be considered totally devoid of artistic, historic, scientific or any practical value. Obviously the defendants here used someone's script in preparing and producing their photoplay. That script must have had value to them. As will be hereinafter shown, it closely resembles plaintiff's synopsis. Ergo, plaintiff's synopsis appears to be a valuable literary composition. Defendants had an unassailable right to have their own employes conduct the research into the Floyd Collins tragedy-an historical event in the public domain-and prepare a story based on those facts and to translate it into a script for the play. But equally unassailable (assuming the verity of the facts which plaintiff asserts) is plaintiff's position that defendants had no right-except by purchase on the terms he offered-to acquire and use the synopsis prepared by him.

The proposition which seems to be implicit in some of the contentions of defendants and their related amici-that a producer, to whom a literary composition or idea is offered for sale for its reasonable value if used, may state that he will not agree to purchase the proffered literary composition, or idea for one, until he knows what the composition or idea is, may then, when it is submitted to him on those terms, consider it and say, in words or by his acts, "Yes, it is indeed valuable and I shall use it but I will not pay you for it because now I have it"-does not commend itself to us. If a producer is not commercially soliciting, and is not willing to accept an obligation to pay for, valuable ideas, or for compositions adapting and implementing them, which ideas and compositions are offered to be conveyed only upon the assumption of such an obligation, he does not need to read manuscripts which he knows are submitted on those terms, or to have his secretary take dictated synopses of stories offered on those conditions, and then use them. (See *Elfenbein v. Luckenbach Terminals,* (1933), *supra,* 111 N.J.L. 67 [166 A. 91, 93]; *cf. Matarese v. Moore-McCormick Lines* (1946, C.C.A. 2d), *supra,* 158 F.2d 631, 634.) We are satisfied that, for the purposes of this appeal, plaintiff's dictation to defendant Wilder's secretary of the synopsis of his composition, embodying the core of his idea and his concept of a desirable entertainment media adaptation of it, is equivalent to submission of the synopsis in typed form.

Under the principles of law which have been stated it appears that for plaintiff to prevail on this appeal the record must indicate either that the evidence favors plaintiff, or that there is a triable issue of fact, in respect to the following questions: Did plaintiff prepare a literary composition on the Floyd Collins tragedy? Did he submit the composition to the defendants for sale? Did the defendants, knowing that it was offered to them for sale, accept and use that composition or any part thereof? If so, what was the reasonable value of the composition?

It is not essential to recovery that plaintiff's story or synopsis possess the elements of copyright protectibility if the fact of consensual contract be found. (*Weitzenkorn v. Lesser* (1953), *supra,* 40 Cal.2d 778, 791-792.) Neither can we hold, on the state of the record, that plaintiff's synopsis is devoid of the elements necessary to give it some measure of such protectibility. While the trial court, or an appellate court on a sufficient record, may determine the specific extent of an author's property right in any particular work (*Nichols v. Universal Pictures Corp.* (1930, C.C.A.2d), 45 F.2d 119, 121-122) it is unnecessary on this appeal to define the limits more exactly than has already been done, *supra,* pages 806-808 (see also *infra,* pp. 814-815).

The Law Applied to the Facts. Here, as conceded by defendants for purposes of their summary judgment motion, plaintiff, in accordance with his testimony, submitted his synopsis to them through defendant Wilder's secretary and such submission included a declaration by both plaintiff and the secretary that defendants were to pay for his story if they used it. The mere fact that at the time of plaintiff's first telephone call to Wilder's office he described the central idea of the story to the secretary in response to her insistence that he explain the purpose of his call would not as a matter of law deprive plaintiff of the right to payment for the story as discussed by him and the secretary when he again spoke with her two days later and at her request read his synopsis to her, for her to take down in shorthand for defendants' consideration; the two conversations appear to have been parts of a single transaction and must be construed as such. The affidavits submitted on behalf of defendants by Wilder and by an officer of Paramount to the effect that neither Wilder nor Wilder's secretary had authority to negotiate contracts for the purchase of scripts do not compel the conclusion as a matter of law that an implied (inferred) contract binding defendants to pay for plaintiff's story was not created if (as is hereinafter shown) the record discloses any substantial evidence indicating that defendants did accept and make use of plaintiff's composition.

Factually it would be inconsistent, and legally it would be untenable, for the defendant corporations to deny that Paramount's employes, Wilder and the secretary, had authority to negotiate contracts for the purchase of literary material and at the same time to permit them to act as agents for the procurement of material offered for sale, and to use the material so acquired while disavowing the authority of the agents. Certainly if the secretary had accepted from plaintiff any other item of merchandise, such, for example, as office supplies, which plaintiff left with her with the statement that he was offering them for sale and that if used by defendants plaintiff expected to be paid therefor, defendants' subsequent use of such property would be held to give rise to an inferred or so-called implied-in-fact promise on their part to make payment. As hereinabove shown (*supra,* p. 802), Civil Code, section 1589, provides: "A voluntary acceptance of the benefit of a transaction is equivalent to a consent to all the obligations arising from it, so far as the facts are known, or ought to be known, to the person accepting." If the secretary had authority to receive and transmit messages to her employer-such as messages offering to sell a story embodying a writer's idea for a photoplay-and to take down in shorthand for transmission to her employer the script of a synopsis, she also necessarily had authority to receive and transmit the conditions and terms of the offer. Her knowledge of those terms and conditions is the knowledge of her employers "He who takes the benefit must bear the burden.") On this issue the evidence would support a finding that plaintiff's synopsis reached defendants through the secretary, and that they are chargeable with knowledge of the conditions on which the synopsis was offered.

With respect to whether defendants used plaintiff's composition, it may be first noted that defendants presented no affidavits in any way denying such use, but merely exhibited their photoplay to the court for purposes of comparison between plaintiff's synopsis and defendants' production. Defendants also produced extracts from a magazine and newspaper to which plaintiff had already freely testified in his deposition that he had referred in preparing his story. A script of the photoplay was, however, attached to plaintiff's complaint as an exhibit, and plaintiff has provided an outline comparing his synopsis with defendants' scenario. Defendants in their brief have likewise outlined the story of their photoplay.

In defendants' motion picture script the trapped man expresses a fear of the curse of dead Indians, as did Collins in the fictional portion of plaintiff's synopsis...

For the purposes of appellate review of this summary judgment proceeding it is apparent from the comparisons above tabulated, and from the outlines which are set out in the margin, that a factual issue, rather than one of law, is presented as to whether defendants used plaintiff's synopsis or developed their production independently thereof. Particularly does this appear true in view of the fact that plaintiff submitted his synopsis to defendants in November, 1949, and that as early as July, 1950, the latter were producing their photoplay which, despite their assertion that it "does not purport to be a biography of the life of Floyd Collins ... Its characters, plot and development are wholly imaginative," obviously does bear a remarkable similarity to plaintiff's story both in respect to the historical data and the fictional material originated by plaintiff.

It has been suggested that this court view the photoplay (which defendants in their brief offer to make available) in order to determine whether a triable issue of fact exists. The scope of the implications in that suggestion is persuasive to us that the issues here are not for summary disposition. In the light of the conclusions we have reached on the evidence already discussed it appears that viewing the photoplay would relate merely to the weight of the evidence. (See *Kurlan v. Columbia Broadcasting System* (1953), *supra,* 40 Cal.2d 799, 806-807.) We therefore find it unnecessary to view the film.

At the trial the trier of fact should proceed with nicety of discrimination in applying the evidence to resolve the issues. Inasmuch as plaintiff's story is taken from the public domain, and as both his story and that of defendants are in principal substance historically accurate, it must be borne in mind that the mere facts that plaintiff submitted and offered to sell to defendants a synopsis containing public domain material and that thereafter defendants used the same public domain material, will not support an inference that defendants promised to pay for either the synopsis or for the idea of using the public domain material. The plaintiff can have no property right in the public domain facts concerning Floyd Collins or in the abstract idea of making a photoplay dramatizing those facts. On the other hand, the fact that plaintiff used the public domain material in constructing his story and synopsis would afford no justification whatsoever for defendants to appropriate plaintiff's composition and use it or any part of it in the production of a photoplay—and this, of course, includes the writing of a scenario for it—without compensating plaintiff for the value of his story. And the further fact, if it be a fact, that the basic idea for the photoplay had been conveyed to defendants before they saw plaintiff's synopsis, would not preclude the finding of an implied (inferred-in-fact) contract to pay for the manuscript, including its implemented idea, if they used such manuscript.

The Complaint; Failure of Proof, or Variance; Amendment. Defendants urge in support of the summary judgment that although in plaintiff's amended complaint he alleges a contract by defendants to pay him if they used his entire 65-page story based upon the life of Floyd Collins, plaintiff's testimony is that such story was actually never submitted to defendants, but rather only the synopsis thereof, and that therefore there was a complete failure of proof. Plaintiff, following entry of the summary judgment, moved the court for an order setting aside the judgment and permitting plaintiff to file an amendment to his amended complaint, alleging submission of the synopsis instead of the 65-page story. The motion was denied and defendants argue that the amendment would have substituted a different cause of action after the statute of limitations had run. This contention is without merit.

Section 469 of the Code of Civil Procedure provides that "No variance between the allegation in a pleading and the proof is to be deemed material, unless it has actually misled the adverse party to his prejudice in maintaining his action or defense upon the merits. Whenever it appears that a party has been so misled, the court may order the pleading to be amended upon such terms as may be just." Section 470 states that "Where the variance is not material, as provided in the last section, the court may direct the fact to be found according to the evidence, or may order an immediate amendment, without costs." Section 471: "Where, however, the allegation of the claim or defense to which the proof is directed, is unproved, not in some particular or particulars only, but in its general scope and meaning, it is not to be deemed a case of variance, within the last two sections, but a failure of proof."

The variance between plaintiff's pleading and proof in the present case obviously did not mislead defendants, since when making their motion for summary judgment they relied upon his testimony that he had submitted his synopsis to them, rather than the entire 65-page story. Further, such a variance clearly did not constitute a complete failure of proof of the general scope and meaning of plaintiff's claim, but merely a showing that his story was submitted in shorter form than that alleged in the complaint.

Great liberality is indulged in matters of amendment to the end that lawsuits may be determined upon their merits. (See *Klopstock v. Superior Court* (1941), 17 Cal.2d 13, 19-20 [108 P.2d 906, 135 A.L.R. 318], and cases there cited.) In the Klopstock case it was declared that "In determining whether a wholly different cause of action is introduced by the amendment technical considerations or ancient formulae are not controlling; nothing more is meant than that the defendant not be required to answer a wholly different legal liability or obligation from that originally stated. As the court says in ... [*Frost v. Witter* (1901), 132 Cal. 421, 426 (64 P. 705, 84 Am.St.Rep. 53)], for the purpose of determining whether amendment is possible, the 'cause of action' referred to as furnishing the test means only the legal obligation which it is sought to enforce against the defendant. Other courts have used almost identical language; the test is not whether under technical rules of pleading a new cause of action is introduced, but rather, the test is whether an attempt is made to state facts which give rise to a wholly distinct and different legal obligation against the defendant. The power to permit amendment is denied only if a change is made in the liability sought to be enforced against the defendant. [Citation.]"

In the present case it is obvious that the proposed amendment would not constitute an attempt to state facts which would give rise to a wholly distinct and different legal obligation against defendants, but would only make the pleading conform to the plaintiff's testimony as to the manner in which his story was submitted to defendants. It is for defendants' claimed use of the same story as that already alleged that plaintiff still would be seeking recovery under the proposed amendment. Such amendment should have been allowed.

Plaintiff has also attempted to appeal from an order denying his motion to set aside the summary judgment and to permit him to file an amendment to his amended complaint. Such order is not appealable, and the attempted appeal therefrom will be dismissed.

The attempted appeal from the order denying plaintiff's motion to set aside the summary judgment and to permit him to file the amendment to his amended complaint is dismissed. The judgment is affirmed as to the second and third counts of the complaint, but as to the first count it is reversed and the cause is remanded for further proceedings not inconsistent with the views expressed in this opinion.

GIBSON, C. J., SHENK, J., TRAYNOR, J., SPENCE, J., and MCCOMB, J., concurred.

CARTER, J.

LAKE v. UNIVERSAL PICTURES CO.
United States District Court for the Southern District of California, Central Division
December 29, 1950
95 F.Supp. 768

WESTOVER, District Judge.

Plaintiff herein wrote a story, entitled 'Winchester, 73', and sold the story to the defendants. He entered into a written contract with defendants by which he assigned to them his rights in said story. The contract, in part, was contained in a letter written by Universal Pictures Company, Inc. to the plaintiff, which letter is as follows:

Los Angeles, California February 14, 1946
'Mr. Stuart N. Lake
% Paul Kohner, Inc.
9169 Sunset Boulevard
Los Angeles 46, California

'Dear Mr. Lake:

'Your signature in the space below will confirm the following agreement made between us this date:

'Concurrently herewith you have delivered to us the following:

'(a) Assignment of all rights, dated as of even date, in connection with that certain story written by you and entitled 'Winchester, 73.'

'(b) Employment Agreement between you and us with respect to your services in the writing of a treatment based upon said story.

'It is agreed that in the event we cause said story to be published in magazine or book form, we shall pay to you a sum equal to one-half of the net proceeds actually received by us from such publication after deducting all commissions and other expenses incurred by us relative to such publication. In connection with such publication, we agree that you shall receive credit as the author of said story.

'Yours very truly, Universal Pictures Company, Inc. By Edward Muhl
Assistant Secretary
Approved and Accepted:
Stuart N. Lake
(Stewart N. Lake)'

In his complaint plaintiff alleges defendants 'caused to be published said story, 'Winchester, 73,' in the August, 1950 issue of 'Movie Story,' * * * ' magazine; that plaintiff, in violation of his agreement with defendants, did not receive any credit or any mention whatsoever as the author of 'Winchester, 73' and that defendants have failed to pay plaintiff any part of the 'net proceeds' realized by them as the result of such publication.

Some time after defendants purchased the story, they engaged Robert L. Richards and Borden Chase to write a screen play based on the plaintiff's original story. The motion picture, 'Winchester '73', was made from the screen play as prepared by Robert L. Richards and Borden Chase.

Three main issues are raised by defendants:

(1) That the story as published in 'Movie Story' magazine was not plaintiff's story.

(2) That if it were plaintiff's story, defendants did not cause it to be published; and

(3) That defendants received no payment whatsoever for such publication, since the publication was for advertising purposes.

A perusal of the original story as sold by plaintiff to defendants and of the script as prepared by Robert L. Richards and Borden Chase indicates that the stories are substantially the same. Both are the stories of a gun— 'One of a Thousand'; both have the same locale, and both use the same characters. It is well known by those familiar with the motion picture industry that very infrequently, if ever, does a producer use a story purchased for filming in its original form as prepared by the writer. Producers evidently deem themselves better judges than writers are of what is necessary to make a successful motion picture. As a result, in nearly every instance the author's version is modified or changed.

In the handling of 'Winchester '73' defendants followed the usual procedure of producers and changed the story as they saw fit to meet the requirements of their particular studio. Although there have been many changes, and characters have been realigned, nevertheless there is sufficient evidence to justify the Court's holding that the story as published in 'Movie Story' was and is substantially plaintiff's story.

Defendants contend they did not cause such publication. Their affidavits indicate that defendants furnished to 'Movie Story' magazine a copy of the final shooting script of 'Winchester '73' as written by Richards and Chase, the authors of the screen play. These affidavits also disclose it is the custom of the motion picture industry to exploit and advertise motion pictures by publication of synopses in national motion picture magazines, such as 'Movie Story.' It seems to the Court there is sufficient evidence to justify the finding that defendants caused the publication.

It is defendants' further contention that the contract makes defendants liable only if the publication is in toto and, inasmuch as the publication is a synopsis, there has not been a publication. Again the Court must find against defendants' contention.

Defendants allege further that they have not received any payment from the magazine. Defendants evidently limit the definition of the term 'net proceeds' to money payment only. The letter quoted above was written by Universal Pictures Company, Inc. to the plaintiff. The defendants chose the terminology of the letter. They could have, had they so desired, specified that 'net proceeds' meant money. It would also have been possible for the defendants to have incorporated in the contract a definition of the word 'published'; but defendants did not attempt to limit the meaning of the word 'published' nor of the term 'net proceeds.'

As a general rule, a contract is to be more strictly construed against the party preparing it and using the specific terms than against the party who did not prepare the contract. Therefore, interpretation of the letter in this case must be construed more strictly against the defendant who prepared it than against plaintiff. Plaintiff argues that the term 'net proceeds' is not limited to money but applies to any proceeds which defendants obtained and further contends that part of the proceeds obtained by defendants was advertising and publicity, and that advertising and publicity have a monetary value of which plaintiff is entitled to one-half, whatever the amount may be.

We do not believe the Court would be justified in holding that the term 'net proceeds' is restricted to money, for 'Proceeds are not necessarily money.' Phelps v. Harris, 101 U.S. 370, at page 380, 25 L.Ed. 855. The Court is satisfied that the term 'net proceeds' as used in the letter quoted above means any proceeds realized and, consequently, plaintiff is entitled to one-half of the value of advertising and publicity realized by defendants.

Plaintiff asserts that as he was not given credit for the story appearing in 'Movie Story' magazine he has been damaged thereby. Defendants, as already pointed out, allege they did not cause the story to be published, but we have held contrary to that contention. Defendants further contend it was not plaintiff's story which was published but the story of the two writers employed by defendants. The Court also holds against the defendants on that controversy.

Defendants allege further that it was not the custom to give author-credit for such a story. Perusal of 'Movie Story' for August, 1950, in which 'Winchester '73' appeared, is illuminating. The following motion pictures are reviewed in that issue of the magazine: 1. The Glass Menagerie; 2. Treasure Island; 3. Stella; 4. The Furies; 5. The Asphalt Jungle; 6. Winchester '73; 7. Rogues of Sherwood Forest; 8. Once a Thief.

The following notations appear in these reviews:

1. The Glass Menagerie * * * 'from the original stage play by Tennessee Williams.'

2. Treasure Island * * * 'from the novel by Robert Louis Stevenson.'

3. Stella * * * 'based on a novel by Doris Miles Disney.'

4. The Furies * * * 'screenplay by Charles Schnee; from a novel by Niven Busch.'

5. The Asphalt Jungle * * * 'screenplay by Ben Maddow and John Huston; from a novel by W. R. Burnett.'

6. Winchester '73. 'Produced by Aaron Rosenberg; directed by Anthony Mann; screenplay by Robert L. Richards and Borden Chase.'

7. Rogues of Sherwood Forest '* * * screenplay by George Bruce; story by Ralph Bettinson.'

8. Once a Thief '* * * screenplay by Richard S. Conway; based on a story by Max Colpet and Hans Wilhelm.'

Of the eight movies reviewed by 'Movie Story' magazine, only in 'Winchester '73' is author credit omitted. The other seven reviews give such credit.

Author credit may have been deleted in 'Winchester '73' through oversight, but there is certainly evidence on which a finding may be made that the deletion was based on the theory that 'Winchester '73', as reviewed, was not plaintiff's story. That has been the contention of the defendants in these proceedings; that is, in the rewriting, the story became that of the rewriters. Possibly that is the reason plaintiff is not given credit for authorship.

Defendants rely on the case of Field v. True Comics, Inc., D.C., 89 F.Supp. 611, 612. We are of the opinion the cited case does not help defendants in any particular. In the Field case, DiMaggio wrote an original book entitled "Lucky to be a Yankee"; plaintiff obtained from DiMaggio 'the sole and exclusive right to publish, print and market in book' form the story entitled "Lucky to be a Yankee". Defendant published and placed on the market a magazine, entitled 'True Comics', which contained a story of 'Joe DiMaggio, the Yankee Clipper'. The Court pointed out that the right obtained by the plaintiff to publish, print and market 'in book form' a story "Lucky to be a Yankee" did not include the publication of a comic magazine, particularly as two publishers of books submitted affidavits as to the meaning of the term 'in book form', stating that such term did not include a publication like that in 'True Comics.' Also, the author appeared at the hearing and alleged that he had rights and claims against 'True Comics' superior to those of the plaintiff.

From the foregoing it is clearly evident plaintiff is entitled to a judgment against the defendants upon the question of liability only. The question of damages will be reserved for a further proceeding. Counsel for plaintiff is instructed to prepare Findings and Judgment in conformity with this memorandum.

ZORICH v. PETROFF
Court of Appeal of California, Second Appellate District, Division Three
July 26, 1957
Civ. No. 22050
152 Cal.App.2d 806, 313 P.2d 118

SHINN, P. J.

Steve Zorich appeals from an adverse judgment after a court trial in an action whereby he sought a recovery of money and a declaration that he has an interest in a motion picture by virtue of an alleged partnership or joint venture agreement entered into with defendants Boris Petroff, Annabelle Sterling and J. Donald Patton.

The complaint alleges that on May 28, 1952, a written agreement designated 'Temporary Agreement' was executed by plaintiff, Petroff, Mrs. Sterling and Patton by which the parties agreed to form a motion picture company for the purpose of producing, selling and distributing a motion picture devoted to the folk dances of various nations and to be entitled 'World Dances.' Petroff was to produce and direct the picture in consideration of 50 per cent of the net profits; Mrs. Sterling was to be secretary-treasurer of the company and agreed to advance $4,000 toward the cost of production in consideration of 15 per cent of the profits; Patton was to be the general manager. Plaintiff was to have the title of associate producer and 'to share equally with J. Donald Patton of the remainder of the profits after the percentage is allowed the parties contributing the remainder of the monies necessary for the completion of the picture, estimated cost at this time to be roughly between $15,000 and $20,000.'

The complaint also alleges that by a contemporaneous oral agreement the parties formed a joint venture or partnership with respect to said motion picture and that they agreed to organize a corporation to conduct the business of the joint venture or partnership enterprise. The picture went into production in August 1952 and during the next four months plaintiff rendered numerous services to the enterprise as associate producer of 'World Dances,' which services are of the reasonable value of $225,000. It is also alleged that Petroff caused defendant Festival Pictures, Inc., to be incorporated in September 1952; the corporation is merely the *alter ego* of Petroff, who is its president; Petroff transferred 'World Dances' to the corporation; no stock in the corporation has ever been issued to plaintiff, despite the fact that the parties did not intend the partnership or joint enterprise to be dissolved upon the formation of the company. Plaintiff further alleges that Mrs. Sterling agreed to advance the remainder of the completion money to the corporation, that the corporation later agreed to repay her the amount advanced in consideration of her release to Festival Pictures, Inc., of all her interest in the film, and that the company executed to her a chattel mortgage on 'World Dances' as security for the repayment of the amount. Plaintiff also alleges that the transactions among Petroff, Mrs. Sterling and Festival Pictures, Inc., were in derogation of the rights of the joint venture or partnership enterprise and of plaintiff. He further alleges that defendant Albert J. Gabaig has invested $100,000 in the corporation and claims an interest in 'World Dances' adverse to him. The prayer is for $225,000 as the reasonable value of plaintiff's services as associate producer and for breach of contract, for an accounting, the appointment of a receiver of Festival Pictures, Inc., and for a declaration that plaintiff has an interest in the enterprise and in 'World Dances.'

The answer admits the execution of the May 28, 1952 agreement, but alleges that it was mutually cancelled, terminated and rescinded by the parties thereto; alleges that the company agreed to pay $18,000 to Mrs. Sterling in consideration of a release of all liability to her under the May agreement; admits that she transferred her interest in the film to the corporation and that it mortgaged the film to her as security for repayment of the completion money. It denies the existence of a joint venture or partnership, denies that plaintiff has an interest in 'World Dances' and alleges that plaintiff has been paid in full for the services he rendered.

Upon the trial a motion for nonsuit was granted as to defendant Gabaig. Annabelle Sterling did not appear in the action, having been served by publication outside the state; her default was entered but plaintiff's counsel conceded at the trial that the court did not have jurisdiction to enter a personal judgment against her. After a trial on the merits the court made findings and entered judgment for defendants.

The court found that under the written agreement of May 28, 1952, plaintiff's percentage of the profits was to be left for further negotiations in case he obtained the completion money and that there was no agreement to give him 10 per cent of the profits; that in September 1952 plaintiff, Mrs. Sterling, Petroff and Patton agreed that Mrs. Sterling would advance the completion money in consideration of 50 per cent of the profits from 'World Dances' and that plaintiff would receive 5 per cent to be taken from her share; early in 1953 Mrs. Sterling sold her interest in the picture to defendant Albert J. Gabaig for a valuable consideration, and Gabaig had no knowledge of the above agreements with plaintiff; plaintiff knew of the sale to Gabaig and made no objection thereto, but completely disassociated himself from the enterprise; at the time of the commencement of the present action Annabelle Sterling had no right, title or interest in the film or its profits; production of the film commenced in the autumn of 1952; plaintiff performed certain jobs in connection therewith, but had no right of management or control over the same; no profits have been realized from the production or sale of 'World Dances'; defendants did not agree to pay plaintiff a salary for his work on the picture and he has been fairly and adequately compensated for the work he did; although plaintiff did not receive screen credit as associate producer of 'World Dances' he has suffered no damage thereby; Annabelle Sterling caused Festival Pictures, Inc., to be incorporated and the rights of Sterling and Petroff were transferred to the corporation; the corporation is not the *alter ego* of Boris Petroff.

In its conclusions of law the court determined that the agreement of May 28, 1952, did not create a partnership, that no partnership or joint venture was formed by the parties, and that plaintiff has no interest either in the film, Festival Pictures, Inc., or the property of the corporation.

The sole contention advanced by plaintiff Zorich is that the findings are unsupported by the evidence. Since the evidence at the trial was in conflict, our review of the judgment is limited to determining whether there was any substantial evidence to support the questioned findings

Plaintiff argues the following points: (1) The court erred in concluding that the parties did not enter into a partnership or joint venture; (2) the court should have found that there was a breach of contract by defendants because (a) the evidence established that plaintiff had an interest in the picture; (b) he was entitled to screen credit as associate producer of 'World Dances'; and (c) defendants transferred the assets of the venture to the corporation to the exclusion of plaintiff; (3) the finding that defendants did not agree to pay plaintiff a salary was without support in the evidence; (4) it was error to construe the temporary agreement as providing for no definite interest of plaintiff in the picture; (5) there was insufficient evidence to support the finding that defendant knew of the sale of Sterling's interest to Gabaig and failed to object to it.

As to the first point, Zorich contends that the court should have found that a partnership or joint venture existed. We cannot agree. It was not established as a matter of law that the parties entered into a partnership or joint venture. The written agreement was in evidence, and upon the basis of the agreement and evidence of the later agreements, the court properly concluded that the parties did not enter into a partnership or joint venture. Plaintiff assumed none of the financial risks of the enterprise; the court could reasonably have inferred from plaintiff's own testimony that the services he performed were limited to assisting other members of the company at Petroff's direction and that he had no right of control over the production of 'World Dances' or its business affairs. The fact that he was to receive an interest in the profits of the picture in consideration for his services did not, as a matter of law, make him a partner or joint adventurer.

However, it is immaterial whether plaintiff became a partner or joint adventurer with defendants. The court found that he entered into certain written and oral agreements with defendants, and that defendants kept their promises. If supported by the evidence, these findings require an affirmance of the judgment.

With respect to the finding that there was an oral modification of the temporary agreement by which the interest of Sterling was to be increased from 15 per cent to 50 per cent and a further agreement that plaintiff was to receive 5 per cent out of her 50 per cent, it is conceded by plaintiff that both Petroff and Patton testified that all parties entered into those oral agreements in September 1952. Mrs. Sterling advanced $12,000 after the agreements were made. Plaintiff merely argues that the testimony of Petroff and Patton was unworthy of belief and that there was sufficient evidence from which the court should have found that he was entitled to a 10 per cent interest in the profits. Inasmuch as there was positive evidence that plaintiff's interest was reduced by the oral agreements to the receipt of 5 per cent out of Mrs. Sterling's 50 per cent, and the court saw fit to rely upon the testimony of Petroff and Patton as against plaintiff's denials of those agreements, it is unnecessary to say more than that it is not our function to reweigh the testimony of the witnesses, and that we are bound by the trial court's determination of the facts.

With respect to the second point, the most that could be claimed by plaintiff is that at the time Mrs. Sterling sold her interest to Gabaig he had some intangible interest in the profits that might be realized from 'World Dances.' However, the court found, as mentioned later, that while it was agreed that plaintiff would receive 5 per cent of the profits out of Sterling's 50 per cent, he stood by without objection when Mrs. Sterling announced her intention to sell her interest. She had a right to sell her interest. The other defendants would have had no right to prevent her from selling it, and the fact that she did so constituted no breach of contract on the part of the other defendants.

With respect to the claim of Zorich that he was entitled to screen credit, the court impliedly found that he was entitled to credit, but if he has not received it and does not receive it, he has suffered and will suffer no damage. It is sufficient to say on this point that there was no evidence from which the court could have placed a value upon the screen credit to be given plaintiff as an associate producer. (Civ. Code, § 3301.) It is undisputed that no profits have been realized from the picture and there was apparently a $36,000 deficit. Upon the evidence that was before the court as to the lack of success of the picture, receipt of screen 'credit' by plaintiff could reasonably have been regarded as a detriment to him.

Defendants did not breach their contract by transferring the assets of the enterprise to the corporation. The written agreement provided that the parties would form a company to carry on the enterprise and implied that they contemplated a transfer to it of the story idea by Petroff and a division of profits earned by the company. The corporation was such a company. This was not a breach of the agreement and no detriment was suffered by plaintiff.

As to the third point, it is stated in plaintiff's brief that 'Petroff testified that there never were any discussions about salaries except for Sterling and himself. However, he admits that it was agreed to pay appellant a salary of $25 per week. The trial court chose to believe Petroff in this regard and denied appellant any compensation for the services he rendered for three months in connection with the production of the picture.' During that time plaintiff was paid $150 for his services. Plaintiff testified that he was to be paid $150 a week as associate producer and that he only agreed to accept $25 a week for expenses. The fact that the court believed the testimony of Petroff rather than that of plaintiff disposes of plaintiff's assertion that the denial of his claim for compensation was arbitrary, unjust or without support in the evidence.

As to point 4, there was no error in the court's construction of the temporary agreement as one under which plaintiff's share of the profits was to be left to future arrangements. It provided that plaintiff was to share equally with Patton 'of the remainder of the profits after the percentage is allowed the parties contributing the remainder of the monies necessary for the completion of the picture, estimated cost at this time to be roughly between $15,000 and $20,000.' Necessarily, plaintiff's share of the profits was left uncertain as to percentage or amount, since no limit was placed upon the sums that might be required for completion of the picture, or the share that would be given to the one who financed it. But the subsequent oral agreements did establish what plaintiff's share of the profits might be and those agreements were controlling.

Upon the fifth point, namely, the alleged lack of knowledge of plaintiff of the sale of Sterling's interest to Gabaig, plaintiff says that the finding that he had knowledge and registered no objection is unsupported by any evidence. This criticism is not borne out by the record. There was direct evidence that the sale of Mrs. Sterling's interest was discussed and agreed upon at a meeting of the parties, plaintiff being present, held in December 1952 at the office of Sterling's attorney. Plaintiff does not attempt any statement of the evidence as to what took place during that meeting. He merely asserts that Gabaig's name was never mentioned. But he testified that he and his attorney were both present when Mrs. Sterling declared her intention of selling her interest and that he (plaintiff) took no part in the conversation. Knowing of Mrs. Sterling's intentions plaintiff made no objection. It is of no consequence that Gabaig had not at that time been unearthed as a purchaser, or, if his identity was known, that it was not disclosed. There is no merit whatever in the contention that plaintiff did not know of the proposed sale of Mrs. Sterling's interest, and it is conceded that he offered no objection to it. He testified that he had nothing more to do with the production after the meeting in December 1952. His silence was acquiescence and estopped him from complaining of the sale of Mrs. Sterling's interest after it had been made.

In view of what we have said, there was no error in denying plaintiff an accounting of the corporate affairs.

Plaintiff's presentation of his appeal ignores two fundamental rules pertaining to the review of judgments, namely, that this court is not vested with jurisdiction to retry questions of fact, and that claims of insufficiency of the evidence to support the findings must be accompanied by a fair statement of the relevant evidence. The well-prepared brief of the defendants has simplified our consideration of the appeal.

The judgment is affirmed. WOOD (Parker), J., concurred.

WELCH v. METRO-GOLDWYN-MAYER FILM CO.
Court of Appeal of California, Second Appellate District, Division Four
December 23, 1988
No. B022873
207 Cal.App.3d 164,
254 Cal.Rptr. 645

ARLEIGH M. WOODS, Presiding Justice.

This lawsuit arises from the firing of the motion picture actress Raquel Welch from her starring role in the film "Cannery Row." The jury found in favor of Welch and Raquel Welch Productions, Inc. (hereinafter sometimes collectively referred to as Welch) on counts of breach of contract, conspiracy to induce breach of contract, slander, and breach of the implied covenant of good faith and fair dealing (bad faith). Welch recovered $2 million in compensatory damages and over $8 million in punitive damages from appellants Metro–Goldwyn–Mayer Film Co. (MGM), several successor corporations to MGM (TBS Entertainment Co., Production, Inc., Lab, Inc., and Lot, Inc.), David Begelman (the president of MGM), and Michael Phillips (the producer of the film).

Welch filed a cross-appeal from the trial court's granting of summary judgment on a count of intentional infliction of emotional distress, but has abandoned the cross-appeal in her briefing.

Appellants raise numerous issues on appeal, including that (1) there is no basis for a conspiracy between Phillips and MGM because Phillips's actions were privileged as a matter of law; (2) Welch as an individual lacked standing to sue for conspiracy to induce breach of contract or bad faith because the contract for her services was between MGM and Raquel Welch Productions, Inc.; (3) the trial court should not have permitted the bad faith count to be added at the close of Welch's case-in-chief as an amendment to conform to proof; (4) the bad faith cause of action cannot stand because there was no evidence of a special relationship between Welch and MGM similar to that of an insured to an insurer, and/or because the jury was not instructed on that issue; (5) there was insufficient evidence to show either a conspiracy to induce breach of contract or a bad faith breach of contract; (6) there was insufficient evidence of slander; (7) Welch's counsel committed misconduct in his closing argument; (8) the successor corporations cannot be held liable for the wrongful acts of MGM; and (9) various errors occurred in the jury's award of compensatory and punitive damages.

We find no error, and affirm.

The evidence showed that Welch appeared in about 30 films between 1965 and 1980 and had a reputation as a strong willed professional actress who sometimes clashed with directors. She was considered a sex symbol, and the only serious dramatic role was as a roller derby queen in "Kansas City Bomber." She turned down all film offers between 1977 and 1980, concentrating during that period on a television special and a television drama about an American Indian woman, for which she served as producer as well as actress.

Prior to 1980, Michael Phillips and David Ward had collaborated on two films, one of which was the Academy Award winner, "The Sting." Over several years, Phillips and Ward developed a film package based on the John Steinbeck novellas "Cannery Row" and "Sweet Thursday." Ward wrote the screenplay and was to be the director, although he had never directed a commercial film before. Phillips was to be the producer. An actor named Nick Nolte was to portray the leading male character.

Phillips and Ward had difficulty finding financing for the film. In early 1980, the project was finally accepted by David Begelman, who had just become president of MGM. Phillips and Ward signed contracts with MGM which gave the studio the right to replace either of them if their service proved unsatisfactory.

Begelman insisted that an actress with a recognizable name be selected for the leading female character, a prostitute named Suzy. Numerous actresses were considered, among whom were Welch and Debra Winger.

At 40 years old, Welch relished the chance to direct her career towards more serious roles. She agreed to audition for the part, which was not customary for an established actress, and to perform nude scenes, which she had previously refused to do in any film.

When Welch first met with Ward and Phillips, they asked her about rumors of problems with the director of the television drama. She assured them the problems had concerned her dual role as both producer and actress, not temperament. She agreed with them that Suzy should be a nonglamorous, natural-looking girl with little or no makeup. Ward and Phillips were impressed with Welch's enthusiasm and her reading of the role. They decided they wanted her for the film.

On October 8, 1980, Raquel Welch Productions, Inc. (RWPI), a "loan-out" company utilized by Welch for tax purposes, entered into a contract with MGM to provide Welch's services on the film. Welch was promised $250,000, with payment divided into weekly increments during filming. She agreed to participate in nine weeks of actual filming, and to be available for rehearsals and wardrobe fittings for two weeks before shooting began.

The contract included a standard "pay or play" clause, under which the studio could terminate Welch from the film at any time, but was obligated to pay her the full contract price, unless she failed to fulfill her contractual obligations. It further required that Welch be provided a fully equipped, "star-type" trailer for makeup purposes; her choice of hairdresser and makeup artist, on first call to her; and a wardrobe assistant.

Before filming began, Welch participated in all but one and one-half days of the two-week rehearsal period. She also prepared for her role by going to vintage clothing shops with the costume designer, talking to Ward about her character, and studying historical pictures. She told Begelman that she was delighted to be working on the film, and that if Ward, as a first-time director, was nervous about discussing her performance with her, Begelman could call her directly.

The production company gave the performers a call sheet at the end of each day of filming, indicating which scenes to prepare for and what time to report for makeup and for shooting on the set the next day. Shooting began at 8:00 or 8:30 a.m. each day. In general, the other actors had makeup calls of 7:00 or 7:30 a.m., and set calls of 8 or 8:30 a.m. Welch had requested, and was given, three hours in which to makeup. She actually needed only two hours for makeup and hair, but had a preparatory routine which included yoga and exercise. The call sheets gave her makeup times of 6:00, 6:30 or 7:00 a.m., and set times three hours later, except for one day on which the makeup period was two and one-half hours.

Welch was initially provided a trailer which lacked enough room for a makeup chair in front of the mirror. She asked Kurt Neumann, the production manager, for a larger trailer. She was given a larger, attractive trailer in which a makeup mirror and chair were installed. In her opinion, the new trailer still did not meet her needs. Its narrowness meant that it became very crowded when her assistants were preparing her, and the makeup artist could not move around the makeup chair without climbing over her or the television set. The television set was eventually removed at Welch's request. She also had dark tinting taken off the windows so that natural light could be used. She asked for, and received, a small empty trailer for exercise purposes.

Principal photography began on December 1, 1980. Welch was first called for shooting on Thursday, December 4. The picture was already behind schedule and $84,000 over budget. Welch arrived at her trailer for her scheduled makeup call at 7 a.m., was ready for her 10 a.m. set call, and waited until 5 p.m. before she was used. She had only a long shot and no lines that day.

Welch had no acting call for the next day, December 5. She came into the studio for some publicity photographs, again making up at her trailer.

Welch's next scheduled call was on Monday, December 8. She arrived at the studio early for her 7 a.m. makeup call, was on time for her 10 a.m. set call, and was not asked to perform a scene until after lunch.

The next day, December 9, she was at the studio early for makeup, but her makeup artist arrived late. As they began their preparations, the director,

David Ward, came in and asked if she could be ready for an over-the-shoulder shot in about 45 minutes. She agreed, and told him that she was willing to waive the 12-hour period the Screen Actors Guild normally required between performances. Her work that day involved only a few lines of dialogue.

On the next day of filming, December 10, Welch awoke with severe cramps. She had the hairdresser come to her home that morning. She put on her own makeup there with an MGM makeup mirror which Kurt Neumann had had delivered to her home. She arrived at the studio at 9 a.m., one hour before her set call. She told Neumann that she had been able to get ready much faster at home, and that she would like to speed up her makeup time by doing it at home until the trailer problem was sorted out. Neumann said it was "okay" for her to make up at home. Neither Phillips nor Ward told her anything to the contrary.

Actually, Phillips and Ward were not happy about the making up at home, and agreed to it only to avoid a confrontation with Welch. Ward was also unhappy about Welch's late set calls, as he had to begin work each day on scenes which did not require her presence, tended to begin filming her scenes late in the day, and had to cut down on the number of takes of her scenes. According to him, but not Welch, Welch told him that the over-the-shoulder shot on December 9 was the only time she would ever agree to come out of makeup to rehearse or block scenes. Phillips thought that three hours for makeup was too long, and that Welch's late availability for shooting would cause problems when filming of her major scenes began. There was no question, however, that Welch was not forbidden to make up at home, received three hours for makeup in the call sheets, was always on the set in time for her set call, and was not the cause of the film's budget problems. Phillips even called Welch at home, early in the filming, to compliment her on how she looked in the dailies.

Welch was not involved in the next few days of shooting, which involved a big production sequence which went greatly over budget.

On Welch's next days of filming, Wednesday, December 17 and Thursday, December 18, the makeup artist and hairdresser reported to her home at the instruction of an assistant director of the film. She arrived ready at the studio long before her set call, and had to wait for filming. Shooting ran until around 7 p.m. on Thursday the 18th. Welch went home to prepare for the next day, which would involve her first major dramatic scene.

Meanwhile, about 5:30 p.m. on Thursday the 18th, Begelman met in his office with Phillips and David Chasman, MGM's head of film production. Begelman was dissatisfied with the dailies he had seen of the film, but not with Welch's performance. He called the meeting because of a memorandum he had received from MGM's chairman of the board, expressing concern that the film was over budget and was in the hands of a first-time director, and suggesting that Begelman pay special attention to the problem.

Begelman began the meeting by asking Phillips, "What the hell's going on?" He also said that Phillips's and Ward's jobs were in jeopardy if the problems continued. Phillips said that shooting was beginning late because of Welch's unusual three-hour makeup period, that she had told Ward she would not come out of makeup for rehearsal, and that she had been making up at home. He further stated that he had not confronted Welch about the problem because he hoped a new makeup room which would be available the following Monday would be acceptable to her. He did not mention that Welch had made up at home for only three days.

Begelman and Chasman thought that Phillips and Ward had been intimidated by Welch. It was against studio policy for an actress to make up at home, both because it was an advantage to the production to have her available for rehearsal during the makeup period, and because of potential problems with liability and Teamster's Union drivers. Begelman ordered Phillips to tell Welch that she would be sent a letter declaring her in breach of contract, unless she made up at the studio the next morning. This was not to be deferred until Monday, and her makeup time was henceforth limited to two hours.

After the meeting, Phillips immediately called Welch. He hysterically told her that Begelman was "a killer" who believed Welch was responsible for the production delays, was not going to work around her makeup call, and was sending out a letter stating that she was in breach of contract. Welch responded that somebody must have lied to Begelman, as Phillips knew she had always been ready early for shooting. She dissolved into tears and gave the telephone to her husband, Andre Weinfeld.

Phillips told Weinfeld that Begelman was a killer and a crazy man who had put a gun at Phillips's head. He said Begelman had just dictated a breach of contract letter which was being sent "right now," and had ordered that Welch appear for makeup at the studio the next morning and shorten her makeup time. Weinfeld answered that since Welch was extremely upset and was facing her first major scene, he did not know if she could comply. Later calls that evening among Weinfeld, Phillips, Welch's attorney (Marc Stein) and Chasman reiterated that Welch had to make up at the studio the following morning (Friday), and a breach of contract letter was "going out."

Around 8 p.m. that night, the assistant director ordered the makeup artist and hairdresser to report to the studio rather than to Welch's home as previously instructed.

Welch was ill and barely slept that night. She arose at 4 a.m. on Friday, December 19, to prepare for filming. She claimed that she did not understand that she had been ordered to make up at the studio that morning, and was surprised when the makeup artist and hairdresser did not arrive at 6:30 a.m.

She got ready by herself and arrived at the studio with Weinfeld at 8:30 a.m., one hour earlier than her set call, and, as usual, without any delay to the company. She performed as an actress throughout that day.

Phillips reported to Chasman and Begelman at 9 a.m. that Welch had disobeyed the instruction to make up at the studio that morning. Begelman called Welch's agent, Michael Levy, to say that the breach of contract letter might be sent. This was the studio's first contact with Levy, even though the usual first step in resolving a serious problem with an actress is to call her agent. Levy called Phillips, who said the studio was pressuring him and that Welch had caused no delays.

Chasman and Begelman met that morning with MGM's general counsel, Karla Davidson. They decided to immediately send out a letter stating that Welch was in substantial breach of her obligations under the October 8 agreement. The letter read: "Artist has failed to comply with our instructions in connection with her performance of her services in the Photoplay by continually refusing and failing to report to the MGM Studio at the hour designated by us for make-up for her role.... [¶] This will notify you that if Artist continues to refuse to perform in accordance with our instructions, we intend to exercise any and all of our rights and remedies with respect to such breach, including our right to terminate the Agreement."

Welch learned of the breach letter around noon, but continued working. Levy called Begelman to complain that the letter was unnecessary. Begelman told Levy not to tell him how to run his business, and that he was not going to let Welch continue her past history of toughness with studio directors. He said the problem was curable if Welch would make up at the studio. Levy assured Begelman, and, later that day, Chasman, that he would make sure that Welch was at the studio at 6:30 a.m. on Monday morning for two hours of makeup. Levy thought the problem was resolved at that point.

At the end of the day's filming, Welch was shown a long-unused studio makeup room which she accepted. Weinfeld told Neumann that the room was satisfactory. Welch planned to report for make up in that room on Monday morning at 6:30 a.m., for the two-hour period specified on that day's call sheet.

Phillips did not discuss the makeup problem with Welch on Friday. According to Phillips, Welch avoided talking to him that day. According to Weinfeld, he told Phillips to speak directly to Welch, and Phillips made no such attempt.

The next day, Saturday the 20th, Phillips left an urgent message on Welch's answering machine that she should call him. Welch got the call at 2 p.m. As she had again not slept well and was upset, she had Levy return the call. A series of telephone calls ensued in which Phillips and Levy spoke over the telephone. Levy would then call Weinfeld to report what Phillips had said.

Weinfeld in turn talked to Welch and relayed her responses to Levy, who relayed them to Phillips.

During these conversations, Phillips repeatedly asked to meet with Welch over the weekend. Welch promised, through Levy, to obey the studio's orders. She was willing to meet with Phillips at the studio at 6:30 a.m. Monday morning, but wanted to rest over the weekend. Phillips said he wanted Welch to be upset, as they would be filming a tense scene on Monday. Finally, between 10 and 12 a.m. on Sunday the 21st, Levy told Phillips that Welch had agreed to Phillips's proposal of a meeting on Monday at 9 a.m. in Phillips's office. Welch and Levy thought the problem was resolved.

Chasman called Davidson later that Sunday morning and told her that neither Welch nor her agent had made an unequivocal commitment to follow the studio's orders.

Phillips called Ward and told him that Welch might be replaced because Phillips had not been able to get in touch with her all weekend. Ward was displeased, as he had never suggested that Welch be terminated.

Later on Sunday, Phillips telephoned Chasman, complaining that he still did not know if Welch agreed to comply with the studio's orders. Chasman called Begelman, who decided to terminate Welch because she had disobeyed the order to make up at the studio on Friday morning and had refused to talk to Phillips over the weekend. Welch's lawyer called her and told her she had been fired from the picture. She was devastated. About one-sixth of her role had been shot at that time.

A letter from MGM dated the next day, December 22, indicated that the employment agreement was terminated due to Welch's failure to comply with her contractual obligations. Welch responded with a letter threatening to sue unless MGM paid the balance of $194,444 which remained due under the agreement. MGM refused.

Welch was replaced by Debra Winger in the film. Winger received $150,000 for the role. It cost almost $200,000 to replace Welch with Winger and reshoot the scenes in which Welch had appeared.

Welch received numerous inquiries from the press regarding what had happened. Many people seemed to believe that she had failed to show up for work. Industry newspapers reported that she had been fired.

An article about the incident appeared in the April 2, 1981, issue of Rolling Stone, a magazine with a weekly circulation of over 700,000 and wide readership in the motion picture industry. According to the article, Ward said that Welch was a casting mistake who was not necessarily a bad actress but was not delivering a performance he could live with. Begelman was quoted as saying: " 'We had a general feeling she had not lived up to her contract.... We had no alternative. It is up to the executives to tell the people in this business we will not stand for that. The producer gave her appropriate directions and she failed to obey.' "

Negative reviews of the film which appeared in Variety and the New York Times in February 1982 stated that Welch should feel happy she had been fired from it. The film was a major failure at the box office, and MGM lost almost $16 million on it.

The evidence established that an accusation of breaking a contract would be very damaging to an actress's reputation, as people in the industry would assume she was undependable. Welch never made another movie because of her firing from "Cannery Row." One deal fell through due to a lack of financing and the only other offers she received, to portray a Nazi and a vampire, were unacceptable. In contrast, she had made about six films between 1973 and 1980, with compensation ranging between $150,000 and $350,000. At the time of trial, in 1986, film actresses routinely received twice the 1980 level of compensation. Some stars were making from $2 to $5 million per film.

Having no offers in Hollywood, Welch moved to New York City. For two weeks at the end of 1981 and six months in 1982, she had a very successful run in the Broadway musical "Woman of the Year," for which she earned $25,000 per week. She later signed two $1 million contracts, one for food commercials and the other for a concert tour. She also made hundreds of thousands of dollars from a best-selling health and beauty book and accompanying videotape. These activities would not have prevented her from accepting a film role.

Welch also presented evidence concerning secret meetings between MGM representatives and representatives of Debra Winger prior to Welch's firing.

On either December 17 or 18, David Chasman had called Arlyne Rothberg, Winger's personal manager, wanting to know if Winger was available to start a film. Rothberg said that Winger had just left for a vacation in New Mexico, and was available. She asked Chasman what project he had in mind. Chasman said he could not tell her, but would get back to her shortly. On Sunday the 21st, he called and told her that Welch had left the film and that the studio wanted Winger to return to Los Angeles as soon as possible. Rothberg reached Winger at her New Mexico cabin on Sunday the 21st. Winger accepted the offer.

On either Saturday the 20th or Sunday the 21st, Rothberg called Winger's attorney, Barry Hirsch, and asked him to negotiate the deal for Winger with Frank Davis, MGM's head of business affairs. Hirsch and Davis negotiated Winger's contract over the weekend. Almost all the details were resolved by Sunday. The deal closed on Monday the 22nd.

On the night of Sunday the 21st, Winger called her agent, Gary Salt, from New Mexico to say that she was replacing Welch in the film. Initial contacts regarding a role are usually made with an actor's agent. Salt worked for the same agency that represented Welch.

Begelman, Chasman, Phillips, Ward, Davidson and Davis denied that there were any discussions regarding Winger or contacts with her or her representatives prior to Monday, December 22.

I

Count II of the first amended complaint alleged that MGM, Phillips and Ward formed a conspiracy to induce MGM to breach the employment contract with RWPI, for the purported purposes of replacing Welch with another actress and making it appear that Welch, rather than Phillips and Ward, was responsible for the picture's budget problems. Welch and RWPI sought $194,444 in actual damages (the amount remaining under the contract), and $5 million in punitive damages. The jury awarded $194,444 in compensation against MGM and Phillips, $500,000 punitive damages against Phillips, and $3,750,000 punitive damages against MGM. Ward was exonerated.

Appellants maintain that there is no legal basis for the conspiracy count because Phillips had a privilege to induce breach of the contract as a matter of law, and there was no other party outside the contract with whom MGM could have conspired.

"[W]hile a party to a contract may not be held liable in tort for interfering with his own contract by breaching it, he may be held liable in tort for interference with his own contract if he conspires with a third party to breach it. [Citation.]" The contracting party's liability is derived from the wrongful interference of the third party coconspirator and is based on "the principle that all who are involved in the common scheme are jointly and severally responsible for the ensuing wrong."

Special rules govern whether the manager or agent of a contracting party can constitute the third party for the purpose of the conspiracy.
"One who is in a confidential relationship with a party to a contract is privileged to induce the breach of that contract. [Citations.]"

"The privilege to induce an otherwise apparently tortious breach of contract is extended by law to further certain social interests deemed of sufficient importance to merit protection from liability. Thus, a manager or agent may, with impersonal or disinterested motive, properly endeavor to protect the interests of his principal by counseling the breach of a contract with a third party which he reasonably believes to be harmful to his employer's best interests." (See Prosser, Law of Torts (4th ed. 1971) § 129, pp. 943–944.) On the other hand, "[i]t is well established ... that a person is not justified in inducing a breach of contract simply because he is in competition with one of the parties to the contract and seeks to further his own economic advantage at the expense of the other. [Citations.]" "Obviously, when a manager induces a breach in the hopes that he himself might fill the resultant economic void, he acts not as a servant, i.e., as one upholding his master's best interests, but rather as a naked competitor, devoid of the protections accorded those who labor under standards of fidelity, good faith and fiduciary responsibility."

Under *Olivet,* the privilege applies where the manager acts solely in the employer's interest and does not apply where the manager acts solely in his or her own interest...

Appellants maintain that the evidence here established that Phillips was acting from mixed motives, so his actions were privileged as a matter of law. We disagree. The evidence contained several possible explanations for Phillips's behavior. Welch's evidence suggested that Phillips reacted to the threat of losing his job, and consequent damage to his career, by making Welch the scapegoat for the film's budget problems. Phillips maintained that Welch was creating a problem for him and MGM which could potentially damage the film. MGM's covert contacts with Winger, and Ward's statement to Rolling Stone Magazine that he was dissatisfied with Welch's portrayal of the role, suggested other possible motives for replacing her. Resolution of the existence of the privilege was "peculiarly a question for determination by the trier of fact. [Citation.]"

The jury was specially instructed that if Phillips gave MGM "truthful information or honest advice within the scope of a request for the advice, or if [he was] materially motivated by a desire to benefit MGM," then he was not liable for conspiracy to induce breach of contract. The jury's finding against Phillips necessarily means that it determined that he was not acting in a privileged capacity. Given the jury's resolution of the conflicting evidence, we cannot find, as a matter of law, that the privilege existed.

II

Appellants next maintain that Welch lacked standing to sue for either conspiracy to induce breach of contract or bad faith, as MGM contracted with Welch's loan-out company, RWPI, rather than with Welch as an individual. The argument lacks merit.

Appellants did not raise this issue below. They maintained in their trial brief that Welch and RWPI had "indistinguishable" interests, and repeatedly argued to the jury that the contract was between "Miss Welch" and MGM.

The contract defined Ms. Welch, individually, as the "artist," and contained numerous specific obligations owed by MGM to the "artist." There was no significant difference between the company Welch utilized for tax purposes and Welch herself.

Moreover, the signature page of the contract shows that Welch signed twice, both as the president of RWPI and as an individual who "ACCEPTED AND AGREED" to the terms. She therefore is presumed to have joint and several liability under the contract. (Civ.Code, § 1660; 1 Witkin, Summary of Cal. Law (9th ed. 1987) Contracts, § 675.)

MGM's reliance on *C & H Foods Co. v. Hartford Ins. Co.* (1984) 163 Cal.App.3d 1055, 211 Cal.Rptr. 765, and *Hatchwell v. Blue Shield of California* (1988) 198 Cal.App.3d 1027, 1034, 244 Cal.Rptr. 249, is misplaced. We held in *C & H Foods* that individuals who were the shareholders and employees of a corporation were not proper plaintiffs in the corporation's bad faith action against its insurance company, as they were not named insureds, additional insureds or beneficiaries under the insurance policy. Similarly, *Hatchwell* held that a spouse who was neither a party nor an express third party beneficiary to the insurance contract between her husband and his insurance company lacked standing to sue for bad faith denial of her husband's benefits. Here, in contrast, Welch signed the employment contract, and it detailed the mutual obligations which she and MGM owed to each other. We therefore conclude that a contractual relationship existed between MGM and Welch which gave Welch standing to sue to enforce her contractual rights.

III

The count of breach of the implied covenant of good faith and fair dealing (bad faith) was alleged solely against MGM. The jury awarded Welch $400,000 in lost contract benefits, $1 million in lost professional income, $750,000 in damages to reputation, nothing for emotional distress, and $3,750,000 in punitive damages.

Appellants complain that the trial court should not have permitted this count to be added at the close of Welch's evidence as an amendment to conform to proof.

Due to the policy that cases should be decided on their merits, amendments to conform to proof are liberally allowed where the "same general set of facts" are involved. (*Austin v. Massachusetts Bonding & Insurance Co.* (1961) 56 Cal.2d 596, 601, 15 Cal.Rptr. 817, 364 P.2d 681; *Grudt v. City of Los Angeles* (1970) 2 Cal.3d 575, 585, 86 Cal.Rptr. 465, 468 P.2d 825.) A trial court's decision to permit such an amendment will be affirmed on appeal unless an abuse of discretion is shown. (*Godfrey v. Steinpress* (1982) 128 Cal.App.3d 154, 174, 180 Cal.Rptr. 95.) Here, no abuse has been shown.

Appellants complain they were prejudiced by the amendment, as they would have prepared and tried the case differently had they known it included a bad faith count. Welch stated at the time of the December 1984 settlement conference, however, that she would seek leave of the trial court to amend the breach of contract count to seek punitive damages. She cited *Seaman's Direct Buying Service, Inc. v. Standard Oil Co.* (1984) 36 Cal.3d 752, 206 Cal.Rptr. 354, 686 P.2d 1158, which had been decided several months earlier, and held that punitive damages were possible where the party who breached a contract adopted a "stonewall," "see you in court" attitude with no real belief in the existence of a defense. While no such amendment had been added by the time the trial started, appellants knew that evidence of emotional damage and lost earnings would be admitted on the conspiracy count, which included a claim for punitive damages. The evidence which supported the bad faith count was introduced without objection throughout Welch's case-in-chief, as it also proved the conspiracy count. Appellants have simply failed to establish that there is anything they would have done differently had they known they faced an allegation of bad faith as well as punitive damages arising from conspiracy. The only possible prejudice was in the possibility of duplicative damages, which we discuss and reject in section X, *infra.*

IV

Appellants contend that the award on the bad faith count must be reversed because one of the essential elements of bad faith, a "special relationship" similar to the relationship between an insurance company and an insured, was lacking as a matter of law. Alternatively, they maintain that, if there was a triable issue as to the existence of a special relationship, the trial court should not have refused their requested instruction on the necessary criteria for the relationship. Welch maintains that because her contract made her an employee of MGM, a special relationship existed as a matter of law.

The record shows that the trial court gave a series of instructions based on existing law involving bad faith termination of employment contracts. (*Koehrer v. Superior Court* (1986) 181 Cal.App.3d 1155, 226 Cal.Rptr. 820.) The jury was told that appellants were guilty of bad faith breach of contract if they sought "to avoid all liability on a meritorious contract claim by denying that liability without probable cause and with no good faith belief in the existence of a defense, ..." The trial court refused to instruct that a prerequisite to a finding of bad faith was the existence of the factors which make the contractual relationship a special relationship as set forth in *Wallis v. Superior Court* (1984) 160 Cal.App.3d 1109, 1118, 207 Cal.Rptr. 123. We must decide whether there were unique features of the employment relationship here which justify an exception to the usual rule that only bad faith and lack of probable cause need be shown in the employment context.

The employment contract for Welch's services was arrived at through careful negotiations between MGM's representatives on one side and Welch's agent and attorney on the other. In addition to compensation, the contract provided for a series of conditions negotiated on behalf of Welch, such as billing; approval of nude scenes and nude stills; effect of changes in the screenplay; effect of replacement of Nolte, Ward, or Phillips; approval, as discussed, of dressing room, hairdresser and make-up artist; a wardrobe assistant and double (actress); and no make up call earlier than 6 a.m. The contract otherwise incorporated all of MGM's Standard Terms, including the "pay or play" clause, and the Basic Agreement of the Screen Actors Guild.

While our Supreme Court has not directly addressed the issue of bad faith termination of employment contracts, some guidance can be found in *Tameny v. Atlantic Richfield Co.* (1980) 27 Cal.3d 167, 164 Cal.Rptr. 839, 610 P.2d 1330, and *Seaman's Direct Buying Service, Inc. v. Standard Oil Co., supra,* 36 Cal.3d 752, 206 Cal.Rptr. 354, 686 P.2d 1158.

In *Tameny v. Atlantic Richfield Co., supra,* 27 Cal.3d 167, 164 Cal.Rptr. 839, 610 P.2d 1330, the plaintiff maintained that he was discharged after 15 years of employment because he refused to participate in an illegal price-fixing scheme. Although the employment contract was of indefinite duration and therefore was terminable at the will of either party, *Tameny* held that the plaintiff properly stated a cause of action in tort for wrongful discharge, since a discharge cannot be based on reasons which contravene public policy. (*Id.,* at pp. 172, 178, 164 Cal.Rptr. 839, 610 P.2d 1330.) That conclusion made it unnecessary to decide whether the employee could also maintain an action for bad faith breach of the employment contract. The court went on to say: "We do note in this regard, however, that authorities in other jurisdictions have on occasion found an employer's discharge of an at-will employee violative of the employer's 'good faith and fair dealing' obligations [citations], and past California cases [in the insurance realm] have held that a breach of this implied-at-law covenant sounds in tort as well as in contract. [Citations.] Since neither plaintiff nor defendants suggest that the elements of a cause of action for breach of the implied covenant in this context would differ from the elements of an ordinary wrongful discharge action, however, we believe that a separate discussion of the 'good faith and fair dealing' covenant in this case is unnecessary." (*Id.,* at p. 179, fn. 12, 164 Cal.Rptr. 839, 610 P.2d 1330.)...

We agree with appellants that the nature of the relationship between Welch and MGM would be subject to challenge under the factors identified by *Seaman's* as justifying extension of bad faith principles outside the realm of insurance contracts. Indeed, the *Wallis* court noted in a footnote that "the characteristics of the insurance contract which give rise to an action sounding in tort are also present in *most* [not all] employer-employee relationships." (160 Cal.App.3d at p. 1116, fn. 2, 207 Cal.Rptr. 123, emphasis added.) We have declined to apply the *Seaman's–Wallis* criteria to the case before us because this is a bad faith discharge case and the trial court followed well-established law that no special relationship beyond the employer-employee relationship is necessary in a bad faith discharge case. Permitting distinctions to be drawn based upon perceived relative bargaining power in an employment relationship would create whole new areas of litigation in the already confused bad faith area.

V

Appellants further contend that there was insufficient evidence to establish either a conspiracy to induce breach of contract or a breach of the implied covenant of good faith and fair dealing. We disagree.

The record suggests that the defendants may have had different underlying motivations. Phillips wanted to protect himself from removal from the film, Begelman needed to protect his new position at MGM and show his strength in dealing with stars, and MGM wanted a different actress for the role. The end result was the same: a conspiracy to falsely blame Welch for the production's problems and to create a pretext for firing her which would provide a basis for not paying her under her contract. That conspiracy explained the studio's insistence on Welch's making up at the studio on Friday morning rather than the following Monday, even though she had previously had permission to make up at home, had never been late for filming, was upset by the talk of breach, and was facing her first major dialogue scene. The conspiracy and bad faith counts were further supported by: (1) the repudiation by Winger's manager and attorney of the testimony of numerous MGM witnesses regarding when the negotiations for Winger began; (2) Phillips's statements to Welch, Weinfeld and Stein on Thursday night that a breach letter was going out, even though Welch had not yet disobeyed the studio's make up order for Friday morning; (3) the failure to contact Levy before threatening the breach letter, when even MGM's expert testified that problems with a star are usually handled through her agent; (4) Phillips's and Neumann's insistence, contrary to the testimony of Weinfeld and Levy, that they were never told that Welch would use the new make up room on Monday; (5) Phillips's emphasis on Welch's refusal to meet with him over the weekend, when she had repeatedly communicated with him through Levy, and had agreed to a Monday meeting; and (6) the abrupt firing of Welch on Sunday, without waiting to see if she would fulfill her promises regarding Monday, and at a time when 98 percent of the details of Winger's contract had been agreed upon.

VI

The slander cause of action was based upon Begelman's statement to the Rolling Stone reporter that, " 'We had a general feeling she had not lived up to her contract, ... We had no alternative. It's up to the executives to tell the people in this business we will not stand for that. The producer gave her appropriate directions and she failed to obey.' "

On this cause of action, the jury returned $300,000 in compensatory damages against MGM, $25,000 in compensatory damages against Begelman, $150,000 in punitive damages against MGM, and $2,500 in punitive damages against Begelman.

Appellants maintain that there were errors in the trial court's instructions on slander and that there was insufficient evidence of slander because (1) Begelman's statement was one of opinion rather than fact and (2) there was no evidence of malice. The contentions lack merit.

The jury was instructed that slander is a false and unprivileged publication which tends to cause injury; if the statement is not slanderous on its face, all the surrounding circumstances should be considered in determining whether it would have a defamatory effect on the average reader; since Welch was a public figure, a published statement about her was absolutely privileged, even if false, unless made with knowledge of falsity or reckless disregard for the truth; there was no privilege if the statement was motivated by ill will or without a good faith belief in its truth; truth was a defense. They were further instructed that to be slanderous, the statement had to be one of fact rather than opinion; and, in determining whether the statement was one of fact or opinion, the jury should consider whether the average reader would consider it to be fact or opinion in the context of all the circumstances shown by the evidence.

Begelman's statement included words which sounded like an expression of opinion ("We had a general feeling") and words which sounded like a description of facts ("she failed to obey") which were communicated to him, the head of the studio, by the film's producer. It therefore was appropriate under the foregoing cases to leave it to the jury to decide whether the statement was one of opinion or fact.

There was sufficient evidence of malice through Welch's evidence, which the jury believed, that Begelman knew that Welch had complied with her obligations, manufactured a pretext to fire her, and therefore must have known that his statement to the Rolling Stone reporter was false.

VII

Appellants also maintain that three statements by Welch's counsel in closing argument constituted improper references to inadmissible settlement negotiations. The statements were that MGM knew for the six years which preceded the trial that Welch had been wrongly fired and still did not pay her. The argument lacks merit. First, there was no objection to any of the statements appellants now contend were improper (*Whitfield v. Roth* (1974) 10 Cal.3d 874,

892, 112 Cal.Rptr. 540, 519 P.2d 588), and the references were not so extreme that an admonition would have been insufficient. Second, as the trial court recognized at the hearing on the motion for new trial, counsel's argument was not improper when taken in context. The references were to a failure to pay the contract price and not an alleged refusal to negotiate. We cannot consider declarations from the jurors regarding how they construed counsel's argument, as evidence of jurors' subjective reasoning processes is inadmissible.

VIII

MGM further contends that the successor corporations to MGM cannot be held liable for punitive damages because they did not perform the alleged wrongful acts and MGM ceased to exist five months before the trial. There is no merit to the argument. MGM's attorney and some of its witnesses represented at trial that they were employed by MGM. There was no mention of the fact that MGM no longer existed until after the trial. A successor corporation may not avoid liability for punitive damages when the issue was not raised before the trier of fact.

IX

We next consider appellants' claims of error in the awards of compensatory damages.

Appellants raise a variety of relatively minor issues regarding the wording of some of the instructions. We see no error in the instructions as a whole.

Appellants maintain that there was insufficient evidence to support an award of $1 million for loss of professional income on the bad faith count, as Welch did not have a reasonably certain future career as a serious film actress. We disagree. The lost income award was supported by the amount of money Welch had made from previous film work, the absence of film offers subsequent to Cannery Row, the expert testimony that she would have obtained additional film roles but for the Cannery Row firing, and the amount of money film stars were making at the time of trial. The $1 million the jury awarded for lost income was considerably less than the $3,200,000 for which her counsel argued.

We similarly reject appellant's argument that there was insufficient evidence to support damages of $750,000 for loss of reputation on the bad faith count. Appellants ignore the difference between Welch's pre-Cannery Row reputation as a somewhat difficult but professional actress and her post-Cannery Row reputation as a contract breaker who had been fired for cause.

Appellants also maintain that MGM cannot be liable for $300,000 of compensatory damages for slander when Begelman, who made the slanderous statement, was found liable for only $25,000 of such damages. We disagree. The jury was instructed that MGM's liability depended upon whether Begelman was speaking solely as an individual or was expressing MGM's official corporate position. The verdict shows that the jury believed that Begelman was speaking on behalf of the studio and that the statement caused more damage coming from the studio than from an individual.

Appellants further complain that the various categories of compensatory damages which were awarded on the bad faith count were duplicative of each other or duplicated the compensatory damages which were awarded on other counts.

On the bad faith count, the jury was instructed to consider: (1) lost contract benefits, including the agreed compensation and loss of value of appearing in the film; (2) loss of professional income; (3) damage to reputation; and (4) emotional distress. The jury verdict form on the bad faith count mirrored the factors in that instruction. As to the other counts, the jury was simply asked to determine the amount of compensatory damages which applied, without specification of the source of the damages.

Appellants never objected to the form of the verdicts, and never contended at the trial court level that there were duplications within the damages on the bad faith count. After the verdicts were returned, they raised some, but not all, of the contentions of duplication which they now make before us. By acquiescing in the measure of damages which was presented to the jury, appellants waived the right to raise this issue on appeal. Moreover, as to those issues of duplication which the trial court was asked to consider, the record supports the trial court's determinations that the only duplication was in the $194,000 awarded both for breach of contract and conspiracy to induce breach of contract; the other damages compensated for different types of losses. The $194,000 duplication was corrected at the trial court level.

X

Finally, we consider appellants' contentions that the punitive damages are excessive or duplicative as a matter of law.

As previously indicated, the jury awarded $3,750,000 against MGM and $500,000 against Phillips as punitive damages on count II (conspiracy to induce breach of contract); $150,000 against MGM and $2,500 against Begelman as punitive damages on count III (slander); and $3,750,000 against MGM as punitive damages against MGM on count IV (breach of the implied covenant of good faith and fair dealing).

An award of punitive damages will be found excessive on appeal only if the record shows that it was so grossly disproportionate that it resulted from passion or prejudice Among the pertinent factors are the reprehensibility of the conduct, the relationship between the amounts of compensatory and punitive damages, and the wealth of the particular defendant. (*Id.,* at p. 928, 148 Cal.Rptr. 389, 582 P.2d 980.) Great weight is given to the determination of a trial court on motion for new trial that the damages were not excessive. Such a ruling was made here.

The punitive damages the jury awarded were substantially less than Welch requested. As to MGM, her counsel asked the jury for $7,500,000 on the slander count and that same amount on the bad faith count. The $500,000 awarded against Phillips for bad faith was exactly what counsel requested. Counsel argued for $700,000 on the slander count, based on one dollar for each Rolling Stone subscriber.

It was stipulated below that MGM had a net worth of $215 million and Phillips of $5 million. The punitive damages thus represented 3.6 percent of MGM's net worth and 10 percent of Phillips's net worth as an individual. As to MGM, the ratio of punitive damages to compensatory damages was 2.8:1. The same ratio as to Phillips was 2.1:1.

As shown by the cases summarized in *Devlin v. Kearny Mesa AMC/Jeep/Renault, Inc., supra,* 155 Cal.App.3d 381, 202 Cal.Rptr. 204, the size of the punitive damage awards here was not inconsistent with or disproportionate to awards which have been affirmed in the past. (See also *Goshgarian v. George* (1984) 161 Cal.App.3d 1214, 1228, 208 Cal.Rptr. 321.) We realize that MGM lost money on the film, and Phillips's salary for producing it was $200,000. Still, given the net worths of the defendants, their complete disregard of the likelihood that the unjustified firing would ruin Welch's film career, and the relatively high actual damages, the jury could properly conclude that appellants' conduct justified the amount of punitive damages which was awarded.

As to duplication, appellants maintain that punitive damages could be assessed either on the conspiracy/slander theory of counts II and III, or on the bad faith theory of count IV, but not on both, as they can not be punished twice for the same conduct. They emphasize that the pleading allegations of Count IV incorporated the paragraphs of Counts II and III which described the alleged acts of conspiracy and slander, and that count IV was added in mid-trial after Welch's counsel argued that it was based on the "identical set of facts" which had already been presented in support of counts II and III.

In denying the motion for new trial, the trial court did not expressly state why it saw no duplication problem. It apparently relied on the argument in Welch's opposition that the torts had different elements and were viewed separately by the jury, which reached a verdict on bad faith a day and a half before its verdict on conspiracy.

Appellants rely primarily on cases which preclude simultaneous imposition of a statutory penalty and punitive damagesCalifornia case law has, however, permitted dual awards of punitive damages from different causes of action arising from the same course of conduct. (*Godfrey v. Steinpress* (1982) 128 Cal.App.3d 154, 181–184, 180 Cal.Rptr. 95 [punitive damages both for intentional infliction of emotional distress and fraudulent concealment]; *Fletcher v. Western National Life Ins. Co.* (1970) 10 Cal.App.3d 376, 402–404, 89 Cal.Rptr. 78 [punitive damages possible both for intentional infliction of emotional distress and tortious interference by an insurance company with a protected property interest of its insured].)

Since the various causes of action here had different elements and relied on different facts for their proof, the separate punitive damage awards were appropriate.

In any event, appellants waived this issue by permitting the case to go to the jury under a theory in which the punitive damages were to be added together.

The jury was instructed that punitive damages are designed for example and punishment. It was told there was no fixed standard for determining the appropriate amount, and that it should consider the reprehensibility of the conduct, deterrence in light of the defendant's financial condition, and a reasonable relationship between punitive damages and actual damages.

As indicated, Welch's counsel asked the jury to award $7,500,000 punitive damages for conspiracy and the same amount for bad faith. The total damage request was for over $20 million. Appellants' counsel argued that $20 million was an "extraordinary amount of money" and that there was no basis for awarding any punitive damages at all, as Welch was fired without malice and in good faith. Appellants did not suggest until their post-verdict motions that the punitive damage awards on the conspiracy and bad faith counts could not be added together.

In awarding $3,500,000 separately on the conspiracy and bad faith counts, the jury determined that a total of $7 million, about half of what Welch had requested, was the appropriate figure to serve the underlying goals of punitive damages. If appellants had suggested prior to the verdict that the punitive damages on the two counts could not be aggregated, the trial court could have resolved that issue in a timely manner. If it ruled in appellants' favor, the jury would have been informed that the two awards could not be aggregated, and might well have awarded additional damages. Instead, appellants acquiesced in a measure of damages which permitted the punitive damages to be added together. They are now precluded from attacking that measure of damages.

The judgment is affirmed.

On Rehearing

Six days after our decision in this case was filed, the Supreme Court held in *Foley v. Interactive Data Corp.*, 47 Cal.3d 654, 254 Cal.Rptr. 211, 765 P.2d 373, that "tort remedies are not available for breach of the implied covenant [of good faith and fair dealing] in an employment contract to employees who allege they have been discharged in violation of the covenant." 47 Cal.3d at 700, 254 Cal.Rptr. 211, 765 P.2d 373.

Chief Justice Lucas's majority opinion in *Foley* expressly left open the question of whether the decision is retroactive or prospective, that issue not having been briefed. (Fn. 43, p. 700, 254 Cal.Rptr. 211, 765 P.2d 373.) The concurring and dissenting opinion by Justice Broussard noted that a similar pattern of past reliance had caused the Supreme Court to make prospective its holding in *Moradi–Shalal v. Fireman's Fund Ins. Co.* (1988) 46 Cal.3d 287, 305, 250 Cal.Rptr. 116, 758 P.2d 58 that section 790.03 of the California Insurance Code does not provide a private right of action against insurance companies. (Fn. 3, 47 Cal.3d at p. 706, 254 Cal.Rptr. 211, 765 P.2d 373.)

Before our decision was final, we requested supplemental briefing on the question of whether *Foley* should be retroactive or prospective. We have concluded that, as occurred with *Moradi–Shalal, Foley* should not apply to cases filed prior to the date on which *Foley* became final.

In *Moradi–Shalal,* the Supreme Court reversed its previous holding in *Royal Globe Ins. Co. v. Superior Court* (1979) 23 Cal.3d 880, 153 Cal.Rptr. 842, 592 P.2d 329, which had created a private cause of action under section 790.03. On the question of retroactivity, Chief Justice Lucas' majority opinion stated: "The general rule is that 'a decision of a court of supreme jurisdiction overruling a former decision is retrospective in its operation. [Fn. & citation omitted.] We have recognized exceptions to that rule when considerations of fairness and public policy preclude full retroactivity. [Citation.] For example, where a ... statute has received a given construction by a court of last resort, and contracts have been made or property rights acquired in accordance with the prior decision, neither will the contracts be invalidated nor will vested rights be impaired by applying the new rule retroactively. [Citation.]' (*Peterson v. Superior Court* (1982) 31 Cal.3d 147, 151–152 [181 Cal.Rptr. 784, 642 P.2d 1305], fn. omitted.) [¶] Without implying any broad exception to the general rule of retrospectivity described above, and in the interest of fairness to the substantial number of plaintiffs who have already initiated their suits in reliance on *Royal Globe,* we hold that our decision overruling that case will not apply to those cases seeking relief under section 790.03 filed before our decision here becomes final." (*Moradi–Shalal v. Fireman's Fund Ins. Co., supra,* 46 Cal.3d at p. 305, 250 Cal.Rptr. 116, 758 P.2d 58; fns. omitted.)

Similarly here, the interest of fairness to the substantial number of plaintiffs who have already initiated their suits in reliance on the long-standing case law recognizing a tort cause of action for bad faith discharge requires that the *Foley* decision be prospective only. It is true that the Supreme Court had never previously expressly held that such a cause of action is available. Its dicta, however, in *Tameny v. Atlantic Richfield Co.* (1980) 27 Cal.3d 167, 179, footnote 12, 164 Cal.Rptr. 839, 610 P.2d 1330, and *Seaman's Direct Buying Service, Inc. v. Standard Oil Co.* (1984) 36 Cal.3d 752, 769, footnote 6, 206 Cal.Rptr. 354, 686 P.2d 1158, strongly suggested that the similarities between the insurer/insured and employer/employee relationships justified extending the bad faith tort to the employment context. A long line of Court of Appeal decisions followed that dicta in recognizing the existence of a tort remedy for bad faith discharge. (*Cleary v. American Airlines* (1980) 111 Cal.App.3d 443, 168 Cal.Rptr. 722; *Crosier v. United Parcel Service, Inc.* (1983) 150 Cal.App.3d 1132, 198 Cal.Rptr. 361; *Shapiro v. Wells Fargo Realty Advisors* (1984) 152 Cal.App.3d 467, 199 Cal.Rptr. 613; *Rulon–Miller v. International Business Machines Corp.* (1984) 162 Cal.App.3d 241, 208 Cal.Rptr. 524; *Khanna v. Microdata Corp.* (1985) 170 Cal.App.3d 250, 215 Cal.Rptr. 860; *Gray v. Superior Court* (1986) 181 Cal.App.3d 813, 226 Cal.Rptr. 570; *Koehrer v. Superior Court* (1986) 181 Cal.App.3d 1155, 226 Cal.Rptr. 820; *Huber v. Standard Ins. Co.* (9th Cir.1988) 841 F.2d 980.) Prior to *Foley,* there was disagreement regarding the ramifications of the tort cause of action for bad faith discharge, but unanimous agreement that the cause of action existed.

Foley's holding that the employer/employee relationship is too different from the insurer/insured relationship to justify applying the bad faith tort in the employment context thus constitutes a dramatic break from long-standing previous authority, including statements by the Supreme Court itself.

Based on the similarities between prior reliance on the existence of a *Royal Globe* cause of action and prior reliance on the existence of a tort cause of action for bad faith discharge, we follow the example of the *Moradi–Shalal* court in holding that *Foley* does not apply to tort actions for bad faith discharge which were filed prior to the finality of *Foley.* That holding means that *Foley* is inapplicable to the case at bench.

MGM's petition for rehearing raises a new issue, that the punitive damages awarded in this case violate the Eighth Amendment's prohibition against excessive fines. We do not reach that issue, as MGM has waived it by not asserting it earlier and no good cause to relieve it of that waiver has been shown.

The petition for rehearing has been denied.

McCLOSKY and GOERTZEN, JJ., concur.

BLAUSTEIN v. BURTON
Court of Appeal of California, Second Appellate District, Division Five
May 28, 1970
Civ. No. 34751
9 Cal.App.3d 161,
88 Cal.Rptr. 319

FRAMPTON, J.

Statement of the Case

Plaintiff, on November 14, 1967, filed his complaint against the defendants Richard Burton, Elizabeth Taylor Burton, Franco Zeffirelli, and Does I through X, wherein he sought damages for (1) breach of contract, (2) unjust enrichment, (3) breach of confidential relationship and (4) services rendered and benefits conferred. Answer to the complaint was filed by the Burtons on January 16, 1968, and no other defendant was served or appeared in the action.

On March 20, 1968, respondents (Burtons) took appellant's (Blaustein's) deposition, and on June 18, 1968, respondents filed their notice of motion for summary judgment based solely upon appellant's deposition. The motion was noticed for hearing on July 17, 1968, but by stipulation, hearing thereon was continued first to July 31, 1968, and ultimately to October 21, 1968.

On July 29, 1968, appellant filed his own affidavit and the deposition of Martin Gang, taken on March 26, 1968, in opposition to the motion. On .ctober 17, 1968, respondents filed the declarations of Richard McWhorter and Norman G. Rudman, and the affidavit of Kenneth L. Maidment in support of the motion.

The matter was argued and submitted and the court announced its decision granting the motion on November 19, 1968. Motion for reconsideration was denied January 10, 1969, and summary judgment was entered in favor of respondents on January 16, 1969. The appeal is from the judgment.

Statement of Facts

Appellant, in his deposition, testified that he had been in the motion picture business since 1935. After serving as a reader, a story editor, the head of a story department, and an editorial supervisor, he became a producer of motion picture films in 1949. The films he has produced include "Broken Arrow"; "Mr. 880"; "Half Angel"; "Just One More Chance"; "Take Care of My Little Girl"; "The Day the Earth Stood Still"; "The Outcasts of Poker Flat"; "Don't

Bother to Knock"; "Desiree"; "The Racers"; "Storm Center"; "Cowboy"; "Bell, Book and Candle"; "The Wreck of the Mary Deare"; "Two Loves"; "The Four Horsemen of the Apocalypse"; and "Khartoum." The functions of a producer of a motion picture are to (1) generate the enthusiasm of the various creative elements as well as to bring them together: (2) search out viable locations which would be proper for the artistic side of the production and would be proper from the logistic physical production side; (3) create a budget that would be acceptable from the physical point of view as well as satisfactory from the point of view of implementing the requirements of the script; (4) make arrangements with foreign government where the photography would take place; (5) supervise the execution of the script, the implementation of it onto film; (6) supervise the editing of all the production work down through the dubbing process and the release printing process, at least through the answer print process with Technicolor in this case; (7) the obligation of consulting with the United Artists people on advertising and publicity; (8) arrange casting; (9) engage the interests of the kind of star or stars that they (the United Artists' people) would find sufficiently attractive to justify an investment, and (10) develop the interest of a proper director.

During 1964, appellant conceived an idea consisting of a number of constituent elements including the following: (a) the idea of producing a motion picture based upon William Shakespeare's play "the Taming of the Shrew"; (b) the idea of casting respondents Richard Burton and Elizabeth Taylor Burton as the stars of this motion picture; (c) the idea of using as the director of the motion picture Franco Zeffirelli, a stage director, who at that time had never directed a motion picture and who was relatively unknown in the United States; (d) the idea of eliminating from the film version of the play the so-called "frame" (i.e., the play within a play device which Shakespeare employed), and beginning the film with the main body of the story; (e) the idea of including in the film version the two key scenes (i.e., the wedding scene and the wedding night scene) which in Shakespeare's play occur offstage and are merely described by a character on stage; (f) the idea of filming the picture in Italy, in the actual Italian settings described by Shakespeare.

On April 6, 1964, appellant met with Hugh French, an established motion picture agent who was then, and was at the time of the taking of the deposition (March 20, 1968), the agent for respondent Richard Burton. Prior to such meeting, appellant knew that Mr. French was Mr. Burton's agent and Mr. French knew that appellant was a motion picture producer, as appellant and Mr. French had been involved in business dealings together in the past. At such meeting, appellant first asked Mr. French "if he could tell me anything about the availability of Mr. and Mrs. Burton." Mr. French replied: "Well, they have many commitments; but, as you know, they are always interested in good ideas or good scripts or good projects." Appellant then replied: "Well, I have a thought about a picture for the Burtons, but it makes no sense to discuss it unless you would be interested in it or unless you tell me that they would be available to consider a production beyond their current commitments." Mr. French responded: "No, indeed, I would like to hear what you have in mind." Appellant then said that he thought there would be something uniquely attractive at that time to do a film based on Shakespeare's "Taming of the Shrew" with respondents as the stars of the picture. Mr. French's reaction was "instantaneous and affirmative." Appellant then asked Mr. French if the idea had ever been previously discussed, and Mr. French replied no, that to his knowledge it had not been. Mr. French further stated that he would discuss appellant's idea with Mr. Burton, and would try to arrange a meeting in New York between appellant and the Burtons.

Thereafter, at Mr. French's suggestion and with tickets arranged for by Mr. French, appellant attended the opening of Mr. Burton's stage production of "Hamlet" in New York City on April 9, 1964. At that time, Mr. French introduced appellant to Mr. Burton as "the man who had been talking about Taming of the Shrew." Because of Mr. Burton's preoccupation with his stage production, it was not possible at that time for appellant to have a private meeting with the Burtons, so appellant proceeded on to London, where he was engaged in production work on another motion picture.

Upon arriving in London, appellant decided to explore the possibility of using the services of Franco Zeffirelli as the director of "The Taming of the Shrew" motion picture. Accordingly, on May 11, 1964, appellant met with John Van Eyssen, Mr. Zeffirelli's agent, in London. Appellant related his idea to Mr. Van Eyssen, and his disclosure thereof to Mr. French. To appellant's inquiry as to the possible availability of Mr. Zeffirelli, Mr. Van Eyssen replied "that he thought it was just a splendid idea, that he was absolutely certain that his client would agree with his reaction, but that he would telephone him in France and discuss it with him as quickly as he could reach him. ..." Thereafter, appellant, together with Mr. Van Eyssen, met with Mr. Zeffirelli in Paris on May 22, 1964. Appellant there related his idea in some detail to Mr. Zeffirelli, and Mr. Zeffirelli's response was: "I can't tell you how much I would like to do it, but why would the Burtons accept me?" Appellant replied "... that is my job, to generate their enthusiasm for you, ... [and] I think there is a very good chance of my persuading them to accept you."

On May 25, 1964, appellant, while still in London, telephoned to Mr. French in Los Angeles, suggested the idea of Mr. Zeffirelli acting as director of the proposed motion picture, told of the meeting with Zeffirelli, and suggested that this information be communicated to Mr. and Mrs. Burton. The possibility of a meeting between appellant and Mr. and Mrs. Burton was also discussed in this telephone conversation. On May 27, 1964, appellant sent the following cable to Mr. French: "Leaving in few days. Please cable about Burton meeting so can plan New York stopover. Julian Blaustein." On May 30, 1964, Mr. French cabled the following reply: "Sorry for delay reply but as cannot give you definite answer suggest you return California most convenient route. If this via New York, will try to arrange meeting. Hugh." On May 31, 1964, Mr. French sent the following cable to appellant: "Now have definite reaction, Richard delighted meet you New York. Let me know when you expect arrive. Will try be there if you feel can help. Hugh." En route from London to Los Angeles, appellant stopped over in New York City until June 3, 1964. He was unable during this time to meet with Mr. and Mrs. Burton.

Upon his return to Los Angeles, appellant met with Martin Gang on June 25, 1964. Mr. Gang at that time was appellant's lawyer. Mr. Gang's firm was also the attorneys for respondents Richard Burton and Elizabeth Taylor Burton. Aaron Frosch, a New York lawyer, acted as general counsel for Mr. and Mrs. Burton. At the meeting between appellant and Mr. Gang, appellant disclosed his above described idea, and related his dealings up to that point with Mr. French. Appellant told Mr. Gang that "Mr. French has so far been unable to arrange a meeting" with Mr. and Mrs. Burton. Mr. Gang offered to attempt to arrange such a meeting. Mr. Gang thereupon phoned Aaron Frosch and informed him of appellant's desire to meet with Mr. and Mrs. Burton and of the reasons for such a meeting. Mr. Frosch stated that he believed that he could arrange such a meeting, suggesting that appellant phone him upon appellant's arrival in New York.

Upon his arrival in New York, appellant phoned Mr. Frosch's secretary on June 29, 1964, and was told to contact Richard Hanley, appointments secretary for Mr. and Mrs. Burton. Appellant did phone Mr. Hanley, who recognized him and stated "It looks fine. Richard and Elizabeth know you are here and we will get it set up as quickly as we can." On the afternoon of June 30, 1964, Mr. Hanley phoned appellant and said: "Can you come up to see them?" Appellant proceeded to Mr. and Mrs. Burton's hotel suite, was introduced to Mr. Burton by Mr. Hanley, and then met for a period alone with Mr. Burton. Later, Mrs. Burton joined them. At the beginning of the conversation between appellant and Mr. Burton regarding "The Taming of the Shrew," Mr. Burton commented upon what a good idea it was for Mrs. Burton and him to make such a motion picture, adding, "I don't know how come we hadn't thought of it."

After Mrs. Burton joined them, appellant explained in full his ideas regarding the proposed project. This included the use of Mr. Zeffirelli as the director. Mr. Burton said of Zeffirelli "I think he is a marvelous idea. The idea of who directs this picture is naturally very important, and I just think you have made a very good choice. And you have met with him?", to which appellant replied in the affirmative. They then discussed the cost of the film, and of appellant's prior discussion with Mr. Zeffirelli relative to the cost area. Mr.

Burton stated "Well, certainly with you as an experienced producer, you can contribute that part of it to him."

There then was a discussion of possible conflicting commitments, and Mr. Burton stated with reference to another project, "Well, look, we are not actually committed to that, and I do believe that could be pushed back anyway. This idea is such a good one and this picture is so important that we do it that I think we should plan on doing it. And we can try to juggle our other productions to fit this." Toward the end of the meeting, Mr. Burton stated, "Well, let's plan to go ahead now. Elizabeth and I would like to do this. We think Zeffirelli is a good idea. We will accept him. You tell me you have worked out a potential deal with him." Appellant had discussed Mr. Zeffirelli's connection with the proposal with Mr. Van Eyssen. Mr. Burton instructed appellant to work out appropriate arrangements with Aaron Frosch. The meeting ended with a mutual expression of looking forward to working together.

After the above meeting, and before appellant left the United States, he called Martin Gang in California from New York City. In this telephone conversation, he told Mr. Gang "Look, you do whatever you think is right about structuring a deal with Aaron Frosch, and you know I am not going to be difficult about my end of this because this is a very important picture to me and I don't want you to feel that we have got to fight with anybody, whatever might come up, about any fees and my participation and so forth. It's a picture I want very badly to do, and please keep me in touch." Mr. Gang replied, "Congratulations. I will get onto it right away and keep you informed."

Upon appellant's return to London, where he was working on another motion picture, he met with Mr. Van Eyssen and proceeded further with the negotiation of a deal for the services of Mr. Zeffirelli as director. Appellant reported progress made in these negotiations in a letter dated July 7, 1964, which he sent to Martin Gang.

On August 11, 1964, appellant received a phone call in London from Mickey Rudin, who was then a partner in Mr. Gang's law firm. Mr. Rudin worked in close contact with Mr. Frosch in connection with "The Taming of the Shrew." Mr. Rudin represented Mr. and Mrs. Burton in connection with "The Taming of the Shrew," and as far as Mr. Gang knows, has continued to do so even after Mr. Rudin disassociated from the Gang firm. In the phone call of August 11, 1964, appellant asked Mr. Rudin what percentage share of the gross receipts from the motion picture "The Taming of the Shrew" appellant would receive if he were paid no guaranteed fee; what percentage share he would receive if he were paid a guaranteed fee of $50,000, and what percentage share he would receive if he were paid a guaranteed fee of $100,000. Mr. Rudin replied that he would think about it and let appellant know.

About November 27, 1964, appellant "felt that there was nothing to do but wait until the Burtons are in a position to and have an inclination to make a commitment."

On December 30, 1964, appellant met with Mr. Gang and Mr. Rudin in Mr. Gang's office in Los Angeles. At this meeting appellant learned that his position in the project was in jeopardy. At this time both Mr. Rudin and Mr. Gang advised appellant that he had no legal rights in the project, and appellant "simply accepted that."

In March 1965, a meeting was held in Dublin, Ireland, where Mr. Burton was filming another motion picture, attended by Mickey Rudin, among others. The meeting concerned "The Taming of the Shrew" project, including appellant's participation in connection therewith. Following this meeting, Mr. Rudin stopped off in London, en route back to Los Angeles, and on March 18, 1965, phoned appellant. In that phone conversation, Mr. Rudin stated to appellant that "[he] might not be the producer if the picture is ever made." Mr. Rudin further stated, "under any conditions, however, there would be a reward for your contribution to the project." On March 20, 1965, appellant addressed a letter to Messrs. Rudin and Gang in which he said in part: "There's no point rehashing the various elements involved; nor is there any point attempting to 'try the case,' particularly with my own attorney. I realize I must simply accept whatever Aaron Frosch and you agree is proper 'reward' for my contribution. But it's important to me, Mickey, that you understand I can never consider any such payment to be a satisfactory substitute for the function that has been denied me on a project I initiated." In conversations with Mr. Van Eyssen (face to face) and with Mr. Zeffirelli (via telephone) on March 25, 1965, appellant was advised that the suggestion that appellant not be the producer of the film had come from "the other side" and from "the Burton lawyer." Appellant understood this reference to be directed toward Mr. Aaron Frosch and so advised both Mr. Zeffirelli and Messrs. Gang and Rudin.

Upon Mr. Rudin's return to Los Angeles, he reported events at the Dublin meeting to his then partner, Martin Gang. Mr. Gang wrote to appellant on April 27, 1965, stating that Mr. Rudin had reported to him that "there is no question in anybody's mind that this was your idea, of 'Taming of the Shrew' and bringing Zeffirelli in was your idea, and this is so recognized by all the principals, including Mr. Burton and Mr. Zeffirelli."

In December 1965, appellant heard rumors of a "deal" being made for the production of "The Taming of the Shrew" involving the respondents and was informed by Mr. Gang that discussions to this effect were then taking place with Columbia Pictures Corporation. In a letter to Mr. Gang dated January 3, 1965, but, in fact, written and sent on January 3, 1966, appellant suggested the possibility of informing Columbia of his participation in the project, noting that "Burton has acknowledged the obligation involved," and stating, "I should imagine Columbia wouldn't hesitate to acknowledge Burton's (and Zeffirelli's) obligation to me as an obligation of the production - provided it's discussed at the proper time, which is during the negotiations of the entire deal." Mr. Gang's response to this suggestion was to advise appellant against contacting Columbia since by doing so "he might upset the possibility of any deal being made because Columbia wouldn't want to get involved in litigation, and that if he wanted to get any rewards out of it for any reason, without giving any legal opinions, that it would be best not to upset that apple cart." Appellant did not communicate with Columbia.

Thereafter, a motion picture based upon William Shakespeare's play "The Taming of the Shrew" was produced and exhibited commencing in or about March 1967. The motion picture stars respondents Richard Burton and Elizabeth Taylor Burton, and is directed by Franco Zeffirelli. The motion picture was financed and distributed by Columbia Pictures Corporation, although at the time of taking Mr. Gang's deposition (March 26, 1968), the formal contract between Columbia and the respondents remained to be completed. Mr. Rudin has represented Mr. and Mrs. Burton in the negotiations with Columbia. The motion picture as completed utilizes the following ideas disclosed by appellant to respondents: (1) It is based upon the Shakespearean play "The Taming of the Shrew"; (2) it stars Elizabeth Taylor Burton and Richard Burton in the roles of Katherine and Petruchio, respectively; (3) the director is Franco Zeffirelli; (4) it eliminates the "frame," i.e., the play within a play device found in the original Shakespearean play, and begins with the main body of the story; and (5) it includes an enactment of the two key scenes previously referred to by appellant which in Shakespeare's play occur off-stage.

In addition, the film was photographed in Italy, although not in the actual locales in Italy described by Shakespeare.

Respondents have paid no monies to appellant, nor have they accorded him any screen or advertising credit.

Respondents, while not challenging the foregoing statement of facts, except to say that they do not acquiese in the claimed "characterizations" and "conclusions" contained therein, urge that critical facts have been omitted therefrom. These critical facts, according to respondents, as revealed by the record, are as follows: In connection with appellant's meeting on April 6, 1964, with Hugh French, motion picture agent for respondent Richard Burton, appellant, was, according to his own testimony, familiar with the function of an agent for an established star in the motion picture industry. Appellant was aware of the role usually played by an agent for an established star, which was to screen projects submitted to the star, in turn submitting them to the star for a determination of interest. If there is interest, the agent usually pursues it further on the star's behalf.

Appellant was aware that an agent for a major star cannot commit the star without the star's approval. This is the practice in very close to 100 percent of the cases and in that sense differs from other agencies. The "few cases" in which the star permits his agent to make commitments on his behalf "are very rare."

Appellant testified in his deposition that there is nothing unique about doing Shakespeare on the screen. It has been done many times. It has been done by leading stars of the calibre of Laurence Olivier. Respondent Richard Burton has himself previously appeared in a motion picture made of Shakespeare's "Hamlet." Shakespearean productions in motion picture form have been made in the United States, with leading stars, and also in England, the Soviet Union and other countries of the World.

Appellant testified that there is nothing unique about the idea of making a motion picture entitled "The Taming of the Shrew," based on Shakespeare's play of that title. Such has been done in the United States before the making of the film here in issue, and the earlier film featured in its leading roles (Petruchio and Katherine) stars who were then married to each other and who were perhaps the leading idols of the screen at the time, Mary Pickford and Douglas Fairbanks. The Pickford-Fairbanks film "The Taming of the Shrew" was done in the 1930's. The declaration of Norman B. Rudman filed in support of the motion disclosed that the earlier version of the film also (1) eliminated the "frame" (the play within a play device utilized by Shakespeare), and (2) depicted on screen the wedding night scenes which in the Shakespearean original occurs off-stage and are merely described by narration.

Appellant testified in his deposition that there was nothing unique or unusual about doing "The Taming of the Shrew" with two of the leading actors of the time, in the sense that it had been done once before, but "there was something unusual about the particular notion of doing it under other circumstances." There is nothing unique about a stage director of good repute coming directly from the stage to motion pictures and directing a major motion picture. Such has been done often in the past by such directors as Ruben Mamoulian, Josh Logan, Danny Mann, Orson Welles, Eliah Kazan, and by Mike Nichols, who directed the film "Who's Afraid of Virginia Woolf," which starred the respondents in its leading roles, as his first film production.

Appellant testified further in his deposition that there is nothing unique about a non-American director directing English speaking actors in a film. Zeffirelli speaks quite good English, was distinguished for his directorial work in the field of opera and had done many stage productions in different languages in Italy, France and England. Zeffirelli was well known and distinguished as a director of at least one Shakespearean production, "Romeo and Juliet," prior to his direction of the respondents in "The Taming of the Shrew."

Appellant testified further, by way of deposition, that he asked Mr. French to communicate with the Burtons to ascertain whether or not they would be interested in doing "The Taming of the Shrew." Appellant was interested in this from a business point of view so that he might have an interest in the film as a producer. One of appellant's objects was to negotiate a co-production or joint venture agreement with respondents under which he would be engaged as producer of the film under specific terms and conditions, and respondents would be committed to star in the film, their services to begin on a given start date. Appellant's company and respondents or their company would be co-venturers and co-owners of the film. The negotiations did not result in a co-production or joint venture agreement.

Appellant testified further, by way of deposition, that his interest in the possibility of using the services of Franco Zeffirelli as director of the motion picture was based upon Zeffirelli's potential in contributing to the commercial success of the picture to such extent that appellant could point out its commercial potential to a possible distributor whose prime interest would be commercialism. The key elements of the picture, so far as appellant was concerned, besides the play itself, were Mr. and Mrs. Burton to play the leads. In appellant's letter of July 11, 1964, addressed to Mr. Martin Gang, his attorney, he stated that if Mr. Zeffirelli were not available as director of the film, respondent Burton might himself direct the film; the only requirement was that there be a top-flight director.

In appellant's first meeting with John Van Eyssen, Zeffirelli's agent, which occurred in London on May 11, 1964, he told Van Eyssen that interest in the project had been expressed by the Burtons' agent, and by the Burtons through their agent, but that nothing had been done beyond that and that appellant had not yet met with the Burtons personally to discuss the subject. Appellant urged Mr. Van Eyssen to discuss the matter with Zeffirelli, but did not enjoin the former from discussing it with others as such an injunction is implict in any discussion with an agent. Before meeting the Burtons, ap-appellant had possibly discussed the matter of the picture informally with one David Chasman of United Artists.

When Mr. Gang, at appellant's request, telephoned Aaron Frosch on June 25, 1964, to assist appellant in obtaining an audience with the Burtons, Mr. Frosch had already known about the proposal of the Burtons doing a film "The Taming of the Shrew" because of appellant's approach to Mr. Zeffirelli, who was also a client of Mr. Frosch's office.

Appellant, since the meeting with respondents of June 30, 1964, has not seen them personally nor had any conversations with them. He has no written contract in connection with the proposed project signed by respondents, or either of them, or any agent of the respondents wherein he was promised the position of producer of the film "The Taming of the Shrew."

Contentions on Appeal

Appellant urges that (1) there are triable issues of fact as to whether a contract was entered into between appellant and respondents pursuant to which appellant is entitled to compensation by reason of respondents' utilization of the idea disclosed to them by appellant; (2) there are triable issues of fact as to whether appellant is entitled to recover from respondents under quasi-contract for services rendered and benefits conferred, and (3) there are triable issues of fact as to whether appellant is entitled to recover from respondents for breach of a confidential relationship.

Respondents urge (1) that appellant's action is barred by the statute of frauds and the statute of limitations under California law; that the substantive law of the State of New York should be invoked in determination of the parties rights, and that under the application of the law of either state, appellant's claim is equally untenable; (2) there is no triable issue of fact raised by the declarations and affidavits, and (3) respondents were not unjustly enriched at appellant's expense, nor did respondents breach any confidential relationship such as to require the law to impose a quasi-contractual obligation upon respondents to pay any sums to appellant.

The issue to be determined by the trial court in ruling on a motion for summary judgment is whether or not the party opposing the motion has presented any facts which give rise to a triable issue or defense, and not to pass upon a determine the issue itself, that is, the true facts in the case. The facts alleged in the affidavits of the party against whom the motion is made must be accepted as true, and that such affidavits to be sufficient need not necessarily be composed wholly of strictly evidentiary facts. A summary judgment is proper only if the affidavits in support of the moving party would be sufficient to sustain judgment in his favor, and his opponent does not by affidavit show such facts as may be deemed by the judges hearing the motion sufficient to present a triable issue of fact. The affidavits are to be construed with all intendments in favor of the party opposing the motion. (*Desny* v. *Wilder*, 46 Cal.2d 715, 725 [299 P.2d 257].) The use of depositions in support of, or in opposition to a motion for summary judgment is proper. (*Kramer v. Barnes*, 212 Cal.App.2d 440, 444 [27 Cal.Rptr. 895].) In examining the sufficiency of affidavits filed in connection with the motion, the affidavits of the moving party are strictly construed and those of his opponent liberally construed and doubts as to the propriety of granting the motion should be resolved in favor of the party opposing the motion. Such summary procedure is drastic and should be used with caution so that it does not become a substitute for the open trial method of determining the facts. (*Wilson v. Bittick*, 63 Cal.2d 30, 34-35 [45 Cal.Rptr. 31, 403 P.2d 159].)

The rights of an idea discloser to recover damages from an idea recipient under an express or implied contract to pay for the idea in event the idea recipient uses such idea after disclosure is discussed in *Desny* v. *Wilder*, 46 Cal.2d 715, 731-739 [299 P.2d 257], as follows: "*The Law Pertaining to Ideas.* Generally speaking, ideas are as free as the air and as speech and the senses, and as potent or weak, interesting or drab, as the experiences, philosophies, vocabularies, and other variables of speaker and listener may combine to produce, to portray, or to comprehend. But there can be circumstances when neither air nor ideas may be acquired without cost. The diver who goes deep in the sea, even as the pilot who ascends high in the troposphere, knows full well that for life itself he, or someone on his behalf, must arrange for air (or its respiration-essential element, oxygen) to be specially provided at the time and place of need. The theatrical producer likewise may be dependent for his business life on the procurement of ideas from other persons as well as the dressing up and portrayal of his self-conceptions; he may not find his own sufficient for survival. As counsel for the Writers Guild aptly say, ideas 'are not freely usable by the entertainment media until the latter are made aware of them.' The producer may think up the idea himself, dress it and portray it; or he may purchase either the conveyance of the idea alone or a manuscript embodying the idea in the author's concept of a literary vehicle giving it form, adaptation and expression. It cannot be doubted that some ideas are of value of a producer.

"An idea is usually not regarded as property, because all sentient beings may conceive and evolve ideas throughout the gamut of their powers of cerebration and because our concept of property implies something which may be owned and possessed to the exclusion of all other persons. We quote as an accurate statement of the law in this respect the following language of Mr. Justice Brandeis, dissenting in *International News Service v. Associated Press* (1918), *supra*, 248 U.S. 215, 250 [39 S.Ct. 68, 76, 63 L.Ed. 211, 225]: 'An essential element of individual property is the legal right to exclude others from enjoying it. If the property is private, the right of exclusion may be absolute; if the property is affected with a public interest, the right of exclusion is qualified. But the fact that a product of the mind has cost its producer money and labor, and has a value for which others are willing to pay, is not sufficient to ensure to it this legal attribute of property. The general rule of law is, that the noblest of human productions—knowledge, truths ascertained, conceptions, and ideas—become, after voluntary communication to others, free as the air to common use.' Of similar import, but stated negatively: 'The doctrine that an author has a property right in his ideas and is entitled to demand for them the same protection which the law accords to the proprietor of personal property generally finds no recognition either in the common law or in the statutes of any civilized country.' Whether the theory upon which this court sustained recovery in the *Golding* case may properly be classed as a property rights theory is not clear (see pp. 694-695 of 35 Cal.2d and pp. 831, 836-837 of 40 Cal.2d) but it is clear that California does not now accord individual property type protection to abstract ideas. (*Weitzenkorn v. Lesser* (1953), 40 Cal.2d 778, 788-789 [256 P.2d 947].) This accords with the general weight of authority. (See generally, Nimmer, '*The Law of Ideas*,' (1954) 27 So.Cal.L.Rev. 120 et seq. and cases cited.) 'There may be literary property in a particular combination of ideas [and this must presuppose an expression thereof] or in the form in which ideas are embodied. There can be none in the ideas.' (*Fendler* v. *Morosco* (1930) 253 N.Y. 281, 287 [171 N.E. 56, 58].) Neither common law nor statutory copyright extends protection to an idea as such. '[O]nly in the "expression" of a copyrighted work does any monopoly inhere; the "theme," the "plot," the " ideas" may always be freely borrowed.' (*Dellar v. Samuel Goldwyn, Inc.* (1945, 2d C.C.A.), 150 F.2d 612.)

"The principles above stated do not, however, lead to the conclusion that ideas cannot be a subject of contract. As Mr. Justice Traynor stated in his dissenting opinion in *Stanley v. Columbia Broadcasting System* (1950), *supra*, 35 Cal.2d 653, 674 [221 P.2d 73, 23 A.L.R.2d 216]: 'The policy that precludes protection of an abstract idea by copyright does not prevent its protection by contract. Even though an idea is not property subject to exclusive ownership, its disclosure may be of substantial benefit to the person to whom it is disclosed. That disclosure may therefore be consideration for a promise to pay ... Even though the idea disclosed may be " widely known and generally understood" [citation], it may be protected by an express contract providing that it will be paid for regardless of its lack of novelty.' (*Cf. Brunner v. Stix, Baer & Fuller Co.* (1944), 352 Mo. 1225 [181 S.W.2d 643, 646]; *Schonwald v. F. Burkart Mfg. Co.* (1947), 356 Mo. 435 [202 S.W.2d 7].) Amici supporting plaintiff add, 'If a studio wishes to have an idea disclosed to it and finds that idea of sufficient value to make use of it, it is difficult to see how any hardship is involved in requiring payment of the reasonable value of the material submitted.' The principles enunciated in the above quotation from Justice Traynor's dissent are accepted as the law of California (*Weitzenkorn* v. *Lesser* (1953), *supra*, 40 Cal.2d 778, 791-792) and we have no quarrel with amici's postulation. This case, however, remains to be resolved.

"The lawyer or doctor who applies specialized knowledge to a state of facts and gives advice for a fee is selling and conveying an idea. In doing that he is rendering a service. The lawyer and doctor have no property rights in their ideas, as such, but they do not ordinarily convey them without solicitation by client or patient. Usually the parties will expressly contract for the performance of and payment for such services, but, in the absence of an express contract, when the service is requested and rendered the law does not hesitate to infer or imply a promise to compensate for it. In other words the recovery may be based on contract either express or implied. The person who can and does convey a valuable idea to a producer who commercially solicits the service or who voluntarily accepts it knowing that it is tendered for a price should likewise be entitled to recover. In so holding we do not fail to recognize that free-lance writers are not necessarily members of a learned profession and as such bound to the exalted standards to which doctors and lawyers are dedicated. So too we are not oblivious of the hazards with which producers of the class represented here by defendants and their related amici are confronted through the unsolicited submission of numerous scripts on public domain materials in which public materials the producers through their own initiative may well find nuclei for legitimately developing the 'stupendous and colossal.' The law, however, is dedicated to the proposition that for every wrong there is a remedy (Civ. Code, § 3523) and for the sake of protecting one party it must not close the forum to the other. It will hear both and seek to judge the cause by standards fair to both. To that end the law of implied contracts assumes particular importance in literary idea and property controversies.

"*The Law Pertaining to Contracts, Express, Implied-in-Fact and Implied by Law, and Quasi Contractual Obligations, as Related to Ideas and Literary Property*. The parties and amici, from their several viewpoints, discuss the law of contracts and caution us not to confuse the rules insofar as such rules may differentiate respectively among contracts which are express or implied-in-fact or implied-in-law, meaning by the latter expression to denote a quasi-contractual obligation imposed by law. We agree that whether a contract be properly identified as express or as implied-in-fact or inferred from circumstances; or whether the bargain meets the subjective test of a meeting of minds or is held to reside in the objective evidence of words and acts with or without a meeting of minds; or whether the obligation be recognized as implied by law from acts having consensual aspects (and therefore often termed implied-in-fact); or whether the obligation be imposed by law because of acts and intents which, although tortious rather than consensual, should in justice give rise to an obligation resembling that created by contract and, hence, should be termed quasi-contractual, is important here to the extent that we recognize the situations and discriminate appropriately in the governing rules.

"An eminent writer says that 'The elements requisite for an informal contract ... are identical whether they are expressly stated or implied in fact,' citing e.g., *Lombard v. Rahilly* (1914), 127 Minn. 449 [149 N.W. 950], holding 'A "contract implied in fact" requires a meeting of the minds, an agreement, just as much as an "express contract"; the difference between the two being largely in the character of the evidence by which they are established'; see also *Silva v. Providence Hospital of Oakland* (1939) 14 Cal.2d 762, 773 [97 P.2d 798]. (Williston on Contracts, rev. ed., vol. 1, p. 8.) The same author describes quasi contracts by declaring that 'as quasi contractual obligations are imposed by the law for the purpose of bringing about justice without reference to the intention of the parties, the only apparent restriction upon the power of the law to create such obligations is that they must be of such a sort as would have been appropriately enforced under common-law procedure by a contractual action. Indeed even this limitation is too narrow, for a bill in equity or a libel in admiralty might be the appropriate means of enforcing some quasi contractual obligations. As the law may impose any obligations that justice requires, the only limit in the last analysis to the category of quasi contracts is that the obligation in question more closely resembles those created by contract than those created by tort. On the other hand, a true contract cannot exist, however desirable it might be to have one, unless there is a manifestation of assent to the making of a promise. Furthermore, the measure of damages appropriate to contractual obligations differs from that applicable to quasi contracts ... It is also true that quasi contractual obligations are not so universally based on unjust enrichment or benefit as is sometimes supposed. There are many cases where the law enforces in a contractual action a duty to restore the plaintiff to a former status—not merely to surrender the benefit which the defendant has received.'

"If it were not for precedent we should hesitate to speak of an implied-in-fact contract. In truth, contracts are either made in fact or the obligation is implied in law. If made in fact, contracts may be established by direct evidence or they may be inferred from circumstantial evidence. The only difference is in the method of proof. In either case they would appear to be express contracts. Otherwise, it would seem that they, or the presumed contractual obligation, must be implied at law. A so-called 'implied-in-fact' contract, however, as the term is used by some writers, may be found although there has been no meeting of the minds. Even an express contract may be found where there has been no meeting of minds. The classic example of this situation is set up by the parol evidence rule. The law accepts the objective evidence of the written contract as constituting the contract and, subject, of course, to certain exceptions, precludes oral evidence to show that the minds of the parties did not meet in the writing. Professor Williston recognizes in effect, if not specifically, that the law implies (or construes) contractual obligations in many cases where there is no true contract in the historically conventional sense and that such implied obligations are of the nature of, and governed by the rules applicable to, contracts termed implied-in-fact by many writers. In a paper published in 14 Illinois Law Review 85, 90, Mr. Williston says: 'The parties may be bound by the terms of an offer even though the offeree expressly indicated dissent, provided his action could only lawfully mean assent. A buyer who goes into a shop and asks and is given [told] the price of an article, cannot take it and say "I decline to pay the price you ask, but will take it at its fair value." He will be liable, if the seller elects to hold him so liable, not simply as a converter for the fair value of the property, but as a buyer for the stated price.' (See *Lucy v. Mouflet* (1860), 5 H. & N. 229, 232; *Wilcox, Ives & Co.* v. *Rogers* (1913), 13 Ga.App. 410 [79 S.E. 219]; Rest., Contracts, § 5, p. 7; § 72(2), p. 77.) Concerning the same subject Professor Costigan, in a paper published in 33 Harvard Law Review 376, at 398, states his view: 'Professor Williston is absolutely right in his contention tht the no-meeting-of-the-minds express contracts—the objective but not subjective test contracts—are properly to be denominated contracts instead of quasi-contracts, and the reason for that concession was that on their breach the normal contract measure of damages is applied. But that same reason has led us to the further conclusion that there are genuine implied-in-fact contracts of both the meeting-of-the-minds and the no-meeting-of-the-minds varieties.'

"Whether the resulting 'contract' in the cases discussed by the learned professors is classified as express (as may be fictionized by the law's objective test) or as implied-in-fact (as also may be fictionized by the law) or whether in the same or slightly differing circumstances an obligation shall be 'implied' and denominated 'quasi contractual' because it is strong-armed by the law from nonconsensual acts and intents, is probably important in California—and for the purposes of resolving the problems now before us—principally as an aid to understanding the significance of rulings and discussions in authorities from other jurisdictions. Here, our terminology and the situations for application of the pertinent rules are simplied by codification.

"Our Civil Code declares that 'A contract is either express or implied'; (§ 1620) 'An express contract is one, the terms of which are stated in words' and 'An implied contract is one, the existence and terms of which are manifested by conduct.' The same code further provides that '[T]he acceptance of the consideration offered with a proposal, is an acceptance of the proposal'; (§ 1589) 'A voluntary acceptance of the benefit of a transaction is equivalent to a consent to all the obligations arising from it, so far as the facts are known, or ought to be known, to the persons accepting'; (§ 1605) 'Any benefit conferred ... upon the promisor, by any other person, to which the promisor is not lawfully entitled ... is a good consideration for a promise'; and (§ 1606) '[A] moral obligation originating in some benefit conferred upon the promisor ... is also a good consideration for a promise, to an extent corresponding with the extent of the obligation, but no further or otherwise.' (See also *Silva v. Providence Hospital of Oakland* (1939), *supra*, 14 Cal.2d 762, 773, and cases there cited; *Horacek v. Smith* (1948), 33 Cal.2d 186, 194[11] [199 P.2d 929]; *Yadkoe v. Fields* (1944), 66 Cal.App.2d 150, 158-159 [151 P.2d 906]; Rest., Contracts, §§ 5, 72(2); 12 Cal.Jur.2d 186-189.)

"From what has been shown respecting the law of ideas and of contracts we conclude that conveyance of an idea can constitute valuable consideration and can be bargained for before it is disclosed to the proposed purchaser, but once it is conveyed, i.e., disclosed to him and he has grasped, it, it is henceforth his own and he may work with it and use it as he sees fit. In the field of entertainment the producer may properly and validly agree that he will pay for the service of conveying to him ideas which are valuable and which he can put to profitable use. Furthermore, where an idea has been conveyed with the expectation by the purveyor that compensation will be paid if the idea is used, there is no reason why the producer who has been the beneficiary of the conveyance of such an idea, and who finds if valuable and is profiting by it, may not then for the first time, although he is not at that time under any legal obligation so to do, promise to pay a reasonable compensation for that idea - that is, for the past service of furnishing it to him - and thus create a valid obligation. As said in 12 American Jurisprudence 603, section 110, 'there is considerable authority with supports the view that the moral obligation arising from a benefit of a material or pecuniary kind conferred upon the promisor by past services, rendered in the expectation that they were to be paid for - or, at least, if rendered upon the assumption by the person rendering them, though mistaken, that they would create a real liability—and, otherwise, in circumstances creating a moral obligation on the part of the promisor to pay for the same, will support an executory promise to do so, although there was, previous to such promise, no legal liability or promise, perfect or imperfect.' But, assuming legality of consideration, the idea purveyor cannot prevail in an action to recover compensation for an abstract idea unless (a) before or after disclosure he has obtained an express promise to pay, or (b) the circumstances preceding and attending disclosure, together with the conduct of the offeree acting with knowledge of the circumstances, show a promise of the type usually referred to as 'implied' or 'implied-in-fact.' (See *Weitzenkorn v. Lesser* (1953), *supra*, 40 Cal.2d 778, 794-795; *Elfenbein v. Luckenbach Terminals* (1933), 111 N.J.L. 67 [166 A. 91, 93].) That is, if the idea purveyor has clearly conditioned his offer to convey the idea upon an obligation to pay for it if it is used by the offeree and the offeree, knowing the condition before he knows the idea, voluntarily accepts its disclosure (necessarily on the specified basis) and finds it valuable and uses it, the law will either apply the objective test (discussed, *supra*, pp. 801-802) and hold that the parties have made an express (sometimes called implied-in-fact) contract, or under those circumstances, as some writers view it, the law itself, to prevent fraud and unjust enrichment, will imply a promise to compensate.

"Such inferred or implied promise, if it is to be found at all, must be based on circumstances which were known to the producer at and preceding the time of disclosure of the idea to him and he must voluntarily accept the disclosure, knowing the conditions on which it is tendered. Section 1584 of the Civil Code ('[T]he acceptance of the consideration offered with a proposal, is an acceptance of the proposal') can have no application unless the offeree has an opportunity to reject the consideration—the proffered conveyance of the idea—before it is conveyed. Unless the offeree has opportunity to reject he cannot be said to accept. The idea man who blurts out his idea without having first made his bargain has no one but himself to blame for the loss of his bargaining power. The law will not in any event, from demands stated subsequent to the unconditioned disclosure of an abstract idea, imply a promise to pay for the idea, for its use, or for its previous disclosure. The law will not imply a promise to pay for an idea from the mere facts that the idea has been conveyed, is valuable, and has been used for profit; this is true even though the conveyance has been made with the hope or expectation that some obligation will ensue. So, if the plaintiff here is claiming only for the conveyance of the idea of making a dramatic production out of the life of Floyd Collins he must fail unless in conformity with the above stated rules he can establish a contract to pay." (*Desny v. Wilder, supra*, 46 Cal.2d 715, 731-739.)

It is held that "... if a producer obligates himself to pay for the disclosure of an idea, whether it is for protectible or unprotectible material, in return for a disclosure thereof he should be compelled to hold to his promise. There is nothing unreasonable in the assumption that a producer would obligate himself to pay for the disclosure of an idea which he would otherwise be legally free to use, but which in fact, he would be unable to use but for the disclosure."

"The producer and the writer should be free to make any contract they desire to make with reference to the buying of the ideas of the writer; the fact that the producer may later determine, with a little thinking, that he could have had the same ideas and could thereby have saved considerable money for himself, is no defense against the claim of the writer. This is so even though the material to be purchased is abstract and unprotected material." (*Chandler v. Roach*, 156 Cal.App.2d 435, 441-442 [319 P.2d 776].) An idea which can be the subject matter of a contract need not be novel or concrete.

It may be noted here that the law of the State of New York no longer requires that an idea be "novel" in order to be the subject of contract protection. As stated in *Frederick Chusid & Co.* v. *Marshall Leeman & Co.* (S.D.N.Y. 1968) 279 F.Supp. 913, 917: "Under New York law the parties have the right by contract to prevent disclosure of such materials, even though they are not secret or confidential and may indeed be a matter of public knowledge." The court in *Krisel v. Duran* (S.D.N.Y. 1966) 258 F.Supp. 845, 860 stated: "Under New York law, an idea, if valuable, even though it does not contain novel, secret or confidential material, may be protected by such an agreement. This doctrine applies even when the subject matter of the idea is common or open to public knowledge."

We are of the opinion that appellant's idea of the filming of Shakespeare's play "The Taming of the Shrew" is one which may be protected by contract.

Express or implied contracts both are based upon the intention of the parties and are distinguishable only in the manifestation of assent. The making of an agreement may be inferred by proof of conduct as well as by proof of the use of words. (12 Cal.Jur.2d, Contracts, § 4, p. 186.) Whether or not the appellant and respondents here, by their oral declarations and conduct, as shown by the depositions and affidavits, entered into a contract whereby respondents agreed to compensate appellant in the event respondents used appellant's idea, is a question of fact which may not be properly resolved in a summary judgment proceeding, but must be resolved upon a trial of the issue. (Cf. *Silva* v. *Providence Hospital of Oakland*, 14 Cal.2d 762, 774 [97 P.2d 798].) Even where a question of interpretation of contractual provisions is involved on a motion for summary judgment, it is settled that, if the opposing interpretations are both reasonable, a question of fact is raised which precludes summary judgment. (*Walsh v. Walsh*, 18 Cal.2d 439, 443-444 [116 P.2d 62].)

Statute of Frauds. Respondents urge that the agreement is barred by the statute of frauds, section 1624 subdivision 1 of the Civil Code.

The application of section 1624 subdivision 1 of the Civil Code to the transaction here under consideration rests upon a triable issue of fact. The trier of fact might conclude that from the negotiations and conduct of the parties and their agents there was an implied contract. That is, the respondents may be found to have made an implied promise of payment, conditioned upon subsequent use, in return for appellant's act of disclosing his idea - not in return for his promise to disclose such idea. This being a unilateral contract (a promise for an act—see Rest., Contracts, §§ 12 and 55), it does not fall within the section of the statute of frauds dealing with contracts not to be performed within one year. (Rest., Contracts, § 198, com. a.) If the trial court should find that appellant disclosed his idea to respondents on the condition that respondents would not use the idea unless they compensated appellant for such use, and respondents accepted the disclosure on that condition, then the compensation would, at respondents' option, take one of two forms: they would engage appellant as producer of the film or pay him the monetary equivalent. Since it appears from the record that appellant has made his disclosure and respondents have elected not to engage him as producer of the film, all that remains to be done is payment by respondents. Where a contract has been fully performed by one party and nothing remains to be done except the payment of money by the other party, the statute of frauds is inapplicable. (*Dutton v. Interstate Inv. Corp.*, 19 Cal.2d 65, 70 [119 P.2d 138]; 1 Witkin, Summary of Cal. Law (1960) Contracts, § 97, p. 105.) Furthermore, to fall under the bar of subdivision 1 of section 1624 of the Civil Code, the contract must, by its terms, be impossible of performance within a year. If it is unlikely that it will be so performed, or the period of performance is indefinite, the statute does not apply. (1 Witkin, Summary of Cal. Law (1954) Contracts, § 95, p. 103.)

Statute of Limitations. Respondents urge that the action is barred by the provisions of section 339 subdivision 1 of the Code of Civil Procedure.

This raises the question as to when the cause of action accrued. This depends on the nature of respondents' obligation, if any, to appellant.

Appellant, in his affidavit, filed in opposition to the motion for summary judgment, states: "However, when I disclosed my ideas to defendants and their representatives, I did not intend to confer a gratuity on them. Nor did I intend to make them a gift of my services. They were not merely actors but competitors of mine in the business of producing films. I made the disclosures and rendered the services with the expectation and understanding that in the event defendants used my ideas and went forwards with production of a film version of The Taming of the Shrew, I would be engaged as producer of the film at my then going rate and receive the usual screen and advertising credits as such producer, or I would receive the monetary equivalent of such compensation and credit. By their words and acts, defendants and their representatives demonstrated—at the various times they solicited my disclosures and services—that they knew I expected to be the producer and receive compensation and credit therefor, or receive the monetary equivalent thereof."

If the trial court should find that the condition under which appellant disclosed his idea, and the condition which was impliedly agreed to by respondents was "that in the event defendants used my ideas and went forword with production of a film version of The Taming of the Shrew, I would be engaged as producer of the film at my then going rate and receive the usual screen and advertising credits as such producer, or I would receive the monetary equivalent of such compensation and credit," then appellant would not have a right to actually participate as the producer, but would only have the obligation so to do as a condition of his right to payment. But as long as he was prepared to render such services, respondents remained obligated to pay the monetary equivalent of what he would have received had he, in fact, rendered such services, even if respondents elected not to use his services. Respondents' obligation to pay is triggered not by the use of appellant's services as a producer, but rather by their use of appellant's idea.

The question arises as to when, within the meaning of the implied promise, if the court should find such a promise, respondents may be held to have used appellant's idea. This again raises an issue of fact turning on the manifested intent of the parties. A trier of fact might conclude that such a use was intended to occur the moment a preliminary script is written embodying appellant's idea, even if in fact no motion picture production, based upon such script, ever occurs. The court might also find that the implied promise to pay arose upon respondents' disclosure of the idea to a substantial segment of the public since such use would tend to destroy any further marketability of the idea. (See *Thompson v. California Brewing Co.*, 191 Cal.App.2d 506, 510 [12

Cal.Rptr. 783]; *Donahue* v. *Ziv Television Programs, Inc.*, 245 Cal.App.2d 593, 611 [54 Cal.Rptr. 130].) The record discloses that the motion picture "The Taming of the Shrew" was first released to the public in or about March 1967. Appellant's action was commenced November 14, 1967. Since the trier of fact might conclude that the date of release of the picture to the general public was the use intended by the parties to trigger respondents' obligation to pay, it is impermissible to find on motion for summary judgment that appellant's cause of action is barred by the two year statute of limitations.

Confidential Relationship. Respondents urge that the record is devoid of any evidence tending to establish the fact that they breached a duty of confidence owed to appellant.

Appellant, in his affidavit, stated: "Because I knew Mr. French to be a highly reputable agent, had had prior dealings with him, had the same firm of attorneys as the Burtons and had been the recipient of an invitation, constantly renewed, to disclose my ideas and render services on the project, I reposed trust and confidence in the Burtons and their representatives and expected that my ideas would be kept in confidence by them. I did not expect or intend that defendants would go forward with production of "Shrew" and make use of my ideas without my participation."

Under the rules governing the granting of a summary judgment, the foregoing declaration on the part of appellant, made in opposition to the motion for summary judgment, is sufficient to raise a triable issue of fact as to whether the disclosure of his idea to respondents was made in confidence, and was accepted by respondents upon the understanding that they would not use it without the consent of appellant. (Cf. *Thompson* v. *California Brewing Co.*, 150 Cal.App.2d 469, 474 [310 P.2d 436.].)

The judgment is reversed.

STEPHENS, Acting P. J., and AISO, J., concurred.

ELLIOTT-MCGOWAN PRODUCTIONS v. REPUBLIC PRODUCTIONS, INC.
United States District Court for the Southern District of New York
September 29, 1956
145 F.Supp. 48

DIMOCK, District Judge.

Plaintiff, Elliott-McGowan Productions, producer of a motion picture photoplay entitled 'Hellfire' brings this action against the distributors, Republic Pictures, Inc., and Republic Pictures Corporation, for a direction that Samuel Hacker & Co., certified public accountants, be permitted to inspect and audit the books of defendants relating to the distribution of the photoplay, for an accounting of all transactions with respect to the distribution of the photoplay and other relief. There are now three motions before me: one by defendants for a partial summary judgment pursuant to Rule 56 F.R.C.P., 28 U.S.C., and two by plaintiff, respectively for discovery and for a direction that questions on an examination be answered.

Defendants' motion for partial summary judgment is based on the contention that any claim arising more than two years prior to the commencement of this suit, August 10, 1953, is barred by the provisions of the contract between the parties. The pertinent part, Paragraph 7 of Section XI, provides:

> 'None of the parties hereto shall have or assert any claim, demand or cause of action for or because of any act or omission or other thing with regard to this contract, or growing out of it, or institute or maintain any action, suit or proceeding at law or in equity based on or growing out of or in reference to any such act or omission or other thing, unless such claim or demand shall have been asserted and such action, suit or proceeding shall have been commenced within two (2) years after the date of the act, omission or other thing to which it refers.'

This action was commenced on August 10, 1953. Therefore the provisions of the contract would appear to bar all claims arising prior to August 10, 1951. Plaintiff presents two principal contentions why this should not be so, first because the provisions should not be so construed and second because defendants' conduct precludes their reliance thereon.

Plaintiff contends that the paragraph limits the time within which suit may be commenced after demand is made. Under this construction demand could be made at any time and suit could be commenced within two years after the demand. In effect this limitation would be no limitation at all. I read the agreement as requiring that demand be made and suit instituted within two years of the 'act, omission or other thing' to which it refers.

Plaintiff also contends that, as the defendants broke the contract by issuing false reports, they cannot invoke the protection of the contractual limitation. The result of such a rule would be that a party could never set up a time limitation except in a case where he was proved blameless and where he would not need the time limitation. I reject the contention.

The parties may by agreement shorten the period limiting the time for bringing suit. The defense of a contractual time limitation may be given effect by a summary judgment motion where it can be established by indisputable proof. If there is any dispute as to when a particular act or omission took place it can be determined at the trial, but everything prior to August 10, 1951 is barred.

Plaintiff cross-moves for an order requiring defendant to answer certain questions propounded to defendant's treasurer on an examination of defendant and to compel the discovery of certain records pursuant to Rule 34 F.R.C.P. Defendant opposes this motion for the reason, among others, that the motion is an attempt to circumvent the procedure established by contract between the parties for any examination of defendants' books.

Paragraph 3 of Section X of the contract between the parties provides:

> 'The producer shall have the right, at its sole cost and expense, through any national firm of certified public accountants of standing comparable to Price, Waterhouse and Company, at all reasonable times during business hours, to inspect and audit and make extracts from said books and records and supporting documents and vouchers with reference to all such gross receipts and expenses and all other matters entering into the computations to be shown on the statements to be furnished by the distributor as hereinafter provided, but only insofar as such books, records, documents and vouchers relate to the distribution of said photoplay.'

Paragraph 3 of Section X of the contract further provides:

> 'No claim of the producer that any charge, computation or deduction shown or reflected in any statement rendered to the producer by the distributor as hereinafter provided is improper or inaccurate shall be asserted or maintained by the producer unless made in writing to the distributor within one (1) year after the date such statement is rendered, nor shall the producer have any right to audit or inspect any such books, records, documents or vouchers relating to transactions reported in any such statement unless such audit or inspection be commenced within one (1) year from the date that such statement is rendered.'

The provision in this paragraph against inspection of any records relating to a statement more than a year old shows that the contract provisions for discovery were intended to the exclusive, for the one-year limitation would be completely nugatory if the producer retained the right of discovery under Rule 34 F.R.C.P.

I see no objection to giving effect to a party's agreement to contract away his right to discovery where the circumstances make such an agreement reasonable. Courts have upheld reasonable agreements for a short statute of limitations, Riddlesbarger v. Hartford Insurance Co., supra, or consenting that the courts of a foreign country should have exclusive jurisdiction over a claim, Wm. H. Muller & Co. v. Swedish-American Line, Ltd., 2 Cir., 224 F.2d 806.

The distributor's position is that the records are so confidential that only someone like a Price, Waterhouse accountant should be permitted to look at them and that the distributor therefore insisted when the contract was drafted that there should be no general right of discovery. In view of the legitimate objections to full discovery in this case and the reasonably effective substitute afforded I hold that the waiver is valid.

The result of the agreement between the parties is that the producer cannot have the benefit of the records until it is established that its candidate for auditor is of standing comparable to Price, Waterhouse & Company. The distributors have refused to permit the audit on the ground that the producer's candidate does not meet this standard. The producer has been well advised to seek a direction in this action that the distributor permit an audit by the producer's candidate. Until it has been established that the candidate has the requisite standing, the distributor's refusal to approve the producer's candidate does not, however, entitle the producer to discovery under Rule 34.

The producer's motion for a direction that defendant Republic Pictures Corporation answer the questions which its treasurer said he could not answer without the records is granted insofar as the questions relate to transactions within the period beginning on August 10, 1951. A party defendant cannot evade answering proper questions, as the witness here attempted, by refusing to consult its records.

Motion for partial summary judgment granted to extent of dismissing claim insofar as it is based on liabilities arising out of acts or omissions which took place prior to August 10, 1951.

Motion for discovery denied.

Motion to compel answers granted insofar as questions relate to matters which took place within the period beginning on August 10, 1951, otherwise denied.

WOOD v. LUCY, LADY DUFF-GORDON
Court of Appeals of New York
November 14, 1917, Argued
December 4, 1917, Decided
222 N.Y. 88, 118 N.E. 214

CARDOZO, J.

The defendant styles herself 'a creator of fashions.' Her favor helps a sale. Manufacturers of dresses, millinery and like articles are glad to pay for a certificate of her approval. The things which she designs, fabrics, parasols and what not, have a new value in the public mind when issued in her name. She employed the plaintiff to help her to turn this vogue into money. He was to have the exclusive right, subject always to her approval, to place her indorsements on the designs of others. He was also to have the exclusive right to place her own designs on sale, or to license others to market them. In return, she was to have one-half of 'all profits and revenues' derived from any contracts he might make. The exclusive right was to last at least one year from April 1, 1915, and thereafter from year to year unless terminated by notice of ninety days. The plaintiff says that he kept the contract on his part, and that the defendant broke it. She placed her indorsement on fabrics, dresses and millinery without his knowledge, and withheld the profits. He sues her for the damages, and the case comes here on demurrer.

The agreement of employment is signed by both parties. It has a wealth of recitals. The defendant insists, however, that it lacks the elements of a contract. She says that the plaintiff does not bind himself to anything. It is true that he does not promise in so many words that he will use reasonable efforts to place the defendant's indorsements and market her designs. We think, however, that such a promise is fairly to be implied. The law has outgrown its primitive stage of formalism when the precise word was the sovereign talisman, and every slip was fatal. It takes a broader view to-day. A promise may be lacking, and yet the whole writing may be 'instinct with an obligation,' imperfectly expressed (SCOTT, J., in *McCall Co. v. Wright,* 133 App. Div. 62; *Moran v. Standard Oil Co.,* 211 N. Y. 187, 198). If that is so, there is a contract.

The implication of a promise here finds support in many circumstances. The defendant gave an *exclusive* privilege. She was to have no right for at least a year to place her own indorsements or market her own designs except through the agency of the plaintiff. The acceptance of the exclusive agency was an assumption of its duties (*Phœnix Hermetic Co. v. Filtrine Mfg. Co.,* 164 App. Div. 424; *W. G. Taylor Co. v. Bannerman,* 120 Wis. 189; *Mueller v. Bethesda Mineral*

Spring Co., 88 Mich. 390). We are not to suppose that one party was to be placed at the mercy of the other (*Hearn v. Stevens & Bro.,* 111 App. Div. 101, 106; *Russell v. Allerton,* 108 N. Y. 288). Many other terms of the agreement point the same way. We are told at the outset by way of recital that 'the said Otis F. Wood possesses a business organization adapted to the placing of such indorsements as the said Lucy, Lady Duff-Gordon has approved.' The implication is that the plaintiff's business organization will be used for the purpose for which it is adapted. But the terms of the defendant's compensation are even more significant. Her sole compensation for the grant of an exclusive agency is to be one-half of all the profits resulting from the plaintiff's efforts. Unless he gave his efforts, she could never get anything. Without an implied promise, the transaction cannot have such business 'efficacy as both parties must have intended that at all events it should have' (BOWEN, L. J., in *The Moorcock,* 14 P. D. 64, 68). But the contract does not stop there. The plaintiff goes on to promise that he will account monthly for all moneys received by him, and that he will take out all such patents and copyrights and trademarks as may in his judgment be necessary to protect the rights and articles affected by the agreement. It is true, of course, as the Appellate Division has said, that if he was under no duty to try to market designs or to place certificates of indorsement, his promise to account for profits or take out copyrights would be valueless. But in determining the intention of the parties, the promise *has* a value. It helps to enforce the conclusion that the plaintiff *had* some duties. His promise to pay the defendant one-half of the profits and revenues resulting from the exclusive agency and to render accounts monthly, was a promise to use reasonable efforts to bring profits and revenues into existence. For this conclusion, the authorities are ample (*Wilson v. Mechanical Orguinette Co.,* 170 N. Y. 542; *Phœnix Hermetic Co. v. Filtrine Mfg. Co., supra; Jacquin v. Boutard,* 89 Hun, 437; 157 N. Y. 686; *Moran v. Standard Oil Co., supra; City of N. Y. v. Paoli,* 202 N. Y. 18; *M'Intyre v. Belcher,* 14 C. B. [N. S.] 654; *Devonald v. Rosser & Sons,* 1906, 2 K. B. 728; *W. G. Taylor Co. v. Bannerman, supra; Mueller v. Bethesda Mineral Spring Co., supra; Baker Transfer Co. v. Merchants' R. & I. Mfg. Co.,* 1 App. Div. 507).

The judgment of the Appellate Division should be reversed, and the order of the Special Term affirmed, with costs in the Appellate Division and in this court.

CUDDEBACK, MCLAUGHLIN and ANDREWS, JJ., concur; HISCOCK, Ch. J., CHASE and CRANE, JJ., dissent.

Judgment reversed, etc.

ARTICLE: OH, WHAT A TANGLED WEB WE WEAVE: REALITY TV SHINES A FALSE LIGHT ON LADY DUFF-GORDON

Walter T. Champion, Jr.

[reprinted by permission of the author]
15 Seton Hall J. of Sports & Ent. L. 27 (2005)

I. Introduction

The problem with popular culture and its symbol of the day, 'Reality TV,' is not the fact of its existence, but the possibility that it is emblematic of a fading society. The potential for depravity in Reality TV appears endless. For example, from tasteless to bizarre, from voyeuristic to sadistic, "reality television has made stars of barely dressed people competing for $1 million, singers competing for recording contracts, and bachelors and bachelorettes competing for love." This diversity has spawned a frenetic competition for newer and riskier plots and scenarios. For example, "[m]ore than three years after CBS began airing the reality phenomenon Survivor, Showtime Networks wants to launch a simulated presidential campaign, to be shown when the actual presidential campaign is heating up next summer."

These "cutting-edge" shows increase the risk of lawsuits. The rights of the participants will be protected by a diverse variety of causes of actions which might include the following: breach of contract, defamation, false light, invasion of privacy, tortious interference with a business relationship, statutory and constitutional violations, publication of private facts, commercial appropriations of a name or likeness, intrusion in public places, breach of confidence, and intentional infliction of emotional distress. An example of Reality TV's legal boundaries is a recent lawsuit by a participant in Doggy Fizzle Televizzle:

> An actress has sued rapper Snoop Dogg and MTV over an episode of the television show Doggy Fizzle Televizzle, in which she claimed she was unwittingly made to appear as if she were naked and engaging in sexual relations with another actor. In a lawsuit filed Friday, Doris Burns accuses Snoop Dogg, whose real name is Calvin Broadus, and MTV of breach of contract, fraud, invasion of privacy and defamation.

The two causes of action that might synergize to create the best protection for maligned participants is breach of contract based on implied terms, as famously exemplified by Wood v. Lucy, Lady Duff-Gordon, and false light invasion of privacy. The vigorous advocate will use Lady Duff-Gordon to assert that implied in the Reality TV contract is the producer's good faith obligation to refrain from purposefully exposing the participant to implied false light publicity.

II. Background: Reality TV and the Law

The so-called privacy torts are the logical choice to begin the analysis of the interaction between Reality TV and the law. "One who intentionally intrudes, physically or otherwise, upon the solitude or seclusion of another or his private affairs or concerns, is subject to liability to the other for invasion of his privacy, if the intrusion would be highly offensive to a reasonable person." The "invasion may be by physical intrusion into a place in which the plaintiff has secluded himself, as when the defendant forces his way into the plaintiff's room in a hotel or insists over the plaintiff's objection in entering his home." Also,

[o]ne who gives publicity to a matter concerning the private life of another is subject to liability to the other for invasion of his privacy, if the matter publicized is of a kind that (a) would be highly offensive to a reasonable person, and (b) is not a legitimate concern to the public.

In A.A. Dietemann v. Time, Inc., the court found Time Magazine liable for invasion of privacy. Defendant's photographers entered the office portion of plaintiff's house by subterfuge, and photographed and recorded plaintiff's conversations with a third person. Additionally, in Miller v. National Broadcasting Co., the court held that a heart attack victim's wife could sue a local television news producer when a camera crew entered her bedroom along with paramedics. A valid cause of action existed against the television network and the news producer for invasion of privacy. Reasonable people could see this intrusion as highly offensive.

Moreover, the Dietemann court extended privacy to cover the case where a reasonable person might expect that a defendant should be excluded. In Miller, a private matter was publicized. For example, publishing a nude photograph may be sufficient to base a "public disclosure" claim. Also, filming nude prison inmates constitutes an invasion of privacy. An individual's privacy warrants some form of protection against an overzealous intrusion into one's private life. Lastly, filming individuals in instances where they no longer consent to be filmed and in times when they are undergoing a personal crisis might be viewed as offensive to a reasonable person.

The most prevalent context of the present legal analysis into Reality TV are those cases where the media accompanies law enforcement personnel in some variation of a "ride-along." Primarily, in Wilson v. Layne, the Supreme Court held that media ride-alongs violate the Fourth Amendment when media accompanies law enforcement officers. Also, in Food Lion, Inc. v. ABC, Inc., the operator of grocery stores sued a television network alleging fraud, trespass, negligent supervision, and civil conspiracy for damages resulting from a PrimeTime Live undercover story that exposed unsanitary food conditions. The court disallowed a motion for summary judgments on the basis that a factual question existed as to the misrepresentation by network employees masquerading as potential employees, on their employment contracts with Food Lion.

Additionally in Howell v. Tribune Entertainment Co., a sixteen-year-old girl who appeared on a television talk show with her sister and stepmother to participate in discussion of problems with stepparents brought an action for invasion of privacy against the show's producer. The court found against the plaintiff on the grounds that she waived any privacy right that attached to the police report filed against her by making statements during the show that accused her stepmother of adultery and mistreatment.

No liability was found in an unauthorized surfing documentary. However, the family of an executive obtained injunctive relief against television reporters for placing their home under surveillance. Also, the Supreme Court of California held that triable issues of fact existed in reference to a documentary rescue program. A triable issue existed as to whether both plaintiffs had an objectively reasonable expectation of privacy in the interior of the rescue helicopter. Likewise, the mother was entitled to a degree of privacy in her conversations with the rescue nurse and other medical rescuers at the accident scene. The nurse's conversations conveying medical information to the hospital commanded privacy as well.

III. Analysis: The Right to Privacy and Lady Duff-Gordon Meet in the False Light of Reality TV

A. The Right to Privacy

In 1890, in their famous essay, Right to Privacy, Louis Brandeis and Samuel Warren commented that the press's "instantaneous photographs" and new "business methods" would be "overstepping in every direction the obvious bounds of propriety and of decency." They observed that "numerous mechanical devices threaten to make good the prediction that 'what is whispered in the closet shall be proclaimed from the housetops.' "

[T]oday a vast number of books, journals, television and radio stations, cable channels and Internet content sources all compete to satisfy our thirst for knowledge and our need for news of political, economic and cultural events as well as our love of gossip, [and] our curiosity about the private lives of others. This "curiosity" segues into morbidity and includes "that weak side of human nature which is never wholly cast down by the misfortunes and frailties of our neighbors." Since 1890, "the United States has also seen a series of revolutions in mores and conventions that has moved, blurred and, at times, seemingly threatened to erase the line between public and private life." Even in 1890, "the details of sexual relations [were] broadcast in the columns of the daily papers." Today, our society is voyeuristic and quite capable of recounting in detail every nuance of what were formerly private matters because they have been depicted on Reality TV.

However, "the desire for privacy must at many points give way before our right to know, and the news media's right to investigate and relate, facts about the events and individuals of our time." Justices Brandeis and Warren recognized that a line must be drawn between private matters and those of "public and general interest" because there is a "legitimate concern" in the latter. In 1931, a California appellate court observed that the right of privacy "does not exist in the dissemination of news and news events." The freedom of the press, as protected by the First and Fourteenth Amendments to the United States Constitution, is extensive and far ranging.

The guarantees for speech and press are not the preserve of political expression or comment on public affairs, essential as those are to a healthy government. One need only pick up any newspaper or magazine to comprehend the vast range of published matter which exposes persons to public view, both private citizens and public officials. Exposure of the self to others in varying degrees is concomitant of life in a civilized community. The risk of this exposure is an essential incident of life in a society which places a primary value on freedom of speech and of press.

The "right to keep information private was bound to clash with the right to disseminate information to the public." Some scholars have suggested that Warren and Brandeis exaggerated the sensationalism of the newspapers of that era. Regardless, they certainly perceived the need to protect personal privacy. In short, Warren and Brandeis were the de facto parents of today's privacy torts.

B. False Light Invasion of Privacy

According to Prosser, there are four forms of invasion of privacy: intrusion upon seclusion or solitude, publication of embarrassing private facts, appropriation of name or likeness, and publicity placing an individual in a false light before the public eye. False light invasion of privacy, the most relevant of privacy torts to Reality TV, involves exposing an otherwise private individual to unwanted and false publicity. Reality TV that places a participant in a "false light" may be subject to tort liability. An employer who publicized a matter that created a false conception about an employee may also be liable. To recover, a plaintiff must show that the defendant employer widely publicized misinformation Publication is an essential element. The published information must be false, and the defendant must publicize the information either with knowledge of its falsity, or with reckless disregard as to its truth or falsity. Some courts adhere to the reckless disregard standard; others adhere to a negligence standard. The standard for false light publicity is that it is highly offensive to a reasonable person. The misrepresentation(s) must be major and refer to a person's character, history, activities, or beliefs. The plaintiff must demonstrate that the misinformation was unreasonable and highly offensive, and if the plaintiff fails to do so the claim will fail.

C. Lady Duff-Gordon

Like Reality TV and its aspiring millionaire participants, Lucy, Lady Duff-Gordon, "employed the plaintiff to help her to turn this vogue into money." Justice Cardozo implied terms into the contract to make it work:

> The agreement of employment is signed by both parties. It has a wealth of recitals. The defendant insists, however, that it lacks the elements of a contract. She says that the plaintiff does not bind himself to anything. It is true that he does not promise in so many words that he will use reasonable efforts to place the defendant's endorsements and market her designs. We think, however, that such a promise is fairly to be implied. The law has outgrown its primitive stage of formalism when the precise word was the sovereign talisman, and every slip was fatal. It takes a broader view today. A promise may be lacking, and yet the whole writing may be instinct with an obligation, imperfectly expressed. If that is so, there is a contract.

"But in determining the intention of the parties, the promise has a value. It helps to enforce the conclusion that the plaintiff had some duties." The intention of the parties implies an obligation of good faith to avoid fraudulent misrepresentation.

The parties' intent also implies that they must use their best efforts to exploit "the number of people watching a specific television show." "The obligation to exploit is at the heart of, and is the very essence of, the 'business' of show business." The "best efforts" to exploit requirement in an agreement can either be expressed or read into the agreement by the court. A part of the "best efforts" obligation would be to avoid fraudulent misrepresentation in a Reality TV contract.

As aforementioned, the linchpin behind looking for reality in Reality TV contracts is the seminal case of Wood v. Lucy, Lady Duff-Gordon. Otis F. Wood sued Lucy, Lady Duff-Gordon for breach of an agreement signed in 1915, which allegedly gave Wood an exclusive right to place Lucy's endorsements on products. When Lucy herself placed the endorsements, Wood contended that he should receive a share of those profits. Lucy argued that the agreement was unenforceable because it did not impose obligations on both parties; thus, no duties were imposed on Wood. The trial judge interpreted the agreement as requiring Wood to exercise his "bona fide judgment." The judge thought bona fide judgment was sufficient to create an obligation to make the agreement enforceable. However, the appellate division unanimously reversed. Next, the court of appeals, by a 4-3 vote, reversed the Appellate Division and agreed with the trial judge. Noticeably, Justice Cardozo's opinion used the phrase "reasonable efforts" to describe Wood's obligations.

The significance of the decision was that the judge sought to preserve some of the values of the past by requiring that the contracts be performed in good faith, the "bona fide judgment" required by the trial judge in Wood. The key characteristic of the new content for the old form was that the courts, not the parties or the market, would have the primary role in determining what was good faith. Consequently, the courts had both a new focus for their deliberations (performance rather than obligation) and a new standard for judgment (good faith).

The Lady Duff-Gordon good faith standard should direct the parties in a Reality TV contract to abstain from fraudulent misstatements that would result in false light damages to plaintiff/participant.

IV. Conclusion

False light invasion of privacy recognizes a civil action for the dissemination of information to the public that makes inaccurate statements or creates false implications about the plaintiff. The focus is on the resulting damage to the plaintiff's feelings, measured by the standard of whether the false light implication would be highly offensive to a reasonable person. Additionally, the potential for false light damages to Reality TV participants is obvious and oftentimes intentional. Lady Duff-Gordon implies an obligation of good faith on the part of the producers in a Reality TV/participation agreement to avoid inaccurate statements or situations. As well, the agreement prohibits purposefully placing the plaintiff in a false light so false inferences can be made from the situation or false inferences (from statements or situations) that purposefully place plaintiffs in a false light. [Footnotes omitted.]

WAVERLY PRODUCTIONS, INC.V. RKO GENERAL, INC.
Court of Appeal of California, Second Appellate District, Division Two
June 28, 1963
Civ. No. 26523
217 Cal.App.2d 721, 32 Cal.Rptr. 73

ASHBURN, J.

Plaintiff, Waverly Productions, Inc., appeals from an adverse judgment in favor of defendant RKO General, Inc., rendered in an action for declaratory relief which grew out of a motion picture distribution agreement between the two companies dated October 14, 1957. Plaintiff agreed to produce two pictures having release titles "Enchanted Island" and "From the Earth to the Moon," and defendant was constituted distributor for both, its license to cover the entire world. Performance of the agreement would require expenditure of large sums of money by each party.

Appellant's major contention is that the instrument did not authorize defendant to enter into sublicenses for distribution in foreign countries and that the trial court erred in excluding parol evidence designed to establish and to resolve an ambiguity in the contract concerning said matter.

Under article (or paragraph) 3 of section IV of the instrument, defendant was given the exclusive right, license and privilege to distribute, exhibit and otherwise exploit the two pictures, "and to license others to do any of the foregoing." Distributor agreed to "use its best efforts to distribute each Picture covered by this agreement throughout the distribution territories in such manner as to obtain the greatest proper gross receipts from the distribution of the Picture that is justified by the quality of the Picture. The Distributor will distribute the Picture in accordance with its regular distribution practice which is current at the time involved. ... In no event shall the Distributor incur any liability to the Producer hereunder based upon any claim by the Producer that the Distributor has failed to realize receipts or revenues which could or should have been realized, unless the Producer alleges and proves that such failure was due solely to the Distributor's action in bad faith."

Article 2 of section V: "... The Distributor may grant to other parties the right to make foreign versions at their own expense, to distribute such foreign versions in specified foreign countries and to deduct the expenses in connection with the preparation of such versions from the gross receipts before remitting the gross receipts to the Distributor."

Article 4 of section IV gives distributor the right to refrain from distributing or causing to be distributed either or both of the pictures in any foreign country if in its judgment such distribution would be unsound economically, or to discontinue such distribution when deemed by it economically desirable, or because of censorship or political difficulties.

Article 4 also provides: "Subject to the provisions of Article 3 of this Section, the Distributor or any distributor in its stead shall have sole and complete control over the distribution, exploitation and exhibition of each Picture covered by this agreement, which may be distributed under any plans which the Distributor deems expedient."

Article 9 of section IX: "Except as herein specifically provided, neither party hereto may assign this agreement in whole or in part, without the consent of the other. ..." Then follow certain specified instances in which the producer may assign or either party may dispose of its right to receive or retain receipts from a picture or its interest in a picture.

Article 4A of section IV furnishes the subject matter around which this controversy mainly revolves. It says: "It is expressly understood and agreed that Distributor may assign or sub-license the distribution rights for a Picture to any distributor of motion pictures for distribution in any territory or territories other than the domestic territory [United States and Canada], or may enter into any plan or plans providing for joint distribution of the Pictures in such territories by Distributor and any such assignee or licensee. It is further expressly understood and agreed that Distributor may so assign, sub-license or transfer the distribution rights for a Picture for distribution in the domestic territory to any one or more of the following named distributors only: Loew's Incorporated, Twentieth Century-Fox Film Corporation, Paramount Pictures Corporation, Warner Bros. Pictures, Inc., Columbia Pictures Corporation, Universal Pictures Company, Inc., United Artists Corporation, or Buena Vista Film Distributors Corporation. In the event that Distributor is unable to arrange for domestic distribution of a Picture by any one or more of said designated distributors upon terms at least as favorable as those provided in Article 2(a) of Section VI hereof, then Distributor may so assign, sub-license or otherwise transfer the domestic distribution rights, or any portion thereof, for such Picture to any other distributor of motion pictures. ..."

In March and June of 1958, defendant entered into sublicense agreements with Rank Film Distributors, Ltd., authorizing it to do the distributing of plaintiff's pictures in numerous European, Asian and South American countries. These were followed by similar concessions to Loew's International Corporation and to certain others for distribution in foreign countries. Plaintiff concluded that defendant was withdrawing entirely from distribution in foreign lands and instructed Technicolor, Inc. (which was processing the films) to make no prints for RKO for distribution in foreign countries. This was about the 1st of October 1958, and was followed by this lawsuit which was filed on October 9, 1958.

As above indicated, plaintiff's major contention is that the first sentence of article 4A of section IV (quoted again in the footnote for convenience) is ambiguous when read in the light of other provisions of the contract, and that the trial court's refusal to receive extrinsic evidence on that subject was prejudicially erroneous; that the real intention of same was that RKO would itself do the distributing in foreign countries.

The agreement concludes with the following paragraph: "13. This agreement constitutes the entire agreement between the parties and can be modified only by a written instrument duly executed by the authorized officers or representatives of each of the parties. No person has any authority to make any representation or promise on behalf of either party not contained herein and this agreement has not been executed in reliance on any such representation or promise."

There is no specific argument in appellant's opening brief that the language of 4A, standing alone, is ambiguous. Responsive to respondent's emphasis upon this matter, appellant's reply brief does essay an exposition of ambiguity within the confines of 4A, but finds uncertainty only in respects which do not bear upon the question of a right to make sublicenses for foreign territories.

Certainly this provision of the agreement does not present a patent ambiguity for the phraseology is not susceptible of two different meanings, especially is it not subject to the construction, standing alone, that RKO cannot sublicense the distribution in foreign countries.

When the words are susceptible to opposing interpretations, a form of latent (or mixed) ambiguity is said to arise (18 Cal.Jur.2d § 276, p. 765) and parol evidence may be received "not to vary or modify the terms of the agreement but to aid the court in ascertaining the true intent of the parties [citation], not to show that 'the parties meant something other *than* what they said' but to show 'what they meant *by* what they said.' " (*Barham v. Barham,* 33 Cal.2d 416, 423 [202 P.2d 289].)

Upon the theory that a true latent ambiguity is raised by extrinsic evidence and hence can be removed by the same type of proofs, appellant's counsel approach the problem from two directions, first, that the contract must be read in its entirety and if uncertain of meaning after such a reading may be subject to parol proofs, and second, that the circumstances surrounding the execution of this agreement show that the intent of the parties was that RKO could not divest itself of an obligation to itself make distribution by sublicensing the distribution to others-an intent directly contrary to the language under discussion.

It is true that the agreement contains numerous provisions imposed upon RKO as distributor which require its personal performance, but those provisions presuppose that RKO will continue to do the distributing and they are all subject to the sublicensing provision of article 4A; when that privilege is exercised and a sublicensee takes over the distribution in a given area he necessarily becomes the active performer of the distributor's obligations *pro tanto,* but RKO as the primary distributor remains obligated to the producer to see that all those obligations are properly performed unless it procures a release thereof from Waverly, and there was no such release here. Incidentally, the agreement provides that RKO shall not be liable to Waverly upon any claim that it has "failed to realize receipts or revenues which could or should have been realized, unless the Producer alleges and proves that such failure was due solely to the Distributor's action in bad faith." The court found upon sufficient evidence that defendant was guilty of no bad faith in the premises.

Appellant's second approach toward resolving the asserted ambiguity is an arraying of negotiations (which in fact were merged into the contract) and an attempt thus to show the understanding and intention of Mr. Tevlin who negotiated the contract on behalf of Waverly. After negotiations extending over months and the ordinary drafts and redrafts of such an elaborate contract (62 pages in this instance) he examined the final draft and pronounced it satisfactory. But the defense nevertheless sought to show that his understanding was that RKO was to distribute directly in foreign countries-not through sublicensees.

Out of all the qualifications and uncertainties of the parol evidence rule one proposition emerges clear and decisive, namely, that the exclusionary rule is applicable "where the *intention* of the parties with respect to their obligations and rights is clearly stated in the writing, and parol evidence of a *contrary intention* is offered." (Witkin, California Evidence, § 374, p. 417.)

Sensing the heavy burden of establishing their major proposition that 4A forbids sublicensing of foreign exhibition although its language is unmistakably to the contrary, counsel for appellant advance the secondary argument that their claim of an obligation on RKO to itself distribute in foreign territory "is subject to the limited qualification that RKO was permitted to make sub-distribution agreements" and that that term has a "special and extremely limited meaning," namely, "the testimony would have been to the effect that sub-distribution refers to arrangements for the marketing of pictures in territories where for political or economic reasons the distributor has difficulty in distributing directly." This seems to be a reference to the sentence of article 4 reading: "It may refrain from distributing any Picture in any country or portion thereof or may withdraw it from distribution in any country or portion thereof if, in its discretion, it seems advisable because of censorship or political difficulties." This matter of "sub-distribution" in the special sense of appellant is not mentioned in the complaint, or in the joint pretrial statement or order and has no substantial basis in logic or in the terms of the agreement.

The language of article 4A here under consideration is so crystal clear that he who runs may read. There was no error in excluding the parol evidence in question.

Appellant insists that the sublicenses granted by respondent for foreign territories were not sublicenses at all, inferentially claims they are assignments and as such forbidden by the agreement constituting defendant the main distributor for plaintiff's two pictures. We think it immaterial whether they are sublicenses or partial assignments. It appears that the joint statement on pretrial does refer to them as assignments. Appellant relies upon the provision of article 9 of section IX: "Except as herein specifically provided, neither party hereto may assign this agreement in whole or in part, without the consent of the other. ..." Obviously an assignment of part of an agreement means transfer to another of less than all of its benefits or burdens. Article 9 says this cannot be done "except as herein specifically provided." One such specific provision is found in article 4A: "It is expressly understood and agreed that Distributor may assign or sub-license the distribution rights for a Picture to any distributor of motion pictures for distribution in any territory or territories other than the domestic territory. ..." Plainly this contemplates transfer of benefits or burdens. It is the burdens with which appellant is concerned. But such a transfer of burden does not relieve the assignor of the obligation unless the other contracting party consents thereto (*Britschgi v. McCall,* 41 Cal.2d 138, 144 [257 P.2d 977]), and there was no such consent here. The court found in effect that no release of RKO resulted from an assignment, and respondent's brief says: "RKO has never contended that it absolved itself from liability to Waverly when it executed the sub-license agreements." Whether a sublicense or a partial assignment, the result is the same so far as this case is concerned.

Appellant endeavors to hold RKO as a trustee or other fiduciary which has not borne its burden of accounting and proving that it has acted in good faith. It is argued that RKO completely withdrew from foreign distribution (the court found to the contrary) and did so in order to avoid further losses from that phase of its business. The court held it acted in good faith and that it was not a fiduciary except with respect to accounting for rentals received from its sublicensees. This is undoubtedly correct.

The contract is an elaborate one which undertakes to define the respective rights and duties of the parties, and specifically confers upon defendant the sublicensing privilege, exercise of which forms the basis of appellant's charge of violation of fiduciary duty. A mere contract or a debt does not constitute a trust or create a fiduciary relationship.

New v. New, 148 Cal.App.2d 372 [306 P.2d 987], is in point. It involved a property settlement agreement through which the husband (defendant and "second party") received participation interests in Continental Corporation and Continental Development Corporation and agreed to " 'pay first party twenty-five per cent (25%) of any and all sums, proceeds, benefits, remunerations, compensation and emoluments of whatsoever kind or nature ... paid to second party or that second party may receive, or paid to or received by others for the use and benefit of second party, directly or indirectly, from the said Continental Corporation, the Continental Development Corporation, their successors, subsidiaries or assigns, or from any of them by virtue of any interest which second party presently has in said Continental Corporation, Continental Development Corporation or which he may have. ...' " (P. 376.) The wife claimed that this made the husband a trustee or other fiduciary for her and that he had acquired for himself a profitable business opportunity which he should have obtained for the corporation and that hence he violated his duty to her. The court said, at pages 381-382: "Counsel for appellant concede in their briefs that 'since the property settlement agreement did not contain a declaration of trust, it was not an express trust.' But they insist upon some implied fiduciary obligation in the nature of a trust,-a 'voluntary trust.' We perceive no basis for this. Defendant's obligation to plaintiff was to pay her a percentage of anything received by him from Continental or Development, directly or indirectly. When received, he owed her 25 per cent of it, just as if he had agreed to pay her $500 cash per month if he received that much from any source. Defendant was not obligated to create a " 'corporate opportunity' or to remain a corporate officer or director or so to manage the corporation as to make the stock lucrative. His primary obligation was negative, to refrain from conduct calculated to deprive plaintiff of the legitimate fruits of her bargain." At page 382: " 'There was and at all times has been, an implied term in said Property Settlement Agreement, and particularly in paragraph 14 thereof as embodied in said Interlocutory Judgment of Divorce, that neither party would do anything to deprive the other of the fruits and benefits thereof.' " And the court then said: "This is an implied term of every contract. 'In every contract there is an implied covenant that neither party shall do anything which will have the effect of destroying or injuring the right of the other party to receive the fruits of the contract, which means that in every contract there exists an implied covenant of good faith and fair dealing. (17 C.J.S. 778, § 328.)' (*Universal Sales Corp. v. California etc. Mfg. Co.,* 20 Cal.2d 751, 771 [128 P.2d 665].) Being of universal prevalence it cannot create a fiduciary relationship; it affords basis for redress for breach of contract and that is all. (See *Gonsalves v. Hodgson,* 38 Cal.2d 91, 97-98 [237 P.2d 656].) The trial judge properly ruled that the stock in Continental and Development was not held by defendant for the use or benefit of plaintiff." (Pp. 382-383.)

Gonsalves v. Hodgson, 38 Cal.2d 91 [237 P.2d 656], an action for breach of contract to construct a fishing vessel. "Taken in its entirety, this cause of action appears to be for breach of a contract based upon a fiduciary relationship." (P.94.) The court said, in part: "The conclusion is inescapable that no trust relationship was created by the contract, or by the dealings of the parties under it." (P. 97.) And: "The contention of Gonsalves and his associates seems to be that a fiduciary relationship arose out of the promise to construct the vessel in a 'workmanlike' manner, in dependence upon the special knowledge and skill of Hodgson. But his knowledge or skill was not property which might be held in trust. It could be the subject only of a contractual obligation.

"Nor was there here any fiduciary relationship between the parties. As is said in 1 Bogert, Trusts and Trustees, section 17, '... there is no fiduciary relation in the case of debt or other contract duty. The rights and duties of parties to a contract may generally be freely transferred. The trustee cannot assign his trusteeship or delegate the performance of his duties. ... There is no rule that parties to a contract may not act for their own interest during the execution of the contract. They have no duty of loyal representation of the opposing party in the relationship.'

"The parties here were engaged in a course of arms-length dealing. Hodgson was to use his knowledge and skill in the supervision of the construction. Gonsalves and his associates were given, and exercised, a supervisory check on all phases of construction. They retained rights of control which completely negative any implication of a fiduciary relationship.

"There being no trust or fiduciary relationship, the only breach which could have occurred would have been one of a strictly contractual obligation." (Pp. 98-99.)

Downey v. Humphreys, 102 Cal.App.2d 323 [227 P.2d 484], was an action brought by the liquidator of an insurance company against an agent to recover unremitted insurance premiums. A nonsuit was granted, the trial court holding that the agent was not a trustee and had a right to offset unearned premiums. The court said, at page 332: "A debt is not a trust and there is not a fiduciary relation between debtor and creditor as such. If a person receives money and it is the intention that he shall have the unrestricted use thereof, being liable to pay a similar amount to a third person, a debt is created. [Citations.] If funds held by an agent are commingled with the knowledge and consent of his principal, in the absence of an agreement to the contrary, the inference is that the agent becomes a debtor to the amount received for the principal." (See also, 48 Cal.Jur.2d § 17, p. 666; 89 C.J.S. § 59, p. 828; Rest. 2d Trusts, § 12, p. 35.)

We think it clear that RKO was not a fiduciary with respect to the performance of the terms of this contract (except as to accounting for rentals received) and that arguments predicated on the assumption that it was are directed to a false issue.

We cover herein the three questions which, according to appellant's reply brief, present the essence of this appeal. Numerous subsidiary arguments of appellant must fall of their own weight because they rest upon the assumption that RKO, not Waverly, defaulted in performance of its obligations under the agreement.

After the two pictures were completed and the facilities for making reprints for exhibition purposes had been turned over to Technicolor, Inc., "RKO ordered foreign release prints from Technicolor, and Waverly, claiming that RKO was in violation of the Distribution Agreement, instructed Technicolor not to honor RKO's orders," as stated in appellant's opening brief. This claim was based upon the primary one that RKO had no right to sublicense the distribution of the pictures in foreign countries. As heretofore shown, this latter contention is unsound. Hence Waverly, without legal cause, made it impossible for RKO or its sublicensees to exhibit the pictures or to earn the contemplated revenues, thus violating the settled principle that "[i]n every contract there is an implied covenant that neither party shall do anything which will have the effect of destroying or injuring the right of the other party to receive the fruits of the contract, which means that in every contract there exists an implied covenant of good faith and fair dealing." (*Universal Sales Corp. v. California etc. Mfg. Co.,* 20 Cal.2d 751, 771 [128 P.2d 665].) Clearly plaintiff violated its agreement and is in no position to complain of alleged deficiencies in defendant's preliminary and partial performance upon which appellant did not rely when obstructing defendant's reaping the proceeds of exhibiting the pictures through its sublicensees.

Appellant further says in its brief that "the case went to trial on the fundamental question as to whether RKO could insist upon having Technicolor honor its orders for the preparation of release prints for release in the foreign territory." The trial judge correctly answered this question in the affirmative. It is unnecessary for this opinion to follow and discuss the many divagations of appellant's main arguments; they are adequately disposed of through the treatment of its principal contentions.

Waverly refused and failed to pay the sum of $25,589.03 which Technicolor claims and the court found to be a production cost. Plaintiff had agreed to pay all costs of production and defendant "all direct distribution expenses." The joint statement on pretrial, which was incorporated in the court's order, says: "Technicolor Corporation has rendered certain laboratory services in connection with said photoplays, and has demanded payment of the sum of $25,589.03 in payment thereof. Neither RKO nor Waverly has made any payment on account of said demand. Technicolor Corporation has asserted a lien upon certain physical properties of said photoplays in order to enforce said demand." Appellant claims the finding is erroneous because not supported by any evidence. The argument overlooks the fact that the agreement provides that Waverly shall deliver to RKO answer prints, picture negatives, protective master positive prints, sound track negatives, dubbing prints and minus dialogue sound track negatives, same to be prepared "by the laboratory which is to do the production laboratory work." It was stipulated that Technicolor prepared a composite negative and one answer print for each picture. Mr. Bogeaus, president of Waverly, testified that Technicolor had also prepared the protective master positive prints and the foreign sound track negative. In the absence of other evidence the foregoing was sufficient to sustain the court's finding: "That the aforestipulated charge of $25,589.03 asserted by Technicolor is not an expense of distribution of the Pictures which RKO is obligated to advance under the Distribution Agreement; said charge is a part of the cost of production of the Pictures which Waverly was obligated to pay under the Distribution Agreement."

It is to be remembered that this is a controversy between Waverly and RKO, that Technicolor is not a party to the action or bound by its result. The question is whether, as between themselves, plaintiff or defendant should discharge this obligation. Even if it be conceded *arguendo* that this was a direct distribution expense, it is plain that RKO was required to advance such cost (sec. V, art. 5) and "be reimbursed as provided in Article 3 of Section VI hereof," which reads: "After the Distributor recoups the distribution fees (other than deferred fees) referred to in Article 2 above, the remainder of the gross receipts of a Picture covered by this agreement shall be applied to reimburse the Distributor for the direct distribution expenses in connection with such Picture." Plaintiff having made it impossible for defendant to procure the prints necessary to produce those gross receipts and having thereby breached its agreement, it necessarily follows that, as between the parties to this action, plaintiff must bear the expense in question.

Judgment affirmed.

FOX, P. J., and HERNDON, J., concurred.

LLOYD v. CALIFORNIA PICTURES CORP.
Court of Appeal of California, Second Appellate District, Division One
October 31, 1955
Civ. No. 20959
136 Cal. App.2d 638,
289 P.2d 295

DORAN, J.

On September 10, 1945, a contract was entered into between the Lloyd Corporation, plaintiff's assignor, and the defendant California Pictures, for the services of Harold Lloyd in a photoplay later known as "Mad Wednesday." On the same day, in connection therewith, Harold Lloyd contracted with Lloyd Corporation to furnish to California Pictures "artistic and stellar services," the agreement provided that plaintiff must "receive star billing and screen credit, advertising credit, and publicity credit as star" of the photoplay.

According to plaintiff's complaint, California Pictures agreed with Lloyd Corporation to be bound by the contractual undertakings of the Lloyd Corporation to Harold Lloyd, and expressly agreed to "give and guarantee the giving, directly and personally to the plaintiff, Harold Lloyd, of star billing and screen credit, advertising credit, publicity credit, and exploitation credit as the star" of the photoplay. These obligations were made binding on California's successors, assigns, licensees, distributors and exhibitors. Plaintiff Harold Lloyd guaranteed performance by Lloyd Corporation, agreed to complete the picture and gave California the right to use plaintiff's name, likeness and voice in connection with the photoplay.

It is further alleged that in return for such guarantee and undertaking, California Pictures agreed on behalf of its successors or assigns, that it would "mention the name of Harold Lloyd as star on the positive prints of, and in all paid advertising and publicity thereafter issued in connection with the production or distribution of said motion picture photoplay." It is alleged that plaintiff, and plaintiff's assignor, Lloyd Corporation, fully performed all obligations under the contracts.

The complaint avers that California released the film in 1947 through United Artists, at which time all contractual obligations were complied with by California. However, the film was withdrawn from release prior to December 1, 1947, and was not again publicly shown until October 10, 1950, after respondent RKO Radio Pictures took over distribution of the picture. It is alleged that about December 13, 1947, California Pictures entered into a written security contract with the defendant Hughes Tool Company which agreed to pay certain debts of California; that as a part of such agreement California assigned the photoplay "Mad Wednesday" to Hughes as security, with rights of distribution, "subject to the duties and obligations of said rights and contracts assigned as aforesaid."

The complaint, as amended, alleges that on November 10, 1950, defendants Hughes and R.K.O. "confirmed by letter agreement in writing a previous and pre-existing oral agreement entered into prior to October 11, 1950, wherein and whereby Hughes granted to R.K.O." world-wide distribution rights to the photoplay, "upon substantially the same terms and conditions as those contained in the distribution agreement dated December 19, 1944, previously entered into between California and United Artists Corporation."

As stated in respondent's brief, "In respect to many matters, including screen credits, advertising and publicity ... RKO agreed to follow 'the wishes and instructions' of Hughes." RKO is alleged to have had knowledge of the California-Lloyd contract and Hughes' assumption thereof; in reference to "Mad Wednesday," the defendants RKO, Hughes and California are alleged to have "jointly participated in or authorized or concurred in or ratified each and every action taken, and things done."

It is also to be noted that Howard Hughes is alleged to be the sole stockholder in California Pictures, as well as being a majority stockholder, president and director of the defendant Hughes Tool Company, and controlling stockholder, director of and in control of the defendant RKO, "particularly with respect to the distribution, exploitation, publicity and advertising of the photoplay 'Mad Wednesday.' "

There are allegations that about October 11, 1950, plaintiff and the Lloyd Corporation notified defendants that objection would be made to any departure from the original contracts "with respect to the advertising and publicity credit to be given Harold Lloyd as the star." Defendant RKO replied by letter on October 18, 1950, that RKO had received "full notice, advice and knowledge" of the provisions in question, and that RKO "had complied and would continue to comply with, and to faithfully keep and perform the terms and provisions of said contract," and that all advertising and publicity would be in accordance with the original contract, which acknowledgments and assurances were made by RKO "for the purpose of inducing plaintiff and plaintiff's assignor to forego and forebear" the commencement of legal or equitable proceedings, which representations were relied upon. In this connection it is claimed that the defendant RKO is therefore "estopped to deny that it is bound by said provisions."

The defendants, and each of them, are alleged to have "impaired, and diminished the value of the name and reputation of the plaintiff, Harold Lloyd, in the motion picture industry and in the mind of the general public ... by subordinating or eliminating the name ... from advertising and publicity issued and caused to be issued ... and in such a manner as to conceal from the entertainment industry and from the general public throughout the world that the plaintiff, Harold Lloyd, was the 'star' of and in said motion picture photoplay," to plaintiff's damage in the sum of $250,000.

Defendants demurred generally and specially to the complaint; the trial court deferred submission of the demurrer pending the filing of amendments by plaintiff, and thereafter sustained the demurrer of RKO without leave to amend. The case is at issue in respect to the other two defendants, and RKO is the only respondent on this appeal.

Four theories are presented by appellant on which recovery might be had, namely, (I) "Respondent, having acquired only the right and license to distribute the photoplay, is bound by notice and knowledge to the obligations of billing and credit connected with the use of plaintiff's name, likeness and voice"; (II) "Respondent was contractually bound, under the rules of promissory estoppel, to give plaintiff star billing"; (III) "Respondent has assumed the obligation to give plaintiff star billing in all paid advertising and publicity," and is liable for having failed to do so; and (IV) "Respondent, having directly caused a breach of contract, is liable."

It is the respondent's contention that RKO, not being a party to the original Lloyd-California contract, and never having assumed liability thereunder, was under no duty to perform the obligations thereof; that the complaint states no cause of action either on the theory of promissory estoppel, or otherwise; that the complaint shows on its face that it is incapable of amendment, and therefore there was no abuse of discretion in sustaining the demurrer without leave to amend.

As hereinbefore indicated, the merits of plaintiff's complaint, and likewise the merits of any defense offered by the defendants, are matters in no manner involved in the present appeal. According to the long established rule, as stated in *Roberts v. Wachter,* 104 Cal.App.2d 281 [231 P.2d 540], and elsewhere, "On appeal from a judgment sustaining a demurrer to a complaint the allegations of the complaint must be regarded as true. ... All that is necessary as against a general demurrer is to plead facts entitling the plaintiff to some relief." The reviewing court in such an appeal "is confined to the allegations of the complaint," and as said in *San Juan Gold Co. v. San Juan Ridge Mut. Water Assn.,* 34 Cal.App.2d 159, 174 [93 P.2d 582]: "the evidence plays no part in determining the correctness of a ruling on a demurrer."

It is appellant's contention that the ruling in the instant case, sustaining the demurrer without leave to amend, resulting in a dismissal as to the respondent RKO, determines as a matter of law, issues of fact which should only be decided after a plenary hearing on the merits. The case is at issue as to the other defendants. If this dismissal as to RKO be sustained, appellant points out that "the other two defendants will be perfectly free to claim that RKO is the wrongdoer and that they endeavored mightily to obtain performance by RKO."

Perfection in pleading is no more expected or required than in other realms of endeavor. As said in *Kauffman v. Bobo & Wood,* 99 Cal.App.2d 322, 323 [221 P.2d 750], "It is well established that a general demurrer must be overruled if, on any theory, it states a cause of action." The same case points out that "pleadings and amendments thereto should be allowed and construed liberally with the object of affording every litigant his day in court and to render substantial justice between the parties." And "Generally, it is held to be an abuse of discretion to sustain without leave to amend a demurrer to an original complaint unless the complaint shows on its face that it is incapable of amendment." (*Temescal Water Co. v. Department of Public Works,* 44 Cal.2d 90 [280 P.2d 1].)

An application of the rule of liberal construction leads to the conclusion that plaintiff's amended complaint sufficiently states a cause of action on one or more of several theories. The sustaining of defendant RKO's demurrer without leave to amend was therefore reversible error. As before indicated, whether the plaintiff will be able to prove the allegations made, is entirely immaterial on the present appeal since against a demurrer the allegations of the complaint must be taken as true.

As is often the case, plaintiff in the present litigation is confronted with the activities of several different defendants, and at a trial on the merits might recover judgment against one or more defendants, or against none. In a case such as the present, where it appears from the complaint that all three defendants were in some manner involved in causing the alleged loss, plaintiff should be accorded the opportunity to confront all of such defendants in court and present the case in its entirety. This course of procedure would not only benefit the plaintiff but would be of inestimable aid in enabling the trial court to view the entire picture and to thus arrive at the correct result.

To require RKO to go to trial along with the other two defendants seems particularly fitting in view of plaintiff's allegations as to the interlocking nature of the three corporate defendants, in all of which Howard Hughes is alleged to be a majority or controlling stockholder. Proof of this relation between the three defendants might conceivably be of importance in reference to plaintiff's theory of promissory estoppel. RKO is likewise charged with having induced a breach of contract by the other defendants. The knowledge and conduct of RKO, as alleged by plaintiff, forms an integral part of the general picture. To limit plaintiff's litigation to a two-thirds survey of the situation by dismissing the case against RKO without trial, would, under the peculiar circumstances here present, deprive the plaintiff of substantial rights.

No case has been cited by either party dealing with either an identical or parallel situation. Indeed the fundamental law of the case seems to be reasonably well settled; its final application to the facts of this case should be left to the trial court or jury at a hearing on the merits, participated in by all defendants. Nor is it necessary to now determine which, if any, of plaintiff's theories may bear fruit. If however, plaintiff is able to prove the facts alleged, recovery on one or more of such theories would follow.

Promissory estoppel, one of the theories relied upon in the plaintiff's complaint, is expounded in the Restatement of Contracts, section 90 (1932), as follows: "A promise which the promissor should reasonably expect to induce action or forbearance of a definite and substantial character on the part of the promisee and which does induce such action or forbearance is binding if injustice can be avoided only by enforcement of the promise."

The courts of this state have adopted this doctrine, as evidenced by the opinion in *Edmonds v. County of Los Angeles,* 40 Cal.2d 642, 653 [255 P.2d 772]: "By their conduct they led everyone to believe that the exception had been granted. Plaintiffs made an oral promise on which defendants relied to their detriment, and justice can be done only by the enforcement of the promise. The situation presented is therefore the ordinary one of promissory estoppel."

Plaintiff's amended complaint has pleaded facts from which such an estoppel could arise. RKO is alleged to have given assurance to plaintiff that the terms of the Lloyd-California contract would be complied with, which assurance is claimed to have been relied upon to plaintiff's detriment. Whether plaintiff's forbearance to sue was or was not requested by RKO, would appear to be immaterial. It is unnecessary to enter into a detailed discussion of the various theories presented in the complaint. As against the demurrer, the complaint is sufficient.

The judgment is reversed with instructions to overrule the demurrer, and allow a reasonable time for respondent RKO to file an answer.

WHITE, P. J., and DRAPEAU, J., concurred.

PARAMOUNT PRODUCTIONS, INC.v. SMITH
Circuit Court of Appeals, Ninth Circuit
July 26, 1937
No. 8288
91 F.2d 863

HANEY, Circuit Judge.

Judgment was rendered for appellee in his action against appellant for breach of contract, and the latter appealed.

It is admitted by the pleadings that appellee is the sole author of a story entitled 'Cruise to Nowhere'; that appellee sold the story to appellant on April 29, 1933, for $2,500, as evidenced by a written contract containing the terms and conditions of the sale. This contract contains the following provisions:

'Second: The Author hereby grants to the Purchaser all the motion picture rights throughout the world, in and to and in connection with the said story, together with the sole and exclusive rights to use, adapt, translate, subtract from, add to and change the said story and the title thereof in the making of motion picture photoplays and/or as a part of and/or in conjunction with any motion picture photoplay and/or to combine the said story with any other work, to use the said title and/or any similar title in conjunction with motion picture photoplays based upon the said story and/or other literary, dramatic and/or dramatico-musical workds (works). * * * '

'Eighth: The Purchaser agrees to announce on the film of the motion picture photoplays that may be produced pursuant hereto that such motion picture photoplays are based upon or adapted from a story written by the Author, or words to that effect.'

In paragraph 'Second,' supra, by the use of the recondite and occult typographical jumble 'and/or,' a near approach to totality of confusion and unintelligibility has been accomplished, but, inasmuch as the determination of this appeal is dependent upon the construction of the eighth paragraph of the contract rather than the second, we abandon without regret all effort to determine, by reference to its written word, the meaning, if any there be, of the provisions of the second paragraph aforesaid.

The complaint alleged that in 1934 appellant completed the production and thereafter exhibited generally throughout the United States a 'talking motion picture' under the title of 'We're Not Dressing,' which 'was based upon, and adapted from, said original story of plaintiff herein, entitled 'Cruise to Nowhere' * * * '; that appellant violated the eighth provision of the contract quoted, in that appellant 'wholly failed to announce upon said films, or at any of the public exhibitions thereof, that the same was either written by plaintiff, or that it was based upon, or adapted from, a story written by' appellee. Appellant admitted production and exhibition of the picture 'We're Not Dressing,' but denied the remainder of these allegations.

At the trial appellee introduced into evidence over appellant's objections a sheet showing production cost prepared by appellant's accounting department. This sheet contained the following:

'Production No. 983.

'Title 'We're Not Dressing'.

'From Story 'Cruise to Nowhere'.'

The objection was 'upon the ground that no proper foundation is laid to show that anyone connected with the accounting or auditing department, or that department itself, had anything to do with selecting either the title for a given picture, or determining whether a given picture should be based upon or adapted from a given story or not.'

Appellee also offered in evidence an item released by the publicity department of appellant dated September 7, 1933, which contained the following statement: ' 'We're Not Dressing' is an original story by Walton Hall Smith.' Appellee also offered in evidence a similar item dated December 13, 1933, which stated in part:

'Francis Martin * * * today was assigned to write the screen adaptation of 'We're Not Dressing' to be produced soon * * *

'Others working on the story, an original by Walton Hall Smith called 'A Cruise to Nowhere,' are * * * '

Objection was made to both items on grounds identical with those urged against the admission of the production cost sheet, and counsel also stated: ' * * * There is no foundation whereby the corporation may be bound, because, in order for the evidentiary matter to be an admission properly received as such, it must be made by one within the scope of his authority, and it must pertain to authority which he has.'

The objections were overruled.

The trial court gave the following instruction to the jury: 'Now, gentlemen, upon the evidence that the court has discussed a moment or so ago, upon the testimony as to earnings and the testimony as to failure on the part of the plaintiff to minimize the damages, there is an experience table of mortality that is applicable, and that may be used because in cases of this kind it is necessary to utilize the instruments that are possible or capable of utilization. One of these is that the experience table of mortality may be used if the jury concludes that it is proper to use it in the particular case; and under the American Experience Table of Mortality the expectant age of the defendant, under the stipulation that he is now 37 years of age, is 30.35 years. So that if you reach this question of damages you have the right to consider that together with all of the other elements that have been included in all of the instructions that have been heretofore given or that will be hereafter given in this case.'

Upon the issues, the jury found in favor of appellee in the sum of $7,500. Judgment was entered on the verdict, from which judgment this appeal was taken.

Appellant contends that it was incumbent on appellee to prove that the accounting department and the publicity department were authorized to determine whether or not the picture produced was based upon or adapted from appellee's story. Appellant urges that, 'in order to be binding upon the principal, admissions must be made by an agent while acting within the scope of his authority and must relate to matters to which that authority extends. The same rule is applicable with respect to admissions of an officer of the corporation. Beasley v. S. J. Fruit-Packing Co., supra, 92 Cal. 388, 392, 28 P. 485. None of these cases is strictly in point. In each of them the person who made the admission was identified before the evidence was offered, or, in other words, it was known who made the admission. Here it is not denied that the admission was in fact made by some one for the corporation, but it did not appear who made the statement.

At the time the cost sheet was offered, there was no evidence as to the origin of the sheet, nor its content. There was proof that it was taken from the files of appellant, and produced by it. There was no proof, at the time it was offered, that it was made by or on behalf of any department. So far as the record shows, it might have been made by or on behalf of the board of directors, or by or on behalf of the production department, which appellant admits had authority to make such an admission. In other words, at the time the cost sheet was offered, the proof showed it was made for the corporation. If one agent or officer made it, it would have been made within his authority; if another agent or officer made it, it would not have been made within his authority.

There seems to be good ground for an exception to the rule mentioned. For example, suppose a prospectus is issued by a large corporation, which contains simply the corporate name at the end thereof, and in which an admission is made. If the rule mentioned is extended, then the person offering the prospectus would have to first prove who made the prospectus, before he could prove such person's authority. It is difficult to see how the party could prove such identity, short of questioning each officer, agent, and employee. Many corporations employ thousands of people. Such a rule would be impractical. Logic would compel admission as evidence of the admission so made, and, if the identity of the person who made the admission is thereafter proven, then the authority of the person should be proven, or the admission, on motion, stricken.

However, assuming without deciding, that the rule relied upon by appellant is applicable here, then we believe the error did not affect the substantial rights of appellant. 28 U.S.C.A. § 391.

Appellant also contends that the cost sheet had no evidentiary value because the later evidence showed 'that it was the practice of the accounting department to charge a story to a production when it had been bought for it, or for a specified star, whether the story was actually used or not. * * *' In the first place, this contention relates to the weight of the evidence and not to the admissibility thereof. In the second place, when such fact was proven, there was no renewal of the objection or a motion to strike. Therefore, no ruling of the trial court exists for review.

With respect to the publicity items it should be noted that both of them were issued before filming, and before the screen adaptation was written. We believe the error, if any, was cured by the repeated instructions of the trial court that the finished picture must have been based upon or adapted from appellee's story, since it was apparent to the jury that appellant may have changed its program. If the error was not cured, then it did not affect appellant's substantial rights. 28 U.S.C.A. § 391.

Appellant specified the admission of certain other evidence as error, in specifications numbered 7 to 13, both inclusive. With respect to these appellant says in its brief: 'We have no desire unduly to prolong this brief and hence the matters dealing with asserted error in the admission of evidence * * * detailed in (the specifications mentioned) will be submitted without argument.' Under such circumstances, error is not shown, and we treat these specifications as abandoned.

With reference to the instruction hereinabove set forth, appellant says that mortality tables are inadmissible as evidence in such a case as this, and relies on Johnson v. Richards, 50 Idaho, 150, 294 P. 507, Snyder v. Great Northern Ry. Co., 88 Wash. 49, 152 P. 703, and Swope v. City of Seattle, 36 Wash. 113, 78 P. 607. Appellee contends that the instruction was proper on the authority of Turner v. Jackson, 139 Or. 539, 4 P.(2d) 925, 11 P. (2d) 1048. The California courts seem not to have passed on the question.

We believe the error, if any, did not affect the substantial rights of the parties, but was a technical error. 28 U.S.C.A. § 391. The mortality table was not introduced into evidence. The court, judicially noting the table, simply instructed the jury to consider it with all the other evidence 'if the jury concludes that it is proper to use it in the particular case.'

Appellant says that the primary question is whether or not the picture was based upon or adapted from appellee's story. That statement is only partially true. Our function is to ascertain whether or not there is any substantial evidence to sustain the verdict. Specifically, the question presented is whether or not there is any substantial evidence to sustain the finding of the jury that the picture 'We're Not Dressing' was based upon or adapted from appellee's story, 'Cruise to Nowhere.'

An examination of the record discloses that the evidence was conflicting. Three of appellant's witnesses defined and distinguished between 'based upon' and 'adapted from.' There was evidence showing that the picture produced was not based upon or adapted from appellee's story. We are not interested in such evidence, however, but only in the evidence of the opposite fact.

The cost sheet hereinabove discussed is some evidence of the fact found by the jury. Correspondence between officers of appellant had some months before filming was started indicates that appellant may have used the story. Appellee introduced a manuscript of his story into evidence, and read it to the jury. During the trial, the court and its attendants, the jury, appellee, and counsel for the parties saw a showing of the picture. The jury was able to make a comparison. Afterward, appellee testified, 'I saw in the picture much of the plot which I originally had in mind; much of the basic idea.' We believe this is sufficient to warrant submission of the issue to the jury, and, since the jury believed it, the verdict is supported thereby.

Finally appellant urges that there is a lack of evidence to support the award of damages, in that there was no standard by which damages could be gauged. Appellee contends that the true rule on uncertainty of damages is that the prohibition is directed against uncertainty as to cause, rather than uncertainty as to measure or extent.

We do not believe the evidence is subject to the charge of uncertainty. Appellee testified that he and another writer collaborated in writing a story and sold it without screen credit for $10,000, which the two writers divided. Appellee's story was sold for $2,500, but under a contract that required that he be given screen credit. From these figures, the jury might easily compute the advertising value of the screen credit. He also testified that he received screen credit for a play; that prior thereto his salary was $250 per week; and that afterward he received $350 per week at one time, and $500 per week for a period of two weeks, due to the screen credit he had received. That evidence is, if believed, likewise sufficient as a gauge for the measure of the damages.

Finding no error affecting the substantial rights of appellant, the judgment is affirmed.

WILBUR, Circuit Judge (dissenting)...

LUSTER ENTERPRISES, INC. v. JACOBS
United States District Court for the Southern District of New York
November 6, 1967
No. 66-Civ. 1914
278 F. Supp. 73

CROAKE, District Judge.

MEMORANDUM

This is a motion for a temporary restraining order brought on by an Order to Show Cause. The plaintiffs, Luster Enterprises, Inc., and Helen Winston ask this court for an injunction restraining the defendants Arthur Jacobs, APJAC Productions, Inc., and their agents and assigns from producing, distributing, showing, exhibiting, advertising in the mass communications media, including but not limited to newspapers, radio, television and billboards or causing the production, distribution, showing or exhibition, etc., of any motion picture film or photoplay based on the 'Doctor Doolittle' stories for any commercial purpose unless suitable credit is given to Helen Winston. As it is claimed that Helen Winston was the architect of the present screen play, the suitable credit suggested is to take the form of an acknowledgment 'Conceived by Helen Winston.'

The present application flows from the plaintiffs' amended complaint where it is alleged in substance that the named defendants and Twentieth Century Fox Film Corp. (FOX) have plagiarized and intend to present the plaintiffs' screen play without the permission and without recognizing the contribution of Helen Winston. The plaintiffs in their amended complaint seek damages of $4,500,000.

Rule 65, Fed.R.Civ.P., enunciates the applicable standards for the relief requested in this case. It is a restrictive rule. It requires among other things that a showing be made that if an injunction is not granted, irreparable harm will result. See Grove Press Inc. v. Collectors Publication, Inc., 264 F.Supp. 603 (C.D.Cal.1967); Dino De Laurentiis Cinematografia v. D-150, Inc., 258 F.Supp. 459 (S.D.N.Y.1966); Federal Maritime Comm. v. Atlantic & Gulf Panama Can. Zone, 241 F.Supp. 766 (S.D.N.Y.1965). In considering whether to issue a preliminary injunction, the court must consider the relative importance of the rights asserted, the acts sought to be enjoined, the irreparable nature of the injury allegedly flowing from denial of preliminary relief, probability of ultimate success or failure of the suit and balancing of damages and convenience generally. See e.g., Securities & Exchange Comm. v. Investment Bankers of America, Inc., 181 F.Supp. 346 (D.C.D.C.1960).

In this particular case we find the determinative aspect is the nature of the irreparable harm claimed. The plaintiff, Helen Winston, states that if a preliminary injunction is not issued by this court she will suffer irreparable injury. Dealing with the substance of this claim, we find it to be without merit. Helen Winston is apparently a successful and talented screen play author. If a screen credit is improperly denied her by the defendants she has an action in damages. One of the forgotten functions of the damage remedy is to apprise members of the community of the rights which the court has adjudicated in the plaintiffs' favor. If the plaintiffs prevail in this action the attendant publicity and the subsequent damage award will make Helen Winston whole within her professional community. Outside of this small professional community, screen credits have little or no significance and any resulting harm by failure to include her name in the credits will be minimal.

On the other hand, if this court grants the preliminary injunction, FOX will be required to include Helen Winston's name in the screen credits or forego its plans to premiere the film in early December. In short, as FOX has engaged in extensive advertising with this December date in mind it would in effect be forced to include Helen Winston's name in the screen credits. As Justice Telesford noted in his opinion directed to essentially the same issues (see Luster Enterprises, Inc. v. Twentieth Century Fox Film Corp., No. 16114/1967 (Sup.Ct.New York, Oct. 18, 1967)) '* * * such credit * * * (would) be but the first step in the building of a claim for damages.' On balance, then, in weighing the equities, we find that if the preliminary injunction issues, the plaintiffs will have in fact been granted a large part of the relief requested in advance of any trial on the merits and will be in a superior position to press their damage claims. See Dino De Laurentiis Cinematografia v. D-150, Inc., 258 F.Supp. 459, 464 (S.D.N.Y.1966). If this court grants the requested preliminary injunction, it will not be preserving the status quo but will be tipping the scales of justice in favor of the plaintiff.

Finally, the plaintiffs were aware for some time that there was a dispute as to ownership of the literary property of the screen play because they commenced their action in this court in July of 1966. It was certainly within their power to put the case in issue before this time. The plaintiffs state that the reason it took over one year from the filing of the original complaint until the service of the answer was primarily that the defendants delayed answering the complaint. We note that the time to answer was extended by stipulation ten times. From this it appears that the plaintiffs were not anxious for a speedy determination of the issues now presented.

By its determination of this motion the court implies no view on the merits of plaintiffs' action for damages. The decision is only a reflection of this court's belief that the injunctive remedy should be reserved for those urgent matters which require immediate relief.

One other matter remains to be considered. Defendants have moved to dismiss this action pursuant to Rule 12(b)(6), Fed.R.Civ.P., on the ground that neither of the plaintiffs in this action has legal title to or beneficial ownership of the literary property involved. If this is true, the complaint fails to state a claim upon which relief can be granted. See Hoffman v. Santly-Joy, Inc., 51 F.Supp. 778 (S.D.N.Y.1943); Manning v. Miller Music Corp., 174 F.Supp. 192 (S.D.N.Y.1959). The court feels that it has insufficient information to determine the precise relationship between the parties who are before it and those who are not with regard to rights in this material. Accordingly, the motion to dismiss is denied as is the application for a preliminary injunction.

So ordered.

TAMARIND LITHO, WORKSHOP v. SANDERS
Court of Appeal of California, Second Appellate District, Division Five
April 28, 1983
Civ. No. 66492
143 Cal. App.3d 571, 193 Cal. Rptr. 409

STEPHENS, J.

The essence of this appeal concerns the question of whether an award of damages is an adequate remedy at law in lieu of specific performance for the breach of an agreement to give screen credits. Our saga traces its origin to March of 1969, at which time appellant, and cross-complainant below, Terry Sanders (hereinafter Sanders or appellant), agreed in writing to write, direct and produce a motion picture on the subject of lithography for respondent, Tamarind Lithography Workshop, Inc. (hereinafter referred to as Tamarind or respondent).

Pursuant to the terms of the agreement, the film was shot during the summer of 1969, wherein Sanders directed the film according to an outline/treatment of his authorship, and acted as production manager by personally hiring and supervising personnel comprising the film crew. Additionally, Sanders exercised both artistic control over the mixing of the sound track and overall editing of the picture.

After completion, the film, now titled "Four Stones for Kanemitsu," was screened by Tamarind at its 10th anniversary celebration on April 28, 1970. Thereafter, a dispute arose between the parties concerning their respective rights and obligations under the original 1969 agreement. Litigation ensued and in January 1973 the matter went to trial. Prior to the entry of judgment, the parties entered into a written settlement agreement, which became the premises for the instant action. Specifically, this April 30, 1973, agreement provided that Sanders would be entitled to a screen credit entitled "A Film by Terry Sanders."

Tamarind did not comply with its expressed obligation pursuant to that agreement, in that it failed to include Sanders' screen credits in the prints it distributed. As a result a situation developed wherein Tamarind and codefendant Wayne filed suit for declaratory relief, damages due to breach of contract, emotional distress, defamation and fraud.

Sanders cross-complained, seeking damages for Tamarind's breach of contract, declaratory relief, specific performance of the contract to give Sanders screen credits, and defamation. Both causes were consolidated and brought to trial on May 31, 1977. A jury was impaneled for purposes of determining damage issues and decided that Tamarind had breached the agreement and awarded Sanders $25,000 in damages.

The remaining claims for declaratory and injunctive relief were tried by the court. The court made findings that Tamarind had sole ownership rights in the film, that "both June Wayne and Terry Sanders were each creative producers of the film, that Sanders shall have the right to modify the prints in his personal possession to include his credits." All other prayers for relief were denied.

It is the denial of appellant's request for specific performance upon which appellant predicates this appeal.

Since neither party is contesting the sufficiency of Sanders' $25,000 jury award for damages, the central issue thereupon becomes whether that award is necessarily preclusive of additional relief in the form of specific performance, i.e., that Sanders receive credit on all copies of the film. Alternately expressed, the issue is whether the jury's damage award adequately compensates Sanders, not only for injuries sustained as a result of the prior exhibitions of the film without Sanders' credits, but also for future injuries which may be incurred as a result of any future exhibitions of the film without his credit. Commensurate with our discussion below, we find that the damages awarded raise an issue that justifies a judgment for specific performance. Accordingly, we reverse the judgment of the lower court and direct it to award appellant the injunctive relief he now seeks.

Our first inquiry deals with the scope of the jury's $25,000 damage award. More specifically, we are concerned with whether or not this award compensates Sanders not only for past or preexisting injuries, but also for future injury (or injuries) as well.

Indeed, it is possible to categorize respondent's breach of promise to provide screen credits as a single failure to act from which all of Sanders' injuries were caused. However, it is also plausible that damages awarded Sanders were for harms already sustained at the date of trial, and did not contemplate injury as a result of future exhibitions of the film by respondent, without appropriate credit to Sanders.

Although this was a jury trial, there are findings of facts and conclusions of law necessitated by certain legal issues that were decided by the court. Finding of fact No. 12 states:

"By its verdict the jury concluded that Terry Sanders and the Terry Sanders Company are entitled to the sum of $25,000.00 in damages for all damages suffered by them arising from Tamarind's breach of the April 30th agreement." The exact wording of this finding was also used in conclusion of law No. 1. Sanders argues that use of the word "suffered" in the past tense is positive evidence that the jury assessed damages only for breach of the contract up to time of trial and did not award possible future damages that might be suffered if the film was subsequently exhibited without the appropriate credit. Tamarind, on the other hand, contends that the jury was instructed that if a breach occurred the award would be for *all* damages past and future arising from the breach. The jury was instructed: "For the breach of a contract, the measure of damages is the amount which will compensate the party aggrieved, for the economic loss, directly and proximately caused by the breach, or which, in the ordinary course of things, would be likely to result therefrom" and "... economic benefits including enhancement of one's professional reputation resulting in increased earnings as a result of screen credit, if their loss is a direct and natural consequence of the breach, may be recovered for breach of an agreement that provides for screen credit. Economic benefits lost through breach of contract may be estimated, and where the plaintiff [Tamarind], by its breach of the contract, has given rise to the difficulty of proving the amount of loss of such economic benefit, it is proper to require of the defendant [Sanders] only that he show the amount of damages with reasonable certainty and to resolve uncertainty as to the amount of economic benefit against the plaintiff [Tamarind]."

The trial court agreed with Tamarind's position and refused to grant the injunction because it was satisfied that the jury had awarded Sanders all the damages he was entitled to including past and possible future damages. The record does not satisfactorily resolve the issue. However, this fact is not fatal to this appeal because, as we shall explain, specific performance as requested by Sanders will solve the problem.

The availability of the remedy of specific performance is premised upon well established requisites. These requisites include: A showing by plaintiff of (1) the inadequacy of his legal remedy; (2) an underlying contract that is both reasonable and supported by adequate consideration; (3) the existence of a mutuality of remedies; (4) contractual terms which are sufficiently definite to enable the court to know what it is to enforce; and (5) a substantial similarity of the requested performance to that promised in the contract. (See *Henderson v. Fisher* (1965) 236 Cal.App.2d 468, 473 [46 Cal.Rptr. 173], and Civ. Code, §§ 3384, 3386, 3390, 3391.)

It is manifest that the legal remedies available to Sanders for harm resulting from the future exhibition of the film are inadequate as a matter of law. The primary reasons are twofold: (1) that an accurate assessment of damages would be far too difficult and require much speculation, and (2) that any future exhibitions might be deemed to be a continuous breach of contract and thereby create the danger of an untold number of lawsuits.

There is no doubt that the exhibition of a film, which is favorably received by its critics and the public at large, can result in valuable advertising or publicity for the artists responsible for that film's making. Likewise, it is unquestionable that the nonappearance of an artist's name or likeness in the form of screen credit on a successful film can result in a loss of that valuable publicity. However, whether that loss of publicity is measurable dollar wise is quite another matter.

By its very nature, public acclaim is unique and very difficult, if not sometimes impossible, to quantify in monetary terms. Indeed, courts confronted with the dilemma of estimating damages in this area have been less than uniform in their disposition of same. Nevertheless, it is clear that any award of damages for the loss of publicity is contingent upon those damages being reasonably certain, specific, and unspeculative. (See *Ericson v. Playgirl, Inc.* (1977) 73 Cal.App.3d 850 [140 Cal.Rptr. 921, 96 A.L.R.3d 427].)

The varied disposition of claims for breach of promise to provide screen credits encompasses two schools of thought. On the one hand, there is the view that damages can be ascertained (to within a reasonable degree of certainty) if the trier of fact is given sufficient factual data. (See *Paramount Productions, Inc. v. Smith* (9th Cir. 1937) 91 F.2d 863, cert. den. 302 U.S. 749 [82 L.Ed. 579, 58 S.Ct. 266].) On the other hand, there is the equally strong stance that although damages resulting from a loss of screen credits might be identifiable, they are far too imponderable and ethereal to define in terms of a monetary award. (See *Poe v. Michael Todd Co.* (S.D.N.Y. 1957) 151 F.Supp. 801.) If these two views can be reconciled, it would only be by an independent examination of each case on its particular set of facts.

In *Paramount Productions, Inc. v. Smith, supra.*, 91 F.2d 863, 866-867, the court was provided with evidence from which the "... jury might easily compute the advertising value of the screen credit." (*Id.*, at p. 867.) The particular evidence presented included the earnings the plaintiff/writer received for his work on a previous film in which he did not contract for screen credits. This evidence was in turn easily compared with earnings that the writer had received for work in which screen credits were provided as contracted. Moreover, evidence of that artist's salary, prior to his receipt of credit for a play when compared with earnings received subsequent to his actually receiving credit, was "... if believed, likewise sufficient as a gauge for the measure of damages." (*Id.*, at p. 867.)

In another case dealing with a request for damages for failure to provide contracted-for screen credits, the court in *Zorich v. Petroff* (1957) 152 Cal.App.2d 806 [313 P.2d 118] demonstrated an equal awareness of the principle. The court emphasized "... that there was no evidence from which the [trial] court could have placed a value upon the screen credit to be given plaintiff as an associate producer. (Civ. Code, § 3301.)" (*Id.*, at p. 811.) Incident to this fact, the court went on to surmise that because the motion picture which was at the root of the litigation was an admitted financial failure, screen credit, if given, "... could reasonably have been regarded as a detriment to him." (*Id.*, at p. 811.)

At the other extreme, it has been held that failure to give an artist screen credit *would* constitute irreparable injury. In *Poe v. Michael Todd Co., supra.*, 151 F.Supp. 801, the New York district court was similarly faced with an author's claim that his contractual right to screen credit was violated. The court held: "Not only would money damages be difficult to establish, but at best they would hardly compensate for the real injury done. A writer's reputation, which would be greatly enhanced by public credit for authorship of an outstanding picture, is his stock in trade, it is clear that irreparable injury would follow the failure to give screen credit if in fact he is entitled to it." (*Id.*, at p. 803.)

Notwithstanding the seemingly inflexible observation of that court as to the compensability of a breach of promise to provide screen credits, all three cases equally demonstrate that the awarding of damages must be premised upon calculations, inferences or observations that are logical. Just how logical or reasonable those inferences are regarded serves as the determining factor. Accordingly, where the jury in the matter sub judice was fully apprised of the favorable recognition Sanders' film received from the Academy of Motion Picture Arts and Sciences, the Los Angeles International Film Festival, and public television, and further, where they were made privy to an assessment of the value of said exposure by three experts, it is reasonable for the jury to award monetary damages for that ascertainable loss of publicity. However, pecuniary compensation for Sanders' future harm is not a fully adequate remedy. (See Rest., Contracts, § 361, p. 648.)

We return to the remaining requisites for Sanders' entitlement to specific performance. The need for our finding the contract to be reasonable and supported by adequate consideration is obviated by the jury's determination of respondent's breach of that contract. The requisite of mutuality of remedy has been satisfied in that Sanders had fully performed his obligations pursuant to the agreement (i.e., release of all claims of copyright to the film and dismissal of his then pending action against respondents). (See Civ. Code, § 3386.) Similarly, we find the terms of the agreement sufficiently definite to permit enforcement of the respondent's performance as promised.

In the present case it should be obvious that specific performance through injunctive relief can remedy the dilemma posed by the somewhat ambiguous jury verdict. The injunction disposes of the problem of future damages, in that full compliance by Tamarind moots the issue. Of course, violation of the injunction by Tamarind would raise new problems, but the court has numerous options for dealing with the situation and should choose the one best suited to the particular violation.

In conclusion, the record shows that the appellant is entitled to relief consisting of the damages recovered, and an injunction against future injury.

Subsequent to the initial filing of this opinion, it was brought to this court's attention that Terry Sanders entered into a settlement agreement which it is alleged may have a mooting effect on the instant action.

The subject agreement, which was executed approximately one day after the initial posting of this opinion, is assertedly a general release from liability of both respondents and various insurance companies for both the instant action and a related action not a part of this appeal. Respondents submit that the import of the agreement, which is captioned "Full Release of All Claims," is to make the instant action moot, thus disposing of the issues before this court. Accordingly, respondents petitioned this court to dismiss the instant appeal or alternatively allow them to produce evidence in addition to their supporting declarations.

In opposition to respondents' request, appellants (Terry Sanders and the Terry Sanders Company) submit, by way of opposition declarations, that the subject settlement agreement did not in any way act as a release of their asserted rights to screen credits which comprise the core of this appeal. Specifically, appellants argue that the agreement only states that its effect is to release and discharge respondents from the *monetary* judgment in the instant action and makes no mention whatsoever concerning this appeal or the rights to screen credits. Appellants suggest by way of argument supported by documentation that said agreement was the product of negotiations in which appellants specifically made known that the agreement was not to affect or otherwise encompass the right to specific performance of the agreement to provide the screen credits involved in this appeal.

Considering the extent of this controversy, in conjunction with our decision to reverse the judgment below, we think it in the best interests of all parties concerned for the trial court to determine what effect, if any, the agreement should have on the action. In effect, respondents' petition is tantamount to a motion to dismiss the entire action, as opposed to the mere dismissal of this appeal. It would appear that the trial court is the more appropriate forum to receive evidence and adjudicate the merits of this issue. If it were to reach a determination unfavorable to petitioners, it would be in position to grant the relief we have determined appellants are entitled to. On the other hand, a contrary determination by the trial court would still leave that court with the authority to take the action requested by petitioners.

The judgment denying appellants' prayer for injunctive relief is hereby reversed and the action, with the addition of this new issue, is remanded to the trial court to take appropriate action in conformity with the views expressed in this opinion, including the taking of additional evidence, oral or written, if deemed appropriate, on the motion to dismiss.

FEINERMAN, P. J., and HASTINGS, J., concurred.

CNA INT'L REINSURANCE CO.V. PHOENIX

Court of Appeal of Florida, First District
July 2, 1996, Filed
Case No. 95-401, 95-2309
678 So.2d 378

JOANOS, Judge.

In these consolidated appeals from final orders granting appellee's motions to dismiss, appellants raise two issues: (1) whether the defense of impossibility of performance due to death applies when the impossibility is, allegedly, the fault of the person obligated to perform the personal services contract, and (2) whether the trial court erred in ruling that the effective dates of the policies of insurance involved here were in November, 1993, after the widely publicized death in question. We affirm in part and reverse in part.

The case arises from the unfortunate death of the young actor, River Phoenix, originally of Gainesville, Florida, apparently due to an overdose of illegal drugs, before completion of two films, "Dark Blood" and "Interview With the Vampire," in which he had contracted to appear. As a result of the death, the "Dark Blood" project was totally abandoned. "Interview With the Vampire" was completed with another actor replacing Phoenix. CNA and American Casualty, which are both members of the CNA group of insurance companies, had written entertainment package insurance policies covering various aspects of the two productions. After paying the policy holders, CNA and American Casualty became subrogated to the claims the insureds had against the estate.

CNA attempted to state a cause of action for breach of contract against Phoenix's estate, based on an "actor loanout agreement," between Jude Nile, a corporation owned and run by Phoenix and his mother, Arlyn Phoenix, and Scala Productions. The agreement, signed by Phoenix, allegedly included a general obligation not to do anything which would deprive the parties to the agreement of its benefits. CNA further alleged that by deliberately taking illegal drugs in quantities in excess of those necessary to kill a human being, Phoenix deprived the parties of his services and breached his obligation. American Casualty also couched its complaint for declaratory judgment in terms of breach of contract based on an actor loanout agreement between Jude Nile and Geffen Pictures, which gave Geffen the right to loan Phoenix to Time Warner. In addition to the count for breach of contract, the CNA complaint contained a second count, for fraud and misrepresentation, based on an allegedly false representation in a medical certificate, allegedly signed by Phoenix, denying that Phoenix had ever used "LSD, heroin, cocaine, alcohol in excess, or any other narcotics, depressants, stimulants or psychedelics whether prescribed or not prescribed by a physician."

The estate moved to dismiss both complaints, contending there could be no cause of action for breach of contract because the personal services contracts were rendered impossible to perform due to the death. The estate further alleged that reliance on any representation in the medical certificate was unreasonable as a matter of law as of the effective dates of the policies, which it contended were in November, 1993, after the widely publicized death on October 31, 1993. After hearings, the trial court granted the motions to dismiss with prejudice.

On appeal, CNA and American Casualty contend that the defense of impossibility of performance does not apply in this case because that doctrine requires that the impossibility be fortuitous and unavoidable, and that it occur through no fault of either party. They contend that because the death occurred from an intentional, massive overdose of illegal drugs, that this is not a situation in which neither party was at fault. The trial court very clearly ruled that even if the death was a suicide (there is no indication in the record that it was) or the result of an intentional, self-inflicted act, the doctrine of impossibility of performance applied.

Appellants have candidly conceded that no case authorities exist in support of their position concerning fault in a case of impossibility due to death. Appellants ask this court to find support for their theory in the following language of the Restatement of Contracts 2d §§ 261 and 262:

> § 261 Where, after a contract is made, a party's performance is made impracticable without his fault by the occurrence of an event the non-occurrence of which was a basic assumption on which the contract was made, his duty to render that performance is discharged, unless the language or the circumstances indicate the contrary.
>
> § 262 If the existence of a particular person is necessary for the performance of a duty, his death or such incapacity as makes performance impracticable is an event the nonoccurrence of which was a basic assumption on which the contract was made.

Appellants contend the Restatement dictates that impossibility of performance due to the destruction of one's own health is not the sort of conduct that will excuse performance, citing *Handicapped Children's Education Board v. Lukaszewski,* 112 Wis.2d 197, 332 N.W.2d 774 (Wis.1983), and that the same reasoning should apply in a case of self-induced death. Appellants also suggest a policy basis for the ruling they advocate, arguing that in a society dealing with increasing problems created by illegal drug abuse, such conduct should not excuse the performance of the contract.

At oral argument of this case, it became apparent that any attempt to discern fault in a death case such as this one, or in a similar case, perhaps involving the use of tobacco or alcohol would create another case by case and hard to interpret rule of law. Being mindful that there are already too many of these in existence, we are not persuaded by the facts or the arguments presented to depart from the clear and unambiguous rule that death renders a personal services contract impossible to perform. *See* 17A Am.Jur.2d "Contracts" § 688 (1991). In such contracts, "there is an implied condition that death shall dissolve the contract." *Id.* With this implied condition in mind, we believe the parties to the agreements could have provided specifically for the contingency of loss due to the use of illegal drugs, as they provided for other hazardous or life threatening contingencies. We affirm the trial court's ruling that the doctrine of impossibility of performance applies in this case.

We reverse the trial court's ruling that, as a matter of law, the policies were not effective until the issuance date, November 12, 1993, after Phoenix's death on October 31, 1993. The policies, as well as pertinent endorsements, clearly reflect earlier effective dates of July 23, 1993, and August 15, 1993 on their faces. Generally, the parties to a contract are competent to fix the effective date. *See* John A. Appleman and Jean Appleman, Insurance Law and Practice § 105 (1981). At the very least, further development of the record is in order on this issue.

AFFIRMED in part, REVERSED in part, and REMANDED for further proceedings consistent with this opinion.

BOOTH and VAN NORTWICK, JJ., concur.

SHELDON v. METRO-GOLDWYN PICTURES CORP.
Circuit Court of Appeals, Second Circuit
January 17, 1936
No. 118
81 F.2d 49

L. HAND, Circuit Judge.

The suit is to enjoin the performance of the picture play, 'Letty Lynton,' as an infringement of the plaintiffs' copyrighted play, 'Dishonored Lady.' The plaintiffs' title is conceded, so too the validity of the copyright; the only issue is infringement. The defendants say that they did not use the play in any way to produce the picture; the plaintiffs discredit this denial because of the negotiations between the parties for the purchase of rights in the play, and because the similarities between the two are too specific and detailed to have resulted from chance. The judge thought that, so far as the defendants had used the play, they had taken only what the law allowed, that is, those general themes, motives, or ideas in which there could be no copyright. Therefore he dismissed the bill.

An understanding of the issue involves some description of what was in the public demesne, as well as of the play and the picture. In 1857 a Scotch girl, named Madeleine Smith, living in Glasgow, was brought to trial upon an indictment in three counts; two for attempts to poison her lover, a third for poisoning him. The jury acquitted her on the first count, and brought in a verdict of 'Not Proven' on the second and third. The circumstances of the prosecution aroused much interest at the time not only in Scotland but in England; so much indeed that it became a cause celebre, and that as late as 1927 the whole proceedings were published in book form. An outline of the story so published, which became the original of the play here in suit, is as follows: The Smiths were a respectable middle-class family, able to send their daughter to a 'young ladies' boarding school'; they supposed her protected not only from any waywardness of her own, but from the wiles of seducers. In both they were mistaken, for when at the age of twenty-one she met a young Jerseyman of French blood, Emile L'Angelier, ten years older, and already the hero of many amorous adventures, she quickly succumbed and poured out her feelings in letters of the utmost ardor and indiscretion, and at times of a candor beyond the standards then, and even yet, permissible for well-nurtured young women. They wrote each other as though already married, and he assuming to dictate her conduct and even her feelings; both expected to marry, she on any terms, he with the approval of her family. Nevertheless she soon tired of him and engaged herself to a man some twenty years older who was a better match, but for whom she had no more than a friendly complaisance. L'Angelier was not, however, to be fobbed off so easily; he threatened to expose her to her father by showing her letters. She at first tried to dissuade him by appeals to their tender memories, but finding this useless and thinking herself otherwise undone, she affected a return of her former passion and invited him to visit her again. Whether he did, was the turning point of the trial; the evidence, though it really left the issue in no doubt, was too indirect to satisfy the jury, perhaps in part because of her advocate's argument that to kill him only insured the discovery of her letters. It was shown that she had several times bought or tried to buy poison,— prussic acid and arsenic,— and that twice before his death L'Angelier became violently ill, the second time on the day after her purchase. He died of arsenical poison, which the prosecution charged that she had given him in a cup of chocolate. At her trial, Madeleine being incompetent as a witness, her advocate proved an alibi by the testimony of her younger sister that early on the night of the murder as laid in the indictment, she had gone to bed with Madeleine, who had slept with her throughout the night. As to one of the attempts her betrothed swore that she had been with him at the theatre.

This was the story which the plaintiffs used to build their play. As will appear they took from it but the merest skeleton, the acquittal of a wanton young woman, who to extricate herself from an amour that stood in the way of a respectable marriage, poisoned her lover. The incidents, the characters, the mis en scene, the sequence of events, were all changed; nobody disputes that the plaintiffs were entitled to their copyright. All that they took from the story they might probably have taken, had it even been copyrighted. Their heroine is named Madeleine Cary; she lives in New York, brought up in affluence, if not in luxury; she is intelligent, voluptuous, ardent and corrupt; but, though she has had a succession of amours, she is capable of genuine affection. Her lover and victim is an Argentinian, named Moreno, who makes his living as a dancer in night-clubs. Madeleine has met him once in Europe before the play opens, has danced with him, has excited his concupiscence; he presses presents upon her. The play opens in his rooms, he and his dancing partner who is also his mistress, are together; Madeleine on the telephone recalls herself to him and says she wishes to visit him, though it is already past midnight. He disposes of his mistress by a device which does not deceive her and receives Madeleine; at once he falls to wooing her, luring her among other devices by singing a Gaucho song. He finds her facile and the curtain falls in season.

The second act is in her home, and introduces her father, a bibulous dotard, who has shot his wife's lover in the long past; Laurence Brennan, a self-made man in the fifties, untutored, self-reliant and reliable, who has had with Madeleine a relation, half paternal, half-amorous since she grew up; and Denis Farnborough, a young British labor peer, a mannekin to delight the heart of well ordered young women. Madeleine loves him; he loves Madeleine; she will give him no chance to declare himself, remembering her mottled past and his supposedly immaculate standards. She confides to Brennan, who makes clear to her the imbecility of her self-denial; she accepts this enlightenment and engages herself to her high-minded paragon after confessing vaguely her evil life and being assured that to post-war generations all such lapses are peccadillo.

In the next act Moreno, who has got wind of the engagement, comes to her house. Disposing of Farnborough, who chances to be there, she admits Moreno, acknowledges that she is to marry Farnborough, and asks him to accept the situation as the normal outcome of their intrigue. He refuses to be cast off, high words pass, he threatens to expose their relations, she raves at him, until finally he knocks her down and commands her to go to his apartment that morning as before. After he leaves full of swagger, her eye lights on a bottle of strychnine which her father uses as a drug; her fingers slowly close upon it; the audience understands that she will kill Moreno. Farnborough is at the telephone; this apparently stiffens her resolve, showing her the heights she may reach by its execution.

The scene then shifts again to Moreno's apartment; his mistress must again be put out, most unwillingly for she is aware of the situation; Madeleine comes in; she pretends once more to fell warmly, she must wheedle him for he is out of sorts after the quarrel. Meanwhile she prepares to poison him by putting the strychnine in coffee, which she asks him to make ready. But in the course of these preparations during which he sings her again his Gaucho song, what with their proximity, and this and that, her animal ardors are once more aroused and drag her, unwillingly and protesting, from her purpose. The play must therefore wait for an hour or more until, relieved of her passion, she appears from his bedroom and while breakfasting puts the strychnine in his coffee. He soon discovers what has happened and tries to telephone for help. He does succeed in getting a few words through, but she tears away the wire and fills his dying ears with her hatred and disgust. She then carefully wipes away all traces of her finger prints and manages to get away while the door is being pounded in by those who have come at his call.

The next act is again at her home on the following evening. Things are going well with her and Farnborough and her father, when a district attorney comes in, a familiar of the household, now in stern mood; Moreno's mistress and a waiter have incriminated Madeleine, and a cross has been found in Moreno's pocket, which he superstitiously took off her neck the night before. The district attorney cross-questions her, during which Farnborough several times fatuously intervenes; she is driven from point to point almost to an avowal when as a desperate plunge she says she spent the night with Brennan. Brennan is brought to the house and, catching the situation after a moment's delay, bears her out. This puts off the district attorney until seeing strychnine brought to relieve the father, his suspicions spring up again and he arrests

Madeleine. The rest of the play is of no consequence here, except that it appears in the last scene that at the trial where she is acquitted, her father on the witness stand accounts for the absence of the bottle of strychnine which had been used to poison Moreno.

At about the time that this play was being written an English woman named Lowndes wrote a book called Letty Lynton, also founded on the story of Madeleine Smith. Letty Lynton lives in England; she is eighteen years old, beautiful, well-reared and intelligent, but wayward. She has had a more or less equivocal love affair with a young Scot, named McLean, who worked in her father's chemical factory, but has discarded him, apparently before their love-making had gone very far. Then she chances upon a young Swede— half English—named Ekebon, and their acquaintance quickly becomes a standardized amour, kept secret from her parents, especially her mother, who is an uncompromising moralist, and somewhat estranged from Letty anyway. She and her lover use an old barn as their place of assignation; it had been fitted up as a play house for Letty when she was a child. Like Madeleine Smith she had written her lover a series of indiscreet letters which he has kept, for though he is on pleasure bent Ekebon has a frugal mind, and means to marry his sweetheart and set himself up for life. They are betrothed and he keeps pressing her to declare it to her parents, which she means never to do. While he is away in Sweden Letty meets an unmarried peer considerably older than she, poor, but intelligent and charming; he falls in love with her and she accepts him, more because it is a good match than for any other reason, though she likes him well enough, and will make him suppose that she loves him.

Thereupon Ekebon reappears, learns of Letty's new betrothal, and threatens to disclose his own to her father, backing up his story with her letters. She must at once disown her peer and resume her engagement with him. His motive, like L'Angelier's, is ambition rather than love, though conquest is a flattery and Letty a charming morsel. His threats naturally throw Letty into dismay; she has come to loathe him and at any cost must get free, but she has no one to turn to. In her plight she thinks of her old suitor, McLean, and goes to the factory only to find him gone. He has taught her how to get access to poisons in his office and has told of their effect on human beings. At first she thinks of jumping out the window, and when she winces at that, of poisoning herself; that would be easier. So she selects arsenic which is less painful and goes away with it; it is only when she gets home that she thinks of poisoning Ekebon. Her mind is soon made up, however, and she makes an appointment with him at the barn; she has told her father, she writes, and Ekebon is to see him on Monday, but meanwhile on Sunday they will meet secretly once more. She has prepared to go on a week-end party and conceals her car near the barn. He comes; she welcomes him with a pretence of her former ardors, and tries to get back her letters. Unsuccessful in this she persuades him to drink a cup of chocolate into which she puts the arsenic. After carefully washing the pans and cups, she leaves with him, dropping him from her car near his home; he being still unaffected. On her way to her party she pretends to have broken down and by asking the help of a passing cyclist establishes an alibi. Ekebon dies at his home attended by his mistress; the letters are discovered and Letty is brought before the coroner's inquest and acquitted chiefly through the alibi, for things look very bad for her until the cyclist appears.

The defendants, who are engaged in producing speaking films on a very large scale in Hollywood, California, had seen the play and wished to get the rights. They found, however, an obstacle in an association of motion picture producers presided over by Mr. Will Hays, who thought the play obscene; not being able to overcome his objections, they returned the copy of the manuscript which they had had. That was in the spring of 1930, but in the autumn they induced the plaintiffs to get up a scenario, which they hoped might pass moral muster. Although this did not suit them after the plaintiffs prepared it, they must still have thought in the spring of 1931 that they could satisfy Mr. Hays, for they then procured an offer from the plaintiffs to sell their rights for $30,000. These negotiations also proved abortive because the play continued to be objectionable, and eventually they cried off on the bargain. Mrs. Lowndes' novel was suggested to Thalberg, one of the vice-presidents of the Metro-Goldwyn Company, in July, 1931, and again in the following November, and he bought the rights to it in December. At once he assigned the preparation of a play to Stromberg, who had read the novel in January, and thought it would make a suitable play for an actress named, Crawford, just then not employed. Stromberg chose Meehan, Tuchock and Brown to help him, the first two with the scenario, the third with the dramatic production. All these four were examined by deposition; all denied that they had used the play in any way whatever; all agreed that they had based the picture on the story of Madeleine Smith and on the novel, 'Letty Lynton.' All had seen the play, and Tuchock had read the manuscript, as had Thalberg, but Stromberg, Meehan and Brown swore that they had not; Stromberg's denial being however worthless, for he had originally sworn the contrary in an affidavit. They all say that work began late in November or early in December, 1931, and the picture was finished by the end of March. To meet these denials, the plaintiffs appeal to the substantial identity between passages in the picture and those parts of the play which are original with them.

The picture opens in Montevideo where Letty Lynton is recovering from her fondness for Emile Renaul. She is rich, luxurious and fatherless, her father having been killed by his mistress's husband; her mother is seared, hard, selfish, unmotherly, and Letty has left home to escape her, wandering about in search of excitement. Apparently for the good part of a year she has been carrying on a love affair with Renaul; twice before she has tried to shake loose, has gone once to Rio where she lit another flame, but each time she has weakened and been drawn back. Though not fully declared as an amour, there can be no real question as to the character of her attachment. She at length determines really to break loose, but once again her senses are too much for her and it is indicated, if not declared, that she spends the night with Renaul. Though he is left a vague figure only indistinctly associated with South America somewhere or other, the part was cast for an actor with a marked foreign accent, and it is plain that he was meant to be understood, in origin anyway, as South American, like Moreno in the play. He is violent, possessive and sensual; his power over Letty lies in his strong animal attractions. However, she escapes in the morning while he is asleep, whether from his bed or not is perhaps uncertain; and with a wax figure in the form of a loyal maid— Letty in the novel had one— boards a steamer for New York. On board she meets Darrow, a young American, the son of a rich rubber manufacturer, who is coming back from a trip to Africa. They fall in love upon the faintest provocation and become betrothed before the ship docks, three weeks after she left Montevideo. At the pier she finds Renaul who has flown up to reclaim her. She must in some way keep her two suitors apart, and she manages to dismiss Darrow and then to escape Renaul by asking him to pay her customs duties, which he does. Arrived home her mother gives her a cold welcome and refuses to concern herself with the girl's betrothal. Renaul is announced; he has read of the betrothal in the papers and is furious. He tries again to stir her sensuality by the familiar gambit, but this time he fails; she slaps his face and declares that she hates him. He commands her to come to his apartment that evening; she begs him to part with her and let her have her life; he insists on renewing their affair. She threatens to call the police; he rejoins that if so her letters will be published, and then he leaves. Desperate, she chances on a bottle of strychnine, which we are to suppose is an accouterment of every affluent household, and seizes it; the implication is of intended suicide, not murder. Then she calls Darrow, tells him that she will not leave with him that night for his parents' place in the Adirondacks as they had planned; she renews to him the pledge of her love, without him she cannot live, an intimation to the audience of her purpose to kill herself.

That evening she goes to Renaul's apartment in a hotel armed with her strychnine bottle, for use on the spot; she finds him cooling champagne, but in bad temper. His caresses which he bestows plentifully enough, again stir her disgust not her passions, but he does not believe it and assumes that she will spend the night with him. Finding that he will not return the letters, she believes herself lost and empties the strychnine into a wine glass. Again he embraces her; she vilifies him; he knocks her down; she vilifies him again. Ignorant of the poison he grasps her glass, and she, perceiving it, lets him drink. He woos her again, this time with more apparent success, for she is terrified; he sings a Gaucho song to her, the same one that has been heard at Montevideo. The poison begins to work and, at length supposing that she has meant to murder him, he reaches for the telephone; she forestalls him, but she does not tear out the wire. As he slowly dies, she stands over him and vituperates him. A waiter enters; she steps behind a curtain; he leaves thinking Renaul drunk; she comes out, wipes off all traces of her fingerprints and goes out, leaving however her rubbers which Renaul had taken from her when she entered.

Next she and Darrow are found at his parents' in the Adirondacks; while there a detective appears, arrests Letty and takes her to New York; she is charged with the murder of Renaul; Darrow goes back to New York with her. The finish is at the district attorney's office; Letty and Darrow, Letty's mother, the wax serving maid are all there. The letters appear incriminating to an elderly rather benevolent district attorney; also the customs slip and the rubbers. Letty begins to break down; she admits that she went to Renaul's room, not to kill him but to get him to release her. Darrow sees that that story will not pass, and volunteers that she came to his room at a hotel and spent the night with him. Letty confirms this and mother, till then silent, backs up their story; she had traced them to the hotel and saw the lights go out, having ineffectually tried to dissuade them. The maid still further confirms them and the district attorney, not sorry to be discomfited, though unbelieving, discharges Letty.

We are to remember that it makes no difference how far the play was anticipated by works in the public demesne which the plaintiffs did not use. The defendants appear not to recognize this, for they have filled the record with earlier instances of the same dramatic incidents and devices, as though, like a patent, a copyrighted work must be not only original, but new. That is not however the law as is obvious in the case of maps or compendia, where later works will necessarily be anticipated. At times, in discussing how much of the substance of a play the copyright protects, courts have indeed used language which seems to give countenance to the notion that, if a plot were old, it could not be copyrighted. London v. Biograph Co. (C.C.A.) 231 F. 696; Eichel v. Marcin (D.C.) 241 F. 404. But we understand by this no more than that in its broader outline a plot is never copyrightable, for it is plain beyond peradventure that anticipation as such cannot invalidate a copyright. Borrowed the work must indeed not be, for a plagiarist is not himself pro tanto an 'author'; but if by some magic a man who had never known it were to compose anew Keats's Ode on a Grecian Urn, he would be an 'author,' and, if he copyrighted it, others might not copy that poem, though they might of course copy Keats's. Bleistein v. Donaldson Lithographing Co., 188 U.S. 239, 249, 23 S.Ct. 298, 47 L.Ed. 460; Gerlach-Barklow Co. v. Morris & Bendien, Inc., 23 F.(2d) 159, 161 (C.C.A. 2); Weil, Copyright Law, p. 234. But though a copyright is for this reason less vulnerable than a patent, the owner's protection is more limited, for just as he is no less an 'author' because others have preceded him, so another who follows him, is not a tort-feasor unless he pirates his work. Jewelers' Circular Publishing

Co. v. Keystone Co., 281 F. 83, 92, 26 A.L.R. 571 (C.C.A. 2); General Drafting Co. v. Andrews, 37 F.(2d) 54, 56 (C.C.A. 2); Williams v. Smythe (C.C.) 110 F. 961; American, etc., Directory Co. v. Gehring Pub. Co. (D.C.) 4 F.(2d) 415; New Jersey, etc., Co. v. Barton Business Service (D.C.) 57 F.(2d) 353. If the copyrighted work is therefore original, the public demesne is important only on the issue of infringement; that is, so far as it may break the force of the inference to be drawn from likenesses between the work and the putative piracy. If the defendant has had access to other material which would have served him as well, his disclaimer becomes more plausible.

In the case at bar there are then two questions: First, whether the defendants actually used the play; second, if so, whether theirs was a 'fair use.' The judge did not make any finding upon the first question, as we said at the outset, because he thought the defendants were in any case justified; in this following our decision in Nichols v. Universal Pictures Corporation, 45 F.(2d) 119. The plaintiffs challenge that opinion because we said that 'copying' might at times be a 'fair use'; but it is convenient to define such a use by saying that others may 'copy' the 'theme,' or 'ideas,' or the like, of a work, though not its 'expression.' At any rate so long as it is clear what is meant, no harm is done. In the case at bar the distinction is not so important as usual, because so much of the play was borrowed from the story of Madeleine Smith, and the plaintiffs' originality is necessarily limited to the variants they introduced. Nevertheless, it is still true that their whole contribution may not be protected; for the defendants were entitled to use, not only all that had gone before, but even the plaintiffs' contribution itself, if they drew from it only the more general patterns; that is, if they kept clear of its 'expression.' We must therefore state in detail those similarities which seem to us to pass the limits of 'fair use.' Finally, in concluding as we do that the defendants used the play pro tanto, we need not charge their witnesses with perjury. With so many sources before them they might quite honestly forget what they took; nobody knows the origin of his inventions; memory and fancy merge even in adults. Yet unconscious plagiarism is actionable quite as much as deliberate. Buck v. Jewell-La Salle Realty Co., 283 U.S. 191, 198. 51 S.Ct. 410, 75 L.Ed. 971, 76 A.L.R. 1266; Harold Lloyd Corporation v. Witwer, 65 F.(2d) 1, 16 (C.C.A. 9); Fred Fisher, Inc., v. Dillingham (D.C.) 298 F. 145.

The defendants took for their mis en scene the same city and the same social class; and they chose a South American villain. The heroines had indeed to be wanton, but Letty Lynton 'tracked'Madeleine Cary more closely than that. She is overcome by passion in the first part of the picture and yields after announcing that she hates Renaul and has made up her mind to leave him. This is the same weakness as in the murder scene of the play, though transposed. Each heroine's waywardness is suggested as an inherited disposition; each has had an errant parent involved in scandal; one killed, the other becoming an outcast. Each is redeemed by a higher love. Madeleine Cary must not be misread; it is true that her lust overcomes her at the critical moment, but it does not extinguish her love for Farnborough; her body, not her soul, consents to the lapse. Moreover, her later avowal, which she knew would finally lose her her lover, is meant to show the basic rectitude of her nature. Though it does not need Darrow to cure Letty of her wanton ways, she too is redeemed by a nobler love. Neither Madeleine Smith, nor the Letty of the novel, were at all like that; they wished to shake off a clandestine intrigue to set themselves up in the world; their love as distinct from their lust, was pallid. So much for the similarity in character.

Coming to the parallelism of incident, the threat scene is carried out with almost exactly the same sequence of event and actuation; it has no prototype in either story or novel. Neither Ekebon nor L'Angelier went to his fatal interview to break up the new betrothal; he was beguiled by the pretence of a renewed affection. Moreno and Renaul each goes to his sweetheart's home to detach her from her new love; when he is there, she appeals to his better side, unsuccessfully; she abuses him, he returns the abuse and commands her to come to his rooms; she pretends to agree, expecting to finish with him one way or another. True, the assault is deferred in the picture from this scene to the next, but it is the same dramatic trick. Again, the poison in each case is found at home, and the girl talks with her betrothed just after the villain has left and again pledges him her faith. Surely the sequence of these details is pro tanto the very web of the authors' dramatic expression; and copying them is not 'fair use.'

The death scene follows the play even more closely; the girl goes to the villain's room as he directs; from the outset he is plainly to be poisoned while they are together. (The defendants deny that this is apparent in the picture, but we cannot agree. It would have been an impossible denoument on the screen for the heroine, just plighted to the hero, to kill herself in desperation, because the villain has successfully enmeshed her in their mutual past; yet the poison is surely to be used on some one.) Moreno and Renaul each tries to arouse the girl by the memory of their former love, using among other aphrodisiacs the Gaucho song; each dies while she is there, incidentally of strychnine not arsenic. In extremis each makes for the telephone and is thwarted by the girl; as he dies, she pours upon him her rage and loathing. When he is dead, she follows the same ritual to eradicate all traces of her presence, but forgets telltale bits of property. Again these details in the same sequence embody more than the 'ideas' of the play; they are its very raiment.

Finally in both play and picture in place of a trial, as in the story and the novel, there is substituted an examination by a district attorney; and this examination is again in parallel almost step by step. A parent is present; so is the lover; the girl yields progressively as the evidence accumulates; in the picture, the customs slip, the rubbers and the letters; in the play, the cross and the witnesses, brought in to confront her. She is at the breaking point when she is saved by substantially the same most unexpected alibi; a man declares that she has spent the night with him. That alibi there introduced is the turning point in each drama and alone prevents its ending in accordance with the classics canon of tragedy; i.e., fate as an inevitable consequence of past conduct, itself not evil enough to quench pity. It is the essence of the authors' expression, the very voice with which they speak.

We have often decided that a play may be pirated without using the dialogue. Daly v. Palmer, Fed. Cas. No. 3,552, 6 Blatch. 256; Daly v. Webster, 56 F. 483, 486, 487; Dam v. Kirke La Shelle Co., 175 F. 902, 907, 41 L.R.A.(N.S.) 1002, 20 Ann.Cas. 1173; Chappell & Co. v. Fields, 210 F. 864. Dymow v. Bolton, 11 F.(2d) 690; and Nichols v. Universal Pictures Corporation, supra, 45 F.(2d) 119, do not suggest otherwise. Were it not so, there could be no piracy of a pantomime, where there cannot be any dialogue; yet nobody would deny to pantomime the name of drama. Speech is only a small part of a dramatist's means of expression; he draws on all the arts and compounds his play from words and gestures and scenery and costume and from the very looks of the actors themselves. Again and again a play may lapse into pantomime at its most poignant and significant moments; a nod, a movement of the hand, a pause, may tell the audience more than words could tell. To be sure, not all this is always copyrighted, though there is no reason why it may not be, for those decisions do not forbid which hold that mere scenic tricks will not be protected. Serrana v. Jefferson (C.C.) 33 F. 347; Barnes v. Miner (C.C.) 122 F. 480; Bloom et al. v. Nixon (C.C.) 125 F. 977. The play is the sequence of the confluents of all these means, bound together in an inseparable unity; it may often be most effectively pirated by leaving out the speech, for which a substitute can be found, which keeps the whole dramatic meaning. That as it appears to us is exactly what the defendants have done here; the dramatic significance of the scenes we have recited is the same, almost to the letter. True, much of the picture owes nothing to the play; some of it is plainly drawn from the novel; but that is entirely immaterial; it is enough that substantial parts were lifted; no plagiarist can excuse the wrong by showing how much of his work he did not pirate. We cannot avoid the conviction that, if the picture was not an infringement of the play, there can be none short of taking the dialogue.

The decree will be reversed and an injunction will go against the picture together with a decree for damages and an accounting. The plaintiffs will be awarded an attorney's fee in this court and in the court below, both to be fixed by the District Court upon the final decree.

Decree reversed.

POE v. MICHAEL TODD CO.
United States District Court for the Southern District of New York
February 11, 1957
No. Number in Original
151 F. Supp. 801

WEINFELD, District Judge.

The plaintiff, a professional writer of screen plays and scripts for motion pictures, seeks a preliminary injunction to enjoin the exhibition of a motion picture entitled 'Around the World in 80 Days' based upon the novel by Jules Verne, unless the defendants give him screen play writing credit.

One S. J. Perelman is given sole credit on the film, which currently is being exhibited in various cities throughout the country. The plaintiff contends the screen play is based upon a script prepared by him and that in acordance with a well-established and recognized practice in the motion picture industry he is entitled to credit on the film as well as on all promotional advertising.

That the plaintiff was engaged to and did write some portion of the screen play cannot be seriously disputed. Indeed, the corporate defendant in its answer admits that in May, 1955 it engaged the plaintiff to render services in connection with the screen play at a fixed salary for ten weeks. Plaintiff contends he completed the script in collaboration with the defendant's director-producer, one Farrow, on June 29, 1955. What is in dispute is the portion of the plaintiff's script which went into the final play. Subsequent to June 29, 1955 the defendants engaged S. J. Perelman who made revisions in the dialogue and changes in the script previously prepared by the plaintiff—this the plaintiff concedes, but claims that they were only incidental revisions and additions which did not change the basic structure of his script.

The defendants say they gave and are giving Perelman sole screen credit because he, of all the script writers, made the substantial and major contribution to the ultimate screen play; that it was his changes of dialogue, revisions, eliminations and writing of new scenes which in large measure resulted in the ultimate success of the picture, the concept of which the individual defendant claims credit, as well as credit for important contributions to the script proper. Thus immediately there is a challenge to the plaintiff's contention of a major contribution to the picture.

Other matters are also in dispute. The employment of plaintiff was by oral contract. Upon his examination before trial he made no contention, nor does he appear to do so on this application, that the oral contract included an express undertaking to give him screen credit. He relies, as already noted, upon an alleged established practice in the motion picture industry to give public credit to an author both on the film and in advertising, and contends that the parties intended to observe this practice.

The defendants in resisting plaintiff's plea deny that any agreement, express or implied, was made to give him authorship credit. Additionally they attack his claim that a custom or practice to give screen credits exists in the trade and assert that it is done only when expressly agreed upon; further, they contend that absent a contractual obligation to give screen credit, there is no inherent right in an author thereto, and the producer may, if he sees fit, omit it.

Finally, the plaintiff contends that the issue as to whether he was entitled to screen credit was submitted for arbitration to the Writers Guild of America, West, Inc., which rendered a decision that credits for the pictures were to be given to three persons, the plaintiff, Farrow, the director-producer, and Perelman. The defendants vigorously deny they ever consented to submit or did submit the matter for arbitration to the Writers Guild. The corporate defendant points out that it resisted membership in the Guild; that its only contact with that body in this matter was when, in response to the Guild's request for information after plaintiff, who was a member, asserted a claim for credit, it (the corporate defendant) notified the Guild of its intention to give sole credit to S. J. Perelman. In submitting this information it set forth the names of others, including that of plaintiff, all of whom it admitted participated 'in the early preparation and treatment of the screen play * * * to some extent; though in our (defendant's) opinion there remains a negligible amount of such contribution of ideas or writing in the final edited picture as it will be released for exhibition.'

In any event, the defendant denies that the information it sent to the Writers Guild was a contract for or submission to arbitration of any question of screen credit or that it agreed to be bound by this determination. Significantly the defendant points out that if in fact there were such an award under an arbitration agreement it would be enforceable as such and no proceeding of any kind with respect thereto has been taken.

I have pointed out these substantial matters in controversy since obviously they do have a bearing on plaintiff's application. To grant the motion for the requested extraordinary injunctive relief would alter rather than preserve the status quo and yield to the plaintiff the full measure of relief which normally he would be entitled to after a trial on the merits and then only in the event he had successfully carried his burden of proof as to the controverted issues as well as others in the case. Under the circumstances here presented, the granting of the requested relief is not warranted— and indeed in the face of the sharply controverted issues of fact would not be a wise exercise of discretion.

Another factor which militates against the granting of this motion is that although the plaintiff was fully aware the picture was to be released on October

17, 1956 without credit to him and he filed this action on that day, no motion for injunctive relief was made until three months thereafter.

The plaintiff, however, has made a sufficient showing to warrant a prompt trial since if he should sustain his burden of proof the failure to give him credit would constitute irreparable injury. Not only would money damages be difficult to establish, but at best they would hardly compensate for the real injury done. A writer's reputation, which would be greatly enhanced by public credit for authorship of an outstanding picture, is his stock in trade; it is clear that irreparable injury would follow the failure to give him screen credit if in fact he is entitled to it.

Accordingly the denial of the motion is without prejudice to an application for a preference pursuant to Local Calendar Rule 11.

Settle order on notice.

AUTRY v. REPUBLIC PRODUCTIONS, INC.
United States Court of Appeals for the Ninth Circuit
June 4, 1954
No. 13522
213 F.2d 667

BONE, Circuit Judge.

Appellant brought this action for an injunction, to restrain appellees from exhibiting motion pictures in connection with commercially sponsored or sustaining television broadcasts, where those motion pictures contain appearances of appellant. In its opinion below, 104 F.Supp. 918, the District Court gave judgment to appellees, holding that the contracts between appellees and appellant placed no restrictions upon appellees' use or exhibition of the motion pictures. There were five contracts executed over a period of a dozen years, but the contracts are sufficiently similar that they need not be discussed individually. The trial judge used paragraph 9 of the 1938 contract as an example. That was fair to both parties, and we shall do likewise:

> "9. The producer shall have the right to photograph and/or otherwise reproduce any and all of the acts, poses, plays and appearances of the artist * * * during each employment period, and to record for motion picture purposes the voice of the artist * * * and to reproduce and/or transmit the same in connection with such acts, poses, plays and appearances as the producer may desire, and the producer shall own solely and exclusively all rights of every kind and character whatsoever in and to the same perpetually, including the right to use and exploit all or any part of the same in such manner as the producer may desire, and including, as well, the perpetual right to use the name and likeness of the artist and recordations and reproductions of his voice in connection with the advertising and exploitation thereof. The artist does hereby also grant to the producer the right to make use of and to allow others to make use of his name (in addition to and other than in connection with the acts, poses, plays and appearances for the artist hereunder) for the purpose of advertising, exploiting and/or publicizing photoplays in which the artist appears, as well as the right to make use of and distribute his physical likeness and his voice for the like purpose. * * *."

This contract, like the contracts in Republic Pictures Corp. v. Rogers, 9 Cir., 213 F.2d 662 contains the descriptive words (1) "acts, poses, plays and appearances" and (2) "name, voice, and likeness." As set forth in our opinion in the Rogers case, we interpret these two sets of words as applying to two different and distinct subject matters. The former refers to the artist's activities or appearances in a motion picture as such; the latter set of words refers to a reproduction of the name, voice or likeness of the artist apart from his activities or appearances in the former, and lacking the motion and dynamic and dramatic qualities contained in motion pictures. There are limitations placed upon appellees' use of the latter, but appellant granted for valuable consideration all rights, unrestricted to appellees in their ownership of the former.

Although appellees unquestionably have the right to cut and edit the motion pictures, and to license others to do the same, we can conceive that some such cutting and editing could result in emasculating the motion pictures so that they would no longer contain substantially the same motion and dynamic and dramatic qualities which it was the purpose of the artist's employment to produce. And although appellees unquestionably have the right to exhibit the motion pictures in connection with or for the purpose of advertising commercial products of all sorts, we can conceive that some such exhibitions could be so "doctored" as to make it appear that the artist actually endorses the products of the programs' sponsors.

The record in this case shows that the appellees proposed to license motion pictures featuring appellant, which said picture would be edited to 53 or 53 ½ minutes each, in length, thus permitting approximately 7 minutes of advertising in an hour television program. It was this proposed use that was alleged in appellant's complaint and as to which an injunction was asked. The parties stipulated that the License Agreement through which the pictures were proposed to be exhibited, expressly prohibited "* * * any advertising * * * [or] any statements which * * * may be understood to be an endorsement of any sponsor * * * [etc.] by * * * any actor or actress appearing therein * * * or * * * that any such person is connected or associated with * * * Station or any Sponsor. * * * All advertising issued * * * relating to any picture shall give cast and due credits in the same manner * * * as such credits appear in the main title of the respective picture."

The issue here, is whether appellees should be enjoined from cutting the appellant's performances to approximately 53 minutes, and showing them in connection with commercial advertising over television, pursuant to a License Agreement such as that above quoted. The judgment from which the appeal is taken goes farther than the printed opinion, in that it expressly permits appellees:

"* * * to cut, edit and otherwise revise and to license others [to do likewise] * * * in any manner, to any length and for any purpose * * *."

Appellant has put in issue the breadth and sweep of this judgment. We agree with appellant that this broad language nullifies all of the clauses in the employment contracts which were introduced therein for the protection of appellant wit reference to the type and quality of photoplays in which he rendered his services. The issue tendered to the trial court was whether appellees could make use of the motion pictures in the manner proposed; the issue was not one of ascertaining what other uses could be made of them, or how far appellees might go. Because this part of the judgment goes beyond the issues presented to the trial court, we hereby disapprove of it. We simply hold that appellees should not be enjoined from cutting the appellant's performances to approximately 53 minutes, and showing them in connection with commercial advertising over television, pursuant to a License Agreement such as that above quoted.

Appellant has raised the issue of unfair competition and the possible application of the Lanham Act, Title 15 U.S.C.A. §§ 1125 and 1126. Even aside from the consent which we find was given by appellant to appellees in the contracts, appellant argues that appellees might so alter or emasculate the motion pictures as to render them substantially different from the product which the artist produced. Further, that the exhibition of old pictures which depict appellant in clothes which are no longer in style, and in autos which are no longer modern, could be quite harmful to his modern reputation. As to the latter point, the consent which we have found in the contracts extends to this risk. As to the question of appellees' emasculating the pictures, we have attempted to leave that question open, to be properly presented when and if the occasion arises; we have disapproved that part of the lower court judgment which could be considered authority for such possible abuse, although our disapproval should not be taken as passing on the merits of what was there said. Appellant is not in a position to further urge unfair competition, since it is our interpretation of the contracts that appellant consented to such exhibition of the pictures as is proposed here.

As herein modified, the judgment of the trial court is affirmed.

LOREN v. SAMUEL BRONSTON PRODUCTIONS, INC.
Supreme Court of New York, Special Term, New York County
January 24, 1962
32 Misc.2d 602,
224 N.Y.S.2d 959

Samuel H. Hofstadter, J.

The egocentricity which appears to be indigenous to "show business" is here manifested by the passionate insistence of a well-known motion-picture actress to have her name emblazoned on Broadway not only in the same type of the same size, but also on the same line, as that of her male lead. Such vanity—"the frail estate of human things", a "splendid but destructive egotism", as it has variously been called—doubtless is due in measurable part to the adulation which the public showers on the denizens of the entertainment world in a profusion wholly disproportionate to the instrinsic contribution which they make to the scheme of things when seen in correct perspective. For that matter often in disproportion to any true talent, latent or apparent!

Sophia Loren, the world-famed winner of the New York Film Critics' Award as the outstanding motion picture actress of 1961, and a corporation, owning the exclusive right to her services, of which her husband, Carlo Ponti is the president and sole stockholder, as plaintiffs, have brought this action for an injunction against the producer and the distributor of the epic motion picture "El Cid", which opened at the Warner Theatre in this city on December 14, 1961 and is being shown there to capacity houses. The owner and operator of the Warner Theatre is also a defendant in the action. The plaintiffs now move for injunctive relief during the pendency of the action substantially the same as they would obtain if successful at the trial.

Sophia Loren plays the leading female role of Chimene in "El Cid"; the part of "El Cid", a national hero of Spain, is taken by Charlton Heston. The plaintiffs' asserted grievance is that Miss Loren has not received the billing to which a written agreement of October 14, 1960, entitles her. This agreement provides that in all paid advertising of "El Cid" Miss Loren is to be accorded "second (2nd) star billing above the title, 100% the size and type of the title, on the same line, same size, same prominence as that used for Charlton Heston, who received first (1st) star billing." The plaintiffs complain of noncompliance with the foregoing provisions, especially in the design of electrically illuminated upright signs, on which the name of Sophia Loren appears below that of Charlton Heston, and the type of their names is different and smaller than that of the title "El Cid". The names of the two top stars on these signs, are, however, in the same size type and there is no differentiation in prominence, except insofar as the position of one above the other may imply. Moreover, on the marquee in front of the Warner Theatre facing Broadway their names are on the same line. The defendants dispute that they are doing anything in derogation of the plaintiffs' rights; they rely on the billing clause of a later employment agreement fully complied with, which, they say, either binds the plaintiffs contractually or which, in the light of their conduct, equity and good conscience will not permit the plaintiffs now to disavow.

In view of the disposition to be made, further statement of the facts or detailed analysis of the conflicting contentions of the parties will not be fruitful. It suffices for present purposes that study of the papers persuades me that the case presents substantial issues as to the plaintiffs' ultimate rights. There is also a genuine question whether, even if the plaintiffs' claims under the billing clause of the October 14, 1960 agreement are upheld, Miss Loren is really in danger of suffering the loss of prestige and other damage attributed to its nonobservance. The injunction prayed for would do far more than preserve the *status quo*, for the plaintiffs demand the removal of the electric signs and changes in the advertising program for the picture. Under established authority, the plaintiffs' rights at this juncture are not so clear as to warrant such an injunction and the motion therefor is denied (*Bachman v. Harrington*, 184 N. Y. 458; *Gilbert v. Burnside*, 6 A D 2d 834, 835; *Durante v. Paramount Pictures Corp.*, 111 N. Y. S. 2d 138).

However, an early trial is indicated. The case is placed at the head of the General Equity Calendar of February 19, 1962, for which date the Clerk is directed to accept a note of issue on payment of his fees. Statement of readiness is dispensed with.

QUESTIONS AND DISCUSSION

1. The case of Wood v. Lucy, Lady Duff-Gordon, 222 N.Y. 88, 118 N.E. 214 (1917), is Justice Cardozo's famous rendering of an implied-in-fact contract. Defendant is a "creator of fashions" and plaintiff is sort of an artist manager. Is the implied promise of plaintiff sufficient to constitute consideration for contract and support his cause against defendant for breach? Justice Cardozo comes up with a compromise: "instinct with an obligation." (Is that like friends with benefits?) This case stands for the proposition that this type of entertainment contract calls for an obligation of implied good faith.

What do you think of all of these "punk'd" reality TV stars? Shows like *Punk'd* seem to be a mean-spirited version of Alan Funk's beloved *Candid Camera*. If there are contracts in these shows, shouldn't there be an obligation of good faith, or at least an obligation to refrain from outright lies and deceptions? Have you ever heard of the phrase, "It's not worth the paper it's printed on"? In entertainment law, there should be a modicum of trust. How would you write a good faith clause (in the style of Wood v. Lucy, Lady Duff-Gordon) in an entertainment employment contract?

2. In Waverly Productions, Inc. v. RKO General, Inc., 217 Cal.App.2d 721, 32 Cal.Rptr., 73 (1963), there was found to be an implied covenant not to destroy prints in a motion picture distribution agreement. Plaintiff produced *Enchanted Island* and *From the Earth to the Moon*. As always, the parol evidence rule is used if the interpretation is needed to decipher contract ambiguities. Sublicenses were granted for foreign territories. The charge from the lab to make foreign prints is not an expense of the distributor; rather, it is an expense of the motion pictures' producer. Could this controversy have been avoided with sharper contractual language? What would you add?

3. The legendary comic actor Harold Lloyd sued for screen credit in Lloyd v. California Pictures Corp., 136 Cal.App.2d 638, 789 P.2d 295 (1955). He alleged promissory estoppel. (Credit is more important than money.) Is promissory estoppel the most effective legal maneuver?

4. In Luster Enterprises, Inc. v. Jacobs, 278 F.Supp. 73 (S.D.N.Y. 1967), plaintiff Helen Winston, the architect of a screenplay, wanted the credit of "conceived by Helen Winston" in the movie version of *Dr. Doolittle*. The request for a preliminary injunction was denied but so was the motion to dismiss. For injunctive relief, you must show irreparable harm. What harm was done to plaintiff here?

5. But, in Tamarind Litho Workshop v. Sanders, 143 Cal.App.3d 571, 193 Cal.Rptr. 409 (1983), specific performance was deemed to be the proper remedy with the result that the credit was styled as "A Film by Terry Sanders." What's the difference between this case and Luster?

6. In CNA Int"l Reinsurance Co. v. Phoenix, 676 So.2d 378 (Fla. App. 1976), there was an actor loan-out agreement involving the actor River Phoenix, who died allegedly of a drug overdose before the two movie projects were completed. Since he died, it was impossible to complete the films (the defense of impossibility), but was his death his fault or just a tragic accident? Of course, there was an insurance policy, which was paid. The movie *Dark Blood* was abandoned but the second film, *Interview With a Vampire* was completed with a different actor. The question is this: When were the policies effective? The court held that further development of the record was necessary. After the untimely death of Phoenix, should the different conclusions of the two movie projects affect the calculation of damages?

7. In Sheldon v. Metro-Goldwyn Pictures, 81 F.2d 49 (2d Cir. 1936), Judge Learned Hand, in an attempt to enjoin the defendant from producing a movie allegedly based on plaintiff's screenplay, famously opined that "no plagiarist can excuse the wrong by showing how much of the work he did not pirate" (at 81 F.2d 49, 55). With that type of language, who would win this contest? Provide a judicial-like explanation of how you would bolster your decision.

8. In Poe v. Michael Todd Co., 151 F.Supp. 801 (S.D.N.Y. 1957), plaintiff sought a preliminary injunction to secure a screenplay writing credit for the block buster, *Around the World in 80 Days* (the original). Plaintiff did not get the injunction but he did get a prompt trial setting. The judge concluded that "[a] writer's reputation which would be greatly enhanced by public credit for authorship of an outstanding picture is his stock in trade; it is clear that irreparable injury would follow the failure to give him screen credit if in fact he is entitled to it" (151 F.Supp. 801, 802-803). Should whether the movie was "outstanding" or a disappointment matter?

CHAPTER 5
TELEVISION

In a section entitled "Common Provisions of Entertainment Contracts" (pp. 5-17) in Contracts for Film and Television Industry, by Mark Litwak (Los Angeles: Silman-James Press, 3rd expanded ed., 2012), Attorney Litwak delineates certain standard provisions: assignment, collection account, ownership of picture, work for hire, right of last refusal, additional documentation notices, force majeure, incapacity, default, effect of suspension, termination rights, effect of termination, right to cure, indemnification, name and likeness, publicity restrictions, morals, remedies, guilds and unions, credits, insurance, employment of others, governing law, captions service of process illegality, employment eligibility, confidentiality, entire agreement, arbitration (Independent Film and Television Alliance [IFTA], IFTA with personal rider, long form, American Arbitration Association [AAA], short form), arbitration jams, optional arbitration provisions, and counterparts.

Television is regulated by the Federal Communications Commission (FCC) and federal statutes. It is not the way it used to be; cable TV, satellite TV, pay-for-view, etc., have dramatically altered the playing field. Since there are so many options for TV broadcasts and re-broadcasts, the syndication of shows has become extremely lucrative. Think "Seinfeld." There are literally thousands of channel options, not to mention reality TV (which to my mind is the bane of our existence).

There are five basic types of TV employment contracts: contracts for loan-out companies, writers, directors, actors, and producers. The most typical TV employment contract that would cross a would-be entertainment attorney's desk would concern actors. A TV actor's employment contract will grant the producer of the TV (or reality TV) show the right to use the actor's name and likeness in the TV show. He or she will usually be paid a percentage of the producer's revenue. These contracts may also contain permission to use the actor's name and likeness in merchandising and marketing. Actor employment contracts may contain a "morals" clause that stipulates inappropriate behavior, with the possible termination as a remedy. A medical examination is usually a prerequisite for employment. The producer of a TV series will often want an option contract for that actor's services for five to seven years. It is very important to scrutinize this exclusive services provision of the TV employment contract while drafting or reviewing a contract. Do not be afraid to move this section to fit the needs and requirements of your client both now and in the future. In negotiations, some entertainment lawyers press for a "favored-nations" clause, which ensures that no other actor in the TV series receives more advantageous terms; for example, credit, billing, use of trailers, hair stylists, time off (for good behavior), per diems, etc. It is somewhat comparable to the escalator clause in sports, through which your client (usually a QB)might receive a better salary than any new quarterbacks who join the league (Mark Litwak, Dealmaking in the Film and Television Industry: From Negotiations to Final Contracts 136-137 (L.A. Silman-James, expanded & updated 2nd ed., 2002)).

Attorney and author Mark Litwak explains the entertainment business for a young actor:

> When a novice signs a service deal, he has little bargaining power. The agreement will set the amount of compensation due in future years. If the series becomes a hit, the actor may become a star, and he may assert under the terms of an agreement that he now thinks does not compensate him fairly. With his newfound clout, he might try to renegotiate the deal and achieve more favorable terms. Sometimes the star will refuse to work or become uncooperative or "sick" to pressure the employer to sweeten the deal. The employer may threaten to sue, but often a compromise is reached as neither parts wants to kill the golden goose. Litwak, Dealmaking in the Film and Television Industries 137.

The first contract is similar in scope to an adhesion contract (take-it-or-leave-it), but since everyone can mature into a star, make sure that you draft the contract with enough flexibility to respond to your new star status.

In Jacobs v. CBS Broadcasting, Inc., 291 F.3d 1173 (9th Cir. 2002), plaintiff Michael Givens is a script writer and member of the Writers' Guild of America (WGA), who wrote *The Fourth Estate* in the hope of securing a TV commitment from a network. Givens was to receive appropriate credit. CBS acquired the broadcast rights to *Early Edition*. Givens seeks "participating writer" credit.

JACOBS v. CBS BROAD., INC.
United States Court of Appeals for the Ninth Circuit
April 11, 2002, Argued and Submitted; June 3, 2002, Filed
No. 01-55478
291 F.3d 1173

GRABER, Circuit Judge.

Plaintiffs Mike Jacobs, Jr., William Webb, and Westwind Releasing Corporation filed this action against Defendant CBS Broadcasting, Inc., alleging that CBS had breached a contract to give Plaintiffs production credit when it produced a television series called *Early Edition.* The district court granted summary judgment to CBS on the ground that an earlier nonjudicial proceeding precluded Plaintiffs from bringing their claim to court. We reverse because that nonjudicial proceeding was too informal to have preclusive effect.

FACTUAL AND PROCEDURAL BACKGROUND

Michael Givens is a script writer and a member of the Writers' Guild of America (WGA). Givens wrote a script titled *The Fourth Estate a/k/a/ Final Edition* (*Final Edition*). Westwind optioned *Final Edition* for the purpose of securing a television broadcast commitment from a network. Under the agreement between Givens and Westwind, any writing credit to be accorded Givens was to be determined pursuant to the WGA's Minimum Basic Agreement (MBA) credit-determination procedures. Givens was entitled to additional compensation under the contract only if the WGA awarded him a "written by" or "screenplay by" credit.

CBS later agreed with Westwind to acquire the broadcast rights to *Final Edition* (First Agreement). In a second contract, CBS bought all rights to *Final Edition* from Westwind *and* Givens (Second Agreement). The Second Agreement provided that, "*[i]f a project is produced based upon the literary property,* CBS agrees ... to provide credit to William Webb and Mike Jacobs, Jr. as Co Executive Producers (or Executive Producers at CBS' election) on a shared card." (Emphasis added.) The Second Agreement also incorporated the provision in the original contract between Givens and Westwind stating that any writing credit for Givens would be governed by the WGA's credit-determination procedures.

CBS eventually participated in the production of a series called *Early Edition,* which shared a common premise with Givens' *Final Edition* script. However, when the Notice of Tentative Writing Credits for *Early Edition* was issued, Givens was not listed as a "participating writer" who was entitled to receive credit. Givens complained to the WGA, citing those provisions of the

MBA setting forth the circumstances under which WGA members such as Givens are entitled to writing credit. The WGA responded by suspending the credits process and informing Columbia Tristar, one of the producers of *Early Edition,* that if *Early Edition* aired with credits different from those that the WGA ultimately found to be proper, the WGA would pursue damages on behalf of the WGA-credited writers.

The WGA undertook an investigation and concluded that Givens was not a "participating writer" of *Early Edition.* Givens sought review of the participating-writer decision but, after engaging in additional investigation, the WGA reaffirmed its conclusion that Givens was not entitled to writing credit. After this second determination, Givens asked the WGA to reconsider its decision. The WGA again decided that Givens was not entitled to credit. In a letter to Givens, the WGA noted that its determination that Givens was not a participating writer precluded it from representing him in any subsequent writing-credit arbitration against CBS.

While Givens was pursuing his WGA appeals, Givens, Jacobs, Webb, and Westwind filed this action in Los Angeles County Superior Court. They argued that the *Early Edition* project was "based upon" the literary property *Final Edition* and that, accordingly, CBS had breached its contract by not providing them with writing and production credit. CBS removed the action to federal court. Next, CBS filed a Notice of Initiation of Arbitration, which sought a decision pursuant to the WGA's arbitration procedure on two questions: (1) whether Givens had a right to enforce the contractual provisions of the Second Agreement with respect to *Early Edition* independently of the processes and standards for determining writing credit set forth in the MBA, and (2) whether Givens had a right to pursue a writing-credit claim in a judicial forum. The district court stayed proceedings in federal court pending the outcome of the arbitration.

The WGA arbitrator ruled in favor of CBS. The arbitrator held that allowing Givens to litigate his claims would undermine the finality of the MBA's "fast, fair, and effective system for determining credit." Givens stipulated to an order confirming the arbitration award. Accordingly, Givens is not a party to this appeal.

CBS then filed a motion for summary judgment against the remaining Plaintiffs, who seek production credit regardless of who actually wrote the *Early Edition* scripts. Arguing that Plaintiffs' claims for production credit were entirely derivative of Givens' claim for writing credit, CBS asserted that the formal WGA arbitration had a preclusive effect on Plaintiffs' federal action. The district court rejected that argument, but nonetheless granted summary judgment on the alternate ground that the earlier WGA participating-writer determination involving Givens had a nonmutual collateral estoppel effect on Plaintiffs' action. Plaintiffs filed a timely notice of appeal.

STANDARD OF REVIEW

We review de novo the district court's grant of summary judgment. *Delta Sav. Bank v. United States,* 265 F.3d 1017, 1021 (9th Cir.2001), *cert. denied,* 534 U.S. 1082, 122 S.Ct. 816, 151 L.Ed.2d 700 (2002). We also review de novo the district court's determination that a prior decision has preclusive effect. *Bates v. Union Oil Co.,* 944 F.2d 647, 649 (9th Cir.1991).

DISCUSSION

A. *California Law on Collateral Estoppel (Issue Preclusion) Applies.*

CBS argues that the WGA's determination that Givens was not a participating writer precludes Plaintiffs from litigating whether *Early Edition* is "based upon" *Final Edition.* To prevail, CBS must establish that the WGA participating-writer proceeding satisfies the requirements for application of collateral estoppel. *Lucido v. Superior Court,* 51 Cal.3d 335, 272 Cal.Rptr. 767, 795 P.2d 1223, 1225 (1990) ("The party asserting collateral estoppel bears the burden of establishing these requirements" under California law.); *Hydranautics v. FilmTec Corp.,* 204 F.3d 880, 885 (9th Cir.2000) (same under federal law).

Because this is a diversity action, state law controls whether the WGA participating-writer determination has a preclusive effect on Plaintiffs' claims for production credit. *See Pardo v. Olson & Sons, Inc.,* 40 F.3d 1063, 1066 (9th Cir.1994) ("Because this is a diversity case, we apply the collateral estoppel rules of the forum state...."); *Costantini v. Trans World Airlines,* 681 F.2d 1199, 1201 (9th Cir.1982) (holding that "a federal court sitting in diversity must apply the res judicata law of the state in which it sits"); *Priest v. Am. Smelting & Ref. Co.,* 409 F.2d 1229, 1231 (9th Cir.1969) ("Since federal jurisdiction in this case is based upon diversity of citizenship, the district court and this court must apply the substantive law of the forum state, ... includ[ing] the law pertaining to collateral estoppel."); *see also BBS Norwalk One, Inc. v. Raccolta, Inc.,* 117 F.3d 674, 677 (2d Cir.1997) ("The governing law in this diversity case is that of New York, where the district court sits: specifically, New York's law on the collateral estoppel effect of an arbitration award.").

Despite those precedents, CBS argues that federal law should govern the issue preclusion analysis in this case. CBS bases its argument on the fact that the district court confirmed the result of the second, more formal arbitration. Because the second arbitration award was confirmed, CBS reasons, that award must be construed as if it were a federal judgment. Under California law, the preclusive effect of a prior *federal* judgment is a matter governed by federal law. *Younger v. Jensen,* 26 Cal.3d 397, 161 Cal.Rptr. 905, 605 P.2d 813, 822 (1980) ("A federal judgment has the same effect in the courts of this state as it would have in a federal court." (citation and internal quotation marks omitted)).

CBS's theory has no application, however, because the potentially preclusive effect of the second arbitration is not at issue in this appeal. The district court held that the WGA's earlier participating-writer determination, which was *not* confirmed, precludes the present action, and it is that holding that CBS seeks to defend. Further, the second arbitration cannot have a preclusive effect on Plaintiffs' claims for production credit, because the arbitrator did not address whether the *Early Edition* project was "based upon" the literary property *Final Edition.* Thus, we need not decide whether federal law would determine the preclusive effect of the second arbitration. Only the WGA's initial participating-writer determination is at issue. Accordingly, we look to California law for the governing principles.

B. *The WGA Participating—Writer Proceeding Is Not Entitled to Preclusive Effect.*

Under California law, CBS must demonstrate that the WGA participating-writer determination was adjudicatory in nature before that determination can have collateral estoppel effect. *See Vandenberg v. Superior Court,* 21 Cal.4th 815, 88 Cal.Rptr.2d 366, 982 P.2d 229, 237 (1999) (stating criterion). Additionally, CBS must show that: (1) the issue decided in the WGA proceeding is identical to that presented in Plaintiffs' action; (2) the issue was actually litigated in the WGA proceeding; (3) the issue was necessarily decided in the WGA proceeding; (4) there was a final judgment on the merits in the WGA proceeding; and (5) Plaintiffs were a party or in privity with a party to the WGA proceeding. *Lucido,* 272 Cal.Rptr. 767, 795 P.2d at 1225. Plaintiffs argue that the first of these factors is dispositive and that the district court erred in giving the WGA participating-writer determination preclusive effect because that determination lacked the procedural safeguards that California courts require. We agree.

In order to have an issue-preclusive effect in a later judicial action in California, an arbitration must have been conducted with certain procedural safeguards. As the California Supreme Court recently explained:

> Whether collateral estoppel is fair and consistent with public policy in a particular case depends in part upon the character of the forum that first decided the issue later sought to be foreclosed. In this regard, courts consider the judicial nature of the prior forum, i.e., its legal formality, the scope of its jurisdiction, and its procedural safeguards, particularly including the opportunity for judicial review of adverse rulings.

Vandenberg, 88 Cal.Rptr.2d 366, 982 P.2d at 237. The California Courts of Appeal have similarly noted that it is "appropriate to give collateral estoppel effect to findings made during an arbitration, *so long as the arbitration had the elements of an adjudicatory procedure.*" *Kelly v. Vons Cos.,* 67 Cal.App.4th 1329,

79 Cal.Rptr.2d 763, 767 (1998) (emphasis added); *see also Camargo v. Cal. Portland Cement Co.,* 86 Cal.App.4th 995, 103 Cal.Rptr.2d 841, 853 (2001) ("[C]ollateral estoppel is appropriately applied to arbitration as a matter of policy where the arbitration had the elements of *an adjudicatory procedure.*" (emphasis added)). The need for procedural safeguards and legal formality is especially acute in the circumstances of this case because "collateral estoppel is invoked by a nonparty to the prior litigation. Such cases require close examination to determine whether nonmutual use of the doctrine is fair and appropriate." *Vandenberg,* 88 Cal.Rptr.2d 366, 982 P.2d at 237 (citations omitted); *see also Benasra v. Mitchell Silberberg & Knupp,* 96 Cal.App.4th 96, 116 Cal.Rptr.2d 644, 652 (2002) (same).

When deciding whether an arbitration was sufficiently adjudicatory in nature, courts apply the same standards used to determine whether an administrative proceeding should have collateral estoppel effect. *See* Restatement (Second) of Judgments, §§ 83(2), 84(3)(b) (1980); *Kelly,* 79 Cal.Rptr.2d at 767; *see also Vandenberg,* 88 Cal.Rptr.2d 366, 982 P.2d at 237 (relying on cases discussing the collateral estoppel effect of administrative proceedings). Accordingly, courts must examine such factors as whether

> (1) the [arbitration] was conducted in a judicial-like adversary proceeding; (2) the proceedings required witnesses to testify under oath; (3) the [arbitral] determination involved the adjudicatory application of rules to a single set of facts; (4) the proceedings were conducted before an impartial hearing officer; (5) the parties had the right to subpoena witnesses and present documentary evidence; and (6) the [arbitrator] maintained a verbatim record of the proceedings. Additional factors include whether the hearing officer's decision was adjudicatory and in writing with a statement of reasons. Finally, [whether] that reasoned decision [was] adopted by the director of the agency with the potential for later judicial review.

Imen v. Glassford, 201 Cal.App.3d 898, 247 Cal.Rptr. 514, 518 (1988) (citing *People v. Sims,* 32 Cal.3d 468, 186 Cal.Rptr. 77, 651 P.2d 321, 328–29 (1982)); *see also Kelly,* 79 Cal.Rptr.2d at 767 (explaining that an arbitration should provide parties "the opportunity for a hearing before an impartial and qualified officer, at which they may give formal recorded testimony under oath, cross-examine and compel the testimony of witnesses, and obtain a written statement of decision"); *cf. Plaine v. McCabe,* 797 F.2d 713, 720 (9th Cir.1986) (giving an administrative proceeding collateral estoppel effect because "[t]he fairness hearing was conducted similarly to a court proceeding. It was an adversary proceeding in which opposing parties were present and represented by counsel and were allowed to call, examine, cross-examine, and subpoena witnesses.... [T]estimony was to be submitted under oath or affirmation and a verbatim transcript was required.").

The WGA participating-writer determination did not provide the requisite procedural safeguards to give it issue-preclusive effect in California. The determination was made after an informal "investigation" into Givens' claims. The WGA did not take formal testimony from interested parties but, instead, engaged in "discussions" with Givens, his agent, CBS, and Columbia Tristar. Givens had no opportunity to cross-examine witnesses. Neither did Jacobs or Webb. Further, none of them had a right to examine the evidence presented by CBS and others. Givens and CBS simply provided the WGA with relevant information about the development of each project, and the WGA arrived at its conclusions through an examination of those materials. Finally, the WGA's participating-writer determination was subject to only very limited judicial review.

Thus, although undoubtedly conducted with care and in good faith, the WGA participating-writer proceeding was insufficiently formal and provided too few procedural safeguards to constitute an adjudicatory proceeding. Because the remaining Plaintiffs did not agree to litigate their entitlement to production credit in an informal arbitral forum, under California law the WGA's decision on writing credit does not preclude the litigation of Plaintiffs' claims in a judicial proceeding.

REVERSED and REMANDED for further proceedings consistent with this opinion.

TWENTIETH CENTURY FOX FILM CORP. v. MARVEL ENTERS
United States District Court for the Southern District of New York
August 9, 2001, Decided; August 10, 2001, Filed
01 Civ. 3016 (AGS), 01 Civ. 3017 (AGS)
155 F.Supp.2d 1

SCHWARTZ, District Judge.

In this action, plaintiff alleges breach of contract, trademark infringement, copyright infringement and related claims arising out of a proposed television series that is currently being developed and produced by defendants. Before the Court is plaintiff's motion for preliminary injunction, and defendants' cross-motion to dismiss the Amended Complaint. For the reasons set forth below, both motions are granted in part and denied in part.

I. Factual Background
A. Parties

Plaintiff Twentieth Century Fox Film Corporation ("Fox"), a Delaware corporation with its principal place of business in Los Angeles, California, creates, produces, distributes and markets motion pictures and television shows throughout the world. (Fox Amend. Compl. ¶ 10.) Defendant Marvel Enterprises, Inc. ("Marvel"), a Delaware corporation with its principal place of business in New York, is purportedly the largest publisher of comic books in the United States, and creates, distributes, and markets comic books and related goods and merchandise throughout the world. (*Id.* ¶ 11; Defendants' Joint Memorandum in Opposition to Plaintiff's Motion for Preliminary Injunction ("Def.Mem.") at 5.) On occasion, Marvel also licenses to third parties the right to create, produce, distribute, and market motion pictures and television shows based on Marvel's comic book characters, concepts, themes, and storylines, and collaborates on such projects. (Fox Amend. Compl. ¶ 11.) As more fully explained below, Marvel licensed to Fox certain rights in its X–Men comic book series so that Fox could create, in association with Marvel, theatrical motion pictures based on such property. Marvel also has licensed certain rights to defendant Tribune Entertainment Co. ("Tribune") so that it may create, in cooperation with Marvel and defendants Fireworks Communications, Inc. and Fireworks Television (US), Inc. (collectively "Fireworks"), a live-action television series called Mutant X. Tribune, a Delaware corporation with its principal place of business in Los Angeles, California, creates, produces, distributes, and markets television shows throughout the United States; the Fireworks companies, which are subsidiaries of Can West Global Communications Corp., a

Canadian media concern, both have their principal places of business in California, and create, produce, distribute, and market television shows in the United States and Canada. (*Id.* ¶¶ 12–13.) Defendants Marvel, Tribune, and Fireworks are hereinafter collectively referred to as "defendants."

B. X–Men Property

In 1963, Marvel began publishing a comic book series called X–Men. In a book entitled *Ultimate X–Men,* co-published by Marvel in 2000, the premise of the X–Men story is described as follows:

> [The X–Men] were mutants: people born genetically different from the rest of humankind. Some people saw the rise of these superhuman mutants as the next step in human evolution. Many, however, regarded mutants as dangerous freaks, threatening the existence of the 'normal' human race. The growing numbers of mutants needed a champion, and they found one in a visionary named Charles Xavier. A mutant himself, Xavier had a dream of a future in which 'normal' humans and mutants would live together in peace and harmony. It was to make this dream a reality that Xavier created his organization of young mutants, the X–Men.

Peter Sanderson, *Ultimate X–Men* 9 (2000). The original six characters of the X–Men series were Professor Charles Xavier (aka Professor X), Scott Summers (aka Cyclops), Jean Grey/Marvel Girl (aka Phoenix), the Beast, Bobby Drake (aka Iceman), and Angel (aka Archangel). Also appearing in the original series were villains comprising the Brotherhood of Evil Mutants, in particular Magneto, the nemesis of Professor X, who believed that mutants should adopt violent and revolutionary means in order to claim their rightful place in society. (Fox Amend. Compl. ¶ 17; Declaration of Avi Arad dated June 18, 2001 ("Arad Decl.") ¶¶ 6, 8(a).) As conceived by Marvel, the X–Men are "metaphors for minorities and other disenfranchised groups ... spanning from the Civil War to Auschwitz to the gay community." Furthermore, "the philosophical divide between Professor X and Magneto can be likened to that between Martin Luther King, Jr. and Malcolm X, in terms of the way each believes they should pursue their objectives for the mutant population." (Arad Decl. ¶ 7; *see also* Transcript of Oral Argument dated July 3, 2001 ("Tr.") at 59:24–25.)

Marvel has "create[d] many new titles spawned from the original X–Men series," which introduced new characters to the existing universe. (Arad Decl. ¶ 8.) Such additional titles include (i) Giant Size X–Men, released in 1975, (ii) The Uncanny X–Men, released in 1980, which supplanted the X–Men title and still continues, (iii) New Mutants, released in 1983, (iv) Alpha Fight, released in 1983, (v) X–Factor, released in 1986, (vi) Wolverine, released in 1988, (vii) Excalibur, released in 1988, (viii) X–Terminator, released in 1988, (ix) X–Force, released in 1991, (x) X–Men Unlimited, a series of short stories released in 1993,

(xi) Generation X, released in 1994, (xii) X–Man, released in 1995, and (xiii) Mutant X, which was released in 1998 and ran through 2001. (*Id.;* Declaration of Joseph Witek, Ph.D. dated June 25, 2001 ("Witek Decl.") ¶¶ 23–25.) According to Marvel, it routinely registers copyrights in its comic books with the United States Copyright Office, and its character names and comic books with the United States Patent and Trademark Office. (Marvel Compl. ¶ 13.) It currently possesses at least ten federal trademark registrations for or incorporating its X–Men mark in connection with various goods and services, including its comic books, magazines, and illustrated stories. (*Id.* ¶ 16, Ex. A.)

C. 1993 Agreement

In October 1993, Fox and Marvel entered into an agreement (the "1993 Agreement" or "Agreement") pursuant to which Marvel licensed to Fox the exclusive right to create, produce, distribute and market theatrical motion pictures based on the "X–Men Property" (or "Property"), which refers to the "X–Men comic book series." (1993 Agreement ¶ 6.) The scope of the grant of rights was broad, although the media within which they could be exploited (i.e. theatrical motion pictures) was narrow. Paragraph 6 of the Agreement, entitled "Granted Rights," states that Property to which Fox obtained rights included (i) certain characters specified in Exhibit A to the Agreement, (ii) the so-called "origin stories" of those characters appearing in the story or screenplay of the film, (iii) all individual storylines from individual comic books other than the origin stories, and, in a catch-all provision, (iv) "all other elements relating to the Property and the Characters." (*Id.*) (emphasis added). This paragraph also specifies that the rights "include the right to use the title (or subtitle or portion of the title) of the Property or any component of the Property as the title of any Picture or related exploitation." (*Id.*) In addition to the $1.6 million purchase price, (Declaration of Thomas Rothman dated June 26, 2001 ("Rothman Decl.") ¶ 10), and a percentage of gross proceeds, (1993 Agreement ¶¶ 4, 5), Marvel was able to reserve, in Paragraph 7 of the Agreement, certain rights for itself in connection with the films to be developed by Fox. Other ancillary rights, which define the scope of Fox's granted rights as applied to other media, are treated in Paragraph 8, the content of which is at the center of the parties' contractual dispute in this case. Paragraph 8, entitled "Other Rights," reads in pertinent part:

> Marvel reserves all television rights [based on the Property] (other than television rights with respect to the Pictures produced hereunder). However, prior to the reversion (if any) of the Rights ... Marvel shall not, without Fox's prior written consent, which consent may be withheld in Fox's sole discretion, produce, distribute or exploit or authorize the production, distribution or exploitation of any live-action motion picture

> for free television exhibition, pay television exhibition, non-theatrical exhibition, or home video exhibition (on cassettes or discs) or any feature-length animated motion picture for non-theatrical exhibition or home video exhibition (on cassettes or discs).

(1993 Agreement ¶ 8.) The possible reversion of rights to Marvel is addressed in Paragraph 9. In effect, this paragraph sets control dates by which Fox must create sequels by requiring reversion where "Subsequent Pictures" are not made within a certain time. (*Id.* ¶ 9.) The reversion dates set forth in this Paragraph were extended by an amendment to the Agreement signed by the parties on or about October 10, 2000. (*See* "X–Men II" Amendment/Extension ¶ 2(d).)

Paragraph 11 further defines the logistics of the production of Fox's films, by requiring that Marvel must approve: (i) the "fundamental elements" of the story, namely the basic storyline, character integrity, living habitat, and conformity with the so-called "X–Men Handbook" written by Marvel; (ii) the screenplay, to the extent it substantially alters a fundamental element; (iii) costumes; (iv) the photography of scenes, to the extent it substantially alters a fundamental element; and (v) the content of director's cuts, to the extent it substantially alters a fundamental element.

Particularly given the catch-all provision in Paragraph 6, the scope of the license to Fox is broad, encompassing any property contained in the "X–Men Universe" of comic books that Fox "may require" in order to create and produce its films, including the right to use Marvel's copyrights and trademarks in such property as Marvel would as owner of such rights. However, Exhibit A to the Agreement limits the characters which Fox may exploit to (i) certain "Initial Characters," comprising the principal and featured characters in the approved story, screenplay, or Marvel's publications, as well as 15 other "Core Characters" from the X–Men Universe of comics, and (ii) certain "Additional Characters," who are among the characters from a limited "X–Universe" of seven comic books, which Fox may add by written notice to Marvel. (Ex. A to 1993 Agreement ¶¶ 1, 3, 4.)

Finally, Paragraph 18 of the Agreement incorporates certain "Other Terms and Conditions" into the Agreement "[i]n accordance with Fox's standard Option/Purchase Agreement, but as such agreement would have been modified following good faith negotiation within Fox's usual parameters taking into account Marvel's and the Property's stature." (1993 Agreement ¶ 18.) While such provisions are generally designed to eliminate the future need for negotiation, this vague provision leaves additional terms and conditions largely open for negotiation based only on unspecified elements of custom.

D. X–Men Film

Following the 1993 Agreement, Fox spent nearly seven years developing "a story that offered the excitement of mutant superheroes, yet also addressed serious issues of intolerance and bigotry toward them in an entertaining way." (Plaintiff's Reply Memorandum of Law in Support of its Motion for Preliminary Injunction ("Pl.Rep.") at 2; Rothman Decl. ¶ 10.) In 1999, Fox began shooting an X–Men film, and, in June and July 2000, launched an extensive media promotional effort as part of a $90 million campaign to "market and distribute 'X–Men' theatrically using distinctive imagery and messages." (Fox Amend. Compl. ¶¶ 24, 26; Pl. Rep. at 3.) As part of its publicity efforts, Fox created and released numerous theatrical and television trailers, which featured clips from the film. (Fox Amend Compl. ¶ 26.) On July 14, 2000, Fox released the theatrical motion picture "X–Men" to national audiences. (*Id.* ¶ 28.)

Fox estimates that the X–Men film has since generated $290 million in gross receipts from sales in the United States and abroad, grossed "tens of millions of dollars more" from sales of videotapes, digital versatile disks (DVDs), and associated merchandising, and that it will net a profit of approximately $160 million. (Pl. Rep. at 3; Rothman Decl. ¶ 14.) Fox also estimates that Marvel will receive approximately $6 million over the life of the film from "back end contingent compensation." (Pl. Rep. at 3–4; Rothman Decl. ¶ 16.) Describing X–Men as the "crown jewel of Fox's current properties," (Rothman Decl. ¶ 24), Fox intends to make it a "franchise film" by developing and producing sequels. (*Id.* ¶¶ 21–23.)

Fox has obtained copyright registrations for both the trailers and the film. (Fox Amend. Compl. ¶ 26, Ex. G.) Fox also created X–Men logos and associated artwork in connection with the film. In particular, Fox has used a three-dimensional, metallic, futuristic letter "X," at the center of which the term "X–Men" is prominently placed. Fox has also used the letter "X" logo without the superimposed "X–Men" term. (*Id.* ¶ 27, Exs. H–I.)

E. Creation and Promotion of the Mutant X Series

1. Mutant X Comic Book

Between November 1998 and May 2001, Marvel published a comic book series entitled Mutant X. This series featured Alex Summers (aka Havok), the mutant brother of Scott Summers (aka Cyclops), one of the original X–Men team members and a principal character in the X–Men film. (Witek Decl. ¶ 25, Ex. 14.) As depicted in the Mutant X comic book, Havok is transported to an alternate world and takes the name Mutant X. In that world, Havok encounters alternate versions of certain X–Men characters.

2. Mutant X Series

a. Creation

In or about July 2000, as the X–Men film was being marketed and distributed, Marvel developed the idea for a live-action television series called Mutant X, which, according to Marvel, was intended to feature "new, never-before-seen, Marvel characters." (Arad Decl. ¶ 25; Declaration of Richard E. Ungar dated June 18, 2001 ("Ungar Decl.") ¶ 2.) Drawing from recent developments in science surrounding the mapping of the human genome and genetic engineering, Marvel decided to tell the story of "various young men and women who were part of genetic 'splicing' experiments conducted many years earlier." (Ungar Decl. ¶ 2.) "As a result of errors in the experimentation, these genetically-augmented individuals underwent physical mutations, thereby developing unexpected abilities," and later, unexpected problems. (*Id.;* Genome X Television Series Concept, Ex. H to Arad Decl.) Because of such problems, the directors of the experiments realized a "product recall" was necessary. Adam, the principal character of the series and a scientist on the experiment team, "realized he had to leave the [team] and use his time and resources to try and locate these babies, who were now adults, either to cure them, help them cope, or assist them in understanding what to expect." (Arad Decl. ¶¶ 30–31.) On the other hand, Adam's partner, who is named Mason Eckhart, believed that the team had to cover its tracks by destroying or imprisoning the mutants. (*Id.* ¶ 31.) Thus, each episode would revolve around the search for a new mutant. (Declaration of Howard Chaykin ("Chaykin Decl.") ¶ 18.) As originally conceived, the series was to be called "Genome X." (Arad Decl. ¶ 28.)

Marvel developed a formal treatment for the new series, and contacted Tribune about producing and distributing the show. (Declaration of Richard H. Askin, Jr. dated June 15, 2001 ("Askin Decl.") ¶ 6.) On August 9, 2000, Marvel and Tribune entered into a production and syndication agreement for a weekly, live-action television series of hour-long shows based on the Genome X concept. However, Richard Askin, Tribune's president, disagreed with the choice of Genome X as the name of the series, because he was concerned that too few people in the target demographic would know what "genome" meant. (Askin Decl. ¶ 9.) Later, "after considerable discussion among representatives of Tribune and Marvel, [they] all eventually agreed upon the name 'Mutant X' for the television series." (Ungar Decl. ¶ 7.) Thereafter, an amended agreement was drafted to reflect this change, in which Marvel licensed the Mutant X name to Tribune for development of the television series. (Ex. D to Askin Decl.). On November 15, 2000, Tribune and Fireworks signed an agreement pursuant to which the two companies would cooperate on the financing, production, and distribution of the new series. (Askin Decl. ¶ 10.)

According to defendants, "the characters portrayed and the stories to be told in the 'Mutant X' television series have absolutely no involvement whatsoever with [the Mutant X] comic book series ...." (Ungar Decl. ¶ 7.) Defendants hired an executive consultant responsible for refining the overall story for the series, based upon Marvel's original treatment, and for the writing of the scripts and supervision of others involved in that process. Part of the consultant's refining job, according to defendants, is to "eliminate any elements arguably reminiscent of the 'X–Men' property contained in [the] treatments." (Askin Decl. ¶ 11.) The record reflects that the characters and storylines in the show being produced as of the date of this Opinion ***11** substantially vary from those presented in the initial concept and treatments.

b. Promotion

Notwithstanding the divergences in characters and storylines between the new Mutant X series and the X–Men Property or Mutant X comic book series, the record reflects that defendants' have made numerous references to the X–Men Property and the X–Men film in promoting the new series.

First, in or about January 2001, defendants placed advertisements in various entertainment industry publications promoting the proposed series. (Fox Amend. Compl. ¶ 31, Ex. J.) The advertisements featured a Mutant X logo developed by defendants, consisting of a three-dimensional green metallic X, at the center of which the term "Mutant X" is prominently placed. (*Id.*) Second, defendants have met with numerous television station licensees and advertisers throughout the United States in an effort to promote and license the new series. (Askin Decl. ¶¶ 17–19.) The sales presentation slides which were shown to these television industry personnel stated, *inter alia,* that the show is "[b]ased on the box office smash, *X–Men,*" and makes reference to "X–Men The Movie" in connection with its $300 million in gross revenue and home video/DVD sales of $50 million "in its first weekend alone!" (Ex. B to Fox Amend. Compl.; Askin Decl. ¶ 21.) Third, defendants created certain a sales presentation videotape for the Mutant X series that appropriated clips from Fox's copyrighted X–Men film and/or trailers, which, according to Fox, creates an association between the new series and the film. (Fox Amend. Compl. ¶¶ 34, 35; Askin Decl. ¶ 22.) According to Fox, defendants have also created and distributed shorter versions of such sales presentation videotapes, including a compilation tape of shows produced by Tribune. (Fox Amend. Compl. ¶ 36.) Fourth, defendants have allegedly made certain public statements linking the new series to the X–Men film. (*Id.* ¶¶ 38, 39.)

Defendants' promotional efforts have been successful. According to Tribune, as of June 15, 2001, it had entered into broadcast licenses with television stations in 161 markets across the country, thus covering approximately 94 percent of all U.S. households. (Askin Decl. ¶ 28; Fox Amend. Compl. ¶ 37.) The company is currently in the process of selling advertising time for the first season of the show. (Askin Decl. ¶ 28.) Filming of the series began on June 4, 2001, and the director's cut of an initial episode, entitled "Russian Roulette," was finalized a few weeks later. (Declaration of Maura J. Wogan with Respect to the Mutant X Director's Rough Cut of "Russian Roulette" dated June 28, 2001 ("Wogan Decl. Roulette"), Ex. B.) The first episode of the series is scheduled to air in late September or early October 2001, with the rest of the fall lineup. (Askin Decl. ¶ 29.) Tribune has apparently committed to two years of production, with each year comprising 22 episodes, (Askin Decl. ¶ 8, Ex. C; Ungar Decl. ¶ 5, Ex. C.), and expects the series to run for at least five seasons, which, according to its calculations, will likely result in net profits of $74.3 million. (Askin Decl. ¶¶ 32–33.)

F. Instant Action

Fox filed the instant action, by order to show cause, on April 10, 2001, alleging claims for (i) breach of contract against Marvel; (ii) breach of the implied covenant of good faith and fair dealing against Marvel; (iii) tortious interference with contractual relations against Tribune and Fireworks; (iv) unfair competition and/or false designation of origin under Section 43(a) of the Lanham Act, 15 U.S.C. § 1125(a), against all defendants; (v) copyright infringement, pursuant to 17 U.S.C. § 101 *et seq.*, against all defendants; (vi) deceptive trade practices, pursuant to New York General Business Law § 349 ("Section 349"), against all defendants; and (vii) common law unfair competition against all defendants. (Fox Amend. Compl. ¶¶ 49–72.) Within minutes of the filing of Fox's Complaint, Marvel filed a reciprocal declaratory judgment action against Fox, and the two actions were thereafter consolidated. (Marvel Compl.) Fox filed an Amended Complaint on May 16, 2001. (Fox Amend. Compl.) The instant motions followed, and oral argument was held on such motions on July 3, 2001.

II. Motion to Dismiss

A. Legal Standard

On a motion to dismiss, the Court must accept the factual allegations contained in the complaint as true, and draw all reasonable inferences in favor of the non-movant; it should not dismiss the complaint "unless it appears beyond doubt that the plaintiff can prove no set of facts in support of his claim which would entitle him to relief."...

B. Breach of Contract

1. Choice of Law

Fox states that California law should apply to its breach of contract claim, because (i) the 1993 Agreement was primarily negotiated in California and drafted by attorneys practicing in California, and (ii) the "acts necessary for performance" [i.e. the creation of the X–Men film] took place in part in California. (Plaintiff's Memorandum of Law in Support of its Motion for a Preliminary Injunction ("Pl.Mem.") at 12 n. 1.) While defendants do not dispute Fox's facts regarding the Agreement's negotiation or performance, and do not address the choice of law issue directly in their papers with regard to the contract claim, they apply New York case law in support of their arguments.

The Court applies California law to the breach of contract claim. Because jurisdiction in this case is based on diversity of citizenship as well as the presence of a federal question, we follow the choice of law rules of New York, the forum state. In contract matters, New York courts apply a "center of gravity" or "grouping of contacts" approach, pursuant to which courts may consider a spectrum of significant contacts, including the place of contracting, the places of negotiation and performance, the location of the subject matter, and the domicile or place of business of the contracting parties...

2. Scope of Marvel's Television Rights

Although Marvel reserved "all television rights" in Paragraph 8 of the Agreement, Fox must consent in writing to Marvel's "production, distribution, or exploitation of any live-action motion picture for free television exhibition, pay television exhibition, non-theatrical exhibition, or home video exhibition ...." (1993 Agreement ¶ 8.) In practice, this so-called "freeze" provision brings such live-action motion pictures within the ambit of Fox's rights under the Agreement, as it permits Fox to preclude Marvel from making such motion pictures when they are based on the X–Men Property. The scope of Marvel's television rights as elaborated within this framework is at the heart of the parties' dispute, as they specifically disagree as to whether a live-action television series is encompassed by the freeze.

While both sides contend that the provision in question is unambiguous as written, they disagree as to what precise media the provision encompasses. Fox contends that Paragraph 8, as a whole, prohibits Marvel from exploiting the X–Men Property "in *any* audio-visual medium without either obtaining Fox's consent or providing Fox a right of first refusal ...." (Opposition to Defendant's Motion to Dismiss Plaintiff's First Amended Complaint ("Pl.Opp.Dis.") at 5, 10.) Adopting a broad reading of the term "motion picture," Fox concludes that the phrase "live-action motion pictures for free television exhibition" effects a freeze on all of Marvel's live-action television rights, including the Mutant X live-action television series. Thus, Fox concludes, Marvel breached the Agreement when it chose to produce and market Mutant X without obtaining Fox's consent.

In support of its position, Fox relies on the context of the Agreement, in particular (i) the broad grant of rights in Paragraph 6 and character preemption rights in Exhibit A, (ii) the use of the term "motion picture" in Paragraph 8 and elsewhere in the Agreement, and (iii) the "overriding purpose" of the Agreement to protect Fox against competition from other X–Men exploitations. (*Id.* at 4–11.) Fox also relies on certain definitions contained in the glossary of Fox's standard Option/Purchase Agreement (the "Fox Glossary") which, Fox claims, like the Option/Purchase Agreement itself, was incorporated by reference in Paragraph 18 of the 1993 Agreement. Specifically, Fox points out that the Fox Glossary defines: "Motion Picture" as "[p]ictures of any kind whatsoever ... and their accompanying devices and processes whereby pictures ... are recorded or otherwise preserved for ... exhibition ... by any means or media ... in such manner as to appear in motion or sequence"; "Television Motion Picture" as a "Motion Picture primarily intended to be initially distributed for [t]elevision [e]xhibition"; Episode as an "individual Television Motion Picture which is part of a Television Series"; and "Television Series" as "related episodes intended to be distributed as a group ...." (Smokler Decl. ¶¶ 40–43, Ex. L.)

In contrast, defendants assert that the term "live-action motion picture" clearly refers to a "long-form movie," namely, a feature-length "movie of the week" or direct-to-video motion picture. (Defendants' Joint Memorandum In Support of Cross Motion to Dismiss Plaintiff's Complaint ("Def.Mem.Dis.") at 9; Def. Mem. at 20.) Because live-action television series like Mutant X do not fall within such definition, then, defendants argue, Fox's breach of contract claim fails as a matter of law; Marvel may proceed with the series, and any other live-action television series whether or not based upon the X–Men Property, without prior written consent from Fox. (Def. Mem. Dis. at 7; Tr. at 39:10–24, 70:2–24.) Defendants assert that this interpretation is consistent with (i) the underlying bargain, whereby Fox contracted for limited rights to produce and distribute "theatrical motion pictures" based on the X–Men property, and Marvel "reserv[ed] all television rights" with the sole exception of live-action motion pictures for television, (ii) Marvel's superior bargaining power derived from its "special stature" in relation to the X–Men Property, (iii) the parties' separate treatment of television series rights in Paragraph 7(f) of the Agreement with respect to animated productions, and the distinction between "motion pictures and television series rights" made in Exhibit A, and (iv) the overall sophistication of the parties. (Def. Mem. Dis. at 8–12; Def. Mem. at 20;

Declaration of Jonathan D. Reichman Regarding Contract Interpretation dated June 17, 2001 ("Reichman Decl.") ¶ 50.)

Under California law, judgment on the pleadings in a breach of contract action may be appropriate when the terms of the contract at issue are unambiguous. This is a question of law, and the Court must determine whether any ambiguity exists by reading the terms in question in light of the overall context of the agreement... Under California's statutory rules of contract interpretation, the mutual intention of the parties at the time the contract is formed governs its interpretation... Where the parties' intentions are clear, and there is no reasonable basis for difference of opinion, no ambiguity exists.

In this case, the Court finds that the phrase "live-action motion picture for free television exhibition," read in the context of the provision in which it is contained and the Agreement as a whole, is ambiguous; in so finding, the Court disagrees with the positions of both parties. Given the varied uses of the term "motion picture" in the 1993 Agreement, and bearing in mind the alternative views presented by the parties concerning the meaning of the relevant phrase in the context of the Agreement, the Court finds that there is a reasonable basis for a difference of opinion as to the scope of the freeze of Marvel's television rights in relation to the X–Men Property. Accordingly, because defendants have failed to show that Fox can prove no facts in support of its breach of contract claim, the Court declines to dismiss this claim. Fox's success on its contract claim will therefore depend on an examination of extrinsic evidence.

C. Implied Covenant of Good Faith and Fair Dealing

Fox's second claim alleges that Marvel breached the implied covenant of good faith and fair dealing by (i) creating, producing, distributing, and marketing the Mutant X series without Fox's consent, and (ii) concealing its actions from Fox while attempting to mislead Fox about the nature of the series.

Under California law, a claim for breach of the implied covenant of good faith and fair dealing is an outgrowth of alleged improper conduct by a defendant under a contract between the parties, and is designed to prevent a party from acting in bad faith to frustrate the contract's actual benefits... Such a claim must be dismissed as duplicative where it merely restates the contract claim. However, a claim for breach of the implied covenant may be sufficiently alleged where additional conduct by the defendant, separate and apart from the conduct resulting in the breach, frustrates the plaintiff's right to benefits due under the contract.

In this case, Fox's allegations of bad faith are merely conclusory. The Amended Complaint sets forth facts germane to a finding that defendants produced and distributed the Mutant X series without Fox's consent. (Fox Amend. Compl. ¶¶ 31–39.) However, Fox asserts no facts reflecting that Marvel acted in bad faith in creating, and authorizing the production of, the series. Fox states that it "found out about the proposed 'Mutant X' series not from [defendants] ... but rather, from public articles and advertisements ...." (*Id.* ¶ 42.) However, such allegation does not suggest that Marvel purposely concealed its actions or somehow misled Fox. The fact that Marvel may not have discussed Mutant X with Fox at the early stages of its development may merely reflect its belief that its conduct did not implicate the 1993 Agreement. Moreover, the considerable publicity associated with the new series in the months following its creation, (Fox Amend. Compl. ¶ 41), runs counter to a finding of purposeful concealment. Because Fox has not alleged, and the record gives the Court no reason to infer, conduct beyond that which would constitute a breach of contract, the Court dismisses Fox's claim for breach of the implied covenant of good faith and fair dealing as duplicative of its contract claim.

D. Tortious Interference

1. Choice of Law

The parties disagree as to which state's law should apply to the tortious interference claim. Fox asserts that California law should apply based on the domicile of Tribune and Fireworks and the location of the alleged tort; defendants claim that the domicile of Marvel and the purported conduct of the other defendants in New York dictates that New York law apply. In tort cases, New York courts apply the law of the jurisdiction with the greatest interest in the litigation. In determining such interest, the courts look "almost exclusively" to the parties' domiciles and locus of the tort. Here, three of the four parties impacted by the tort, including the two allegedly responsible for committing it—Fox, Tribune, and Fireworks—are domiciled in California. The August 9, 2000 Agreement between Marvel and Tribune, and its amendment, which are both letter agreements, are directed to Rick Ungar, President of Marvel Characters Group, at Marvel studios in California, and probably signed by him there. (Exs. C and D to Askin Decl.) Moreover, although, as defendants point out, Tribune and Fireworks are alleged to have significant contacts with New York, (Fox Amend. Compl. ¶ 8), their actions in creating, producing and marketing the Mutant X series, (*Id.* ¶ 56), the record reflects, appear to have occurred in California, rather than New York. Accordingly, the Court applies California law to Fox's tortious interference claim.

2. Merits

Fox asserts that Tribune and Fireworks tortiously interfered with the 1993 Agreement by participating in the creation, production, distribution, and marketing of the Mutant X series, despite their awareness of the existence and terms of the 1993 Agreement. (Fox Amend. Compl. ¶ 56.) Fox further asserts that "[a]s a direct and proximate result of [such] tortious interference ... [Fox] has suffered immediate and irreparable injury for which there is no adequate remedy at law." (*Id.* ¶ 57.)

In this case, Fox's claim is insufficient for three reasons. First, Fox has failed to allege that Tribune's and/or Fireworks' actions were taken with the intent to induce a breach of the 1993 Agreement. A defendant's mere knowledge of an agreement is not enough; Fox must allege and prove that Tribune and/or Fireworks intentionally interfered with Fox's rights under the Agreement without justification. Second, Fox fails to allege that Tribune's and/or Fireworks' actions were the proximate cause of Marvel's alleged breach; the Amended Complaint merely alleges that Fox suffered injury as a direct and proximate result of their actions. (Fox Amend. Compl. ¶ 57); Pl. Opp. Dis. at 16–17 (acknowledging that the causation element is properly pled under California law "by alleging that defendants were the proximate cause of the breach"). Third, even if Fox had sufficiently alleged these two elements, the facts asserted in the Amended Complaint do not support them, therefore requiring dismissal of the claim. Nothing in the Amended Complaint, or, for that matter, in the evidence submitted in support of Fox's motion for preliminary injunction, indicates that the actions of Tribune and/or Fireworks, in assisting in the creation and production of the new series, suggests that it was their intent to induce a breach. Nor do the facts alleged reflect that either Tribune or Fireworks was the proximate cause of the alleged breach. Accordingly, the Court dismisses Fox's claim for tortious interference with contract.

E. Lanham Act

Fox's Lanham Act claim, for "unfair competition and false designation of origin," is grounded in its assertion that defendants "have sold 'Mutant X' by falsely associating it with Fox's 'X–Men'." (Pl. Rep. at 25.) Specifically, Fox asserts that defendants improperly marketed the new series by (i) infringing Fox's unregistered trademarks in its "unique logo" used in the film, and (ii) falsely promoting Mutant X as affiliated with the X–Men film. It alleges that such promotion has caused potential purchasers to confuse the source of the series and the film, which is demonstrated by comments from such purchasers and articles from those in the entertainment industry stating that the two productions are related. (Fox Amend. Compl. ¶¶ 31–41, 59.)...

It is a broad federal unfair competition provision which protects unregistered marks similar to the way that Section 32(1), 15 U.S.C. § 1114(1), protects registered marks. The section prohibits two forms of unfair competition: (i) the infringement of unregistered marks, names, and/or trade dress; and (ii) false advertising, that is, misleading or deceptive representations as to the quality or characteristics of the defendant's goods or services. Under the trademark infringement prong of Section 43(a), upon which Fox bases its allegations concerning defendants' Mutant X logo, the applicable standard is substantially the same as that under Section 32(1); that is, a plaintiff must allege (i) the existence of a valid mark, and (ii) that the defendant's actions are likely to confuse the buying public, that is, "an appreciable number of ordinarily prudent purchasers ...." *E.G.L. Gem Lab Ltd. v. Gem Quality Inst., Inc.,* 90 F.Supp.2d 277, 292 (S.D.N.Y.2000). Under the false advertising prong, the basis for Fox's allegations concerning defendants' promotional activities more generally, a plaintiff must allege that the defendant made materially false or misleading statements of fact in advertisements or promotional materials that are likely to influence the purchasing decisions of ordinarily prudent purchasers. Under either prong, the likelihood of confusion relates to either the source of the product or to affiliation with or sponsorship of the defendant by the plaintiff. *Gem Lab,* 90 F.Supp.2d at 292.

The disposition of Fox's Lanham Act claim is grounded in its limited rights as a trademark licensee. Under the 1993 Agreement, specifically Paragraph 6 and Exhibit A as incorporated therein, Marvel licensed a set of rights to Fox which included the right to use Marvel's X–Men trademarks in commerce. Critically, however, Fox neither obtained a transfer of such trademarks nor the benefit of their associated goodwill, which had inured to Marvel over several decades. Where no goodwill has been transferred with the license, a trademark licensee cannot independently develop its own goodwill in a licensed mark, as such goodwill inures solely to the benefit of the licensor... This principle applies even where, as here, the licensee creates a new product on the basis of the license that enhances such goodwill. "A licensee that wishes to create rights in a mark separate from the licensed mark has an affirmative obligation to choose a mark sufficiently different from the licensed mark to avoid confusion—the licensee trades upon the goodwill of the licensor at the licensee's peril."

Fox's principal X–Men logo consists of a three-dimensional, metallic, futuristic letter "X," at the center of which the name "X–Men" is prominently placed. Fox also uses the letter "X" logo without the superimposed "X–Men" name. (Fox Amend. Compl. ¶ 27, Ex. H.) As licensee of the X–Men mark, and the letter "X" insofar as it refers to such mark, Fox is unable to establish the existence of its own valid mark for the purposes of its Lanham Act claim. Such logos are not sufficiently distinct from the licensed mark so as to create independent trademark rights, as they are mere depictions of Marvel's trademarked name, which Marvel itself approved as the title of Fox's film pursuant to the 1993 Agreement. In fact, defendants assert that Fox's logos were derived from Marvel's own designs as they have appeared in Marvel's comic books over the past several decades. Defendants correctly point out that there is no derivative work concept in trademark law, as there is in copyright law, that would allow Fox to exploit the trademark license as provided under the 1993 Agreement, because such concept would contravene the principle that a trademark is to signal a single source of a product's origin to the relevant consumers.

A similar analysis applies to Fox's false advertising claim, which is based on the purported goodwill Fox has captured in the X–Men film. Because Fox is a trademark licensee, its creation and distribution of the X–Men did not give Fox any additional trademark rights to the X–Men Property, or any element of it (e.g. character names), than that conveyed in the 1993 Agreement. Marvel did not assign its trademarks and copyrights in the X–Men Property in the 1993 Agreement; it granted Fox limited rights to produce a theatrical motion picture based upon such Property, long owned by Marvel. As defendants point out, "[a]ny success that Fox's film enjoyed simply strengthens *Marvel's* trademark rights in X–Men."

Accordingly, the Court dismisses Fox's Lanham Act claim.

F. Copyright

Fox claims that defendants have infringed its copyrights (i) in the X–Men film by using video clips from the film and trailers in promoting the Mutant X series, and (ii) in the X–Men logos created by Fox in connection with the film by creating and using a logo that is confusingly and deceptively similar. (Fox Amend. Compl. ¶ 64.) While defendants do not move to dismiss the copyright claim based on their alleged use of the video clips, (Def. Rep. Dis. at 12 n. 8), they contend that Fox has failed to sufficiently allege a copyright claim with respect to the logos, because the logos are derivative works, and Fox allegedly failed to notify the Copyright Office thereof when applying for its registration certificate. (Def. Mem. Dis. at 26–28.)

In order to plead a cause of action for copyright infringement, a plaintiff must allege: (i) which original works are the subject of the copyright claim; (ii) that the plaintiff owns the copyrights in those works; (iii) that the copyrights have been registered in accordance with the statute; and (iv) "by what acts during what time" the defendant infringed the copyright. The registration of a copyright is prima facie evidence of its validity. *Id.* at 251 n. 10. The Copyright Act requires that the registration application include "in the case of a compilation or derivative work, an identification of any preexisting work or works that it is based on or incorporates, and a brief, general statement of the additional material covered by the copyright claim being registered." 17 U.S.C. § 409(9). Because a derivative work is only copyrightable to the extent that it is original, 17 U.S.C. § 103(b), it is important that the Copyright Office be informed of the preexisting work so that it may determine if the author of the derivative work has made an original contribution...

In this case, Fox has sufficiently alleged the elements of a copyright cause of action with respect to its copyrighted X–Men logos. Moreover, defendants have failed to set forth sufficient grounds on its motion to dismiss to demonstrate that Fox's logos are derivative of Marvel's works. In particular, defendants do not describe, nor have they presented any evidence of, the existence and scope of Marvel's preexisting copyrights. Nor does the record enable the Court to discern which aspects of Fox's copyrighted artwork have allegedly been derived from Marvel's works. Even were the Court to consider the affidavits and exhibits presented by defendants on the preliminary injunction motion and in their reply on the motion to dismiss, and conclude that Fox's works were derivative, dismissal of the claim would still be improper because (i) the record does not reflect that Fox knowingly omitted the derivative work classification from its copyright registration application, and (ii) the work has the requisite degree of originality to be copyrightable as a derivative work, which right Fox obtained in the 1993 Agreement.

G. Common Law Unfair Competition

Fox claims that defendants have misappropriated Fox's labors and expenditures in violation of New York law by marketing and promoting Mutant X so as to create an improper association with the X–Men film. Defendants contend that the claim is barred for the same reasons as Fox's Lanham Act claim.

The New York law of unfair competition is broad and encompasses claims involving the misappropriation of a plaintiff's creative efforts as well as claims for false designation of origin. Fox's allegation that defendants' actions in promoting Mutant X are an attempt to "free-rid[e] on Fox's creativity and investment" and "profit at Fox's expense by allowing Defendants to market 'Mutant X' for much less than it otherwise would have cost" is merely an allegation of copying. (Fox does not allege any additional facts that would warrant the maintenance of its unfair competition claim under a misappropriation theory. Thus, to the extent that Fox's unfair competition claim alleges misappropriation, the Court dismisses the claim as preempted by the copyright laws.

Although claims that allege a false designation of origin or false advertising "are not asserting rights equivalent to those protected by copyright and therefore do not encounter preemption," *Warner Bros.,* 720 F.2d at 246, this aspect of Fox's unfair competition claim is precluded for the same reasons as Fox's Lanham Act claim, namely, that Fox has accrued no goodwill in the X–

Men film, logos, or the marks it was assigned under the 1993 Agreement that may have been misappropriated.

Accordingly, the Court dismisses Fox's common law unfair competition claim.

H. Section 349

Fox's claim that defendants engaged in deceptive business practices under New York law through their promotional activities is unavailing for related reasons...

In this case, Fox's claim must fail because it does not allege, nor does the record reflect, that defendants' actions caused public harm. In fact, as of the date of this Order, there has been very limited public exposure to Mutant X marketing. Defendants' sales presentation slides and videotapes were presented only to a handful of television station and advertising personnel, and according to defendants, all clips from, and references to the X–Men film have been removed from such sales materials. (Def. Mem. at 30 & n. 20; Ex. 3 to Def. Rep. Dis.) Defendants' original, green metallic Mutant X logo purportedly appeared in certain entertainment industry publications in early 2001. However, while such publication may have infringed Fox's copyrights, any harm to the public as a result of its association of Mutant X with the X–Men is illusory, because the goodwill associated with the X–Men is Marvel's alone. The allegation of false association or "public confusion" upon which Fox's claim is based is therefore unavailing, (Pl. Rep. at 25 n. 69), as the public would merely be associating two Marvel products. *Cf. Avon Prods.,* 984 F.Supp. at 800 (dismissing Section 349 claim on the ground that Lanham Act claim had been dismissed, and noting that the pleading standards under the two provisions are "substantially the same"). Defendants' alleged actions at most give rise to, and have in fact given rise to, a private contract dispute. Accordingly, the Court dismisses Fox's Section 349 claim.

III. Motion for Preliminary Injunction

Fox moves for a preliminary injunction based on defendants' promotional activities as described above. Its position is succinctly expressed by Thomas Rothman, Chairman of Fox Filmed Entertainment, Fox's parent, as follows:

> "Mutant X" is a rip-off. That is precisely why the Defendants do not want to change the title or the substance of their series. On behalf of the hundreds of Fox employees who worked tirelessly over the years to make the "X–Men" film and who will continue to create its sequels, I

respectfully implore the Court as a matter of law and basic justice to stop the Defendants before it is too late.

Accordingly, Fox proposes an order that (i) enjoins Marvel from taking any actions which directly or indirectly breach the 1993 Agreement, and (ii) enjoins all defendants from (a) creating a false association between Mutant X and the X–Men, and/or (b) infringing on the copyrighted or trademarked elements of the footage, trailers, and logos of the X–Men film. (Proposed Order Granting Injunctive Relief.) Fox's proposed order calls for, *inter alia,* (i) removal of the Mutant X title, the terms "Mutants," "New Mutants" or the letter "X," characters substantially similar to X–Men characters, and storylines referring to the existence of mutants or new mutants or other storylines or elements derived from the X–Men Property, and (ii) prohibiting defendants' from using Fox's film clips or logos, or indicating in any way that their television series is related to the X–Men. (*Id.*) Downplaying the scope of its request, Fox asserts that it "is not asking that the [Mutant X] program be stopped entirely, only that Defendants modify it to eliminate the title, logo, and story elements that rightfully belong to Fox and denote 'Mutant X' as an X–Men program."...

A. Breach of Contract Claim

The Court applies the heightened standard for preliminary relief with respect to Fox's breach of contract claim. *Tom Doherty,* 60 F.3d at 34–35. Fox's casual characterization of its requested relief aside, the scope of the proposed injunction is broad and would clearly require defendants to change their proposed series in such a way that could not be undone after a trial on the merits.

1. Likelihood of Success

The Court has declined to dismiss Fox's breach of contract claim on the ground that the meaning of the phrase "live-action motion picture for free television exhibition" in Paragraph 8 of the 1993 Agreement is ambiguous when read in the context of the entire Agreement. In determining Fox's likelihood of success on this claim, the Court must first consider whether such phrase encompasses a live-action television series. If such a series is covered by the Agreement, the Court must then consider whether the Mutant X series violates the terms of the Agreement, based on Fox's specific allegations concerning the title, characters, and storylines of the new series.

a. Scope of Marvel's Television Rights

In determining whether live-action television series are within the scope of Paragraph 8's freeze provision, the Court considers the extrinsic evidence submitted by the parties. *Int'l Brotherhood of Elec. Workers v. South. California Edison Co.,* 880 F.2d 104, 107 (9th Cir.1989) (same). Having examined such evidence, the Court agrees with Fox that live-action television series are within the scope of the freeze. The Court is particularly persuaded by the evidence presented by Fox concerning the (i) negotiation of the 1993 Agreement, including previous drafts thereto, and (ii) the understanding of the term "motion picture" in the entertainment industry with respect to television rights.

Fox has submitted testimony from those individuals involved in negotiating the terms of the 1993 Agreement on its behalf. Such evidence reveals that throughout the negotiations, the parties agreed that neither Fox nor Marvel could produce a live-action television series, or any other form of live-action television production, without the other's consent. The material terms of the Agreement were negotiated by Melinda Benedek, then head of Business Affairs at Fox, and Ken Ziffren, an entertainment industry lawyer representing Marvel. (Declaration of Melinda Benedek dated June 23, 2001 ("Benedek Decl.") ¶ 8; Reichman Decl. ¶ 17.) According to Benedek, the agreement they reached in late June 1993 included, *inter alia,* a freeze on all live-action television exploitation. (Benedek Decl. ¶¶ 8–11.) In the initial draft of the 1993 Agreement, composed by Mark Resnick, then Senior Vice President of Business Affairs at Fox, and circulated on July 6, 1993, Fox was granted live-action television rights but could not exercise them without Marvel's written consent. No objections to such provision were made by Ziffren, or his partner Paul Brindze, who was also involved in the negotiating process Resnick then turned over the final negotiating and drafting tasks to Sandra Smokler, an attorney in Fox's Legal Affairs Department, whose counterpart representing Marvel was Brindze. (*Id.* ¶ 9; Smokler Decl. ¶ 4; Reichman Decl. ¶ 21.) During the course of subsequent negotiations and drafts, the parties agreed that Marvel would reserve live-action television rights for itself, but in keeping with the general understanding of the parties, acknowledged that Marvel could not exercise such rights without Fox's written consent. By September 12, 1993, the last date on which Fox received any written comments from Marvel, Marvel had not indicated a disagreement with a freeze on all forms of live-action television rights. (Smokler Decl. ¶ 29, Ex. I.)

In the penultimate draft, circulated by Smokler on September 17, 1993, Paragraph 8 read, in pertinent part, as follows:

> Marvel reserves all television rights ... However, prior to the reversion (if any) of the Rights ... Marvel shall not, without Fox's prior written consent ... exploit *any rights of live-action free television or pay television*

> *exhibition, any rights in connection with motion pictures made for non-theatrical exhibition or any rights in connection with motion pictures made for home video exhibition on cassettes or discs.*

(Smokler Decl. ¶ 30, Ex. J) (emphasis added). According to Fox, no comments were made to this version of Paragraph 8, and defendants do not provide evidence of any exchange. The changes that Fox subsequently made to this version in order to produce the final draft for signature were apparently the result of a grammatical change that was not discussed with Marvel. Specifically, Smokler states that she moved the term "motion picture," which she considered to be the subject of the relevant clause, to the front of the clause to yield its current form...

Both Benedek and Smokler further assert that no one at Marvel ever expressed a desire to have live-action television series rights unfrozen. (Benedek Decl. ¶ 13; Smokler Decl. ¶ 15.) However, defendants assert that in the late stages of the negotiations, Marvel "was unwilling to agree to any broad freeze on television rights, given the 'X–Men' property's stature at the time and the extraordinary value of television rights." (Reichman Decl. ¶¶ 7, 22.) While defendants recognize that the typical film licensing deal for Fox includes a freeze on television rights, it claims that the repute of X–Men made it an "A-plus" property, which provided Marvel with significant leverage in the negotiations. (*Id.* ¶¶ 8–11.) Defendants also assert that live-action television rights were appreciating in value at the time of the negotiations because of the success of a Fox series called the "Might Morphin Power Rangers," which made such rights as important to Marvel as animated television rights, which Marvel was eventually able to secure pursuant to Paragraph 7(f) of the Agreement. Because Marvel perceived that there was no longer a "commercial distinction" between animated and live-action television series, it believed that "it no longer made commercial sense to preserve the freedom to produce an 'X–Men' animated television series, yet give Fox veto power over a live-action television series." (Def. Mem. at 19–20; Reichman Decl. ¶¶ 33–34.)

While the record reflects that Marvel's stature may have enabled it to bargain successfully for substantial rights and monetary compensation in exchange for licensing the X–Men Property, defendants have failed to adduce support for their contention that Marvel's rights included unrestricted live-action television series rights. Defendants have offered a logical explanation, in hindsight, for why Marvel may have wanted such rights in exclusivity. (Reichman Decl. ¶¶ 22, 33–34; Brindze Dep. at 104:24–105:16, 107:16–109:12.) However, the construction of the freeze in Paragraph 8 advanced by defendants contradicts the clear language of the draft agreements. Further, aside from Brindze's conclusory statement that he "requested" changes to eliminate live-action television series from the scope of the freeze after the penultimate draft was circulated, (Def. Mem. at 19; Reichman Decl. ¶ 36; Brindze Dep. at 105:19–

24), and Brindze's and Ziffren's testimony concerning what they now believe Paragraph 8 to mean, (Reichman Decl. ¶¶ 36, 37, 39 (citing excerpts from Brindze Dep. and Ziffren Dep.)), defendants have failed to offer any concrete evidence to rebut the extensive evidence of the negotiation process presented by Fox, or Fox's contention that the fundamental understanding of the parties never changed. Defendants' suggestion that Marvel only became aware of the importance of live-action television rights at the point of final negotiation appears implausible, (Brindze Dep. at 104:24–110:22), and their suggestion that Fox simply accommodated this view in the final draft of the Agreement ignores the possibility that Fox also may have attached significant value to such rights... Further, given the significant changes to the existing understanding of the parties that defendants' interpretation would have produced, and the ambiguity of the term "motion picture" in the industry acknowledged by Brindze, (Brindze Dep. at 115:5–14; 138:15–22), the absence of correspondence concerning such change is noteworthy, and suggests that Fox's interpretation is the correct one.

The Court also finds irrelevant to the instant case defendants' assertions that Marvel (i) had not negotiated a freeze of television series rights in a 1993 draft agreement with Columbia Pictures which preceded the negotiations in the instant case, (ii) refused to agree to a freeze on live-action television series rights in 1992 when it licensed animated television series rights to Fox Children's Network, and (iii) produced a live-action movie of the week called Generation X in 1995 based on an X–Men comic book series of the same title without complaint from Fox, where Fox itself exhibited the show. (Reichman Decl. ¶¶ 14–16, 18; Def. Rep. Dis. at 1–2.)

The industry custom and practice concerning the use of the term "motion picture" in connection with television and other rights also supports Fox's claims. The record reflects that the term "motion picture," as commonly understood in the entertainment industry at the time of the Agreement, referred to "moving pictures," or more precisely to the exhibition of a series of pictures in rapid succession with objects shown in successive positions slightly changed so as to impart the impression of a continuous picture in which the objects move. (Pl. Rep. at 15 (citing declarations).) According to the basic agreements between the studios and the talent guilds, which are heavily negotiated, motion pictures are neither described in terms of length nor confined to certain media. (Kamon Decl. ¶¶ 35–38.) They include feature-length movies, short films, and programs or episodes of a series produced for television, cable, or satellite distribution. (*Id.* ¶ 32.) In order to distinguish between types of motion pictures, studio contracts generally specify the medium in which a motion picture is to be exhibited, and/or the length of such picture. (*Id.* ¶ 33.) Such specification is evident in the 1993 Agreement; in Paragraph 6, the parties specified that Fox obtained rights necessary to produce "*theatrical* motion pictures;" and in Paragraph 8, they defined the freeze of animated non-theatrical rights to encompass "*feature-length* animated motion picture[s]." (1993 Agreement ¶¶ 6, 8.)

Fox contends that when the parties agreed in Paragraph 8 that the freeze would also encompass "live-action motion pictures for free television exhibition," with no prescription for length, they intended the term to be construed broadly to refer to television series such as Mutant X. (Pl. Rep. at 16–17.) Without contesting the industry usage of the term "motion picture" as described above, defendants' two experts focus, respectively, on the phrases "live-action motion picture for free television exhibition" and "motion picture for television." Unfortunately, their focus on these phrases is no less abstract, and far less grounded, than Fox's discussion of the term "motion picture." The conclusion of the first expert, Todd Leavitt, that "live-action motion picture for free television exhibition" does not include television series is based solely on his opinion that Fox "would have been well aware of the distinction between made-for-television movies and television series production ... [and] would be expected to use the specific terms 'series', 'episode series programming', or similar words if that were its intent." (This assessment ignores the possibility, which is supported by a review of the negotiating history in this case, that Fox used a term commonly used in the industry to refer to a broad spectrum of rights, i.e. "motion picture," to encompass both types of productions. Moreover, although Leavitt provides a chronology of the negotiations, he neglects to discuss the nature of the underlying bargain, stating, in conclusory fashion that the editing change in the final draft clearly "limit[ed] the application of the consent requirement over free and pay television exhibition to the made-for-television movie genre." (*Id.* ¶¶ 22–24.) Also, in contrast to the examples Fox has provided of industry usage of the term "motion picture," Leavitt provides no examples of the use of the phrase "live action motion picture for free television exhibition" in an agreement or documents where its scope could be more clearly assessed.

While carefully reasoned, the conclusions of defendants' second expert on this point, Penelope Glass, are also unpersuasive as applied here, because they are based on industry usage of the phrase "motion picture for television."... Accordingly, for the foregoing reasons, the Court finds that the 1993 Agreement's freeze on "live-action motion pictures for free television exhibition" encompasses television series rights. It now considers whether Mutant X itself falls within the scope of the Agreement, that is, to what extent, if at all, Marvel may have breached the Agreement by failing to obtain Fox's consent before creating and authorizing the production of the series.

b. Mutant X Title

Fox claims that defendants breached the terms of the 1993 Agreement by calling the proposed series Mutant X. In so arguing, Fox relies on Paragraph 6 of the Agreement, which provides that the X–Men Property includes "all ... elements relating to the Property and the Characters," and gives Fox the "right to use the title (or subtitle or portion of the title) of the Property or any component of the Property as the title of any Picture or related exploitation." (Pl. Opp. Dis. at 11.) Fox also relies on Paragraph 6(d) of Exhibit A, which prohibits a third party from using titles derived from the X–Men Property as the title of a motion picture when Marvel licenses to such third party a character of the X–Universe that Fox has not previously claimed. (*Id.*) Without addressing Paragraph 6, defendants argue that Paragraph 6(d) of Exhibit A is inapplicable because (i) Marvel has not licensed any X–Universe characters to Tribune, and (ii) Mutant X is not a motion picture. (Def. Mem. Dis. at 15–16.)...

In its motion papers and at oral argument, Fox asserted that defendants' use of either "Mutant" or "X," standing alone in the title of the series, would constitute a breach of the Agreement. This contention is unavailing. The term "mutant" is often employed in science fiction literature and media to describe individuals or entities with special powers. Such individuals or entities are also depicted without the explicit use of the word "mutant." Likewise, the letter "X" is commonly used to designate an unknown or mysterious quality or entityMarvel has used "X" in comic books other than those of the X–Men series to indicate such a quality, in particular "Earth X," "Universe X," "X–51," and a planned series, "Paradise X." Fox itself uses the letter for such a designation in certain of its own television series, including the "X Files," which treats supernatural and unknown elements or entities, and the upcoming reality television mystery "Murder in Small Town X." Under a similar rationale, the fact that either the term "mutant" or the letter "X" is used in the title of a story concerning mutants would not constitute a breach, as Fox suggests

c. Characters and Storylines

The Court arrives at a different conclusion with regard to that portion of Fox's breach of contract claim based on the characters and storylines of the Mutant X series.

i. Characters

Fox claims that Marvel has breached the 1993 Agreement because of "numerous similarities" between the Mutant X characters and those licensed to

Fox and portrayed in the "X–Men" film, such that the two share virtually the "very same core characters." In so arguing, Fox presents evidence concerning (i) defendants' original conception of the Mutant X characters, as reflected in an early treatment and comments by certain of the creators, and (ii) the overlap in names and traits between the X–Men and Mutant X characters.

Fox points out that a Mutant X treatment draft revised in August 2000 included references to X–Men characters that appear in the X–Men film, including Charles Xavier (aka Professor X) and Senator Robert Kelly, the principal opponent of mutants within the U.S. Congress. (Cendali Decl. ¶ 4, Ex. 4; Chaykin Decl. ¶ 10, Ex. B.) Fox also points to communications, during the development of Mutant X, between representatives of defendants, indicating that they intended to adopt characteristics of certain X–Men characters in creating the Mutant X characters. (*Id.* ¶¶ 5, 9–12, 22(a), (e), 23, Exs. 5, 9–12, 22.23.) Although Fox acknowledges that Marvel has since removed all direct references to X–Men characters, it nevertheless takes the position that the current characters are derived from the X–Men characters. Fox first contends that defendants use of the terms "mutant" or "New Mutants" to describe the characters conveys an impermissibly strong association with the X–Men. Second, Fox asserts that, on an individual level, there are extensive similarities between (Mutant X character first) (i) Adam and Professor Xavier, (ii) Shalimar Fox and Wolverine, (iii) Brennan Mulwray and Storm and Jubilee, (iv) Jesse Kilmartin and Shadowcat, Colossus and the Blob, and (v) Emma Delauro and Jean Grey and Rogue. (Witek Decl. ¶¶ 45–60.) Defendants defend their "mutant" denominations on the ground that mutants are pervasive in stories of the science fiction genre, and in the Marvel Universe of characters in particular. They also claim that they have removed all similarities between the Mutant X characters and the X–Men in order to make the former a truly original product. At present, defendants state, the characters from the two works share at most generic similarities that are present in several works of the same genre. Finally, defendants state that the process of producing a television series is "immensely plastic, and the 'Mutant X' story is constantly being molded, revised, and reinterpreted up until the moment that the camera begins to roll." (Chaykin Decl. ¶ 11.) Accordingly, "every element of the bible and scripts is subject to change at any time." (*Id.*)

As an initial matter, the Court finds that defendants' use of the terms "mutant" or "new mutants" to refer to the Mutant X characters does not constitute a breach of the 1993 Agreement. As discussed in the previous section, the term "mutant" is commonly used to describe individuals or entities with special powers, which are commonplace in science fiction literature and media. Moreover, while Fox claims that defendants' reference to the Mutant X characters as "new mutants" clearly suggests the X–Men by begging the question, "Who are the old mutants?,", the Mutant X characters are clearly a new form of mutant, that is "those who had been genetically enhanced by [Genomex]." One of Fox's experts acknowledges that the available scripts of the new series refer to "mutants as a whole (i.e. the individuals created by the Genomex program, and to the Mutant X team.") Adopting this view, the "old" mutants may include the X–Men, as well as other mutant individuals or entities who were created before the advent of genome mapping or sophisticated genetic engineering. However, were defendants to either (i) denominate Mutant X characters as a group as the "New Mutants," as they appear to have done in the series' initial treatments and bibles (Ex. B, C to Chaykin Decl.), or, (ii) as noted *infra,* entitle the series "New Mutants," then such designation would impinge on Fox's contractual rights, as the "New Mutants" was the title of a discontinued X–Men comic book series that was a spinoff of the X–Men.

Further, the Court agrees with defendants that the Mutant X characters are distinct from those portrayed in the X–Men Property and the X–Men film. Fox describes its character similarities at a general level of abstraction, emphasizing basic similarities common to many characters, and ignoring pronounced differences. To begin with, the characters' names are entirely distinct from one another, and the Mutant X characters neither have code names such as "Professor X," "Wolverine," "Storm," or "Rogue," nor do they wear comic-book style costumes. Adam and Professor Xavier are each intelligent leaders of a group of mutants with a mysterious past, and each has spent money to build a form of sanctuary for them. However, intelligent, older leaders are far from unique to the X–Men. Further, the differences in character traits are substantial. Unlike Professor Xavier, Adam is not a mutant, is of middle rather than advanced age, and is physically active rather than confined to a wheelchair. (Marschall Decl. ¶ 27(a).) While Adam has a powerful memory and ability to reason, Professor Xavier excels as a telepath. (Witek Decl. ¶ 47.) As to Shalimar Fox and Wolverine, their only common ground is a linkage to the animal kingdom, and the occasional recklessness and acute sensory perception derived therefrom. (*Id.* ¶ 52.) Otherwise, the differences are overwhelming. While Wolverine is a "loner and rough neck with a vicious temper," Shalimar is a "sexy, extroverted blonde with a kittenish sense of humor." (Chaykin Decl. ¶ 36(b).) While Wolverine has the ability to heal himself almost instantaneously and has an implanted metal skeleton, including distinctive metal claws, Shalimar is graced with superhuman strength and speed, and excellent night vision. (*Id.*) Further, while Brennan Mulwray's ability to shoot lightning bolts and sparks from his hands is similar to Storm's ability to generate lightning by controlling the weather, and Jubilee, who can create fireworks with her hands, the power to generate and discharge electricity is commonplace in comic book and science fiction genres. (Marschall Decl. ¶ 27(d); Chaykin Decl. ¶ 36(e).) Moreover, Brennan is male (both Storm and Jubilee are female), is unable to fly (Storm flies), can use his powers anywhere (Storm must use her powers outside), and his power is limited to sparks and bolts (Jubilee creates fireworks in various shapes, colors, and strengths and Storm controls all forms of weather). (Series Bible; X–Men Character Descriptions, Ex. C to Witek Decl.) Jesse Kilmartin's power to change his body density may resemble certain powers held by Shadowcat, who can pass through solid objects, and Colossus, who can turn his body into steel. However, the ability to change body form or density is a common trait of superheroes; defendants point out, for example, that the Vision, a character from the Avengers comic book series, like Jesse, could make himself intangible or impermeable. (Marschall Decl. ¶ 27(e); Chaykin Decl. ¶ 36(d).) Also, Fox's assertion regarding Brennan's similarities to Colossus is wholly conclusory, and the record does not reflect that Colossus is part of the X–Universe of characters to which Fox obtained rights. Finally, contrary to Fox's contention, Emma Delauro's powers are not comparable to those of Rogue or Jean Grey, beyond the fact that her powers are mental rather than physical. Emma is a so-called "telempath" or "empath," which allows her to sense the emotions of others and compel others to feel a particular way, while Jean Grey, like Professor Xavier, is telepathic (read minds) and also telekinetic (move objects), and Rogue absorbs the life force, or mutant powers, of anyone she touches. (Marschall Decl. ¶ 27(c); Witek Decl. ¶¶ 57–59; Marvel Compl. ¶ 20.) Defendants also point out that Emma is outgoing, while Rogue is "almost obsessively shy" and Jean Grey is considered an intellectual. (Chaykin Decl. ¶ 36(c).)

More generally, defendants also point out differences in overall character portrayal. Specifically, the Mutant X characters do not display their special abilities at each available opportunity, as is typical of the X–Men film characters, because the television series revolves less around the characters' mutations than their personal stories and individual identities. (Chaykin Decl. ¶¶ 23–24, 34.) Because the Mutant X series is designed to be "dramatically lighter than the 'X–Men' and most comic books," the Mutant X characters often have fun, e.g. by using their special abilities to play light-hearted pranks on fellow team members, activity which is not reflected in the X–Men Property. (*Id.* ¶ 25.)

Because the Mutant X characters are not based on or derived from the X–Men Property licensed to Fox in the 1993 Agreement, the Court finds that Fox is not likely to succeed on its contract claim to the extent it is grounded in similarities between such characters and licensed X–Men characters.

ii. Storylines

Fox points out that it has the exclusive right to X–Men storylines because Paragraph 6 of the 1993 Agreement includes within the definition of the X–Men Property "all storylines from individual comic books ... which are contained in a Story or Screenplay approved by Marvel ..." (1993 Agreement ¶¶

6, 11(a).) Fox then contends that both the overall storyline, or premise, of Mutant X and certain specific storylines are sufficiently similar to those encompassed by the X–Men Property to constitute a breach of the 1993 Agreement.

Fox contends that in both works, a super-intelligent and wealthy good mutant seeks out young mutants, trains them to use their powers, and protects them from a potentially hostile world, consisting of bad mutants and humans who seek to control them. (Fox Opp. Dis. at 14.) In addition to misrepresenting certain aspects of the Mutant X premise (Adam is not a mutant and there is no team of bad mutants), the generalized plot scenario represented by this premise is common to fiction in general and science fictional works in particular. One example is the nurturing of the gifted Luke Skywalker by Obi–Wan ("Ben") Kenobi in *Star Wars,* of which the Court takes judicial notice. Moreover, the fact that the Mutant X characters, like the X–Men, may "struggle with their status as mutants" and "fight[ ] against societal prejudice and government persecution" does not indicate a breach of contract, because such struggles are also typical of superheroes. (Witek Decl. ¶ 40; Marschall Decl. ¶ 15 (noting that "relationships and conflicts between [ ] superhuman characters and ordinary members of society," and the former's alienation from society as a result of their powers, are common themes in Marvel comics).) Further, "complicated personal relations" are typical of any drama. (Witek Decl. ¶ 40.)

Beyond the above generalities, the premise of Mutant X is admittedly novel. The Mutant X characters are at the center of society's current moral debate concerning the mapping of the human genome and genetic engineering, and their powers are due to genetic experimentation. In contrast, the powers of the X–Men are naturally occurring, and, as noted *supra,* the central allegory of the series is to historically oppressed or disenfranchised groups. Further, Mutant X involves neither a full-scale conflict between humans and thousands of mutants, nor between good and evil mutants; rather, it features a much smaller number of mutants (i.e. few hundred) who are unknown to the public and are attempting to evade Eckhart and certain "guest villains" working for him. (Chaykin Decl. ¶ 15.) The premise of mutant individuals seeking to evade the government entity that created them is parallel to the plot of Fox's Dark Angel television series. (Chernin Dep. at 21:11–22:16, 26:18–25.) Moreover, while the U.S. government is a primary antagonist in the X–Men, Eckhart's Genomex, a privately held company affiliated with the government's secret Genetic Security Agency, is "rarely the central antagonist, as each episode contains its own guest villains." (Chaykin Dep. ¶ 15, Ex. D; Witek Decl. ¶ 39 & n. 4.) Further, unlike the X–Men's Professor Xavier, Adam does not train the Mutant X team to be a fighting force, but simply to lead normal lives, and seeks to assist other mutants in doing the same. (Arad Decl. ¶ 38.)

With regard to specific storylines, Fox contends that elements of certain X–Men **2** storylines appear in three planned Mutant X episodes. Specifically, Fox states that (i) the concept of a prototype gun designed to neutralize the powers of its targets, first exploited in a story in the Uncanny X–Men comic book series, is the centerpiece of the Mutant X "Russian Roulette" episode; (ii) the story of the "Legacy Virus," which kills mutants by causing their powers to go out of control until they are consumed from within, first exploited in several X–Men comics between 1993 and early 2001, is paralleled in a Mutant X episode entitled "The Meaning of Death"; and (iii) the occasional portrayal of mutants in concentration camps in the X–Men series is paralleled in a Mutant X episode entitled "I Scream the Body Electric." (Witek Decl. ¶¶ 61–67; Tr. at 11:12–12:8.) However, the purportedly similar elements, i.e., weapons that neutralize power, powerful viruses, and imprisonment in internment camps, are general themes running through literature and do not demonstrate an exploitation of the X–Men Property by defendants.

iii. Other Elements Related to Storylines

Fox finally contends that defendants have appropriated certain distinctive X–Men elements, namely a "VTOL" (vertical take-off and landing) jet aircraft for transport of the team and a hideout or sanctuary, denominated in the X–Men as the "danger room" and in Mutant X as the "Sanctuary." (Witek Decl. ¶¶ 68–70.) However, as defendants point out, VTOL jets have been used by other Marvel superheroes, including the Fantastic Four (VTOL Fantasticar) and the Avengers (VTOL Quinn Jets). (Marschall Decl. ¶¶ 12, 28.) Moreover, defendants have recognized the potential for confusion potentially posed by use of a jet of similar size, shape or color, and, accordingly, are in the process of designing a jet that is distinct from the X–Men's "Blackbird" with respect to such elements.

Sanctuaries are also commonly used by teams of superheroes, and specifically by both Marvel's Fantastic Four and the Avengers. (Marschall Decl. ¶¶ 11, 28.) Moreover, on the basis of the pictorial and video evidence that the parties have submitted, the designs of the sanctuaries in Mutant X and the X–Men are considerably different, the former containing a mix of Asian and Spanish styles conveying a feeling of warmth and the latter metallic, futuristic, and cold. (Chaykin Decl. ¶ 38, Ex. E; Ex. 50 to Witek Decl.; Ex. B to Wogan Decl. Roulette; X–Men Film.) Further, while both sanctuaries apparently contain training rooms with the capability of three-dimensional holographic projection, the "Virtual Dojo" of Mutant X is designed for meditation, while X–Men's danger room is designed to prepare team members for battle. (Chaykin Decl. ¶¶ 39–40; Witek Decl. ¶ 70, Ex. 50.)

In sum, the Court finds that Fox is not likely to succeed on its breach of contract claim to the extent it alleges misappropriation of X–Men storylines and related elements.

2. Irreparable Harm

In its moving papers, Fox asserts that it would suffer incalculable irreparable harm if the Court declined to enjoin the broadcast of Mutant X, because the series will dilute the value of the "X–Men film franchise." (Pl. Mem. at 20 ("Fox will suffer irreparable harm if Defendants are not barred from proceeding with their proposed 'Mutant X' series"); Pl. Rep. at 32–38.) The focus of Fox's concerns are X–Men sequels. However, neither the nature nor quality of the alleged harm is precisely explained. Each side presents equally plausible, yet equally indeterminate, views concerning the impact of a television series, in particular a live-action series, on the value of a theatrical motion picture based on the same underlying property which is produced after the television series is released. (*Compare* Kamon Decl. ¶¶ 21–26 (noting that there is a "potential for harm" if the television production is of poor or lesser quality than the film, which potential is "more severe when the program at issue is a series, rather than a one-time show or even a mini-series with a limited number of episodes") and Rothman Decl. ¶¶ 34–35 (stating that audiences would be less inclined to pay to see a theatrical motion picture when they can see a similar program for free every week on television, and that Mutant X will tarnish the X–Men Property because it has a lower budget), *with* Leavitt Decl. ¶¶ 28–30 (stating that genres other than made-for-television movies do not compete with, and would not threaten the market for, a feature film), and Declaration of Shelly Schwab dated June 17, 2001 ("Schwab Decl.") ¶¶ 1, 5–6, 8–10, 15 (noting that television and film audiences have different expectations as to the quality of the respective productions, and opining that it is probable that a Mutant X television series based on the X–Men Property would increase, not decrease, the value of Fox's theatrical motion pictures by widening the X–Men viewing audience); *see also* Deposition of Joseph Calamari at 91:23–94:7 (stating that live-action television would not interfere with the market for theatrical motion pictures).) Each side presents differing opinions concerning the relative success of specific television series and theatrical motion pictures which have been produced based on the same property; and neither side has pointed to an example precisely analogous to this case, that is, the production of a theatrical motion picture sequel following the release of a live- action television series. Moreover, such views are based on the assumption that the series in question is substantially similar to the film in substance, which is not the case here.

Even assuming Fox were correct that a television series posed a competitive threat to a movie sequel derived from the same Property, the record does not suggest that any harm to Fox is actual or imminent. While the Mutant X series, like all television series, has a more limited budget than a feature film, and requires fewer days to shoot, (*see, e.g.,* Rothman Decl. ¶ 35; Askin Decl. ¶ 13), nothing in the record indicates that the new series will be of low quality. While Fox's assertions of irreparable harm relate to the future "X–Men franchise" (Cohen Decl. ¶ 35), the proposed X–Men sequel, referred to as X–2, is currently at the earliest stages of development. (Wogan Decl. ¶ 5.) Moreover, given the fact that Fox owns goodwill in neither the X–Men films in general nor the Mutant X name in particular, *see supra,* the possibility of unquantifiable losses of goodwill or reputation from the production of a lower quality series is irrelevant here. Rather, the record reflects that the sole measure of damages to Fox from defendants' use of the Mutant X name would be loss of profits, which, although difficult to precisely quantify,... Accordingly, because the Court cannot conclude that a "Mutant X" series will irreparably harm Fox's interest in the X–Men films, it denies Fox's motion for preliminary injunction with respect to its breach of contract claim.

This ruling does not eliminate the possibility of permanent injunctive relief following a trial on the merits, particularly in light of Fox's allegations concerning defendants' use of the Mutant X name as the title of their series. Fox's proposed order for injunctive relief requests that the Court enjoin the production of any live-action television motion picture that "bears the title 'Mutant X', or any other similar title which causes confusion with the 'X–Men', including but not limited to titles using the term 'Mutant' or the letter 'X'." (Proposed Order Granting Injunctive Relief.) For the reasons stated in the previous section, the Court is of the opinion that neither the term "Mutant," nor the term "X," standing alone as incorporated in the series title, would warrant a finding of breach of contract. Consequently, an alternative name need only eliminate either "Mutant" or "X," not both, provided that neither the new name, nor any of its components, is itself part of the X–Men Property.

B. Copyright Claim

Fox's copyright claim consists of two elements: (i) defendants' alleged use, in Mutant X sales presentation videotapes, of clips from Fox's copyrighted X–Men film and trailers; and (ii) defendants' alleged promotional use of a Mutant X logo that is substantially similar to Fox's copyrighted X–Men logos. The Court applies the traditional standard for preliminary relief to this claim. Defendants state that they have replaced the allegedly infringing videos and logo with new non-infringing promotional materials; thus, the requested injunction would be designed to preserve the status quo. *Tom Doherty,* 60 F.3d at 34. Even if defendants have not removed such materials, a limited injunction ordering such removal and preventing further use of the material would not deprive them of a meaningful remedy should they prevail at a trial on the merits. *Id.* at 35.

1. Likelihood of Success

To demonstrate likelihood of success on a copyright claim, a plaintiff must establish prima facie infringement by showing that it owns a valid copyright and that the defendant has engaged in unauthorized copying. Fox has established a substantial likelihood of success on its claim with respect to defendants' use of the video clips, because defendants' have conceded such use. The Court finds unavailing defendants' argument that Fox is not likely to succeed based on the "fair use" doctrine, on the ground that defendants' use is *de minimis* and/or an accepted practice in the entertainment industry.

First, the *de minimis* concept, which is considered separately from, and in advance of, the fair use analysis, focuses on whether "copying has occurred to such a trivial extent as to fall below the quantitative threshold of substantial similarity, which is always required as an element of actionable copying." *Ringgold v. Black Entertainment Television, Inc.,* 126 F.3d 70, 74 (2d Cir.1997). In cases like the instant one involving visual works, the substantial similarity analyses centers on the observability of the copied work, which includes the length of time the copied work is observable in the allegedly infringing work and such factors as focus, lighting, camera angles, and prominence. *Id.* at 75. Here, defendants have incorporated substantial portions of Fox's X–Men trailers, and certain highlights of the film, directly into their advertising tapes. Although the clips are each of a short duration, of three seconds or less, they appear prominently and are plainly observable to the lay viewer.

Second, defendants' fair use defense is inapplicable here. In determining whether an alleged infringement constitutes a fair use, courts consider: (i) the purpose and character of the use, including whether such use is of a commercial nature or is for nonprofit educational purposes; (ii) the nature of the copyrighted work; (iii) the amount and substantiality of the portion used in relation to the copyrighted work as a whole; and (iv) the effect of the use upon the potential market for or value of the copyrighted work. Here, defendants' use, like Fox's use, is commercial and is not transformative of either the X–Men film or its trailers. The X–Men film and its associated trailers are clearly works deserving of copyright protection because they are highly creative, expressive works, from which defendants have directly copied... Further, although the appropriated segments are each individually brief, collectively their presence is significant; in particular, Fox points out that on the shorter of the Mutant X sales tapes, the X–Men material comprises more than a quarter of the tape. (Pl. Rep. at 7.) The clips are plainly observable and depict substantial, and among the most memorable, highlights of the trailers and the film, which collectively go to the "heart" of Fox's copyrighted works. Finally, while there is a question as to whether defendants' use of the clips would harm the existing market for Fox's X–Men film or trailers, Fox has established that the market for excerpts of such works has been, and will continue to be, negatively affected by defendants' use of the infringing clips without a license.

The mere fact that use of footage from pre-existing films or television shows is commonplace to convey the general concept of a syndicated television series—for which pilots are not yet available—does not minimize the potential harm resulting from infringement, and therefore does not support the defense of fair use here. If use of such footage is indeed commonplace, it would also seem that obtaining a license to use such footage would, or should, likewise be an industry convention. Fox asserts that such is the general practice with respect to Fox's property, and that Marvel itself has recently licensed certain clips of the X–Men film from Fox for use at a video game trade show.

Although Fox has established that it owns valid copyrights in the X–Men logos, the Court cannot conclude that Fox is likely to succeed on the merits of its claim with respect to the logos, given the outstanding questions with regard to Fox's creation of the works (i.e. whether it is derivative) and observable dissimilarities between the two logos in question. Nevertheless, for the reasons the Court discussed in denying defendants' motion to dismiss Fox's copyright claim, there are sufficiently serious questions as to the infringement of Fox's copyrights in the logos to constitute a fair ground for litigation. Moreover, given the potential harm the allegedly infringing logo could cause to Fox's rights, and the fact that defendants represent that they are in the process of discontinuing use of such logo, the balance of equities clearly favors Fox on this aspect of its copyright claim.

2. Irreparable Harm

Because Fox has demonstrated prima facie infringement as to the video clips, a presumption of irreparable harm arises as to this aspect of its copyright claim. *See ABKCO Music,* 96 F.3d at 64. Defendants attempt to rebut such presumption by asserting that they have (i) voluntarily removed all X–Men clips from their sales presentation materials, and do not intend to reuse such clips, and (ii) affirmatively requested that the television stations return all "pitch kits" that contain the allegedly infringing clips. (Def. Mem. at 30 & n. 20; Ex. 3 to Def. Rep. Dis.; Urick Decl. ¶ ¶ 11–13.) Similarly, defendants assert that Fox cannot establish irreparable harm with regard to the X–Men logos, because defendants have changed the design of the Mutant X logo to avoid any substantial similarity with Fox's logos.

Although defendants claim that the allegedly infringing clips have been recalled, they have not submitted any proof that all clips have been eliminated from the market. Nor is their expressed intention not to use such clips sufficient to eliminate the possibility of irreparable harm, given the nature of the copying in this case. Even if the tapes have been totally recalled, an award of preliminary relief is not moot; defendants have not provided the Court with a consent injunction or other enforceable assurance that their alleged infringement will not be repeated. Moreover, as of the date of this Opinion, the original Mutant X logo is still featured prominently on the Internet website used to promote the new series. (*See also* Rock Dep. at 66:11–19 (affirming that there has been no official decision as to whether to change the original Mutant X logo)). Accordingly, the Court finds that an injunction, albeit a limited one, is warranted. It therefore grants Fox's motion for preliminary injunction to the extent that defendants are prohibited from using (a) video clips from the X–Men film and/or trailers in order to promote defendants' new series, and (b) a logo that is substantially similar to that used by Fox in connection with the X–Men film, including the three-dimensional green metallic logo currently used to promote Mutant X.

C. Other Claims

The Court has granted defendants' motion to dismiss Fox's claims for breach of the implied covenant of good faith and fair dealing, tortious interference, violation of the Lanham Act, common law unfair competition, and Section 349. Accordingly, as to these claims, Fox's motion for preliminary injunction is denied as moot.

IV. Conclusion

For the foregoing reasons, the Court (i) grants defendants' motion to dismiss as to each of Fox's claims except its breach of contract and copyright claims, and (ii) grants Fox's motion for preliminary injunction, but only as to defendants' use of (a) video clips from the X–Men film and/or trailers in order to promote defendants' new series, and (b) a logo that is substantially similar to that used by Fox in connection with the X–Men film, including the green metallic logo currently used to promote Mutant X.

SO ORDERED.

SMITHERS v. METRO-GOLDWYN-MAYER STUDIOS, INC.
Court of Appeal of California, Second Appellate District, Division Four
February 1, 1983
Civ. No. 65508

H.P. NELSON, Associate Justice.

Metro-Goldwyn-Mayer Studios, Inc. (MGM), Harris Katleman (Katleman), and Bernard Weitzman (Weitzman) appeal from the judgment (as well as from the denial of a motion for judgment notwithstanding the verdict) in this action by William Smithers (Smithers). A cross-appeal from the trial court's remittitur of punitive damages was filed by Smithers.

Smithers sued MGM, Katleman and Weitzman for breach of contract, tortious breach of contract (covenant of good faith and fair dealing), and fraud. The jury returned its verdict as follows:

1. For Smithers against MGM, damages in the sum of $500,000, for breach of contract (count I);

2. For Smithers against MGM, for tortious breach of contract (covenant of good faith and fair dealing), damages in the sum of $300,000 (count II);

3. For Smithers against MGM, Katleman and Weitzman for fraud damages of $200,000 (count III);

4. For Smithers against MGM, punitive damages of $2 million (count IV).

The trial judge denied the motions of MGM, Katleman and Weitzman for judgment notwithstanding the verdict, and for new trial on Smithers' acceptance of reduction of damage for fraud (count III) from $200,000 to $1, and punitive damages from $2 million to $1 million. MGM, Katleman, and Weitzman appeal. Smithers cross-appeals.

Beginning in January 1976, MGM produced a television series entitled "Executive Suite." Harris Katleman was president of MGM Television and Bernard Weitzman was vice president of MGM in charge of Business Affairs. MGM hired an independent casting agency, the Melnick/Holstra Agency, to hire actors for the "Executive Suite" series. Through the Melnick/Holstra Agency, MGM negotiated with Smithers' agent, the William Morris Agency, to cast Smithers in the role of Anderson Galt in the series.

William Smithers is a professional actor of more than 30 years' experience. He has appeared in motion pictures, theater, and radio productions, and has been a regular or cast member in several television series. For approximately 11 years he has been billed as a "guest star," usually with his name and possibly his picture appearing alone on the screen. Appellants concede, as was established by numerous witnesses, that Smithers is a highly regarded actor.

In the course of negotiations between Smithers' agent and the casting agency, the casting director offered a provision known as a "Most-Favored-Nations" billing arrangement. This provision ultimately read as follows:

"Except for the parts of DON WALLING, HELEN WALLING, and HOWARD RUTLEDGE, this deal is on a Most Favored Nations basis, i.e., if any other performer receives greater compensation than Artist, Artist shall receive that compensation.

"Additionally, no other performer shall receive more prominent billing or a better billing provision than Artist (except with respect to where his name is placed alphabetically on the crawl)."

This Most-Favored-Nations provision was offered by the casting director for MGM since Smithers was being offered a lower than usual compensation rate. Further, MGM by this provision could "get some good people to work for reasonably low money and to not have to take up a great deal of space in the main titles." Because of the provision, and in hopes of an improved role, Smithers accepted the role. An interim agreement, called the Outline Deal Memo, was signed by the casting director for MGM and Smithers' agent setting forth the above, being binding pending the execution of a long form contract. Smithers' understanding was that he would get billing at the end of the show, name alphabetically, but that only three other actors would be given more prominent billing at the front of the show.

At a screening of the pilot film, Smithers saw that there were *four* actors with "up-front" billing, instead of the agreed upon three actors. The casting agency had employed another actor for the series during the filming of the pilot film, and had given him "star billing." Smithers saw that his billing remained the same, but preferred to wait until he was in a better bargaining position to complain. Ultimately, ten or eleven actors were given "up-front" billing, while Smithers' end-of-show-name-only billing remained the same.

When the series "Executive Suite" was sold to the CBS network, Smithers' contract provided that he would perform in at least seven of the thirteen episodes. He actually performed in ten of the episodes. Beginning in September 1976, the program was broadcast over the CBS television network. Owing to poor ratings, MGM decided to make several changes, including the "story line" and the billing of the actors. After being informed of these changes, Smithers complained that his billing was not in conformity with the most-favored-nations provision. Upon perusal by Smithers and his agency, it was discovered that the provision had been changed in the long-form contract (which was then—November 1976—still unsigned). The change would allow any number of actors to be billed more prominently than Smithers. MGM's attorney in charge of drafting the contracts testified concerning the change: "There were only two plausible explanations. Either I made a mistake or someone told me to do it," and "Generally somebody who had more authority than I told me to change it."

In mid-December Smithers was told that his role was to be written out of the series. In late December of 1976, Smithers' agent was told that the most-favored-nations provision had been a mistake, and that Smithers should waive the provision. Upon Smithers' refusal to agree to the change, Katleman told Smithers' agent, "... if he didn't, that he (Katleman) would be hard pressed to use Mr. Smithers again on any shows that he (Katleman) was involved with, and that if he (Katleman) were to tell this to Bud Grant, who was then the head of CBS for programing, if he (Katleman) were to tell him (Grant) this, that he (Katleman) was certain he (Grant) would go along as well with not using Mr. Smithers." This threat was reported to Smithers, who ultimately again refused to go along with the change. MGM then went ahead and changed Smithers to an end-of-show billing, however, on a separate card from the rest of the end-of-show billing.

The testimony was considerable on the importance of billing to an actor. Several witnesses testified that billing reflects the actor's stature in the industry, and affects his negotiations for roles, since it reflects what his status and compensation has been in the past. Billing reflects recognition by the producer and the public of the actor's importance or "star quality," and in turn affects the actor's compensation in present and future roles.

ISSUES ON MGM'S APPEAL

MGM contends that Smithers was not entitled to proceed on a theory of a tortious breach of an implied covenant of good faith and fair dealing (tortious breach of contract); that damages for breach of contract were not shown, but if shown, were speculative, uncertain, and excessive; that there was no evidence of fraud, but if there were, damages should not have been allowed for emotional distress on that theory, so that no basis exists for punitive damages, which were also excessive; and that the trial court erred in refusing to give certain instructions. Our approach is, as always, to determine whether substantial evidence supports the judgment in the trial court, viewing that evidence in the light most favorable to respondent.

A. *Tortious Breach of Duty of Good Faith and Fair Dealing.*

The jury found that Katleman issued what amounted to a threat to blacklist Smithers and to encourage others to blacklist him also unless he would forgo his contractual rights. The question is whether the act gave rise to an action in tort. Prior to trial, Judge Cole ruled that such conduct, if proved, fit "to a T" the definition enunciated in *Sawyer v. Bank of America* (1978) 83

Cal.App.3d 135, 139, 145 Cal.Rptr. 623: "[T]he tort of breaching an implied covenant of good faith and fair dealing consists in bad faith action, extraneous to the contract, with the motive intentionally to frustrate the obligee's enjoyment of contract rights." This developing, and confusing, area of the law has had much discussion... (MGM takes the position that the rule is clearly established; however, it has an applicability limited to insurance cases or contracts of adhesions...

The trial judge, on the motion for judgment notwithstanding the verdict, found the evidence on the issue sufficient, and we agree. Further, it is clear that the threat was extraneous to the contract, not only intending to bludgeon Smithers into foregoing his contractual rights but also threatening action directly affecting the practice of his art and damaging to his future earning power. (We agree with Judge Cole that such bad faith conduct fits the *Sawyer* definition. The jury's verdict is supported by substantial evidence.

B. *Breach of Contract.*

MGM concedes that its contract with Smithers was breached, but takes the position that damages arising from such breach were speculative and incapable of ascertainment. Damages for breach of contract must, of course, be clearly ascertainable as to their nature and origin. (Civ.Code § 3301.) However, it is clear that one who wilfully breaches the contract bears the risk as to the uncertainty or the difficulty of computing the amount of damages. A number of witnesses established the relationship between billing and the actor's future negotiations for compensation. The jury could reasonably conclude from the evidence that Smithers suffered an economic loss by reason of MGM's failure to live up to its agreement. Although witnesses were unable to estimate with precision how much Smithers had lost or how much he would earn in future years, the jury was provided a reasonable basis upon which to calculate damages. That fulfills the requirement of Civil Code section 3301.

C. *Fraud.*

The evidence, viewed most favorably for Smithers, adequately showed that MGM, based upon later actions of its agents, had no intention of living up to its most-favored-nations provision, which was offered to induce Smithers to accept a lower than usual compensation rate. The evidence is further sufficient to sustain the jury's determination that Smithers relied upon the promise when he entered the contract. MGM's main point here is that damages were improperly allowed for emotional distress based upon a fraud theory... Here the jury, based upon substantial evidence, determined that actual damage had been suffered by Smithers as a result of MGM's fraud and deceit. Following precedent, as we must, that determination will be upheld.

SMITHERS' CROSS APPEAL

Two basic contentions are urged by Smithers: The trial court should not have found the damages awarded under the fraud theory to be duplicative, and the punitive damages award should not have been reduced. Smithers, therefore, would have us reinstate the jury's verdict in its entirety.

Since the trial court, on a motion to reduce damages, sits as an independent trier of fact, we are required to accord to its order respecting damages the same deference as is given to juries' verdicts on appeal. Therefore every presumption is in favor of the correctness of that order, in the absence of an abuse of discretion.

I

The trial court, reviewing the evidence, concluded that the damages awarded on the fraud theory duplicated those found on the theories of breach of contract and tortious breach of the covenant of good faith and fair dealing. One may have many theories, but one recovery. The trial court's order respecting the duplication of damages reviewed the evidence, noting the overlapping and interweaving of the facts as they supported the various theories, concluded that such interdependence warranted essentially one recovery. That independent judgment was fully justified by the evidence, since, indeed, the summation of Smithers' counsel (though that is not dispositive) wove this very tapestry of facts for the jury. The trial court's exercise of discretion in this regard was sound.

II

Concerning the reduction of punitive damages, we again accord the presumption of correctness to the trial court's order. Here the trial court found punitive damages to be justified, and the record supports that conclusion. The trial court's judgment as to the gravity of MGM's acts, the amount of damages awarded, and MGM's wealth rests on substantial evidence. Reducing damages to a nominal amount on the fraud theory created a facial disproportion between that nominal amount and the punitive damages before and after such reduction. That, however, is of no consequence.

Smithers' real contention is that the trial court, in contrast to its specifications as required by Code of Civil Procedure section 657 on the reduction of damages for emotional distress, did not meet those requirements concerning the reduction of punitive damages. Specification is adequate, according to *Neal,* when "it makes reference to those aspects of the trial proceedings which, in the trial court's view, improperly led the jury to inflate its award." *Id.* at 932, 148 Cal.Rptr. 389, 582 P.2d 980. The trial court noted that such damages were "justifiable," and that the evidence "fully supported the conclusion that the conduct of the defendants was 'extreme and outrageous.' " Fairly read, the specification notes that MGM's threat was neither carried out nor communicated to CBS, and apparently did not cause economic loss, although it caused emotional distress. Then the trial court found $1 million in punitive damages to be more reasonable than $2 million. We cannot say that the punitive damages, as ultimately awarded, did not bear a reasonable relation to the actual damages as we have affirmed them.

We therefore affirm the judgment on the appeal and on the cross-appeal. Neither party shall recover costs on appeal.

KINGSLEY, Acting P.J., and McCLOSKY, J., concur.

OUT OF CHAOS, LTD v. AON CORP.
United States Court of Appeals for the Fourth Circuit
June 6, 2001, Argued
August 3, 2001, Decided
No. 00-2592
15 Fed. Appx. 137

PER CURIAM.

Appellant, Out of Chaos, Ltd ("OCL"), a "start up" film production company, filed a multi-count lawsuit against Appellees Aon Corporation and AON/Albert G. Ruben Insurance Services (hereinafter, jointly, "AON/AGR"), an insurance agency, and other entities not parties to this appeal, in the United States District Court for the Eastern District of Virginia, seeking substantial damages for losses OCL incurred in connection with an aborted film production. The district court granted judgment on the pleadings in favor of Appellees on OCL's claims for fraud and conversion. Subsequently, at the conclusion of discovery, the district court granted summary judgment in favor of Appellees on OCL's negligence claims. We discern no error in the district court's rulings; accordingly, we affirm.

I

Brothers James and Randall Starrett formed OCL and entered into a one million dollar contract with Discovery Communications, Inc. ("Discovery"), to film "Tournament of Shadows," a docudrama about the British explorer Sir Francis Younghusband's expedition into the mountains of central Asia.

On Discovery's recommendation, the Starretts contacted Kristi Jones, a broker with AON/AGR, to secure insurance for their undertaking, as the contract required. Jones advised the Starretts that OCL would be eligible to obtain insurance under the Discovery blanket policy with Chubb. Jones faxed to OCL a document which stated as follows: "The following brief description of motion picture and television production insurance is general in nature and is not meant to be a complete explanation of the policy terms. Specimen policies are available through our firm." (J.A. 336.) The Starretts never requested specimen policies prior to paying the necessary premiums. Randy Starrett testified on deposition that he understood that the policies "cover[ed] all risk [sic] except those risks which are excepted." (J.A. 339.)

In fact, AON/AGR procured coverage for that part of OCL's production of "Tournament of Shadows" that would not be based in Pakistan under a package of insurance provided by Federal Insurance Company, Vigilant Insurance

Company and Pacific Indemnity Company, three companies affiliated with Chubb Corporation (hereinafter, collectively, "Chubb"). AON/AGR obtained on OCL's behalf a separate foreign policy from the Insurance Company for the State of Pennsylvania ("ICSOP") to provide workers' compensation, automobile and commercial general liability insurance for filming in Pakistan.

In her communications with the Starretts, Jones did not explain every policy exclusion. Specifically, she did not explain that there was an employee infidelity exception in the Chubb coverage. Significantly, neither of the Starretts advised Jones that OCL faced any special risk of misconduct by employees or representatives. Moreover, James Starrett specifically stated on deposition that he would not have attempted to purchase different or additional insurance had he known beforehand about the employee infidelity exclusion.

AON/AGR faxed OCL confirmation that it had bound OCL's insurance effective in June 1997. The fax transmission included a declarations page stating that all standard exclusions applied.

After it had obtained the insurance, OCL hired Pavel Lounguine to develop the screenplay and direct the film; shortly thereafter, filming began in Pakistan. Relations between Lounguine and the Starretts soon soured. By the time principal photography in Pakistan had been completed in December 1997, the project was seriously over budget. Lounguine and his editor went to Paris to process and assemble the film. In February 1998, after he had completed this work, Lounguine absconded with the computer disks containing the film assembly and announced he would no longer work for OCL.

In March 1998, Lounguine filed a lawsuit against OCL in Paris ("the French lawsuit"), and the bailiff of the French court seized the film. Discovery advised OCL that it must settle the French lawsuit and cease all production activity. By April 1998, OCL's counsel had negotiated a settlement of the French lawsuit "upon terms dictated by" Discovery. Discovery obtained possession of the film, which it retains. Pursuant to the French settlement, OCL paid $7,000 unconditionally, and it deposited an additional $45,875 in escrow. When the French lawsuit was not dismissed as required by the settlement, the French court dismissed the case. Virtually all of the escrowed settlement funds were returned to OCL. Discovery advised OCL that before OCL could regain possession of the film and complete the production, it had to pay the extra expenses the project had incurred, totaling $975,510. (J.A. 125.) OCL has not paid these extra costs and has never completed the film.

A portion of the damages OCL sought in this action allegedly resulted directly from the French lawsuit and its surrounding circumstances, while other claimed damages resulted indirectly. In particular, OCL alleged that it incurred $63,057 in defense costs in connection with the French lawsuit. According to OCL, its other damages claims against AON/AGR are rooted in (1) the "undisclosed" employee infidelity exclusion in the Chubb coverage and (2) the confusion and delay (which OCL asserts resulted in the failure of the entire production) attending AON/AGR's awkward efforts to process and deliver to the appropriate insurers OCL's claims for indemnity under the policies that AON/AGR had obtained on OCL's behalf from the various insurers.[2] In short, OCL has sought to assign as a cause of the collapse of the film project AON/AGR's acts and omissions.

Ultimately, OCL filed this suit in April 2000. OCL joined as defendants all of the insurers with whom AON/AGR had placed insurance, as well as AON/AGR. Eventually, all defendants except AON/AGR were dismissed from the lawsuit. Specifically, ICSOP settled with OCL and paid it $113,097.32. According to the uncontradicted affidavit of ICSOP's vice-president, even if ISCOP had received timely notice of the French lawsuit, ISCOP would have merely provided OCL a defense through a reasonable period (i.e., September 1998) in order to effect a reasonable settlement, which OCL had indeed achieved on its own, albeit under pressure from Discovery. Chubb also settled the claims asserted by OCL's in this action, but the terms of that settlement are not in the record.

II

As relevant to this appeal, in its amended complaint OCL asserted three claims against AON/AGR: (1) fraud; (2) conversion; and negligence.

The district court entered judgment on the pleadings in respect to the claims for fraud and conversion. The court noted that under *Richmond Metropolitan Authority v. McDevitt, Street, Bovis, Inc.*, 256 Va. 553, 507 S.E.2d 344 (Va.1998), a claim for an alleged misrepresentation as to a duty or obligation that was specifically required by a contract sounds in contract. The district court observed that fraud in the inducement would be an exception to the rule in that case, and repeatedly indicated that if OCL could, within "the strictures of Rule 11," allege that AON/AGR "told you something, never intending to perform it," then OCL could further amend its complaint. (J.A. 245, 262–63, 269.) OCL never attempted further to amend its complaint.

The parties proceeded with discovery as to the contract and negligence claims and Aon/AGR filed a motion for summary judgment. During oral argument on AON/AGR's motion, counsel for OCL conceded that it was "clear that [AON/AGR] bought insurance for my client that's been produced in discovery and it is there," and that the issue OCL "tried to raise is whether it was the appropriate insurance," which was "more of a negligence question than a contract claim." (J.A. 396.)

Accordingly, the district court granted summary judgment for AON/AGR on the breach of contract claim because it was clear AON/AGR had procured insurance. The surviving claims concerned the adequacy of that insurance and the reasonableness of AON/AGR's handling of the claim processing efforts it undertook. The district court granted summary judgment on the negligence claims, as well, however, ruling that the undisputed facts established that the insurance policies that OCL obtained were essentially the standard sort of policies ordinarily obtained by, or for, Discovery, if not also the entire film industry, and that OCL had communicated no unique or special issues which could have placed AON/AGR on notice that it had a duty to obtain a policy that would provide coverage for losses occasioned by employee infidelity. Furthermore, the district court concluded that OCL had failed to establish that any of the damages that it suffered were proximately caused by a breach of duty chargeable to AON/AGR in its handling of the claims processing functions.

III

We review *de novo* a district court's grant of judgment on the pleadings under Federal Rule of Civil Procedure 12(c)...

IV

OCL's amended complaint alleged that AON/AGR committed fraud and conversion when it did not obtain the insurance it agreed to obtain and when it utilized OCL's insurance premiums for its own purposes. Under Virginia law, "a party can, in certain circumstances, show both a breach of contract and a tortious breach of duty." *Richmond Metropolitan Authority v. McDevitt, Street, Bovis, Inc.,* 256 Va. 553, 507 S.E.2d 344, 347 (Va.1998) (internal quotations omitted). The Virginia Supreme Court further held that "the duty tortiously or negligently breached must be a common law duty, not one existing between the parties solely by virtue of the contract." *Id.* (internal quotations omitted).

A claim for "fraud in the inducement" is not foreclosed by the rule of *McDevitt, Street, Bovis, Inc.,* 507 S.E.2d at 348 (*citing Flip Mortgage Corp. v. McElhone,* 841 F.2d 531 (4th Cir.1988)). To make out such a claim, the plaintiff must allege facts that demonstrate the defendant's intent (at the time the promises are made) never to abide by the terms of the contract. *Id.* When, as in the instant case, the allegations of fraud or conversion "are nothing more than allegation[s] of negligent performance of contractual duties," such alleged breaches of duty are not actionable in tort. *Id.* at 347.

Essentially, OCL alleged that it had a contract with AON/AGR that OCL would pay premiums and AON/AGR would secure insurance for "Tournament of Shadows." OCL alleged that AON/AGR did not secure insurance as the contract required, and made fraudulent statements and issued fraudulent documents stating that it had. In addition, OCL alleged that AON/AGR converted OCL's premiums for its own use. Each of these alleged wrongful acts arise from AON/AGR's contractual duty to OCL, i.e., to use OCL's payments to buy insurance. AON/AGR had no separate common law duty to do these things for OCL; rather, such duties inhere solely in AON/AGR's contractual undertakings.

Plainly, as the district court correctly concluded, OCL did not plead that it had been fraudulently induced to enter into the (oral) contract with AON/AGR for the procurement of insurance. Nor is there a scintilla of evidence that AON/AGR misapplied funds intended for use as premium payments. Thus, the district court properly entered judgment on the pleadings as to the claims for fraud and conversion.

V

We are likewise satisfied that the district court did not err in granting summary judgment to AON/AGR on OCL's negligence claims. OCL theorized that AON/AGR negligently "fail[ed] to procure [adequate] insurance" and negligently "fail[ed] to professionally process" OCL's claims for coverage. Even if AON/AGR had an independent tort duty to comply with a relevant standard of care which required, specifically, that it disclose and explain to the Starretts the employee infidelity exclusion, or to expeditiously process OCL's claims, and even if we assume that AON/AGR breached these duties, there is no genuine dispute of material fact whether OCL suffered any damages proximately caused by these ostensible breaches. It did not.

A

The district court correctly granted summary judgment to AON/AGR on the adequacy of insurance issue because the record stands undisputed that even if James Starrett had obtained actual possession of the policy documents (as he was invited to do) and discussed with Jones, the AON/AGR broker, the employee infidelity clause in the Chubb coverage, he would not have sought substitute coverage or otherwise done anything differently. Thus, the fact that the Chubb coverage obtained by AON/AGR contained an employee infidelity exclusion was not a proximate cause of injury to OCL.

B

Similarly unavailing is OCL's contention that AON/AGR's breach of its duty to process OCL's claims in a professionally reasonable manner and to provide timely notice of loss to the respective insurance companies proximately caused injury to OCL. Even if AON/AGR had an independent duty to provide timely notice to the insurers of OCL's claims, the breach of which would give rise to a claim sounding in tort, OCL failed to generate a genuine dispute of material fact as to whether a breach of such duty caused it injury or damage.

It is undisputed that ICSOP's policy covered third party claims for personal injury or property damage, and that the French lawsuit included a claim for personal injury to Lounguine. Thus, there was a potentiality of coverage. ICSOP, though belatedly notified of the French litigation, has settled with OCL, paying recompense for the direct damages caused by the French lawsuit. (J.A. 378.) Without contradiction, ICSOP's vice-president has attested that had ICSOP known about the French lawsuit while it was pending,[7] it would have covered OCL's defense costs only for the purpose of securing a prompt settlement of that action. (J.A. 379.) OCL alleges it was forced to settle the French lawsuit because no insurance company came forward to defend it; however, the most that OCL would have obtained from ICSOP would have been assistance in settling the case. More to the point, it was Discovery that insisted that OCL cease film production and settle the French case immediately. Pursuant to the French settlement, OCL paid $7,000 unconditionally and deposited an additional $45,875 in escrow. When Lounguine failed to dismiss the French lawsuit in accordance with the terms of the settlement, virtually all of the escrowed funds were returned to OCL. As a matter of law, therefore, as the district court correctly concluded, OCL suffered no cognizable damage from the delay in ICSOP's receipt of notice of the claim.

OCL alleges that Discovery canceled production of "Tournament of Shadows" because of the French lawsuit, and that AON/AGR's failure to deliver timely notice to ICSOP of the French lawsuit was therefore the proximate cause of the damages flowing from the production cancellation. These bald allegations are unsupported by any evidence in the summary judgment record and therefore lack merit. First, as explained above, even if AON/AGR had notified ICSOP sooner, this possibility would not have altered the consequences to OCL of the seizure of the film and the institution of the French lawsuit. ICSOP, like Discovery, would have insisted on prompt settlement, which is precisely what occurred.

Second, OCL has failed to generate a factual dispute as to whether the film production was actually canceled as a result of the French lawsuit. The undisputed evidence in the record shows that, in accordance with the French settlement, the film was returned to Discovery, which retains possession of it. Discovery informed OCL that it would not allow it to complete the film until OCL paid Discovery $975,510 in cost overruns. Plainly, it is because OCL has never paid this sum to Discovery that the production was canceled.

OCL insists that the $975,510 should have been paid by Chubb or ICSOP. But there is no factual support in the record for OCL's assertion that the policies with these companies did or would have required any such payments. Accordingly, the issue of whether AON/AGR unreasonably failed to provide timely notice to the insurers of OCL's losses resulting from the cancellation of the production is immaterial to the issue that is dispositive of OCL's damages claims based on its negligence theories.

In sum, the district court correctly concluded that OCL failed to produce evidence that AON/AGR's acts or omissions were a proximate cause of OCL's damages.

AFFIRMED.

WARNER BROS., INC. v. AMERICAN BROADCASTING COS.
United States Court of Appeals for the Second Circuit
March 16, 1983; October 6, 1983, Decided
Nos. 82-7152, 82-7794, No. 850—August Term, 1982

NEWMAN, Circuit Judge:

The primary issue raised by this appeal is whether as a matter of law the fictional character Ralph Hinkley, the principal figure in a television series, "The Greatest American Hero," is not sufficiently similar to the fictional character Superman, the hero of comic books, television, and more recently films, so that claims of copyright infringement and unfair competition may be dismissed without consideration by a jury. The appeal is from a January 22, 1982, judgment of the District Court for the Southern District of New York (Constance Baker Motley, Chief Judge) dismissing claims of plaintiffs Warner Bros., Inc., Film Export, A.G., and DC Comics, Inc. against defendant American Broadcasting Companies, Inc. (ABC) and third-party defendant Stephen J. Cannell Productions upon the granting of defendants' motion for summary judgment. Defendants cross-appeal from the denial of their motion to amend the judgment to award attorney's fees and additional costs beyond those allowed under Fed.R.Civ.P. 54(d). For the reasons that follow, we affirm the judgment.

I.

Many of the significant facts are set out in our prior opinion affirming the denial of plaintiffs' motion for a preliminary injunction. *Warner Bros. Inc. v. American Broadcasting Companies, Inc.,* 654 F.2d 204 (2d Cir.1981). Plaintiffs own the copyrights in various works embodying the character Superman and have thereby acquired copyright protection for the character itself. *See Detective Comics, Inc. v. Bruns Publications, Inc.,* 111 F.2d 432 (2d Cir.1940). Since the creation of Superman in 1938, plaintiffs have exploited their rights with great success, portraying Superman in several media and licensing the character for a variety of merchandising purposes. Through plaintiffs' efforts, Superman has attained an extremely high degree of exposure and recognition.

In 1978, building on previous Superman works, plaintiff Warner Bros., Inc. released a motion picture entitled "Superman, The Movie" (*Superman I*) and more recently two sequels...

In *Superman I* and in previous Superman works, Superman is portrayed as a brave, fearless hero, endowed with superhuman powers. His strength, speed, vision, and hearing far exceed the physical capabilities of mere mortals. He is impervious to bullets. In early works, Superman displayed extraordinary leaping ability,... in later works this skill had become the power of flight, as Superman is regularly seen soaring through the sky, arms stretched ahead, then landing agilely on his feet ready for action...

Descriptions of Superman and lines of dialogue in the Superman works have become as well known as the Superman character. He is described as "faster than a speeding bullet," "more powerful than a locomotive," and "able to leap tall buildings in a single bound," and he always fights for "truth, justice, and the American way." From the early comic books continuing through the modern films, startled pedestrians have shouted, "Look! Up in the sky! ... It's a bird! ... It's a plane! ... It's Superman!"

The substantial commercial success of *Superman I* and the attendant publicity prompted many requests for licenses permitting use of the Superman character in connection with the merchandising of toys, greeting cards, apparel, and other products. It also led ABC to seek a license for production of a television series about "Superboy" based on the early adventures of Superman. Plaintiffs, who were planning to make their own sequels and derivative works, refused ABC permission to proceed with its proposed project.

Unable to obtain this license, ABC assigned to Cannell, the principal of the third-party defendant production company, the task of creating a "pilot" program for a TV series involving a superhero. Cannell produced a program, and subsequently a weekly series, entitled "The Greatest American Hero" (*Hero*), which he described as being about "what happens when you [the average person] become Superman." *Hero's* protagonist, Ralph Hinkley, was given attributes intended to identify him as an "ordinary guy." Hinkley is portrayed as a young high school teacher attempting to cope with a recent divorce, a dispute over the custody of his son, and the strain that his domestic problems place upon his work and his relationship with his girlfriend. Although Hinkley is attractive, his physical appearance is not imposing: he is of medium height with a slight build and curly, somewhat unkempt, blond hair...

Hinkley's magical costume endows him with superhuman speed and strength, the ability to fly, imperviousness to bullets, and what Cannell calls "holographic vision," the power to perceive sights and sounds occurring out of his line of vision...

The *Hero* series contains several visual effects and lines that inevitably call Superman to mind, sometimes by way of brief imitation, sometimes by mention of Superman or another character from the Superman works, and sometimes by humorous parodying or ironic twisting of well-known Superman phrases...

In the three weeks before the first episode of *Hero* was televised, ABC conducted one of the most extensive promotional campaigns in the network's history, airing nearly 200 commercials, or "promos," each running five, ten, twenty, or thirty seconds. Most were slight variations of thirteen basic "promos." By multiplying the number of "promos" by the estimated television audience at the time each was shown, plaintiffs estimate that the promotional campaign registered more than 2.4 billion viewer impressions...

II.

The basic issues concerning the copyright infringement claim are whether the *Hero* and *Superman* works are substantially similar so as to support an inference of copying and whether the lack of substantial similarity is so clear as to fall outside the range of reasonably disputed fact questions requiring resolution by a jury. The similarity to be assessed must concern the expression of ideas, not the ideas themselves...

The "parody" branch of the "fair use" doctrine is itself a means of fostering the creativity protected by the copyright law. It also balances the public interest in the free flow of ideas with the copyright holder's interest in the exclusive use of his work. Especially in an era of mass communications, it is to be expected that phrases and other fragments of expression in a highly successful copyrighted work will become part of the language. That does not mean they lose all protection in the manner of a trade name that has become generic...

Applying these principles to this case, we conclude that Chief Judge Motley correctly entered summary judgment for the defendants on the claim of copyright infringement. Plaintiffs make no claim that the *Hero* pilot, subsequent episodes, or "promos" infringed the story of any Superman works. Their contention is that the *Hero* character, Ralph Hinkley, is substantially similar to Superman and that the *Hero* works impermissibly copied what plaintiffs call the "indicia" of Superman, a concept broad enough to include Superman's costume, his abilities, the well-known lines associated with him—in short, anything occurring in the *Hero* works that might remind a viewer of Superman.

The total perception of the Hinkley character is not substantially similar to that of Superman. On the contrary, it is profoundly different. Superman looks and acts like a brave, proud hero, who has dedicated his life to combating the forces of evil. Hinkley looks and acts like a timid, reluctant hero, who accepts his missions grudgingly and prefers to get on with his normal life. Superman performs his superhuman feats with skill, verve, and dash, clearly the master of his own destiny. Hinkley is perplexed by the superhuman powers his costume confers and uses them in a bumbling, comical fashion. In the genre of superheros, Hinkley follows Superman as, in the genre of detectives, Inspector Clouseau follows Sherlock Holmes.

However, when a trial judge has correctly ruled that two works are not substantially similar as a matter of law, that conclusion is not to be altered by the availability of survey evidence indicating that some people applying some standard of their own were reminded by one work of the other. Courts have an important responsibility in copyright cases to monitor the outer limits within which juries may determine reasonably disputed issues of fact. If a case lies beyond those limits, the contrary view of a properly drawn sample of the population, or even of a particular jury, cannot be permitted to enlarge (or diminish) the scope of statutory protection enjoyed by a copyright proprietor.

III.

The unfair competition and trademark dilution claims present slightly different issues, but, as will appear, we agree with Chief Judge Motley that defendants were entitled to summary judgment on these claims as well as on the infringement claims. Preliminarily, plaintiffs contend that summary judgment was procedurally improper because it was entered by the District Court "sua sponte" and without consideration of all of the evidence they proposed to offer had the unfair competition claims gone to trial. We disagree.

Defendants moved for summary judgment with respect to the entire complaint, affording plaintiffs a full opportunity to submit memoranda and affidavits in opposition. After the District Court's initial denial of the motion, which was made prior to viewing all of the pertinent works, defendants appear to have renewed the motion orally, at least with respect to the infringement claims. Thereafter Chief Judge Motley granted the defendants partial summary judgment with respect to the infringement claims and expressed an intention to certify that ruling for appeal pursuant to 28 U.S.C. § 1292(b) (1976). Upon further reflection and with the opportunity to consider the mass of plaintiffs' evidence presented during the two-week pretrial session, the District Court entered summary judgment for defendants on all of the claims.

Though we find no procedural error, we think the plaintiffs' point is not answered, as defendants contend, by the provision of Fed.R.Civ.P. 54(b) specifying that "any order or other form of decision ... which adjudicates fewer than all of the claims ... is subject to revision at any time before the entry of judgment adjudicating all the claims ...." The District Court's initial ruling denying summary judgment on all claims was not an order "adjudicating" any of them; it simply left them for adjudication at trial.

The judgment of the District Court is affirmed.

The next case looks into a different but related area, namely the confluence of public access cable TV and the First Amendment's mandate to protect children from pornography. Denver Area Educ. Telcoms. Consortium v. FCC, 518 U.S. 727 (1996). The case analyzes the Cable Television Consumer Protection and Competition Act of 1992.

DENVER AREA EDUC. TELCOMS. CONSORTIUM v. FCC
Supreme Court of the United States
February 21, 1996, Argued; June 28, 1996, Decided
No. 95-124

Justice BREYER announced the judgment of the Court and delivered the opinion of the Court with respect to Part III, an opinion with respect to Parts I, II, and V, in which Justice STEVENS, Justice O'CONNOR, and Justice SOUTER join, and an opinion with respect to Parts IV and VI, in which Justice STEVENS and Justice SOUTER join.

These cases present First Amendment challenges to three statutory provisions that seek to regulate the broadcasting of "patently offensive" sex-related material on cable television. Cable Television Consumer Protection and Competition Act of 1992 (1992 Act or Act), 106 Stat. 1486, §§ 10(a), 10(b), and 10(c), 47 U.S.C. §§ 532(h), 532(j), and note following § 531. The provisions apply to programs broadcast over cable on what are known as "leased access channels" and "public, educational, or governmental channels." Two of the provisions essentially permit a cable system operator to prohibit the broadcasting of "programming" that the "operator reasonably believes describes or depicts sexual or excretory activities or organs in a patently offensive manner." 1992 Act, § 10(a); see § 10(c)... The remaining provision requires cable system operators to segregate certain "patently offensive" programming, to place it on a single channel, and to block that channel from viewer access unless the viewer requests access in advance and in writing. 1992 Act, § 10(b); 47 CFR § 76.701(g) (1995).

We conclude that the first provision—which *permits* the operator to decide whether or not to broadcast such programs on *leased* access channels—is consistent with the First Amendment. The second provision, which *requires* leased channel operators to segregate and to block that programming, and the third provision, applicable to public, educational, and governmental channels, violate the First Amendment, for they are not appropriately tailored to achieve the basic, legitimate objective of protecting children from exposure to "patently offensive" material.

I

Cable operators typically own a physical cable network used to convey programming over several dozen cable channels into subscribers' houses. Program sources vary from channel to channel. Most channels carry programming produced by independent firms, including "many national and regional cable programming networks that have emerged in recent years," *Turner Broadcasting System, Inc. v. FCC,* 512 U.S. 622, 629, 114 S.Ct. 2445, 2452, 129 L.Ed.2d 497 (1994), as well as some programming that the system operator itself (or an operator affiliate) may provide. Other channels may simply retransmit through cable the signals of over-the-air broadcast stations. *Ibid.* Certain special channels here at issue, called "leased channels" and "public, educational, or governmental channels," carry programs provided by those to whom the law gives special cable system access rights.

A "leased channel" is a channel that federal law requires a cable system operator to reserve for commercial lease by unaffiliated third parties...

The FCC, carrying out this statutory instruction, promulgated regulations defining "sexually explicit" in language almost identical to that in the statute's leased channel provision, namely, as descriptions or depictions of "sexual or excretory activities or organs in a patently offensive manner" as measured by the cable viewing community. See § 76.702 (1995) (incorporating definition from 47 CFR § 76.701(g)).

The upshot is, as we said at the beginning, that the federal law before us (the statute as implemented through regulations) now *permits* cable operators either to allow or to forbid the transmission of "patently offensive" sex-related materials over both leased and public access channels, and *requires* those operators, at a minimum, to segregate and to block transmission of that same material on leased channels.

II

We turn initially to the provision that *permits* cable system operators to prohibit "patently offensive" (or "indecent") programming transmitted over leased access channels. 1992 Act, § 10(a).

The history of this Court's First Amendment jurisprudence, however, is one of continual development, as the Constitution's general command that "Congress shall make no law ... abridging the freedom of speech, or of the press," has been applied to new circumstances requiring different adaptations of prior principles and precedents. The essence of that protection is that Congress may not regulate speech except in cases of extraordinary need and with the exercise of a degree of care that we have not elsewhere required.

This tradition teaches that the First Amendment embodies an overarching commitment to protect speech from government regulation through close judicial scrutiny, thereby enforcing the Constitution's constraints, but without imposing judicial formulas so rigid that they become a straitjacket that disables government from responding to serious problems. This Court, in different contexts, has consistently held that government may directly regulate speech to address extraordinary problems, where its regulations are appropriately tailored to resolve those problems without imposing an unnecessarily great restriction on speech.

Rather than decide these issues, we can decide these cases more narrowly, by closely scrutinizing § 10(a) to assure that it properly addresses an extremely important problem, without imposing, in light of the relevant interests, an unnecessarily great restriction on speech. The importance of the interest at stake here—protecting children from exposure to patently offensive depictions of sex; the accommodation of the interests of programmers in maintaining access channels and of cable operators in editing the contents of their channels; the similarity of the problem and its solution to those at issue in *Pacifica;* and the flexibility inherent in an approach that *permits* private cable operators to make editorial decisions, lead us to conclude that § 10(a) is a sufficiently tailored response to an extraordinarily important problem.

First, the provision before us comes accompanied with an extremely important justification, one that this Court has often found compelling—the need to protect children from exposure to patently offensive sex-related material.

Second, the provision arises in a very particular context—congressional *permission* for cable operators to regulate programming that, but for a previous Act of Congress, would have had no path of access to cable channels free of an operator's control. The First Amendment interests involved are therefore complex, and require a balance between those interests served by the access requirements themselves (increasing the availability of avenues of expression to programmers who otherwise would not have them), H.R.Rep. No. 98–934, at 31–36, and the disadvantage to the First Amendment interests of cable operators and other programmers (those to whom the cable operator would have assigned the channels devoted to access). See *Turner,* 512 U.S., at 635–637, 114 S.Ct., at 2455–2456.

Third, the problem Congress addressed here is remarkably similar to the problem addressed by the FCC in *Pacifica,* and the balance Congress struck is commensurate with the balance we approved there. In *Pacifica* this Court considered a governmental ban of a radio broadcast of "indecent" materials, defined in part, like the provisions before us ...

The Court found this ban constitutionally permissible primarily because "broadcasting is uniquely accessible to children" and children were likely listeners to the program there at issue—an afternoon radio broadcast. 438 U.S., at 749–750, 98 S.Ct., at 3040.

For the reasons discussed, we conclude that § 10(a) is consistent with the First Amendment.

III

The statute's second provision significantly differs from the first, for it does not simply permit, but rather requires, cable system operators to restrict speech—by segregating and blocking "patently offensive" sex-related material appearing on leased channels (but not on other channels). 1992 Act, § 10(b)...

These requirements have obvious restrictive effects. The several up-to-30-day delays, along with single channel segregation, mean that a subscriber cannot decide to watch a single program without considerable advance planning and without letting the "patently offensive" channel in its entirety invade his household for days, perhaps weeks, at a time.

This device—the "lockbox"—would help protect children by permitting their parents to "lock out" those programs or channels that they did not want their children to see. See FCC 85–179, ¶ 132, 50 Fed.Reg. 18637, 18655 (1985)...

Consequently, we cannot find that the "segregate and block" restrictions on speech are a narrowly, or reasonably, tailored effort to protect children. Rather, they are overly restrictive, "sacrific[ing]" important First Amendment interests for too "speculative a gain." *Columbia Broadcasting,* 412 U.S., at 127, 93 S.Ct., at 2099; see *League of Women Voters,* 468 U.S., at 397, 104 S.Ct., at 3126. For that reason they are not consistent with the First Amendment.

IV

The statute's third provision, as implemented by FCC regulation, is similar to its first provision, in that it too *permits* a cable operator to prevent transmission of "patently offensive" programming, in this case on public access channels. 1992 Act, § 10(c); 47 CFR § 76.702 (1995)...

This system of public, private, and mixed nonprofit elements, through its supervising boards and nonprofit or governmental access managers, can set programming policy and approve or disapprove particular programming services. And this system can police that policy by, for example, requiring indemnification by programmers, certification of compliance with local standards, time segregation, adult content advisories, or even by prescreening individual programs...

The upshot, in respect to the public access channels, is a law that could radically change present programming-related relationships among local community and nonprofit supervising boards and access managers, which relationships are established through municipal law, regulation, and contract. In doing so, it would not significantly restore editorial rights of cable operators, but would greatly increase the risk that certain categories of programming (say, borderline offensive programs) will not appear. At the same time, given present supervisory mechanisms, the need for this particular provision, aimed directly at public access channels, is not obvious. Having carefully reviewed the legislative history of the Act, the proceedings before the FCC, the record below, and the submissions of the parties and *amici* here, we conclude that the Government cannot sustain its burden of showing that § 10(c) is necessary to protect children or that it is appropriately tailored to secure that end. See, *e.g., Columbia Broadcasting,* 412 U.S., at 127, 93 S.Ct., at 2098–2099; *League of Women Voters,* 468 U.S., at 398–399, 104 S.Ct., at 3126–3127; *Sable,* 492 U.S., at 126, 109 S.Ct., at 2836–2837. Consequently, we find that this third provision violates the First Amendment.

V

Finally, we must ask whether § 10(a) is severable from the two other provisions...

VI

For these reasons, the judgment of the Court of Appeals is affirmed insofar as it upheld § 10(a); the judgment of the Court of Appeals is reversed insofar as it upheld § 10(b) and § 10(c).

It is so ordered.

Justice STEVENS, concurring.

Similarly, the next case, Loce v. Time Warner Entertainment Advance/Newhouse Pshp., 191 F.3d 256 (2d Cir. 1999), analyzes the Cable Television Consumer Protection and Competition Act of 1992. This is a question of the retransmission of certain leased access channels on the basis that the programs violated TimeWarner's policy against indecent programming.

LOCE v. TIME WARNER ENTERTAINMENT ADVANCE/NEWHOUSE PSHP
Second Circuit Court of Appeals
November 4, 1998, Argued; June 14, 1999, Decided
Docket Nos. 97-9601, 98-7040
191 F.3d 256

KEARSE, Circuit Judge:

Plaintiffs Thomas Loce and Ed Richter, individually and doing business as Life Without Shame, appeal from so much of a final judgment of the United States District Court for the Western District of New York, Michael A. Telesca, *Judge,* as dismissed their claims under the First Amendment of the Constitution and § 612 of the Communications Act of 1934, as amended by the Cable Communications Policy Act of 1984 (the "1984 Act"), by the Cable Television Consumer Protection and Competition Act of 1992 ("Cable Act of 1992" or "1992 Act"), and by Title V of the Telecommunications Act of 1996 (collectively the "Cable Act" or "Act"), *codified at* 47 U.S.C. § 532 (1994 & Supp. II 1996), against defendants Time Warner Entertainment Advance/Newhouse Partnership *et al.* (collectively "Time Warner" or "TW") for (a) refusing to transmit certain of plaintiffs' television programs on defendants' leased access channels on the ground that the programs violated defendants' policy against indecent programming, and (b) refusing to specify what parts of the submitted programs defendants found objectionable. The district court granted partial summary judgment dismissing plaintiffs' First Amendment claims on the ground that Time Warner is not a state actor and dismissing in part their statutory claims on the ground that Time Warner's refusals to transmit or assist in editing the programs in question were not unreasonable and hence did not violate the Cable Act. Plaintiffs challenge these rulings on appeal. The district court also ruled that Time Warner's policies of (a) requiring programmers to certify that they would not submit programs that Time Warner would consider indecent, and (b) suspending programmers who had submitted programs that Time Warner considered indecent, and refusing to allow further program submissions by such programmers, violated the Act. Time Warner cross-appeals from so much of the judgment as granted declaratory and injunctive relief against its policy of suspending programmers. For the reasons that follow, we affirm the judgment.

I. BACKGROUND

Most of the facts are undisputed. Pursuant to franchise agreements with municipalities in and around Rochester, New York, and Syracuse, New York,

Time Warner offers cable television service in the Rochester and Syracuse areas. Time Warner offers its subscribers, for a monthly fee, "standard-tier" programming containing several dozen channels, as well as optional "premium" channels for which a subscriber pays an additional monthly fee, and "pay-per-view" programs, for each of which a subscriber must make a specific request and pay a one-time fee. The vast majority of Time Warner's customers in the Rochester and Syracuse areas subscribe only to standard-tier programming.

Standard-tier programming includes "leased access" channels for commercial use by unaffiliated programmers, as required by the 1984 Act, *see* 47 U.S.C. § 532(b) (1994). Standard-tier programming is unscrambled at all times, and a subscriber cannot avoid receiving the leased access channels except by obtaining an addressable converter capable of blocking specific channels or by having Time Warner install a physical device called a "trap" on the subscriber's cable line. Programs containing nudity and sexually explicit content, when provided by Time Warner or its affiliates, are not shown on standard-tier channels but are confined to the optional premium or pay-per-view channels. The present case involves the contents of programs provided by independent programmers on leased access channels, which, as part of standard-tier programming, are transmitted to all subscribers and are not scrambled.

Loce and Richter are independent producers of cable television programming doing business as Life Without Shame (collectively "plaintiffs" or "LWS"). During the period 1993-1996, pursuant to lease agreements with Time Warner, plaintiffs' television program "Life Without Shame" was broadcast on leased access channels in the Rochester and Syracuse areas. Airing from midnight to 1 a.m., the program principally featured scenes of female nude dancers in various adult clubs in those areas, along with commentary and interviews by Loce and Richter as the show's hosts. The hosts' commentary typically focused on a stripper's physique and the hosts' fantasies about that woman or any number of other women. The program became a source of controversy, as area subscribers and community members petitioned Time Warner to cease carrying the show.

A. *Time Warner's Indecency Policy*

In 1996, following the Supreme Court's decision in *Denver Area Educational Telecommunications Consortium, Inc. v. FCC*, 518 U.S. 727, 116 S.Ct. 2374, 135 L.Ed.2d 888 (1996), upholding the constitutionality of a provision of the Cable Act of 1992, 47 U.S.C. § 532(h) (1994), which allows cable operators to exercise limited editorial control over programs on leased access channels, *see* Part II.A, below, Time Warner adopted a written policy forbidding "indecent" material on leased access channels (the "Indecency Policy" or "Policy") in its

Rochester and Syracuse divisions ("TW Rochester" and "TW Syracuse" respectively).

The Indecency Policy required any program provider seeking use of leased access channel capacity to "certify in its application (a) that the program provider is responsible for the content of the programming; and (b) that the program provider will not submit for cablecast any programming that is obscene or indecent as defined herein." Time Warner "reserve [d] the right to determine whether programming exhibited or sought to be exhibited is indecent."...

B. *The Rejected LWS Programs*

In 1997, LWS submitted to Time Warner three episodes of "Life Without Shame," whose rejection by Time Warner prompted the present lawsuit. In January 1997, LWS submitted to TW Syracuse an episode entitled "The Best of Lookers." The program was filmed at a Syracuse adult club called "Lookers" and contained, *inter alia,* scenes of women dancing topless, fondling their breasts, pressing their breasts against customers' faces, or simulating acts of sex and masturbation. The episode also contained advertisements for various other nude and topless dance clubs in Syracuse, as well as advertisements for an "escort service" promising "we make house and hotel calls." One or more of the commercials showed women topless, contained lines such as "Bring your hard dicks down here," and depicted a topless woman performing a "lap dance" on Richter...

C. *The Present Action*

Following notification of Time Warner's refusal to telecast "The All Black Special," plaintiffs commenced the present action, principally seeking a judgment declaring that the application of Time Warner's Indecency Policy to the three rejected episodes violated plaintiffs' rights under the First Amendment and the Cable Act, and requesting preliminary and permanent injunctions forbidding Time Warner from engaging in pre-screening and censorship pursuant to the Policy. Pointing to the Cable Act's requirement that the terms of leased access use not be "unreasonable," 47 U.S.C. § 532(d) (1994), plaintiffs contended that Time Warner had violated that provision by failing to respond to requests for clarification of whether the Policy forbade depictions of topless women and by refusing to specify the parts of the rejected tapes it considered indecent in order to give programmers an opportunity to edit and resubmit modified versions of the tapes. With regard to "A Tribute to Violence," plaintiffs contended that the Act did not authorize Time Warner to ban programming other than that which violated its written Indecency Policy, and that the show did not violate the Policy because it contained no sexual content.

Plaintiffs sought a preliminary injunction requiring Time Warner to transmit "The Best of Lookers," "The All Black Special," and "A Tribute to Violence" in their entirety.

Plaintiffs also argued that if cable operators deem programming to be indecent, the Cable Act authorizes them to bar only the program, not the persons who provide the programs, and they requested an injunction against Time Warner's enforcement of its suspensions of LWS and a judgment declaring that the suspension provisions of the TW Indecency Policy violated the Act.

Time Warner opposed the requests for declaratory and injunctive relief and moved for judgment on the pleadings or for summary judgment dismissing the complaint. It contended that the First Amendment was not applicable because, *inter alia,* Time Warner is not a state actor. It contended that the Cable Act permitted it to refuse to air the three programs because they were "patently offensive" as judged by contemporary community standards in the Rochester and Syracuse areas...

In a comprehensive Decision and Order dated September 11, 1997 ("Decision"), the district court granted summary judgment dismissing most of plaintiffs' claims, but upheld their challenge to the suspension provisions. It dismissed the First Amendment claims on the ground that Time Warner was not a state actor because its contested action had not been "compelled by the State." Decision at 18. It dismissed plaintiffs' statutory challenges to Time Warner's rejections of "The Best of Lookers" and "The All Black Special" pursuant to its Indecency Policy, reasoning that the 1992 Act requires reviewing courts to accord a "presumption of reasonableness" to the decisions of cable operators, Decision at 31, that determinations of "indecency" are essentially factual in nature...

The court held that Time Warner's refusal to telecast "A Tribute to Violence" was likewise a reasonable exercise of Time Warner's general authority under the 1992 Act to refuse to transmit programming that is "filthy" or "indecent"...Decision at 35 (quoting Webster's Ninth New Collegiate Dictionary).

The district court also rejected plaintiffs' contentions that Time Warner's procedures with respect to its consideration of proffered programs were unreasonable. The court held that Time Warner had no obligation to "serve as assistant editors" in order to allow programmers to edit and resubmit rejected programs...

However, the court upheld plaintiffs' claims that the Indecency Policy's provision for suspensions of program suppliers, not just for the rejection of programming, violated the Cable Act.

The district court also found flawed the Indecency Policy requirement that programmers certify that they would "not submit for cablecast any programming that is obscene or indecent as defined herein" (Indecency Policy ¶ 4), given that the Policy defined "indecent programming" in terms of what "*the cable operator reasonably believes* describes or depicts" patently offensive material (Indecency Policy ¶ 2 (emphasis added)). The court found this certification requirement unreasonable because it required a programmer to guess how Time Warner would feel about his program and exposed him to a penalty for simply guessing wrong...

The district court dismissed all of plaintiffs' other claims. The final judgment "permanently enjoin[s defendants] from enforcing the suspension provisions of its written policy prohibiting broadcast of indecent material." These appeals followed.

II. DISCUSSION

On their appeal, plaintiffs challenge so much of the district court's judgment as dismissed their claims under the First Amendment and their claims asserting that Time Warner violated the Cable Act by rejecting the three programs in question and by not facilitating resubmission of the programs after modification. Time Warner, on its cross-appeal, challenges so much of the judgment as declares the suspension provisions unlawful and enjoins their application. For the reasons that follow, we reject both sides' challenges.

A. *The Statutory Provisions Governing Leased Access Channels*

Under 47 U.S.C. § 532(b) (1994), which was part of the 1984 Act, a cable operator is required to allocate a certain percentage of its system's capacity for leased access channels, *i.e.,* channels for commercial use by programmers not affiliated with the cable operator. Congress's stated purpose in requiring leased access channels was "to assure that the widest possible diversity of information sources are [*sic*] made available to the public from cable systems in a manner consistent with growth and development of cable systems." 47 U.S.C. § 532(a) (1994). Programmers using leased access channels may include commercial advertising in their programs and must pay a fee to the cable operator for use of the channel. Cable operators may also be required, by the franchising authority, to reserve a certain amount of channel capacity for "public, educational, or governmental use." *Id.* § 531(a). Public access channels are available at low or no cost to members of the public, and programs on those channels generally do not include commercial advertising.

The 1984 Act included two provisions with regard to editorial control over programs cablecast on leased access channels. It provided that "[a] cable operator shall not exercise any editorial control over any video programming [on leased access channels], or in any other way consider the content of such programming," 47 U.S.C. § 532(c)(2) (1994); and it provided that "the franchising authority" could prohibit or impose conditions on the transmission of material that "in the judgment of the franchising authority is obscene, or is in conflict with community standards in that it is lewd, lascivious, filthy, or indecent or is otherwise unprotected by the Constitution of the United States," 47 U.S.C. § 532(h) (1988).

In section 10(a) of the Cable Act of 1992, Congress amended § 532(h) to give cable operators limited authority to control editorial content of programs transmitted on leased access channels. *See* 1992 Act, Pub.L. No. 102-385, § 10(a), 106 Stat. 1460, 1486...

Consistent with this 1992-amended version of § 532(h), Congress in 1996 amended § 532(c)(2) (which theretofore had forbidden cable operators to exercise any editorial control over or to consider the content of programming on leased access channels), by adding the exception that "a cable operator may refuse to transmit any leased access program or portion of a leased access program which contains obscenity, indecency, or nudity," 47 U.S.C. § 532(c)(2) (Supp. II 1996).

In 1996, in *Denver Area Educational Telecommunications Consortium, Inc. v. FCC*, 518 U.S. 727, 116 S.Ct. 2374, 135 L.Ed.2d 888 ("*Denver Area*"), the Supreme Court rejected a facial challenge to the constitutionality of the 1992-amended version of § 532(h) that granted limited editorial control to cable operators. *See* 518 U.S. at 737-53, 116 S.Ct. 2374 (plurality opinion of Breyer, J.); *id.* at 819-26, 116 S.Ct. 2374 (Thomas, J., concurring in the judgment in part and dissenting in part). It was in the wake of the *Denver Area* decision that Time Warner adopted its Indecency Policy pursuant to § 532(h).

B. *Plaintiffs' Claims Under the First Amendment*

The First Amendment applies only to state actors. In order to establish a First Amendment claim against a private entity based on the entity's relationship to the state, a plaintiff must demonstrate, *inter alia,* "a sufficiently close nexus between the State and the challenged action of the regulated entity so that the action of the latter may be fairly treated as that of the State itself."...

Section 532(h) does not compel cable operators to exercise editorial control over leased-access-channel program content. Notwithstanding the language of the first sentence of subsection (h), stating that if the franchising authority or the cable operator judges the program to be obscene or in conflict with community standards, a leased-access-channel program "shall not" be transmitted or "shall" be transmitted only subject to conditions, 47 U.S.C. § 532(h) (1994), the second sentence of that subsection indicates that, with respect to cable operators, the subsection is permissive. That second sentence says "[t]his subsection shall *permit* a cable operator to enforce prospectively a written and published policy" of banning programs it reasonably believes to contain obscene or patently offensive matter as measured by contemporary community standards. *Id.* (emphasis added). Accordingly, in upholding § 532(h), the *Denver Area* Court described that subsection as merely permitting, not requiring, the cable operator to ban programs as to which it held such a reasonable belief. *See, e.g.,* 518 U.S. at 733, 745-46, 116 S.Ct. 2374 (plurality opinion of Breyer, J.); *id.* at 768, 771, 116 S.Ct. 2374 (Stevens, J., concurring); *id.* at 779, 116 S.Ct. 2374 (O'Connor, J., concurring in part and dissenting in part); *id.* at 783, 797, 116 S.Ct. 2374 (Kennedy J., concurring in part and dissenting in part). *See also Implementation of Section 10 of the Cable Consumer Protection and Competition Act of 1992,* 8 F.C.C.R. 998, 1003 (1993). The interpretation of § 532(h) as permissive is also supported by clear legislative history. Senator Helms, author of the amendment containing the language that would eventually be added to § 532(h), stated that "[t]he pending amendment merely gives cable operators the legal right to make that decision. The amendment does not require cable operators to do anything." 138 Cong. Rec. 985 (1992).

In the present case, the district court correctly ruled that there was no basis on which to infer that Time Warner's Indecency Policy or its treatment of LWS constituted state action. The fact that federal law requires a cable operator to maintain leased access channels and the fact that the cable franchise is granted by a local government are insufficient, either singly or in combination, to characterize the cable operator's conduct of its business as state action. Nor does it suffice that cable operators, in their management of leased access channels, are subject to statutory and regulatory limitations.

Plaintiffs argue that Time Warner is a state actor because cable operators and local franchising authorities act as joint venturers in the administration of leased access channels. But that conclusory assertion is not supported. The record offers no evidence that Time Warner and the municipal franchising authorities jointly administer leased access channels. Nor is there any suggestion that the franchise agreements reserve to the franchising municipalities control over Time Warner's editorial decisions. As indicated above, Time Warner itself is permitted by 47 U.S.C. § 532(h) (1994) and 47 U.S.C. § 532(c)(2) (Supp. II 1996) to refuse to transmit leased access programming that, in its judgment, is obscene, or is in conflict with community standards in that it is lewd, lascivious, filthy, or indecent. Time Warner presented evidence as to its formulation and implementation of the Indecency Policy; there is no indication in the record of any assistance from or supervision by municipal, state, or federal authorities, and plaintiffs presented no evidence of any governmental participation. Similarly, there is no evidence that Time Warner's determinations that the three shows in question were indecent were made with any input or influence from a government. Although Time Warner received complaints from civic leaders, there is no indication in the record that it received any order, instruction, or request for editorial control from the franchising municipalities or any other government.

In sum, plaintiffs presented no evidence from which a rational factfinder could infer joint action between Time Warner and any government with respect to the content of leased-access-channel programming. We conclude that the district court properly dismissed plaintiffs' First Amendment claims.

C. *Plaintiffs' Claims Under the Cable Act*

The Cable Act provides that "[a]ny person aggrieved by the failure or refusal of a cable operator to make channel capacity available for use pursuant to" § 532 may bring an action in federal court "to compel that such capacity be made available." 47 U.S.C. § 532(d) (1994). In such an action, the court may order appropriate relief if it "finds that the channel capacity sought by such person has not been made available in accordance with [§ 532], or finds that the price, terms, or conditions established by the cable operator are unreasonable." *Id.* The Act also provides that in such an action, "there shall be a presumption that the price, terms, and conditions for use of [leased access] channel capacity ... are reasonable and in good faith unless shown by clear and convincing evidence to the contrary." *Id.* § 532(f) (1994).

Plaintiffs contend that the district court erred in ruling that Time Warner's refusals to transmit the three episodes in question were permissible under the Cable Act. They argue principally that "The Best of Lookers" and "The All Black Special" could not properly be rejected because they do not contain depictions of oral sex, bestiality, or rape, and because the shows would have been telecast late at night with minimal risk that children would be watching; and they argue that "A Tribute to Violence" could not properly be rejected because it included no sexual or excretory depictions or descriptions. They also contend that Time Warner's refusal to identify for LWS the objectionable portions of the submitted programs, to facilitate editing and resubmission, was unreasonable. We disagree.

1. *Reasonableness of Rejection*

As detailed in Part II.A. above, by 1997, when plaintiffs submitted the episodes in question to Time Warner, the Cable Act allowed a cable operator to refuse to transmit on a leased access channel any program that "contains obscenity, indecency, or nudity," 47 U.S.C. § 532(c)(2) (Supp. II 1996); it allowed the operator to deny leased-channel access or to provide access "subject to conditions" if the proffered program "in the judgment of ... the cable operator is obscene, or is in conflict with community standards in that it is lewd, lascivious, filthy, or indecent or is otherwise unprotected by the Constitution of the United States," *id.* § 532(h) (1994)...

In amending § 532(h) in 1992, Congress sought to address, *inter alia,* "sexually explicit programs" such as "depict[ions of] men and women stripping completely nude," "explicit sex ads," "incest, beastiality [*sic*], even rape," "oral sex," and "strip shows,"

The FCC has noted that the Cable Act confers on cable operators "wide discretion to determine the manner in which they may enforce a policy of prohibiting indecent leased access programming." *Implementation of Section 10 of the Cable Consumer Protection and Competition Act of 1992,* 8 F.C.C.R. at 1002-03. Thus, although material that is patently offensive may be less so if shown in late-night hours when children are less likely to see it, *see, e.g., Denver Area,* 518 U.S. at 752, 116 S.Ct. 2374 (plurality opinion of Breyer, J.); *Pacifica II,* 438 U.S. at 750, 98 S.Ct. 3026, section 532(h) permits cable operators not only to confine indecent material to late-night programming but also permits them to prohibit such material entirely, *see Denver Area,* 518 U.S. at 746, 116 S.Ct. 2374 (plurality opinion of Breyer, J.).

Whether offensive material can be prohibited under § 532(h) depends, in large part, on its context. *See Denver Area,* 518 U.S. at 752, 116 S.Ct. 2374 (plurality opinion of Breyer, J.); *see also Pacifica II,* 438 U.S. at 750, 98 S.Ct. 3026; *Infinity Broadcasting Corp.,* 2 F.C.C.R. 2705, 2705 (1987) ("*Infinity I*") ("what is indecent 'is largely a function of context' and cannot adequately be judged in the abstract"). In addition, the FCC has noted that while the indecency concept does not justify a ban of an entire program because of "the isolated use of an offensive word," *Infinity I* 2 F.C.C.R. at 2705, neither need there be a constant stream of sexual or excretory depictions before a program may be banned, *see Pacifica Foundation, Inc.,* 2 F.C.C.R. 2698, 2699 (1987) ("*Pacifica III*"). That agency has declined to "attempt to provide [broadcasters] with a comprehensive index or thesaurus of indecent words or pictorial depictions that will be considered patently offensive," *Infinity Broadcasting Corp.,* 3 F.C.C.R. 930, 931-32 (1987) ("*Infinity II*"), and it has noted that the assertion that sexually-oriented programming involves merely innuendo or double entendre does not mean that it falls outside the category of the patently offensive and indecent. *See Infinity I,* 2 F.C.C.R. at 2705-06.

Within this framework, the district court properly concluded that there was no genuine issue of fact to be tried as to the reasonableness of Time Warner's rejection of the three LWS episodes in question. "The Best of Lookers" and "The All Black Special" included the scenes described in Part I.B. above, and plaintiffs did not dispute Time Warner's Rule 56 Statement assertion that those episodes contained such features as repeated nudity, including close-up camera shots of unclothed breasts and buttocks; simulated acts of sex and masturbation; advertisements for strip clubs, "escort" services, "1-800" telephone-sex hotlines, and stores selling sexual devices; and double-entendre highly suggestive of sexual acts, as well as repeated use of language such as "tits," "ass," "dick," and "shit." On this record, no rational factfinder could find that Time Warner's belief that "The Best of Lookers" and "The All Black Special" depicted sexual activities or organs in a patently offensive manner as measured by contemporary community standards was not reasonable.

Nor are we persuaded by plaintiffs' argument that Time Warner's rejection of "A Tribute to Violence" was not reasonable because that episode concerned only violence and not sex, for plaintiffs' factual premise is belied by the tape itself. In addition to being laced with advertisements for strip clubs and an "escort" service, the episode is replete with blatantly sexual innuendo. For example, in narrating one scene, Loce and Richter refer to a " 'Pedophile' organization." In the scene from "The Gore Gore Girls," the woman shown being savaged is wearing a partially see-through bikini; Loce repeatedly refers to her "ass"; and when the beaten woman lies bent over a table, Richter states, and Loce agrees, "that's my favorite position of a woman." Similarly, in the scene depicting the fight between amputees, Loce and Richter discuss Richter's penchant for amputees; and Richter states his view that "amputees are the best" and that "[u]ntil you've gone with an amputee, you haven't gone," and his rationale that with a woman "you don't have to hold the legs back."

Plaintiffs did not adduce any evidence from which a rational factfinder could find that Time Warner's rejection of "A Tribute to Violence" on the ground of indecency was not reasonable. No rational factfinder could fail to see the sexual connotations in "A Tribute to Violence," and neither the fact that its sexual content is less constant than in "The Best of Lookers" and "The All Black Special," nor the fact that it consists largely of double-entendres and innuendo rather the sexually oriented or scatological words used in "The Best of Lookers" and "The All Black Special," sufficed to undermine Time Warner's view of "A Tribute to Violence" as patently offensive under the prevailing community standards or to make rejection of the episode unreasonable.

We conclude that the district court properly ruled that plaintiffs were not entitled to either declaratory or injunctive relief requiring Time Warner to transmit the three episodes in question.

2. *The Reasonableness of Time Warner's Procedures*

Plaintiffs also contend that the district court erred in rejecting their claims that Time Warner's procedures are unreasonable because Time Warner does not identify for programmers what parts of the submission it deems obscene or indecent in order to allow the programmer to edit and resubmit the program. The district court rejected this claim on the ground that the Cable Act imposes no obligation on a cable operator to work with a programmer in the program editing process. We agree substantially for the reasons stated in the district court's Decision.

We note, in passing, however, that we do not regard the district court as having given Time Warner carte blanche to refuse even to consider programming that has been rejected, has thereafter been substantially edited to remove the obscene or patently offensive material, and is then resubmitted. The question of whether such a refusal would be permissible was not squarely presented. The Time Warner Indecency Policy, though containing (the now invalidated) provisions for the suspension of programmers who had submitted programs that Time Warner rejected pursuant to the Policy, did not state that a once-rejected program could not be edited to remove the offending material and then resubmitted. Nor did plaintiffs make any effort to resubmit any of the three rejected episodes. (Plaintiffs advised the district court that if the portions of "The Best of Lookers" and "The All Black Special" depicting topless women were removed, there would be little left.) And although the district court referred to the Time Warner Indecency Policy as not allowing resubmissions, the court's rationale for dismissing this claim was simply that the Cable Act gives cable companies "the right to censor leased access programs, not the obligation to serve as assistant editors to program providers" or the obligation "to work with program providers to ensure that material submitted to the company is decent." Decision at 30.

D. *The Suspension Provisions*

In its cross appeal, Time Warner contends that the district court erred in construing the Cable Act as not authorizing cable operators to suspend persons who have submitted indecent programming. TW argues that that interpretation of § 532 unduly restricts its flexibility in enforcing the Indecency Policy and that a practice of tape-by-tape review would be unduly expensive. We reject these contentions substantially for the reasons stated in the district court's Decision.

As discussed in the preceding sections, the editorial control given to cable operators under §§ 532(c)(2) and 532(h) is limited. As this Court has noted with respect to the public access counterpart to § 532(c)(2), *i. e.,* 47 U.S.C. § 531(e) (Supp. II 1996), a "refusal to broadcast ***all*** of [a programmer's] future programming," far from exercising limited control, would constitute "the strongest and broadest possible form of editorial control." *McClellan v. Cablevision of Connecticut, Inc.,* 149 F.3d 161, 168 n. 14 (2d Cir.1998) (emphasis in original). We see no indication that Congress, in fashioning § 532(h) to give a cable operator limited authority to prohibit "programming" described by that section, intended that section or any other to authorize the cable operator to impose a blanket ban on all programs (irrespective of content) of a given program supplier. Indeed, in requiring cable operators to provide leased access channels, Congress sought principally to assure the widest possible diversity of information sources on cable systems. *See* 47 U.S.C. § 532(a) (1994). A cable operator's exclusion of a given supplier would, instead, plainly limit the number of potential program sources. Finally, we see no indication that Congress meant to imply that a cable operator could reasonably believe any given program to be patently offensive solely because of its source. Nor does the present record suggest that Time Warner could be justified in such a belief with respect to LWS. As noted in Part I.B. above, LWS for a period of time submitted shows to TW Rochester that were not deemed indecent under TW's Indecency Policy.

In sum, we reject Time Warner's contention that the Act authorizes it to foreclose the submission of programs based solely on source, without regard to whether they contain material whose prohibition is authorized by §§ 532(c)(2) and (h)...

Finally, although Time Warner argues that a tape-by-tape review process will be unduly expensive, we note that § 532(c)(1) allows a cable operator to "establish, consistent with the purpose of [§ 532]" and with such rules as are prescribed by the FCC, "price, terms and conditions of [leased-access-channel] use which are at least sufficient to assure that such use will not adversely affect the operation, financial condition, or market development of the cable system." 47 U.S.C. § 532(c)(1) (1994). (*See also* Plaintiffs' brief on appeal at 40 (suggesting, as an "appropriate" approach, "a regime of fines or penalties to cover additional costs for a second screening").) In light of § 532 as a whole, we cannot conclude that Congress intended to permit cable operators to exclude program suppliers because of the expense of determining whether their products should be excluded in accordance with §§ 532(c)(2) and (h).

We conclude that the district court properly ruled that the suspension provisions violated the Act. Time Warner remains free in accordance with §§ 532(c)(2) and (h) to reject any program it reasonably believes is obscene or patently offensive as measured by contemporary community standards.

CONCLUSION

We have considered all of the parties' contentions in support of their respective appeals and have found them to be without merit. The judgment of the district court is affirmed.

QUESTIONS AND DISCUSSION

1. Here's a long quote from one of the author's law review articles on the subject of the implied covenant of good faith and fair dealing:

> [T]he linchpin behind looking for reality in Reality TV contracts is the seminal case of Wood v. Lucy, Lady Duff-Gordon, [222 N.Y. 88 (1917)]. Otis F. Wood sued Lucy, Lady Duff-Gordon for breach of an agreement signed in 1915, which allegedly gave Wood an exclusive right to place Lucy's endorsements on products. When Lucy herself placed the endorsements, Wood contended that he should receive a share of those profits. Lucy argued that the agreement was unenforceable because it did not impose obligations on both parties; thus, no duties were imposed on Wood. The trial judge interpreted the agreement as requiring Wood to exercise his "bona fide judgment." The judge thought bona fide judgment was sufficient to create an obligation to make the agreement enforceable. However, the appellate division unanimously reversed. Next, the court of appeals, by a 4-3 vote, reversed the Appellate Division and agreed with the trial judge. Noticeably, Justice Cardozo's opinion used the phrase "reasonable efforts" to describe Wood's obligations.
>
> The significance of the decision was that the judge sought to preserve some of the values of the past by requiring that the contracts be performed in good faith, the "bona fide judgment" required by the trial judge in Wood. The key characteristic of the new content for the old form was that the courts, not the parties or the market, would have the primary role in determining what was good faith. Consequently, the courts had both new focus for their deliberations (performance rather than obligation) and a new standard for judgment (good faith). The Lady Duff-Gordon good faith standard should direct the parties in a Reality TV contract to abstain from fraudulent misstatements that would result in false light damages to plaintiff/participant.

Champion, "...Reality TV Shines a False Light on Lady Duff-Gordon," 15 Seton Hall J. Sports & Ent. L. 27 (2005) (footnotes omitted). Should this implied covenant of good faith and fair dealing be the Bible for entertainment contracts?

2. Should there be civil (and criminal) penalties (both state and federal) to police bad behavior and stop "contract bullying" in entertainment contracts?

3. Look at the following TV/FCC/First Amendment/cable TV cases. Is there a bottom line of appropriate programming? Should there be? Remember Janet Jackson's Super Bowl wardrobe malfunction? (Ultimately the FCC was unable to fine the network.) What is good taste? If the moral of implied good faith and fair dealing controlled the TV business, would most of these problems wither and die?

In the antitrust case NCAA v. Board of Regents, 468 U.S. 85 (1984), the Supreme Court declared that the NCAA's football TV program was unlawful under a rule of reason analysis. The NCAA's TV package was an unreasonable restraint of trade. The NCAA's plan restricted the total number of football games an NCAA member could televise and also stopped member schools from selling TV rights except in accordance with the NCAA plans. This opinion immediately set the networks free to negotiate TV contracts with the major football schools. Should the TV package monies be distributed evenly among all Division 1A schools?

See also Red Lion Broadcasting Co. v. FCC, 395 U.S. 367 (1969) ("fairness doctrine" requires that each side of public issues presented by broadcasters to be given fair coverage); TBS v. FCC, 512 U.S. 622 (1994) (the Cable TV Consumer Protection & Competition Act of 1992 subjects the TV cable industry to rate regulation by the FCC; their "must carry" provisions earn intermediate scrutiny); and TBS v. FCC, 520 U.S. 180 (1997) (must carry provisions are consistent with First Amendment's free speech guarantee).

CHAPTER 6
RADIO

Radio these days is different. Employment contract remuneration is based on popularity and ratings. Popular radio shows will be syndicated. Talk shows, however, can be controversial. Popular satellite radio offers such programming a viable home. (Think Howard Stern.)

The Federal Communications Commission (FCC) controls the radio. The FCC is also the arbitrator of "good taste and high morals." In CBS v. U.S., 316 U.S. 407 (1942), CBS tried to enjoin the enforcement of an FCC order where the FCC and the Mutual Broadcasting System were permitted to invervene as defendants. The failure to comply with an FCC order that penalizes licensed radio stations, allows those stations to review the order under the Urgent Deficiencies Act, 28 U.S.C. §§ 1253, 2101, 2284, 2325. The radio network's standing to sue was based on the fact that the regulations purported to alter and adversely affect the network's contractual rights with the radio station's owners. The network sought to enjoin the FCC's order promulgating chain broadcasting regulations alleging that their affiliates were cancelling or threatening to cancel contracts in order to conform to FCC regulations, which would have caused irreparable injury. See also America Manufacturers Mutual Insurance Co. v. American Broadcasting-Paramount Theatres Inc., 87 S.Ct. 1 (1966) (radio broadcasting sponsorship contract entailed illegal "tying" arrangement).

PROUTY V. NATIONAL BROADCASTING CO.

District Court, D. Massachusetts
January 9, 1939
No. 39
26 F. Supp. 265

BREWSTER, District Judge.

This bill of complaint was filed September 17, 1938. Plaintiff concedes that it is a civil action and not an infringement suit brought under 17 U.S.C.A. § 25, and is, therefore, governed by the new Federal Rules of Civil Procedure, 28 U.S.C.A. following section 723c.

Defendant has moved to dismiss, under Rule 12(b)(6), for failure to state a claim upon which relief can be granted.

The question now presented, therefore, is whether the allegations of the complaint, if proved, would entitle the plaintiff to relief without the aid of section 25 of the Copyright Law.

Plaintiff has obviously endeavored to follow Rule 8(e) in stating her claim, and it not easy to summarize in a few words the allegations of the bill.

After alleging jurisdictional prerequisites, she says that she is the author and present owner of an original novel entitled 'Stella Dallas' and of the copyright of both the work and the title thereto; that the novel is in a uniform text known to the defendant.

In the third paragraph of her complaint she alleges facts which tend to show that the novel, as a work of art, has a present and potential value, adding that she has in contemplation the writing of a sequel in which the character 'Stella Dallas' will feature.

In the fourth paragraph, the alleged wrong of the defendant is set forth as follows: 'The respondent, in return for money compensation and in violation of the rights of the complainant and without the approval or consent of the complainant, is engaged in broadcasting throughout the United States and Canada and to reception throughout the world skits as episodes in the life of Stella Dallas in the character portrayed in said novel under that name and title. These are a degradation in artistic quality and harmonious consistency from the said novel or from any play based thereon. They are not an adaption, change, addition, subtraction, use or treatment of said novel or of any play based thereon. They are improvisations of a person or persons unknown to the complainant. They are of inferior artistic and commercial quality. In this way, the respondent is misappropriating the title 'Stella Dallas' and the complainant's rights therein and to the imaginatively created personality Stella Dallas and to the complainant's established goodwill developed by the complainant's successful authorship, to matter of such inferior grade as to imperil the further sale of said novel and of any sequel thereto, and the reputation of the complainant as the well known author of Stella Dallas and thereby to imperil the further sale of other works which the complainant has written and is writing, whose future sales is dependent on the continued maintenance of the high reputation as an author which the complainant now has.'

The plaintiff also by reference has incorporated the text of broadcasts made by the defendant since November 1, 1937. A demand to discontinue the broadcasts and a refusal are also alleged.

If it should appear that in these broadcasts the defendant had appropriated, without plaintiff's consent, the plot and principal characters of the novel, and that the use being made of her literary production was such as to injure the reputation of the work and of the author, and to amount to a deception upon the public, it may well be that relief would be afforded by applying well-recognized principles of equity which have been developed in the field known as 'unfair competition.'

It may be true, as the defendant contends, that on the pleadings it must be found that there is no competition between the plaintiff, as a writer of novels, and the defendant as a broadcasting station. The absence of the element of competition, however, is not necessarily fatal to the plaintiff's claim. Wall v. Rolls-Royce of America, Inc., 3 Cir., 4 F.2d 333; Yale Electric Corp. v. Robertson, Com'r of Patents, 2 Cir., 26 F.2d 972; Alfred Dunhill, of London, Inc., v. Dunhill Shirt Shop, Inc., D.C., 3 F.Supp. 487, Vogue Co. v. Thompson-Hudson Co., 6 Cir., 300 F. 509.

In Vogue Co. v. Thompson-Hudson Co., supra, the Court observed that unfair competition is only a 'convenient name for the doctrine that no one should be allowed to sell his goods as those of another. * * * There is no fetish in the word 'competition.' The invocation of equity rests more vitally upon the unfairness.' (Page 512.) It is the injury to the author and a fraud upon the reading public that constitute the real offense alleged. Until there has been a hearing upon the merits, when the Court will have before it the text of the broadcasts, it is impossible to determine whether the plaintiff is entitled to the relief for which she has prayed.

The motion to dismiss, therefore, is denied without prejudice to any defense that may be set up in answer to the merits.

WARING v.DUNLEA
E.D. North Carolina
January 25, 1939
26 F.Supp. 838

This case involves the famous band leader in the 1930s who had a unique, civilized style of orchestra music. Fred Waring sought to enjoin radio station WMFD from playing "certain electrical transcriptions of musical interpretations or renditions of complainant's orchestra" (at 2 F.Supp. 338, 339). A Notice appears on the record or electrical transcription that the record is to be used only on the Ford Motor Program and limited to such use on the part of the distributee. [Id.] The radio station was a distributee and the record was played on a program other than the Ford Motor Program. Fred Waring successfully enjoined the radio station from playing his orchestra's record where he had a property right in the orchestra's performance, and a corresponding right to prohibit its unauthorized public performance. Fred's orchestra for a consideration distributed his composition over the radio on a special program. The radio station played one of Fred Waring's musical numbers, without the permission of Fred Waring or the Ford Motor Company, and without being one of the licensees. The court held that Fred Waring had an interest in his unique renditions—"Music in the Waring Style."

COLUMBIA BROADCASTING SYSTEM, INC., v. UNITED STATES ET AL.
Supreme Court of the United States.
No. 1026
Argued May 1, 1942
Decided June 1, 1942
62 S.Ct. 1194, 86 L.Ed. 1563

Mr. Chief Justice STONE delivered the opinion of the Court.

The Federal Communications Commission, by its order of May 2, 1941, as amended by its order of October 11, 1941, promulgated regulations which purport to require the Commission to refuse to grant a license to any broadcasting station which enters into certain defined types of contract with any broadcasting network organization. These regulations, it is alleged, affect adversely appellant's contractual relations with broadcasting stations and impair its ability to carry on its business in maintaining and operating its nationwide broadcasting network. The regulations as amended on October 11, 1941, together with a supplemental 'minute' promulgated by the Commission on October 31, 1941, are set forth at the end of this opinion. The question for our decision is whether appellant is entitled to secure a judicial review of the order by a suit brought under § 402(a) of the Communications Act of 1934, 48 Stat. 1093, 47 U.S.C. § 402(a), 47 U.S.C. § 402(a), and the Urgent Deficiencies Act, 38 Stat. 219, 220, 28 U.S.C. § 47, 28 U.S.C. § 47.

Pursuant to § 402(a) appellant brought the present suit against the United States in the Southern District of New York, to enjoin enforcement of the Commission's order as contrary to the public interest and beyond the Commission's statutory authority, and on the further ground, if the order be deemed within that authority, that the statute is an unconstitutional delegation of legislative power by Congress in violation of Article I, § 1 of the Constitution, and operates to deprive appellant of property without due process of law in violation of the Fifth Amendment. The case was heard by a court of three judges, which permitted the Commission and the Mutual Broadcasting Company to intervene as defendants. It granted appellees' motion to dismiss the complaint for want of jurisdiction, D.C., 44 F.Supp. 688, and stayed the operation of the Commission's order pending direct appeal to this Court.

In 1938 the Communications Commission authorized an investigation 'to determine what special regulations applicable to radio stations engaged in chain or other broadcasting are required in the public interest, convenience, or necessity'. Extensive hearings were held by a committee consisting of three members of the Commission, at whose request the national networks, including appellant, intervened. In June, 1940, the committee made a report, on the basis of which briefs were filed and oral argument was presented before the full Commission by the three national networks and other interested parties. In May, 1941, the Commission issued its 'Report on Chain Broadcasting' and ordered the adoption of the regulations which, in their amended form, are the subject of the present controversy.

The relevant facts stated in the bill of complaint are as follows: Appellant or its predecessor has been engaged in the business of nationwide network or chain broadcasting since 1927. It has a large amount of physical property used in the business and has built up a valuable goodwill. For its broadcasts it maintains a staff of employees and expends large amounts for musicians and broadcasting performers. It has commitments by long-term contracts aggregating more than $4,000,000 for broadcasting expenditures, including those for the use of land and buildings and for the furnishing of news and broadcasting programs in the next few years. Appellant's total property devoted to its broadcasting business exceeds $18,000,000 in value; its earnings from the network exceeded $3,000,000 in both 1939 and 1940.

Chain broadcasting is the means by which radio programs are made available to all or a large part of the nationwide radio audience. It is defined by the Communications Act, 47 U.S.C. § 153(p), 47 U.S.C.A. § 153(p), as the 'simultaneous broadcasting of an identical program by two or more connected stations'. The chain broadcaster prepares radio programs, for which it engages performers in advance, and simultaneously broadcasts them over a large number of radio stations to which the programs are transmitted from some central point of origination by wire telephone lines leased by the broadcaster, here the appellant. The programs, which are prepared well in advance of the broadcast and given by persons employed for the purpose by appellant, are of two classes—commercial programs sponsored and paid for by advertisers, and sustaining programs furnished by appellant and not paid for by any advertiser.

Appellant's network comprises 123 stations in 122 cities in the United States. It is so operated as to enable ninety per cent of the radio audience of the United States to listen simultaneously to programs provided by appellant and broadcasted over these stations. Appellant owns and operates seven of the stations and leases an eighth, all licensed by the Commission. With the remaining 115 stations it enters into individual contracts usually for periods of five years, terminable in some instances by appellant on twelve months' notice. By these contracts appellant undertakes to furnish each station with an average of at least sixty hours per week of network sustaining and sponsored programs. The sustaining programs are furnished without charge, the station being free to use them or not as it chooses. Appellant undertakes to furnish the station with all commercial programs which the sponsor requests the station to broadcast and to pay the station a specified hourly rate for the use of its facilities in broadcasting such programs. Appellant agrees not to furnish its programs to other stations in the same city; the affiliated station, with exceptions not now material, agrees not to broadcast the program of any other network. Of critical importance in the present litigation is the stipulation of the affiliated station that it will, upon not less than twenty-eight days' notice from appellant, broadcast the sponsored or commercial program furnished to it by appellant for at least fifty 'converted' hours (averaging seventy-nine regular clock hours) per week.

These provisions of appellant's contracts are alleged to be indispensable to the maintenance and efficient operation of its network and to the existence of a strong and efficient network broadcasting system, and necessary to enable appellant to compete with other advertising media. On May 2, 1941 the Commission issued its order which, as amended by its order of October 11, 1941, promulgated the 'Chain Broadcasting Regulations' of which appellant complains, and which the Commission characterized in its Report as 'the expression of the general policy we will follow in exercising our licensing power'.[1] The regulations provide that no license shall be granted to a broadcast station having contracts with a network organization, containing any of several provisions which are characteristic of appellant's contracts with its affiliates. These included provisions by which the station is prevented from broadcasting the programs of any other network organization (3.101); or which prevent another station serving substantially the same area from broadcasting the network programs not taken by the station applying for license, or prevent another station serving a substantially different area from broadcasting any program of the network organization (3.102); or by which the station contracts for affiliation with the network for a period longer than two years (3.103); or by which the station 'options for network programs any time subject to call on less than 56 days' notice or more time than a total of three hours' within each of four specified segments of the broadcast day, the regulation declaring 'such options may not be exclusive as against other network organizations and may not prevent or hinder the station from optioning or selling any or all of the time covered by the option, or other time, to other network organizations' (3.104); or which prevent the station (a) from rejecting network programs which the station reasonably believes to be unsatisfactory or unsuitable or (b) from substituting for the network program a program of outstanding local or national importance (3.105).

After making its order of May 2, 1941, the Commission deferred its effective date until further order. By its order of October 11, 1941, the Commission fixed the effective date as November 15, 1941, and directed 'that the effective date of Regulation 3.106 with respect to any station may be extended from time to time in order to permit the orderly disposition of properties', and 'that the effective date of Regulation 3.107 shall be suspended indefinitely and any further order of the Commission placing said Regulation

3.107 in effect shall provide for not less than six months' notice and for further extension of the effective date from time to time in order to permit the orderly disposition of properties.'

The bill of complaint also alleges that the purpose and effect of the regulations are to prohibit station licensees from having agreements of the kind which appellant has with its affiliates; that prior to the order of May 2, 1941, it was the practice of the Commission to renew the licenses of stations annually and that the licensed stations have had a reasonable expectancy of the annual renewal of their licenses; that 115 licensed stations have such contracts with appellant expiring at various times between the original effective date of the regulations and December 31, 1947. It is alleged that when their current licenses expire, at the latest, and perhaps earlier through the revocation of existing licenses, such stations face the loss of their licenses if they perform or continue in force or renew any existing contracts containing the described provisions.

The bill alleges that since the stations fear the loss of their licenses, as a result of the regulations, they will not negotiate for or renew affiliation contracts containing such provisions. And because they fear the loss of their licenses the stations have threatened to cancel and repudiate their affiliation contracts, and many have notified appellant that they will not be bound by their contracts after the regulations become effective. As a consequence appellant's ability to conduct its business and maintain its public broadcasting service is seriously impaired and the regulations will make the operation of appellant's business more costly, reduce its earnings and render its property and business less valuable.

The bill of complaint was filed October 30, 1941. The following day the Commission promulgated a supplemental 'minute' setting up a procedure by which the validity of the regulations might be tested upon application for a license by an individual licensee. The minute declared that if a station wished to challenge the regulations the Commission would grant a temporary extension of its license until there had been a final court determination of the issues. In the event of such litigation, and if the validity of the regulations were sustained, 'the Commission will nevertheless grant a regular license to the licensee, otherwise entitled thereto, who has unsuccessfully litigated that issue, if the licensee thereupon conforms to the decision'.

An affidavit subsequently submitted by appellant in support of its motion for a temporary injunction states that since the Commission's minute of October 31st, appellant has continued to receive indications that its affiliates will cancel and repudiate their contracts and refuse to renew them, and has received no indication that the minute has or will have the effect of inducing stations to assume the burden of testing the validity of the regulations. Attached to the affidavit are letters from five affiliates, written after October

31st, indicating their intention not to be bound by the contracts. The affidavit also states appellant's belief that it would have received more such letters had it not been for its circulation of information concerning the pendency of this suit.

Accepting the allegations of the complaint as true, as for present purposes we must, it is evident that application by the Commission of its regulations in accordance with their terms would disrupt appellant's broadcasting system and seriously disorganize its business. As the bill alleges, station licenses have been renewable by the Commission annually, whereas appellant's contracts are for five year periods and many of them will survive the expiration of the existing licenses to the affiliated stations. Under Regulations 3.101, 3.102, 3.103 and 3.104, each affiliate must repudiate his contract or be denied the renewal of his license. In either case this would deprive appellant of the station's participation in its network, for which its contracts call.

Regulation 3.104 not only requires all options by appellant to be exercised on 56 days' rather than 28 days' notice as at present, but provides that no option time is exclusive of other networks, and thus allows to appellant no option time within which it can command the use of affiliated stations for any program for broadcasting on a national scale. These sections together thus operate to break down the network enterprise in which appellant and its affiliates are by their contracts cooperating, and to substitute a system in which every station is available to every network on a 'first come first served basis'.

The Commission concedes by its brief that as provided by § 312(a) 'Any station license may be revoked * * * because of conditions revealed by such statements of fact as may be required (of a licensee) from time to time which would warrant the Commission in refusing to grant a license on an original application'. Consequently the regulations by their terms, read in conjunction with § 312(a), expose licensees, who renew their affiliation contracts, to revocation proceedings by the Commission whenever upon a statement which the Commission may require it appears that the licensee has entered into an affiliation contract which the regulations proscribe.

A proceeding to set aside an order of the Commission under § 402(a) and the Urgent Deficiencies Act is a plenary suit in equity. Hence the questions raised by the motion to dismiss are whether the Commission's order is an 'order', review of which is authorized by § 402(a) of the Act, and if so whether the bill states a cause of action in equity. The suit cannot be maintained unless both questions are answered in the affirmative.

Section 402(a) makes applicable the provisions of the Urgent Deficiencies Act to 'suits to enforce, enjoin, set aside, annul, or suspend any order of the Commission' except orders 'granting or refusing an application for a construction permit for a radio station, or for a radio station license, or for renewal of an existing radio station license, or for modification of an existing radio station license, or suspending a radio operator's license'. Review of the orders excepted from § 402(a) is by appeal to the Court of Appeals of the District of Columbia under the provisions of § 402(b). See Scripps-Howard Radio, Inc., v. Federal Communications Comm., 316 U.S. 4, 62 S.Ct. 875, 86 L.Ed. —. Since the Commission's order neither grants, denies nor modifies any license, any review in advance or independently of an application for a station license must be under § 402(a), and then only if the Commission's order promulgating the regulations is an 'order' within the meaning of this section. The particular label placed upon it by the Commission is not necessarily conclusive, for it is the substance of what the Commission has purported to do and has done which is decisive. Powell v. United States, 300 U.S. 276, 284, 285, 57 S.Ct. 470, 474, 475, 81 L.Ed. 643; A.F. of L. v. Labor Board, 308 U.S. 401, 408, 60 S.Ct. 300, 303, 84 L.Ed. 347.

The Commission's investigation of the contractual relations between the networks and the stations, which resulted in the order now under attack, was for the stated purpose of prescribing regulations of such relationships. The order authorizing the investigation recited that the proceeding was taken under § 303(i) of the Act, which gives the Commission 'authority to make special regulations applicable to radio stations engaged in chain broadcasting'. Since the Commission is not in terms given authority to regulate contractual relations between the stations and the networks, regulation of them could be accomplished only by regulating licensed radio stations which participate in chain broadcasting. It was by regulations in terms applicable to such stations that the Commission sought to control their contractual relationships with the networks.

The order is thus in its genesis and on its face, and in its practical operation, an order promulgating regulations which operate to control such contractual relationships, and it was adopted by the Commission in the avowed exercise of its rule-making power. Such regulations which affect or determine rights generally even though not directed to any particular person or corporation, when lawfully promulgated by the Interstate Commerce Commission, have the force of law and are orders reviewable under the Urgent Deficiencies Act. Assigned Car Cases, 274 U.S. 564, 47 S.Ct. 727, 71 L.Ed. 1204; United States v. Baltimore & O.R. Co., 293 U.S. 454, 55 S.Ct. 268, 79 L.Ed. 587. And regulations of like character, by which the Communications Commission has prescribed generally the records and accounts to be kept by telephone companies subject to its jurisdiction, are similarly reviewable under § 402(a). American T. & T. Co. v. United States, 299 U.S. 232, 57 S.Ct. 170, 81 L.Ed. 142.

The regulations here prescribe rules which govern the contractual relationships between the stations and the networks. If the applicant for a license has entered into an affiliation contract, the regulations require the Commission to reject his application. If a licensee renews his contract, the regulations, with the sanction of § 312(a), authorize the Commission to cancel his license. In a proceeding for revocation or cancellation of a license, the decisive question is whether the station, by entering into a contract, has forfeited its right to a license as the regulations prescribe. It is the signing of the contract which, by virtue of the regulations alone, has legal consequences to the stations and to appellant. The regulations are not any the less reviewable because their promulgation did not operate of their own force to deny or cancel a license. It is enough that failure to comply with them penalizes licensees, and appellant, with whom they contract. If an administrative order has that effect it is reviewable and it does not cease to be so merely because it is not certain whether the Commission will institute proceedings to enforce the penalty incurred under its regulations for non-compliance. Assigned Car Cases, supra; American T. & T. Co. v. United States, supra.

The regulations are rules which in proceedings before the Commission require it to reject and authorize it to cancel licenses on the grounds specified in the regulations without more. If the regulations are valid they alter the status of appellant's contracts and thus determine their validity in advance of such proceedings. By striking them down by a determination proclaimed in advance that licenses shall be cancelled or refused because of a previous failure to comply with the regulations, they impose a penalty and sanction for noncompliance far more drastic than the fines customarily inflicted for breach of reviewable administrative orders.

Most rules of conduct having the force of law are not self-executing but require judicial or administrative action to impose their sanctions with respect to particular individuals. Unlike an administrative order or a court judgment adjudicating the rights of individuals, which is binding only on the parties to the particular proceeding, a valid exercise of the rule-making power is addressed to and sets a standard of conduct for all to whom its terms apply. It operates as such in advance of the imposition of sanctions upon any particular individual. It is common experience that men conform their conduct to regulations by governmental authority so as to avoid the unpleasant legal consequences which failure to conform entails. And in this case it is alleged without contradiction that numerous affiliated stations have conformed to the regulations to avoid loss of their licenses with consequent injury to appellant.

Such regulations have the force of law before their sanctions are invoked as well as after. When as here they are promulgated by order of the Commission and the expected conformity to them causes injury cognizable by a court of equity, they are appropriately the subject of attack under the provisions of § 402(a) and the Urgent Deficiencies Act. American T. & T. Co. v. United States, supra; Rochester Tel. Corp. v. United States, 307 U.S. 125, 59 S.Ct. 754, 83 L.Ed. 1147; Interstate Commerce Commission v. Goodrich Transit Co., 224 U.S. 194, 32 S.Ct. 436, 56 L.Ed. 729; Kansas City So. Ry. v. United States, 231 U.S. 423, 34 S.Ct. 125, 58 L.Ed. 296, 52 L.R.A., N.S., 1; Assigned Car Cases, supra;

Chicago, R.I. & P. Ry. Co. v. United States, 284 U.S. 80, 52 S.Ct. 87, 76 L.Ed. 177; United States v. Baltimore & O.R. Co., supra.

It is no answer to say that the regulations are addressed only of the Commission and merely prohibit it from granting—and authorize it to cancel—licenses in the case of all stations entering into such contracts, and that accordingly all stations are left free to enter into contracts or not as they choose. They are free only in the sense that all those who do not choose to conform to regulations which may be determined to be lawful are free by their choice to accept the legal consequences of their acts. Failure to comply with the regulations entails such consequences to the station owner and to appellant. These are the loss of the affiliated stations' licenses if they adhere to their contracts, and disruption of appellant's network through the declared unlawfulness of the contracts, if the regulations are valid.

The purposes sought to be accomplished by § 402(a) and the Urgent Deficiencies Act would be defeated if a suitor were unable to resort to them to avoid reasonably anticipated irreparable injury resulting from such legal consequences of the Commission's order, merely because the Commission as yet has neither refused to renew a license, as the regulations require, nor cancelled a license, as the regulations permit. Such an argument addressed to the form rather than the substance of the order was rejected in Powell v. United States, supra; cf. A.F. of L. v. Labor Board, supra, 308 U.S. 408, 60 S.Ct. 303, 84 L.Ed. 347. The Powell case likewise repudiates the suggestion that merely because the order is not in terms addressed to those whose rights are affected, they cannot seek its review. See also Western Pacific C.R. Co. v. Southern Pac. Co., 284 U.S. 47, 52 S.Ct. 56, 76 L.Ed. 160; Claiborne-Annapolis Ferry Co. v. United States, 285 U.S. 382, 52 S.Ct. 440, 76 L.Ed. 808.

The order here is not one, as the Government argues and as the court below seemed to think, where the complainant's rights are affected only on the contingency of future administrative action as in United States v. Los Angeles & S.L.R.R., 273 U.S. 299, 47 S.Ct. 413, 71 L.Ed. 651; cf. Rochester Telephone Corp. v. United States, supra, 307 U.S. 130, 59 S.Ct. 757, 83 L.Ed. 1147. As the Court declared in the Los Angeles case, 273 U.S. 309, 310, 47 S.Ct. 414, 71 L.Ed. 651, reviewable orders are 'an exercise either of the quasi judicial function of determining controversies or of the delegated legislative function of rate making and rule making'. And the Court pointed out that the 'so-called order' in that case did not 'determine any right or obligation' or change the plaintiff's 'existing or future status or condition', and that it was 'merely the formal record of conclusions reached after a study of data collected in the course of extensive research conducted by the Commission' and 'is the exercise solely of the function of investigation.'

Here the Commission exercised its rule-making power by adopting regulations whose operation is not made subject to future administrative determinations, save only as the Commission may be called on to decide in any given case whether a station's contract with a network is within the regulations. The regulations' applicability to all who are within their terms does not depend upon future administrative action. Instead they operate to control such action and to determine in advance the rights of others affected by it. The Commission gave its own recognition that such is their operation by its successive postponements of the effective date of the order for a period now expired, and by its suspension of Regulations 3.106 and 3.107, in order to enable the networks to dispose of their properties.

Of course the Commission was at liberty to follow a wholly different procedure. Instead of proclaming general regulations applicable to all licenses, in advance of any specific contest over a license, it might have awaited such a contest to declare that the policy which these regulations embody represents its concept of the public interest. As a matter of sound administrative practice, both the rule-making proceeding and the specific license proceeding undoubtedly have much to commend them. But they are by no means the same, nor do they necessarily give rise to the same kind of judicial review. Having adopted this order under its rule-making power, the Commission cannot insist that the appellant be relegated to that judicial review which would be exclusive if the rule-making power had never been exercised and consequently had never subjected appellant to the threatened irreparable injury.

The court below assumed that if appellant had any equitable cause of action, it must be prosecuted in an ordinary suit and not under the provisions of the Urgent Deficiencies Act. But we think this mistakes both the nature of the regulations and the purpose of suits under that Act, as incorporated in § 402(a). Such a cause of action obviously can arise only because of the operation of the regulations. The regulations are the effective implement by which the injury complained of is wrought, and hence must be the object of the attack. It is because they are an exercise of the rule-making power, and because they presently determine rights on the basis of which the Commission is required to withhold licenses and authorized to cancel them, that there is an order within the meaning of § 402(a) and the Urgent Deficiencies Act.

The Commission argues that since its Report characterized the regulations as announcements of policy, the order promulgating them is no more subject to review than a press release similarly announcing its policy. Undoubtedly regulations adopted in the exercise of the administrative rule-making power, like laws enacted by legislatures, embody announcements of policy. But they may be something more. When, as here, the regulations are avowedly adopted in the exercise of that power, couched in terms of command and accompanied by an announcement of the Commission that the policy is one 'which we will follow in exercising our licensing power', they must be taken by those entitled to rely upon them as what they purport to be—an exercise of the delegated legislative power—which, until amended, are controlling alike upon the Commission and all others whose rights may be affected by the Commission's execution of them. The Commission's contention that the regulations are no more reviewable than a press release is hardly reconcilable with its own recognition that the regulations afford legal basis for cancellation of the license of a station if it renews its contract with appellant.

Appellant's standing to maintain the present suit in equity is unaffected by the fact that the regulations are not directed to appellant and do not in terms compel action by it or impose penalties upon it because of its action or failure to act. It is enough that, by setting the controlling standards for the Commission's action, the regulations purport to operate to alter and affect adversely appellant's contractual rights and business relations with station owners whose applications for licenses the regulations will cause to be rejected and whose licenses the regulations may cause to be revoked. Chicago Junction Case, 264 U.S. 258, 266—268, 44 S.Ct. 317, 320, 68 L.Ed. 667; Western Pacific C.R. Co. v. Southern Pac. Co. supra; Claiborne-Annapolis Ferry Co. v. United States, supra; compare, in the case of an attack upon the validity of a statute, Truax v. Raich, 239 U.S. 33, 38, 39, 36 S.Ct. 7, 9, 60 L.Ed. 131, L.R.A.1916D, 545, Ann.Cas.1917B, 283; Pierce v. Society of Sisters, 268 U.S. 510, 45 S.Ct. 571, 69 L.Ed. 1070, 39 A.L.R. 468.

What we have said of the allegations of the complaint, and of the effect of the Commission's order if those allegations are sustained upon the trial, is enough to establish the threat of irreparable injury to appellant's business and to show also that the injury can not be avoided, as the Commission suggests, by appellant's intervention in proceedings upon applications for renewal of licenses by its affiliates or in proceedings to cancel their licenses, if and when such proceedings are instituted. Appellant has sufficiently alleged that the affiliates are cancelling or threatening to cancel their contracts in order to conform to the regulations. It is to avoid the irreparable injury which would result from such wholesale cancellations of its contracts, induced by the force of the regulations, that appellant makes its attack on them now rather than in later proceedings on the individual applications for licenses in those cases, if any, in which the stations are willing to seek licenses without complying with the prerequisites laid down by the regulations.

The issues in such a proceeding are not necessarily the same as the issues here. Intervention in it would afford appellant no assurance either of an adjudication of appellant's contentions or that the action of other stations would be governed by it. Moreover, if the Commission's order is as we hold a reviewable order, appellant is free to seek review under § 402(a). It is not thereby, as the court below seemed to think, improperly substituting a different procedure and court for that which Congress has prescribed for the trial of like issues so far as they may be raised on review of an order denying a license. Such issues may likewise be involved in a proceeding, upon the Commission's own motion, for modification or cancellation of a license, which concededly is reviewable under § 402(a). See Scripps-Howard Radio, Inc., v. Federal Communications Commission, supra. But review of the order by a licensee in such a proceeding affords no adequate remedy. If ever instituted, which is uncertain, it would come too late to save appellant from the injury wrought by the outlawry of its contracts.

Nor does the Commission's minute, filed after the present suit was brought, afford an adequate basis for requiring appellant to seek relief by intervention in a proceeding on application for a license reviewable under § 402(b). In that event the minute would not operate to broaden the issues involved in the renewal application. Nor would it afford a basis for restraining enforcement of the regulations as to other affiliated stations, pending adjudication of the validity of the regulations. Without full exploration of the subject, such as can be had only at the trial, we cannot say that the minute will afford a sufficient inducement to persuade the affiliated stations to cease cancellations and assume the initiative in litigating the validity of the regulations and of the contracts which they undertake to condemn. The affidavit filed in the court below on the application for a stay is to the contrary. And in any case we are of the opinion that there are no equitable principles by which the right of appellant, upon the showing made by its complaint and affidavit, to test the order under § 402(a) can justly be suspended to await action which the station owners may or may not take in assuming the burden of challenging the regulations.

We need not stop to discuss here the great variety of administrative rulings which, unlike this one, are not reviewable—either because they do not adjudicate rights or declare them legislatively, or because there are adequate administrative remedies which must be pursued before resorting to judicial remedies, or because there is no occasion to resort to equitable remedies. But we should not for that reason fail to discriminate between them and this case in which, because of its peculiar circumstances, all the elements prerequisite to judicial review are present. The ultimate test of reviewability is not to be found in an overrefined technique, but in the need of the review to protect from the irreparable injury threatened in the exceptional case by administrative rulings which attach legal consequences to action taken in advance of other hearings and adjudications that may follow, the results of which the regulations purport to control.

We conclude that the Commission's promulgation of the regulations is an order reviewable under § 402(a) of the Act, and that the bill of complaint states a cause of action in equity. The stay now in effect will be continued, on terms to be settled by the court below.

Reversed.

Mr. Justice BLACK took no part in the consideration or decision of this case...

THE MINUTE OF OCTOBER 31, 1941

The Commission today adopted the following minute setting forth the procedure that it will follow in applying the policies announced in the Chain Broadcasting Regulations:

If a station wishes to contest the validity of the Chain Broadcasting Regulations adopted in Docket No. 5060, or the reasonableness of their application to the particular station, its license will be set for hearing. In order to insure that the station may remain on the air and be in no way injured by any such Commission proceeding and appeal to court from a decision in such proceeding, the Commission will grant such licensee a temporary extension of its license, with renewals from time to time until there has been a final determination of the issues raised at such hearing. In the event of such litigation, and if the validity of the application of the Chain Broadcasting Regulations to such licensee is sustained by the courts, the Commission will nevertheless grant a regular license to the licensee, otherwise entitled thereto, who has unsuccessfully litigated that issue, if the licensee thereupon conforms to the decision.

The supplementary decision and order in Docket No. 5060 indefinitely suspended Regulation 3.107, relating to the operation of more than one network by a single network organization. No similar suspension was made of that portion of Regulation 3.106, relating to network operation of more than one standard broadcast station with substantially overlapping service areas. The Commission will postpone indefinitely any action to prevent such dual station operation if it is shown that the operation of two stations in any city is indispensable to the continued operation of two networks by a single network organization.

The adoption of the foregoing procedure is without prejudice to the rights of any person who may petition the Commission for modification or stay of the Chain Broadcasting Regulations.

Mr. Justice FRANKFURTER, dissenting.

Mr. Justice REED and Mr. Justice DOUGLAS join in this dissent.

AMERICAN MANUFACTURERS MUTUAL INSURANCE CO. V. AMERICAN BROADCASTING-PARAMOUNT THEATRES, INC.

Supreme Court of the United States
Aug. 1, 1966
87 S.Ct. 1

Memorandum of Mr. Justice HARLAN.

This is an application for a stay, pending certiorari, of the enforcement of a New York Supreme Court, 48 Misc.2d 397, 265 N.Y.S.2d 76, money judgment awarded against petitioners in an action for breach of a radio broadcasting sponsorship contract. The questions sought to be brought to this Court for review all relate to the state court's disallowance of a defense predicated on the alleged illegality of this contract under federal antitrust laws. Having carefully considered the papers on both sides, and mindful that what is here involved is a state judgment and state cause of action, I conclude that the requested stay should issue, conditioned, however, as hereafter indicated.

The claim that the contract in suit entailed a federally illegal 'tying' arrangement cannot be regarded as lacking in substance in light of Associated Press v. Taft-Ingalls Corp., 340 F.2d 753, cert. denied, 382 U.S. 820, 86 S.Ct. 47, 15 L.Ed.2d 66 and does not appear to be precisely controlled by any decision of this Court. The posture of federal law relating to the availability of the asserted antitrust defense in this contract action is to say the least highly debatable. See Continental Wall Paper Co. v. Voight & Sons Co., 212 U.S. 227, 29 S.Ct. 280, 53 L.Ed. 486; Bruce's Juices, Inc. v. American Can Co., 330 U.S. 743, 67 S.Ct. 1015, 91 L.Ed. 1219; Kelly v. Kosuga, 358 U.S. 516, 79 S.Ct. 429, 3 L.Ed.2d 475. And the view of the state court that it could render judgment for the respondent without adjudicating the merits of petitioners' antitrust defense also presents a federal question which cannot be deemed devoid of substance. In these circumstances I am unable to say that the case bears no reasonable chance of review by this Court.

I have also deemed it incumbent upon me to consider two further questions, although they have been little if at all pressed in respondent's papers. The first is the failure of petitioners to show what ultimate damage they will suffer by reason of having to pay the judgment pending certiorari. The second is the ambiguity that exists as to whether petitioners sought a stay pending certiorari from the state courts before coming to me. I conclude that neither of these points prevents issuance of the requested stay.

With respect to a case arising in the federal system it seems to be accepted that a party taking an appeal from the District Court is entitled to a stay of a money judgment as a matter of right if he posts a bond in accordance with Fed.R.Civ.P. 62(d) and 73(d), see In re Federal Facilities Realty Trust, 7 Cir., 227 F.2d 651, 655; 7 Moore, Federal Practice 62.06 (2d ed. 1955); 3 Barron & Holtzoff, Federal Practice and Procedure § 1374 (rules ed. 1958), and I perceive no substantial countervailing reason why at the certiorari stage this federal policy should not be applied to state cases presenting arguably substantial federal questions. As to the other question, I am disposed to accept Judge Van Voorhis' stay of judgment pending the making of this application as entailing sufficient compliance on the part of petitioners with this Court's Rule 27, and respondent does not argue to the contrary.

An order will issue staying enforcement of the New York judgment pending the timely filing of the petition for certiorari. Should such petition be so timely filed, this stay is to remain in effect pending the action of this Court on such petition. In the event the petition is denied, this stay shall terminate automatically. Should the petition for writ of certiorari be granted, this stay is to remain in effect pending the issuance of the mandate of this Court. This stay is conditioned upon the posting of a good and sufficient surety bond in the principal amount of the judgment and providing for costs, interest and damages for delay. Compare Supreme Court Rule 18. Such bond is to be posted with and approved by the Supreme Court of New York County, or a judge thereof, and when so posted and approved to be filed with the clerk of that court.

In reaching this decision I imply no view whatever upon any phase of the ultimate merits of the underlying controversy.

COMMUNICATIONS ACT OF 1934

An Act to provide for the regulation of interstate and foreign communication by wire or radio, and for other purposes.

Be it enacted by the Senate and House of Representatives of the United States of America in Congress assembled.

TITLE I—GENERAL PROVISIONS

SEC. 1. [47 U.S.C. 151] PURPOSES OF ACT, CREATION OF FEDERAL COMMUNICATIONS COMMISSION.

For the purpose of regulating interstate and foreign commerce in communication by wire and radio so as to make available, so far as possible, to all the people of the United States, without discrimination on the basis of race, color, religion, national origin, or sex, a rapid, efficient, Nationwide, and world-wide wire and radio communication service with adequate facilities at reasonable charges, for the purpose of the national defense, for the purpose of promoting safety of life and property through the use of wire and radio communication, and for the purpose of securing a more effective execution of this policy by centralizing authority heretofore granted by law to several agencies and by granting additional authority with respect to interstate and foreign commerce in wire and radio communication, there is hereby created a commission to be known as the "Federal Communications Commission," which shall be constituted as hereinafter provided, and which shall execute and enforce the provisions of this Act.

SEC. 2. [47 U.S.C. 152] APPLICATION OF ACT.

(a) The provisions of this Act shall apply to all interstate and foreign communication by wireor radio and all interstate and foreign transmission of energy by radio, which originates and/or is received within the United States, and to all persons engaged within the United States in such communication or such transmission of energy by radio, and to the licensing and regulating of all radio stations as hereinafter provided; but it shall not apply to persons engaged in wire or radio communication or transmission in the Canal Zone, or to wire or radio communication or transmission wholly within the Canal Zone. The provisions of this Act shall apply with respect to cable service, to all persons engaged within the United States in providing such service, and to the facilities of cable operators which relate to such service, as provided in title VI.

(b) Except as provided in sections 223 through 227, inclusive, and section 332, and subjectto the provisions of section 301 and title VI, nothing in this Act shall be construed to apply or to give the Commission jurisdiction with respect to (1) charges, classifications, practices, services, facilities, or regulations for or in connection with intrastate communication service by wire or radio of any carrier, or (2) any carrier engaged in interstate or foreign communication solely through physical connection with the facilities of another carrier not directly or indirectly controlling or controlled by, or under direct or indirect common control with such carrier, or (3) any carrier engaged in interstate or foreign communication solely through connection by radio, or by wire and radio, with facilities, located in an adjoining State or in Canada or Mexico (where they adjoin the State in which the carrier is doing business), of another carrier not directly or indirectly controlling or controlled by, or under direct or indirect common control with such carrier, or (4) any carrier to which clause (2) or clause (3) would be applicable except for furnishing interstate mobile radio communication service or radio communication service to mobile stations on land vehicles in Canada or Mexico; except that sections 201 through 205 of this Act, both inclusive, shall, except as otherwise provided therein, apply to carriers described in clauses (2), (3), and (4).

SEC. 3. [47 U.S.C. 153] DEFINITIONS.

For the purposes of this Act, unless the context otherwise requires—

(1) AFFILIATE.—The term "affiliate" means a person that (directly or indirectly) owns or controls, is owned or controlled by, or is under common ownership or control with, another person. For purposes of this paragraph, the term "own" means to own an equity interest (or the equivalent thereof) of more than 10 percent.

(2) AMATEUR STATION.—The term "amateur station" means a radio station operated by a duly authorized person interested in radio technique solely with a personal aim and without pecuniary interest.

(3) AT&T CONSENT DECREE.—The term "AT&T Consent Decree" means the order entered August 24, 1982, in the antitrust action styled United States v. Western Electric, Civil Action No. 82-0192, in the United States District Court for the District of Columbia, and includes any judgment or order with respect to such action entered on or after August 24, 1982.

(4) BELL OPERATING COMPANY.—The term "Bell operating company"—

(A) means any of the following companies: Bell Telephone Company ofNevada, Illinois Bell Telephone Company, Indiana Bell Telephone Company, Incorporated, Michigan Bell Telephone Company, New England Telephone and Telegraph Company, New Jersey Bell Telephone Company, New York Telephone Company, U S West Communications Company, South Central Bell Telephone

Company, Southern Bell Telephone and Telegraph Company, Southwestern Bell Telephone Company, The Bell Telephone Company of Pennsylvania, The Chesapeake and Potomac Telephone Company, The Chesapeake and Potomac Telephone Company of Maryland, The Chesapeake and Potomac Telephone Company of Virginia, The Chesapeake and Potomac Telephone Company of West Virginia, The Diamond State Telephone Company, The Ohio Bell Telephone Company, The Pacific Telephone and Telegraph Company, or Wisconsin Telephone Company; and

(B) includes any successor or assign of any such company that provides wireline telephone exchange service; but

(C) does not include an affiliate of any such company, other than an affiliatedescribed in subparagraph (A) or (B).

(5) BROADCAST STATION.—The term "broadcast station," "broadcasting station," or "radio broadcast station" means a radio station equipped to engage in broadcasting as herein defined.

(6) BROADCASTING.—The term "broadcasting " means the dissemination of radio communications intended to be received by the public, directly or by the intermediary of relay stations.

(7) CABLE SERVICE.—The term "cable service" has the meaning given such term in section 602.

(8) CABLE SYSTEM.—The term "cable system" has the meaning given such term in section 602.

(9) CHAIN BROADCASTING.—The term "chain broadcasting" means simultaneous broadcasting of an identical program by two or more connected stations.

(10) COMMON CARRIER.—The term "common carrier " or "carrier" means any person engaged as a common carrier for hire, in interstate or foreign communication by wire or radio or in interstate or foreign radio transmission of energy, except where reference is made to common carriers not subject to this Act; but a person engaged in radio broadcasting shall not, insofar as such person is so engaged, be deemed a common carrier.

(11) CONNECTING CARRIER.—The term "connecting carrier" means a carrier described in clauses (2), (3), or (4) of section 2(b).

(12) CONSTRUCTION PERMIT.—The term "construction permit" or "permit for construction" means that instrument of authorization required by this Act or the rules and regulations of the Commission made pursuant to this Act for the construction of a station, or the installation of apparatus, for the transmission of energy, or communications, or signals by radio, by whatever name the instrument may be designated by the Commission.

(13) CORPORATION.—The term "corporation" includes any corporation, joint-stock company, or association.

(14) CUSTOMER PREMISES EQUIPMENT.—The term "customer premises equipment" means equipment employed on the premises of a person (other than a carrier) to originate, route, or terminate telecommunications.

(15) DIALING PARITY.—The term "dialing parity" means that a person that is not an affiliate of a local exchange carrier is able to provide telecommunications services in such a manner that customers have the ability to route automatically, without the use of any access code, their telecommunications to the telecommunications services provider of the customer's designation from among 2 or more telecommunications services providers (including such local exchange carrier).

(16) EXCHANGE ACCESS.—The term "exchange access" means the offering of access to telephone exchange services or facilities for the purpose of the origination or termination of telephone toll services.

(17) FOREIGN COMMUNICATION.—The term "foreign communication" or "foreign transmission" means communication or transmission from or to any place in the United States to or from a foreign country, or between a station in the United States and a mobile station located outside the United States.

(18) GREAT LAKES AGREEMENT.—The term "Great Lakes Agreement" means the Agreement for the Promotion of Safety on the Great Lakes by Means of Radio in force and the regulations referred to therein.

(19) HARBOR.—The term "harbor" or "port" means any place to which ships may resort for shelter or to load or unload passengers or goods, or to obtain fuel, water, or supplies. This term shall apply to such places whether proclaimed public or not and whether natural or artifical.

(20) INFORMATION SERVICE.—The term "information service" means the offering of a capability for generating, acquiring, storing, transforming, processing, retrieving, utilizing, or making available information via telecommunications, and includes electronic publishing, but does not include any use of any such capability for the management, control, or operation of a telecommunications system or the management of a telecommunications service.

(21) INTERLATA SERVICE.—The term "interLATA service" means telecommunications between a point located in a local access and transport area and a point located outside such area.

(22) INTERSTATE COMMUNICATION.—The term "interstate communication" or "interstate transmission" means communication or transmission (A) from any State, Territory, or possession of the United States (other than the Canal Zone), or the District of Columbia, to any other State, Territory, or possession of the United States (other than the Canal Zone), or the District of Columbia, (B) from or to the United States to or from the Canal Zone, insofar as such communication or transmission takes place within the United States, or (C) between points within the United States but through a foreign country; but

shall not, with respect to the provisions of title II of this Act (other than section 223 thereof), include wire or radio communication between points in the same State, Territory, or possession of the United States, or the District of Columbia, through any place outside thereof, if such communication is regulated by a State commission.

(23) LAND STATION.—The term "land station" means a station, other than a mobile station, used for radio communication with mobile stations.

(24) LICENSEE.—The term "licensee" means the holder of a radio station license granted or continued in force under authority of this Act.

(25) LOCAL ACCESS AND TRANSPORT AREA.—The term "local access and transport area" or "LATA" means a contiguous geographic area—

(A) established before the date of enactment of the Telecommunications Actof 1996 by a Bell operating company such that no exchange area includes points within more than 1 metropolitan statistical area, consolidated metropolitan statistical area, or State, except as expressly permitted under the AT&T Consent Decree; or

(B) established or modified by a Bell operating company after such date ofenactment and approved by the Commission.

(26) LOCAL EXCHANGE CARRIER.—The term "local exchange carrier" means any person

that is engaged in the provision of telephone exchange service or exchange access. Such term does not include a person insofar as such person is engaged in the provision of a commercial mobile service under section 332(c), except to the extent that the Commission finds that such service should be included in the definition of such term.

(27) MOBILE SERVICE.—The term "mobile service" means a radio communication service carried on between mobile stations or receivers and land stations, and by mobile stations communicating among themselves, and includes (A) both one-way and two-way radio communication services, (B) a mobile service which provides a regularly interacting group of base, mobile, portable, and associated control and relay stations (whether licensed on an individual, cooperative, or multiple basis) for private one-way or two-way land mobile radio communications by eligible users over designated areas of operation, and (C) any service for which a license is required in a personal communications service established pursuant to the proceeding entitled "Amendment to the Commission's Rules to Establish New Personal Communications Services" (GEN Docket No. 90-314; ET Docket No. 92-100), or any successor proceeding.

(28) MOBILE STATION.—The term "mobile station" means a radio-communication station capable of being moved and which ordinarily does move.

(29) NETWORK ELEMENT.—The term "network element" means a facility or equipment used in the provision of a telecommunications service. Such term also includes features, functions, and capabilities that are provided by means of such facility or equipment, including subscriber numbers, databases, signaling systems, and information sufficient for billing and collection or used in the transmission, routing, or other provision of a telecommunications service.

(30) NUMBER PORTABILITY.—The term "number portability" means the ability of users of telecommunications services to retain, at the same location, existing telecommunications numbers without impairment of quality, reliability, or convenience when switching from one telecommunications carrier to another.

(31)(A) OPERATOR.—The term "operator" on a ship of the United States means, for the purpose of parts II and III of title III of this Act, a person holding a radio operator 's license of the proper class as prescribed and issued by the Commission.

(B) "Operator" on a foreign ship means, for the purpose of part II of title III of this Act, a person holding a certificate as such of the proper class complying with the provision of the radio regulations annexed to the International Telecommunication Convention in force, or complyng with an agreement or treaty between the United States and the country in which the ship is registered.

(32) PERSON.—The term "person" includes an individual, partnership, association, joint-stock company, trust, or corporation.

(33) RADIO COMMUNICATION.—The term "radio communication" or "communication by radio" means the transmission by radio of writing, signs, signals, pictures, and sounds of all kinds, including all instrumentalities, facilities, apparatus, and services (among other things, the receipt, forwarding, and delivery of communications) incidental to such transmission.

(34)(A) RADIO OFFICER.—The term "radio officer" on a ship of the United States means, for the purpose of part II of title III of this Act, a person holding at least a first or second clase radiotelegraph operator 's license as prescribed and issued by the Commission. When such person is employed to operate a radiotelegraph station aboard a ship of the United States, he is also required to be licensed as a "radio officer" in accordance with the Act of May 12, 1948 (46 U.S.C. 229a-h).

(B) "Radio officer" on a foreign ship means, for the purpose of part II of title III of this Act, a person holding at least a first or second class radiotelegraph operator 's certificate complying with the provisions of the radio regulations annexed to the International Telecommunication Convention in force.

(35) RADIO STATION.—The term "radio station" or "station" means a station equipped to engage in radio communication or radio transmission of energy.

(36) RADIOTELEGRAPH AUTO ALARM.—The term "radiotelegraph auto alarm" on a ship of the United States subject to the provisions of part II of title

III of this Act means an automatic alarm receiving apparatus which responds to the radiotelegraph alarm signal and has been approved by the Commission. "Radiotelegraph auto alarm" on a foreign ship means an automatic alarm receiving apparatus which responds to the radiotelegraph alarm signal and has been approved by the government of the country in which the ship is registered : Provide, That the United States and the country in which the ship is registered are parties to the same treaty, convention, or agreement prescribing the requirements for such apparatus. Nothing in this Act or in any other provision of law shall be construed to require the recognition of a radiotelegraph auto alarm as complying with part II of title III of this Act, on a foreign ship subject to such part, where the country in which the ship is registered and the United States are not parties to the same treaty, convention, or agreements prescribing the requirements for such apparatus.

(37) RURAL TELEPHONE COMPANY.—The term "rural telephone company" means a local exchange carrier operating entity to the extent that such entity—

(A) provides common carrier service to any local exchange carrier study areathat does not include either—

(i) any incorporated place of 10,000 inhabitants or more, or any partthereof, based on the most recently available population statistics of the Bureau of the Census; or

(ii) any territory, incorporated or unincorporated, included in anurbanized area, as defined by the Bureau of the Census as of August 10, 1993;

(B) provides telephone exchange service, including exchange access, to fewerthan 50,000 access lines;

(C) provides telephone exchange service to any local exchange carrier studyarea with fewer than 100,000 access lines; or

(D) has less than 15 percent of its access lines in communities of more than50,000 on the date of enactment of the Telecommunications Act of 1996.

(38) SAFETY CONVENTION.—The term "safety convention" means the International Convention for the Safety of Life at Sea in force and the regulations referred to therein.

(39)(A) SHIP.—The term "ship" or "vessel" includes every description of watercraft or

other artificial contrivance, except aircraft, used or capable of being used as a means of transportation on water, whether or not it is actually afloat.

(B) A ship shall be considered a passenger ship if it carries or is licensed or certificatedto carry more than twelve passengers.

(C) A cargo ship means any ship not a passenger ship.

(D) A passenger is any person carried on board a ship or vessel except (1) the officersand crew actually employed to man and operate the ship, (2) persons employed to carry on the business of the ship, and (3) persons on board a ship when they are carried, either because of the obligation laid upon the master to carry shipwrecked, distressed, or other persons in like or similar situations or by reason of any circumstance over which neither the master, the owner, nor the charterer (if any) has control.

(E) "Nuclear ship" means a ship provided with a nuclear powerplant.

(40) STATE.—The term "State" includes the District of Columbia and the Territories and possessions.

(41) STATE COMMISSION.—The term "State commission" means the commission, board, or official (by whatever name designated) which under the laws of any State has regulatory jurisdiction with respect to intrastate operations of carriers.

(42) STATION LICENSE.—The term "station license," "radio station license," or "license" means that instrument of authorization required by this Act or the rules and regulations of the Commission made pursuant to this Act, for the use or operation of apparatus for transmission of energy, or communications, or signals by radio by whatever name the instrument may be designated by the Commission.

(43) TELECOMMUNICATIONS.—The term "telecommunications" means the transmission, between or among points specified by the user, of information of the user 's choosing, without change in the form or content of the information as sent and received.

(44) TELECOMMUNICATIONS CARRIER.—The term "telecommunications carrier" means any provider of telecommunications services, except that such term does not include aggregators of telecommunications services (as defined in section 226). A telecommunications carrier shall be treated as a common carrier under this Act only to the extent that it is engaged in providing telecommunications services, except that the Commission shall determine whether the provision of fixed and mobile satellite service shall be treated as common carriage.

(45) TELECOMMUNICATIONS EQUIPMENT.—The term "telecommunications equipment" means equipment, other than customer premises equipment, used by a carrier to provide telecommunications services, and includes software integral to such equipment (including upgrades).

(46) TELECOMMUNICATIONS SERVICE.—The term "telecommunications service" means the offering of telecommunications for a fee directly to the public, or to such classes of users as to be effectively available directly to the public, regardless of the facilities used.

(47) TELEPHONE EXCHANGE SERVICE.—The term "telephone exchange service" means (A) service within a telephone exchange, or within a connected system of telephone exchanges within the same exchange area operated to furnish to subscribers intercommunicating service of the character ordinarily furnished by a single exchange, and which is covered by the exchange service charge, or (B) comparable service provided through a system of switches,

transmission equipment, or other facilities (or combination thereof) by which a subscriber can originate and terminate a telecommunications service.

(48) TELEPHONE TOLL SERVICE.—The term "telephone toll service" means telephone service between stations in different exchange areas for which there is made a separate charge not included in contracts with subscribers for exchange service.

(49) TRANSMISSION OF ENERGY BY RADIO.—The term "transmission of energy by radio" or "radio transmission of energy" includes both such transmission and all instrumentalities, facilities, and services incidental to such transmission.

(50) UNITED STATES.—The term "United States" means the several States and Territories, the District of Columbia, and the possessions of the United States, but does not include the Canal Zone.

(51) WIRE COMMUNICATION.—The term "wire communication" or "communication by wire" means the transmission of writing, signs, signals, pictures, and sounds of all kinds by aid of wire, cable, or other like connection between the points of origin and reception of such transmission, including all instrumentalities, facilities, apparatus, and services (among other things, the receipt, forwarding, and delivery of communications) incidental to such transmission.

TITLE II—COMMON CARRIERS

PART I—COMMON CARRIER REGULATION

SEC. 201. [47 U.S.C. 201] SERVICE AND CHARGES.

(a) It shall be the duty of every common carrier engaged in interstate orforeign communication by wire or radio to furnish such communication service upon reasonable request therefor; and, in accordance with the orders of the Commission, in cases where the Commission, after opportunity for hearing, finds such action necessary or desirable in the public interest, to establish physical connections with other carriers, to establish through routes and charges applicable thereto and the divisions of such charges, and to establish and provide facilities and regulations for operating such through routes.

(b) All charges, practices, classifications, and regulations for and inconnection with such communication service, shall be just and reasonable, and any such charge, practice, classification, or regulation that is unjust or unreasonable is hereby declared to be unlawful: *Provided*, That communications by wire or radio subject to this Act may be classified into day, night, repeated, unrepeated, letter, commercial, press, Government and such other classes as the Commission may decide to be just and reasonable, and different charges may be made for the different classes of comunications: *Provided further*, That nothing in this Act or in any other provision of law shall be construed to prevent a common carrier subject to this Act from entering into or operating under any contract with any common carrier not subject to this Act, for the exchange of their services, if the Commission is of the opinion that such contract is not contrary to the public interest: *Provided further*, That nothing in this Act or in any other provision of law shall prevent a common carrier subject to this Act from furnishing reports of positions of ships at sea to newspapers of general circulation, either at a nominal charge or without charge, provided the name of such common carrier is displayed along with such ship position reports. The Commissioner may prescribe such rules and regulations as may be necessary in the public interest to carry out the provisions of this Act.

SEC. 202. [47 U.S.C. 202] DISCRIMINATION AND PREFERENCES.

(a) It shall be unlawful for any common carrier to make any unjust orunreasonable discrimination in charges, practices, classifications, regulations, facilities, or services for or in connection with like communication service, directly or indirectly, by any means or device, or to make or give any undue or unreasonable preference or advantage to any particular person, class of persons, or locality, or to subject any particular person, class of persons, or locality to any undue or unreasonable prejudice or disadvantage.

(b) Charges or services, whenever referred to in this Act, include chargesfor, or services in connection with, the use of common carrier lines of communication, whether derived from wire or radio facilities, in chain broadcasting or incidental to radio communication of any kind.

Any carrier who knowingly violates the provisions of this section shall forfeit to the United States the sum of $6,000 for each such offense and $300 for each and every day of the continuance of such offense.

SEC. 204. [47 U.S.C. 204] HEARING AS TO LAWFULNESS OF NEW CHARGES; SUSPENSION.

(a)(1) Whenever there is filed with the Commission any new or revised charge, classification, regulation, or practice, the Commission may either upon complaint or upon its own initiative without complaint, upon reasonable notice, enter upon a hearing concerning the lawfulness thereof; and pending such hearing and the decision thereon the Commission, upon delivering to the carrier or carriers affected thereby a statement in writing of its reasons for such suspension, may suspend the operation of such charge, classification, regulation, or practice, in whole or in part but not for a longer period than five months beyond the time when it would otherwise go into effect; and after full hearing the Commission may make such order with reference thereto as would be proper in a proceeding initiated after such charge, classification, regulation, or practice had become effective. If the proceeding has not been concluded and an order made within the period of the suspension, the proposed new or revised charge, classification, regulation, or practice shall go into effect at the end of such period; but in case of a proposed charge for a new service or a revised charge, the Commission may by order require the interested carrier or carriers to keep accurate account of all amounts received by reason of such charge for a new service or revised charge, specifying by whom and in whose behalf such amounts are paid, and upon completion of the hearing and decision may by further order require the interested carrier or carriers to refund, with interest, to the persons in whose behalf such amounts were paid, such portion of such charge for a new service or revised charges as by its decision shall be found not justified. At any hearing involving a new or revised charge, or a proposed new or revised charge, the burden of proof to show that the new or revised charge, or proposed charge, is just and reasonable shall be upon the carrier, and the Commission shall give to the hearing and decision of such questions preference over all other questions pending before it and decide the same as speedily as possible.

(2)(A) Except as provided in subparagraph (B), the Commission shall, with respect to any hearing under this section, issue an order concluding such hearing within 5 months after the date that the charge, classification, regulation, or practice subject to the hearing becomes effective.

(B) The Commission shall, with respect to any such hearing initiated priorto the date of enactment of this paragraph, issue an order concluding the hearing not later than 12 months after such date of enactment.

(C) Any order concluding a hearing under this section shall be a final orderand may be appealed under section 402(a).

(3) A local exchange carrier may file with the Commission a new or
revised charge, classification, regulation, or practice on a streamlined basis. Any such charge, classification, regulation, or practice shall be deemed lawful and shall be effective 7 days (in the case of a reduction in rates) or 15 days (in the case of an increase in rates) after the date on which it is filed with the Commission unless the Commission takes action under paragraph (1) before the end of that 7-day or 15-day period, as is appropriate.

(b) Notwithstanding the provisions of subsection (a) of this section, the Commission may allow part of a charge, classification, regulation, or practice to go into effect, based upon a written showing by the carrier or carriers affected, and an opportunity for written comment thereon by affected persons, that such partial authorization is just, fair, and reasonable. Additionally, or in combination with a partial authorization, the Commission, upon a similar showing, may allow all or part of a charge, classification, regulation, or practice to go into effect on a temporary basis pending further order of the Commission. Authorizations of temporary new or increased charges may include an accounting order of the type provided for in subsection (a).

SEC. 211. [47 U.S.C. 211] COPIES OF CONTRACTS TO BE FILED.

(a) Every carrier subject to this Act shall file with the Commission copiesof all contracts, agreements, or arrangements with other carriers, or with common carriers not subject to the provisions of this Act, in relation to any traffic affected by the provisions of this Act to which it may be a party.

(b) The Commission shall have authority to require the filing of any othercontracts of any carrier, and shall also have authority to exempt any carrier from submitting copies of such minor contracts as the Commission may determine.

TITLE III—PROVISIONS RELATING TO RADIO

PART I—GENERAL PROVISIONS

SEC. 301. [47 U.S.C. 301] LICENSE FOR RADIO COMMUNICATION OR TRANSMISSION OF ENERGY

It is the purpose of this Act, among other things, to maintain the control of the United States over all the channels of radio transmission; and to provide for the use of such channels, but not the ownership thereof, by persons for limited periods of time, under licenses granted by Federal authority, and no such license shall be construed to create any right, beyond the terms, conditions, and periods of the license. No person shall use or operate any apparatus for the transmission of energy or communications or signals by radio (a) from one place in any State, Territory, or possession of the United States or in the District of Columbia to another place in the same State, Territory, possession, or District; or (b) from any State, Territory, or possession of the United States, or from the District of Columbia to any other State, Territory, or possession of the United States; or (c) from any place in any State, Territory, or possession of the United States, or in the District of Columbia, to any place in any foreign country or to any vessel; or (d) within any State when the effects of such use extend beyond the borders of said State, or when interference is caused by such use or operation with the transmission of such energy, communications, or signals from within said State to any place beyond its borders, or from any place beyond its borders to any place within said State, or with the transmission or reception of such energy, communications, or signals from and/or to places beyond the borders of said State; or (e) upon any vessel or aircraft of the United States (except as provided in section 303(t)); or (f) upon any other mobile stations within the jurisdiction of the United States, except under and in accordance with this Act and with a license in that behalf granted under the provisions of this Act.

SEC. 302. [47 U.S.C. 302] DEVICES WHICH INTERFERE WITH RADIO RECEPTION.

(a) The Commission may, consistent with the public interest, convenience,and necessity, make reasonable regulations (1) governing the interference potential of devices which in their operation are capable of emitting radio frequency energy by radiation, conduction, or other means in sufficient degree to cause harmful interference to radio communications; and (2) establishing minimum performance standards for home electronic equipment and systems to reduce their susceptibility to interference from radio frequency energy. Such regulations shall be applicable to the manufacture, import, sale, offer for sale, or shipment of such devices and home electronic equipment and systems, and to the use of such devices.

(b) No person shall manufacture, import, sell, offer for sale, or ship devicesor home electronic equipment and systems, or use devices, which fail to comply with regulations promulgated pursuant to this section.

(c) The provisions of this section shall not be applicable to carrierstransporting such devices or home electronic equipment and systems without trading in them, to devices or home electronic equipment and systems manufactured solely for export, to the equipment manufacturer, assembly, or installation of devices or home electronic and systems for its own use by a public utility engaged in providing electric service, or to devices or home electronic equipment and systems for use by the Government of the United States or any agency thereof. Devices and home electronic equipment and systems for use by the Government of the United States or any agency thereof shall be developed, procured, or otherwise acquired, including offshore procurement, under United States Government criteria, standards, or specifications designed to achieve the objectives of reducing interference to radio reception and to home electronic equipment and systems, taking into account the unique needs of national defense and security.

(d)(1) Within 180 days after the date of enactment of this subsection, the Commission shall prescribe and make effective regulations denying equipment authorization (under part 15 of title 47, Code of Federal Regulations, or any other part of that title) for any scanning receiver that is capable of—

(A) receiving transmissions in the frequencies allocated to thedomestic cellular radio telecommunications service,

(B) readily being altered by the user to receive transmissions in suchfrequencies, or

(C) being equipped with decoders that convert digital cellulartransmissions to analog voice audio.

(2) Beginning 1 year after the effective date of the regulations adopted pursuant to paragraph (1), no receiver having the capabilities described in subparagraph (A), (B), or (C) of paragraph (1), as such capabilities are defined in such

regulations, shall be manufactured in the United States or imported for use in the United States.

(e) The Commission may—

(1) authorize the use of private organizations for testing andcertifying the compliance of devices or home electronic equipment and systems with regulations promulgated under this section;

(2) accept as prima facie evidence of such compliance thecertification by any such organization; and

(3) ,establish such qualifications and standards as it deemsappropriate for such private organizations, testing, and certification.

SEC. 303. [47 U.S.C. 303] GENERAL POWERS OF COMMISSION.

Except as otherwise provided in this Act, the Commission from time to time, as public convenience, interest, or necessity requires shall—

(a) Classify radio stations;

(b) Prescribe the nature of the service to be rendered by each class oflicensed stations and each station within any class; (c) Assign bands of frequencies to the various classes of stations, and assign frequencies for each individual station and determine the power which each station shall use and the time during which it may operate;

(d) Determine the location of classes of stations or individual stations;

(e) Regulate the kind of apparatus to be used with respect to its externaleffects and the purity and sharpness of the emissions from each station and from the apparatus therein;

(f) Make such regulations not inconsistent with law as it may deemnecessary to prevent interference between stations and to carry out the provisions of this Act: *Provided, however,* that changes in the frequencies, authorized power, or in the times of operation of any station, shall not be made without the consent of the station licensee unless the Commission shall determine that such changes will promote public convenience or interest or will serve public necessity, or the provisions of this Act will be more fully complied with;

(g) Study new uses for radio, provide for experimental uses of frequencies,and generally encourage the larger and more effective use of radio in the public interest;

(h) Have authority to establish areas or zones to be served by any station;

(i) Have authority to make special regulations applicable to radio stationsengaged in chain broadcasting;

(j) Have authority to make general rules and regulations requiring stationsto keep such records of programs, transmissions of energy, communications or signals as it may deem desirable;

(k) Have authority to exclude from the requirements of any regulations inwhole or in part any radio station upon railroad rolling stock, or to modify such regulations in its discretion;

(l)(1) Have the authority to prescribe the qualifications of station operators, to classify them according to the duties to be performed, to fix the forms of such licenses, and to issue them to persons who are found to be qualified by the Commission and who otherwise are legally eligible for employment in the United

States, except that such requirement relating to eligibility for employment in the

United States shall not apply in the case of licenses issued by the Commission to (A) persons holding United States pilot certificates; or (B) persons holding foreign aircraft pilot certificates which are valid in the United States, if the foreign government involved has entered into a reciprocal agreement under which such foreign government does not impose any similar requirement relating to eligibility for employment upon citizens of the United States;

(2) Notwithstanding paragraph (1) of this subsection, an individual to whom a radio station is licensed under the provisions of this Act may be issued an operator's license to operate that station.

(3) In addition to amateur operator licenses which the Commission may issue to aliens pursuant to paragraph (2) of this subsection, and notwithstanding section 301 of this Act and paragraph (1) of this subsection, the Commission may issue authorizations, under such conditions and terms as it may prescribe, to permit an alien licensed by his government as an amateur radio operator to operate his amateur radio station licensed by his government in the United States, its possessions, and the Commonwealth of Puerto Rico provided there is in effect a multilateral or bilateral agreement, to which the United States and the alien 's government are parties, for such operation on a reciprocal basis by United States amateur radio operators. Other provisions of this Act and of the Administrative Procedure Act shall not be applicable to any request or application for or modification, suspension or cancellation of any such authorization.

(m)(1) Have authority to suspend the license of any operator upon proof sufficient to satisfy the Commission that the licensee—

(a) Has violated, or caused, aided, or abetted the violation of, any provision of any Act, treaty, or convention binding on the United States, which the Commission is authorized to administer, or any regulation made by the Commission under any such Act, treaty, or convention; or

(B) Has failed to carry out a lawful order of the master or person lawfully in charge of the ship or aircraft on which he is employed; or

(C) Has willfully damaged or permitted radio apparatus or installations tobe damaged; or

(D) Has transmitted superfluous radio communications or signals orcommunications containing profane or obscene words, language, or meaning, or has knowingly transmitted—

(1) False or deceptive signals or communications; or

(2) A call signal or letter which has not been assigned by proper authorityto the station he is operating; or

(E) Has willfully or maliciously interfered with any other radiocommunications or signals; or

(F) Has obtained or attempted to obtain, or has assisted another to obtainor attempt to obtain, an operator's license by fraudulent means.

(2) No order of suspension of any operator's license shall take effect until fifteen days' notice in writing thereof, stating the cause for the proposed suspension, has been given to the operator licensee who may make written application to the Commission at any time within said fifteen days for hearing upon such order. The notice to the operator licensee shall not be effective until actually received by him, and from that time he shall have fifteen days in which to mail the said application. In the event that physical conditions prevent mailing of the application at the expiration of the fifteen-day period, the application shall then be mailed as soon as possible thereafter, accompanied by a satisfactory explanation of the delay. Upon receipt by the Commission of such application for hearing, said order of suspension shall be held in abeyance until the conclusion of the hearing which shall be conducted under such rules as the Commission may prescribe. Upon the conclusion of said hearing the Commission may affirm, modify, or revoke said order of suspension.

SEC. 307. [47 U.S.C. 307] ALLOCATION OF FACILITIES; TERM OF LICENSES.

(a) The Commission, if public convenience, interest, or necessity will beserved thereby, subject to the limitations of this Act, shall grant to any applicant therefor a station license provided for by this Act.

(b) In considering applications for licenses, and modifications and renewals thereof, when and insofar as there is demand for the same, the Commission shall make such distribution of licenses, frequencies, hours of operation, and of power among the several States and communities as to provide a fair, efficient, and equitable distribution of radio service to each of the same.

(c) TERMS OF LICENSES.—

(1) INITIAL AND RENEWAL LICENSES.—Each license granted for the operation of a broadcasting station shall be for a term of not to exceed 8 years. Upon application therefor, a renewal of such license may be granted from time to time for a term of not to exceed 8 years from the date of expiration of the preceding license, if the Commission finds that public interest, convenience, and necessity would be served thereby. Consistent with the foregoing provisions of

this subsection, the Commission may by rule prescribe the period or periods for which licenses shall be granted and renewed for particular classes of stations, but the Commission may not adopt or follow any rule which would preclude it, in any case involving a station of a particular class, from granting or renewing a license for a shorter period than that prescribed for stations of such class if, in its judgment, the public interest, convenience, or necessity would be served by such action.

(2) MATERIALS IN APPLICATION.—In order to expedite action on applications for renewal of broadcasting station licenses and in order to avoid needless expense to applicants for such renewals, the Commission shall not require any such applicant to file any information which previously has been furnished to the Commission or which is not directly material to the considerations that affect the granting or denial of such application, but the Commission may require any new or additional facts it deems necessary to make its findings.

(3) CONTINUATION PENDING DECISION.—Pending any hearing and final decision on such an application and the disposition of any petition for rehearing pursuant to section 405, the Commission shall continue such license in effect.

(d) No renewal of an existing station license in the broadcast or the common carrier services shall be granted more than thirty days prior to the expiration of the original license.

(e)(1) Notwithstanding any license requirement established in this Act, if the Commission determines that such authorization serves the public interest, convenience, and necessity, the Commission may by rule authorize the operation of radio stations without individual licenses in the following radio services: (A) the citizens band radio service; (B) the radio control service; (C) the aviation radio service for aircraft stations operated on domestic flights when such aircraft are not otherwise required to carry a radio station; and (D) the maritime radio service for ship stations navigated on domestic voyages when such ships are not otherwise required to carry a radio station.

(2) Any radio station operator who is authorized by the Commission tooperate without an individual license shall comply with all other provisions of this Act and with rules prescribed by the Commission under this Act.

(3) For purposes of this subsection, the terms "citizens band radio service", "radio control service", "aircraft station" and "ship station" shall have the meanings given them by the Commission by rule.

SEC. 309. [47 U.S.C. 309] ACTION UPON APPLICATIONS; FORM OF AND CONDITIONS ATTACHED TO LICENSES.

(a) Subject to the provisions of this section, the Commission shalldetermine, in the case of each application filed with it to which section 308 applies, whether the public interest, convenience, and necessity will be served by the granting of such application, and, if the Commission, upon examination of such application and upon consideration of such other matters as the Commission may officially notice, shall find that public interest, convenience, and necessity would be served by the granting thereof, it shall grant such application.

(b) Except as provided in subsection (c) of this section, no suchapplication—

(1) for an instrument of authorization in the case of a station in thebroadcasting or common carrier services, or

(2) for an instrument of authorization in the case of a station in anyof the following categories:

(A) industrial radio positioning stations for whichfrequencies are assigned on an exclusive basis,

(B) aeronautical en route stations,

(C) aeronautical advisory stations,

(D) airdrome control stations,

(E) aeronautical fixed stations, and

(F) such other stations or classes of stations, not in thebroadcasting or common carrier services, as the Commission shall by rule prescribe,

shall be granted by the Commission earlier than thirty days following issuance of public notice by the Commission of the acceptance for filing of such application or of any substantial amendment thereof.

(c) Subsection (b) of this section shall not apply—

(1) to any minor amendment of an application to which suchsubsection is applicable, or

(2) to any application for—

(A) a minor change in the facilities of an authorized station,

(B) consent to an involuntary assignment or transfer undersection 310(b) or to an assignment or transfer thereunder which does not involve a substantial change in ownership or control,

(C) a license under section 319(c) or, pending applicationfor or grant of such license, any special or temporary authorization to permit interim operation to facilitate completion of authorized construction or to provide substantially the same service as would be authorized by such license,

(D) extension of time to complete construction ofauthorized facilities,

(E) an authorization of facilities for remote pickups, studiolinks and similar facilities for use in the operation of a broadcast station,

(F) authorizations pursuant to section 325(c) where theprograms to be transmitted are special events not of a continuing nature,

(G) a special temporary authorization for nonbroadcastoperation not to exceed thirty days where no application for regular operation is contemplated to be filed or not to exceed sixty days pending the filing of an application for such regular operation, or

(H) an authorization under any of the proviso clauses ofsection 308(a).

(d)(1) Any party in interest may file with the Commission a petition to deny any application (whether as originally filed or as amended) to which subsection (b) of this section applies at any time prior to the day of Commission grant thereof without hearing or the day of formal designation thereof for hearing; except that with respect to any classification of applications, the Commission from time to time by rule may specify a shorter period (no less than thirty days following the issuance of public notice by the Commission of the acceptance for filing of such application or of any substantial amendment thereof), which shorter period shall be reasonably related to the time when the applications would normally be reached for processing. The petitioner shall serve a copy of such petition on the applicant. The petition shall contain specific allegations of fact sufficient to show that the petitioner is a party in interest and that a grant of the application would be prima facie inconsistent with subsection (a) (or subsection (k) in the case of renewal of any broadcast station license). Such allegations of fact shall, except for those of which official notice may be taken, be supported by affidavit of a person or persons with personal knowledge thereof. The applicant shall be given the opportunity to file a reply in which allegations of fact or denials thereof shall similarly be supported by affidavit.

(2) If the Commission finds on the basis of the application, the pleadings filed, or other matters which it may officially notice that there are no substantial and material questions of fact and that a grant of the application would be consistent with subsection (a) (or subsection (k) in the case of renewal of any broadcast station license), it shall make the grant, deny the petition, and issue a concise statement of the reasons for denying the petition, which statement shall dispose of all substantial issues raised by the petition. If a substantial and material question of fact is presented or if the Commission for any reason is unable to find that grant of the application would be consistent with subsection (a) (or subsection (k) in the case of renewal of any broadcast station license), it shall proceed as provided in subsection (e).

(e) If, in the case of any application to which subsection (a) of this section applies, a substantial and material question of fact is presented or the Commission for any reason is unable to make the finding specified in such subsection, it shall formally designate the application for hearing on the ground or reasons then obtaining and shall forthwith notify the applicant and all other known parties in interest of such action and the ground and reasons therefor, specifying with particularity the matters and things in issue but not including issues or requirements phrased generally. When the Commission has so designated an application for hearing, the parties in interest, if any, who are not notified by the Commission of such action may acquire the status of a party to the proceeding thereon by filing a petition for intervention showing the basis for their interest not more than thirty days after publication of the hearing issues or any substantial amendment thereto in the Federal Register. Any hearing subsequently held upon such application shall be a full hearing in which the applicant and all other parties in interest shall be permitted to participate. The burden of proceeding with the introduction of evidence and the burden of proof shall be upon the applicant, except that with respect to any issue presented by a petition to deny or a petition to enlarge the issues, such burdens shall be as determined by the Commission. (f) When an application subject to subsection (b) has been filed, the Commission, notwithstanding the requirements of such subsection, may, if the grant of such application is otherwise authorized by law and if it finds that there are extraordinary circumstances requiring temporary operations in the public interest and that delay in the institution of such temporary operations would seriously prejudice the public interest, grant a temporary authorization, accompanied by a statement of its reasons therefor, to permit such temporary operations for a period not exceeding 180 days, and upon making like findings may extend such temporary authorization for additional periods not to exceed 180 days.

When any such grant of a temporary authorization is made, the Commission shall give expeditious treatment to any timely filed petition to deny such application and to any petition for rehearing of such grant filed under section 405.

(g) The Commission is authorized to adopt reasonable classifications ofapplications and amendments in order to effectuate the purposes of this section.

(h) Such station licenses as the Commission may grant shall be in suchgeneral form as it may prescribe, but each license shall contain, in addition to other provisions, a statement of the following conditions to which such license shall be subject: (1) The station license shall not vest in the licensee any right to operate the station nor any right in the use of the frequencies designated in the license beyond the term thereof nor in any other manner than authorized therein; (2) neither the license nor the right granted thereunder shall be assigned or otherwise transferred in violation of this Act; (3) every license issued under this Act shall be subject in terms to the right of use or control conferred by section 706 of this Act.

(i) RANDOM SELECTION.-(1) GENERAL AUTHORITY.—If—

(A) there is more than one application for any initial licenseor construction permit which will involve a use of the
electromagnetic spectrum; and

(B) the Commission has determined that the use is notdescribed in subsection (j)(2)(A);

then the Commission shall have the authority to grant such license or permit to a qualified applicant through the use of a system of random selection.

(2) No license or construction permit shall be granted to an applicant selected pursuant to paragraph (1) unless the Commission determines the qualifications of such applicant pursuant to subsection (a) and section 308(b). When substantial and material questions of fact exist concerning such qualifications, the Commission shall conduct a hearing in order to make such determinations. For the purposes of making such determinations, the Commission may, by rule, and notwithstanding any other provision of law—

(A) adopt procedures for the submission of all or part of theevidence in written form;

(B) delegate the function of presiding at the taking of writtenevidence to Commission employees other than administrative law judges; and

(C) omit the determination required by subsection (a) with respectto any application other than the one selected pursuant to paragraph (1).

(3)(A) The Commission shall establish rules and procedures to ensure that, in the administration of any system of random selection under this subsection used for granting licenses or construction permits for any media of mass communications, significant preferences will be granted to applicants or groups of applicants, the grant to which of the license or permit would increase the diversification of ownership of the media of mass communications. To further diversify the ownership of the media of mass communications, an additional significant preference shall be granted to any applicant controlled by a member or members of minority group.

(B) The Commission shall have authority to require each qualifiedapplicant seeking a significant preference under subparagraph (A) to submit to the Commission such information as may be necessary to enable the Commission to make a determination regarding whether such applicant shall be granted such preference. Such information shall be submitted in such form, at such times, and in accordance with such procedures, as the Commission may require.

(C) For purposes of this paragraph:

(i) The term "media of mass communication" includes television, radio, cable television, multipoint distribution service, direct broadcast satellite service, and other services, the licensed facilities of which may be substantially devoted toward providing programming or other information services within the editorial control of the licensee.

(ii) The term "minority group" includes Blacks, Hispanics, AmericanIndians, Alaska Natives, Asians, and Pacific Islanders.

(4)(A) The Commission shall, after notice and opportunity for hearing, prescribe rules establishing a system of random selection for use by the Commission under this subsection in any instance in which the Commission, in its discretion, determines that such use is appropriate for the granting of any license or permit in accordance with paragraph (1).

(B) The Commission shall have authority to amend such rules from time totime to the extent necessary too carry out the provisions of this subsection. Any such amendment shall be made after notice and opportunity for hearing.

(C) Not later than 180 days after the date of enactment of this subparagraph, the Commission shall prescribe such transfer disclosures and antitrafficking restrictions and payment schedules as are necessary to prevent the unjust enrichment of recipients of licenses or permits as a result of the methods employed to issue licenses under this subsection.

(j) USE OF COMPETITIVE BIDDING.—

(1) GENERAL AUTHORITY.—If mutually exclusive applications are accepted for filing for any initial license or construction permit which will involve a use of the electromagnetic spectrum described in paragraph (2), then the Commission shall have the authority, subject to paragraph (10), to grant such license or permit to a qualified applicant through the use of a system of competitive bidding that meets the requirements of this subsection.

(2) USES TO WHICH BIDDING MAY APPLY.—A use of the electromagnetic spectrum is described in this paragraph if the Commission determines that—

(A) the principal use of such spectrum will involve, or is reasonably likely to involve, the licensee receiving compensation from subscribers in return for which the licensee—

(i) enables those subscribers to receive communications signals that are transmitted utilizing frequencies on which the licensee is licensed to operate; or

(ii) enables those subscribers to transmit directly communications signals utilizing frequencies on which the licensee is licensed to operate; and

(B) a system of competitive bidding will promote theobjectives described in paragraph (3).

(3) DESIGN OF SYSTEMS OF COMPETITIVE BIDDING.—For each class of licenses or permits that the Commission grants through the use of a competitive bidding system, the Commission shall, by regulation, establish a competitive bidding methodology. The Commission shall seek to design and test multiple alternative methodologies under appropriate circumstances. In identifying classes of licenses and permits to be issued by competitive bidding, in specifying eligibility and other characteristics of such licenses and permits, and in designing the methodologies for use under this subsection, the Commission shall include safeguards to protect the public interest in the use of the spectrum and shall seek to promote the purposes specified in section 1 of this Act and the following objectives:

(A) the development and rapid deployment of newtechnologies, products, and services for the benefit of the public, including those residing in rural areas, without administrative or judicial delays;

(B) promoting economic opportunity and competition andensuring that new and innovative technologies are readily accessible to the American people by avoiding excessive concentration of licenses and by disseminating licenses among a wide variety of applicants, including small businesses, rural telephone companies, and businesses owned by members of minority groups and women;

(C) recovery for the public of a portion of the value of thepublic spectrum resource made available for commercial use and avoidance of unjust enrichment through the methods employed to award uses of that resource; and

(D) efficient and intensive use of the electromagneticspectrum.

(4) CONTENTS OF REGULATIONS.—In prescribing regulations pursuant to paragraph (3), the Commission shall—

(A) consider alternative payment schedules and methods of calculation, including lump sums or guaranteed installment payments, with or without royalty payments, or other schedules or methods that promote the objectives described in paragraph (3)(B), and combinations of such schedules and methods;

(B) include performance requirements, such as appropriatedeadlines and penalties for performance failures, to ensure prompt delivery of service to rural areas, to prevent stockpiling or warehousing of spectrum by licensees or permittees, and to promote investment in and rapid deployment of new technologies and services;

(C) consistent with the public interest, convenience, andnecessity, the purposes of this Act, and the characteristics of the proposed service, prescribe area designations and bandwidth assignments that promote (i) an equitable distribution of licenses and services among geographic areas, (ii) economic opportunity for a wide variety of applicants, including small businesses, rural telephone companies, and businesses owned by members of minority groups and women, and (iii) investment in and rapid deployment of new technologies and services;

(D) ensure that small businesses, rural telephone companies,and businesses owned by members of minority groups and women are given the opportunity to participate in the provision of spectrum-based services, and, for such purposes, consider the use of tax certificates, bidding preferences, and other procedures; and

(E) require such transfer disclosures and antitraffickingrestrictions and payment schedules as may be necessary to prevent unjust enrichment as a result of the methods employed to issue licenses and permits.

(5) BIDDER AND LICENSEE QUALIFICATION.—No person shall be permitted to participate in a system of competitive bidding pursuant to this subsection

unless such bidder submits such information and assurances as the Commission may require to demonstrate that such bidder's application is acceptable for filing. No license shall be granted to an applicant selected pursuant to this subsection unless the Commission determines that the applicant is qualified pursuant to subsection (a) and sections 308(b) and 310. Consistent with the objectives described in paragraph (3), the Commission shall, by regulation, prescribe expedited procedures consistent with the procedures authorized by subsection (i)(2) for the resolution of any substantial and material issues of fact concerning qualifications.

(6) RULES OF CONSTRUCTION.—Nothing in this subsection, or in the use of competitive bidding, shall—

(A) alter spectrum allocation criteria and proceduresestablished by the other provisions of this Act;

(B) limit or otherwise affect the requirements of subsection(h) of this section, section 301, 304, 307, 310, or 706, or any other provision of this Act (other than subsections (d)(2) and (e) of this section);

(C) diminish the authority of the Commission under theother provisions of this Act to regulate or reclaim spectrum licenses;

(D) be construed to convey any rights, including anyexpectation of renewal of a license, that differ from the rights that apply to other licenses within the same service that were not issued pursuant to this subsection;

(E) be construed to relieve the Commission of theobligation in the public interest to continue to use engineering solutions, negotiation, threshold qualifications, service regulations, and other means in order to avoid mutual exclusivity in application and licensing proceedings;

(F) be construed to prohibit the Commission from issuing nationwide, regional, or local licenses or permits;

(G) be construed to prevent the Commission from awardinglicenses to those persons who make significant contributions to the development of a new telecommunications service or technology; or

(H) be construed to relieve any applicant for a license orpermit of the obligation to pay charges imposed pursuant to section 8 of this Act.

(7) CONSIDERATION OF REVENUES IN PUBLIC INTEREST DETERMINATIONS.—

(A) CONSIDERATION PROHIBITED.—In making a decision pursuant to section 303(c) to assign a band of frequencies to a use for which licenses or permits will be issued pursuant to this subsection, and in prescribing regulations pursuant to paragraph (4)(C) of this subsection, the Commission may not base a finding of public interest, convenience, and necessity on the expectation of Federal revenues from the use of a system of competitive bidding under this subsection.

(B) CONSIDERATION LIMITED.—In prescribing regulations pursuant to paragraph (4)(A) of this subsection, the Commission may not base a finding of public interest, convenience, and necessity solely or predominantly on the expectation of Federal revenues from the use of a system of competitive bidding under this subsection.

(C) CONSIDERATION OF DEMAND FOR SPECTRUM NOT AFFECTED.—Nothing in this paragraph shall be construed to prevent the Commission from continuing to consider consumer demand for spectrum-based services.

(8) TREATMENT OF REVENUES.—

(A) GENERAL RULE.—Except as provided in subparagraph (B), all proceeds from the use of a competitive bidding system under this subsection shall be deposited in the Treasury in accordance with chapter 33 of title 31, United States Code.

(B) RETENTION OF REVENUES.—Notwithstanding subparagraph (A), the salaries and expenses account of the Commission shall retain as an offsetting collection such sums as may be necessary from such proceeds for the costs of developing and implementing the program required by this subsection. Such offsetting collections shall be available for obligation subject to the terms and conditions of the receiving appropriations account, and shall be deposited in such accounts on a quarterly basis. Any funds appropriated to the Commission for fiscal years 1994 through 1998 for the purpose of assigning licenses using random selection under subsection (i) shall be used by the Commission to implement this subsection. Such offsetting collections are authorized to remain available until expended.

(C) DEPOSIT AND USE OF AUCTION ESCROW ACCOUNTS.—Any deposits the Commission may require for the qualification of any person to bid in a system of competitive bidding pursuant to this subsection shall be deposited in an interest bearing account at a financial institution designated for purposes of this subsection by the Commission (after consultation with the Secretary of the Treasury). Within 45 days following the conclusion of the competitive bidding—

(i) the deposits of successful bidders shall be paid tothe Treasury;

(ii) the deposits of unsuccessful bidders shall bereturned to such bidders; and

(iii) the interest accrued to the account shall betransferred to the Telecommunications Development Fund established pursuant to section 714 of this Act.

(9) USE OF FORMER GOVERNMENT SPECTRUM.—The Commission shall, not later than 5 years after the date of enactment of this subsection, issue licenses and permits pursuant to this subsection for the use of bands of frequencies that—

(A) in the aggregate span not less than 10 megahertz; and

(B) have been reassigned from Government use pursuant to part B of the National Telecommunications and Information Administration Organization Act.

(10) AUTHORITY CONTINGENT ON AVAILABILITY OF ADDITIONAL SPECTRUM.—
(A) INITIAL CONDITIONS.—The Commission's authority to issue licenses or permits under this subsection shall not take effect unless—
(i) the Secretary of Commerce has submitted to the Commission the report required by section 113(d)(1) of the National Telecommunications and Information Administration Organization Act;
(ii) such report recommends for immediatereallocation bands of frequencies that, in the aggregate, span not less than 50 megahertz;
(iii) such bands of frequencies meet the criteriarequired by section 113(a) of such Act; and
(iv) the Commission has completed the rulemaking required by section 332(c)(1)(D) of this Act.
(B) SUBSEQUENT CONDITIONS.—The Commission's authority to issue licenses or permits under this subsection on and after 2 years after the date of the enactment of this subsection shall cease to be effective if—
(i) the Secretary of Commerce has failed to submit the report required by section 113(a) of the National Telecommunications and Information Administration
Organization Act;
(ii) the President has failed to withdraw and limit assignments of frequencies as required by paragraphs (1) and (2) of section 114(a) of such Act;
(iii) the Commission has failed to issue the regulations required by section 115(a) of such Act;
(iv) the Commission has failed to complete andsubmit to Congress, not later than 18 months after the date of enactment of this subsection, a study of current and future spectrum needs of State and local government public safety agencies through the year 2010, and a specific plan to ensure that adequate frequencies are made available to public safety licensees; or
(v) the Commission has failed under section 332(c)(3) to grant or deny within the time required by such section any petition that a State has filed within 90 days after the date of enactment of this subsection; until such failure has been corrected.
(11) TERMINATION.—The authority of the Commission to grant a license or permit under this subsection shall expire September 30, 1998.
(12) EVALUATION.—Not later than September 30, 1997, the Commission shall conduct a public inquiry and submit to the Congress a report—
(A) containing a statement of the revenues obtained, and a projection of the future revenues, from the use of competitive bidding systems under this subsection;
(B) describing the methodologies established by the Commission pursuant to paragraphs (3) and (4);

(C) comparing the relative advantages and disadvantages of such methodologies in terms of attaining the objectives described in such paragraphs;

(D) evaluating whether and to what extent—

(i) competitive bidding significantly improved the efficiency and effectiveness of the process for granting radio spectrum licenses;

(ii) competitive bidding facilitated the introductionof new spectrum-based technologies and the entry of new companies into the telecommunications market;

(iii) competitive bidding methodologies have secured prompt delivery of service to rural areas and have adequately addressed the needs of rural spectrum users; and

(iv) small businesses, rural telephone companies, and businesses owned by members of minority groups and women were able to participate successfully in the competitive bidding process; and

(E) recommending any statutory changes that are needed toimprove the competitive bidding process.

(13) RECOVERY OF VALUE OF PUBLIC SPECTRUM IN CONNECTION WITH PIONEER PREFERENCES.—

(A) IN GENERAL.—Notwithstanding paragraph (6)(G), the Commission shall not award licenses pursuant to a preferential treatment accorded by the Commission to persons who make significant contributions to the development of a new telecommunications service or technology, except in accordance with the requirements of this paragraph.

(B) RECOVERY OF VALUE.—The Commission shall recover for the public a portion of the value of the public spectrum resource made available to such person by requiring such person, as a condition for receipt of the license, to agree to pay a sum determined by—

(i) identifying the winning bids for the licenses that the Commission determines are most reasonably comparable in terms of bandwidth, scope of service area, usage restrictions, and other technical characteristics to the license awarded to such person, and excluding licenses that the Commission determines are subject to bidding anomalies due to the award of preferential treatment;

(ii) dividing each such winning bid by the populationof its service area (hereinafter referred to as the per capita
bid amount);

(iii) computing the average of the per capita bidamounts for the licenses identified under clause (i);

(iv) reducing such average amount by 15 percent;and

(v) multiplying the amount determined under clause(iv) by the population of the service area of the license obtained by such person.

(C) INSTALLMENTS PERMITTED.—The Commission shall require such person to pay the sum required by subparagraph (B) in a lump sum or in guaranteed installment payments, with or without royalty payments, over a period of not more than 5 years.

(D) RULEMAKING ON PIONEER PREFERENCES.—Except with respect to pending applications described in clause (iv) of this subparagraph, the Commission shall prescribe regulations specifying the procedures and criteria by which the Commission will evaluate applications for preferential treatment in its licensing processes (by precluding the filing of mutually exclusive applications) for persons who make significant contributions to the development of a new service or to the development of new technologies that substantially enhance an existing service. Such regulations shall—

(i) specify the procedures and criteria by which thesignificance of such contributions will be determined, after an opportunity for review and verification by experts in the radio sciences drawn from among persons who are not employees of the Commission or by any applicant for such
preferential treatment;

(ii) include such other procedures as may benecessary to prevent unjust enrichment by ensuring that the value of any such contribution justifies any reduction in the amounts paid for comparable licenses under this subsection;

(iii) be prescribed not later than 6 months after thedate of enactment of this paragraph;

(iv) not apply to applications that have beenaccepted for filing on or before September 1, 1994; and

(v) cease to be effective on the date of the expirationof the Commission 's authority under subparagraph (F).

(E) IMPLEMENTATION WITH RESPECT TO PENDING APPLICATIONS.—In applying this paragraph to any broadband licenses in the personal communications service awarded pursuant to the preferential treatment accorded by the Federal Communications Commission in the Third Report and Order in
General Docket 90-314 (FCC 93-550, released February 3, 1994)—

(i) the Commission shall not reconsider the award ofpreferences in such Third Report and Order, and the Commission shall not delay the grant of licenses based on such awards more than 15 days following the date of enactment of this paragraph, and the award of such preferences and licenses shall not be subject to administrative or judicial review;

(ii) the Commission shall not alter the bandwidth orservice areas designated for such licenses in such Third Report and Order;

(iii) except as provided in clause (v), theCommission shall use, as the most reasonably comparable licenses for purposes of subparagraph (B)(i), the broadband licenses in the personal communications service for blocks A and B

for the 20 largest markets (ranked by population) in which no applicant has obtained preferential treatment; (iv) for purposes of subparagraph (C), the Commission shall permit guaranteed installment payments
over a period of 5 years, subject to—
(I) the payment only of interest on unpaidbalances during the first 2 years, commencing not later than 30 days after the award of the license (including any preferential treatment used in making such award) is final and no longer subject to administrative or judicial review, except that no such payment shall be required prior to the date of completion of the auction of the comparable licenses described in clause (iii); and
(II) payment of the unpaid balance andinterest thereon after the end of such 2 years in accordance with the regulations prescribed by the
Commission; and
(v) the Commission shall recover with respect to broadband licenses in the personal communications service an amount under this paragraph that is equal to not less than $400,000,000, and if such amount is less than $400,000,000, the Commission shall recover an amount equal to $400,000,000 by allocating such amount among the holders of such licenses based on the population of the license areas held by each licensee.
The Commission shall not include in any amounts required to be collected under clause (v) the interest on unpaid balances required to be collected under clause (iv).
(F) EXPIRATION.—The authority of the Commission to provide preferential treatment in licensing procedures (by precluding the filing of mutually exclusive applications) to persons who make significant contributions to the development of a new service or to the development of new technologies that substantially enhance an existing service shall expire on September 30, 1998.
(G) EFFECTIVE DATE.—This paragraph shall be effective on the date of its enactment and apply to any licenses issued on or after August 1, 1994, by the Federal Communications Commission pursuant to any licensing procedure that provides preferential treatment (by precluding the filing of mutually exclusive applications) to persons who make significant contributions to the development of a new service or to the development of new technologies that substantially enhance an existing service.
(k) BROADCAST STATION RENEWAL PROCEDURES.—
(1) STANDARDS FOR RENEWAL.—If the licensee of a broadcast station submits an application to the Commission for renewal of such license, the Commission shall grant the application if it finds, with respect to that station, during the preceding term of its license—
(A) the station has served the public interest, convenience, and necessity;
(B) there have been no serious violations by the licensee of this Act or the rules and regulations of the Commission; and

(C) there have been no other violations by the licensee of this Act or the rules and regulations of the Commission which, taken together, would constitute a pattern of abuse.

(2) CONSEQUENCE OF FAILURE TO MEET STANDARD.—If any licensee of a broadcast station fails to meet the requirements of this subsection, the Commission may deny the application for renewal in accordance with paragraph (3), or grant such application on terms and conditions as are appropriate, including renewal for a term less than the maximum otherwise permitted.

(3) STANDARDS FOR DENIAL.—If the Commission determines, after notice and opportunity for a hearing as provided in subsection (e), that a licensee has failed to meet the requirements specified in paragraph (1) and that no mitigating factors justify the imposition of lesser sanctions, the Commission shall—

(A) issue an order denying the renewal application filed by such licensee under section 308; and

(B) only thereafter accept and consider such applications fora construction permit as may be filed under section 308 specifying the channel or broadcasting facilities of the former licensee.

(4) COMPETITOR CONSIDERATION PROHIBITED.—In making the determinations specified in paragraph (1) or (2), the Commission shall not consider whether the public interest, convenience, and necessity might be served by the grant of a license to a person other than the renewal applicant.

SEC. 310. [47 U.S.C. 310] LIMITATION ON HOLDING AND TRANSFER OF LICENSES.

(a) The station license required under this Act shall not be granted to orheld by any foreign government or the representative thereof.

(b) No broadcast or common carrier or aeronautical en route oraeronautical fixed radio station license shall be granted to or held by—

(1) any alien or the representative of any alien;

(2) any corporation organized under the laws of any foreigngovernment;

(3) any corporation of which more than one-fifth of the capitalstock is owned of record or voted by aliens or their representatives or by a foreign government or representative thereof or by any corporation organized under the laws of a foreign country;

(4) any corporation directly or indirectly controlled by any othercorporation of which more than one-fourth of the capital stock is owned of record or voted by aliens, their representatives, or by a foreign government or representative thereof, or by any corporation organized under the laws of a

foreign country, if the Commission finds that the public interest will be served by the refusal or revocation of such license.

(c) In addition to amateur station licenses which the Commission may issueto aliens pursuant to this Act, the Commission may issue authorizations, under such conditions and terms as it may prescribe, to permit an alien licensed by his government as an amateur radio operator to operate his amateur radio station licensed by his government in the United States, its possessions, and the Commonwealth of Puerto Rico provided there is in effect a multilateral or bilateral agreement, to which the United States and the alien's government are parties, for such operation on a reciprocal basis by United States amateur radio operators. Other provisions of this Act and of the Administrative Procedure Act shall not be applicable to any request or application for or modification, suspension, or cancellation of any such authorization.

(d) No construction permit or station license, or any rights thereunder, shall be transferred, assigned, or disposed of in any manner, voluntarily or involuntarily, directly or indirectly, or by transfer of control of any corporation holding such permit or license, to any person except upon application to the Commission and upon finding by the Commission that the public interest, convenience, and necessity will be served thereby. Any such application shall be disposed of as if the proposed transferee or assignee were making application under section 308 for the permit or license in question; but in acting thereon the Commission may not consider whether the public interest, convenience, and necessity might be served by the transfer, assignment, or disposal of the permit or license to a person other than the proposed transferee or assignee.

(e)(1) In the case of any broadcast station, and any ownership interest therein, which is excluded from the regional concentration rules by reason of the savings provision for existing facilities provided by the First Report and Order adopted March 9, 1977 (docket No. 20548; 42 Fed. Reg. 16145), the exclusion shall not terminate solely by reason of changes made in the technical facilities of the station to improve its service.

(2) For purposes of this subsection, the term "regional concentration rules" means the provisions of sections 73.35, 73.240, and 73.636 of title 47, Code of Federal Regulations (as in effect June 1, 1983), which prohibit any party from directly or indirectly owning, operating, or controlling three broadcast stations in one or several services where any two of such stations are within 100 miles of the third (measured city-to-city), and where there is a primary service contour overlap of any of the stations.

SEC. 311. [47 U.S.C. 311] SPECIAL REQUIREMENTS WITH RESPECT TO CERTAIN APPLICATIONS IN THE BROADCASTING SERVICE.

(a) When there is filed with the Commission any application to whichsection 309(b)(1) applies, for an instrument of authorization for a station in the broadcasting service, the applicant—

(1) shall give notice of such filing in the principal area which isserved or is to be served by the station; and

(2) if the application is formally designated for hearing in accordance with section 309, shall give notice of such hearing in such area at least ten days before commencement of such hearing.

The Commission shall by rule prescribe the form and content of the notices to be given in compliance with this subsection, and the manner and frequency with which such notices shall be given.

(b) Hearings referred to in subsection (a) may be held at such places as theCommission shall determine to be appropriate, and in making such determination in any case the Commission shall consider whether the public interest, convenience, or necessity will be served by conducting the hearing at a place in, or in the vicinity of, the principal area to be served by the station involved.

(c)(1) If there are pending before the Commission two or more applications for a permit for construction of a broadcasting station, only one of which can be granted, it shall be unlawful, without approval of the Commission, for the applicants or any of them to effectuate an agreement whereby one or more of such applicants withdraws his or their application or applications.

(2) The request for Commission approval in any such case shall be made inwriting jointly by all the parties to the agreement. Such request shall contain or be accompanied by full information with respect to the agreement, set forth in such detail, form, and manner as the Commission shall by rule require.

(3) The Commission shall approve the agreement only if it determines that (A) the agreement is consistent with the public interest, convenience, or necessity; and (B) no party to the agreement filed its application for the purpose of reaching or carrying out such agreement.

(4) For the purposes of this subsection an application shall be deemed to be "pending" before the Commission from the time such application is filed with the Commission until an order of the Commission granting or denying it is no longer subject to rehearing by the Commission or to review by any court.

(d)(1) If there are pending before the Commission an application for the renewal of a license granted for the operation of a broadcasting station and one or more applications for a construction permit relating to such station, only one of which can be granted, it shall be unlawful, without approval of the Commission, for the applicants or any of them to effectuate an agreement whereby one or more of such applicants withdraws his or their application or applications in exchange for the payment of money, or the transfer of assets or any other thing of value by the remaining applicant or applicants.

(2) The request for Commission approval in any such case shall be made inwriting jointly by all the parties to the agreement. Such request shall contain or be accompanied by full information with respect to the agreement, set forth in such detail, form, and manner as the Commission shall require.

(3) The Commission shall approve the agreement only if it determines that (A) the agreement is consistent with the public interest, convenience, or necessity; and (B) no party to the agreement filed its application for the purpose of reaching or carrying our such agreement.

(4) For purposes of this subsection, an application shall be deemed to bepending before the Commission from the time such application is filed with the Commission until an order of the Commission granting or denying it is no longer subject to rehearing by the Commission or to review by any court.

SEC. 312. [47 U.S.C. 312] ADMINISTRATIVE SANCTIONS.

(a) The Commission may revoke any station license or construction permit–

(1) for false statements knowingly made either in the application orin any statement of fact which may be required pursuant to section 308;

(2) because of conditions coming to the attention of the Commission which would warrant it in refusing to grant a license or permit on an original application;

(3) for willful or repeated failure to operate substantially as set forthin the license;

(4) for willful or repeated violation of, or willful or repeated failure to observe any provision of this Act or any rule or regulation of the Commission authorized by this Act or by a treaty ratified by the United States;

(5) for violation of or failure to observe any final cease and desistorder issued by the Commission under this section;

(6) for violation of section 1304, 1343, or 1464 of title 18 of the United States Code; or

(7) for willful or repeated failure to allow reasonable access to or to permit purchase of reasonable amounts of time for the use of a broadcasting station by a legally qualified candidate for Federal elective office on behalf of his candidacy.

(b) Where any person (1) has failed to operate substantially as set forth in a license, (2) has violated or failed to observe any of the provisions of this Act, or section 1304, 1343, or 1464 of title 18 of the United States Code, or (3) has violated or failed to observe any rule or regulation of the Commission authorized by this Act or by a treaty ratified by the United States, the Commission may order such person to cease and desist from such action.

(c) Before revoking a license or permit pursuant to subsection (a), orissuing a cease and desist order pursuant to subsection (b), the Commission shall serve upon the licensee, permittee, or person involved an order to show cause why an order of revocation or a cease and desist order should not be issued. Any such order to show cause shall contain a statement of the matters with respect to which the Commission is inquiring and shall call upon said licensee, permittee, or person to appear before the Commission at a time and place stated in the order, but in no event less than thirty days after the receipt of such order, and give evidence upon the matter specified therein; except that where safety of life or property is involved, the Commission may provide in the order for a shorter period. If after hearing, or a waiver thereof, the Commission determines that an order of revocation or a cease and desist order should issue, it shall issue such order, which shall include a statement of the findings of the Commission and the grounds and reasons therefor and specify the effective date of the order, and shall cause the same to be served on said licensee, permittee, or person.

(d) In any case where a hearing is conducted pursuant to the provisions ofthis section, both the burden of proceeding with the introduction of evidence and the burden of proof shall be upon the Commission.

(e) The provisions of section 9(b) [5 U.S.C. 558(c)(1) and (2)] of theAdministrative Procedure Act which apply with respect to the institution of any proceeding for the revocation of a license or permit shall apply also with respect to the institution, under this section, of any proceeding for the issuance of a cease and desist order.

(f) For purposes of this section:

(1) The term "willful", when used with reference to the commissionor omission of any act, means the conscious and deliberate commission or omission of such act, irrespective of any intent to violate any provision of this Act or any rule or regulation of the Commission authorized by this Act or by a treaty ratified by the United States.

(2) The term "repeated", when used with reference to thecommission or omission of any act, means the commission or omission of such act more than once or, if such commission or omission is continuous, for more than one day.

(g) If a broadcasting station fails to transmit broadcast signals for anyconsecutive 12-month period, then the station license granted for the operation of that broadcast station expires at the end of that period, notwithstanding any provision, term, or condition of the license to the contrary.

SEC. 313. [47 U.S.C. 313] APPLICATION OF ANTITRUST LAWS; REFUSAL OF LICENSES AND PERMITS IN CERTAIN CASES.

(a) All laws of the United States relating to unlawful restraints andmonopolies and to combinations, contracts or agreements in restraint of trade are hereby declared to be applicable to the manufacture and sale of and to trade in radio apparatus and devices entering into or affecting interstate or foreign commerce and to interstate or foreign radio communications. Whenever in any suit, action, or proceeding, civil or criminal, brought under the provisions of any of said laws or in any proceedings brought to enforce or to review findings and orders of the Federal Trade Commission or other governmental agency in respect of any matters as to which said Commission or other governmental agency is by law authorized to act, any licensee shall be found guilty of the violation of the provisions of such laws or any of them, the court, in addition to the penalties imposed by said laws, may adjudge, order, and/or decree that the license of such licensee shall, as of the date the decree or judgment becomes finally effective or as of such date as the said decree shall fix, be revoked and that all rights under such license shall thereupon cease: *Provided, however,* That such licensee shall have the same right of appeal or review, as is provided by law in respect of other decrees and judgments of said court.

(b) The Commission is hereby directed to refuse a station license and/or thepermit hereinafter required for the construction of a station to any person (or to any person directly or indirectly controlled by such person) whose license has been revoked by a court under this section.

SEC. 314. [47 U.S.C. 314] PRESERVATION OF COMPETITION IN COMMERCE.

After the effective date of this Act no person engaged directly, or indirectly through any person directly or indirectly controlling or controlled by, or under direct or indirect common control with, such person, or through an agent, or otherwise, in the business of transmitting and/or receiving for hire energy, communications, or signals by radio in accordance with the terms of the license issued under this Act, shall by purchase, lease, construction, or otherwise, directly or indirectly, acquire, own, control, or operate any cable or wire telegraph or telephone line or system between any place in any State, Territory, or possession of the United States or in the District of Columbia, and any place in any foreign country, or shall acquire, own, or control any part of the stock or other capital share or any interest in the physical property and/or other assets of any such cable, wire, telegraph, or telephone line or system, if in either case the purpose is and/or the effect thereof may be to substantially lessen competition or to restrain commerce between any place in any State, Territory, or possession of the United States, or in the District of Columbia, and any place in any foreign country, or unlawfully to create monopoly in any line of commerce; nor shall any person engaged directly, or indirectly through any person directly or indirectly controlling or controlled by, or under direct or indirect common control with, such person, or through an agent, or otherwise, in the business of transmitting and/or receiving for hire messages by any cable, wire, telegraph, or telephone line or system (a) between any place in any State, Territory, or possession of the United States, or in the District of Columbia, and any place in any other State, Territory, or possession of the United States; or (b) between any place in any State, Territory, or possession of the United States, or in the District of Columbia, and any place in any foreign country, by purchase, lease, construction, or otherwise, directly or indirectly acquire, own, control, or operate any station or the apparatus therein, or any system for transmitting and/or receiving radio communications or signals between any place in any State, Territory, or possession of the United States, or in the District of Columbia, and any place in any foreign country, or shall acquire, own, or control any part of the stock or other capital share of any interest in the physical property and/or other assets of any such radio station, apparatus, or system, if in either case, the purpose is and/or the effect thereof may be to substantially lessen competition or to restrain commerce between any place in any State, Territory, or possession of the United States, or in the District of Columbia, and any place in any foreign country, or unlawfully to create monopoly in any line of commerce.

TITLE IV—PROCEDURAL AND ADMINISTRATIVE PROVISIONS

SEC. 401. [47 U.S.C. 401] JURISDICTION TO ENFORCE ACT AND ORDERS OF COMMISSION.

(a) The district courts of the United States shall have jurisdiction, upon application of the Attorney General of the United States at the request of the Commission, alleging a failure to comply with or a violation of any of the provisions of this Act by any person, to issue a writ or writs of mandamus commanding such person to comply with the provisions of this Act.

(b) If any person fails or neglects to obey any order of the Commission other than for the payment of money, while the same is in effect, the Commission or any party injured thereby, or the United States, by its Attorney General, may apply to the appropriate district court of the United States for the enforcement of such order. If, after hearing, that court determines that the order was regularly made and duly served, and that the person is in disobedience of the same, the court shall enforce obedience to such order by a writ of injunction or other proper process, mandatory or otherwise, to restrain such person or the officers, agents, or representatives of such person, from further disobedience of such order, or to enjoin upon it or them obedience to the same.

(c) Upon the request of the Commission it shall be the duty of any district attorney of the United States to whom the Commission may apply to institute in the proper court and to prosecute under the direction of the Attorney General of the United States all necessary proceedings for the enforcement of the provisions of this Act and for the punishment of all violations thereof, and the costs and expenses of such prosecutions shall be paid out of the appropriations for the expenses of the courts of the United States.

SEC. 402. [47 U.S.C. 402] PROCEEDINGS TO ENJOIN, SET ASIDE, ANNUL, OR SUSPEND ORDERS OF THE COMMISSION.

(a) Any proceeding to enjoin, set aside, annul, or suspend any order of the Commission under this Act (except those appealable under subsection (b) of this section) shall be brought as provided by and in the manner prescribed in chapter 158 of title 28, United States Code.

(b) Appeals may be taken from decisions and orders of the Commission to the United States Court of Appeals for the District of Columbia in any of the following cases:

(1) By any applicant for a construction permit or station license, whose application is denied by the Commission.

(2) By any applicant for the renewal or modification of any such instrument of authorization whose application is denied by the Commission.

(3) By any party to an application for authority to transfer, assign, or dispose of any such instrument of authorization, or any rights thereunder, whose application is denied by the Commission.

(4) By any applicant for the permit required by section 325 of this act whose application has been denied by the Commission, or by any permittee under said section whose permit has been revoked by the Commission.

(5) By the holder of any construction permit or station license which has been modified or revoked by the Commission.

(6) By any other person who is aggrieved or whose interests are adversely affected by any order of the Commission granting or denying any application described in paragraphs (1), (2), (3), (4), and (9) hereof.

(7) By any person upon whom an order to cease and desist has been served under section 312 of this Act.

(8) By any radio operator whose license has been suspended by theCommission.

(9) By any applicant for authority to provide interLATA services under section 271 of this Act whose application is denied by the Commission.

(c) Such appeal shall be taken by filing a notice of appeal with the courtwithin thirty days from the date upon which public notice is given of the decision or order complained of. Such notice of appeal shall contain a concise statement of the nature of the preceedings as to which the appeal is taken; a concise statement of the reasons on which the appellant intends to rely, separately stated and numbered; and proof of service of a true copy of said notice and statement upon the Commission. Upon filing of such notice, the court shall have jurisdiction of the proceedings and of the questions determined therein and shall have power, by order, directed to the Commission or any other party to the appeal, to grant such temporary relief as it may deem just and proper. Orders granting temporary relief may be either affirmative or negative in their scope and application so as to permit either the maintenance of the status quo in the matter in which the appeal is taken or the restoration of a position or status terminated or adversely affected by the order appealed from and shall, unless otherwise ordered by the court, be effective pending hearing and determination of said appeal and compliance by the Commission with the final judgment of the court rendered in said appeal.

(d) Upon the filing of any such notice of appeal the appellant shall, not later than five days after the filing of such notice, notify each person shown by the records of the Commission to be interested in said appeal of the filing and pendency of the same. The Commission shall file with the court the record upon which the order complained of was entered, as provided in section 2112 of Title 28, United States Code.

(e) Within thirty days after the filing of any such appeal any interested person may intervene and participate in the proceedings had upon said appeal by filing with the court a notice of intention to intervene and a verified statement showing the nature of the interest of such party, together with proof of service of true copies of said notice and statement, both upon appellant and upon the Commission. Any person who would be aggrieved or whose interest would be adversely affected by a reversal or modification of the order of the Commission complained of shall be considered an interested party.

(f) The record and briefs upon which any such appeal shall be heard and determined by the court shall contain such information and material, and shall be prepared within such time and in such manner as the court may by rule prescribe.

(g) The court shall hear and determine the appeal upon the record before it in the manner prescribed by section 706 of title 5.

(h) In the event that the court shall render a decision and enter an order reversing the order of the Commission, it shall remand the case to the Commission to carry out the judgment of the court and it shall be the duty of the Commission, in the absence of the proceedings to review such judgment, to forth with give effect thereto, and unless otherwise ordered by the court, to do so upon the basis of the proceedings already had and the record upon which said appeal was heard and determined.

(i) The court may, in its discretion, enter judgment for costs in favor of or against an appellant, or other interested parties intervening in said appeal, but not against the Commission, depending upon the nature of the issues involved upon said appeal and the outcome thereof.

(j) The court 's judgment shall be final, subject, however, to review by the Supreme Court of the United States upon writ of certiorari on petition therefor under section 1254 of title 28 of the United States Code, by the appellant, by the Commission, or by any interested party intervening in the appeal, or by certification by the court pursuant to the provisions of that section.

SEC. 403. [47 U.S.C. 403] INQUIRY BY COMMISSION ON ITS OWN MOTION.

The Commission shall have full authority and power at any time to institute an inquiry, on its own motion, in any case and as to any matter or thing concerning which complaint is authorized to be made, to or before the Commission by any provision of this Act, or concerning which any question may arise under any of the provisions of this Act, or relating to the enforcement of any of the provisions of this Act. The Commission shall have the same powers and authority to proceed with any inquiry instituted on its own motion as though it had been appealed to by complaint or petition under any of the provisions of this Act, including the power to make and enforce any order or orders in the case, or relating to the matter or thing concerning which the inquiry is had, excepting orders for the payment of money.

SEC. 404. [47 U.S.C. 404] REPORTS OF INVESTIGATIONS.

Whenever an investigation shall be made by the Commission it shall be its duty to make a report in writing in respect thereto, which shall state the conclusions of the Commission, together with its decision, order, or requirements in the premises; and in case damages are awarded such report shall include the findings of fact on which the award is made.

SEC. 405. [47 U.S.C. 405] RECONSIDERATIONS.

(a) After an order, decision, report, or action has been made or taken in any proceeding by the Commission, or by any designated authority within the Commission pursuant to a delegation under section 5(c)(1), any party thereto, or any other person aggrieved or whose interests are adversely affected thereby, may petition for reconsideration only to the authority making or taking the order, decision, report, or action; and it shall be lawful for such authority, whether it be the Commission or other authority designated under section 5(c)(1), in its discretion, to grant such a reconsideration if sufficient reason therefor be made to appear. A petition for reconsideration must be filed within thirty days from the date upon which public notice is given of the order, decision, report, or action complained of. No such application shall excuse any person from complying with or obeying any order, decision, report, or action of the Commission, or operate in any manner to stay or postpone the enforcement thereof, without the special order of the Commission. The filing of a petition for reconsideration shall not be a condition precedent to judicial review of any such order, decision, report, or action, except where the party seeking such review (1) was not a party to the proceedings resulting in such order, decision, report, or action, or (2) relies on questions of fact or law upon which the Commission, or designated authority within the Commission, has been afforded no opportunity to pass. The Commission, or designated authority within the Commission, shall enter an order, with a concise statement of the reasons therefor, denying a petition for reconsideration or granting such petition, in whole or in part, and ordering such further proceedings as may be appropriate: *Provided,* That in any case where such petition relates to an instrument of authorization granted without a hearing, the Commission, or designated authority within the Commission, shall take such action within ninety days of the filing of such petition. Reconsiderations shall be governed by such general rules as the Commission may establish, except that no evidence other than newly discovered evidence, evidence which has become available only since the original taking of evidence, or evidence which the Commission or designated authority within the Commission believes should have been taken in the original proceeding shall be taken on any reconsideration. The time within which a petition for review must be filed in a proceeding to which section 402(a) applies, or within which an appeal must be taken under section 402(b) in any case, shall be computed from the date upon which the Commission gives public notice of the order, decision, report, or action complained of.

(b)(1) Within 90 days after receiving a petition for reconsideration of an order concluding a hearing under section 204(a) or concluding an investigation under section 208(b), the Commission shall issue an order granting or denying such petition.

(2) Any order issued under paragraph (1) shall be a final order and may be appealed under section 402(a).

TITLE V—PENAL PROVISIONS-FORFEITURES
SEC. 501. [47 U.S.C. 501] GENERAL PENALTY.

Any person who willfully and knowingly does or causes or suffers to be done any act, matter, or thing, in this Act prohibited or declared to be unlawful, or who willfully and knowingly omits or fails to do any act, matter, or thing in this Act required to be done, or willfully and knowingly causes or suffers such omission or failure, shall upon conviction thereof, be punished for such offense, for which no penalty (other than a forfeiture) is provided in this Act, by a fine of not more than $10,000 or by imprisonment for a term not exceeding one year, or both; except that any person, having been once convicted of an offense punishable under this section, who is subsequently convicted of violating any provision of this Act punishable under this section, shall be punished by a fine of not more than $10,000 or by imprisonment for a term not exceeding two years, or both.

SEC. 502. [47 U.S.C. 502] VIOLATION OF RULES, REGULATIONS, AND SO FORTH.

Any person who willfully and knowingly violates any rule, regulation, restriction, or condition made or imposed by the Commission under authority of this Act, or any rule, regulation, restriction, or condition made or imposed by any international radio or wire communications treaty or convention, or regulations annexed thereto, to which the United States is or may hereafter become a party, shall, in addition to any other penalties provided by law, be punished, upon conviction thereof, by a fine of not more than $500 for each and every day during which such offense occurs.

SEC. 503. [47 U.S.C. 503] FORFEITURES IN CASES OF REBATES AND OFFSETS.

(a) Any person who shall deliver messages for interstate or foreign transmission to any carrier, or for whom as sender or receiver, any such carrier shall transmit any interstate or foreign wire or radio communication, who shall knowingly by employee, agent, officer, or otherwise, directly or indirectly, by or through any means or device whatsoever, receive or accept from such common carrier any sum of money or any other valuable consideration as a rebate or offset against the regular charges for transmission of such messages as fixed by the schedules of charges provided for in this Act, shall in addition to any other penalty provided by this Act forfeit to the United States a sum of money three times the amount of money so received or accepted and three times the value of any other consideration so received or accepted, to be ascertained by the trial court; and in the trial of said action all such rebates or other considerations so received or accepted for a period of six years prior to the commencement of the action, may be included therein, and the amount recovered shall be three times the total amount of money, or three times the total value of such consideration, so received or accepted, or both, as the case may be.

(b)(1) Any person who is determined by the Commission, in accordance with paragraph (3) or (4) of this subsection, to have—

(A) willfully or repeatedly failed to comply substantially with theterms and conditions of any license, permit, certificate, or other instrument or authorization issued by the Commission;

(B) willfully or repeatedly failed to comply with any of theprovisions of this Act or of any rule, regulation, or order issued by the Commission under this Act or under any treaty, convention, or other agreement to which the United States is a party and which is binding upon the United States;

(C) violated any provision of section 317(c) or 508(a) of this Act;

or

(D) violated any provision of section 1304, 1343, or 1464 of title 18, United States Code; shall be liable to the United States for a forfeiture penalty. A forfeiture penalty under this subsection shall be in addition to any other penalty provided for by this Act; except that this subsection shall not apply to any conduct which is subject to forfeiture under title II, part II or III of title III, or section 506 of this Act.

(2)(A) If the violator is (i) a broadcast station licensee or permittee, (ii) a cable television operator, or (iii) an applicant for any broadcast or cable television operator license, permit, certificate, or other instrument or authorization issued by the Commission, the amount of any forfeiture penalty determined under this section shall not exceed $25,000 for each violation or each day of a continuing violation, except that the amount assessed for any continuing violation shall not exceed a total of $250,000 for any single act or failure to act described in paragraph (1) of this subsection.

(B) If the violator is a common carrier subject to the provisions of this Actor an applicant for any common carrier license, permit, certificate, or other instrument of authorization issued by the Commission, the amount of any forfeiture penalty determined under this subsection shall not exceed $100,000 for each violation or each day of a continuing violation, except that the amount assessed for any continuing violation shall not exceed a total of $1,000,000 for any single act or failure to act described in paragraph (1) of this subsection.

(C) In any case not covered in subparagraph (A) or (B), the amount of any forfeiture penalty determined under this subsection shall not exceed $10,000 for each violation or each day of a continuing violation, except that the amount assessed for any continuing violation shall not exceed a total of $75,000 for any single act or failure to act described in paragraph (1) of this subsection.

(D) The amount of such forfeiture penalty shall be assessed by the Commission, or its designee, by written notice. In determining the amount of such a forfeiture penalty, the Commission or its designee shall take into account the nature, circumstances, extent, and gravity of the violation and, with respect to the violator, the degree of culpability, any history of prior offenses, ability to pay, and such other matters as justice may require.

(3)(A) At the discretion of the Commission, a forfeiture penalty may be determined against a person under this subsection after notice and an opportunity for a hearing before the Commission or an administrative law judge thereof in accordance with section 554 of title 5, United States Code. Any person against whom a forfeiture penalty is determined under this paragraph may obtain review thereof pursuant to section 402(a).

(B) If any person fails to pay an assessment of a forfeiture penalty determined under subparagraph (A) of this paragraph, after it has become a final and unappealable order or after the appropriate court has entered final judgment in favor of the Commission, the Commission shall refer the matter to the Attorney General of the United States, who shall recover the amount assessed in any appropriate district court of the United States. In such action, the validity and appropriateness of the final order imposing the forfeiture penalty shall not be subject to review.

(4) Except as provided in paragraph (3) of this subsection, no forfeiture penalty shall be imposed under this subsection against any person unless and until—

(A) the Commission issues a notice of apparent liability, in writing, with respect to such person;

(B) such notice has been received by such person, or until the Commission has sent such notice to the last known address of such person, by registered or certified mail; and

(C) such person is granted an opportunity to show, in writing,within such reasonable period of time as the Commission prescribes by rule or regulation, why no such forfeiture penalty should be imposed.

Such a notice shall (i) identify each specific provision, term, and condition of any Act, rule, regulation, order, treaty, convention, or other agreement, license, permit, certificate, instrument, or authorization which such person apparently violated or with which such person apparently failed to comply; (ii) set forth the nature of the act or omission charged against such person and the facts upon which such charge is based; and (iii) state the date on which such conduct occurred. Any forfeiture penalty determined under this paragraph shall be recoverable pursuant to section 504(a) of this Act.

(5) No forfeiture liability shall be determined under this subsection againstany person, if such person does not hold a license, permit, certificate, or other authorization issued by the Commission, and if such person is not an applicant for a license, permit, certificate, or other authorization issued by the Commission, unless, prior to the notice required by paragraph (3) of this subsection or the notice of apparent liability required by paragraph (4) of this subsection, such person (A) is sent a citation of the violation charged; (B) is

given a reasonable opportunity for a personal interview with an official of the Commission, at the field office of the Commission which is nearest to such person's place of residence; and (C) subsequently engages in conduct of the type described in such citation. The provisions of this paragraph shall not apply, however, if the person involved is engaging in activities for which a license, permit, certificate, or other authorization is required, or is a cable television system operator, if the person involved is transmitting on frequencies assigned for use in a service in which individual station operation is authorized by rule pursuant to section 307(e), or in the case of violations of section 303(q), if the person involved is a nonlicensee tower owner who has previously received notice of the obligations imposed by section 303(q) from the Commission or the permittee or licensee who uses that tower. Whenever the requirements of this paragraph are satisfied with respect to a paricular person, such person shall not be entitled to receive any additional citation of the violation charged, with respect to any conduct of the type described in the citation sent under this paragraph.

(6) No forfeiture penalty shall be determined or imposed against any personunder this subsection if—

(A) such person holds a broadcast station license issued under titleIII of this Act and if the violation charged occurred—

(i) more than 1 year prior to the date of issuance of therequired notice or notice of apparent liability; or

(ii) prior to the date of commencement of the current termof such license, whichever is earlier; or

(B) such person does not hold a broadcast station license issuedunder title III of this Act and if the violation charged occurred more than 1 year prior to the date of issuance of the required notice or notice of apparent liability. For purposes of this paragraph, "date of commencement of the current term of such license" means the date of commencement of the last term of license for which the licensee has been granted a license by the Commission. A separate license term shall not be deemed to have commenced as a result of continuing a license in effect under section 307(c) pending decision on an application for renewal of the license.

SEC. 504. [47 U.S.C. 504] PROVISIONS RELATING TO FORFEITURES.

(a) The forfeitures provided for in this Act shall be payable into theTreasury of the United States, and shall be recoverable, except as otherwise provided with respect to a forfeiture penalty determined under section 503(b)(3) of this Act, in a civil suit in the name of the United States brought in the district where the person or carrier has its principal operating office or in any district through which the line or system of the carrier runs: *Provided,* That any suit for the recovery of a forfeiture imposed pursuant to the provisions of this Act shall be a trial de novo: *Provided further,* That in the case of forfeiture by a ship, said forfeiture may also be recoverable by way of libel in any district in which such ship shall arrive or depart. Such forfeitures shall be in addition to any other general or specific penalties herein provided. It shall be the duty of the various district attorneys, under the direction of the Attorney General of the United States, to prosecute for the recovery of forfeitures under this Act. The costs and expenses of such prosecutions shall be paid from the appropriation for the expenses of the courts of the United States.

(b) The forfeitures imposed by title II, parts II and III of title III, andsections 503(b) and 506 of this Act shall be subject to remission or mitigation by the Commission, under such regulations and methods of ascertaining the facts as may seem to it advisable, and, if suit has been instituted, the Attorney General, upon request of the Commission, shall direct the discontinuance of any prosecution to recover such forfeitures: *Provided, however,* That no forfeiture shall be remitted or mitigated after determination by a court of competent jurisdiction.

(c) In any case where the Commission issues a notice of apparent liabilitylooking toward the imposition of a forfeiture under this Act, that fact shall not be used, in any other proceeding before the Commission, to the prejudice of the person to whom such notice was issued, unless (i) the forfeiture has been paid, or (ii) a court of competent jurisdiction has ordered payment of such forfeiture, and such order has become final.

SEC. 505. [47 U.S.C. 505] VENUE OF OFFENSES.

The trial of any offense under this Act shall be in the district in which it is committed; or if the offense is committed upon the high seas, or out of the jurisdiction of any particular State or district, the trial shall be in the district where the offender may be found or into which he shall be first brought. Whenever the offense is begun in one jurisdiction and completed in another it may be dealt with, inquired of, tried, determined, and punished in either jurisdiction in the same manner as if the offense had been actually and wholly committed therein.

TITLE VI—CABLE COMMUNICATIONS
PART I—GENERAL PROVISIONS
SEC. 601. [47 U.S.C. 521] PURPOSES.

The purposes of this title are to—

(1) establish a national policy concerning cable communications;

(2) establish franchise procedures and standards which encourage the growth and development of cable systems and which assure that cable systems are responsive to the needs and interests of the local community;
(3) establish guidelines for the exercise of Federal, State, and local authority with respect to the regulation of cable systems;
(4) assure that cable communications provide and are encouraged to provide the widest possible diversity of information sources and services to the public;
(5) establish an orderly process for franchise renewal which protects cable operators against unfair denials of renewal where the operator's past performance and proposal for future performance meet the standards established by this title; and
(6) promote competition in cable communications and minimizeunnecessary regulation that would impose an undue economic burden on cable systems.

RED LION BROADCASTING CO. v. FCC
Supreme Court of the United States
April 2-3, 1969; June 9, 1969, Decided
No. 2
395 U.S. 367; 89 S.Ct. 1794; 23 L.Ed.2d 371

Mr. Justice WHITE delivered the opinion of the Court.

The Federal Communications Commission has for many years imposed on radio and television broadcasters the requirement that discussion of public issues be presented on broadcast stations, and that each side of those issues must be given fair coverage. This is known as the fairness doctrine, which originated very early in the history of broadcasting and has maintained its present outlines for some time. It is an obligation whose content has been defined in a long series of FCC rulings in particular cases, and which is distinct from the statutory requirement of § 315 of the Communications Act that equal time be allotted all qualified candidates for public office. Two aspects of the fairness doctrine, relating to personal attacks in the context of controversial public issues and to political editorializing, were codified more precisely in the form of FCC regulations in 1967. The two cases before us now, which were decided separately below, challenge the constitutional and statutory bases of the doctrine and component rules. Red Lion involves the application of the fairness doctrine to a particular broadcast, and RTNDA arises as an action to review the FCC's 1967 promulgation of the personal attack and political editorializing regulations, which were laid down after the Red Lion litigation had begun.

I.

A.

The Red Lion Broadcasting Company is licensed to operate a Pennsylvania radio station, WGCB. On November 27, 1964, WGCB carried a 15-minute broadcast by the Reverend Billy James Hargis as part of a 'Christian Crusade' series. A book by Fred J. Cook entitled 'Goldwater—Extremist on the Right' was discussed by Hargis, who said that Cook had been fired by a newspaper for making false charges against city officials; that Cook had then worked for a Communist-affiliated publication; that he had defended Alger Hiss and attacked J. Edgar Hoover and the Central Intelligence Agency; and that he had now written a 'book to smear and destroy Barry Goldwater.' When Cook heard of the broadcast he concluded that he had been personally attacked and demanded free reply time, which the station refused. After an exchange of letters among Cook, Red Lion, and the FCC, the FCC declared that the Hargis broadcast constituted a personal attack on Cook; that Red Lion had failed to meet its obligation under the fairness doctrine as expressed in Times-Mirror Broadcasting Co., 24 P & F Radio Reg. 404 (1962), to send a tape, transcript, or summary of the broadcast to Cook and offer him reply time; and that the station must provide reply time whether or not Cook would pay for it. On review in the Court of Appeals for the District of Columbia Circuit, the FCC's position was upheld as constitutional and otherwise proper. 127 U.S.App.D.C. 129, 381 F.2d 908 (1967).

B.

Not long after the Red Lion litigation was begun, the FCC issued a Notice of Proposed Rule Making, 31 Fed.Reg. 5710, with an eye to making the personal attack aspect of the fairness doctrine more precise and more readily enforceable, and to specifying its rules relating to political editorials. After considering written comments supporting and opposing the rules, the FCC adopted them substantially as proposed, 32 Fed.Reg. 10303. Twice amended, 32 Fed.Reg. 11531, 33 Fed.Reg. 5362, the rules were held unconstitutional in the RTNDA litigation by the Court of Appeals for the Seventh Circuit, on review of the rulemaking proceeding, as abridging the freedoms of speech and press. 400 F.2d 1002 (1968).

As they now stand amended, the regulations read as follows:

'Personal attacks; political editorials.

'(a) When, during the presentation of views on a controversial issue of public importance, an attack is made upon the honesty, character, integrity or like personal qualities of an identified person or group, the licensee shall, within a reasonable time and in no event later than 1 week after the attack, transmit to the person or group attacked (1) notification of the date, time and identification of the broadcast; (2) a script or tape (or an accurate summary if a script or tape is not available) of the attack, and (3) an offer of a reasonable opportunity to respond over the licensee's facilities.

'(b) The provisions of paragraph (a) of this section shall not be applicable (1) to attacks on foreign groups or foreign public figures; (2) to personal attacks which are made by legally qualified candidates, their authorized spokesmen, or those associated with them in the campaign, on other such candidates, their authorized spokesmen, or persons associated with the candidates in the campaign; and (3) to bona fide newscasts, bona fide news interviews, and on-the-spot coverage of a bona fide news event (including commentary or analysis contained in the foregoing programs, but the provisions of paragraph (a) of this section shall be applicable to editorials of the licensee).

'NOTE: The fairness doctrine is applicable to situations coming within ((3)), above, and, in a specific factual situation, may be applicable in the ((2)), above. See, section 315(a) of the Act, 47 U.S.C. § 315(a); Public Notice: Applicability of the Fairness Doctrine in the Handling of Controversial Issues of Public Importance. 29 F.R. 10415. The categories listed in ((3)) are the same as those specified in section 315(a) of the Act.

'(c) Where a licensee, in an editorial, (i) endorses or (ii) opposes a legally qualified candidate or candidates, the licensee shall, within 24 hours after the editorial, transmit to respectively (i) the other qualified candidate or candidates for the same office or (ii) the candidate opposed in the editorial (1) notification of the date and the time of the editorial; (2) a script or tape of the editorial; and (3) an offer of a reasonable opportunity for a candidate or a spokesman of the candidate to respond over the licensee's facilities: Provided, however, That where such editorials are broadcast within 72 hours prior to the day of the election, the licensee shall comply with the provisions of this paragraph sufficiently far in advance of the broadcast to enable the candidate or candidates to have a reasonable opportunity to prepare a response and to present it in a timely fashion.' 47 CFR §§ 73.123, 73.300, 73.598, 73.679 (all identical).

C.

Believing that the specific application of the fairness doctrine in Red Lion, and the promulgation of the regulations in RTNDA, are both authorized by Congress and enhance rather than abridge the freedoms of speech and press protected by the First Amendment, we hold them valid and constitutional, reversing the judgment below in RTNDA and affirming the judgment below in Red Lion.

II.

The history of the emergence of the fairness doctrine and of the related legislation shows that the Commission's action in the Red Lion case did not exceed its authority, and that in adopting the new regulations the Commission was implementing congressional policy rather than embarking on a frolic of its own.

A.

Before 1927, the allocation of frequencies was left entirely to the private sector, and the result was chaos. It quickly became apparent that broadcast frequencies constituted a scarce resource whose use could be regulated and rationalized only by the Government. Without government control, the medium would be of little use because of the cacophony of competing voices, none of which could be clearly and predictably heard.[5] Consequently, the Federal Radio Commission was established to allocate frequencies among competing applicants in a manner responsive to the public 'convenience, interest, or necessity.'

Very shortly thereafter the Commission expressed its view that the 'public interest requires ample play for the free and fair competition of opposing views, and the commission believes that the principle applies * * * to all discussions of issues of importance to the public.' Great Lakes Broadcasting Co., 3 F.R.C.Ann.Rep. 32, 33 (1929), rev'd on other grounds, 59 App.D.C. 197, 37 F.2d 993, cert. dismissed, 281 U.S. 706, 50 S.Ct. 467, 74 L.Ed., 1129 (1930). This doctrine was applied through denial of license renewals or construction permits, both by the FRC, Trinity Methodist Church, South v. FRC, 61 App.D.C. 311, 62 F.2d 850 (1932), cert. denied, 288 U.S. 599, 53 S.Ct. 317, 77 L.Ed. 975 (1933), and its successor FCC, Young People's Association for the Propagation of the Gospel, 6 F.C.C. 178 (1938). After an extended period during which the licensee was obliged not only to cover and to cover fairly the views of others, but also to refrain from expressing his own personal views, Mayflower Broadcasting Corp., 8 F.C.C. 333 (1940), the latter limitation on the licensee was abandoned and the doctrine developed into its present form.

There is a twofold duty laid down by the FCC's decisions and described by the 1949 Report on Editorializing by Broadcast Licensees, 13 F.C.C. 1246 (1949). The broadcaster must give adequate coverage to public issues, United Broadcasting Co., 10 F.C.C. 515 (1945), and coverage must be fair in that it accurately reflects the opposing views. New Broadcasting Co., 6 P & F Radio Reg. 258 (1950). This must be done at the broadcaster's own expense if sponsorship is unavailable. Cullman Broadcasting Co., 25 P & F Radio Reg. 895 (1963). Moreover, the duty must be met by programming obtained at the licensee's own initiative if available from no other source... The Federal Radio Commission had imposed these two basic duties on broadcasters since the outset... and in particular respects the personal attack rules and regulations at issue here have spelled them out in greater detail.

When a personal attack has been made on a figure involved in a public issue both the doctrine of cases such as Red Lion and Times-Mirror Broadcasting Co., 24 P & F Radio Reg. 404 (1962), and also the 1967 regulations at issue in RTNDA require that the individual attacked himself be offered an opportunity to respond. Likewise, where one candidate is endorsed in a political editorial, the other candidates must themselves be offered reply time to use personally or through a spokesman. These obligations differ from the general fairness requirement that issues be presented, and presented with coverage of competing views, in that the broadcaster does not have the option of presenting the attacked party's side himself or choosing a third party to represent that side. But insofar as there is an obligation of the broadcaster to see that both sides are presented, and insofar as that is an affirmative obligation, the personal attack doctrine and regulations do not differ from the preceding fairness doctrine. The simple fact that the attacked men or unendorsed candidates may respond themselves or through agents is not a critical distinction, and indeed, it is not unreasonable for the FCC to conclude that the objective of adequate presentation of all sides may best be served by allowing those most closely affected to make the response, rather than leaving the response in the hands of the station which has attacked their candidacies, endorsed their opponents, or carried a personal attack upon them.

B.

The statutory authority of the FCC to promulgate these regulations derives from the mandate to the 'Commission from time to time, as public convenience, interest, or necessity requires' to promulgate 'such rules and regulations and prescribe such restrictions and conditions * * * as may be necessary to carry out the provisions of this chapter * * *.' 47 U.S.C. § 303 and § 303(r). The Commission is specifically directed to consider the demands of the public interest in the course of granting licenses. 47 U.S.C. ss 307(a), 309(a); renewing them, 47 U.S.C. § 307; and modifying them. Ibid. Moreover, the FCC has included among the conditions of the Red Lion license itself the requirement that operation of the station be carried out in the public interest, 47 U.S.C. § 309(h). This mandate to the FCC to assure that broadcasters operate in the public interest is a broad one, a power 'not niggardly but expansive,' It is broad enough to encompass these regulations.

The fairness doctrine finds specific recognition in statutory form, is in part modeled on explicit statutory provisions relating to political candidates, and is approvingly reflected in legislative history.

In 1959 the Congress amended the statutory requirement of § 315 that equal time be accorded each political candidate to except certain appearances on news programs, but added that this constituted no exception 'from the obligation imposed upon them under this Act to operate in the public interest and to afford reasonable opportunity for the discussion of conflicting views on issues of public inportance.' Act of September 14, 1959, § 1, 73 Stat. 557, amending 47 U.S.C. § 315(a) (emphasis added). This language makes it very plain that Congress, in 1959, announced that the phrase 'public interest,' which had been in the Act since 1927, imposed a duty on broadcasters to discuss both sides of controversial public issues. In other words, the amendment vindicated the FCC's general view that the fairness doctrine inhered in the public interest standard. Subsequent legislation declaring the intent of an earlier statute is entitled to great weight in statutory construction. And here this principle is given special force by the equally venerable principle that the construction of a statute by those charged with its execution should be followed unless there are compelling indications that it is wrong, especially when Congress has refused to alter the administrative construction. Here, the Congress has not just kept its silence by refusing to overturn the administrative construction, but has ratified it with positive legislation. Thirty years of consistent administrative construction left undisturbed by Congress until 1959, when that construction was expressly accepted, reinforce the natural conclusion that the public interest language of the Act authorized the Commission to require licensees to use their stations for discussion of public issues, and that the FCC is free to implement this requirement by reasonable rules and regulations which fall short of abridgment of the freedom of speech and press, and of the censorship proscribed by § 326 of the Act.

The objectives of § 315 themselves could readily be circumvented but for the complementary fairness doctrine ratified by § 315. The section applies only to campaign appearances by candidates, and not by family, friends, campaign managers, or other supporters. Without the fairness doctrine, then, a licensee could ban all campaign appearances by candidates themselves from the air and proceed to deliver over his station entirely to the supporters of one slate of candidates, to the exclusion of all others. In this way the broadcaster could have a far greater impact on the favored candidacy than he could by simply allowing a spot appearance by the candidate himself. It is the fairness doctrine as an aspect of the obligation to operate in the public interest, rather than § 315, which prohibits the broadcaster from taking such a step.

The legislative history reinforces this view of the effect of the 1959 amendment. Even before the language relevant here was added, the Senate report on amending § 315 noted that 'broadcast frequencies are limited and, therefore, they have been necessarily considered a public trust. Every licensee who is fortunate in obtaining a license is mandated to operate in the public interest and has assumed the obligation of presenting important public questions fairly and without bias.'

Rather than leave this approval solely in the legislative history, Senator Proxmire suggested an amendment to make it part of the Act. 105 Cong.Rec. 14457. This amendment, which Senator Pastore, a manager of the bill and a ranking member of the Senate Committee, considered 'rather surplusage,' 105 Cong.Rec. 14462, constituted a positive statement of doctrine and was altered to the present merely approving language in the conference committee. In explaining the language to the Senate after the committee changes, Senator Pastore said: 'We insisted that that provision remain in the bill, to be a continuing reminder and admonition to the Federal Communications Commission and to the broadcasters alike, that we were not abandoning the philosophy that gave birth to section 315, in giving the people the right to have a full and complete disclosure of conflicting views on news of interest to the people of the country.' 105 Cong.Rec. 17830. Senator Scott, another Senate manager, added that: 'It is intended to encompass all legitimate areas of public importance which are controversial,' not just politics. 105 Cong.Rec. 17831.

It is true that the personal attack aspect of the fairness doctrine was not actually adjudicated until after 1959, so that Congress then did not have those rules specifically before it. However, the obligation to offer time to reply to a personal attack was presaged by the FCC's 1949 Report on Editorializing, which the FCC views as the principal summary of its ratio decidendi in cases in this area:

'In determining whether to honor specific requests for time, the station will inevitably be confronted with such questions as * * * whether there may not be other available groups or individuals who might be more appropriate spokesmen for the particular point of view than the person making the request. The latter's personal involvement in the controversy may also be a factor which must be considered, for elementary considerations of fairness may dictate that time be allocated to a person or group which has been specifically attacked over the station, where otherwise no such obligation would exist.' 13 F.C.C., at 1251—1252.

When the Congress ratified the FCC's implication of a fairness doctrine in 1959 it did not, of course, approve every past decision or pronouncement by the Commission on this subject, or give it a completely free hand for the future. The statutory authority does not go so far. But we cannot say that when a station publishes personal attacks or endorses political candidates, it is a misconstruction of the public interest standard to require the station to offer time for a response rather than to leave the response entirely within the control of the station which has attacked either the candidacies or the men who wish to reply in their own defense. When a broadcaster grants time to a political candidate, Congress itself requires that equal time be offered to his opponents. It would exceed our competence to hold that the Commission is unauthorized by the statute to employ a similar device where personal attacks or political editorials are broadcast by a radio or television station.

In light of the fact that the 'public interest' in broadcasting clearly encompasses the presentation of vigorous debate of controversial issues of importance and concern to the public; the fact that the FCC has rested upon that language from its very inception a doctrine that these issues must be discussed, and fairly; and the fact that Congress has acknowledged that the analogous provisions of § 315 are not preclusive in this area, and knowingly preserved the FCC's complementary efforts, we think the fairness doctrine and its component personal attack and political editorializing regulations are a legitimate exercise of congressionally delegated authority. The Communications

Act is not notable for the precision of its substantive standards and in this respect the explicit provisions of § 315, and the doctrine and rules at issue here which are closely modeled upon that section, are far more explicit than the generalized 'public interest' standard in which the Commission ordinarily finds its sole guidance, and which we have held a broad but adequate standard before. We cannot say that the FCC's declaratory ruling in Red Lion, or the regulations at issue in RTNDA, are beyond the scope of the congressionally conferred power to assure that stations are operated by those whose possession of a license serves 'the public interest.'

III.

The broadcasters challenge the fairness doctrine and its specific manifestations in the personal attack and political editorial rules on conventional First Amendment grounds, alleging that the rules abridge their freedom of speech and press. Their contention is that the First Amendment protects their desire to use their allotted frequencies continuously to broadcast whatever they choose, and to exclude whomever they choose from ever using that frequency. No man may be prevented from saying or publishing what he thinks, or from refusing in his speech or other utterances to give equal weight to the views of his opponents. This right, they say, applies equally to broadcasters.

A.

Although broadcasting is clearly a medium affected by a First Amendment interest, United States v. Paramount Pictures, Inc., 334 U.S. 131, 166, 68 S.Ct. 915. 333, 92 L.Ed. 1260 (1948), differences in the characteristics of new media justify differences in the First Amendment standards applied to them. Joseph Burstyn, Inc. v. Wilson, 343 U.S. 495, 503, 72 S.Ct. 777, 781, 96 L.Ed. 1098 (1952). For example, the ability of new technology to produce sounds more raucous than those of the human voice justifies restrictions on the sound level, and on the hours and places of use, of sound trucks so long as the restrictions are reasonable and applied without discrimination. Kovacs v. Cooper, 336 U.S. 77, 69 S.Ct. 448, 93 L.Ed. 513 (1949).

Just as the Government may limit the use of sound-amplifying equipment potentially so noisy that it drowns out civilized private speech, so may the Government limit the use of broadcast equipment. The right of free speech of a broadcaster, the user of a sound truck, or any other individual does not embrace a right to snuff out the free speech of others. Associated Press v. United States, 326 U.S. 1, 20, 65 S.Ct. 1416, 1424, 89 L.Ed. 2013 (1945).

When two people converse face to face, both should not speak at once if either is to be clearly understood. But the range of the human voice is so limited that there could be meaningful communications if half the people in the United States were talking and the other half listening. Just as clearly, half the people might publish and the other half read. But the reach of radio signals is incomparably greater than the range of the human voice and the problem of interference is a massive reality. The lack of know-how and equipment may keep many from the air, but only a tiny fraction of those with resources and intelligence can hope to communicate by radio at the same time if intelligible communication is to be had, even if the entire radio spectrum is utilized in the present state of commercially acceptable technology.

It was this fact, and the chaos which ensued from permitting anyone to use any frequency at whatever power level he wished, which made necessary the enactment of the Radio Act of 1927 and the Communications Act of 1934, as the Court has noted at length before. National Broadcasting Co. v. United States, 319 U.S. 190, 210—214, 63 S.Ct. 997, 1006—1009, 87 L.Ed. 1344 (1943). It was this reality which at the very least necessitated first the division of the radio spectrum into portions reserved respectively for public broadcasting and for other important radio uses such as amateur operation, aircraft, police, defense, and navigation; and then the subdivision of each portion, and assignment of specific frequencies to individual users or groups of users. Beyond this, however, because the frequencies reserved for public broadcasting were limited in number, it was essential for the Government to tell some applicants that they could not broadcast at all because there was room for only a few.

Where there are substantially more individuals who want to broadcast than there are frequencies to allocate, it is idle to posit an unabridgeable First Amendment right to broadcast comparable to the right of every individual to speak, write, or publish. If 100 persons want broadcast licenses but there are only 10 frequencies to allocate, all of them may have the same 'right' to a license; but if there is to be any effective communication by radio, only a few can be licensed and the rest must be barred from the airwaves. It would be strange if the First Amendment, aimed at protecting and furthering communications, prevented the Government from making radio communication possible by requiring licenses to broadcast and by limiting the number of licenses so as not to overcrowd the spectrum.

This has been the consistent view of the Court. Congress unquestionably has the power to grant and deny licenses and to eliminate existing stations. FRC v. Nelson Bros. Bond & Mortgage Co., 289 U.S. 266, 53 S.Ct. 627, 77 L.Ed. 1166 (1933). No one has a First Amendment right to a license or to monopolize a radio frequency; to deny a station license because 'the public interest' requires it 'is not a denial of free speech.' National Broadcasting Co. v. United States, 319 U.S. 190, 227, 63 S.Ct. 997, 1014, 87 L.Ed. 1344 (1943).

[12] By the same token, as far as the First Amendment is concerned those who are licensed stand no better than those to whom licenses are refused. A license permits broadcasting, but the lisensee has no constitutional right to be the one who holds the license or to monopolize a radio frequency to the exclusion of his fellow citizens. There is nothing in the First Amendment which prevents the Government from requiring a licensee to share his frequency with others and to conduct himself as a proxy or fiduciary with obligations to present those views and voices which are representative of his community and which would otherwise, by necessity, be barred from the airwaves.

This is not to say that the First Amendment is irrelevant to public broadcasting. On the contrary, it has a major role to play as the Congress itself recognized in § 326, which forbids FCC interference with 'the right of free speech by means of radio communication.' Because of the scarcity of radio frequencies, the Government is permitted to put restraints on licensees in favor of others whose views should be expressed on this unique medium. But the people as a whole retain their interest in free speech by radio and their collective right to have the medium function consistently with the ends and purposes of the First Amendment. It is the right of the viewers and listeners, not the right of the broadcasters, which is paramount. It is the purpose of the First Amendment to preserve an uninhibited marketplace of ideas in which truth will ultimately prevail, rather than to countenance monopolization of that market, whether it be by the Government itself or a private licensee. It is the right of the public to receive suitable access to social, political, esthetic, moral, and other ideas and experiences which is crucial here. That right may not constitutionally be abridged either by Congress or by the FCC.

B.

Rather than confer frequency monopolies on a relatively small number of licensees, in a Nation of 200,000,000, the Government could surely have decreed that each frequency should be shared among all or some of those who wish to use it, each being assigned a portion of the broadcast day or the broadcast week. The ruling and regulations at issue here do not go quite so far. They assert that under specified circumstances, a licensee must offer to make available a reasonable amount of broadcast time to those who have a view different from that which has already been expressed on his station. The expression of a political endorsement, or of a personal attack while dealing with a controversial public issue, simply triggers this time sharing. As we have said, the First Amendment confers no right on licensees to prevent others from broadcasting on 'their' frequencies and no right to an unconditional monopoly of a scarce resource which the Government has denied others the right to use.

In terms of constitutional principle, and as enforced sharing of a scarce resource, the personal attack and political editorial rules are indistinguishable from the equal-time provision of § 315, a specific enactment of Congress requiring stations to set aside reply time under specified circumstances and to which the fairness doctrine and these constituent regulations are important complements. That provision, which has been part of the law since 1927, Radio Act of 1927, § 18, 44 Stat. 1170, has been held valid by this Court as an obligation of the licensee relieving him of any power in any way to prevent or censor the broadcast, and thus insulating him from liability for defamation. The constitutionality of the statute under the First Amendment was unquestioned.

Nor can we say that it is inconsistent with the First Amendment goal of producing an informed public capable of conducting its own affairs to require a broadcaster to permit answers to personal attacks occurring in the course of discussing controversial issues, or to require that the political opponents of those endorsed by the station be given a chance to communicate with the public Otherwise, station owners and a few networks would have unfettered power to make time available only to the highest bidders, to communicate only their own views on public issues, people and candidates, and to permit on the air only those with whom they agreed. There is no sanctuary in the First Amendment for unlimited private censorship operating in a medium not open to all. 'Freedom of the press from governmental interference under the First Amendment does not sanction repression of that freedom by private interests.'

C.

It is strenuously argued, however, that if political editorials or personal attacks will trigger an obligation in broadcasters to afford the opportunity for expression to speakers who need not pay for time and whose views are unpalatable to the licensees, then broadcasters will be irresistibly forced to self-censorship and their coverage of controversial public issues will be eliminated or at least rendered wholly ineffective. Such a result would indeed be a serious matter, for should licensees actually eliminate their coverage of controversial issues, the purposes of the doctrine would be stifled.

At this point, however, as the Federal Communications Commission has indicated, that possibility is at best speculative. The communications industry, and in particular the networks, have taken pains to present controversial issues in the past, and even now they do not assert that they intend to abandon their efforts in this regard. It would be better if the FCC's encouragement were never necessary to induce the broadcasters to meet their responsibility. And if experience with the administration of those doctrines indicates that they have the net effect of reducing rather than enhancing the volume and quality of coverage, there will be time enough to reconsider the constitutional implications. The fairness doctrine in the past has had no such overall effect.

That this will occur now seems unlikely, however, since if present licensees should suddenly prove timorous, the Commission is not powerless to insist that they give adequate and fair attention to public issues. It does not violate the First Amendment to treat licensees given the privilege of using scarce radio frequencies as proxies for the entire community, obligated to give suitable time and attention to matters of great public concern. To condition the granting or renewal of licenses on a willingness to present representative community views on controversial issues is consistent with the ends and purposes of those constitutional provisions forbidding the abridgment of freedom of speech and freedom of the press. Congress need not stand idly by and permit those with licenses to ignore the problems which beset the people or to exclude from the airways anything but their own views of fundamental questions. The statute, long administrative practice, and cases are to this effect.

Licenses to broadcast do not confer ownership of designated frequencies, but only the temporary privilege of using them. 47 U.S.C. § 301. Unless renewed, they expire within three years. 47 U.S.C. § 307(d). The statute mandates the issuance of licenses if the 'public convenience, interest, or necessity will be served thereby.' 47 U.S.C. § 307(a). In applying this standard the Commission for 40 years has been choosing licensees based in part on their program proposals. In FRC v. Nelson Bros. Bond & Mortgage Co., 289 U.S. 266, 279, 53 S.Ct. 627, 634, 77 L.Ed. 1166 (1933), the Court noted that in 'view of the limited number of available broadcasting frequencies, the Congress has authorized allocation and licenses.' In determining how best to allocate frequencies, the Federal Radio Commission considered the needs of competing communities and the programs offered by competing stations to meet those needs; moreover, if needs or programs shifted, the Commission could alter its allocations to reflect those shifts. Id., at 285, 53 S.Ct. at 636. In the same vein, in FCC v. Pottsville Broadcasting Co., 309 U.S. 134, 137—138, 60 S.Ct. 437, 439, 84 L.Ed. 656 (1940), the Court noted that the statutory standard was a supple instrument to effect congressional desires 'to maintain * * * a grip on the dynamic aspects of radio transmission' and to allay fears that 'in the absence of governmental control the public interest might be subordinated to monopolistic domination in the broadcasting field.' Three years later the Court considered the validity of the Commission's chain broadcasting regulations, which among other things forbade stations from devoting too much time to network programs in order that there be suitable opportunity for local programs serving local needs. The Court upheld the regulations, unequivocally recognizing that the Commission was more than a traffic policeman concerned with the technical aspects of broadcasting and that it neither exceeded its powers under the statute nor transgressed the First Amendment in interesting itself in general program format and the kinds of programs broadcast by licensees. National

Broadcasting Co. v. United States, 319 U.S. 190, 63 S.Ct. 997, 87 L.Ed. 1344 (1943).

D.

The litigants embellish their First Amendment arguments with the contention that the regulations are so vague that their duties are impossible to discern. Of this point it is enough to say that, judging the validity of the regulations on their face as they are presented here, we cannot conclude that the FCC has been left a free hand to vindicate its own idiosyncratic conception of the public interest or of the requirements of free speech. Past adjudications by the FCC give added precision to the regulations; there was nothing vague about the FCC's specific ruling in Red Lion that Fred Cook should be provided an opportunity to reply. The regulations at issue in RTNDA could be employed in precisely the same way as the fairness doctrine was in Red Lion. Moreover, the FCC itself has recognized that the applicability of its regulations to situations beyond the scope of past cases may be questionable, 32 Fed.Reg. 10303, 10304 and n. 6, and will not impose sanctions in such cases without warning. We need not approve every aspect of the fairness doctrine to decide these cases, and we will not now pass upon the constitutionality of these regulations by envisioning the most extreme applications conceivable, United States v. Sullivan, 332 U.S. 689, 694, 68 S.Ct. 331, 334, 92 L.Ed. 297 (1948), but will deal with those problems if and when they arise.

We need not and do not now ratify every past and future decision by the FCC with regard to programming. There is no question here of the Commission's refusal to permit the broadcaster to carry a particular program or to publish his own views; of a discriminatory refusal to require the licensee to broadcast certain views which have been denied access to the airwaves; of government censorship of a particular program contrary to § 326; or of the official government view dominating public broadcasting. Such questions would raise more serious First Amendment issues. But we do hold that the Congress and the Commission do not violate the First Amendment when they require a radio or television station to give reply time to answer personal attacks and political editorials.

E.

It is argued that even if at one time the lack of available frequencies for all who wished to use them justified the Government's choice of those who would best serve the public interest by acting as proxy for those who would present differing views, or by giving the latter access directly to broadcast facilities, this condition no longer prevails so that continuing control is not justified. To this there are several answers.

Scarcity is not entirely a thing of the past. Advances in technology, such as microwave transmission, have led to more efficient utilization of the frequency spectrum, but uses for that spectrum have also grown apace. Portions of the spectrum must be reserved for vital uses unconnected with human communication, such as radio-navigational aids used by aircraft and vessels. Conflicts have even emerged between such vital functions as defense preparedness and experimentation in methods of averting midair collisions through radio warning devices. 'Land mobile services' such as police, ambulance, fire department, public utility, and other communications systems have been occupying an increasingly crowded portion of the frequency spectrum and there are, apart from licensed amateur radio operators' equipment, 5,000,000 transmitters operated on the 'citizens' band' which is also increasingly congested. Among the various uses for radio frequency space, including marine, aviation, amateur, military, and common carrier users, there are easily enough claimants to permit use of the whole with an even smaller allocation to broadcast radio and television uses than now exists.

Comparative hearings between competing applicants for broadcast spectrum space are by no means a thing of the past. The radio spectrum has become so congested that at times it has been necessary to suspend new applications. The very high frequency television spectrum is, in the country's major markets, almost entirely occupied, although space reserved for ultra high frequency television transmission, which is a relatively recent development as a commercially viable alternative, has not yet been completely filled.

The rapidity with which technological advances succeed one another to create more efficient use of spectrum space on the one hand, and to create new uses for that space by ever growing numbers of people on the other, makes it unwise to speculate on the future allocation of that space. It is enough to say that the resource is one of considerable and growing importance whose scarcity impelled its regulation by an agency authorized by Congress. Nothing in this record, or in our own researches, convinces us that the resource is no longer one for which there are more immediate and potential uses than can be accommodated, and for which wise planning is essential. This does not mean, of course, that every possible wavelength must be occupied at every hour by some vital use in order to sustain the congressional judgment. The substantial capital investment required for many uses, in addition to the potentiality for confusion and interference inherent in any scheme for continuous kaleidoscopic reallocation of all available space may make this unfeasible. The allocation need not be made at such a breakneck pace that the objectives of the allocation are themselves imperiled.

Even where there are gaps in spectrum utilization, the fact remains that existing broadcasters have often attained their present position because of their initial government selection in competition with others before new technological advances opened new opportunities for further uses. Long experience in broadcasting, confirmed habits of listeners and viewers, network affiliation, and other advantages in program procurement give existing broadcasters a substantial advantage over new entrants, even where new entry is technologically possible. These advantages are the fruit of a preferred position conferred by the Government. Some present possibility for new entry by competing stations is not enough, in itself, to render unconstitutional the Government's effort to assure that a broadcaster's programming ranges widely enough to serve the public interest.

In view of the scarcity of broadcast frequencies, the Government's role in allocating those frequencies, and the legitimate claims of those unable without governmental assistance to gain access to those frequencies for expression of their views, we hold the regulations and ruling at issue here are both authorized by statute and constitutional. The judgment of the Court of Appeals in Red Lion is affirmed and that in RTNDA reversed and the causes remanded for proceedings consistent with this opinion.

It is so ordered.

Not having heard oral argument in these cases, Mr. Justice DOUGLAS took no part in the Court's decision

HOWARD STERN SIGNS NEW FIVE-YEAR CONTRACT WITH SIRIUS XM
Agreement Includes Rights for SIRIUS XM to Transmit Howard Stern's Programming to Mobile Devices

New York, Dec. 9, 2010/PRNewswire-FirstCall/—Howard Stern and SIRIUS XM Radio) (Nasdaq: SIRI) today announced a new five year agreement. The news was first reported by Howard during his show this morning. (Logo: http://photos.prnewswire.com/prnh/NY82093LOGO)

"On my first day in satellite radio SIRIUS had approximately 600,000 subscribers. Today the two companies have 20 million; and, in my view, we have just scratched the surface of how many people will get on board," said Howard Stern. "I am especially excited that my show ill now be heard through SIRIUS XM on mobile devices. Access to my show on mobile devices will open up additional opportunities for my fans to hear me wherever they are."

"Howard is a great talent and we are thrilled that he will continue to provoke, engage and entertain on SIRIUS XM. Our agreement is good news on all fronts—it is good for SIRIUS XM subscribers and good for SIRIUS stockholders. Howard forever changed radio and was instrumental in putting SIRIUS on the map when he first launched on satellite radio. He is one of the few 'one-name' entertainers in the country and our 20 million subscribers are lucky to have him," said Mel Karmzin, Chief Executive Officer, SIRIUS XM.

The world-renowned Stern is credited with revolutionizing the talk radio format. Known for his large and extremely loayal fan base and for his unequalled ability to migrate fans to other media, Stern has embarked on numerous highly successful ventures over the years. Stern has written two best selling books—Private Parts, which was Simon & Schuster's fastest-selling book ever, and Miss America, the fastest-selling book in publishing history. He later starred in the highly successful motion picture adaptation of Private Parts, orchestrated on the fastest-selling soundtracks in motion picture history and has starred in one of the most watched entertainment pay-per-view of all time.

Howard's new contract will run through December 31, 2015. Under the terms of the new contract, SIRIUS XM will now have the right to transmit Howard's exclusive programming to mobile devices. Additional terms of the contract will not be disclosed.

About SIRIUS XM Radio

SIRIUS XM is America's satellite radio company, broadcasting more than 135 channels of commercial-free music, and premier sports, news, talk, entertainment, traffic, weather, and data services to more than 20 million subscribers in cars, trucks, boats and aircraft, and through a wide range of mobile devices.

SIRIUS XM offers an array of content from some of the biggest names in entertainment, as well as from professional sports leagues, major colleges, and national news and talk providers. SIRIUS XM programming is also available at sirius.com and xmradio.com, and on Apple iPhone and iPodtouch, Blackberry and Android-powered mobile devices using the SIRIUS XM Premium Online App.

SIRIUS XM has arrangements with every major automaker and its radio products are available at retail locations nationwide, as well as shop.sirius.com and shop.xmradio.com.

This communication contains "forward-looking statements" within the meaning of the Private Securities Litigation Reform Act of 1995. Such statements include, but are not limited to, statements about future financial and operating results, the combined company's plans, objectives, expectations and intentions with respect to future operations, products and services; and other statements identified by words such as "will likely result," "are expected to," "will continue," "is anticipated," "estimated," "intend," "plan," "projection," "outlook," or words of similar meaning. Such forward-looking statements are based upon the current beliefs and expectations of SIRIUS SM's management and are inherently subject to significant business, economic and competitive uncertainties and contingencies, many of which are difficult to predict and generally beyond the control of SIRIUS and XM. Actual results may differ materially from the results anticipated in these forward-looking statements.

The following facts, among others, could cause acual results to differ materially from the anticipated results or other expectations expressed in the forward-looking statement: our dependence upon automakers and other third parties, the substantial indebtness of SIRIUS and XM; the useful life of our satellites; and our competitive position versus other forms of audio and video entertainment. Additional factors that could cause SIRIUS' and XM's results to differ materially from those described in the forward-looking statements can be found in SIRIUS' Annual Report on form 10-K for the year ended December 31, 2009 and its Quarterly Report on Form 10-Q for the period ending September 30, 2010, which are filed with the Securities and Exchange Commission (the "SEC") and available at the SEC's Internet site (http:/www.sec.gov (Http://www.sec.gov)). The information set forth herein speaks only as of the date hereof, and XM disclaim any intention or obligation to update any forward looking statements as a result of developments occurring after the date of this communication.

P-SIRI

Contact Information for Media

Media

Patrick Reilly

212-901-6646
Patrick.reilly@siriusxm.com
News Provided by Acquire Media
[Published with permission for educational purposes]

SIRIUS XM AND HOWARD STERN IN A CONTRA 'DANCE'

Brian Stelter, CNN Money, (N.Y.), March 11, 2015
Htttp://money.cnn.com/2015/03/11/media/howard-stern-sirius-xm-contract-speculation/
[reprinted for educational purposes]

Sirius are once again negotiating in public law.

It's a "dance we're in," "Sirius CEO Jim Meyer told investors at a Deutsche Bank conference on Tuesday, "and we'll keeping working at it."

Does Stern want to sign up for a second decade on satellite radio? Or will the famously controversial talk show host decide to do something else, somewhere else?

In a Bloomberg Businessweek profile published on Wednesday, Meyer said he is eager to renew Stern's contract, but acknowledges the unknowns.

"If you listen to [Stern's] show, he always talks how happy he is, "Meyer told reporter Felix Gillette. But "just like your 12-year-old, he's always happy until something else comes along."

The Internet gives Stern more options than ever. Then again, no outlet may pay as handsomely as Sirius, which lured Stern away from traditional radio and into satellite radio back in 2006. It came at an extraordinary cost: about $100 million a year in cash and stock for Stern.

After five years and $500 million, Stern renewed his contract at the end of 2010. Neither side divulged the value of the new deal, but analysis estimated that Stern would make roughly $80 million a year.

Would he make more or less with a new contract? Meyer won't say.

"I want Howard Stern for as long as Howard Stern wants to work," he told Businessweek. "I'm only willing to pay so much. I know what the number is. But even if I was in an al-Qaeda camp, no one is going to know what that number is but me.

Meyer also commented that he's hoping the "roar of the crowd" convinces Stern to keep going, putting it this way: "Why is Peyton Manning maybe going to play another year? It's not the money."

Stern has a reputation for fighting publicly with Sirius and talking openly on the radio about his business dealings. Already this year, he has mused about leaving the radio and retiring.

But that could be seen as predictable posturing ahead of official negotiations.

At the Deutsche Bank conference on Tuesday, Meyer told investors, "You should assume we're working hard on trying to get Howard to renew."

Meyer quipped that since Stern has a home a few miles away from the site of the conference in Florida, he had emailed Stern and offered to "trim the hedges or anything else while I was down here."

"I don't know what Howard may or may not choose to do," Meyer added. "You know, on his radio show, about two months ago, he did say, 'if I'm going to stay on radio, I would prefer to stay at Sirius.' We're going to work really hard on keeping him. And we'll see."

RADIO SYNDICATION CONTRACT

EMPLOYMENT AGREEMENT

THIS EMPLOYMENT AGREEMENT (the "Agreement") is made and entered into as of March ___, 2015, by and between **JOHN DOE** (a/k/a "Big Johnny Jon"), a Texas resident ("Performer"), and **ELITE RADIO CORPORATION**, an Texas corporation, as the operator of a radio station in Houston, Texas using the call letters GZTB-FM (such corporation and radio station, collectively, the "Station"), relating to the engagement of Performer as on-air talent for Station according to the terms and subject to the conditions set forth in this Agreement.

RECITALS

In consideration of the mutual promises and covenants set forth in this Agreement, and for other good and valuable consideration, the receipt and sufficiency of which are hereby acknowledged, the parties agree as follows:

AGREEMENT

1. Duties and Services.

(a) General. During the Term (as defined below), Performer shall serve Station as on-air talent and perform such other or different duties as may be reasonably assigned to Performer by Station. Upon the terms and subject to the conditions set forth in this Agreement, Performer shall furnish Performer's exclusive radio broadcast services and related radio promotional services to Station during the Term in the Market. For purposes of this Agreement, the "Market" shall mean the Houston Total Survey Area (as defined by Arbitron Ratings Company, or any successor thereto ("Arbitron")), as specified in the most recently issued Arbitron Ratings Quarterly Report (the "Report"). Performer shall perform on-air duties during the hours of 5:00 a.m. through 10:00 a.m. Monday through Friday each week during the Term (the "Program"). Station has the right to produce a "Best Of" program on a recorded basis for use on weekends or during the week when Performers (as hereinafter defined) are not providing a live show due to vacation or other approved time off.

(b) Other Agreement. This Agreement is predicated upon the premise that Performer shall serve as part of a radio announcer team. In connection therewith, Station is, as of even date herewith, entering into an Agreement ("Other Agreement") with Robert Smith (a/k/a "Big Smith") ("Other Performer" and, when referred to together with the Performer, the "Performers") as the other member of the on-air talent team for the Program.

(c) Services-Related Matters. Certain other material terms and conditions relating to Performer's duties and obligations under this Agreement are set forth on Exhibit A, attached hereto and made a part hereof.

(d) No Obligation to Utilize Services. Station shall not be liable to Performer in any way for any failure or refusal by Station to utilize Performer's services in whole or in part. Notwithstanding anything to the contrary contained in this Agreement, Station will have fully performed, satisfied and discharged all of its obligations to Performer under this Agreement by making the payments to Performer provided for in Section 2(a).

(e) Transfer Rights. Performer acknowledges and agrees that Station shall have the right to require Performer to provide to other station(s) within the Market some or all of the services Performer is required herein to provide to Station. If Station so elects, Performer shall negotiate in good faith such changes to this Agreement as are necessary or appropriate in connection with such transfer, yet which are consistent with the spirit and intent of this Agreement. Upon reaching agreement as to such matters, the parties shall execute an amendment to this Agreement setting forth the amended provisions.

2. Compensation.

(a) Base Salary. During the Term, Station shall pay or cause to be paid to Performer an annualized base salary ("Base Salary") as follows:

Dates:	Base Salary:
January 1, 2015–December 31, 2015	$170,000
January 1, 2016–December 31, 2016	$180,000
January 1, 2017–December 31, 2017	$190,000

All Base Salary paid hereunder shall be subject to withholding for applicable taxes and as otherwise required by law. Additionally, Performer acknowledges and agrees that: (i) ten percent (10%) of all Base Salary paid hereunder is being paid in consideration of Employer's exclusive rights set forth in Paragraph 7, including without limitation the right to post-term protection set forth in Paragraph 7(d); and (ii) Station may pay Performer, a portion of Performer's Base Salary hereunder in stock or equity pursuant to a plan adopted for Station employees (not to exceed 10% of Base Salary). Additionally, all cash sums payable to Performer pursuant to Paragraphs 2(a), 2(b) and 2(c) of this Agreement shall be subject to a deduction in the amount of ten percent (10%) for commissions (the "Commissions") payable to Performer's representative, Big Smith Enterprises, Inc. ("BSE"). Performer hereby authorizes Station to make such deductions and remit such Commissions to BSE (P.O. Box 113, Houston, Texas 77077) each pay period during the Term; provided, however, that the Commissions attributable to the Signing Bonus paid pursuant to Paragraph 2(b) shall be paid in four (4) equal installments of $2,125 each to be deducted from the first four (4) pay periods immediately following the execution of this Agreement.

(b) Signing Bonus. Performer acknowledges receipt of a signing bonus in the amount of Eighty Five Thousand Dollars ($85,000) that was paid to Performer by Station on or about June 9, 2014. Performer acknowledges and agrees that Performer shall be required to refund to Station a prorated portion of such signing bonus if Station terminates this Agreement for "cause" pursuant to Section 13(a) of this Agreement.

(c) Performance Bonus. In addition to Performer's Base Salary, Performer shall be eligible to receive one (1) bonus in an amount up to a maximum of Twenty Three Thousand Dollars ($23,000) for each full Arbitron quarterly booking period during the Term during which Performer provides live, on-air broadcast services pursuant to this Agreement (each, a "Performance Bonus"). The amount of the Performance Bonus for any given quarter during the Term, if any, shall equal the amount set forth opposite the Station's Average Quarter Hour Rank for the daypart during which Performer regularly provided such services as stated in the Report as follows:

Bonus Schedule

Adults 18–34:

Rank:	Bonus (not cumulative):
#1	$ 8,500
#2	$ 7,500
#3	$ 6,500
#4	$ 5,500

Adults 25–54:

Rank:	Bonus (not cumulative):
#1	$14,500
#2	$13,500
#3	$11,500
#4	$10,500

It is understood and agreed that Station may, at its sole election, pay any Performance Bonus amounts, if any, in cash or Shares (as defined below). In the event Station elects pursuant to this Section 2(c) to pay a Performance Bonus in Shares, the exact number of Shares to be awarded to Performer shall be determined by dividing the total dollar amount of the applicable Performance Bonus by the average of the reported high and low Share price on the last day of the applicable quarter, as reported by NASDAQ. Performer shall receive any Performance Bonus amounts within sixty (60) days after the conclusion of the applicable quarter during which such Performance Bonus was earned pursuant to the terms and conditions of this Agreement. It is understood and agreed that, in the event one or more radio stations in the Market tie the Station for a particular ranking, Performer shall receive the average of the amount set forth opposite the ranking for which the tie occurred and the next lowest ranking (e.g., in the event of a tie for the #2 ranking, Performer shall receive $7,000 (the average of $7,500 and $6,500).

(d) Personal Appearances and Live Spots. Performer shall make up to a maximum of ten (10) non-Station-related personal appearances each year during the Term. Performer shall receive a flat rate of $250.00 per hour ($500.00 minimum per appearance) for all non-Station-related personal appearances, such payment made in arrears on a monthly basis. Station shall pay Performer $35.00 for each live spot, such payment to be made in arrears on a monthly basis. Additionally, the Performer shall appear at no cost to Station up to a maximum of ten (10) Station-related appearances each year during the Term. For the purposes of this Section 2(d), a "Station-related personal appearance " shall mean any personal appearance by Performer that is reasonably designated by the Station for the benefit of Station as opposed to the benefit of one or more of the Station's advertisers. Station shall be responsible for obtaining payment from clients and otherwise coordinating such personal appearances. Performer agrees to comply with all applicable policies of Station at such personal appearances.

(e) Equity Incentive Compensation. In the event that, during the Term, Station's actual broadcast cash flow (as determined and reported by Station) equals or exceeds its budgeted broadcast cash flow goal (as determined by Station) for the immediately preceding Station fiscal year, Performer shall receive an option ("Option") to acquire Five Hundred (500) shares (the "Shares") of Class A Common Stock of Elite Communications Corporation ("Elite") on or about such date or dates on which Elite awards equity incentive compensation to its employees (each, an "Award Date") pursuant to the terms and subject to the conditions of the applicable Elite Equity Incentive Plan; provided, however, in the event Station's actual broadcast cash flow exceeds its budgeted broadcast cash flow goal by ten percent (10%) or more, Performer shall be granted an additional Option to acquire an additional One Thousand (1,000) Shares pursuant to the terms and conditions set forth above in this sentence. It is understood and agreed that in the event of any change in the outstanding Shares by reason of any reorganization, recapitalization, stock split, reverse stock split, stock dividend, share combination, consolidation or similar event, the number and class of Shares awarded pursuant to this Agreement or covered by an Option granted pursuant to this Paragraph 2(e) (and any applicable Option exercise price) shall be adjusted by the Compensation Committee of Elite Communications Corporation (the "Committee") in its sole discretion and in accordance with the terms of the applicable Elite Equity Incentive Plan and the Option agreement evidencing the grant of the Option. The determination of the Committee shall be conclusive and binding.

(f) Fringe Benefits. During the Term, Performer shall be entitled to receive the fringe benefit package (including provisions for insurance and leave time) generally available to other full-time, non-management Station employees with a comparable length of service. Performer shall be eligible to take up to five (5) weeks of vacation each year during the Term pursuant to Station policy or practices.

(g) Life Insurance. During the Term, Station shall, subject to the insurability of Performer, obtain and maintain a term life insurance policy in the face amount of $500,000 for which Station shall be the owner and Performer shall be the insured and the beneficiary; provided, that the annual premium costs incurred by Station shall in no event exceed $1,600. Station agrees to provide Performer with a copy of said policy and any amendments or other material correspondence not later than sixty (60) days following execution of this Agreement.

(h) Conferences. Upon submission of receipts, Station shall reimburse Performer for reasonable expenses actually incurred while attending "The Morning Show Boot-Camp" once each year during the Term. Such expenses shall include registration fees, daily meal allowance ($40 per person per day maximum), reasonable hotel expenses and coach class airfare. Performer shall utilize Station's travel agent to make the requisite travel arrangements.

3. Term. The term of this Agreement shall be for a period of three (3) years commencing on January 1, 2015, through and including December 31, 2017, unless earlier terminated in accordance with the terms of this Agreement (the "Term"). Notwithstanding anything to the contrary contained in this Agreement, it is understood and agreed that Station may, in its sole discretion, terminate this Agreement without any further obligation on or anytime after July 1, 2016, by providing Performer with five (5) months' prior written notice or five (5) months' pay in lieu of such notice.

4. Program Format. The program format is described on Exhibit B, attached hereto and made a part hereof, along with certain other material terms and conditions of this Agreement relating to Performer's duties and obligations. Station and Performer may, from time-to-time during the Term, jointly develop and determine program format changes and modifications. Station acknowledges that Performer shall maintain creative input regarding the non-commercial or non-promotional content and style of the Program; however, Performer acknowledges and recognizes the necessity for Station to exercise final control and authority over the format consistent with the Station's public interest and licensee obligations and responsibilities. Accordingly, Performer agrees to perform Performer's services in a diligent, competent and artistic manner, and to comply with all Station rules and policies which apply to Station and its employees, and with the rules and regulations of the Federal Communications Commission and any other governmental body having jurisdiction in the premises. Performer also agrees to devote such time to

rehearsal and/or preparation as may be reasonably required, to abide by all written instructions of the Station concerning the commercial and promotional content of performances on which Performer appears (including but not limited to instructions limiting the number and content of on-air mentions of commercial ventures in which Performer has an interest), and to perform the services contemplated hereunder in a capable, professional and efficient manner.

5. Expenses. Station shall reimburse Performer for reasonable expenses actually incurred by Performer directly related to the performance of Performer's duties to the extent authorized in writing in advance by the Station or otherwise incurred in accordance with Station's written policies.

6. Conduct. At all times during the Term Performer's conduct shall be with due regard to public and social conventions of good conduct, good morals and decency, and Performer shall refrain from committing any act which brings Performer or Station, or Station's advertisers, sponsors or advertising agencies, or any officer, director, employee or representative of the Station or Elite or any of its affiliated or related companies (collectively, "Affiliated Group Members") into public disrepute, scandal, contempt or ridicule, or which disparages or reflects adversely upon any Affiliated Group Members. Furthermore, Performer shall refrain from engaging in any activities which, directly or indirectly, interfere with, or adversely impact upon, Performer's services to be provided to Station under the terms of this Agreement without first obtaining Station's written consent to do so. Without limiting the generality of the foregoing, Exhibit A includes specific obligations and remedies pertaining to the subject matter of this Section.

7. Exclusivity; Rights of First Refusal and Negotiation; and Post-Term Protection.

(a) Exclusive Employment During Term. During the Term, Performer shall not, without the prior written consent of Station (i) perform, broadcast, or appear on, or for the benefit of, any radio station (other than the Station) or on any radio network or syndicated radio program (other than one affiliated with the Station), or (ii) negotiate or enter into any agreement (other than with the Station) regarding Performer's performance, broadcast, or appearance on, or for the benefit of, any radio station or on any radio network or syndicated radio program (other than one affiliated with the Station); provided, however, that Performer may negotiate with any third party during the last ninety (90) days of the Term, subject to Station's rights under Section 7(c) and Section 7(d). Prior to Performer engaging in any television or other entertainment industry services for third parties not otherwise prohibited by this Agreement, Performer shall obtain Station's prior written consent for such engagements, which consent shall not be unreasonably withheld. In the event Performer seeks Station's consent pursuant to this provision, Station agrees to use its reasonable efforts to provide a response in a timely manner.

(b) Right of First Negotiation. During the one hundred eighty (180) days prior to the expiration of the Term, Performer agrees to negotiate in good faith a new employment agreement for Performer's services with Station for a subsequent term. If, ninety (90) days from the end of the Term, Station and Performer have not entered into a new agreement for the engagement of Performer's services, Performer shall furnish to Station in writing the least favorable terms of employment Performer is willing to accept for Performer's services. Station shall have five (5) business days from its receipt of such terms within which to notify Performer of Station's decision regarding the engagement of Performer to provide Performer's services on such terms. Thereafter, if Station accepts such terms, the parties shall enter into a new agreement substantially similar to this Agreement, as expressly modified by the terms of the Performer's notice. If Station elects not to accept such terms, Performer may negotiate with any third party subject to the limitations set forth in this Section 7.

(c) Right of First Refusal. Performer agrees that if, as of the date ninety (90) days from the end of the Term, Performer and Station have not entered into an extension of this Agreement or otherwise agreed as to the continued employment of services by Performer, Performer shall not, during the last ninety (90) days of the Term and for ninety (90) days immediately following the end of the Term (the "Refusal Period "), directly or indirectly make or enter into any agreement, understanding or option with any person or entity (other than Station) regarding Performer's performance, broadcast, or appearance on or for the benefit of any radio station or any radio network or syndicated radio program on terms less favorable to Performer than those last offered by Performer to Station under the terms of Paragraph 7(b) above without giving Station the first opportunity to enter into an exclusive agreement with Performer for Performer's services on terms and conditions substantially similar to those offered to Performer by any such other person or entity which Performer is willing to accept or to those offered by Performer to such other person or entity which such person or entity is willing to accept (collectively, the "Offer"). Station will have five (5) business days from the date of its receipt of Performer's written notice of any Offer (which notice shall contain a true, complete and un-redacted copy of the Offer to Performer and a written summary of all oral terms or conditions of the Offer) in which to agree to match the Offer on terms that are substantially similar to the Offer when taken as a whole. If Station agrees to match the Offer as provided above, the parties will enter into a new agreement substantially similar to this Agreement, as modified by the terms of the Station's matching offer. If Station fails or refuses to match the Offer within the time specified above, then and only then will Performer be free to furnish or agree to furnish such other person or entity with Performer's services on the terms contained in such Offer (subject to the restriction set forth in Paragraph 7(d) below). If Performer does not accept such Offer, the terms of this subsection will apply to any subsequent offer received or made by Performer during the Refusal Period.

(d) Post-Term Protection. Performer recognizes that the Station has invested, and will continue to invest, substantial amounts of money and professional efforts to secure and retain audiences for the Station and for the Program and other programs on which Performer appears; that Performer's standing as a radio personality will be enhanced by reason of Performer's appearances and broadcasts before such audiences; and that Performer's standing as a radio personality will have a unique and extraordinary character which is and will be of substantial and unique value to the Station in retaining its audiences. Performer further recognizes that irreparable harm will occur if Performer, following the expiration or termination of this Agreement, uses Performer's standing as a radio personality against the interests of the Station and that the Station is entitled to reasonable protection against the loss or impairment of its investment and promotional efforts in connection with Performer's radio broadcasting services and activities under this Agreement in the Market, which would result from Performer providing, rendering, furnishing or engaging in any radio broadcasting service or activity in competition with the Station. Consequently, for a period of three (3) months immediately following the expiration or earlier termination of the Term for any reason (except Performer's breach of this Agreement), Performer shall not directly or indirectly engage or participate in any performance, broadcast, promotion or appearance on, or for the benefit of, any radio station located within the Market. In the event Station elects not to use Performer's services pursuant to Paragraph 1(d) above, the foregoing restriction shall be reduced by one (1) day for each day during which Station elects not to use Performer's services.

(e) Non-Solicitation. Performer agrees that for a period of one (1) year immediately following the expiration or early termination of the Term for any reason, Performer shall refrain from, either directly or indirectly, soliciting, inducing, recruiting or encouraging any of Station's employees to leave their employment with Station for the benefit of Performer or on behalf of or for the benefit of any other person or entity.

(f) Remedies. Notwithstanding the arbitration requirement in Section 18, because Performer's services are of a special, unique, unusual and extraordinary character, and because the loss of Performer's services will result in damages to Station for which Station cannot reasonably or adequately be compensated, Station will have the unrestricted and unqualified right to seek and obtain (without posting any bond or other security) equitable, injunctive or other relief (whether at law or equity or both) in any court of competent jurisdiction to enforce the provisions of this Section 7 and each of its subsections. Station shall not, as a result of the time involved in obtaining such relief, be deprived of the benefit of the full period of post-term protection or non-solicitation set forth herein. Accordingly, the obligations set forth in Sections 7(d) and 7(e) shall be deemed to have the duration set forth therein, computed from the date such relief is granted but reduced by the time expired between the date the restrictive period began to run and the date of the first violation of the obligations by Performer.

(g) Construction. Despite the express agreement herein between Station and Performer, in the event that any of the provisions set forth in this Section 7 shall be determined by any court or other tribunal of competent jurisdiction to be unenforceable for any reason whatsoever, the parties agree that this Section 7 shall be interpreted to extend only to the maximum extent as to which it may be enforceable, and that this Section 7 shall be severable into its component parts, all as determined by such court or tribunal.

8. Syndication.

(a) General. Performer, Other Performer and Station (collectively, the "Syndication Owners ") shall jointly own the rights to syndicate or otherwise act to acquire contractual rights to broadcast the Program (which for purposes of this Section 8 shall mean the Program and any other program for which Performer and Other Performer provide on-air talent services) on radio broadcast facilities (other than the Station, and after the expiration of this Agreement, not more than one radio broadcasting station for which Performer and Other Performer provide on-air talent services) and over the Internet, wherever located. In connection therewith, Station shall own a fifty percent (50.0%) ownership interest, Performer shall own a twenty-five percent (25.0%) ownership interest, and Other Performer shall own the remaining twenty-five percent (25.0%) ownership interest. Performer acknowledges that in undertaking such activities, Station may appoint such agents or representatives (including affiliates of Station) as Station deems reasonably appropriate and in the best interests of the syndication of the Program. Further, Station agrees to consult with Performer and Other Performer before appointing such agents or representatives. Also, Station shall have the sole and exclusive right to enter into agreements, bill and accept payments, and otherwise act in connection with such syndication efforts; provided, that Station acts reasonably and consults with the Performer from time-totime regarding such matters or as requested by Performer.

(b) Revenues. The net revenues earned from such syndication activities, including but not limited to those earned from programming payments and from the sale of advertising, shall be split pro-rata based on the ownership described above in Section 8(a). For these purposes, "net revenues" shall consist of all syndication-related revenue earned, less expenses incurred directly in connection with such syndication activities including, but not limited to commissions. In connection therewith, Station agrees that it will not, and it will not permit its affiliates, to incur or charge against such revenues overhead or other administrative expenses not directly related to the Station's syndication efforts pursuant to this Section 8 or substantially in excess of commercially reasonable amounts based on then-current industry data. Net revenues for each month shall be distributed to all of the Syndication Owners within thirty (30) days after the end of each month during the Term.

(c) Audit Rights. Station shall keep accurate and complete books and records of all transactions relating to the syndication efforts. Performer or Performer's representatives may, at any time during the Term and for a period of one (1) year thereafter, during business hours and upon reasonable notice, have full access to audit, and make copies of, all such books and records related thereto. The exercise by Performer of any right to audit or the acceptance by Performer of any accounting statement or payment shall be without prejudice to the Performer's rights and remedies and shall not bar Performer from thereafter disputing the accuracy of such accounting statement or payment, and Station shall remain fully liable for all balances due under this Section 8. If an audit reveals that Station has under reported or has misrepresented any item bearing upon the computation of the amount payable to Performer pursuant to this Section 8 and the discrepancy is ten percent (10%) or more, Station agrees, in addition to re-computing and making immediate payment of the amounts due based on the actual and true items, to pay all reasonable, out-of pocket costs and expenses incurred by Performer in connection with the audit and an amount equal to twenty percent (20.0%) of the discrepancy. In any case, all amounts due Performer shall accrue interest from the date the payment should have been made at a rate equal to 8.0% per annum, and Station shall pay all costs, fees and expenses (other than audit expenses which shall be paid in accordance with the preceding sentence, but including any attorneys' fees and expenses) incurred by Performer in connection with the collection of any past due amounts.

(d) Right of First Refusal. For the period from the date of expiration or termination of the Term (for whatever reason) and for one year thereafter, if the Performer is part of a radio program broadcast during the same or approximately the same (e.g., 6:00 A.M.–10:00 A.M. (Monday–Friday)) time period as the Program, Station shall have the right to broadcast such program within the Market, at the Station's election, (i) on such economic terms as are "market" and on such other terms as are considered to be industry-standard for syndication agreements, in each case as negotiated in good faith between Performer and Station or (ii) on the same terms offered to any other broadcaster within the Market. If Station elects sub-item (i) in the preceding sentence, Station shall give written notice to Performer, and Performer and Station shall promptly negotiate such terms within thirty (30) days after Performer's receipt of such notice. Prior to entering into a binding agreement with any other broadcaster within the Market, Performer shall provide a full and complete description of all the agreed-upon terms for the syndicated broadcast of such new program within the Market, and Station shall have thirty (30) days upon receipt of the written description of such terms within which to notify Performer of acceptance of such terms.

(e) Buy-Out. If this Agreement is terminated (other than by a breach of this Agreement by Performer) or is not renewed or Performer does not enter into a new agreement whereby the syndication arrangement provided for in this Section 8 is continued, Performer may, at Performer's sole option and in Performer's sole discretion, purchase all of the Station's syndication ownership interests by giving Station written notice of his purchase within ninety (90) days after the expiration or other termination of this Agreement, which notice unconditionally guarantees payment to Station, in twelve (12) equal monthly installments commencing on the first day of the month immediately following termination, of an aggregate amount equal to forty percent (40.0%) of the total net revenues for syndication of the Program pursuant to this Section 8 during the last-completed full calendar year of the Term (the "Syndication Buy-Out Price"). (The total amount payable pursuant to this Section 8(e) is the total amount payable for the buyout of Station's syndication rights both under this Agreement and under the Other Agreement. In the event that Performer and Other Performer both desire to purchase the Station's syndication ownership interests, each shall be entitled to purchase fifty percent (50%) of Station's syndication ownership interests by paying one-half of the Syndication Buy-Out Price in twelve equal installments in accordance with the payment schedule stated above. However, in the event that Performer and Other Performer both elect to purchase the Station's syndication ownership interests, Station may seek payment pursuant to either this Agreement or under the Other Agreement if there is a default in payment by either Performer or by Other Performer. It is understood and agreed that the percentage of Station's ownership interest ultimately transferred to Performer and Other Performer shall be in proportion to the payment received by Station from each such person.

9. Website. Station re-affirms that, pursuant to the previous employment agreement between the parties, Station has assigned and transferred any and all of its rights to own and operate a website currently known as "JohnAndRobert.com" (the "Website"), as well as all of its rights and interests in the domain name "JohnandRobert.com", to Performer and Other Performer, or their respective business entities. It is understood and agreed that nothing herein shall obligate either the Performer or any entity owned wholly or partially by the Performer to operate the Website for any period of time or to incur any costs in connection with the operation of the Website; it being the agreement of the parties hereto that the operation of the Website shall be at the sole and absolute discretion and option of Performer's entity owning same. In any case, Station shall have the right to pre-approve or consent to the

content provided by Performer, including, but not limited to, trademarks, trade names, logos and other intellectual property of Station, on such Website through the end of the Term; provided, that such consent or approval is not unreasonably withheld or delayed. Performer agrees to abide by all Station policies and/or directions of which Performer is advised regarding the content contained or presented on the Website, and at Station's request, shall remove any content deemed by Station, in its discretion, to be inappropriate or in violation of Station policy.

10. Name and Likeness. During the Term, Performer grants Station the exclusive right to use Performer's name, likeness, sobriquet, biography, picture, voice and recorded performances in connection with the Program and all other programs and broadcasts on which Performer appears in connection with Station and in advertising and publicizing Station and its programs and the products or services of the sponsor or sponsors thereof; provided, however, that such use shall not be in the form of endorsements or testimonials of any product or sponsor (other than Station) without Performer's consent, which consent shall not be unreasonably withheld. Specifically, during the Term, Performer shall not appear in any advertisement, testimonial, endorsement, or promotion or otherwise endorse or publicize any product or service without the express prior written consent of Station, which consent shall not be unreasonably withheld. The parties agree that such written consent may be withheld by Station if it is reasonably likely that Performer's appearance in any such advertisement, testimonial, endorsement, or promotion would have a negative or adverse impact or result on the Station's or any Affiliate Group Member's image, revenues, sponsors or advertisers. Notwithstanding the arbitration provisions set forth in Section 18, Station shall have the unrestricted and unqualified right to seek and obtain (without posting any bond or other security) equitable, injunctive or other relief (whether at law or equity or both) in any court of competent jurisdiction to enforce the provisions of this Section 10. Furthermore, it is understood and agreed that Station's rights pursuant to this provision shall expire immediately upon the expiration of the Term; provided, that Station shall have the non-exclusive right to continue to use Performer's name and likeness while removing billboards, posters, and other advertising materials and uses of such name and likeness. Station agrees to use its' reasonable efforts to effect such removal in a prompt manner.

11. Ownership of Materials. Station shall solely and exclusively own all rights of every kind and nature in perpetuity and throughout the universe in the programs and broadcasts on which Performer appears or renders services on Station, as well as all of the results and proceeds of Performer's services rendered for the Station pursuant to the terms of this Agreement. Any work in connection with the Program or specially ordered by Station for use as part of any radio broadcast programs of Station shall be considered to be "work made

for hire" for the Station. Station shall be the author and copyright owner of the programs on which Performer appears and the broadcasts and tapes or recordings thereof for all purposes without limitation of any kind; provided, however, that Performer shall own the rights to all of the characters, materials, trademarks, and service marks developed by Performer that are set forth on Exhibit C, attached hereto and made a part hereof. All characters developed for the programs and broadcasts on which Performer appears for Station during the Term shall be solely and exclusively owned by Station, including all rights, title and interest thereto, unless the parties have otherwise agreed in writing. The exclusive legal title to all of the aforesaid "works made for hire", programs and broadcasts, and all secondary and derivative rights therein shall be in the Station which shall have the right to copyright the same and apply for copyright registrations and copyright renewal registrations and to make whatever use thereof Station deems advisable, including, but not limited to, use of any portions of any program in the production and broadcast of other programs consistent with the terms of this Paragraph 11. Notwithstanding the arbitration provisions set forth in Section 18, Station shall have the unrestricted and unqualified right to seek and obtain (without posting any bond or other security) equitable, injunctive or other relief (whether at law or equity or both) in any court of competent jurisdiction to enforce the provisions of this Section. Notwithstanding the foregoing, it is understood and agreed that after the expiration of the Term, Station may not rebroadcast any of the programs described above without obtaining Performer's prior written consent; provided, however, that Station may use portions of such programs for Station special programming (e.g., seasonal or "retro" shows), reference or archival purposes without obtaining Performer's consent to do so.

12. Representations, Warranties and Covenants. Performer hereby represents, warrants and covenants that:

(a) Original Materials. Any and all scripts, and all literary, artistic, production, creative or musical materials written or furnished by Performer which Performer uses or authorizes others to use on broadcasts or programs of the Station will be original works of Performer (unless Performer has obtained, or confirmed in writing that Station has obtained, valid, written consents or licenses for such use from third parties) or exist in the public domain, and any use of such materials will not violate any common law, statutory, copyright, proprietary right, or other right of any kind of any person or other entity whatsoever.

(b) Right to Enter Into Agreement. Performer: (i) has the full and unqualified right to enter into and fully perform this Agreement; (ii) has not made any contract or commitment in contravention of the terms of this Agreement; (iii) has the right to grant the rights herein granted to Station; (iv) is free and clear from any obligation whatsoever to perform services for any other person, firm, entity or corporation that would hinder Performer's rendition of services hereunder; and (v) is at full liberty, and is willing and able, to perform all of the services required by this Agreement.

(c) Consideration for Broadcast. Performer has not accepted, nor agreed to accept, and will not solicit, receive, accept or agree to accept, directly or indirectly, from any person or entity, other than Station, any money, service or other valuable consideration for the inclusion of any matter as a part of any program or broadcast on which Performer appears or will appear for Station or on behalf of, and Performer shall not, for consideration other than from Station, mention, use or identify on any program or broadcast on which Performer appears for or on behalf of Station any product, service, material, trademark or brand name other than those of Station or its sponsors. Furthermore, Performer agrees to execute Station's customary "Payola/Plugola" certification each year during the Term when requested to do so.

(d) FCC Requirements. Performer shall refrain from violating any of the provisions of the Communications Act of 1934, as amended, or any of the rules or regulations of the FCC promulgated thereunder. Without limiting the generality of the foregoing, Performer has not, and shall not, accept or pay any consideration, or agree to do so, in contravention of the requirements of such laws and regulations. In the event such consideration has been or is offered, accepted, or paid, voluntarily or involuntarily, full disclosure must be promptly made to Station. Any breach of this provision shall give Station the right to terminate this Agreement, including all payments to be made hereunder. Station shall not assert a breach of this Section 12(d) as a result of Performer conducting "phone shams" unless Station has previously given Performer written notice that it has determined that a "phone sham" constitutes a violation of this Section 12(d).

13. Termination.

(a) Termination by Station for Cause. Station may terminate this Agreement at any time during the Term for cause. For purposes of this Agreement, "cause" shall consist of: (i) actual or threatened violence against another employee; (ii) sexual or other prohibited harassment of others; (iii) use or possession of illegal drugs during working hours or drug or alcohol abuse off duty if such use adversely affects the performance of Performer's duties or the Station's interests; (iv) any material and repeated failure by Performer to comply with written program and format instructions, or failure or refusal to comply with the Station's rules, policies or directives, when Performer has been given notice of such failure and a reasonable opportunity to cure such failure; (v) any breach of the material terms of this Agreement by Performer when Performer has been given notice of such breach and a reasonable opportunity to cu re such breach; (vi) any conviction of Performer for a felony or other crime of moral turpitude; provided, that Station may suspend Performer with or without pay during any investigation of such matter; and (vii) any act or omission constituting cause or gross misconduct under applicable laws.

(b) Termination by Station Due to Death or Disability. This Agreement shall automatically terminate upon (i) the death of Performer; or (ii) Performer becoming wholly or partially disabled for any cumulative period in excess of twelve (12) weeks within any twelve (12) month period. For purposes of this Agreement, a "disability" shall include the (1) inability to substantially perform the services required hereunder, or (2) any material impairment of Performer's voice. In the event this Agreement is terminated pursuant to this Section 13(b), neither party shall have any further obligation to the other except (i) Station's obligation to pay any unpaid Base Salary prior to Performer's date of disability or death, whichever the case may be, and (ii) Performer's obligations set forth in Section 7 which are specifically intended to survive the termination of this Agreement.

(c) Termination of Other Agreement. Station may, in its discretion, terminate this Agreement immediately upon written notice to Performer due to the death or disability of the Other Performer or due to the breach of the Other Agreement by Other Performer. Upon termination due to the death or disability of the Other Performer, Station shall pay Performer the remaining amount of Base Salary to be paid during the Term pursuant to Section 2(a) and all bonuses previously earned but unpaid as of the termination date. Upon termination of this Agreement due to termination of the Other Agreement as a result of a breach of the Other Agreement by Other Performer, Station shall pay to Performer, in a lump sum payment: fifty percent (50%) of the Base Salary payable to Performer pursuant to Section 2(a) for the remainder of the Term, as well as all bonuses previously earned but unpaid as of the termination date. Furthermore, upon termination of this Agreement pursuant to this Section 13(c), all of the restrictive covenants set forth in Section 7 shall automatically expire as of the date of such termination and Performer may immediately enter into agreements with third parties to provide any or all of the same or similar services provided for Station prior to the termination date including, but not limited to, broadcasting and appearing on radio stations located within the Market.

(d) Events Upon Termination. Upon any early termination of this Agreement pursuant to this Section 13 or upon the expiration of the Term of this Agreement, Performer shall promptly return to Station any and all Station property in Performer's custody or control. After termination of this Agreement, Station shall have no further obligations or liabilities hereunder except to pay any unpaid Base Salary and bonuses earned through the date of termination in accordance with Section 2(a)or 2(c).

14. Force Majeure. If Station is prevented from broadcasting by reason of fire, casualty, accident, war, act of terrorism, act of God, strike, defect in its Station

broadcasting equipment or apparatus, or any other cause beyond Station's control, whether of the same or of any kind or character, neither party hereto shall be in breach of its obligations under this Agreement, but Station shall not be relieved of the obligation to make any payments of Base Salary required pursuant to this Agreement during the continuance of such interruption of broadcasting; provided, however, that if the interruption of broadcasting continues for a period of more than thirty (30) days, Station may terminate this Agreement effective as of the thirtieth (30th) day of such interruption of broadcasting, by giving written notice on or about the thirtieth (30th) day to Performer of its desire to do so, provided that Station shall pay Performer such vacation and other Base Salary as of such thirtieth (30th) day.

15. Indemnification; Notice of Claim.

(a) By Performer. Performer hereby agrees to fully indemnify, defend and hold harmless Station and each of the Affiliate Group Members, and each of their respective officers, directors, employees, agents, attorneys, insurers and representatives, from and against any and all damages, losses, costs, expenses (including without limitation, reasonable attorneys' fees and expenses), actions, liabilities, and claims in connection with, arising out of, or in any way related to: (i) any breach by Performer of any of the material representations, warranties or covenants made by Performer in this Agreement; or (ii) any material furnished by Performer for broadcast that (a) is determined to be defamatory (whether libel or slander) by a court of competent jurisdiction, (b) infringes upon any trade names or trademarks of any third party, (c) results in liability for product disparagement, (d) violates the rights of privacy of any third party, (e) infringes upon any copyrights, or other intellectual or proprietary rights of any third party, (f) violates any common law or statutory provision, (g) constitutes unfair competition, or (h) violates any prior written instructions or notices given to Performer by Station, which prior written instructions or notices specifically relate to the conduct giving rise to the third party claim or action. It is understood and agreed that the immediately foregoing indemnification obligation shall not apply so long as Performer's action or conduct giving rise to any such damage, loss, cost, expense, action, liability or claim was reasonable and in the good faith performance of Performer's duties pursuant to this Agreement. In all instances whereby Performer indemnifies, defends or holds harmless Station pursuant to this Section 15(a), Station shall be entitled to select legal counsel in Station's sole discretion.

(b) By Station. Station hereby agrees to fully indemnify, defend and hold harmless Performer from and against any and all damages, losses, costs, expenses (including without limitation, reasonable attorneys' fees and expenses), actions, liabilities, and claims relating to: (i) any broadcast on which Performer appears containing material solely provided by Station and specifically authorized by Station to be broadcast; or (ii) any action or conduct by Performer that is reasonable and in the good faith performance of Performer's duties pursuant to this Agreement. Performer agrees to fully cooperate with Station in each instance in which the Station indemnifies, defends or holds harmless Performer pursuant to this Section 13(b), and hereby permits Station to select legal counsel in Station's sole discretion; provided, that Station shall consult with Performer regarding its selection of counsel.

(c) Notice of Claim. Any party seeking indemnification pursuant to this Paragraph 15 shall promptly notify the other party in writing of any claim, notice or demand to which any indemnification obligation hereunder may apply.

16. Retractions. In the event that Performer, in the course of Performer's employment by Station, utters, disseminates, publishes, broadcasts or otherwise communicates any matters, materials or speech which contain, or may contain, or otherwise give rise to, claims of libel, slander, product disparagement, infringement of trade names or of trademarks, violation of rights of privacy, infringement of copyrights or any proprietary rights, or of unfair competition, or which contradict or violate any written instructions or notices given to Performer by Station, Station may request in writing that Performer issue, broadcast, or publish a retraction or correction of the foregoing. Upon receipt of such request, Performer shall promptly, in consultation with Station, and in good faith, issue, broadcast and/or publish a retraction or correction. Performer shall have the right to review the text, terminology and phraseology of any such retractions or corrections in advance. In the event of any dispute regarding the text of any retraction, Station's determination with regard to such text shall be final and binding. Notwithstanding the arbitration provisions set forth in Section 18, Station may enforce the provisions of this Section by an order of specific performance, injunctive or other relief issued by a court of competent jurisdiction.

17. Failure to Perform. If Performer fails or refuses to render services or to perform any of Performer's duties and obligations under the terms of this Agreement, Station shall, in addition to any other rights or remedies available to Station, (i) not be required to pay Performer any compensation under this Agreement relating to the period of such non-performance, and (ii) have the right, but not the obligation, to extend the Term for a period equal to that of the non-performance, unless the nonperformance is the result of pre-approved absences, verified sick days, or as otherwise provided in this Agreement.

18. Arbitration. Except as otherwise provided herein, any controversy or claim of either party hereto arising out of, or in any way relating to this Agreement, or any breach thereof, shall be settled by final and binding arbitration before a single arbitrator in Houston, Texas in accordance with the applicable rules of the American Arbitration Association, and judgment upon the award rendered may be entered by the prevailing party in any court having jurisdiction thereof. It is understood and agreed that the costs of such arbitration shall be borne equally

by the parties; provided, however, that each party shall be responsible for its own attorneys' fees and expenses in connection therewith.

19. <u>Station Warranty.</u> Station hereby represents and warrants that it is authorized to enter into this Agreement and that nothing in its Articles of Incorporation, By-Laws or other organizational documents or contractual commitments prohibits this Agreement from being enforceable in accordance with its terms.

20. <u>Notices.</u> Any notices hereunder shall be deemed to have been duly given if in writing and delivered personally or by pre-paid guaranteed overnight delivery service, or sent postage prepaid by United States certified mail, return receipt requested, to the Performer at the Performer's then-current address provided by the Performer to the Station and listed in Station's records, with a copy to Big Smith Enterprises, Attn: Big Smith, 1376 Elm Street, Houston, Texas 77077, or to the Station at the then-current address of the Station, with a copy to Elite Communications Corporation, 8581 Maydale Street, Houston, Texas 77077, Attention: Brian James, Esq. Any such notice shall be effective on the date of delivery if delivered personally, on the next business day following delivery to the guaranteed overnight delivery service if the notice was so delivered and the charges were prepaid, or on the date the recipient signed for the notice if sent by certified mail.

21. <u>Miscellaneous.</u> In the event any provision of this Agreement shall be held to be invalid or unenforceable, in whole or in part, neither the validity nor the enforceability of the remainder of this Agreement shall be affected in any way. This Agreement may be changed only by an instrument in writing signed by the parties hereto. This Agreement may be executed in counterparts, including facsimile or photocopy counterparts, each of which shall be deemed an original but all of which taken together shall constitute a single document. This Agreement shall be construed by and interpreted in accordance with the laws and judicial decisions of the State of Texas. No waiver by either party of a breach of any provision of this Agreement shall be deemed to be a waiver of any preceding or succeeding breach of the same or similar nature or of any other provision of this Agreement. The headings of the paragraphs and subparagraphs of this Agreement are solely for the purpose of convenience, and they are not a part of this Agreement and shall not be used in the construction or interpretation of any provision thereof. The exhibits referred to herein are attached hereto and are hereby incorporated by reference and made a part hereof as if fully set forth herein. This Agreement, and Performer's rights and obligations hereunder, may not be assigned by Performer without the prior written consent of Station, which consent may be granted or withheld in station's sole and absolute discretion. Station may assign all or any portion of its rights and obligations hereunder to any subsidiary, affiliate or related entity, or any third party by way of merger, corporate reorganization, acquisition of

substantially all of the assets or stock of Station, or otherwise. This Agreement shall be binding upon and inure to the benefit of the parties hereto and any successor to Station, but neither this Agreement nor any rights of payment hereunder shall be assignable by Performer. Performer agrees that no representation of any kind has been made to Performer by the Station or by any of its agents and that no understanding has been had or agreement entered into other than as set forth herein and that all prior agreements, oral or written, are merged herein.

IN WITNESS WHEREOF, the parties hereto have caused this Agreement to be executed as of the date first above written.

JOHN DOE	**ELITE RADIO CORPORATION d/b/a**
("Performer")	**GZTB-FM** ("Station")

By:______________________
John Doe

By:______________________
Josh Dunbar, Senior Vice President and Market Manager

Exhibit A
Services-Related Matters

1. Spots.
(a) During the Program, Performer shall perform such live (i.e., read by Performer on the air or taped) commercial spots as reasonably requested by Station. (To have for use in Performer's absence, Performer shall make a tape for one of the first times a spot is read by Performer on the air.) In performing spots, Performer shall read all copy points included in the script for each such spot. All spots, live or prerecorded, shall be done in a professional manner.
(b) Performer acknowledges that Station sells a certain number of thirty-second and sixty-second commercial spots to be broadcast during each hour of the Program. Performer agrees to run all such spots (no less than 16) within the hour of the Program as scheduled in increments of no less than three (3) commercial breaks per hour. Also, Performer agrees, that for each spot scheduled to be broadcast during a particular hour of the Program which is broadcast between one minute and 20 minutes after that hour, Station shall be entitled to setoff $35.00 against amounts otherwise payable pursuant to Section 2. Similarly, Station shall be entitled to setoff $50.00 for each such spot broadcast more than 20 minutes after the end of that hour. The aforementioned penalties shall not be applicable if the running of a scheduled

spot after the end of the hour is due to a Station emergency, defects or damage to equipment or broadcasting apparatus, or any other cause beyond Performer 's reasonable control.

(c) If during a fiscal quarter of Station Performer broadcasts ninety-five percent (95.0%) or more of the aggregate number of commercial spots scheduled to be broadcast during the particular hours of the Program during a quarter subject to a Report, the Performance Bonus payable for the Daypart pursuant to the terms and conditions of <u>Section 2(c)</u> (as to adults 25-54), if any, shall be increased by $1,525.00.

2.<u>Equipment.</u>

<u>(a) Purchase of Equipment.</u> During the Term, Performer may submit reasonable equipment requests, and Station will use reasonable efforts to obtain budgeting approval for such equipment acquisitions. All such purchased equipment shall be the property of Station, and such equipment may be used by other personnel of Station from time to time during the Term.

<u>(b) Maintenance of Equipment.</u> Performer agrees to transport to Station any "home studio" equipment that may require maintenance or repair so long as equipment is portable.

<u>3. Promotional Budget.</u> Station agrees to spend up to $1,000 each month during the Term for promotional items (T-shirts, mugs, etc.) in support of the Program as reasonably requested by Performers. Any requested expenditures in excess of that amount shall be borne solely by Performers. Station agrees to provide Performers with a monthly accounting of the year-to-date total upon written request to do so.

<u>4. Number of Weeks of Programming.</u> Each year during the Term, Performer shall provide forty-seven (47) weeks (Monday through Friday) of live episodes of the Program. The dates on which such programming are to be provided shall be mutually determined by Performers and Station (with regard to Performers requested vacation time); provided, however, that Station may require live programming during any ratings period. Performer shall not be required to perform live services on the following holidays: Christmas, New Year's Day, Memorial Day, Fourth of July, Labor Day, and Thanksgiving Day, or in the event of verified sick days consistent with Station policy or as otherwise agreed upon with Station.

<u>5. Subscriptions.</u> Station agrees to provide Performers with the following subscriptions each year during the Term at Station's sole expense: Bit Board, Radio Star, The Complete Sheet, The Shipper Report, and Radio & Records.

<u>6. Sporting Events.</u> Performers shall have reasonable access to Station tickets for local sporting events upon request and based on availability as determined by Station in its sole discretion.

<u>7. Support Staff.</u> During the Term, Station agrees to provide one (1) producer, one (1) production technician, and one (1) newsperson to perform services in

connection with the Program at Station's sole expense, such employees to be selected in Station's discretion after reasonable input from Performers.

8. Material Terms and Conditions of Employment. Each of the following provisions represents a material term and condition of Performers' employment with Station (each, a "Material Employment Term"; collectively, the "Material Employment Terms"). Performers jointly understand and agree that Station shall have the right, at all times during the Term, to insist on strict compliance with such Material Employment Terms, and that Performers' failure to comply with any Material Employment Term following written notice by Station of Performers' non-compliance, as determined by Station in its sole discretion, and a reasonable opportunity to cure such noncompliance, shall result in disciplinary action by Station, including without limitation suspension without payment of Base Salary for up two (2) weeks for each violation, and termination of Performers' employment.

(a) Performers agree to meet and confer regularly with Station's program director regarding the content of the Program (no less than on a weekly basis for at least one hour each week), and use good faith efforts to make changes to the Program Format as suggested by the Station's program director.

(b) Performers agree to only play music during the Program that has been pre-approved by Station's program director.

(c) Performers agree to implement recommendations for the Program requested by Station as a result of a Coleman Research study analysis of the Program.

(d) Performers agree to minimize any religious content and/or references from the Program consistent with the terms of Exhibit B. Notwithstanding anything to the contrary contained in this Agreement, including without limitation the terms set forth in Exhibit B, in the event that Station management determines that all religious content and/or references should be eliminated from the Program, Performers shall comply with such request.

(e) Performers agree to discuss and coordinate all promotions with the station's promotion director and program director.

(f) At all times during the Term, Performers agree to promote the station in a positive and meaningful way, and to endorse the Station and the Station's music and format. Similarly, Performers also agree to cross promote the Station and Station features and programs during the Program on a regular basis.

(g) Performers agree to run all advertising spots within the hour as scheduled pursuant to the terms and conditions set forth in paragraph 1(b) of this Exhibit A.

(h) At all times during the Term, Performers agree to use good faith efforts to assist the Station in its sales efforts. Accordingly, Performers agree to set aside reasonable amounts of time to meet with Station sales personnel after the conclusion of the Program if requested to do so. Furthermore, Performers agree to make sales calls with Station sales personnel as reasonably requested to do so and agree that, if an on air interview is scheduled with a customer or client of the Station, Performers shall use their best efforts to put the customer or client on the air within 15 minutes of their scheduled broadcast time.

(i) Performers agree to refrain from conducting prize giveaways until Performers are aware that the requisite prizes are on Station premises.

(j) At all times during the Term, Performers agree to use good faith efforts to comply with all provisions of this Agreement and to cooperate with Station management in the performance of their duties and obligations pursuant to this Agreement.

Exhibit B

Program Format and Related Matters

The Program is a mainstream topical entertainment show which is broadcast Mondays through Fridays from 5:00 a.m. through 9:00 a.m. on both the John & Robert syndication network and the Station. The show may be broadcast locally for an additional hour from 9 a.m. through 10 a.m. so long as a minimum of four (4) songs from the Station's play list are played and it includes local content.

The Program is locally broadcast on GTBZ, 103.1 FM, and on a number of affiliate stations via satellite.

The Program consists of talk, comedy, guests, and music from the 80's and 90's. The Program also includes news, sports, traffic time checks and weather reports each hour. The weather is provided by KTTK-TV Chief meteorologist Dave Kruger. The Program is designed to appeal to the 25-54 year old men and women demographic in the Market. The talk subjects covered on the Program are driven by what is on the minds of the 25-54 year old male & female demographic of the Station. These subjects are often exhibited by subjects covered on television & radio news, local & national mainstream newspapers and magazines for the day and week or month.

When, for any reason, John & Robert cannot be present to perform the John & Robert show, the show's production director, after notifying the Program Director and the Sales Manager, will run a "Best of John & Robert Show". The "Best of the John & Robert Show" is a recorded compilation of the best shows that John & Robert have done. In addition the show's production director will run "live like" recorded spots to replace the ones that would have been performed live by John & Robert had they been there. Live spots during a best of John & Robert show are subject to provisions described in Exhibit A.

A show called "The Worst of the John & Robert Show" will run each Saturday between 6:00am and 9:00 am. This is a recorded show very similar to the "Best of Show" described above.

The Program is a mainstream topical entertainment show on an 80's/90's radio station. Station acknowledges that Performers have strong religious beliefs. We also acknowledge that a nominal amount of the morning show content will include, from time to time, sporadic mentions of certain religious beliefs. However, there shall be no proselytizing or praying on the show or any emphasis of religious material or content.

While we understand and accept reasonable and limited mention of religious beliefs on the air, we are concerned that present audiences that do not share these beliefs may no longer listen to the show if the religious content becomes too extensive. It is the Station's belief that while religious content in limited amounts may be acceptable to listeners, anything more than limited amounts of this content may have the opposite effect because it may unnecessarily offend present and potential audiences that do not share Performers' religious beliefs. Station has invested substantial sums of money to market the Program as a mainstream comedy and conversational entertainment show, and as such, the Program has acquired large audiences. If the Program should take the form of religious entertainment show we are not confident that the ratings will be maintained and grow and therefore our investment in the Program will be materially diminished.

Therefore, Performers agree to keep the religious content of the Program to a bare minimum and to use their best efforts maintain the Program's identity as a mainstream comedy and entertainment show. Station reserves the right to demand a reduction of the religious content of the Program at any time during the Term. In the event that Station management determines that all religious content and/or references should be eliminated from the Program, Performers shall comply with such request.

Exhibit C
Performer's Materials

All right, title and interest in and to the following characters (together with any materials, trademarks, or copyrights associated with the characters) is solely and exclusively owned by Robert Smith and/or John Doe:

1. The Henry Brothers
2. Jack Walker
3. Ellie Jefferson
4. Ron Morrow
5. Edmond Berry
6. The Mad Doctor
7. Russell Danger

Additionally, Station acknowledges and agrees that all right, title and interest in and to the domain name "JohnandRobert.com", and the name

"JohnandRobert", and any derivations or variations of said names as used in connection with the performance of Performer's services pursuant to this Agreement belong exclusively to Robert Smith and/or John Doe.

QUESTIONS AND DISCUSSION

1. Radio was big at one time; there was no TV. FDR had fireside chats on the radio! Everyone tuned in to their favorite radio shows. People listened to baseball games. It was the most important medium of its era. Do you think shock radio talk shows are detrimental to the image of radio?

2. In Waring v. Dunlea plaintiff successfully enjoined a radio station from playing his compositions. Would this work today?

3. Read the Federal Communication Act of 1934. This was promulgated when radio was at its zenith. Does the FCC have too much power?

4. In Red Lion Broadcasting Co. v. FCC., 395 U.S. 367 (1969), the court looked at the fairness doctrine, which allows a response when a personal attack has been made on the radio involving a public issue; this also mandates a response when a political candidate is backed by a radio station. In Red Lion, the broadcasting company carried as a part of its Christian Crusade series, a 15-minute broadcast in which a third person's honesty and integrity were impugned. The FCC ordered the radio station to supply free reply time. Are there any limits to the FCC's fairness doctrine?

5. Howard Stern! Private Parts! Satellite radio's bad boy. SIRIUS XM is described as "America's satellite radio company, broadcasting more than 135 channels of commercial-free music and premier sports, news, talk, entertainment, traffic, weather, and data services to more than, 20 million subscribers in cars, trucks, boats and aircraft, and through a wide range of mobile devices." They, of course, have an online app. Is this the wave of the future for radio? Do you see the FCC seriously limiting satellite radio?

CHAPTER 7
COPYRIGHT IN FILMS, TV, AND RADIO

And now on to copyright and Mickey Mouse, since he has flourished in every medium.

Mickey Mouse is an American icon. From Steamboat Willie to pornographic replications of Mickey with Snow White, Minnie, and the Seven Dwarfs, Mickey Mouse is America personified. Mickey Mouse is emblematic of America's dance macabre with intellectual property. Just think of how many patents, copyrights, and trademarks are associated with Mickey and the Disney Empire. Forget the light bulb; it's Mickey that coalesces the many rationales associated with the protections established by intellectual property. The Sonny Bono Copyright Extension Act could just as easily be designated as the Mickey Mouse Copyright Extension Act because that was the animus for its unprecedented extension. It extended copyright protection by an additional seven years, which coincidentally began when Mickey's copyright protection was expiring. The question is how long Congress will extend Mickey's copyright. Walt Disney, et al., have vigorously pursued any perceived infringement or weakening of the copyright of all things Mickey. The Disney Co. is especially vigilant in protecting Mickey from scandalous and lewd characterizations and associations that, in their minds, besmirch Mickey's alleged family values (and, ultimately, the literal keys to the kingdom).

Mickey and Walt started out humbly enough. But at least by 1939 and Fantasia, which featured Mickey's bravura performance in Dukas's "Sorcerer's Apprentice," Mickey's brand was conspicuously, purposefully, and specifically attached to Walt's burgeoning empire. Those of us of a certain age remember Mickey's Playhouse—*those ears, that hat, Mickey's lunchbox, religious pilgrimages to California and then later to Florida, and, of course, "Who's the leader of the gang that's made for you and me, Mickey Mouse..." This was revisited 30 years later in an eerie rendition in Stanley Kubrick's* Full Metal Jacket. *It is difficult to imagine anything, anybody, or any idea that pervades American society like Mikey; presidents and cars go out fashion, but Mickey prevails. Outsiders think of Mickey Mouse as representative of our culture. It is no wonder that Premier Nikita Khrushchev had a fit when he was told he could not visit Disney World because of security concerns. But is there anything even remotely comparable to Disney World in the U.S.S.R. of the Cold War Era? Nyet.*

Mickey Mouse, of course, is only a cartoon character. In fact, he is only a cartoon representation of a lowly mouse, albeit with anthropomorphic implications. But he's still a mouse. Why a mouse? Why should a mouse be a "leader"? Is it the mouse that roared, or something comparable to Teddy

Roosevelt's, "Speak softly and carry a big stick"? Mickey was used by the Allied Forces as a morale booster; he was even enlisted at one time. And he was certainly America's number one bond salesman. He reminded us that a "slip of the lips sink ships" and urged us to save tin and obey blackouts. Did Mickey win the war? (Yes, but not single-handedly.) Maybe the extension of Mickey's copyright was a recompense for his meritorious wartime service. It is not suggested that Ike Eisenhower and Walt Disney indulged in some Machiavellian connivance but, in truth, no other cartoon character has been afforded such an honor.

Although Mickey Mouse began as a celluloid cartoon character, he has morphed into every conceivable medium: TV, newspaper, film, video games, marketing, cyberspace, clay figures, stop-action, radio, comic books, amusement parks, animatronic, Internet, ring tones, etc. He is ubiquitous and, seemingly, neverending. Three-year-olds born today are obsessed with Mickey. Is it in our DNA? Is that the reason for the copyright extension?

If Mickey is one of a kind in many conceivable and inconceivable ways, is it not appropriate that we celebrate his uniqueness by stretching, and maybe breaking, the copyright laws? Although he is undoubtedly unique, he does not appear to be legally unique. Perhaps there should be a new type of intellectual property right that protects this wily military veteran/entrepreneur/movie star/cultural icon.

The more interesting question is whether the copyright extension begins with Steamboat Willie or if the extension should attach to the year of each incantation and morphing of "Willie" in different roles and mediums: Mickey the movie star, Mickey the TV star, Mickey the newspaper cartoon, Mickey the iTune, Mickey the Internet warrior, Mickey the board game, Mickey the video game, Mickey the amusement park, Mickey the marketing icon, etc. Is Mickey Mouse for everything, or are these discernible specific representations or medium collages that also merit particular copyright protection for the maximum length of time allowable by law? It is an interesting question and one unique to American jurisprudence; something is definitely going on. One wonders if the H-bomb would merit such protection.

[Champion, Intellectual Property Law in the Sports and Entertainment Industries 62-63, reprinted with permission of the authors for educational purposes].

The Supreme Court Protects Mickey in Eldred v. Ashcroft

This 20-year increase under CTEA came under fire in Eldred v. Ashcroft. It was alleged that CTEA was unconstitional under the Copyright Clauses's "limited times" prescription and First Amendment free speech. The district court found that the CTEA did not violate the "limited times" restriction because the CTEA's terms, though longer than the 1976 Act's terms, were still limited an not perpetual. The Court of Appeals affirmed the district court's ruling. The Appeals Court found that the case of Harper & Row, Publishers, Inc. v. National Enterprises foreclosed the petitioners' First Amendment challenge. The Appeals Court reasoned that copyright does not impressibly restrict free speech because it grants the author an exclusive right to only the specified form of expression. The court further held that the copyright does not shield any idea or fact contained in the copyrighted work and allows for "fair use" even of the expression itself. The Court of Appeals also found that Congress did not exceed the scope of its Constitutional powers.

In Eldred, the Supreme Court of the United States affirmed the decision of the Appeals Court and the district court and found for respondents. The issue was whether to extend the protection of an already existing copyright. The court emphasized that copyright's goal should be the promotion of scientific progess. Congress should have the say on the way in which the objectives of the Copyright Clause in the Constitution are pursued. The court noted that the term "limited," as found in the Copyright Clause of the Constitution, did not mean "inalterable" or "fixed." Following this case, the standard duration for copyright has been set as the life of the author plus 70 years. However, if the actual works are anonymous, pseudonymous, or works for hire, the copyright duration will be determined by looking at the date of publication or date of creation. The copyright duration for these works is either 95 years from the first publication or 120 years from creation, whichever occurs first. Id., at 67 (footnotes omitted).

Copyright law not only affords protection and fully expanded rights to the owners of copyrights, but it also limits the powers of non-holders regarding copyrighted instruments. The reason it is important to have an understanding of copyright law is not necessarily because you want to get something copyrighted; it is more so because you need to know what privileges and restrictions you have regarding currently copyrighted material.

Copyright literally means "the right to copy." Article I of the Untied States Constitution introduces the idea of copyright by mandating that Congress shall have the power to promote the progress of science and useful arts by securing for limited time to authors and investors the exclusive right to their respective writings and discoveries. Copyright protection exists in the original works of authorship fixed in a tangible medium of expression, now known or later developed, from which they can be perceived, reproduced, or otherwise communicated, either directly or with the aid of a machine or device. Copyright law exiss to protect works of authorship including literary works, including accompanying words; pantomimes and choreographic works; pictorial, graphic, and sculptural works, motion picture and other audio visual works; sound recordings; and architectural works. Though the protections afforded by copyright laws are extensive, such protections are not designed to extend to any idea, procedure, process, system, method of operation, illustrated, or embodied in such work. Essentially, the laws are designed to protect the actual work itself, not any byproducts that may be a result of that which is contained in it.

The ability to copyright one's material is best identified as an intangible property right. In distinguishing the right to the intangible property from the actual physical property itself, the original Copyright Act of 1976 explained: Ownership of copyright, or of any of the exclusive rights under a copyright, is distinct from ownership of any material object in which the work is embodied. Transfer of ownership of any material object, including the copy of phonorecord in which the work is first fixed, does not of itself convey any rights in the copyrighted work embodied in the object. The right to copyright something is an authorship right, and it exists separately and independently from its ultimate physical expression. Congress has granted exclusive rights to such authors upon acquiring ownership of a copyright. Congress has explicitly exercised its Article I power to identify the scope and application of copyright protection and to designate the rights granted to those who carry them.

The first discussion of the Constitution's copyright clause was at the Constitutional Convention on September 5, 1787. The clause was unanimously approved. The first federal copyright laws were adopted in 1790. Congress passed the Copyright Act of 1790, which provided copyright protection against only the copying of certain types of printed material. It was not until 1889 that performance rights were granted statutory protection. It took an additional 20 years for the right of mechanical reproduction of phonograph records to be added in 1909; this occurred at a time when piano rolls were prominent.

Works which are not fixed in a sheet music, song folios, phonorecords, or any tangible medium of expression do not qualify for statutory protection under the federal copyright laws. When these particular forms of unpublished works exist and they have not ben submitted for federal copyright registration and protection, they are protected by state common law. The protections of common law copyright are applicable without any sort of formalities, registration, or notice. This copyright system affords an artist, composer, or author complete protection against any unauthorized commercialization of his or her work. However, common law copyright extends to protect "live" television, or radio presentation of a song, as long as it is not recorded simultaneously with transmission. Federal copyright laws create a uniform method for establishing, protecting, and owning rights to one's work. The common law copyright protection acts as a safety net, catching all forms which may have fallen through the federal spider web.

By the middle of 1950s, the Copyright Act of 1909 appeared to be completely outdated. The tremendous amount of technological innovations and industrial advancements that occurred in the years following the establishment of the Copyright Act in 1909, until the mid-1950s, provided the courts with very little knowledge on how to cope with the vast changes. Certain innovations such as television, cable television, transcripts, synchronization with film, offset printing, Xerox reprography, and long-playing records were not contemplated in the Copyright Act of 1909; for that reason, as was the case several times before then, the Act was in desperate need of a revision. During this period of innovation, in 1955, the United States Copyright Office initiated and conducted a series of valuable studies specifically designed in preparation for necessary revisions to the antiquated Copyright Act. Additionally, the United States Copyright Office distributed 34 reports on a multitude of problems to an established panel of consultants on the matter; these reports were also disseminated to the general public. Following the distribution of the reports, the United States Copyright Office circulated preliminary drafts of the new copyright statute for review. After circulating the many preliminary drafts, the United States Copyright Office submitted a general revision of the Copyright Act of 1909 to Congress in 1964. There were several groups who opposed certain provisions of the revised copyright act, and the opposition led to an extended deliberation period referencing the the proposed revisions to the statute. However, after twelve long years of discussions, hearing, and compromises in the industry, Congress passed the Copyright Act of 1976.

The Copyright Act of 1970 provided for a copyright duration of 14 years. This duration allowed for additional 14-year period if, in the fourteenth year of the original copyright, the owner exercised the right to renew it. The Copyright Act of 1909 allowed for a total copyright term of 56 years. In the ealy 1960s, Congress extended the renewal term by one year during that time period. This, however, was not the only revision; the Copyright Act of 1976 distinguished between pre-1978, and post-1977 copyrights. Since the Act went into effect on January 1, 1978, the year separating the applicable rules for copyright was set at 1978. This Act differed from its predecessors by listing the renewal term for pre-1978 works at 47 years. This created a total of 75 years of copyright protection tacked onto the original protection of 28 years. This version of the Act completely abolished the requirements of renewal for works after 1977 and instead imposed a copyright duration for the length of the life of the author plus an additional 50 years. This Act also listed a 75 year copyright term for works created for hire. Included in the Copyright Renewal Act of 1992 was an automatic extension for works whose copyrights were filed between January 1, 1964, and December 31, 1977. This automatic extension increased the term to 67 years. In 1998, the copyright Term Extension Act (CETA) increased the term by an additional 20 years and provided for copyright duration for the life of the author plus 70 years. [From Walter T. Champion, chapter 5, "Mickey Mouse and Copyrights," in Champion and Willis, Intellectual Property Law on the Sports and Entertainment Industries 64-67 (Santa Barbara: ABC-CLIO, 2014) (footnotes omitted) [reprinted with permission of the authors for educational purposes]; see also M.L. Cross, annot., "Literary and artistic rights for purposes of, and their infringement by or in connection with, motion picures, radio, and television," 23 A.L.R. 244.]]

DETECTIVE COMICS, INC. v. BRUNS PUBLICATIONS, INC.
United States Court of Appeals for the Second Circuit
April 29, 1940
No. 203
111 F.2d 432

AUGUSTUS N. HAND, Circuit Judge.

The complainant is the owner of eleven copyrights for a like number of monthly issues of a periodical known as 'Action Comics'. Judge Woolsey found that these copyrights were infringed by a magazine of the defendant Bruns Publications Inc., (hereinafter called Bruns) and known as 'Wonderman.' He found infringement both by Bruns and by the defendants Kable News Company and Interborough News Co., who were the distributing agents of Bruns. The defendants all had access to complainant's periodicals, which had a wide sale.

We have compared the alleged infringing magazine of Bruns with the issues of 'Action Comics' and are satisfied that the finding that Bruns copied the pictures in the complainant's periodical is amply substantiated. Each publication portrays a man of miraculous strength and speed called 'Superman' in 'Action Comics' and 'Wonderman' in the magazine of Bruns. The attributes and antics of 'Superman' and 'Wonderman' are closely similar. Each at times conceals his strength beneath ordinary clothing but after removing his cloak stand revealed in full panoply in a skintight acrobatic costume. The only real difference between them is that 'Superman' wears a blue uniform and 'Wonderman' a red one. Each is termed the champion of the oppressed. Each is shown running toward a full moon 'off into the night', and each is shown crushing a gun in his powerful hands. 'Superman' is pictured as stopping a bullet with his person and 'Wonderman' as arresting and throwing back shells. Each is depicted as shot at by three men, yet as wholly impervious to the missiles that strike him. 'Superman' is shown as leaping over a twenty story building, and 'Wonderman' as leaping from building to building. 'Superman' and 'Wonderman' are each endowed with sufficient strength to rip open a steel door. Each is described as being the strongest man in the world and each as battling against 'evil and injustice.'

Defendants attempt to avoid the copyright by the old argument that various attributes of 'Superman' find prototypes or analogues among the heroes of literature and mythology. But if the author of 'Superman' has portrayed a comic Hercules, yet if his production involves more than the presentation of a general type he may copyright it and say of it: 'A poor thing but mine own'. Perhaps the periodicals of the complainant are foolish rather than comic, but they embody an original arrangement of incidents and a pictorial and literary form which preclude the contention that Bruns was not copying the antics of 'superman' portrayed in 'Action Comics'. We think it plain that the defendants have used more than general types and ideas and have appropriated the pictorial and literary details embodied in the complainant's copyrights.

We have repeatedly held that irrespective of the sources from which the author of a work may derive the material which he uses, a picture or writing which is his own production cannot be copied. The prior art is only relevant as bearing on the question whether an alleged infringer has copied the author or has taken his material directly from the prior art. Sheldon v. Metro-Goldwyn Pictures Corporation, 2 Cir., 81 F.2d 49, 53.

So far as the pictorial representations and verbal descriptions of 'Superman' are not a mere delineation of a benevolent Hercules, but embody an arrangement of incidents and literary expressions original with the author, they are proper subjects of copyright and susceptible of infringement because of the monopoly afforded by the act. Since the complainant is not entitled to a monopoly of the mere character of a 'Superman' who is a blessing to mankind (Nichols v. Universal Pictures Corp., 2 Cir., 45 F.2d (119), we think the language of clause 4(c) of the decree somewhat too sweeping. It should be modified so as to read as follows: '(c) From printing, publishing, offering for sale or selling, or in any way distributing any cartoon or cartoons, or any periodical or book portraying any of the feats of strength or powers performed by 'Superman' or closely imitating his costume or appearance in any feat whatever.'

Clause (d) of Article 4, which merely adjures the defendants to obey the law, should be deleted.

The decree modified as provided in this opinion is affirmed, but without costs or any allowance for counsel fees upon this appeal.

MUSTO v. MEYER
United States District Court for the Southern District of New York
June 24, 1977
No. 75 Civ. 6411
434 F.Supp.

BONSAL, District Judge.

As the late Sir Arthur Conan Doyle wrote in The Yellow-Face, which appears in The Memoirs of Sherlock Holmes published by Penguin Books, "(s)ave for the occasional use of cocaine he (Holmes) had no vices, and he only turned to the drug as a protest against the monotony of existence when cases were scanty and the papers uninteresting." This passage provides a backdrop for this lawsuit.

Plaintiff, David F. Musto ("Musto"), author of an article entitled "A Study in Cocaine: Sherlock Holmes and Sigmund Freud" which appeared in the April 1, 1968 edition of the Journal of the American Medical Association (volume 204, No. 1) (the "article") is suing the defendants for damages alleging that the defendants infringed upon his copyright by publishing, distributing and selling in 1974 a hard-cover and paperback edition of a book entitled The Seven Per Cent Solution (the "book"), and by making and producing a feature length film of the book known by the same name. The defendants include the editor of the book, Nicholas Meyer; the publisher of the hard-cover edition, E. P. Dutton & Co., Inc.; the publisher of the paperback edition, Ballantine Books; and the makers of the film, Universal Pictures. Musto alleges that a substantial portion of the book and film is copied from his article and that the writing and publishing of the book and the subsequent making of the motion picture infringes upon his copyright and is therefore actionable at law.

The defendants deny the allegations in the complaint and move pursuant to Rule 12(c) of the Federal Rules of Civil Procedure for an order dismissing the complaint for failure to state a cause of action upon which relief may be granted.

General Background

Musto's article is a brief but interesting history of the use of cocaine in Europe and America in the 19th century. The article is highlighted by Musto's speculation, somewhat tongue-in-cheek on the use of cocaine by the fictional character Sherlock Holmes and by the famous psychiatrist Sigmund Freud. Musto suggests that Holmes may have been a heavy user of the drug and that his addiction led him to believe that Professor Moriarty, the alleged master criminal, was after him. Musto hypothesizes that Holmes' mysterious disappearance between 1891 and 1894, described in Sir Arthur Conan Doyle's The Final Problem, may have been for the reason that Holmes was being treated for his chronic overuse of cocaine, possibly by Freud. Musto concludes with an exposition of Freud's apparent fascination with and study of the effects of cocaine, and the use of cocaine in America.

The book purports to be an edited version of a recently discovered manuscript written in 1939 by the late John H. Watson, M.D. the alleged biographer and friend of Holmes. The book opens with a scene in which Watson learns that his friend, Holmes, is suffering from overuse of the drug cocaine. In an effort to rid Holmes of his habit, Watson engages the services of Holmes' brother, Mycroft, to trick Holmes into pursuing the notorious Professor Moriarty to Vienna, Austria where Sigmund Freud can hopefully cure Holmes of his addiction. Once in Vienna, Freud cures Holmes of the habit by use of hypnosis and the two then embark upon a Holmesian adventure involving political intrigue that culminates in a high-speed train chase across the Bavarian countryside. At the end of the book, we are told that Holmes' antipathy for Professor Moriarty stems from the fact that Moriarty, as Holmes' mathematics tutor, carried the sad news to Holmes that Holmes' father had killed his mother because of an illicit love affair. The book has become a bestseller and is the subject of a motion picture.

Musto contends that Meyer, and by implication the other defendants, copied both literal and non-literal portions of his article and thus violated his copyright. After oral argument on defendants' motion for judgment on the pleadings, the Court directed Musto's attorney to submit a memorandum outlining in detail the alleged copying, and granted defendants' attorneys time to respond. Both parties have complied with the Court's directions. Since the parties have had ample opportunity to address themselves to the issues at hand and since the Court has been supplied with a copy of the article and the alleged infringing book, the Court, in its discretion, will consider defendants' motion for judgment on the pleadings as a motion for summary judgment pursuant to Rule 56. See Fed.R.Civ.P. 12(c).

The Copyright Claims

In a copyright infringement action the plaintiff must first prove ownership of the copyright and then copying by the defendant. See Nimmer, The Law of Copyright § 141 (1976). Generally speaking, a copyright registration certificate constitutes prima facie evidence of ownership. 17 U.S.C. § 209; Edward B. Marks Music Corp. v. Wonnell, 61 F.Supp. 722 (S.D.N.Y.1945). Here, there does not appear to be any dispute between the parties that Musto is the owner of the copyright on the article.

Copying is generally established by proof of access by the defendant and substantial similarity between the works. Access is ordinarily defined as the opportunity to copy, Detective Comics, Inc. v. Bruns Publications, Inc., 28 F.Supp. 399 (S.D.N.Y.1939), modified, 111 F.2d 432 (2d Cir. 1940) and, here again, there does not appear to be any dispute that Meyer had access to the article. In the book's acknowledgments, Meyer states that "(p)sychiatrist Dr. David F. Musto, in a brilliant essay published in Journal of the American Medical Association plausibly connected Holmes with Dr. Sigmund Freud through the all-important link of cocaine." Meyer also acknowledges that he incorporated into the book's plot the imaginative theories of other writers who have analyzed the works of Sir Arthur Conan Doyle and the exploits of his imaginary figure, Sherlock Holmes.

Substantial similarity, on the other hand, is a more difficult concept to define. See Nimmer, supra at § 143.1. Here, the parties vigorously contest the existence of substantial similarity between the two works.

Substantial Similarity

The Copyright Act does not protect against the borrowing of the ideas contained in a copyrighted work but only against the copying of the "expression of the idea" contained in such works. 17 U.S.C. § 1; see Holmes v. Hurst, 174 U.S. 82, 19 S.Ct. 606, 43 L.Ed. 904 (1899); Mazer v. Stein, 347 U.S. 201, 217, 74 S.Ct. 460, 98 L.Ed. 630 (1954); Dymow v. Bolton, 11 F.2d 690 (2d Cir. 1926); MacDonald v. Du Maurier, 144 F.2d 696 (2d Cir. 1944); Peter Pan Fabrics, Inc. v. Martin Weiner Corp., 274 F.2d 487 (2d Cir. 1960); Fuld v. National Broadcasting Company, 390 F.Supp. 877 (S.D.N.Y.1975). While the distinction between an "idea" and "expression of an idea" is necessarily vague, Peter Pan Fabrics, Inc. v. Martin Weiner Corp., supra, 274 F.2d at 489, the courts over the years have developed approaches to the problem that have been commonly referred to as the "abstractions test," Nichols v. Universal Pictures Corp., 45 F.2d 119, 121 (2d Cir.), cert. denied, 282 U.S. 902, 51 S.Ct. 216, 75 L.Ed. 795 (1930); Burnett v. Lambino, 204 F.Supp. 327 (S.D.N.Y.1962), and the so-called "pattern" test. See Nimmer, supra at § 143.11; see also Sorenson and Sorenson, Re-examining the Traditional Legal Test of Literary Similarity: A Proposal for Content Analysis, 37 Corn.L.Q. 638 (1952).

Here, Musto appears to rely on the "pattern" test in alleging that Meyer copied original and non-historical elements from his article. For instance, Musto contends that the following elements in his article reappear in the book: (1) the reading public had been misled by Sir Arthur Conan Doyle in The Final Problem as to what really happened to Holmes during his three-year absence in Central Europe; (2) Watson diagnosed Holmes in The Final Problem as suffering from cocaine induced paranoia; (3) Watson does not believe Holmes' "fantastic" talk about Moriarty but instead is "pained" by it; (4) Watson writes a letter to Sigmund Freud in the magazine Lancet in an effort to secure help for Holmes; (5) Freud has withdrawn his initial advocacy of cocaine and is now treating victims of the drug; (6) Holmes' trip to Europe was not to follow Moriarty but to receive medical attention from Freud; (7) Freud successfully treated Holmes for cocaine addiction; and (8) in return for this help Holmes revealed to Freud his style of reasoning. While certain of these elements in the article do appear in the book, the similarity between the two appears to end there.

For instance, in the article, Musto attempts to connect episodes in Holmes' earlier career to the theory that Holmes was addicted to cocaine. Musto refers freely to Doyle's earlier writings, especially the opening scenes from The Final Problem, to support the theory that Holmes was suffering ". . . from the side effect of chronic cocaine use which often induces an extremely suspicious cast of mind and leads the sufferer to weave elaborate schemes to explain facts of whose significance only he is aware." (Article at 29). Musto then refers to the possibility that Holmes received treatment for his addiction from Freud before beginning a discussion of Freud's association with the drug. On the whole, it appears that the article is directed primarily to a discussion of the use and effects of cocaine in the 19th century with the added dimension of a connection between Freud and Holmes through the link of cocaine.

The book, on the other hand, attempts to set straight the record as to what really happened to Holmes during his alleged wanderings through Central Europe. While borrowing heavily at the beginning and at times copying verbatim from Doyle's The Final Problem, Meyer links Holmes to cocaine to introduce the setting of another Holmesian adventure, only this time with Sigmund Freud in Central Europe. The adventure starts out with Holmes following Professor Moriarty from London to Vienna with the aid of Toby, the remarkable bloodhound, who picks up an enduring trail of vanilla extract. The trail leads Holmes to the home of Sigmund Freud where Holmes realizes that he has been tricked by his friend, Watson. After a somewhat testy exchange of mental prowess with Freud, Holmes finally succumbs to Freud's arduous and painful cure of cocaine addiction. Holmes remains in a depressed state of mind following the cure until Freud encroaches upon him to come to the aid of Nancy Osborn Slater Von Leinsdorf, the American wife of Baron Von Leinsdorf. The mystery is rather elementary by Holmesian standards, but it provides a challenge to Freud's deductive reasoning and stimulates Holmes sufficiently so that he soon returns to his normal self.

Musto contends that the literal similarities between the book and his article are such that it appears that Meyer copied passages verbatim, including the following:

Musto concedes, however, that he borrowed the above quotations for his article from Sir Arthur Conan Doyle's The Final Problem which is in the public domain. Nevertheless, he contends that he is protected by his copyright as against an infringer who copies primary material from a secondary source, and that in any event the Court must presume against the defendants, not only access but copying of all common material, including public domain matter. See MacDonald v. Du Maurier, supra.

The protection afforded by a copyright extends generally only to those elements of a work which are original. See 17 U.S.C. § 1; Chamberlin v. Uris Sales Corp., 150 F.2d 512 (2d Cir. 1945). If a copyrighted work is derivative in the sense that it is based in whole or part upon a prior or underlying work, the copyright on the derivative work will not necessarily protect the underlying work. If, for instance, the underlying work is in the public domain, as is Sir Arthur Conan Doyle's The Final Problem, the copyright on the derivative work will not protect the underlying work. See Nimmer, supra at § 41; American Code Co. v. Bensinger, 282 F. 829 (2d Cir. 1922).

Assuming there was direct copying by Meyer of portions of Musto's article, see Dellar v. Samuel Goldwyn, Inc., 104 F.2d 661, 662 (2d Cir. 1939); Collins v. Metro-Goldwyn Pictures Corp., 106 F.2d 83 (1939), it does not appear that the book contains anything similar other than the "idea" that Holmes was addicted to cocaine and that his addiction was cured by Sigmund Freud. Certainly there is no similarity between the article and the book as to the objective or type of reader appeal, the fashioning of a plot, the delineation of characters, or the literary skill employed to reach the final objective. See MacDonald v. Du Maurier, supra, 144 F.2d at 702 (dissenting opinion). Musto's article, although somewhat tongue-in-check, was written for a professional journal with a bent toward informing his readership of the uses of cocaine in the 19th century. Meyer's book, meanwhile, was written as a revised version of an earlier Doyle story on the adventures of Sherlock Holmes with a view toward capturing the imagination of Holmes' followers. Since ideas and basic plots, or even isolated incidents are not protected by the copyright laws, 17 U.S.C. § 1; Holmes v. Hurst, supra; Dymow v. Bolton, supra; Nichols v. Universal Pictures Corp., supra; Shipman v. R.K.O. Radio Pictures, 100 F.2d 533 (2d Cir. 1938), it would appear that Musto's claim must fail.

The Instant Motion

Motions for judgment on the pleadings or summary judgment in copyright infringement cases have been generally frowned upon in this Circuit, Dellar v. Samuel Goldwyn, Inc., supra; MacDonald v. Du Maurier, supra; Arnstein v. Porter, 154 F.2d 464 (2d Cir. 1946). However, such motions may be granted for the defendant if, after assuming copying, the Court finds that any similarity between the works is insubstantial or that undisputed facts raise a complete defense as a matter of law. Nimmer, supra at § 138; See, Fuld v. National

Broadcasting Co., supra; Buckler v. Paramount Pictures, Inc., 133 F.Supp. 223 (S.D.N.Y.1955); see also, Meeropol v. Nizer, 417 F.Supp. 1201 (S.D.N.Y.1976).

Here, the similarity between the article and the book is limited to the idea that Sir Arthur Conan Doyle misled the reading public in The Final Problem as to the real activities of Sherlock Holmes in Central Europe, that Holmes was really addicted to cocaine at the time, and that Holmes' friend, Watson, tricked Holmes into following Professor Moriarty to Vienna so that he could be cured of his habit by Sigmund Freud. Even assuming the "idea" of Holmes' cocaine addition was copied by Meyer from Musto's article without any reference to Sir Arthur Conan Doyle's earlier works, the Court finds as a matter of law that the copying involved only an "idea" and not an "expression of an idea" and therefore is not actionable under the copyright laws. See Mazer v. Stein, supra; Baker v. Selden, 101 U.S. 99 (1879); Reyher v. Children's Television Workshop, 533 F.2d 87 (2d Cir. 1976); Fuld v. National Broadcasting Co., supra.

Since the defendants have a complete defense as a matter of law with respect to Musto's claim of infringement by the publication of the book, defendants' motion for judgment on the pleadings will be granted as to the first claim contained in Musto's complaint.

The second claim relates to the motion picture film which has not been furnished to the Court. Accordingly, defendants' motion for judgment on the pleadings as to the second claim is denied without prejudice.

Settle judgment on notice.

WARNER BROS., INC. v. AMERICAN BROADCASTING COS.
United States Court of Appeals for the Second Circuit
March 16, 1983, Argued; October 6, 1983, Decided
Nos. 82-7152, 82-7794, No. 850 – August Term, 1982
720 F.2d 231

NEWMAN, Circuit Judge:

The primary issue raised by this appeal is whether as a matter of law the fictional character Ralph Hinkley, the principal figure in a television series, "The Greatest American Hero," is not sufficiently similar to the fictional character Superman, the hero of comic books, television, and more recently films, so that claims of copyright infringement and unfair competition may be dismissed without consideration by a jury. The appeal is from a January 22, 1982, judgment of the District Court for the Southern District of New York (Constance Baker Motley, Chief Judge) dismissing claims of plaintiffs Warner Bros., Inc., Film Export, A.G., and DC Comics, Inc. against defendant American Broadcasting Companies, Inc. (ABC) and third-party defendant Stephen J. Cannell Productions upon the granting of defendants' motion for summary judgment. Defendants cross-appeal from the denial of their motion to amend the judgment to award attorney's fees and additional costs beyond those allowed under Fed.R.Civ.P. 54(d). For the reasons that follow, we affirm the judgment.

I.

Many of the significant facts are set out in our prior opinion affirming the denial of plaintiffs' motion for a preliminary injunction. *Warner Bros. Inc. v. American Broadcasting Companies, Inc.,* 654 F.2d 204 (2d Cir.1981). Plaintiffs own the copyrights in various works embodying the character Superman and have thereby acquired copyright protection for the character itself. *See Detective Comics, Inc. v. Bruns Publications, Inc.,* 111 F.2d 432 (2d Cir.1940). Since the creation of Superman in 1938, plaintiffs have exploited their rights with great success, portraying Superman in several media and licensing the character for a variety of merchandising purposes. Through plaintiffs' efforts, Superman has attained an extremely high degree of exposure and recognition.

In 1978, building on previous Superman works, plaintiff Warner Bros., Inc. released a motion picture entitled "Superman, The Movie" (*Superman I*) and more recently two sequels. Our prior opinion in this case summarizes the manner in which *Superman I* recounts the Superman legend:

> The character is depicted as a superhuman being from a fictional planet, Krypton, who was sent to earth to escape the fatal consequences of the

> imminent destruction of his planet. Superman is found by the Kents, a midwestern couple, who name the boy Clark and raise him as their son in a bucolic setting. The Kents instill in Clark a strong sense of moral conviction and faith in the "American way," and counsel the boy not to reveal his superhuman powers to anyone. Clark matures into a tall, well-built, dark-haired, and strikingly handsome young man. Ultimately, Clark leaves his pastoral home, finding himself drawn by a mysterious force to a place where he encounters the image of his deceased father, Jor-El. There, Jor-El informs him of his true identity and instructs him to use his superpowers to protect the world from evil. Clark emerges from his fantastic encounter with Jor-El wearing for the first time his Superman costume—a skin-tight blue leotard with red briefs, boots and cape, and a large "S" emblazoned in red and gold upon the chest and cape.
>
> Clark subsequently obtains a position as a reporter for the *Daily Planet,* but reveals his true identity to no one, assuming instead the appearance of a shy, bumbling, but well-intentioned young man. There he soon meets and becomes infatuated with a beautiful colleague, Lois Lane. Later he appears clad in his Superman regalia to perform amazing feats of strength and courage which immediately attract wide attention, acclaim, and the amorous interest of Lois Lane.
>
> Superman is continually confronted by villains in all of his adventures, but eventually overcomes all evil opponents by exploiting his superpowers of self-propelled flight, imperviousness to bullets, blinding speed, X-ray vision, fantastic hearing, and seemingly immeasurable strength.

654 F.2d at 206.

In *Superman I* and in previous Superman works, Superman is portrayed as a brave, fearless hero, endowed with superhuman powers. His strength, speed, vision, and hearing far exceed the physical capabilities of mere mortals. He is impervious to bullets. In early works, Superman displayed extraordinary leaping ability, *see Detective Comics, Inc. v. Bruns Publications, Inc., supra,* 111 F.2d at 433; in later works this skill had become the power of flight, as Superman is regularly seen soaring through the sky, arms stretched ahead, then landing agilely on his feet ready for action. Superman engages in a series of exploits against assorted criminals and villains who pose threats not only to public safety but also to national security and even world peace. Regardless of his adversary, Superman always prevails.

Descriptions of Superman and lines of dialogue in the Superman works have become as well known as the Superman character. He is described as "faster than a speeding bullet," "more powerful than a locomotive," and "able to leap tall buildings in a single bound," and he always fights for "truth, justice, and the American way." From the early comic books continuing through the modern films, startled pedestrians have shouted, "Look! Up in the sky! ... It's a bird! ... It's a plane! ... It's Superman!"

The substantial commercial success of *Superman I* and the attendant publicity prompted many requests for licenses permitting use of the Superman character in connection with the merchandising of toys, greeting cards, apparel, and other products. It also led ABC to seek a license for production of a television series about "Superboy" based on the early adventures of Superman. Plaintiffs, who were planning to make their own sequels and derivative works, refused ABC permission to proceed with its proposed project.

Unable to obtain this license, ABC assigned to Cannell, the principal of the third-party defendant production company, the task of creating a "pilot" program for a TV series involving a superhero. Cannell produced a program, and subsequently a weekly series, entitled "The Greatest American Hero" (*Hero*), which he described as being about "what happens when you [the average person] become Superman." *Hero's* protagonist, Ralph Hinkley, was given attributes intended to identify him as an "ordinary guy." Hinkley is portrayed as a young high school teacher attempting to cope with a recent divorce, a dispute over the custody of his son, and the strain that his domestic problems place upon his work and his relationship with his girlfriend. Although Hinkley is attractive, his physical appearance is not imposing: he is of medium height with a slight build and curly, somewhat unkempt, blond hair.

In the pilot show, as described on the prior appeal:

> Hinkley's van breaks down en route to a high school field trip in the desert. While walking along a road in search of help, Hinkley is nearly run over by an out-of-control automobile driven by Bill Maxwell, an American undercover agent. Maxwell has been searching the desert for his missing FBI partner who, unbeknownst to Maxwell, has been murdered by a band of extremists. Maxwell and Hinkley are suddenly approached by a brightly glowing spaceship from which descends the image of Maxwell's deceased partner. Hinkley is handed a magical caped costume—a red leotard with a tunic top, no boots, and a black cape—which, when worn, endows him with fantastic powers. Unfortunately, however, Hinkley loses the instruction book that accompanied the intergalactic gift and is left only with the verbal instruction that he should use his powers to save the world from self-destruction. Hinkley grudgingly accepts the mission after being importuned to do so by Maxwell.

654 F.2d at 206–07.

Hinkley's magical costume endows him with superhuman speed and strength, the ability to fly, imperviousness to bullets, and what Cannell calls "holographic vision," the power to perceive sights and sounds occurring out of his line of vision. Partly for lack of the instruction book that accompanied the costume and partly because some of his character traits remain dominant when he is wearing the suit, Hinkley as a superhero is not an unqualified success. He uses his superpowers awkwardly and fearfully. When flying, Hinkley shouts with fright and makes crash-landings, sometimes crumpling in a heap or skidding nearly out of control to a stop. Though protected from bullets by his costume, Hinkley cringes and cowers when shot at by villains.

In the pilot episode of *Hero,* the reaction of the first man who sees Hinkley in his costume, which he has put on in a gas station washroom, is fear that Hinkley is some sort of pervert who may harm the man or his seven-year-old son, Jerry. While the man calls for the police, Jerry notices that Hinkley is trying to fly but does not know how. The youngster patiently explains that Hinkley must take three steps and jump vigorously into the air. Hinkley manages to get airborne, has difficulty steering, barely avoids colliding with a fire escape, and finally crashes into a brick wall, knocking himself out. Police officers arrest him and take him to a hospital, where he protests in vain to a nurse that he is not crazy.

Goaded by FBI Agent Maxwell into using his superpowers to combat villains, Hinkley, remains a reluctant hero. When Maxwell urges him to intercept the President's helicopter to warn the President of impending danger, Hinkley protests, "I'm Captain Crash! I navigate like I got hit by a can of Raid. This suit belongs in the Smithsonian. How'm I gonna buzz that chopper?" Despite his apprehensiveness, Hinkley saves the President's helicopter, then loses control of his flying ability, and crash-lands, skidding to a stop on his chest.

The *Hero* series contains several visual effects and lines that inevitably call Superman to mind, sometimes by way of brief imitation, sometimes by mention of Superman or another character from the Superman works, and sometimes by humorous parodying or ironic twisting of well-known Superman phrases. Hinkley's suit invests him with most of Superman's powers, and the suit, like Superman's, is a tight-fitting leotard with a chest insignia and a cape. Their outfits differ in that Superman wears a blue leotard with red briefs, boots, and cape, while Hinkley's costume is a red leotard with a tunic top, no boots, and a black cape. In one scene, as Hinkley is running at super speed, smoke emerges from his footsteps, and the sound of a locomotive is heard. A similar scene occurs in *Superman I,* though even without seeing the movie it would be difficult not to be reminded by the *Hero* scene of Superman, who is regularly described as "more powerful than a locomotive." When Hinkley first views himself in a mirror holding his costume in front of him, he says, "It's a bird ... it's a plane ... it's Ralph Hinkley." The youngster, Jerry, watching Hinkley's unsuccessful first effort to fly, tells him, "Superman wouldn't do it that way." In a scene with his girlfriend, who is aware of the powers that come with the magic costume, Hinkley says, "Look at it this way ... you're already one step up on Lois Lane. She never found out who Clark Kent really was."

In the three weeks before the first episode of *Hero* was televised, ABC conducted one of the most extensive promotional campaigns in the network's history, airing nearly 200 commercials, or "promos," each running five, ten, twenty, or thirty seconds. Most were slight variations of thirteen basic "promos." By multiplying the number of "promos" by the estimated television audience at the time each was shown, plaintiffs estimate that the promotional campaign registered more than 2.4 billion viewer impressions. Some of the "promos" contained scenes created specially for the commercial, a departure from what plaintiffs contend is the normal industry practice of using only action scenes excerpted from episodes to be shown in the series.

Like the pilot episode, the "promos" show Hinkley displaying some Superman-like abilities in a decidedly unSuperman-like way. For example, Hinkley has the ability to fly, but does so carrying a large lantern and, on occasion, waves his arms wildly to maintain his course or crash lands into a treetop. He has superhuman strength, but, before succeeding in crashing through a wall to surprise the villians, his first attempt nearly knocks him out. Though protected from bullets by his suit, he cringes and covers his face with his arms when shots are fired. The "promos" also preview the *Hero* series device of referring to Superman characters or well-known Superman lines. Hinkley is shown admiring himself in his suit, saying, "It's a bird! It's a plane. It's Ralph!" In one of the basic "promos" an announcer gives this description of Hinkley:

> He may be unable to leap tall buildings in a single bound, he may be slower than a speeding bullet and he may be less powerful than a locomotive ... but he's working on it. Give the poor guy a chance. He's just getting started. But when he gets it going there's no stopping him.

During this "promo" the viewer sees Hinkley crash into a tree and then a wall, and hears a bystander call him "butterfingers."

The "promos" include three other devices that plaintiffs assert provide special support for their copyright infringement and unfair competition claims. First, some of the "promos" show Hinkley flying (with his lantern) in outer space, with the earth as a background; plaintiffs contend this is an attempt to copy a scene from *Superman I* in which Superman performs exploits in outer space. Second, some of the "promos" show the Statue of Liberty, which plaintiffs contend is an attempt to copy a movie scene of Superman flying around the Statue. Third, in one of the "promos" Hinkley is shown watching a television set on which appears a brief clip from the television cartoon "Superfriends" showing the animated cartoon figure of Superman. In addition, plaintiffs assert that a special videotape prepared to promote the *Hero* series, which was shown to ABC's sponsors and affiliated stations, used excerpts from the music soundtrack of *Superman I*.

The complaint alleged copyright infringement in violation of section 101 of the Copyright Act of 1976, 17 U.S.C. § 501 (Supp. V 1981), unfair competition in violation of the common law of New York, and impairment of the value of plaintiffs' trademarks and indicia associated with the Superman character in violation of New York's "anti-dilution" statute, N.Y.Gen.Bus.Law § 368–d (McKinney 1968). Chief Judge Motley denied a preliminary injunction that would have barred the showing of the *Hero* series, 523 F.Supp. 611, and this Court affirmed, 654 F.2d 204. The defendants then moved for summary judgment and dismissal of the complaint. Chief Judge Motley initially denied that motion, and prepared the case for bifurcated jury trials of the copyright infringement and unfair competition claims, Fed.R.Civ.P. 42(b). Two specific copyright claims, those concerning the use of the *Superman I* music soundtrack in the special promotional videotape and the use of the clip from the "Superfriends" cartoon in one of the televised "promos," were ruled to be outside the scope of the litigation. The holder of the copyright in the *Superman I* music was not a party to this suit, and the claim concerning the "Superfriends" cartoon clip was not made until the eve of trial. Though the District Judge referred to these two claims as "severed," it is apparent that Chief Judge Motley simply declined to permit their addition to this lawsuit and left them available for determination in another case.

Prior to the start of the trial the District Judge, apparently harboring doubts as to the need for a trial, conducted an extended pretrial conference, lasting two weeks, to afford an opportunity to review the evidence to be offered by the plaintiffs. In the course of the pretrial conference, Chief Judge Motley ruled that the responses to an audience survey commissioned by the plaintiffs were inadmissible, "because they were too general to be of any benefit to the jury with respect to ... the copyright claim." The District Judge also excluded all expert testimony on the copyright claim, including testimony, sought to be introduced by plaintiffs, offered to show the inability of young children to perceive the differences between Hinkley and Superman.

On December 9, 1981, Chief Judge Motley granted partial summary judgment to defendants on the claim that their "promos" infringed plaintiffs' copyrights, but on all other issues reaffirmed her prior denial of summary judgment. On December 16, 1981, the District Judge concluded that no reasonable jury could find that the parties' works were substantially similar and granted summary judgment to defendants on the entire copyright claim. Chief Judge Motley initially expressed an intention to certify the latter ruling for appeal, 28 U.S.C. § 1292(b) (1976), and to stay proceedings on the unfair competition claims pending this Court's disposition of the copyright issue. However, after reconsidering the matter, she concluded that public confusion as to the origin of *Hero* was unlikely as a matter of law, and relied on this latter finding to preclude trial on the Lanham Act and common law unfair competition claims, and also on the New York "anti-dilution" claim. On January 20, 1982, the District Judge dismissed plaintiffs' complaint in a comprehensive opinion. 530

F.Supp. 1187. On September 27, 1982, the Court denied defendants' motion to amend the judgment to include an award of attorney's fees and additional costs.

II.

The basic issues concerning the copyright infringement claim are whether the *Hero* and *Superman* works are substantially similar so as to support an inference of copying and whether the lack of substantial similarity is so clear as to fall outside the range of reasonably disputed fact questions requiring resolution by a jury. The similarity to be assessed must concern the expression of ideas, not the ideas themselves, a distinction easier to assert than to apply... Before assessing the District Court's determination that summary judgment was appropriate in this case, we consider the principles that guide decision in this area.

It is a fundamental objective of the copyright law to foster creativity. However, that law has the capacity both to augment and diminish the prospects for creativity. By assuring the author of an original work the exclusive benefits of whatever commercial success his or her work enjoys, the law obviously promotes creativity. At the same time, it can deter the creation of new works if authors are fearful that their creations will too readily be found to be substantially similar to preexisting works. The idea-expression dichotomy originated in the case law and is now codified in the statute, 17 U.S.C. § 102(b) (Supp. V 1981), in an effort to enable courts to adjust the tension between these competing effects of copyright protection. Though imprecise, it remains a useful analytic tool for separating infringing from non-infringing works, especially when the essence of the work sought to be protected is a story and the allegedly infringing work is accused of what Professor Nimmer calls "comprehensive nonliteral similarity," 3 *Nimmer* § 13.03 [A][1], duplicating the "fundamental essence or structure" of a work, *id.* Confronting a claim of that sort, courts have often invoked Learned Hand's "abstractions" test, or Professor Chaffee's "pattern" test.

When, as in this case, the claim concerns infringement of a character, rather than a story, the idea-expression distinction has proved to be especially elusive. In *Nichols,* Hand applied his "abstractions" test in determining that neither the plot nor the characters of "Abie's Irish Rose" were infringed by a similar play called "The Cohens and the Kellys." He noted that no case then decided had found infringement of a character described only by written word, although he recognized the possibility that a literary character could be sufficiently delineated to support a claim of infringement by a second comer, 45 F.2d at 121. Copyrightability of a literary character has on occasion been recognized, *Burroughs v. Metro-Goldwyn-Mayer, Inc.,* 519 F.Supp. 388, 391

(S.D.N.Y.1981) (Tarzan), *aff'd with issue expressly left open,* 683 F.2d 610, 621 (2d Cir.1982). However, there has been no doubt that copyright protection is available for characters portrayed in cartoons...

In determining whether a character in a second work infringes a cartoon character, courts have generally considered not only the visual resemblance but also the totality of the characters' attributes and traits. *See Detective Comics, Inc. v. Bruns Publications, Inc., supra,* 111 F.2d at 433; *Warner Brothers, Inc. v. Film Ventures International,* 403 F.Supp. 522, 525 (C.D.Cal.1975); *see also Sid & Marty Krofft Television Productions, Inc. v. McDonald's Corp.,* 562 F.2d 1157, 1167 n. 9, 1169 (9th Cir.1977) (H.R. Pufnstuf puppets created for children's television series). A pertinent consideration, formulated in a case concerning greeting cards in which characters were one element of the art work, is the extent to which the allegedly infringing character captures the "total concept and feel" of the copyrighted character...

The tension between these two propositions perhaps results from their formulation in the context of literary works and their subsequent application to graphic and three-dimensional works. A story has a linear dimension: it begins, continues, and ends. If a defendant copies substantial portions of a plaintiff's sequence of events, he does not escape infringement by adding original episodes somewhere along the line. A graphic or three-dimensional work is created to be perceived as an entirety. Significant dissimilarities between two works of this sort inevitably lessen the similarity that would otherwise exist between the total perceptions of the two works. The graphic rendering of a character has aspects of both the linear, literary mode and the multi-dimensional total perception. What the character thinks, feels, says, and does and the descriptions conveyed by the author through the comments of other characters in the work episodically fill out a viewer's understanding of the character. At the same time, the visual perception of the character tends to create a dominant impression against which the similarity of a defendant's character may be readily compared, and significant differences readily noted.

Ultimately, care must be taken to draw the elusive distinction between a substantially similar character that infringes a copyrighted character despite slight differences in appearance, behavior, or traits, and a somewhat similar though non-infringing character whose appearance, behavior, or traits, and especially their combination, significantly differ from those of a copyrighted character, even though the second character is reminiscent of the first one. Stirring one's memory of a copyrighted character is not the same as appearing to be substantially similar to that character, and only the latter is infringement. *See Ideal Toy Corp. v. Kenner Products Division of General Mills Fun Group, Inc.,* 443 F.Supp. 291, 305 (S.D.N.Y.1977).

An entirely separate issue of infringement, also posed by this case, concerns what Professor Nimmer calls "fragmented literal similarity," 3 Nimmer

§ 13.03[A][2], duplicating the exact or nearly exact wording of a fragment of the protected work, *id.* With respect to such claims, courts have invoked two distinct doctrines. First, a *de minimis* rule has been applied, allowing the literal copying of a small and usually insignificant portion of the plaintiff's work...

The "parody" branch of the "fair use" doctrine is itself a means of fostering the creativity protected by the copyright law. It also balances the public interest in the free flow of ideas with the copyright holder's interest in the exclusive use of his work. Especially in an era of mass communications, it is to be expected that phrases and other fragments of expression in a highly successful copyrighted work will become part of the language. That does not mean they lose all protection in the manner of a trade name that has become generic. No matter how well known a copyrighted phrase becomes, its author is entitled to guard against its appropriation to promote the sale of commercial products. That doctrine enabled the proprietors of the Superman copyright to prevent a discount chain from using a television commercial that parodied well-known lines associated with Superman.

Applying these principles to this case, we conclude that Chief Judge Motley correctly entered summary judgment for the defendants on the claim of copyright infringement. Plaintiffs make no claim that the *Hero* pilot, subsequent episodes, or "promos" infringed the story of any Superman works. Their contention is that the *Hero* character, Ralph Hinkley, is substantially similar to Superman and that the *Hero* works impermissibly copied what plaintiffs call the "indicia" of Superman, a concept broad enough to include Superman's costume, his abilities, the well-known lines associated with him—in short, anything occurring in the *Hero* works that might remind a viewer of Superman.

The total perception of the Hinkley character is not substantially similar to that of Superman. On the contrary, it is profoundly different. Superman looks and acts like a brave, proud hero, who has dedicated his life to combating the forces of evil. Hinkley looks and acts like a timid, reluctant hero, who accepts his missions grudgingly and prefers to get on with his normal life. Superman performs his superhuman feats with skill, verve, and dash, clearly the master of his own destiny. Hinkley is perplexed by the superhuman powers his costume confers and uses them in a bumbling, comical fashion. In the genre of superheros, Hinkley follows Superman as, in the genre of detectives, Inspector Clouseau follows Sherlock Holmes.

An infringement claim would surely be within the range of reasonable jury fact issues if a character strongly resembled Superman but displayed some trait inconsistent with the traditional Superman image. If a second comer endowed his character with Superman's general appearance, demeanor, and skills, but portrayed him in the service of the underworld, a jury would have to make the factual determination whether the second character was Superman gone astray or a new addition to the superhero genre. In this case, however, a reasonable jury could not conclude that Hinkley is substantially similar to the Superman character with only a change of name. The overall perception of the way Hinkley looks and acts marks him as a different, non-infringing character who simply has some of the superhuman traits popularized by the Superman character and now widely shared within the superhero genre.

The same considerations make evident the correctness of Chief Judge Motley's ruling that the "promos" for the *Hero* series present no jury issue concerning infringement of the Superman character. By aggregating the total number of viewer impressions made by all the showings of the thirteen basic "promos" and their minor variations, appellants imply, and we agree, that the visual impact of the series of "promos" should be primarily assessed. A viewer of an adequate sampling of the "promos" would necessarily be exposed to the Hinkley characteristics that distinguish him from Superman. In six of the thirteen basic "promos" Hinkley either flies out of control, crash lands, or cringes in cowardly fashion at the firing of bullets. In six other "promos" his flying, though uneventful, is aided (either for vision or balance) by carrying in one hand a large lantern. It may be that within a series of generally non-infringing "promos" a single "promo" could be so substantially similar to a copyrighted character as to establish infringement or at least create a fair factual issue for jury consideration. Here, however, no single "promo" is that similar to the Superman character, and whatever recollections of Superman may be stirred by the "promos" showing Hinkley flying without incident are quickly dispelled by the remainder of the series in which his flying skills are decidedly not super. Nor does infringement arise because one "promo" shows the Statue of Liberty and another shows Hinkley flying in outer space with the earth in the background. Appellants' claim that these shots infringe scenes from *Superman I* is too extravagant to be maintained. The Statue of Liberty is a widely recognized symbol of the United States, available for portrayal in any fictional work, and Superman has no monopoly among fictional heroes on self-propelled flight in outer space.

That leaves for consideration on the infringement claim the use in the *Hero* episodes and "promos" of lines that either mention Superman and other characters from the Superman saga or incorporate phrases associated with Superman. The use of such lines is manifestly not infringement. In each instance the lines are used, not to create a similarity with the Superman works, but to highlight the differences, often to a humorous effect. Appellants acknowledge the contrasting point made by some of the *Hero* lines, but insist nevertheless that the point may not be appreciated by some of the viewers, especially young viewers who make up a significant share of the television audience for the *Hero* series. Appellants were prepared to offer expert testimony to show that some children would not perceive the negatives when the announcer says that Hinkley "may be unable to leap tall buildings in a single bound," "may be slower than a speeding bullet," and "may be less powerful than a locomotive." We do not doubt that some viewers may miss the point, but their misunderstanding does not establish infringement. Perhaps if *Hero* were a children's series, aired on Saturday mornings among the cartoon programs, we would have greater concern for the risk that lines intended to contrast Hinkley with Superman might be mistakenly understood to suggest that *Hero* was a Superman program. *Cf. Ideal Toy Corp. v. Fab-Lu, Ltd.,* 261 F.Supp. 238, 241–42 (S.D.N.Y.1966) (children's perception of television commercial for dolls). But when a work is presented to a general audience of evening television viewers, the possible misperception of some young viewers cannot prevent that audience from seeing a program that will readily be recognized by the "average lay observer," *Ideal Toy Corp. v. Fab-Lu Ltd.,* 360 F.2d 1021, 1022 (2d Cir.1966), as poking fun at, rather than copying, a copyrighted work.

Our conclusion is not altered by plaintiffs' proffered evidence of a survey of persons who viewed the *Hero* pilot. The survey reported, among other things, that of the 45% of those interviewed who said Hinkley reminded them of some other character, 74% (33% of the entire sample) said they were reminded of Superman. We appreciate the problem plaintiffs confronted in designing the survey. If they asked too pointed a question, *e.g.,* "Do you think Hinkley is substantially similar to Superman?", they would have been faulted for using a leading question. On the other hand, their open-ended questions caused Chief Judge Motley to rule the entire survey inadmissible because the responses were "too general." 530 F.Supp. at 1197 n. 3. That dilemma simply illustrates the problems that arise when surveys are sought to be used as an aid in determining issues of copyright infringement. *See Ideal Toy Corp. v. Kenner Products Division of General Mills Fun Group, Inc., supra,* 443 F.Supp. at 304 (cautioning against "the dangerous precedent of allowing trial by the court to be replaced by trial by public opinion poll"). The "substantial similarity" that supports an inference of copying sufficient to establish infringement of a copyright is not a concept familiar to the public at large. It is a term to be used in a courtroom to strike a delicate balance between the protection to which authors are entitled under an act of Congress and the freedom that exists for all others to create their works outside the area protected against infringement. We need not and do not decide whether survey evidence of the sort tendered in this case would be admissible to aid a jury in resolving a claim of substantial similarity that lies within the range of reasonable factual dispute. However, when a trial judge has correctly ruled that two works are not substantially similar as a matter of law, that conclusion is not to be altered by the availability of survey evidence indicating that some people applying some standard of their own were reminded by one work of the other. Courts have an important responsibility in copyright cases to monitor the outer limits within which juries may determine reasonably disputed issues of fact. If a case lies beyond those limits, the contrary view of a properly drawn sample of the population, or even of a particular jury, cannot be permitted to enlarge (or diminish) the scope of statutory protection enjoyed by a copyright proprietor.

III.

The unfair competition and trademark dilution claims present slightly different issues, but, as will appear, we agree with Chief Judge Motley that defendants were entitled to summary judgment on these claims as well as on the infringement claims. Preliminarily, plaintiffs contend that summary judgment was procedurally improper because it was entered by the District Court "sua sponte" and without consideration of all of the evidence they proposed to offer had the unfair competition claims gone to trial. We disagree.

Defendants moved for summary judgment with respect to the entire complaint, affording plaintiffs a full opportunity to submit memoranda and affidavits in opposition. After the District Court's initial denial of the motion, which was made prior to viewing all of the pertinent works, defendants appear to have renewed the motion orally, at least with respect to the infringement claims. Thereafter Chief Judge Motley granted the defendants partial summary judgment with respect to the infringement claims and expressed an intention to certify that ruling for appeal pursuant to 28 U.S.C. § 1292(b) (1976). Upon further reflection and with the opportunity to consider the mass of plaintiffs' evidence presented during the two-week pretrial session, the District Court entered summary judgment for defendants on all of the claims...

The District Court's initial ruling denying summary judgment on all claims was not an order "adjudicating" any of them; it simply left them for adjudication at trial. Normally, a trial court's reconsideration of a denial of summary judgment occurs upon presentation of a renewed motion for summary judgment.

Turning to the merits of the unfair competition claims, we have noted that "the absence of substantial similarity leaves little basis for asserting a likelihood of confusion or palming off" for purposes of a claim under section 43(a) of the Lanham Act, 15 U.S.C. § 1125(a) (1976), We do not doubt that the image of a cartoon character and some indicia of that character can function as a trademark to identify the source of a work of entertainment, *see DC Comics, Inc. v. Filmation Associates,* 486 F.Supp. 1273 (S.D.N.Y.1980). But, as with claims of copyright infringement, courts retain an important authority to monitor the outer limits of substantial similarity within which a jury is permitted to make the factual determination whether there is a likelihood of confusion as to source. Though likelihood of confusion is frequently a fairly disputed issue of fact on which reasonable minds may differ...

We agree with Chief Judge Motley that a visual comparison of the Superman works with the *Hero* series and "promos" establishes as a matter of law a lack of substantial similarity that would create a likelihood of confusion as to source. Our discussion of the differences in "total concept and feel" of the central characters of Superman and Hinkley applies to the issue of likelihood of confusion as well as to copyright infringement. We do not doubt that there may be some viewers among the television audience who think that the *Hero* series was produced or authorized by those responsible for the Superman movies, television series, or comics. Some may come to that conclusion with respect to every film or television program portraying a character with superhuman abilities. Perhaps some viewers think that every program with a dramatic courtroom lawyer was made by the producers of the Perry Mason series, or that every show featuring a doctor is a spin-off of the Marcus Welby series. The "average lay observer" test, however, must be applied by fact-finders within an outer limit of reasonable fact-finding marked by the courts. Otherwise the scope of protection a competitor is entitled to enjoy would be expanded far beyond what Congress prescribed in the Lanham Act. Thus, as we concluded with respect to the copyright claim, the availability of survey evidence indicating that some viewers associated the *Hero* series with Superman does not create a *reasonably* disputed factual issue of likelihood of confusion as to source when the works are as different as those in this case.

Appellants contend that summary judgment was inappropriate on the unfair competition claims because of the existence of evidence offered to show that defendants intended to make the *Hero* series confusingly similar to the Superman works. For example, plaintiffs cite the fact that Cannell rejected the first proposal for Hinkley's costume, a beige and yellow outfit with a white collar and "fold-up wings," and selected instead a red and black outfit with a cape, somewhat similar to Superman's red and blue costume. We have recognized that evidence of intentional copying raises a presumption that a second comer intended to create a confusing similarity of appearance and succeeded. *Perfect Fit Industries, Inc. v. Acme Quilting Co.,* 618 F.2d 950, 954 (2d Cir.1980) (applying New York law). But if comparison of the works reveals no fair jury issue concerning likelihood of confusion, then intent to copy, even if found from the proffered evidence, would not establish a Lanham Act violation...

We also recognize that lack of substantial similarity is not a complete answer to a Lanham Act claim, since a second comer can violate section 43(a) by falsely representing his goods as those of the trademark owner, *see Sutton Cosmetics (P.R.) Inc. v. Lander Co.,* 455 F.2d 285, 287–88 (2d Cir.1972). A claim of "passing off" or "palming off" may be established even if the goods are not confusingly similar; the wrong is in the misrepresentation of a common source. However, in this case this aspect of the section 43(a) claim is also defeated as a matter of law by visual comparison of the works in question. Whether a television viewer could be misled into thinking that the *Hero* series was produced or authorized by those responsible for the Superman films depends on the extent to which the *Hero* programs and "promos" convey such a misrepresentation, even if it was not intended.

Plaintiffs fare no better to the extent that their claims are based on New York's common law of unfair competition or the state anti-dilution statute. We have recognized the breadth of New York's common law tort of unfair competition and have not hesitated to apply it to pirated audio-visual works, so long as the cause of action was not preempted by the Copyright Act of 1976...

Finally, to whatever extent plaintiffs' claims under New York's anti-dilution statute, N.Y.Gen.Bus.Law § 368–d (McKinney 1968), do not involve rights equivalent to those protected by copyright and thereby escape preemption, they too fail on the merits as a matter of law. Though an anti-dilution claim may be established in the absence of likely confusion as to source, there must be a mark of sufficient distinction to warrant the statute's special protection and there must be a blurring or tarnishing of the plaintiff's mark sufficient to constitute dilution. *Sally Gee, Inc. v. Myra Hogan, Inc.,* 699 F.2d 621, 624–26 (2d Cir.1983). Even if we assume that the Superman character and related indicia function as trademarks with the requisite distinctiveness, plaintiffs have failed as a matter of law to present a triable issue as to the blurring or tarnishing of their marks. *Cf. Dallas Cowboys Cheerleaders, Inc. v. Pussycat Cinema, Ltd.,* 604 F.2d 200, 204–05 & n. 8 (2d Cir.1979) (dilution by showing "sexually depraved film" using distinctive uniforms "almost identical" with those of plaintiffs). Even if Superman's trademarks are not as indestructible as the character that spawned them, no reasonable jury could find that the *Hero* series or "promos" blurred or tarnished those marks.

IV.

The cross-appeal need not detain us. Though defendants were surely entitled to urge the District Judge that creativity and competition could be chilled by the prospect of defending litigation like this suit and that defendants should therefore be awarded attorney's fees under the Copyright and Lanham Acts, 17 U.S.C. § 505 (Supp. V 1981); 15 U.S.C. § 1117 (1976), for having to resist plaintiffs' claims, Chief Judge Motley's decision not to award fees and added costs was not an abuse of discretion.

The judgment of the District Court is affirmed.

BERKIC v. CRICHTON
United States Court of Appeals for the Ninth Circuit
January 10, 1985, Argued and Submitted; March 11, 1985
No. 84-57333
761 F.2d 1289

SNEED, Circuit Judge.

The plaintiff appeals the district court's judgment disposing by various means of his copyright and Lanham Act claims. We affirm.

I.
FACTS AND PROCEEDINGS BELOW

In 1968, the plaintiff wrote a 54 page screen treatment that he called *Reincarnation, Inc.* Hoping to interest a studio in producing a film based on his work, he gave the screen treatment to a literary agent, defendant Marvin Moss, and asked for his help. Moss read *Reincarnation* and suggested that the plaintiff collaborate with defendant Michael Crichton on a "shared-credit" basis. The plaintiff declined the offer.

In 1978, defendant MGM/UA Entertainment Co. released the movie *Coma,* written and directed by Crichton, and based on a novel by the same title written by defendant Robin Cook. The novel is still in print and the movie has been and continues to be shown on cable television and is available on videocassettes and videodiscs. The plaintiff alleges that both the movie and the book *Coma* were largely "adapted, derived, or copied" from his screen treatment *Reincarnation.*

In December 1980, the plaintiff brought suit in California state court alleging plagiarism, breach of implied-in-fact contract, and several other state causes of action. That complaint was dismissed on a demurrer and the dismissal was affirmed on appeal.

In March 1983, the plaintiff filed this lawsuit in federal district court alleging that *Coma* infringed his copyright in *Reincarnation,* and that by failing to credit his contribution to the novel or the movie, the defendants marketed their works under a false designation of origin and thus violated the Lanham Act's prohibition of unfair competition.

On July 1, 1983, the district court dismissed the copyright claim as time-barred to the extent that it was based on actions occurring more than three years before the claim was filed in federal court. The district court then dismissed the Lanham Act claim in its entirety. Although the court's order did not state the reason for the dismissal, the district judge explained at the hearing on the defendants' motion to dismiss that the plaintiff had failed to state a claim on which relief could be granted because he could not establish the requisite element of "secondary meaning."

On December 16, 1983, the district court disposed of the remainder of the plaintiff's copyright claim by granting summary judgment for the defendants on the ground that no reasonable jury could conclude that *Coma* and *Reincarnation* were substantially similar.

We shall address the substantial similarity issue. Because we affirm the district court's disposition of this issue, we need not reach the other issues raised by the plaintiff on this appeal.

II.
SUBSTANTIAL SIMILARITY

To establish a successful copyright claim, a plaintiff must show: (1) his ownership of the copyright; (2) the defendant's access to his work; and (3) "substantial similarity" between the defendant's work and his own. *See Sid & Marty Krofft Television Productions, Inc. v. McDonald's Corp.,* 562 F.2d 1157, 1162 (9th Cir.1977). For purposes of their summary judgment motion only, the defendants stipulated the plaintiff's ownership of the copyright and their access to his work, but argued that, as a matter of law, there was no substantial similarity between *Reincarnation* and *Coma.* On appeal, the district court's judgment granting that motion, and the findings that support it, are subject to our *de novo* review. *Twentieth Century-Fox Film Corp. v. MCA, Inc.,* 715 F.2d 1327, 1328 (9th Cir.1983).

A. *The Test for Substantial Similarity.*

We have broken the test for substantial similarity into two parts. The first part, the "extrinsic test," is used to determine whether two works are substantially similar in their "general ideas." ...

The extrinsic test compares the individual features of the works; it looks to find specific, articulable similarities between the plot, themes, dialogue, mood, setting, pace, characters, and sequence of events. *Litchfield v. Spielberg,* 736 F.2d 1352, 1356-57 (9th Cir.1984).

The second part of the substantial similarity inquiry, the "intrinsic test," is used to determine whether two works are substantially similar in their "forms of expression." The intrinsic test is subjective; it depends solely "on the response of the ordinary reasonable person." *Krofft,* 562 F.2d at 1164. To that extent, expert testimony or the comparison of individual features of the works is inappropriate in applying the intrinsic test. Rather, the trier of fact ordinarily decides whether the "total concept and feel" of the two works is substantially similar. In comparing two films, for example, or a film with a written work, the proper question in applying the intrinsic test is whether the ordinary, reasonable audience would recognize the defendant's work as a "dramatization" or "picturization" of the plaintiff's work. *Litchfield,* 736 F.2d at 1357.

To prevail on a copyright claim, a plaintiff must show substantial similarity of *both* ideas and expression. *Id.* at 1356. In this case, the district court found as a matter of law that *Coma* and *Reincarnation* were substantially *dissimilar,* both in idea and in expression. We agree.

B. *Disposition by Summary Judgment.*

It is true that as a general rule, summary judgment is not highly favored on the substantial similarity issue in copyright cases... But the plaintiff is wrong to suggest that summary judgment can never be properly granted on the substantial similarity issue. Indeed, "no special standard is employed in determining whether summary judgment is appropriate on the issue of substantial similarity of expression in a copyright case." *See v. Durang,* 711 F.2d 141, 142 (9th Cir.1983). *Krofft* emphasized that the question whether there is substantial similarity of ideas between two works "may often be decided as a matter of law." 562 F.2d at 1164. And, since *Krofft,* we have frequently affirmed summary judgments in favor of copyright defendants on the substantial similarity issue... Our independent review of *Reincarnation* and *Coma* leads us to the same result today.

C. *The Extrinsic Test for Similarity of Ideas.*

At a very high level of generality, the works do show a certain gruesome similarity. Both deal with criminal organizations that murder healthy young people, then remove and sell their vital organs to wealthy people in need of organ transplants. To some extent, both works take their general story from the adventures of a young professional who courageously investigates, and finally exposes, the criminal organization. But this degree of similarity between the basic plots of two works cannot sustain a plaintiff's claim that the works are "substantially similar." No one can own the basic idea for a story. General plot ideas are not protected by copyright law; they remain forever the common property of artistic mankind. *See Litchfield,* 736 F.2d at 1357 (no copyright protection for general plot ideas); 3 *M. Nimmer on Copyright* § 13.03[A] (1984).

The test for "substantial similarity of ideas" compares, not the basic plot ideas for stories, but the actual concrete elements that make up the total sequence of events and the relationships between the major characters. The extrinsic test for similarity of ideas looks beyond the vague, abstracted idea of a general plot and instead "focuses on ... the objective details of the works.... The extrinsic test requires a comparison of plot, theme, dialogue, mood, setting, pace, and sequence." *Litchfield,* 736 F.2d at 1356. *See also Jason,* 526 F.Supp. at 777. In this case, we believe that the district court was correct in its judgment that no jury could reasonably conclude that plaintiff's *Reincarnation* and defendants' *Coma* were substantially similar in ideas.

In *Reincarnation,* for example, the main character does not, until very late in the story, participate in the investigation that exposes the criminal organization. Indeed, for most of *Reincarnation,* the plaintiff's Dr. Lamkin is a dupe of the criminal conspiracy. In *Coma,* Dr. Wheeler, who investigates the unexplained brain deaths of young, healthy patients, is moved to action by purely personal concerns: early in the story her best friend falls victim to the organization during a routine surgical procedure. In *Reincarnation,* on the other hand, Lieutenant DeNove, who investigates the mysterious disappearance of young women, is seeking to advance his career as a police detective.

The settings of both works are also dissimilar. Most of the events in *Coma* take place in a large metropolitan hospital. Only a few, relatively minor scenes in *Reincarnation* are set in a hospital. *Coma* is replete with references to sophisticated medical technology. *Reincarnation* is a less technically intimidating, if more traditionally satisfying detective story.

The major romantic relationship in *Reincarnation,* between Lieutenant DeNove and his wife, is a significant part of the story, and is used by the plaintiff to discuss the racial problems of the 1960s. The only romantic relationship in *Coma,* between Dr. Wheeler and her boyfriend, is not a major part of the story and is not used to treat larger social concerns.

Nevertheless, we recognize that there are some similarities between the works. The plaintiff argues that they raise at least a triable issue of fact on the substantial similarity of ideas issue. We believe that the plaintiff's argument rests on a misunderstanding of the nature of the protection afforded by copyright law. It is well established that, as a matter of law, certain forms of literary expression are not protected against copying. As noted earlier, the general idea for a story is among these. So too are all situations and incidents which flow naturally from a basic plot premise, so-called scenes a faire. *See Jason,* 526 F.Supp. at 777. Many of the similarities the plaintiff finds between *Coma* and his own work fall into this category of unprotectible expression. Many of the other similarities he lists-including depictions of the small miseries of domestic life, romantic frolics at the beach, and conflicts between ambitious young people on one hand, and conservative or evil bureaucracies on the other-are also unprotectible. These familiar scenes and themes are among the very staples of modern American literature and film. The common use of such stock cannot raise a triable issue of fact on the plaintiff's copyright claim. It merely reminds us that in Hollywood, as in the life of men generally, there is only rarely anything new under the sun. Taken separately or together, the common features of *Coma* and *Reincarnation* do not allow a reasonable inference that the works are substantially similar in their ideas.

D. *The Intrinsic Test for Similarity of Expression.*

Nor did the district court err in the application of the intrinsic test. We agree that *Coma* and *Reincarnation* are not substantially similar in their form of expression. Our own, independent review of the works satisfies us that they are substantially dissimilar in "the mood evoked ... as a whole," *see See v. Durang,* 711 F.2d at 144, and in the "total concept and feel of the works," *see Litchfield,* 736 F.2d at 1357. We are confident that no reasonable reader or moviegoer would recognize either the book or movie *Coma* as a "picturization" or "dramatization" of *Reincarnation. See id.* at 1357.

AFFIRMED.

Berkic looked at the "substantial similarity of ideas" test. Most important to the movie industry is the distribution of these films. In U.S. v. Paramont Pictures, Inc., 334 U.S. 131 (1948), the United States sued five major film distributors for violating the Sherman Antitrust Act; the court held that the question of conspiracy was a question for the district court.

WALKER v. TIME LIFE FILMS, INC.
United States Court of Appeals for the Second Circuit
November 20, 1985, Argued; January 7, 1986
No. 85-7690
784 F.2d 1634

FEINBERG, Chief Judge:

Plaintiff Thomas Walker, author of the book "Fort Apache," appeals from an order of the United States District Court for the Southern District of New York, David N. Edelstein, J., granting summary judgment for defendants in plaintiff's copyright action against Time Life Films, Inc., David Susskind, Gill Champion and Martin Richards, producers of the film "Fort Apache: The Bronx," and Heywood Gould, the film's screenwriter. The district court held as a matter of law that the book and the film were not substantially similar in their copyrightable aspects, 615 F.Supp. 430. Appellant argues that substantial similarity remained a genuine factual issue, and contends that the district court made several evidentiary errors in comparing the two works. We conclude that no reasonable observer could find substantial similarity between the protectible elements of plaintiff's book and defendants' movie, and that the district court did not abuse its discretion in its other rulings. Accordingly, we affirm.

I.

This litigation arises out of two works depicting the violence and urban decay of the 41st Precinct of the New York City Police Department. The 41st Precinct, located in the South Bronx, has been known among police officers by the nickname "Fort Apache" since the late 1960's for its high incidence of violent crime, which has drawn the attention of the press and other news media. Appellant Walker, a former New York City police officer, was assigned there as a lieutenant from May 1971 until August 1972. Based upon his experiences, he wrote a book entitled "Fort Apache," published in 1976 in hardcover and in paperback, which sold in excess of 100,000 copies.

As its author describes it, "Fort Apache" is a chronicle of true events. Narrated by Walker, it begins on his first day at the precinct station house, where he is shocked by its squalor, an attack on the station house by an angry mob, and the apparent inability of the police to maintain its security. On his first day, he also witnesses several violent crimes, and notes that much of the area's housing is ruined or dilapidated. Successive chapters give Walker's harrowing impressions of dozens of ugly and sometimes bizarre murders, suicides, robberies and other crimes, as well as of the drug-dealing, prostitution and physical devastation that characterize the neighborhood. Through his accounts, he illustrates some of the social patterns of the South Bronx, including family life and the popularity of youth gangs. Through anecdotes, the book also illustrates the morale of the precinct's officers and the ways they respond to the stresses of their work.

The book unfolds as a chronicle of police work and daily life in a violent neighborhood. Several chapters focus on specific topics, such as attacks on policemen. Throughout the book, Walker expresses compassion for those he considers the victims of the South Bronx, hopelessness regarding the prospects for basic improvement there, and a sense that the officers of the 41st Precinct will continue to fight a rearguard action against lawlessness with very limited success. The book ends with his transfer to another precinct.

Defendants produced and wrote the screenplay for the film entitled "Fort Apache: The Bronx," which is set in the same milieu as plaintiff's book. In 1973, Heywood Gould made a contract with the newly formed Fort Apache Company to write a screenplay for a film set in the South Bronx. The following year, the Company filed a draft screenplay written by Gould with the United States Copyright Office. In 1976, defendants placed an advertisement in the trade journal "Variety" announcing the production of a film. "Fort Apache: The Bronx" was released in 1981.

The movie focuses on Connolly, the newly arrived captain of the 41st Precinct, and Murphy, a rank-and-file veteran of 12 years there, and their responses to the crime and decay of the South Bronx. The film also portrays the close relationship of Murphy and his partner, Corelli. The film opens with the motiveless murder of two rookie policemen by a deranged prostitute. Much of the film shows the extensive, finally unsuccessful efforts of the police to locate the killer. The prostitute, in the meantime, is rescued by Murphy from a beating by her pimp, and thereafter murders another man. While engaged in the search, Murphy and Corelli respond to a bewildering variety of other South Bronx characters, crises and crimes, including a fleet-footed mugger, the birth of a child to a teenage mother and mob attacks on firefighters and policemen. The film centers around Murphy's affair with a drug-addicted nurse, who eventually is killed by drug dealers trafficking in narcotics at the hospital where she works. In addition, Murphy and Corelli witness the murder of a Hispanic teenager by fellow officers who throw the boy off a roof. After agonizing over whether to denounce the officers, Murphy does so against the advice of the nurse and Corelli, but tenders his resignation to Connolly at the same time. Connolly, however, asks Murphy to reconsider. Meanwhile, the drug dealers, who have given the nurse a fatal overdose, barricade themselves with hostages in the hospital. At the movie's climax, Murphy rescues the hostages. He then succeeds in catching the mugger, displaying a pride in his work that implies he will return to his job.

Walker contends that defendants infringed his copyright by copying from the manuscript for his book. He claims that Heywood Gould, then a reporter, met Walker on a visit in late 1971 or early 1972 to the 41st Precinct, and learned that Walker was working on a book. Walker then, he says, showed Gould the manuscript on the condition that Gould not take notes on it. Gould, however, examined the manuscript for several hours and took notes. Shortly thereafter, the manuscript disappeared from the station house. Gould denies ever having met Walker or read any version of his book, and contends that he received the idea for the screenplay from news reports describing a crime in the area and from two other officers.

In 1980, while defendants' film was still in production, Walker sued defendants in New York state court for infringement, common law copyright, fraud, conversion, unfair competition and conspiracy to commit fraud. The New York Supreme Court dismissed the infringement claim on the ground that the federal courts had exclusive jurisdiction over copyright actions. Holding that Walker's other legal theories merely duplicated his infringement claim, the court dismissed the entire action for lack of jurisdiction. *Walker v. Time Life Films, Inc.,* No. 8938/80 (N.Y.Sup.Ct.1983).

Subsequently, Walker brought this action in federal court under 28 U.S.C. § 1338(a), alleging copyright infringement, Lanham Act violations, unfair competition and breach of a confidential and fiduciary relationship. No demand was made for a jury trial. After the parties agreed to a pre-trial order incorporating stipulated facts, defendants moved for summary judgment. Defendants conceded for the purpose of their motion that Gould had had access to Walker's manuscript, but argued that the book and the film were so different that no reasonable trier of fact could find them substantially similar under the copyright laws. In support of this argument, defendants offered affidavits, some of which were prepared by an expert in literary analysis, analyzing and comparing the structure, mood, characters, themes and episodes of the two works. In response, Walker also submitted affidavits by an expert, highlighting and listing similarities between the works. In addition, Walker offered documentary evidence purportedly showing that lay observers believed the film to be derived from the book, as well as a videotape of the film, with voiceovers drawing attention to similar events or passages in the book and the first portion of the film (the voiceover version).

After reading the book and viewing the movie, and considering the experts' affidavits, Judge Edelstein granted defendants' motion. The judge rejected the claim of infringement because no reasonable observer could find the works substantially similar, and whatever similarities existed were trivial, abstract or related to noncopyrightable material. The judge refused, however, to view the voiceover version or to compare the works on the basis of Walker's proffered lists of similarities. Concluding that the movie and the book were not confusingly similar and that defendants had not attempted to "pass off" the film as derived from the book, the court granted summary judgment on the Lanham Act claim, and found the pendent state law claims barred for failure to state a cause of action and preempted by the copyright laws. Accordingly, the judge dismissed the entire complaint on the merits in a well-reasoned opinion, reported at 615 F.Supp. 430. This appeal followed.

II.

It is undisputed that appellant Walker has a valid copyright in his book. To prove infringement, he must also show copying by defendants. *Warner Brothers v. American Broadcasting Co.,* 654 F.2d 204, 207 (2d Cir.1981) (Warner I). Copying may be inferred where a plaintiff establishes that the defendant had access to the copyrighted work and that substantial similarities exist as to protectible material in the two works. *Reyher v. Children's Television Workshop,* 533 F.2d 87, 90 (2d Cir.), cert. denied, 429 U.S. 980, 97 S.Ct. 492, 50 L.Ed.2d 588 (1976). Put another way, Walker must show that his book was "copied," by proving access and substantial similarity between the works, and also show that his expression was "improperly appropriated," by proving that the similarities relate to copyrightable material. *Hoehling v. Universal City Studios, Inc.,* 618 F.2d 972, 977 (2d Cir.), cert. denied, 449 U.S. 841, 101 S.Ct. 121, 66 L.Ed.2d 49 (1980); *Arnstein v. Porter,* 154 F.2d 464, 468 (2d Cir.1946); *Davis v. United Artists, Inc.,* 547 F.Supp. 722, 723 (S.D.N.Y.1982).

A. *General Claims of Similarity.*

In moving for summary judgment, defendants conceded access to Walker's manuscript, thus narrowing the issues to the similarity between the works. In response, Walker argued that "Fort Apache" and "Fort Apache: The Bronx" were similar in plot, theme, dialogue, mood, setting, pace and sequence. He now asserts that these parallels, akin to what the late Professor Nimmer termed "comprehensive nonliteral similarity," 3 Nimmer on Copyright § 13.03[A][1] (1985) (hereinafter Nimmer), raised questions of fact that could not be resolved on a motion for summary judgment. However, a district court may determine noninfringement as a matter of law on a motion for summary judgment either when the similarity concerns only noncopyrightable elements of plaintiff work, or when no reasonable trier of fact could find the works substantially similar. *Warner Brothers v. American Broadcasting Co.,* 720 F.2d 231, 240 (1983) (Warner II). To determine whether the grant of summary judgment was proper, we must decide whether the lack of substantial similarity between the protectible aspects of the works was "so clear as to fall outside the range of disputed fact questions" requiring resolution at trial. *Id.* at 239.

The copyright protection granted to appellant's book extends only to its particular expression of ideas, not to the ideas themselves, 17 U.S.C. § 102(b), a distinction easier to state than to apply. In assessing claims of substantial similarity, courts therefore must decide "whether the similarities shared by the works are something more than mere generalized idea or themes," *Warner I, supra,* 654 F.2d at 208, a task generally performed after detailed examination of the works themselves, see, e.g., *Sheldon v. Metro-Goldwyn Pictures Corp.,* 81 F.2d 49 (2d Cir.), cert. denied, 298 U.S. 669, 56 S.Ct. 835, 80 L.Ed. 1392 (1936). Judge Learned Hand articulated this distinction in his often-quoted "abstractions" test:

> Upon any work, ... a great number of patterns of increasing generality will fit equally well, as more and more of the incident is left out. The last may perhaps be no more than the most general statement of what the [work] is about, and at times consist only of its title; but there is a point in this series of abstractions where they are no longer protected....

Nichols v. Universal Picture Corp., 45 F.2d 119, 121 (2d Cir.), cert. denied, 282 U.S. 902, 51 S.Ct. 216, 75 L.Ed. 795 (1931).

Each of the panel members has read the book and viewed the film. Applying these principles to appellant's claim that the film replicates the fundamental structure, setting and pace of his book, we conclude from a comparison of the two works that no reasonable observer could find them substantially similar beyond the level of generalized or otherwise nonprotectible ideas. We note at the outset that Walker's book, by Walker's own description, is an account of actual events. This renders proof of infringement more difficult, because copyright protection in this circuit does not extend to facts or to true events, even if they are discovered through original research. Appellees therefore were free to avail themselves of any facts contained in Walker's book, see *Hoehling, supra,* 618 F.2d at 979–80, so long as they did not appropriate his unique expression of those facts.

At the most general level, the movie and the book tell the same story. Both recount the experiences of policemen battling the hostile environment of the 41st Precinct. But, in moving to the next level of specificity, differences in plot and structure far outweigh this general likeness. "Fort Apache: The Bronx" is intensely plotted. Much of the work is dedicated to several vivid, interrelated story lines. Throughout the film the police engage in an extensive manhunt for the killer of their fellow officers, making mass arrests and sweeping the South Bronx for leads. Murphy begins a love affair that first blossoms, but ends tragically. He experiences moral doubts, which he eventually resolves, in deciding whether to testify against fellow officers who have committed a crime. Connolly struggles, with sometimes unfortunate consequences, to transform the precinct and the station house into an orderly "house of law" enjoying the respect of the area's residents. The book, on the other hand, is organized topically, moves anecdotally from one event to another, and has little plot or story line. As a nonstop recounting of brutal crimes and police action, it achieves its effects by creating a depressing, somewhat impressionistic, cumulative portrait of life in a crime-ridden and poverty-stricken urban neighborhood.

Thus, the works differ radically in pace and dramatic structure. The story lines of "Fort Apache: The Bronx" impart a continuity and suspense entirely missing from the book. In the film, each subplot and set of characters also relates to all the others. For example, the drug dealers who traffic in narcotics at the hospital first appear as targets of an undercover investigation. Later, they encounter the deranged prostitute who, unknown to them, has killed the two police officers in the movie's opening scenes. She attempts unsuccessfully to kill one of the two dealers as well, and he stabs her fatally. The dealers next discover that the drug-addicted nurse is Murphy's lover, and, fearing that she will expose their operation, decide to kill her by selling her pure heroin. After carrying out their plan, they are caught selling narcotics in the hospital and barricade themselves in a room there, taking doctors and nurses as hostages. Murphy, believing that the nurse is in the room, leads a bloody rescue of the hostages. On finding that the nurse is not among them, he rushes to find her, only to be confronted by the sight of her dead body in the emergency room. The book contains no such plot intricacies. Rather, diary-like, it presents a series of randomly-ordered sketches of police life and work, without significant character or plot development. Although individual vignettes sometimes carry suspense, no continuing story emerges to engage the reader's attention.

To be sure, the book and the film share an identical setting, and police officers are central characters in both works. But the South Bronx and the 41st Precinct are real places known to the public through media reportage. Accordingly, the notion of telling a police story that takes place there cannot be copyrightable. As to Walker's claim that the film misappropriates characters from his book, we must consider the "totality of [their] attributes and traits" as well as the extent to which the defendants' characters capture the "total concept and feel" of figures in the book. *Warner II, supra,* 720 F.2d at 241. The characters of "Fort Apache: The Bronx," however, are quite different from those in the book. In the film, Murphy is an independent-minded, cynical, divorced patrolman contemptuous of authority, once demoted for insubordination. Murphy's romantic scenes reveal tenderness; his soul-searching over whether to denounce fellow officers reveal both integrity and loyalty. By contrast, his boss, Captain Connolly, is a hard-driving disciplinarian eager to "go by the book" and establish the rule of law in the South Bronx. Walker, the book's narrator, is a pragmatic, happily-married lieutenant who never disobeys an order or questions his superiors. In his life history, outlook, rank and marital status he bears little resemblance to any of the film's characters.

B. *Specific Claims of Similarity.*

In the district court, appellant proffered lists of specific alleged similarities in an attempt to prove, in Professor Nimmer's term, "fragmented literal similarity" between the book and the film. 3 Nimmer, supra, § 13.03 [A] [2]. None of these claims alters our conclusion that the district court properly held that as a matter of law no substantial similarity exists between the protectible elements of the works. For example, appellant notes that both the book and the film begin with the murder of a black and a white policeman with a handgun at close range; both depict cockfights, drunks, stripped cars, prostitutes and rats; both feature as central characters third-or fourth-generation Irish policemen who live in Queens and frequently drink; both show disgruntled, demoralized police officers and unsuccessful foot chases of fleeing criminals.

These similarities, however, relate to uncopyrightable material. The killing of the two police officers actually occurred and was reported in the news media, which placed the historical fact of the murders in the public domain and beyond the scope of copyright protection. *Hoehling, supra,* 618 F.2d at 978–79. Elements such as drunks, prostitutes, vermin and derelict cars would appear in any realistic work about the work of policemen in the South Bronx. These similarities therefore are unprotectible as "scenes a faire," that is, scenes that necessarily result from the choice of a setting or situation. See *Reyher, supra,* 533 F.2d at 92. Neither does copyright protection extend to copyright or "stock" themes commonly linked to a particular genre. Foot chases and the morale problems of policemen, not to mention the familiar figure of the Irish cop, are venerable and often-recurring themes of police fiction. As such, they are not copyrightable except to the extent they are given unique—and therefore protectible—expression in an original creation.

Appellant lists other events claimed to occur in both works. Leaving aside the difficulty of comparing unified artistic works on the basis of such scattered analogies, we find that when the works are examined the claimed similarities either fail to materialize or prove entirely insubstantial. Appellant correctly notes, for instance, that in both works a person is thrown off a roof. But the differences between the two incidents are overwhelming. In the book, two children hurl a third from a rooftop. He falls wounded into a narrow space between two buildings, where Walker finds and rescues him. In the movie, two police officers throw a teenager from a building to his death in a street crowded with people, and the incident leads to Murphy's struggle with himself over whether to identify the culprits. We conclude that none of appellant's claims of related events in the book and the movie raised a material issue as to their similarity.

None of appellant's other documentary evidence was sufficient to bar summary judgment. He argues that evidence he offered tended to show that lay observers considered the movie to be derived from the book and therefore raised a genuine issue as to their similarity. In particular, he claims that three newspaper articles demonstrated that reporters believed that the book and the film were related. Even assuming that the articles were relevant on the question of similarity, they had no probative value. One was the creation of a movie reviewer who later admitted that he had never read Walker's book. Both the others were accounts of a visit to Florida of the doctor who delivered Walker at birth, and mentioned Walker only in passing as the author of both the book and the film. Appellant contends that similarities between a review of his book and the analysis of his book prepared by the defendants' expert witness raise questions concerning similarities in the works themselves. But comparison of secondary or descriptive materials cannot prove substantial similarity under the copyright laws, cf. *Davis, supra,* 547 F.Supp. at 724–25, because the works themselves, not descriptions or impressions of them, are the real test for claims of infringement.

Appellant makes several claims of evidentiary error. He contends that the district court erred in considering the affidavit of a literary expert submitted by defendants, which analyzed the plot, themes, structure, characters and pace of both works. District courts, appellant claims, routinely exclude such expert testimony when entertaining motions for summary judgment on the question of similarity.

The relevance, and hence the admissibility, of expert analysis on this issue depends on the standard for determining substantial similarity. We note that some confusion surrounds the standard to be applied. The formula most favored by courts, see *Nimmer, supra,* § 13.03[E][1], and often expressed in our circuit, see, e.g., *Herbert Rosenthal Jewelry Corp. v. Honora Jewelry Co.,* 509 F.2d 64 (2d Cir.1974); *Ideal Toy Corp. v. Fab-Lu Ltd.,* 360 F.2d 1021 (2d Cir.1966), is that substantial similarity should be judged by the spontaneous response of the ordinary lay observer. Taken literally, such a standard would altogether bar expert analysis and "dissection" of creative works. See *Nichols, supra,* 45 F.2d at 123 ("We hope that in this class of cases [expert] evidence may in the future be entirely excluded."). However, our opinion in Arnstein v. Porter, supra, indicated that such literalness is not required. That decision framed a two-part test for similarity by drawing a distinction between noninfringing "copying," on the one hand, which may be inferred from substantial similarities between the two works, and infringing "illicit copying," on the other, which demands that such similarities relate to protectible material...

We do not believe that Judge Edelstein's consideration of the affidavits was improper under *Arnstein.* Assuming arguendo that some of the "dissection" was improper, which we do not believe to have been the case, any error made in this regard was harmless since we find that no trier of fact could find the works substantially similar in their protectible aspects.

In addition, appellant asserts that the district court erred in refusing to consider the voiceover version of the film, and in refusing to compare the book and the film on the basis of appellant's list of purported similarities. We disagree. Fed.R.Evid. 1006, despite appellant's contentions, did not require that the voiceover version be admitted. The Rule is designed to deal with the problem of writings, recordings or photographs "which cannot conveniently be examined in court" by allowing them to be presented in "chart [or] summary form," and does not apply to the movie, which could be viewed in its undistorted entirety by the use of standard projection equipment. Moreover, as the district court noted, in copyright infringement cases the works themselves supersede and control contrary descriptions of them. As the finally released version of the film was the best and most relevant evidence on substantial similarity, the judge was not required to consider the voiceover version in deciding the motion for summary judgment. In any event, the voiceover version adds nothing of significance to the briefs.

Appellant's argument that Judge Edelstein should have compared the book and the film on the basis of a list of similarities is similarly without merit. Courts customarily decide infringement cases, once access is decided, primarily through detailed viewing or reading of the works themselves. See, e.g., *Warner II, supra; Hoehling, supra; Nichols, supra.* While it might be an abuse of discretion to bar a plaintiff from using such lists in arguing on a summary judgment motion that similarities exist, appellant's objection has no force because Judge Edelstein had the alleged similarities called to his attention and focused on them carefully in his excellent opinion.

Finally, we need not decide whether Judge Edelstein erred in excluding from his consideration early drafts of the screenplay of the film. Generally, such early drafts might be useful to show that defendants had gained access to plaintiff's work, borrowed from it, and later made changes in order to conceal that borrowing. Although defendants conceded access in this case, early drafts could still have been evidence that some borrowing occurred. However, since we conclude as a matter of law that, even assuming borrowing or copying, no substantial similarity exists between the protectible portions of the final versions of the works, any error in exclusion of the early drafts was harmless.

III.

In pressing his claim under the Lanham Act, Walker argued that appellees had attempted to confuse the public into believing that the film was derived from his book, in order to trade on the book's popularity. The district court's conclusion that the works were not substantially similar seriously undermines the theory that the film itself was designed to mislead viewers into associating it with Walker's book. See *Warner II, supra,* 720 F.2d at 246–47. Appellant also contends that the advertisement appellees placed in "Variety" in 1976 was itself an attempt to wrongfully "pass off" the film as a work created by Walker or derived from his work. The district court found, however, that no reasonable observer could infer from the advertisement that the film derived from "Fort Apache," or that the two works came from a common source. From our examination of the film and the "Variety" advertisement, which do not even mention Walker or his book, we agree. To bolster his argument that the public could not tell the book and the film apart, appellant offered the three newspaper articles described above. As already indicated, the articles were so unreliable and isolated as to deserve very little weight. The Lanham Act claim was therefore properly dismissed.

In addition, the district court was correct to dismiss appellant's pendent state law allegations of unfair competition and breach of a confidential relationship. As the New York Supreme Court found in appellant's state court action, Walker's cause of action for unfair competition is preempted by the federal copyright laws to the extent it seeks protection against copying of Walker's book. 17 U.S.C. § 301(a); see *Oboler v. Goldin,* 714 F.2d 211 (2d Cir.1983). We also agree that summary judgment was appropriate on Walker's claim that Heywood Gould breached a confidential or fiduciary relationship with Walker, because Walker failed to produce facts sufficient to show that Walker and Gould ever made any such agreement or that such a relationship otherwise existed between them.

Last of all, we conclude that the district court acted properly in dismissing Walker's state law claims on the merits after disposing of the federal claims. While federal courts, absent exceptional circumstances, should abstain from exercising pendent jurisdiction when federal claims in a case can be disposed of by summary judgment, see *Kavit v. A.L. Stamm & Co.,* 491 F.2d 1176, 1180 (1974), we think that the circumstances here were exceptional. Many issues critical to appellant's state law claims, including their relationship to federal law, overlap considerably with the issues central to his claim of infringement. Moreover, the New York state courts have already considered appellant's state law causes of action, and found them to be "equivalent to" the federal claims. Considerations of "judicial economy, convenience and fairness to litigants," *United Mine Workers v. Gibbs,* 383 U.S. 715, 726, 86 S.Ct. 1130, 1139, 16 L.Ed.2d 218 (1966), therefore made it proper for the district court to retain jurisdiction over the state law claims and to decide them on the merits. The order granting summary judgment is affirmed.

In the following case, MGM v. American Honda, Inc., 900 F.Supp. 1287 (C.D. Cal. 1995), the court found that the Honda commercials infringed on the

James Bond copyrights since the ads captured the total concept and feel of the James Bond films.

METRO-GOLDWYN-MAYER, INC. v. AMERICAN HONDA MOTOR CO.

United States District Court for the Central District of California
March 29, 1995, Dated; March 31, 1995, Entered, Docketed;
March 29, 1995, Filed
CV 94-87-8732-KN (MCX)
900 F.Supp. 1287

KENYON, District Judge.

Based on the papers submitted and the brief arguments presented at the March 13, 1995 hearing, the Court **GRANTS** Plaintiffs' motion for a preliminary injunction and **DENIES** Defendants' motion for summary judgment for the reasons set forth below. Plaintiffs are **ORDERED** to post a bond in the amount of $6,000,000 for this preliminary injunction to issue.

The Court **ORDERS** that Defendants, their agents, employees, representatives, and all others purporting to work, or working, on their behalf, be, and by this order are, enjoined from continuing to infringe on Plaintiffs' copyrighted works by displaying or exhibiting in any manner, or causing to be displayed or exhibited in any manner, the Honda del Sol commercial which is the subject of this action, in any medium, including network or cable television or movie theaters.

I. *Introduction*

This case arises out of Plaintiffs Metro–Goldwyn–Mayer's and Danjaq's claim that Defendants American Honda Motor Co. and its advertising agency Rubin Postaer and Associates, violated Plaintiffs' "copyrights to sixteen James Bond films and the exclusive intellectual property rights to the James Bond character and the James Bond films" through Defendants' recent commercial for its Honda del Sol automobile. *Plaintiffs' Opening Memo re: Preliminary Injunction Motion,* at 3.

Premiering last October 1994, Defendants' "Escape" commercial features a young, well-dressed couple in a Honda del Sol being chased by a high-tech helicopter. A grotesque villain with metal-encased arms jumps out of the helicopter onto the car's roof, threatening harm. With a flirtatious turn to his companion, the male driver deftly releases the Honda's detachable roof (which Defendants claim is the main feature allegedly highlighted by the commercial), sending the villain into space and effecting the couple's speedy get-away.

Plaintiffs move to enjoin Defendants' commercial pending a final trial on the merits, and Defendants move for summary judgment.

II. *Factual Background*

In 1992, Honda's advertising agency Rubin Postaer came up with a new concept to sell the Honda del Sol convertible with its detachable rooftop. For what was to become the commercial at issue, Rubin Postaer vice-president Gary Yoshida claims that he was initially inspired by the climax scene in "Aliens," wherein the alien is ejected from a spaceship still clinging onto the spacecraft's door. From there, Yoshida and coworker Robert Coburn began working on the storyboards for the "Escape" commercial. As the concept evolved into the helicopter chase scene, it acquired various project names, one of which was "James Bob," which Yoshida understood to be a play on words for James Bond. *Yoshida Depo.* at 45. In addition, David Spyra, Honda's National Advertising Manager, testified the same way, gingerly agreeing that he understood "James Bob to be a pun on the name James Bond." *Spyra Depo.* at 91.

While the commercial was initially approved by Honda in May 1992, it was put on hold because of financing difficulties. Actual production for the commercial did not begin until after July 8, 1994, when Honda reapproved the concept. Defendants claim that, after the initial May 1992 approval, they abandoned the "James Bob" concept, whiting out "James" from the title on the commercial's storyboards because of the implied reference to "James Bond." However, Plaintiffs dispute this assertion, pointing to the fact that when casting began on the project in the summer of 1994, the casting director specifically sent requests to talent agencies for "James Bond"-type actors and actresses to star in what conceptually could be "the next James Bond film."

With the assistance of the same special effects team that worked on Arnold Schwarzenegger's "True Lies," Defendants proceeded to create a sixty- and thirty-second version of the Honda del Sol commercial at issue: a fast-paced helicopter chase scene featuring a suave hero and an attractive heroine, as well as a menacing and grotesque villain.

The commercial first aired on October 24, 1994, but was apparently still not cleared for major network airing as late as December 21, 1994. Plaintiffs first viewed the film during the weekend of December 17 and 18, 1994; they demanded that Defendants pull the commercial off the air on December 22; Defendants refused on December 23; and Plaintiffs filed this action on December 30, 1994. After a brief telephone conference with this Court on January 4, 1995, the Court allowed Plaintiffs to conduct expedited discovery in this matter.

On January 15, 1995, in an effort to accommodate Plaintiffs' demands without purportedly conceding liability, Defendants changed their commercial by: (1) altering the protagonists' accents from British to American; and (2) by changing the music to make it less like the horn-driven James Bond theme. This version of the commercial was shown during the Superbowl, allegedly the most widely viewed TV event of the year.

Plaintiffs filed the instant motion for preliminary injunction on January 23, 1995, and Defendants filed their summary judgment motion on February 21, 1995.

III. *Legal Analysis*
A. *Plaintiffs' Preliminary Injunction Motion*
1. *The Preliminary Injunction Standard*

In the Ninth Circuit, "[a] preliminary injunction may be granted if the moving party shows either (1) a combination of probable success on the merits and the possibility of irreparable harm, or (2) the existence of serious questions going to the merits, the balance of hardships tipping sharply in its favor, and at least a fair chance of success on the merits." *Senate of State of California v. Mosbacher,* 968 F.2d 974, 977 (9th Cir.1992). In essence, this test requires looking at two key elements in deciding whether an injunction should issue: the relative *merits* of the claim, and the relative *harms* to be suffered by the parties.

2. *Merits of Plaintiff's Copyright Infringement Claim*

The required showing of likelihood of success on the merits is examined in the context of injuries to the parties and the public, and is not reducible to a mathematical formula. *See, e.g., Dataphase Systems, Inc. v. C L Systems, Inc.,* 640 F.2d 109, 113 (8th Cir.1981) (rejecting idea that "likelihood" requires moving party to show better than 50–50 chance of prevailing on merits). To satisfy the "merits" prong of the preliminary injunction standard, Plaintiffs must show a "reasonable probability," at one end of the spectrum, or "fair chance," on the other, of success on the merits. *Gilder v. PGA Tour, Inc.,* 936 F.2d 417, 422 (9th Cir.1991). Of course, a lesser showing of probability of success requires a greater showing of harm, and vice-versa. *See, e.g., id.* at 422–23.

A claim for copyright infringement requires that the plaintiff prove (1) its ownership of the copyright in a particular work, and (2) the defendant's copying of a substantial, legally protectable portion of such work. *Pasillas v. McDonald's Corp.,* 927 F.2d 440, 442 (9th Cir.1991). "An author can claim to 'own' only an original manner of expressing ideas or an original arrangement of facts." *Cooling Systems and Flexibles, Inc. v. Stuart Radiator, Inc.,* 777 F.2d 485, 491 (9th Cir.1985). The plaintiff need only show that the defendant copied the protectable portion of its work to establish a prima facie case of infringement.

a. *Plaintiffs' Ownership of the Copyrights*

Plaintiffs claim that the Honda commercial: (1) "infringes [P]laintiffs' copyrights in the James Bond films by intentionally copying numerous specific scenes from the *films;*" and (2) "independently infringes [P]laintiffs' copyright in the *James Bond character as expressed and delineated in those films." Plaintiffs' Opening Memo,* at 14.

Neither side disputes that Plaintiffs own registered copyrights to each of the sixteen films which Plaintiffs claim "define and delineate the James Bond character." *Plaintiffs' Opening Memo re: Preliminary Injunction Motion,* at 14. However, Defendants argue that because Plaintiffs have not shown that they own the copyright to the James Bond character in particular, Plaintiffs cannot prevail. *Defendants' Opposition Memo re: Preliminary Injunction Motion,* at 22 (citing *Warner Bros. Pictures, Inc. v. Columbia Broadcasting System, Inc.,* 216 F.2d 945, 949–50 (9th Cir.1954), *cert. denied,* 348 U.S. 971, 75 S.Ct. 532, 99 L.Ed. 756 (1955) (evidence at bar suggesting that assignment from author to plaintiffs did not include copyrights to author's characters) [the *Sam Spade* case]). Specifically, Defendants claim that James Bond has appeared in two films in which Plaintiffs hold no copyright—"Casino Royale" and "Never Say Never Again"—and therefore, Plaintiffs cannot have exclusive rights to the James Bond character.

It appears that Defendants misconstrue Plaintiffs' claim. First, Plaintiffs do not allege that Defendants have violated Plaintiffs' copyright in the James Bond character itself, but rather in the James Bond character *as expressed and delineated in Plaintiffs' sixteen films.* To the extent that copyright law only protects original *expression,* not *ideas,* Plaintiffs' argument is that the James Bond character as developed in the sixteen films is the copyrighted work at issue, not the James Bond character generally. *See, e.g., Anderson v. Stallone,* 11 U.S.P.Q.2d 1161, 1989 WL 206431, *6 (C.D.Cal.1989) (holding that Rocky characters as developed in three "Rocky" movies "constitute expression protected by copyright independent from the story in which they are contained"). Second, there is sufficient authority for the proposition that a plaintiff who holds copyrights in a film series acquires copyright protection as well for the expression of any significant characters portrayed therein. *See, e.g., New Line Cinema Corp. v. Bertlesman Music Group,* 693 F.Supp. 1517, 1521 n. 5 (S.D.N.Y.1988) ("Because New Line has valid copyrights in the Nightmare [on Elm Street film] series, it is clear that it has acquired copyright protection as well *for the character of Freddy.*") (emphasis added); *Warner Bros. Inc. v. American Broadcasting Cos.,* 720 F.2d 231, 235 (2d Cir.1983) (same). And third, the *Sam Spade* case, 216 F.2d at 949–50, on which Defendants' rely, is distinguishable on its facts because *Sam Spade* dealt specifically with the transfer of rights from author to film producer rather than the copyrightability of a character as developed and expressed in a series of films.

Accordingly, Plaintiffs will likely satisfy the "ownership" prong of the test. *See also infra* discussion re: Plaintiffs' copyright ownership in context of summary judgment discussion, at 27–29.

b. *What Elements Of Plaintiffs' Work Are Protectable Under Copyright Law*

Plaintiffs contend that Defendants' commercial infringes in two independent ways: (1) by reflecting specific scenes from the 16 films; and (2) by the male protagonist's possessing James Bond's unique character traits as developed in the films.

Defendants respond that Plaintiffs are simply trying to gain a monopoly over the "action/spy/police hero" genre which is contrary to the purposes of copyright law. Specifically, Defendants argue that the allegedly infringed elements identified by Plaintiffs are not protectable because: (1) the helicopter chase scene in the Honda commercial is a common theme that naturally flows from most action genre films, and the woman and villain in the film are but stock characters that are not protectable; and (2) under the Ninth Circuit's *Sam Spade* decision, the James Bond character does not constitute the "story being told," but is rather an unprotected dramatic character.

Whether Film Scenes Are Copyrightable

In their opening brief, Plaintiffs contend that each of their sixteen films contains distinctive scenes that together comprise the classic James Bond adventure: "a high-thrill chase of the ultra-cool British charmer and his beautiful and alarming sidekick by a grotesque villain in which the hero escapes through wit aided by high-tech gadgetry." *Plaintiffs' Opening Memo re: Preliminary Injunction Motion,* at 20. Defendants argue that these elements are naturally found in any action film and are therefore unprotected "scenes-a-faire."

Both sides provide expert testimony to support their claims that such scenes are distinctive or generic, and both sides question the qualifications—and hence, the testimony—of the others' experts. Indeed, there is a notable difference in the backgrounds of the parties' experts. Plaintiffs' impressive array of James Bond experts includes: (1) Lee Pfeiffer, a writer and James Bond expert whose 1992 book is entitled "The Incredible World of 007"—he has appeared on many radio and television programs as a James Bond expert; (2) Richard B. Jewell, a professor at the USC School of Cinema–Television who recently taught a course on James Bond films in the Spring of 1994; (3) Mark Cerulli, a writer/producer at HBO who has written articles and film reviews of many of the Bond films; (4) Drew Casper, a professor and film historian at the USC School of Cinema–Television; and (5) Irwin Coster, president of Coster Music Research Enterprises, Inc. Defendants' less-impressive expert list includes: (1) Arnold Margolin, a writer and producer, who considers himself to be "conversant with the genre to which James Bond and his films belong," because he has been a fan of Bond films since 1959 and has written several screenplays in the "spy film" genre; and (2) Hal Needham, a movie director responsible for the "Cannonball Run" and "Smokey and the Bandit" comedy film series.

Plaintiffs' experts describe in a fair amount of detail how James Bond films are the source of a genre rather than imitators of a broad "action/spy film" genre as Defendants contend. Specifically, film historian Casper explains how the James Bond films represented a fresh and novel approach because they "hybridize[d] the spy thriller with the genres of adventure, comedy (particularly, social satire and slapstick), and fantasy. This amalgam ... was also a departure from the series' literary source, namely writer Ian Fleming's novels." *Casper Decl.,* ¶ 9. Casper also states: "I also believe that this distinct melange of genres, which was also seminal ... created a protagonist, antagonist, sexual consort, type of mission, type of exotic setting, type of mood, type of dialogue, type of music, etc. that was not there in the subtype of the spy thriller films of that ilk hitherto." *Id.,* ¶ 11. In addition, Professor Jewell and Lee Pfeiffer describe the aforementioned elements in more detail and how these are in essence copied by the Honda commercial.

Based on Plaintiffs' experts' greater familiarity with the James Bond films, as well as a review of Plaintiffs' James Bond montage and defense expert Needham's video montage of the "action/spy" genre films, it is clear that James Bond films are unique in their expression of the spy thriller idea. A filmmaker could produce a helicopter chase scene in practically an indefinite number of ways, but only James Bond films bring the various elements Casper describes together in a unique and original way.

Thus, the Court believes that Plaintiffs will likely succeed on their claim that their expression of the action film sequences in the James Bond films is copyrightable as a matter of law.

Whether James Bond Character Is Copyrightable

The law in the Ninth Circuit is unclear as to when visually-depicted characters such as James Bond can be afforded copyright protection. In the landmark *Sam Spade* case, *Warner Bros.,* 216 F.2d at 950, the Ninth Circuit held that the *literary* character Sam Spade was not copyrightable because he did not constitute "the story being told." The court opined: "It is conceivable that the character really constitutes the story being told, but if the character is only the chessman in the game of telling the story he is not within the area of the protection afforded by the copyright." *Id.*

Two subsequent Ninth Circuit decisions have cast doubt on the continued viability of the *Sam Spade* holding as applied to graphic characters. In *Walt Disney Productions v. Air Pirates,* 581 F.2d 751, 755 (9th Cir.1978), *cert. denied,* 439 U.S. 1132, 99 S.Ct. 1054, 59 L.Ed.2d 94 (1979), the circuit panel held that several Disney comic book characters were protected by copyright. In acknowledging the *Sam Spade* opinion, the court reasoned that because "comic book characters ... are distinguishable from literary characters, the [*Sam Spade*] language does not preclude protection of Disney's characters." *Id.* The *Air Pirates* decision may be viewed as either: (1) following *Sam Spade* by implicitly holding that Disney's graphic characters constituted the story being told; or (2) applying a less stringent test for the protectability of graphic characters. *See Anderson,* 1989 WL 206431, at *6–7 (identifying two views and citing 1 M. Nimmer, *The Law of Copyright,* § 2–12, at 2–176 (1988) (interpreting *Air Pirates* as limiting the "story being told" test to word portraits, not graphic depictions)). One rationale for adopting the second view is that, "[a]s a practical matter, a graphically depicted character is much more likely than a literary character to be fleshed out in sufficient detail so as to warrant copyright protection." *Anderson,* 1989 WL 206431, at *7. However, as one district court warned, "this fact does not warrant the creation of separate analytical paradigms for protection of characters in the two mediums." *Id.*

A second Ninth Circuit opinion issued in 1988 did little to clarify *Air Pirates'* impact on the *Sam Spade* test. In *Olson v. National Broadcasting Co.,* 855 F.2d 1446, 1451–52 n. 6 (9th Cir.1988), the court cited with approval the *Sam Spade* "story being told" test and declined to characterize this language as dicta. Later in the opinion, the court cited the *Air Pirates* decision along with Second Circuit precedent, recognizing that "cases subsequent to [the *Sam Spade* decision] have allowed copyright protection for characters who are especially distinctive." *Id.* at 1452. *Olson* also noted that "copyright protection may be afforded to characters visually depicted in a television series or in a movie." *Id.* However, later in the opinion, the court distanced itself from the character delineation test applied by these other cases, referring to it as "the more lenient standard adopted elsewhere." *Id.*

There have been no Ninth Circuit cases on the protectability of visually-depicted characters since *Olson,* and therefore, it behooves this Court to analyze James Bond's status under the *Sam Spade/Olson/*Ninth Circuit "story being told" test, as well as under the *Air Pirates/*Second Circuit "character delineation" test.

Predictably, Plaintiffs claim that under either test, James Bond's character as developed in the sixteen films is sufficiently unique and deserves copyright protection, just as Judge Keller ruled that Rocky and his cohorts were sufficiently unique. *See Anderson,* 1989 WL 206431, at *7–8. Plaintiffs point to various character traits that are specific to Bond—i.e. his cold-bloodedness; his overt sexuality; his love of martinis "shaken, not stirred;" his marksmanship; his "license to kill" and use of guns; his physical strength; his sophistication—some of which, Plaintiffs' claim, appear in the Honda commercial's hero.

On the other hand, Defendants assert that, like Sam Spade, James Bond is not the "story being told," but instead "has changed enormously from film to film, from actor to actor, and from year to year." *Defendants' Opp. Memo re: Preliminary Injunction Motion,* at 22. Moreover, Defendants contend that even if Bond's character is sufficiently delineated, there is so little character development in the Honda commercial's hero that Plaintiffs cannot claim that Defendants copied more than the broader outlines of Bond's personality. *See, e.g., Smith v. Weinstein,* 578 F.Supp. 1297, 1303 (S.D.N.Y.), *aff'd,* 738 F.2d 419 (2d Cir.1984) ("no character infringement claim can succeed unless plaintiff's original conception sufficiently developed the character, and defendants have copied this development and not merely the broader outlines").

Reviewing the evidence and arguments, the Court believes that James Bond is more like Rocky than Sam Spade—in essence, that James Bond is a copyrightable character under either the *Sam Spade* "story being told test" or the Second Circuit's "character delineation" test. Like Rocky, Sherlock Holmes, Tarzan, and Superman, James Bond has certain character traits that have been developed over time through the sixteen films in which he appears. Contrary to Defendants' assertions, because many actors can play Bond is a testament to the fact that Bond is a unique character whose specific qualities remain constant despite the change in actors. *See* Pfeiffer and Lisa, *The Incredible World of 007,* at 8 ("[Despite the different actors who have played the part] James Bond is like an old reliable friend."). Indeed, audiences do not watch Tarzan, Superman, Sherlock Holmes, or James Bond for the story, they watch these films to see their heroes at work. A James Bond film without James Bond is *not* a James Bond film. Moreover, as discussed more specifically below, the Honda Man's character, from his appearance to his grace under pressure, is substantially similar to Plaintiffs' Bond.

Accordingly, the Court concludes that Plaintiffs will probably succeed on their claim that James Bond is a copyrightable character under either the "story being told" or the "character delineation" test.

c. *Defendants' Alleged Infringement*

After identifying the scope of Plaintiffs' copyrightable work, the Court must focus on whether Defendants copied Plaintiffs' work. Since direct evidence of actual copying is typically unavailable, the plaintiff may demonstrate copying circumstantially by showing: (1) that the defendant had *access* to the plaintiff's work, and (2) that the defendant's work is *substantially similar* to the plaintiff's. *Shaw v. Lindheim,* 919 F.2d 1353, 1356 (9th Cir.1990).

Access

To demonstrate access, the plaintiff must show that the defendant had "an opportunity to view or to copy plaintiff's work." *Sid & Marty Krofft Television Productions, Inc. v. McDonald's Corp.,* 562 F.2d 1157, 1172 (9th Cir.1977). Access may not be inferred through mere "speculation or conjecture." *Ferguson v. National Broadcasting Co.,* 584 F.2d 111, 113 (5th Cir.1978). There must be a reasonable possibility to view plaintiff's work, not just a bare possibility. *See Meta–Film Associates, Inc. v. MCA, Inc.,* 586 F.Supp. 1346, 1355 (C.D.Cal.1984).

In this case, Plaintiffs contend that Defendants conceded access during the telephone conference with the Court on January 4, 1995. Defendants raise access as an issue, arguing that the inventor of the Honda commercial, Gary Yoshida, states in his declaration that he has never watched more than a few minutes of any one James Bond film, and that he got the idea for the commercial from the climax scene in "Aliens."

The Court notes that: (1) Yoshida's admission that he has at least viewed portions of the James Bond films on television; (2) the "Honda man's" having been referred to as "James Bob"; and (3) the casting director's desire to cast "James Bond"-type actors and actresses, are factors sufficient to establish Defendants' access to Plaintiffs' work. Moreover, the sheer worldwide popularity and distribution of the Bond films allows the Court to indulge a presumption of access. *See, e.g., Warner Bros. Inc.,* 654 F.2d at 208 (holding that access to Superman character assumed based on character's worldwide popularity).

Thus, the Court concludes that Plaintiffs will probably succeed on their claim that Defendants had access to Plaintiffs' work.

Substantial Similarity Test

The Ninth Circuit has established a two-part process for determining "substantial similarity" by applying both the "extrinsic" and "intrinsic" tests. *Krofft,* 562 F.2d at 1164–65. "The [*Krofft*] test permits a finding of infringement only if a plaintiff proves *both* substantial similarity of general ideas under the 'extrinsic test' and substantial similarity of the protectable expression of those ideas under the 'intrinsic test.' " *Shaw,* 919 F.2d at 1356 (emphasis in original). This "idea-expression" dichotomy is particularly elusive to courts and the substantial similarity test necessarily involves decisions made on a case-by-case basis. *Peter Pan Fabrics, Inc. v. Martin Weiner Corp.,* 274 F.2d 487, 489 (2d Cir.1960) ("Obviously, no principle can be stated as to when an imitator has gone beyond the 'idea,' and has borrowed its 'expression.' Decisions must therefore inevitably be *ad hoc.*").

(a) *Extrinsic Test*

The "extrinsic" test compares specific, objective criteria of two works on the basis of an analytic dissection of the following elements of each work—plot, theme, dialogue, mood, setting, pace, characters, and sequence of events. *Shaw,* 919 F.2d at 1359. Evidence is usually supplied by expert testimony comparing the works at issue. Because the extrinsic test relies on objective analytical criteria, "this question may often be decided as a matter of law." *Krofft,* 562 F.2d at 1164.

Here, both Plaintiffs' and Defendants' experts go through specific analyses of the similarities in ideas between the James Bond films and the Honda commercial. Plaintiffs contend that the commercial illegally copies specific protected portions of the James Bond films and the James Bond character itself. Defendants claim that the commercial depicts a generic action scene with a generic hero, all of which is not protected by copyright. Alternatively, Defendants argue that they did not copy a substantial portion of any one James Bond work to be liable for infringement as a matter of law.

Viewing Plaintiffs' and Defendants' videotapes and examining the experts' statements, Plaintiffs will likely prevail on this issue because there is substantial similarity between the specific protected elements of the James Bond films and the Honda commercial: (1) the *theme, plot, and sequence* both involve the idea of a handsome hero who, along with a beautiful woman, lead a grotesque villain on a high-speed chase, the male appears calm and unruffled, there are hints of romance between the male and female, and the protagonists escape with the aid of intelligence and gadgetry; (2) the *settings* both involve the idea of a high-speed chase with the villain in hot pursuit; (3) the *mood and pace* of both works are fast-paced and involve hi-tech effects, with loud, exciting horn music in the background; (4) both the James Bond and Honda commercial *dialogues* are laced with dry wit and subtle humor; (5) the *characters* of Bond and the Honda man are very similar in the way they look and act—both heros are young, tuxedo-clad, British-looking men with beautiful women in tow and grotesque villains close at hand; moreover, both men exude uncanny calm under pressure, exhibit a dry sense of humor and wit, and are attracted to, and are attractive to, their female companions.

In addition, several specific aspects of the Honda commercial appear to have been lifted from the James Bond films:

(1) In "The Spy Who Loved Me," James Bond is in a white sports car, a beautiful woman passenger at his side, driving away down a deserted road from some almost deadly adventure, when he is suddenly attacked by a chasing helicopter whose bullets he narrowly avoids by skillfully weaving the car down the road at high speed. At the beginning of the Honda commercial, the Honda man turns to his companion and says, "That wasn't so bad"; to which the

woman replies, "Well, I wouldn't congratulate yourself quite yet"—implying that they had just escaped some prior danger. Suddenly, a helicopter appears from out of nowhere and the adventure begins.

(2) In "Dr. No.," the villain has metal hands. In the Honda commercial, the villain uses his metal-encased hands to cling onto the roof of the car after he jumps onto it.

(3) In "Goldfinger," Bond's sports car has a roof which Bond can cause to detach with the flick of a lever. In the Honda commercial, the Honda del Sol has a detachable roof which the Honda man uses to eject the villain.

(4) In "Moonraker," the villainous henchman, Jaws, sporting a broad grin revealing metallic teeth and wearing a pair of oversized goggles, jumps out of an airplane. In the Honda commercial, the villain, wearing similar goggles and revealing metallic teeth, jumps out of a helicopter.

(5) In "The Spy Who Loved Me," Jaws assaults a vehicle in which Bond and his female sidekick are trying to make their escape. In the Honda commercial, the villain jumps onto the roof of the Honda del Sol and scrapes at the roof, attempting to hold on and possibly get inside the vehicle.

(6) In "You Only Live Twice," a chasing helicopter drops a magnetic line down to snag a speeding car. In the Honda commercial, the villain is dropped down to the moving car and is suspended from the helicopter by a cable.

In sum, the extrinsic ideas that are inherent parts of the James Bond films appear to be substantially similar to those in the Honda commercial.

(b) *Intrinsic Test*

The "intrinsic" test asks whether the "total concept and feel" of the two works is also substantially similar. *Litchfield v. Spielberg,* 736 F.2d 1352, 1357 (9th Cir.1984), *cert. denied,* 470 U.S. 1052, 105 S.Ct. 1753, 84 L.Ed.2d 817 (1985). This is a subjective test that requires a determination of whether the ordinary reasonable audience could recognize the Defendants' commercial as a picturization of Plaintiffs' copyrighted work. *See Berkic v. Crichton,* 761 F.2d 1289, 1292 (9th Cir.), *cert. denied,* 474 U.S. 826, 106 S.Ct. 85, 88 L.Ed.2d 69 (1985).

Because this is a subjective determination, the comparison during the intrinsic test is left for the trier of fact. This would involve showing the Honda commercial to the members of the jury so that they may compare the same with the sixteen Bond films at issue. Viewing the evidence, it appears likely that the average viewer would immediately think of James Bond when viewing the Honda commercial, even with the subtle changes in accent and music.

As in this Court's *Jaws* opinion, *Universal,* 543 F.Supp. at 1141, the Court finds that Defendants' attempt to characterize all of the alleged similarities between the works as scenes-a-faire to be unavailing. There are many ways to express a helicopter chase scene, but only Plaintiffs' Bond films would do it the way the Honda commercial did with these very similar characters, music, pace, and mood. Plaintiffs are therefore likely to prevail on the "intrinsic test."

(3) *Independent Creation*

After the plaintiff has satisfied both the "access" and "substantial similarity" prongs of the test, the burden then shifts to the defendant to show that the defendant's work was not a copy but rather was *independently created. Kamar Int'l, Inc. v. Russ Berrie and Co.,* 657 F.2d 1059, 1062 (9th Cir.1981).

Defendants claim that their commercial was independently created, as evidenced from the Yoshida declaration stating that he was inspired not by James Bond, but by "Aliens." Moreover, Defendants claim that their intent is irrelevant in determining whether their commercial infringes or not.

Plaintiffs raise two points in response: (1) there is other evidence before the Court to suggest that Honda never abandoned the idea of using James Bond as the basis for its commercial—for example, the casting director's notes, Yoshida's reference in his deposition to the Honda Man as "James," etc.; and (2) this evidence of intent is relevant to counter Defendants' claim of independent creation. *See, e.g., New Line Cinema,* 693 F.Supp. at 1530.

For the reasons discussed above, Defendants' evidence is neither very strong nor credible; it is highly unlikely that Defendants will be able to show that they created their commercial separate and apart from the James Bond concept. Accordingly, Plaintiffs should prevail on this issue.

(4) *The Fair Use Doctrine*

Finally, as a separate defense to copyright infringement, Defendants claim that their use of Plaintiffs' work is protected under the fair use doctrine, which protects parodies, for example. Under the Supreme Court's recent decision in *Campbell v. Acuff–Rose Music, Inc.,* —— U.S. ——, 114 S.Ct. 1164, 127 L.Ed.2d 500 (1994), a subsequent work may not infringe on an original upon examining the following four-prong statutory factors: (1) the purpose and character of the use, including whether such use is of a commercial nature or is for nonprofit educational purposes; (2) the nature of the copyrighted work; (3) the amount and substantiality of the portion used in relation to the copyrighted work as a whole; and (4) the effect of the use on the potential for, or value of, the copyrighted work. The Court shall analyze each factor in turn below.

First, the Court must look to whether Defendants' use is of a commercial nature and whether, and to what extent, the infringing work is transformative of the original. *Id.,* 510 U.S. at ——, 114 S.Ct. at 1171. In *Campbell,* the Supreme Court noted that a purported parody would not be protected if it is "commentary that has no critical bearing on the substance or style of the original composition, which the alleged infringer merely uses to get attention or to avoid the drudgery in working up something fresh...." *Id.,* 114 S.Ct. at 1172. Here, Plaintiffs contend that the Honda ad is completely commercial in its nature and does not comment on the earlier Bond films. Defendants claim that their commercial is a parody on the action film genre, and further, is more than simply a commercial because of its artistic merit. On balance, Plaintiffs should prevail on this issue—the Supreme Court in *Campbell* notes that "[t]he use ... of a copyrighted work to advertise a product, even in parody, will be entitled to less indulgence under the first factor of the fair use enquiry, than the sale of the parody for its own sake...." 114 S.Ct. at 1174. *See also Tin Pan Apple, Inc. v. Miller Brewing Co.,* 737 F.Supp. 826, 832 (S.D.N.Y.1990) (beer commercial copying music video); *D.C. Comics, Inc. v. Crazy Eddie, Inc.,* 205 U.S.P.Q. 1177 (S.D.N.Y.1979) (commercial copying Superman).

Second, the Court must recognize that "some works are closer to the core of intended copyright protection than others," and thus are more deserving of protection. *Campbell,* 510 U.S. at ——, 114 S.Ct. at 1175 & cases cited therein (e.g. fictional works are closer to the core than fact-based works). Plaintiffs view their films as just such core-predictable work, while Defendants see their work as generic, spy thriller fare. Again, Plaintiffs should prevail on this issue because their work has created its own unique niche in the larger "action film" genre.

Third, the Court must look to the quantitative and qualitative extent of the copying involved. A parodist may appropriate only that amount of the original necessary to achieve his or her purpose. *See Fisher v. Dees,* 794 F.2d 432, 438 (9th Cir.1986). The amount that may be used diminishes the less the purpose is to critique the original and the more that the parody serves as a substitute for the original. *Campbell,* 510 U.S. at ——, 114 S.Ct. at 1176. Plaintiffs claim that the Honda commercial is a total appropriation; Defendants describe the two versions of their commercial as "de minimis" appropriation, if at all. Plaintiffs should prevail on this issue: as mentioned above, the brevity of the infringing work when compared with the original does not excuse copying.

And fourth, the Court must measure " 'the effect of the use upon the potential market for or value of the copyrighted work.' " *Campbell,* 114 S.Ct. at 1177 (*citing* 17 U.S.C. § 107(4)). The task is to distinguish between " 'biting criticism [that merely] suppresses demand [and] copyright infringement [which] usurps it.' " *Id.,* 114 S.Ct. at 1178 (*citing Fisher,* 794 F.2d at 438). Where the appropriation involves "mere duplication for commercial purposes," market harm is presumed. *Id.,* 510 U.S. at ——, 114 S.Ct. at 1177. Plaintiffs allege that "one of the most commercially lucrative aspects of the copyrights is their value as lending social cachet and upscale image to cars" and that Defendants' commercial unfairly usurps this benefit. *Plaintiffs' Opening Memo re:*

Preliminary Injunction Motion, at 32. Defendants counter that Plaintiffs present no evidence that their commercial will dissuade viewers from watching the Bond films. Plaintiffs should win on this issue as well; it is likely that James Bond's association with a low-end Honda model will threaten its value in the eyes of future upscale licensees.

It is clear from the foregoing discussion that Plaintiffs will likely succeed on this issue and Defendants will be unable to show fair use or parody.

3. *Balance of Relative Harms*

It is well-settled in this circuit that once a copyrightholder has shown a likelihood of success on the merits based on access and substantial similarity, irreparable injury is presumed, warranting a preliminary injunction. *See, e.g., Universal,* 543 F.Supp. at 1139. Irreparable injury is presumed because the copyright owner's right to exploit its work is unique. *Robert Stigwood Group, Ltd. v. Sperber,* 457 F.2d 50, 55 (2d Cir.1972).

As discussed above, Plaintiffs have established a likelihood of success on the merits and therefore, the Court presumes irreparable injury. Moreover, the Court notes that Plaintiffs have shown they have been specifically harmed by the continued airing of Defendants' commercial in two ways: (1) prolonged lost licensing revenue (purportedly in the millions of dollars); and (2) dilution of the copyrights' long-term value. The latter is especially true given Plaintiffs' own deal with BMW for a special movie tie-in in conjunction with Plaintiffs' release of the first James Bond movie in six years, "Goldeneye"—a fact undisputed by Defendants. *See Stolber Depo.,* at 81:9–84:2. Indeed, the Court can very well imagine that a majority of the public, upon viewing the Honda commercial and a future BMW ad, would come to the conclusion that James Bond was endorsing two automobile companies. Such a scenario would drastically decrease the long-term value of Plaintiffs' James Bond franchise.

In response, Defendants assert that aside from the fact that Plaintiffs will not prevail on the merits of their claim, the balance of equities tips in Defendants' favor for three reasons: (1) Plaintiffs have waited too long before seeking an injunction—Defendants began airing the commercial on October 24, 1994, Plaintiffs did not complain until mid-December 1994 and did not move for a preliminary injunction until January 23, 1995; (2) Plaintiffs have waived their rights to equitable relief by not objecting to the use of the Bond character in "Cannonball Run," "Casino Royale," and "Never Say Never Again"; and (3) unlike Plaintiffs' speculative losses, Defendants have already poured in over $6 million into the Honda commercial ($2 million in production costs plus $4 million in media placement) and stand to lose much more because of the seasonal sales of the Honda del Sol, should the injunction issue.

All three of Defendants' arguments fail because: (1) Plaintiff's counsel states in his declaration that the commercial was not approved by any of the major networks as of December 21, 1994, and therefore, Plaintiffs' discovery of the commercial during the weekend of December 17–18, 1994 was reasonable; (2) Plaintiffs did not equitably waive their rights in the James Bond character as to "Cannonball Run" (an obvious parody), "Casino Royale" (Ian Fleming had sold the rights to "Casino Royale" before Plaintiffs acquired their movie rights to make their 16 films and Plaintiffs do not claim that the James Bond character in "Casino Royale" is the same as theirs), and "Never Say Never Again" (Plaintiffs tried to assert their rights in a British court, but the court allowed for the release of "Never Say Never Again" as a remake of Plaintiffs' "Thunderball"); and (3) the amount of Defendants' alleged loss, while relevant to determining the size of the bond Plaintiffs must post, does not change the Court's conclusion that the injunction should issue based on its finding that Plaintiffs are likely to prevail on their copyright claim.

B. *Defendants' Summary Judgment Motion*

As stated above, Defendants move for summary judgment on Plaintiffs' copyright infringement claim on three grounds: (1) Plaintiffs are not the exclusive owners of the elements of the James Bond character they seek to protect; (2) Plaintiffs' alleged similarities are not protected by copyright; and (3) their commercial is not substantially similar to any of Plaintiffs' films or characters.

1. *The Summary Judgment Standard*

Under Rule 56(c) of the Federal Rules of Civil Procedure, a court may grant summary judgment upon finding that "there is no genuine issue as to any material fact and that the moving party is entitled to judgment as a matter of law." Fed.R.Civ.Proc. 56(c). Under Rule 56, a non-moving party must set forth specific facts showing that there exists a genuine issue of material fact for trial. *See Kaiser Cement Corp. v. Fischbach and Moore, Inc.,* 793 F.2d 1100, 1103–04 (9th Cir.), *cert. denied,* 479 U.S. 949, 107 S.Ct. 435, 93 L.Ed.2d 384 (1986). Any inferences to be drawn from the underlying facts must be viewed in the light most favorable to the party opposing the summary judgment motion. *See Matsushita Elec. Indus. Co. v. Zenith Radio Corp.,* 475 U.S. 574, 587, 106 S.Ct. 1348, 1356, 89 L.Ed.2d 538 (1986).

2. *Defendants' Motion Fails on Its Merits*

a. *Plaintiffs Own the Copyrights to the James Bond Character as Well as the 16 Films at Issue*

Defendants first contend that Plaintiffs do not exclusively own a copyright in "James Bond" because this visually-depicted character appeared in at least three other productions: the film and television versions of "Casino Royale" and the film version of "Never Say Never Again." Defendants primarily argue that because Plaintiffs admit that the James Bond character in "Never Say Never Again" is exactly the same character depicted in Plaintiffs' 16 films, Plaintiffs do not have exclusive ownership, under *Krofft,* of the James Bond character as expressed and delineated in these films.

Defendants' arguments fail for several reasons. First, the *Krofft* case does not stand for the proposition that a copyrightholder must have "exclusive" ownership of the copyright at issue, but only "ownership" of such a right. *Krofft,* 562 F.2d at 1162. Indeed, if this were the case, joint ownership of copyrights could never be recognized—in fact, Plaintiffs herein assert co-ownership of these rights. Second, as stated above, ownership of a copyright in a film confers copyright ownership of any significant characters as delineated therein. And third, any claim that Plaintiffs abandoned or waived their rights in the James Bond character must be accompanied by a showing of an "intentional relinquishment of a known right with knowledge of its existence and the intent to relinquish it." *United States v. King Features Entertainment, Inc.,* 843 F.2d 394, 399 (9th Cir.1988).

There is no evidence to suggest that Plaintiffs have ever relinquished their rights to the James Bond character as expressed in their films. First, Plaintiffs do not assert that the character in either of the two "Casino Royale" productions is the same as their James Bond portrayal; and second, Plaintiffs heavily litigated their right to enjoin "Never Say Never Again" from ever being made—the fact that Plaintiffs lost that litigation does not mean that they waived their copyright claims, and Defendants have not cited, nor is the Court aware of, any case that stands for this proposition.

Thus, based on the evidence before it, the Court **FINDS** as a matter of law that Plaintiffs own the copyright to the James Bond character as expressed and delineated in their 16 films.

b. *The Alleged Similarities Between the Works Are Protected by Copyright*

Next, Defendants claim, as they did in opposing Plaintiffs' preliminary injunction motion, that the similarities between the works alleged by Plaintiffs are not protectable under copyright law. Defendants' arguments are largely repetitive of those made and discussed above; however, Defendants also argue that, as a matter of law, Plaintiffs' works are entitled to only "thin" protection based on Defendants' citation to cases wherein courts have required nearly identical copying for the copyrightholder to prevail. *See, e.g., Apple Computer, Inc. v. Microsoft Corp.,* 35 F.3d 1435, 1442–44 (9th Cir.1994), *cert. denied,* 513

U.S. 1184, 115 S.Ct. 1176, 130 L.Ed.2d 1129 (1995) (requiring copying of computer program to be nearly identical because Apple had freely licensed 90% of allegedly infringing program); *Worth v. Selchow & Righter Co.,* 827 F.2d 569, 572 (9th Cir.1987), *cert. denied,* 485 U.S. 977, 108 S.Ct. 1271, 99 L.Ed.2d 482 (1988) (requiring greater showing of similarity between factually-based works as opposed to between works of fiction).

But as Plaintiffs correctly point out, Defendants' cases are distinguishable on their facts and as a matter of policy. While it is understandable to require less protection of expressions of factual events or widely-licensed computer programs, conversely, it is important that this Court require greater protection for original works of fiction and the expression of the characters contained therein.

Thus, the Court **FINDS** that the instant case, which involves a careful visual delineation of a fictional character as developed over sixteen films and three decades, requires greater protection of the fictional works at issue than that accorded more factually-based or scientific works.

c. *Issues Of Material Fact Exist Precluding This Court From Concluding That The Works Are Substantially Similar*

Finally, Defendants contend that the Honda commercial is not substantially similar—both extrinsically and intrinsically—to Plaintiffs' protected works. The Court **FINDS,** for the reasons set forth above, that Plaintiffs have presented sufficient expert testimony on the extrinsic test to create a triable issue as to whether the ideas expressed in the Honda commercial are substantially similar to those protected ideas that appear in Plaintiffs' films.

Moreover, because it finds that summary judgment is inappropriate under the extrinsic test, the Court is further precluded from granting summary judgment under the intrinsic test, because, at bottom, the jury must make a factual determination as to whether the Honda commercial captures the total "concept and feel" of Plaintiffs' Bond films. As the Ninth Circuit explained in *Shaw:* "Because each of us differs, to some degree, in our capability to reason, imagine, and react emotionally, subjective comparisons of literary works [and films] that are objectively similar in their expression of ideas must be left to the trier of fact." 919 F.2d at 1361. IT IS SO ORDERED.

In many "copyright" cases, other intellectual property is often included as a cause of action (e.g., the Monty Python trademarks).

GILLIAM v. AMERICAN BROADCASTING CO.
United States Court of Appeals for the Second Circuit
April 13, 1976, Argued; June 30, 1976, Decided
Nos. 75-7693, 76-7023, Nos. 913, 1058—September Term, 1975
538 F.2d 14

LUMBARD, Circuit Judge:

Plaintiffs, a group of British writers and performers known as "Monty Python," appeal from a denial by Judge Lasker in the Southern District of a preliminary injunction to restrain the American Broadcasting Company (ABC) from broadcasting edited versions of three separate programs originally written and performed by Monty Python for broadcast by the British Broadcasting Corporation (BBC). We agree with Judge Lasker that the appellants have demonstrated that the excising done for ABC impairs the integrity of the original work. We further find that the countervailing injuries that Judge Lasker found might have accrued to ABC as a result of an injunction at a prior date no longer exist. We therefore direct the issuance of a preliminary injunction by the district court.

Since its formation in 1969, the Monty Python group has gained popularity primarily through its thirty-minute television programs created for BBC as part of a comedy series entitled "Monty Python's Flying Circus." In accordance with an agreement between Monty Python and BBC, the group writes and delivers to BBC scripts for use in the television series. This scriptwriters' agreement recites in great detail the procedure to be followed when any alterations are to be made in the script prior to recording of the program. The essence of this section of the agreement is that, while BBC retains final authority to make changes, appellants or their representatives exercise optimum control over the scripts consistent with BBC's authority and only minor changes may be made without prior consultation with the writers. Nothing in the scriptwriters' agreement entitles BBC to alter a program once it has been recorded. The agreement further provides that, subject to the terms therein, the group retains all rights in the script.

Under the agreement, BBC may license the transmission of recordings of the television programs in any overseas territory. The series has been broadcast in this country primarily on non-commercial public broadcasting television stations, although several of the programs have been broadcast on commercial stations in Texas and Nevada. In each instance, the thirty-minute programs have been broadcast as originally recorded and broadcast in England in their entirety and without commercial interruption.

In October 1973, Time-Life Films acquired the right to distribute in the United States certain BBC television programs, including the Monty Python series. Time-Life was permitted to edit the programs only "for insertion of commercials, applicable censorship or governmental . . . rules and regulations, and National Association of Broadcasters and time segment requirements." No similar clause was included in the scriptwriters' agreement between appellants and BBC. Prior to this time, ABC had sought to acquire the right to broadcast excerpts from various Monty Python programs in the spring of 1975, but the group rejected the proposal for such a disjoined format. Thereafter, in July 1975, ABC agreed with Time-Life to broadcast two ninety-minute specials each comprising three thirty-minute Monty Python programs that had not previously been shown in this country.

Correspondence between representatives of BBC and Monty Python reveals that these parties assumed that ABC would broadcast each of the Monty Python programs "in its entirety." On September 5, 1975, however, the group's British representative inquired of BBC how ABC planned to show the programs in their entirety if approximately 24 minutes of each 90 minute program were to be devoted to commercials. BBC replied on September 12, "we can only reassure you that ABC have decided to run the programmes 'back to back,' and that there is a firm undertaking not to segment them."

ABC broadcast the first of the specials on October 3, 1975. Appellants did not see a tape of the program until late November and were allegedly "appalled" at the discontinuity and "mutilation" that had resulted from the editing done by Time-Life for ABC. Twenty-four minutes of the original 90 minutes of recording had been omitted. Some of the editing had been done in order to make time for commercials; other material had been edited, according to ABC, because the original programs contained offensive or obscene matter.

In early December, Monty Python learned that ABC planned to broadcast the second special on December 26, 1975. The parties began negotiations concerning editing of that program and a delay of the broadcast until Monty Python could view it. These negotiations were futile, however, and on December 15 the group filed this action to enjoin the broadcast and for damages. Following an evidentiary hearing, Judge Lasker found that "the plaintiffs have established an impairment of the integrity of their work" which "caused the film or program . . . to lose its iconoclastic verve." According to Judge Lasker, "the damage that has been caused to the plaintiffs is irreparable by its nature." Nevertheless, the judge denied the motion for the preliminary injunction on the grounds that it was unclear who owned the copyright in the programs produced by BBC from the scripts written by Monty Python; that there was a question of whether Time-Life and BBC were indispensable parties to the litigation; that ABC would suffer significant financial loss if it were enjoined a week before the scheduled broadcast; and that Monty Python had displayed a "somewhat disturbing casualness" in their pursuance of the matter.

Judge Lasker granted Monty Python's request for more limited relief by requiring ABC to broadcast a disclaimer during the December 26 special to the effect that the group dissociated itself from the program because of the editing. A panel of this court, however, granted a stay of that order until this appeal could be heard and permitted ABC to broadcast, at the beginning of the special, only the legend that the program had been edited by ABC. We heard argument on April 13 and, at that time, enjoined ABC from any further broadcast of edited Monty Python programs pending the decision of the court.

I

In determining the availability of injunctive relief at this early stage of the proceedings, Judge Lasker properly considered the harm that would inure to the plaintiffs if the injunction were denied, the harm that defendant would suffer if the injunction were granted, and the likelihood that plaintiffs would ultimately succeed on the merits. See Hamilton Watch Co. v. Benrus Watch Co., 206 F.2d 738 (2d Cir. 1953). We direct the issuance of a preliminary injunction because we find that all these factors weigh in favor of appellants.

There is nothing clearly erroneous in Judge Lasker's conclusion that any injury suffered by appellants as a result of the broadcast of edited versions of their programs was irreparable by its nature. ABC presented the appellants with their first opportunity for broadcast to a nationwide network audience in this country. If ABC adversely misrepresented the quality of Monty Python's work, it is likely that many members of the audience, many of whom, by defendant's admission, were previously unfamiliar with appellants, would not become loyal followers of Monty Python productions. The subsequent injury to appellants' theatrical reputation would imperil their ability to attract the large audience necessary to the success of their venture. Such an injury to professional reputation cannot be measured in monetary terms or recompensed by other relief. See Coca-Cola Co. v. Gemini Rising, Inc., 346 F.Supp. 1183, 1189 (E.D.N.Y.1972); Estee Lauder, Inc. v. Watsky, 323 F.Supp. 1064, 1067 (S.D.N.Y.1970).

In contrast to the harm that Monty Python would suffer by a denial of the preliminary injunction, Judge Lasker found that ABC's relationship with its affiliates would be impaired by a grant of an injunction within a week of the scheduled December 26 broadcast. The court also found that ABC and its affiliates had advertised the program and had included it in listings of forthcoming television programs that were distributed to the public. Thus a last minute cancellation of the December 26 program, Judge Lasker concluded, would injure defendant financially and in its reputation with the public and its advertisers.

However valid these considerations may have been when the issue before the court was whether a preliminary injunction should immediately precede the broadcast, any injury to ABC is presently more speculative. No rebroadcast of the edited specials has been scheduled and no advertising costs have been incurred for the immediate future. Thus there is no danger that defendant's relations with affiliates or the public will suffer irreparably if subsequent broadcasts of the programs are enjoined pending a disposition of the issues.

We then reach the question whether there is a likelihood that appellants will succeed on the merits. In concluding that there is a likelihood of infringement here, we rely especially on the fact that the editing was substantial, i.e., approximately 27 per cent of the original program was omitted, and the editing contravened contractual provisions that limited the right to edit Monty Python material. It should be emphasized that our discussion of these matters refers only to such facts as have been developed upon the hearing for a preliminary injunction. Modified or contrary findings may become appropriate after a plenary trial.

Judge Lasker denied the preliminary injunction in part because he was unsure of the ownership of the copyright in the recorded program. Appellants first contend that the question of ownership is irrelevant because the recorded program was merely a derivative work taken from the script in which they hold the uncontested copyright. Thus, even if BBC owned the copyright in the recorded program, its use of that work would be limited by the license granted to BBC by Monty Python for use of the underlying script. We agree.

Section 7 of the Copyright Law, 17 U.S.C. § 7, provides in part that "adaptations, arrangements, dramatizations . . . or other versions of . . . copyrighted works when produced with the consent of the proprietor of the copyright in such works . . . shall be regarded as new works subject to copyright . . . ." Manifestly, the recorded program falls into this category as a dramatization of the script, and thus the program was itself entitled to copyright protection. However, section 7 limits the copyright protection of the derivative work, as works adapted from previously existing scripts have become known, to the novel additions made to the underlying work, Reyher v. Children's Television Workshop, 533 F.2d 87 (2d Cir.1976), and the derivative work does not affect the "force or validity" of the copyright in the matter from which it is derived. See Grove Press, Inc. v. Greenleaf Publishing Co., 247 F.Supp. 518 (S.D.N.Y.1965). Thus, any ownership by BBC of the copyright in the recorded program would not affect the scope or ownership of the copyright in the underlying script.

Since the copyright in the underlying script survives intact despite the incorporation of that work into a derivative work, one who uses the script, even with the permission of the proprietor of the derivative work, may infringe the underlying copyright.

If the proprietor of the derivative work is licensed by the proprietor of the copyright in the underlying work to vend or distribute the derivative work to third parties, those parties will, of course, suffer no liability for their use of the underlying work consistent with the license to the proprietor of the derivative work. Obviously, it was just this type of arrangement that was contemplated in this instance. The scriptwriters' agreement between Monty Python and BBC specifically permitted the latter to license the transmission of the recordings made by BBC to distributors such as Time-Life for broadcast in overseas territories.

One who obtains permission to use a copyrighted script in the production of a derivative work, however, may not exceed the specific purpose for which permission was granted. Most of the decisions that have reached this conclusion have dealt with the improper extension of the underlying work into media or time, i.e., duration of the license, not covered by the grant of permission to the derivative work proprietor. Appellants herein do not claim that the broadcast by ABC violated media or time restrictions contained in the license of the script to BBC. Rather, they claim that revisions in the script, and ultimately in the program, could be made only after consultation with Monty Python, and that ABC's broadcast of a program edited after recording and without consultation with Monty Python exceeded the scope of any license that BBC was entitled to grant.

The rationale for finding infringement when a licensee exceeds time or media restrictions on his license the need to allow the proprietor of the underlying copyright to control the method in which his work is presented to the public applies equally to the situation in which a licensee makes an unauthorized use of the underlying work by publishing it in a truncated version. Whether intended to allow greater economic exploitation of the work, as in the media and time cases, or to ensure that the copyright proprietor retains a veto power over revisions desired for the derivative work, the ability of the copyright holder to control his work remains paramount in our copyright law. We find, therefore, that unauthorized editing of the underlying work, if proven, would constitute an infringement of the copyright in that work similar to any other use of a work that exceeded the license granted by the proprietor of the copyright.

If the broadcast of an edited version of the Monty Python program infringed the group's copyright in the script, ABC may obtain no solace from the fact that editing was permitted in the agreements between BBC and Time-Life or Time-Life and ABC. BBC was not entitled to make unilateral changes in the script and was not specifically empowered to alter the recordings once made;

Monty Python, moreover, had reserved to itself any rights not granted to BBC. Since a grantor may not convey greater rights than it owns, BBC's permission to allow Time-Life, and hence ABC, to edit appears to have been a nullity. See Hampton v. Paramount Pictures Corp., 279 F.2d 100 (9th Cir.), cert. denied, 364 U.S. 882, 81 S.Ct. 170, 5 L.Ed.2d 103 (1970); Ilyin v. Avon Publications, 144 F.Supp. 368, 372 (S.D.N.Y.1956).

ABC answers appellants' infringement argument with a series of contentions, none of which seems meritorious at this stage of the litigation. The network asserts that Monty Python's British representative, Jill Foster, knew that ABC planned to exclude much of the original BBC program in the October 3 broadcast. ABC thus contends that by not previously objecting to this procedure, Monty Python ratified BBC's authority to license others to edit the underlying script.

Although the case of Ilyin v. Avon Publications, Inc., 144 F.Supp. 368, 373 (S.D.N.Y.1956), may be broadly read for the proposition that a holder of a derivative copyright may obtain rights in the underlying work through ratification, the conduct necessary to that conclusion has yet to be demonstrated in this case. It is undisputed that appellants did not have actual notice of the cuts in the October 3 broadcast until late November. Even if they are chargeable with the knowledge of their British representative, it is not clear that she had prior notice of the cuts or ratified the omissions, nor did Judge Lasker make any finding on the question. While Foster, on September 5, did question how ABC was to broadcast the entire program if it was going to interpose 24 minutes of commercials, she received assurances from BBC that the programs would not be "segmented." The fact that she knew precisely the length of material that would have to be omitted to allow for commercials does not prove that she ratified the deletions. This is especially true in light of previous assurances that the program would contain the original shows in their entirety. On the present record, it cannot be said that there was any ratification of BBC's grant of editing rights. ABC, of course, is entitled to attempt to prove otherwise during the trial on the merits.

ABC next argues that under the "joint work" theory adopted in Shapiro, Bernstein & Co. v. Jerry Vogel Music, Inc., 221 F.2d 569 (2d Cir.1955), the script produced by Monty Python and the program recorded by BBC are symbiotic elements of a single production. Therefore, according to ABC, each contributor possesses an undivided ownership of all copyrightable elements in the final work and BBC could thus have licensed use of the script, including editing, written by appellants.

The joint work theory as extended in Shapiro has been criticized as inequitable unless "at the time of creation by the first author, the second author's contribution (is envisaged) as an integrated part of a single work," and the first author intends that the final product be a joint work. See 1 M. Nimmer,

Copyright ss 67-73. Furthermore, this court appears to have receded from a broad application of the joint work doctrine where the contract which leads to collaboration between authors indicates that one will retain a superior interest. See Szekely v. Eagle Lion Films, Inc., 242 F.2d 266 (2d Cir.), cert. denied, 354 U.S. 922, 77 S.Ct. 1382, 1 L.Ed.2d 1437 (1957). In the present case, the screenwriters' agreement between Monty Python and BBC provides that the group is to retain all rights in the script not granted in the agreement and that at some future point the group may license the scripts for use on television to parties other than BBC. These provisions suggest that the parties did not consider themselves joint authors of a single work. This matter is subject to further exploration at the trial, but in the present state of the record, it presents no bar to issuance of a preliminary injunction.

Aside from the question of who owns the relevant copyrights, ABC asserts that the contracts between appellants and BBC permit editing of the programs for commercial television in the United States. ABC argues that the scriptwriters' agreement allows appellants the right to participate in revisions of the script only prior to the recording of the programs, and thus infers that BBC had unrestricted authority to revise after that point. This argument, however, proves too much. A reading of the contract seems to indicate that Monty Python obtained control over editing the script only to ensure control over the program recorded from that script. Since the scriptwriters' agreement explicitly retains for the group all rights not granted by the contract, omission of any terms concerning alterations in the program after recording must be read as reserving to appellants exclusive authority for such revisions.

Finally, ABC contends that appellants must have expected that deletions would be made in the recordings to conform them for use on commercial television in the United States. ABC argues that licensing in the United States implicitly grants a license to insert commercials in a program and to remove offensive or obscene material prior to broadcast. According to the network, appellants should have anticipated that most of the excised material contained scatological references inappropriate for American television and that these scenes would be replaced with commercials, which presumably are more palatable to the American public.

The proof adduced up to this point, however, provides no basis for finding any implied consent to edit. Prior to the ABC broadcasts, Monty Python programs had been broadcast on a regular basis by both commercial and public television stations in this country without interruption or deletion. Indeed, there is no evidence of any prior broadcast of edited Monty Python material in the United States. These facts, combined with the persistent requests for assurances by the group and its representatives that the programs would be shown intact belie the argument that the group knew or should have known that deletions and commercial interruptions were inevitable.

Several of the deletions made for ABC, such as elimination of the words "hell" and "damn," seem inexplicable given today's standard television fare. If, however, ABC honestly determined that the programs were obscene in substantial part, it could have decided not to broadcast the specials at all, or it could have attempted to reconcile its differences with appellants. The network could not, however, free from a claim of infringement, broadcast in a substantially altered form a program incorporating the script over which the group had retained control.

Our resolution of these technical arguments serves to reinforce our initial inclination that the copyright law should be used to recognize the important role of the artist in our society and the need to encourage production and dissemination of artistic works by providing adequate legal protection for one who submits his work to the public. See Mazer v. Stein, 347 U.S. 201, 74 S.Ct. 460, 98 L.Ed. 630 (1954). We therefore conclude that there is a substantial likelihood that, after a full trial, appellants will succeed in proving infringement of their copyright by ABC's broadcast of edited versions of Monty Python programs. In reaching this conclusion, however, we need not accept appellants' assertion that any editing whatsoever would constitute infringement. Courts have recognized that licensees are entitled to some small degree of latitude in arranging the licensed work for presentation to the public in a manner consistent with the licensee's style or standards. That privilege, however, does not extend to the degree of editing that occurred here especially in light of contractual provisions that limited the right to edit Monty Python material.

II

It also seems likely that appellants will succeed on the theory that, regardless of the right ABC had to broadcast an edited program, the cuts made constituted an actionable mutilation of Monty Python's work. This cause of action, which seeks redress for deformation of an artist's work, finds its roots in the continental concept of droit moral, or moral right, which may generally be summarized as including the right of the artist to have his work attributed to him in the form in which he created it. See 1 M. Nimmer, supra, at § 110.1.

American copyright law, as presently written, does not recognize moral rights or provide a cause of action for their violation, since the law seeks to vindicate the economic, rather than the personal, rights of authors. Nevertheless, the economic incentive for artistic and intellectual creation that serves as the foundation for American copyright law, Goldstein v. California, 412 U.S. 546, 93 S.Ct. 2303, 37 L.Ed.2d 163 (1973); Mazer v. Stein, 347 U.S. 201, 74 S.Ct. 460, 98 L.Ed. 630 (1954), cannot be reconciled with the inability of artists to obtain relief for mutilation or misrepresentation of their work to the public on which the artists are financially dependent. Thus courts have long granted relief for misrepresentation of an artist's work by relying on theories outside the statutory law of copyright, such as contract law, Granz v. Harris, 198 F.2d 585 (2d Cir.1952) (substantial cutting of original work constitutes misrepresentation), or the tort of unfair competition, Prouty v. National Broadcasting Co., 26 F.Supp. 265 (D.Mass.1939). See Strauss, The Moral Right of the Author 128-138, in Studies on Copyright (1963). Although such decisions are clothed in terms of proprietary right in one's creation, they also properly vindicate the author's personal right to prevent the presentation of his work to the public in a distorted form. See Gardella v. Log Cabin Products Co., 89 F.2d 891, 895-96 (2d Cir. 1937); Roeder, The Doctrine of Moral Right, 53 Harv.L.Rev. 554, 568 (1940).

Here, the appellants claim that the editing done for ABC mutilated the original work and that consequently the broadcast of those programs as the creation of Monty Python violated the Lanham Act § 43(a), 15 U.S.C. § 1125(a). This statute, the federal counterpart to state unfair competition laws, has been invoked to prevent misrepresentations that may injure plaintiff's business or personal reputation, even where no registered trademark is concerned. See Mortellito v. Nina of California, 335 F.Supp. 1288, 1294 (S.D.N.Y.1972). It is sufficient to violate the Act that a representation of a product, although technically true, creates a false impression of the product's origin. See Rich v. RCA Corp., 390 F.Supp. 530 (S.D.N.Y.1975) (recent picture of plaintiff on cover of album containing songs recorded in distant past held to be a false representation that the songs were new); Geisel v. Poynter Products, Inc., 283 F.Supp. 261, 267 (S.D.N.Y.1968).

These cases cannot be distinguished from the situation in which a television network broadcasts a program properly designated as having been written and performed by a group, but which has been edited, without the writer's consent, into a form that departs substantially from the original work. "To deform his work is to present him to the public as the creator of a work not his own, and thus makes him subject to criticism for work he has not done." Roeder, supra, at 569. In such a case, it is the writer or performer, rather than the network, who suffers the consequences of the mutilation, for the public will have only the final product by which to evaluate the work. Thus, an allegation that a defendant has presented to the public a "garbled," Granz v. Harris, supra (Frank, J., concurring), distorted version of plaintiff's work seeks to redress the very rights sought to be protected by the Lanham Act, 15 U.S.C. § 1125(a), and should be recognized as stating a cause of action under that statute.

During the hearing on the preliminary injunction, Judge Lasker viewed the edited version of the Monty Python program broadcast on December 26 and the original, unedited version. After hearing argument of this appeal, this panel also viewed and compared the two versions. We find that the truncated version at times omitted the climax of the skits to which appellants' rare brand of humor was leading and at other times deleted essential elements in the schematic development of a story line. We therefore agree with Judge Lasker's conclusion that the edited version broadcast by ABC impaired the integrity of appellants' work and represented to the public as the product of appellants what was actually a mere caricature of their talents. We believe that a valid cause of action for such distortion exists and that therefore a preliminary injunction may issue to prevent repetition of the broadcast prior to final determination of the issues.

III

We do not share Judge Lasker's concern about the procedures by which the appellants have pursued this action. The district court indicated agreement with ABC that appellants were guilty of laches in not requesting a preliminary injunction until 11 days prior to the broadcast. Our discussion above, however, suggests that the group did not know and had no reason to believe until late November that editing would take place. Several letters between BBC and Monty Python's representative indicate that appellants believed that the programs would be shown in their entirety. Furthermore, the group did act to prevent offensive editing of the second program immediately after viewing the tape of the first edited program. Thus we find no undue delay in the group's failure to institute this action until they were sufficiently advised regarding the facts necessary to support the action. In any event, ABC has not demonstrated how it was prejudiced by any delay. See Emle Industries, Inc. v. Patentex, Inc., 478 F.2d 562, 574 (2d Cir.1973).

Finally, Judge Lasker denied a preliminary injunction because Monty Python had failed to join BBC and Time-Life as indispensable parties. We do not believe that either is an indispensable party. ABC argues that joinder of both was required because it acted in good faith pursuant to its contractual rights with Time-Life in broadcasting edited versions of the programs, and Time-Life, in turn, relied upon its contract with BBC. Furthermore, ABC argues, BBC must be joined since it owns the copyright in the recorded programs.

Even if BBC owns a copyright relevant to determination of the issues in this case, the formalistic rule that once required all owners of a copyright to be parties to an action for its infringement has given way to equitable considerations. See Jaeger v. American International Pictures, supra, 330 F.Supp. at 279; 7 C. Wright & A. Miller, Federal Practice and Procedure, § 1614. In this case, the equities to be considered under Fed.R.Civ.P. 19(a) strongly favor appellants. Monty Python is relying solely on its copyright in the script and on its rights as an author. No claim is being made that Monty Python has rights derived from the copyright held by another. Compare First Financial Marketing Services Group, Inc. v. Field Promotions, Inc., 286 F.Supp. 295 (S.D.N.Y.1968).

One of the parties is an English corporation, and any action that appellants, a group of English writers and performers, might have against that potential defendant would be better considered under English law in an English court.

Complete relief for the alleged infringement and mutilation complained of may be accorded between Monty Python and ABC, which alone broadcast the programs in dispute. If ABC is ultimately found liable to appellants, a permanent injunction against future broadcasts and a damage award would satisfy all of appellants' claims. ABC's assertion that failure to join BBC and Time-Life may leave it subject to inconsistent verdicts in a later action against its licensors may be resolved through the process of impleader, which ABC has thus far avoided despite a suggestion from the district court to use that procedure. Finally, neither of the parties considered by ABC to be indispensable has claimed any interest in the subject matter of this litigation. See Fed.R.Civ.P. 19(a)(2).

For these reasons we direct that the district court issue the preliminary injunction sought by the appellants.

GURFEIN, Circuit Judge (concurring):

I concur in my brother Lumbard's scholarly opinion, but I wish to comment on the application of Section 43(a) of the Lanham Act, 15 U.S.C. § 1125(a).

I believe that this is the first case in which a federal appellate court has held that there may be a violation of Section 43(a) of the Lanham Act with respect to a common-law copyright. The Lanham Act is a trademark statute, not a copyright statute. Nevertheless, we must recognize that the language of Section 43(a) is broad. It speaks of the affixation or use of false designations of origin or false descriptions or representations, but proscribes such use "in connection with any goods or services." It is easy enough to incorporate trade names as well as trademarks into Section 43(a) and the statute specifically applies to common law trademarks, as well as registered trademarks. Lanham Act § 45, 15 U.S.C. § 1127.

In the present case, we are holding that the deletion of portions of the recorded tape constitutes a breach of contract, as well as an infringement of a common-law copyright of the original work. There is literally no need to discuss whether plaintiffs also have a claim for relief under the Lanham Act or for unfair competition under New York law. I agree with Judge Lumbard, however, that it may be an exercise of judicial economy to express our view on the Lanham Act claim, and I do not dissent therefrom. I simply wish to leave it open for the District Court to fashion the remedy.

The Copyright Act provides no recognition of the so-called droit moral, or moral right of authors. Nor are such rights recognized in the field of copyright law in the United States. See 1 Nimmer on Copyright, § 110.2 (1975 ed.). If a distortion or truncation in connection with a use constitutes an infringement of copyright, there is no need for an additional cause of action beyond copyright infringement. Id. at § 110.3. An obligation to mention the name of the author carries the implied duty, however, as a matter of contract, not to make such changes in the work as would render the credit line a false attribution of authorship, Granz v. Harris, 198 F.2d 585 (2d Cir.1952).

So far as the Lanham Act is concerned, it is not a substitute for droit moral which authors in Europe enjoy. If the licensee may, by contract, distort the recorded work, the Lanham Act does not come into play. If the licensee has no such right by contract, there will be a violation in breach of contract. The Lanham Act can hardly apply literally when the credit line correctly states the work to be that of the plaintiffs which, indeed it is, so far as it goes. The vice complained of is that the truncated version is not what the plaintiffs wrote. But the Lanham Act does not deal with artistic integrity. It only goes to misdescription of origin and the like. See Societe Comptoir De L'Industrie Cotonniere Etablissements Boussac v. Alexander's Dept. Stores, Inc., 299 F.2d 33, 36 (2d Cir.1962).

The misdescription of origin can be dealt with, as Judge Lasker did below, by devising an appropriate legend to indicate that the plaintiffs had not approved the editing of the ABC version. With such a legend, there is no conceivable violation of the Lanham Act. If plaintiffs complain that their artistic integrity is still compromised by the distorted version, their claim does not lie under the Lanham Act, which does not protect the copyrighted work itself but protects only against the misdescription or mislabelling.

So long as it is made clear that the ABC version is not approved by the Monty Python group, there is no misdescription of origin. So far as the content of the broadcast itself is concerned, that is not within the proscription of the Lanham Act when there is no misdescription of the authorship.

I add this brief explanation because I do not believe that the Lanham Act claim necessarily requires the drastic remedy of permanent injunction. That form of ultimate relief must be found in some other fountainhead of equity jurisprudence.

SID & MARTY KROFFT TELEVISION PRODUCTIONS, INC. v. MCDONALD'S CORP.
United States Court of Appeals for the Ninth Circuit
October 12, 1977
Nos. 75-1203, 75-1202

JAMES M. CARTER, Circuit Judge:

This is a copyright infringement action. Plaintiffs Sid and Marty Krofft Television Productions, Inc., and Sid and Marty Krofft Productions, Inc. were awarded $50,000.00 in their action against defendants McDonald's Corporation and Needham, Harper & Steers, Inc. Defendants were found to have infringed plaintiffs' "H. R. Pufnstuf" children's television show by the production of their "McDonaldland" television commercials.

Plaintiffs argue on appeal that the district court erred in awarding damages pursuant to 17 U.S.C. § 101(b). They contend that the court should have ordered an accounting of profits by defendants or, alternatively, should have awarded statutory "in lieu" damages.

Defendants cross-appeal. They contend that their television commercials did not infringe upon plaintiffs' television series as a matter of law. To find infringement, they suggest, would abridge their first amendment rights. They also refute plaintiffs' contentions as to damages.

We believe that the district court's finding of infringement was not clearly erroneous, and see no merit to defendants' first amendment claims, We find, however, that the district court was in error in awarding damages. We therefore affirm in part, reverse in part, and remand for further proceedings.

Facts

In 1968, Sid and Marty Krofft were approached by the NBC television network to create a children's television program for exhibition on Saturday morning. The Kroffts spent the next year creating the H. R. Pufnstuf television show, which was introduced on NBC in September 1969. The series included several fanciful costumed characters, as well as a boy named Jimmy, who lived in a fantasyland called "Living Island," which was inhabited by moving trees and talking books. The television series became extremely popular and generated a line of H. R. Pufnstuf products and endorsements.

In early 1970, Marty Krofft, the President of both Krofft Television and Krofft Productions and producer of the show, was contacted by an executive from Needham, Harper & Steers, Inc., an advertising agency. He was told that Needham was attempting to get the advertising account of McDonald's hamburger restaurant chain and wanted to base a proposed campaign to

McDonald's on the H. R. Pufnstuf characters. The executive wanted to know whether the Kroffts would be interested in working with Needham on a project of this type.

Needham and the Kroffts were in contact by telephone six or seven more times. By a letter dated August 31, 1970, Needham stated it was going forward with the idea of a McDonaldland advertising campaign based on the H. R. Pufnstuf series. It acknowledged the need to pay the Kroffts a fee for preparing artistic designs and engineering plans. Shortly thereafter, Marty Krofft telephoned Needham only to be told that the advertising campaign had been cancelled.

In fact, Needham had already been awarded McDonald's advertising account and was proceeding with the McDonaldland project. Former employees of the Kroffts were hired to design and construct the costumes and sets for McDonaldland. Needham also hired the same voice expert who supplied all of the voices for the Pufnstuf characters to supply some of the voices for the McDonaldland characters. In January 1971, the first of the McDonaldland commercials was broadcast on network television. They continue to be broadcast.

Prior to the advent of the McDonaldland advertising campaign, plaintiffs had licensed the use of the H. R. Pufnstuf characters and elements to the manufacturers of toys, games, lunch boxes, and comic books. In addition, the H. R. Pufnstuf characters were featured in Kellogg's cereal commercials and used by the Ice Capades. After the McDonaldland campaign, which included the distribution of toys and games, plaintiffs were unable to obtain new licensing arrangements or extend existing ones. In the case of the Ice Capades, the H. R. Pufnstuf characters were actually replaced by the McDonaldland characters.

Plaintiffs filed suit in September 1971. The complaint alleged, inter alia, that the McDonaldland advertising campaign infringed the copyrighted H. R. Pufnstuf television episodes as well as various copyrighted articles of Pufnstuf merchandise. By way of relief, plaintiffs sought compensatory damages of $250,000, an order for an accounting of profits attributable to the infringements, or, in the alternative, statutory "in lieu" damages, as provided by 17 U.S.C. § 101(b). Prior to trial, the district court signed a Pre-Trial Conference Order that was "approved as to form and content" by counsel for both sides. It provided that "(t)he prayer for relief raises issues of injunctive relief and an accounting which are questions for the Court."

The three week jury trial began on November 27, 1973. The jurors were shown for their consideration on the question of infringement: (1) two H. R. Pufnstuf television episodes; (2) various items of H. R. Pufnstuf merchandise, such as toys, games, and comic books; (3) several 30 and 60 second McDonaldland television commercials; and (4) various items of McDonaldland merchandise distributed by McDonald's, such as toys and puzzles. The jury was instructed that it was not to consider defendants' profits in determining damages, but could consider the value of use by the defendants of plaintiffs' work.

A verdict in favor of plaintiffs was returned and damages of $50,000.00 assessed. After the verdict, the parties briefed the question of whether plaintiffs were entitled to additional monetary recovery in the form of profits or statutory "in lieu" damages. The district court denied plaintiffs' claim for such relief. The court found that these matters were properly for the jury to consider so that it would not exercise its discretion in hearing further evidence. These appeals followed.

I. INFRINGEMENT

Proof of Infringement

It has often been said that in order to establish copyright infringement a plaintiff must prove ownership of the copyright and "copying" by the defendant. "Copying," in turn, is said to be shown by circumstantial evidence of access to the copyrighted work and substantial similarity between the copyrighted work and defendant's work. Reyher v. Children's Television Workshop, supra, 533 F.2d at 90; 2 Nimmer § 141.2 at 613. But an analysis of the cases suggests that these statements frequently serve merely as boilerplate to copyright opinions.

Under such statements, infringement would be established upon proof of ownership, access, and substantial similarity. Application of this rule, however, would produce some untenable results. For example, a copyright could be obtained over a cheaply manufactured plaster statue of a nude. Since ownership of a copyright is established, subsequent manufacturers of statues of nudes would face the grave risk of being found to be infringers if their statues were substantially similar and access were shown. The burden of proof on the plaintiff would be minimal, since most statues of nudes would in all probability be substantially similar to the cheaply manufactured plaster one.

Clearly the scope of copyright protection does not go this far. A limiting principle is needed. This is provided by the classic distinction between an "idea" and the "expression" of that idea. It is an axiom of copyright law that the protection granted to a copyrighted work extends only to the particular expression of the idea and never to the idea itself. This principle attempts to reconcile two competing social interests: rewarding an individual's creativity and effort while at the same time permitting the nation to enjoy the benefits and progress from use of the same subject matter.

The real task in a copyright infringement action, then, is to determine whether there has been copying of the expression of an idea rather than just the idea itself. "(N)o one infringes, unless he descends so far into what is concrete (in a work) as to invade . . . (its) expression." National Comics

Publications v. Fawcett Publications, 191 F.2d 594, 600 (2 Cir. 1951). Only this expression may be protected and only it may be infringed.

The difficulty comes in attempting to distill the unprotected idea from the protected expression. No court or commentator in making this search has been able to improve upon Judge Learned Hand's famous "abstractions test" articulated in Nichols v. Universal Pictures Corporation, 45 F.2d 119 (2 Cir. 1930), cert. denied, 282 U.S. 902, 51 S.Ct. 216, 75 L.Ed. 795 (1931):

"Upon any work, and especially upon a play, a great number of patterns of increasing generality will fit equally well, as more and more of the incident is left out. The last may perhaps be no more than the most general statement of what the play is about, and at times might consist of only its title; but there is a point in this series of abstractions where they are no longer protected, since otherwise the playwright could prevent the use of his 'ideas,' to which, apart from their expression, his property is never extended." 45 F.2d at 121. See also Chafee, Reflections on the Law of Copyright, 45 Colum.L.Rev. 503 (1945); Esezobar, Concepts in Copyright Protection, 23 Bull.Cprt.Soc. 258 (1976); Note, "Expression" and "Originality" in Copyright Law, 11 Washburn L.J. 400 (1972).

The test for infringement therefore has been given a new dimension. There must be ownership of the copyright and access to the copyrighted work. But there also must be substantial similarity not only of the general ideas but of the expressions of those ideas as well. Thus two steps in the analytic process are implied by the requirement of substantial similarity.

The determination of whether there is substantial similarity in ideas may often be a simple one. Returning to the example of the nude statue, the idea there embodied is a simple one a plaster recreation of a nude human figure. A statue of a horse or a painting of a nude would not embody this idea and therefore could not infringe. The test for similarity of ideas is still a factual one, to be decided by the trier of fact. See International Luggage Registry v. Avery Products Corp., 541 F.2d 830, 831 (9 Cir. 1976); Williams v. Kaag Manufacturers, Inc., 338 F.2d 949, 951 (9 Cir. 1964).

We shall call this the "extrinsic test." It is extrinsic because it depends not on the responses of the trier of fact, but on specific criteria which can be listed and analyzed. Such criteria include the type of artwork involved, the materials used, the subject matter, and the setting for the subject. Since it is an extrinsic test, analytic dissection and expert testimony are appropriate. Moreover, this question may often be decided as a matter of law.

The determination of when there is substantial similarity between the forms of expression is necessarily more subtle and complex. As Judge Hand candidly observed, "Obviously, no principle can be stated as to when an imitator has gone beyond copying the 'idea,' and has borrowed its 'expression.' Decisions must therefore inevitably be ad hoc." Peter Pan Fabrics, Inc. v. Martin Weiner Corp., 274 F.2d 487, 489 (2 Cir. 1960). If there is substantial similarity in ideas, then the trier of fact must decide whether there is substantial similarity in the expressions of the ideas so as to constitute infringement.

The test to be applied in determining whether there is substantial similarity in expressions shall be labeled an intrinsic one depending on the response of the ordinary reasonable person. See International Luggage Registry v. Avery Products Corp., supra, 541 F.2d at 831; Harold Lloyd Corp. v. Witwer, 65 F.2d 1, 18-19 (9 Cir. 1933). See generally Nimmer § 143.5. It is intrinsic because it does not depend on the type of external criteria and analysis which marks the extrinsic test. As this court stated in Twentieth Century-Fox Film Corp. v. Stonesifer, 140 F.2d 579, 582 (9 Cir. 1944):

> "The two works involved in this appeal should be considered and tested, not hypercritically or with meticulous scrutiny, but by the observations and impressions of the average reasonable reader and spectator."

Because this is an intrinsic test, analytic dissection and expert testimony are not appropriate.

This same type of bifurcated test was announced in Arnstein v. Porter, 154 F.2d 464, 468-69 (2 Cir. 1946), cert. denied, 330 U.S. 851, 67 S.Ct. 1096, 91 L.Ed. 1294 (1947). The court there identified two separate elements essential to a plaintiff's suit for infringement: copying and unlawful appropriation...

We believe that the court in Arnstein was alluding to the idea-expression dichotomy which we make explicit today. When the court in Arnstein refers to "copying" which is not itself an infringement, it must be suggesting copying merely of the work's idea, which is not protected by the copyright. To constitute an infringement, the copying must reach the point of "unlawful appropriation," or the copying of the protected expression itself. We analyze this distinction in terms both of the elements involved idea and expression and of the tests to be used extrinsic and intrinsic in an effort to clarify the issues involved.

The Tests Applied

In the context of this case, the distinction between these tests is important. Defendants do not dispute the fact that they copied the idea of plaintiffs' Pufnstuf television series basically a fantasyland filled with diverse and fanciful characters in action. They argue, however, that the expressions of this idea are too dissimilar for there to be an infringement. They come to this conclusion by dissecting the constituent parts of the Pufnstuf series characters, setting, and plot and pointing out the dissimilarities between these parts and those of the McDonaldland commercials.

This approach ignores the idea-expression dichotomy alluded to in Arnstein and analyzed today. Defendants attempt to apply an extrinsic test by the listing of dissimilarities in determining whether the expression they used was substantially similar to the expression used by plaintiffs.

Defendants contest the continued viability of Arnstein. It is true that Arnstein's alternative holding that summary judgment may not be granted when there is the slightest doubt as to the facts has been disapproved.

As a finding of fact, a conclusion as to the question of copying is subject to the "clearly erroneous" standard. Fed.R.Civ.P. 52(a). But it follows that this court will be less likely to find clear error when the subjective test for copying of expression has been applied.

The present case demands an even more intrinsic determination because both plaintiffs' and defendants' works are directed to an audience of children. This raises the particular factual issue of the impact of the respective works upon the minds and imaginations of young people.

The H. R. Pufnstuf series became the most popular children's show on Saturday morning television. This success led several manufacturers of children's goods to use the Pufnstuf characters. It is not surprising, then, that McDonald's hoped to duplicate this peculiar appeal to children in its commercials. It was in recognition of the subjective and unpredictable nature of children's responses that defendants opted to recreate the H. R. Pufnstuf format rather than use an original and unproven approach.

Defendants would have this court ignore that intrinsic quality which they recognized to embark on an extrinsic analysis of the two works. For example, in discussing the principal characters Pufnstuf and Mayor McCheese defendants point out:

> " 'Pufnstuf' wears what can only be described as a yellow and green dragon suit with a blue cummerband from which hangs a medal which says 'mayor'. 'McCheese' wears a version of pink formal dress 'tails' with knicker trousers. He has a typical diplomat's sash on which is written 'mayor', the 'M' consisting of the McDonald's trademark of an 'M' made of golden arches."

So not only do defendants remove the characters from the setting, but dissect further to analyze the clothing, colors, features, and mannerisms of each character. We do not believe that the ordinary reasonable person, let alone a child, viewing these works will even notice that Pufnstuf is wearing a cummerbund while Mayor McCheese is wearing a diplomat's sash.

Duplication or near identity is not necessary to establish infringement. Runge v. Lee, 441 F.2d 579, 582 (9 Cir. 1971); Williams v. Kaag Manufacturers, Inc., supra, 338 F.2d at 951.

And, as Judge Learned Hand put it, copyright "cannot be limited literally to the text, else a plagiarist would escape by immaterial variations." Nichols v. Universal Pictures Corp., 45 F.2d 119, 121 (2 Cir. 1930).

We have viewed representative samples of both the H. R. Pufnstuf show and McDonaldland commercials. It is clear to us that defendants' works are substantially similar to plaintiffs'. They have captured the "total concept and feel" of the Pufnstuf show. Roth Greeting Cards v. United Card Co., 429 F.2d 1106, 1110 (9 Cir. 1970). We would so conclude even if we were sitting as the triers of fact. There is no doubt that the findings of the jury in this case are not clearly erroneous.

Unity of Idea and Expression

Defendants argue that dissection is proper and that duplication or near identity is necessary because the competing works are things, rather than dramatic works. They cite numerous cases in which infringement was found because the defendants' works were nearly identical to those of the plaintiffs. Defendants fail to perceive, however, that near identity may be required in some cases not because the works are things, but because the expression of those works and the idea of those works are indistinguishable.

The idea and the expression will coincide when the expression provides nothing new or additional over the idea. Thus, the expression of a jeweled bee pin contains nothing new over the idea of a jeweled bee pin. Returning to our own example, the idea of a plaster statute of a nude will probably coincide with the expression of that idea when an inexpensive manufacturing process is used. There will be no separately distinguishable features in the statute's expression over the idea of a plaster nude statute.

The complexity and artistry of the expression of an idea will separate it from even the most banal idea. Michaelangelo's David is, as an idea, no more than a statute of a nude male. But no one would question the proposition that if a copyrighted work it would deserve protection even against the poorest of imitations. This is because so much more was added in the expression over the idea.

When idea and expression coincide, there will be protection against nothing other than identical copying of the work. When other defendants made jeweled bees from the same molds as plaintiffs, they were held liable. See Herbert Rosenthal Jewelry Corp. v. Grossbardt, 436 F.2d 315 (2 Cir. 1970). Therefore, the scope of copyright protection increases with the extent expression differs from the idea.

The coincidence of idea and expression may occur in works other than "things." Baker v. Selden, supra, held that blank accounting books are not subject to copyright protection. Yet if any information is contained in those blanks, copyright protection is available.

There is no special standard of similarity required in the case of "things." Nor is any such standard suggested by any of the cases cited by defendants. For example, in Monogram Models, Inc. v. Industro Motive Corp., 492 F.2d 1281, 1284 (6 Cir. 1974), the issue was one of copyright infringement of scale model airplane kits. Defendant admitted copying, but argued lack of substantial copying. The court affirmed a jury finding of infringement, citing the ordinary reasonable observer test. Id. at 1286.

No standard more demanding than that of substantial similarity should be imposed here. This is not a case where the idea is indistinguishable as a matter of law from the expression of that idea. See Goodson-Todman Enterprises, Inc. v. Kellogg Co., supra, 513 F.2d at 914. The expression inherent in the H. R. Pufnstuf series differs markedly from its relatively simple idea. The characters each have developed personalities and particular ways of interacting with one another and their environment. The physical setting also has several unique features.

Lest we fall prey to defendants' invitation to dissect the works, however, we should remember that it is the combination of many different elements which may command copyright protection because of its particular subjective quality.

Copyright and the First Amendment

Defendants argue that the first amendment operates in this case to limit the protection for plaintiffs' works. They seem to suggest that a more demanding standard than that of substantial similarity should be imposed, and that the threshold question about copying becomes one of "constitutional fact" to be reviewed de novo on appeal. Defendants attempt to analogize the copyright area to those of obscenity and defamation in suggesting that prior law must be modified to accommodate expanding first amendment rights.

The constitutionality of the copyright law was settled long ago by the Supreme Court. In Kalem Co. v. Harper Brothers, 222 U.S. 55, 32 S.Ct. 20, 56 L.Ed. 92 (1911), the defendant argued that the copyright law could not grant an author an exclusive right to dramatize his works. In rejecting this contention, the Court stated:

> "It is argued that the law, construed as we have construed it, goes beyond the power conferred upon Congress by the Constitution, to secure to authors for a limited time the exclusive right to their writings. Art. I, § 8, cl. 8. It is suggested that to extend the copyright to a case like this is to extend it to the ideas, as distinguished from the words in which the ideas are clothed. But there is no attempt to make a monopoly of the ideas expressed. The law confines itself to a particular, cognate, and well-known form of reproduction. If to that extent a grant of monopoly is thought a proper way to secure the right to the writings, this court cannot say that Congress was wrong." Id. at 63, 32 S.Ct. at 22.

The Court recognized that the protection of the copyright laws is necessary to provide an incentive for artistic creation which ultimately advances the public good. See Twentieth Century Music Corp. v. Aiken, 422 U.S. 151, 156, 95 S.Ct. 2040, 45 L.Ed.2d 84 (1975).

But the impact, if any, of the first amendment on copyright has not been discussed by the Court. We believe this silence stems not from neglect but from the fact that the idea-expression dichotomy already serves to accommodate the competing interests of copyright and the first amendment. The "marketplace of ideas" is not limited by copyright because copyright is limited to protection of expression.

Ideas which may be of public interest are not subject to copyright; the specific form of expression of these ideas are. Thus, the political views of Dr. Martin Luther King may be widely disseminated. But the precise expression of these views in a speech may be protected. Similarly, the facts about a historical figure are available to all to use. But if the expression of those facts in a biography is substantially copied infringement will be found.

With the law of copyright permitting the free use of ideas, it is not surprising that the few courts addressing the issue have not permitted defendants who copy a work's expression to hide behind the first amendment.

The district court in Disney recognized that the expression inherent in plaintiff's works differs from the mere idea of those works. The "idea" of Mickey Mouse is, after all, no more than a mouse. Yet the particular expression of that mouse has phenomenal commercial value and is recognized worldwide. Defendants there could have chosen any number of ways to express their idea of a mouse, but chose to copy Disney's. So too the defendants in this case had many ways to express the idea of a fantasyland with characters, but chose to copy the expression of plaintiffs'. The first amendment will not protect such imitation.

There may be certain rare instances when first amendment considerations will operate to limit copyright protection for graphic expressions of newsworthy events. For example, in Time, Inc. v. Bernard Geis Associates, 293 F.Supp. 130 (S.D.N.Y.1968), Life magazine sued a historian for copying frames of the Zapruder films of the assassination of John F. Kennedy. Although the court did not expressly invoke the first amendment, it did justify the defendant's right to copy frames of the film on the ground of the "public interest in having the fullest information available on the murder of President Kennedy." Id. at 146. Plaintiffs' work in this case is neither a graphic expression nor concerning newsworthy events. Therefore, no first amendment considerations operate.

Access

In addition to substantial similarity, a plaintiff must show access in order to prove infringement. Reyher v. Children's Television Workshop, supra, 533 F.2d at 90; Access is proven when the plaintiff shows that the defendant had an opportunity to view or to copy plaintiff's work. Arrow Novelty Co. v. Enco National Corp., 393 F.Supp. 157, 160 (S.D.N.Y.), aff'd, 515 F.2d 504 (2 Cir. 1975); Universal Athletic Sales Co. v. Salkeld, 340 F.Supp. 899, 901 (W.D.Pa.1972). In this case, there is no dispute as to defendants' access to plaintiffs' work. Indeed, defendants were engaged in negotiations with plaintiffs for licensing of the works even while preparing the McDonaldland commercials.

No amount of proof of access will suffice to show copying if there are no similarities. Williams v. Kaag Manufacturers, Inc., supra, 338 F.2d at 951; Arnstein v. Porter, supra, 154 F.2d at 468. This is not to say, however, that where clear and convincing evidence of access is presented, the quantum of proof required to show substantial similarity may not be lower than when access is shown merely by a preponderance of the evidence...

In this case, representatives of Needham actually visited the Kroffts' headquarters in Los Angeles to discuss the engineering and design work necessary to produce the McDonaldland commercials. They did this after they had been awarded the contract by McDonald's and apparently with no intention to work with the Kroffts. We believe that this degree of access justifies a lower standard of proof to show substantial similarity. Since the subjective test applies, it is impossible to quantify this standard. But there is no question it is met here.

II. DAMAGES

Awarding Damages

Section 101(b), 17 U.S.C., provides that a copyright infringer shall be liable as follows:

> "(b) Damages and profits; amount; other remedies.
> To pay to the copyright proprietor such damages as the copyright proprietor may have suffered due to the infringement, as well as all the profits which the infringer shall have made from such infringement, and in proving profits the plaintiff shall be required to prove sales only, and the defendant shall be required to prove every element of cost which he claims. . . ."

Thus, a court in making an award for infringement must determine both actual damages suffered by a plaintiff and profits from the infringement made by defendant.

While there is disagreement as to whether both damages and profits are to be included in the award, an issue we will take up shortly, there is agreement that a successful plaintiff is entitled to at least the greater of damages or profits...

The jury assessed damages of $50,000 against defendants in this case. Subsequent to the return of the verdict, counsel for both sides, at the district court's request, briefed the question of whether plaintiffs were entitled to additional monetary recovery either in the form of profits or statutory "in lieu" damages. After considering this question, the district court concluded that plaintiffs were not entitled to any additional recovery and denied plaintiffs' motion for an accounting of profits by defendants.

The issues on appeal are threefold: (1) whether the jury considered profits in assessing damages; (2) if not, whether plaintiffs are entitled to recovery of damages and profits or merely damages or profits; and (3) whether, if profits cannot accurately be determined, plaintiffs are entitled to statutory "in lieu" damages.

Consideration of Profits by the Jury

Two weeks before trial, the district court signed the Pre-Trial Conference Order that was prepared and "approved as to form and content" by counsel for both sides. It provided...

Rule 16 of the Federal Rules of Civil Procedure expressly provides that a Pre-Trial Conference Order "when entered controls the subsequent course of the action, unless modified at the trial to prevent manifest injustice." There was no modification of this Order at trial or at any other time. Rule 39(a) of the Federal Rules further provides that issues will not be given to the jury when reserved for the court by "written stipulation filed with the court."

Defendants argue that plaintiffs' original demand for a jury trial meant that all issues had to go to the jury. See Fed.R.Civ.P. 38(c). But the clear language of the Pre-Trial Conference Order and the subsequent conduct of the parties contradict any claimed general demand for a jury trial. We conclude that the parties intended to withhold the issue of profits from the jury...

The record also shows that inquiry from the court elicited agreement with this instruction from counsel for both sides.

Defendants argue that this instruction was designed only to prevent the jury from considering the corporate profits of McDonald's, which are derived from the purveying of food. ... Defendants claim that the value of use provided in this instruction is equivalent to defendant's profits from the infringement.

The value of use reference in Instruction No. 49 is defined as a part of the reasonable value of plaintiffs' work. It amounts to a determination of what a willing buyer would have been reasonably required to pay to a willing seller for plaintiffs' work. That is a different measure than the determination of defendants' actual profits from the infringement. An author might license the use of his copyright either for a lump sum based on the reasonable value of the work or for a royalty derived from the licensee's profits, or for a combination of both.

The district court recognized the potential for confusion between these two instructions. It agreed upon an explanation offered by counsel for plaintiffs: "I think that the difference would be that a person may pay to use 'Living Island' and the characters, and then, even though they have paid for them, they may have suffered a loss and suffered no profit." It was only because the district court concluded that there was a difference between profits and value of use that both Instructions 26 and 49 were delivered to the jury. We agree with this distinction.

Defendants argue further that profits in fact were considered by the jury. The record does not support this conclusion. No exhibits regarding either defendants' profits were submitted to the jury in the infringement action. We therefore find that the issue of profits was neither submitted to nor considered by the jury.

An Accounting of Profits as a Legal Remedy

In denying plaintiffs' motion for an accounting of profits, the district court relied upon Dairy Queen v. Wood, 369 U.S. 469, 82 S.Ct. 894, 8 L.Ed.2d 44 (1962). That case involved claims for breach of contract and trademark infringement in which the plaintiffs also asked for an accounting. The Court ruled that the wording of the claim for relief is not dispositive. The plaintiffs sought money damages and had a right to trial by jury... But a right is not an obligation. Dairy Queen only decided when a party has a right to a jury trial. It certainly cannot be read to hold that the parties are required to have a jury determination even if they do not wish it. It is clear from our analysis of the Pre-Trial Conference Order and jury instructions that the parties did not intend the jury to consider profits. The district court therefore was in error in concluding that Dairy Queen compelled the jury to consider profits in this case.

Conclusion

The judgment of the district court finding infringement is affirmed. The McDonald commercials are based on the same ideas as the H. R. PufnStuf series. The expression of that idea is sufficiently similar so that a jury applying an intrinsic test could find infringement. This is especially true here since there was strong evidence of access.

SNEED, Circuit Judge [concur]...

PECLARSKY v. AMERICAN BROADCASTING CO.
United States District Court for the District of Columbia
December 6, 1984
Civ. A. No. 81-2482
603 F.Supp. 688

HAROLD H. GREENE, District Judge.

In this action plaintiff, a free-lance journalist and attorney who is appearing *pro se,* has sued defendants American Broadcasting Company (ABC), *et al.,* for their alleged breach of an agreement concerning his 1978 article, "The Selling of the President." The claims asserted against the defendants include common-law breach of contract (Count I), unfair trade practices (Count III), unfair competition (Count IV), fraudulent misrepresentation (Count V), negligent misrepresentation (Count VII), and trade secret conversion (Count VIII) claims, as well as federal copyright (Count II) and civil RICO (Count VI) claims. Plaintiff has moved for summary judgment against various defendants with respect to several of the counts asserted in the complaint; defendants have cross-moved for summary judgment and dismissal of the complaint in its entirety. For the reasons stated below, the Court will deny plaintiff's motion, and it will grant defendants' motion with respect to Counts II, III, IV, VI, and VIII.

I

Most of the material facts concerning the incidents involved in this case are not in dispute. In July, 1978 plaintiff brought a copy of his copyrighted seventeen page article, "The Selling of the President", to defendant ABC's Washington, D.C. headquarters. The article focused on a series of alleged irregularities and improprieties in then-President Jimmy Carter's personal finances. Defendants George Watson, the Washington Bureau Chief of ABC News, and C. Robert Zelnick, the Bureau's Director of News Coverage, thought the allegations sufficiently newsworthy to merit further investigation. Watson therefore directed Zelnick to negotiate with plaintiff concerning the use of the article, and Zelnick did so.

There is no dispute between the parties concerning most of the terms of the verbal agreement reached between plaintiff and Zelnick. ABC was to have exclusive rights to the information contained in plaintiff's article for a period of three weeks (between approximately August 7 to August 27, 1978). During that time, ABC was to investigate the allegations contained in the article with the assistance of plaintiff, who was retained as a consultant at a fee of $500 per week for the three-week period. If ABC broadcast reports based on the article, plaintiff was to be paid $1,000 for each television spot and $100 for each radio spot.

It is also undisputed that both parties substantially performed these terms. Plaintiff provided defendants with exclusive access to his article; he assisted in undertaking additional investigations; and defendants paid plaintiff his $1,500 consulting fee. Defendants also paid plaintiff $2,000 after they broadcast two spot reports—one on the October 19, 1978 edition of "World News Tonight", and the other on the October 20, 1978 edition of "Good Morning America"—concerning alleged discrepancies in President Carter's valuation of farm equipment for federal income and local property tax purposes that had been reported in plaintiff's article.

The contest here revolves primarily around ABC's alleged promise to give plaintiff audio and video credit on any spots based on his article. Plaintiff has produced an August 7, 1978 letter from himself to Zelnick which purports to memorialize the agreement between the parties, and which includes the disputed credit provision. The letter also includes a request that Zelnick notify plaintiff if the letter did not accurately reflect the parties' agreement, and a handwritten note by plaintiff, apparently in reference to a telephone conversation with Zelnick, that the letter accurately reflects the agreement. Defendants, for their part, vigorously deny, both in their papers and in their depositions, that Zelnick or any other ABC employee agreed that plaintiff would receive audio-visual credit on any spots, although they admit that plaintiff sought such credit and that he and Zelnick discussed the matter several times. In the event, ABC never performed the contested term of the agreement—that is, plaintiff never received any sort of on-air credit in the television spots that concerned allegations contained in the article.

It should also be noted that in his most recent amendment to the complaint, plaintiff alleged for the first time that defendants also breached the terms of the agreement requiring that he be paid for each radio and television spot based on his article. Specifically, he claims that ABC broadcast five additional spots based on his article for which he was never paid and on which he received no on-air credit. Defendants admit both that they have not paid plaintiff for the additional broadcasts, and that they did not provide him with on-air credit, but they deny that they had any obligation to do so.

II

The two breach of contract claims in Count I of the complaint—one relating to defendants' alleged failure to pay plaintiff for the later television spots based on his article, and the other to their failure to provide him with audio-video credit on all seven television spots—form the heart of this case.

A. Defendants' motion for summary judgment with respect to the failure to credit claim proceeds on the grounds (1) that Zelnick never agreed on behalf of ABC to provide plaintiff with on-air credit, and (2) that even if Zelnick made such a promise, he lacked authority to do so and he therefore he could not bind the other defendants.

It appears from the affidavits submitted by defendants and from the deposition testimony that Zelnick did lack actual authority to bind ABC to an agreement to provide on-air credit. But even absent actual authority, an on-air credit promise by Zelnick—if one was made—could have bound ABC if Zelnick possessed apparent authority to do so. See 1 *Restatement (2d) of Agency* §§ 8, 48, 140, 159 (1958). The issues of the precise scope of Zelnick's authority, of plaintiff's contemporaneous belief concerning that authority, and of the reasonableness of his beliefs in light of industry custom and practice all involve unresolved questions of material fact.

Assuming that plaintiff is able to prove that, under agency principles, Zelnick's promises bind ABC, the factual question remains what promises Zelnick actually made with respect to on-air credit to plaintiff. This question involves both intent and credibility—clearly matters for the finders of fact and therefore inappropriate for summary judgment. See *Centronics Financial Corp. v. El Conquistador Hotel Corp.,* 573 F.2d 779, 782 (2d Cir.1978). Defendants' summary judgment motion with respect to the failure to credit claim must accordingly be denied.

B. Defendants' motion with regard to the later newscasts proceeds on two premises: (1) that the claim is barred by the statute of limitations; and (2) that those newscasts concerned only Carter Administration reactions to the original stories and that, as such, they were not covered by the agreement.

Clearly, the claims concerning the five additional October and November, 1978 broadcasts were first asserted well beyond the statute of limitations period. The applicable District of Columbia limitations period, which governs this common-law diversity contract claim, is three years. D.C.Code Ann. §§ 12–301(7) (contracts) and 12–308 (other unenumerated claims). Since the alleged breaches occurred in 1978, plaintiff's assertion of these claims in his 1984 amended complaint came more than two years after the statutory filing period. Accordingly, plaintiff's claims concerning these later broadcasts are time-barred unless saved by a doctrine that mitigates the statutory bar.

The Court finds that these particular claims "relate back" under Fed.R.Civ.P. 15(c) to the date of plaintiff's original complaint and are therefore timely. Under Rule 15(c), Fed.R.Civ.P., amendments relate back to the date of the original pleading if they arise out of the same "conduct, transaction or occurrence" set forth in the original pleading. In this Circuit (as elsewhere), policies of notice pleading and judicial economy favor the liberal use of relation back as long as the original pleading provided sufficient notice to defendant so that he will not be prejudiced by the assertion of the new claim. See *Columbia Plaza Corp. v. Security National Bank,* 525 F.2d 620, 626 (D.C.Cir.1975); see generally, 6 C. Wright & A. Miller, *Federal Practice and Procedure* Civil § 1497 (1971 and Supp.1984).

Here the later broadcasts occurred close in time to the broadcasts identified in the original complaint, and the breach of contract claims concerning those broadcasts involve failure to credit claims identical to those asserted concerning the earlier identified broadcasts. To be sure, the claim that defendants failed to compensate plaintiff for the later broadcasts represents a different breach than the previously asserted on-air credit breach. But that is not conclusive. Plaintiff's assertion of the on-air credit issue required defendants to review five additional newscast tapes, as they have already done during discovery. That is also the only factual preparation necessary to address the new factual issues posed by the non-payment claim—*i.e.,* whether the television spots mentioned the allegations contained in plaintiff's article.

The crux of all of these claims is the proper construction of one agreement, which is now asserted to have been violated basically in two respects rather than in one. To require defendants to address these additional claims on the merits will neither unduly complicate the case nor prejudice them. Accordingly, the Court holds that the claims with respect to the latter five broadcasts relate back and are therefore not time-barred.

With regard to the merits of the non-payment claims, there exist genuine, controverted issues of material fact that preclude the granting of summary judgment on this issue to either party. An examination of the broadcast transcripts submitted to the Court reveals that they are indeed concerned with Carter Administration reactions to the earlier broadcasts (for which plaintiff was paid) or are follow-up reports on new developments not reported in plaintiff's article. However, the content of the broadcasts is not alone determinative in assessing this claim. Rather, its resolution requires determinations as to the parties' original intent, the scope of the payment provision of their agreement, and indeed, whether the agreement necessary to form a contract ever existed. All of these are material questions of fact. See *Davis v. Chevy Chase Financial, Ltd.,* 667 F.2d 160, 170–71 (D.C.Cir.1981); *Martin Ice Cream Co. v. Chipwich, Inc.,* 554 F.Supp. 933, 937–39 (S.D.N.Y.1983); see generally, 10A C. Wright & A. Miller, *Federal Practice and Procedure* Civil § 2730.1. Accordingly, both parties' motions for summary judgment on this aspect of the contract claim will be denied.

III

The Court's conclusion with respect to the contract claim also disposes of the parties' motions regarding the fraudulent misrepresentation claim (Count

V of the complaint). To establish the common law tort of fraudulent misrepresentation, a plaintiff must prove that defendants (1) made a false representation (2) with respect to a material fact, (3) with knowledge of its falsity, (4) with the intent to deceive plaintiff, and (5) that plaintiff acted in reliance on the false representation. Plaintiff's allegations, read as they must be in the light most favorable to him, as well as the deposition testimony, indicate that, if plaintiff's claims that defendants agreed to provide him with on-air credit and payment even for Carter Administration "reaction" stories are true, then plaintiff may be able to establish the elements of the fraudulent misrepresentation claim. Since, as indicated, the facts concerning the provisions of plaintiff's agreement with defendants remain disputed, the fraudulent misrepresentation claim, which largely turns on the same facts as the contract claim, is similarly unripe for summary judgment. Accordingly, both parties' summary judgment motions must and will be denied as to this claim.

Plaintiffs common-law claim of negligent misrepresentation (Count VII), to the effect that defendants "owed plaintiff a duty not to mislead him concerning their proposed use of his proprietary, copyrighted material," Complaint at paragraph 56, is similarly unripe for summary judgment. Defendants have moved for summary judgment on the grounds that no misrepresentations were made. However, as noted above, the nature and truth of the representations made to plaintiff remain very much contested issues of material fact. Accordingly, defendants' motion for summary judgment will be denied with respect to this claim.

IV

Both parties have moved for summary judgment on the copyright claim: plaintiff on the ground that defendants copied his work without authorization by broadcasting infringing news spots without compensating him, and defendants on the basis that no reasonable jury could find that defendants infringed the copyright.

It is well recognized that the federal copyright laws provide only limited protection for news reports. Although a reporter's mode of expression is protected by copyright, the facts reported are not themselves so protected. Similarly, the Copyright Act does not extend copyright protection to ideas contained within the article. The Act thus strikes a careful balance, protecting authors' original expression without impeding the public's access to information and ideas.

A comparison of plaintiff's articles with transcripts of the allegedly infringing newscasts compels the conclusion that no copyright infringement occurred. To be sure, the later newscasts reported some facts concerning former President Carter's taxes that were similar to those reported by plaintiff.

But such material was distinctly subordinate to the theme of the newscasts. Plaintiff's article contains numerous allegations of irregularities and improprieties concerning Carter family finances, and it suggests that loans received from Saudi Arabian and domestic sources constitute conflicts of interest and raise substantial doubts about the President's integrity. The ABC broadcasts, by contrast, reported only a single allegation similar to those raised in the article, and, significantly, they raised no conflict of interest questions whatsoever. The broadcasts reported numerous additional facts based on ABC's own investigations, and their thrust was to question the consistency of the President's actions with his statements about the federal tax system.

In short, the references to plaintiff's work were entirely incidental to the publication of ideas and news reports of benefit to the public. To hold that plaintiff had a copyright on this material would be inconsistent with copyright law precepts and entirely inimical to First Amendment principles. Defendants' motion for summary judgment will accordingly be granted with respect to Count II of the complaint.

V

Defendants have moved for summary judgment with respect to the unfair trade practices claims (Count III) and the unfair competition claims (Count IV) on the basis that these common law claims are pre-empted by the Copyright Act.

Section 301 of the Copyright Act, 17 U.S.C. § 301, provides a broad statutory basis for the pre-emption of state claims equivalent to copyright that extend to works within the scope of federal copyright law. The purpose of this broad statutory pre-emption scheme is to further the Copyright Act's goal of encouraging contributions to recorded knowledge by precluding the use of state law to prevent the copying of material that Congress has determined should be left in the public domain.

Plaintiff's copyrighted article is plainly within the subject matter of the Copyright Act. The seventeen-page article is an "original work of authorship fixed in a tangible medium of expression". 17 U.S.C. §§ 102(a), 301. It is also clear from the allegations of the complaint that the thrust of his unfair competition and unfair trade practices charges is that ABC improperly made unauthorized use of the material contained in his article and failed to provide him with compensation and on-air credit therefor. The rights to control the use or reproduction of copyrighted work are explicitly protected by section 106 of the Copyright Act. Although section 106 does not explicitly protect the right of attribution of authorship, assertion of such a claim in an otherwise pre-empted common law action will not save the common law claim from pre-emption. See *Suid v. Newsweek Magazine, Inc.*, 503 F.Supp. 146, 149 (D.D.C.1980).

Plaintiff's unfair competition and unfair trade practices claims thus fall squarely within the pre-emption provisions of § 301 of the Copyright Act. Accordingly, defendants' motion for summary judgment will be granted with respect to Counts III and IV of the complaint.

VI

Plaintiff has alleged in count VI that the non-corporate defendants committed numerous acts of wire and mail fraud in furtherance of their alleged scheme to defraud him, and that they are therefore liable under the Racketeer Influenced and Corrupt Organizations (RICO) Act, 18 U.S.C. § 1961 *et seq.* To prevail on his RICO claim, plaintiff is required to prove (1) the existence of an enterprise (2) affecting interstate commerce (3) with which defendants were associated (4) and in the affairs of which they participated (5) through a pattern of racketeering activity. *Martin-Trigona v. Smith,* 712 F.2d 1421, 1426 n. 6 (D.C.Cir.1983). Certainly, as defendants concede, the first four elements are satisfied here. It is equally clear, however, that plaintiff has not satisfied the fifth element.

Plaintiff has failed to develop any facts tending to prove the two predicate criminal acts necessary to establish the requisite pattern of racketeering activity, and his RICO claim therefore cannot stand. Assuming the truth of plaintiff's allegations that Zelnick engaged in fraudulent misrepresentations in their August 1, 1978 telephone conversation—allegations which, it may be noted, are very much disputed—this conversation between plaintiff in Virginia and Zelnick in the District of Columbia could in theory be found to be within the federal wire fraud statute, which constitutes one of the predicate RICO felonies. However, despite his allegations that defendants engaged in numerous interstate telephone conversations with each other in furtherance of the fraud, extensive discovery has produced not the slightest factual support for these claims. The Court will not require defendants to contest at trial so serious a charge on grounds which are so flimsy as to be non-existent.

Similarly defective is the allegation that the ABC television news spots constituted acts of wire fraud: if any fraud occurred, it was consummated prior to the broadcasts, when defendants obtained plaintiff's services and access to his article, and the broadcasts therefore cannot be considered acts in the furtherance or execution of the alleged fraudulent scheme, as is required for coverage under the wire fraud statute. See 18 U.S.C. § 1343; *United States v. Alston,* 609 F.2d 531, 536 (D.C.Cir.1976). The Court will therefore grant summary judgment to defendants with respect to this claim.

VII

Finally, plaintiff claims that defendants converted his alleged trade secrets (Count VIII). Defendants' motion argues (1) that the information contained in the article does not constitute a trade secret, and (2) that plaintiff's intangible property rights in the article cannot be the subject of conversion.

Plaintiff's contention that his article, or the information contained therein, constituted a trade secret is frivolous. Plaintiff's compilation of facts, the overwhelming majority of which consisted of publicly available information, cannot reasonably be characterized as a "formula, pattern, device or compilation of information" regularly used in his business. The compilation of facts was not used by plaintiff as a means for conducting his business as an investigative reporter; rather, it was the product of his efforts as a reporter.

Beyond that, neither the article nor the facts contained therein were secret. At the time plaintiff showed the article to Zelnick, he had already shown it to editors at *Penthouse* magazine, and earlier drafts had been shown to several other journalistic organizations. Indeed, most of the facts contained in the article were available in the public record; ascertainment of these facts certainly required effort, but hardly the sort of effort and expense normally associated with the development of trade secrets. See *Ashland Oil, supra,* 409 F.Supp. at 303. Defendants' motion for summary judgment will accordingly be granted as to Count VIII.

VIII

As the foregoing analysis has suggested, plaintiff has transformed a relatively simple contract claim into major federal litigation through the addition of numerous common law and federal statutory claims, most of which are legally unsupportable. Accordingly, defendants' motion for summary judgment will be granted with respect to these inappropriate additional claims (set forth in counts II, III, IV, VI, and VIII of the complaint), which will be dismissed. The parties' motions for summary judgment will be denied as to the contract and misrepresentation claims (set forth in counts I, V, and VII), which involve factual disputes appropriate for resolution at trial. It is the Court's expectation that, now that the scope of this lawsuit has been properly narrowed, a prompt resolution can be anticipated. Accordingly, the Court will schedule a status call in order that the Court and the parties can set final discovery cut-off, pretrial, and trial dates, and bring this case to an expeditious resolution on the merits.

OLSON v. NATIONAL BROADCASTING CO.
United States Court of Appeals for the Ninth Circuit
May 2, 1988, Argued and Submitted; September 1, 1988, Filed
Nos. 86-6325, 87-5606, 87-5664

GOODWIN, Circuit Judge:

Plaintiff Ernest Olson appeals a judgment notwithstanding the verdict granted to National Broadcasting Company (NBC) on his claim that NBC's television series "The A–Team" infringed his copyright.

Olson sued NBC, Stephen J. Cannell (individually and dba Stephen J. Cannell Productions), MCA Inc. and MCA Television Ltd. for infringement of his treatment and screenplay for a television series pilot entitled "Cargo." Olson also alleged pendent state-law claims, which were dismissed before trial.

The jury found by special verdict that "The A–Team" was substantially similar to the treatment and screenplay for "Cargo" and that the substantial similarity resulted from copying of Olson's works. It found that the Cannell defendants, who wrote and developed "The A–Team," had not copied Olson's works. However, the jury found that NBC had copied "Cargo."

NBC moved for j.n.o.v., and, in the alternative, for a new trial. Cannell and the MCA defendants moved for a protective order reversing the jury's finding of substantial similarity, and, in the alternative, for a new trial.

The district court granted each of the defendants' motions. In the memorandum decision explaining its judgment, the court found that Olson had failed to prove that the defendants who created the allegedly infringing work had access to his work. It also found that "The A–Team" was not substantially similar to the "Cargo" works under either the extrinsic test or the intrinsic test. Finally, it found that no reasonable person could conclude that NBC copied the general ideas or protectable expression of "Cargo."

On appeal, Olson does not attack the jury's finding that the Cannell defendants did not have access to his works. He asks the panel to overturn the district court's grant of j.n.o.v. and to reinstate the jury's findings that NBC had access to his works and that "The A–Team" was substantially similar to "Cargo." He asks that the jury's finding of substantial similarity be made binding upon the Cannell defendants.

A district court may grant j.n.o.v. only "if the evidence permits of only one reasonable conclusion as to the verdict."

I. *Copyright Claim.*

"[I]n order to establish copyright infringement a plaintiff must prove ownership of the copyright and 'copying' by the defendant." *Sid & Marty Krofft Television Prods., Inc. v. McDonald's Corp.,* 562 F.2d 1157, 1162 (9th Cir.1977). Because the defendants do not dispute Olson's ownership of the copyright, Olson may prevail by demonstrating that the defendants copied his works. Copying is "shown by circumstantial evidence of access to the copyrighted work and substantial similarity between the copyrighted work and defendant's work." *Id.* Because we affirm the district court's grant of j.n.o.v. on the ground that there existed no substantial similarity between "The A–Team" and "Cargo," we do not reach the question whether the jury properly could have found that NBC had access to Olson's works.

The jury found by special verdict that "The A–Team" was substantially similar to Olson's works in both ideas and protectable expression. The district court granted j.n.o.v., finding that there existed no substantial similarity under either the extrinsic or intrinsic test.

Krofft sets forth a two-part test for determining whether one work is substantially similar to another. *See Krofft,* 562 F.2d at 1164; *see also Aliotti v. R. Dakin & Co.,* 831 F.2d 898, 900 (9th Cir.1987). The "extrinsic" test, which is used to determine whether there is a substantial similarity in ideas, "depends not on the responses of the trier of fact, but on specific criteria which can be listed and analyzed." *Krofft,* 562 F.2d at 1164. The "intrinsic" test, which is used to compare forms of expression, "depend[s] on the response of the ordinary reasonable person." *Id.* Although analytic dissection and expert testimony are appropriate under the extrinsic test, they are not appropriate under the intrinsic test. *See id.* To demonstrate substantial similarity, Olson must prove both substantial similarity of general ideas under the extrinsic test and substantial similarity of the protectable expression of those ideas under the intrinsic test. *See id.; Litchfield v. Spielberg,* 736 F.2d 1352, 1356 (9th Cir.1984), *cert. denied,* 470 U.S. 1052, 105 S.Ct. 1753, 84 L.Ed.2d 817 (1985).

"Cargo" features a unit of three Vietnam veterans—Van Druten, Tronski and Brown—who developed a group practice of conducting scams in Vietnam and continue to conduct such scams as civilians. While in Vietnam, they alienated Col. Kilgore and Lt. Brite by humiliating them in order to prevent them from uncovering a scam. Today, Tronski and Brown work together for an air cargo business in Miami. Tronski is romantically involved with Marsha Bainwright, the daughter of the owner of the air freight company.

Olson provides three- to four-line descriptions of each of his characters. He compares Van Druten to John Ritter, describing him as an old-money New York intellectual who has studied medicine; he was the group's navigator in Vietnam, and he is reluctant to become involved in the group's scams but agrees to participate. Tronski, who is compared to Nick Nolte, is an impulsive, quick-thinking "good old boy" from the South; he was a pilot in Vietnam and serves as the trio's leader and strategist. Brown, described as a "Rosie Greer [*sic*] type," is depicted as a physically large, athletic, sensitive, emotionally deep man from the deep South. Kilgore is a "militaristic, extremist, schizoid" Southerner. Marsha Bainwright, who resembles Kate Jackson, is said to be wealthy and elegant.

"Cargo" is set in the present. Kilgore and Brite, who are now corrupt Drug Enforcement agents, threaten Tronski and Brown with unjustified smuggling charges, which are to be dropped if they cooperate in breaking up a large Colombian cocaine smuggling ring. Because Van Druten closely resembles the ringleader's son, the DEA agents force Tronski and Brown to enlist his help. After a series of plot episodes that lead the trio to New York City, Florida, Colombia, and much of the adjacent airspace, the unit escapes in a cargo plane carrying a load of drugs, unaware that Kilgore and Brite have sabotaged the plane. After the trio crash lands the plane in the ocean, Kilgore and Brite take them captive, then send divers to salvage the drugs from the plane. The Coast Guard arrives and arrests Kilgore and Brite. The trio flies clothes and gifts to a children's mission in South America.

"The A–Team" includes three members—Peck, Baracus, and Smith—who were wrongly faced with a court martial because, acting under orders from a colonel who died without verifying their story, they robbed the Bank of Hanoi of 100 million yen shortly after the end of the Vietnam war. A fourth man, Murdock, was the trio's pilot in Vietnam. Colonel Lynch, who ran the prison from which the group escaped more than 10 years before, still seeks to find them.

Peck is a suave con artist who is reluctant to participate in the A–Team's adventures. Baracas is a huge, mohawked, pugnacious, mechanical genius. Smith, the leader of the unit in Vietnam, continues to lead the group here. Murdock serves as the group's eccentric, possibly insane pilot. Lynch is a career military man. Amy Allen is an impetuous, dedicated newspaper reporter.

"The A–Team" is set in the present. In the pilot episode, Allen hires the A–Team to help her find a reporter who is missing in Mexico. The A–Team goes to Mexico and, with the reporter's assistance, accomplishes its mission. In the process, it rescues a terrorized town from a band of Mexican revolutionaries.

At trial, Olson presented the testimony of an expert witness, William Talbot, who dissected the works and listed and analyzed similarities involving specific criteria such as characters, character relationships, plot incidents, scenes, theme, pace and mood. Talbot explained a chart and a 90-minute film montage which consisted of scenes from 27 episodes of "The A–Team." The district court found that Talbot's testimony and montage were entitled to little weight, given that he deemphasized any dissimilarities between plaintiff's and defendants' works and that his montage in effect compared unprotectable scenes a faire—that is, stock scenes. The district court's decision to discount this testimony was correct under *Litchfield,* 736 F.2d at 1356, which observes that such "lists of similarities" are "inherently subjective and unreliable," especially where they "emphasize random similarities scattered throughout the works."

"The A–Team" and Olson's works share a common idea: Both are group action-adventure series designed to show Vietnam veterans in a positive light. This idea, standing alone, is not protectable. *See Berkic v. Crichton,* 761 F.2d 1289, 1293 (9th Cir.), *cert. denied,* 474 U.S. 826, 106 S.Ct. 85, 88 L.Ed.2d 69 (1985) (finding no substantial similarity of ideas where two works dealt "with criminal organizations that murder healthy young people, then remove and sell their vital organs to wealthy people in need of organ transplants" and both works took "their general story from the adventures of a young professional who courageously investigates, and finally exposes, the criminal organization"); *see Jason v. Fonda,* 526 F.Supp. 774, 777 (C.D.Cal.1981), *incorp'd by reference,* 698 F.2d 966, 967 (9th Cir.1982) (observing that no copyright protection may be afforded to ideas "deal[ing] generally with subjects such as morality and the effects of war on women, injured veterans and soldiers").

Berkic sets forth the type of more specific analysis that is appropriate under the extrinsic test:

> The test for "substantial similarity of ideas" compares, not the basic plot ideas for stories, but the actual concrete elements that make up the total sequence of events and the relationships between the major characters. The extrinsic test for similarity of ideas looks beyond the vague, abstracted idea of a general plot and instead "focuses on ... the objective details of the works.... The extrinsic test requires a comparison of plot, theme, dialogue, mood, setting, pace, and sequence."

Berkic, 761 F.2d at 1293 (quoting *Litchfield,* 736 F.2d at 1356); *see Jason,* 526 F.Supp. at 777.

We begin our analysis by applying these factors. We observe first that there is little similarity between "The A–Team" and the "Cargo" works in terms of overall plot, sequence, dialogue or setting. The "Cargo" crew is coerced by DEA agents into breaking up a drug-smuggling ring. The A–Team, in the pilot episode, is hired by a reporter to help her find a fellow reporter who is missing somewhere in Mexico. While some episodes of "The A–Team" may have included some of the plot incidents presented in "Cargo," such similarities were insufficient to constitute the type of congruence of plot relevant to the substantial similarity inquiry. *See Berkic,* 791 F.2d at 1293 (observing that no protection may be afforded to "situations and incidents which flow naturally from a basic plot premise"). Nor has Olson demonstrated the type of extended similarity of dialogue needed to support a claim of substantial similarity based upon this issue. The settings of the two works are too dissimilar to be relevant to the issue of substantial similarity.

Given this lack of similarity in plot, it is apparent that Olson's claim of substantial similarity is based primarily on the theory that "The A–Team" infringed "Cargo's" "series concept" and characters. Olson argues that he may show substantial similarity of ideas without showing similarity as to each of the factors deemed relevant by *Berkic* and *Litchfield. See Bevan v. Columbia Broadcasting System, Inc.,* 329 F.Supp. 601, 605 (S.D.N.Y.1971) (suggesting that copyright infringement may be found in the absence of similarity in the overall plots based upon similarities in "dramatic mood, the details and interplay of the characters, and the dynamic of events"). Without resolving this issue, we now determine whether those similarities that do exist demonstrate substantial similarity.

"The A–Team" and "Cargo" are similar in terms of theme, mood, and pace. The two shows emphasize action and lack identifiable themes. Both shows may be broadly described as comic, and they therefore have similar moods. Both works are quickly paced. However, these similarities are common to the genre of action-adventure television series and movies and therefore do not demonstrate substantial similarity. *Cf. Berkic,* 761 F.2d at 1293–94 (denying protection to "familiar scenes and themes [which] are among the very staples of modern American literature and film"); *Walker v. Time Life Films, Inc.,* 784 F.2d 44, 50 (2d Cir.) (denying protection to " 'stock' themes commonly linked to a particular genre"), *cert. denied,* 476 U.S. 1159, 106 S.Ct. 2278, 90 L.Ed.2d 721 (1986).

Olson's claim of substantial similarity is supported most strongly by a comparison between the characters in "Cargo" and those in "The A–Team." It is possible to find loose correspondences among the characters of the two works by comparing Van Druten to Peck, Brown to Baracus, Tronski to Murdock and Smith, Marsha to Amy, and Kilgore to Lynch.

However, we find that Olson may not maintain a claim of substantial similarity based upon these similarities in characters. *See Warner Bros. Pictures, Inc. v. Columbia Broadcasting System, Inc.,* 216 F.2d 945, 950 (9th Cir.1954) (stating that characters ordinarily may not be copyrighted), *cert. denied,* 348 U.S. 971, 75 S.Ct. 532, 99 L.Ed. 756 (1955). *Warner Bros.* concerned a dispute arising out of Dashiell Hammett's assignment of the motion picture rights to his book, "The Maltese Falcon." Hammett subsequently wrote other stories using "Falcon" characters. The court concluded first that Hammett had not contracted away the rights to his characters. *See id.* at 949–50. In what is arguably dicta, the court then stated that "if the character is only the chessman in the game of telling the story he is not within the area of the protection afforded by the copyright." *Id. See Columbia Pictures Corp. v. National Broadcasting Co.,* 137 F.Supp. 348, 353 (S.D.Cal.1955) (stating that characters ordinarily are not protectable). Under *Warner Bros.,* Olson's claim of substantial similarity based upon a comparison of characters appears doomed.

We recognize that cases subsequent to *Warner Bros.* have allowed copyright protection for characters who are especially distinctive. For example, cartoon characters may be afforded copyright protection notwithstanding *Warner Bros. See Walt Disney Prods. v. Air Pirates,* 581 F.2d 751, 755 (9th Cir.1978), *cert. denied,* 439 U.S. 1132, 99 S.Ct. 1054, 59 L.Ed.2d 94 (1979). "[M]any literary characters may embody little more than an unprotected idea [while] a comic book character, which has physical as well as conceptual qualities, is more likely to contain some unique elements of expression." *Id. See Warner Bros., Inc. v. American Broadcasting Cos., Inc.,* 720 F.2d 231, 240–45 (2d Cir.1983) (finding that copyright protection was available for the character of Superman although defendants' parody did not infringe copyright). For similar reasons, copyright protection may be afforded to characters visually depicted in a television series or in a movie. *See Silverman v. CBS, Inc.,* 632 F.Supp. 1344, 1355 (S.D.N.Y.1986) (finding that the personifications of the characters from "Amos 'n' Andy" on television were distinctive enough to be afforded copyright protection); *Ideal Toy Corp. v. Kenner Prods. Div. of General Mills Fun Group, Inc.,* 443 F.Supp. 291, 301 (S.D.N.Y.1977) (finding that the characters in the movie "Star Wars" were protected from infringement).

Even if the statements in *Warner Bros.* concerning the unprotectability of characters are considered to be dicta, the "Cargo" characters are not protectable even under the more lenient standards adopted elsewhere. In the classic formulation of the doctrine, Judge Learned Hand stated that it was possible that two characters may correspond closely enough for infringement, "quite independently of the 'plot' proper, though, as far as we know, such a case has never arisen."

> If Twelfth Night were copyrighted, it is quite possible that a second comer might so closely imitate Sir Toby Belch or Malvolio as to infringe, but it would not be enough that for one of his characters he cast a riotous knight who kept wassail to the discomfort of the household, or a vain and foppish steward who became amorous of his mistress.... [T]he less developed the characters, the less they can be copyrighted; that is the penalty an author must bear for marking them too indistinctly.

Nichols v. Universal Pictures Corp., 45 F.2d 119, 121 (2d Cir.1930), *cert. denied,* 282 U.S. 902, 51 S.Ct. 216, 75 L.Ed. 795 (1931). *See Warner Bros. Inc. v. Film Ventures Int'l,* 403 F.Supp. 522, 525 (C.D.Cal.1975) (recognizing the need for distinctive delineation of a character).

Van Druten is neither Malvolio nor Mickey Mouse; Brown is neither Sir Toby Belch nor Superman. The "Cargo" characters are depicted only by three- or four-line summaries in the "Cargo" treatment and screenplay, plus whatever insight into their characters may be derived from their dialogue and action.

Although such lightly sketched characters may be descriptive enough to sustain a finding of infringement where other *Berkic* factors are also copied, "Cargo" contained no descriptions which could be sufficient to afford copyright protection to a character taken alone. Olson's argument that substantial similarity should be found because of similarities between the ensemble of characters in "Cargo" and the characters in "The A–Team" also fails under *Warner Bros. Warner Bros.* found no possibility of infringement even though the author used the group of characters that he had employed in the "The Maltese Falcon." *See id.* at 948, 950.

We therefore uphold the district court's grant of j.n.o.v. to defendants on the ground that "The A–Team" and "Cargo" are not substantially similar under the extrinsic test.

Olson claims, in essence, that the defendants took his characters and his format for an action-adventure series. However, copyright law affords no protection to the format proposed by Olson. Nor may we find copyright infringement based upon a comparison of the characters in "Cargo" to those in "The A–Team," both because the "Cargo" characters were drawn so thinly and because the characters of "The A–Team" differed in significant ways from those in "Cargo."

There thus existed no substantial similarity under the extrinsic test. The intrinsic test likewise produces no basis for recovery. Although a reasonable jury might have found substantial similarity in "the total concept and feel of the works," *Litchfield,* 736 F.2d at 1357, and considerable deference is due to a jury's finding of substantial similarity under the intrinsic test, *Krofft,* 562 F.2d at 1166, "no substantial similarity may be found under the intrinsic test where analytic dissection demonstrates that all similarities in expression arise from the use of common ideas," *Aliotti,* 831 F.2d at 901 (*citing McCulloch v. Albert E. Price, Inc.,* 823 F.2d 316, 320–21 (9th Cir.1987)). Because those similarities that do exist arose from unprotectable scenes a faire, there exists no substantial similarity of protectable expression under the intrinsic test.

II. *The Cannell Defendants' Claim for Attorneys' Fees.*

The Cannell defendants appeal the district court's denial of their request for attorneys' fees of $352,365, claiming that the court erred by failing to apply an "even-handed" approach to attorneys' fees in copyright cases. They do not argue that the district court erred in concluding that they were not entitled to attorneys' fees under a standard requiring a showing of bad faith or frivolity.

The Cannell defendants claim that Olson has waived his claim that the district court erroneously granted them an extension of time to file their notice of appeal because he failed to include this claim in his opening brief. However, claims of defects in subject matter jurisdiction may be raised at any time, either by the parties or sua sponte by the court...

We find that the Cannell defendants timely sought and obtained an extension under Fed.R.App.P. 4(a)(5). Although the district court filed its nunc pro tunc j.n.o.v. on December 8, 1986, the judgment was not entered until December 15, 1986. Under Fed.R.App.P. 4(a)(1), a party must appeal within 30 days of the time that the judgment is entered. Under Fed.R.App.P. 4(a)(5), the district court "upon a showing of excusable neglect or good cause" may within 30 days after expiration of the time for filing extend the time for filing a notice of appeal, subject to certain time limitations. The district court, in an order stating that good cause had been shown, on February 11, 1987 extended the period in which notice of appeal could be filed until February 13, 1987. Because February 11, 1987 was within 60 days of December 15, 1986, the district court had power to grant an extension; the two extra days did not exceed the permissible period of extension. We therefore find that the notice of appeal was timely filed and that we have jurisdiction to consider the appeal...

Any decision to overrule these cases and to adopt an even-handed approach must be made by an en banc court. We therefore affirm the district court's decision to deny attorneys' fees to the Cannell defendants.

III. *Conclusion.*

We affirm the district court's grant of j.n.o.v. to defendants on the ground that there existed no substantial similarity of ideas or protectable expression. Our ruling makes it unnecessary for us to determine whether Olson could seek to have the Cannell defendants held liable as innocent infringers, whether the district court properly granted a new trial in the alternative, or whether certain evidence and testimony should be admitted at any new trial. We also affirm the district court's order refusing the Cannell defendants' request for attorneys' fees.

AFFIRMED.

NASH v. CBS, INC.
United States Court of Appeals for the Seventh Circuit
January 24, 1990, Argued; April 23, 1990, Decided
No. 89-1823
899 F.2d 1537

EASTERBROOK, Circuit Judge.

John Dillinger, Public Enemy No. 1, died on July 22, 1934, at the Biograph Theater in Chicago. He emerged from the air conditioned movie palace into a sweltering evening accompanied by two women, one wearing a bright red dress. The "lady in red", Anna Sage, had agreed to betray his presence for $10,000. Agents of the FBI were waiting. Alerted by Polly Hamilton, the other woman, Dillinger wheeled to fire, but it was too late. A hail of bullets cut him down, his .45 automatic unused. William C. Sullivan, *The Bureau* 30–33 (1979). Now a national historic site, the Biograph bears a plaque commemorating the event. It still shows movies, and the air conditioning is no better now than in 1934.

Jay Robert Nash believes that Dillinger did not die at the Biograph. In *Dillinger: Dead or Alive?* (1970), and *The Dillinger Dossier* (1983), Nash maintains that Dillinger learned about the trap and dispatched Jimmy Lawrence, a small-time hoodlum who looked like him, in his stead. The FBI, mortified that its set-up had no sting, kept the switch quiet. Nash points to discrepancies between Dillinger's physical characteristics and those of the corpse: Dillinger had a scar on his upper lip and the corpse did not; Dillinger lacked a tooth that the corpse possessed; Dillinger had blue eyes, the corpse brown eyes; Dillinger's eyebrows were thicker than those of the corpse. Although Dillinger's sister identified the dead man, Nash finds the circumstances suspicious, and he is struck by the decision of Dillinger's father to encase the corpse in concrete before burial. As part of the cover-up, according to Nash, the FBI planted Dillinger's fingerprints in the morgue. After interviewing many persons connected with Dillinger's gang and the FBI's pursuit of it, Nash tracked Dillinger to the west coast, where Dillinger married and lay low. Nash believes that he survived at least until 1979. *The Dillinger Dossier* contains pictures of a middle-aged couple and then an elderly man who, Nash believes, is Dillinger in dotage. Nash provides capsule versions of his conclusions in his *Bloodletters and Badmen: A Narrative Encyclopedia of American Criminals from the Pilgrims to the Present* (1973), and his exposé *Citizen Hoover* (1972).

Nash's reconstruction of the Dillinger story has not won adherents among historians—or the FBI. Someone in Hollywood must have read *The Dillinger Dossier,* however, because in 1984 CBS broadcast an episode of its

Simon and Simon series entitled *The Dillinger Print. Simon and Simon* featured brothers Rick and A.J. Simon, private detectives in San Diego. The district court summarized the episode, 704 F.Supp. 823, 828–29 (N.D.Ill.1989):

The opening scene of The [Dillinger] Print shows Ty Becker, a retired FBI agent, telling his grandchildren about Dillinger's life and the shooting outside the Biograph Theater on July 22, 1934. Ty also mentions that he doubts Dillinger was the man who was shot that night and vows to track him down some day. After the grandchildren leave with his daughter Addie, an intruder breaks into Ty's home, steals an old gun which once belonged to Dillinger, and kills Ty with the gun.

Concerned that the police would regard Ty's death as a typical murder incident to burglary rather than related to moonlighting she suspected he was performing for the FBI, Addie hires the Simons. Next, Addie goes to the bank to remove her father's safety deposit box. While she is in the vault, a masked man, wearing 1930s-style spectator shoes, shoots tear gas into the bank and steals Ty's safety deposit box. The Simons arrive at the bank soon thereafter and pick up the thief's gun, which turns out to be the Dillinger gun stolen from Ty's house. Police investigation later reveals that the gun bears the fresh fingerprint of John Dillinger.

The Simons are next seen purchasing newspapers which are carrying the story that Dillinger may be alive. As the Simons discuss the case, A.J. reads from a book entitled "Twentieth Century Desperadoes." He implies that some evidence supports the idea Dillinger is alive and relates to Rick several physical discrepancies between Dillinger and the corpse described in the 1934 autopsy. Nash cites the same discrepancies in his books.

Numerous Dillinger impostors soon come forward, and the FBI enters the case. However, FBI Agent Kinneman, who is a friend of A.J.'s, informs the Simons that Ty Becker was not working for the FBI at the time of his death.

The scene then switches to a health club. As A.J. and Kinneman are playing racquetball, a man wearing a trench coat and spectator shoes enters the club and, from the viewing area, sprays a salvo of bullets over A.J. and Kinneman. Afterwards, A.J. solemnly swears revenge against Dillinger or whoever tried to shoot him.

The next day, the Simons visit the police station and discover that "leads" regarding Dillinger's whereabouts have poured in from all over the world. They agree to check out a few leads, including one that takes them to a dentist in San Diego. The dentist rejects the Simons' suggestion that Dillinger lives in his house and attributes the police tip to a crazy woman who lives across the street.

The Simons and Addie then pay a visit to Ty Becker's old secretary, who informs them that Ty was working on an internal FBI investigation at the time he was killed. Immediately thereafter, the Simons and Addie receive a call from

Kinneman, who tells them that "there is more truth to this" Dillinger affair than anyone had imagined and that the Simons should meet him at a closed-down theater.

When the Simons and Addie enter the theater, a gangster documentary is playing. Kinneman and a man wearing spectator shoes shoot at the trio. The Simons eventually kill the man in spectator shoes. They then subdue Kinneman, who admits to killing Ty Becker in order to stop the internal investigation which, it turns out, was directed at Kinneman, and to leaving the fake Dillinger fingerprint on the gun at the bank.

In the penultimate scene, the FBI thanks the Simons for their help in arresting Kinneman and solving the Dillinger mystery. Rick nevertheless insists Dillinger may be alive and perhaps living in Oregon.... The episode closes with a teaser: the dentist, one of the leads whom the Simons had interviewed earlier in the program, is seen pushing his elderly father in a wheelchair and admonishing him to refrain from discussing the "old days in Chicago" anymore.

Nash filed this suit seeking damages on the theory that *The Dillinger Print* violates his copyrights in the four books setting out his version of Dillinger's escape from death and new life on the west coast. The district court determined that the books' copyrighted material consists in Nash's presentation and exposition, not in any of the historical events. 691 F.Supp. 140 (N.D.Ill.1988). CBS then moved for summary judgment, conceding for this purpose both access to Nash's books and copying of the books' factual material. The court granted this motion, 704 F.Supp. 823, holding that *The Dillinger Print* did not appropriate any of the material protected by Nash's copyrights.

CBS's concession removes from this case two questions that bedevil copyright litigation. See *Selle v. Gibb,* 741 F.2d 896, 901–02 (7th Cir.1984). It leaves the questions whether the copier used matter that the copyright law protects and, if so, whether it took "too much" (that is, more than allowed by the "fair use" doctrine codified in 17 U.S.C. § 107). See *Atari, Inc. v. North American Philips Consumer Electronics Corp.,* 672 F.2d 607, 614–17 (7th Cir.1982); *Toksvig v. Bruce Pub. Co.,* 181 F.2d 664 (7th Cir.1950). These latter questions have proven especially difficult when, as in this case, the copier works in a medium different from the original.

Learned Hand, whose opinions still dominate this corner of the law, observed in *Nichols v. Universal Pictures Corp.,* 45 F.2d 119, 121 (2d Cir.1930), that all depends on the level of abstraction at which the court conceives the interest protected by the copyright. If the court chooses a low level (say, only the words the first author employed), then a copier may take the plot, exposition, and all other original material, even though these may be the most important ingredients of the first author's contribution. As a practical matter this would mean that anyone could produce the work in a new medium without compensating the original author, despite the statute's grant to the author of the privilege to make "derivative works". If on the other hand the court should select a high level of abstraction, the first author may claim protection for whole genres of work ("the romantic novel" or, more modestly, any story involving doomed young lovers from warring clans, so that a copyright on *Romeo and Juliet* would cover *West Side Story* too)... Sometimes called the "abstractions test", Hand's insight is not a "test" at all. It is a clever way to pose the difficulties that require courts to avoid either extreme of the continuum of generality. It does little to help resolve a given case, even when melded with Hand's further observation, in cases such as *Peter Pan Fabrics, Inc. v. Martin Weiner Corp.,* 274 F.2d 487, 489 (2d Cir.1960), that one may ask what the "ordinary observer" would think are the essential parts of the two works' "aesthetic appeal". See also *Selle,* 741 F.2d at 903–05. Who is the "ordinary" observer, and how does this person choose the level of generality? Ordinary observers, like reasonable men in torts, are fictitious characters of the law, reminders that judges must apply objective tests rather than examine their own perceptions. They do not answer the essential question: at what level of generality? After 200 years of wrestling with copyright questions, it is unlikely that courts will come up with the answer any time soon, if indeed there is "an" answer, which we doubt.

Hand returned again and again to the opposing forces that make the formulation of a single approach so difficult. Intellectual (and artistic) progress is possible only if each author builds on the work of others. No one invents even a tiny fraction of the ideas that make up our cultural heritage. Once a work has been written and published, any rule requiring people to compensate the author slows progress in literature and art, making useful expressions "too expensive", forcing authors to re-invent the wheel, and so on. Every work uses scraps of thought from thousands of predecessors, far too many to compensate even if the legal system were frictionless, which it isn't. Because any new work depends on others even if unconsciously, broad protection of intellectual property also creates a distinct possibility that the cost of litigation—old authors trying to get a "piece of the action" from current successes—will prevent or penalize the production of new works, even though the claims be rebuffed. Authors as a group therefore might prefer limited protection for their writings—they gain in the ability to use others' works more than they lose in potential royalties. See William M. Landes & Richard A. Posner, *An Economic Analysis of Copyright Law,* 18 J. Legal Studies 325, 332–33, 349–59 (1989).

Yet to deny authors all reward for the value their labors contribute to the works of others *also* will lead to inefficiently little writing, just as surely as excessively broad rights will do. The prospect of reward is an important stimulus for thinking and writing, especially for persons such as Nash who are full-time authors. Before the first work is published, broad protection of intellectual property seems best; after it is published, narrow protection seems best. At each instant some new works are in progress, and every author is simultaneously a creator in part and a borrower in part. In these roles, the same person has different objectives. Yet only one rule can be in force. This single rule must achieve as much as possible of these inconsistent demands. Neither Congress nor the courts has the information that would allow it to determine which is best. Both institutions must muddle through, using not a fixed rule but a sense of the consequences of moving dramatically in either direction.

If Nash had written a novel that another had translated into a screenplay, this would be a difficult case. Although *The Dillinger Print* is substantially original, it does not matter that almost all of the second author's expression is new. "[N]o plagiarist can excuse the wrong by showing how much of his work he did not pirate." *Sheldon v. Metro–Goldwyn Pictures Corp.,* 81 F.2d 49, 56 (2d Cir.1936) (L. Hand, J.). The TV drama took from Nash's works the idea that Dillinger survived and retired to the west coast, and employed many of the ingredients that Nash used to demonstrate that the man in the Cook County morgue was not Dillinger. CBS even used one of Nash's books as a prop: "Twentieth Century Desperadoes" in *The Dillinger Print* is a ringer for Nash's *Bloodletters and Badmen.* To see that *The Dillinger Print* is in a sense a "derivative work", we need only imagine how we would react if Nash had written a short story based on the premise that Dillinger was really a woman masquerading as a man, and CBS had used a switch in sex roles as the centerpiece of a drama. In such an event we would need to decide, as Hand did in *Sheldon,* whether the portions CBS took over were qualitatively so important that the original author's market would be diminished excessively by a rule allowing similar appropriations in the regular course.

Nash does not portray *The Dillinger Dossier* and its companion works as fiction, however, which makes all the difference. The inventor of Sherlock Holmes controls that character's fate while the copyright lasts; the first person to conclude that Dillinger survived does not get dibs on history. If Dillinger survived, that fact is available to all. Nash's rights lie in his expression: in his words, in his arrangement of facts (his deployment of narration interspersed with interviews, for example), but not in the naked "truth". *The Dillinger Print* does not use any words from *The Dillinger Dossier* or Nash's other books; it does not take over any of Nash's presentation but instead employs a setting of its own invention with new exposition and development. Physical differences between Dillinger and the corpse, planted fingerprints, photographs of Dillinger and other gangsters in the 1930s, these and all the rest are facts as Nash depicts them. (Nash did not take the photographs and has no rights in them; *The Dillinger Print* used the photos but not Nash's arrangement of them.)

The cases closest to ours are not plays translated to the movie screen (as in *Sheldon*) but movies made from speculative works representing themselves as fact. For example, Universal made a motion picture based on the premise that an idealistic crewman planted a bomb that destroyed the dirigible

Hindenburg on May 6, 1937. The theory came straight from A.A. Hoehling's *Who Destroyed the Hindenburg?* (1962), a monograph based on exhaustive research. The motion picture added sub-plots and development, but the thesis and the evidence adduced in support of it could be traced to Hoehling. Nonetheless, the Second Circuit concluded that this did not infringe Hoehling's rights, because the book placed the facts (as opposed to Hoehling's exposition) in the public domain. *Hoehling v. Universal City Studios, Inc.,* 618 F.2d 972 (1980). See also *Miller v. Universal City Studios* (facts about a notorious kidnapping are not protected by copyright). Cf. *Musto v. Meyer,* 434 F.Supp. 32 (S.D.N.Y.1977) (idea for *The Seven Per Cent Solution* derived from article in medical journal).

Hoehling suggested that "[t]o avoid a chilling effect on authors who contemplate tackling an historical issue or event, broad latitude must be granted to subsequent authors who make use of historical subject matter, including theories or plots". 618 F.2d at 978. As our opinion in *Toksvig* shows, we are not willing to say that "anything goes" as long as the first work is about history. *Toksvig* held that the author of a biography of Hans Christian Andersen infringed the copyright of the author of an earlier biography by using portions of Andersen's letters as well as some of the themes and structure. *Hoehling* rejected *Toksvig,* see 618 F.2d at 979, concluding that "[k]nowledge is expanded ... by granting new authors of historical works a relatively free hand to build upon the work of their predecessors." *Id.* at 980 (footnote omitted). With respect for our colleagues of the east, we think this goes to the extreme of looking at incentives only *ex post.* The authors in *Hoehling* and *Toksvig* spent years tracking down leads. If all of their work, right down to their words, may be used without compensation, there will be too few original investigations, and facts will not be available on which to build.

In *Toksvig* the first author, who knew Danish, spent three years learning about Andersen's life; the second author, who knew no Danish, wrote her biography in less than a year by copying out of the first book scenes and letters that the original author discovered or translated. Reducing the return on such effort, by allowing unhindered use, would make the initial leg-work less attractive and so less frequent. Copyright law does not protect hard work (divorced from expression), and hard work is not an essential ingredient of copyrightable expression (see *Rockford Map*); to the extent *Toksvig* confuses work or ideas with expression, it has been justly criticized. *Rosemont Enterprises, Inc. v. Random House, Inc.,* 366 F.2d 303, 310 (2d Cir.1966); *Miller v. Universal City Studios,* 650 F.2d at 1371; William F. Patry, *The Fair Use Privilege in Copyright Law* 65–70 (1985). See also *Eisenschiml v. Fawcett Publications, Inc.,* 246 F.2d 598, 604 (7th Cir.1957) (recognizing both that any two treatments of the same historical subject will be similar because the facts limit the author's freedom, and that a scholar is entitled to use a predecessor's work). We need not revisit *Toksvig* on its own facts to know that it is a mistake to hitch up at *either* pole of the continuum between granting the first author a right to forbid all similar treatments of history and granting the second author a right to use anything he pleases of the first's work. Cf. *New Era Publications v. Henry Holt & Co.,* 873 F.2d 576 (2d Cir.), rehearing en banc denied, 884 F.2d 659 (1989).

Authors of fiction do not (necessarily) need greater incentives than authors of non-fiction. Users of and elaborators on works of non-fiction are not (necessarily) more easily dissuaded than are those who use or elaborate on works of fiction. Decisions such as *Hoehling* do not come straight from first principles. They depend, rather, on the language of what is now 17 U.S.C. § 102(b): "In no case does copyright protection for an original work ... extend to any idea, ... or discovery, regardless of the form in which it is described, explained, illustrated, or embodied in such work." Long before the 1976 revision of the statute, courts had decided that historical facts are among the "ideas" and "discoveries" that the statute does not cover. *International News Service v. Associated Press,* 248 U.S. 215, 234, 39 S.Ct. 68, 71, 63 L.Ed. 211 (1918). This is not a natural law; Congress could have made copyright broader (as patent law is). But it is *law,* which will come as no surprise to Nash. His own books are largely fresh expositions of facts looked up in other people's books...

The producers of *Simon and Simon* used Nash's work as Nash has used others': as a source of facts and ideas, to which they added their distinctive overlay. As the district court found, CBS did no more than § 102(b) permits. Because *The Dillinger Print* uses Nash's analysis of history but none of his expression, the judgment is

AFFIRMED.

SHAW v. LINDHEIM

United States District Court for the Central District of California
September 4, 1992, Decided; September 4, 1992, Filed
CV 87-06926 AHS
809 F.Supp. 1393

Like his character "The Equalizer," plaintiff Lou Shaw has been attempting to "equalize the odds" against him in a five-year court battle that has taken him from this Court to the Ninth Circuit and back again.

Lou Shaw is a well-known writer and producer in Hollywood; defendant Richard Lindheim is an entertainment industry executive who was in the Dramatic Programming Division of NBC Television when he entered into a February, 1978 option contract with Shaw granting NBC the option to develop a pilot script created by Shaw, "The Equalizer," into a television series; defendant Michael Sloan wrote the pilot script for defendants' television series "The Equalizer" in 1982, the pilot episode of which aired on CBS in 1985.

As this Court described previously, "[t]he theme of both [plaintiff's script and defendants' pilot episode] revolves around the main character, the Equalizer—'a man who will equalize the odds, a lone man working outside the system to protect his underdog clients and to resolve their predicaments as a part of his rough notion of justice ...' both works involve a cover up/ blackmail conspiracy and a woman who is in jeopardy, however, in defendants' work the main character takes on two cases whereas [Shaw's] Equalizer has only one client ... both works involve a criminal organization that blackmails a public official. The defendants' Equalizer, however, involves a tight blackmail ring, operated out of the corporate headquarters of a telecommunications company in New York City, whereas [Shaw's] criminal organization is described as a Mafia that controls the Boyle Heights Chicano Community of Los Angeles." *Shaw v. Lindheim,* 919 F.2d 1353, 1357–58 (9th Cir.1990) (quoting this Court's Order). The lead characters in both plaintiff's and defendants' works also contain various similarities: "[i]n defendants' story, McCall, the former spy turned Equalizer is motivated by past wrongs and seems intent on helping any underprivileged person who face insurmountable odds. [Shaw's] lead character, Jericho, also seeks to prevent injustice ... both are well educated, wealthy and have expensive tastes...." *Id.* at 1358 (quoting this Court's Order).

On November 17, 1987, Shaw filed this action for, among other claims, copyright infringement, alleging that defendants Sloan and Lindheim copied his 1978 script to produce "The Equalizer" television series, which was substantially similar to the script he submitted to Lindheim. Defendants moved for summary judgment on August 8, 1988. This Court granted defendants' motion on October

28, 1988, finding that as a matter of law the protectible expression in the works was not substantially similar under the intrinsic or subjective test of *Sid & Marty Krofft Television Prods. Inc. v. McDonald's Corp.,* 562 F.2d 1157, 1164 (9th Cir.1977).

The Ninth Circuit reversed and remanded, concluding that since Shaw had "satisfied the extrinsic [or objective] test for [copyright infringement] of literary works" he "presented a triable issue of fact regarding substantial similarity of protected expression." *Shaw,* 919 F.2d at 1363.

On remand, plaintiff pursued only his copyright infringement claim and the parties stipulated that plaintiff's action was based solely on the alleged infringement of his "Equalizer" script by defendants' pilot episode of "The Equalizer" television series.

II.
THE TRIAL

At trial upon remand, the parties presented the following stipulated facts to the jury: (1) that Lou Shaw wrote a script entitled "The Equalizer," which he registered at the Copyright Office on September 25, 1987; (2) that Mr. Shaw filed a supplemental registration for the work on October 20, 1988, advising the Copyright Office that his script was derived from an earlier outline or "treatment" also authored by him, a fact which was not known to or considered by this Court or the Court of Appeals when it reviewed this Court's grant of summary judgment; (3) that Universal City Studios, Inc., registered the pilot episode of "The Equalizer" television series with the Copyright Office on November 26, 1985, listing Universal as the author; and (4) defendant Sloan received sole "written by" credit while Sloan and Lindheim both received co-"created by" credit for the pilot episode of "The Equalizer" which aired September 28, 1985.

In order to prove the works' "substantial similarity," plaintiff presented the following evidence during the liability phase of trial: the testimony of expert witness Linda Seger, who asserted that a cumulation of various individual similarities between plaintiff's script and defendants' pilot episode existed, i.e., both have "similar settings[:] ... a high rise apartment, ... an elegant living room, a restaurant, a roof top, a formal party, a police station, truck on the road ... a large city," both characters are described in terms of contradictions such as " 'ruthless,' 'deadly,' 'sympathetic,' 'comforter,' 'sentimentalist,' 'realist,' 'idealist,' and 'cynic,' " both start with "a very strong action scene, then [ ] a relationship scene," and both contain a "killing of a Hispanic man" within the first twenty seconds. R.T. at 601–02, 610, 615.

In order to prove actual copying of his script by the author of defendants' work, plaintiff produced the following: (1) the testimony of

Lindheim that he had read plaintiff's script at NBC (R.T. at 498); (2) the testimony of Peter Andrews, who worked with Lindheim at NBC, which indicated that Lindheim intended to take "The Equalizer" script with him when he left NBC (R.T. at 145, 148); and (3) an argument in closing that since the 1981 Lindheim/Sloan story outline or treatment contained similar ideas to those included in the Shaw 1978 treatment, impermissible copying of plaintiff's script by defendants was established (R.T. at 208).

In rebuttal, defendants (1) offered the deposition testimony of plaintiff, in which he indicated that he had "pretty well developed what would be the lead character, and the supporting characters, and the villains, and the basic plot" in his treatment for later use in the allegedly infringed script (R.T. at 312); (2) elicited an admission from plaintiff on cross-examination that he never showed his script to defendant Sloan and had no knowledge that the script was ever shown to anyone but Lindheim (R.T. at 322); and (3) relied on the testimony of Lindheim that he had never seen plaintiff's treatment, he took no scripts with him when he left NBC, he never stated, as Mr. Andrews testified, that he would not leave NBC with such "gems" as Shaw's "Equalizer" or that he "had plans for 'The Equalizer' " himself upon leaving NBC and he provided only the rough concept of the pilot episode's script to defendant Sloan, who was the sole author of that script (R.T. at 497, 507, 545, 560, 568, 576). Moreover, as to the issue of substantial similarity, defendants proffered the expert testimony of Arnold Margolin to the effect that no "significant or meaningful similarities [ ] existed outside of the genre ... outside of commonplace scenes or scenes a faire. That is, scenes that [ ] follow out of the genre ... scenes that you would necessarily expect to see in the movie, given the subject matter of the movie." (R.T. at 849).

At the close of the evidence, the Court instructed the jury that in order for plaintiff Shaw to prevail, he "must prove: (1) that he is the owner of a federal copyright in the script that he claims was infringed; (2) that the actual concrete elements of the pilot episode of the television series 'The Equalizer' (that is, its plot, theme, characters, dialogue, mood, setting, pace and sequence of events) are substantially similar to the actual concrete elements in plaintiff's script; (3) that the pilot episode of the television series 'The Equalizer' is substantially similar to the protectible expression in plaintiff's script, that is, that a reasonable lay viewer watching the pilot episode of 'The Equalizer' would find that it had captured the 'total concept and feel' of plaintiff's script, i.e., it was a 'dramatization' or 'picturization' of the protectible expression in plaintiff's script; and (4) that the author or authors of the pilot episode of 'The Equalizer' actually copied substantial original and protectible expression from the plaintiff's script in creating the pilot episode, rather than creating the pilot episode independently of plaintiff's script."

Specifically, the Court instructed that "[i]n order for the plaintiff to prove that his script and [the] TV Pilot are substantially similar with regard to the protectible expression contained in plaintiff's script, a two-part test must be satisfied.... Under [the objective] test, you should focus on the various concrete elements of the two works, that is, the objective manifestations of creativity, which include plot, theme, dialogue, mood, setting, pace, character and sequence of events. Under the 'objective' test, analytic dissection and expert testimony are appropriate. [The subjective] test requires you, as an audience of ordinary, reasonable persons, to make a subjective judgment as to whether the two works are or are not similar. You must determine if the defendants' TV Pilot captured the 'total concept and feel' of plaintiff's script, that is, whether the TV Pilot constitutes a dramatization or picturization of the protectible expression in plaintiff's script."

With regard to the element of copying, the Court instructed that "even where two works are substantially similar under both the objective and subjective tests, no amount of substantial similarity will suffice to prove infringement unless the defendant actually copied protectible expression from plaintiff's script. An inference of copying may arise if plaintiff proves (a) that the author of defendants' episode had access to plaintiff's script, and (b) that plaintiff's script and the defendants' episode contain similarities that in the normal course of events could not be expected to arise independently in the two works."

In the first (liability) phase of trial, the jury returned a verdict in favor of plaintiff on the remaining claim of copyright infringement. On the Special Verdict Form, the jury answered in the affirmative to the following interrogatories: (1) "[d]o you find that the TV Episode of 'The Equalizer' against which the plaintiff alleges copyright infringement ... is substantially similar to the original and protectible expression in Plaintiff's Script, when compared and analyzed *objectively* under the law?"; (2) "[d]o you find that its intended audience would consider that the TV Episode captured the 'total concept and feel' of Plaintiff's Script, that is, whether the TV Episode constitutes a 'dramatization' or 'picturization' of the original and protectible expression in Plaintiff's Script, when compared *subjectively* under the law?"; and (3) "[i]f you find that the TV Episode is substantially similar to the original and protectible expression in Plaintiff's Script, do you find that such substantial similarity resulted from copying of Plaintiff's Script by the author or authors of the TV Episode under the law?"

Defendants brought a motion for judgment as a matter of law thereafter on April 21, 1992, and a motion for new trial on April 22, 1992, both before the second (damages) phase of trial. Plaintiff filed opposition to both motions on April 29, 1992. Defendants filed replies on May 6, 1992. The Court heard oral argument on the motions on May 11, 1992. At the hearing, the Court granted defendants' motion for judgment as a matter of law and conditionally granted their motion for new trial.

The Court now issues this opinion in order to clarify the circumstances under which a trial court may grant judgment as a matter of law in a copyright infringement action under *Shaw.*

III.
THE APPLICABLE STANDARDS

Fed.R.Civ.P. 50(b) states that a motion for judgment as a matter of law made at the close of the evidence may be "renewed by service and filing not later than 10 days after entry of judgment."

IV.
THE PARTIES' CONTENTIONS
A. Motion for Judgment as a Matter of Law

Defendants argued that judgment as a matter of law should be entered in their favor because there was insufficient evidence for a reasonable jury applying the appropriate legal principles to have found that the parties' works were substantially similar under the objective test or that defendant Sloan, the author of defendants' TV episode, had access to the protectible expression embodied in plaintiff's script. They urged that juror confusion was inevitable, based on plaintiff counsel's arguments which confused the issues of substantial similarity with copying and indicated that the jurors should compare the parties' two unregistered treatments rather than the relevant script and TV episode.

With regard to their contention that insufficient similarities between the protected expression in the parties' works were evidenced to support the jury's verdict, defendants argued that: (1) under *Feist Publications, Inc. v. Rural Telephone Service Company, Inc.,* 499 U.S. 340, ——, 111 S.Ct. 1282, 1289, 113 L.Ed.2d 358, 371 (1991), copyright protection extends only to those protectible aspects of plaintiff's script which are original to the script, and pursuant to 17 U.S.C. § 103(b), these aspects did not include those which were original to the underlying work from which it was derived, i.e., plaintiff's treatment; and (2) since plaintiff never registered the underlying treatment, a prerequisite to bringing suit for copyright infringement in accordance with 17 U.S.C. § 411(a), he cannot assert a claim or recover for infringement of protectible expression original to that treatment. Finally, they contended that plaintiff's expert Dr. Seger's testimony missed the point of the extrinsic test for substantial similarity, since it (1) focused on the cumulative nature of individual similarities rather than the substantial similarity of protectible expression and (2) suggested that evidence of actual copying of unprotected elements would support a finding of substantial similarity as to elements of protectible expression.

Dr. Seger's testimony was particularly confusing and irrelevant, defendants contended, because: (1) in contravention of *Feist,* 499 U.S. at ——, 111 S.Ct. at 1294, 113 L.Ed.2d at 377 and *Berkic v. Crichton,* 761 F.2d 1289, 1293 (9th Cir.1985), she focused on the similarity of discrete concrete elements rather than the similarity of the selection, coordination, arrangement or total sequence of events created by those elements; (2) she relied on comparisons of unprotected ordinary phrases to show similarity (*See Narell v. Freeman,* 872 F.2d 907, 911 (9th Cir.1989) (cliche phrases not protected)); (3) she relied on plaintiff's word pictures of characters who merely served to move the story along, and therefore were not protectible elements under *Warner Brothers, Inc. v. ABC, Inc.,* 720 F.2d 231, 240 (2d Cir.1983) and *Columbia Pictures Corp. v. NBC, Inc.,* 137 F.Supp. 348, 353 (S.D.Cal.1955); (4) she impermissibly "split characters" in fragmented comparisons of characters in both works in contravention of *Rose v. Connelly,* 38 F.Supp. 54, 55–56 (S.D.N.Y.1941) and *Twentieth Century Fox Film Corp. v. MCA, Inc.,* 715 F.2d 1327, 1330 (9th Cir.1983); (5) she used a montage of photographs arranged out of sequence to support her conclusions of similarity, a practice which the court in *Litchfield v. Spielberg,* 736 F.2d 1352, 1356 (9th Cir.1984) deemed "inherently suggestive and unreliable;" (6) she failed to limit her testimony to a comparison of protectible expression; and (7) she relied on "impressions" created by reading between the lines of the script or imagining what plaintiff could have created through a rewrite.

In short, defendants argued that (1) plaintiff has very little protectible expression in his script, as most of it flows from the genre and constitutes unprotectible scenes a faire; (2) if any protectible expression exists, it was derived from the treatment and therefore is not original to the script (and cannot be sued upon); and (3) even if the derivative works argument is not accepted, as a matter of law the script does not contain any protectible expression which was infringed by defendants' episode.

Moreover, they contended that plaintiff has produced no evidence that the author of the protectible expression in the TV episode (Sloan) had a reasonable opportunity to access plaintiff's registered script so that he could have actually copied it. *See Meta–Film Associates, Inc. v. MCA, Inc.,* 586 F.Supp. 1346, 1355 (C.D.Cal.1984). At the most, defendants urged, plaintiff showed that Lindheim had access to plaintiff's script, but the evidence showed that he was not responsible for creating the protectible expression in defendants' script for the TV episode, since his treatment and contributions to Sloan's writing efforts concerned only very general matters and ideas which were not entitled to copyright protection.

Finally, they distinguished the case's posture at this juncture, and ripeness for decision as a matter of law, from its posture at the summary judgment stage by pointing out that: (1) neither this Court on summary judgment nor the Ninth Circuit on review was presented with the derivative work issue, since plaintiff had not filed his amended certificate of copyright registration with regard to his script describing it as a work derivative of his previous treatment until after the motions had been briefed for this Court; (2) the Ninth Circuit's decision expanded the extrinsic test applied by this Court on summary judgment from a comparison of "general ideas" to a comparison of protectible expression in the case of literary works, 919 F.2d at 1357; and (3) the Supreme Court's decision in *Feist,* 499 U.S. at ——, ——, 111 S.Ct. at 1287, 1295, 113 L.Ed.2d at 369, 379, makes clear that (a) the "inverse ratio rule" (the more evidence of uncanny similarities, the less evidence of actual physical access is needed to prove copying) and (b) the Ninth Circuit's consideration in *Shaw* of unprotectible similarities relevant only to the issue of copying when applying the extrinsic test for similarity of protectible expression are both no longer permissible in copyright infringement actions involving literary works.

In opposition, plaintiff argued that the Ninth Circuit's decision in *Shaw* is law of the case, and must be followed by this Court. In other words, he contended that this Court cannot find that plaintiff may not prevail on the basis of substantial similarity when the Ninth Circuit has already indicated that a triable issue of fact exists as to it....

Moreover, plaintiff urged that this case is no different than when the Ninth Circuit considered it: (1) the law at that time provided that a plaintiff must show a defendant had copied protected elements of a work and that the similarity between their works extended to protectible expression, *Shaw,* 919 F.2d at 1356; (2) *Shaw* did not rely on unprotectible similarities such as titles in applying the extrinsic test, and this Court did not instruct the jury to do so either; (3) whether the extrinsic test applied by the Ninth Circuit in *Shaw* was "new" or not, the Ninth Circuit applied it to the facts presented here and found that a triable issue of fact existed as to substantial similarity; and (4) plaintiff's treatment was unregistered at all relevant times during this proceeding, even at the time this court originally considered defendants' motion for summary judgment, so that defendants' "derivative work" argument was always available to them.

Plaintiff refuted on policy grounds defendants' argument that those elements which first appeared in plaintiff's treatment and reappear in the script do not constitute protectible expression when they are included in plaintiff's script, the work derived from plaintiff's treatment. Plaintiff argued that if the contents of all working outlines are unprotected once incorporated into their final form, copyright protection (at least for literary works, where multiple drafts are the norm) would be emasculated. As a general proposition, plaintiff also stated that defendants cannot now expect to succeed on this motion since the jury made all factual findings after being "correctly" instructed with regard to the law, as requested by the defendants.

Finally, plaintiff contended that pursuant to *Bevan v. Columbia Broadcasting System, Inc.,* 329 F.Supp. 601 (S.D.N.Y.1971), the jury had sufficient evidence to find that Sloan had access to plaintiff's work vicariously through Lindheim, who had heard plaintiff "pitch" his treatment and probably obtained a copy of plaintiff's script.

In reply, defendants contended that two exceptions to the law of the case doctrine apply here because: after the Ninth Circuit's decision in *Shaw,* the Supreme Court decided *Feist,* a decision by a higher, controlling authority which "clarified" the law and therefore renders the law of the case doctrine inapplicable in accordance with *Dean v. Trans World Airlines, Inc.,* 924 F.2d 805, 810 (9th Cir.1991) (noting that the doctrine does not bar reconsideration of an issue where controlling authority has since made a contrary decision of law); and this trial has produced substantially different evidence than that which was presented to the Ninth Circuit upon the appeal of this Court's grant of summary judgment. *See United States v. Robinson,* 690 F.2d 869, 872 (11th Cir.1982). Defendants further noted that plaintiff's own testimony at trial supports their position that the script added little protectible expression to that which was already included in his treatment, and therefore the script's copyright protection was extremely limited to that protectible expression which did not appear first in the underlying work. R.T. at 310, 312, 323–24. Moreover, defendants asserted that the Ninth Circuit's recent decision in *Brown Bag Software v. Symantec Corp.,* 960 F.2d 1465, 1477 (9th Cir.1992) indicates that the circuit has backed away from an extreme interpretation of *Shaw* (that summary judgment or judgment as a matter of law is almost never available in a copyright case) to adopt Nimmer's position: "the decision [in *Shaw*] is better viewed as standing for the unremarkable proposition that when objectively speaking a triable case of expressive similarity exists, the case must be sent to the trier of fact." Nimmer § 13.03 [E][3] at 13–78.20. Finally, defendants added that the Supreme Court's opinion in *Feist* has clarified that the focus of copyright protection in works that incorporate pre-existing or unprotectible elements (not just facts in compilations like the one at issue in *Feist,* but stock characters and scenes a faire in literary works) should be whether the arrangement of individual similarities is sufficiently original, and here plaintiff's expert Dr. Seger has only illustrated that disparate similarities as to isolated elements exist.

B. Motion for New Trial

Defendants based their motion for new trial on identified errors of law, misconduct by plaintiff's counsel, insufficiency of the evidence and the existence of accident or surprise which could not have been guarded against through due diligence. Specifically, they urged that: (1) there was insufficient evidence to support the jury's finding of substantial similarity under the objective test; (2) the jury's verdict with regard to the subjective test was against the weight of the evidence, which was probably the result of the jury's confusion over the use of the "total concept and feel" language in the jury instructions, as it intimated that similarity between the two concepts rather than their protectible expression was sufficient to support a finding of substantial similarity; (3) the only evidence of access to plaintiff's script was by Lindheim, a nonwriter of the allegedly infringing TV episode, which is insufficient under *Jason v. Fonda,* 698 F.2d 966, 967 (9th Cir.1982) (a finding of access by an allegedly infringing author must be based on a reasonable possibility of access rather than speculation or conjecture); (4) closing statements made by plaintiff's counsel with regard to "David and Goliath" analogies and plaintiff's as well as his expert witness' inability to work in the entertainment industry again after this trial due to anticipated "industry" retaliation constituted prejudicial misconduct under *Draper v. Airco, Inc.,* 580 F.2d 91, 95 (3d Cir.1978) and *Brownlee v. United Fidelity Insurance Co.,* 117 F.R.D. 383, 386–87 (S.D.Miss.1987), *aff'd without opinion,* 854 F.2d 1319 (5th Cir.1988); (5) the Court's exclusion of Shaw's "Have Gun Will Travel" scripts impaired Lindheim and Margolin's testimony, since the jurors were not able to note for themselves the extent to which plaintiff "borrowed" from the character therein in creating his "Equalizer;" and (6) plaintiff's failure to comply with Fed.R.Civ.P. 26(e)(2) in responding to interrogatories with regard to his witness Mr. Andrews and knowing concealment of Mr. Andrews' address once plaintiff revealed he would call Andrews as a witness prejudiced the defense in the preparation of its case (since they could not reach him to depose him and thereby discover the content of his testimony with regard to defendant Lindheim's reputed admissions that he intended to take plaintiff's "gem," i.e., script, with him when he left Universal).

In opposition, plaintiff asserted: (1) that the evidence of plagiarism was overwhelming, so that both the objective and subjective tests for substantial similarity were supported by the evidence; (2) there was evidence that Lindheim acted as Sloan's intermediary in gaining access to plaintiff's script in order to copy it; (3) plaintiff counsel's closing argument was perfectly accurate as to the relative size of the parties (industry giant defendants versus lone plaintiff writer), but at any rate defendants waived any objection to the argument by not objecting to counsel's remarks at the time they were made and by not requesting a curative instruction be made to the jury, citing *Gonzalez v. Volvo of America Corp.,* 752 F.2d 295, 298 (7th Cir.1985); (4) the Court properly excluded the "Have Gun Will Travel" scripts as cumulative and unduly time consuming; and (5) plaintiff's counsel did not act improperly with regard to Andrews, since

Andrews' previous declaration did not render any documents previously produced untrue and therefore need not have been disclosed pursuant to Fed.R.Civ.P. 26(e)(2)(B) and the correctness of Andrews' local address was of no moment to the defense's case since they did not even search for Andrews in earnest until after the first phase of trial.

In reply, defendants contended that plaintiff's counsel added to the jury's confusion and ensured a verdict against the weight of the evidence by focusing his expert witness' testimony and his closing argument on the evidence of actual copying rather than on the substantial similarity of the protectible expression in both works. Moreover, they stated that they did not waive any objections to plaintiff's closing argument by choosing to address the issue after closing argument and out of the presence of the jury. Finally, they stated that the Andrews situation is prejudicial due to plaintiff counsel's acts of concealment, that the defense's failure to search earnestly for Andrews until after the trial is of no moment and therefore plaintiff's "no harm no foul" argument should not be tolerated.

V.
ANALYSIS
A. Motion for Judgment as a Matter of Law
1. *Summary of Elements of Copyright Infringement*

To prove copyright infringement, plaintiff must prove that his work and defendants' are substantially similar with regard to their protectible expression under both an objective/extrinsic and subjective/intrinsic test, and that the author of defendants' work had a reasonable opportunity to gain access to plaintiff's work in order to actually copy it....

The extrinsic test for substantial similarity of protectible expression in the allegedly infringed and infringing works is an objective analysis of the similarity of the expression of plot, themes, characters, dialogue, mood, setting, pace and sequence of events in the two works, measured by analytic dissection and expert testimony. *Shaw,* 919 F.2d at 1356–57. The intrinsic test measures substantial similarity of protectible expression based on the response of the ordinary reasonable person as to whether the defendants' work captured the "total concept and feel" of plaintiff's work, in other words, whether the allegedly infringing work constituted a "picturization" or "dramatization" of plaintiff's. *Id.* at 1356, 1358. *See also, Litchfield,* 736 F.2d at 1356. A presumption of copying of plaintiff's work by defendants arises where plaintiff offers proof that the author of defendants' work had a reasonable opportunity to gain access to plaintiff's work and the two works are substantially similar in their protectible expression; to rebut the presumption, defendants then must produce evidence which offers an alternative reason for the similarity other than copying (i.e., independent creation). *See Granite Music,* 532 F.2d at 720–721. *See also, Meta–Film Associates,* 586 F.Supp. at 1354–55.

2. *No Evidence as to Similarity or Access*

Plaintiff has failed to produce evidence that the parties' works are substantially similar under the extrinsic test, whether or not plaintiff's script is a "derivative work" of his earlier script. Plaintiff's analysis of alleged similarities between the works, introduced through the testimony of Dr. Seger, indicates that the similarities are between ideas, concepts and other unprotected elements such as stock scenes and aspects of characters which flow naturally from the particular genre or primarily serve a plot function. *See Olson v. National Broadcasting Co., Inc.,* 855 F.2d 1446, 1452–53 (9th Cir.1988) (the less developed the character, the less copyright protection exists).

Moreover, the *script* on which plaintiff sues does not contain protectible expression to the extent it contains elements of protectible expression contained in the *treatment* or underlying work, based on its registered "derivative work" status. *See* 17 U.S.C. § 103(b) ("[t]he copyright in a ... derivative work extends only to the material contributed by the author of such work, as distinguished from the preexisting material employed in the work, and does not imply any exclusive right in the preexisting material.") Contrary to plaintiff's contention that a "work in progress" or draft like plaintiff's treatment cannot be deemed an underlying work and a final product like plaintiff's script a derivative one, 17 U.S.C. § 101 states that "[a] work consisting of editorial revisions, annotations, elaborations or other modifications which, as a whole, represent an original work of authorship, is a derivative work." Even disregarding the derivative work status of plaintiff's script, however, whatever the treatment contributed to the script either constituted mere uncopyrightable ideas or unprotectible scenes a faire. *See* 17 U.S.C. § 102(b) ("[i]n no case does copyright protection for an original work of authorship extend to any idea ... concept, principle or discovery, regardless of the form in which it is described ...").

Plaintiff has also failed to produce evidence of actual copying by the author of defendants' TV episode, defendant Sloan. The evidence presented at trial indicated that defendant Lindheim had read plaintiff's script, although he had not retained it, and that Lindheim added only broad-based verbal suggestions to Sloan when Sloan was writing the script for defendants. R.T. at 497, 545–546, 560, 568, 576. Plaintiff produced no evidence like that adduced in *Bevan,* 329 F.Supp. at 604, 609–10, to the effect that a particular defendant must have received plaintiff's script based on the defendant's (1) placement in the chain of command in an entertainment company that had considered plaintiff's script and (2) participation in the development of the allegedly infringing program. At most, plaintiff Shaw has shown that Lindheim succeeded in transferring what uncopyrightable ideas and concepts he could recall from plaintiff's script to Sloan's. Aside from the identity of the title, which Lindheim testified plaintiff gave him the right to use, plaintiff produced no evidence of striking similarities that would bespeak copying and preclude the possibility of Sloan's independent creation of his script. *See Id.* at 609. In short, plaintiff did not present sufficient evidence for a reasonable jury to find that Sloan had "a reasonable opportunity to view or read plaintiff's [allegedly infringed] work." *Id.* at 604.

3. *Judgment as a Matter of Law at this Juncture*

The Ninth Circuit's decision in *Shaw* does not constitute "law of the case" for purposes of this Court's ruling on defendants' motion for judgment as a matter of law, in light of the substantially different evidence presented at trial upon remand. *See United States v. Robinson,* 690 F.2d 869, 872 (11th Cir.1982). Moreover, judgment as a matter of law at this juncture is consistent with the Ninth Circuit's opinion in *Shaw,* even though the Court determined that in light of the evidence before it at that point this Court's grant of summary judgment in favor of defendants was improper. *Feist,* 499 U.S. 340, —— - ——, 111 S.Ct. 1282, 1295–96, 113 L.Ed.2d 358, 379–80, made clear that a lack of similarity between original protected expression is fatal to a plaintiff's copyright claim; in other words, substantial similarities between unprotected elements, like those presented by plaintiff's expert witness at trial in this case, cannot be used to find substantial similarities in the protectible expression of two works. The Ninth Circuit also has stated recently in *Brown Bag* that *Shaw* merely asserts that when a triable issue of substantial similarity under the objective test exists, a case must be sent to the trier of fact. 960 F.2d at 1476–1477. This indicates that *Shaw* should not be read so stringently as to preclude judgment as a matter of law under all circumstances, particularly in the case of a post-trial judgment as a matter of law where a plaintiff has had the opportunity to present all his evidence to the trier of fact and it still proves insufficient to support his claim.

B. Motion for New Trial

The Court also finds that a conditional grant of the motion for new trial is appropriate since the jury had insufficient evidence to support a finding of similarity under the objective test or access to copy on the part of the defendant author Sloan.

VI.
CONCLUSION

1. The Court grants defendants' motion for judgment as a matter of law. Plaintiff failed to produce sufficient evidence at trial to support a finding by a reasonable jury that plaintiff's script and defendants' TV episode were substantially similar under the extrinsic test or that defendant Sloan, the author of the protectible expression in defendants' allegedly infringing work, had a reasonable opportunity to gain access to plaintiff's script and actually copy it.

Plaintiff's analysis of alleged similarities between the works, introduced through the testimony of Dr. Seger, showed that any similarities between the two works exist with regard to ideas, concepts and other unprotected elements such as stock scenes and aspects of characters which flow naturally from the particular genre or primarily serve a plot function. Moreover, to the extent plaintiff's script contains elements of protectible expression that first appeared in the underlying work (plaintiff's treatment), the script does not enjoy independent copyright protection and plaintiff cannot recover for infringement of those aspects in this action, in light of the script's registered "derivative work" status.

Plaintiff also failed to produce evidence of actual copying by the author of defendants' TV episode, defendant Sloan. The evidence presented at trial indicated that defendant Lindheim had read plaintiff's script, although he had not retained it, and that Lindheim added only broad-based verbal suggestions to Sloan when Sloan was writing the script for defendants. Aside from the identity of the title, plaintiff also lacked evidence of striking similarities that bespeak copying. Accordingly, the Court grants defendants' motion for judgment as a matter of law.

2. The Court conditionally grants defendants' motion for new trial as well, in light of its grant of defendants' motion for judgment as a matter of law and its finding that the jury's verdict was not sufficiently supported by the evidence. *See* Fed.R.Civ.P. 59; Local Rule 15.1.

IT IS SO ORDERED.

FISHER v. VIACOM INT'L INC.
United States District Court for the District of Maryland
August 16, 2000, Decided
Civil No. JFM-00-357
115 F.Supp.2d 535

MOTZ, District Judge.

This case is before the Court on a motion to dismiss filed by the Defendants, Viacom International Inc. and MTV Networks, Inc. [collectively "MTVN"]. The Plaintiff, Steven Fischer, filed a complaint in the Circuit Court for Anne Arundel County, Maryland, on December 4, 1999, asserting claims for breach of contract, violation of the Lanham Act, and breach of confidence. MTVN removed the case to this court on February 4, 2000, and filed its motion to dismiss on April 3, 2000.

I.

In the late 1970s, Steven Fischer created an animated character team called "Steve & Bluey," comprised of "a guy named 'Steve' and his blue dog named 'Bluey.' " This character team served as the basis for numerous copyrighted works between 1989 and 1993, including an unpublished manuscript, *Bluey and His Friend the Bluester,* and a published collection of comic strips titled *There's a Blue Dog Under My Bed.* In 1990, Fischer incorporated Blue Dog Productions, Inc., to publish "Steve & Bluey" stories, and the following year he created a television show for Blue Dog Productions to produce. Over the next three years, Blue Dog Productions searched for production partners and financiers to support the project.

While he was living in London in June 1993, Fischer created a written proposal for a children's animated television series featuring "Steve & Bluey" and submitted the proposal to James Baker, Director of Programmes for Nickelodeon U.K. On July 1, 1993, Baker sent Fischer a letter acknowledging receipt of the proposal and requesting that Viacom be allowed to keep "the details of the series on file for future reference." Fischer responded to Baker's letter on July 7, 1993, with a "more detailed written description of the program, a script for a pilot episode for a half hour children's animated television series, a model sheet (with the characters drawn in different poses), and a character description."

Over the next two months, Viacom and Fischer exchanged correspondence and telephone calls. Viacom allegedly expressed interest in Fischer's idea and encouraged him to develop it. On September 17, 1993, Peter

Press, Vice President and Managing Director of Viacom International Inc., wrote to Fischer suggesting that he contact Nickelodeon representatives in Middlesex, England, to pursue the production of his series. Fischer contacted Kathy Fairbairn, Nickelodeon's Acquisitions and Scheduling Manager, in Middlesex, then produced a five-minute "animatic" videotape of "Steve & Bluey" with Nickelodeon's encouragement. He sent the videotape to Fairbairn on December 15, 1993. On January 14, 1994, Fischer received a letter from Fairbairn, thanking him for the videotape and referring him to Linda Simensky at Nickelodeon in New York, where the bulk of Nickelodeon's animation work occurs. Fischer wrote to Simensky ten days later, and Nickelodeon responded by sending a release for Fischer's signature. At that point, Fischer broke off communications with Nickelodeon. Neither the videotape nor the other materials were ever returned to Fischer.

From 1994 to 1996, Fischer continued to produce "Steve & Bluey" programs for radio and television. A five-part "Steve & Bluey" radio program aired on a Utah radio station in June 1996, and fourteen animated episodes featuring "Steve & Bluey" appeared on TCI–TV between October 1996 and May 1999.

In January 1997, a member of Fischer's family informed him that "his show had been aired on Nickelodeon under the title of 'Blue's Clues' and inquired as to why his name did not appear in the credits." "Blue's Clues" appears on the Nickelodeon channel five days a week and has become one of the most successful children's television programs in history. As described by MTVN, the program is an "interactive play along show" where the host, Steve Burns, asks children to solve puzzles presented by his animated sidekick, a female puppy named Blue. Fischer wrote to Nickelodeon in February 1997 concerning use of his ideas in the "Blue's Clues" program, but MTVN denied any wrongdoing. Fischer alleges that MTVN unlawfully appropriated his ideas to develop the highly successful "Blue's Clues" program, and falsely took credit for the creation of the characters on that show. Moreover, Fischer claims that MTVN's actions[3] amount to a breach of implied contract, breach of confidence, and a violation of the Lanham Act.

II.

MTVN argues first that Fischer's breach of contract and breach of confidence claims must be dismissed on limitations grounds. This case was removed from state court, in part, on diversity grounds. Federal courts exercising diversity jurisdiction must apply the choice-of-law rules of the forum state. Maryland courts generally adhere to the doctrine of *lex loci delicti,* and will apply their own procedural rules, including statutes of limitations, to claims that arise under the substantive law of other states. Fischer's claims, therefore, are subject to Maryland's three-year statute of limitations.

The Maryland Code provides that "[a] civil action at law shall be filed within three years from the date it accrues unless another provision of the Code" applies. Md. Code Ann. Cts. & Judicial Proceedings § 5–101 (1998 & 1999 Supp.). A cause of action "accrues" when the plaintiff had actual knowledge of the wrong or an "awareness implied from a knowledge of circumstances which ought to have put a person of ordinary prudence on inquiry" of the wrong. *See Poffenberger v. Risser,* 290 Md. 631, 635–37, 431 A.2d 677 (1981). This standard, also known as the "discovery rule," is satisfied when: (1) the plaintiff had knowledge of circumstances that would have led a reasonable person in the same circumstances to undertake an investigation; and (2) the investigation, if pursued with reasonable diligence, would have led to knowledge of the alleged wrong. Whether a cause of action is barred by the statute of limitations is usually a mixed question of law and fact that may be taken from the jury when the court determines, as a matter of law, that the plaintiff did not file the suit within the prescribed time.

Here, Fischer's complaint alleges that he became aware of the alleged breaches in January 1997, when a family member told him that "Blue's Clues" had aired on Nickelodeon. Compl. ¶ 30. In contrast, MTVN contends that Fischer must be charged with constructive knowledge of the first airing of "Blue's Clues" on Nickelodeon in September 1996. I must, however, accept Fischer's factual allegations as true for the purposes of the present motion. Because it is far from clear that Fischer had knowledge of circumstances that would have put him on inquiry notice concerning "Blue's Clues" prior to February 1997, MTVN's motion to dismiss on this issue is unmeritorious.

Fischer's Lanham Act claim is also subject to a three-year limitations period. Where a federal statute, such as the Lanham Act, contains no limitations period, courts routinely borrow the equivalent limitations period from the law of the forum state. *See Wilson v. Garcia,* 471 U.S. 261, 267, 105 S.Ct. 1938, 85 L.Ed.2d 254 (1985). In the context of a Lanham Act claim brought in this court, the appropriate state law equivalent is Maryland's three-year limitations period. The accrual of the relevant cause of action, however, remains a matter of federal law. *See Cox v. Stanton,* 529 F.2d 47, 50 (4th Cir.1975). As a general matter, the time for accrual under federal law is when the plaintiff knows or has reason to know of the injury underlying the cause of action...

III.

A.

MTVN also contends that the Copyright Act preempts Fischer's state law claims. The Copyright Act provides:

> all legal or equitable rights that are equivalent to any of the exclusive rights within the general scope of copyright as specified by section 106 in works of authorship that are fixed in a tangible medium of expression and come within the subject matter of copyright as specified by sections 102 and 103 ... are governed exclusively by this title. [After January 1, 1978], no person is entitled to any such right or equivalent right in any such work under the common law or statutes of any State.

17 U.S.C. § 301(a). To determine whether a state claim is preempted by the Act, courts must make a two-part inquiry: (1) the work must be within the scope of the subject matter of copyright; and (2) the state law rights must be equivalent to any exclusive rights within the scope of federal copyright.

Under the first prong of this test, the scope of the subject matter of copyright encompasses "original works of authorship fixed in any tangible medium of expression[,]" including literary, pictorial, and audiovisual works. 17 U.S.C. § 102(a). The Copyright Act, however, does not extend its protections to ideas or concepts. 17 U.S.C. § 102(b). Fischer alleges that he originally submitted a "written proposal for a children's animated television series featuring 'Steve and Bluey' " to Nickelodeon, then followed up with "a more detailed written description of the program, a script for a pilot episode for a half hour children's animated television series, a model sheet ... and a character description." Clearly, these tangible works fall within the scope of copyright and, therefore, satisfy the first prong of the preemption inquiry.

Fischer argues, however, that his state law claims are based on his "idea" for an animated children's program featuring Steve & Bluey. Compl. ¶¶ 40, 43. Because ideas are not protected by copyright, Fischer contends his claims based on this idea are not preempted by the Act.

This argument is unpersuasive. In *Berge,* the Fourth Circuit rejected a nearly identical argument in the course of finding the Copyright Act preempted a state law action for conversion of a doctoral dissertation. *See* 104 F.3d at 1463. Responding to the author's argument that her "ideas and methods" were excluded from the scope of copyright protections, the court concluded that the author suggested a "fallacious interpretation of the Copyright Act." *Id.* "Berge wants to argue that ideas embodied in a work covered by the Copyright Act do not fall within the scope of the Act because the Act specifically excludes them from protection. But scope and protection are not synonyms. Moreover, the shadow actually cast by the Act's preemption is notably broader than the wing of its protection." *Id.* In other words, the scope of the subject matter of copyright extends beyond those works actually protected by the Copyright Act, as expressed in section 102(a); it may, in fact, extend to include uncopyrightable material, such as ideas...Applying these standards to the present case, I find that Fischer's asserted "idea" for an animated children's program is indistinguishable from the copyrightable "written proposal for a children's animated television series featuring 'Steve and Bluey' " and the detailed written description of the program he submitted to Nickelodeon. Consequently, this idea falls within the scope of the subject matter of copyright, even if the idea itself would not be protected by the Copyright Act. The first prong of the preemption test is therefore satisfied.

B.

The second prong of the preemption inquiry requires a court to examine the rights a plaintiff claims under state law to determine whether these rights are equivalent to the exclusive rights granted by the Copyright Act. Preemption is appropriate unless there is an "extra element" that renders the state law claim "qualitatively different from a copyright infringement claim." Put differently, preemption will occur unless the state law violation "is predicated upon an act incorporating elements beyond mere reproduction or the like...." The state law right "is equivalent to one of the rights comprised by a copyright if it is infringed by the mere act of reproduction, performance, distribution, or display." *Baltimore Orioles, Inc. v. Major League Baseball Players Ass'n,* 805 F.2d 663, 677 (7th Cir.1986)(internal quotations omitted).

Here, Fischer asserts that his two state law[5] causes of action are distinct from the exclusive rights granted under by copyright. The first cause of action is Fischer's claim for breach of an implied-in-fact contract arising from his submissions to Nickelodeon and Viacom. Compl. ¶¶ 39–46. Assuming an implied contract may arise from these facts, *see Werlin v. Reader's Digest Assoc., Inc.,* 528 F.Supp. 451, 465 (S.D.N.Y.1981), the question is whether Fischer's claim for breach of such a contract contains an "extra element" that makes this claim qualitatively different from a copyright infringement action. Fischer argues that a breach of contract claim involves the extra element of a promise between the parties, thus removing it from preemption. MTVN, on the other hand, asserts that Fischer's claim is not qualitatively different from a copyright claim because the alleged contract is essentially an implied promise to pay Fischer for use of his ideas.

Although courts have generally held that the Copyright Act does not preempt actions for breach of contract,...[a]n examination of the case law, however, reveals that a categorical rule for preemption of implied-in-fact contracts would be inappropriate. A more sensible approach requires a court to examine "the specific contractual rights at issue to determine whether they [are] equivalent to exclusive rights under the Copyright Act." *Wrench,* 51 F.Supp.2d at 852. The outcome depends, as it must, on "the precise contract right being asserted." *Id.* at 853; *see American Movie Classics Co. v. Turner Entertainment Co.,* 922 F.Supp. 926, 931 (S.D.N.Y.1996). If in a given case this right arises simply from an implied promise not to use another's ideas without paying for them, then the state law action is qualitatively equivalent to an action for copyright infringement and, therefore, will be preempted.... Here, the allegations in the Complaint make clear that Fischer's breach of contract claim is preempted. He asserts that he submitted his idea and materials to MTVN with an expectation that MTVN would pay him and give him credit if it chose to use his idea. Compl. ¶ 41. Fischer further claims that his interactions with MTVN created an implied contract "that if [MTVN] used the ideas, Fischer would be compensated and given the appropriate recognition for his work." Compl. ¶ 43. This implied contract was allegedly breached when Fischer's "idea for an animated television show ... was used without compensation to develop the currently successful 'Blue's Clues' television program[.]" Compl. ¶ 45.

In short, the gravamen of Fischer's claim is that MTVN took his ideas and used them without proper compensation or attribution. Morever, the implied contract he alleges is no more than an agreement not to use his ideas without permission or payment. Because this alleged contract did not regulate the parties' conduct beyond the mere use of Fischer's ideas, the rights protected by the implied contract are equivalent to the exclusive rights protected by the Copyright Act. *See Selby,* 96 F.Supp.2d at 1062.

IV.

Fischer's second state law claim is that MTVN breached a confidential arrangement by "using and disclosing [Fischer's] idea for the purpose of creating, developing, and producing the television series based on Fischer's idea." Compl. ¶ 58. As a general rule, courts have found that the Copyright Act does not preempt such claims because they involve the extra element of a confidential promise or duty of trust between the parties. The central issue, therefore, is whether Fischer has properly pleaded the existence of such a relationship in this case.

To establish a breach of confidence claim, Fischer must show that the parties either stood in a relationship imposing a duty of trust or confidentiality, or that they made a promise to keep Fischer's ideas and materials confidential. Of course, for a breach to occur, there must be some duty in the first place, whether that duty arises from the relationship between the parties or from a promise. Under New York law, a confidential relationship is "synonymous with fiduciary relationship and .... exists between trustee and cestui que trust, guardian and ward, attorney and client, principal and agent or employer and employee and generally where the parties do not deal on equal terms and one trusts and relies on the other." Courts will find a duty not to reveal confidential information only when the recipient has accepted the confidential relationship. *See Smith,* 578 F.Supp. at 1307. Such a relationship may arise either explicitly by contract, or implicitly by the actions of the parties or other circumstances....

Here, Fischer does not allege that the parties formed an explicit agreement of trust or confidentiality. To the contrary, Fischer simply contends that he "submitted his idea in confidence to [MTVN] who accepted the disclosures in confidence and with the understanding that they would not use or disclose the idea without Fischer's knowledge and approval." Compl. ¶ 57. Fischer seems to argue, however, that the dealings and relationships between the parties gave rise to an implied duty of confidentiality. As noted, New York law recognizes an implied duty of confidentiality in circumstances where the parties deal on unequal terms, the transaction is more than an arm's length deal, and one party trusts and relies on the other. *See Sachs,* 39 N.Y.S.2d at 856. Courts must be wary, however, of claims for idea theft "predicated on the existence of an 'implied' confidential relationship, because ... artful pleading and presentation of evidence seemingly may create a pendant state law claim that in actuality is nothing more than a dressed up version of a copyright infringement claim."

In *Markogianis v. Burger King Corp.,* No. 95 Civ. 4627, 1997 WL 167113 *3–4 (S.D.N.Y. Apr.8, 1997), the court granted Burger King's motion to dismiss a breach of confidentiality claim strikingly similar to Fischer's. After the plaintiffs contacted Burger King to "pitch" an educational marketing concept, Burger King invited them to submit a presentation. *See id.* at *3. The plaintiffs submitted their materials and the parties exchanged telephone calls and correspondence, but Burger King eventually decided not to pursue the plaintiffs' concept. *See id.* The court found that "this level of activity between the parties, who were complete strangers to one another, does not give rise to any fiduciary or confidential relationship." *Id.* Furthermore, the court noted that the parties had no prior dealings and never met to discuss the concept. *See id.* The court concluded, therefore, that the complaint failed to allege a relationship between the parties that would give rise to a confidential or fiduciary duty. *See id.*

Similarly, in this case, Fischer has failed to allege a relationship giving rise to a duty of confidentiality. To the contrary, the facts alleged by Fischer describe the commonplace give-and-take between those who "pitch" ideas and those who listen and consider. Fischer does not allege that he had any prior dealings with MTVN, and the parties appear to have been complete strangers. Although Fischer allegedly submitted materials to both Nickelodeon and Viacom, he never met with them to discuss his ideas. Instead, Fischer claims he communicated with at least three different people at Viacom and Nickelodeon, who referred him at least twice to different offices. Rather than establishing a relationship of trust and confidentiality with MTVN, Fischer merely contacted Nickelodeon U.K. to pitch his idea, then Nickelodeon asked to keep "the details of the series on file." Compl. ¶¶ 15–24. Fischer further alleges that Viacom and Nickelodeon "expressed interest" and "encouraged" development of his ideas, Compl. ¶ 17, 20, but he does not allege (as did the plaintiff in *Markogianis*) that either company made him an explicit promise of confidentiality. Fischer finally "broke off communication with Nickelodeon" when it sent him a release for his signature. Compl. ¶ 25. These alleged facts describe parties acting at arm's length, with no prior dealings, no promise of confidentiality, and no employment or personal relationship that could give rise to a duty of trust. Accordingly, there is no support for the formation of a confidential relationship between Fischer and MTVN, and Fischer's breach of confidence claim must be dismissed.

V.

For these reasons, MTVN's motion to dismiss will be granted in part and denied in part.

Remember, a stock character, or basic character-type (e.g., the sleazy sports agent, etc.) is not entitled to copyright protection.

WILLIS v. HBO
United States District Court for the Southern District of New York
November 5, 2001, Decided; November 5, 2001, Filed
00 Iv. 2500 (JSM)
2001 U.S. Dist. LEXIS 17887; 60 U.S.P.Q.2d (BNA) 1916

MARTIN, District J.

Many people would consider the phrase "sleazy talent agent" to be redundant. While this is no doubt as unfair a stereotype as is the "sleazy lawyer," no one could reasonably claim a copyright in the concept of a sleazy talent agent. The question presented here is what degree of detail must an author add to such a well-recognized stock character in order to obtain copyright protection.

In this case, Plaintiff prepared an outline for a television situation comedy-known in the trade as a "treatment"-that proposed a series to be called "Schmoozers" "that lampoons the lives of two smarmy 'east coast' Agents concurrently laughing at the 'show-bizzification' of everyday discourse in mainstream America." Schmoozers Treatment, Snyder Aff. Ex. D at 1. Plaintiff's Treatment somehow found its way into the files of an employee of Defendant HBO, which sometime thereafter produced a popular series entitled "Arli," whose central character is a smarmy west coast sports agent.

Defendant now moves for summary judgment contending that the only similarity between Arli and Schmoozers is that both employ well-known concepts which no one may copyright. Plaintiff contends, however, that there are such significant similarities in the details of her Treatment for Schmoozers and the series Arli that a trier of fact could conclude that Arli violates her Schmoozers copyright. To support her claim she relies upon the report of an "expert" in television studies who details what he considers to be the significant similarities between Schmoozers and Arli and concludes that the two series are "uniquely alike."

DISCUSSION

To establish her claim of copyright infringement Plaintiff must establish that Defendant had access to her copyrighted work and that substantial similarities exist as to protectible material in the two works. Although Defendant offers substantial evidence that the creators of Arli never had access to Plaintiff's work, the existence of a copy of Plaintiff's Schmoozers Treatment in HBO's files creates an issue of fact that precludes summary judgment on that issue. Thus, the question that remains is whether the "protectible expression in [the plaintiff's work] is substantially similar to the equivalent portions of [the defendant's work]." *Cooling Systems & Flexibles, Inc. v. Stuart Radiator, Inc.,* 777 F.2d 485, 493 (9th Cir.1985). *See Hoehling v. Universal City Studios, Inc.,* 618 F.2d 972, 977 (2d Cir.1980).

In order to determine the extent to which Arli employed copyrightable elements of the Schmoozers Treatment, the Court read the Treatment and Plaintiff's expert's report and viewed the first five episodes of Arli and a videotape prepared by Plaintiff which compared specific portions of the Treatment with segments from various Arli episodes. The Court did not consider it essential to view all fifty-nine Arli episodes that have been submitted, since it is reasonable to conclude that the basic theme of the series and the unique traits of each of the characters would be developed in the first few episodes or in the segments submitted by Plaintiff. On the basis of this review, the Court concludes that summary judgment is appropriate because comparison of the two works at issue shows that the only similarities between them relate to non-copyrightable elements. *See generally Ring v. Estee Lauder, Inc.,* 874 F.2d 109 (2d Cir.1989).

The problem with Plaintiff's claim and her "expert's" report is that, to the extent that there are similarities, they are found either in stock characters, or themes that are common to the talent agency business, or to situation comedies in general or in trivial detail that are not essential to either series. Plaintiff's arguments also ignore the significant differences between the two series and strain to find similarities where none exist.

As Judge Scheindlin observed in *Hogan v. DC Comics,* 48 F.Supp.2d 298, 310 (S.D.N.Y.1999):

A stock character or basic character type ... is not entitled to copyright protection. *Robinson v. Viacom International, Inc.,* 93 Civ. 2539, 1995 WL 417076, at *9 (S.D.N.Y. Jan. 4, 1995); *Sinicola v. Warner Bros.,* 948 F.Supp. 1176, 1185 (E.D.N.Y.1996). 'No character infringement claim can succeed unless plaintiff's original conception sufficiently developed the character, and defendants have copied this development and not merely the broader outlines.' *Smith v. Weinstein,* 578 F.Supp. 1297, 1303, *aff'd mem.,* 738 F.2d 419 (2d Cir.1984); *see also Nichols v. Universal Pictures Corp.,* 45 F.2d 119, 121 (2d Cir.1930) ("the less developed the characters, the less they can be copyrighted; that is the penalty an author must bear for marking them too indistinctly").

The strongest similarity between the two works at issue is that they both involve talent agents who operate in a "bottom-dwelling ethical nether world, where lying is an art form; insincerity, a science, and personal convictions are as commonplace as nose rings." Treatment at 1. This concept is not original or protectible under the copyright law. It does not strain the concept of judicial notice to observe that books, movies and television series are full of such unethical men and women in a variety of businesses and, as noted above, this is a not uncommon perception of talent agents.

Plaintiff argues, however, that Arli copied more than her theme and misappropriated her use of a male side-kick, a female assistant and an African American character with a business background. The concept of a male sidekick and female assistant is not new. While the Court is not *au courant* with today's television scene, an earlier generation was entertained by Perry Mason, his side-kick Paul Drake and his assistant Della Street. Matt Dillon had Chester and Miss Kitty. The interplay of male and female characters in television sitcoms was essential to the comedy of Sid Caesar, Dick Van Dyke, Jackie Gleason and Lucille Ball. None of the creators of these televison classics would have thought of suing the others for copyright infringement.

Plaintiff argues that the personality traits, physical characteristics and personal histories of the Schmoozers characters and their interaction in the series are so similar to those of the Arli characters that they establish an infringement of her work. While some similarities do exist, there are significant differences between the two sets of characters and the overall concept of the two shows.

Schmoozers is about Randee Crouch and Tym Barker, two partners in the StarTrack talent agency who grew up in the same town in Indiana and have been friends since childhood. Their principal assistant is Tym's sister, Maricait, described in the Treatment as a persistently horn-rimmed dishwater blonde who evokes the "warmth and flaky brilliance of a young Diane Keaton." Treatment at 10. The other principal characters are a client, Jack O'Shaunessey, a not very successful comedian; a secretary named Carter Palen Campbell, a woman with a prep school background who is described as politically passionate and somewhat dramatic in her personal conduct; Tym's girlfriend, Gillian Landry, a successful television actress; and Fred Stovall, another client who is a radio shock-jock. The treatment lists as secondary characters Randee and Tym's parents, each of whom is individually described. The Treatment describes the primary sets as a "downtown restaurant", "a showcase club", the steam room at a health club, and a tanning parlor.

Arli is about a sports agent who grew up in New Jersey and has his own agency. Arliss has an assistant named Kirby, a former All-American and professional football player who was Arliss's first client; an Asian American secretary named Rita Wu; and the agency's chief financial officer, an African American, Stanley Babson. These four characters are the mainstays of the program. There are no roles similar to that envisioned in Schmoozers for Jack O'Shaunessey, Carter Palen Campbell, Gillian Landry, Fred Stovall or the four parents of the two main characters. The primary setting for the Arli show is the offices of the Arliss Michaels Agency and there is no regular restaurant, showcase club, health club or tanning parlor.

Despite the substantial differences between the characters in the two shows and their locales, Plaintiff, with the aid of her expert, attempts to demonstrate that the similarities between the characters in Schmoozers and the cast of Arli are substantial enough to establish copyright infringement. While there are some similarities between Arliss Michaels and Tym Barker-they both wear gold-rimmed glasses and designer suits, and are utterly amoral in their approach to their businesses-these characteristics of Plaintiff's Tym Barker are not inherently distinctive. Arliss Michaels and Tym Barker are not the same character; they are both stereotypes of the amoral talent agent. The most that could be said is that the Arliss character embodies "the broader outlines" of Tym Barker. *Hogan,* 48 F.Supp.2d at 310. However, this is not a protectible element of Plaintiff's work.

In large measure, the similarities cited by Plaintiff in an attempt to support her claim are so strained that all they prove is how little real evidence there is of a copyright violation. Perhaps the clearest example of this is Plaintiff's wholly unsuccessful attempt to demonstrate that Arliss' sidekick Kirby was copied from the character Randee Crouch in Schmoozers.

Plaintiff's "expert" states that "Schmoozers proposes a supporting male agent character named Randee Crouch and Arli executes a supporting male agent character named Kirby Carlisle who are substantially similar." Expert's Report, Snyder Aff. Ex. E at 23. When the two series are compared, all that this statement demonstrates is the sad fact that one can apparently get an "expert" to swear to anything.

In the Treatment, Randee Crouch is not a supporting character. He is the first character described in the Treatment and one of two equal partners in the StarTrack Agency. Like his lifelong friend Tym, he is a failed athlete who dresses in Armani suits. Kirby, on the other hand, is a supporting character who refers to Arliss as "boss" and is clearly in an inferior position within the Arliss Michaels Agency. In addition, unlike Arliss, who does dress in designer suits, Kirby usually appears in casual clothes. Far from being a failed athlete, Kirby is a former All-American and professional football player and he did not know Arliss until he became his fist client. No reasonable fact finder could conclude that the characters of Randee and Kirby are substantially similar.

Almost as unsuccessful is Plaintiff's expert's attempt to prove that Arliss's secretary Rita Wu is substantially similar to Maricait Barker. Aside from the fact that they are both female there is little that Rita and Maricait have in common. While Maricait is described as "a persistently horn-rimmed dishwater blonde who evokes the warmth and flaky brilliance of a young Diane Keaton," Treatment at 10, Rita is a with-it Asian American who would remind no one of Diane Keaton. Rita does wear dark rimmed glasses but they are stylish and would not ordinarily be described as horn-rimmed. While Maricait is described as "good-hearted, yet cerebral" and "happiest with her face in a book",

Treatment at 10, no one but Plaintiff's expert would describe Rita as "cerebral" or think of her as happiest with her face in a book. In asserting that Rita, like Maricait, serves "as the 'moral voice' of the series", Expert's Report at 31, Plaintiff's expert apparently overlooks those episodes in which Rita is shown attempting to overhear the conversations in Arliss's office by kneeling outside his office with a glass to the door, and other instances where she lies without compunction and sleeps with a variety of his clients.

Perhaps the greatest stretch in Plaintiff's argument is found in the contention that Arliss's African American chief financial officer was copied from a reference in the Treatment to an African American attorney employed at Goldman Sachs in mergers and acquisitions. This attorney is not a character in Schmoozers and he is not described or even given a name in the Treatment; he is simply mentioned in the description of the character Carter Palen Campbell as her romantic interest. One would have hoped that we were well past the day when someone would urge that it should be considered "creative" to conceive of an African American male involved in finance.

Plaintiff's attempt to pull isolated segments out of the fifty-nine Arli episodes to prove copying of her creative work is equally unsuccessful. It is not surprising that in this substantial number of episodes there are instances where themes outlined in the Schmoozers Treatment are found present in a show about a sports agent. As Judge Haight observed in *CK Comp. v. Burger King Corp.,* No. 92 Civ. 1488, 1994 WL 533253, at *4 (S.D.N.Y. Sept. 30, 1994):

'The essence of infringement lies in taking not a general theme, but its particular expression through similarities of treatment, details, scenes, events and characterization.' *Reyher,* 533 F.2d at 91. '[T]he law will not grant an author a monopoly over the unparticularized expression of an idea at such a level of abstraction or generality as unduly to inhibit independent creation by others.' *Gund, Inc. v. Smile Int'l, Inc.,* 691 F.Supp. 642, 644 (S.D.N.Y.1988), *aff'd mem.,* 872 F.2d 1021 (2d Cir.1989). Consistent with these principles, copyright law does not protect stock characters, incidents or settings that are as a practical matter indispensable or standard in the treatment of a given topic. *Hoehling v. Universal City Studios, Inc.,* 618 F.2d 972, 979 (2d Cir.), *cert. denied,* 449 U.S. 841 (1980).

Plaintiff also argues that two dramatic devices used in Arli were copied from Schmoozers: 1) a character who talks directly to the audience, and 2) celebrities appearing as themselves. There is nothing novel about either of these devices. Ancient Greek tragedy employed a chorus that spoke to the audience and this device is far from unique in modern theater, film and television. Celebrities have appeared as themselves in numerous films and television shows and it is not surprising that someone creating a series about a talent agent would think it appropriate to have actual celebrities appearing as clients. Thus, even if HBO copied these devices from Plaintiff's Treatment there is no copyright violation. It should also be noted that the use of a character speaking to the audience is substantially different in the Treatment than as employed in Arli. In the Treatment, Maricait is the character who addresses the audience, but she does so as "Audience Ambassador to Schmoozers", challenging "the reigning Dictatorship of Bad Taste." Treatment at 22a. While Arli uses a voice over, it is Arliss reading an excerpt from his autobiography. This voice over is designed to contrast the image of himself that Michaels has set forth in the book with the sleazy conduct he engages in every day. Thus, the use of this device in the two works is entirely different and there is no reason to conclude that the use of this device in Arli

In sum, Plaintiff has failed to show that protectible portions of her Treatment were substantially reproduced in the Arli series. Thus, even if we accept her assumption that the creators of Arli had her Schmoozers Treatment and copied all of the similar ideas that may be found in the two works, Plaintiff cannot prevail.

For the foregoing reasons, Defendant's motion for summary judgment is granted and the complaint is dismissed.

SO ORDERED.

The following case, Waring v. Dunlea, 26 F.Supp. 338 (E.D.N.C. 1939), concerns the copyright of "music in the Waring manner"; that is, the Fred Waring Orchestra and Waring's successful attempts to stop the rebroadcast of his music on a radio station that did not have the license to do so.

WARING v. DUNLEA
District Court, E.D. North Carolina, Wilmington Division
January 25, 1939
No. Number in Original
26 F.Supp.338

MEEKINS, District Judge.

This is an Equity Cause in which Complainant seeks to enjoin Respondent from using or playing on Respondent's radio station W M F D, certain electrical transcriptions of musical interpretations or renditions of Complainant's orchestra. A Notice appears on the record or electrical transcription that the record is to be used only on the Ford Motor Program and limited to such use on the part of the distributee. Respondent was not a distributee and the record was played by Respondent on a program other than the Ford Motor Program.

There is diversity of citizenship and the jurisdictional amount is present. Complainant is the owner of an orchestra, nationally known and he made certain electrical transcriptions of his unique interpretations of different musical numbers, which for a consideration he distributed over the radio on a special program, known as the Ford Motor Program.

The transcriptions contained a notice or legend that the use was limited to the distributee station for the purpose only of being played on a definite program.

Respondent without the consent of Complainant, and not being one of the licensed distributees, played one of Complainant's musical numbers 'Wa-Hoo' on his radio station, this number being one of the presentations of a musical number contracted for on the special program.

Both Complainant and Respondent are engaged in a business of selling musical entertainment to the public.

It appears to the Court that Complainant has created by his efforts and talents a distinctive style known as his style, in the interpretations of musical numbers. He desires to sell or license such renditions. This presents the first question: Does Complainant have such an interest in his unique rendition that it is a distinct and separable property right? My answer is, Yes.

Rights in personal property are of no less importance than rights in real property. To say that personal property cannot be divided in its uses and distribution of its uses would be like saying that real property can only be conveyed in fee simple. The other course has been definitely established. Land is subject to restrictions, and chattels are likewise subject to restrictive uses.

'Just as modern needs have brought equitable restrictions on land, of which the old common law knew nothing, into existence, they may also call for a limited departure from the free transfer of chattels for the sake of promoting desirable business practices wholly strange to Coke's day.' 31 Harvard Law Review 945, 983.

Complainant has a property right in his performance. Complainant by mental labor creates something which is the subject of sale, for he has contracted for its rendition with the Ford Motor Company. It is his work, his property, and so recognized.

'Nothing can with greater propriety be called a man's property than the fruit of his brain.' Copinger's Law of Copyright, 5th Ed., Pg. 1.

A dramatic performance gives life to the story, and is the property of the interpreter. The great singers and actors of this day give something to the composition that is particularly theirs, and to say that they could not limit its use is to deny them the right to distribute their art, as they may see fit, when they see fit. Surely, their labors and talents are entitled to the privilege of distribution, especially where, as here, the privilege is subject to definite terms and bounds. They have an exclusive right in their property and thus have a right to prohibit its unauthorized public performance. Ferris v. Frohman, 1912, 223 U.S. 424, 32 S.Ct. 263, 56 L.Ed. 492; Palmer v. DeWitt, 1872, 47 N.Y. 532, 7 Am.Rep. 480; Tompkins v. Halleck, 1882, 133 Mass. 32, 43 Am.Rep. 480.

Performance is not a publication. Uproar Co. v. Nat. Broadcasting Co., D.C., 1934, 8 F.Supp. 358; Ferris v. Frohman, 1912, 223 U.S. 424, 32 S.Ct. 263, 56 L.Ed. 492.

The distribution of intellectual property or work is capable of limitation. Press Pub. Co. v. Monroe, 2 Cir., 1896, 73 F. 196, 51 L.R.A. 353.

The restrictions of the use of Complainant's interpretations are not unreasonable nor are they against public policy. If anything, they tend to create value, and develop interest in the arts, instead of interfering with the course of trade, which it does not since his works have never been placed in trading media, and since the artist by his restrictive covenant increases the uses and is more able to give his works and art to the public within proper limitations.

The radio, Motion picture, and television have great value and are the subject of popular demand and are as much the subject of property rights and deserve the protection of equity as the more concrete and definite easements in land.

'It requires but little argument to show that, since a man has a right to withhold from all dissemination his thoughts, sentiments, and emotions, no matter what their media or expression, he has a right to restrict or limit this dissemination. * * *

'Applying that principle to the instant case it is my view that the plaintiff is entitled 'to decide whether, and when, and how, and for whose advantage,' his rendition of musical compositions shall be mechanically reproduced. ' Waring v. W D A S, 327 Pa. 433, at pages 459, 461, 194 A. 631, at page 643; Edison v. Edison Polyform & Mfg. Co., 73 N.J.Eq. 136, 67 A. 392; Foster-Milburn Co. v. Chinn, 134 Ky. 424, 120 S.W. 364, 34 L.R.A., N.S., 1137, 135 Am.St.Rep. 417; Kunz v. Allen, 102 Kan. 883, 172 P. 532, L.R.A. 1918D, 1151; 70 U.S. L. Rev. 435; 51 Harvard Law Review 171; 38 Columbia Law Review 181; 86 Univ. of Penn. Law Rev. 217; 23 Washington Law Rev. Quarterly 283; 15 NYU Law Quart. Rev. 275.

To allow Respondent to benefit financially by Complainant's work and skill would be an unfair trade practice and equity will enjoin such an effort on the part of Respondent.

Relief prayed by Complainant allowed, and Decree signed in accord herewith.

The following case, Eldred v. Ashcroft, 537 U.S. 186 (2002), famously declared the Copyright Term Extension Act (CTEA) was constitutional. Blame it on Mickey; both existing and future copyrights "from the time of the work's creation until 50 years after the author's death" are extended to "the time of the work's creation until 70 years after the author's death."

ELDRED v. ASHCROFT
Supreme Court of the United States
October 9, 2002, Argued; January 15, 2003, Decided
No. 01-618
537 U.S. 186; 123 S. Ct. 769; 154 L.Ed.2d 683

Justice GINSBURG delivered the opinion of the Court.

This case concerns the authority the Constitution assigns to Congress to prescribe the duration of copyrights. The Copyright and Patent Clause of the Constitution, Art. I, § 8, cl. 8, provides as to copyrights: "Congress shall have Power ... [t]o promote the Progress of Science ... by securing [to Authors] for limited Times ... the exclusive Right to their ... Writings." In 1998, in the measure here under inspection, Congress enlarged the duration of copyrights by 20 years. Copyright Term Extension Act (CTEA), Pub.L. 105–298, §§ 102(b) and (d), 112 Stat. 2827–2828 (amending 17 U.S.C. §§ 302, 304). As in the case of prior extensions, principally in 1831, 1909, and 1976, Congress provided for application of the enlarged terms to existing and future copyrights alike.

Petitioners are individuals and businesses whose products or services build on copyrighted works that have gone into the public domain. They seek a determination that the CTEA fails constitutional review under both the Copyright Clause's "limited Times" prescription and the First Amendment's free speech guarantee. Under the 1976 Copyright Act, copyright protection generally lasted from the work's creation until 50 years after the author's death. Pub.L. 94–553, § 302(a), 90 Stat. 2572 (1976 Act). Under the CTEA, most copyrights now run from creation until 70 years after the author's death. 17 U.S.C. § 302(a). Petitioners do not challenge the "life–plus–70–years" timespan itself. "Whether 50 years is enough, or 70 years too much," they acknowledge, "is not a judgment meet for this Court." Brief for Petitioners 14. Congress went awry, petitioners maintain, not with respect to newly created works, but in enlarging the term for published works with existing copyrights. The "limited Tim[e]" in effect when a copyright is secured, petitioners urge, becomes the constitutional boundary, a clear line beyond the power of Congress to extend. See *ibid.* As to the First Amendment, petitioners contend that the CTEA is a content-neutral regulation of speech that fails inspection under the heightened judicial scrutiny appropriate for such regulations.

In accord with the District Court and the Court of Appeals, we reject petitioners' challenges to the CTEA. In that 1998 legislation, as in all previous copyright term extensions, Congress placed existing and future copyrights in parity. In prescribing that alignment, we hold, Congress acted within its authority and did not transgress constitutional limitations.

I

A

We evaluate petitioners' challenge to the constitutionality of the CTEA against the backdrop of Congress' previous exercises of its authority under the Copyright Clause. The Nation's first copyright statute, enacted in 1790, provided a federal copyright term of 14 years from the date of publication, renewable for an additional 14 years if the author survived the first term. Act of May 31, 1790, ch. 15, § 1, 1 Stat. 124 (1790 Act). The 1790 Act's renewable 14-year term applied to existing works (*i.e.,* works already published and works created but not yet published) and future works alike. *Ibid.* Congress expanded the federal copyright term to 42 years in 1831 (28 years from publication, renewable for an additional 14 years), and to 56 years in 1909 (28 years from publication, renewable for an additional 28 years). Act of Feb. 3, 1831, ch. 16, §§ 1, 16, 4 Stat. 436, 439 (1831 Act); Act of Mar. 4, 1909, ch. 320, §§ 23–24, 35 Stat. 1080–1081 (1909 Act). Both times, Congress applied the new copyright term to existing and future works, 1831 Act §§ 1, 16; 1909 Act §§ 23–24; to qualify for the 1831 extension, an existing work had to be in its initial copyright term at the time the Act became effective, 1831 Act §§ 1, 16.

In 1976, Congress altered the method for computing federal copyright terms. 1976 Act §§ 302–304. For works created by identified natural persons, the 1976 Act provided that federal copyright protection would run from the work's creation, not—as in the 1790, 1831, and 1909 Acts—its publication; protection would last until 50 years after the author's death. § 302(a). In these respects, the 1976 Act aligned United States copyright terms with the then-dominant international standard adopted under the Berne Convention for the Protection of Literary and Artistic Works. See H.R.Rep. No. 94–1476, p. 135 (1976), U.S.Code Cong. & Admin.News 1976, p.5659. For anonymous works, pseudonymous works, and works made for hire, the 1976 Act provided a term of 75 years from publication or 100 years from creation, whichever expired first. § 302(c).

These new copyright terms, the 1976 Act instructed, governed all works not published by its effective date of January 1, 1978, regardless of when the works were created. §§ 302–303. For published works with existing copyrights as of that date, the 1976 Act granted a copyright term of 75 years from the date of publication, §§ 304(a) and (b), a 19-year increase over the 56-year term applicable under the 1909 Act.

The measure at issue here, the CTEA, installed the fourth major duration extension of federal copyrights. Retaining the general structure of the 1976 Act, the CTEA enlarges the terms of all existing and future copyrights by 20 years. For works created by identified natural persons, the term now lasts from creation until 70 years after the author's death. 17 U.S.C. § 302(a). This standard harmonizes the baseline United States copyright term with the term adopted by the European Union in 1993. See Council Directive 93/98/EEC of 29 October 1993 Harmonizing the Term of Protection of Copyright and Certain Related Rights, 1993 Official J. Eur. Coms. (L290), p. 9 (EU Council Directive 93/98). For anonymous works, pseudonymous works, and works made for hire, the term is 95 years from publication or 120 years from creation, whichever expires first. 17 U.S.C. § 302(c).

Paralleling the 1976 Act, the CTEA applies these new terms to all works not published by January 1, 1978. §§ 302(a), 303(a). For works published before 1978 with existing copyrights as of the CTEA's effective date, the CTEA extends the term to 95 years from publication. §§ 304(a) and (b). Thus, in common with the 1831, 1909, and 1976 Acts, the CTEA's new terms apply to both future and existing copyrights.

B

Petitioners' suit challenges the CTEA's constitutionality under both the Copyright Clause and the First Amendment. On cross-motions for judgment on the pleadings, the District Court entered judgment for the Attorney General (respondent here). 74 F.Supp.2d 1 (D.D.C.1999). The court held that the CTEA does not violate the "limited Times" restriction of the Copyright Clause because the CTEA's terms, though longer than the 1976 Act's terms, are still limited, not perpetual, and therefore fit within Congress' discretion. *Id.,* at 3. The court also held that "there are no First Amendment rights to use the copyrighted works of others." *Ibid.*

The Court of Appeals for the District of Columbia Circuit affirmed. 239 F.3d 372 (2001). In that court's unanimous view, *Harper & Row, Publishers, Inc. v. Nation Enterprises,* 471 U.S. 539, 105 S.Ct. 2218, 85 L.Ed.2d 588 (1985), foreclosed petitioners' First Amendment challenge to the CTEA. 239 F.3d, at 375. Copyright, the court reasoned, does not impermissibly restrict free speech, for it grants the author an exclusive right only to the specific form of expression; it does not shield any idea or fact contained in the copyrighted work, and it allows for "fair use" even of the expression itself. *Id.,* at 375–376.

A majority of the Court of Appeals also upheld the CTEA against petitioners' contention that the measure exceeds Congress' power under the Copyright Clause. Specifically, the court rejected petitioners' plea for interpretation of the "limited Times" prescription not discretely but with a view to the "preambular statement of purpose" contained in the Copyright Clause: "To promote the Progress of Science." *Id.,* at 377–378. Circuit precedent, *Schnapper v. Foley,* 667 F.2d 102 (C.A.D.C.1981), the court determined, precluded that plea. In this regard, the court took into account petitioners' acknowledgment that the preamble itself places no substantive limit on Congress' legislative power. 239 F.3d, at 378.

The appeals court found nothing in the constitutional text or its history to suggest that "a term of years for a copyright is not a 'limited Time' if it may later be extended for another 'limited Time.' " *Id.,* at 379. The court recounted that "the First Congress made the Copyright Act of 1790 applicable to subsisting copyrights arising under the copyright laws of the several states." *Ibid.* That construction of Congress' authority under the Copyright Clause "by [those] contemporary with [the Constitution's] formation," the court said, merited "very great" and in this case "almost conclusive" weight. *Ibid.* (quoting *Burrow–Giles Lithographic Co. v. Sarony,* 111 U.S. 53, 57, 4 S.Ct. 279, 28 L.Ed. 349 (1884)). As early as *McClurg v. Kingsland,* 1 How. 202, 11 L.Ed. 102 (1843), the Court of Appeals added, this Court had made it "plain" that the same Clause permits Congress to "amplify the terms of an existing patent." 239 F.3d, at 380. The appeals court recognized that this Court has been similarly deferential to the judgment of Congress in the realm of copyright. *Ibid.* (citing *Sony Corp. of America v. Universal City Studios, Inc.,* 464 U.S. 417, 104 S.Ct. 774, 78 L.Ed.2d 574 (1984); *Stewart v. Abend,* 495 U.S. 207, 110 S.Ct. 1750, 109 L.Ed.2d 184 (1990)).

Concerning petitioners' assertion that Congress might evade the limitation on its authority by stringing together "an unlimited number of 'limited Times,' " the Court of Appeals stated that such legislative misbehavior "clearly is not the situation before us." 239 F.3d, at 379. Rather, the court noted, the CTEA "matches" the baseline term for "United States copyrights [with] the terms of copyrights granted by the European Union." *Ibid.* "[I]n an era of multinational publishers and instantaneous electronic transmission," the court said, "harmonization in this regard has obvious practical benefits" and is "a 'necessary and proper' measure to meet contemporary circumstances rather than a step on the way to making copyrights perpetual." *Ibid.*

Judge Sentelle dissented in part. He concluded that Congress lacks power under the Copyright Clause to expand the copyright terms of existing works. *Id.,* at 380–384. The Court of Appeals subsequently denied rehearing and rehearing en banc. 255 F.3d 849 (2001).

We granted certiorari to address two questions: whether the CTEA's extension of existing copyrights exceeds Congress' power under the Copyright Clause; and whether the CTEA's extension of existing and future copyrights violates the First Amendment. 534 U.S. 1126 and 1160, 122 S.Ct. 1062 and 1170, 151 L.Ed.2d 966 and 152 L.Ed.2d 115 (2002). We now answer those two questions in the negative and affirm.

II

A

We address first the determination of the courts below that Congress has authority under the Copyright Clause to extend the terms of existing copyrights. Text, history, and precedent, we conclude, confirm that the Copyright Clause empowers Congress to prescribe "limited Times" for copyright protection and to secure the same level and duration of protection for all copyright holders, present and future.

The CTEA's baseline term of life plus 70 years, petitioners concede, qualifies as a "limited Tim[e]" as applied to future copyrights. Petitioners contend, however, that existing copyrights extended to endure for that same term are not "limited." Petitioners' argument essentially reads into the text of the Copyright Clause the command that a time prescription, once set, becomes forever "fixed" or "inalterable." The word "limited," however, does not convey a meaning so constricted. At the time of the Framing, that word meant what it means today: "confine[d] within certain bounds," "restrain[ed]," or "circumscribe[d]." S. Johnson, A Dictionary of the English Language (7th ed. 1785); see T. Sheridan, A Complete Dictionary of the English Language (6th ed. 1796) ("confine[d] within certain bounds"); Webster's Third New International Dictionary 1312 (1976) ("confined within limits"; "restricted in extent, number, or duration"). Thus understood, a timespan appropriately "limited" as applied to future copyrights does not automatically cease to be "limited" when applied to existing copyrights. And as we observe, *infra,* at 783, there is no cause to suspect that a purpose to evade the "limited Times" prescription prompted Congress to adopt the CTEA.

To comprehend the scope of Congress' power under the Copyright Clause, "a page of history is worth a volume of logic." *New York Trust Co. v. Eisner,* 256 U.S. 345, 349, 41 S.Ct. 506, 65 L.Ed. 963 (1921) (Holmes, J.). History reveals an unbroken congressional practice of granting to authors of works with existing copyrights the benefit of term extensions so that all under copyright protection will be governed evenhandedly under the same regime. As earlier recounted, see *supra,* at 775, the First Congress accorded the protections of the Nation's first federal copyright statute to existing and future works alike. 1790 Act § 1.[5] Since then, Congress has regularly applied duration extensions to both existing and future copyrights. 1831 Act §§ 1, 16; 1909 Act §§ 23–24; 1976 Act §§ 302–303; 17 U.S.C. §§ 302–304.

Because the Clause empowering Congress to confer copyrights also authorizes patents, congressional practice with respect to patents informs our inquiry. We count it significant that early Congresses extended the duration of numerous individual patents as well as copyrights. See, *e.g.,* Act of Jan. 7, 1808, ch. 6, 6 Stat. 70 (patent); Act of Mar. 3, 1809, ch. 35, 6 Stat. 80 (patent); Act of

Feb. 7, 1815, ch. 36, 6 Stat. 147 (patent); Act of May 24, 1828, ch. 145, 6 Stat. 389 (copyright); Act of Feb. 11, 1830, ch. 13, 6 Stat. 403 (copyright); see generally Ochoa, Patent and Copyright Term Extension and the Constitution: A Historical Perspective, 49 J. Copyright Soc. 19 (2001). The courts saw no "limited Times" impediment to such extensions; renewed or extended terms were upheld in the early days, for example, by Chief Justice Marshall and Justice Story sitting as circuit justices. See *Evans v. Jordan,* 8 F. Cas. 872, 874 (No. 4,564) (CC Va. 1813) (Marshall, J.) ("Th[e] construction of the constitution which admits the renewal of a patent, is not controverted. A renewed patent ... confers the same rights, with an original."), aff'd, 9 Cranch 199, 3 L.Ed. 704 (1815); *Blanchard v. Sprague,* 3 F. Cas. 648, 650 (No. 1,518) (CC Mass. 1839) (Story, J.) ("I never have entertained any doubt of the constitutional authority of congress" to enact a 14-year patent extension that "operates retrospectively"); see also *Evans v. Robinson,* 8 F. Cas. 886, 888 (No. 4,571) (CC Md. 1813) (Congresses "have the exclusive right ... to limit the times for which a patent right shall be granted, and are not restrained from renewing a patent or prolonging" it.).[7]

Further, although prior to the instant case this Court did not have occasion to decide whether extending the duration of existing copyrights complies with the "limited Times" prescription, the Court has found no constitutional barrier to the legislative expansion of existing patents. *McClurg v. Kingsland*, 1 How. 202, 11 L.Ed. 102 (1843), is the pathsetting precedent. The patentee in that case was unprotected under the law in force when the patent issued because he had allowed his employer briefly to practice the invention before he obtained the patent. Only upon enactment, two years later, of an exemption for such allowances did the patent become valid, retroactive to the time it issued. *McClurg* upheld retroactive application of the new law. The Court explained that the legal regime governing a particular patent "depend[s] on the law as it stood at the emanation of the patent, together with such changes as have been since made; for though they may be retrospective in their operation, that is not a sound objection to their validity." *Id.*, at 206. Neither is it a sound objection to the validity of a copyright term extension, enacted pursuant to the same constitutional grant of authority, that the enlarged term covers existing copyrights.

Congress' consistent historical practice of applying newly enacted copyright terms to future and existing copyrights reflects a judgment stated concisely by Representative Huntington at the time of the 1831 Act: "[J]ustice, policy, and equity alike forb[id]" that an "author who had sold his [work] a week ago, be placed in a worse situation than the author who should sell his work the day after the passing of [the] act." 7 Cong. Deb. 424 (1831); accord, Symposium, The Constitutionality of Copyright Term Extension, 18 Cardozo Arts & Ent. L.J. 651, 694 (2000) (Prof.Miller) ("[S]ince 1790, it has indeed been Congress's policy that the author of yesterday's work should not get a lesser reward than the author of tomorrow's work just because Congress passed a statute lengthening the term today."). The CTEA follows this historical practice by keeping the duration provisions of the 1976 Act largely in place and simply adding 20 years to each of them. Guided by text, history, and precedent, we cannot agree with petitioners' submission that extending the duration of existing copyrights is categorically beyond Congress' authority under the Copyright Clause.

Satisfied that the CTEA complies with the "limited Times" prescription, we turn now to whether it is a rational exercise of the legislative authority conferred by the Copyright Clause. On that point, we defer substantially to Congress. *Sony,* 464 U.S., at 429, 104 S.Ct. 774 ("[I]t is Congress that has been assigned the task of defining the scope of the limited monopoly that should be granted to authors ... in order to give the public appropriate access to their work product.").

The CTEA reflects judgments of a kind Congress typically makes, judgments we cannot dismiss as outside the Legislature's domain. As respondent describes, see Brief for Respondent 37–38, a key factor in the CTEA's passage was a 1993 European Union (EU) directive instructing EU members to establish a copyright term of life plus 70 years. EU Council Directive 93/98, Art. 1(1), p. 11; see 144 Cong. Rec. S12377–S12378 (daily ed. Oct. 12, 1998) (statement of Sen. Hatch). Consistent with the Berne Convention, the EU directed its members to deny this longer term to the works of any non-EU country whose laws did not secure the same extended term. See Berne Conv. Art. 7(8); P. Goldstein, International Copyright § 5.3, p. 239 (2001). By extending the baseline United States copyright term to life plus 70 years, Congress sought to ensure that American authors would receive the same copyright protection in Europe as their European counterparts. The CTEA may also provide greater incentive for American and other authors to create and disseminate their work in the United States. See Perlmutter, Participation in the International Copyright System as a Means to Promote the Progress of Science and Useful Arts, 36 Loyola (LA) L.Rev. 323, 330 (2002) ("[M]atching th[e] level of [copyright] protection in the United States [to that in the EU] can ensure stronger protection for U.S. works abroad and avoid competitive disadvantages vis-à-vis foreign rightholders."); see also *id.,* at 332 (the United States could not "play a leadership role" in the give-and-take evolution of the international copyright system, indeed it would "lose all flexibility," "if the only way to promote the progress of science were to provide incentives to create new works").

In addition to international concerns, Congress passed the CTEA in light of demographic, economic, and technological changes, Brief for Respondent 25–26, 33, and nn. 23 and 24, and rationally credited projections that longer terms would encourage copyright holders to invest in the restoration and public distribution of their works, *id.,* at 34–37; see H.R.Rep. No. 105–452, p. 4 (1998) (term extension "provide[s] copyright owners generally with the incentive to restore older works and further disseminate them to the public").

In sum, we find that the CTEA is a rational enactment; we are not at liberty to second-guess congressional determinations and policy judgments of this order, however debatable or arguably unwise they may be. Accordingly, we cannot conclude that the CTEA—which continues the unbroken congressional practice of treating future and existing copyrights in parity for term extension purposes—is an impermissible exercise of Congress' power under the Copyright Clause.

B

Petitioners' Copyright Clause arguments rely on several novel readings of the Clause. We next address these arguments and explain why we find them unpersuasive.

1

Petitioners contend that even if the CTEA's 20-year term extension is literally a "limited Tim[e]," permitting Congress to extend existing copyrights allows it to evade the "limited Times" constraint by creating effectively perpetual copyrights through repeated extensions. We disagree.

As the Court of Appeals observed, a regime of perpetual copyrights "clearly is not the situation before us." 239 F.3d, at 379. Nothing before this Court warrants construction of the CTEA's 20-year term extension as a congressional attempt to evade or override the "limited Times" constraint. Critically, we again emphasize, petitioners fail to show how the CTEA crosses a constitutionally significant threshold with respect to "limited Times" that the 1831, 1909, and 1976 Acts did not. See *supra,* at 775–776; Austin, *supra* n. 13, at 56 ("If extending copyright protection to works already in existence is constitutionally suspect," so is "extending the protections of U. S copyright law to works by foreign authors that had already been created and even first published when the federal rights attached."). Those earlier Acts did not create perpetual copyrights, and neither does the CTEA.

2

Petitioners dominantly advance a series of arguments all premised on the proposition that Congress may not extend an existing copyright absent new consideration from the author. They pursue this main theme under three headings. Petitioners contend that the CTEA's extension of existing copyrights

(1) overlooks the requirement of "originality," (2) fails to "promote the Progress of Science," and (3) ignores copyright's *quid pro quo.*

Petitioners' "originality" argument draws on *Feist Publications, Inc. v. Rural Telephone Service Co.,* 499 U.S. 340, 111 S.Ct. 1282, 113 L.Ed.2d 358 (1991). In *Feist,* we observed that "[t]he *sine qua non* of copyright is originality," *id.,* at 345, 111 S.Ct. 1282, and held that copyright protection is unavailable to "a narrow category of works in which the creative spark is utterly lacking or so trivial as to be virtually nonexistent," *id.,* at 359, 111 S.Ct. 1282. Relying on *Feist,* petitioners urge that even if a work is sufficiently "original" to qualify for copyright protection in the first instance, any extension of the copyright's duration is impermissible because, once published, a work is no longer original.

Feist, however, did not touch on the duration of copyright protection. Rather, the decision addressed the core question of copyrightability, *i.e.,* the "creative spark" a work must have to be eligible for copyright protection at all. Explaining the originality requirement, *Feist* trained on the Copyright Clause words "Authors" and "Writings." *Id.,* at 346–347, 111 S.Ct. 1282. The decision did not construe the "limited Times" for which a work may be protected, and the originality requirement has no bearing on that prescription.

More forcibly, petitioners contend that the CTEA's extension of existing copyrights does not "promote the Progress of Science" as contemplated by the preambular language of the Copyright Clause. Art. I, § 8, cl. 8. To sustain this objection, petitioners do not argue that the Clause's preamble is an independently enforceable limit on Congress' power. See 239 F.3d, at 378 (Petitioners acknowledge that "the preamble of the Copyright Clause is not a substantive limit on Congress' legislative power." (internal quotation marks omitted)). Rather, they maintain that the preambular language identifies the sole end to which Congress may legislate; accordingly, they conclude, the meaning of "limited Times" must be "determined in light of that specified end." Brief for Petitioners 19. The CTEA's extension of existing copyrights categorically fails to "promote the Progress of Science," petitioners argue, because it does not stimulate the creation of new works but merely adds value to works already created.

As petitioners point out, we have described the Copyright Clause as "both a grant of power and a limitation," *Graham v. John Deere Co. of Kansas City,* 383 U.S. 1, 5, 86 S.Ct. 684, 15 L.Ed.2d 545 (1966), and have said that "[t]he primary objective of copyright" is "[t]o promote the Progress of Science," *Feist,* 499 U.S., at 349, 111 S.Ct. 1282. The "constitutional command," we have recognized, is that Congress, to the extent it enacts copyright laws at all, create a "system" that "promote[s] the Progress of Science." *Graham,* 383 U.S., at 6, 86 S.Ct. 684.

We have also stressed, however, that it is generally for Congress, not the courts, to decide how best to pursue the Copyright Clause's objectives. See

Stewart v. Abend, 495 U.S., at 230, 110 S.Ct. 1750 ("Th[e] evolution of the duration of copyright protection tellingly illustrates the difficulties Congress faces .... [I]t is not our role to alter the delicate balance Congress has labored to achieve."); *Sony,* 464 U.S., at 429, 104 S.Ct. 774 ("[I]t is Congress that has been assigned the task of defining the scope of [rights] that should be granted to authors or to inventors in order to give the public appropriate access to their work product."); *Graham,* 383 U.S., at 6, 86 S.Ct. 684 ("Within the limits of the constitutional grant, the Congress may, of course, implement the stated purpose of the Framers by selecting the policy which in its judgment best effectuates the constitutional aim."). The justifications we earlier set out for Congress' enactment of the CTEA, *supra,* at 781–782, provide a rational basis for the conclusion that the CTEA "promote[s] the Progress of Science."

On the issue of copyright duration, Congress, from the start, has routinely applied new definitions or adjustments of the copyright term to both future works and existing works not yet in the public domain. Such consistent congressional practice is entitled to "very great weight, and when it is remembered that the rights thus established have not been disputed during a period of [over two] centur[ies], it is almost conclusive." *Burrow–Giles Lithographic Co. v. Sarony,* 111 U.S., at 57, 4 S.Ct. 279. Indeed, "[t]his Court has repeatedly laid down the principle that a contemporaneous legislative exposition of the Constitution when the founders of our Government and framers of our Constitution were actively participating in public affairs, acquiesced in for a long term of years, fixes the construction to be given [the Constitution's] provisions." *Myers v. United States,* 272 U.S. 52, 175, 47 S.Ct. 21, 71 L.Ed. 160 (1926). Congress' unbroken practice since the founding generation thus overwhelms petitioners' argument that the CTEA's extension of existing copyrights fails *per se* to "promote the Progress of Science."

Closely related to petitioners' preambular argument, or a variant of it, is their assertion that the Copyright Clause "imbeds a quid pro quo." Brief for Petitioners 23. They contend, in this regard, that Congress may grant to an "Autho[r]" an "exclusive Right" for a "limited Tim[e]," but only in exchange for a "Writin[g]." Congress' power to confer copyright protection, petitioners argue, is thus contingent upon an exchange: The author of an original work receives an "exclusive Right" for a "limited Tim[e]" in exchange for a dedication to the public thereafter. Extending an existing copyright without demanding additional consideration, petitioners maintain, bestows an unpaid-for benefit on copyright holders and their heirs, in violation of the *quid pro quo* requirement.

We can demur to petitioners' description of the Copyright Clause as a grant of legislative authority empowering Congress "to secure a bargain—this for that." *Id.,* at 16; see *Mazer v. Stein,* 347 U.S. 201, 219, 74 S.Ct. 460, 98 L.Ed. 630 (1954) ("The economic philosophy behind the clause empowering Congress to grant patents and copyrights is the conviction that encouragement of individual effort by personal gain is the best way to advance public welfare through the talents of authors and inventors in 'Science and useful Arts.' "). But the legislative evolution earlier recalled demonstrates what the bargain entails. Given the consistent placement of existing copyright holders in parity with future holders, the author of a work created in the last 170 years would reasonably comprehend, as the "this" offered her, a copyright not only for the time in place when protection is gained, but also for any renewal or extension legislated during that time. Congress could rationally seek to "promote ... Progress" by including in every copyright statute an express guarantee that authors would receive the benefit of any later legislative extension of the copyright term. Nothing in the Copyright Clause bars Congress from creating the same incentive by adopting the same position as a matter of unbroken practice. See Brief for Respondent 31–32.

Neither *Sears, Roebuck & Co. v. Stiffel Co.,* 376 U.S. 225, 84 S.Ct. 784, 11 L.Ed.2d 661 (1964), nor *Bonito Boats, Inc. v. Thunder Craft Boats, Inc.,* 489 U.S. 141, 109 S.Ct. 971, 103 L.Ed.2d 118 (1989), is to the contrary. In both cases, we invalidated the application of certain state laws as inconsistent with the federal patent regime. *Sears,* 376 U.S., at 231–233, 84 S.Ct. 784; *Bonito,* 489 U.S., at 152, 109 S.Ct. 971. Describing Congress' constitutional authority to confer patents, *Bonito Boats* noted: "The Patent Clause itself reflects a balance between the need to encourage innovation and the avoidance of monopolies which stifle competition without any concomitant advance in the 'Progress of Science and useful Arts.' " *Id.,* at 146, 109 S.Ct. 971. *Sears* similarly stated that "[p]atents are not given as favors ... but are meant to encourage invention by rewarding the inventor with the right, limited to a term of years fixed by the patent, to exclude others from the use of his invention." 376 U.S., at 229, 84 S.Ct. 784. Neither case concerned the extension of a patent's duration. Nor did either suggest that such an extension might be constitutionally infirm. Rather, *Bonito Boats* reiterated the Court's unclouded understanding: "It is for Congress to determine if the present system" effectuates the goals of the Copyright and Patent Clause. 489 U.S., at 168, 109 S.Ct. 971. And as we have documented, see *supra,* at 779–781, Congress has many times sought to effectuate those goals by extending existing patents.

We note, furthermore, that patents and copyrights do not entail the same exchange, and that our references to a *quid pro quo* typically appear in the patent context. See, *e.g., J.E.M. Ag Supply, Inc. v. Pioneer Hi–Bred International, Inc.,* 534 U.S. 124, 142, 122 S.Ct. 593, 151 L.Ed.2d 508 (2001) ("The disclosure required by the Patent Act is 'the *quid pro quo* of the right to exclude.' " (quoting *Kewanee Oil Co. v. Bicron Corp.,* 416 U.S. 470, 484, 94 S.Ct. 1879, 40 L.Ed.2d 315 (1974))); *Bonito Boats,* 489 U.S., at 161, 109 S.Ct. 971 ("the *quid pro quo* of substantial creative effort required by the federal [patent] statute"); *Brenner v. Manson,* 383 U.S. 519, 534, 86 S.Ct. 1033, 16 L.Ed.2d 69 (1966) ("The basic *quid pro quo* ... for granting a patent monopoly is the benefit derived by the public from an invention with substantial utility."); *Pennock v. Dialogue,* 2 Pet. 1, 23, 7 L.Ed. 327 (1829) (If an invention is already commonly known and used when the patent is sought, "there might be sound reason for presuming, that the legislature did not intend to grant an exclusive right," given the absence of a "*quid pro quo.*"). This is understandable, given that immediate disclosure is not the objective of, but is *exacted from,* the patentee. It is the price paid for the exclusivity secured. See *J.E.M. Ag Supply,* 534 U.S., at 142, 122 S.Ct. 593. For the author seeking copyright protection, in contrast, disclosure is the desired objective, not something exacted from the author in exchange for the copyright. Indeed, since the 1976 Act, copyright has run from creation, not publication. See 1976 Act § 302(a); 17 U.S.C. § 302(a).

Further distinguishing the two kinds of intellectual property, copyright gives the holder no monopoly on any knowledge. A reader of an author's writing may make full use of any fact or idea she acquires from her reading. See § 102(b). The grant of a patent, on the other hand, does prevent full use by others of the inventor's knowledge. See Brief for Respondent 22; *Alfred Bell & Co. v. Catalda Fine Arts,* 191 F.2d 99, 103, n. 16 (C.A.2 1951) (The monopoly granted by a copyright "is not a monopoly of knowledge. The grant of a patent does prevent full use being made of knowledge, but the reader of a book is not by the copyright laws prevented from making full use of any information he may acquire from his reading." (quoting W. Copinger, Law of Copyright 2 (7th ed.1936))). In light of these distinctions, one cannot extract from language in our patent decisions—language not trained on a grant's duration—genuine support for petitioners' bold view. Accordingly, we reject the proposition that a *quid pro quo* requirement stops Congress from expanding copyright's term in a manner that puts existing and future copyrights in parity.

3

As an alternative to their various arguments that extending existing copyrights violates the Copyright Clause *per se,* petitioners urge heightened judicial review of such extensions to ensure that they appropriately pursue the purposes of the Clause. See Brief for Petitioners 31–32. Specifically, petitioners ask us to apply the "congruence and proportionality" standard described in cases evaluating exercises of Congress' power under § 5 of the Fourteenth Amendment. See, *e.g., City of Boerne v. Flores,* 521 U.S. 507, 117 S.Ct. 2157, 138 L.Ed.2d 624 (1997). But we have never applied that standard outside the § 5 context; it does not hold sway for judicial review of legislation enacted, as copyright laws are, pursuant to Article I authorization.

Section 5 authorizes Congress to *enforce* commands contained in and incorporated into the Fourteenth Amendment. Amdt. 14, § 5 ("The Congress shall have power to *enforce,* by appropriate legislation, the provisions of this article." (emphasis added)). The Copyright Clause, in contrast, empowers Congress to *define* the scope of the substantive right. See *Sony,* 464 U.S., at 429, 104 S.Ct. 774. Judicial deference to such congressional definition is "but a corollary to the grant to Congress of any Article I power." *Graham,* 383 U.S., at 6, 86 S.Ct. 684. It would be no more appropriate for us to subject the CTEA to "congruence and proportionality" review under the Copyright Clause than it would be for us to hold the Act unconstitutional *per se.*

For the several reasons stated, we find no Copyright Clause impediment to the CTEA's extension of existing copyrights.

III

Petitioners separately argue that the CTEA is a content-neutral regulation of speech that fails heightened judicial review under the First Amendment. We reject petitioners' plea for imposition of uncommonly strict scrutiny on a copyright scheme that incorporates its own speech-protective purposes and safeguards. The Copyright Clause and First Amendment were adopted close in time. This proximity indicates that, in the Framers' view, copyright's limited monopolies are compatible with free speech principles. Indeed, copyright's purpose is to *promote* the creation and publication of free expression. As *Harper & Row* observed: "[T]he Framers intended copyright itself to be the engine of free expression. By establishing a marketable right to the use of one's expression, copyright supplies the economic incentive to create and disseminate ideas." 471 U.S., at 558, 105 S.Ct. 2218.

In addition to spurring the creation and publication of new expression, copyright law contains built-in First Amendment accommodations. See *id.,* at 560, 105 S.Ct. 2218. First, it distinguishes between ideas and expression and makes only the latter eligible for copyright protection. Specifically, 17 U.S.C. § 102(b) provides: "In no case does copyright protection for an original work of authorship extend to any idea, procedure, process, system, method of operation, concept, principle, or discovery, regardless of the form in which it is described, explained, illustrated, or embodied in such work." As we said in *Harper & Row,* this "idea/expression dichotomy strike[s] a definitional balance between the First Amendment and the Copyright Act by permitting free communication of facts while still protecting an author's expression." 471 U.S., at 556, 105 S.Ct. 2218 (internal quotation marks omitted). Due to this distinction, every idea, theory, and fact in a copyrighted work becomes instantly available for public exploitation at the moment of publication. See *Feist,* 499 U.S., at 349–350, 111 S.Ct. 1282.

Second, the "fair use" defense allows the public to use not only facts and ideas contained in a copyrighted work, but also expression itself in certain circumstances. Codified at 17 U.S.C. § 107, the defense provides: "[T]he fair use of a copyrighted work, including such use by reproduction in copies ..., for purposes such as criticism, comment, news reporting, teaching (including multiple copies for classroom use), scholarship, or research, is not an infringement of copyright." The fair use defense affords considerable "latitude for scholarship and comment," *Harper & Row,* 471 U.S., at 560, 105 S.Ct. 2218, and even for parody, see *Campbell v. Acuff–Rose Music, Inc.,* 510 U.S. 569, 114 S.Ct. 1164, 127 L.Ed.2d 500 (1994) (rap group's musical parody of Roy Orbison's "Oh, Pretty Woman" may be fair use).

The CTEA itself supplements these traditional First Amendment safeguards. First, it allows libraries, archives, and similar institutions to "reproduce" and "distribute, display, or perform in facsimile or digital form" copies of certain published works "during the last 20 years of any term of copyright ... for purposes of preservation, scholarship, or research" if the work is not already being exploited commercially and further copies are unavailable at a reasonable price. 17 U.S.C. § 108(h); see Brief for Respondent 36. Second, Title II of the CTEA, known as the Fairness in Music Licensing Act of 1998, exempts small businesses, restaurants, and like entities from having to pay performance royalties on music played from licensed radio, television, and similar facilities. 17 U.S.C. § 110(5)(B); see Brief for Representative F. James Sensenbrenner, Jr., et al. as *Amici Curiae* 5–6, n. 3.

Finally, the case petitioners principally rely upon for their First Amendment argument, *Turner Broadcasting System, Inc. v. FCC,* 512 U.S. 622, 114 S.Ct. 2445, 129 L.Ed.2d 497 (1994), bears little on copyright. The statute at issue in *Turner* required cable operators to carry and transmit broadcast stations through their proprietary cable systems. Those "must-carry" provisions, we explained, implicated "the heart of the First Amendment," namely, "the principle that each person should decide for himself or herself the ideas and beliefs deserving of expression, consideration, and adherence." *Id.,* at 641, 114 S.Ct. 2445.

The CTEA, in contrast, does not oblige anyone to reproduce another's speech against the carrier's will. Instead, it protects authors' original expression from unrestricted exploitation. Protection of that order does not raise the free speech concerns present when the government compels or burdens the communication of particular facts or ideas. The First Amendment securely protects the freedom to make—or decline to make—one's own speech; it bears less heavily when speakers assert the right to make other people's speeches. To the extent such assertions raise First Amendment concerns, copyright's built-in free speech safeguards are generally adequate to address them. We recognize that the D.C. Circuit spoke too broadly when it declared copyrights "categorically immune from challenges under the First Amendment." 239 F.3d, at 375. But when, as in this case, Congress has not altered the traditional contours of copyright protection, further First Amendment scrutiny is unnecessary. See *Harper & Row,* 471 U.S., at 560, 105 S.Ct. 2218; cf. *San Francisco Arts & Athletics, Inc. v. United States Olympic Comm.,* 483 U.S. 522, 107 S.Ct. 2971, 97 L.Ed.2d 427 (1987).

IV

If petitioners' vision of the Copyright Clause held sway, it would do more than render the CTEA's duration extensions unconstitutional as to existing works. Indeed, petitioners' assertion that the provisions of the CTEA are not severable would make the CTEA's enlarged terms invalid even as to tomorrow's work. The 1976 Act's time extensions, which set the pattern that the CTEA followed, would be vulnerable as well.

As we read the Framers' instruction, the Copyright Clause empowers Congress to determine the intellectual property regimes that, overall, in that body's judgment, will serve the ends of the Clause. See *Graham,* 383 U.S., at 6, 86 S.Ct. 684 (Congress may "implement the stated purpose of the Framers by selecting the policy which *in its judgment* best effectuates the constitutional aim." (emphasis added)). Beneath the facade of their inventive constitutional interpretation, petitioners forcefully urge that Congress pursued very bad policy in prescribing the CTEA's long terms. The wisdom of Congress' action, however, is not within our province to second-guess. Satisfied that the legislation before us remains inside the domain the Constitution assigns to the First Branch, we affirm the judgment of the Court of Appeals.

It is so ordered.

Justice STEVENS, dissenting...

See also Eldred v. Reno, 239 F.3d 372 (D.D.C. 2001) (the work of a subsisting copyright has already passed the originality test, so it automatically acquires CETA's 20 extra years of copyright protection).

QUESTIONS AND DISCUSSION

1. In King Features Syndicate v. Fleischer, 299 F. 533 (2d Cir.1924), the copyright holder of cartoons sued a doll manufacturer. You cannot avoid infringement of a copyright by taking its substance or idea and then produce it through a different medium. If it is similar, even though you are omitting the work of the artisan, you are still appropriating the genius of the artist. And, anyhow, copyright law should have a liberal construction to give effect to the inherent right of the author in his or her work. Genius and creativity should be protected, right? Mickey Mouse is in a million different mediums, but he is still Mickey (for copyright purposes). What do you think of that? Is there a similar and comparable "genius" in moving "an idea in a form" to another medium?

2. Walt Disney Prods v. Air Pirates, 281 F.2d 751 (9th Cir.1978), is one of my favorite cases. Mickey Mouse (et al.) protected his copyright against pornographic cartoon recreations! [As an aside, a co-author's sister had a risqué poster of Disney characters; she gave it away and now it's a collector's item!] Mickey and Walt won as to copyright infringement but were reversed and remanded as to trademark infringement, unfair competition, and trade disparagement. Don't mess with the Mouse! The Walt Disney Empire polices their many copyrights, trademarks, trade secrets, etc., vociferously. Because it is their brand and, therefore, it's who they are. Have we gone too far in protecting the intellectual property of this photographic rodent?

3. In Nichols v. Universal Pictures Corp., 45 F.2d 119 (2d Cir.1930), a copyrighted play was made into a motion picture. Again, different mediums. Were there substantial similarities? This case concerns a play, "Abie's Irish Rose" and a motion picture, "The Cohens and the Kellys." The bottom line is that the less developed a character in a play is, the less it can be copyrighted. This is the penalty the author must accept for drawing characters too indistinctly; stock characters are not protected. What could we add to these stock characters to make them more distinct, and hence more likely to be copyrightable? A lisp?

4. Look at Sheldon v. MGM, 81 F.2d 49 (2d Cir.1936). The broader outline of a plot is never copyrightable. Take time in the creation of your work. Harry Potter was copyrightable because, among other reasons of course, author Rowling imagined seven books! The question in Sheldon is whether the movie, "Letty Lymon" infringes on the copyrighted play, "Dishonored Lady." This case is famous for the aphorism, "No plagiarist can excuse the wrong by showing how much of the work he did not pirate" (at 55). That makes sense, doesn't it? Look at the indices of similarity first.

5. In King v. Mister Maestro, Inc., 224 F. Supp. 101 (S.D.N.Y.1963), Martin Luther King seeks copyright protection for his speeches. If his speeches are in the public domain, they are not copyrightable. He was granted a preliminary injunction. That's certainly appropriate, but isn't the point to get the word out,

if it's done in a proper, accurate, and respectful manner? Remember the nomenclature, "for educational purposes only"? What does that mean? Isn't everything educational?

6. Ditto with Estate of Hemingway v. Random House, Inc., 268 N.Y.S.D. 531 (N.Y. Supr., Spec. Term, N.Y. Cty.). Ernest Hemingway's widow tried to enjoin publication of a biography. She lost basically because the widow's right of privacy was not violated by references to her as the wife of the central figure. Genius, even if it's in the form of a biography, must be protected. Is there any way that we can keep her name out of this?

7. In Warner Bros. Pictures, Inc. v. CBS, Inc., 216 F.2d 945 (9th Cir.1954), the court ruled that even if Dashiell Hammett, the author of *The Maltese Falcon,* assigned his complete rights in the copyright, it still did not prevent him from using those characters (e.g., Sam Spade) in other stories. If this negative practice was allowed, there would be no sequels, prequels, etc., and life as we know it would cease to exist. But, is this a correct interpretation of the law?

8. Ideal Toy Corp. v. Kenner Products Div. of General Mills fun Group, Inc., 443 F.Supp. 291 (S.D.N.Y.1977), merges the concepts of film copyright, trademark, and unfair competition in the lucrative world of marketing. (Think *Star Wars* figurines.) Ideal sold "Star Team" toys; Ideal won. It is pure speculation as to whether Ideal's toys weakened the market for Kenner's copyrighted *Star Wars* toys. Good advice: Prove your case with statistics. Would this case have been winnable with better preparation?

CHAPTER 8
COPYRIGHT AND MUSIC

In a copyright infringement suit, a federal jury in Los Angeles awarded the heirs of Marvin Gaye an unprecedented $7.3 million dollars for the plagiarism by Robin Thicke and Pharell Williams, who share a writing credit, for Thicke's mega 2013 hit "Blurred Lines." Remember, "War is not the answer..." Robin Thicke saw "Blurred Lines" as an homage to his idol. According to the jury's decision, Nona and Frankie Gaye, two of Marvin Gaye's children, are to receive $4 million in damages, plus $3.3 million in profits attributed to Thicke and Williams, as well as about $9,000 in statutory damages for infringement of copyright. Clifford Harris, Jr., better known as T.L., who contributed a rap in the song, was found not liable (Ben Sisario and Noah Smith, N.Y. Times, "Jury: Blurred Lines' clearly plagiarism. Thicke, Williams ordered to pay Gaye's children $7.3 million for song." Houston Chronicle at A2 (March 11, 2015)). This was one of the largest damages awards for copyright infringement ever, including a $5.4 million awards against Michael Bolton and Sony for infringement of a 1960s Isley Brothers song. This is an important, groundbreaking case which included airing industry dirty laundry on percentage splits in royalty deals, embarrassing drug use, unearned songwriting credits (what's new?), and the intentional obfuscation and deception of the news media (again, what's new?). Pharrell said that the song had a similar "feel" but it was not a copy of "Got to Give It Up." It was stated at trial that "Blurred Lines" earned an estimated $16 million in profits.

BRIGHT TUNES MUSIC CORP v. HARRISONGS MUSIC, LTD.
United States District court for the Southern District of New York
August 31, 1976
No. 71 Civ. 602
420 F.Supp. 177

OWEN, District Judge.

This is an action in which it is claimed that a successful song, My Sweet Lord, listing George Harrison as the composer, is plagiarized from an earlier successful song, He's So Fine, composed by Ronald Mack, recorded by a singing group called the "Chiffons," the copyright of which is owned by plaintiff, Bright Tunes Music Corp.

He's So Fine, recorded in 1962, is a catchy tune consisting essentially of four repetitions of a very short basic musical phrase, "sol-mi-re," (hereinafter motif A), altered as necessary to fit the words, followed by four repetitions of another short basic musical phrase, "sol-la-do-la-do," (hereinafter motif B). While neither motif is novel, the four repetitions of A, followed by four repetitions of B, is a highly unique pattern. In addition, in the second use of the motif B series, there is a grace note inserted making the phrase go "sol-la-do-la-re-do."

My Sweet Lord, recorded first in 1970, also uses the same motif A (modified to suit the words) four times, followed by motif B, repeated three times, not four. In place of He's So Fine's fourth repetition of motif B, My Sweet Lord has a transitional passage of musical attractiveness of the same approximate length, with the identical grace note in the identical second repetition. The harmonies of both songs are identical.

George Harrison, a former member of The Beatles, was aware of He's So Fine. In the United States, it was No. 1 on the billboard charts for five weeks; in England, Harrison's home country, it was No. 12 on the charts on June 1, 1963, a date upon which one of the Beatle songs was, in fact, in first position. For seven weeks in 1963, He's So Fine was one of the top hits in England.

According to Harrison, the circumstances of the composition of My Sweet Lord were as follows. Harrison and his group, which include an American black gospel singer named Billy Preston, were in Copenhagen, Denmark, on a singing engagement. There was a press conference involving the group going on backstage. Harrison slipped away from the press conference and went to a room upstairs and began "vamping" some guitar chords, fitting on to the chords he was playing the words, "Hallelujah" and "Hare Krishna" in various ways. During the course of this vamping, he was alternating between what musicians call a Minor II chord and a Major V chord.

At some point, germinating started and he went down to meet with others of the group, asking them to listen, which they did, and everyone began to join in, taking first "Hallelujah" and then "Hare Krishna" and putting them into four part harmony. Harrison obviously started using the "Hallelujah," etc., as repeated sounds, and from there developed the lyrics, to wit, "My Sweet Lord," "Dear, Dear Lord," etc. In any event, from this very free-flowing exchange of ideas, with Harrison playing his two chords and everybody singing "Hallelujah" and "Hare Krishna," there began to emerge the My Sweet Lord text idea, which Harrison sought to develop a little bit further during the following week as he was playing it on his guitar. Thus developed motif A and its words interspersed with "Hallelujah" and "Hare Krishna."

Approximately one week after the idea first began to germinate, the entire group flew back to London because they had earlier booked time to go to a recording studio with Billy Preston to make an album. In the studio, Preston was the principal musician. Harrison did not play in the session. He had given Preston his basic motif A with the idea that it be turned into a song, and was back and forth from the studio to the engineer's recording booth, supervising the recording "takes." Under circumstances that Harrison was utterly unable to recall, while everybody was working toward a finished song, in the recording studio, somehow or other the essential three notes of motif A reached polished form.

"Q. (By the Court): . . . you feel that those three notes . . . the motif A in the record, those three notes developed somewhere in that recording session?

"Mr. Harrison: I'd say those three there were finalized as beginning there."

"Q. (By the Court): Is it possible that Billy Preston hit on those (notes comprising tif A)?

"Mr. Harrison: Yes, but it's possible also that I hit on that, too, as far back as the dressing room, just scat singing."

Similarly, it appears that motif B emerged in some fashion at the recording session as did motif A. This is also true of the unique grace note in the second repetition of motif B.

"Q. (By the Court): All I am trying to get at, Mr. Harrison, is if you have a recollection when that (grace) note popped into existence as it ends up in the Billy Preston recording.

"Mr. Harrison: . . . (Billy Preston) might have put that there on every take, but it just might have been on one take, or he might have varied it on different takes at different places."

The Billy Preston recording, listing George Harrison as the composer, was thereafter issued by Apple Records. The music was then reduced to paper by someone who prepared a "lead sheet" containing the melody, the words and the harmony for the United States copyright application.

Seeking the wellsprings of musical composition why a composer chooses the succession of notes and the harmonies he does whether it be George Harrison or Richard Wagner is a fascinating inquiry. It is apparent from the extensive colloquy between the Court and Harrison covering forty pages in the transcript that neither Harrison nor Preston were conscious of the fact that they were utilizing the He's So Fine theme. However, they in fact were, for it is perfectly obvious to the listener that in musical terms, the two songs are virtually identical except for one phrase. There is motif A used four times, followed by motif B, four times in one case, and three times in the other, with the same grace note in the second repetition of motif B.

What happened? I conclude that the composer, in seeking musical materials to clothe his thoughts, was working with various possibilities. As he tried this possibility and that, there came to the surface of his mind a particular combination that pleased him as being one he felt would be appealing to a prospective listener; in other words, that this combination of sounds would work. Why? Because his subconscious knew it already had worked in a song his conscious mind did not remember. Having arrived at this pleasing combination of sounds, the recording was made, the lead sheet prepared for copyright and the song became an enormous success. Did Harrison deliberately use the music of He's So Fine? I do not believe he did so deliberately. Nevertheless, it is clear that My Sweet Lord is the very same song as He's So Fine with different words, and Harrison had access to He's So Fine. This is, under the law, infringement of copyright, and is no less so even though subconsciously accomplished. Sheldon v. Metro-Goldwyn Pictures Corp., 81 F.2d 49, 54 (2d Cir. 1936); Northern Music Corp. v. Pacemaker Music Co., Inc., 147 U.S.P.Q. 358, 359 (S.D.N.Y.1965).

Given the foregoing, I find for the plaintiff on the issue of plagiarism, and set the action down for trial on November 8, 1976 on the issue of damages and other relief as to which the plaintiff may be entitled. The foregoing constitutes the Court's findings of fact and conclusions of law.

So Ordered.

SYSTEMS XIX, INC. v. PARKER
United States District Court for the Nothern District of California
November 6, 1998, Decided; November 6, 1998, Filed
No. C97-3983 SI
30 F.Supp.2d 1225

ILLSTON, District Judge.

On November 6, 1998, the Court heard argument on defendants' motion for summary judgment. Having carefully considered the moving and opposing papers and the arguments of counsel, and for the reasons set out below, the motion is GRANTED in part and DENIED in part.

BACKGROUND

Plaintiff Maritime Hall Productions (Maritime) owns Maritime Hall, a combined amphitheater and recording studio in San Francisco, California. Defendants are Lawrence Parker (Parker), a performer of rap music who performs under the name "KRS–ONE", and Zomba Recording Corporation (Zomba), the record company responsible for the marketing and distribution of Parker's songs. Zomba is the copyright owner of Parker's musical compositions and recordings.

In mid-January 1997, Albert Cook, a concert promoter, contacted Maritime's president, Boots Hughston, to arrange a concert involving Parker at the Maritime Hall. Over the course of the next four weeks, Cook, Hughston, and Wesley Powell, Parker's road manager, negotiated the terms of the performance contract.

According to Hughston, Cook explained to Hughston during the negotiations that Parker was creating a new album and that if Maritime were to record Parker's performance, those recordings might be used on the new album. Hughston Decl. ¶ 21. Hughston informed Cook that Maritime would require compensation and producer credits if Parker included a Maritime Hall recording on an album Although the parties' negotiations were reduced to an Artist Engagement Contract, neither party signed the agreement due, in part, to an inability to agree on terms relating to the production and recording of Parker's live performance. Hughston Decl. ¶ 20.

Parker states that he customarily records his performances for purposes of self-evaluation. Parker Decl. ¶ 9. On March 15, 1997, the day of the concert, Parker claims that since Parker's own sound engineer was absent, Powell requested Maritime to record the concert. *Id.* at 18. Maritime proceeded to set up its recording equipment, including stage and audience microphones, audio lines and video cameras. Powell and Hughston then discussed the recording process for the concert. According to Hughston, Powell observed the pre-concert recording set-up, asked some questions about the video cameras, but appeared primarily concerned with receiving "the master" of the performance. Hughston Decl. ¶¶ 33–34.

Maritime recorded the concert and provided Powell with a master tape of the concert after the show. In the summer of 1997, Parker released an album "I Got Next" (the album). Two tracks on the album were taken from the sound recording of the concert on March 15, 1997. Although each of the remaining sixteen tracks on the album listed producer credits, the two tracks from the Maritime Hall concert sound recording contained no reference to producer credits or venue. Following the release of the album, Maritime requested compensation and producer credit listing from Zomba for its use of the sound recording on the album. Zomba did not reply to Maritime's request.

Maritime filed this action for declaratory relief and damages against Parker and Zomba on October 30, 1997. Maritime seeks a judicial determination of its rights under the Copyright Act with respect to the sound recording. In the alternative, Maritime seeks recovery in *quantum meruit* for Zomba's allegedly unauthorized use of the sound recording. Defendants filed the instant motion for summary judgment on August 7, 1998.

LEGAL STANDARD

The Federal Rules of Civil Procedure provide for summary adjudication when "the pleadings, depositions, answers to interrogatories, and admissions on file, together with affidavits, if any, show that there is no genuine issue as to any material fact and that the moving party is entitled to a judgment as a matter of law." Fed.R.Civ.P. 56(c).

In a motion for summary judgment, "[if] the moving party for summary judgment meets its initial burden of identifying for the court those portions of the materials on file that it believes demonstrate the absence of any genuine issues of material fact, the burden of production then shifts so that the non-moving party must set forth, by affidavit or as otherwise provided in Rule 56, 'specific facts showing that there is a genuine issue for trial.' " ...

In judging evidence at the summary judgment stage, the Court does not make credibility determinations or weigh conflicting evidence, and draws all inferences in the light most favorable to the nonmoving party...

DISCUSSION

1. Maritime's rights under the Copyright Act

Maritime claims joint copyright ownership of the sound recordings. Defendants respond that Maritime is not a joint author of the sound recordings because Zomba and Parker lacked the requisite intent to create a joint work and never authorized Maritime to use the underlying musical compositions to make the sound recording.

Section 101 of the Copyright Act of 1976(Act) defines a 'joint work' as: "a work prepared by two or more authors with the intention that their contributions be merged into inseparable or interdependent parts of a unitary whole." A party claiming joint authorship must establish that the authors 1) intended to merge their contributions into a unitary whole and 2) contributed copyrightable subject matter to the joint work. 17 U.S.C. § 101; *Ashton–Tate Corp. v. Ross,* 916 F.2d 516, 520–21 (9th Cir.1990).

A. Intention of the parties

i. The applicable standard

For a joint work to exist, the putative authors must have intended to merge their respective contributions into a unitary whole. 17 U.S.C. § 101. Defendants first argue that under *Childress v. Taylor,* 945 F.2d 500 (2d Cir.1991), the parties' intent turns on their *subjective* expectations. *Id.* at 507. Maritime responds that the courts scrutinize the subjective intent of the parties under the heightened *Childress* test only where the copyright claimant does not occupy a traditional authorship role as contemplated by Congress. In the case of sound recordings, Maritime argues that since Congress explicitly recognized the potential joint authorship roles of producer and artist, the *Childress* test is inapplicable to the instant facts. Rather than a subjective standard, Maritime contends that the parties' intent should be measured against an objective, factual standard as contemplated by the Act.

The Court agrees with Maritime that the subjective standard under *Childress* does not apply to the instant facts. *Childress* involved an actress/research assistant who claimed joint authorship of a play. The *Childress* court evaluated the intention of the parties based on a subjective standard to prevent the extension of "joint authorship status to many persons who are not likely to have been within the contemplation of Congress." *Id.*

In contrast to the playwright/research assistant relationship in *Childress,* the producer/performer relationship here was under the specific contemplation of Congress as joint authors of a sound recording under the Act. Congress discussed in the Act's legislative history that "[t]he copyrightable elements of a sound recording will usually, though not always, involve 'authorship' both on the part of the performers whose performance is captured and on the part of the *record producer* responsible for setting up the session, capturing and electronically processing the sounds, and compiling and editing them to make a final sound recording." H.R.Rep. No. 94–1476, 94th Cong., 2nd Sess. 56 (1976) (emphasis added)

The standard by which the intent of the parties is measured is not strictly subjective as urged by Defendants. Rather, the requisite intent will be found if, based on an objective, factual standard, the parties prepared the sound recording "with the intention that their contributions be merged into inseparable or interdependent parts of a unitary whole." 17 U.S.C. § 101; P. Goldstein, *Copyright,* 2nd ed., § 4.2.1 (1998).

ii. Did Zomba possess the requisite intent to create a joint work?

Defendants contend that they did not share a mutual intent with Maritime to create a joint work in the sound recordings. Defendants argue that since neither Zomba nor Parker ever had any direct communication with Maritime, much less asked Maritime to professionally record the concert, defendants could not have intended the creation of a joint work with Maritime.

Maritime responds that defendants did share an intention with Maritime to co-author the sound recording, as demonstrated by copyright practice, industry custom, and the factual circumstances in which the sound recording was produced.

Maritime first argues that sound recordings by their nature are usually joint works. For example, according to the United States Copyright Office, "[s]ound recording authorship may be contributed by the performer or the record producer. Usually, authorship is contributed by both performer and producer." Compendium of Copyright Office Practices, United States Copyright Office, § 495.01 at 400–37 (1984).

Maritime next argues that as an experienced artist, Parker understood the inherently collaborative nature of producing a live performance. Parker was aware of both the technical and creative efforts that are customarily required of producers, as well as the acknowledgment of those efforts through the industry practice of 1) crediting producers on an album for their contribution in recording a particular track and 2) requesting third party producers to transfer their rights in the track in exchange for royalty payments.

Finally, Maritime contends that when Parker requested, through his road manager, that Maritime record his performance, Parker intended to create a collaborative joint work with Maritime, in accordance with copyright practice and industry custom. Powell, the road manager, claims that he did not request a professional recording, but merely asked Maritime to activate a tape recorder. Maritime points out, however, that both Parker and Powell knew prior to the concert that Parker was going to be professionally recorded because the recording equipment, including large microphones and video cameras, was plainly visible from the stage.

After the concert, Parker's road manager left with the "master" tape. Parker and Zomba ultimately used the sound recording on the album. Maritime concludes that by requesting a recording of the concert, which was later commercially released, defendants intended that the parties merge their creative efforts in the production of a sound recording.

The Court finds that Maritime has demonstrated the existence of triable issues of fact with respect to the intention of the parties. Contrary to defendants' contentions, whether Zomba or Parker ever directly asked Maritime to record the concert is not dispositive of the question of the parties' intent.... Maritime has submitted evidence that Parker requested Maritime to record him. Parker knew Maritime was employing professional equipment while he was being recorded. Parker, through his road manager, sought out the tape after the concert, and ultimately used the tape on his album. From these circumstances a jury could reasonably conclude that Parker/Zomba and Maritime shared an implied agreement to jointly create a sound recording of the concert through the interdependent contributions of Parker's performance and Maritime's recordation and production thereof.

B. Copyrightable contribution

Copyright protection applies only to those claimants that have made an original contribution. 17 U.S.C. 102(a). Maritime argues that it contributed copyrightable subject matter to the sound recordings through the arrangement and administration of recording equipment, the electronic processing of sounds, and the balancing, equalization, and integration of vocal, instrumental and audience components into a blended whole....

Defendants contend, however, that as a matter of law, Maritime is precluded from making copyrightable contributions to the sound recording because Maritime did not have Zomba's consent to make those contributions. *See Pamfiloff v. Giant Records, Inc.,* 794 F.Supp. 933, 938 (N.D.Cal.1992). Zomba owns the exclusive copyright to the musical compositions that form the basis of the sound recording. Defendants correctly maintain that to assert a claim of joint authorship over the sound recordings, Maritime must have obtained Zomba's permission to use Parker's musical compositions in the sound recordings. 17 U.S.C. § 103(a). Defendants conclude that since Zomba did not authorize Maritime to use the underlying compositions in the sound recording, Maritime had no legal right to make copyrightable contributions in the production of the sound recording.

Permission to employ pre-existing copyrighted material in a sound recording need not be in writing, but can be granted orally or implied from conduct in the form of a non-exclusive license. *Pamfiloff,* 794 F.Supp. at 938–39; M. Nimmer & D. Nimmer, *Nimmer on Copyright* § 10.03[A][7]. Maritime argues that it received a non-exclusive license from defendants to use Parker's underlying musical compositions in the sound recording. Maritime contends that its license was implied from the following conduct: 1) Parker's road manager asked Maritime to record the performance; 2) Parker performed in front of two highly conspicuous audience microphones; and 3) Parker and Zomba accepted and released the sound recordings.

Defendants argue that since Zomba owned the copyrights to Parker's musical compositions, only Zomba could grant Maritime a license to use the compositions. Defendants contend that Maritime has presented evidence of an implied license based only on the conduct of Powell and Parker, and not of Zomba.

The Court finds that whether Maritime had an implied license to use Parker's musical compositions based on the conduct of Zomba or its agents is a question of fact that cannot be resolved on summary judgment. It is true that Zomba owns the copyright to Parker's musical compositions. Zomba, however, also vested Parker with the authority to perform those compositions at Maritime's venue. At the venue, Parker requested that Maritime record his musical compositions. Since Parker states that he "customarily" records his own performances, it should have come as no surprise to Zomba that Parker asked Maritime to record the concert. Parker Decl. ¶ 9.

From these facts, a jury could reasonably conclude that Parker, vested with Zomba's authority to perform the copyrighted compositions, acted as Zomba's agent when he requested Maritime to record the concert.... In light of Zomba's later acceptance and commercial exploitation of the sound recordings, it is a question of fact whether Parker's request to record the performance constituted an implied license for Maritime to use the underlying compositions to produce the sound recording.

2. Maritime's unjust enrichment claim

Defendants contend that Maritime's equitable claim for unjust enrichment is preempted by the Copyright Act under 17 U.S.C. § 301. Maritime responds that preemption does not apply because the subject matter of its state law claim falls outside the scope of the Act.

Section 301(a) of the Act provides a three-part test to determine whether a state law claim is preempted by federal copyright law. First, the work on which the state claim is based must be fixed in a tangible medium of expression. Second, the work must fall within the subject matter of copyright as defined in §§ 102 and 103 of the Act. Third, the state cause of action must protect rights that are qualitatively equivalent to copyright protection as defined under § 106 of the Act. 17 U.S.C. § 301(a).

Under the first prong, neither party disputes that the sound recordings are fixed in the tangible medium of an audio cassette tape. Under the second prong, defendants argue that the work on which the claim for unjust enrichment is based is the sound recording, which falls within the subject matter of the Act under § 102(a)(7). Maritime responds that the work at issue is not the sound recording, but rather the physical tape in which the sound recording is fixed. Maritime contends that the tape itself is a chattel, specifically a "phonorecord," that falls outside the scope of protection under the Act. 17 U.S.C. § 101.

The Court agrees with defendants that the work at issue is the sound recording rather than the tape in which the recording is fixed. Maritime's quasi-contract claim is not that defendants have been unjustly enriched by the retention of an audio cassette, but by the retention of a sound recording embodied in the audio cassette. The value to either party rests not in the tape, but in the sounds captured in the tape.

Under the third prong, defendants claim that the rights which Maritime seeks to vindicate in its unjust enrichment claim are qualitatively equivalent to the copyright protection embodied in § 106(1) and 106(2) of the Act. In its opposition, Maritime does not dispute defendant's argument

The Court finds that the rights which Maritime seeks to enforce in its claim for unjust enrichment is equivalent to the rights of a copyright owner under § 106(1) and 106(3) of the Act. Section 106(1) ensures a copyright owner the right "to reproduce the copyrighted work in copies or phonorecords." Section 106(3) protects the right of copyright owners to distribute those copies to the public for sale.

In its state law claim, Maritime seeks recovery from defendants for their wrongful profits from Maritime's interest in the sound recording. Under the Act, Maritime, as putative joint author, possesses the right under § 106(1) and 106(3) to share in the profits of Zomba's reproduction and distribution of the sound recordings[.] Under federal copyright law or in *quantum meruit,* Maritime is seeking the same thing: compensation for the reproduction and distribution of the sound recordings. Under the third prong, therefore, the rights Maritime asserts under its state law claim are equivalent to rights within the general scope of copyright as specified in § 106.

The sound recording is a work of authorship fixed in a tangible medium of expression and the work comes within the subject matter of copyright under § 102(a)(7). Further, the rights sought to be vindicated in Maritime's unjust enrichment claim are rights involving reproduction and distribution that are clearly equivalent to the rights prescribed by § 106(1) and 106(3). Consequently, § 301(a) preempts Maritime's unjust enrichment claim.

CONCLUSION

For the foregoing reasons, the Court DENIES defendants' motion for summary judgment of Maritime's claims under the Copyright Act, and GRANTS defendants' motion for summary judgment of Maritime's claims of unjust enrichment.

IT IS SO ORDERED.

STEELE v. TURNER BROAD SYS.
United States District Court for the District of Massachusetts
August 19, 2009, Decided
Civil Action No. 08-11727-NMG
646 F. Supp.2d 185

GORTON, District Judge.

The plaintiff, acting *pro se,* brings this case against numerous defendants for alleged copyright infringement. He alleges that a song he wrote about the Boston Red Sox was unlawfully copied and used to create an advertisement promoting Major League Baseball post-season telecasts.

I. *Background*

A. Factual Background

The plaintiff, Samuel Bartley Steele ("Steele"), along with two "unincorporated business organizations," Steele Publishing Company and Steele Recordz (for convenience, all of the plaintiffs are hereinafter collectively referred to as "Steele" or "plaintiff"), are residents of Chelsea, Massachusetts. Steele is a songwriter and musician who asserts that, in 2004, he wrote a "love anthem" about the Boston Red Sox ("the Red Sox") entitled "Man I Really Love This Team" ("the Steele Song"). Not surprisingly, Steele's song gained popularity around Fenway Park, the Red Sox historic stadium, in the fall of 2004 as the team played toward its first World Series Championship in 86 years.

Steele's claim for copyright infringement arises from an advertisement produced and aired by the defendant Turner Broadcasting System, Inc. ("TBS") during the 2007 Major League Baseball ("MLB") post-season ("the TBS Promo"). The TBS Promo features a song by the popular band Bon Jovi entitled "I Love This Town" ("the Bon Jovi Song") along with baseball video footage. In addition to TBS, Steele's complaint names Bon Jovi front-man John Bongiovi and guitarist Richard Sambora as defendants. Also sued were William Falcone, Time Warner Corporation, Major League Baseball Properties, the Red Sox, A & E Television Networks, AEG Live, Mark Shimmel Music, Universal Music Publishing ("Universal Music"), Universal Polygram International Publishing, The Bigger Picture Cinema Company, Island Def Jam Records ("Island Records"), Kobalt Music Publishing America, Inc. ("Kobalt"), Fox Broadcasting Company ("Fox"), Sony ATV Tunes LLC ("Sony") and Vector 2 LLC ("Vector").

Steele asserts that the Bon Jovi Song and the TBS Promo infringe his copyright. With respect to the TBS Promo, Steele contends that it was unlawfully derived from his work through a method called "temp tracking."

According to Steele, that term refers to the use of a song as a template to create an audiovisual work which, in turn, is used to create a final soundtrack. Steele alleges that much of the visual portion of the TBS Promo is derived from his song and that the Bon Jovi Song was then based upon that Promo, the Steele Song or both.

B. Procedural History

Steele filed his initial complaint alleging copyright infringement and violation of the Lanham Act on October 8, 2008. On January 30, 2009, Steele amended his complaint to add the Red Sox as a defendant and a claim pursuant to the Massachusetts Consumer Protection Act, M.G.L. c. 93A ("Chapter 93A"). The amended complaint did not include a Lanham Act claim or some of the original defendants but, at Steele's urging and in light of his *pro se* status, this Court considered both complaints together in deciding the defendants' motions to dismiss.

On April 3, 2009, 607 F.Supp.2d 258 (D.Mass.2009), this Court issued a Memorandum and Order dismissing the claims brought under the Lanham Act and Chapter 93A and all claims against the defendants Universal Music, Fox, Sony and Vector. *Steele v. Turner Broadcasting Sys., Inc.,* 607 F.Supp.2d 258 (D.Mass.2009). The Court declined to dismiss Steele's copyright infringement claims against the remaining defendants and instead permitted limited discovery to allow Steele to "gather and present evidence of substantial similarity" including expert analysis of his song and the alleged infringing works. *Id.* at 265. The Court indicated that, following such discovery, it would entertain motions for summary judgment on the issue of substantial similarity.

On June 10, 2009, the remaining defendants, with the exception of Kobalt and Island Records, moved for summary judgment.[1] In support of their motion they included an expert report from musicologist Anthony Ricigliano ("the Ricigliano Report"). Kobalt separately moves for summary judgment incorporating by reference the arguments made by its co-defendants.

On July 17, 2009, Steele opposed the defendants' motions for summary judgment. He also has submitted an (unsigned) report from a musicologist, reports from various other purported experts, affidavits from "ordinary listeners" who claim to detect similarity between the Steele Song and the alleged infringing works and an affidavit of his own. On July 30, the defendants (with the exception of Kobalt and Island Records and with leave of Court) submitted a reply memorandum. Although a hearing on the motion is scheduled for September 10, 2009, this Court concludes that a decision can be rendered based on the thorough submissions currently before it.

II. *Analysis*
A. Legal Standard

The role of summary judgment is "to pierce the pleadings and to assess the proof in order to see whether there is a genuine need for trial." *Mesnick v. Gen. Elec. Co.,* 950 F.2d 816, 822 (1st Cir.1991) (quoting *Garside v. Osco Drug, Inc.,* 895 F.2d 46, 50 (1st Cir.1990)). The burden is upon the moving party to show, based upon the pleadings, discovery and affidavits, "that there is no genuine issue as to any material fact and that the moving party is entitled to a judgment as a matter of law." Fed.R.Civ.P. 56(c).

A fact is material if it "might affect the outcome of the suit under the governing law." *Anderson v. Liberty Lobby, Inc.,* 477 U.S. 242, 248, 106 S.Ct. 2505, 91 L.Ed.2d 202 (1986). "Factual disputes that are irrelevant or unnecessary will not be counted." *Id.* A genuine issue of material fact exists where the evidence with respect to the material fact in dispute "is such that a reasonable jury could return a verdict for the nonmoving party." *Id.*

Once the moving party has satisfied its burden, the burden shifts to the non-moving party to set forth specific facts showing that there is a genuine, triable issue. *Celotex Corp. v. Catrett,* 477 U.S. 317, 324, 106 S.Ct. 2548, 91 L.Ed.2d 265 (1986). The court must view the entire record in the light most hospitable to the non-moving party and indulge all reasonable inferences in that party's favor. *O'Connor v. Steeves,* 994 F.2d 905, 907 (1st Cir.1993). If, after viewing the record in the non-moving party's favor, the court determines that no genuine issue of material fact exists and the moving party is entitled to judgment as a matter of law, summary judgment is appropriate.

B. Copyright Infringement

To succeed on a claim for copyright infringement, a plaintiff must prove "(1) ownership of a valid copyright, and (2) copying of constituent elements of the work that are original." *Feist Publ'ns, Inc. v. Rural Tel. Serv. Co., Inc.,* 499 U.S. 340, 361, 111 S.Ct. 1282, 113 L.Ed.2d 358 (1991). As part of the second prong, a plaintiff must prove that the copyrighted and alleged infringing works are "substantially similar." *Johnson v. Gordon,* 409 F.3d 12, 18 (1st Cir.2005) (citation and internal quotation marks omitted).

In determining substantial similarity, courts apply the "ordinary observer," or, "in musical milieu, the ordinary listener test." *Id.* (internal quotation marks omitted). A defendant's work is substantially similar to the copyrighted work only if

> an ordinary person of reasonable attentiveness would, upon listening to both, conclude that the defendant unlawfully appropriated the plaintiff's protectable expression.

Id.

Importantly, for a plaintiff to succeed the substantial similarity must relate to *original* elements of the copyrighted work. *See id.* at 18–19 (citing *Feist,* 499 U.S. at 361, 111 S.Ct. 1282). Thus, before examining the similarity between the works,

> a court must engage in dissection of the copyrighted work by separating its original, protected expressive elements from those aspects that are not copyrightable.

Id. Accordingly, "an overall impression of similarity may not be enough" if "such an impression flows from similarities as to elements that are not themselves copyrightable." *Id.* at 19.

Among the elements that must be dissected out are ideas and concepts which are not protected by copyright law. 17 U.S.C. § 102(b). Nor are common phrases or *scene a faire,* meaning "stock scenes or elements that necessarily flow from a common idea," protected.

Although ordinarily an issue for the factfinder, substantial similarity (or lack thereof) can be decided by the Court as a matter of law.

C. Application

The defendants assert that Steele's copyright infringement claim fails as a matter of law because there is no substantial similarity between his song and the alleged infringing works. In considering the issue this Court has reviewed the expert reports and other affidavits submitted by both sides. It has also carefully listened to the Steele Song and the Bon Jovi Song and viewed both the original TBS Promo and the version provided by the plaintiff in which the audio has been replaced with the Steele Song.

1. Musical Similarity

Applying the "ordinary listener" standard this Court detects no musical similarity between the Steele Song and the Bon Jovi Song. The expert analyses by opposing musicologists support that conclusion. The opinion of plaintiff's musicologist is particularly relevant because, on a motion for summary judgment, this Court considers the facts in the light most favorable to the non-moving party. *See id.* at 19 (concentrating on the views of plaintiff's chosen expert).

Plaintiff has submitted an unsigned report from musicologist Alexander Stewart ("the Stewart Report") which states, in part:

> This case is not strong musicologically: Melody of "hook" has only one note in common (1). Three words in common, but not the most distinctive word, "team." Harmony is commonplace. Both tunes consist

> primarily of I, IV, and V chords-the most commonly used chords in harmony. Moreover, "Team" [the Steele Song] is a 12-bar blues. One of the most distinctive harmonic figures in "Team," the chromatic chord change (D–D#–E) at the end of the hook, is not found in "Town" [the Bon Jovi Song]. Hook in "Town" begins on the IV chord (progression IV V I); hook of "Team" begins on V (progression V IV I). Bon Jovi song has somewhat irregular structure: 5-bar "B section"; "Team" is regular 4- and 8-bar sections[.]

Not surprisingly, the Ricigliano Report (submitted by the defendants) reaches a similar conclusion, noting that the songs

> do not share any significant similarity and are not substantially similar in lyric content, melodic content (pitch series, rhythm or rhythmic patterns, melodic development and structure), or harmonic content....

In response to such damaging testimony, Steele asserts that musicologists (including his own expert) are not helpful in this case because they are not qualified to compare the video evidence presented in the form of the TBS Promo. Nevertheless, this Court concludes, based upon the musicologist reports and its own review of the songs, that no reasonable jury applying the correct legal standard could find substantial similarity between the musical elements of the two works.

2. Lyrical Similarity

A comparison of the lyrics in the Steele Song and the Bon Jovi song also reveals no substantial similarity with respect to original elements. Before engaging in comparison, however, the Court must first dissect the lyrical elements of Steele's song that are not copyrightable. In this case, that turns out to be most, if not all, of the similarities.

For example, although both songs use the phrase "I love this ..." in their title and chorus, common expressions and cliches are not copyrightable. *See Johnson,* 409 F.3d at 24 (phrase "You're the One for Me" too common to be copyrightable). As defendants point out, online databases reveal nearly 100 songs that use the phrase "I love this ..." in some form in their title. Although plaintiff argues that none of those songs is about baseball, neither is the Bon Jovi Song.

The phrases "come on" and "here we go" are likewise too trite and common too warrant protection. *See id.* Another purported similarity, the fact that both songs rhyme "round" with "town," is also commonplace as evinced by the fact that it is found in the popular children's song "The Wheels on the Bus". When those unprotected elements are filtered out, the Steele Song and Bon Jovi Song display little lyrical similarity, and certainly not the substantial similarity required to prove a claim of copyright infringement. As plaintiff's own musicologist observes, the songs have "[o]nly three words in common ('I' 'love' 'this')." Moreover, the subject of the Steele Song "is clearly baseball and specifically the Red Sox" while the Bon Jovi song is about a town and "without the video, there would be no connection to baseball."

In an effort to show lyrical similarity, plaintiff relies on "reports" from Jonathan Yasuda ("the Yasuda Report"), a law student with an undergraduate degree in music, and Mark Ferraguto ("the Ferraguto Report"), a musicology Ph.D. candidate. Both reports identify purported similarities between the structure and rhyme scheme of the Steele Song and the Bon Jovi Song.

Even assuming those individuals are qualified to render opinions on the subject, their conclusions do not create a genuine issue of material fact concerning substantial similarity. A common rhyme scheme or structure does not qualify as original expression protectable under federal copyright law. *See id.* at 23 (holding that a particular harmonic progression "is a stereotypical building block of musical composition, [which] lacks originality"). Furthermore, considered as a whole, differences between the two songs (as recognized by plaintiff's own musicologist) overwhelmingly eclipse any similarity in structure and rhyme scheme. *See id.* at 18 (noting that "[t]he substantial similarity requirement focuses holistically on the works in question"). Accordingly, even crediting the assertions of plaintiff's experts, no reasonable jury could conclude that the Bon Jovi Song is substantially similar to the original lyrical elements of the Steele Song.

3. The TBS Promo

Much of Steele's argument focuses not on similarity between the Bon Jovi Song and his own work (although he does maintain that the two are substantially similar) but, rather, on the TBS Promo, which features the Bon Jovi song along with baseball video footage and scenes from in and around major league ballparks. Steele asserts that the images in the TBS Promo bear a striking resemblance to the scenes described in his song and that, together with similarities between the two songs, the Promo conclusively demonstrates that his work was unlawfully copied.

According to Steele, his song was used as a template for the creation of the video portion of the TBS Promo. Through a process he calls "temp tracking," the defendants allegedly created the video based on the Steele Song and then replaced the audio with the Bon Jovi Song (which is based on the video, the Steele Song or both).

In an effort to show similarity (and that the TBS Promo was derived from his song) Steele has submitted a version of the TBS Promo in which the audio has been replaced with the Steele Song. He maintains that in many places the lyrics of his song correspond to the images in the TBS Promo. In particular,

Steele notes the following similarities:

1) At the exact moment Steele sings "Word is out on Yawkey Way," the TBS Promo shows a Yawkey Way street sign;

2) when Steele mentions the Detroit Tigers the TBS Promo shows a Tiger's player rounding the bases;

3) when Steele sings "You got to keep believin', gotta stay tough" the Promo shows players "chest butting" and acting tough; and

4) when Steele exhorts fans to "Get up off your seats" the Promo shows fans standing and cheering.

Again, before conducting the substantial similarity analysis, the Court must dissect the unprotected elements from Steele's work. Here, the Steele Song's references to Fenway Park and Yawkey Way are classic *scene a faire*; they are stock scenes that flow from the idea of baseball. *CMM Cable Rep, Inc.*, 97 F.3d at 1522 n. 25. Steele does not enjoy a monopoly over the use of those images simply because he references them in a copyrighted song. *See id.* (doctrine of *scene a faire* is "concerned with preventing a monopoly on commonplace ideas").

Furthermore, although the Steele Song does appear to match some of the images in the TBS Promo, it is inevitable that a song about baseball will at times correspond with a baseball promotional advertisement. For example, there are over a dozen scenes in the TBS Promo that display a cheering crowd (at either a ballpark or a Bon Jovi concert). Consequently, it is unsurprising that one of those scenes parallels one of the four points in the Steele Song where he encourages fans to "Get up off your seats."

As the defendants point out, the number of places in which the TBS Promo corresponds to the lyrics of the Bon Jovi Song vastly outnumber any parallels with the Steele Song. More importantly, however, the issue is not whether the video portion of the TBS Promo is more similar to the Bon Jovi Song or the Steele Song but, rather, whether the TBS Promo is *substantially similar* to the original elements of the Steele Song. Because no reasonable jury could find substantial similarity between the two works, the defendants are entitled to summary judgment.

4. Other Issues

Steele raises a number of other arguments that do not change this Court's conclusion but are, nonetheless, worthy of addressing. First, to the extent that Steele maintains that the defendants stole his "marketing concept" of a baseball song that could be adapted to any team or city, such an idea or concept explicitly is unprotected by federal copyright law. 17 U.S.C. § 102(b) ("In no case does copyright protection for an original work of authorship extend to any idea ... [or] concept....").

Second, Steele's effort to show a genuine issue of material fact by submitting affidavits from assorted "ordinary listeners," although understandable given his *pro se* status and the relevant legal standard, is misguided for a number of reasons. First, the "ordinary listeners" upon whom Steele asks the Court to rely are all his personal friends or acquaintances. Second, there is no evidence that those ordinary listeners were "correctly applying the pertinent legal standards." *See Johnson,* 409 F.3d at 18. Most importantly, those affidavits present inadmissable lay opinion and therefore are not appropriate for consideration. *See* Fed.R.Civ.P. 56(e)(1) (affidavits must "set out facts that would be admissible in evidence"); Fed.R.Evid. 701 (lay opinion is inadmissible unless it is "helpful" to the factfinder).

Finally, Steele's assertions that the defendants violated his synchronization, or "synch," rights (by allegedly timing the display of images in the TBS Promo to his song) is also unpersuasive. A synch right is the "right to record a copyrighted song in synchronization with [a] film or videotape, and is obtained separately from the right to perform the music." *Broad. Music, Inc. v. Columbia Broad. Sys., Inc.,* 441 U.S. 1, 33 n. 23, 99 S.Ct. 1551, 60 L.Ed.2d 1 (1979) (Stevens, J., dissenting). Thus, synch rights are an additional right that a user must acquire when it seeks not only to perform the protected work but also to use it in timed-relation with an audiovisual work. *See ABKCO Music, Inc. v. Stellar Records, Inc.,* 96 F.3d 60, 62 n. 4 (2d Cir.1996). Although Steele has submitted a report from a purported music and film expert that asserts that 96% of the video sequences in the TBS Promo are synchronized to the Steele Song's quarter-note beat, intervals of time are not original expression protectable under federal copyright law. Accordingly, no reasonable juror could conclude that the TBS Promo violates plaintiff's synch rights.

In sum, because no reasonable juror applying the correct standards could find that the original elements of the Steele Song are substantially similar to the Bon Jovi Song or the TBS Promo, summary judgment will enter in favor of the defendants.

ORDER

In accordance with the foregoing, the defendants' motions for summary judgment (Docket Nos. 92 and 98) are **ALLOWED.**

So ordered.

ROGER MILLER MUSIC, INC. v. SONY/ATV PUBL'G, LLC
United States Court of Appeals for the Sixth Circuit
October 12, 2011, Argued; February 22, 2012, Decided; February 22, 2012, Filed
File Name: 12a0049p.06
No. 10-5363
672 F.3d 434

KAREN NELSON MOORE, Circuit Judge.

Defendant–Appellant Sony/ATV Publishing, LLC ("Sony") appeals the district court's judgment in favor of Plaintiffs–Appellees Mary Miller and Roger Miller Music, Inc. (collectively, "RMMI") on their copyright infringement claim and the award of $903,349.17 in damages. Because the Copyright Act makes clear that the renewal copyright vested with Roger Miller, and thus with Sony as his assignee, we REVERSE the district court's judgment and REMAND with instructions to enter judgment in favor of Sony.

I. BACKGROUND

Famed singer and songwriter Roger Miller, best known for the hit song "King of the Road," assigned the original and renewal copyrights to his songs to Tree Publishing Co. (Sony's predecessor-in-interest) in a series of contracts in the 1960s. In exchange for this assignment, Miller was entitled to receive royalty payments from the use of his songs. Relevant to this litigation are the songs originally copyrighted in 1964, for which the renewal copyright term began January 1, 1993.

Sony filed applications to register the renewal copyrights for the 1964 songs with the United States Copyright Office in January and April 1992 and subsequently registered these copyrights. Miller died on October 25, 1992. In his will, he granted all interests in his intellectual property to his wife, Mary; Mary Miller assigned these interests to Roger Miller Music, Inc. Over the next twelve years, Sony continued to exploit the 1964 songs and pay royalties to RMMI.

In December 2004, RMMI brought suit against Sony for copyright infringement, seeking damages and a declaration that RMMI was the owner of the renewal copyrights to the songs Miller composed between 1958 and 1964. At this stage in the litigation, Sony did not contend that it owned the renewal copyrights to the 1964 songs or dispute RMMI's contention that ownership vested in RMMI due to Miller's death prior to the start of the renewal term. The district court granted Sony's motion for judgment on the pleadings, holding that Sony owned the renewal copyrights to the 1958–1963 songs and that it held an implied, non-exclusive license to exploit the 1964 songs based on RMMI's actions and inactions in accepting royalty payments without objection. *Roger Miller Music, Inc. v. Sony/ATV Publishing, LLC,* No. 04–1132, 2005 WL 5351103, at *1 (M.D.Tenn. July 11, 2005) (*RMMI I*). Sony subsequently filed a motion to alter or amend the judgment under Federal Rule of Civil Procedure 59(e), arguing that it owned the renewal copyrights to the 1964 songs because it had applied to register them prior to Miller's death. The district court treated Sony's previous position regarding the 1964 songs as a binding judicial admission and refused to hear Sony's arguments on the issue.

Both parties appealed, and a previous panel of this court affirmed as to Sony's ownership of the copyrights to the 1958–1963 songs, but reversed the holding that Sony's previous statements regarding the 1964 songs constituted judicial admissions. *Roger Miller Music, Inc. v. Sony/ATV Publishing, LLC,* 477 F.3d 383, 391–95 (6th Cir.2007) (*RMMI II*). We remanded for a determination of whether the district court should hear arguments on ownership of the renewal copyrights to the 1964 songs.

On remand, the district court concluded that Sony did not own the renewal copyrights, because Roger Miller had died prior to the vesting of the renewal rights and assignees were not included in the list of statutory successors, and the court thus denied Sony's Rule 59(e) motion. The court incorporated its previous decision that Sony held an implied license to exploit the 1964 songs, but nonetheless appointed a Special Master to conduct an accounting of the infringement damages owed to RMMI. Sony objected to the Special Master's report on the grounds that Sony's status as a licensee precluded any liability for infringement. In response, the district court reversed its prior holding on the license issue and awarded RMMI $903,349.17 in damages. *Roger Miller Music, Inc. v. Sony/ATV Publishing, LLC,* No. 04–1132, 2010 WL 1026980, at *3 (M.D.Tenn. Mar. 18, 2010) (*RMMI III*). Sony timely appealed, arguing that it owned the renewal copyrights to the 1964 songs and, alternatively, that the district court's sua sponte reversal of its previous holding on the license issue was both procedurally impermissible and substantively incorrect.

II. ANALYSIS

A. Standard of Review

" 'A matter requiring statutory interpretation is a question of law,' " which we review de novo. *Roberts v. Hamer,* 655 F.3d 578, 582 (6th Cir.2011) (quoting *United States v. Brown,* 639 F.3d 735, 737 (6th Cir.2011)).

B. Copyright Infringement

This case presents an interstitial issue of copyright law. Miller's assignment of the renewal copyright would indisputably have been made effective if he had still been living at the commencement of the renewal term on January 1, 1993. Equally indisputable is that the assignment would have been rendered ineffective if Miller had died before 1992. This case is before us because Miller was still living at the time in 1992 that his assignee applied to register the copyright, but Miller died before the start of the renewal term. RMMI contends that Miller must have been living at the start of the renewal term to effectuate his assignment to Sony, but Sony counters that Miller needed to survive only until the time at which the application was filed. Sony is correct that the Copyright Act supports the effectiveness of assignments in such circumstances.

1. The Renewal Copyright

Under the Copyright Act, an artistic work has an original copyright term of twenty-eight years followed by a renewal term of an additional sixty-seven years. 17 U.S.C. § 304(a)(1)(A), (a)(2)(B). A renewal copyright can be registered with the U.S. Copyright Office at any point in the final year of the original term (the "renewal year"), *id.* § 304(a)(3)(A)(i), or at any time within the renewal term itself, *id.* § 304(a)(3)(A)(ii); without registration, the copyright renews automatically at the start of the renewal term, *id.* § 304(a)(3)(B).

The Copyright Act provides that, if an application to register the renewal copyright is filed within the renewal year, the renewal copyright "shall vest, upon the beginning of such further term, in any person who is entitled under paragraph (1)(C) to the renewal and extension of the copyright at the time the application is made." *Id.* § 304(a)(2)(B)(i). If no application is filed, the renewal copyright "shall vest, upon the beginning of such further term, in any person entitled under paragraph (1)(C), as of the last day of the original term of copyright, to the renewal and extension of the copyright." *Id.* § 304(a)(2)(B)(ii).

Paragraph (1)(C) establishes a hierarchy of who is entitled to the renewal copyright:

(i) the author of such work, if the author is still living,

(ii) the widow, widower, or children of the author, if the author is not living,

(iii) the author's executors, if such author, widow, widower, or children are not living, or

(iv) the author's next of kin, in the absence of a will of the author.

Id. § 304(a)(1)(C).

The original and renewal copyrights are distinct legal interests. An author who sells the original copyright to his work thus has a second chance to claim ownership at the end of the original term. This system protects an author who was in a weak bargaining position at the outset but whose work ultimately proved successful. *Stewart v. Abend,* 495 U.S. 207, 218–19, 110 S.Ct. 1750, 109 L.Ed.2d 184 (1990). The statutory succession provision likewise provides a deceased author's family with a new chance to receive remuneration for a valuable creation. *Id.* at 218, 110 S.Ct. 1750.

2. Assignments

Notwithstanding this author-protecting policy, an author can assign his interest in the renewal copyright, either before or after the start of the renewal term. *Miller Music Corp. v. Charles N. Daniels, Inc.,* 362 U.S. 373, 375, 80 S.Ct. 792, 4 L.Ed.2d 804 (1960) (citing *Fred Fisher Music Co. v. M. Witmark & Sons,* 318 U.S. 643, 63 S.Ct. 773, 87 L.Ed. 1055 (1943)); *Fred Fisher Music Co.,* 318 U.S. at 647, 655–56, 63 S.Ct. 773. However, the author has only a contingency interest in the renewal, which is all he can assign, "until the renewal period arrives." *Miller Music Corp.,* 362 U.S. at 375–78, 80 S.Ct. 792. If the author dies prior to that point, ownership of the renewal copyright passes to the statutory successors, regardless of whether the author had otherwise previously assigned or devised it. *Id.* at 375, 80 S.Ct. 792. This result follows from the fact that, as in other contractual relationships, a copyright assignee stands in the shoes of the assignor and thus is entitled to the copyright only if the assigning author would otherwise be entitled to it. *See id.* at 377–78, 80 S.Ct. 792; *see also Plumb v. Fluid Pump Serv., Inc.,* 124 F.3d 849, 864 (7th Cir.1997) (" '[E]lementary contract law provides that upon a valid and unqualified assignment the assignee stands in the shoes of the assignor and assumes the same rights, title and interest possessed by the assignor.' " (quoting *Moutsopoulos v. Am. Mut. Ins. Co.,* 607 F.2d 1185, 1189 (7th Cir.1979))).

Neither *Fred Fisher Music* nor *Miller Music* identified the point at which a pre-renewal-term assignment of a renewal copyright is no longer contingent and is therefore guaranteed to vest in the assignee. The Court did not define "renewal period" or otherwise specify whether an assignment sheds its contingent status upon commencement of the renewal year, registration, or commencement of the renewal term. *See Stewart,* 495 U.S. at 220 n. 2, 110 S.Ct. 1750 (recognizing the open question). Because the author in *Miller Music* had died more than one year before the termination of the original term, and thus outside of any potential definition of renewal period, the need for further clarity did not arise. *See Miller Music Corp. v. Charles N. Daniels, Inc.,* 158 F.Supp. 188, 190 (S.D.N.Y.1957).

3. The Statutory Language Supports Sony

Despite its somewhat convoluted syntax, the statutory language enacted in 1992 provides an answer. An author is "entitled under paragraph (1)(C) to the renewal and extension of the copyright," 17 U.S.C. § 304(a)(2)(B)(i), if he is still living, *see id.* § 304(a)(1)(C)(i). The renewal copyright vests in any party entitled to it "at the time the application is made." *Id.* § 304(a)(2)(B)(i). The author (and therefore any of his assignees) thus secures an interest in the renewal copyright so long as he is still living at the time of application for renewal with the Copyright Office. This interest is not lost even if the author subsequently dies prior to the commencement of the renewal term. The House Judiciary Committee Report for the 1992 Act confirms this reading, explaining that "[r]egistration during the final year would assure the author or other claimant that his or her right to the renewal term vested on registration, even if he or she died later that year." H. Rep. 102–379(I), at 13, 1992 U.S.C.C.A.N. 166, 172.

Roger Miller was entitled to the renewal copyright because he was living at the time the application for registration was made. Sony was in turn entitled as Miller's assignee, and thus took ownership at the time the interest vested on January 1, 1993.

The fact that the interest in the renewal copyright vests "upon the beginning of such further term," 17 U.S.C. § 304(a)(2)(B)(i), does not dictate a contrary result. The date of vesting is not dispositive as to who owns the copyright, as the 1992 Act "separate[d] the inquiry of who is entitled to the renewal rights from the inquiry of who is alive when renewal vests." *Dimensional Music Publ'g,* 435 F.Supp.2d at 457; *see also* 3 Nimmer on Copyright § 9.05(C)(2) (describing the two concepts as "uncoupled"). Instead, the date of the renewal application determines entitlement to ownership. Accordingly, a party can become entitled to ownership of the renewal copyright prior to the time it actually vests.

The district court (and RMMI) cited language in *Broadcast Music, Inc. v. Roger Miller Music, Inc.,* 396 F.3d 762 (6th Cir.2005), and the prior panel's opinion in this case as support for its conclusion that an assignee has no interest in a renewal copyright if the assigning author dies prior to vesting. In both cases, this language is dicta. The issue in *Broadcast Music* was whether an author's widow and children take equal shares in the renewal interest upon statutory succession; the opinion mentioned vesting only in the course of an overview of the law regarding renewal copyrights. *Id.* at 763–64, 768–69. Moreover, *Broadcast Music* cited *Miller Music,* which, as described above, did not address this issue and, of course, was decided before the 1992 amendments. *RMMI II* remanded to the district court on the very issue of Sony's ownership interest in the 1964 songs and thus did not rule on that issue. 477 F.3d at 395.

4. RMMI's Position Is Inconsistent with the Statute

If Congress intended to condition all assignments on the author's survival to the start of the renewal term, it would not have split § 304(a)(2)(B) into two subparagraphs; ownership in all cases would be determined "as of the last day of the original term of copyright," 17 U.S.C. § 304(a)(2)(B)(ii). Under this interpretation, the "at the time the application is made" language in § 304(a)(2)(B)(i) would be meaningless. In accordance with the rules of statutory construction, however, we "must 'giv[e] effect to each word' " and do not interpret a statute in a way that renders a provision " 'meaningless or superfluous.' " *Nat'l Air Traffic Controllers Ass'n v. Sec'y of Dep't of Transp.,* 654 F.3d 654, 657 (6th Cir.2011) (quoting *Menuskin v. Williams,* 145 F.3d 755, 768 (6th Cir.1998)). Instead, the two subparagraphs articulate different rules for two different sets of circumstances; only if no application is filed is ownership determined "as of the last day of the original term of copyright."

RMMI's reading of § 304(a)(2)(B)(i) as a provision that "simply freezes the eligible statutory successors so that the only successors who may be entitled to the renewal interest on the first day of the renewal period are those who qualified as statutory successors at the time the application was filed," Appellee Br. at 9, finds no support in caselaw or commentary. More damning is RMMI's failure to explain why the then-living Roger Miller would not be included in the closed class of statutory successors. A living author is the first person entitled to the renewal copyright under § 304(a)(1)(C). If the class closes at the time of application, and the author is alive at the time of application, then the author is included within the closed class and the copyright vests in him at the start of the renewal term. The renewal copyright passes to the author's assignee, even if the author has died in between the filing of the application and the renewal term. By describing § 304(a)(1)(C) as "expressly limited to the author's relatives" and thus rejecting Sony's argument as an attempt "to amend Section 304(a)(1)(C) to include an author's assignees," the district court made a similar error. *RMMI III,* 2010 WL 1026980, at *2.

Nor does the statute support RMMI's contention that the statutory successors hold concurrent contingent interests along with the author's assignees from the time of application until the commencement of the renewal term and thereupon receive sole ownership of the copyright if the author has died in the interim. The statement in *Broadcast Music* that "renewal copyright interests can be held simultaneously by numerous parties" was made in the context of a dispute between an author's widow and child, both of whom occupy the same tier in the statutory successor hierarchy. 396 F.3d at 768. By contrast, a living author is the sole member of the top tier in that hierarchy. A spouse is not "entitled under paragraph (1)(C)," 17 U.S.C. § 304(a)(2)(B)(i), if the author is still living, and thus does not share the renewal interest with him.

Because Roger Miller was "entitled under paragraph (1)(C) to the renewal and extension of the copyright at the time the application [wa]s made," 17 U.S.C. § 304(a)(2)(B)(i), the renewal interest vested in him at the commencement of the renewal period. And because he had previously made an otherwise valid assignment of the renewal interest to Sony, the copyright thus vested in Sony.

III. CONCLUSION

Because Sony owns the renewal copyrights to the 1964 songs as the assignee of an author who was living at the time of the application for renewal registration, we REVERSE the judgment of the district court holding Sony liable for copyright infringement and awarding damages to RMMI. We REMAND for entry of judgment in favor of Sony.

MIDLER v. FORD MOTOR CO.
United States Court of Appeals for the Ninth Circuit
February 4, 1988, Argued and Submitted; June 22, 1988, Filed
No. 87-6168
849 F.2d 460

NOONAN, Circuit Judge:

This case centers on the protectibility of the voice of a celebrated chanteuse from commercial exploitation without her consent. Ford Motor Company and its advertising agency, Young & Rubicam, Inc., in 1985 advertised the Ford Lincoln Mercury with a series of nineteen 30 or 60 second television commercials in what the agency called "The Yuppie Campaign." The aim was to make an emotional connection with Yuppies, bringing back memories of when they were in college. Different popular songs of the seventies were sung on each commercial. The agency tried to get "the original people," that is, the singers who had popularized the songs, to sing them. Failing in that endeavor in ten cases the agency had the songs sung by "sound alikes." Bette Midler, the plaintiff and appellant here, was done by a sound alike.

Midler is a nationally known actress and singer. She won a Grammy as early as 1973 as the Best New Artist of that year. Records made by her since then have gone Platinum and Gold. She was nominated in 1979 for an Academy award for Best Female Actress in *The Rose,* in which she portrayed a pop singer. *Newsweek* in its June 30, 1986 issue described her as an "outrageously original singer/comedian." *Time* hailed her in its March 2, 1987 issue as "a legend" and "the most dynamic and poignant singer-actress of her time."

When Young & Rubicam was preparing the Yuppie Campaign it presented the commercial to its client by playing an edited version of Midler singing "Do You Want To Dance," taken from the 1973 Midler album, "The Divine Miss M." After the client accepted the idea and form of the commercial, the agency contacted Midler's manager, Jerry Edelstein. The conversation went as follows: "Hello, I am Craig Hazen from Young and Rubicam. I am calling you to find out if Bette Midler would be interested in doing ...? Edelstein: "Is it a commercial?" "Yes." "We are not interested."

Undeterred, Young & Rubicam sought out Ula Hedwig whom it knew to have been one of "the Harlettes" a backup singer for Midler for ten years. Hedwig was told by Young & Rubicam that "they wanted someone who could sound like Bette Midler's recording of [Do You Want To Dance]." She was asked to make a "demo" tape of the song if she was interested. She made an a capella demo and got the job.

At the direction of Young & Rubicam, Hedwig then made a record for the commercial. The Midler record of "Do You Want To Dance" was first played to her. She was told to "sound as much as possible like the Bette Midler record," leaving out only a few "aahs" unsuitable for the commercial. Hedwig imitated Midler to the best of her ability.

After the commercial was aired Midler was told by "a number of people" that it "sounded exactly" like her record of "Do You Want To Dance." Hedwig was told by "many personal friends" that they thought it was Midler singing the commercial. Ken Fritz, a personal manager in the entertainment business not associated with Midler, declares by affidavit that he heard the commercial on more than one occasion and thought Midler was doing the singing.

Neither the name nor the picture of Midler was used in the commercial; Young & Rubicam had a license from the copyright holder to use the song. At issue in this case is only the protection of Midler's voice. The district court described the defendants' conduct as that "of the average thief." They decided, "If we can't buy it, we'll take it." The court nonetheless believed there was no legal principle preventing imitation of Midler's voice and so gave summary judgment for the defendants. Midler appeals.

The First Amendment protects much of what the media do in the reproduction of likenesses or sounds. A primary value is freedom of speech and press. *Time, Inc. v. Hill,* 385 U.S. 374, 388, 87 S.Ct. 534, 542, 17 L.Ed.2d 456 (1967). The purpose of the media's use of a person's identity is central. If the purpose is "informative or cultural" the use is immune; "if it serves no such function but merely exploits the individual portrayed, immunity will not be granted." Felcher and Rubin, "Privacy, Publicity and the Portrayal of Real People by the Media," 88 Yale L.J. 1577, 1596 (1979). Moreover, federal copyright law preempts much of the area. "Mere imitation of a recorded performance would not constitute a copyright infringement even where one performer deliberately sets out to simulate another's performance as exactly as possible." Notes of Committee on the Judiciary, 17 U.S.C.A. § 114(b). It is in the context of these First Amendment and federal copyright distinctions that we address the present appeal.

Nancy Sinatra once sued Goodyear Tire and Rubber Company on the basis of an advertising campaign by Young & Rubicam featuring "These Boots Are Made For Walkin'," a song closely identified with her; the female singers of the commercial were alleged to have imitated her voice and style and to have dressed and looked like her. The basis of Nancy Sinatra's complaint was unfair competition; she claimed that the song and the arrangement had acquired "a secondary meaning" which, under California law, was protectible. This court noted that the defendants "had paid a very substantial sum to the copyright proprietor to obtain the license for the use of the song and all of its arrangements." To give Sinatra damages for their use of the song would clash with federal copyright law. Summary judgment for the defendants was affirmed. *Sinatra v. Goodyear Tire & Rubber Co.,* 435 F.2d 711, 717-718 (9th Cir.1970), *cert. denied,* 402 U.S. 906, 91 S.Ct. 1376, 28 L.Ed.2d 646 (1971). If Midler were claiming a secondary meaning to "Do You Want To Dance" or seeking to prevent the defendants from using that song, she would fail like Sinatra. But that is not this case. Midler does not seek damages for Ford's use of "Do You Want To Dance," and thus her claim is not preempted by federal copyright law. Copyright protects "original works of authorship fixed in any tangible medium of expression." 17 U.S.C. § 102(a). A voice is not copyrightable. The sounds are not "fixed." What is put forward as protectible here is more personal than any work of authorship.

Bert Lahr once sued Adell Chemical Co. for selling Lestoil by means of a commercial in which an imitation of Lahr's voice accompanied a cartoon of a duck. Lahr alleged that his style of vocal delivery was distinctive in pitch, accent, inflection, and sounds. The First Circuit held that Lahr had stated a cause of action for unfair competition, that it could be found "that defendant's conduct saturated plaintiff's audience, curtailing his market." *Lahr v. Adell Chemical Co.,* 300 F.2d 256, 259 (1st Cir.1962). That case is more like this one. But we do not find unfair competition here. One-minute commercials of the sort the defendants put on would not have saturated Midler's audience and curtailed her market. Midler did not do television commercials. The defendants were not in competition with her. *See Halicki v. United Artists Communications, Inc.,* 812 F.2d 1213 (9th Cir.1987).

California Civil Code section 3344 is also of no aid to Midler. The statute affords damages to a person injured by another who uses the person's "name, voice, signature, photograph or likeness, in any manner." The defendants did not use Midler's name or anything else whose use is prohibited by the statute. The voice they used was Hedwig's, not hers. The term "likeness" refers to a visual image not a vocal imitation. The statute, however, does not preclude Midler from pursuing any cause of action she may have at common law; the statute itself implies that such common law causes of action do exist because it says its remedies are merely "cumulative." *Id.* § 3344(g).

The companion statute protecting the use of a deceased person's name, voice, signature, photograph or likeness states that the rights it recognizes are "property rights." *Id.* § 990(b). By analogy the common law rights are also property rights. Appropriation of such common law rights is a tort in California. *Motschenbacher v. R.J. Reynolds Tobacco Co.,* 498 F.2d 821 (9th Cir.1974). In that case what the defendants used in their television commercial for Winston cigarettes was a photograph of a famous professional racing driver's racing car. The number of the car was changed and a wing-like device known as a "spoiler" was attached to the car; the car's features of white pinpointing, an oval medallion, and solid red coloring were retained. The driver, Lothar Motschenbacher, was in the car but his features were not visible. Some persons, viewing the commercial, correctly inferred that the car was his and that he was in the car and was therefore endorsing the product. The defendants were held to have invaded a "proprietary interest" of Motschenbacher in his own identity. *Id.* at 825.

Midler's case is different from Motschenbacher's. He and his car were physically used by the tobacco company's ad; he made part of his living out of giving commercial endorsements. But, as Judge Koelsch expressed it in *Motschenbacher,* California will recognize an injury from "an appropriation of the attributes of one's identity." *Id.* at 824. It was irrelevant that Motschenbacher could not be identified in the ad. The ad suggested that it was he. The ad did so by emphasizing signs or symbols associated with him. In the same way the defendants here used an imitation to convey the impression that Midler was singing for them.

Why did the defendants ask Midler to sing if her voice was not of value to them? Why did they studiously acquire the services of a sound-alike and instruct her to imitate Midler if Midler's voice was not of value to them? What they sought was an attribute of Midler's identity. Its value was what the market would have paid for Midler to have sung the commercial in person.

A voice is more distinctive and more personal than the automobile accouterments protected in *Motschenbacher.* A voice is as distinctive and personal as a face. The human voice is one of the most palpable ways identity is manifested. We are all aware that a friend is at once known by a few words on the phone. At a philosophical level it has been observed that with the sound of a voice, "the other stands before me." D. Ihde, *Listening and Voice* 77 (1976). A fortiori, these observations hold true of singing, especially singing by a singer of renown. The singer manifests herself in the song. To impersonate her voice is to pirate her identity. *See* W. Keeton, D. Dobbs, R. Keeton, D. Owen, *Prosser & Keeton on Torts* 852 (5th ed. 1984).

We need not and do not go so far as to hold that every imitation of a voice to advertise merchandise is actionable. We hold only that when a distinctive voice of a professional singer is widely known and is deliberately imitated in order to sell a product, the sellers have appropriated what is not theirs and have committed a tort in California. Midler has made a showing, sufficient to defeat summary judgment, that the defendants here for their own profit in selling their product did appropriate part of her identity.

REVERSED AND REMANDED FOR TRIAL.

GREENWICH FILM PRODS. S.A. v. DRG RECORDS, INC.
United States District Court for the Southern District of New York
September 18, 1992; Decided; September 25, 1992, Filed
91 Civ. 0546 (JSM)
1992 U.S. Dist. LEXIS 14770; 25 U.S.P.Q.2d (BNA 1435; Copy L. Rep. (CCH) P27, 004

MARTIN, District Judge.

Plaintiff Greenwich Film Productions, S.A. commenced this action seeking a permanent injunction prohibiting defendants from publishing, distributing, manufacturing, selling, marketing or otherwise exploiting the soundtrack from the motion picture "DIVA." In addition to injunctive relief, the Plaintiff seeks compensatory damages for breach of contract, copyright infringement, trademark infringement, and unfair competition. The Defendants now move pursuant to Fed.R.Civ.P. 56 for summary judgment dismissing several of these claims. Greenwich Film Productions, S.A. cross-moves on the issue of copyright infringement.

FACTUAL BACKGROUND

At the beginning of the film "DIVA," the protagonist, an opera aficionado, sits in the shadows of a concert hall, surreptitiously recording the vocal recital of a beautiful diva. It is this bootleg recording which spurs the plot, setting off a chain of events that include murder, white slavery, and unrequited love. Interestingly, a similar recording has spurred another plot, this one occurring behind the scenes of the film. And while this plot perhaps lacks the intrigue of the film, it presents legal issues at least as interesting.

The behind the scenes story of "DIVA" begins, for our purposes, in 1980, when Plaintiff Greenwich Film Productions, S.A. ("Greenwich") began production of the film "DIVA" and contracted Vladimir Cosma (the "Composer") to compose the soundtrack.

The story continues through the film's release in 1981, and the similar release of a "single" from the soundtrack. The film was an immediate success, both commercially and critically.

Hoping to duplicate the film's success outside of France, Plaintiff began worldwide distribution of the film in 1982. At the same time, Plaintiff entered into negotiations with Defendant DRG Records, Inc. ("DRG") concerning distribution rights in the soundtrack. These negotiations resulted in a licensing agreement (the "License") granting DRG the exclusive right for a term of five years to manufacture and distribute the "DIVA" soundtrack.

By its terms, this License expired on June 22, 1987. However, instead of surrendering the "master" to the Plaintiff as required by the terms of the License, DRG continued manufacturing and distributing "DIVA" recordings. Furthermore, DRG entered into agreements with third parties to further exploit the "DIVA" soundtrack.

On December 17, 1991, Plaintiff registered its copyright in the soundtrack and commenced the present action seeking compensatory and injunctive relief for breach of contract, copyright infringement, trademark infringement, and unfair competition.

DISCUSSION

Summary Judgment

Summary judgment is proper when there is no genuine issue of material fact and, based upon facts not in dispute, the moving party is entitled to judgment as a mater of law. Fed.R.Civ.P. 56(c); *Celotex Corp. v. Catrett,* 477 U.S. 317, 322–23, 106 S.Ct. 2548 (1986). The court's role on a motion for summary judgment is not to decide disputed issues of fact but only to determine whether there is a genuine issue to be tried. *Rattner v. Netburn,* 930 F.2d 204, 209 (2d Cir.1991). Moreover, the court must resolve all ambiguities and draw all factual inferences in favor of the nonmoving party. *Rattner,* 930 F.2d at 209 (citing *Anderson v. Liberty Lobby, Inc.,* 477 U.S. 242, 255, 106 S.Ct. 2505 (1986)). Summary judgment may be granted "against a party who fails to make a showing sufficient to establish the existence of an element essential to that party's case." *Celotex,* 477 U.S. at 322, 106 S.Ct. at 2552.

I. The Copyright Claim

To prevail on a copyright claim, a plaintiff must establish i) ownership of a valid copyright in an original work in a tangible form; ii) compliance with statutory prerequisites to suit; and iii) unauthorized copying by defendants.... DRG moves for summary judgment on the ground that Plaintiff cannot establish any of these elements. Plaintiff counters that it has established these elements, and cross-moves for summary judgment on the issue of liability.

A. Ownership of Copyright

The first element Plaintiff must establish to prevail on its copyright claim is that it owns a copyright in the work at issue. Here, Plaintiff rests its claim of ownership on two grounds: i) Plaintiff claims ownership in the work as a work for hire; and, in the alternative ii) Plaintiff claims ownership as a transferee of rights assigned by the Composer.

Plaintiff's claim that it owns the copyright in the work by virtue of it being a work for hire clearly lacks support under U.S. law. Section 101 of the Copyright Act defines a "work made for hire" as:

> (1) a work prepared by an employee within the scope of his or her employment; or
> (2) a work specially ordered or commissioned for use as a contribution to a collective work, as a part of a motion picture or other audiovisual work ... if the parties expressly agree in a written instrument signed by them that the work shall be considered a work made for hire.

17 U.S.C. § 101. Here, the compositions and soundtracks were clearly commissioned for a motion picture, thus triggering subsection (2). Furthermore, Plaintiff concedes that there is no agreement between it and the Composer designating the work as a work for hire. As such, under U.S. law, the compositions and soundtrack cannot be claimed as work for hire....

The argument is made, however, that U.S. law should not govern the determination of title. Specifically, Plaintiff notes that it is a French entity asserting copyright ownership in work commissioned in France for a French film. As such, it is suggested that French law should govern the determination of ownership. This argument is not without some legal support.

However, we need not resolve these arguments today. The agreements between Plaintiff and Composer adequately support Plaintiff's alternate ground for ownership, that it owns certain rights by virtue of a transfer. Specifically, these agreements establish that Plaintiff has the exclusive license to exploit the compositions and soundtrack through the film "DIVA." The August 7, 1980 Agreement provides:

> 1. [Composer] grants Publisher on an exclusive basis and Publisher accepts pursuant to the terms and conditions hereinafter set forth, his intangible right of ownership both to the work entitled ... "LA DIVA" ... and to the title of the work.
> 2. The assigned right of ownership includes in its entirety the exclusive right to exploit the work in any form and by any means whatsoever (including, in particular, all the publishing, reproduction, representation and public performance rights).
> 3. This assignment also includes ownership of the manuscript of the work delivered by [Composer] to Publisher.

August 7, 1980 Agreement, Article 1, ¶¶ 1–3. The August 7, 1980 Agreement further states that this right includes "the right in all forms and by all means to publish all or extracts of the work covered hereunder, or cause to be published, through sound recordings or any analogous processes, including but not limited to tape, computer or satellites." *Id.* at Article 7, ¶ 2. While the March 26, 1981 "clarification" of this agreement provides that the Composer remains owner of the individual compositions "for any other form of exploitation," nothing in this modification derogates Plaintiff's exclusive rights in the compositions and the soundtrack in connection with the film "DIVA." Based on these agreements, we conclude that plaintiff has established ownership rights in both the "DIVA" compositions and soundtrack.

B. Compliance with Statutory Prerequisites to Suit

The second element Plaintiff must establish to prevail on its copyright claim is that it has complied with statutory prerequisites to suit. Here, DRG argues that Plaintiff's claim must be dismissed as Plaintiff has i) failed to register certain copyrights and ii) failed to record the transfer of rights it received from the Composer.

While registration is no longer a prerequisite to bringing an infringement action for works whose country of origin is not the United States, *see* 17 U.S.C. § 411(a), it remains a prerequisite for Berne works published prior to March 1, 1989. Absent such registration, courts cannot exercise jurisdiction and the claim must be dismissed. 17 U.S.C. § 411(a); *Pristine Indus., Inc. v. Hallmark Cards, Inc.,* 753 F.Supp. 140, 148 (S.D.N.Y.1990); *Techniques, Inc. v. Rohn,* 592 F.Supp. 1195, 1197 (S.D.N.Y.1984).

Similarly, DRG points out that Plaintiff has not recorded the rights it received from the Composer. Such recordation remains a prerequisite to bringing suit for causes of action arising prior to March 1, 1989....

Here, Plaintiff concedes that it has neither registered its rights in the compositions nor recorded any transfer of rights from the Composer. However, Plaintiff argues that the Court should grant Plaintiff permission to register and record late and thus cure the asserted defect.

We note, first of all, that courts have routinely allowed late registrations and recordations to cure jurisdictional defects....

We note secondly that under paragraphs 7.2.4 and 8 of the License, DRG obligated itself to be solely responsible for the fulfillment of all United States copyright requirements regarding the "DIVA" compositions and soundtrack. As such, Plaintiff argues that DRG should be estopped from asserting Plaintiff's failure to register or record as a defense.

Because we conclude that DRG obligated itself to perfect Plaintiff's copyright, and that prejudice to DRG would be minimal, we grant Plaintiff permission to file a supplemental pleading upon registering and recording the transfer of rights it received from the Composer.

C. Unauthorized Copying

The third and final element of a copyright infringement claim is unauthorized copying by the defendant. DRG raises two arguments in its defense.

First, DRG argues that Plaintiff should be estopped from asserting that defendant's conduct was unauthorized. DRG contends that estoppel is proper in that Plaintiff impliedly consented to DRG's continued exploitation of the soundtrack after the License expired in 1987. While there is some factual support for this argument, we nonetheless conclude that DRG cannot establish an estoppel defense. Specifically, in order to establish an estoppel defense, a defendant must show i) that plaintiff knew of defendant's infringing conduct; ii) that plaintiff intended that its conduct be relied upon or that plaintiff acted so that the defendants had a right to believe that it was so intended; iii) that defendants were ignorant of the true facts; and iv) that defendants relied on plaintiff's conduct to their detriment. *Lottie Joplin Thomas Trust v. Crown Publishers, Inc.,* 456 F.Supp. 531, 535 (S.D.N.Y.1977), *aff'd,* 592 F.2d 651 (2d Cir.1978). Here, as DRG was aware that the License expired in 1987, DRG was aware of the true facts and cannot establish the third element of an estoppel defense. Accordingly, the defense must fail.

DRG next argues that the soundtrack to "DIVA" has entered the public domain and, as such, DRG cannot be liable for unauthorized copying. Specifically, DRG contends that the release of a "single" from the soundtrack in 1981 without copyright notice as required by § 405(a) injected the single, as well as the entire soundtrack, into the public domain.

For works published prior to March 1, 1989, the effective date of the Berne Implementation Amendments, notice is a condition to protection of the work. Absent notice, the work is forfeited and enters, by operation of law, the public domain. *Shapiro & Son Bedspread Corp. v. Royal Mills Assocs,* 764 F.2d 69, 72 (2d Cir.1985); *Beacon Looms, Inc. v. S. Lichtenberg & Co.,* 552 F.Supp. 1305, 1309–10 (S.D.N.Y.1982).

Here, Plaintiff concedes that over a thousand copies of a single containing the two selections from the "DIVA" soundtrack were distributed in France without the requisite notice. Because none of the cure provisions of § 405 are applicable, the recording of these two selections was clearly injected into the public domain.

The question remains, however, whether publication of the single placed the entire soundtrack into the public domain. We answer this question in the negative. A similar question was addressed by the Supreme Court in *Mifflin v. Dutton,* 190 U.S. 265, 23 S.Ct. 771 (1903). *Mifflin* involved the serialized publication, without notice, of the first twenty-nine chapters of Harriet Beecher Stowe's novel the "Minister's Wooing." These chapters were published in the

"Atlantic Monthly" prior to the publication of the full length book, for which copyright protection had been obtained. As such, the Supreme Court held that these chapters had lost copyright protection and become public property. *Mifflin,* 190 U.S. at 266, 23 S.Ct. at 772. Importantly, the Court further noted that but for the subsequent publication without notice of the last thirteen chapters, these chapters would undoubtedly have been protected by Stowe's copyright in the book. *Mifflin,* 190 U.S. at 266, 23 S.Ct. at 772. *Cf. Wrench v. Universal Pictures Co.,* 104 F.Supp. 374, 378 (S.D.N.Y.1952) (copyright in short story collection not lost where one story had appeared without notice). Applying this reasoning to the case sub judice, we conclude that publication of the single injected only the recordings contained on the single into the public domain and not the recordings contained on the entire soundtrack. Accordingly, to the extent Plaintiff's claim is premised on infringement of the recordings contained in the single, the claim is dismissed.

As to Plaintiff's infringement claim based on the underlying compositions and the remaining soundtrack, we think that Plaintiff has established both ownership and unlawful copying. Accordingly, DRG's motion for summary judgment dismissing this claim is denied. Because Plaintiff has not yet complied with all statutory prequisites to suit, however, we similarly deny DRG's motion for summary judgment on this claim. Plaintiff, however, may renew its motion upon completion of registration and recordation.

II. The Trademark Infringement Claim

DRG next moves for summary judgment dismissing Plaintiff's claim for trademark infringement. Ownership of a registered mark is a prerequisite to bringing a trademark infringement claim under § 43(a) of the Lanham Act. *See* 15 U.S.C. § 1114; *Bayshore Group, Ltd. v. Bay Shore Seafood Brokers, Inc.,* 762 F.Supp. 404, 409 (D.Mass.1991). *Cf. Centaur Communications, Ltd. v. A/S/M Communications, Inc.,* 830 F.2d 1217, 1221 (2d Cir.1987). As Plaintiff concedes that no federal trademark registration for the "DIVA" name has been obtained, this claim is dismissed.

III. The Federal Unfair Competition Claims

Plaintiff's federal unfair competition claim is similarly dismissed.

In order to establish a claim for unfair competition, a plaintiff must show that its mark has acquired secondary meaning and that there exists a likelihood of confusion by the public as to the source or sponsorship of the product....

As a rule, an unauthorized sale of authorized goods cannot, without more, constitute unfair competition, since there is no possibility of deception or confusion....

The rationale articulated in *Monte Carlo* bears repeating:

> A showing of likely buyer confusion as to the source, origin or sponsorship of goods is part of a cause of action for infringement of a registered trademark. No such confusion was possible in this case. The goods sold by [defendants] were not imitations of [plaintiff's] shirts; they were the genuine product, planned and sponsored by [plaintiff] and produced for it on contract for future sale.

Monte Carlo, 707 F.2d at 1058.

Here, the "DIVA" recordings distributed by DRG were genuine in that they were identical copies of the original "master" provided by Plaintiff. Because the recordings were genuine, there can be no confusion as to source and the unfair competition claim must be dismissed.

IV. State Unfair Competition Claim

Lastly, we turn to Plaintiff's unfair competition claim brought under state law. To the extent that Plaintiff's claim seeks protection against DRG's copying, it is a claim based on a right equivalent to "exclusive rights within the ... scope of copyright" and is thus preempted. 17 U.S.C.§ 301(a). Accordingly, the state law claim for unfair competition is dismissed.

SO ORDERED.

HIP HOP AND INTELLECTUAL PROPERTY

[Ch. 20 in Champion, Intellectual Property in the Sports and Entertainment Industries 236-238; reprinted with permission of the authors, for educational purposes.]

"I sit alone in my four-cornered room staring at candles" (Ghetto Boyz, "My Mind's Playing Tricks on Me"). Hip-hop is life today. It's music, it's culture, it's a way of life. It also permeates with intellectual property concerns, mostly because of its tendency to "sample" from other songs, motifs, logos, etc. Hip-hop is rife with free speech, First Amendment, and intellectual property concerns. Copyright law affects hip-hop's creativity and accessibility by requiring licenses for even "de minimus" sampling of music.

There is deep distrust of the law in the urban hip hop community. Sometimes, such as Ice-T's "Cop-Killer" and Dr. Dre and Snoop Dogg's "Deep Cover," the form of expression takes a desire to inflict violence upon police. In Skywalker Records, Inc. v. Navarro, 737 F.Supp. 578 (S.D. Fla. 1990), a complaint was made to the Broward County Sheriff concerning the graphic nature of 2 Live Crew's "As Nasty as They Wanna Be" then being sold in local retail music stores. The deputy assigned to investigate the complaint prepared an affidavit concerning his findinds and filed it, along with a tape cassette of the album and transcript of six of the tape's 18 songs, in the county circuit court. The judge agreed and issued an order finding probable cause to believe that the recording was obscene under Florida Law. Local law enforcement "visioned" several of the music store managers, provided them with a copy of the order, and warned them " as a matter of courtesy" that any further sale of the album would result in arrest. While the district court agreed that the recording was obscene under Florida law, it also found that the Sheriff's Office violated the First and Fourteenth Amendments by prior restraint of speech. The Eleventh Circuit Court disagreed, however, and found the district court's decision that the album "had no artistic value" was arbitrary.

"Hip-hop" is more than just a style of music. It is the manner of dress, dialect, and language preferred by a large segment of the population born between 1965 and 1984. Three of its four principal elements are grounded in music: emceeing (or "MCing," sometimes "rapping"), disc jokeyiing ("DJing"), break dancing, and graffiti. Its essence, however, is MCling and DJing. A form of verbal expression deeply rooted in ancient African culture and oral tradition shaped by contributions from the R&B, Caribbean, and other forms in the early 1970s; MCing or rapping is the performance of complex rhyming lyrics that often are spoken against a backdrop of music or a beat rather than sung. Generally,

the hip-hop artist composes his or her own lyrics and uses the lyrics of others only to show respect or to call out the author to battle.

"The sampler is a tool and a music instrument. That's how I always thought about it...[T]he sampler is an instrument that I play." RZA, from the WuTang Clan, continues, "I've always been into using the sampler more like a painter's palette than a Xerox" (The RZA, The Wu-Tang Manual 192 [2005]). The sampler is like a musical instrument or an artistic tool. Sampling is hip-hop; it creates its unique collage-like artistry which is very similar to the oral tradition of adding and supplementing, as witnessed in African-american spirituals and chants.

In Campbell v. Acuff Rose, Inc., 510 U.S. 569 (1994), the Supreme Court ruled in favor of hip-hop artists 2Live Crew's mocking version of Roy Orbison's "Oh, Pretty Woman." 1 Live Crew parodied (or mocked) Orbison's "Oh, Pretty Woman." 2 Live Crew parodied (or Mocked) Orbison's haunting ballad. Parody is just another version of sampling. This parody was without the consent of the original copyright owner. Here, 2 Live Crew actually offered to pay royalties for the use of the song but was refused. However, 2 Live Crew included "Pretty Woman" in their 1980 LP release "As Clean as They Wanna Be" with the same opening lyrics, drum bear, and bass riff but transmorphing Roy's icon of feminist beauty into a "big hairy woman."

Sampling and Copyrights

In Newton v. Diamond, 349 F.3d 591 (9th Cir. 2003), the famous Beastie Boys sampled a six-second, three-note segment from jazz flautist James Newton. The Beastie Boys, however, obtained a license to sample from Newton's sound recording, but they did not obtain a license to sample from the musical composition. As regards copyright infringement, the standard for hip-hop sampling appears to be measuring the similarity of the two works.

De minimus copying is allowed, and the test is whether the average audience would recognize the appropriation. Bridgeport Music, Inc. v. Dimension Films, 401 F.3d 647 (6th Cir. 2003) involved a two-second sample of an arpeggiated guitar chord from a song by George Clinton and the Funkadelics; the sample was lowered, looped, and extended to sixteen beats, extended to seven seconds, and repeated five times in the song "100 Miles and Runnin," which was used in the movie soundtrack for "I Got the Hook Up." This de minimus sampling was allowed, at least in the Sixth Circuit.

In Grand Upright v. Warner Bros. Records, 780 F.Supp. 182 (S.D.N.Y. 1991), old school hip-hop artist Biz Markie sampled Gilbert O'Sullivan's song "Alone Again Naturally." The court found that Biz Markie requested but was denied permission to sample and had infringed Gilbert O'Sullivan's copyright. The court saw this sampling as "theft."

In Williams v. Broadus, 2001 WL 894714 (S.D.N.Y.), rapper Snooop Dogg was sued over his use of an allegedly unauthorized sample. The court utilizes a "substantial similarity" test and finds that a sample that is not qualitatively or quantitatively similar to the sampled sound recording is not a violation of the copyright holder's right to create a derivative work.

In summary of the major digital sampling cases: "In Grand Upright, one person owned both the copyright in the underlying composition and the copyright in the master recording, permission was sought by Biz Markie and not received, and the final court ruling was in favor of the original artist. In Newton, the Beastie Boys paid for the rights to sample the sound recording but did not obtain a license for the underlying musical composition from the original recording artist, but still won the case defendant-sampler had entered into a license agreement for the musical composition copyright but did not get a copyright to sample the digital sound recording, and eventually lost against the company owning the sound recording copyright under the theory that any sampling of a sound recording is per se infringement" (22 St. Johns J. Legal Comment at 406.) [footnotes omitted]

CAMPBELL v. ACUFF-ROSE MUSIC
Supreme Court of the United States
November 9, 1993, Argued; March 7, 1994, Decided
No. 92-1292
510 U.S. 569; 114 S.Ct. 1164; 127 L.Ed.2d 500

Justice SOUTER delivered the opinion of the Court.

We are called upon to decide whether 2 Live Crew's commercial parody of Roy Orbison's song, "Oh, Pretty Woman," may be a fair use within the meaning of the Copyright Act of 1976, 17 U.S.C. § 107 (1988 ed. and Supp. IV). Although the District Court granted summary judgment for 2 Live Crew, the Court of Appeals reversed, holding the defense of fair use barred by the song's commercial character and excessive borrowing. Because we hold that a parody's commercial character is only one element to be weighed in a fair use enquiry, and that insufficient consideration was given to the nature of parody in weighing the degree of copying, we reverse and remand.

I

In 1964, Roy Orbison and William Dees wrote a rock ballad called "Oh, Pretty Woman" and assigned their rights in it to respondent Acuff–Rose Music, Inc. See Appendix A, *infra,* at 1179. Acuff–Rose registered the song for copyright protection.

Petitioners Luther R. Campbell, Christopher Wongwon, Mark Ross, and David Hobbs are collectively known as 2 Live Crew, a popular rap music group. In 1989, Campbell wrote a song entitled "Pretty Woman," which he later described in an affidavit as intended, "through comical lyrics, to satirize the original work...." App. to Pet. for Cert. 80a. On July 5, 1989, 2 Live Crew's manager informed Acuff–Rose that 2 Live Crew had written a parody of "Oh, Pretty Woman," that they would afford all credit for ownership and authorship of the original song to Acuff–Rose, Dees, and Orbison, and that they were willing to pay a fee for the use they wished to make of it. Enclosed with the letter were a copy of the lyrics and a recording of 2 Live Crew's song. See Appendix B, *infra,* at 1179–80. Acuff–Rose's agent refused permission, stating that "I am aware of the success enjoyed by 'The 2 Live Crews', but I must inform you that we cannot permit the use of a parody of 'Oh, Pretty Woman.' " App. to Pet. for Cert. 85a. Nonetheless, in June or July 1989, 2 Live Crew released records, cassette tapes, and compact discs of "Pretty Woman" in a collection of songs entitled "As Clean As They Wanna Be." The albums and compact discs identify the authors of "Pretty Woman" as Orbison and Dees and its publisher as Acuff–Rose.

Almost a year later, after nearly a quarter of a million copies of the recording had been sold, Acuff–Rose sued 2 Live Crew and its record company, Luke Skyywalker Records, for copyright infringement. The District Court granted summary judgment for 2 Live Crew, reasoning that the commercial purpose of 2 Live Crew's song was no bar to fair use; that 2 Live Crew's version was a parody, which "quickly degenerates into a play on words, substituting predictable lyrics with shocking ones" to show "how bland and banal the Orbison song" is; that 2 Live Crew had taken no more than was necessary to "conjure up" the original in order to parody it; and that it was "extremely unlikely that 2 Live Crew's song could adversely affect the market for the original." 754 F.Supp. 1150, 1154–1155, 1157–1158 (MD Tenn.1991). The District Court weighed these factors and held that 2 Live Crew's song made fair use of Orbison's original. *Id.,* at 1158–1159.

The Court of Appeals for the Sixth Circuit reversed and remanded. 972 F.2d 1429, 1439 (1992). Although it assumed for the purpose of its opinion that 2 Live Crew's song was a parody of the Orbison original, the Court of Appeals thought the District Court had put too little emphasis on the fact that "every commercial use ... is presumptively ... unfair," *Sony Corp. of America v. Universal City Studios, Inc.,* 464 U.S. 417, 451, 104 S.Ct. 774, 792, 78 L.Ed.2d 574 (1984), and it held that "the admittedly commercial nature" of the parody "requires the conclusion" that the first of four factors relevant under the statute weighs against a finding of fair use. 972 F.2d, at 1435, 1437. Next, the Court of Appeals determined that, by "taking the heart of the original and making it the heart of a new work," 2 Live Crew had, qualitatively, taken too much. *Id.,* at 1438. Finally, after noting that the effect on the potential market for the original (and the market for derivative works) is "undoubtedly the single most important element of fair use," *Harper & Row, Publishers, Inc. v. Nation Enterprises,* 471 U.S. 539, 566, 105 S.Ct. 2218, 2233, 85 L.Ed.2d 588 (1985), the Court of Appeals faulted the District Court for "refus[ing] to indulge the presumption" that "harm for purposes of the fair use analysis has been established by the presumption attaching to commercial uses." 972 F.2d, at 1438–1439. In sum, the court concluded that its "blatantly commercial purpose ... prevents this parody from being a fair use." *Id.,* at 1439.

We granted certiorari, 507 U.S. 1003, 113 S.Ct. 1642, 123 L.Ed.2d 264 (1993), to determine whether 2 Live Crew's commercial parody could be a fair use.

II

It is uncontested here that 2 Live Crew's song would be an infringement of Acuff–Rose's rights in "Oh, Pretty Woman," under the Copyright Act of 1976, 17 U.S.C. § 106 (1988 ed. and Supp. IV), but for a finding of fair use through parody. From the infancy of copyright protection, some opportunity for fair use of copyrighted materials has been thought necessary to fulfill copyright's very purpose, "[t]o promote the Progress of Science and useful Arts...." U.S. Const., Art. I, § 8, cl. 8. For as Justice Story explained, "[i]n truth, in literature, in science and in art, there are, and can be, few, if any, things, which in an abstract sense, are strictly new and original throughout. Every book in literature, science and art, borrows, and must necessarily borrow, and use much which was well known and used before." *Emerson v. Davies,* 8 F.Cas. 615, 619 (No. 4,436) (CCD Mass.1845). Similarly, Lord Ellenborough expressed the inherent tension in the need simultaneously to protect copyrighted material and to allow others to build upon it when he wrote, "while I shall think myself bound to secure every man in the enjoyment of his copy-right, one must not put manacles upon science." *Carey v. Kearsley,* 4 Esp. 168, 170, 170 Eng.Rep. 679, 681 (K.B.1803). In copyright cases brought under the Statute of Anne of 1710, English courts held that in some instances "fair abridgements" would not infringe an author's rights, see W. Patry, The Fair Use Privilege in Copyright Law 6–17 (1985) (hereinafter Patry); Leval, Toward a Fair Use Standard, 103 Harv.L.Rev. 1105 (1990) (hereinafter Leval), and although the First Congress enacted our initial copyright statute, Act of May 31, 1790, 1 Stat. 124, without any explicit reference to "fair use," as it later came to be known, the doctrine was recognized by the American courts nonetheless.

In *Folsom v. Marsh,* 9 F.Cas. 342 (No. 4,901) (CCD Mass. 1841), Justice Story distilled the essence of law and methodology from the earlier cases: "look to the nature and objects of the selections made, the quantity and value of the materials used, and the degree in which the use may prejudice the sale, or diminish the profits, or supersede the objects, of the original work." *Id.,* at 348. Thus expressed, fair use remained exclusively judge-made doctrine until the passage of the 1976 Copyright Act, in which Justice Story's summary is discernible:

"§ 107. Limitations on exclusive rights: Fair use

"Notwithstanding the provisions of sections 106 and 106A, the fair use of a copyrighted work, including such use by reproduction in copies or phonorecords or by any other means specified by that section, for purposes such as criticism, comment, news reporting, teaching (including multiple copies for classroom use), scholarship, or research, is not an infringement of copyright. In determining whether the use made of a work in any particular case is a fair use the factors to be considered shall include—

"(1) the purpose and character of the use, including whether such use is of a commercial nature or is for nonprofit educational purposes;

"(2) the nature of the copyrighted work;

"(3) the amount and substantiality of the portion used in relation to the copyrighted work as a whole; and

"(4) the effect of the use upon the potential market for or value of the copyrighted work.

"The fact that a work is unpublished shall not itself bar a finding of fair use if such finding is made upon consideration of all the above factors." 17 U.S.C. § 107 (1988 ed. and Supp. IV).

Congress meant § 107 "to restate the present judicial doctrine of fair use, not to change, narrow, or enlarge it in any way" and intended that courts continue the common-law tradition of fair use adjudication. H.R.Rep. No. 94–1476, p. 66 (1976) (hereinafter House Report); S.Rep. No. 94–473, p. 62 (1975) U.S.Code Cong. & Admin.News 1976, pp. 5659, 5679 (hereinafter Senate Report). The fair use doctrine thus "permits [and requires] courts to avoid rigid application of the copyright statute when, on occasion, it would stifle the very creativity which that law is designed to foster." *Stewart v. Abend,* 495 U.S. 207, 236, 110 S.Ct. 1750, 1767, 109 L.Ed.2d 184 (1990) (internal quotation marks and citation omitted).

The task is not to be simplified with bright-line rules, for the statute, like the doctrine it recognizes, calls for case-by-case analysis. *Harper & Row,* 471 U.S., at 560, 105 S.Ct., at 2230; *Sony,* 464 U.S., at 448, and n. 31, 104 S.Ct., at 792, & n. 31; House Report, pp. 65–66; Senate Report, p. 62. The text employs the terms "including" and "such as" in the preamble paragraph to indicate the "illustrative and not limitative" function of the examples given, § 101; see *Harper & Row, supra,* 471 U.S., at 561, 105 S.Ct., at 2230, which thus provide only general guidance about the sorts of copying that courts and Congress most commonly had found to be fair uses. Nor may the four statutory factors be treated in isolation, one from another. All are to be explored, and the results weighed together, in light of the purposes of copyright. See Leval 1110–1111; Patry & Perlmutter, Fair Use Misconstrued: Profit, Presumptions, and Parody, 11 Cardozo Arts & Ent.L.J. 667, 685–687 (1993) (hereinafter Patry & Perlmutter).

A

The first factor in a fair use enquiry is "the purpose and character of the use, including whether such use is of a commercial nature or is for nonprofit educational purposes." § 107(1). This factor draws on Justice Story's formulation, "the nature and objects of the selections made." *Folsom v. Marsh, supra,* at 348. The enquiry here may be guided by the examples given in the preamble to § 107, looking to whether the use is for criticism, or comment, or news reporting, and the like, see § 107. The central purpose of this investigation is to see, in Justice Story's words, whether the new work merely "supersede[s] the objects" of the original creation, *Folsom v. Marsh, supra,* at 348; accord, *Harper & Row, supra,* 471 U.S., at 562, 105 S.Ct., at 2231 ("supplanting" the original), or instead adds something new, with a further purpose or different character, altering the first with new expression, meaning, or message; it asks, in other words, whether and to what extent the new work is "transformative." Leval 1111. Although such transformative use is not absolutely necessary for a finding of fair use, *Sony, supra,* 464 U.S., at 455, n. 40, 104 S.Ct., at 795, n. 40, the goal of copyright, to promote science and the arts, is generally furthered by the creation of transformative works. Such works thus lie at the heart of the fair use doctrine's guarantee of breathing space within the confines of copyright, see, *e.g., Sony, supra,* at 478–480, 104 S.Ct., at 807–808 (BLACKMUN, J., dissenting), and the more transformative the new work, the less will be the significance of other factors, like commercialism, that may weigh against a finding of fair use.

This Court has only once before even considered whether parody may be fair use, and that time issued no opinion because of the Court's equal division. *Benny v. Loew's Inc.,* 239 F.2d 532 (CA9 1956), aff'd *sub nom. Columbia Broadcasting System, Inc. v. Loew's Inc.,* 356 U.S. 43, 78 S.Ct. 667, 2 L.Ed.2d 583 (1958). Suffice it to say now that parody has an obvious claim to transformative value, as Acuff–Rose itself does not deny. Like less ostensibly humorous forms of criticism, it can provide social benefit, by shedding light on an earlier work, and, in the process, creating a new one. We thus line up with the courts that have held that parody, like other comment or criticism, may claim fair use under § 107. See, *e.g., Fisher v. Dees,* 794 F.2d 432 (CA9 1986) ("When Sonny Sniffs Glue," a parody of "When Sunny Gets Blue," is fair use*Elsmere Music, Inc. v. National Broadcasting Co.,* 482 F.Supp. 741 SDNY), aff'd, 623 F.2d 252 (CA2 1980) ("I Love Sodom," a "Saturday Night Live" television parody of "I Love New York," is fair use); see also House Report, p. 65; Senate Report, p. 61, U.S.Code Cong. & Admin.News 1976, pp. 5659, 5678 ("[U]se in a parody of some of the content of the work parodied" may be fair use).

The germ of parody lies in the definition of the Greek *parodeia,* quoted in Judge Nelson's Court of Appeals dissent, as "a song sung alongside another." 972 F.2d, at 1440, quoting 7 Encyclopedia Britannica 768 (15th ed. 1975). Modern dictionaries accordingly describe a parody as a "literary or artistic work that imitates the characteristic style of an author or a work for comic effect or ridicule," or as a "composition in prose or verse in which the characteristic turns of thought and phrase in an author or class of authors are imitated in such a way as to make them appear ridiculous." For the purposes of copyright law, the nub of the definitions, and the heart of any parodist's claim to quote from existing material, is the use of some elements of a prior author's composition to create a new one that, at least in part, comments on that author's works. See, *e.g., Fisher v. Dees, supra,* at 437; *MCA, Inc. v. Wilson,* 677 F.2d 180, 185 (CA2 1981). If, on the contrary, the commentary has no critical bearing on the substance or style of the original composition, which the alleged infringer merely uses to get attention or to avoid the drudgery in working up something fresh, the claim to fairness in borrowing from another's work diminishes accordingly (if it does not vanish), and other factors, like the extent of its commerciality, loom larger. Parody needs to mimic an original to make its point, and so has some claim to use the creation of its victim's (or collective victims') imagination, whereas satire can stand on its own two feet and so requires justification for the very act of borrowing. See *ibid.;* Bisceglia, Parody and Copyright Protection: Turning the Balancing Act Into a Juggling Act, in ASCAP, Copyright Law Symposium, No. 34, p. 25 (1987).

The fact that parody can claim legitimacy for some appropriation does not, of course, tell either parodist or judge much about where to draw the line. Like a book review quoting the copyrighted material criticized, parody may or may not be fair use, and petitioners' suggestion that any parodic use is presumptively fair has no more justification in law or fact than the equally hopeful claim that any use for news reporting should be presumed fair, see *Harper & Row,* 471 U.S., at 561, 105 S.Ct., at 2230. The Act has no hint of an evidentiary preference for parodists over their victims, and no workable presumption for parody could take account of the fact that parody often shades into satire when society is lampooned through its creative artifacts, or that a work may contain both parodic and nonparodic elements. Accordingly, parody, like any other use, has to work its way through the relevant factors, and be judged case by case, in light of the ends of the copyright law.

Here, the District Court held, and the Court of Appeals assumed, that 2 Live Crew's "Pretty Woman" contains parody, commenting on and criticizing the original work, whatever it may have to say about society at large. As the District Court remarked, the words of 2 Live Crew's song copy the original's first line, but then "quickly degenerat[e] into a play on words, substituting predictable lyrics with shocking ones ... [that] derisively demonstrat[e] how bland and banal the Orbison song seems to them." 754 F.Supp., at 1155 (footnote omitted). Judge Nelson, dissenting below, came to the same conclusion, that the 2 Live Crew song "was clearly intended to ridicule the white-bread original" and "reminds us that sexual congress with nameless streetwalkers is not necessarily the stuff of romance and is not necessarily without its consequences. The singers (there are several) have the same thing on their minds as did the lonely man with the nasal voice, but here there is no hint of wine and roses." 972 F.2d, at 1442. Although the majority below had difficulty discerning any criticism of the original in 2 Live Crew's song, it assumed for purposes of its opinion that there was some. *Id.,* at 1435–1436, and n. 8.

We have less difficulty in finding that critical element in 2 Live Crew's song than the Court of Appeals did, although having found it we will not take the further step of evaluating its quality. The threshold question when fair use is raised in defense of parody is whether a parodic character may reasonably be perceived. Whether, going beyond that, parody is in good taste or bad does not and should not matter to fair use. As Justice Holmes explained, "[i]t would be a dangerous undertaking for persons trained only to the law to constitute themselves final judges of the worth of [a work], outside of the narrowest and most obvious limits. At the one extreme some works of genius would be sure to miss appreciation. Their very novelty would make them repulsive until the public had learned the new language in which their author spoke." *Bleistein v. Donaldson Lithographing Co.,* 188 U.S. 239, 251, 23 S.Ct. 298, 300, 47 L.Ed. 460 (1903) (circus posters have copyright protection); cf. *Yankee Publishing Inc. v. News America Publishing, Inc.,* 809 F.Supp. 267, 280 (SDNY 1992)

While we might not assign a high rank to the parodic element here, we think it fair to say that 2 Live Crew's song reasonably could be perceived as commenting on the original or criticizing it, to some degree. 2 Live Crew juxtaposes the romantic musings of a man whose fantasy comes true, with degrading taunts, a bawdy demand for sex, and a sigh of relief from paternal responsibility. The later words can be taken as a comment on the naiveté of the original of an earlier day, as a rejection of its sentiment that ignores the ugliness of street life and the debasement that it signifies. It is this joinder of reference and ridicule that marks off the author's choice of parody from the other types of comment and criticism that traditionally have had a claim to fair use protection as transformative works.

The Court of Appeals, however, immediately cut short the enquiry into 2 Live Crew's fair use claim by confining its treatment of the first factor essentially to one relevant fact, the commercial nature of the use. The court then inflated the significance of this fact by applying a presumption os tensibly culled from *Sony,* that "every commercial use of copyrighted material is presumptively ... unfair...." *Sony,* 464 U.S., at 451, 104 S.Ct., at 792. In giving virtually dispositive weight to the commercial nature of the parody, the Court of Appeals erred.

The language of the statute makes clear that the commercial or nonprofit educational purpose of a work is only one element of the first factor enquiry into its purpose and character. Section 107(1) uses the term "including" to begin the dependent clause referring to commercial use, and the main clause speaks of a broader investigation into "purpose and character." As we explained in *Harper & Row,* Congress resisted attempts to narrow the ambit of this traditional enquiry by adopting categories of presumptively fair use, and it urged courts to preserve the breadth of their traditionally ample view of the universe of relevant evidence. 471 U.S., at 561, 105 S.Ct. at 2230; House Report,

p. 66, U.S.Code Cong. & Admin.News 1976, pp. 5659, 5679. Accordingly, the mere fact that a use is educational and not for profit does not insulate it from a finding of infringement, any more than the commercial character of a use bars a finding of fairness. If, indeed, commerciality carried presumptive force against a finding of fairness, the presumption would swallow nearly all of the illustrative uses listed in the preamble paragraph of § 107, including news reporting, comment, criticism, teaching, scholarship, and research, since these activities "are generally conducted for profit in this country." *Harper & Row, supra,* at 592, 105 S.Ct., at 2246 (Brennan, J., dissenting). Congress could not have intended such a rule, which certainly is not inferable from the common-law cases, arising as they did from the world of letters in which Samuel Johnson could pronounce that "[n]o man but a blockhead ever wrote, except for money." 3 Boswell's Life of Johnson 19 (G. Hill ed. 1934).

Sony itself called for no hard evidentiary presumption. There, we emphasized the need for a "sensitive balancing of interests," 464 U.S., at 455, n. 40, 104 S.Ct., at 795, n. 40, noted that Congress had "eschewed a rigid, bright-line approach to fair use," *id.,* at 449, n. 31, 104 S.Ct., at 792, n. 31, and stated that the commercial or nonprofit educational character of a work is "not conclusive," *id.,* at 448–449, 104 S.Ct., at 792, but rather a fact to be "weighed along with other[s] in fair use decisions," *id.,* at 449, n. 32, 104 S.Ct. at 792, n. 32, (quoting House Report, p. 66) U.S.Code Cong. & Admin.News 1976, pp. 5659, 5679. The Court of Appeals's elevation of one sentence from *Sony* to a *per se* rule thus runs as much counter to *Sony* itself as to the long common-law tradition of fair use adjudication. Rather, as we explained in *Harper & Row, Sony* stands for the proposition that the "fact that a publication was commercial as opposed to nonprofit is a separate factor that tends to weigh against a finding of fair use." 471 U.S., at 562, 105 S.Ct., at 2231. But that is all, and the fact that even the force of that tendency will vary with the context is a further reason against elevating commerciality to hard presumptive significance. The use, for example, of a copyrighted work to advertise a product, even in a parody, will be entitled to less indulgence under the first factor of the fair use enquiry than the sale of a parody for its own sake, let alone one performed a single time by students in school. See generally Patry & Perlmutter 679–680; *Fisher v. Dees,* 794 F.2d, at 437; *Maxtone–Graham v. Burtchaell,* 803 F.2d 1253, 1262 (CA2 1986); *Sega Enterprises Ltd. v. Accolade, Inc.,* 977 F.2d 1510, 1522 (CA9 1992).

B

The second statutory factor, "the nature of the copyrighted work," § 107(2), draws on Justice Story's expression, the "value of the materials used." *Folsom v. Marsh,* 9 F.Cas., at 348. This factor calls for recognition that some works are closer to the core of intended copyright protection than others, with the consequence that fair use is more difficult to establish when the former works are copied.... This fact, however, is not much help in this case, or ever likely to help much in separating the fair use sheep from the infringing goats in a parody case, since parodies almost invariably copy publicly known, expressive works.

C

The third factor asks whether "the amount and substantiality of the portion used in relation to the copyrighted work as a whole," § 107(3) (or, in Justice Story's words, "the quantity and value of the materials used," *Folsom v. Marsh, supra,* at 348) are reasonable in relation to the purpose of the copying. Here, attention turns to the persuasiveness of a parodist's justification for the particular copying done, and the enquiry will harken back to the first of the statutory factors, for, as in prior cases, we recognize that the extent of permissible copying varies with the purpose and character of the use. See *Sony, supra,* 464 U.S., at 449–450, 104 S.Ct., at 792–793 (reproduction of entire work "does not have its ordinary effect of militating against a finding of fair use" as to home videotaping of television programs); *Harper & Row, supra,* 471 U.S., at 564, 105 S.Ct., at 2232 ("[E]ven substantial quotations might qualify as fair use in a review of a published work or a news account of a speech" but not in a scoop of a soon-to-be-published memoir). The facts bearing on this factor will also tend to address the fourth, by revealing the degree to which the parody may serve as a market substitute for the original or potentially licensed derivatives. See Leval 1123.

The District Court considered the song's parodic purpose in finding that 2 Live Crew had not helped themselves overmuch. 754 F.Supp., at 1156–1157. The Court of Appeals disagreed, stating that "[w]hile it may not be inappropriate to find that no more was taken than necessary, the copying was qualitatively substantial.... We conclude that taking the heart of the original and making it the heart of a new work was to purloin a substantial portion of the essence of the original." 972 F.2d, at 1438.

The Court of Appeals is of course correct that this factor calls for thought not only about the quantity of the materials used, but about their quality and importance, too. In *Harper & Row,* for example, the Nation had taken only some 300 words out of President Ford's memoirs, but we signaled the significance of the quotations in finding them to amount to "the heart of the book," the part most likely to be newsworthy and important in licensing serialization. 471 U.S., at 564–566, 568, 105 S.Ct., at 2232–2234, 2234 (internal quotation marks omitted). We also agree with the Court of Appeals that whether "a substantial portion of the infringing work was copied verbatim" from the copyrighted work is a relevant question, see *id.,* at 565, 105 S.Ct., at

2232, for it may reveal a dearth of transformative character or purpose under the first factor, or a greater likelihood of market harm under the fourth; a work composed primarily of an original, particularly its heart, with little added or changed, is more likely to be a merely superseding use, fulfilling demand for the original.

Where we part company with the court below is in applying these guides to parody, and in particular to parody in the song before us. Parody presents a difficult case. Parody's humor, or in any event its comment, necessarily springs from recognizable allusion to its object through distorted imitation. Its art lies in the tension between a known original and its parodic twin. When parody takes aim at a particular original work, the parody must be able to "conjure up" at least enough of that original to make the object of its critical wit recognizable. See, *e.g., Elsmere Music,* 623 F.2d, at 253, n. 1; *Fisher v. Dees,* 794 F.2d, at 438–439. What makes for this recognition is quotation of the original's most distinctive or memorable features, which the parodist can be sure the audience will know. Once enough has been taken to assure identification, how much more is reasonable will depend, say, on the extent to which the song's overriding purpose and character is to parody the original or, in contrast, the likelihood that the parody may serve as a market substitute for the original. But using some characteristic features cannot be avoided.

We think the Court of Appeals was insufficiently appreciative of parody's need for the recognizable sight or sound when it ruled 2 Live Crew's use unreasonable as a matter of law. It is true, of course, that 2 Live Crew copied the characteristic opening bass riff (or musical phrase) of the original, and true that the words of the first line copy the Orbison lyrics. But if quotation of the opening riff and the first line may be said to go to the "heart" of the original, the heart is also what most readily conjures up the song for parody, and it is the heart at which parody takes aim. Copying does not become excessive in relation to parodic purpose merely because the portion taken was the original's heart. If 2 Live Crew had copied a significantly less memorable part of the original, it is difficult to see how its parodic character would have come through. See *Fisher v. Dees, supra,* at 439.

This is not, of course, to say that anyone who calls himself a parodist can skim the cream and get away scot free. In parody, as in news reporting, see *Harper & Row, supra,* context is everything, and the question of fairness asks what else the parodist did besides go to the heart of the original. It is significant that 2 Live Crew not only copied the first line of the original, but thereafter departed markedly from the Orbison lyrics for its own ends. 2 Live Crew not only copied the bass riff and repeated it, but also produced otherwise distinctive sounds, interposing "scraper" noise, overlaying the music with solos in different keys, and altering the drum beat. See 754 F.Supp., at 1155. This is not a case, then, where "a substantial portion" of the parody itself is composed of a "verbatim" copying of the original. It is not, that is, a case where the parody is so insubstantial, as compared to the copying, that the third factor must be resolved as a matter of law against the parodists.

Suffice it to say here that, as to the lyrics, we think the Court of Appeals correctly suggested that "no more was taken than necessary," 972 F.2d, at 1438, but just for that reason, we fail to see how the copying can be excessive in relation to its parodic purpose, even if the portion taken is the original's "heart." As to the music, we express no opinion whether repetition of the bass riff is excessive copying, and we remand to permit evaluation of the amount taken, in light of the song's parodic purpose and character, its transformative elements, and considerations of the potential for market substitution sketched more fully below.

D

The fourth fair use factor is "the effect of the use upon the potential market for or value of the copyrighted work." § 107(4). It requires courts to consider not only the extent of market harm caused by the particular actions of the alleged infringer, but also "whether unrestricted and widespread conduct of the sort engaged in by the defendant ... would result in a substantially adverse impact on the potential market" for the original. Nimmer § 13.05[A] [4], p. 13–102.61 (footnote omitted); accord, *Harper & Row,* 471 U.S., at 569, 105 S.Ct., at 2235; Senate Report, p. 65; *Folsom v. Marsh,* 9 F.Cas., at 349. The enquiry "must take account not only of harm to the original but also of harm to the market for derivative works." *Harper & Row, supra,* 471 U.S. at 568, 105 S.Ct., at 2234.

Since fair use is an affirmative defense, its proponent would have difficulty carrying the burden of demonstrating fair use without favorable evidence about relevant markets. In moving for summary judgment, 2 Live Crew left themselves at just such a disadvantage when they failed to address the effect on the market for rap derivatives, and confined themselves to uncontroverted submissions that there was no likely effect on the market for the original. They did not, however, thereby subject themselves to the evidentiary presumption applied by the Court of Appeals. In assessing the likelihood of significant market harm, the Court of Appeals quoted from language in *Sony* that " '[i]f the intended use is for commercial gain, that likelihood may be presumed. But if it is for a noncommercial purpose, the likelihood must be demonstrated.' " 972 F.2d, at 1438, quoting *Sony,* 464 U.S., at 451, 104 S.Ct., at 104 S.Ct., at 793. The court reasoned that because "the use of the copyrighted work is wholly commercial, ... we presume that a likelihood of future harm to Acuff–Rose exists." 972 F.2d, at 1438. In so doing, the court resolved the fourth factor against 2 Live Crew, just as it had the first, by applying a presumption about the effect of commercial use, a presumption which as applied here we hold to be error.

No "presumption" or inference of market harm that might find support in *Sony* is applicable to a case involving something beyond mere duplication for commercial purposes. *Sony's* discussion of a presumption contrasts a context of verbatim copying of the original in its entirety for commercial purposes, with the noncommercial context of *Sony* itself (home copying of television programming). In the former circumstances, what *Sony* said simply makes common sense: when a commercial use amounts to mere duplication of the entirety of an original, it clearly "supersede[s] the objects," *Folsom v. Marsh, supra,* at 348, of the original and serves as a market replacement for it, making it likely that cognizable market harm to the original will occur. *Sony, supra,* 464 U.S., at 451, 104 S.Ct., at 793. But when, on the contrary, the second use is transformative, market substitution is at least less certain, and market harm may not be so readily inferred. Indeed, as to parody pure and simple, it is more likely that the new work will not affect the market for the original in a way cognizable under this factor, that is, by acting as a substitute for it ("supersed[ing] [its] objects"). See Leval 1125; Patry & Perlmutter 692, 697–698. This is so because the parody and the original usually serve different market functions. Bisceglia, ASCAP, Copyright Law Symposium, No. 34, at 23.

We do not, of course, suggest that a parody may not harm the market at all, but when a lethal parody, like a scathing theater review, kills demand for the original, it does not produce a harm cognizable under the Copyright Act. Because "parody may quite legitimately aim at garroting the original, destroying it commercially as well as artistically," B. Kaplan, An Unhurried View of Copyright 69 (1967), the role of the courts is to distinguish between "[b]iting criticism [that merely] suppresses demand [and] copyright infringement[, which] usurps it." *Fisher v. Dees,* 794 F.2d, at 438.

This distinction between potentially remediable displacement and unremediable disparagement is reflected in the rule that there is no protectible derivative market for criticism. The market for potential derivative uses includes only those that creators of original works would in general develop or license others to develop. Yet the unlikelihood that creators of imaginative works will license critical reviews or lampoons of their own productions removes such uses from the very notion of a potential licensing market. "People ask ... for criticism, but they only want praise." S. Maugham, Of Human Bondage 241 (Penguin ed. 1992). Thus, to the extent that the opinion below may be read to have considered harm to the market for parodies of "Oh, Pretty Woman," see 972 F.2d, at 1439, the court erred. Accord, *Fisher v. Dees, supra,* at 437; Leval 1125; Patry & Perlmutter 688–691.

In explaining why the law recognizes no derivative market for critical works, including parody, we have, of course, been speaking of the later work as if it had nothing but a critical aspect (*i.e.*, "parody pure and simple," *supra*, at 1177). But the later work may have a more complex character, with effects not only in the arena of criticism but also in protectible markets for derivative works, too. In that sort of case, the law looks beyond the criticism to the other elements of the work, as it does here. 2 Live Crew's song comprises not only parody but also rap music, and the derivative market for rap music is a proper focus of enquiry, see *Harper & Row, supra*, 471 U.S., at 568, 105 S.Ct., at 2234; Nimmer § 13.05 [B]. Evidence of substantial harm to it would weigh against a finding of fair use, because the licensing of derivatives is an important economic incentive to the creation of originals. See 17 U.S.C. § 106(2) (copyright owner has rights to derivative works). Of course, the only harm to derivatives that need concern us, as discussed above, is the harm of market substitution. The fact that a parody may impair the market for derivative uses by the very effectiveness of its critical commentary is no more relevant under copyright than the like threat to the original market.

Although 2 Live Crew submitted uncontroverted affidavits on the question of market harm to the original, neither they, nor Acuff–Rose, introduced evidence or affidavits addressing the likely effect of 2 Live Crew's parodic rap song on the market for a nonparody, rap version of "Oh, Pretty Woman." And while Acuff–Rose would have us find evidence of a rap market in the very facts that 2 Live Crew recorded a rap parody of "Oh, Pretty Woman" and another rap group sought a license to record a rap derivative, there was no evidence that a potential rap market was harmed in any way by 2 Live Crew's parody, rap version. The fact that 2 Live Crew's parody sold as part of a collection of rap songs says very little about the parody's effect on a market for a rap version of the original, either of the music alone or of the music with its lyrics. The District Court essentially passed on this issue, observing that Acuff–Rose is free to record "whatever version of the original it desires," 754 F.Supp., at 1158; the Court of Appeals went the other way by erroneous presumption. Contrary to each treatment, it is impossible to deal with the fourth factor except by recognizing that a silent record on an important factor bearing on fair use disentitled the proponent of the defense, 2 Live Crew, to summary judgment. The evidentiary hole will doubtless be plugged on remand.

III

It was error for the Court of Appeals to conclude that the commercial nature of 2 Live Crew's parody of "Oh, Pretty Woman" rendered it presumptively unfair. No such evidentiary presumption is available to address either the first factor, the character and purpose of the use, or the fourth, market harm, in determining whether a transformative use, such as parody, is a fair one. The court also erred in holding that 2 Live Crew had necessarily copied excessively from the Orbison original, considering the parodic purpose of the use. We therefore reverse the judgment of the Court of Appeals and remand the case for further proceedings consistent with this opinion.

It is so ordered.

APPENDIX A TO OPINION OF THE COURT
"Oh, Pretty Woman" by Roy Orbison and William Dees

Pretty Woman, walking down the street,
Pretty Woman, the kind I like to meet,
Pretty Woman, I don't believe you, you're not the truth,
No one could look as good as you
Mercy
Pretty Woman, won't you pardon me,
Pretty Woman, I couldn't help but see,
Pretty Woman, that you look lovely as can be
Are you lonely just like me?
Pretty Woman, stop a while,
Pretty Woman, talk a while,
Pretty Woman give your smile to me
Pretty Woman, yeah, yeah, yeah
Pretty Woman, look my way,
Pretty Woman, say you'll stay with me
'Cause I need you, I'll treat you right
Come to me baby, Be mine tonight
Pretty Woman, don't walk on by,
Pretty Woman, don't make me cry,
Pretty Woman, don't walk away,
Hey, O.K.
If that's the way it must be, O.K.
I guess I'll go on home, it's late
There'll be tomorrow night, but wait!
What do I see
Is she walking back to me?
Yeah, she's walking back to me!
Oh, Pretty Woman.

APPENDIX B TO OPINION OF THE COURT
"Pretty Woman" as Recorded by 2 Live Crew

Pretty woman walkin' down the street
Pretty woman girl you look so sweet
Pretty woman you bring me down to that knee

Pretty woman you make me wanna beg please
Oh, pretty woman
Big hairy woman you need to shave that stuff
Big hairy woman you know I bet it's tough
Big hairy woman all that hair it ain't legit
'Cause you look like 'Cousin It'
Big hairy woman
Bald headed woman girl your hair won't grow
Bald headed woman you got a teeny weeny afro
Bald headed woman you know your hair could look nice
Bald headed woman first you got to roll it with rice
Bald headed woman here, let me get this hunk of biz for ya
Ya know what I'm saying you look better than rice a roni
Oh bald headed woman
Big hairy woman come on in
And don't forget your bald headed friend
Hey pretty woman let the boys
Jump in
Two timin' woman girl you know you ain't right
Two timin' woman you's out with my boy last night
Two timin' woman that takes a load off my mind
Two timin' woman now I know the baby ain't mine
Oh, two timin' woman
Oh pretty woman

Justice KENNEDY, concurring.

NEWTON v. DIAMOND
United States Court of Appeals for the Ninth Circuit
November 4, 2003, Filed
No. 02-55983
349 F.3d 591

Opinion by Chief Judge SCHROEDER. Dissent by Judge GRABER.

SCHROEDER, Chief Judge:

This appeal raises the difficult and important issue of whether the incorporation of a short segment of a musical recording into a new musical recording, i.e., the practice of "sampling," requires a license to use both the performance and the composition of the original recording. The particular sample in this case consists of a six-second, three-note segment of a performance of one of his own compositions by plaintiff, and accomplished jazz flutist, James W. Newton. The defendants, the performers who did the sampling, are the members of the musical group Beastie Boys. They obtained a license to sample the sound recording of Newton's copyrighted performance, but they did not obtain a license to use Newton's underlying composition, which is also copyrighted.

The district court granted summary judgment to the defendants. In a scholarly opinion, it held that no license to the underlying composition was required because, as a matter of law, the notes in question—C–D flat—C, over a held C note—lacked sufficient originality to merit copyright protection. *Newton v. Diamond,* 204 F.Supp.2d 1244, 1256 (C.D.Cal.2002). The district court also held that even if the sampled segment of the composition were original, Beastie Boys' use was de minimis and therefore not actionable. *Id.* at 1259. We affirm on the ground that the use was de minimis.

Background and Procedural History

The plaintiff and appellant in this case, James W. Newton, is an accomplished avant-garde jazz flutist and composer. In 1978, he composed the song "Choir," a piece for flute and voice intended to incorporate elements of African–American gospel music, Japanese ceremonial court music, traditional African music, and classical music, among others. According to Newton, the song was inspired by his earliest memory of music, watching four women singing in a church in rural Arkansas. In 1981, Newton performed and recorded "Choir" and licensed all rights in the sound recording to ECM Records for $5000. The license covered only the sound recording, and it is undisputed that Newton retained all rights to the composition of "Choir." Sound recordings and their underlying compositions are separate works with their own distinct copyrights. 17 U.S.C. § 102(a)(2), (7).

The defendants and appellees include the members of the rap and hip-hop group Beastie Boys, and their business associates. In 1992, Beastie Boys obtained a license from ECM Records to use portions of the sound recording of "Choir" in various renditions of their song "Pass the Mic" in exchange for a one-time fee of $1000. Beastie Boys did not obtain a license from Newton to use the underlying composition.

The portion of the composition at issue consists of three notes, C–D flat—C, sung over a background C note played on the flute. When played on the sound recording licensed by Beastie Boys, the segment lasts for approximately six seconds. The score to "Choir" also indicates that the entire song should be played in a "largo/senza-misura" tempo, meaning "slowly/without-measure." Apart from an instruction that the performer sing into the flute and finger simultaneously, the score is not further orchestrated.

The dispute between Newton and Beastie Boys centers around the copyright implications of the practice of sampling, a practice now common to many types of popular music. Sampling entails the incorporation of short segments of prior sound recordings into new recordings. The practice originated in Jamaica in the 1960s, when disc jockeys (DJs) used portable sound systems to mix segments of prior recordings into new mixes, which they would overlay with chanted or 'scatted' vocals. *See* Robert M. Szymanski, *Audio Pasitiche: Digital Sampling, Intermediate Copying, Fair Use,* 3 U.C.L.A. Ent. L. Rev. 271, 277 (Spring 1996). Sampling migrated to the United States and developed throughout the 1970s, using the analog technologies of the time. *Id.* The digital sampling involved here developed in the early 1980s with the advent of digital synthesizers having MIDI (Musical Instrument Digital Interface) keyboard controls. These digital instruments allowed artists digitally to manipulate and combine sampled sounds, expanding the range of possibilities for the use of pre-recorded music. Whereas analog devices limited artists to "scratching" vinyl records and "cutting" back and forth between different sound recordings, digital technology allowed artists to slow down, speed up, combine, and otherwise alter the samples. *See id.*

Pursuant to their license from ECM Records, Beastie Boys digitally sampled the opening six seconds of Newton's sound recording of "Choir." Beastie Boys repeated or "looped" this six-second sample as a background element throughout "Pass the Mic," so that it appears over forty times in various renditions of the song. In addition to the version of "Pass the Mic" released on their 1992 album, "Check Your Head," Beastie Boys included the "Choir" sample in two remixes, "Dub the Mic" and "Pass the Mic (Pt. 2, Skills to Pay the Bills)." It is unclear whether the sample was altered or manipulated, though Beastie Boys' sound engineer stated that alterations of tone, pitch, and rhythm are commonplace, and Newton maintains that the pitch was lowered slightly.

Newton filed the instant action in federal court on May 9, 2000, alleging violations of his copyright in the underlying composition, as well as Lanham Act violations for misappropriation and reverse passing off. The district court dismissed Newton's Lanham Act claims on September 12, 2000, and granted summary judgment in favor of Beastie Boys on the copyright claims on May 21, 2002. *Newton v. Diamond,* 204 F.Supp.2d 1244 (C.D.Cal.2002). The district court held that the three-note segment of the "Choir" composition could not be copyrighted because, as a matter of law, it lacked the requisite originality. 204 F.Supp.2d at 1256. The court also concluded that even if the segment were copyrightable, Beastie Boys' use of the work was de minimis and therefore not actionable. *Id.* at 1259. Newton appealed.

Whether Defendants' Use was De Minimis

We may affirm the grant of summary judgment on any basis supported by the record and need not reach each ground relied upon by the district court.... Assuming that the sampled segment of the composition was sufficiently original to merit copyright protection, we nevertheless affirm on the ground that Beastie Boys' use was de minimis and therefore not actionable.

For an unauthorized use of a copyrighted work to be actionable, there must be substantial similarity between the plaintiff's and the defendants' works.... This means that even where the fact of copying is conceded, no legal consequences will follow from that fact unless the copying is substantial.... The principle that trivial copying does not constitute actionable infringement has long been a part of copyright law. Indeed, as Judge Learned Hand observed over 80 years ago: "Even where there is some copying, that fact is not conclusive of infringement. Some copying is permitted. In addition to copying, it must be shown that this has been done to an unfair extent." *West Publ'g Co. v. Edward Thompson Co.,* 169 F. 833, 861 (E.D.N.Y.1909). This principle reflects the legal maxim, *de minimis non curat lex* (often rendered as, "the law does not concern itself with trifles"). *See Ringgold,* 126 F.3d at 74–75.

The leading case on de minimis infringement in our circuit is *Fisher v. Dees,* 794 F.2d 432 (9th Cir.1986), where we observed that a use is de minimis only if the average audience would not recognize the appropriation. *See id.* at 434 n.2 ("[A] taking is considered de minimis only if it is so meager and fragmentary that the average audience would not recognize the appropriation."). This observation reflects the relationship between the de minimis maxim and the general test for substantial similarity, which also looks to the response of the average audience, or ordinary observer, to determine whether a use is infringing. *See, e.g., Cavalier v. Random House, Inc.,* 297 F.3d

815, 822 (9th Cir.2002); *Castle Rock Entm't, Inc. v. Carol Publ'g Group, Inc.,* 150 F.3d 132(2d Cir.1998) ("Two works are substantially similar where 'the ordinary observer, unless he set out to detect the disparities, would be disposed to overlook them, and regard [the] aesthetic appeal [of the two works] as the same.' " (quoting *Arica Inst., Inc. v. Palmer,* 970 F.2d 1067, 1072 (2d Cir.1992) (quoting *Peter Pan Fabrics, Inc. v. Martin Weiner Corp.,* 274 F.2d 487, 489 (2d Cir.1960) (L. Hand, J.)))). To say that a use is de minimis because no audience would recognize the appropriation is thus to say that the works are not substantially similar.

On the facts of *Fisher,* this court rejected the de minimis defense because the copying was substantial: the defendant had appropriated the main theme and lyrics of the plaintiff's song, both of which were easily recognizable in the defendant's parody. 794 F.2d at 434 & n.2. Specifically, the defendant copied six of the thirty-eight bars to the 1950s standard, "When Sunny Gets Blue," to make the parody, "When Sonny Sniffs Glue," and paralleled the original lyrics with only minor variations. *Id.* However, despite the works' substantial similarities, we held that the use was nevertheless non-infringing because, as a parody, it was "fair use" under 17 U.S.C. § 107. *Id.* at 440. We explained that the defendant's successful fair use defense precluded a finding that the use was insubstantial or unrecognizable because "the parodist must appropriate a substantial enough portion of [the original] to evoke recognition." *Id.* at 435 n.2.

This case involves not only use of a composition, as was the case in *Fisher,* but also use of a sound recording of a performance of that composition. Because the defendants licensed the sound recording, our inquiry is confined to whether the unauthorized use of the composition itself was substantial enough to sustain an infringement claim. Therefore, we may consider only Beastie Boys' appropriation of the song's compositional elements and must remove from consideration all the elements unique to Newton's performance. Stated another way, we must "filter out" the licensed elements of the sound recording to get down to the unlicensed elements of the composition, as the composition is the sole basis for Newton's infringement claim. *See Cavalier,* 297 F.3d at 822; *Apple Computer, Inc. v. Microsoft Corp.,* 35 F.3d 1435, 1446 (9th Cir.1994).

In filtering out the unique performance elements from consideration, and separating them from those found in the composition, we find substantial assistance in the testimony of Newton's own experts. His experts reveal the extent to which the sound recording of "Choir" is the product of Newton's highly developed performance techniques, rather than the result of a generic rendition of the composition. As a general matter, according to Newton's expert Dr. Christopher Dobrian, "[t]he contribution of the performer is often so great that s/he in fact provides as much musical content as the composer." This is particularly true with works like "Choir," given the nature of jazz performance and the minimal scoring of the composition. Indeed, as Newton's expert Dr. Oliver Wilson explained:

> [T]he copyrighted score of "Choir", as is the custom in scores written in the jazz tradition, does not contain indications for all of the musical subtleties that it is assumed the performer-composer of the work will make in the work's performance. The function of the score is more mnemonic in intention than prescriptive.

And it is clear that Newton goes beyond the score in his performance. For example, Dr. Dobrian declared that "Mr. Newton blows and sings in such a way as to emphasize the upper partials of the flute's complex harmonic tone, [although] such a modification of tone color is not explicitly requested in the score." More generally, Dr. Wilson explained Newton's performance technique as follows:

> [T]he Newton technique produces a musical event in which the component sounds resulting from the simultaneous singing of one or more pitches and the interaction of this pitch or pitches with the various components of the multiphonic array of pitches produced on the flute create a relatively dense cluster of pitches and ambient sounds that sometimes change over time.

Whatever copyright interest Newton obtained in this "dense cluster of pitches and ambient sounds," he licensed that interest to ECM Records over twenty years ago, and ECM Records in turn licensed that interest to Beastie Boys. Thus, regardless of whether the average audience might recognize "the Newton technique" at work in the sampled sound recording, those performance elements are beyond consideration in Newton's claim for infringement of his copyright in the underlying composition. Having licensed away his interest in the recording of his performance, Newton's only claim is for a violation of his rights in the three-note sequence transcribed in the composition.

Once we have isolated the basis of Newton's infringement action—the "Choir" composition, devoid of the unique performance elements found only in the sound recording—we turn to the nub of our inquiry: whether Beastie Boys' unauthorized use of the composition, as opposed to their authorized use of the sound recording, was substantial enough to sustain an infringement action. In answering that question, we must distinguish between the degree and the substantiality of the works' similarity. *Cf. Ringgold,* 126 F.3d at 74–75; 4 Nimmer § 13.03[A][2], at 13–45. The practice of music sampling will often present cases where the degree of similarity is high. Indeed, unless the sample has been altered or digitally manipulated, it will be identical to the original. Yet as Nimmer explains, "[if] the similarity is only as to nonessential matters, then a finding of no substantial similarity should result." 4 Nimmer § 13.03[A][2], at 13–48; *cf. Warner Bros. v. Am. Broad. Cos.,* 720 F.2d 231, 242 (2d Cir.1983). This reflects the principle that the substantiality requirement applies throughout the law of copyright, including cases of music sampling, even where there is a high degree of similarity.

The high degree but limited scope of similarity between the works here place Newton's claim for infringement into the class of cases that allege what Nimmer refers to as "fragmented literal similarity." 4 Nimmer § 13.03[A][2], at 13–45. Fragmented literal similarity exists where the defendant copies a portion of the plaintiff's work exactly or nearly exactly, without appropriating the work's overall essence or structure. *Id.* Because the degree of similarity is high in such cases, the dispositive question is whether the similarity goes to trivial or substantial elements. The substantiality of the similarity is measured by considering the qualitative and quantitative significance of the copied portion in relation to the plaintiff's work as a whole. This focus on the sample's relation to the plaintiff's work as a whole embodies the fundamental question in any infringement action, as expressed more than 150 years ago by Justice Story: whether "so much is taken[ ] that the value of the original is sensibly diminished, or the labors of the original author are substantially to an injurious extent appropriated by another." *Folsom v. Marsh,* 9 F.Cas. 342, 348 (C.C.Mass.1841) (No. 4901). Courts also focus on the relationship to the plaintiff's work because a contrary rule that measured the significance of the copied segment in the defendant's work would allow an unscrupulous defendant to copy large or qualitatively significant portions of another's work and escape liability by burying them beneath non-infringing material in the defendant's own work, even where the average audience might recognize the appropriation. *Cf. Sheldon v. Metro–Goldwyn Pictures Corp.,* 81 F.2d 49, 56 (2d Cir.1936) ("[I]t is enough that substantial parts were lifted; no plagiarist can excuse the wrong by showing how much of his work he did not pirate."). Thus, as the district court properly concluded, the fact that Beastie Boys "looped" the sample throughout "Pass the Mic" is irrelevant in weighing the sample's qualitative and quantitative significance. *See Newton,* 204 F.Supp.2d at 1257.

When viewed in relation to Newton's composition as a whole, the sampled portion is neither quantitatively nor qualitatively significant. Quantitatively, the three-note sequence appears only once in Newton's composition. It is difficult to measure the precise relationship between this segment and the composition as a whole, because the score calls for between 180 and 270 seconds of improvisation. When played, however, the segment lasts six seconds and is roughly two percent of the four-and-a-half-minute "Choir" sound recording licensed by Beastie Boys. Qualitatively, this section of the composition is no more significant than any other section. Indeed, with the exception of two notes, the entirety of the scored portions of "Choir" consist of notes separated by whole and half-steps from their neighbors; the remainder of the composition calls for sections of improvisation that range between 90 and 180 seconds in length. Although the sampled section may be representative of the scored portions of the composition, Newton has failed to offer any evidence as to this section's particular significance in the composition as a whole. Instead, his experts emphasize the significance of Newton's performance, the unique elements of which Beastie Boys properly licensed.

Yet Newton maintains that the testimony of his experts creates a genuine issue of material fact on the substantiality of the copying. To the extent the expert testimony is relevant, it is not helpful to Newton. On the key question of whether the sample is quantitatively or qualitatively significant in relation to the composition as a whole, his experts are either silent or fail to distinguish between the sound recording, which was licensed, and the composition, which was not. Moreover, their testimony on the composition does not contain anything from which a reasonable jury could infer the segment's significance in relation to the composition as a whole: rather, Dr. Dobrian described the three-note sequence at issue as "a simple 'neighboring tone' figure." The district court cited two pieces by Gyorgy Ligeti and Jacob Druckman employing similar figures. *Newton,* 204 F.Supp.2d at 1255. This evidence is consistent with the opinion of Beastie Boys' expert, Dr. Lawrence Ferrara, who stated that the sampled excerpt from the "Choir" composition "is merely a common, trite, and generic three-note sequence, which lacks any distinct melodic, harmonic, rhythmic or structural elements." Dr. Ferrara also described the sequence as "a common building block tool" used over and over again by major composers in the 20th century, particularly the '60s and '70s, just prior to James Newton's usage.

Having failed to demonstrate any quantitative or qualitative significance of the sample in the "Choir" composition as a whole, Newton is in a weak position to argue that the similarities between the works are substantial, or that an average audience would recognize the appropriation. In this respect, the minimal scoring of the "Choir" composition bears emphasis, as does the relative simplicity of the relevant portion of the composition. On the undisputed facts of this case, we conclude that an average audience would not discern Newton's hand as a composer, apart from his talent as a performer, from Beastie Boys' use of the sample. The works are not substantially similar: Beastie Boys' use of the "Choir" composition was de minimis. There is no genuine issue of material fact, and the grant of summary judgment was appropriate.

Conclusion

Because Beastie Boys' use of the sound recording was authorized, the sole basis of Newton's infringement action is his remaining copyright interest in the "Choir" composition. We hold today that Beastie Boys' use of a brief segment of that composition, consisting of three notes separated by a half-step over a background C note, is not sufficient to sustain a claim for copyright infringement. We affirm the district court's grant of summary judgment on the ground that Beastie Boys' use of the composition was de minimis and therefore not actionable.

AFFIRMED.

GRAND UPRIGHT MUSIC, LTD. v. WARNER BROS. RECORDS, INC.
United States District Court for the Southern District of New York
December 16, 1991, Decided; December 17, 1991, Filed
91 Civ. 7648 (KTD)
780 F.Supp. 182

KEVIN THOMAS DUFFY, District Judge:

"Thou shalt not steal."[1] has been an admonition followed since the dawn of civilization. Unfortunately, in the modern world of business this admonition is not always followed. Indeed, the defendants in this action for copyright infringement would have this court believe that stealing is rampant in the music business and, for that reason, their conduct here should be excused. The conduct of the defendants herein, however, violates not only the Seventh Commandment, but also the copyright laws of this country.

This proceeding was instituted by Order To Show Cause to obtain a preliminary injunction against the defendants for the improper and unlicensed use of a composition "Alone Again (Naturally)" written and performed on records by Raymond "Gilbert" O'Sullivan. Defendants admit "that the Biz Markie album 'I Need A Haircut' embodies the rap recording 'Alone Again' which uses three words from 'Alone Again (Naturally)' composed by Gilbert O'Sullivan and a portion of the music taken from the O'Sullivan recording." Defendants' Post–Hearing Memorandum at 2. The only issue, therefore, seems to be who owns the copyright to the song "Alone Again (Naturally)" and the master recording thereof made by Gilbert O'Sullivan.

Three categories of proof lead me to the conclusion that the plaintiff is the true owner of these copyrights: (1) copies of the original copyrights made out to NAM Music, Inc., along with a deed vesting title to the copyrights in Gilbert O'Sullivan and another deed transferring the copyrights to the plaintiff corporation; and (2) the testimony of Gilbert O'Sullivan the acknowledged writer of the composition "Alone Again (Naturally)" and the performer who is featured on the master recording pirated by the defendants; and (3) the defendants' actions both before and after the issuance of the defendant album in contacting Gilbert O'Sullivan and his brother/agent in an attempt to obtain a license to use the copyrighted material.

Defense counsel objected to the admission of copies of the certificates of copyright because they were not "authenticated." It was apparent that defense counsel was not using this term "authenticated" in the sense that it is normally used in the law, particularly in the law of evidence. Since the original copyright was in the name of NAM Music, Inc., defense counsel seemed to argue that someone authorized by NAM Music, Inc. would have to identify the certificates in order to "authenticate" them.

Of course, the reader should be aware that NAM Music, Inc. had long been dissolved, as defense counsel knew. It was clear to me that the use of the word "authenticate" by defense counsel had nothing whatsoever to do with self-authentication of public records under Rule 902 of the Federal Rules of Evidence. Nor did counsel believe that the certificate was anything less than a true and complete copy of the public record.

Counsel for the defendants also attempted to keep out evidence of the transfer to the plaintiff of copyrights in the work at issue. Defense counsel did not conduct any discovery in the time between the institution of this lawsuit and the hearing on the preliminary injunction and claimed to be surprised when the plaintiff produced documentation of the transfer. However, that defense counsel did not adequately prepare for this hearing does not give the court cause to reject evidence of the transfer.

Defense counsel also objected to the admission of the transfer documents on the grounds that, since they had not been filed with the Registrar of Copyrights, they were without legal effect. This is not the law and the specific section upon which the defense counsel relied has long been repealed. These documents, taken together, prove valid copyrights vested in the plaintiff.

In addition to the documents offered into evidence by the plaintiff, Gilbert O'Sullivan—who the defendants acknowledge was the composer, lyricist and first performer of the piece at issue—testified that plaintiff is the owner of the copyright. There can be no one more interested in the question of valid copyright than a person in Gilbert O'Sullivan's position and he was a thoroughly credible and believable witness. Defense counsel did not effectively controvert O'Sullivan's testimony in any way. Indeed, the thrust of the cross-examination of O'Sullivan went to the artist's motive for refusing to give the defendants a license to use the song.

However, the most persuasive evidence that the copyrights are valid and owned by the plaintiff comes from the actions and admissions of the defendants. Prior to the time that Biz Markie's album was released, the various defendants apparently discussed among themselves the need to obtain a license. They decided to contact O'Sullivan and wrote to his brother/agent, enclosing a copy of the tape. In this letter, an attorney for the defendant states:

This firm represents a recording artist professionally known as Biz Markie, who has recorded a composition for Cold Chillin' Records entitled "Alone Again" which incorporates portions of the composition entitled "Alone Again Naturally" originally recorded by Gilbert O'Sullivan (the "Original Composition").

Biz Markie would like to obtain your consent to the use of the "Original Composition."

In writing this letter, counsel for Biz Markie admittedly was seeking "terms" for the use of the material. One would not agree to pay to use the material of another unless there was a valid copyright! What more persuasive evidence can there be!

Each defendant who testified knew that it is necessary to obtain a license—sometimes called a "clearance"—from the holder of a valid copyright before using the copyrighted work in another piece. Warner Bros. Records, Inc. had a department set up specifically to obtain such clearances. Brown Deposition of 11/19/91 at 30 et seq.; Tillman Deposition of 11/22/91 at 7. WEA International, Inc. knew it had to obtain "consents, permissions or clearances...." Rossi Deposition of 11/22/91 at 10–11. Cold Chillin' Records, Inc. knew that such clearances were necessary. Fitchelberg Deposition of 11/21/91 at 34 et seq.

Clearly, the attorneys representing Biz Markie and acting on his behalf also knew of this obligation. Biz Markie's attorneys sent copies of an August 16 letter, addressed to counsel for Cold Chillin' Records, Inc., to the other defendants. That letter contains the following:

In light of the fact that Cold Chillin' knew that other sample clearance requests were pending at that time, it follows that Cold Chillin' should have known that similar denials of permission by rightsholders of other samples used on the album and single might be forthcoming, for which similar action would have been appropriate. Nevertheless, instead of continuing to communicate with our client and us and otherwise cooperating to ensure that all rights were secured prior to release of the album and single, as it did in the situation involving the Eagles samples, Cold Chillin' unilaterally elected to release the album and single, perhaps with the thought that it would look to Biz for resolution of any problems relating to sampling rights, or the failure to secure such rights, that may arise in the future.

Consequently, if any legal action arises in connection with the samples in question, such action will not arise due to the fact that Biz used the samples in his recorded compositions, but rather, due to the fact that Cold Chillin' released such material prior to the appropriate consents being secured in connection with such samples.

From all of the evidence produced in the hearing, it is clear that the defendants knew that they were violating the plaintiff's rights as well as the rights of others. Their only aim was to sell thousands upon thousands of records. This callous disregard for the law and for the rights of others requires not only the preliminary injunction sought by the plaintiff but also sterner measures.

The application for the preliminary injunction is granted. The plaintiff is to submit within five (5) days hereof an appropriate decree. This matter is respectfully referred to the United States Attorney for the Southern District of

New York for consideration of prosecution of these defendants under 17 U.S.C. § 506(a) and 18 U.S.C. § 2319.

SO ORDERED.

BRIDGEPORT MUSIC, INC. v. DIMENSION FILMS
United States Court of Appeals for the Sixth Circuit
April 28, 2004, Argued; September 7, 2004, Decided; September 7, 2004, Filed
Nos. 02-6521; 03-5738
401 F.3d 647

RALPH B. GUY, JR., Circuit Judge.

Plaintiffs, Bridgeport Music, Inc., Westbound Records, Inc., Southfield Music, Inc., and Nine Records, Inc., appeal from several of the district court's findings with respect to the copyright infringement claims asserted against No Limit Films.[1] This action arises out of the use of a sample from the composition and sound recording "Get Off Your Ass and Jam" ("Get Off") in the rap song "100 Miles and Runnin" ("100 Miles"), which was included in the sound track of the movie *I Got the Hook Up* (*Hook Up*). Specifically, Westbound appeals from the district court's decision to grant summary judgment to defendant on the grounds that the alleged infringement was *de minimis* and therefore not actionable. Bridgeport, while not appealing from the summary judgment order, challenges instead the denial of its motion to amend the complaint to assert new claims of infringement based on a different song included in the sound track of *Hook Up.* Finally, Bridgeport, Southfield, and Nine Records appeal from the decision to award attorney fees and costs totaling $41,813.30 to No Limit Films under 17 U.S.C. § 505. For the reasons that follow, we reverse the district court's grant of summary judgment to No Limit on Westbound's claim of infringement of its sound recording copyright, but affirm the decision of the district court as to the award of attorney fees and the denial of Bridgeport's motion to amend.

I.

The claims at issue in this appeal were originally asserted in an action filed on May 4, 2001, by the related entities Bridgeport Music, Southfield Music, Westbound Records, and Nine Records, alleging nearly 500 counts against approximately 800 defendants for copyright infringement and various state law claims relating to the use of samples without permission in new rap recordings. In August 2001, the district court severed that original complaint into 476 separate actions, this being one of them, based on the allegedly infringing work and ordered that amended complaints be filed.

The claims in this case were brought by all four plaintiffs: Bridgeport and Southfield, which are in the business of music publishing and exploiting musical composition copyrights, and Westbound Records and Nine Records, which are in the business of recording and distributing sound recordings. It was conceded at the time of summary judgment, however, that neither Southfield Music nor Nine Records had any ownership interest in the copyrights at issue in this case. As a result, the district court ordered that they be jointly and severally liable for 10% of the attorney fees and costs awarded to No Limit Films.

Bridgeport and Westbound claim to own the musical composition and sound recording copyrights in "Get Off Your Ass and Jam" by George Clinton, Jr. and the Funkadelics. We assume, as did the district court, that plaintiffs would be able to establish ownership in the copyrights they claim. There seems to be no dispute either that "Get Off" was digitally sampled or that the recording "100 Miles" was included on the sound track of *I Got the Hook Up.* Defendant No Limit Films, in conjunction with Priority Records, released the movie to theaters on May 27, 1998. The movie was apparently also released on VHS, DVD, and cable television. Fatal to Bridgeport's claims of infringement was the Release and Agreement it entered into with two of the original owners of the composition "100 Miles," Ruthless Attack Muzick (RAM) and Dollarz N Sense Music (DNSM), in December 1998, granting a sample use license to RAM, DNSM, and their licensees. Finding that No Limit Films had previously been granted an oral synchronization license to use the composition "100 Miles" in the sound track of *Hook Up,* the district court concluded Bridgeport's claims against No Limit Films were barred by the unambiguous terms of the Release and Agreement. *Bridgeport Music, Inc. v. Dimension Films LLC,* 230 F.Supp.2d 830, 833–38 (M.D.Tenn.2002). Although Bridgeport does not appeal from this determination, it is relevant to the district court's later decision to award attorney fees to No Limit Films.

Westbound's claims are for infringement of the sound recording "Get Off." Because defendant does not deny it, we assume that the sound track of *Hook Up* used portions of "100 Miles" that included the allegedly infringing sample from "Get Off." The recording "Get Off" opens with a three-note combination solo guitar "riff" that lasts four seconds. According to one of plaintiffs' experts, Randy Kling, the recording "100 Miles" contains a sample from that guitar solo. Specifically, a two-second sample from the guitar solo was copied, the pitch was lowered, and the copied piece was "looped" and extended to 16 beats. Kling states that this sample appears in the sound recording "100 Miles" in five places; specifically, at 0:49, 1:52, 2:29, 3:20 and 3:46. By the district court's estimation, each looped segment lasted approximately 7 seconds. As for the segment copied from "Get Off," the district court described it as follows:

> The portion of the song at issue here is an arpeggiated chord—that is, three notes that, if struck together, comprise a chord but instead are played one at a time in very quick succession—that is repeated several times at the opening of "Get Off." The arpeggiated chord is played on an

> unaccompanied electric guitar. The rapidity of the notes and the way they are played produce a high-pitched, whirling sound that captures the listener's attention and creates anticipation of what is to follow.

Bridgeport, 230 F.Supp.2d at 839. No Limit Films moved for summary judgment, arguing (1) that the sample was not protected by copyright law because it was not "original"; and (2) that the sample was legally insubstantial and therefore does not amount to actionable copying under copyright law.

Mindful of the limited number of notes and chords available to composers, the district court explained that the question turned not on the originality of the chord but, rather, on "the use of and the aural effect produced by the way the notes and the chord are played, especially here where copying of the sound recording is at issue." *Id.* (citations omitted). The district court found, after carefully listening to the recording of "Get Off," "that a jury could reasonably conclude that the way the arpeggiated chord is used and memorialized in the 'Get Off' sound recording is original and creative and therefore entitled to copyright protection." *Id.* (citing *Newton v. Diamond,* 204 F.Supp.2d 1244, 1249–59 (C.D.Cal.2002)) (later affirmed on other grounds at 349 F.3d 591 (9th Cir.2003)). No Limit Films does not appeal from this determination.

Turning then to the question of *de minimis* copying in the context of digital sampling, the district court concluded that, whether the sampling is examined under a qualitative/quantitative *de minimis* analysis or under the so-called "fragmented literal similarity" test, the sampling in this case did not "rise to the level of a legally cognizable appropriation." 230 F.Supp.2d at 841. Westbound argues that the district court erred both in its articulation of the applicable standards and its determination that there was no genuine issue of fact precluding summary judgment on this issue.

On October 11, 2002, the district court granted summary judgment to No Limit Films on the claims of Bridgeport and Westbound; dismissed with prejudice the claims of Southfield and Nine Records; denied as moot the motion of Bridgeport and Westbound for partial summary judgment on the issue of copyright ownership; and entered final judgment accordingly. Bridgeport and Westbound appealed. The facts relevant to the earlier denial of Bridgeport's motion to amend the complaint will be discussed below. No Limit Films filed a post-judgment motion for attorney fees and costs, which the district court granted for the reasons set forth in its memorandum opinion and order of April 24, 2003. Bridgeport, Southfield Music, and Nine Records appealed from that award.

II.

The district court's decision granting summary judgment is reviewed *de novo. Smith v. Ameritech,* 129 F.3d 857, 863 (6th Cir.1997). In deciding a motion for summary judgment, the court must view the evidence and reasonable inferences in the light most favorable to the nonmoving party. *Matsushita Elec. Indus. Co. v. Zenith Radio Corp.,* 475 U.S. 574, 587, 106 S.Ct. 1348, 89 L.Ed.2d 538 (1986). Summary judgment is appropriate when there are no genuine issues of material fact in dispute and the moving party is entitled to judgment as a matter of law. Fed.R.Civ.P. 56(c).

In granting summary judgment to defendant, the district court looked to general *de minimis* principles and emphasized the paucity of case law on the issue of whether digital sampling amounts to copyright infringement. Drawing on both the quantitative/qualitative and "fragmented literal similarity" approaches, the district court found the *de minimis* analysis was a derivation of the substantial similarity element when a defendant claims that the literal copying of a small and insignificant portion of the copyrighted work should be allowed. After listening to the copied segment, the sample, and both songs, the district court found that no reasonable juror, even one familiar with the works of George Clinton, would recognize the source of the sample without having been told of its source. This finding, coupled with findings concerning the quantitatively small amount of copying involved and the lack of qualitative similarity between the works, led the district court to conclude that Westbound could not prevail on its claims for copyright infringement of the sound recording.

Westbound does not challenge the district court's characterization of either the segment copied from "Get Off" or the sample that appears in "100 Miles." Nor does Westbound argue that there is some genuine dispute as to any material fact concerning the nature of the protected material in the two works. The heart of Westbound's arguments is the claim that no substantial similarity or *de minimis* inquiry should be undertaken at all when the defendant has not disputed that it digitally sampled a copyrighted sound recording. We agree and accordingly must reverse the grant of summary judgment.

A. Digital Sampling of Copyrighted Sound Recordings

At the outset it is important to make clear the precise nature of our decision. Our conclusions are as follows:

1. The analysis that is appropriate for determining infringement of a musical composition copyright, is not the analysis that is to be applied to determine infringement of a sound recording. We address this issue only as it pertains to sound recording copyrights.

2. Since the district court decision essentially tracked the analysis that is made if a musical composition copyright were at issue, we depart from that analysis.

3. We agree with the district court's analysis on the question of originality. On remand, we assume that Westbound will be able to establish it has a copyright in the sound recording and that a digital sample from the copyrighted sound recording was used in this case.

4. This case involves "digital sampling" which is a term of art well understood by the parties to this litigation and the music industry in general. Accordingly, we adopt the definition commonly accepted within the industry.

5. Because of the court's limited technological knowledge in this specialized field, our opinion is limited to an instance of digital sampling of a sound recording protected by a valid copyright. If by analogy it is possible to extend our analysis to other forms of sampling, we leave it to others to do so.

6. Advances in technology coupled with the advent of the popularity of hip hop or rap music have made instances of digital sampling extremely common and have spawned a plethora of copyright disputes and litigation.

7. The music industry, as well as the courts, are best served if something approximating a bright-line test can be established. Not necessarily a "one size fits all" test, but one that, at least, adds clarity to what constitutes actionable infringement with regard to the digital sampling of copyrighted sound recordings.

B. Analysis

We do not set forth the arguments made by Westbound since our analysis differs somewhat from that offered by the plaintiff. Our analysis begins and largely ends with the applicable statute. Section 114(a) of Title 17 of the United States Code provides:

> The exclusive rights of the owner of copyright in a sound recording are limited to the rights specified by clauses (1), (2), (3) and (6) of section 106, and do not include any right of performance under section 106(4).
>
> Section 106 provides:
>
> Subject to sections 107 through 122, the owner of copyright under this title has the exclusive rights to do and to authorize any of the following:
>
> (1) to reproduce the copyrighted work in copies or phonorecords;
>
> (2) to prepare derivative works based upon the copyrighted work;
>
> (3) to distribute copies or phonorecords of the copyrighted work to the public by sale or other transfer of ownership, or by rental, lease, or lending;

(4) in the case of literary, musical, dramatic, and choreographic works, pantomimes, and motion pictures and other audiovisual works to perform the copyrighted work publicly;

(5) in the case of literary, musical, dramatic, and choreographic works, pantomimes, and pictorial, graphic, or sculptural works, including the individual images of a motion picture or other audiovisual work, to display the copyrighted work publicly; and

(6) in the case of sound recordings, to perform the copyrighted work publicly by means of a digital audio transmission.

Section 114(b) states:

(b) The exclusive right of the owner of copyright in a sound recording under clause (1) of section 106 is limited to the right to duplicate the sound recording in the form of phonorecords or copies that directly or indirectly recapture the actual sounds fixed in the recording. The exclusive right of the owner of copyright in a sound recording under clause (2) of section 106 is limited to the right to prepare a derivative work in which the actual sounds fixed in the sound recording are rearranged, remixed, or otherwise altered in sequence or quality. The exclusive rights of the owner of copyright in a sound recording under clauses (1) and (2) of section 106 do not extend to the making or duplication of another sound recording that consists entirely of an independent fixation of other sounds, even though such sounds imitate or simulate those in the copyrighted sound recording. The exclusive rights of the owner of copyright in a sound recording under clauses (1), (2), and (3) of section 106 do not apply to sound recordings included in educational television and radio programs (as defined in section 397 of title 47) distributed or transmitted by or through public broadcasting entities (as defined by section 118(g)): *Provided,* That copies or phonorecords of said programs are not commercially distributed by or through public broadcasting entities to the general public.

Before discussing what we believe to be the import of the above quoted provisions of the statute, a little history is necessary. The copyright laws attempt to strike a balance between protecting original works and stifling further creativity. The provisions, for example, for compulsory licensing make it possible for "creators" to enjoy the fruits of their creations, but not to fence them off from the world at large. 17 U.S.C. § 115. Although musical compositions have always enjoyed copyright protection, it was not until 1971 that sound recordings were subject to a separate copyright. If one were to analogize to a book, it is not the book, *i.e.,* the paper and binding, that is copyrightable, but its contents. There are probably any number of reasons why the decision was made by Congress to treat a sound recording differently from a book even though both are the medium in which an original work is fixed rather than the creation itself.

None the least of them certainly were advances in technology which made the "pirating" of sound recordings an easy task. The balance that was struck was to give sound recording copyright holders the exclusive right "to duplicate the sound recording in the form of phonorecords or copies that directly or indirectly recapture the actual sounds fixed in the recording." 17 U.S.C. § 114(b). This means that the world at large is free to imitate or simulate the creative work fixed in the recording so long as an actual copy of the sound recording itself is not made. That leads us directly to the issue in this case. If you cannot pirate the whole sound recording, can you "lift" or "sample" something less than the whole. Our answer to that question is in the negative.

Section 114(b) provides that "[t]he exclusive right of the owner of copyright in a sound recording under clause (2) of section 106 is limited to the right to prepare a derivative work in which the actual sounds fixed in the sound recording are rearranged, remixed, or otherwise altered in sequence or quality." In other words, a sound recording owner has the exclusive right to "sample" his own recording. We find much to recommend this interpretation.

To begin with, there is ease of enforcement. Get a license or do not sample. We do not see this as stifling creativity in any significant way. It must be remembered that if an artist wants to incorporate a "riff" from another work in his or her recording, he is free to duplicate the sound of that "riff" in the studio. Second, the market will control the license price and keep it within bounds. The sound recording copyright holder cannot exact a license fee greater than what it would cost the person seeking the license to just duplicate the sample in the course of making the new recording. Third, sampling is never accidental. It is not like the case of a composer who has a melody in his head, perhaps not even realizing that the reason he hears this melody is that it is the work of another which he had heard before. When you sample a sound recording you know you are taking another's work product.

This analysis admittedly raises the question of why one should, without infringing, be able to take three notes from a musical composition, for example, but not three notes by way of sampling from a sound recording. Why is there no *de minimis* taking or why should substantial similarity not enter the equation. Our first answer to this question is what we have earlier indicated. We think this result is dictated by the applicable statute. Second, even when a small part of a sound recording is sampled, the part taken is something of value. No further proof of that is necessary than the fact that the producer of the record or the artist on the record intentionally sampled because it would (1) save costs, or (2) add something to the new recording, or (3) both. For the sound recording copyright holder, it is not the "song" but the sounds that are fixed in the medium of his choice. When those sounds are sampled they are taken directly from that fixed medium. It is a physical taking rather than an intellectual one.

This case also illustrates the kind of mental, musicological, and technological gymnastics that would have to be employed if one were to adopt a *de minimis* or substantial similarity analysis. The district judge did an excellent job of navigating these troubled waters, but not without dint of great effort. When one considers that he has 800 other cases all involving different samples from different songs, the value of a principled bright-line rule becomes apparent. We would want to emphasize, however, that considerations of judicial economy are not what drives this opinion. If any consideration of economy is involved it is that of the music industry. As this case and other companion cases make clear, it would appear to be cheaper to license than to litigate.

Since our holding arguably sets forth a new rule, several other observations are in order. First, although there were no existing sound recording judicial precedents to follow, we did not pull this interpretation out of thin air. Several law review and text writers, some of whom have been referenced in this opinion, have suggested that this is the proper interpretation of the copyright statute as it pertains to sound recordings. Since digital sampling has become so commonplace and rap music has become such a significant part of the record industry, it is not surprising that there are probably a hundred articles dealing with sampling and its ramifications. It is also not surprising that the viewpoint expressed in a number of these articles appears driven by whose ox is being gored. As is so often the case, where one stands depends on where one sits. For example, the sound recording copyright holders favor this interpretation as do the studio musicians and their labor organization. On the other hand, many of the hip hop artists may view this rule as stifling creativity. The record companies and performing artists are not all of one mind, however, since in many instances, today's sampler is tomorrow's samplee. The incidence of "live and let live" has been relatively high, which explains why so many instances of sampling go unprotested and why so many sampling controversies have been settled.

Second, to pursue further the subject of stifling creativity, many artists and record companies have sought licenses as a matter of course. Since there is no record of those instances of sampling that either go unnoticed or are ignored, one cannot come up with precise figures, but it is clear that a significant number of persons and companies have elected to go the licensing route. Also there is a large body of pre- 1972 sound recordings that is not subject to federal copyright protection. Additionally, just as many artists and companies choose to sample and take their chances, it is likely that will continue to be the case.

Third, the record industry, including the recording artists, has the ability and know-how to work out guidelines, including a fixed schedule of license fees, if they so choose.

Fourth, we realize we are announcing a new rule and because it is new, it should not play any role in the assessment of concepts such as "willful" or "intentional" in cases that are currently before the courts or had their genesis before this decision was announced.

Finally, and unfortunately, there is no Rosetta stone for the interpretation of the copyright statute. We have taken a "literal reading" approach. If this is not what Congress intended or is not what they would intend now, it is easy enough for the record industry, as they have done in the past, to go back to Congress for a clarification or change in the law. This is the best place for the change to be made, rather than in the courts, because as this case demonstrates, the court is never aware of much more than the tip of the iceberg. To properly sort out this type of problem with its complex technical and business overtones, one needs the type of investigative resources as well as the ability to hold hearings that is possessed by Congress.

These conclusions require us to reverse the entry of summary judgment entered in favor of No Limit Films on Westbound's claims of copyright infringement. Since, the district judge found no infringement, there was no necessity to consider the affirmative defense of "fair use." On remand, the trial judge is free to consider this defense and we express no opinion on its applicability to these facts.

III.

Bridgeport's substantive appeal is from the denial of leave to file a second amended complaint that would have asserted new claims of infringement based on the inclusion of a different song, called "How Ya Do Dat," in the sound track of *Hook Up.*[19] We review the denial of a motion to amend for abuse of discretion, except to the extent that it is based on a legal determination that the amendment would not withstand a motion to dismiss.

A. Facts

Plaintiffs commenced this action in May 2001, and filed an amended complaint in September 2001. In November 2001, the district court entered a scheduling order which required that any motion to amend pleadings be filed far enough in advance of April 1, 2002, to allow briefing to be completed by that date. Discovery was to be completed by May 21, 2002. On March 18, 2002, the district court extended the time for amending pleadings with the proviso that it would have to be done in time to avoid extending discovery beyond May 21, 2002.

On April 15, 2002, plaintiffs' counsel received a "cue sheet" for *Hook Up* that apparently alerted Bridgeport to the presence of another song in which it held a copyright interest. Specifically, Bridgeport claims 37% interest in the composition "How Ya Do Dat" ("How Ya") under a Release and Agreement dated October 21, 1998, that granted permission to use a sample from the composition "One of Those Funky Things" in "How Ya." While there was disagreement about whether discovery made available as early as October 2001 should have alerted Bridgeport of this claim, there is no dispute that the presence of "How Ya" was readily observable from watching the movie. In fact, the magistrate judge noted that the "cue sheet" appears to be a list of credits from the end of the film.

Plaintiffs moved to amend on April 19, 2002, and No Limit Films opposed the motion in a response filed on April 26, 2002. On May 6, 2002, the magistrate judge recommended that the motion be denied. Plaintiffs filed objections on May 16, 2002, and defendant responded on May 30, 2002. The discovery cutoff date, May 21, had passed, but the deadline for completing depositions had been extended to June 14, 2002. But, the deadline for filing dispositive motions continued to be June 21, 2002. No Limit Films filed its motion for summary judgment on that date. On August 14, 2002, the district court entered its order overruling plaintiffs' objections, denying plaintiffs' motion to amend, and denying plaintiffs' further motion to certify the issue for appeal.

B. Analysis

Bridgeport maintains the district court abused its discretion by denying leave to amend on the grounds of unjustified delay and in the absence of a finding of prejudice to the defendant. It is true that, ordinarily, delay alone will not justify the denial of leave to amend the complaint. *Morse v. McWhorter,* 290 F.3d 795, 800 (6th Cir.2002). Delay, however, will become "undue" at some point, "placing an unwarranted burden on the court," or " 'prejudicial,' placing an unfair burden on the opposing party." *Morse,* 290 F.3d at 800 (citing *Adams v. Gould Inc.,* 739 F.2d 858, 863 (3d Cir.1984)).

Had the district court made an explicit finding of prejudice, very little would need to be said in affirming the denial of leave in this case. The district court's order, although brief, touched on undue delay and prejudice, explaining: To the extent that this brief discussion leaves doubt that a finding of prejudice was made, we may sustain a denial of leave to amend on grounds that are apparent from the record. *Morse,* 290 F.3d at 801.

Defendant clearly argued that it would be unfairly prejudiced if required to respond to a distinct new claim of infringement with only a few weeks of discovery remaining. Plaintiffs focus on the magistrate judge's mistaken reliance on the April 1 deadline for seeking leave to amend. Nonetheless, as defendant argues, plaintiffs' motion was not timely because the district court required that any amendments be sought in sufficient time that discovery could be completed before May 21. Also, the record reflects that although there were extensions of discovery beyond that date, extensions were only granted to allow the completion of certain depositions and did not affect the deadline for filing dispositive motions. We find no abuse of discretion in the district court's denial of leave to raise new claims based on a different song, by a different artist, in the movie.

IV.

Bridgeport, Southfield Music, and Nine Records appeal from the decision to award $41,813.30 in attorney fees and costs to No Limit Films as a prevailing party under 17 U.S.C. § 505. Apportioning the award between these plaintiffs, the district court ordered that Southfield and Nine Records be held liable, jointly and severally, for 10% of the total. The district court also found that no award was warranted against Westbound Records because its claims were objectively reasonable and based on a developing area of copyright law. As a result, the amount of fees reasonably incurred in defense of this action were reduced by 50%. Plaintiffs do not challenge the calculation of the fees or the inclusion of any particular item.

The discretion to award attorney fees under § 505 is to be exercised in an evenhanded manner with respect to prevailing plaintiffs and prevailing defendants, and in a manner consistent with the primary purposes of the Copyright Act. Several nonexclusive factors may be considered as long as they are "faithful to the purposes of the Copyright Act and are applied to prevailing plaintiffs and defendants in an evenhanded manner." *Id.* at 534 n. 19, 114 S.Ct. 1023. Those nonexclusive factors include: "frivolousness, motivation, objective unreasonableness (both in the factual and in the legal components of the case) and the need in particular circumstances to advance considerations of compensation and deterrence." *Id.* (quoting *Lieb v. Topstone Indus., Inc.,* 788 F.2d 151, 156 (3d Cir.1986)).

Southfield and Nine Records, neither of which had an interest in "Get Off" or "100 Miles," argue that defendant did not truly prevail against them because they were "inadvertently" left in the amended complaint and they did not oppose dismissal in this case. They did not voluntarily dismiss their claims, however, as it was only in response to defendant's dispositive motions that they acquiesced in dismissal. Moreover, the inclusion of Southfield and Nine Records in the amended complaint in this case was less "inadvertent" than a reflection of the plaintiffs' failure to discriminate between defendants and claims. No Limit Films is a prevailing defendant as judgment was entered in its favor on all claims. Concluding that Bridgeport's claim was objectively unreasonable, the district court indicated that the factor weighed heavily in favor of awarding fees.

The district court, relying on its decision granting summary judgment to defendant, specifically found Bridgeport's claims were objectively unreasonable because Bridgeport had no ownership interest in "100 Miles" when the oral synchronization license was granted and offered no evidence to undermine the existence of a valid license. Bridgeport argues that its claim, although unsuccessful, was not objectively unreasonable because it was not aware No Limit would claim it had an oral license that preceded the Release and Agreement. As defendant responds, nothing in this record suggests Bridgeport would not have sued No Limit Films if it had been aware of the oral license.

This brings us to what the district court called the deciding factor—the manner in which the plaintiffs litigated this action. This consideration, plaintiffs maintain, represents nothing more than an attempt to punish Bridgeport and deter the plaintiffs from pursuing reasonable, nonfrivolous claims in other cases under threat of an award of attorney fees. The district court reasoned as follows:

> The initial complaint in this action is so voluminous that, with exhibits, it is almost 1,000 pages long and takes days to read in its entirety. It is replete with diatribes against the music industry, but lacks concrete facts directed at specific defendants. Almost all of the 800 or so defendants in the initial complaint (representing what appeared to be almost the entirety of entities involved in making urban music) were lumped together in broad categories and descriptions of activities. The individual counts described the infringing conduct of the defendants by references to these broad generalizations, without any specific information as to what any individual defendant did to violate the Copyright Act.
>
> From that inauspicious beginning, this action proceeded in a like manner, with heavy emphasis on discovery disputes and motion practice and little attention paid to narrowing the issues and refining the claims. The plaintiffs repeatedly taxed the patience of the Court, from narrowing the margins on their memoranda to circumvent page limits, to filing voluminous pleadings that were long on argument but short on concrete facts or applicable legal authority. The plaintiffs took every opportunity to inundate the Court with paperwork, yet many of these motions were hastily prepared and often lacked sufficient legal or factual support. Most notably, the plaintiffs filed a motion for summary judgment on ownership yet failed to submit certified copies of the registration certificates for the copyrights they claimed to own. When this oversight was pointed out by the Magistrate Judge as being fatal to their summary judgment motion, the plaintiffs, instead of providing the documentation (which could be easily obtained from the U.S. Copyright Office), expended enormous effort in subsequent motion papers trying to convince the Court that the certified copies were unnecessary [until ordered to produce them].

The plaintiffs' tactics have contributed to the multiplication of fees by all parties, including the defendant here. This, combined with the determination that Bridgeport's claim was objectively unreasonable, merits an award for fees and costs against Bridgeport.

To award fees simply because of the length of and lack of specificity in the original complaint or because of the number of claims brought by the plaintiffs would strike us as punitive and inconsistent with the purposes of the Copyright Act. *See Murray Hill,* 264 F.3d at 639–40 (reversing award of attorney fees, despite district court's criticism of the "voluminous burden" the case imposed, noting only that the law was unsettled and the plaintiff presented one or more colorable claims). The district court's criticisms go beyond just that, however, and are tied to conduct that complicated rather than streamlined the issues and contributed to the multiplication of fees for the defendant.

While the district court did not articulate this consideration in terms of the *Fogerty* factors, and was not required to since they are nonexclusive, we see it as related to the recognized factor of deterrence and compensation. The unique posture of this case as one of hundreds brought in the same manner and asserting parallel claims, makes deterrence a particularly relevant and appropriate consideration. It is not the deterrence of objectively reasonable good faith claims, but the interest in motivating plaintiffs to sort through the objectively unreasonable ones and prosecute this at best cumbersome litigation in a way that discriminates between parties and claims.

Plaintiffs charge that the defendant was equally responsible for multiplying fees, particularly by failing to designate a representative for deposition who had knowledge of the facts concerning the use of "Get Off" in *Hook Up.* While there is some suggestion that defendant contributed to increased discovery costs because multiple depositions were required, our review is deferential and the record does not demonstrate clear error in the district court's assessment of plaintiffs' litigation conduct. Ultimately, we cannot say the district court abused its discretion in this case, particularly given the 50% reduction in attorney fees to account for Westbound's claims. Nor should Southfield and Nine Records be relieved of the nominal award of fees in this case, as defendant was required to investigate whether they had any claim and affirmatively move for dismissal of their claims before it was conceded that they had no interest in the copyrighted works.

AFFIRMED in part, **REVERSED** in part, and **REMANDED** for further proceedings consistent with this opinion.

BRIDGEPORT MUSIC, INC. v. DIMENSION FILMS
United States Court of Appeals for the Sixth Circuit
December 20, 2004, Filed
No. 02-6521
401 F.3d 647

ORDER GRANTING PANEL REHEARING

The court having received a petition for rehearing en banc from defendant, No Limit Films, LLC, and the amicus brief filed by the Recording Industry Association of America (RIAA) in support of that petition, and the petition and brief having been circulated not only to the original panel members but also to all other active judges of this court, and no judge of this court having requested a vote on the suggestion for rehearing en banc, the petition for rehearing has been referred to the original panel.

The panel has reviewed the submissions and concludes that the issues raised in the petition and supporting amicus brief are worthy of additional consideration. The panel accordingly grants rehearing on the issues discussed in Section II only of the court's opinion, and also amends certain portions of the opinion to provide greater clarity. Specifically, the panel amends the opinion as follows:

(1) insert the following as footnote 4 at the end of the second paragraph in Section II;

> Were we to follow the analysis used by the district judge, we would agree with the result he reached.

(2) replace the conclusion listed as number 3 under Section II.A., with the following:

> 3. We agree with the district court's analysis on the question of originality. On remand, we assume that Westbound will be able to establish it has a copyright in the sound recording and that a digital sample from the copyrighted sound recording was used in this case.

(3) replace the second sentence in the sixth paragraph from the end of Section II, with the following, including the insertion of a new footnote and amendment to the existing footnote;

> First, although there were no existing sound recording judicial precedents to follow, we did not pull this interpretation out of thin air.

Two prior cases are worthy of mention, however, as they are often cited in discussions of digital sampling. These cases are *Grand Upright Music Ltd. v. Warner Bros. Records, Inc.*, 780 F.Supp. 182 (S.D.N.Y.1991), and *United States v. Taxe*, 540 F.2d 961 (9th Cir.1976).

Although *Grand Upright* applied a bright-line test in a sampling case, we have not cited it as precedent for several reasons. First, it is a district court opinion and as such has no binding precedential value. Second, although it appears to have involved claims for both sound recording and musical composition copyright infringement, the trial judge does not distinguish which he is talking about in his ruling, and appears to be addressing primarily the musical composition copyright. Third, and perhaps most important, there is no analysis set forth to indicate how the judge arrived at his ruling, which has resulted in the case being criticized by commentators. Although often cited in later cases, there appears to be no case involving only the digital sampling of sound recording that has relied on that decision. Nonetheless, it did precipitate a significant increase in licensing requests and changes in the way some artists and recording companies approached the issue of digital sampling.

Taxe involved a criminal prosecution of sound recording "pirates." The defendants were convicted in the district court and on appeal the court held that a jury instruction that characterized "any and all re-recordings as infringements" went too far, but nonetheless found the instructions as a whole to be free of any error requiring reversal. Like *Grand Upright*, there was no analysis to support his conclusion. This is understandable because the court was upholding the instructions given and had no need to dwell on that portion of the instruction the court "believed" "went beyond the law." *Taxe*, 540 F.2d at 965. Although *Taxe* has been cited frequently, it has not been cited for the pronouncement relative to the nature of the copyright protection afforded to sound recordings. It has been cited, however, for the proposition that infringement occurs even though the unauthorized recording makes changes in the sounds duplicated. *Id.* at n. 2.

We have not addressed several of the cases frequently cited in music copyright cases because in the main they involve infringement of the composition copyright and not the sound recording copyright or were decided on other grounds. *Baxter v. MCA, Inc.*, 812 F.2d 421 (9th Cir.1987); *Jarvis v. A&M Records*, 827 F.Supp. 282 (D.N.J.1993); *Tuff 'N' Rumble Mgmt., Inc. v. Profile Records, Inc.*, 42 U.S.P.Q.2d 1398 (S.D.N.Y.1987)(plaintiff did not prove ownership of valid copyright or actual copying); *Williams v. Broadus*, 60 U.S.P.Q.2d 1051 (S.D.N.Y.2001); *Newton v. Diamond*, 349 F.3d 591 (9th Cir.2003), *amended* 388 F.3d 1189 (9th Cir.2004).

(4) replace the third sentence in the fifth paragraph from the end of Section II as follows and insert a new footnote:

> Also there is a large body of pre-1972 sound recordings that is not subject to federal copyright protection.

We speak to federal copyright protection only, and recognize that the Copyright Act provides that "With respect to sound recordings fixed before February 15, 1972, any rights or remedies under the common law or statutes of any States shall not be annulled or limited by this title until February 15, 2067. The preemptive provision of subsection (a) shall apply to any such rights and remedies pertaining to any cause of action arising from undertakings commenced on and after February 15, 2067. Nothwithstanding the provision of section 303, no sound recording fixed before February 15, 1972, shall be subject to copyright under this title before, on, or after February 15, 2067." 17 U.S.C. § 301(c)(1998).

(5) replace the final paragraph at the end of Section II with the following:

> These conclusions require us to reverse the entry of summary judgment entered in favor of No Limit Films on Westbound's claims of copyright infringement. Since the district judge found no infringement, there was no necessity to consider the affirmative defense of "fair use." On remand, the trial judge is free to consider this defense and we express no opinion on its applicability to these facts.

(6) finally, as a result of the additional footnotes, renumber the footnotes beginning with the new footnote 4 and continuing through the remainder of Section II,III, and IV.

The clerk is instructed to set a briefing schedule and a date for telephonic oral arguments.

ENTERED BY ORDER OF THE COURT

OPINION

RALPH B. GUY, JR., Circuit Judge.

Plaintiffs, Bridgeport Music, Inc., Westbound Records, Inc., Southfield Music, Inc., and Nine Records, Inc., appeal from several of the district court's findings with respect to the copyright infringement claims asserted against No Limit Films.[1] This action arises out of the use of a sample from the composition and sound recording "Get Off Your Ass and Jam" ("Get Off") in the rap song "100 Miles and Runnin" ("100 Miles"), which was included in the sound track of the movie *I Got the Hook Up* (*Hook Up*). Specifically, Westbound appeals from the district court's decision to grant summary judgment to defendant on the grounds that the alleged infringement was *de minimis* and therefore not actionable. Bridgeport, while not appealing from the summary judgment order, challenges instead the denial of its motion to amend the complaint to assert new claims of infringement based on a different song included in the sound track of *Hook Up*. Finally, Bridgeport, Southfield, and Nine Records appeal from the decision to award attorney fees and costs totaling $41,813.30 to No Limit Films under 17 U.S.C. § 505. For the reasons that follow, we reverse the district court's grant of summary judgment to No Limit on Westbound's claim of infringement of its sound recording copyright, but affirm the decision of the district court as to the award of attorney fees and the denial of Bridgeport's motion to amend.

I.

The claims at issue in this appeal were originally asserted in an action filed on May 4, 2001, by the related entities Bridgeport Music, Southfield Music, Westbound Records, and Nine Records, alleging nearly 500 counts against approximately 800 defendants for copyright infringement and various state law claims relating to the use of samples without permission in new rap recordings. In August 2001, the district court severed that original complaint into 476 separate actions, this being one of them, based on the allegedly infringing work and ordered that amended complaints be filed.

The claims in this case were brought by all four plaintiffs: Bridgeport and Southfield, which are in the business of music publishing and exploiting musical composition copyrights, and Westbound Records and Nine Records, which are in the business of recording and distributing sound recordings. It was conceded at the time of summary judgment, however, that neither Southfield Music nor Nine Records had any ownership interest in the copyrights at issue in this case. As a result, the district court ordered that they be jointly and severally liable for 10% of the attorney fees and costs awarded to No Limit Films.

Bridgeport and Westbound claim to own the musical composition and sound recording copyrights in "Get Off Your Ass and Jam" by George Clinton, Jr. and the Funkadelics. We assume, as did the district court, that plaintiffs would be able to establish ownership in the copyrights they claim. There seems to be no dispute either that "Get Off" was digitally sampled or that the recording "100 Miles" was included on the sound track of *I Got the Hook Up*. Defendant No Limit Films, in conjunction with Priority Records, released the movie to theaters on May 27, 1998. The movie was apparently also released on VHS, DVD, and cable television. Fatal to Bridgeport's claims of infringement was the Release and Agreement it entered into with two of the original owners of the composition "100 Miles," Ruthless Attack Muzick (RAM) and Dollarz N Sense Music (DNSM), in December 1998, granting a sample use license to RAM, DNSM, and their licensees. Finding that No Limit Films had previously been granted an oral synchronization license to use the composition "100 Miles" in the sound track of *Hook Up*, the district court concluded Bridgeport's claims against No Limit Films were barred by the unambiguous terms of the Release and Agreement. *Bridgeport Music, Inc. v. Dimension Films LLC*, 230 F.Supp.2d 830, 833–38 (M.D.Tenn.2002). Although Bridgeport does not appeal from this determination, it is relevant to the district court's later decision to award attorney fees to No Limit Films.

Westbound's claims are for infringement of the sound recording "Get Off." Because defendant does not deny it, we assume that the sound track of *Hook Up* used portions of "100 Miles" that included the allegedly infringing sample from "Get Off." The recording "Get Off" opens with a three-note combination solo guitar "riff" that lasts four seconds. According to one of plaintiffs' experts, Randy Kling, the recording "100 Miles" contains a sample from that guitar solo. Specifically, a two-second sample from the guitar solo was copied, the pitch was lowered, and the copied piece was "looped" and extended to 16 beats. Kling states that this sample appears in the sound recording "100 Miles" in five places; specifically, at 0:49, 1:52, 2:29, 3:20 and 3:46. By the district court's estimation, each looped segment lasted approximately 7 seconds. As for the segment copied from "Get Off," the district court described it as follows:

> The portion of the song at issue here is an arpeggiated chord—that is, three notes that, if struck together, comprise a chord but instead are played one at a time in very quick succession—that is repeated several times at the opening of "Get Off." The arpeggiated chord is played on an unaccompanied electric guitar. The rapidity of the notes and the way they are played produce a high-pitched, whirling sound that captures the listener's attention and creates anticipation of what is to follow.

Bridgeport, 230 F.Supp.2d at 839. No Limit Films moved for summary judgment, arguing (1) that the sample was not protected by copyright law because it was not "original"; and (2) that the sample was legally insubstantial and therefore does not amount to actionable copying under copyright law.

Mindful of the limited number of notes and chords available to composers, the district court explained that the question turned not on the originality of the chord but, rather, on "the use of and the aural effect produced by the way the notes and the chord are played, especially here where copying of the sound recording is at issue." *Id.* (citations omitted). The district court found, after carefully listening to the recording of "Get Off," "that a jury could reasonably conclude that the way the arpeggiated chord is used and memorialized in the 'Get Off' sound recording is original and creative and therefore entitled to copyright protection." *Id.* (citing *Newton v. Diamond,* 204 F.Supp.2d 1244, 1249–59 (C.D.Cal.2002)) (later affirmed on other grounds at 349 F.3d 591 (9th Cir.2003)). No Limit Films does not appeal from this determination.

Turning then to the question of *de minimis* copying in the context of digital sampling, the district court concluded that, whether the sampling is examined under a qualitative/quantitative *de minimis* analysis or under the so-called "fragmented literal similarity" test, the sampling in this case did not "rise to the level of a legally cognizable appropriation." 230 F.Supp.2d at 841. Westbound argues that the district court erred both in its articulation of the applicable standards and its determination that there was no genuine issue of fact precluding summary judgment on this issue.

On October 11, 2002, the district court granted summary judgment to No Limit Films on the claims of Bridgeport and Westbound; dismissed with prejudice the claims of Southfield and Nine Records; denied as moot the motion of Bridgeport and Westbound for partial summary judgment on the issue of copyright ownership; and entered final judgment accordingly. Bridgeport and Westbound appealed. The facts relevant to the earlier denial of Bridgeport's motion to amend the complaint will be discussed below. No Limit Films filed a post-judgment motion for attorney fees and costs, which the district court granted for the reasons set forth in its memorandum opinion and order of April 24, 2003. Bridgeport, Southfield Music, and Nine Records appealed from that award.

II.

The district court's decision granting summary judgment is reviewed *de novo. Smith v. Ameritech,* 129 F.3d 857, 863 (6th Cir.1997). In deciding a motion for summary judgment, the court must view the evidence and reasonable inferences in the light most favorable to the nonmoving party. *Matsushita Elec. Indus. Co. v. Zenith Radio Corp.,* 475 U.S. 574, 587, 106 S.Ct. 1348, 89 L.Ed.2d 538 (1986). Summary judgment is appropriate when there are no genuine issues of material fact in dispute and the moving party is entitled to judgment as a matter of law. Fed.R.Civ.P. 56(c).

In granting summary judgment to defendant, the district court looked to general *de minimis* principles and emphasized the paucity of case law on the issue of whether digital sampling amounts to copyright infringement. Drawing on both the quantitative/qualitative and "fragmented literal similarity" approaches, the district court found the *de minimis* analysis was a derivation of the substantial similarity element when a defendant claims that the literal copying of a small and insignificant portion of the copyrighted work should be allowed. After listening to the copied segment, the sample, and both songs, the district court found that no reasonable juror, even one familiar with the works of George Clinton, would recognize the source of the sample without having been told of its source. This finding, coupled with findings concerning the quantitatively small amount of copying involved and the lack of qualitative similarity between the works, led the district court to conclude that Westbound could not prevail on its claims for copyright infringement of the sound recording.

Westbound does not challenge the district court's characterization of either the segment copied from "Get Off" or the sample that appears in "100 Miles." Nor does Westbound argue that there is some genuine dispute as to any material fact concerning the nature of the protected material in the two works. The heart of Westbound's arguments is the claim that no substantial similarity or *de minimis* inquiry should be undertaken at all when the defendant has not disputed that it digitally sampled a copyrighted sound recording. We agree and accordingly must reverse the grant of summary judgment.

A. Digital Sampling of Copyrighted Sound Recordings

At the outset it is important to make clear the precise nature of our decision. Our conclusions are as follows:

1.The analysis that is appropriate for determining infringement of a musical composition copyright, is not the analysis that is to be applied to determine infringement of a sound recording. We address this issue only as it pertains to sound recording copyrights.

2. Since the district court decision essentially tracked the analysis that is made if a musical composition copyright were at issue, we depart from that analysis.

3. We agree with the district court's analysis on the question of originality. On remand, we assume that Westbound will be able to establish it has a copyright in the sound recording and that a digital sample from the copyrighted sound recording was used in this case.

4. This case involves "digital sampling" which is a term of art well understood by the parties to this litigation and the music industry in general. Accordingly, we adopt the definition commonly accepted within the industry.

5. Because of the court's limited technological knowledge in this specialized field, our opinion is limited to an instance of digital sampling of a sound recording protected by a valid copyright. If by analogy it is possible to extend our analysis to other forms of sampling, we leave it to others to do so.

6. Advances in technology coupled with the advent of the popularity of hip hop or rap music have made instances of digital sampling extremely common and have spawned a plethora of copyright disputes and litigation.

7. The music industry, as well as the courts, are best served if something approximating a bright-line test can be established. Not necessarily a "one size fits all" test, but one that, at least, adds clarity to what constitutes actionable infringement with regard to the digital sampling of copyrighted sound recordings.

B. Analysis

We do not set forth the arguments made by Westbound since our analysis differs somewhat from that offered by the plaintiff. Our analysis begins and largely ends with the applicable statute. Section 114(a) of Title 17 of the

United States Code provides:

> The exclusive rights of the owner of copyright in a sound recording are limited to the rights specified by clauses (1), (2), (3) and (6) of section 106, and do not include any right of performance under section 106(4).
>
> Section 106 provides:
>
> Subject to sections 107 through 122, the owner of copyright under this title has the exclusive rights to do and to authorize any of the following:
>
> (1) to reproduce the copyrighted work in copies or phonorecords;
>
> (2) to prepare derivative works based upon the copyrighted work;
>
> (3) to distribute copies or phonorecords of the copyrighted work to the public by sale or other transfer of ownership, or by rental, lease, or lending;
>
> (4) in the case of literary, musical, dramatic, and choreographic works, pantomimes, and motion pictures and other audiovisual works to perform the copyrighted work publicly;
>
> (5) in the case of literary, musical, dramatic, and choreographic works, pantomimes, and pictorial, graphic, or sculptural works, including the individual images of a motion picture or other audiovisual work, to display the copyrighted work publicly; and
>
> (6) in the case of sound recordings, to perform the copyrighted work publicly by means of a digital audio transmission.
>
> Section 114(b) states:
>
> (b) The exclusive right of the owner of copyright in a sound recording under clause (1) of section 106 is limited to the right to duplicate the sound recording in the form of phonorecords or copies that directly or indirectly recapture the actual sounds fixed in the recording. The exclusive right of the owner of copyright in a sound recording under clause (2) of section 106 is limited to the right to prepare a derivative work in which the actual sounds fixed in the sound recording are rearranged, remixed, or otherwise altered in sequence or quality. The exclusive rights of the owner of copyright in a sound recording under clauses (1) and (2) of section 106 do not extend to the making or duplication of another sound recording that consists entirely of an independent fixation of other sounds, even though such sounds imitate or simulate those in the copyrighted sound recording. The exclusive rights of the owner of copyright in a sound recording under clauses (1), (2), and (3) of section 106 do not apply to sound recordings included in educational television and radio programs (as defined in section 397 of title 47) distributed or transmitted by or through public broadcasting entities (as defined by section 118(g)): *Provided,* That copies or phonorecords of said programs are not commercially distributed by or through public broadcasting entities to the general public.

Before discussing what we believe to be the import of the above quoted provisions of the statute, a little history is necessary. The copyright laws attempt to strike a balance between protecting original works and stifling further creativity. The provisions, for example, for compulsory licensing make it possible for "creators" to enjoy the fruits of their creations, but not to fence them off from the world at large. 17 U.S.C. § 115. Although musical compositions have always enjoyed copyright protection, it was not until 1971 that sound recordings were subject to a separate copyright. If one were to analogize to a book, it is not the book, *i.e.,* the paper and binding, that is copyrightable, but its contents. There are probably any number of reasons why the decision was made by Congress to treat a sound recording differently from a book even though both are the medium in which an original work is fixed rather than the creation itself. None the least of them certainly were advances in technology which made the "pirating" of sound recordings an easy task. The balance that was struck was to give sound recording copyright holders the exclusive right "to duplicate the sound recording in the form of phonorecords or copies that directly or indirectly recapture the actual sounds fixed in the recording." 17 U.S.C. § 114(b). This means that the world at large is free to imitate or simulate the creative work fixed in the recording so long as an actual copy of the sound recording itself is not made. That leads us directly to the issue in this case. If you cannot pirate the whole sound recording, can you "lift" or "sample" something less than the whole. Our answer to that question is in the negative.

Section 114(b) provides that "[t]he exclusive right of the owner of copyright in a sound recording under clause (2) of section 106 is limited to the right to prepare a derivative work in which the actual sounds fixed in the sound recording are rearranged, remixed, or otherwise altered in sequence or quality." In other words, a sound recording owner has the exclusive right to "sample" his own recording. We find much to recommend this interpretation.

To begin with, there is ease of enforcement. Get a license or do not sample. We do not see this as stifling creativity in any significant way. It must be remembered that if an artist wants to incorporate a "riff" from another work in his or her recording, he is free to duplicate the sound of that "riff" in the studio. Second, the market will control the license price and keep it within bounds. The sound recording copyright holder cannot exact a license fee greater than what it would cost the person seeking the license to just duplicate the sample in the course of making the new recording. Third, sampling is never accidental. It is not like the case of a composer who has a melody in his head, perhaps not even realizing that the reason he hears this melody is that it is the work of another which he had heard before. When you sample a sound recording you know you are taking another's work product.

This analysis admittedly raises the question of why one should, without infringing, be able to take three notes from a musical composition, for example, but not three notes by way of sampling from a sound recording. Why is there no *de minimis* taking or why should substantial similarity not enter the equation. Our first answer to this question is what we have earlier indicated. We think this result is dictated by the applicable statute. Second, even when a small part of a sound recording is sampled, the part taken is something of value. No further proof of that is necessary than the fact that the producer of the record or the artist on the record intentionally sampled because it would (1) save costs, or (2) add something to the new recording, or (3) both. For the sound recording copyright holder, it is not the "song" but the sounds that are fixed in the medium of his choice. When those sounds are sampled they are taken directly from that fixed medium. It is a physical taking rather than an intellectual one.

This case also illustrates the kind of mental, musicological, and technological gymnastics that would have to be employed if one were to adopt a *de minimis* or substantial similarity analysis. The district judge did an excellent job of navigating these troubled waters, but not without dint of great effort. When one considers that he has 800 other cases all involving different samples from different songs, the value of a principled bright-line rule becomes apparent. We would want to emphasize, however, that considerations of judicial economy are not what drives this opinion. If any consideration of economy is involved it is that of the music industry. As this case and other companion cases make clear, it would appear to be cheaper to license than to litigate.

Since our holding arguably sets forth a new rule, several other observations are in order. First, although there were no existing sound recording judicial precedents to follow, we did not pull this interpretation out of thin air. Several law review and text writers, some of whom have been referenced in this opinion, have suggested that this is the proper interpretation of the copyright statute as it pertains to sound recordings. Since digital sampling has become so commonplace and rap music has become such a significant part of the record industry, it is not surprising that there are probably a hundred articles dealing with sampling and its ramifications. It is also not surprising that the viewpoint expressed in a number of these articles appears driven by whose ox is being gored. As is so often the case, where one stands depends on where one sits. For example, the sound recording copyright holders favor this interpretation as do the studio musicians and their labor organization. On the other hand, many of the hip hop artists may view this rule as stifling creativity. The record companies and performing artists are not all of one mind, however, since in many instances, today's sampler is tomorrow's samplee. The incidence of "live and let live" has been relatively high, which explains why so many instances of sampling go unprotested and why so many sampling controversies have been settled.

Second, to pursue further the subject of stifling creativity, many artists and record companies have sought licenses as a matter of course. Since there is no record of those instances of sampling that either go unnoticed or are ignored, one cannot come up with precise figures, but it is clear that a significant number of persons and companies have elected to go the licensing route. Also there is a large body of pre-1972 sound recordings that is not subject to federal copyright protection. Additionally, just as many artists and companies choose to sample and take their chances, it is likely that will continue to be the case.

Third, the record industry, including the recording artists, has the ability and know-how to work out guidelines, including a fixed schedule of license fees, if they so choose.

Fourth, we realize we are announcing a new rule and because it is new, it should not play any role in the assessment of concepts such as "willful" or "intentional" in cases that are currently before the courts or had their genesis before this decision was announced.

Finally, and unfortunately, there is no Rosetta stone for the interpretation of the copyright statute. We have taken a "literal reading" approach. If this is not what Congress intended or is not what they would intend now, it is easy enough for the record industry, as they have done in the past, to go back to Congress for a clarification or change in the law. This is the best place for the change to be made, rather than in the courts, because as this case demonstrates, the court is never aware of much more than the tip of the iceberg. To properly sort out this type of problem with its complex technical and business overtones, one needs the type of investigative resources as well as the ability to hold hearings that is possessed by Congress.

These conclusions require us to reverse the entry of summary judgment entered in favor of No Limit Films on Westbound's claims of copyright infringement. Since, the district judge found no infringement, there was no necessity to consider the affirmative defense of "fair use." On remand, the trial judge is free to consider this defense and we express no opinion on its applicability to these facts.

III.

Bridgeport's substantive appeal is from the denial of leave to file a second amended complaint that would have asserted new claims of infringement based on the inclusion of a different song, called "How Ya Do Dat," in the sound track of *Hook Up.* We review the denial of a motion to amend for abuse of discretion, except to the extent that it is based on a legal determination that the amendment would not withstand a motion to dismiss.

Wade v. Knoxville Utilities Bd., 259 F.3d 452, 459 (6th Cir.2001). Leave to amend a pleading shall be freely given "when justice so requires." FED.R.CIV.P. 15(a).

Undue delay in filing, lack of notice to the opposing party, bad faith by the moving party, repeated failure to cure deficiencies by previous amendments, undue prejudice to the opposing party, and futility of amendment are all factors which may affect the decision. Delay by itself is not sufficient reason to deny a motion to amend. Notice and substantial prejudice to the opposing party are critical factors in determining whether an amendment should be granted. *Head v. Jellico Hous. Auth.,* 870 F.2d 1117, 1123 (6th Cir.1989) (quoting *Hageman v. Signal L.P. Gas, Inc.,* 486 F.2d 479, 484 (6th Cir.1973)). "When amendment is sought at a late stage in the litigation, there is an increased burden to show justification for failing to move earlier." *Wade,* 259 F.3d at 459 (citing *Duggins v. Steak 'N Shake, Inc.,* 195 F.3d 828, 834 (6th Cir.1999)).

A. Facts

Plaintiffs commenced this action in May 2001, and filed an amended complaint in September 2001. In November 2001, the district court entered a scheduling order which required that any motion to amend pleadings be filed far enough in advance of April 1, 2002, to allow briefing to be completed by that date. Discovery was to be completed by May 21, 2002. On March 18, 2002, the district court extended the time for amending pleadings with the proviso that it would have to be done in time to avoid extending discovery beyond May 21, 2002.

On April 15, 2002, plaintiffs' counsel received a "cue sheet" for *Hook Up* that apparently alerted Bridgeport to the presence of another song in which it held a copyright interest. Specifically, Bridgeport claims 37% interest in the composition "How Ya Do Dat" ("How Ya") under a Release and Agreement dated October 21, 1998, that granted permission to use a sample from the composition "One of Those Funky Things" in "How Ya." While there was disagreement about whether discovery made available as early as October 2001 should have alerted Bridgeport of this claim, there is no dispute that the presence of "How Ya" was readily observable from watching the movie. In fact, the magistrate judge noted that the "cue sheet" appears to be a list of credits from the end of the film.

Plaintiffs moved to amend on April 19, 2002, and No Limit Films opposed the motion in a response filed on April 26, 2002. On May 6, 2002, the magistrate judge recommended that the motion be denied. Plaintiffs filed objections on May 16, 2002, and defendant responded on May 30, 2002. The discovery cutoff date, May 21, had passed, but the deadline for completing depositions had been extended to June 14, 2002. But, the deadline for filing dispositive motions continued to be June 21, 2002. No Limit Films filed its motion for summary judgment on that date. On August 14, 2002, the district court entered its order overruling plaintiffs' objections, denying plaintiffs' motion to amend, and denying plaintiffs' further motion to certify the issue for appeal.

B. Analysis

Bridgeport maintains the district court abused its discretion by denying leave to amend on the grounds of unjustified delay and in the absence of a finding of prejudice to the defendant. It is true that, ordinarily, delay alone will not justify the denial of leave to amend the complaint. *Morse v. McWhorter,* 290 F.3d 795, 800 (6th Cir.2002). Delay, however, will become "undue" at some point, "placing an unwarranted burden on the court," or " 'prejudicial,' placing an unfair burden on the opposing party." *Morse,* 290 F.3d at 800 (citing *Adams v. Gould Inc.,* 739 F.2d 858, 863 (3d Cir.1984)).

Had the district court made an explicit finding of prejudice, very little would need to be said in affirming the denial of leave in this case. The district court's order, although brief, touched on undue delay and prejudice, explaining:

> The plaintiffs object to the Magistrate Judge's conclusion that plaintiffs had not offered a sufficient reason for failing to amend their complaint to add claims and parties by the deadline set by the Court. Plaintiffs argue that this deadline was modified by subsequent order, and that the Magistrate Judge erred under Sixth Circuit law by not allowing the amendments in the interests of justice. The defendants respond that [the] Magistrate Judge correctly concluded that, under the circumstances of this case, amendment on the eve of the close of discovery would be prejudicial to defendants and unduly delay trial.

After careful consideration of the entire record, the Court adopts and approves the Magistrate Judge's Report and Recommendation. The plaintiffs' objections are overruled. The interest of justice in this case requires that plaintiffs show good cause why the Court should allow amendment of their complaint to add a claim and parties after the Court's deadline for such amendments, which the plaintiffs have failed to do.

To the extent that this brief discussion leaves doubt that a finding of prejudice was made, we may sustain a denial of leave to amend on grounds that are apparent from the record. *Morse,* 290 F.3d at 801.

Defendant clearly argued that it would be unfairly prejudiced if required to respond to a distinct new claim of infringement with only a few weeks of discovery remaining. Plaintiffs focus on the magistrate judge's mistaken reliance on the April 1 deadline for seeking leave to amend. Nonetheless, as defendant argues, plaintiffs' motion was not timely because the district court required that any amendments be sought in sufficient time that discovery could be completed before May 21. Also, the record reflects that although there were extensions of discovery beyond that date, extensions were only granted to allow the completion of certain depositions and did not affect the deadline for filing dispositive motions. We find no abuse of discretion in the district court's denial of leave to raise new claims based on a different song, by a different artist, in the movie.

IV.

Bridgeport, Southfield Music, and Nine Records appeal from the decision to award $41,813.30 in attorney fees and costs to No Limit Films as a prevailing party under 17 U.S.C. § 505. Apportioning the award between these plaintiffs, the district court ordered that Southfield and Nine Records be held liable, jointly and severally, for 10% of the total. The district court also found that no award was warranted against Westbound Records because its claims were objectively reasonable and based on a developing area of copyright law. As a result, the amount of fees reasonably incurred in defense of this action were reduced by 50%. Plaintiffs do not challenge the calculation of the fees or the inclusion of any particular item.

A court may, in its discretion, award costs, including reasonable attorney fees, to the prevailing party in a civil suit under the Copyright Act. 17 U.S.C. § 505. Our review is for abuse of discretion. *Coles v. Wonder,* 283 F.3d 798, 804 (6th Cir.2002) (affirming award to prevailing defendant); *Murray Hill Publ'ns, Inc. v. ABC Communications, Inc.,* 264 F.3d 622, 639 (6th Cir.2001) (reversing award to prevailing defendant). A district court abuses its discretion when it relies on clearly erroneous factual findings, improperly applies the law, or uses an erroneous legal standard. *Adcock–Ladd v. Sec'y of Treasury,* 227 F.3d 343, 349 (6th Cir.2000).

The discretion to award attorney fees under § 505 is to be exercised in an evenhanded manner with respect to prevailing plaintiffs and prevailing defendants, and in a manner consistent with the primary purposes of the Copyright Act. *Fogerty v. Fantasy, Inc.,* 510 U.S. 517, 114 S.Ct. 1023, 127 L.Ed.2d 455 (1994). " 'There is no precise rule or formula for making these determinations,' but instead equitable discretion should be exercised 'in light of the considerations we have identified.' " *Id.* at 534, 114 S.Ct. 1023 (quoting *Hensley v. Eckerhart,* 461 U.S. 424, 436–37, 103 S.Ct. 1933, 76 L.Ed.2d 40 (1983)). Several nonexclusive factors may be considered as long as they are "faithful to the purposes of the Copyright Act and are applied to prevailing plaintiffs and defendants in an evenhanded manner." *Id.* at 534 n. 19, 114 S.Ct. 1023. Those nonexclusive factors include: "frivolousness, motivation, objective unreasonableness (both in the factual and in the legal components of the case) and the need in particular circumstances to advance considerations of compensation and deterrence." *Id.* (quoting *Lieb v. Topstone Indus., Inc.,* 788 F.2d 151, 156 (3d Cir.1986)).

Southfield and Nine Records, neither of which had an interest in "Get Off" or "100 Miles," argue that defendant did not truly prevail against them because they were "inadvertently" left in the amended complaint and they did not oppose dismissal in this case. They did not voluntarily dismiss their claims, however, as it was only in response to defendant's dispositive motions that they acquiesced in dismissal. Moreover, the inclusion of Southfield and Nine Records in the amended complaint in this case was less "inadvertent" than a reflection of the plaintiffs' failure to discriminate between defendants and claims. No Limit Films is a prevailing defendant as judgment was entered in its favor on all claims Concluding that Bridgeport's claim was objectively unreasonable, the district court indicated that the factor weighed heavily in favor of awarding fees. The district court, relying on its decision granting summary judgment to defendant, specifically found Bridgeport's claims were objectively unreasonable because Bridgeport had no ownership interest in "100 Miles" when the oral synchronization license was granted and offered no evidence to undermine the existence of a valid license. Bridgeport argues that its claim, although unsuccessful, was not objectively unreasonable because it was not aware No Limit would claim it had an oral license that preceded the Release and Agreement. As defendant responds, nothing in this record suggests Bridgeport would not have sued No Limit Films if it had been aware of the oral license.

This brings us to what the district court called the deciding factor—the manner in which the plaintiffs litigated this action. This consideration, plaintiffs maintain, represents nothing more than an attempt to punish Bridgeport and deter the plaintiffs from pursuing reasonable, nonfrivolous claims in other cases under threat of an award of attorney fees. The district court reasoned as follows:

> The initial complaint in this action is so voluminous that, with exhibits, it is almost 1,000 pages long and takes days to read in its entirety. It is replete with diatribes against the music industry, but lacks concrete facts directed at specific defendants. Almost all of the 800 or so defendants in the initial complaint (representing what appeared to be almost the entirety of entities involved in making urban music) were lumped together in broad categories and descriptions of activities. The individual counts described the infringing conduct of the defendants by references to these broad generalizations, without any specific information as to what any individual defendant did to violate the Copyright Act.

From that inauspicious beginning, this action proceeded in a like manner, with heavy emphasis on discovery disputes and motion practice and little attention paid to narrowing the issues and refining the claims. The plaintiffs repeatedly taxed the patience of the Court, from narrowing the margins on their memoranda to circumvent page limits, to filing voluminous pleadings that were long on argument but short on concrete facts or applicable legal authority. The plaintiffs took every opportunity to inundate the Court with paperwork, yet many of these motions were hastily prepared and often lacked sufficient legal or factual support. Most notably, the plaintiffs filed a motion for summary judgment on ownership yet failed to submit certified copies of the registration certificates for the copyrights they claimed to own. When this oversight was pointed out by the Magistrate Judge as being fatal to their summary judgment motion, the plaintiffs, instead of providing the documentation (which could be easily obtained from the U.S. Copyright Office), expended enormous effort in subsequent motion papers trying to convince the Court that the certified copies were unnecessary [until ordered to produce them].

The plaintiffs' tactics have contributed to the multiplication of fees by all parties, including the defendant here. This, combined with the determination that Bridgeport's claim was objectively unreasonable, merits an award for fees and costs against Bridgeport.

To award fees simply because of the length of and lack of specificity in the original complaint or because of the number of claims brought by the plaintiffs would strike us as punitive and inconsistent with the purposes of the Copyright Act. *See Murray Hill,* 264 F.3d at 639–40 (reversing award of attorney fees, despite district court's criticism of the "voluminous burden" the case imposed, noting only that the law was unsettled and the plaintiff presented one or more colorable claims). The district court's criticisms go beyond just that, however, and are tied to conduct that complicated rather than streamlined the issues and contributed to the multiplication of fees for the defendant.

While the district court did not articulate this consideration in terms of the *Fogerty* factors, and was not required to since they are nonexclusive, we see it as related to the recognized factor of deterrence and compensation. The unique posture of this case as one of hundreds brought in the same manner and asserting parallel claims, makes deterrence a particularly relevant and appropriate consideration. It is not the deterrence of objectively reasonable good faith claims, but the interest in motivating plaintiffs to sort through the objectively unreasonable ones and prosecute this at best cumbersome litigation in a way that discriminates between parties and claims.

Plaintiffs charge that the defendant was equally responsible for multiplying fees, particularly by failing to designate a representative for deposition who had knowledge of the facts concerning the use of "Get Off" in *Hook Up.* While there is some suggestion that defendant contributed to increased discovery costs because multiple depositions were required, our review is deferential and the record does not demonstrate clear error in the district court's assessment of plaintiffs' litigation conduct. Ultimately, we cannot say the district court abused its discretion in this case, particularly given the 50% reduction in attorney fees to account for Westbound's claims. Nor should Southfield and Nine Records be relieved of the nominal award of fees in this case, as defendant was required to investigate whether they had any claim and affirmatively move for dismissal of their claims before it was conceded that they had no interest in the copyrighted works.

AFFIRMED in part, **REVERSED** in part, and **REMANDED** for further proceedings consistent with this opinion.

QUESTIONS AND DISCUSSION

1. New Kids on the Block v. News America Pub., Inc., 971 F.2d 302 (9th Cir. 1992), appreciates the fact that boy bands are marketing phenomenons. Two newspapers ran polls in the order of who was the best kid (on the Block). The band's legal attack on the newspapers mostly hinged on intentional interference with prospective economic advantage, but that won't fly. The court found against the New Kids since the newspapers' use of the mark was "fair and reasonable." You must make hay while the sun shines. "New kids" do not have a long shelf-life.

2. Sampling is fun—we all do it—but when does it cross the line and become infringement? A rapper's best defense is that his or her rendition of a classic tune is a parody and protected by the Fair Use Doctrine and the First Amendment. In Campbell v. Acuff-Rose Music, 510 U.S. 569 (1994), the U.S. Supreme Court found for the rap group 2 Live Crew. Why?

3. In Midler v. Ford Motor Co., 849 F.2d 460 (9th Cir. 1988), the court found that Ford's use of a sing-alike impersonator violated Bette Medler's copyright. Her voice was deliberately imitated to sell a product and, as such, appropriated a part of her (commercial) identity. Does it help your understanding of the decision that the impersonation was deliberate (i.e., for gain), and that Bette Midler's voice is distinct and unique and has been used before by the Divine Miss M. herself for her own monetary gain?

4. In Roger Miller Music, Inc. v. Sony/AV Publ'g, LLC, 672 F.3d 434 (6th Cir. 2012), the Court found against the widow of Roger Miller, on the grounds that Sony owns the renewal copyrights of the 1964 songs as the assignee of the author, Roger Miller, who was living at the time of the application for the general registration. That certainly does not seem fair. Music compositions are a form of property; in most cases, property can be bequeathed to your living spouse, right? This case generated a great deal of sympathy and controversy over what seemed like a raw deal against the widow of an iconic music superstar ("King of the Road"). Is this just a technical application of a rather arcane law? Should the wishes of the artist supersede slavish adherence to copyright laws?

CHAPTER 9

ENTERTAINMENT LAWS IN CYBERSPACE

Cyberspace is the universe of information that is available from computer networks and the connective tissue of society-at-large. The question is how authors, inventors, artists, composers, athletes, advertisers, marketers, entertainers, and creative folk in general are going to get paid for the use of their intellectual property. Intellectual property is of course old school, horse and buggy, and printed book (whatever that is), but the information highway changes everything. Those changes are what we must mark, appreciate, and understand to deter infringement and effectively pursue internet copyright violators.

Domain names and cybersquatting are the indicators and signs that mark, symbolize, and police the intellectual property of artists, entertainers, and athletes. The domain names are part of the Internet, home of the World Wide Web. There are many aspects of intellectual property in cyberspace that affect sports and entertainment. For example, e-commerce allows movie- and concert-goers the opportunity to purchase tickets online. Between iTunes, VCast, T.V., PSP, Windows Media, cellular phones, public WiFi, and available broadband Internet access, the consumer is already well on the way towards multiplatform, on-demand access to world-wide content, 16 Media L. & Pol. 165 [Sum. 2007]. And let's not forget mobile entertainment and ringtones. The music business was significantly changed through the advent of digital technology. In the 1980s, there was digital sampling to illegal Internet downloads accompanied by home copying.... Champion, Intellectual Proerty in the Sports and Entertainment Industries 193-194 [reprinted with permission of the author for educational purposes].

A & M RECORDS v. NAPSTER, INC.
United States Court of Appeals for the Ninth Circuit
October 2, 2000, Argued and Submitted, San Francisco, California
February 12, 2001, Filed
No. 00-16401,No. 00-164403
239 F.3d 1004

BEEZER, Circuit Judge:

Plaintiffs are engaged in the commercial recording, distribution and sale of copyrighted musical compositions and sound recordings. The complaint alleges that Napster, Inc. ("Napster") is a contributory and vicarious copyright infringer. On July 26, 2000, the district court granted plaintiffs' motion for a preliminary injunction. The injunction was slightly modified by written opinion on August 10, 2000. *A & M Records, Inc. v. Napster, Inc.,* 114 F.Supp.2d 896 (N.D.Cal.2000). The district court preliminarily enjoined Napster "from engaging in, or facilitating others in copying, downloading, uploading, transmitting, or distributing plaintiffs' copyrighted musical compositions and sound recordings, protected by either federal or state law, without express permission of the rights owner." *Id.* at 927. Federal Rule of Civil Procedure 65(c) requires successful plaintiffs to post a bond for damages incurred by the enjoined party in the event that the injunction was wrongfully issued. The district court set bond in this case at $5 million.

We entered a temporary stay of the preliminary injunction pending resolution of this appeal. We have jurisdiction pursuant to 28 U.S.C. § 1292(a)(1). We affirm in part, reverse in part and remand.

I

We have examined the papers submitted in support of and in response to the injunction application and it appears that Napster has designed and operates a system which permits the transmission and retention of sound recordings employing digital technology.

In 1987, the Moving Picture Experts Group set a standard file format for the storage of audio recordings in a digital format called MPEG-3, abbreviated as "MP3." Digital MP3 files are created through a process colloquially called "ripping." Ripping software allows a computer owner to copy an audio compact disk ("audio CD") directly onto a computer's hard drive by compressing the audio information on the CD into the MP3 format. The MP3's compressed format allows for rapid transmission of digital audio files from one computer to another by electronic mail or any other file transfer protocol.

Napster facilitates the transmission of MP3 files between and among its users. Through a process commonly called "peer-to-peer" file sharing, Napster allows its users to: (1) make MP3 music files stored on individual computer hard drives available for copying by other Napster users; (2) search for MP3 music files stored on other users' computers; and (3) transfer exact copies of the contents of other users' MP3 files from one computer to another via the Internet. These functions are made possible by Napster's MusicShare software, available free of charge from Napster's Internet site, and Napster's network servers and server-side software. Napster provides technical support for the indexing and searching of MP3 files, as well as for its other functions, including a "chat room," where users can meet to discuss music, and a directory where participating artists can provide information about their music.

A. Accessing the System

In order to copy MP3 files through the Napster system, a user must first access Napster's Internet site and download the MusicShare software to his individual computer. *See http://www.Napster.com.* Once the software is installed, the user can access the Napster system. A first-time user is required to register with the Napster system by creating a "user name" and password.

B. Listing Available Files

If a registered user wants to list available files stored in his computer's hard drive on Napster for others to access, he must first create a "user library" directory on his computer's hard drive. The user then saves his MP3 files in the library directory, using self-designated file names. He next must log into the Napster system using his user name and password. His MusicShare software then searches his user library and verifies that the available files are properly formatted. If in the correct MP3 format, the names of the MP3 files will be uploaded from the user's computer to the Napster servers. The content of the MP3 files remains stored in the user's computer.

Once uploaded to the Napster servers, the user's MP3 file names are stored in a server-side "library" under the user's name and become part of a "collective directory" of files available for transfer during the time the user is logged onto the Napster system. The collective directory is fluid; it tracks users who are connected in real time, displaying only file names that are immediately accessible.

C. Searching For Available Files

Napster allows a user to locate other users' MP3 files in two ways: through Napster's search function and through its "hotlist" function.

Software located on the Napster servers maintains a "search index" of Napster's collective directory. To search the files available from Napster users currently connected to the network servers, the individual user accesses a form in the MusicShare software stored in his computer and enters either the name of a song or an artist as the object of the search. The form is then transmitted to a Napster server and automatically compared to the MP3 file names listed in the server's search index. Napster's server compiles a list of all MP3 file names pulled from the search index which include the same search terms entered on the search form and transmits the list to the searching user. The Napster server does not search the contents of any MP3 file; rather, the search is limited to "a text search of the file names indexed in a particular cluster. Those file names may contain typographical errors or otherwise inaccurate descriptions of the content of the files since they are designated by other users." *Napster,* 114 F.Supp.2d at 906.

To use the "hotlist" function, the Napster user creates a list of other users' names from whom he has obtained MP3 files in the past. When logged onto Napster's servers, the system alerts the user if any user on his list (a "hotlisted user") is also logged onto the system. If so, the user can access an index of all MP3 file names in a particular hotlisted user's library and request a file in the library by selecting the file name. The contents of the hotlisted user's MP3 file are not stored on the Napster system.

D. Transferring Copies of an MP3 file

To transfer a copy of the contents of a requested MP3 file, the Napster server software obtains the Internet address of the requesting user and the Internet address of the "host user" (the user with the available files). *See generally Brookfield Communications, Inc. v. West Coast Entm't Corp.,* 174 F.3d 1036, 1044 (9th Cir.1999) (describing, in detail, the structure of the Internet). The Napster servers then communicate the host user's Internet address to the requesting user. The requesting user's computer uses this information to establish a connection with the host user and downloads a copy of the contents of the MP3 file from one computer to the other over the Internet, "peer-to-peer." A downloaded MP3 file can be played directly from the user's hard drive using Napster's MusicShare program or other software. The file may also be transferred back onto an audio CD if the user has access to equipment designed for that purpose. In both cases, the quality of the original sound recording is slightly diminished by transfer to the MP3 format.

This architecture is described in some detail to promote an understanding of transmission mechanics as opposed to the content of the transmissions. The content is the subject of our copyright infringement analysis.

II

We review a grant or denial of a preliminary injunction for abuse of discretion. *Gorbach v. Reno,* 219 F.3d 1087, 1091 (9th Cir.2000) (en banc). Application of erroneous legal principles represents an abuse of discretion by the district court. *Rucker v. Davis,* 237 F.3d 1113, 1118–19 (9th Cir.2001) (en banc). If the district court is claimed to have relied on an erroneous legal premise in reaching its decision to grant or deny a preliminary injunction, we will review the underlying issue of law de novo. *Id.* at 1118 (citing *Does 1–5 v. Chandler,* 83 F.3d 1150, 1152 (9th Cir.1996)).

On review, we are required to determine, "whether the court employed the appropriate legal standards governing the issuance of a preliminary injunction and whether the district court correctly apprehended the law with respect to the underlying issues in the case." *Id.* "As long as the district court got the law right, 'it will not be reversed simply because the appellate court would have arrived at a different result if it had applied the law to the facts of the case.' " *Gregorio T. v. Wilson,* 59 F.3d 1002, 1004 (9th Cir.1995) (quoting *Sports Form, Inc. v. United Press, Int'l,* 686 F.2d 750, 752 (9th Cir.1982)).

Preliminary injunctive relief is available to a party who demonstrates either: (1) a combination of probable success on the merits and the possibility of irreparable harm; or (2) that serious questions are raised and the balance of hardships tips in its favor. *Prudential Real Estate Affiliates, Inc. v. PPR Realty, Inc.,* 204 F.3d 867, 874 (9th Cir.2000). "These two formulations represent two points on a sliding scale in which the required degree of irreparable harm increases as the probability of success decreases." *Id.*

III

Plaintiffs claim Napster users are engaged in the wholesale reproduction and distribution of copyrighted works, all constituting direct infringement. The district court agreed. We note that the district court's conclusion that plaintiffs have presented a prima facie case of direct infringement by Napster users is not presently appealed by Napster. We only need briefly address the threshold requirements.

A. Infringement

Plaintiffs must satisfy two requirements to present a prima facie case of direct infringement: (1) they must show ownership of the allegedly infringed material and (2) they must demonstrate that the alleged infringers violate at least one exclusive right granted to copyright holders under 17 U.S.C. § 106. *See* 17 U.S.C. § 501(a) (infringement occurs when alleged infringer engages in activity listed in § 106); *see also Baxter v. MCA, Inc.,* 812 F.2d 421, 423 (9th Cir.1987); *see, e.g., S.O.S., Inc. v. Payday, Inc.,* 886 F.2d 1081, 1085 n. 3 (9th Cir.1989) ("The word 'copying' is shorthand for the infringing of any of the copyright owner's five exclusive rights...."). Plaintiffs have sufficiently demonstrated ownership. The record supports the district court's determination that "as much as eighty-seven percent of the files available on Napster may be copyrighted and more than seventy percent may be owned or administered by plaintiffs." *Napster,* 114 F.Supp.2d at 911.

The district court further determined that plaintiffs' exclusive rights under § 106 were violated: "here the evidence establishes that a majority of Napster users use the service to download and upload copyrighted music.... And by doing that, it constitutes—the uses constitute direct infringement of plaintiffs' musical compositions, recordings." *A & M Records, Inc. v. Napster, Inc.,* Nos. 99–5183, 00–0074, 2000 WL 1009483, at *1 (N.D.Cal. July 26, 2000) (transcript of proceedings). The district court also noted that "it is pretty much acknowledged ... by Napster that this is infringement." *Id.* We agree that plaintiffs have shown that Napster users infringe at least two of the copyright holders' exclusive rights: the rights of reproduction, § 106(1); and distribution, § 106(3). Napster users who upload file names to the search index for others to copy violate plaintiffs' distribution rights. Napster users who download files containing copyrighted music violate plaintiffs' reproduction rights.

Napster asserts an affirmative defense to the charge that its users directly infringe plaintiffs' copyrighted musical compositions and sound recordings.

B. Fair Use

Napster contends that its users do not directly infringe plaintiffs' copyrights because the users are engaged in fair use of the material. *See* 17 U.S.C. § 107 ("[T]he fair use of a copyrighted work ... is not an infringement of copyright."). Napster identifies three specific alleged fair uses: sampling, where users make temporary copies of a work before purchasing; space-shifting, where users access a sound recording through the Napster system that they already own in audio CD format; and permissive distribution of recordings by both new and established artists.

The district court considered factors listed in 17 U.S.C. § 107, which guide a court's fair use determination. These factors are: (1) the purpose and character of the use; (2) the nature of the copyrighted work; (3) the "amount and substantiality of the portion used" in relation to the work as a whole; and

(4) the effect of the use upon the potential market for the work or the value of the work. *See* 17 U.S.C. § 107. The district court first conducted a general analysis of Napster system uses under § 107, and then applied its reasoning to the alleged fair uses identified by Napster. The district court concluded that Napster users are not fair users. We agree. We first address the court's overall fair use analysis.

1. Purpose and Character of the Use

This factor focuses on whether the new work merely replaces the object of the original creation or instead adds a further purpose or different character. In other words, this factor asks "whether and to what extent the new work is 'transformative.' " *See Campbell v. Acuff–Rose Music, Inc.,* 510 U.S. 569, 579, 114 S.Ct. 1164, 127 L.Ed.2d 500 (1994).

The district court first concluded that downloading MP3 files does not transform the copyrighted work. *Napster,* 114 F.Supp.2d at 912. This conclusion is supportable. Courts have been reluctant to find fair use when an original work is merely retransmitted in a different medium. *See, e.g., Infinity Broadcast Corp. v. Kirkwood,* 150 F.3d 104, 108 (2d Cir.1998) (concluding that retransmission of radio broadcast over telephone lines is not transformative); *UMG Recordings, Inc. v. MP3.com, Inc.,* 92 F.Supp.2d 349, 351 (S.D.N.Y.) (finding that reproduction of audio CD into MP3 format does not "transform" the work), *certification denied,* 2000 WL 710056 (S.D.N.Y. June 1, 2000) ("Defendant's copyright infringement was clear, and the mere fact that it was clothed in the exotic webbing of the Internet does not disguise its illegality.").

This "purpose and character" element also requires the district court to determine whether the allegedly infringing use is commercial or noncommercial. *See Campbell,* 510 U.S. at 584–85, 114 S.Ct. 1164. A commercial use weighs against a finding of fair use but is not conclusive on the issue. *Id.* The district court determined that Napster users engage in commercial use of the copyrighted materials largely because (1) "a host user sending a file cannot be said to engage in a personal use when distributing that file to an anonymous requester" and (2) "Napster users get for free something they would ordinarily have to buy." *Napster,* 114 F.Supp.2d at 912. The district court's findings are not clearly erroneous.

Direct economic benefit is not required to demonstrate a commercial use. Rather, repeated and exploitative copying of copyrighted works, even if the copies are not offered for sale, may constitute a commercial use. *See Worldwide Church of God v. Philadelphia Church of God,* 227 F.3d 1110, 1118 (9th Cir.2000) (stating that church that copied religious text for its members "unquestionably profit[ed]" from the unauthorized "distribution and use of [the text] without having to account to the copyright holder"); *American Geophysical Union v.*

Texaco, Inc., 60 F.3d 913, 922 (2d Cir.1994) (finding that researchers at for-profit laboratory gained indirect economic advantage by photocopying copyrighted scholarly articles). In the record before us, commercial use is demonstrated by a showing that repeated and exploitative unauthorized copies of copyrighted works were made to save the expense of purchasing authorized copies. *See Worldwide Church,* 227 F.3d at 1117–18; *Sega Enters. Ltd. v. MAPHIA,* 857 F.Supp. 679, 687 (N.D.Cal.1994) (finding commercial use when individuals downloaded copies of video games "to avoid having to buy video game cartridges"); *see also American Geophysical,* 60 F.3d at 922. Plaintiffs made such a showing before the district court.

We also note that the definition of a financially motivated transaction for the purposes of criminal copyright actions includes trading infringing copies of a work for other items, "including the receipt of other copyrighted works." *See* No Electronic Theft Act ("NET Act"), Pub.L. No. 105–147, 18 U.S.C. § 101 (defining "Financial Gain").

2. The Nature of the Use

Works that are creative in nature are "closer to the core of intended copyright protection" than are more fact-based works. *See Campbell,* 510 U.S. at 586, 114 S.Ct. 1164. The district court determined that plaintiffs' "copyrighted musical compositions and sound recordings are creative in nature ... which cuts against a finding of fair use under the second factor." *Napster,* 114 F.Supp.2d at 913. We find no error in the district court's conclusion.

3. The Portion Used

"While 'wholesale copying does not preclude fair use per se,' copying an entire work 'militates against a finding of fair use.' " *Worldwide Church,* 227 F.3d at 1118 (quoting *Hustler Magazine, Inc. v. Moral Majority, Inc.,* 796 F.2d 1148, 1155 (9th Cir.1986)). The district court determined that Napster users engage in "wholesale copying" of copyrighted work because file transfer necessarily "involves copying the entirety of the copyrighted work." *Napster,* 114 F.Supp.2d at 913. We agree. We note, however, that under certain circumstances, a court will conclude that a use is fair even when the protected work is copied in its entirety. *See, e.g., Sony Corp. v. Universal City Studios, Inc.,* 464 U.S. 417, 449–50, 104 S.Ct. 774, 78 L.Ed.2d 574 (1984) (acknowledging that fair use of time-shifting necessarily involved making a full copy of a protected work).

4. Effect of Use on Market

"Fair use, when properly applied, is limited to copying by others which does not materially impair the marketability of the work which is copied." *Harper & Row Publishers, Inc. v. Nation Enters.,* 471 U.S. 539, 566–67, 105 S.Ct. 2218, 85 L.Ed.2d 588 (1985). "[T]he importance of this [fourth] factor will vary, not only with the amount of harm, but also with the relative strength of the showing on the other factors." *Campbell,* 510 U.S. at 591 n. 21, 114 S.Ct. 1164. The proof required to demonstrate present or future market harm varies with the purpose and character of the use:

> A challenge to a noncommercial use of a copyrighted work requires proof either that the particular use is harmful, or that if it should become widespread, it would adversely affect the potential market for the copyrighted work.... *If the intended use is for commercial gain, that likelihood [of market harm] may be presumed. But if it is for a noncommercial purpose, the likelihood must be demonstrated.*

Sony, 464 U.S. at 451, 104 S.Ct. 774 (emphases added).

Addressing this factor, the district court concluded that Napster harms the market in "at least" two ways: it reduces audio CD sales among college students and it "raises barriers to plaintiffs' entry into the market for the digital downloading of music." *Napster,* 114 F.Supp.2d at 913. The district court relied on evidence plaintiffs submitted to show that Napster use harms the market for their copyrighted musical compositions and sound recordings. In a separate memorandum and order regarding the parties' objections to the expert reports, the district court examined each report, finding some more appropriate and probative than others. *A & M Records, Inc. v. Napster, Inc.,* Nos. 99–5183 & 00–0074, 2000 WL 1170106 (N.D.Cal. August 10, 2000). Notably, plaintiffs' expert, Dr. E. Deborah Jay, conducted a survey (the "Jay Report") using a random sample of college and university students to track their reasons for using Napster and the impact Napster had on their music purchases. *Id.* at *2. The court recognized that the Jay Report focused on just one segment of the Napster user population and found "evidence of lost sales attributable to college use to be probative of irreparable harm for purposes of the preliminary injunction motion." *Id.* at *3.

Plaintiffs also offered a study conducted by Michael Fine, Chief Executive Officer of Soundscan, (the "Fine Report") to determine the effect of online sharing of MP3 files in order to show irreparable harm. Fine found that online file sharing had resulted in a loss of "album" sales within college markets. After reviewing defendant's objections to the Fine Report and expressing some concerns regarding the methodology and findings, the district court refused to exclude the Fine Report insofar as plaintiffs offered it to show irreparable harm. *Id.* at *6.

Plaintiffs' expert Dr. David J. Teece studied several issues ("Teece Report"), including whether plaintiffs had suffered or were likely to suffer harm in their existing and planned businesses due to Napster use. *Id.* Napster objected that the report had not undergone peer review. The district court noted that such reports generally are not subject to such scrutiny and overruled defendant's objections. *Id.*

As for defendant's experts, plaintiffs objected to the report of Dr. Peter S. Fader, in which the expert concluded that Napster is *beneficial* to the music industry because MP3 music file-sharing stimulates more audio CD sales than it displaces. *Id.* at *7. The district court found problems in Dr. Fader's minimal role in overseeing the administration of the survey and the lack of objective data in his report. The court decided the generality of the report rendered it "of dubious reliability and value." The court did not exclude the report, however, but chose "not to rely on Fader's findings in determining the issues of fair use and irreparable harm." *Id.* at *8.

The district court cited both the Jay and Fine Reports in support of its finding that Napster use harms the market for plaintiffs' copyrighted musical compositions and sound recordings by reducing CD sales among college students. The district court cited the Teece Report to show the harm Napster use caused in raising barriers to plaintiffs' entry into the market for digital downloading of music. *Napster,* 114 F.Supp.2d at 910. The district court's careful consideration of defendant's objections to these reports and decision to rely on the reports for specific issues demonstrates a proper exercise of discretion in addition to a correct application of the fair use doctrine. Defendant has failed to show any basis for disturbing the district court's findings.

We, therefore, conclude that the district court made sound findings related to Napster's deleterious effect on the present and future digital download market. Moreover, lack of harm to an established market cannot deprive the copyright holder of the right to develop alternative markets for the works. *See L.A. Times v. Free Republic,* 54 U.S.P.Q.2d 1453, 1469–71 (C.D.Cal.2000) (stating that online market for plaintiff newspapers' articles was harmed because plaintiffs demonstrated that "[defendants] are attempting to exploit the market for viewing their articles online"); *see also UMG Recordings,* 92 F.Supp.2d at 352 ("Any allegedly positive impact of defendant's activities on plaintiffs' prior market in no way frees defendant to usurp a further market that directly derives from reproduction of the plaintiffs' copyrighted works."). Here, similar to *L.A. Times* and *UMG Recordings,* the record supports the district court's finding that the "record company plaintiffs have already expended considerable funds and effort to commence Internet sales and licensing for digital downloads." 114 F.Supp.2d at 915. Having digital downloads available for free on the Napster system necessarily harms the copyright holders' attempts to charge for the same downloads.

Judge Patel did not abuse her discretion in reaching the above fair use conclusions, nor were the findings of fact with respect to fair use considerations clearly erroneous. We next address Napster's identified uses of sampling and space-shifting.

5. Identified Uses

Napster maintains that its identified uses of sampling and space-shifting were wrongly excluded as fair uses by the district court.

a. Sampling

Napster contends that its users download MP3 files to "sample" the music in order to decide whether to purchase the recording. Napster argues that the district court: (1) erred in concluding that sampling is a commercial use because it conflated a noncommercial use with a personal use; (2) erred in determining that sampling adversely affects the market for plaintiffs' copyrighted music, a requirement if the use is noncommercial; and (3) erroneously concluded that sampling is not a fair use because it determined that samplers may also engage in other infringing activity.

The district court determined that sampling remains a commercial use even if some users eventually purchase the music. We find no error in the district court's determination. Plaintiffs have established that they are likely to succeed in proving that even authorized temporary downloading of individual songs for sampling purposes is commercial in nature. *See Napster,* 114 F.Supp.2d at 913. The record supports a finding that free promotional downloads are highly regulated by the record company plaintiffs and that the companies collect royalties for song samples available on retail Internet sites. *Id.* Evidence relied on by the district court demonstrates that the free downloads provided by the record companies consist of thirty-to-sixty second samples or are full songs programmed to "time out," that is, exist only for a short time on the downloader's computer. *Id.* at 913–14. In comparison, Napster users download a full, free and permanent copy of the recording. *Id.* at 914–15. The determination by the district court as to the commercial purpose and character of sampling is not clearly erroneous.

The district court further found that both the market for audio CDs and market for online distribution are adversely affected by Napster's service. As stated in our discussion of the district court's general fair use analysis: the court did not abuse its discretion when it found that, overall, Napster has an adverse impact on the audio CD and digital download markets. Contrary to Napster's assertion that the district court failed to specifically address the market impact of sampling, the district court determined that "[e]ven if the type of sampling supposedly done on Napster were a non-commercial use, plaintiffs have demonstrated a substantial likelihood that it would adversely affect the potential market for their copyrighted works if it became widespread." *Napster,* 114 F.Supp.2d at 914. The record supports the district court's preliminary determinations that: (1) the more music that sampling users download, the less likely they are to eventually purchase the recordings on audio CD; and (2) even if the audio CD market is not harmed, Napster has adverse effects on the developing digital download market.

Napster further argues that the district court erred in rejecting its evidence that the users' downloading of "samples" increases or tends to increase audio CD sales. The district court, however, correctly noted that "any potential enhancement of plaintiffs' sales ... would not tip the fair use analysis conclusively in favor of defendant." *Id.* at 914. We agree that increased sales of copyrighted material attributable to unauthorized use should not deprive the copyright holder of the right to license the material. *See Campbell,* 510 U.S. at 591 n. 21, 114 S.Ct. 1164 ("Even favorable evidence, without more, is no guarantee of fairness. Judge Leval gives the example of the film producer's appropriation of a composer's previously unknown song that turns the song into a commercial success; the boon to the song does not make the film's simple copying fair."); *see also L.A. Times,* 54 U.S.P.Q.2d at 1471–72. Nor does positive impact in one market, here the audio CD market, deprive the copyright holder of the right to develop identified alternative markets, here the digital download market. *See id.* at 1469–71.

We find no error in the district court's factual findings or abuse of discretion in the court's conclusion that plaintiffs will likely prevail in establishing that sampling does not constitute a fair use.

b. Space-Shifting

Napster also maintains that space-shifting is a fair use. Space-shifting occurs when a Napster user downloads MP3 music files in order to listen to music he already owns on audio CD. *See id.* at 915–16. Napster asserts that we have already held that space-shifting of musical compositions and sound recordings is a fair use. *See Recording Indus. Ass'n of Am. v. Diamond Multimedia Sys., Inc.,* 180 F.3d 1072, 1079 (9th Cir.1999) ("Rio [a portable MP3 player] merely makes copies in order to render portable, or 'space-shift,' those files that already reside on a user's hard drive.... Such copying is a paradigmatic noncommercial personal use."). *See also generally Sony,* 464 U.S. at 423, 104 S.Ct. 774 (holding that "time-shifting," where a video tape recorder owner records a television show for later viewing, is a fair use).

We conclude that the district court did not err when it refused to apply the "shifting" analyses of *Sony* and *Diamond.* Both *Diamond* and *Sony* are inapposite because the methods of shifting in these cases did not also simultaneously involve distribution of the copyrighted material to the general public; the time or space-shifting of copyrighted material exposed the material only to the original user. In *Diamond,* for example, the copyrighted music was transferred from the user's computer hard drive to the user's portable MP3 player. So too *Sony,* where "the majority of VCR purchasers ... did not distribute taped television broadcasts, but merely enjoyed them at home." *Napster,* 114 F.Supp.2d at 913. Conversely, it is obvious that once a user lists a copy of music he already owns on the Napster system in order to access the music from another location, the song becomes "available to millions of other individuals," not just the original CD owner. *See UMG Recordings,* 92 F.Supp.2d at 351–52 (finding space-shifting of MP3 files not a fair use even when previous ownership is demonstrated before a download is allowed); *cf. Religious Tech. Ctr. v. Lerma,* No. 95–1107A, 1996 WL 633131, at *6 (E.D.Va. Oct.4, 1996) (suggesting that storing copyrighted material on computer disk for later review is not a fair use).

c. Other Uses

Permissive reproduction by either independent or established artists is the final fair use claim made by Napster. The district court noted that plaintiffs did not seek to enjoin this and any other noninfringing use of the Napster system, including: chat rooms, message boards and Napster's New Artist Program. *Napster,* 114 F.Supp.2d at 917. Plaintiffs do not challenge these uses on appeal.

We find no error in the district court's determination that plaintiffs will likely succeed in establishing that Napster users do not have a fair use defense. Accordingly, we next address whether Napster is secondarily liable for the direct infringement under two doctrines of copyright law: contributory copyright infringement and vicarious copyright infringement.

IV

We first address plaintiffs' claim that Napster is liable for contributory copyright infringement. Traditionally, "one who, with knowledge of the infringing activity, induces, causes or materially contributes to the infringing conduct of another, may be held liable as a 'contributory' infringer." *Gershwin Publ'g Corp. v. Columbia Artists Mgmt., Inc.,* 443 F.2d 1159, 1162 (2d Cir.1971); *see also Fonovisa, Inc. v. Cherry Auction, Inc.,* 76 F.3d 259, 264 (9th Cir.1996). Put differently, liability exists if the defendant engages in "personal conduct that encourages or assists the infringement." *Matthew Bender & Co. v. West Publ'g Co.,* 158 F.3d 693, 706 (2d Cir.1998).

The district court determined that plaintiffs in all likelihood would establish Napster's liability as a contributory infringer. The district court did not err; Napster, by its conduct, knowingly encourages and assists the infringement of plaintiffs' copyrights.

A. Knowledge

Contributory liability requires that the secondary infringer "know or have reason to know" of direct infringement. *Cable/Home Communication Corp. v. Network Prods., Inc.,* 902 F.2d 829, 845 & 846 n. 29 (11th Cir.1990); *Religious Tech. Ctr. v. Netcom On-Line Communication Servs., Inc.,* 907 F.Supp. 1361, 1373–74 (N.D.Cal.1995) (framing issue as "whether Netcom knew or should have known of" the infringing activities). The district court found that Napster had both actual and constructive knowledge that its users exchanged copyrighted music. The district court also concluded that the law does not require knowledge of "specific acts of infringement" and rejected Napster's contention that because the company cannot distinguish infringing from noninfringing files, it does not "know" of the direct infringement. 114 F.Supp.2d at 917.

It is apparent from the record that Napster has knowledge, both actual and constructive of direct infringement. Napster claims that it is nevertheless protected from contributory liability by the teaching of *Sony Corp. v. Universal City Studios, Inc.,* 464 U.S. 417, 104 S.Ct. 774, 78 L.Ed.2d 574 (1984). We disagree. We observe that Napster's actual, specific knowledge of direct infringement renders *Sony*'s holding of limited assistance to Napster. We are compelled to make a clear distinction between the architecture of the Napster system and Napster's conduct in relation to the operational capacity of the system.

The *Sony* Court refused to hold the manufacturer and retailers of video tape recorders liable for contributory infringement despite evidence that such machines could be and were used to infringe plaintiffs' copyrighted television shows. *Sony* stated that if liability "is to be imposed on petitioners in this case, it must rest on the fact that *they have sold equipment with constructive knowledge of the fact that their customers may use that equipment to make unauthorized copies* of copyrighted material." *Id.* at 439, 104 S.Ct. 774 (emphasis added). The *Sony* Court declined to impute the requisite level of knowledge where the defendants made and sold equipment capable of both infringing and "substantial noninfringing uses." *Id.* at 442 (adopting a modified "staple article of commerce" doctrine from patent law)....

We are bound to follow *Sony,* and will not impute the requisite level of knowledge to Napster merely because peer-to-peer file sharing technology may be used to infringe plaintiffs' copyrights. *See* 464 U.S. at 436, 104 S.Ct. 774 (rejecting argument that merely supplying the " 'means' to accomplish an infringing activity" leads to imposition of liability). We depart from the reasoning of the district court that Napster failed to demonstrate that its system is capable of commercially significant noninfringing uses. *See Napster,* 114 F.Supp.2d at 916, 917–18. The district court improperly confined the use analysis to current uses, ignoring the system's capabilities. *See generally Sony,* 464 U.S. at 442–43, 104 S.Ct. 774 (framing inquiry as whether the video tape recorder is "*capable* of commercially significant noninfringing uses") (emphasis added). Consequently, the district court placed undue weight on the proportion of current infringing use as compared to current and future noninfringing use. *See generally Vault Corp. v. Quaid Software Ltd.,* 847 F.2d 255, 264–67 (5th Cir.1988) (single noninfringing use implicated *Sony*). Nonetheless, whether we might arrive at a different result is not the issue here. *See Sports Form, Inc. v. United Press Int'l, Inc.,* 686 F.2d 750, 752 (9th Cir.1982). The instant appeal occurs at an early point in the proceedings and "the fully developed factual record may be materially different from that initially before the district court...." *Id.* at 753. Regardless of the number of Napster's infringing versus noninfringing uses, the evidentiary record here supported the district court's finding that plaintiffs would likely prevail in establishing that Napster knew or had reason to know of its users' infringement of plaintiffs' copyrights.

This analysis is similar to that of *Religious Technology Center v. Netcom On-Line Communication Services, Inc.,* which suggests that in an online context, evidence of actual knowledge of specific acts of infringement is required to hold a computer system operator liable for contributory copyright infringement. 907 F.Supp. at 1371. *Netcom* considered the potential contributory copyright liability of a computer bulletin board operator whose system supported the posting of infringing material. *Id.* at 1374. The court, in denying Netcom's motion for summary judgment of noninfringement and plaintiff's motion for judgment on the pleadings, found that a disputed issue of fact existed as to whether the operator had sufficient knowledge of infringing activity. *Id.* at 1374–75.

The court determined that for the operator to have sufficient knowledge, the copyright holder must "provide the necessary documentation to show there is likely infringement." 907 F.Supp. at 1374; *cf. Cubby, Inc. v. CompuServe, Inc.,* 776 F.Supp. 135, 141 (S.D.N.Y.1991) (recognizing that online service provider does not and cannot examine every hyperlink for potentially defamatory material). If such documentation was provided, the court reasoned that Netcom would be liable for contributory infringement because its failure to remove the material "and thereby stop an infringing copy from being distributed worldwide constitutes substantial participation" in distribution of copyrighted material. *Id.*

We agree that if a computer system operator learns of specific infringing material available on his system and fails to purge such material from the system, the operator knows of and contributes to direct infringement. *See Netcom,* 907 F.Supp. at 1374. Conversely, absent any specific information which identifies infringing activity, a computer system operator cannot be liable for contributory infringement merely because the structure of the system allows for the exchange of copyrighted material. *See Sony,* 464 U.S. at 436, 442–43, 104 S.Ct. 774. To enjoin simply because a computer network allows for infringing use would, in our opinion, violate *Sony* and potentially restrict activity unrelated to infringing use.

We nevertheless conclude that sufficient knowledge exists to impose contributory liability when linked to demonstrated infringing use of the Napster system. *See Napster,* 114 F.Supp.2d at 919 ("*Religious Technology Center* would not mandate a determination that Napster, Inc. lacks the knowledge requisite to contributory infringement."). The record supports the district court's finding that Napster has *actual* knowledge that *specific* infringing material is available using its system, that it could block access to the system by suppliers of the infringing material, and that it failed to remove the material. *See Napster,* 114 F.Supp.2d at 918, 920–21.

B. Material Contribution

Under the facts as found by the district court, Napster materially contributes to the infringing activity. Relying on *Fonovisa,* the district court concluded that "[w]ithout the support services defendant provides, Napster users could not find and download the music they want with the ease of which defendant boasts." *Napster,* 114 F.Supp.2d at 919–20 ("Napster is an integrated service designed to enable users to locate and download MP3 music files."). We agree that Napster provides "the site and facilities" for direct infringement. *See Fonovisa,* 76 F.3d at 264; *cf. Netcom,* 907 F.Supp. at 1372 ("Netcom will be liable for contributory infringement since its failure to cancel [a user's] infringing message and thereby stop an infringing copy from being distributed worldwide constitutes substantial participation."). The district court correctly applied the reasoning in *Fonovisa,* and properly found that Napster materially contributes to direct infringement.

We affirm the district court's conclusion that plaintiffs have demonstrated a likelihood of success on the merits of the contributory copyright infringement claim. We will address the scope of the injunction in part VIII of this opinion.

V

We turn to the question whether Napster engages in vicarious copyright infringement. Vicarious copyright liability is an "outgrowth" of respondeat superior. *Fonovisa,* 76 F.3d at 262. In the context of copyright law, vicarious liability extends beyond an employer/employee relationship to cases in which a defendant "has the right and ability to supervise the infringing activity and also has a direct financial interest in such activities." *Id.* (quoting *Gershwin,* 443 F.2d at 1162); *see also Polygram Int'l Publ'g, Inc. v. Nevada/TIG, Inc.,* 855 F.Supp. 1314, 1325–26 (D.Mass.1994) (describing vicarious liability as a form of risk allocation).

Before moving into this discussion, we note that *Sony*'s "staple article of commerce" analysis has no application to Napster's potential liability for vicarious copyright infringement. The issues of Sony's liability under the "doctrines of 'direct infringement' and 'vicarious liability' " were not before the Supreme Court, although the Court recognized that the "lines between direct infringement, contributory infringement, and vicarious liability are not clearly drawn." *Id.* at 435 n. 17, 104 S.Ct. 774. Consequently, when the *Sony* Court used the term "vicarious liability," it did so broadly and outside of a technical analysis of the doctrine of vicarious copyright infringement. *Id.* at 435 ("[V]icarious liability is imposed in virtually all areas of the law, and the concept of contributory infringement is merely a species of the broader problem of identifying the circumstances in which it is just to hold one individual accountable for the actions of another.")... .

A. Financial Benefit

The district court determined that plaintiffs had demonstrated they would likely succeed in establishing that Napster has a direct financial interest in the infringing activity. *Napster,* 114 F.Supp.2d at 921–22. We agree. Financial benefit exists where the availability of infringing material "acts as a 'draw' for customers." *Fonovisa,* 76 F.3d at 263–64 (stating that financial benefit may be shown "where infringing performances enhance the attractiveness of a venue"). Ample evidence supports the district court's finding that Napster's future revenue is directly dependent upon "increases in userbase." More users register with the Napster system as the "quality and quantity of available music increases." 114 F.Supp.2d at 902. We conclude that the district court did not err in determining that Napster financially benefits from the availability of protected works on its system.

B. Supervision

The district court determined that Napster has the right and ability to supervise its users' conduct. *Napster,* 114 F.Supp.2d at 920–21 (finding that Napster's representations to the court regarding "its improved methods of blocking users about whom rights holders complain ... is tantamount to an admission that defendant can, and sometimes does, police its service"). We agree in part.

The ability to block infringers' access to a particular environment for any reason whatsoever is evidence of the right and ability to supervise. *See Fonovisa,* 76 F.3d at 262 ("Cherry Auction had the right to terminate vendors for any reason whatsoever and through that right had the ability to control the activities of vendors on the premises."); *cf. Netcom,* 907 F.Supp. at 1375–76 (indicating that plaintiff raised a genuine issue of fact regarding ability to supervise by presenting evidence that an electronic bulletin board service can suspend subscriber's accounts). Here, plaintiffs have demonstrated that Napster retains the right to control access to its system. Napster has an express reservation of rights policy, stating on its website that it expressly reserves the "right to refuse service and terminate accounts in [its] discretion, including, but not limited to, if Napster believes that user conduct violates applicable law ... or for any reason in Napster's sole discretion, with or without cause."

To escape imposition of vicarious liability, the reserved right to police must be exercised to its fullest extent. Turning a blind eye to detectable acts of infringement for the sake of profit gives rise to liability.

The district court correctly determined that Napster had the right and ability to police its system and failed to exercise that right to prevent the exchange of copyrighted material. The district court, however, failed to recognize that the boundaries of the premises that Napster "controls and patrols" are limited.... Put differently, Napster's reserved "right and ability" to police is cabined by the system's current architecture. As shown by the record, the Napster system does not "read" the content of indexed files, other than to check that they are in the proper MP3 format.

Napster, however, has the ability to locate infringing material listed on its search indices, and the right to terminate users' access to the system. The file name indices, therefore, are within the "premises" that Napster has the ability to police. We recognize that the files are user-named and may not match copyrighted material exactly (for example, the artist or song could be spelled wrong). For Napster to function effectively, however, file names must reasonably or roughly correspond to the material contained in the files, otherwise no user could ever locate any desired music. As a practical matter, Napster, its users and the record company plaintiffs have equal access to infringing material by employing Napster's "search function."

Our review of the record requires us to accept the district court's conclusion that plaintiffs have demonstrated a likelihood of success on the merits of the vicarious copyright infringement claim. Napster's failure to police the system's "premises," combined with a showing that Napster financially benefits from the continuing availability of infringing files on its system, leads to the imposition of vicarious liability. We address the scope of the injunction in part VIII of this opinion.

VI

We next address whether Napster has asserted defenses which would preclude the entry of a preliminary injunction.

Napster alleges that two statutes insulate it from liability. First, Napster asserts that its users engage in actions protected by § 1008 of the Audio Home Recording Act of 1992, 17 U.S.C. § 1008. Second, Napster argues that its liability for contributory and vicarious infringement is limited by the Digital Millennium Copyright Act, 17 U.S.C. § 512. We address the application of each statute in turn.

A. Audio Home Recording Act

The statute states in part:

> *No action may be brought under this title alleging infringement of copyright* based on the manufacture, importation, or distribution of a digital audio recording device, a digital audio recording medium, an analog recording device, or an analog recording medium, or *based on the noncommercial use by a consumer of such a device or medium* for making digital musical recordings or analog musical recordings.

17 U.S.C. § 1008 (emphases added). Napster contends that MP3 file exchange is the type of "noncommercial use" protected from infringement actions by the statute. Napster asserts it cannot be secondarily liable for users' nonactionable exchange of copyrighted musical recordings.

The district court rejected Napster's argument, stating that the Audio Home Recording Act is "irrelevant" to the action because: (1) plaintiffs did not bring claims under the Audio Home Recording Act; and (2) the Audio Home Recording Act does not cover the downloading of MP3 files. *Napster,* 114 F.Supp.2d at 916 n. 19.

We agree with the district court that the Audio Home Recording Act does not cover the downloading of MP3 files to computer hard drives. First, "[u]nder the plain meaning of the Act's definition of digital audio recording devices, computers (and their hard drives) are not digital audio recording devices because their 'primary purpose' is not to make digital audio copied recordings." *Recording Indus. Ass'n of Am. v. Diamond Multimedia Sys., Inc.,* 180 F.3d 1072, 1078 (9th Cir.1999). Second, notwithstanding Napster's claim that computers are "digital audio recording devices," computers do not make "digital music recordings" as defined by the Audio Home Recording Act. *Id.* at 1077.

B. Digital Millennium Copyright Act

Napster also interposes a statutory limitation on liability by asserting the protections of the "safe harbor" from copyright infringement suits for "Internet service providers" contained in the Digital Millennium Copyright Act, 17 U.S.C. § 512. *See Napster,* 114 F.Supp.2d at 919 n. 24. The district court did not give this statutory limitation any weight favoring a denial of temporary injunctive relief. The court concluded that Napster "has failed to persuade this court that subsection 512(d) shelters contributory infringers." *Id.*

We need not accept a blanket conclusion that § 512 of the Digital Millennium Copyright Act will never protect secondary infringers. ("[T]he committee reports leave no doubt that Congress intended to provide some relief from vicarious liability").

We do not agree that Napster's potential liability for contributory and vicarious infringement renders the Digital Millennium Copyright Act inapplicable per se. We instead recognize that this issue will be more fully developed at trial. At this stage of the litigation, plaintiffs raise serious questions regarding Napster's ability to obtain shelter under § 512, and plaintiffs also demonstrate that the balance of hardships tips in their favor....

Plaintiffs have raised and continue to raise significant questions under this statute, including: (1) whether Napster is an Internet service provider as defined by 17 U.S.C. § 512(d); (2) whether copyright owners must give a service provider "official" notice of infringing activity in order for it to have knowledge or awareness of infringing activity on its system; and (3) whether Napster complies with § 512(i), which requires a service provider to timely establish a detailed copyright compliance policy. *See A & M Records, Inc. v. Napster, Inc.,* No. 99–05183, 2000 WL 573136 (N.D.Cal. May 12, 2000) (denying summary judgment to Napster under a different subsection of the Digital Millennium Copyright Act, § 512(a)).

The district court considered ample evidence to support its determination that the balance of hardships tips in plaintiffs' favor:

> Any destruction of Napster, Inc. by a preliminary injunction is speculative compared to the statistical evidence of massive, unauthorized downloading and uploading of plaintiffs' copyrighted works-as many as 10,000 files per second by defendant's own admission. *See* Kessler Dec. ¶ 29. The court has every reason to believe that, without a preliminary injunction, these numbers will mushroom as Napster users, and newcomers attracted by the publicity, scramble to obtain as much free music as possible before trial.

114 F.Supp.2d at 926.

VII

Napster contends that even if the district court's preliminary determinations that it is liable for facilitating copyright infringement are correct, the district court improperly rejected valid affirmative defenses of waiver, implied license and copyright misuse. We address the defenses in turn.

A. Waiver

"Waiver is the intentional relinquishment of a known right with knowledge of its existence and the intent to relinquish it." *United States v. King Features Entm't, Inc.,* 843 F.2d 394, 399 (9th Cir.1988). In copyright, waiver or abandonment of copyright "occurs only if there is an intent by the copyright proprietor to surrender rights in his work." 4 Melville B. Nimmer & David Nimmer, *Nimmer on Copyright* ¶ 13.06 (2000); *see also Micro Star v. Formgen, Inc.,* 154 F.3d 1107, 1114 (9th Cir.1998) (discussing abandonment).

Napster argues that the district court erred in not finding that plaintiffs knowingly provided consumers with technology designed to copy and distribute MP3 files over the Internet and, thus, waived any legal authority to exercise exclusive control over creation and distribution of MP3 files. The district court, however, was not convinced "that the record companies created the monster that is now devouring their intellectual property rights." *Napster,* 114 F.Supp.2d at 924. We find no error in the district court's finding that "in hastening the proliferation of MP3 files, plaintiffs did [nothing] more than seek partners for their commercial downloading ventures and develop music players for files they planned to sell over the Internet." *Id.*

B. Implied License

Napster also argues that plaintiffs granted the company an implied license by encouraging MP3 file exchange over the Internet. Courts have found implied licenses only in "narrow" circumstances where one party "created a work at [the other's] request and handed it over, intending that [the other] copy and distribute it." *SmithKline Beecham Consumer Healthcare, L.P. v. Watson Pharms., Inc.,* 211 F.3d 21, 25 (2d Cir.2000) (quoting *Effects Assocs., Inc. v. Cohen,* 908 F.2d 555, 558 (9th Cir.1990)), *cert. denied,* 531 U.S. 872, 121 S.Ct. 173, 148 L.Ed.2d 118 (2000). The district court observed that no evidence exists to support this defense: "indeed, the RIAA gave defendant express notice that it objected to the availability of its members' copyrighted music on Napster." *Napster,* 114 F.Supp.2d at 924–25. The record supports this conclusion.

C. Misuse

The defense of copyright misuse forbids a copyright holder from "secur[ing] an exclusive right or limited monopoly not granted by the Copyright Office." *Lasercomb Am., Inc. v. Reynolds,* 911 F.2d 970, 977–79 (4th Cir.1990), *quoted in Practice Mgmt. Info. Corp. v. American Med. Ass'n,* 121 F.3d 516, 520 (9th Cir.), *amended by* 133 F.3d 1140 (9th Cir.1997). Napster alleges that online distribution is not within the copyright monopoly. According to Napster, plaintiffs have colluded to "use their copyrights to extend their control to online distributions."

We find no error in the district court's preliminary rejection of this affirmative defense. The misuse defense prevents copyright holders from leveraging their limited monopoly to allow them control of areas outside the monopoly. *See Lasercomb,* 911 F.2d at 976–77; *see also Religious Tech. Ctr. v. Lerma,* No. 95–1107A, 1996 WL 633131, at *11 (E.D.Va. Oct.4, 1996) (listing circumstances which indicate improper leverage).[8] There is no evidence here that plaintiffs seek to control areas outside of their grant of monopoly. Rather, plaintiffs seek to control reproduction and distribution of their copyrighted works, exclusive rights of copyright holders. 17 U.S.C. § 106; *see also, e.g., UMG Recordings,* 92 F.Supp.2d at 351 ("A [copyright holder's] 'exclusive' rights, derived from the Constitution and the Copyright Act, include the right, within broad limits, to curb the development of such a derivative market by refusing to license a copyrighted work or by doing so only on terms the copyright owner finds acceptable."). That the copyrighted works are transmitted in another medium-MP3 format rather than audio CD-has no bearing on our analysis. *See id.* at 351 (finding that reproduction of audio CD into MP3 format does not "transform" the work).

VIII

The district court correctly recognized that a preliminary injunction against Napster's participation in copyright infringement is not only warranted but required. We believe, however, that the scope of the injunction needs modification in light of our opinion. Specifically, we reiterate that contributory liability may potentially be imposed only to the extent that Napster: (1) receives reasonable knowledge of specific infringing files with copyrighted musical compositions and sound recordings; (2) knows or should know that such files are available on the Napster system; and (3) fails to act to prevent viral distribution of the works. *See Netcom,* 907 F.Supp. at 1374–75. The mere existence of the Napster system, absent actual notice and Napster's demonstrated failure to remove the offending material, is insufficient to impose contributory liability. *See Sony,* 464 U.S. at 442–43, 104 S.Ct. 774.

Conversely, Napster may be vicariously liable when it fails to affirmatively use its ability to patrol its system and preclude access to potentially infringing files listed in its search index. Napster has both the ability to use its search function to identify infringing musical recordings and the right to bar participation of users who engage in the transmission of infringing files.

The preliminary injunction which we stayed is overbroad because it places on Napster the entire burden of ensuring that no "copying, downloading, uploading, transmitting, or distributing" of plaintiffs' works occur on the system. As stated, we place the burden on plaintiffs to provide notice to Napster of copyrighted works and files containing such works available on the Napster system before Napster has the duty to disable access to the offending content. Napster, however, also bears the burden of policing the system within the limits of the system. Here, we recognize that this is not an exact science in that the files are user named. In crafting the injunction on remand, the district court should recognize that Napster's system does not currently appear to allow Napster access to users' MP3 files.

Based on our decision to remand, Napster's additional arguments on appeal going to the scope of the injunction need not be addressed. We, however, briefly address Napster's First Amendment argument so that it is not reasserted on remand. Napster contends that the present injunction violates the First Amendment because it is broader than necessary. The company asserts two distinct free speech rights: (1) its right to publish a "directory" (here, the search index) and (2) its users' right to exchange information. We note that First Amendment concerns in copyright are allayed by the presence of the fair use doctrine. *See* 17 U.S.C. § 107; *see generally Nihon Keizai Shimbun v. Comline Business Data, Inc.*, 166 F.3d 65, 74 (2d Cir.1999); *Netcom,* 923 F.Supp. at 1258 (stating that the Copyright Act balances First Amendment concerns with the rights of copyright holders). There was a preliminary determination here that Napster users are not fair users. Uses of copyrighted material that are not fair uses are rightfully enjoined. *See Dr. Seuss Enters. v. Penguin Books USA, Inc.*, 109 F.3d 1394, 1403 (9th Cir.1997) (rejecting defendants' claim that injunction would constitute a prior restraint in violation of the First Amendment).

IX

We address Napster's remaining arguments: (1) that the court erred in setting a $5 million bond, and (2) that the district court should have imposed a constructive royalty payment structure in lieu of an injunction.

A. Bond

Napster argues that the $5 million bond is insufficient because the company's value is between $1.5 and $2 billion. We review objections to the amount of a bond for abuse of discretion. *Walczak v. EPL Prolong, Inc.,* 198 F.3d 725 (9th Cir.1999).

We are reluctant to dramatically raise bond amounts on appeal. *See GoTo.com, Inc. v. The Walt Disney Co.,* 202 F.3d 1199, 1211 (9th Cir.2000); *see also* Fed.R.Civ.P. 65(c). The district court considered competing evidence of Napster's value and the deleterious effect that any injunction would have upon the Napster system. We cannot say that Judge Patel abused her discretion when she fixed the penal sum required for the bond.

B. Royalties

Napster contends that the district court should have imposed a monetary penalty by way of a compulsory royalty in place of an injunction. We are asked to do what the district court refused.

Napster tells us that "where great public injury would be worked by an injunction, the courts might ... award damages or a continuing royalty instead of an injunction in such special circumstances." *Abend v. MCA, Inc.,* 863 F.2d 1465, 1479 (9th Cir.1988) (quoting 3 Melville B. Nimmer & David Nimmer, *Nimmer On Copyright* § 14.06[B] (1988)), *aff'd,* 495 U.S. 207, 110 S.Ct. 1750, 109 L.Ed.2d 184 (1990). We are at a total loss to find any "special circumstances" simply because this case requires us to apply well-established doctrines of copyright law to a new technology. Neither do we agree with Napster that an injunction would cause "great public injury." Further, we narrowly construe any suggestion that compulsory royalties are appropriate in this context because Congress has arguably limited the application of compulsory royalties to specific circumstances, none of which are present here. *See* 17 U.S.C. § 115.

The Copyright Act provides for various sanctions for infringers. *See, e.g.,* 17 U.S.C. §§ 502 (injunctions); 504 (damages); and 506 (criminal penalties); *see also* 18 U.S.C. § 2319A (criminal penalties for the unauthorized fixation of and trafficking in sound recordings and music videos of live musical performances). These statutory sanctions represent a more than adequate legislative solution to the problem created by copyright infringement.

Imposing a compulsory royalty payment schedule would give Napster an "easy out" of this case. If such royalties were imposed, Napster would avoid penalties for any future violation of an injunction, statutory copyright damages and any possible criminal penalties for continuing infringement. The royalty structure would also grant Napster the luxury of either choosing to continue and pay royalties or shut down. On the other hand, the wronged parties would be forced to do business with a company that profits from the wrongful use of intellectual properties. Plaintiffs would lose the power to control their intellectual property: they could not make a business decision *not* to license their property to Napster, and, in the event they planned to do business with Napster, compulsory royalties would take away the copyright holders' ability to negotiate the terms of any contractual arrangement.

X

We affirm in part, reverse in part and remand.

We direct that the preliminary injunction fashioned by the district court prior to this appeal shall remain stayed until it is modified by the district court to conform to the requirements of this opinion. We order a partial remand of this case on the date of the filing of this opinion for the limited purpose of permitting the district court to proceed with the settlement and entry of the modified preliminary injunction.

Even though the preliminary injunction requires modification, appellees have substantially and primarily prevailed on appeal. Appellees shall recover their statutory costs on appeal. *See* Fed. R.App. P. 39(a)(4) ("[i]f a judgment is affirmed in part, reversed in part, modified, or vacated, costs are taxed only as the court orders.").

AFFIRMED IN PART, REVERSED IN PART AND REMANDED.

AUTOSKILL, INC. v. NAT'L EDUC. SUPPORT SYS.
United States Court of Appeals for the Tenth Circuit
May 19, 1993, Filed
No. 92-2118
994 F.2d 1476

HOLLOWAY, Circuit Judge.

Autoskill, Inc. (Autoskill), a Canadian corporation, in 1986 obtained a certificate of registration of copyright on a computer program designed to test and train students with reading deficiencies. After National Educational Support Systems, Inc. (NESS), a New Mexico corporation, began marketing similar software in 1990, Autoskill sued for copyright infringement in the District of New Mexico. That court had jurisdiction of the claim of copyright infringement asserted under 28 U.S.C. § 1338(a) and 28 U.S.C. § 1332(a). The district court granted Autoskill a preliminary injunction against NESS covering some portions of Autoskill's program, *Autoskill, Inc. v. National Educational Support Systems Inc.,* 793 F.Supp. 1557, 1573 (D.N.M.1992), and NESS appeals. We have appellate jurisdiction granted by 28 U.S.C. § 1292(a)(1). We affirm.

I. THE FACTUAL BACKGROUND

Beginning in the late 1970s, Dr. Christina Fiedorowicz and Dr. Ronald Trites, the president of Autoskill, developed a computer software program for use in teaching reading skills to students with reading disabilities. After reviewing some research of others, they designed their program to identify students with reading difficulties in three categories or subtypes: Type O, the oral reading subtype; Type A, the intermodal associative deficit subtype; and Type S, the sequential deficit subtype. Autoskill obtained a United States certificate of registration of the copyright on the software Trites and Fiedorowicz developed, effective January 27, 1986, called "Autoskill: Component Reading Subskills Testing and Training Program." 793 F.Supp. at 1559.

NESS was incorporated as a New Mexico corporation in 1989. Two of the principals of NESS, Byron Manning and Ron Neil, were familiar with the Autoskill program. As a salesman for the computer manufacturer UNISYS Corp., Neil sold ICON computers with Autoskill software to educational institutions for about four years between 1986 and 1990. NESS has explained that as "the first alternative for business of the newly organized NESS," Manning and Neil decided to attempt to obtain a license to market the Autoskill program. Brief of

Appellant at 15. However, several months of negotiations between NESS and Autoskill ended in late 1989, without an agreement.

With the licensing negotiations with Autoskill still ongoing, Neil began discussions with a computer programming firm, Automation Consultants, Inc. (ACI), about developing a reading software program for NESS. The president of ACI, Lynn Beckwith, wrote in his notes about his initial conversations with Neil that the NESS software was "to be like AUTOSKILL" and was to be an "AUTOSKILL REPLACEMENT." 793 F.Supp. at 1559.

In January 1990, ACI began programming the NESS reading software. NESS specified the substantive and pedantic content of the NESS program to the programming firm. In addition, NESS gave the programmers copies of some of the published articles that had been used as part of the basis of the Autoskill program, as well as an Autoskill sales brochure. *Id.* By March 1990, the programming firm had produced a preliminary version of the NESS software, called "Nessi: Reading and Language Development Program." Appellant's App. at 391.

With its reading software ready to demonstrate, NESS began a marketing effort in May 1990. *Id.* at 186. A Canadian-based firm, Lifeskills Technology, signed an agreement with NESS to distribute the NESS program in Canada. Both NESS and Lifeskills began hearing rumors that Autoskill was planning to initiate a copyright infringement action against NESS. In April 1991, an attorney for Autoskill sent a letter to Lifeskills stating that Autoskill viewed the NESS software as an infringing program, and warning that Lifeskills could be named in an infringement action. *Id.* at 389–90.

NESS filed a suit in the District of New Mexico in July 1991 for a declaratory judgment that it did not infringe the Autoskill copyright, and other relief. *Id.* at 1, 5–6 (complaint). The district judge issued a temporary restraining order that prohibited Autoskill officers and other employees from interfering with the distribution of the NESS software. On September 25, 1991, Autoskill filed this instant case in the District Court against NESS for copyright infringement and misappropriation of trade secrets, seeking a preliminary injunction, which is at issue here, to prevent continued infringement. Autoskill's action was consolidated with the NESS suit.

On April 21, 1992, the district judge granted Autoskill a preliminary injunction which prohibited NESS from "[m]anufacturing, reproducing, duplicating, copying, marketing, selling, renting, lending, distributing, displaying or demonstrating any portion of any NESSI Program or user manual which is substantially similar to the protectible elements of the Autoskill Program" and "[d]oing any other act which infringes on the protectible portion of the Autoskill Program." 793 F.Supp. at 1573. The judge concluded that Autoskill had shown a substantial likelihood of success on the merits and had prevailed on the other three elements—irreparable harm, proof that the threatened injury outweighed the potential harm to NESS from the injunction, and that the injunction would not be adverse to the public interest. *Id.* at 1572.

II. APPELLATE JURISDICTION

In a motion to dismiss this appeal, Autoskill argued two theories: (1) the automatic bankruptcy stay of 11 U.S.C. § 362 prevented NESS from appealing the preliminary injunction; and (2) NESS' notice of appeal was untimely because it was filed more than 30 days after the order granting the injunction. We reserved judgment on the jurisdictional question for disposition by the hearing panel.

On April 27, 1992, six days after the district judge entered the preliminary injunction, NESS filed a voluntary petition in the Bankruptcy Court for the District of New Mexico in which it sought relief under Chapter 11. Commencement of the voluntary Chapter 11 case constituted an order for relief under the chapter. *See* 11 U.S.C. § 301. Subsequently, on June 3, 1992, memorializing an oral ruling on June 2, the bankruptcy judge granted Autoskill relief from the automatic stay so that Autoskill might enforce the preliminary injunction. None of the bankruptcy judge's orders are before us for review.

NESS initiated this appeal of the preliminary injunction by filing a notice of appeal on June 26, 1992, the sixtieth day after it filed the Chapter 11 petition and the sixty-sixth day after the injunction issued. On July 7, 1992, Autoskill filed the motion to dismiss the appeal for lack of jurisdiction. NESS then sought a ruling in the bankruptcy court on the applicability of the automatic stay to the appeal, or in the alternative a ruling granting it relief from the automatic stay in order to pursue the appeal. *See* Appellant's App. at 162. On July 16, 1992, the bankruptcy judge ruled that the appeal was permissible on two grounds. First, he held that Rule 6009 of the Bankruptcy Rules controlled; thus, NESS had not needed court approval to prosecute the appeal. *Id.* Second, the judge granted NESS relief from the automatic stay to prosecute an appeal of the preliminary injunction. *Id.*

A. 11 U.S.C. § 108(b)(2)

We address first the timeliness of NESS' notice of appeal filed outside the 30 days allowed by Rule 4(a) of the Federal Rules of Appellate Procedure.

In arguing that its notice of appeal was timely, NESS relies on the 60-day time period that 11 U.S.C. § 108(b)(2) provides for certain actions by Chapter 11 trustees or debtors in possession. We must decide whether, when the Rule 4(a) 30-day period for filing a notice of appeal has not expired before the filing of a bankruptcy petition, § 108(b)(2) extends the time for filing a notice of appeal for

60 days after the order for relief is entered. Few courts have addressed the question and the issue is one of first impression in our circuit.

Rule 4(a)(1) of the Federal Rules of Appellate Procedure requires a party appealing as of right in a civil case to file a notice of appeal "within 30 days after the date of entry of the judgment or order appealed from." Since the notice of appeal here was filed outside the 30-day time period, NESS relies on § 108(b)(2) of the Bankruptcy Code. In general terms, § 108(b) embodies a longstanding provision in the bankruptcy statutes that "permit the trustee, when he steps into the shoes of the debtor, an extension of time for filing an action or doing some other act that is required to preserve the debtor's rights." H.R.Rep. No. 595, 95th Cong., 1st Sess. 318 (1977), *reprinted in* 1978 U.S.C.C.A.N. 5963, 6275; *see also* S.Rep. No. 989, 95th Cong., 2d Sess. 30 (1978), *reprinted in* 1978 U.S.C.C.A.N. 5787, 5816 (same). Section 108(b) provides:

> Except as provided in subsection (a) of this section, if applicable nonbankruptcy law, an order entered in a nonbankruptcy proceeding, or an agreement fixes a period within which the debtor or an individual protected under section 1201 or 1301 of this title may file any pleading, demand, notice, or proof of claim or loss, cure a default, or perform any other similar act, and such period has not expired before the date of the filing of the petition, the trustee may only file, cure, or perform, as the case may be, before the later of—
>
> (1) the end of such period, including any suspension of such period occurring on or after the commencement of the case; or
>
> (2) 60 days after the order for relief.

11 U.S.C. § 108(b). For certain types of actions, then, the statute "allows the trustee 'the later of' two periods, one being the end of the period prescribed by applicable nonbankruptcy law, and the other a specific extension granted by this section." 2 *Collier on Bankruptcy* ¶ 108.02, at 108–5 (15th ed. 1992).

One requirement of § 108(b)—that the relevant time period "has not expired before the date of the filing of the petition"—is not at issue. Since NESS filed the Chapter 11 petition just six days after the district judge entered the preliminary injunction, the 30-day period for filing a notice of appeal had just begun to run. We consider instead whether a notice of appeal is within the scope of the actions that Congress inténded to include within the § 108(b) extended period for actions by a trustee or debtor in possession.

Section 108(b) applies generally to fixed periods within which a debtor or trustee "may file any pleading, demand, notice, or proof of claim or loss, cure a default, or perform any other similar act." We agree with the courts holding that § 108(b)'s sweeping language "includes the filing of a notice of appeal." *Production Credit Ass'n v. Burk,* 427 N.W.2d 108, 110 (N.D.1988); *Di Maggio v. Blache,* 466 So.2d 489, 490–91 (La.Ct.App.1985). Although § 108(b) does not specifically refer to notices of appeal, the statute includes a broad catchall extending the time in which a debtor or trustee may "perform *any other similar act* " in addition to the steps listed. § 108(b) (emphasis added); *see In re G–N Partners,* 48 B.R. 462, 467 (Bankr.D.Minn.1985) (that § 108(b) is "broader" than listed items "is obvious from its reading"). Filing a notice of appeal is at least a "similar act" with respect to two of the actions specified, filing a "pleading" or a "notice." Consequently § 108(b) gives a debtor in possession or a trustee an extended period for filing a notice of appeal of up to 60 days, as long as the 30-day time period of Rule 4(a) has not expired when the bankruptcy petition is filed.

We feel that under § 108(b) NESS was required to file a notice of appeal "before the later of" either (1) the period provided by applicable nonbankruptcy law, *or* (2) "60 days after the order for relief." The time period under relevant nonbankruptcy law, Rule 4(a)(1), would have expired 30 days after the district judge entered the preliminary injunction on April 21, 1992 or on May 21, 1992. However, the extended 60-day time period provided by § 108(b)(2) began running on the date of the commencement of the Chapter 11 case—April 27, 1992. The 60-day period extended to and included June 26, 1992, the day NESS filed its notice of appeal. NESS thus commenced the appeal within the extended time period provided by § 108(b).

B. Effect of Rule 4(a) on § 108(b)(2)

Autoskill argues that by extending the time for filing a notice of appeal, § 108(b) would override the explicit language of Rule 4(a)(1) which provides a 30-day period for filing notices of appeal "in all civil cases." Fed.R.App.P. 4(a) advisory committee's note. Autoskill would have us determine the effect of the two provisions, § 108(b) and Rule 4(a)(1), by applying the abrogation clause in the Rules Enabling Act, which provides that "[a]ll laws in conflict with such rules shall be of no further force or effect after such rules have taken effect." 28 U.S.C. § 2072(b).

We cannot agree with Autoskill that Rule 4(a)(1) supersedes § 108(b). The abrogation provision on which such argument is constructed is currently codified at 28 U.S.C. § 2072(b). This statute is generally viewed as applying so as to abrogate conflicting statutes enacted before the rules.

We are persuaded that this interpretation serves the legislative purpose in adopting § 108(b). As is apparent from § 108(b) itself, this bankruptcy provision was included to afford a trustee or debtor in possession a longer period to determine the advisability of further steps in litigation or business transactions to protect the interests of the bankruptcy estate. Both the House and Senate committee reports contained identical, broad statements that § 108(b) permits "the trustee, when he steps into the shoes of the debtor, an extension of time for filing an action or doing some other act that is required to preserve the debtor's rights." H.R.Rep. No. 595, 95th Cong., 1st Sess. 318 (1977) U.S.Code Cong. & Admin.News p. 6275; S.Rep. No. 989, 95th Cong., 2d Sess. 30 (1978) U.S.Code Cong. & Admin.News p. 5816.

C. Effect of the Automatic Stay on § 108(b)(2)

Autoskill contends that even if § 108(b) extended NESS' time for filing the notice of appeal, the automatic stay of § 362 then in effect made the filing a void act. Under § 362(a)(1) a petition in bankruptcy stays the "continuation ... of a judicial, administrative, or other action or proceeding against the debtor that was ... commenced before the commencement" of the bankruptcy proceeding. Autoskill relies upon the rule that § 362 stays "all appeals in proceedings that were *originally brought* against the debtor, regardless of whether the debtor is the appellant or appellee." *Association of St. Croix Condominium Owners v. St. Croix Hotel Corp.,* 682 F.2d 446, 449 (3d Cir.1982) (emphasis original).

We disagree. Autoskill's argument ignores the first ground cited by the bankruptcy judge in recognizing the validity of the appeal: that Rule 6009 of the Bankruptcy Rules supported NESS' prosecution of the appeal. As we read his ruling, the bankruptcy judge felt that Rule 6009 allowed NESS to prosecute its appeal from the preliminary injunction without obtaining relief from the automatic stay of § 362, and we agree.

Rule 6009 allows a trustee or debtor in possession "[w]ith or without court approval" to "enter an appearance and defend any pending action or proceeding by or against the debtor, or commence and prosecute any action or proceeding in behalf of the estate." The plain language of Rule 6009 enabled NESS to "commence" this appeal, which certainly was a "proceeding in behalf of the estate." *See* 8 *Collier on Bankruptcy* ¶ 6009.03 & n. 7, at 6009–3 (15th ed. 1992). "Rule 6009, along with Code section 362 itself, makes it clear that the automatic stay does not apply to the continued prosecution of actions by the trustee or debtor in possession. Those entities may continue or pursue litigation without leave of court (or release of stay under section 362)." *Id.* Rule 6009 enabled NESS to prosecute this appeal without the authorization of the bankruptcy court and the notice of appeal was not a void act.

In its memorandum in support of its motion to dismiss this appeal, Autoskill argues that the automatic bankruptcy stay acts to stay an appeal by the debtor from an adverse decision in a nonbankruptcy suit brought against it, such as Autoskill's suit for copyright infringement, citing *St. Croix, inter alia.* There the pendency of a Chapter 11 reorganization petition was revealed in briefs filed with the Third Circuit. That court entered an order staying the appeal, stating that its order "staying this proceeding is without prejudice to the rights of the parties to apply to the Bankruptcy Court for relief from the provisions of section 362...." *Id.* at 449...

St. Croix does not support NESS' motion that we dismiss this appeal as invalid. It is apparent from the order as quoted above that the validity of the appeal in *St. Croix* was not rejected by the Third Circuit and that the court was merely staying the appellate proceeding, affording the parties an opportunity to have the stay of § 362 lifted. That has already been done in the instant case, by application to the bankruptcy court which granted that relief on July 16, 1992, in addition to holding that Rule 6009 of the Bankruptcy Rules controlled, permitting the prosecution of the appeal by NESS.

In sum, we hold that NESS' appeal was timely and valid and deny the motion to dismiss.

III. THE PRELIMINARY INJUNCTION

We turn now to NESS' claims of error in the granting of the preliminary injunction by the district court.

The Copyright Act authorizes a federal court to "grant temporary and final injunctions on such terms as it may deem reasonable to prevent or restrain infringement of a copyright." 17 U.S.C. § 502(a). A district judge may grant a preliminary injunction if the moving party demonstrates:

> (1) substantial likelihood that the movant will eventually prevail on the merits; (2) a showing that the movant will suffer irreparable injury unless the injunction issues; (3) proof that the threatened injury to the movant outweighs whatever damage the proposed injunction may cause the opposing party; and (4) a showing that the injunction, if issued, would not be adverse to the public interest.

The district judge concluded that Autoskill demonstrated all four factors. We will not set aside a preliminary injunction on appeal "[u]nless the district court abuses its discretion, commits an error of law, or is clearly erroneous in its preliminary factual findings." 846 F.2d at 1270.

A. Likelihood of Success on the Merits

To demonstrate a substantial likelihood of success Autoskill was required to present "a prima facie case showing a reasonable probability that [it] will ultimately be entitled to the relief sought." *Continental Oil Co. v. Frontier Ref. Co.*, 338 F.2d 780, 781 (10th Cir.1964). Autoskill was not required to show to an absolute certainty that it has a right to prevail on the infringement claim at trial. *See id.* at 781. Rather, under our "liberal definition" of the likelihood of success factor, "[w]hen the other three requirements for a preliminary injunction are satisfied, 'it will ordinarily be enough that the plaintiff has raised questions going to the merits so serious, substantial, difficult and doubtful, as to make them a fair ground for litigation and thus for more deliberate investigation.' " *Otero Sav. & Loan Ass'n,* 665 F.2d at 278 (quoting *Hamilton Watch Co. v. Benrus Watch Co.,* 206 F.2d 738, 740 (2d Cir.1953)).

Thus Autoskill was required to present at least a prima facie case of infringement. To prove copyright infringement a plaintiff is required to show: "(1) ownership of a valid copyright, and (2) copying of constituent elements of the work that are original." *Feist Publications, Inc. v. Rural Tel. Serv. Co.,* 499 U.S. 340, ——, 111 S.Ct. 1282, 1296, 113 L.Ed.2d 358 (1991). NESS challenges the district judge's conclusion that Autoskill established these elements.

1. Ownership of Valid Copyright

The Copyright Act provides that a certificate of registration of a copyright "shall constitute prima facie evidence of the validity of the copyright and of the facts stated in the certificate." 17 U.S.C. § 410(c). By presenting a registration certificate a party establishes the validity of the copyright prima facie and the burden to dispute the validity of the copyright then shifts to the party challenging it. *See Harris Market Research v. Marshall Mktg. & Communications, Inc.,* 948 F.2d 1518, 1526 (10th Cir.1991). The district judge ruled that NESS failed to present either argument or evidence sufficient to rebut Autoskill's prima facie showing of the validity of its copyright. 793 F.Supp. at 1563.

As proof of ownership, Autoskill presented evidence of the certificate of registration, No. TX 1 742 632, obtained on its reading program. Appellant's App. at 471–72. In the registration certificate Autoskill identified itself as the author of the work and described the nature of its authorship as *"[h]irer of entire work comprising program and including manual." Id.* (emphasis added). We think the "facts stated in the certificate," to which the statutory presumption of validity extends, logically include the identification of the author and the statement that the entire work was made for hire. By introducing the registration certificate in which it identified itself as the author, then, Autoskill presented prima facie evidence that it was the owner of the copyright. We hold that Autoskill satisfied its initial burden on the ownership element by establishing a prima facie case on this issue.

NESS argues that the district judge erred factually and legally in ruling that Autoskill was the owner of the United States copyright. One principal contention of NESS is that the judge erred in holding that *Community for Creative Non-Violence v. Reid,* 490 U.S. 730, 109 S.Ct. 2166, 104 L.Ed.2d 811 (1989), should not be retroactively applied to this controversy. And under *Reid* NESS says this was not a work made for hire because Autoskill's programmers were not its employees under the common law agency test adopted by *Reid.* Appellant's Brief at 42–43.

On the retroactivity point, we agree with NESS. It is now settled that "[o]nce retroactive application is chosen for any assertedly new rule, it is chosen for all others who might seek its prospective application." *James B. Beam Distilling Co. v. Georgia,* 501 U.S. 529, ——— - ———, 111 S.Ct. 2439, 2447–48, 115 L.Ed.2d 481 (1991); *see Anixter v. Home–Stake Prod. Co.,* 977 F.2d 1533, 1543 (10th Cir.1992), *cert. denied,* 507 U.S. 1029, 113 S.Ct. 1841, 123 L.Ed.2d 467 (1993); *Gray v. Phillips Petroleum Co.,* 971 F.2d 591, 596 (10th Cir.1992). In *Reid* the new rule adopted was applied to the litigants before the Court; hence, selective non-retroactivity is barred in all other cases as to that new rule. Thus *Reid* should be applied here, but this does not carry the day for NESS.

NESS had the burden of rebutting the statutory presumption of Autoskill's ownership of the copyright. NESS says the "uncontroverted evidence at both hearings is that all versions of the Autoskill programs were programmed in Canada by contract programming companies or individuals, none of whom worked for Autoskill." Appellant's Brief at 42 (footnote omitted). We note that Dr. Trites was asked by NESS' counsel about Edfour Education Consultants,[13] the programming firm used by Autoskill and referred to in Autoskill's copyright certificate as a manufacturer. Trites replied that Edfour was paid under an "independent contract" and its people were not "employees" of Autoskill at the time of that work.

The broad assertions by NESS about Autoskill's programming and the sparse evidence it presented on the issue do not address the critical question raised, *i.e.,* whether the Autoskill programmers—companies or individuals—were or were not employees of Autoskill, considering the relevant factors under the "common law agency law meaning." *Reid,* 490 U.S. at 739, 109 S.Ct. at 2172. We have considered the references in NESS' brief which it relies upon, Appellant's Brief at 8–21, 44, and find no substantial evidence identified which addresses the important factors under the common law of agency which NESS relies on. *See supra* note 14. The state of the record is such that this issue—whether the programmers were Autoskill's employees—remains a fair ground for litigation. The prima facie case of Autoskill was not sufficiently rebutted to justify reversal of the preliminary injunction on this point.

Furthermore, we note that there was proof on another basis to establish Autoskill's ownership of the copyright. NESS identified Edfour as the contract programmer on the first version of the Autoskill program. Appellant's Brief at 12. With respect to Edfour, there was testimony by Dr. Trites that Autoskill had received an assignment of rights from Edfour. Appellee's Supp.App. at 211–12. The assignment was not in Dr. Trites' possession at the hearing, but the specific testimony about the assignment was given in response to NESS' questioning, it was not objected to nor contradicted, and it is still undisputed at this point.

In sum, we are not persuaded that the preliminary injunction should be reversed on the basis of the ownership showing.

2. Copying

In a copyright infringement action a "plaintiff may prove defendant's copying either by direct evidence or, as is most often the case, by showing that (1) the defendant had access to the plaintiff's copyrighted work, and (2) defendant's work is substantially similar to the plaintiff's copyrightable material." *Computer Assocs. Int'l, Inc. v. Altai, Inc.,* 982 F.2d 693, 701 (2d Cir.1992); 3 *Nimmer* § 13.01[B], at 13–10 to –11. These two types of circumstantial evidence of infringement are accepted because direct evidence of copying is rarely available. NESS contends that Autoskill demonstrated neither access nor substantial similarity.

a. Access to the Copyrighted Work

Addressing the access prong, the district judge noted that the founders of NESS, Neil and Manning, were "thoroughly familiar with the Autoskill Program." 793 F.Supp. at 1559 (finding No. 14). Neil, the judge found, had sold ICON computers for UNISYS with Autoskill software for four years. *Id.* Further, the court found that the supervisor of the programming of the NESS program had reviewed "a document which describes the Autoskill Program in detail." *Id.* (finding No. 22). The judge concluded "there is no question that NESS had access to the Autoskill Program." *Id.*

On access, a plaintiff may meet his initial burden by showing that the defendant had a "reasonable opportunity to view" or "opportunity to copy" the allegedly infringed work. We agree that defining access as the "opportunity" to view or copy makes sense for the purposes of shifting the burden to the defendant, and we follow this approach. *See* 3 *Nimmer* § 13.02[A] n. 5, at 13–15. NESS makes no argument that the judge's underlying factual findings on this point are clearly erroneous and those findings establish opportunity.

b. Substantial Similarity

As the district judge found, the Autoskill program "is based primarily upon the identification of three reading sub-types of students who are experiencing reading difficulties." 793 F.Supp. at 1559. In general, the Autoskill program is designed to improve the student's rapid automatic responses to training stimuli. The Autoskill program first tests the students in order to identify their subtype for training purposes. Autoskill tests students for "oral reading, audio-visual matching, visual matching and visual scanning," in that order. *Id.*

The tests are presented according to 13 categories of word form types, which are based on different combinations of vowels and consonants. The tests use words and nonwords and record accuracy and speed of response. *Id.* at 1560. Based upon the results of the testing in Autoskill, students are assigned a training program that corresponds to their subtypes. "Training proceeds hierarchically from the simplest skills to the most complex." *Id.* Students receive immediate feedback to their responses, and in order to move to the next subprogram must achieve a 95 percent accuracy rate over three, consecutive 50-trial blocks, with a speed of no slower than 100 milliseconds. *Id.*

Comparing the Autoskill and NESS programs, the district judge found numerous similarities and concluded that NESS had merely changed the names and sequence of the tests and had made minor format changes of "no pedagogical value." *Id.* at 1561. The testing categories in the NESS program have similar names to those in Autoskill: "reading aloud, audio identification, visual identification and visual scanning." *Id.* at 1560. The judge found that the three main sections of each program are testing or diagnosis, profile analysis, and training. In both programs, the judge found, students progress from the simplest skills to the most complex and overall are "trained in substantially the same way." *Id.* He also concluded that in both programs students must attain similar criteria during training in order to move to the next level, and that both programs present similar profiles reflecting student speed and accuracy. *Id.*

Substantial similarity analysis concludes with a comparison of portions of the alleged infringer's works with the portions of the complaining party's works which are determined to be legally protectable under the Copyright Act. To determine whether any portions of Autoskill's computer program were protectable, the district judge used a three-step method of analysis recommended in 3 *Nimmer* § 13.03[F], at 13–80, a variation of which was recently adopted by the Second Circuit in *Altai:* abstraction, filtration, and comparison. In this preliminary injunction appeal we need not decide which is precisely the correct method of analysis for a final copyright judgment, *Plains Cotton Coop. Ass'n v. Goodpasture Computer Serv., Inc.,* 807 F.2d 1256, 1262 (5th Cir.), *cert. denied,* 484 U.S. 821, 108 S.Ct. 80, 98 L.Ed.2d 42 (1987), because we are satisfied that the trial judge used a permissible method of analysis here; moreover Autoskill showed a likelihood of success in defining as protectable the portions of its program for which the judge granted preliminary injunctive relief, after finding there was substantial similarity between the identified portions of the NESS and Autoskill programs which the judge compared. The choice of the precise test for such analysis can await an appeal requiring that choice, perhaps preferably one from a final copyright judgment.

1. The Abstractions Analysis

One of the fundamentals of copyright law is that a copyright does not protect an idea, but only the expression of the idea. *See, e.g., Baker v. Selden,* 101 U.S. 99, 104, 107, 25 L.Ed. 841 (1879); *Mazur v. Stein,* 347 U.S. 201, 217, 74 S.Ct. 460, 470, 98 L.Ed. 630 (1954); *see also* 17 U.S.C. § 102(b) (codifying idea/expression distinction). This idea/expression dichotomy applies to computer programs. *Altai,* 982 F.2d at 703. Thus, in general, the portions of a computer program that are "ideas" are nonprotectable, and the portions that represent "expression" may be protected. "Infringement is shown by a substantial similarity of *protectable expression,* not just an overall similarity between the works." 3 *Nimmer* § 13.03[F], at 13–82 (emphasis in original). Separating idea from expression, then, is one of the basic parts of a substantial similarity analysis.

In order to separate idea from expression, the judge here chose an approach known as the "abstractions" test or analysis. In articulating the approach, Judge Learned Hand explained:

> Upon any work, and especially upon a play, a great number of patterns of increasing generality will fit equally well, as more and more of the incident is left out. The last may perhaps be no more than the most general statement of what the play is about, and at times might consist only of its title; but there is a point in this series of abstractions where they are no longer protected, since otherwise the playwright could prevent the use of his "ideas," to which, apart from their expression, his property is never extended.

Nichols v. Universal Pictures Corp., 45 F.2d 119, 121 (2d Cir.1930), *cert. denied,* 282 U.S. 902, 51 S.Ct. 216, 75 L.Ed. 795 (1931). Because Judge Hand's abstractions approach generally "mirrors" the process that computer programmers use, it is particularly suited to the substantial similarity analysis for computer programs. *See* 3 *Nimmer* § 13.03 [F][1].

The trial judge here recognized that at the "highest and most general" level of abstraction the Autoskill program is "a reading program designed to diagnose, re-mediate and teach reading skills through the use of the computer." 793 F.Supp. at 1566. This level was thus treated as "idea" matter, not entitled to protection. Then the judge also excluded from the area of protection Autoskill's use of the three subtypes of students with reading difficulties—types O, A, and S—explaining that "[b]ecause these particular sub-types are identified and discussed in the literature available to the public, Autoskill is not entitled to protection from their use by others with testing or, diagnosing, profiling and training." *Id.* at 1566. The judge explained that "[t]he identification of those sub-types by researchers would be of little value[ ] if such theories were not allowed practical application to real students" and that to "allow such protection would grant Autoskill a virtual monopoly over those concepts and serve to thwart efforts of others to build upon them." *Id.* (citing *Feist,* 499 U.S. at ——, 111 S.Ct. at 1290).

The judge ruled, however, that "[t]he manner in which Autoskill utilizes those ideas and communicates them to students and teachers in the context of its reading program amounts to expression. Such expression can extend to the organization, structure and sequence if they are original." *Id.* The judge then proceeded to consider "Protectible v. Non-Protectible Expression," *id.,* in his subsequent filtration analysis when he determined which elements of expression survived for protection. We treat filtration below.

NESS essentially makes two complaints about the abstractions analysis of the trial judge. First, there is a generalized criticism that he erred when he "proceeded to examine the similarities in the highest level of abstraction (the functions performed) between Autoskill and NESS' programs." Appellant's Brief at 32.

We disagree. As noted, we feel that the judge used a permissible method of analysis and reached reasonable conclusions, although we are not deciding which precise method of analysis should be followed in a final copyright decision. Under the abstractions analysis outlined in *Altai* a judge essentially retraces, in reverse order, the steps taken by the program's designer, beginning with the code and ending with the program's ultimate function. *Altai,* 982 F.2d at 707. It is true that the trial judge's analysis and conclusions here do not reveal precisely the abstractions analysis outlined in *Altai,* cited by both NESS and Autoskill. However, we feel we should focus on the court's findings and conclusions, and his resulting ruling on protectable areas of expression, rather than on the precise method of analysis the judge used.

We are not persuaded at this preliminary injunction stage that the judge's rulings should be reversed simply because of a lack of any particular detail in his analysis. *See Altai,* 982 F.2d at 714 ("While the facts of a different case might require that a district court draw a more particularized blueprint of a program's overall structure, this description is a workable one for the case at hand."). Moreover, we find no persuasive presentation by NESS of any conflicting abstractions analysis which was presented below. We feel the record amply supports the judge's conclusions made as to the nonprotectable and protectable features of the Autoskill program for the purposes of a preliminary injunction.

We are convinced that the record furnishes an ample factual basis for the trial judge's analysis on the levels of abstraction and his conclusions as to which were idea levels not entitled to protection, and which were in the expression area and possibly eligible for protection after filtration analysis. There was detailed testimony by Autoskill's expert, Dr. Olson, that recognized the highest two levels of abstraction demonstrated in Autoskill's Exhibit AC,

Appellee's Supp.App. at 319, as unprotectable idea levels. Dr. Olson explained that it was below the highest two levels of abstraction that "we are starting to get into some very specific aspects of expression of those top two level ideas." Appellee's Supp.App. at 157. As the judge noted, the experts' opinions may be helpful, but their legal conclusions on these points are not binding. 793 F.Supp. at 1570. The consideration of the experts' views on these matters in drawing the judge's conclusions was within his discretion and not error. *Altai,* 982 F.2d at 713–14.

Second, NESS argues that the judge erroneously prevented the use by others of educational processes, methods and procedures, Appellant's Brief at 23–25, citing 17 U.S.C. § 102(b) and its provision that copyright protection does not extend to "any idea, procedure, or process, [or] system...." We are not persuaded. The judge explicitly dealt with § 102(b) and pointed out that more than literal application of the statute is required. *See Toro Co. v. R & R Prods. Co.,* 787 F.2d 1208, 1211–12 (8th Cir.1986). He faced up to the need to deal with the idea/expression dichotomy, appropriately analyzing the dichotomy as discussed in *Baker v. Selden.* 793 F.Supp. at 1564. In his abstractions analysis and conclusions he excluded from protection the highest two levels of abstraction in the Autoskill program, as we have noted above, and left only the lower levels for further consideration in his filtration discussion and possible protection.

In sum, we are not convinced that NESS has demonstrated any reversible error in the trial judge's abstractions analysis. For purposes of review of a preliminary injunction, on this issue we feel that Autoskill has shown a substantial likelihood of success.

2. The Filtration Analysis

Under the second step of his analysis—filtration—the judge considered whether any of the expression of the Autoskill program should be excluded from copyright protection. The step requires that a court examine the program's "structural components at each level of abstraction" to determine whether they are excludable under traditional copyright doctrines. *Altai,* 982 F.2d at 707. By removing unprotected expression from the analysis, the filtration step "serves 'the purpose of defining the scope of plaintiff's copyright.' " 982 F.2d at 707 (quoting *Brown Bag Software v. Symantec Corp.,* 960 F.2d 1465, 1475 (9th Cir.1992)); *see* 3 *Nimmer* § 13.03[C], at 13–71.

Applying the related copyright doctrines of merger and scènes à faire, the judge filtered out two aspects of the Autoskill program. The merger doctrine excludes expression from copyright protection if it is "merged" inseparably with an idea. 3 *Nimmer* § 13.03[B][3], at 13–65. The judge filtered out the 13 categories of vowel and consonant combinations used in the Autoskill program because he concluded they were an aspect of expression that is dictated by teaching reading in English, and thus is merged with the idea of the reading program. 793 F.Supp. at 1568.

The judge also addressed whether any aspects of the expression in the Autoskill program were merged with the idea of testing and training the three subtypes of readers, and thus were nonprotectable. The judge found "no evidence that the idea of testing, diagnosing and training the particular sub-types could be expressed in only one way." *Id.* at 1560. The judge also found that the "idea of testing, diagnosing and training the particular sub-types is capable of being expressed in more than one way." *Id.* Thus the judge held that the idea of the Autoskill program for testing, diagnosing, and training the three subtypes need not be denied copyright protection under the merger doctrine. *Id.* at 1567.

NESS does not specifically challenge the judge's factual findings on merger, but instead makes a general argument that the judge's ruling conflicts with the merger doctrine. Appellant's Brief at 33. We are not persuaded by this unsupported, vague argument and feel that the judge's findings were not clearly erroneous and that he properly concluded he should deny exclusion on the merger theory.

The scènes à faire doctrine in general excludes from copyright protection material that is "standard," "stock," or "common" to a particular topic, or that "necessarily follow[s] from a common theme or setting." 3 *Nimmer* § 13.03[B][4], at 13–70. Applying this doctrine, the judge also filtered out the "silent sentence" and "silent paragraph" components of the Autoskill program because he concluded they were "so standard to the field that they cannot be afforded protection." 793 F.Supp. at 1568.

NESS further contends that the trial judge erred in the filtration analysis by not finding that the components of the Autoskill program at issue were either scènes à faire matter, or were taken from the public domain. Any components of the program that were taken from the public domain would be "free for the taking." *Altai,* 982 F.2d at 710. "It is axiomatic that material in the public domain is not protected by copyright, even when incorporated into a copyrighted work." 3 *Nimmer* § 13.03[F][4], at 13–98. NESS contends that features of the Autoskill program sought to be protected were taken from the Doehring study upon which the Autoskill program was based and were common and obvious methods of testing subjects. Appellant's Brief at 34–37.

Autoskill argues in response that its program involves substantial additional elements constituting original expression as shown by the testimony of Dr. Olson and Dr. Moya on the uniqueness of the Autoskill program, and by the testimony of Dr. Trites and Dr. Fiedorowicz on necessary changes and differences from Doehring's approach. Appellee's Brief at 42–43.

The trial judge did not discuss the public domain issue in those precise terms, but he made findings dealing with the substance of this contention. His findings stated that he was persuaded by the testimony of Dr. Olson and Dr. Moya. He cited their testimony on the many unique aspects of the Autoskill program and found that the opposing testimony of Dr. Norton of lack of uniqueness of the Autoskill program was less convincing than that of Dr. Olson and Dr. Moya. 793 F.Supp. at 1561 (findings Nos. 53, 54).

One of Autoskill's witnesses, Dr. Trites, explained that Autoskill did not simply use Dr. Doehring's theories in a computerized form, but instead had to make "significant changes" to Dr. Doehring's techniques to develop effective training programs. Appellee's Supp.App. at 24. As an example of the process used in developing the Autoskill program, Dr. Trites explained that the original Autoskill testing to determine the reading subtypes was dependent on having a touch-sensitive screen on the computer. He further explained that the Autoskill system did not simply involve touching keys 1, 2, or 3, but involved looking at the word on the screen and responding with hands on the keyboard, a system that took considerable investigation and research staff work, and also that of statisticians and programmers. *Id.* at 25. This testimony shows that the Autoskill program was unique and was not drawn directly from the Doehring research.

As to uniqueness, Dr. Trites testified that the Autoskill program tested for 39 subskills, which were not the same subskills tested in the Doehring research. Dr. Trites testified that the NESS program used the same 39 subskills, which was not necessary because there were thousands of possible choices that could have been made. For example, he pointed out that while Autoskill used "CVCC" syllables, other skills could have been selected. *Id.* at 27.

Another witness whose testimony was relevant to uniqueness, Dr. Moya, explained that there was uniqueness in the Autoskill program in the manner in which it used the computer to record mastery and speed of response. The automaticity theory that Autoskill utilizes was not found in the other software programs. Dr. Moya also pointed to their manner of continuous reinforcement of the students, offering 50 trials to reinforce a student's response, as unique. He also mentioned Autoskill's presentation of graphs and its immediate feedback which was not found in other software programs. *Id.* at 267. In addition, he described the way that Autoskill assessed the abilities of students and divided them into three distinct subtypes, and then prescribed training according to those subtypes. In reporting to the superintendent, the committee considered this uniqueness of the Autoskill program in its recommendation, feeling that they had finally located a software program that was going to impact the reading instructional program in their school system and in their southwest area where reading scores are very low. *Id.* at 268–69.

As another point of departure from the Doehring research, Dr. Trites explained that the Autoskill program emphasized errors as being more important than latency, a decision based on years of research. *Id.* at 28. Also, Dr. Trites testified that the Autoskill program contained unique aspects in assessing the subtypes of readers; to his knowledge, no programs other than Autoskill do a diagnostic assessment for a profile indicating a subtype of reading difficulty. *Id.* at 35.

Turning to NESS' witnesses, Dr. Norton testified that she operated the Autoskill program for at least an hour. Appellee's Supp.App. at 250. She was asked about the subtype approach as defined by Doehring and Hoshko. She said she knew that concept through the learning disabilities literature and "that there are learner characteristics or subskills to the overall word recognition that draw a different perceptual strength." *Id.* at 253. She agreed that in other reading software she was aware of there is no norm of using the zero and one keys in the same way that they are used in the Autoskill and NESS programs. *Id.* at 256. She also said there are no other marketed programs that pursue a sequence of 13, 14, or 15 skill patterns using sense and nonsense words; but she explained that there was software around that used the sense and nonsense words and Dr. Norton herself designed a program to teach the patterns they were talking about in 1980 or 1981. She found a lack of interest in it because some publishers she contacted "did not see computers in the schools...." *Id.* at 257–58.

We note that the trial judge accepted Dr. Olson's testimony that no other programs of which he was aware used alternating sense and nonsense words. 793 F.Supp. at 1569. In light of the uncertainty in Dr. Norton's testimony on the point we cannot say the judge's acceptance of Olson's testimony was clearly erroneous.

Thus the judge heard considerable testimony that suggests that the Autoskill program was not identical to the testing outlined in the Doehring study. We feel that this evidence refutes NESS' argument that the Autoskill program was taken entirely from the public domain or was so standard to the topic as to be unprotectable scènes à faire material.

NESS also contends that the oral reading test in the Autoskill program is not subject to copyright protection because it is the equivalent of using flash cards, a method which it argues is taken from the public domain or is akin to scènes à faire material. In support of the argument NESS refers, in part, to testimony comparing the "visual training mode" of the Autoskill program to "a computerized version of a human presenting flash cards and holding them up." Appellant's App. at 358. NESS' generalized complaints are not supported by substantial evidence that the Autoskill oral reading test contained no original expression.

In sum, we are convinced that the expert testimony and the exhibits furnish a substantial basis for the trial judge's conclusion that there are protectable elements in the Autoskill program that survive the filtration process.

3. The Comparison

Finally, after conducting an analysis to filter out the nonprotectable material, the judge attempted to compare the remaining "core" of material, the copyrightable expression. *See* 3 *Nimmer* § 13.03[F], at 13–99. "Once a court has sifted out all elements of the allegedly infringed program which are 'ideas' or are [other unprotected material], there may remain a core of protectable expression." *Altai,* 982 F.2d at 710. The analysis at this point "poses essentially a value judgment, involving an assessment of the importance of the material that was copied." 3 *Nimmer* § 13.03[F], at 13–102; *see Altai,* 982 F.2d at 710.

NESS concedes "there are many similarities in the two programs," but contends that after filtration there is no protectable expression remaining to compare. Reply Brief of Appellant at 18. Having rejected NESS' arguments concerning the filtration step, we disagree. We think the judge, after his comparison analysis, had an adequate basis for observing "many significant similarities" in the protectable aspects of the Autoskill program and the allegedly infringing NESS program. 793 F.Supp. at 1569.

The judge identified similarities in the three basic tests used in the programs. The judge concluded that in the oral reading tests in both programs, "a word or words come up on the screen and the student attempts to read it orally" and both programs "require a trainer to decide whether or not the word is read correctly and to record speed and accuracy into the computer." The judge concluded that in the auditory visual matching test, or audio identification test, in both programs "three word choices appear on the screen and an auditory stimulus of a target word or nonsense word is presented to the student. The student must select which word he hears and indicate his response by hitting the 1, 2 or 3 key." *Id.* In the visual match, or visual identification, test in both programs, the judge concluded, "the screen displays four words or nonsense words. The target word is isolated from the other words and the student is expected to choose one of the remaining three words which is identical to the target word." *Id.*

The judge noted that both programs use alternating words and nonsense words. The judge concluded that both programs record speed, or latency of response, and accuracy data and use the information in the same manner. *Id.* Further, the judge concluded that in both programs the students are trained according to the same three testing topics. In both programs, the judge noted, students receive immediate feedback about accuracy. The judge concluded that the criteria for a student's progressing to the next subprogram is similar in both programs. Further, the judge noted that in both programs: the presentation of skills proceeds hierarchically from the simple to the complex; a visual scanning test is administered in combination with the other tests to determine the student's subtype; matrices record student progress within each section; and graphs are used for the same purposes. *Id.*

To show lack of similarity of the Autoskill and NESS programs, a prime witness for NESS was Mr. Johnson–Laird. The trial judge noted his strong background in computer software but said he has no background in the area of reading education or its software. *Id.* at 1561. Johnson–Laird's testimony particularly sought to prove lack of similarity between the NESS and Autoskill programs. He presented charts showing differences in logic flow between the display screens of both programs.

We have examined the testimony of Mr. Johnson–Laird on these points, *e.g.,* Appellant's App. at 317–328, and Ex. 10, photographs of the program screens, *id.* at 473–78, used in his testimony. He said the Autoskill screen does have elements, similar to that of NESS, that were arguably protectable, Appellant's App. at 397, identifying "the matrices here, when you take them as an entire entity." *Id.* at 398; *see also id.* at 400–401. He said, however, that there was not substantial similarity in the look and feel of the Autoskill and NESS screens, stressing the way NESS uses color. *Id.* at 401–03. He referred also to the fact that in the NESS program, one's voice could be recorded and played back, which was not done on the Autoskill program. *Id.* at 442.

The judge explained that he rejected NESS' suggestions of differences because the differences (color in NESS' program absent in Autoskill's, word choices appearing in phases in NESS' program while those on the Autoskill screen appear at the same time) were not important or substantial parts of Autoskill's program. The judge gave greater weight to Dr. Olson's testimony that the differences were not pedagogically significant. 793 F.Supp. at 1570–71. We are satisfied the judge's crediting of the Autoskill witness' testimony over that of NESS' witness was not clearly erroneous or an abuse of discretion.

In sum, we affirm the judge's conclusion that Autoskill satisfied its burden on the substantial similarity requirement for purposes of the preliminary injunction. Having satisfied its burden at this stage on both elements required to show copying—access and substantial similarity—Autoskill thus demonstrated a substantial likelihood of success on the merits. Our ruling, of course, is for purposes of the preliminary injunction alone and does not represent a final determination on the substantial similarity issue.

B. Irreparable Harm

The district judge held that Autoskill had made the requisite showing of irreparable harm on two alternative grounds. First, the judge applied the rule a leading commentary describes as the prevailing one in the circuits: a showing of a prima facie case of copyright infringement or of a reasonable likelihood of success on the merits usually raises a presumption of irreparable harm for preliminary injunction purposes. 3 *Nimmer* § 14.06[A], at 14–78.13 to –78.14; 793 F.Supp. at 1572. We need not decide whether to adopt that test because of the second ground on which the trial judge found irreparable injury—one that is independently sufficient.

In his second holding on irreparable injury, the judge cited testimony that from NESS' conduct, Autoskill "will suffer from a loss of uniqueness in the marketplace." 793 F.Supp. at 1572. The judge also noted testimony that if the NESS program produced poor results, "such results would affect Autoskill's reputation." *Id.* Further, the judge noted testimony that Autoskill "had no way of ascertaining how many customers were lost to NESS." *Id.* On the basis of this evidence, the judge held that Autoskill had demonstrated irreparable harm by presenting evidence that the NESS program "jeopardizes Autoskill's investment and competitive position and thus shows irreparable harm." *Id.*

We are satisfied that the judge's conclusion that a danger of irreparable harm was shown was not in error.

C. Balance of Hardships

Autoskill was also required to demonstrate that the injury it would sustain if the injunction did not issue outweighed the potential harm that the injunction would cause to NESS. *See Tri-State Generation & Transmission Ass'n, Inc. v. Shoshone River Power, Inc.*, 805 F.2d 351, 356–57 (10th Cir.1986). The district judge observed that while NESS argued that the injunction would have a devastating impact on its business, it presented no evidence to support the contention. 793 F.Supp. at 1572. However, even assuming the injunction would have such a devastating effect on NESS, the judge adopted the reasoning of other courts that "a knowing infringer cannot be 'permitted to construct its business around its infringement.' " *Id.* (quoting *Apple Computer, Inc. v. Franklin Computer Corp.*, 714 F.2d 1240, 1255 (3d Cir.1983)). Thus the judge made a primarily legal ruling on the factor.

Autoskill's burden on this factor was to demonstrate that the harm it would sustain without an injunction outweighed the potential harm of an injunction to NESS. Autoskill presented evidence that it would sustain at least some harm; under the usual application of the balancing test, the judge did not make it clear how this potential harm to Autoskill outweighed the harm it assumed NESS would sustain. Instead, the judge recognized that in the copyright context the four factors require sensitive weighing. Stated another way, the district judge adopted the view that the potential injury to an allegedly infringing party caused by an injunction "merits little equitable consideration and is insufficient to outweigh the continued wrongful infringement." *Georgia Television Co. v. TV News Clips of Atlanta, Inc.*, 718 F.Supp. 939, 949 (N.D.Ga.1989). We agree that placing too much weight on this factor would reward infringers. Under the law that the judge applied to the factor, which we rule was correct, Autoskill made a persuasive showing that the balance of the harms weighed in its favor.

D. The Public Interest

On the final factor, Autoskill was required to demonstrate that the issuance of the injunction was not adverse to the public interest. *See Tri-State Generation & Transmission Ass'n, Inc.,* 805 F.2d at 357. The district court implicitly addressed this factor by acknowledging that by granting an injunction it would uphold the rights of the copyright holder. 793 F.Supp. at 1572. In copyright cases, we think this factor normally weighs in favor of the issuance of an injunction because the public interest is the interest in upholding copyright protections. *See* 3 *Nimmer* § 14.06[A], at 14–80. The issuance of the injunction clearly was not adverse to the public interest.

IV. CONCLUSION

In sum, in his filtration analysis the district judge denied copyright protection to two aspects of the Autoskill program, the 13 categories, or skill levels, based on different combinations of vowels and consonants, as well as the "silent sentence" and "silent paragraph" components. 793 F.Supp. at 1568. Further, for the reasons already given, the judge gave preliminary injunctive relief against infringement, due to the likelihood of success which was shown, as to the essential aspects of the Autoskill program, including: the oral reading test; the auditory visual matching test; the visual match test; the visual scanning test; alternating words and nonsense words; utilization of speed and accuracy data; use of speed and accuracy criteria; and hierarchical presentation of skills. *Id.* at 1569.

We hold that we have appellate jurisdiction and the motion to dismiss the appeal is **DENIED.** We hold that the district judge's findings were not clearly erroneous, his grant of the preliminary injunction was not an abuse of discretion, and the injunctive order is **AFFIRMED.** The case is **REMANDED** for further proceedings.

MICRO STAR v. FORMGEN INC.
United States Court of Appeals for the Ninth Circuit
November 4, 1997, Argued and Submitted; September 11, 1998, Filed
No. 96-56426, No.96-56433
154 F.3d 1107
KOZINSKI, Circuit Judge.

Duke Nukem routinely vanquishes Octabrain and the Protozoid Slimer. But what about the dreaded Micro Star?

I

FormGen Inc., GT Interactive Software Corp. and Apogee Software, Ltd. (collectively FormGen) made, distributed and own the rights to Duke Nukem 3D (D/N-3D), an immensely popular (and very cool) computer game. D/N-3D is played from the first-person perspective; the player assumes the personality and point of view of the title character, who is seen on the screen only as a pair of hands and an occasional boot, much as one might see oneself in real life without the aid of a mirror. Players explore a futuristic city infested with evil aliens and other hazards. The goal is to zap them before they zap you, while searching for the hidden passage to the next level. The basic game comes with twenty-nine levels, each with a different combination of scenery, aliens, and other challenges. The game also includes a "Build Editor," a utility that enables players to create their own levels. With FormGen's encouragement, players frequently post levels they have created on the Internet where others can download them. Micro Star, a computer software distributor, did just that: It downloaded 300 user-created levels and stamped them onto a CD, which it then sold commercially as Nuke It (N/I). N/I is packaged in a box decorated with numerous "screen shots," pictures of what the new levels look like when played.

Micro Star filed suit in district court, seeking a declaratory judgment that N/I did not infringe on any of FormGen's copyrights. FormGen counterclaimed, seeking a preliminary injunction barring further production and distribution of N/I. Relying on *Lewis Galoob Toys, Inc. v. Nintendo of Am., Inc.,* 964 F.2d 965 (9th Cir.1992), the district court held that N/I was not a derivative work and therefore did not infringe FormGen's copyright. The district court did, however, grant a preliminary injunction as to the screen shots, finding that N/I's packaging violated FormGen's copyright by reproducing pictures of D/N-3D characters without a license. The court rejected Micro Star's fair use claims. Both sides appeal their losses.

II

A party seeking a preliminary injunction must show "either a likelihood of success on the merits and the possibility of irreparable injury, or that serious questions going to the merits were raised and the balance of hardships tips sharply in its favor." *Johnson Controls, Inc. v. Phoenix Control Systems, Inc.,* 886 F.2d 1173, 1174 (9th Cir.1989). Because "in a copyright infringement claim, a showing of a reasonable likelihood of success on the merits raises a presumption of irreparable harm," *id.,* FormGen need only show a likelihood of success on the merits to get the preliminary injunction it seeks (barring the manufacture and distribution of N/I) and to preserve the preliminary injunction it already won (barring the screen shots on N/I's packaging).

III

To succeed on the merits of its claim that N/I infringes FormGen's copyright, FormGen must show (1) ownership of the copyright to D/N-3D, and (2) copying of protected expression by Micro Star. *See Triad Systems Corp. v. Southeastern Express Co.,* 64 F.3d 1330, 1335 (9th Cir.1995). FormGen's copyright registration creates a presumption of ownership, *see id.,* and we are satisfied that FormGen has established its ownership of the copyright. We therefore focus on the latter issue.

FormGen alleges that its copyright is infringed by Micro Star's unauthorized commercial exploitation of user-created game levels. In order to understand FormGen's claims, one must first understand the way D/N-3D works. The game consists of three separate components: the game engine, the source art library and the MAP files. The game engine is the heart of the computer program; in some sense, it *is* the program. It tells the computer when to read data, save and load games, play sounds and project images onto the screen. In order to create the audiovisual display for a particular level, the game engine invokes the MAP file that corresponds to that level. Each MAP file contains a series of instructions that tell the game engine (and, through it, the computer) what to put where. For instance, the MAP file might say scuba gear goes at the bottom of the screen. The game engine then goes to the source art library, finds the image of the scuba gear, and puts it in just the right place on the screen. The MAP file describes the level in painstaking detail, but it does not actually contain any of the copyrighted art itself; everything that appears on the screen actually comes from the art library. Think of the game's audiovisual display as a paint-by-numbers kit. The MAP file might tell you to put blue paint in section number 565, but it doesn't contain any blue paint itself; the blue paint comes from your palette, which is the low-tech analog of the art library, while you play the role of the game engine. When the player selects one of the N/I levels, the game engine references the N/I MAP files, but still uses the D/N-3D art library to generate the images that make up that level.

FormGen points out that a copyright holder enjoys the exclusive right to prepare derivative works based on D/N-3D. *See* 17 U.S.C. § 106(2) (1994). According to FormGen, the audiovisual displays generated when D/N-3D is run in conjunction with the N/I CD MAP files are derivative works that infringe this exclusivity. Is FormGen right? The answer is not obvious.

The Copyright Act defines a derivative work as

> a work based upon one or more preexisting works, such as a translation, musical arrangement, dramatization, fictionalization, motion picture version, sound recording, art reproduction, abridgment, condensation, or any other form in which a work may be recast, transformed, or adapted. A work consisting of editorial revisions, annotations, elaborations, or other modifications which, as a whole, represent an original work of authorship, is a "derivative work."

Id. § 101. The statutory language is hopelessly overbroad, however, for "[e]very book in literature, science and art, borrows and must necessarily borrow, and use much which was well known and used before." *Emerson v. Davies,* 8 F. Cas. 615, 619 (C.C.D.Mass.1845) (No. 4436), *quoted in 1 Nimmer on Copyright,* § 3.01, at 3–2 (1997). To narrow the statute to a manageable level, we have developed certain criteria a work must satisfy in order to qualify as a derivative work. One of these is that a derivative work must exist in a "concrete or permanent form," *Galoob,* 964 F.2d at 967 (internal quotation marks omitted), and must substantially incorporate protected material from the preexisting work, *see Litchfield v. Spielberg,* 736 F.2d 1352, 1357 (9th Cir.1984). Micro Star argues that N/I is not a derivative work because the audiovisual displays generated when D/N-3D is run with N/I's MAP files are not incorporated in any concrete or permanent form, and the MAP files do not copy any of D/N-3D's protected expression. It is mistaken on both counts.

The requirement that a derivative work must assume a concrete or permanent form was recognized without much discussion in *Galoob.* There, we noted that all the Copyright Act's examples of derivative works took some definite, physical form and concluded that this was a requirement of the Act. *See Galoob,* 964 F.2d at 967–68; *see also* Edward G. Black & Michael H. Page, *Add-On Infringements,* 15 Hastings Comm/Ent. L.J. 615, 625 (1993) (noting that in *Galoob* the Ninth Circuit "re-examined the statutory definition of derivative works offered in section 101 and found an independent fixation requirement of sorts built into the statutory definition of derivative works"). Obviously, N/I's MAP files themselves exist in a concrete or permanent form; they are burned onto a CD-ROM. *See ProCD, Inc. v. Zeidenberg,* 86 F.3d 1447, 1453 (7th Cir.1996) (computer files on a CD are fixed in a tangible medium of expression). But what about the audiovisual displays generated when D/N-3D runs the N/I MAP files—

i.e., the actual game level as displayed on the screen? Micro Star argues that, because the audiovisual displays in *Galoob* didn't meet the "concrete or permanent form" requirement, neither do N/I's.

In *Galoob,* we considered audiovisual displays created using a device called the Game Genie, which was sold for use with the Nintendo Entertainment System. The Game Genie allowed players to alter individual features of a game, such as a character's strength or speed, by selectively "blocking the value for a single data byte sent by the game cartridge to the [Nintendo console] and replacing it with a new value." *Galoob,* 964 F.2d at 967. Players chose which data value to replace by entering a code; over a billion different codes were possible. The Game Genie was dumb; it functioned only as a window into the computer program, allowing players to temporarily modify individual aspects of the game. *See Lewis Galoob Toys, Inc. v. Nintendo of Am., Inc.,* 780 F.Supp. 1283, 1289 (N.D.Cal.1991).

Nintendo sued, claiming that when the Game Genie modified the game system's audiovisual display, it created an infringing derivative work. We rejected this claim because "[a] derivative work must incorporate a protected work in some concrete or permanent form." *Galoob,* 964 F.2d at 967 (internal quotation marks omitted). The audiovisual displays generated by combining the Nintendo System with the Game Genie were not incorporated in any permanent form; when the game was over, they were gone. Of course, they could be reconstructed, but only if the next player chose to reenter the same codes.

Micro Star argues that the MAP files on N/I are a more advanced version of the Game Genie, replacing old values (the MAP files in the original game) with new values (N/I's MAP files). But, whereas the audiovisual displays created by Game Genie were never recorded in any permanent form, the audiovisual displays generated by D/N-3D from the N/I MAP files are in the MAP files themselves. In *Galoob,* the audiovisual display was defined by the original game cartridge, not by the Game Genie; no one could possibly say that the data values inserted by the Game Genie described the audiovisual display. In the present case the audiovisual display that appears on the computer monitor when a N/I level is played is described—in exact detail—by a N/I MAP file.

This raises the interesting question whether an exact, down to the last detail, description of an audiovisual display (and—by definition—we know that MAP files do describe audiovisual displays down to the last detail) counts as a permanent or concrete form for purposes of *Galoob.* We see no reason it shouldn't. What, after all, does sheet music do but describe in precise detail the way a copyrighted melody sounds? *See* 1 William F. Patry, *Copyright Law and Practice* 168 (1994) ("[A] musical composition may be embodied in sheet music...."). To be copyrighted, pantomimes and dances may be "described in sufficient detail to enable the work to be performed from that description." *Id.* at 243 (citing *Compendium II of Copyright Office Practices* § 463); *see also*

Horgan v. Macmillan, Inc., 789 F.2d 157, 160 (2d Cir.1986). Similarly, the N/I MAP files describe the audiovisual display that is to be generated when the player chooses to play D/N-3D using the N/I levels. Because the audiovisual displays assume a concrete or permanent form in the MAP files, *Galoob* stands as no bar to finding that they are derivative works.

In addition, "[a] work will be considered a derivative work only if it would be considered an infringing work if the material which it has derived from a preexisting work had been taken without the consent of a copyright proprietor of such preexisting work." *Mirage Editions v. Albuquerque A.R.T. Co.,* 856 F.2d 1341, 1343 (quoting 1 *Nimmer on Copyright* § 3.01 (1986)) (internal quotation marks omitted). "To prove infringement, [FormGen] must show that [D/N-3D's and N/I's audiovisual displays] are substantially similar in both ideas and expression." *Litchfield v. Spielberg,* 736 F.2d 1352, 1356 (9th Cir.1984) (emphasis omitted). Similarity of ideas may be shown by comparing the objective details of the works: plot, theme, dialogue, mood, setting, characters, etc. *See id.* Similarity of expression focuses on the response of the ordinary reasonable person, and considers the total concept and feel of the works. *See id.* at 1356–57. FormGen will doubtless succeed in making these showings since the audiovisual displays generated when the player chooses the N/I levels come entirely out of D/N-3D's source art library. *Cf. Atari, Inc. v. North Am. Philips Consumer Elec. Corp.,* 672 F.2d 607, 620 (7th Cir.1982) (finding two video games substantially similar because they shared the same "total concept and feel").

Micro Star further argues that the MAP files are not derivative works because they do not, in fact, incorporate any of D/N-3D's protected expression. In particular, Micro Star makes much of the fact that the N/I MAP files reference the source art library, but do not actually contain any art files themselves. Therefore, it claims, nothing of D/N-3D's is reproduced in the MAP files. In making this argument, Micro Star misconstrues the protected work. The work that Micro Star infringes is the D/N-3D story itself—a beefy commando type named Duke who wanders around post-Apocalypse Los Angeles, shooting Pig Cops with a gun, lobbing hand grenades, searching for medkits and steroids, using a jetpack to leap over obstacles, blowing up gas tanks, avoiding radioactive slime. A copyright owner holds the right to create sequels, *see Trust Co. Bank v. MGM/UA Entertainment Co.,* 772 F.2d 740 (11th Cir.1985), and the stories told in the N/I MAP files are surely sequels, telling new (though somewhat repetitive) tales of Duke's fabulous adventures. A book about Duke Nukem would infringe for the same reason, even if it contained no pictures.

Micro Star nonetheless claims that its use of D/N-3D's protected expression falls within the doctrine of fair use, which permits unauthorized use of copyrighted works "for purposes such as criticism, comment, news reporting, teaching (including multiple copies for classroom use), scholarship, or research." 17 U.S.C. § 107; *see Narell v. Freeman,* 872 F.2d 907, 913 (9th Cir.1989). Section

107 instructs courts "determining whether the use made of a work in any particular case is a fair use" to consider four factors: (1) the purpose and character of the use, including whether it is commercial in nature; (2) the nature of the copyrighted work; (3) the amount and substantiality of the copied material in relation to the copyrighted work as a whole; and (4) the effect of the use on the potential market for the copyrighted work. 17 U.S.C. § 107.

As a preliminary matter, Micro Star asks us to focus on the player's use of the N/I CD in evaluating the fair use claim, because-according to Micro Star-the player actually creates the derivative work. In *Galoob,* after we assumed for purposes of argument that the Game Genie did create derivative works, we went on to consider the fair use defense from the player's point of view. *See Galoob,* 964 F.2d at 970. But the fair use analysis in *Galoob* was not necessary and therefore is clearly dicta. More significantly, Nintendo alleged only contributory infringement—that Galoob was helping consumers create derivative works; FormGen here alleges direct infringement by Micro Star, because the MAP files encompass new Duke stories, which are themselves derivative works.

Our examination of the section 107 factors yields straightforward results. Micro Star's use of FormGen's protected expression was made purely for financial gain. While that does not end our inquiry, *see Campbell v. Acuff–Rose Music, Inc.,* 510 U.S. 569, 584, 114 S.Ct. 1164, 127 L.Ed.2d 500 (1994), "every commercial use of copyrighted material is presumptively an unfair exploitation of the monopoly privilege that belongs to the owner of the copyright." *Sony Corp. of Am. v. Universal City Studios, Inc.,* 464 U.S. 417, 451, 104 S.Ct. 774, 78 L.Ed.2d 574 (1984). The Supreme Court has explained that the second factor, the nature of the copyrighted work, is particularly significant because "some works are closer to the core of intended copyright protection than others, with the consequence that fair use is more difficult to establish when the former works are copied." *Campbell,* 510 U.S. at 586, 114 S.Ct. 1164. The fair use defense will be much less likely to succeed when it is applied to fiction or fantasy creations, as opposed to factual works such as telephone listings. *See United Tel. Co. v. Johnson Publ'g Co.,* 855 F.2d 604, 609 (8th Cir.1988); *see also Stewart v. Abend,* 495 U.S. 207, 237, 110 S.Ct. 1750, 109 L.Ed.2d 184 (1990). Duke Nukem's world is made up of aliens, radioactive slime and freezer weapons-clearly fantasies, even by Los Angeles standards. N/I MAP files "expressly use[ ] the [D/N-3D] story's unique setting, characters, [and] plot," *Stewart,* 495 U.S. at 238, 110 S.Ct. 1750; both the quantity and importance of the material Micro Star used are substantial. Finally, by selling N/I, Micro Star "impinged on [FormGen's] ability to market new versions of the [D/N-3D] story." *Stewart,* 495 U.S. at 238, 110 S.Ct. 1750; *see also Twin Peaks Productions, Inc. v. Publications Int'l, Ltd.,* 996 F.2d 1366, 1377 (2d Cir.1993). Only FormGen has the right to enter that market; whether it chooses to do so is entirely its business. "[N/I] neither falls into any of the categories enumerated in section 107 nor meets the four criteria set forth in section 107." *Stewart,* 495 U.S. at 237, 110 S.Ct. 1750. It is not protected by fair use.

Micro Star also argues that it is the beneficiary of the implicit license FormGen gave to its customers by authorizing them to create new levels. Section 204 of the Copyright Act requires the transfer of the exclusive rights granted to copyright owners (including the right to prepare derivative works) to be in writing. *See* 17 U.S.C. § 204(a); *Effects Assocs., Inc. v. Cohen,* 908 F.2d 555, 556 (9th Cir.1990). A nonexclusive license may, however, be granted orally or implied by conduct. *See Effects,* 908 F.2d at 558. Nothing indicates that FormGen granted Micro Star any written license at all; nor is there evidence of a nonexclusive oral license. The only written license FormGen conceivably granted was to players who designed their own new levels, but that license contains a significant limitation: Any new levels the players create "must be offered [to others] solely for free." The parties dispute whether the license is binding, but it doesn't matter. If the license is valid, it clearly prohibits commercial distribution of levels; if it doesn't, FormGen hasn't granted any written licenses at all.

In case FormGen didn't license away its rights, Micro Star argues that, by providing the Build Editor and encouraging players to create their own levels, FormGen abandoned all rights to its protected expression. It is well settled that rights gained under the Copyright Act may be abandoned. But abandonment of a right must be manifested by some overt act indicating an intention to abandon that right. *See Hampton v. Paramount Pictures Corp.,* 279 F.2d 100, 104 (9th Cir.1960). Given that it overtly encouraged players to make and freely distribute new levels, FormGen may indeed have abandoned its exclusive right to do the same. But abandoning some rights is not the same as abandoning all rights, and FormGen never overtly abandoned its rights to profit commercially from new levels. Indeed, FormGen warned players not to distribute the levels commercially and has actively enforced that limitation by bringing suits such as this one.

IV

Because FormGen will likely succeed at trial in proving that Micro Star has infringed its copyright, we reverse the district court's order denying a preliminary injunction and remand for entry of such an injunction. Of course, we affirm the grant of the preliminary injunction barring Micro Star from selling N/I in boxes covered with screen shots of the game.

AFFIRMED in part, REVERSED in part, and REMANDED. Micro Star to bear costs of both appeals.

RECORDING INDUS. ASS'N OF AM. v. DIAMOND MULTIMEDIA SYS.
United States Court of Appeals for the Ninth Circuit
April 15, 1999, Argued and Submitted; June 15, 1999, Filed
No. 98-56727
180 F.3d 1072

O'SCANNLAIN, Circuit Judge:

In this case involving the intersection of computer technology, the Internet, and music listening, we must decide whether the Rio portable music player is a digital audio recording device subject to the restrictions of the Audio Home Recording Act of 1992.

I

This appeal arises from the efforts of the Recording Industry Association of America and the Alliance of Artists and Recording Companies (collectively, "RIAA") to enjoin the manufacture and distribution by Diamond Multimedia Systems ("Diamond") of the Rio portable music player. The Rio is a small device (roughly the size of an audio cassette) with headphones that allows a user to download MP3 audio files from a computer and to listen to them elsewhere. The dispute over the Rio's design and function is difficult to comprehend without an understanding of the revolutionary new method of music distribution made possible by digital recording and the Internet; thus, we will explain in some detail the brave new world of Internet music distribution.

A

The introduction of digital audio recording to the consumer electronics market in the 1980's is at the root of this litigation. Before then, a person wishing to copy an original music recording—e.g., wishing to make a cassette tape of a record or compact disc—was limited to analog, rather than digital, recording technology. With analog recording, each successive generation of copies suffers from an increasingly pronounced degradation in sound quality. For example, when an analog cassette copy of a record or compact disc is itself copied by analog technology, the resulting "second-generation" copy of the original will most likely suffer from the hiss and lack of clarity characteristic of older recordings. With digital recording, by contrast, there is almost no degradation in sound quality, no matter how many generations of copies are made. Digital copying thus allows thousands of perfect or near perfect copies (and copies of copies) to be made from a single original recording. Music "pirates" use digital recording technology to make and to distribute near perfect copies of commercially prepared recordings for which they have not licensed the copyrights.

Until recently, the Internet was of little use for the distribution of music because the average music computer file was simply too big: the digital information on a single compact disc of music required hundreds of computer floppy discs to store, and downloading even a single song from the Internet took hours. However, various compression algorithms (which make an audio file "smaller" by limiting the audio bandwidth) now allow digital audio files to be transferred more quickly and stored more efficiently. MPEG-1 Audio Layer 3 (commonly known as "MP3") is the most popular digital audio compression algorithm in use on the Internet, and the compression it provides makes an audio file "smaller" by a factor of twelve to one without significantly reducing sound quality. MP3's popularity is due in large part to the fact that it is a standard, non-proprietary compression algorithm freely available for use by anyone, unlike various proprietary (and copyright-secure) competitor algorithms. Coupled with the use of cable modems, compression algorithms like MP3 may soon allow an hour of music to be downloaded from the Internet to a personal computer in just a few minutes.

These technological advances have occurred, at least in part, to the traditional music industry's disadvantage. By most accounts, the predominant use of MP3 is the trafficking in illicit audio recordings, presumably because MP3 files do not contain codes identifying whether the compressed audio material is copyright protected. Various pirate websites offer free downloads of copyrighted material, and a single pirate site on the Internet may contain thousands of pirated audio computer files.

RIAA represents the roughly half-dozen major record companies (and the artists on their labels) that control approximately ninety percent of the distribution of recorded music in the United States. RIAA asserts that Internet distribution of serial digital copies of pirated copyrighted material will discourage the purchase of legitimate recordings, and predicts that losses to digital Internet piracy will soon surpass the $300 million that is allegedly lost annually to other more traditional forms of piracy. RIAA fights a well-nigh constant battle against Internet piracy, monitoring the Internet daily, and routinely shutting down pirate websites by sending cease-and-desist letters and bringing lawsuits. There are conflicting views on RIAA's success—RIAA asserts that it can barely keep up with the pirate traffic, while others assert that few, if any, pirate sites remain in operation in the United States and illicit files are difficult to find and download from anywhere online.

In contrast to piracy, the Internet also supports a burgeoning traffic in legitimate audio computer files. Independent and wholly Internet record labels routinely sell and provide free samples of their artists' work online, while many unsigned artists distribute their own material from their own websites. Some free samples are provided for marketing purposes or for simple exposure, while others are teasers intended to entice listeners to purchase either mail order recordings or recordings available for direct download (along with album cover art, lyrics, and artist biographies). Diamond cites a 1998 "Music Industry and the Internet" report by Jupiter Communications which predicts that online sales for pre-recorded music will exceed $1.4 billion by 2002 in the United States alone.

Prior to the invention of devices like the Rio, MP3 users had little option other than to listen to their downloaded digital audio files through headphones or speakers at their computers, playing them from their hard drives. The Rio renders these files portable. More precisely, once an audio file has been downloaded onto a computer hard drive from the Internet or some other source (such as a compact disc player or digital audio tape machine), separate computer software provided with the Rio (called "Rio Manager") allows the user further to download the file to the Rio itself via a parallel port cable that plugs the Rio into the computer. The Rio device is incapable of effecting such a transfer, and is incapable of receiving audio files from anything other than a personal computer equipped with Rio Manager.

Generally, the Rio can store approximately one hour of music, or sixteen hours of spoken material (e.g., downloaded newscasts or books on tape). With the addition of flash memory cards, the Rio can store an additional half-hour or hour of music. The Rio's sole output is an analog audio signal sent to the user via headphones. The Rio cannot make duplicates of any digital audio file it stores, nor can it transfer or upload such a file to a computer, to another device, or to the Internet. However, a flash memory card to which a digital audio file has been downloaded can be removed from one Rio and played back in another.

B

RIAA brought suit to enjoin the manufacture and distribution of the Rio, alleging that the Rio does not meet the requirements for digital audio recording devices under the Audio Home Recording Act of 1992, 17 U.S.C. § 1001 *et seq.* (the "Act"), because it does not employ a Serial Copyright Management System ("SCMS") that sends, receives, and acts upon information about the generation and copyright status of the files that it plays. *See id.* § 1002(a)(2). RIAA also sought payment of the royalties owed by Diamond as the manufacturer and distributor of a digital audio recording device. *See id.* § 1003.

The district court denied RIAA's motion for a preliminary injunction, holding that RIAA's likelihood of success on the merits was mixed and the balance of hardships did not tip in RIAA's favor.

II

The initial question presented is whether the Rio falls within the ambit of the Act. The Act does not broadly prohibit digital serial copying of copyright protected audio recordings. Instead, the Act places restrictions only upon a specific type of recording device. Most relevant here, the Act provides that "[n]o person shall import, manufacture, or distribute any *digital audio recording device* ... that does not conform to the Serial Copy Management System ["SCMS"] [or] a system that has the same functional characteristics." 17 U.S.C. § 1002(a)(1), (2) (emphasis added). The Act further provides that "[n]o person shall import into and distribute, or manufacture and distribute, any *digital audio recording device* ... unless such person records the notice specified by this section and subsequently deposits the statements of account and applicable royalty payments." *Id.* § 1003(a) (emphasis added). Thus, to fall within the SCMS and royalty requirements in question, the Rio must be a "digital audio recording device," which the Act defines through a set of nested definitions.

The Act defines a "digital audio recording device" as:

> any machine or device of a type commonly distributed to individuals for use by individuals, whether or not included with or as part of some other machine or device, the digital recording function of which is designed or marketed for the primary purpose of, and that is capable of, making a *digital audio copied recording* for private use....

Id. § 1001(3) (emphasis added).

A "digital audio copied recording" is defined as:

> a reproduction in a digital recording format of a *digital musical recording,* whether that reproduction is made directly from another digital musical recording or indirectly from a transmission.

Id. § 1001(1) (emphasis added).

A "digital musical recording" is defined as:

> *a material object—*
> (i) in which are fixed, in a digital recording format, *only sounds, and material, statements, or instructions incidental to those fixed sounds,* if any, and
> (ii) from which the sounds and material can be perceived, reproduced, or otherwise communicated, either directly or with the aid of a machine or device.

Id. § 1001(5)(A) (emphasis added).

In sum, to be a digital audio recording device, the Rio must be able to reproduce, either "directly" or "from a transmission," a "digital music recording."

III

We first consider whether the Rio is able directly to reproduce a digital music recording—which is a specific type of material object in which only sounds are fixed (or material and instructions incidental to those sounds). *See id.*

A

The typical computer hard drive from which a Rio directly records is, of course, a material object. However, hard drives ordinarily contain much more than "only sounds, and material, statements, or instructions incidental to those fixed sounds." *Id.* Indeed, almost all hard drives contain numerous programs (e.g., for word processing, scheduling appointments, etc.) and databases that are not incidental to any sound files that may be stored on the hard drive. Thus, the Rio appears not to make copies from digital music recordings, and thus would not be a digital audio recording device under the Act's basic definition unless it makes copies from transmissions.

Moreover, the Act expressly provides that the term "digital musical recording" does not include:

> *a material object—*
>
> (i) in which the fixed sounds consist entirely of spoken word recordings, or
>
> (ii) *in which one or more computer programs are fixed,* except that a digital recording may contain statements or instructions constituting the fixed sounds and incidental material, and statements or instructions to be used directly or indirectly in order to bring about the perception, reproduction, or communication of the fixed sounds and incidental material.

Id. § 1001(5)(B) (emphasis added). As noted previously, a hard drive is a material object in which one or more programs are fixed; thus, a hard drive is excluded from the definition of digital music recordings. This provides confirmation that the Rio does not record "directly" from "digital music recordings," and therefore could not be a digital audio recording device unless it makes copies "from transmissions."

B

The district court rejected the exclusion of computer hard drives from the definition of digital music recordings under the statute's plain language[3] (after noting its "superficial appeal") because it concluded that such exclusion "is ultimately unsupported by the legislative history, and contrary to the spirit and purpose of the [Act]." *RIAA I,* 29 F.Supp.2d at 629. We need not resort to the legislative history because the statutory language is clear. *See City of Auburn v. United States,* 154 F.3d 1025, 1030 (9th Cir.1998) Nevertheless, we will address the legislative history here, because it is consistent with the statute's plain meaning and because the parties have briefed it so extensively.

1

The Senate Report states that "if the material object contains computer programs or data bases that are not incidental to the fixed sounds, then the material object would not qualify" under the basic definition of a digital musical recording. S. Rep. 102–294 (1992), *reprinted at* 1992 WL 133198, at *118–19. The Senate Report further states that the definition "is intended to cover those objects commonly understood to embody sound recordings and their underlying works." *Id.* at *97. A footnote makes explicit that this definition only extends to the material objects in which songs are normally fixed: "[t]hat is recorded compact discs, digital audio tapes, audio cassettes, long-playing albums, digital compact cassettes, and mini-discs." *Id.* at n. 36. There are simply no grounds in either the plain language of the definition or in the legislative history for interpreting the term "digital musical recording" to include songs fixed on computer hard drives.

RIAA contends that the legislative history reveals that the Rio does not fall within the specific exemption from the digital musical recording definition of "a material object in which one or more computer programs are fixed." 17 U.S.C. § 1001(5)(B)(ii). The House Report describes the exemption as "revisions reflecting exemptions for talking books and *computer programs.* " H.R. Rep. 102–873(I) (1992), *reprinted at* 1992 WL 232935, at *35 (emphasis added); *see also id.* at *44 ("In addition to containing an *express exclusion of computer programs* in the definition of 'digital musical recording'....") (emphasis added). We first note that limiting the exemption to computer programs is contrary to the plain meaning of the exemption. As Diamond points out, a computer program is not a material object, but rather, a literary work, *see, e.g., Apple Computer, Inc. v. Franklin Computer Corp.,* 714 F.2d 1240, 1249 (3d Cir.1983) ("[A] computer program ... is a 'literary work.' "), that can be fixed in a variety of material objects, *see* 17 U.S.C. § 101 (" 'Literary works' are works ... expressed in words, numbers, or other verbal or numerical symbols or indicia, *regardless of the nature of the material objects, such as books ... tapes, disks, or cards, in which they are embodied.*") (emphasis added). Thus, the plain language of the exemption at issue does not exclude the copying of programs from coverage by the Act, but instead, excludes copying from various types of material objects. Those objects include hard drives, which indirectly achieve the desired result of excluding copying of programs. But by its plain language, the exemption is not limited to the copying of programs, and instead extends to any copying from a computer hard drive.

Moreover, RIAA's assertion that computer hard drives do not fall within the exemption is irrelevant because, regardless of that portion of the legislative history which addresses the *exemption* from the definition of digital music recording, *see id.* § 1001(5)(B)(ii), the Rio does not reproduce files from something that falls within the plain language of the basic *definition* of a digital music recording, *see id.* § 1001(5)(A).

2

The district court concluded that the exemption of hard drives from the definition of digital music recording, and the exemption of computers generally from the Act's ambit, "would effectively eviscerate the [Act]" because "[a]ny recording device could evade [ ] regulation simply by passing the music through a computer and ensuring that the MP3 file resided momentarily on the hard drive." *RIAA I,* 29 F.Supp.2d at 630. While this may be true, the Act seems to have been expressly designed to create this loophole.

a

Under the plain meaning of the Act's definition of digital audio recording devices, computers (and their hard drives) are not digital audio recording devices because their "primary purpose" is not to make digital audio copied recordings. *See* 17 U.S.C. § 1001(3). Unlike digital audio tape machines, for example, whose primary purpose is to make digital audio copied recordings, the primary purpose of a computer is to run various programs and to record the data necessary to run those programs and perform various tasks. The legislative history is consistent with this interpretation of the Act's provisions, stating that "the typical personal computer would not fall within the definition of 'digital audio recording device,' " S. Rep. 102–294, at *122, because a personal computer's "recording function is designed and marketed primarily for the recording of data and computer programs," *id.* at *121. Another portion of the Senate Report states that "[i]f the 'primary purpose' of the recording function is to make objects other than digital audio copied recordings, then the machine or device is not a 'digital audio recording device,' *even if the machine or device is technically capable of making such recordings." Id.* (emphasis added). The legislative history thus expressly recognizes that computers (and other devices) have recording functions capable of recording digital musical recordings, and thus implicate the home taping and piracy concerns to which the Act is responsive. Nonetheless, the legislative history is consistent with the Act's plain language—computers are *not* digital audio recording devices.

b

In turn, because computers are not digital audio recording devices, they are not required to comply with the SCMS requirement and thus need not send, receive, or act upon information regarding copyright and generation status. *See* 17 U.S.C. § 1002(a)(2). And, as the district court found, MP3 files generally do not even carry the codes providing information regarding copyright and generation status. *See RIAA I,* 29 F.Supp.2d. at 632. Thus, the Act seems designed to allow files to be "laundered" by passage through a computer, because even a device with SCMS would be able to download MP3 files lacking SCMS codes from a computer hard drive, for the simple reason that there would be no codes to prevent the copying.

Again, the legislative history is consistent with the Act's plain meaning. As the Technical Reference Document that describes the SCMS system explains, "[d]igital audio signals ... that have no information concerning copyright and/or generation status *shall be recorded* by the [digital audio recording] device so that the digital copy is copyright asserted and original generation status." *Technical Reference Document for the Audio Home Recording Act of 1992,* II–A, ¶ 10, *reprinted in* H.R. Rep. 102–780(I), 32, 43 (1992) (emphasis added). Thus, the incorporation of SCMS into the Rio would allow the Rio to copy MP3 files lacking SCMS codes so long as it marked the copied files as "original generation status." And such a marking would allow another SCMS device to make unlimited further copies of such "original generation status" files, *see, e.g.,* H.R. Rep. 102–873(I), at *47 ("Under SCMS ... consumers will be able to make an unlimited number of copies from a digital musical recording."), despite the fact that the Rio does not permit such further copies to be made because it simply cannot download or transmit the files that it stores to any other device. Thus, the Rio without SCMS inherently allows *less* copying than SCMS permits.

c

In fact, the Rio's operation is entirely consistent with the Act's main purpose—the facilitation of personal use. As the Senate Report explains, "[t]he purpose of [the Act] is to ensure the right of consumers to make analog or digital audio recordings of copyrighted music for their *private, noncommercial use.*" S. Rep. 102–294, at *86 (emphasis added). The Act does so through its home taping exemption, *see* 17 U.S.C. § 1008, which "protects all noncommercial copying by consumers of digital and analog musical recordings," H.R. Rep. 102–873(I), at *59. The Rio merely makes copies in order to render portable, or "space-shift," those files that already reside on a user's hard drive. *Cf. Sony Corp. of America v. Universal City Studios,* 464 U.S. 417, 455, 104 S.Ct. 774, 78 L.Ed.2d 574 (1984) (holding that "time-shifting" of copyrighted television shows with VCR's constitutes fair use under the Copyright Act, and thus is not an infringement). Such copying is paradigmatic noncommercial personal use entirely consistent with the purposes of the Act.

IV

Even though it cannot directly reproduce a digital music recording, the Rio would nevertheless be a digital audio recording device if it could reproduce a digital music recording "from a transmission." 17 U.S.C. § 1001(1).

A

The term "transmission" is not defined in Act, although the use of the term in the Act implies that a transmission is a communication to the public. *See id.* § 1002(e) (placing restrictions upon "[a]ny person who transmits or *otherwise communicates to the public* any sound recording in digital format") (emphasis added). In the context of copyright law (from which the term appears to have been taken), "[t]o 'transmit' a performance or display is to communicate it by any device or process whereby images or sounds are received beyond the place from which they are sent." 17 U.S.C. § 101. The legislative history confirms that the copyright definition of "transmission" is sufficient for our purposes here. The Act originally (and circularly) provided that "[a] 'transmission' is any audio or audiovisual transmission, now known or later developed, whether by a broadcast station, cable system, multipoint distribution service, subscription service, direct broadcast satellite, or other form of analog or digital communication." S. Rep. 102–294, at *10. The Senate Report provides a radio broadcast as an example of a transmission. *See id.,* at *119 (referring to "a transmission (e.g., a radio broadcast of a commercially released audio cassette)."). The parties do not really dispute the definition of transmission, but rather, whether *indirect* reproduction of a transmission of a digital music recording is covered by the Act.

B

RIAA asserts that indirect reproduction of a transmission is sufficient for the Rio to fall within the Act's ambit as a digital audio recording device. *See* 17 U.S.C. § 1001(1) (digital audio recording devices are those devices that are capable of making "a reproduction in a digital recording format of a digital musical recording, whether that reproduction is made directly from another digital musical recording or *indirectly* from a transmission") (emphasis added). Diamond asserts that the adverb "indirectly" modifies the recording of the underlying "digital music recording," rather than the recording "from the transmission." Diamond effectively asserts that the statute should be read as covering devices that are capable of making a reproduction of a digital musical recording, "whether that reproduction is made directly[,] from another digital musical recording[,] or indirectly[,] from a transmission."

While the Rio can only directly reproduce files from a computer hard drive via a cable linking the two devices (which is obviously not a transmission), the Rio can indirectly reproduce a transmission. For example, if a radio broadcast of a digital audio recording were recorded on a digital audio tape machine or compact disc recorder and then uploaded to a computer hard drive, the Rio could indirectly reproduce the transmission by downloading a copy from the hard drive. Thus, if indirect reproduction of a transmission falls within the statutory definition, the Rio would be a digital audio recording device.

1

RIAA's interpretation of the statutory language initially seems plausible, but closer analysis reveals that it is contrary to the statutory language and common sense. The focus of the statutory language seems to be on the two means of reproducing the underlying digital music recording—either directly from that recording, or indirectly, by reproducing the recording from a transmission. RIAA's interpretation of the Act's language (in which "indirectly" modifies copying "from a transmission," rather than the copying of the underlying digital music recording) would only cover the indirect recording of transmissions, and would omit restrictions on the direct recording of transmissions (e.g., recording songs from the radio) from the Act's ambit. This interpretation would significantly reduce the protection afforded by the Act to transmissions, and neither the statutory language nor structure provides any reason that the Act's protections should be so limited. Moreover, it makes little sense for the Act to restrict the indirect recording of transmissions, but to allow unrestricted direct recording of transmissions (e.g., to regulate second-hand recording of songs from the radio, but to allow unlimited direct recording of songs from the radio). Thus, the most logical reading of the Act extends protection to direct copying of digital music recordings, and to indirect copying of digital music recordings from transmissions of those recordings.

2

Because of the arguable ambiguity of this passage of the statute, recourse to the legislative history is necessary on this point. *Cf. Moyle v. Director, Office of Workers' Compensation Programs,* 147 F.3d 1116, 1120 (9th Cir.1998) ("[I]f the statute is ambiguous, [this court] consult[s] the legislative history, to the extent that it is of value, to aid in [its] interpretation."), *cert.*

denied, 526 U.S. 1064, 119 S.Ct. 1454, 143 L.Ed.2d 541 (1999). The Senate Report states that "a digital audio recording made from a commercially released compact disc or audio cassette, or *from a radio broadcast* of a commercially released compact disc or audio cassette, would be a 'digital audio copied recording.' " S. Rep. 102–294, at *119 (emphasis added). This statement indicates that the recording of a transmission need not be indirect to fall within the scope of the Act's restrictions, and thus refutes RIAA's proposed interpretation of the relevant language. Moreover, the statement tracks the statutory definition by providing an example of direct copying of a digital music recording from that recording, and an example of indirect copying of a digital music recording from a transmission of that recording. Thus the legislative history confirms the most logical reading of the statute, which we adopt: "indirectly" modifies the verb "is made"—in other words, modifies the making of the reproduction of the underlying digital music recording. Thus, a device falls within the Act's provisions if it can indirectly copy a digital music recording by making a copy from a transmission of that recording. Because the Rio cannot make copies from transmissions, but instead, can only make copies from a computer hard drive, it is not a digital audio recording device.

V

For the foregoing reasons, the Rio is not a digital audio recording device subject to the restrictions of the Audio Home Recording Act of 1992. The district court properly denied the motion for a preliminary injunction against the Rio's manufacture and distribution. Having so determined, we need not consider whether the balance of hardships or the possibility of irreparable harm supports injunctive relief.

AFFIRMED.

MOTOWN RECORD CO., LP, ET AL., PLAINTIFFS v. THERESA DEPIETRO, DEFENDANT
2007 WL 576284
Unite States District Court, E.D. Pennsylvania
Civil No. 04-CV-2246 Feb. 16, 2007

CYNTHIA M. RUFE, J.

This is one of many actions filed throughout the nation in which numerous record companies are seeking to protect their copyrighted sound recordings from illegal downloading and sharing over the Internet. Presently before the Court are the parties' Cross-Motions for Summary Judgment and the oppositions thereto. After consideration of the parties' submissions and review of the relevant legal authorities, Defendant's Motion will be denied, and Plaintiffs' Motion will be dismissed without prejudice. The Court will, however, entertain a request for a hearing to make the necessary findings of fact and conclusions of law regarding Defendant's alleged destruction of integral evidence, before any further judgment is rendered.

I. FACTUAL BACKGROUND

Most of the underlying facts of this case are undisputed. On November 18, 2003, at 7:07 a.m., while investigating copyright infringement by users of peer-to-peer file-sharing programs ("P2P programs"), Plaintiffs discovered that substantial copyright infringement was occurring at Internet protocol address ("IP address") 216.15.109.54, through use of KaZaA. At that time, the user at that IP address was distributing 1203 music files, including 31 sound recordings whose copyrights are owned by the Plaintiffs and are at issue in this action. According to Plaintiffs, the user was detected using KaZaA to share copyrighted music files 32 times between November 5, 2003, and April 12, 2004. Each time, the user was notified by instant message that he or she "appeared to be infringing Plaintiffs' copyrights, that distributing or downloading copyrighted music on the internet without permission is illegal, and that by breaking the law the individual risked legal penalties."

Plaintiffs ascertained that RCN Corporation ("RCN") was the Internet service provider ("ISP") for the computer with IP address 216.15.109.54 on the date at issue. Accordingly, they served a subpoena upon RCN requesting information related to that IP address. In response to the subpoena, RCN identified Theresa DePietro, 1121 Folsom Avenue, Prospect Park, Pennsylvania, as the subscriber of record for that IP address on November 18, 2003, at 7:07 a.m.

On April 8, 2004, after Defendant was identified as the alleged infringer, Plaintiffs sent her a letter explaining, among other things, that a "Doe" lawsuit had been filed against her and that she was about to be named as a defendant. That letter specifically explained the need to preserve evidence relating to the claims against Defendant. After Plaintiffs' settlement attempts with Defendant failed, they filed the instant action naming Theresa DiPietro as Defendant in May 2004, and served her in July 2004. Defendant subsequently answered the Complaint in August 2004. Nonetheless, Defendant disposed of the computer allegedly used for the infringement by setting it out for trash collection in or around September 2004. Defendant also disposed of the cable modem allegedly used for the infringement by returning it to RCN sometime in September or October 2004.

Defendant's refusal to cooperate with Plaintiffs has persisted throughout the discovery process. Defendant initially refused to provide any written discovery to Plaintiffs. On at least two different occasions, Defendant refused to answer questions related to the case by asserting her Fifth Amendment privilege against self-incrimination, even though no criminal investigation or charges were pending against her. These refusals to cooperate forced Plaintiffs to seek Orders from this Court compelling Plaintiff to provide written discovery and to be deposed. Thereafter, Plaintiff was deposed a second time and submitted responses to previously issued interrogatories. During discovery, Defendant acknowledged that she was the only person who had access to her computer, that her live-in boyfriend was the only other person in her apartment for any extended period of time, and that she never used a wireless router or wireless service to connect to the Internet.

In support of Defendant's position that someone other than she downloaded the music files at issue here, she submitted a report prepared by her purported expert, Joseph C. Magee, Jr., in December 2005. The first drafts of this report were contested by Plaintiffs for failure to comply with Federal Rule of Civil Procedure 26(b)(2). Defendant has resubmitted a draft that she contends complies with the Rule, though Defendants continue to question the validity of the report and the conclusions offered within it.

On June 15, 2006, after discovery concluded, Defendant made a request for summary judgment. Plaintiffs filed an opposition to Defendant's request on July 6, 2006. On June 22, 2006, Plaintiffs filed their Motion for Summary Judgment. In this Motion, Plaintiffs argued that, even if summary judgment were deemed inappropriate, the Court should sanction Defendant by entering default judgment against her for destroying integral evidence. Defendant filed a bare-bones opposition to Plaintiffs' Motion on July 14, 2006. In that Response, Defendant claimed that she never admitted that "she threw her computer away," despite the fact that she explicitly admitted that fact in responses to interrogatories and requests for production of documents and things. While the

Motion was under review, Plaintiffs sought leave of Court to file a late Reply brief to Defendant's opposition, which was granted, and Plaintiffs filed their Reply on February 2, 2007. Without seeking leave of Court, Defendant filed a Sur-reply on February 15, 2007, in which she repeats her denials of liability and vehemently denies discarding her computer after receiving any letter from Plaintiffs or being named as Defendant in this action. The Cross-Motions for Summary Judgment are now ready for review.

II. LEGAL STANDARD FOR SUMMARY JUDGMENT

Disposition upon motion for summary judgment is appropriate if "the pleadings, depositions, answers to interrogatories, and admissions on file, together with the affidavits, if any, show that there is no genuine issue as to any material fact and that the moving party is entitled to judgment as a matter of law." In this case, the Court is presented with cross-motions for summary judgment. The mere existence of cross-motions does not necessarily dictate that one motion will be granted and the other denied, thereby disposing of the case. If issues of material fact exist, such that a reasonable jury could return a verdict for the non-moving party, then summary judgment is not appropriate, and the case must be allowed to proceed to trial.

III. DISCUSSION

A. Applicable Copyright Law

Under the Copyright Act, the owner of a valid copyright on a sound recording, such as a song, has the exclusive right to, among other things, "reproduce the copyrighted work in copies or phonorecords" and "distribute copies or phonorecords of the copyrighted work to the public." Accordingly, in order to prevail on a cause of action for copyright infringement, a plaintiff must prove: (1) that he or she owns the copyrights in the sound recordings allegedly downloaded and/or distributed by the defendant; and (2) that the defendant actually "copied" those sound recordings. Under the Copyright Act, "[c]opying refers to the act of infringing any of the exclusive rights that accrue to the owner of a valid copyright, as set forth at 17 U.S.C. § 106, including the right to distribute and reproduce copyrighted material." A plaintiff claiming infringement of the exclusive-distribution right can establish infringement by proof of actual distribution or by proof of offers to distribute, that is, proof that the defendant "made available" the copyrighted work.

B. Defendant's Motion for Summary Judgment

Defendant's Request for Summary Judgment demands dismissal with prejudice because "Plaintiff's [sic] have no credible evidence that proves Defendant Theresa DePietro or Defendants [sic] computer to be the perpetrator of the alleged copyright infringement complaints outlined in this case." This one sentence constitutes the entire substance of the request. Defendant does not provide the Court with any evidence, in the form of affidavits, depositions, or otherwise, supporting her claim. Nor does she make any argument informing the Court of the rationale behind her bald assertion that there are no genuine issues of material fact. It is well-established that "a party seeking summary judgment always bears the initial responsibility of informing the district court of the basis for its motion, and identifying those portions of 'the pleadings, depositions, answers to interrogatories, and admissions on file, together with the affidavits, if any,' which it believes demonstrate the absence of a genuine issue of material fact." While the Court acknowledges that it should construe *pro se* filings liberally in the interests ofjustice, no amount of liberality will render Defendant's Motion sufficient. Because Defendant has wholly failed to meet her initial burden of informing the Court of the basis for her request and identifying the evidence supporting her position, her Motion will be denied.

C. Plaintiffs' Motion for Summary Judgment

Plaintiffs argue that they are entitled to summary judgment because they indisputably own the copyrights on the 31 sound recordings at issue in this case, and Defendant has not offered any evidence to rebut their allegations that she infringed those copyrights by distributing the sound recordings through the P2P program, KaZaA. At this stage of the litigation, however, the Court cannot agree.

It is clear and undisputed that Plaintiffs own now, and owned at the time of the alleged infringement, the copyrights on the 31 sound recordings at issue here. There are, however, genuine issues of material fact concerning whether or not Defendant has been misidentified as the infringing user. While a mere assertion of misidentification may not be sufficient to satisfy Defendant's burden to establish the existence of a genuine issue of material fact, Defendant has also supplied the Court with a report from her purported expert. In this report, Defendant's expert offers several theories to explain that, even though Plaintiffs identified a user at Defendant's IP address as the infringer on November 18, 2003, it is possible that Defendant was not the infringing user. At the summary-judgment stage, the Court must accept this report in the light most favorable to Defendant. Doing so, in conjunction with Defendant's repeated denials that she downloaded or distributed the sound recordings at issue in this case, creates a genuine issue of material fact. If Defendant can offer proof at trial that she may not have been the user identified by Plaintiffs, a reasonable jury could find that she is not liable for infringement.

The above analysis is not, however, dispositive as to Plaintiffs' Motion. Plaintiffs have been deprived of the opportunity to fully test, evaluate, and challenge the theories offered in Defendant's expert's report because the computer allegedly used in the infringement has not been made available to Plaintiffs for examination. According to Plaintiffs, and also according to Defendant's own admission, Defendant is responsible for that deprivation because she discarded the computer in or around September 2004 by placing it "out for weekly trash pick up." It appears that this was done approximately five months after receiving the "Doe letter" informing her that she had been identified as an infringer and instructing her to preserve all related evidence, four months after the Complaint was filed in this case, two months after Defendant was served with the Complaint, and a month after Defendant filed her Answer to the Complaint. Moreover, Defendant disposed of the cable modem in use at the time of the alleged infringement by returning it to her provider, RCN, sometime in September or October 2004. As Defendant's expert acknowledged at his deposition, if Plaintiffs had access to the computer and the modem, they could determine: (1) whether KaZaA had ever been downloaded to the computer; (2) whether the MAC address of the computer and the modem matched the MAC address in RCN's logs; (3) whether a virus or worm could be responsible for downloading music files to the computer without her knowledge; and (4) whether Defendant had enabled the remote-desktop feature on her computer, which may have allowed a third party to access her computer remotely. With this information, Plaintiffs may be able to prevail at the summary-judgment stage. Without it, there remain genuine issues of fact such that a reasonable jury could return a verdict in Defendant's favor.

In the face of these disputed facts, the Court does not believe that granting summary judgment is the appropriate remedy, even when the disputes exist only as a result of alleged spoliation. The Court must first determine whether Defendant discarded the computer and modem in bad faith and, if so, the appropriate sanction for such spoliation. The Court will make the appropriate findings of fact and conclusions of law, but only after an appropriate motion is filed, to which Defendant will have the opportunity to respond, and the parties have an opportunity to be heard in Court. In the interim, the Court will dismiss Plaintiffs' Motion without prejudice. Plaintiffs will be permitted to renew their Motion at a later date, if appropriate.

IV. CONCLUSION

For the foregoing reasons, Defendant's Motion for Summary Judgment will be denied, and Plaintiffs' Motion for Summary Judgment will be dismissed without prejudice. Upon appropriate motion, the Court will hold a hearing to consider the spoliation issue.

ORDER

AND NOW, this 16th day of February 2007, upon consideration of Plaintiffs' Motion for Summary Judgment [Doc. # 50], Defendant's Response thereto [Doc. # 54], Plaintiffs' Reply [Doc. # 57], and Defendant's Sur-reply [Doc. # 58], it is hereby **ORDERED** that Plaintiffs' Motion is **DISMISSED** without prejudice, and a renewed motion may be filed at a later date, in accordance with the Court's Memorandum Opinion.

It is **FURTHER ORDERED** that, upon consideration of Defendant's Motion for Summary Judgment [Doc. # 47] and Plaintiffs' Response thereto [Doc. # 53], Defendant's Motion is **DENIED** without prejudice.

It is so **ORDERED.**

MGM STUDIOS, INC. v. GROKSTER, LTD.
United States District Court for the Central District of California
Oct. 16, 2007, Decided; October 16, 2007, Filed, Entered
CV 01-8541 SVW (FMOx), CV 01-9923 SVW (FMOx)
518 F.Supp.2d 1197

STEPHEN V. WILSON, District Judge

I. INTRODUCTION

On September 27, 2006, this Court granted Plaintiffs' motion for summary judgment on the question of liability as against StreamCast Networks, Inc. ("StreamCast"). In that Order, the Court recounted this case's procedural history, and engaged in a detailed analysis of the factual record pertaining to StreamCast's inducement of copyright infringement. *See Metro–Goldwyn–Mayer Studios, Inc. v. Grokster, Ltd.,* 454 F.Supp.2d 966, 971, 975–92 (C.D.Cal.2006). StreamCast is the only defendant remaining in this case. As the parties are well aware, StreamCast operates and distributes the Morpheus System and Software.

Presently before this Court is Plaintiffs' motion for a permanent injunction against StreamCast. StreamCast has vigorously opposed the imposition of a permanent injunction. StreamCast also asks for an evidentiary hearing, additional discovery, or at least a stay of the permanent injunction's enforcement pending appeal.

An initial hearing was held before this Court on February 12, 2007. During the hearing, the Court espoused its concern regarding the specificity and scope of Plaintiffs' proposed permanent injunction. Subsequently, this Court issued an order requiring further briefing, in which it detailed specific questions for the parties to answer. [Docket No. 1234.] On the technology front, the parties were asked to expand on their discussion of filtering technology and StreamCast's ability to coax end-users away from legacy (non-filtered) versions of Morpheus Software. On the legal front, the parties were ordered to analyze exhaustively the history of permanent injunctive relief in the context of patent inducement. This briefing has since been received, and the Court has evaluated the pertinent issues. The Court's analysis and conclusions are specified as follows.

II. BACKGROUND

A. The Proposed Permanent Injunction

Plaintiffs' proposed permanent injunction is composed of several parts. Under § 1(a)(I) and § 1(a)(ii), StreamCast would be enjoined from directly or indirectly infringing Plaintiffs' copyrighted works in any manner, which also includes StreamCast's "enabling, facilitating, permitting, assisting, soliciting, encouraging, authorizing, inducing, or knowingly materially contributing to" such infringement. Pursuant to § 1(b), StreamCast would be barred from operating the Morpheus System and Software, or any other similar peer-to-peer or file-trading system, until there is a "robust and secure means exhaustively to" stop infringement. According to § 1(c), StreamCast would be required to "use all technologically feasible means to prevent or inhibit" the infringement of Plaintiffs' copyrights by end-users through any version of the Morpheus Software in existence.

Until StreamCast is able to "exhaustively" stop all infringement, it would also be barred from displaying advertising on all Morpheus Software versions. StreamCast must give notice to all of StreamCast's agents and employees, as well as to any entity interested in a transfer of StreamCast's ownership interest in the Morpheus System and Software, and all successors or those acting in concert with them. Any successor in interest to any part of StreamCast's business must also submit to this Court's jurisdiction and venue, and agree to be bound by the injunction. StreamCast could be held in contempt for any violation of the permanent injunction.

B. StreamCast's Claimed Initial Filtering Efforts

In the September 27, 2006 Order granting Plaintiffs' motion for summary judgment, this Court held that StreamCast distributed the Morpheus Software with the intent to induce copyright infringement. *Grokster,* 454 F.Supp.2d at 992 ("[N]o reasonable factfinder can conclude that StreamCast provided OpenNap services and distributed Morpheus without the intent to induce infringement."). In support of this conclusion, the record revealed numerous undisputed facts: (1) StreamCast's software was used overwhelmingly for infringing purposes; (2) StreamCast targeted a known community of infringers—former Napster users; (3) StreamCast provided technical assistance to aid users in their enjoyment of illegally downloaded content; (4) StreamCast thwarted enforcement efforts by copyright holders; (5) StreamCast's business model depended on massive infringing use; and (6) StreamCast took no meaningful steps to prevent infringement. *Id.* at 985–92. The Court concluded that "evidence of StreamCast's objective of promoting infringement is overwhelming." *Id.* at 992.

After receiving this Court's Order, StreamCast claims that it decided "to the best of its abilities, it should develop and integrate a robust filtering mechanism ... so that copyrighted works that are not authorized by copyright holders for free downloading or distribution utilizing Morpheus would not be able to be downloaded by Morpheus users." (Weiss Decl. ¶ 4.) Yet, despite taking steps to implement a filter, "StreamCast ... maintains that any requirement to filter is improper and not required under the law. Accordingly, StreamCast reserves the right to cease distribution of a filtered version." (StreamCast Supp. Opp. at 18 n. 2.)

Plaintiffs have reportedly refused to turn over a list of artists that they wish to have filtered. (Weiss Decl. ¶ 6.) Thus, in order to meet its self-imposed deadline of implementing its filtering mechanism by November 17, 2006, StreamCast's CEO (Weiss) instructed its Director of Technology (Kassis) to copy the names of all artists on the RIAA website. (*Id.*) StreamCast asserts that its homemade filter would be even more effective if it were given the "hash values" of files on Morpheus' network that contain Plaintiffs' copyrighted material. (*Id.* ¶¶ 8–9.) Beginning on November 17 and 20, 2006, StreamCast began distributing its new filtering software to Morpheus users. (*Id.* ¶ 7.) On December 15, 2006, StreamCast started sending screenshots to users of "legacy versions" of the Morpheus software stating that it was "strongly recommended" that they click "ok" to accept a software upgrade—this upgrade allegedly contained a filter. (Kassis Decl. ¶ 7.) StreamCast asserts that 92.5% of copyrighted audio and video files were blocked by the filtering versions of the Morpheus Software as of January 14, 2007. (*Id.* ¶ 11.) However, the new filtering software has not replaced all "legacy versions." In fact, StreamCast admits that only about one-third of the downloading sessions in December 2006 and January 2007 were from software that contained this new filter. (*Id.* ¶¶ 8–9.)

In order to develop a list of hash values known to contain infringing content, StreamCast initially ran a "batch process" four times per day. (*Id.* ¶ 16.) These values are derived from the search results generated by end-users. (*Id.*) "Using each artist name as a search term keyword, the batch process scan the P2P networks accessed by Morpheus users and saves all audio and video file hash values obtained from the search results. The hash values are then stored on a hash database server that StreamCast created and maintains." (*Id.* ¶ 19.) When an end-user attempts to download an audio or music video file containing a hash value found in StreamCast's database, the download is "blocked." (*Id.* ¶ 21.) This filtering mechanism is also performed during the uploading process for audio and music video files. (*Id.* ¶ 23.) For TV shows and motion pictures, StreamCast allows the download of any file with DRM protection. (*Id.* ¶ 26.) All other such files are blocked if they either exceed fifteen (15) minutes in running-time (if known) or the file exceeds 100 MB in size. (*Id.* ¶ 27.) All filtering versions of the Morpheus Software are capable of being automatically updated at the end of an individual user's session. (*Id.* ¶ 31.)

During this timeframe, StreamCast also contacted various companies regarding acoustical fingerprinting technology. SNOCAP informed StreamCast that it would be "difficult to determine" the total number of "artist-title pairs" in its collection. Audible Magic allegedly claimed that it could not identify the total number of artist-title pairs in its database. (Weiss Decl. ¶¶ 10–11.) Weiss believes that these two options would, regardless, be "cost-prohibitive." (*Id.* ¶ 12.) StreamCast has also contacted other companies, such as *allmusic.com,* NARM, MUZE, and Gracenote. (*Id.* ¶ 13.) It is not clear from these contacts whether such companies would either be willing to license their information to StreamCast, or if it would be comprehensive enough to cover all copyrighted works owned by Plaintiffs. (*Id.* ¶ 14.)

StreamCast also posts warnings on its websites and within the Morpheus System and Software that end-users should download the new filtering software; they are also warned about their potential legal liability for engaging in illegal file sharing. (*Id.* ¶¶ 18, 20.) "StreamCast urges users of non-filtering versions to upgrade to a filtering version each time a user uses a non-filtering version of Morpheus or Morpheus Ultra." (*Id.* ¶ 22.)

Plaintiffs submitted a declaration indicating that in December 2006, after the institution of StreamCast's new filtering software, it was still possible to illegally download each of the Top 40 songs on the Billboard chart. (Zaman Decl. ¶ 4.) After learning of Plaintiffs' declaration, StreamCast claims to have researched the issue. It determined that the artists' names from the RIAA website only included gold and platinum artists. (Weiss Decl. ¶ 15.) "[I]t was possible that current Top 40 artists who did not reach gold and platinum standings would not be on the RIAA website." (*Id.*) StreamCast has since taken steps to add all "Top 40" artist names to its filtering database. (*Id.* ¶ 16.) Additionally, "StreamCast stands ready to include in its filter any artist names, hash values, or file names that the Plaintiffs provide us. Any information provided to StreamCast by Plaintiffs increases the effectiveness of StreamCast's filter." (*Id.* ¶ 17.)

Furthermore, StreamCast claims in its supplemental briefing that it has instituted various other improvements to its filter (*e.g.,* eliminating "low host count files" from the Gnutella network, Morpheus' "select all" downloading feature, and access to the "G2 Network"). (Kassis Supp. Decl. ¶¶ 4–6.) StreamCast also started collecting information about the files passing through its filtering system, and is now running its batch process twelve (12) times per day as opposed to four (4). (*Id.* ¶¶ 7, 9.) StreamCast further asserts that it has added "popular song titles, movies [sic] titles and television titles" to its keyword filter, as well as common misspellings made known to the company.

(*Id.* ¶¶ 10, 23.) Finally, StreamCast claims that it has disabled access to video files in excess of 10 minutes in length as of January 18, 2007. (*Id.* ¶ 25.)

C. The Purported Effectiveness of StreamCast's Filter

A great deal of effort has been expended by the parties in evaluating whether StreamCast's homemade filter is effective, and whether it has been improved since this Court's Order requiring further briefing. Plaintiffs have submitted several declarations in which it is claimed that Morpheus end-users were able to download numerous popular audio and/or video files during December 2006, January 2007, February 2007, March 2007, and April 2007—all after StreamCast first instituted its filtering software. (*See* Zaman Decl.; Zaman Reply Decl.; Patel Decl.; Boyle Decl.; Patel Second Decl.; Bennett Decl.) Plaintiffs have also submitted the declaration of Ellis Horowitz, a computer science professor at the University of Southern California. (Horowitz Decl. Ex. 1.) Although some of his criticisms regarding StreamCast's filter may have since been partly remedied by StreamCast's efforts, he asserts the following implementation flaws: (1) StreamCast filters only by artist, not by title name; (2) StreamCast does not filter common misspellings or variations; (3) StreamCast only collects hashes for its database four times a day; (4) the size filter of 100 MB does not capture 30-minute television shows, especially when StreamCast cannot identify a file's "runtime"; (5) StreamCast does not filter all file types, including ".rar" files that "can break up large files into numerous pieces, send them in pieces, and then reassemble them on the other end." (*Id.* ¶¶ 27, 32–41.) Horowitz further argues that StreamCast's filter is technologically outdated, substantially because of its failure to incorporate "digital fingerprinting" technology such as acoustical fingerprinting. (*Id.* ¶¶ 42, 47.)

In response, StreamCast claims to have conducted its own in-house testing of the Morpheus filter compared to those utilized by other peer-to-peer networks (in particular, I–Mesh and Kazaa). (Deutscher Decl.; Frawley Decl.; Thompson Decl.) StreamCast has also submitted a statistical analysis of the results. (Mercurio Decl.; Mercurio Supp. Decl.)

D. Plaintiffs' Proposals Regarding Filtering Technology and Legacy Software

1. Filtering Options

Plaintiffs maintain that StreamCast's "homemade filter" is hopelessly ineffective. They believe that StreamCast should be required to employ commercially available state-of-the-art filtering solutions to prevent infringement by end-users. Plaintiffs offer two related but distinct proposals for the filtering of: (1) audio/music video files, and (2) other video files.

a. Audio/Music Video Files
i. File Hashes and Acoustical Fingerprinting

First and foremost, Plaintiffs state that StreamCast should be required to incorporate both "acoustical fingerprint" and "file hash" technology into a filter. According to evidence submitted by Plaintiffs, other companies claim to have employed this filtering duo successfully. (*See generally* Sorenson Decl.; Marco Decl.)

Acoustical fingerprinting is licensed by various companies, including Audible Magic. This technology analyzes the actual content of an audio file, as opposed to a written description of what is contained within it (*e.g.*, "metadata"). (Ikezoye Decl. ¶ 3 ("Audible Magic's technology analyzes the shape of the spectrum represented by a digital audio file.").) This means that the filtering tool "listens" to the sound recording, and creates a twenty-second "fingerprint" that can then be compared against any other file that an end-user is attempting to upload or download. (*Id.* ¶ 8.) If the suspected file has that precise sequence (or spectrum) of sounds, the uploading or downloading of the song will be blocked. According to Plaintiffs, Audible Magic has a database of approximately 6 million acoustical fingerprints of musical sound recordings. (*Id.* ¶ 11.)

The second part of this filtering system is the "file hash." This represents a different type of "fingerprint." "A hash value is a unique multi-character number that is associated with a computer file. Some computer scientists compare a hash value to an electronic fingerprint in that each file has a unique hash value." *United States v. Cartier,* 2007 WL 319648, at *1 (D.N.D. Jan.30, 2007). This fingerprint is not based on the actual sound/content of the recording, but constitutes a mixture of characters that allow the file to be easily identified, and remains the same for *identical* copies of that file (after they are uploaded or downloaded).

The file hash is a fairly limited tool. In order to explain its usefulness, the Court constructs the following hypothetical: assume that there is a two minute sixteen second version of Louis Armstrong singing "What a Wonderful World" available for download through the Morpheus System and Software, which has a hash value of 123456789. If any other individual downloads this precise file, and makes no alterations to it, his/her downloaded copy will contain the same file hash: 123456789. Companies such as Audible Magic claim to have a database of file hashes that are known to contain copyrighted content. Therefore, if file hash 123456789 is already contained in an Audible Magic database, and StreamCast purchases the right to license this information, a Morpheus end-user should be prevented from downloading this precise copy of the song. However, an end-user with this two minute sixteen second copy of "What a Wonderful World" could decide to recopy the song such that it only lasts for two minutes fifteen seconds. This one second alteration would automatically cause the derivative file to be associated with a *different* file hash—for example, 012345678. If StreamCast relied entirely on file hash filtering, then the derivative version of "What a Wonderful World" with hash value 012345678 would evade the filtering gatekeeper mechanism.

The file hash filter serves as a useful starting point according to Plaintiffs. It theoretically gives StreamCast the ability to start with a number of computer files that are known to contain infringing content. This is where the acoustical fingerprinting technology arrives at center stage.

In following from the original hypothetical, the Court presumes that Audible Magic has created a twenty-second audio fingerprint of "What a Wonderful World," which comes from the file containing hash value 123456789. Because this fingerprint is based on the spectrum of sounds contained in the sound recording, it can also be "matched up" with the file associated with hash value 012345678. Thus, the filtering tool would recognize all files, regardless of the hash value, that contain this "acoustical fingerprint" of What a Wonderful World.[7] Audible Magic represents that its acoustical fingerprinting technology "would successfully block well over 99% of the files unauthorized for peer-to-peer distribution." (Ikezoye Decl. ¶ 18.)

ii. Keyword Filtering

Keyword filtering is merely a supplement to the acoustical fingerprinting and hash value filtering tools, and would be ineffective by itself. Every file has "metadata," which contains certain information about itself (*e.g.,* artist, song title, etc.). By having a filter that matches files against certain keywords of known artist/song titles found in the metadata, StreamCast would be better positioned to identify infringing content. (Marco Decl. ¶¶ 11–12; Sorenson Decl. ¶ 17.)

This information can be easily altered. Unknown misspellings of artist names and song titles could escape the filter. But according to Plaintiffs, keyword filtering is sometimes the best method for locating illegally "leaked" pre-release copies of sound recordings that have yet to be added to the acoustical fingerprint database.

iii. "Quality Improvement Process"

Plaintiffs argue that filtering technologies evolve rapidly, and are fine-tuned to incorporate state-of-the-art technology and to overcome the efforts of would-be infringers to defeat the filtering tools. Plaintiffs explain that StreamCast should be required to update the lists of blocked files on a routine basis. This information can be obtained from third-party sources such as Audible

Magic. It can also result from an agreement with StreamCast that would allow the record companies to modify the block list, and require StreamCast to implement it immediately. This would help ensure that the list is not overinclusive or underinclusive.

b. Video Files

The motion picture Plaintiffs begin by noting that commercial vendors are rapidly developing filtering techniques for video downloads. Audible Magic uses the same kind of acoustical fingerprinting for such files. (Izekoye Decl. ¶ 24.) In a declaration, Audible Magic asserts that it has over 1000 acoustic fingerprints for motion pictures and television shows, and in the near future it will likely expand to a large number of Plaintiffs' "most popular" titles. (*Id.* ¶ 26.) Additionally, it appears that technology is developing that may allow for "video fingerprinting." This presumably means that the filter would have in its database a visual "snapshot" of the film, which could then be compared against other files end-users are attempting to upload and download. (*See* Winter Decl. ¶ 7.) Companies such as Philips, Vobile, and Gracenote are in the process of trying to use acoustical fingerprinting, video fingerprinting, or both in order to make filtering more successful. (Plaintiffs' Supp. Brief at 10.)

The motion picture Plaintiffs suggest an injunction in two parts, which would be subject to reexamination after 180 days. First, StreamCast should be ordered to utilize commercially available acoustical fingerprinting technology for those video titles currently protected. To protect works not currently fingerprinted in this manner, Plaintiffs ask that StreamCast perform the following: (1) use commercially available solutions for creating and supplementing a database of hashes that have been verified as infringing or likely to contain infringing content, (2) block files that are longer than 10 minutes in length or larger than 40 megabytes in size, and (3) use a supplemental keyword search based on terms submitted by the Plaintiffs. Second, Plaintiffs ask that this Court order the parties to submit briefing in 180 days after the injunction is entered in order to determine whether a status conference is necessary in light of technological advances.

c. What Happens if the Filter Fails?

Plaintiffs' proposed injunction previously required StreamCast to "exhaustively" stop all infringement. However, this Court questioned whether such language would leave StreamCast liable for infringement even if it accepts a third-party filtering system approved by Plaintiffs, but is not itself "perfect." Plaintiffs assert that they would not hold StreamCast liable in such circumstances, but *only if* StreamCast: (1) properly installs, implements, and maintains the third-party filter and available updates/upgrades, (2) takes into account reasonably foreseeable deficiencies with a filtering solution, and (3) implements technological improvements as they become available.

If Plaintiffs believe that StreamCast has not acted in good faith, then Plaintiffs vaguely suggest that the Court's injunction include a "mandated notice-and-cure procedure pursuant to which Plaintiffs would give StreamCast written notice of such problems and StreamCast would have a certain amount of time to cure the problems or otherwise respond." (Plaintiffs' Supp. Brief at 15.) It is not clear to the Court how exactly this procedure would work. Lastly, Plaintiffs do not believe that they should bear the burden of providing artist-title pairs or hash values to StreamCast for a "homemade filter."

2. Legacy Software

a. Encouraging Morpheus Users to Upgrade

StreamCast states that it cannot require users to upgrade their software to versions containing a filter. Similarly, declarations submitted by *Plaintiffs* reveal that some of StreamCast's apparent competitors, I–Mesh and Kazaa, are unable to do so as well. (Sorenson Decl. ¶ 20 ("Sharman did not have a technical means to force users to upgrade.").; Marco Decl. 119 ("As a result of these efforts, our sense is that there are at most hundreds or thousands of customers still using the legacy software and that small number becomes smaller still over time.").). Plaintiffs do not currently seek such relief. (*See* Plaintiffs' Supp. Brief at 17 n. 7.) Instead, Plaintiffs ask this Court to include three conditions in its forthcoming injunction Order. First, StreamCast should insert aggressive "pop-ups" that would make it difficult (or at least very annoying) for users to continue with the unfiltered versions of the Morpheus software. Second, Plaintiffs ask that StreamCast copiously remove all postings in the "Morpheus Forum" that help users to download non-filtering versions of Morpheus. Third, StreamCast should be forced to distribute do-not-infringe messages as search results, so that users who continue to search for copyrighted material are given a warning not to infringe.

b. Advertising

Plaintiffs ask that StreamCast be denied the right to sell advertising on the legacy versions of the Morpheus software.

III. ANALYSIS

A. Legal Standard

Under 17 U.S.C. § 502(a), this Court is empowered to grant a permanent injunction "as it may deem reasonable to prevent or restrain infringement of a copyright." "It goes without saying that an injunction is an equitable remedy." *Weinberger v. Romero–Barcelo,* 456 U.S. 305, 311, 102 S.Ct. 1798, 72 L.Ed.2d 91 (1982). "An injunction should issue only where the intervention of a court of equity 'is essential in order effectually to protect property rights against injuries otherwise irremediable.' " *Id.* at 312, 102 S.Ct. 1798 (quoting *Cavanaugh v. Looney,* 248 U.S. 453, 456, 39 S.Ct. 142, 63 L.Ed. 354 (1919)).

As recently confirmed by the Supreme Court, Plaintiffs must meet their burden with respect to the traditional four-part test. Plaintiffs "must demonstrate: (1) that it has suffered an irreparable injury; (2) that remedies available at law, such as monetary damages, are inadequate to compensate for that injury; (3) that, considering the balance of hardships between the plaintiff and defendant, a remedy in equity is warranted; and (4) that the public interest would not be disserved by a permanent injunction." *eBay Inc. v. MercExchange, L.L.C.,* 547 U.S. 388, 126 S.Ct. 1837, 1839, 164 L.Ed.2d 641 (2006). "[T]he decision whether to grant or deny injunctive relief rests within the equitable discretion of the district courts." *Id.* at 1841. Further, the Supreme Court "has consistently rejected invitations to replace traditional equitable considerations with a rule that an injunction automatically follows a determination that a copyright has been infringed." *Id.* at 1840.

B. Application of the Four-Part Test

Before applying *eBay,* it must be noted that Plaintiffs also ask this Court first to apply an arguably different (and perhaps more permissive) permanent injunction test. Prior to *eBay,* in *MAI Sys. Corp. v. Peak Computer, Inc.,* 991 F.2d 511, 520 (9th Cir.1993), the Ninth Circuit stated that "[a]s a general rule, a permanent injunction will be granted when liability has been established and there is a threat of continuing violations."

In light of this two-part rule (past infringement + likelihood of future infringements), Plaintiffs have asked for a permanent injunction. However, this Court has doubts that *MAI's* "general rule" regarding permanent injunctions survives *eBay.* In *eBay,* the Supreme Court rejected the Federal Circuit's "general rule" in patent cases that "courts will issue permanent injunctions against patent infringement absent exceptional circumstances." 126 S.Ct. at 1839–40 (citation omitted). As stated in Chief Justice Roberts's concurrence, the "historical practice" of granting permanent injunctive relief in most instances after the establishment of infringement "does not *entitle* a patentee to a permanent injunction or justify a general rule that such injunctions should issue." *Id.* at 1841 (Roberts, C.J., concurring).

The Supreme Court also stated that permanent injunctions issued under the Patent Act should be treated as they are under the Copyright Act, and that the traditional four-part test must be applied. Additionally, the Ninth Circuit has applied *eBay* to the Lanham Act. *See Reno Air Racing Ass'n, Inc. v. McCord,* 452 F.3d 1126, 1137–38 (9th Cir.2006). By implication, the four *eBay* factors are the only relevant considerations for purposes of Plaintiffs' instant motion under the Copyright Act. This Court can identify no place for a separate and distinct two-part MAI test or "general rule" that could circumvent *eBay. See Christopher Phelps & Assocs., LLC v. Galloway,* 492 F.3d 532, 543 (4th Cir.2007) (applying *eBay* and rejecting plaintiff's assertion that "when copyright infringement has been proved and there is a threat of continuing infringement, the copyright holder is '*entitled* to an injunction' ") (citations omitted). See also *Nat'l League of Junior Cotillions, Inc. v. Porter,* 2007 WL 2316823, at *5 (W.D.N.C. Aug. 9, 2007) *MAI* should only be relevant to the extent it informs the *eBay* analysis.

1. Irreparable Harm

The first question to address is whether Plaintiffs "ha[ve] suffered an irreparable injury." *eBay,* 126 S.Ct. at 1839. "The concept of irreparable harm, unfortunately, 'does not readily lend itself to definition.' " *Prairie Band of Potawatomi Indians v. Pierce,* 253 F.3d 1234, 1250 (10th Cir.2001) (citation omitted). According to the Fifth Circuit, "[b]y definition, 'irreparable injury' is that for which compensatory damages are unsuitable." *Wildmon v. Berwick Universal Pictures,* 983 F.2d 21, 24 (5th Cir.1992). Or, as alternatively stated by the Seventh Circuit, "[o]nly harm that the district court cannot remedy following a final determination on the merits may constitute irreparable harm." *Am. Hosp. Ass'n v. Harris,* 625 F.2d 1328, 1331 (7th Cir.1980). In perhaps combining these two statements, the Tenth Circuit has observed that "irreparable harm is often suffered when the injury can[not] be adequately atoned for in money, or when the district court cannot remedy [the injury] following a final determination on the merits." *Prairie Band,* 253 F.3d at 1250 (internal quotation marks and citations omitted). One district court has also recently stated that "the irreparable harm requirement contemplates the inadequacy of alternate remedies available to the plaintiff." *Smith & Nephew, Inc. v. Synthes (U.S.A.),* 466 F.Supp.2d 978, 982–83 (W.D.Tenn.2006), thereby linking the first *eBay* factor with the second. Based on these varying definitions, the Court now proceeds to its irreparable harm analysis.

a. There is no Presumption of Irreparable Harm

The parties dispute whether, in light of *eBay,* irreparable harm can be presumed.

Pre-*eBay* and Post-*eBay Permanent Injunction cases:* Other courts have in the past presumed the existence of irreparable injury upon the establishment of liability in copyright cases. *See,...* (internal citation omitted). As pointed out by Plaintiffs, this Court once essentially agreed with this analysis. *See Warner Bros. Entertainment Inc. v. Caridi,* 346 F.Supp.2d 1068, 1073 (C.D.Cal.2004) (Wilson, J.) (entering a permanent injunction after a default judgment in a copyright action).

Yet, these cases were all decided prior to the Supreme Court's decision in *eBay.* The *eBay* Court held that it is Plaintiffs who "must demonstrate" (meaning, have the burden of proof) that the traditional factors favor a permanent injunction. 126 S.Ct. at 1839 The Supreme Court also highlighted that it has "consistently rejected" the rule that "an injunction automatically follows" an infringement holding. *Id.* at 1840. Given Plaintiffs' burden of proof and the inability of a district court to "automatically" issue injunctions, it is perhaps unclear in *eBay's* wake whether a permanent injunction can be granted based on a rebuttable presumption of irreparable harm. On remand from the Supreme Court, the *eBay* district court highlighted this uncertainty by initially expressing the following concerns:

> [T]he legal standard for issuing an injunction was in flux throughout the appeal of this matter and appears to remain uncertain today in that the Supreme Court did not expressly address whether the presumption of irreparable harm upon a showing of validity and infringement survives the Supreme Court's decision.

Mercexchange, L.L.C. v. eBay, Inc., 467 F.Supp.2d 608, 615 n. 7 (E.D.Va.2006). However, the *eBay* district court has subsequently decided that there can be no presumption of irreparable harm in the permanent injunction context. *See MercExchange, L.L.C. v. eBay, Inc.,* 500 F.Supp.2d 556, 568 (E.D.Va.2007) ("[A] review of relevant caselaw, as well as the language of the Supreme Court's decision, supports defendants' position that such presumption no longer exists."). This view appears to have been followed by perhaps every court expressly considering *eBay.*

This Court agrees with StreamCast, and these district courts, that the presumption of irreparable harm no longer inures to the benefit of Plaintiffs. The *eBay* Court plainly stated that Plaintiffs "must demonstrate" the presence of the traditional factors, and therefore have the burden of proof with regard to irreparable harm. If this Court adopted a presumption of irreparable harm in favor of Plaintiffs, then StreamCast would effectively have the burden of proving the contrary. Such a rule would contravene the Supreme Court's intent that

Plaintiffs establish not merely that infringement causes "harm," but how it amounts to *irreparable* harm.

Analogy to Preliminary Injunction Cases: In arguing for a presumption, Plaintiffs also cite to various preliminary injunction cases within the Ninth Circuit that predate *eBay.* In these cases, the Ninth Circuit held that "a showing of a reasonable likelihood of success on the merits raises a presumption of irreparable harm." *Johnson Controls, Inc. v. Phoenix Control Systems, Inc.,* 886 F.2d 1173, 1174 (9th Cir.1989); *see also LGS Architects, Inc. v. Concordia Homes of Nev.,* 434 F.3d 1150, 1155–56 (9th Cir.2006) (same); *Micro Star v. Formgen Inc.,* 154 F.3d 1107, 1109 (9th Cir.1998) (same). Plaintiffs' citations are unpersuasive. First, prior preliminary injunction cases issued by the Ninth Circuit are of no moment when this Court is faced with a more recent Supreme Court decision that is directly on point, and which requires a different holding.

Second, one might reasonably argue that there is a sensible policy rationale for permitting a presumption of irreparable harm in preliminary injunction, but not permanent injunction, motions.

Preliminary injunctions are typically requested when a lawsuit's factual development is limited and are designed to preserve the status quo pending trial. Relatedly, preliminary injunctions are also temporary in the sense that they will expire once the case's merits are decided. Given these considerations, one could legitimately conclude that a plaintiff should be absolved of proving irreparable harm at such an early stage.

Third, the longstanding rule that irreparable harm can be presumed after a showing of likelihood of success for purposes of a copyright preliminary injunction motion may *itself* have to be reevaluated in light of *eBay.* It is true that post-*eBay,* the Federal Circuit assumed the continued existence of a presumption of irreparable harm for preliminary injunctions. *See Abbott Labs. v. Andrx Pharms., Inc.,* 452 F.3d 1331, 1347 (Fed.Cir.2006) ("First, as noted above, we conclude that Abbott has not established a likelihood of success on the merits. As a result, Abbott is no longer entitled to a presumption of irreparable harm."); *see also Docusign, Inc. v. Sertifi, Inc.,* 468 F.Supp.2d 1305, 1309 n. 6 (W.D.Wash.2006) ("*Abbott,* which came after *eBay,* assumed (without deciding) that such a presumption was still appropriate in the preliminary injunction context, where a strong showing of likely infringement was made."). And some district courts have also rejected *eBay's* application to preliminary injunctions. *E.g., Christiana Industries v. Empire Electronics, Inc.,* 443 F.Supp.2d 870, 884 (E.D.Mich.2006) ("Defendant asserts that in [*eBay*], the Supreme Court eliminated the presumption of irreparable harm for preliminary injunctions upon a showing of validity and infringement. Plaintiff argues, and this Court agrees, that *eBay* did not invalidate the presumption.").

However, a significant number of lower court cases are reaching precisely the contrary conclusion. *See, e.g., Sun Optics, Inc. v. FGX Int'l, Inc.,*

2007 WL 2228569, at *1 (D.Del. Aug.2, 2007) ("Even if the moving party succeeds in demonstrating a likelihood of success on the merits, the notion that there follows a presumption of irreparable harm seems inconsistent with the Supreme Court's holding in [*eBay*]."); *Torspo Hockey Int'l, Inc. v. Kor Hockey Ltd.,* 491 F.Supp.2d 871, 881 (D.Minn.2007) ("[T]he Court finds that it may not presume that a patentee who is likely to succeed on the merits at trial will suffer irreparable harm in the absence of a preliminary injunction."); *Allora, LLC v. Brownstone, Inc.,* 2007 WL 1246448, at *5 (W.D.N.C. Apr.27, 2007) ("Until this issue is clarified by the Fourth Circuit or the Supreme Court, this Court will not *presume* irreparable harm and likelihood of success on the merits following a prima facie showing of copyright infringement, but will instead treat copyright cases in the same manner as any other civil action requesting a preliminary injunction."); *Chamberlain Group, Inc. v. Lear Corp.,* 2007 WL 1017751, at *5 (N.D.Ill. Mar.30, 2007) ("While *eBay* has yet to be completely fleshed out in the lower courts, it has been applied to preliminary, as well as permanent, injunctions, and has been read to limit the presumption of irreparable harm solely upon the finding of infringement.") (internal citation omitted). The law is muddled, and the Court is not aware of a post-*eBay* Ninth Circuit ruling on this point. Certainly, the post-*eBay* legal landscape has created some question as to the viability of these Ninth Circuit preliminary injunction decisions.

Amoco and *eBay:* The argument that *eBay* bars a presumption of irreparable harm with regard to permanent or preliminary injunction motions is strengthened when considered in conjunction with the Supreme Court's prior opinion in *Amoco Production Co. v. Village of Gambell,* 480 U.S. 531, 107 S.Ct. 1396, 94 L.Ed.2d 542 (1987). In *Amoco,* the Ninth Circuit entered a preliminary injunction after determining that the Secretary of the Interior likely violated Section 810 of the Alaska National Interest Lands Conservation Act ("ANILCA"). *Id.* at 534, 107 S.Ct. 1396. In reaching this conclusion, the Ninth Circuit applied a presumption of irreparable harm. The Supreme Court reversed and held that "[t]his presumption is contrary to traditional equitable principles and has no basis in ANILCA." *Id.* at 545, 107 S.Ct. 1396.

Prior to *eBay, Amoco* appears to have had little impact. In *Sierra Club v. United States Forest Service,* 843 F.2d 1190 (9th Cir.1988), the Ninth Circuit signaled that *Amoco* might be limited to ANILCA and should not be extended even to National Environmental Policy Act ("NEPA") cases. *Id.* at 1195; *see also Pub. Serv. Co. of Colo. v. Andrus,* 825 F.Supp. 1483, 1505 (D.Idaho 1993) ("The Ninth Circuit has questioned the applicability of the *Amoco* decision in NEPA cases."). There was perhaps little reason to think that *Amoco* would be relevant to intellectual property cases.

But in *eBay,* the Supreme Court cited to *Amoco* twice. *Amoco* was cited first, as support for the four factors that a plaintiff must demonstrate before district courts can grant a permanent injunction, and second, to help justify the proposition that a departure from traditional equity practice should not be "lightly implied." *eBay*. 126 S.Ct. at 1839 (citing *Amoco,* 480 U.S. at 542, 107 S.Ct. 1396). The *eBay* Court relied on *Amoco* in this manner even though it was a preliminary injunction case. *eBay's* invocation of *Amoco* suggests that permanent and preliminary injunctions should generally be treated alike.

eBay and *Amoco* also have important parallels. *Amoco* held that a presumption of irreparable harm for a preliminary injunction is "contrary to traditional equitable principles." 480 U.S. at 545, 107 S.Ct. 1396. *eBay* does not speak in the language of presumptions and only expressly states that "traditional equitable considerations" militate against the "automatic" issuance of permanent injunctions. 126 S.Ct. at 1840. But as already discussed, *eBay* is in implicit agreement with *Amoco* on the presumption question (in the permanent injunction context) because it clearly places the burden of proof on the plaintiff. *Id.* at 1839.

Furthermore, these cases stand together for the principle that a district court should not depart from a traditional analysis of the relevant equitable factors, whether for a preliminary or a permanent injunction, unless directed to do so by statute. Policy considerations aside, there is nothing in the text of Section 502 evidencing a departure from traditional equitable practices for either a preliminary or a permanent injunction. Section 502(a) merely states that a district court "may ... grant temporary and final injunctions on such terms as it may deem reasonable to prevent or restrain infringement of a copyright." 17 U.S.C. § 502(a). Based on *eBay* and *Amoco,* there is no language in the text of the Copyright Act that would permit a departure from traditional equitable principles such that a presumption of irreparable harm would be allowed in any injunctive context.

Thus, *Amoco* provides additional doctrinal support for rejecting a presumption of irreparable harm in permanent injunction cases, and further reduces the import of Plaintiffs' pre-*eBay* preliminary injunction citations.

b. Irreparable Harm has been Established

Irreparable harm cannot be established solely on the fact of past infringement. Additionally, it must also be true that the mere likelihood of future infringement by a defendant does not by itself allow for an inference of irreparable harm. As to the latter, future copyright infringement can always be redressed via damages, whether actual or statutory. *See* 17 U.S.C. § 504. To the extent that future infringement is relevant to the analysis, the onus is on Plaintiffs to explain why future infringements resulting from StreamCast's inducement would cause *irreparable* harm. It cannot be presumed. For example, in a recent patent infringement case in the Eastern District of Texas, the district court held that the defendant's continued infringement of plaintiff's patent would cause irreparable harm due to the "[l]oss of market share in this nascent market" for digital video recorders. *TiVo Inc.,* 446 F.Supp.2d at 669. Importantly, the *TiVo* Court did not make a finding of irreparable harm based on the simple fact of continued infringement, which could be compensated for with an award of damages.

"[I]rreparable harm may not be presumed[, but] [i]n run-of-the-mill copyright litigation, such proof should not be difficult to establish...." 6 Patry, *supra,* § 22:74. Thus, Plaintiffs may establish an irreparable harm stemming from the infringement (*e.g.,* loss of market share, reputational harm). It is also possible that some qualitative feature about the infringement itself, such as its peculiar nature, could elevate its status into the realm of "irreparable harm."

StreamCast accepts that certain harms caused by infringement, such as loss of brand recognition and market share, can amount to irreparable harm. (StreamCast Opp. at 10.) However, StreamCast rejects the argument that copyright infringement can itself ever represent irreparable harm. StreamCast asserts that "[i]f damages can be calculated, the injury is **not** irreparable ...—the Copyright Act specifically provides for statutory damages, which are calculable assuming Plaintiffs can prove direct infringement of their works, and a basis for the range requested." (*Id.*) This Court has doubts regarding StreamCast's position. In *eBay,* Chief Justice Roberts indicated that irreparable harm can result from the infringement itself, depending upon the circumstances of the case:

> From at least the early 19th century, courts have granted injunctive relief upon a finding of infringement in the vast majority of patent cases. This "long tradition of equity practice" is not surprising, given the difficulty of protecting a right to *exclude* through monetary remedies that allow an infringer to *use* an invention against the patentee's wishes-a difficulty that often implicates the first two factors of the traditional four-factor test.

126 S.Ct. at 1841 (Roberts, C.J., concurring); *see also MercExchange,* 500 F.Supp.2d at 568; *cf. Muniauction, Inc.,* 2007 WL 2225847, at *2

This Court also recognizes that a competing *eBay* concurrence took issue with Chief Justice Roberts's "right to exclude" language. Justice Kennedy explained his view that "the existence of a right to exclude does not dictate the remedy for a violation of that right." *eBay,* 126 S.Ct. at 1842 (Kennedy, J., concurring). This Court agrees, since a contrary conclusion would come close to permitting a presumption of irreparable harm. This Court also observes that Justice Kennedy's statement was made primarily in the context of certain recent developments in the patent field that are wholly inapplicable to this lawsuit. For example, this is simply not a case in which the copyright infringement represents "but a small component of the product the companies seek to produce," such that "legal damages may well be sufficient to compensate for the infringement." *Id.* As this Court previously held, StreamCast's entire business was built around the fundamental premise that Morpheus would be utilized to infringe copyrights, including those owned by Plaintiffs. Furthermore, Justice Kennedy emphasized that "[t]he equitable discretion over injunctions ... is well suited to allow courts to adapt to the rapid technological and legal developments...." *Id.* Given the technological aspects of the infringement induced by StreamCast, and the flexibility conferred by the Copyright Act, this Court is persuaded that its bases for finding irreparable harm, *infra,* are supported by both Chief Justice Roberts's and Justice Kennedy's concurrences.

In light of this authority, the Court concludes that certain qualities pertaining to the nature of StreamCast's inducement of infringement are relevant to a finding of irreparable harm. As stated before, the Court disagrees with the Eighth Circuit's categorical pronouncement in *Taylor* that "irreparable harm inescapably flows from the denial" of "the right to control the use of its copyrighted materials." *See supra* note 13 (quoting *Taylor,* 403 F.3d at 968). After *eBay,* the word "inescapably" simply goes too far. However, infringement may still occur in such a manner that it has the actual effect of irreparably harming a plaintiff's right to control the use of his/her copyrighted material.

The irreparable harm analysis centers on two basic themes: (1) StreamCast has and will continue to induce far more infringement than it could ever possibly redress with damages; and (2) Plaintiffs' copyrights (especially those of popular works) have and will be rendered particularly vulnerable to continuing infringement on an enormous scale due to StreamCast's inducement. The Court agrees with both arguments, and each is independently sufficient to support of finding of irreparable harm in this case.

First, the Court must ask whether a particular defendant's probable inability to pay damage constitutes irreparable harm. In the ordinary case, "merely alleging an opponent's inability to pay damages does not constitute irreparable harm." *Rosewood Apartments Corp. v. Perpignano,* 200 F.Supp.2d 269, 278 (S.D.N.Y.2002). But "[i]n some limited circumstances, parties have demonstrated such a strong likelihood that their opponent will be unable to pay that courts have awarded them equitable relief." *Id.* For example, in another copyright infringement case, the district court found that the harm from infringement "will not be remedied by a damage award that may or may not be collectible." *See Lava Records LLC v. Ates,* 2006 WL 1914166, at *3 (W.D.La. July 11, 2006). The rationale in such cases must be that an award of monetary damages will be meaningless, and the plaintiff will have no substantive relief, where it will be impossible to collect an award for past and/or future infringements perpetrated by a defendant.

Plaintiffs have not yet sought an award of statutory damages. Additionally, Plaintiffs have not provided this Court with specific evidence as part of this motion demonstrating that StreamCast would be unable to pay damages for the infringements it has induced in the past, and could continue to induce in the future. But such evidence is not necessary here. Based on the undisputed evidence at summary judgment of massive end-user infringement, it is highly likely that the award of statutory damages that ultimately befalls StreamCast in this case will be enormous (especially considering the potential relationship between inducement and a finding of willfulness), and would far outstrip the amount of revenue the company has garnered in recent years. *See Grokster,* 454 F.Supp.2d at 982–83. This Court's conclusion would also be the same even if Plaintiffs chose to forgo a damages award as part of this lawsuit. This is because the amount of infringement that StreamCast could induce in the future is so staggering that the recoverable statutory damages would very probably be well beyond StreamCast's anticipated resources. Because it is extremely unlikely that StreamCast will be able to compensate Plaintiffs monetarily for the infringements it has induced in the past, or the infringements it could induce in the future through Morpheus, Plaintiffs have and will continue to suffer irreparable harm.

Second, the Court agrees with Plaintiffs' claim that a substantial number of their copyrighted works have and would continue to become irreparably exposed to infringement on a tremendous scale due to StreamCast's inducement. This inducement greatly erodes Plaintiffs' ability to enforce their exclusive rights. *See A & M Records, Inc. v. Napster, Inc.,* 239 F.3d 1004, 1029 (9th Cir.2001) (rejecting Napster's request for compulsory royalties as opposed to injunctive relief because "Plaintiffs would lose the power to control their intellectual property"). It also promises no realistic mechanism through which statutory damages can be collected for all of the inevitable subsequent infringements occurring outside of the Morpheus System and Software.

In our constitutional system, Congress has been empowered "[t]o promote the progress of science and useful arts, by securing for limited times to authors and inventors the exclusive right to their respective writings and discoveries." U.S. Const. art. I, § 8, cl. 8. Pursuant to this authority, the Copyright Act confers certain exclusive rights to Plaintiffs in their works, such as the rights of reproduction and distribution. 17 U.S.C. §§ 106(1), (3). The exclusive right to engage in such actions also provides the copyright owner the concurrent power, through the legal system, to exclude others from engaging in such activities without authorization. *See Taylor,* 403 F.3d at 968 (copyright owner has right to "control the use of its copyrighted materials").

Importantly, the inducement of infringement via the internet and other digital pathways represents no ordinary infringement:

> When digital works are distributed via the internet, ... every downloader who receives one of the copyrighted works ... is in turn capable of also transmitting perfect copies of the works. Accordingly, the process is

> potentially exponential rather than linear, threatening virtually unstoppable infringement of the copyright.

Elektra, 2004 WL 783123, at *7 n. 5 (internal citation omitted); *see also Streeter,* 438 F.Supp.2d at 1073 n. 2 (same). StreamCast's inducement through the Morpheus Software has "left Plaintiffs' sound recordings vulnerable to massive, repeated, near-instantaneous, and worldwide infringement." ...

When StreamCast induces infringement, Morpheus end-users obtain "perfect copies" of Plaintiffs' work that can be inexpensively reproduced and distributed *ad nauseam.* In fact, through StreamCast's inducement, an entire universe of copyrighted content has been, and can continue to be, made available for unending infringement outside of the Morpheus System and Software. And given the volume of infringement caused by StreamCast's inducement in this particular case, the assault on Plaintiffs' intellectual property rights through further digital transfers by members of the public—Plaintiffs' customer base—is difficult to overstate. StreamCast's inducement has eviscerated Plaintiffs' ability to protect and enforce their statutorily-created property rights.

StreamCast has submitted to this Court an article in which it is claimed that internet file sharing has had a "statistically indistinguishable" effect on music sales. (Baker Decl. Ex. B at 68.) However, this argument misses the mark because it does not matter whether file sharing affects record company sales or not. It would also make no difference if StreamCast's inducement was demonstrated to *increase* Plaintiffs' sales. The Court is not concerned with whether end-users are now less likely, or more likely, to buy Plaintiffs's music or movies as a result of their infringement. This is a policy rationale for a legislature to consider, if it should choose to do so.

As copyright owners, Plaintiffs have the exclusive right to decide when and how their material should be reproduced and/or distributed, regardless of whether their decisions make good business sense. When StreamCast induces infringement, Plaintiffs' copyrighted works can be unstoppably and near-instantaneously infringed throughout the computer-literate world with the files obtained by Morpheus endusers. Plaintiffs' power to control their rights has been so compromised by the means through which StreamCast encouraged end-users to infringe (digital files plus the internet) that the inducement amounts to irreparable harm. This is especially true considering the amount of infringement that occurs on the Morpheus System and Software. Morpheus users have the continued ability to pillage a tremendous quantity of Plaintiffs' intellectual property, and to spread this capacity elsewhere with additional file sharing.

The Court is aware that Plaintiffs can seek an award of statutory damages from StreamCast for infringements occurring through the Morpheus System and Software (ignoring for now the likely reality regarding StreamCast's ability to pay). However, Plaintiffs cannot recover damages from StreamCast for the inevitable derivative infringements that will occur outside of Morpheus, with copyrighted content originally acquired within it, as a consequence StreamCast's inducement. Even numerous lawsuits against direct infringers will necessarily prove to be insufficient under these conditions. Indeed, the very need to file multiple lawsuits as a consequence of StreamCast's inducement is itself supportive of an irreparable harm finding.

In sum, Plaintiffs' have offered two independently sufficient grounds for a finding of irreparable harm. Plaintiffs will suffer irreparable harm because of StreamCast's likely inability to pay for the past and/or future infringements that it has induced. Additionally, StreamCast's inducement has and will continue to irreparably harm Plaintiffs' very ability to enforce its exclusive rights. Relatedly, Plaintiffs cannot possibly recover all damages for the infringements that will occur in the future outside of Morpheus, with files obtained within Morpheus, as a consequence of the inducement.

2. Adequate Remedy at Law

The Court must now consider whether there is an adequate remedy at law for the harm that has or could be caused by StreamCast's inducement. "[T]he requisite analysis for the second factor of the four-factor test inevitably overlaps with that of the first...." *MercExchange,* 500 F.Supp.2d at 582; *see also 800 Adept, Inc. v. Murex Securities, Ltd.,* 505 F.Supp.2d 1327, 1336–37 (M.D.Fla.2007) (quoting *Lewis v. S.S. Baune,* 534 F.2d 1115, 1124 (5th Cir.1976) (" '[o]ften times the concepts of 'irreparable injury' and 'no adequate remedy at law' are indistinguishable' in the context of a permanent injunction.")). As should be expected, this Court's adequate remedy at law analysis parallels that performed for irreparable harm.

First, as discussed above, there is a substantial possibility that StreamCast will be unable to pay a statutory damages award for the infringement it has induced (or will continue to induce).

Second, "[a] legal remedy is inadequate if it would require a 'multiplicity of suits.' " *Id.* at 714. In this case, Plaintiffs will only be entitled to a statutory recovery of those infringements induced through the Morpheus System. However, this award will not compensate Plaintiffs when these same files are subsequently shared outside Morpheus.

Therefore, the second equitable factor weighs in Plaintiffs' favor.

3. Balance of Hardships

As to the third factor, the Court must consider the hardships; that might afflict the parties by the grant or denial of Plaintiffs' motion for a permanent injunction. The Court has already described in detail the substantial costs exacted by StreamCast's inducement, whether in the past or in the future, and need not recapitulate them here in detail. Obviously, "the fact that Plaintiffs' recordings can be replicated into infinity, for free, establishes that a distinct hardship rests with Plaintiffs." *Blake,* 2007 WL 1853956, at *3.

StreamCast has its own claims of hardship. First, StreamCast complains that it will suffer undue harm because Plaintiffs' proposed injunction would "wipe [ ] out" the non-infringing aspects of the Morpheus System and Software. (StreamCast Opp. at 15.) Essentially, StreamCast is concerned that Plaintiffs' proposed injunction would be technologically impossible to comply with and would result in the shutdown of the company. However, as discussed *infra* Part III.D.5, the injunction imagined by this Court alleviates such concerns.

In relation to this argument, StreamCast cites to *Abend v. MCA, Inc.,* 863 F.2d 1465 (9th Cir.1988), where the Ninth Circuit denied an injunction as to further showings of the Alfred Hitchcock film "Rear Window." The Court held that "[i]t would cause a great injustice for the owners of the film" because the "success of the movie resulted in large part from factors completely unrelated to the underlying story." *Id.* at 1479. No such special circumstances are present in this case. StreamCast's inducement of infringement has no separate legitimate business purpose whatsoever. The injunction will be limited to restraining future infringement resulting from StreamCast's inducement, rendering *Abend* inapplicable.

Second, StreamCast argues that it no longer has the intent to induce infringement through its distribution of Morpheus, and that there is no risk that such intent will return:

> "There is no evidence of current or potential future inducement: by StreamCast. StreamCast lacks the requisite specific intent to induce infringement, evidenced by its efforts to discourage infringement, including its development of an effective filter, its messages to users to upgrade to a filtered version, and its testing and license negotiations with ... companies that distribute and license acoustic finger-printing technology/filters."

StreamCast's self-serving statements, and its actions taken post-September 27, 2006, do not change this Court's conclusion. As discussed *infra* Part III.D.5, distribution can itself amount to an act of inducement. StreamCast unquestionably desires to continue its distribution of Morpheus. However, StreamCast now asserts that its "intent" has changed and that its further distribution would not be based on a will to induce. The Court is inherently suspicious of StreamCast's statements, as it is entirely too easy for an adjudicated infringer to claim a reformation once the specter of a permanent injunction looms near. ...

The Court is persuaded that StreamCast would likely engage in further inducement of infringement in the absence of a permanent injunction. As has been stated by the Ninth Circuit in the securities context, "[t]he existence of past violations may give rise to an inference that there will be future violations." *SEC v. Murphy,* 626 F.2d 633, 655 (9th Cir.1980). And in this case, such an inference is warranted based upon various undisputed facts, including: (1) "overwhelming" evidence of StreamCast's illegal objective, which resulted in a "staggering" amount of infringement, Grokster, 454 F.Supp.2d at 985, 992; (2) StreamCast's business model has depended on inducement, *id.* at 988–89, and the company would financially benefit from further infringement based on its continued desire to advertise, ...

Even if this Court gave some credence to StreamCast's alleged reform, it could immediately return to its prior ways after the motion for a permanent injunction is denied. *See LGS Architects,* 434 F.3d at 1153. In a relatively recent case decided by the Seventh Circuit, the defendant was a direct infringer who appealed the district court's grant of a permanent injunction. *Id.* at 893; ... Because StreamCast is likely to induce further infringements without an injunction, the balance of hardships necessarily shifts further in Plaintiffs' favor. The Court therefore holds that the third equitable factor strongly supports a permanent injunction.

4. The Public Interest

The Court finally agrees that the public interest will be served with a permanent injunction, since it will protect Plaintiffs' copyrights against increased infringement. ... The public interest in receiving copyrighted content for free is outweighed by the need to incentivize the creation of original works. ... Certainly, the public does not benefit from StreamCast's inducement of infringement.

StreamCast claims the public will be harmed because Plaintiffs' proposed permanent injunction is so broad that: (1) StreamCast will be forced to discontinue the Morpheus System and Software (including all non-infringing aspects); and (2) StreamCast will not be able to update the non-filtering legacy versions of its software, which are still apparently used by a large number of end-users. However, as discussed *infra,* the injunction in this case will not require StreamCast to immediately shut down. StreamCast will be empowered to update legacy versions of its software as far as it is technologically feasible to do so.

Thus, the Court finds that the four-factor test favors the imposition of an injunction to restrain StreamCast's inducement of infringement. In its discretion, the Court deems it appropriate for a permanent injunction to issue.

C. StreamCast's Other Defenses

StreamCast offers several defenses in an effort to argue that Plaintiffs are not entitled to an injunction in any form. None of these defenses are meritorious.

1. Unclean Hands

StreamCast asserts that Plaintiffs are not entitled to a permanent injunction as a result of their unclean hands.

StreamCast claims that Plaintiffs have acted inequitably by refusing to share the hash values or artist-title pairs of their copyrighted material. Plaintiffs' conduct was not inequitable. Plaintiffs have taken the legal position, since this Court's summary judgment holding in their favor, that StreamCast has the burden of effectively stopping infringement via Morpheus and that Plaintiffs are not required to assist in this process. This is not "hav [ing] it both ways" (StreamCast Opp. at 19), let alone an act of contributing to or condoning the inducement of infringement. As explained *infra* Part III.D.6, the Court ultimately agrees with StreamCast that some form of notice from Plaintiffs is required. In particular, Plaintiffs will be required to provide StreamCast with artist-title pairs before StreamCast's filtering responsibilities will be triggered for each copyrighted work. Nonetheless, the law on this question is not fully clear, meaning that Plaintiffs' legal position was objectively reasonable. As this Court similarly stated in its September 27, 2006 Order, "the Court rejects StreamCast's position that a copyright holder's assertion of what it plausibly believes to be its rights under an ambiguous statute" can amount to an inequitable act. *See Grokster,* 454 F.Supp.2d at 998. The refusal to disclose artist-title pairs to date does not allow StreamCast to succeed on an unclean hands defense...

The Court also fails to understand how StreamCast has suffered any actual harm. StreamCast has only generally argued that due to Plaintiffs' "refusal to share either hash values or Artist–Title information, StreamCast gathered the facts of Artist–Title pair names, even though this process was time-consuming and difficult to track." (StreamCast Opp. at 19.) StreamCast vaguely claims with some uncertainty that this refusal may cause StreamCast's filter to be "more burdensome ... to update." (*Id.*) The fact that a task was possibly made harder by Plaintiffs' refusal to offer assistance does not mean that StreamCast suffered any form of discernible damages. StreamCast's speculative claims of personal injury are totally insufficient. Furthermore, StreamCast has likely benefitted from Plaintiffs' unwillingness to cooperate. ...

Given its inability to allege a plausible harm to its own interest, StreamCast argues that the public will be harmed if it is forced to shut down. First, StreamCast's argument was made in light of Plaintiffs' proposed injunction that would require the company to stop its operations unless direct infringement could be prevented exhaustively. From this premise, StreamCast complained that it would lose the opportunity to update all legacy versions of the Morpheus software, which lack a filtering mechanism at this time. But StreamCast will not have to close its doors for failing to introduce a perfect filter at this time. Additionally, the unclean hands "defense will not apply if the defendant merely establishes harm to the public interest." *McCormick v. Cohn,* 1992 WL 687291, at *4 (S.D.Cal. July 31, 1992); ...

StreamCast's unclean hands defense fails because Plaintiffs have not acted inequitably and StreamCast has suffered no personal harm to date.

2. Waiver and Estoppel

StreamCast raises the defenses of waiver and estoppel. "Waiver is the intentional relinquishment of a known right with knowledge of its existence and the intent to relinquish it." *United States v. King Features Entm't, Inc.,* 843 F.2d 394, 399 (9th Cir.1988). "StreamCast argues that Plaintiffs waived their right to a permanent injunction by: (1) refusing to provide hash values and artist-title pairs to StreamCast, and (2) allowing other peer-to-peer networks such as iMesh to offer unfiltered software. This argument is wrongheaded. First, Plaintiffs' failure to divulge the requested information to StreamCast provides no evidence whatsoever of an "intent" to waive a permanent injunction. This lawsuit has been litigated for numerous years, and the Court even noted in its 2003 Order granting defendants' motion for summary judgment that "Plaintiffs principally seek prospective injunctive relief." *Metro–Goldwyn–Mayer Studios, Inc. v. Grokster, Ltd.,* 259 F.Supp.2d 1029, 1033 (C.D.Cal.2003). Plaintiffs' refusal to assist StreamCast in their filtering efforts, after years of protracted litigation, cannot plausibly be viewed as a waiver.

Furthermore, Plaintiffs' actions with respect to other companies operating peer-to-peer networks are irrelevant. The Court knows of no rule in copyright, and StreamCast has cited no authority for the proposition, that a copyright holder is bound to pursue either all infringers or none at all. The waiver analysis should ordinarily be limited to evaluating the conduct and/or communications that occur between a plaintiff and a defendant claiming the waiver defense. StreamCast's position would create a rule whereby Plaintiffs would be barred from suing any of the millions upon millions of direct infringers utilizing peer-to-peer networks unless all were sued. Even assuming that StreamCast correctly describes Plaintiffs' arrangement with other file sharing companies, it is of no moment.

StreamCast further raises the estoppel argument, based again upon the same two grounds discussed immediately above: (1) Plaintiffs' refusal to assist StreamCast, and (2) Plaintiffs' dealings with iMesh and others. The elements of estoppel in copyright cases were established by the Ninth Circuit in *Hampton v. Paramount Pictures Corp.,* 279 F.2d 100 (9th Cir.1960): ...

D. The Permanent Injunction's Scope and Specificity

A permanent injunction must be carefully crafted. "[T]he scope of the injunction should be coterminous with the infringement." 4 Nimmer & Nimmer, *supra,* § 14.06[C]. This is perhaps partly why "blanket injunctions to obey the law are disfavored." *Mulcahy v. Cheetah Learning LLC,* 386 F.3d 849, 852 n. 1 (8th Cir.2004). Rule 65(d) also requires that injunctions be specific:

> Every order granting an injunction and every restraining order shall set forth the reasons for its issuance; shall be specific in terms; shall describe in reasonable detail, and not by reference to the complaint or other document, the act or acts sought to be restrained.

Fed.R.Civ.P. 65(d). "Injunctive relief should be narrowly tailored to fit specific legal violations." *Waldman Pub. Corp. v. Landoll, Inc.,* 43 F.3d 775, 785 (2d Cir.1994). The devil is in the details.

1. Non-Inducement Theories of Liability...

2. Non-Federal Law...

3. Valid and Subsisting Copyrights...

4. Plaintiffs' Universe of Copyrights

Plaintiffs' proposed injunction also extends to all of Plaintiffs' copyrighted works "whether now in existence or later created." This provision is entirely proper, as confirmed by recent Ninth Circuit law. *See Amazon.com, Inc.,* 487 F.3d at 710 n. 1... The clause also comports with the Copyright Act's express terms. Because the permanent injunction may extend to "any copyright," this includes: (1) all valid and subsisting copyrights in existence at the time the injunction is issued (not simply those a defendant has been held liable for infringement), and (2) any valid and subsisting copyright not yet created. In light of the facts of this case, and that future, popular works created by Plaintiffs would undoubtedly financially benefit StreamCast's inducement of infringement, the clause will be included.

5. Filtering and Updating Legacy Software

The purpose of a permanent injunction in this case is to restrain StreamCast's inducement of infringement, as well as future end-user infringements arising from the inducement. As stated by the Supreme Court, "one who distributes a device with the object of promoting its use to infringe copyright, as shown by clear expression or other affirmative steps taken to foster infringement, is liable for the resulting acts of infringement by third parties." *Grokster,* 545 U.S. at 936–37, 125 S.Ct. 2764. StreamCast fully intends to continue its distribution of the Morpheus System and. Software. While reserving its right to contest the injunction's issuance in the first place, StreamCast concedes that non-distribution acts promoting and encouraging infringement via Morpheus can be enjoined. (*See* StreamCast Supp. Opp. at 9–10 ("[T]he Court must narrowly tailor any injunction to address only the specific acts of inducement for which StreamCast was found to liable....").)

The fundamental dispute between Plaintiffs and StreamCast is whether this Court has the power to regulate StreamCast's distribution of the Morpheus System and Software to end-users. In particular, Plaintiffs request that StreamCast filter the Morpheus System and Software to reduce its infringing capacities as far as possible.

StreamCast asserts that its continued distribution of the Morpheus System and Software is legal, even though it fails to implement any filtering technology to limit Morpheus's infringing capabilities, as long as it does not engage in any additional actions or statements promoting or encouraging end-user infringement. StreamCast concludes that its mere distribution of a product capable of substantial noninfringing uses, going forward, is legal under *Sony* and cannot be regulated with filtering.

The Court recognizes that *in the first instance* one cannot be held liable for contributory infringement under *Sony* merely for distributing a product capable of substantial noninfringing uses, even with knowledge that the product is used to infringe. *See Grokster,* 545 U.S. at 931–32, 125 S.Ct. 2764. Of note, this Court's 2003 Order ruling that Morpheus met the *Sony* standard has never been disturbed. However, *Sony* provides no immunity where a staple's distribution is sufficiently connected to the promotion/encouragement of infringement. *See id.* at 935, 125 S.Ct. 2764.

The Supreme Court's decision in this case did not address the question of remedies. Consequently, analogies must be made with reference to the law of patent inducement and elsewhere. As codified by the Patent Act, "[w]hoever actively induces infringement of a patent shall be liable as an infringer." 35 U.S.C. § 271(b). One leading patent treatise has argued that "the patent owner's remedies under Section 271(b) for active inducement cannot be expanded so as to establish exclusive control over the staple commodity." 5 Donald J. Chisum, *Chisum on Patents,* § 17.04[3]. In patent law, the staple article "is one that was not specifically designed for use with a patented process [or combination] and has substantial, efficient, and feasible uses outside of the patent. If the practice of the patented method [or combination] is incidental and necessary to the practice of the unpatented methods, the device is a staple and there can be no contributory infringement." ...

These cases are of limited assistance to StreamCast, however, because they speak specifically of a proposed total ban on the distribution or sale of a staple. Were this Court to hold that StreamCast could no longer distribute Morpheus in light of its inducement, such a ruling might grant rights to Plaintiffs beyond the limited monopoly permitted under the Copyright Act. But a filtering solution is different. There is a distinction between forbidding distribution of a technology capable of substantial noninfringing uses and simply requiring sufficient efforts to minimize the prospective infringement that would otherwise be induced through the staple's distribution. StreamCast would still be allowed to distribute Morpheus so long as it undertook sufficient measures to mitigate end-user capacity for infringement.

StreamCast argues still that Plaintiffs should not be permitted any "right to control the distribution" of products capable of substantial noninfringing use. However, *Sony* does not create a general rule of immunity against all forms of secondary liability, but provides only a limited safe harbor as to "imputed intent." *See Grokster,* 545 U.S. at 934, 125 S.Ct. 2764. Distributors of products capable of substantial noninfringing uses are often vulnerable to lawsuits for contributory infringement, and injunctions regulating how such products may be subsequently distributed (as opposed to a total ban) have been upheld. StreamCast need only look to its predecessor—Napster—for such confirmation.

On its first appeal to the Ninth Circuit, Napster argued that it could not be held liable for material contribution or vicarious infringement based on the fact that its system was capable of substantial noninfringing uses. In affirming the district court's determination that a preliminary injunction was proper, the Court held that *Sony* was not a bar to liability on either theory. *See Napster,* 239 F.3d at 1020, 1022–23. On remand, the district court ordered Napster to institute "audio fingerprinting" technology (presumably a different term for acoustical fingerprinting) in order to effectuate the terms of the modified preliminary injunction. The Ninth Circuit affirmed this action as a "proper exercise of the district court's supervisory authority." *A & M Records, Inc. v. Napster, Inc.,* 284 F.3d 1091, 1098 (9th Cir.2002). Importantly, Napster was never enjoined from distributing its software to the public. The injunction was solely aimed at stopping the infringement that was effectuated through Napster, and court-ordered filtering was deemed an appropriate mechanism for achieving this task. While the plaintiffs were not given exclusive control over Napster's product, *Sony* was no obstacle to an injunction designed to reduce the infringing capabilities of a product capable of substantial noninfringing use.

Based on the Ninth Circuit's *Napster* decisions, products capable of substantial noninfringing use can be filtered if the failure to do so would constitute either continued contributory infringement (in the form of material contribution) or vicarious infringement. It would therefore be anomalous if such filtering were always unavailable where a defendant has only been held liable for inducement. Thus, there' should not be an *a priori* rule as to whether or not the continued distribution of a product capable of substantial noninfringing uses, in the absence of any further acts promoting its use for infringement, amounts to inducement. Rather, a court should consider the facts of each case before rendering such a determination.

In this Court's view, StreamCast's argument against filtering reflects an overly restrictive vision of inducement...

In effect, the "culpable act," which induces third parties to infringement, certainly manifests itself once two components are present—distribution and promotion/encouragement. *See Amazon.com,* 487 F.3d at 727 n. 11; *Visa,* 494 F.3d at 800–01. It is important to recognize that the Supreme Court did not impose any strict timing relationship between specific acts promoting infringements, distribution, and the direct infringements themselves. For a party to be liable for inducement, distribution may begin prior to any promotion of infringement, distribution and promotion can occur at the same time, and most critically, *distribution can follow past promotion.* This highlighted portion of the above sentence is crucial. As a matter of common sense, a successful inducer will sometimes have no need to repeat the infringing message *ad infinitum.* This is especially likely to be the case where the product in question is overwhelmingly used for infringing purposes, and requires little or no specialized training to operate. At a certain point, the inducer can simply continue to distribute the product without any additional active encouragement, recognizing that the marketplace will respond in turn.

Thus, once the market has internalized the inducer's promotion of infringement, the resulting infringements should be attributable to that defendant even though he/she no longer chooses to actively promote that message. There is no difference between these infringements and those that are consummated while the defendant is still engaging in the active promotion of infringement.

Thus, distribution of a product capable of substantial noninfringing uses, even after the promotion/encouragement of infringement ceases, can by itself constitute inducement.

StreamCast's future distribution is undoubtedly connected to past promotional efforts. In its September 27, 2006 Order, this Court recounted in detail, among other undisputed facts, StreamCast's efforts to promote its software to the Napster market as a mechanism for infringing Plaintiffs' copyrighted works. ...

StreamCast's revenues skyrocketed as a result. Furthermore, StreamCast could not reasonably claim ignorance of the infringements perpetrated by Morpheus endusers. *Grokster,* 454 F.Supp.2d at 992.

StreamCast has etched its niche in the market for infringement.... The fact that a permanent injunction is imposed also does not leave Morpheus magically reborn as a product safe for unfiltered distribution under *Sony.* As stated by Justice Scalia to StreamCast's counsel at oral argument, "the point is that those past acts [of encouragement] are what have developed your client's current clientele."

It is also of no moment that Morpheus's mere distribution, had there never been any promotion of infringement by StreamCast, would have been legal under this Court's prior interpretations of *Sony.* The *Sony* rule is at its height when analyzed in the vacuum of a product's architecture. But once other evidence is in fact considered (*e.g.,* past promotion), mere distribution of a staple can "itself" become the "culpable act" lacking protection under the Copyright Act. *Grokster,* 545 U.S. at 940 n. 13, 125 S.Ct. 2764. StreamCast is not being "punished" for its past actions; rather, StreamCast's past activity is relevant to what future actions constitute inducement going forward.

An unfiltered Morpheus, which StreamCast intends to distribute if provided the opportunity, necessarily capitalizes on and remains inexorably linked to its historical efforts to promote infringement. The bell simply cannot be unrung. Accordingly, Morpheus's connection to the past promotion of infringement means that StreamCast's continued distribution of Morpheus alone constitutes inducement. This Court is empowered to regulate Morpheus under 17 U.S.C. § 502(a) in order to prevent this distribution from causing future harm to Plaintiffs' rights.

Remedy: Given the Court's determination regarding the status of Morpheus's further distribution, the Court must analyze the proper scope of injunctive relief. First, because StreamCast's distribution of Morpheus will induce the infringement of Plaintiffs' copyrights, the Court could potentially bar Morpheus's distribution in its entirety. However, as previously discussed, this remedy could constitute an inappropriate extension of Plaintiffs' copyrights. Plaintiffs should not lightly be given total control over a product capable of substantial noninfringing uses.

Second, Plaintiffs' proposed permanent injunction would bar StreamCast from distributing Morpheus or another peer-to-peer network "unless and until it has demonstrated to the Court's satisfaction that it contains a robust and secure means exhaustively to prevent users from using the applicable system ..." to infringe Plaintiffs' copyrights. ...

In any event, the Court will follow a third path. A permanent injunction will issue requiring StreamCast to reduce Morpheus's infringing capabilities, while preserving its core noninfringing functionality, as effectively as possible. StreamCast's duties will include, but not necessarily be limited to: (1) a filter as part of future Morpheus software distributed to the public; and (2) steps to encourage end-user upgrades from non-filtered legacy software. Such duties represent the proper balance between competing interests. Plaintiffs' copyrights can be protected to the extent feasible, but Morpheus's noninfringing uses will not be completely enjoined....

In defining "effectiveness," StreamCast would likely argue that cost is relevant to the calculus. The Court is aware that Plaintiffs want StreamCast to apply a "state of the art" commercial filter that includes acoustical fingerprinting, which StreamCast has termed "cost-prohibitive." (Weiss Decl. ¶ 12.) The Court is tentatively of the view that affordability is a minor, but potentially relevant, consideration at the fringes. For example, if two competing filtering regimens had identical success rates for purposes of reducing infringement, but the cost of the first option was inordinate compared to the second, the Court might be more inclined to opt for the latter. Cost is not likely to be a controlling factor, as the injunction will be designed primarily to protect Plaintiffs' copyrights. The mere fact that an adjudicated infringer may have to expend substantial resources to prevent the consummation of further induced infringements is not a central concern...

As explained *infra* Part III.F, the Court intends to appoint a special master. The special master will assist this Court in selecting a filtering regimen that reduces Morpheus's infringing capacity, preserves its noninfringing functionality as feasible, and analyzes any potential cost concerns.

6. Notice of Copyrighted Works

StreamCast also argues, as part of a permanent injunction, that it should have no duty to filter Plaintiffs' copyrighted works until it has been provided sufficient notice. The Court agrees.

In *Napster,* the district court enjoined Napster from "engaging in, or facilitating others in copying, downloading, uploading, transmitting, or distributing plaintiffs' copyrighted musical compositions and sound recordings...." 114 F.Supp.2d at 927. The district court determined that "[b]ecause defendant has contributed to illegal copying on a scale that is without precedent, it bears the burden of developing a means to comply with the injunction." *Id.*

While the Ninth Circuit affirmed the injunction generally, its scope was too broad. The Ninth Circuit held...

On remand, the plaintiffs were ordered to provide Napster with certain information regarding their copyrighted works: (1) title; (2) artist; (3) the name(s) of one or more files on Napster's system containing the work; and (4) certification of ownership.

Doctrinally, the notice requirement is of particular interest considering the fact that the district court and Ninth Circuit agreed that Napster would likely be held liable as both a contributory *and* vicarious infringer. The Ninth Circuit's modification is eminently clear when examined solely from a contributory liability perspective, since the Ninth Circuit's affirmance on this theory was based substantially on *Napster's* actual notice. 239 F.3d at 1027 However, Napster was also likely to be found liable at trial as a vicarious infringer, which is based on a defendant's financial benefit and its right and ability to supervise. *See id.,* at 1023–24. *Sony's* knowledge prong is completely irrelevant to whether one can be held liable as a vicarious infringer. *Id.* at 1022 By imposing the notice requirement on the plaintiffs, the Ninth Circuit essentially allowed *Sony* notice concerns to creep back into the vicarious infringement analysis for purposes of an injunction.

Similarly, *Sony* represents no bar to inducement liability. According to the Supreme Court, "where evidence goes beyond a product's characteristics or the knowledge that it may be put to infringing uses, and shows statements or actions directed to promoting infringement, *Sony's* staple-article rule will not preclude liability." *Grokster,* 545 U.S. at 935, 125 S.Ct. 2764. And due to its relationship to StreamCast's past promotion of infringement, the mere continued distribution of Morpheus now by itself amounts to inducement. *See supra* Part III.D.5.

Although actual notice of specific infringing files (and the failure to remove them) is not a prerequisite to inducement liability in the first instance, like vicarious infringement, *Napster* informs this Court that notice is relevant to the injunction. While the continued distribution of an ineffectively filtered Morpheus would violate the injunction, some precautions are necessary to ensure that StreamCast will not be unfairly penalized for the architecture of its staple commodity. For example, by requiring Plaintiffs to provide StreamCast with some notice before the latter's filtering responsibilities for a given copyright are triggered, there will be no threat of contempt proceedings simply because StreamCast failed for a time to filter certain files containing recently released (e.g., illegally "leaked" works) or hardly known copyrighted material.

One might argue that *Napster's* notice requirement should not be followed in light of the Supreme Court's Grokster opinion. At one point, the Supreme Court stated that "*Sony* did not displace other theories of secondary liability," and is confined to cases involving "imputed intent." *Grokster,* 545 U.S. at 934, 125 S.Ct. 2764. It could reasonably be argued, as a result, that *Sony* occupies a much less central position in the copyright field than was previously understood. Since Sony cannot preclude vicarious and inducement liability, the doctrine could now be viewed as irrelevant to injunctions aimed at preventing such violations. However, this Court will not read this implication into the Supreme Court's ruling, nor hold that *Napster* has been overruled *sub silentio* on this question. It must be recognized that the Supreme Court did not reach, or even comment on, the proper scope of an injunctive remedy.

On the other hand, while some form of notice is appropriate, the Court will not require Plaintiffs to provide hash values to StreamCast. As in *Napster,* once Plaintiffs have provided certain basic information sufficient to constitute "notice," the burden of implementing an effective filtering solution rests on StreamCast. 239 F.3d at 1027. *Napster* does not require a copyright owner to disclose to an adjudicated infringer all specialized information in his/her possession that might be helpful to the prevention of further infringement, such as hash values.

Therefore, StreamCast's duty to filter any particular copyrighted work will commence upon Plaintiffs' provision of notice. For each work, Plaintiffs will be required to provide the artist-title pair, a certification of ownership, and some evidence that one or more files containing each work is available on the Morpheus System and Software.

7. Advertising to Users of Legacy Software

Plaintiffs argue that "[i]f StreamCast can earn no profits from users of legacy versions of Morpheus that lack filtering technology it will have a powerful reason promptly to move those users to new versions of Morpheus with filtering technology." (Plaintiffs' Supp. Brief at 18.) The Court tentatively agreed at first. But upon further consideration, the Court will not prohibit StreamCast from displaying advertising through Morpheus to users of legacy software. The Court agrees with StreamCast that this restriction will not have any effect on the quantum of induced infringement. At this point in time, the Court has no reason to believe that StreamCast will disregard the terms of a permanent injunction, including those provisions designed to encourage and/or coax end-user upgrades to Morpheus versions containing a filter.

Of course, if StreamCast fails to comply with its responsibilities under the permanent injunction, the Court has the power to respond. Should the Court later determine that StreamCast has violated the terms of the permanent injunction, the Court can consider what remedies should be imposed in order to coerce compliance and compensate Plaintiffs for the harm caused. *See Shuffler v. Heritage Bank,* 720 F.2d 1141, 1147 (9th Cir.1983) (citations omitted) ("Sanctions for civil contempt can be imposed for one or both of two distinct purposes: (1) to compel or coerce obedience to a court order; and (2) to compensate the contemnor's adversary for injuries resulting from the contemnor's noncompliance."). In order to coerce compliance with the other terms of the permanent injunction, as part of a contempt sanction, this Court could *then* potentially prohibit StreamCast from collecting advertising revenue on legacy software or even issue a shut down order. But in the meantime, Plaintiffs' requested ban on advertising to legacy software is premature.

8. Reservation of Court's Power to Alter Terms

The Court also recognizes that filtering technology is evolving. New products may emerge over time that will be vastly more effective than their predecessors. Consequently, the permanent injunction shall retain a clause that expressly: (1) permits this Court to amend the permanent injunction in light of such new developments; and (2) provides a procedure by which either party may petition the Court for such an adjustment to the permanent injunction's terms. ...

E. Request for an Evidentiary Hearing and Discovery...

Finally, StreamCast seeks discovery (and perhaps an evidentiary hearing) on the technological effectiveness of various measures that could be utilized to reduce Morpheus's infringing capabilities. The Court considers this request to be moot. The special master will be conferred with the power necessary to fully investigate all available filtering tools, as well as the options for updating legacy software.

F. Appointment of a Special Master

Shortly, the Court will separately issue a proposed order defining the special master's powers and responsibilities. The parties will be ordered to meet and confer regarding the selection of a special master.

G. StreamCast's Motion for a Stay Pending Appeal

The Court agrees with Plaintiffs that StreamCast's motion for a stay pending appeal pursuant to Rule 62(c) is premature... . Once the Court finalizes the terms of a permanent injunction, and an appeal is taken, StreamCast can renew its request. StreamCast's motion is therefore DENIED WITHOUT PREJUDICE.

IV. CONCLUSION

For the foregoing reasons, this Court GRANTS IN PART Plaintiffs' motion for a permanent injunction. Importantly, StreamCast will be required to use the most effective means available to reduce the infringing capabilities of the Morpheus System and Software, while preserving its noninfringing uses as feasible. StreamCast's motion for a stay of the permanent injunction pending appeal is DENIED WITHOUT PREJUDICE. A special master will be appointed to assist the Court with further proceedings.

IT IS SO ORDERED.

CAPITOL RECORDS, INC. v. THOMAS-RASSET

United States Court of Appeals, Eighth Circuit
Nos. 11-28020, 11-2858, Submitted : June 12, 2012
Sept. 11, 2012, Filed
692 F.3d 899

COLLOTON, Circuit Judge.

This appeal arises from a dispute between several recording companies and Jammie Thomas–Rasset. There is a complicated procedural history involving three jury trials, but for purposes of appeal, it is undisputed that Thomas–Rasset willfully infringed copyrights of twenty-four sound recordings by engaging in file-sharing on the Internet. After a first jury found Thomas–Rasset liable and awarded damages of $222,000, the district court granted a new trial on the ground that the jury instructions incorrectly provided that the Copyright Act forbids making sound recordings available for distribution on a peer-to-peer network, regardless of whether there is proof of "actual distribution." A second jury found Thomas–Rasset liable for willful copyright infringement under a different instruction, and awarded statutory damages of $1,920,000. The district court remitted the award to $54,000, and the companies opted for a new trial on damages. A third jury awarded statutory damages of $1,500,000, but the district court ultimately ruled that the maximum amount permitted by the Due Process Clause of the Fifth Amendment was $54,000 and reduced the verdict accordingly. The court also enjoined Thomas–Rasset from taking certain actions with respect to copyrighted recordings owned by the recording companies.

The companies appeal two aspects of the remedy ordered by the district court. They object to the district court's ruling on damages, and they seek an award of $222,000, which was the amount awarded by the jury in the first trial. They also seek a broader injunction that bars Thomas–Rasset from making any of their sound recordings available to the public. For tactical reasons, the companies do not seek reinstatement of the third jury's award of $1,500,000. They urge instead that this court should reverse the district court's order granting a new trial, rule that the Copyright Act does protect a right to "making available" sound recordings, reinstate the first jury's award of $222,000, and direct entry of a broader injunction. In a cross-appeal, Thomas–Rasset argues that *any* award of statutory damages is unconstitutional, and urges us to vacate the award of damages altogether.

For reasons set forth below, we conclude that the recording companies are entitled to the remedies they seek: damages of $222,000 and a broadened injunction that forbids Thomas–Rasset to make available sound recordings for distribution. But because the verdicts returned by the second and third juries are sufficient to justify these remedies, it is unnecessary for this court to consider the merits of the district court's order granting a new trial after the first verdict. Important though the "making available" legal issue may be to the recording companies, they are not entitled to an opinion on an issue of law that is unnecessary for the remedies sought or to a freestanding decision on whether Thomas–Rasset violated the law by making recordings available.

I.

Capitol Records, Inc., Sony BMG Music Entertainment, Arista Records LLC, Interscope Records, Warner Bros. Records, and UMG Recordings, Inc., are recording companies that own the copyrights to large catalogs of music recordings. In 2005, they undertook to investigate suspected infringement of these copyrights. MediaSentry, an online investigative firm hired by the recording companies, discovered that an individual with the username "tereastarr" was participating in unauthorized file sharing on the peer-to-peer network KaZaA.

During the relevant time period, KaZaA was a file-sharing computer program that allowed its users to search for and download specific files from other users. KaZaA users shared files using a share folder. A share folder is a location on the user's computer in which the user places files—such as audio or video recordings—that she wants to make available for other users to download. KaZaA allowed its users to access other users' share folders, view the files in the folder, and download copies of files from the folder.

MediaSentry accessed tereastarr's share folder. The investigative firm determined that the user had downloaded copyrighted songs and was making those songs available for download by other KaZaA users. MediaSentry took screen shots of tereastarr's share folder, which included over 1,700 music files, and downloaded samples of the files. But MediaSentry was unable to collect direct evidence that other users had downloaded the files from tereastarr. MediaSentry then used KaZaA to send two instant messages to tereastarr, notifying the user of potential copyright infringement. Tereastarr did not respond to the messages. MediaSentry also determined tereastarr's IP address, and traced the address to an Internet service account in Duluth, Minnesota, provided by Charter Communications. MediaSentry compiled this data in a report that it prepared for the recording companies.

Using the information provided by MediaSentry, the recording companies, through the Recording Industry Association of America (RIAA), issued a subpoena to Charter Communications requesting the name of the person associated with tereastarr's IP address. Charter informed the RIAA that the IP address belonged to Jammie Thomas–Rasset. The RIAA then sent a letter to Thomas–Rasset informing her that she had been identified as engaging in unauthorized trading of music and inviting her to contact them to discuss the situation and settle the matter. Thomas–Rasset contacted the RIAA as directed in the letter and engaged in settlement conversations with the organization. The parties were unable to resolve the matter.

In 2006, the recording companies sued Thomas–Rasset, seeking statutory damages and injunctive relief for willful copyright infringement under the Copyright Act, 17 U.S.C. § 101 *et seq.* They alleged that Thomas–Rasset violated their exclusive right to reproduction and distribution under 17 U.S.C. § 106 by impermissibly downloading, distributing, and making available for distribution twenty-four copyrighted sound recordings.

A jury trial was held in October 2007. At trial, Thomas–Rasset conceded that "tereastarr" is a username that she uses regularly for Internet and computer accounts. She admitted familiarity with and interest in some of the artists of works found in the tereastarr KaZaA account. She also acknowledged that she wrote a case study during college on the legality of Napster—another peer-to-peer file sharing program—and knew that Napster was shut down because it was illegal. Nonetheless, Thomas–Rasset testified that she had never heard of KaZaA before this case, did not have KaZaA on her computer, and did not use KaZaA to download files. The jury also heard evidence from a forensic investigator that Thomas–Rasset removed and replaced the hard drive on her computer with a new hard drive after investigators notified her of her potential infringement. The new hard drive did not contain the files at issue.

At the close of evidence, the district court instructed the jury that one who reproduces or distributes a copyrighted work without license infringes the copyright. The court's instructions defined "reproduction" to include "[t]he act of downloading copyrighted sound recordings on a peer-to-peer network." The court also instructed that the act of "making copyrighted sound recordings available for electronic distribution on a peer-to-peer network, without license from the copyright owners, violates the copyright owners' exclusive right of distribution, regardless of whether actual distribution has been shown." The jury found Thomas–Rasset liable for willful infringement and awarded the recording companies statutory damages of $9,250 per work, for a total of $222,000.

Thomas–Rasset moved for a new trial or, in the alternative, for a remittitur, arguing that the size of the jury's statutory damages award violated her rights under the Due Process Clause. The United States intervened to defend the constitutionality of the statute on statutory damages, 17 U.S.C. § 504(c). The recording companies also filed a post-trial motion, seeking to amend the judgment to include an injunction enjoining Thomas–Rasset from infringing the recording companies' copyrights by "using the Internet or any online media distribution system to reproduce (*i.e.,* download) any of Plaintiffs' Recordings, to distribute (*i.e.,* upload) any of Plaintiffs' Recordings, or to make any of Plaintiffs' Recordings available for distribution to the public."

Several months later, the district court *sua sponte* raised the issue whether it erred by instructing the jury that making sound recordings available for distribution on a peer-to-peer network violates a copyright owners' exclusive right to distribution, "regardless of whether actual distribution has been shown." The parties filed supplemental briefs in which the recording companies defended the court's instruction and Thomas–Rasset argued that the court erred when it instructed the jury on the "making available" issue. After a hearing, the district court granted Thomas–Rasset's motion for a new trial on this alternative ground, holding that making a work available to the public is not "distribution" under 17 U.S.C. § 106(3). The issue whether making copyrighted works available to the public is a right protected by § 106(3) has divided the district courts. *Compare, e.g., Atl. Recording Corp. v. Howell,* 554 F.Supp.2d 976, 981–84 (D.Ariz.2008), *and London–Sire Records v. Doe 1,* 542 F.Supp.2d 153, 176 (D.Mass.2008), *with Motown Record Co. v. DePietro,* No. 04–CV–2246, 2007 WL 576284, at *3 (E.D.Pa. Feb. 16, 2007), *and Warner Bros. Records, Inc., v. Payne,* No. W–06–CA–051, 2006 WL 2844415, at *3 (W.D.Tex. July 17, 2006).

The district court convened a second trial in June 2009, at which the recording companies produced substantially the same evidence of Thomas–Rasset's liability. At this trial, however, Thomas–Rasset attempted to deflect responsibility by suggesting for the first time that her children and former boyfriend might have done the downloading and file-sharing attributed to the "tereastarr" username. The court again instructed the jury that reproduction or distribution constituted copyright infringement. But this time, the court omitted reference to making works available and instructed the jury that "[t]he act of distributing copyrighted sound recordings to other users on a peer-to-peer network, without license from the copyright owners, violates the copyright owners' exclusive distribution right." The jury again found Thomas–Rasset liable for willful infringement, and awarded the recording companies statutory damages of $80,000 per work, for a total of $1,920,000.

Following the second trial, Thomas–Rasset filed a post-trial motion in which she argued that any statutory damages award would be unconstitutional in her case, but in the alternative that the court should reduce the jury's award either through remittitur or based on the Due Process Clause. The district court declined to rule on the constitutional issue and instead remitted damages to $2,250 per work, for a total of $54,000, on the ground that the jury's award was "shocking." The recording companies declined the remitted award and exercised their right to a new trial on damages.

A third trial was held in November 2010, and the only question for the jury was the amount of statutory damages. The jury awarded the recording companies statutory damages of $62,500 per work, for a total of $1,500,000.

Thomas–Rasset then moved to alter or amend the judgment, again arguing that any statutory damages award would be unconstitutional, but alternatively that the district court should reduce the award under the Due Process Clause. The district court, relying in part on the now-vacated decision in *Sony BMG Music Entm't v. Tenenbaum,* 721 F.Supp.2d 85 (D.Mass.2010), *vacated in relevant part by,* 660 F.3d 487 (1st Cir.2011), granted Thomas–Rasset's motion and reduced the award to $2,250 per work, for a total of $54,000. The court ruled that this amount was the maximum award permitted by the Due Process Clause. The district court also entered a permanent injunction against Thomas–Rasset, but refused to include language enjoining her from "making available" copyrighted works for distribution to the public.

The recording companies appeal the judgment of the district court, arguing that the district court erred in (1) granting a new trial based on the "making available" instruction in the first trial, and (2) holding that the Due Process Clause limits statutory damages to $2,250 per infringed work. They request that we reinstate and affirm the first jury's $222,000 award, and remand with instructions to grant an injunction prohibiting Thomas–Rasset from making the copyrighted works available to the public. Thomas–Rasset cross-appeals, arguing that even an award of the minimum statutory damages authorized by the Copyright Act would be unconstitutional.

II.

In their brief on appeal, the record companies urge this court to review the district court's order granting a new trial after the first verdict. The companies argue that the court erred by holding that an individual does not infringe a copyright holder's exclusive rights by making a copyrighted work available to the public without authorization. They argue that accepting their position on that issue would "lead to reversing the District Court's erroneous refusal to enjoin Thomas–Rasset from making Plaintiffs' copyrighted works available, but also would reinstate the first jury's $9,250–per–work verdict," for total damages of $222,000. Although the third jury's verdict awarded $62,500 per work, for a total of $1,500,000, the companies seek only the smaller amount awarded by the first jury, because they want a ruling on the legal issue whether making works available is part of the distribution right protected by the Copyright Act.

In reply, Thomas–Rasset says that she has no objection to reinstatement of the first verdict, subject to her arguments on the constitutionality of the damages. She maintains that she still disagrees with the recording companies about the meaning of "distribute" in the Copyright Act, 17 U.S.C. § 106(3), but she does not object to the relief that the companies request on appeal. She now suggests that this court should reinstate the first jury's verdict on liability (albeit without making precedent on the meaning of "distribute") and then determine whether the first damages award of $222,000 is constitutional. Thomas–Rasset is liable for willful infringement under any of the verdicts, and it suits her fine to cap the maximum possible damages at $222,000 rather than $1,500,000. Thomas–Rasset also offers to acquiesce in the entry of an injunction that forbids her to make copyrighted works available for distribution. In light of these concessions, she suggests that the issue whether making works available is part of the distribution right protected by the Copyright Act is moot.

Our response to these tactical maneuvers is to observe that this court reviews judgments, not decisions on issues. *Thompson v. Mo. Bd. of Prob. & Parole,* 39 F.3d 186, 189 n. 2 (8th Cir.1994); *see California v. Rooney,* 483 U.S. 307, 310, 107 S.Ct. 2852, 97 L.Ed.2d 258 (1987). The record companies appeal the district court's final judgment and seek additional remedies that the district court refused to order. The entitlement of the companies to these remedies—damages of $222,000 and an injunction against making copyrighted works available to the public—are the matters in controversy. That the companies seek these remedies with the objective of securing a ruling on a particular legal issue does not make that legal issue itself the matter in controversy. Once the requested remedies are ordered, the desire of the companies for an opinion on the meaning of the Copyright Act, or for a statement that Thomas–Rasset violated the law by making works available, is not sufficient to maintain an Article III case or controversy. *Chathas v. Local 134 IBEW,* 233 F.3d 508, 512 (7th Cir.2002); *Alliance to End Repression v. City of Chicago,* 820 F.2d 873, 875–76 (7th Cir.1987).

For the reasons set forth below, we conclude that when the district court entered judgment after the verdict in the third trial, the court should have enjoined Thomas–Rasset from making copyrighted works available to the public, whether or not that conduct by itself violates rights under the Copyright Act. We also conclude that statutory damages of at least $222,000 were constitutional, and that the district court erred in holding that the Due Process Clause allowed statutory damages of only $54,000. We therefore will vacate the district court's judgment and remand with directions to enter a judgment that includes those remedies. The question whether the district court correctly granted a new trial after the first verdict is moot.

A.

After the third trial, the district court entered an injunction that prohibits Thomas–Rasset from "using the Internet or any online media distribution system to reproduce (*i.e.,* download) any of Plaintiffs' Recordings, or to distribute (*i.e.,* upload) any of Plaintiff's Recordings." The recording companies urged the district court to amend the judgment to enjoin Thomas–

Rasset from making any of their sound recordings available for distribution to the public through an online media distribution system. The district court declined to do so on the ground that the Copyright Act does not provide an exclusive right to making recordings available. The court further reasoned that the injunction as granted was adequate to address the concerns of the companies. We review the grant or denial of a permanent injunction for abuse of discretion. *Fogie v. THORN Americas, Inc.,* 95 F.3d 645, 649 (8th Cir.1996). "Abuse of discretion occurs if the district court reaches its conclusion by applying erroneous legal principles or relying on clearly erroneous factual findings." *Id.*

We conclude that the district court's ruling was based on an error of law. Even assuming for the sake of analysis that the district court's ruling on the scope of the Copyright Act was correct, a district court has authority to issue a broad injunction in cases where "a proclivity for unlawful conduct has been shown." *See McComb v. Jacksonville Paper Co.,* 336 U.S. 187, 192, 69 S.Ct. 497, 93 L.Ed. 599 (1949). The district court is even permitted to "enjoin certain otherwise lawful conduct" where "the defendant's conduct has demonstrated that prohibiting only unlawful conduct would not effectively protect the plaintiff's rights against future encroachment." *Russian Media Grp., LLC v. Cable America, Inc.,* 598 F.3d 302, 307 (7th Cir.2010) (citing authorities). If a party has violated the governing statute, then a court may in appropriate circumstances enjoin conduct that allowed the prohibited actions to occur, even if that conduct "standing alone, would have been unassailable." *EEOC v. Wilson Metal Casket Co.,* 24 F.3d 836, 842 (6th Cir.1994) (internal quotation omitted).

Thomas–Rasset's willful infringement and subsequent efforts to conceal her actions certainly show "a proclivity for unlawful conduct." The recording companies rightly point out that once Thomas–Rasset makes copyrighted works available on an online media distribution system, she has completed all of the steps necessary for her to engage in the same distribution that the court did enjoin. The record also demonstrates the practical difficulties of detecting actual transfer of recordings to third parties even when a party has made large numbers of recordings available for distribution online. The narrower injunction granted by the district court thus could be difficult to enforce.

For these reasons, we conclude that the district court erred after the third trial by concluding that the broader injunction requested by the companies was impermissible as a matter of law. An injunction against making recordings available was lawful and appropriate under the circumstances, even accepting the district court's interpretation of the Copyright Act. Thomas–Rasset does not resist expanding the injunction to include this relief. We therefore will direct the district court to modify the judgment to include the requested injunction.

B.

[7] On the question of damages, we conclude that a statutory damages award of $9,250 for each of the twenty-four infringed songs, for a total of $222,000, does not contravene the Due Process Clause. The district court erred in reducing the third jury's verdict to $2,250 per work, for a total of $54,000, on the ground that this amount was the maximum permitted by the Constitution.

The Supreme Court long ago declared that damages awarded pursuant to a statute violate due process only if they are "so severe and oppressive as to be wholly disproportioned to the offense and obviously unreasonable." *St. Louis, I. M. & S. Ry. Co. v. Williams,* 251 U.S. 63, 67, 40 S.Ct. 71, 64 L.Ed. 139 (1919). Under this standard, Congress possesses a "wide latitude of discretion" in setting statutory damages. *Id.* at 66, 40 S.Ct. 71. *Williams* is still good law, and the district court was correct to apply it.

Thomas–Rasset urges us to consider instead the "guideposts" announced by the Supreme Court for the review of punitive damages awards under the Due Process Clause. When a party challenges an award of punitive damages, a reviewing court is directed to consider three factors in determining whether the award is excessive and unconstitutional: "(1) the degree of reprehensibility of the defendant's misconduct; (2) the disparity between the actual or potential harm suffered by the plaintiff and the punitive damages award; and (3) the difference between the punitive damages awarded by the jury and the civil penalties authorized or imposed in comparable cases." *State Farm Mut. Auto. Ins. Co. v. Campbell,* 538 U.S. 408, 418, 123 S.Ct. 1513, 155 L.Ed.2d 585 (2003); *see also BMW of N. Am., Inc. v. Gore,* 517 U.S. 559, 574–75, 116 S.Ct. 1589, 134 L.Ed.2d 809 (1996).

The Supreme Court never has held that the punitive damages guideposts are applicable in the context of statutory damages. *See Zomba Enters., Inc. v. Panorama Records, Inc.,* 491 F.3d 574, 586–88 (6th Cir.2007). Due process prohibits excessive punitive damages because " '[e]lementary notions of fairness enshrined in our constitutional jurisprudence dictate that a person receive fair notice not only of the conduct that will subject him to punishment, but also of the severity of the penalty that a State may impose.' " *Campbell,* 538 U.S. at 417, 123 S.Ct. 1513 (quoting *Gore,* 517 U.S. at 574, 116 S.Ct. 1589). This concern about fair notice does not apply to statutory damages, because those damages are identified and constrained by the authorizing statute. The guideposts themselves, moreover, would be nonsensical if applied to statutory damages. It makes no sense to consider the disparity between "actual harm" and an award of statutory damages when statutory damages are designed precisely for instances where actual harm is difficult or impossible to calculate. *See Cass Cnty. Music Co. v. C.H.L.R., Inc.,* 88 F.3d 635, 643 (8th Cir.1996). Nor could a reviewing court consider the difference between an award of statutory damages and the "civil penalties authorized," because statutory damages *are* the civil penalties authorized.

Applying the *Williams* standard, we conclude that an award of $9,250 per each of twenty-four works is not "so severe and oppressive as to be wholly disproportioned to the offense and obviously unreasonable." 251 U.S. at 67, 40 S.Ct. 71. Congress, exercising its "wide latitude of discretion," *id.* at 66, 40 S.Ct. 71, set a statutory damages range for willful copyright infringement of $750 to $150,000 per infringed work. 17 U.S.C. § 504(c). The award here is toward the lower end of this broad range. As in *Williams,* "the interests of the public, the numberless opportunities for committing the offense, and the need for securing uniform adherence to [federal law]" support the constitutionality of the award. *Id.* at 67, 40 S.Ct. 71.

Congress's protection of copyrights is not a "special private benefit," but is meant to achieve an important public interest: "to motivate the creative activity of authors and inventors by the provision of a special reward, and to allow the public access to the products of their genius after the limited period of exclusive control has expired." *Sony Corp. of Am. v. Universal City Studios, Inc.,* 464 U.S. 417, 429, 104 S.Ct. 774, 78 L.Ed.2d 574 (1984). With the rapid advancement of technology, copyright infringement through online file-sharing has become a serious problem in the recording industry. Evidence at trial showed that revenues across the industry decreased by fifty percent between 1999 and 2006, a decline that the record companies attributed to piracy. This decline in revenue caused a corresponding drop in industry jobs and a reduction in the number of artists represented and albums released. *See Sony BMG Music Entm't v. Tenenbaum,* 660 F.3d 487, 492 (1st Cir.2011).

Congress no doubt was aware of the serious problem posed by online copyright infringement, and the "numberless opportunities for committing the offense," when it last revisited the Copyright Act in 1999. To provide a deterrent against such infringement, Congress amended § 504(c) to increase the minimum per-work award from $500 to $750, the maximum per-work award from $20,000 to $30,000, and the maximum per-work award for willful infringement from $100,000 to $150,000. *Id.*

Thomas–Rasset contends that the range of statutory damages established by § 504(c) reflects only a congressional judgment "at a very general level," but that courts have authority to declare it "severe and oppressive" and "wholly disproportioned" in particular cases. The district court similarly emphasized that Thomas–Rasset was "not a business acting for profit, but rather an individual consumer illegally seeking free access to music for her own use." By its terms, however, the statute plainly encompasses infringers who act without a profit motive, and the statute already provides for a broad range of damages that allows courts and juries to calibrate the award based on the nature of the violation. For those who favor resort to legislative history, the record also suggests that Congress was well aware of the threat of noncommercial copyright infringement when it established the lower end of the range. *See* H.R. Rep. 106–216, at 3 (1999), 1999 WL 446444, at *3. Congressional amendments to the criminal provisions of the Copyright Act in 1997 also reflect an awareness that the statute would apply to noncommercial infringement. *See* No Electronic Theft (NET) Act, Pub.L. No. 105–147, § 2(a), 111 Stat. 2678 (1997); *see also* H.R. Rep. 105–339, at 5 (1997), 1997 WL 664424, at *5.

In holding that any award over $2,250 per work would violate the Constitution, the district court effectively imposed a treble damages limit on the $750 minimum statutory damages award. The district court based this holding on a "broad legal practice of establishing a treble award as the upper limit permitted to address willful or particularly damaging behavior." Any "broad legal practice" of treble damages for statutory violations, however, does not control whether an award of statutory damages is within the limits prescribed by the Constitution. The limits of treble damages to which the district court referred, such as in the antitrust laws or other intellectual property laws, represent congressional judgments about the appropriate maximum in a given context. They do not establish a *constitutional* rule that can be substituted for a different congressional judgment in the area of copyright infringement. Although the United States seems to think that the district court's ruling did not question the constitutionality of the statutory damages statute, the district court's approach in our view would make the statute unconstitutional as applied to a significant category of copyright infringers. The evidence against Thomas–Rasset demonstrated an aggravated case of willful infringement by an individual consumer who acted to download and distribute copyrighted recordings without profit motive. If an award near the bottom of the statutory range is unconstitutional as applied to her infringement of twenty-four works, then it would be the rare case of noncommercial infringement to which the statute could be applied.

Thomas–Rasset's cross-appeal goes so far as to argue that *any* award of statutory damages would be unconstitutional, because even the minimum damages award of $750 per violation would be "wholly disproportioned to the offense" and thus unconstitutional. This is so, Thomas–Rasset argues, because the damages award is not based on any evidence of harm caused by her specific infringement, but rather reflects the harm caused by file-sharing in general. The district court similarly concluded that "statutory damages must still bear *some* relation to actual damages." The Supreme Court in *Williams,* however, disagreed that the constitutional inquiry calls for a comparison of an award of statutory damages to actual damages caused by the violation. 251 U.S. at 66, 40 S.Ct. 71. Because the damages award "is imposed as a punishment for the violation of a public law, the Legislature may adjust its amount to the public wrong rather than the private injury, just as if it were going to the state." *Id.* The protection of copyrights is a vindication of the public interest, *Sony Corp. of Am.,* 464 U.S. at 429, 104 S.Ct. 774, and statutory damages are "by definition a substitute for unproven or unprovable actual damages." *Cass Cnty. Music Co.,* 88 F.3d at 643. For copyright infringement, moreover, statutory damages are "designed to discourage wrongful conduct," in addition to providing "restitution of profit and reparation for injury." *F.W. Woolworth Co. v. Contemporary Arts,* 344 U.S. 228, 233, 73 S.Ct. 222, 97 L.Ed. 276 (1952).

Thomas–Rasset highlights that if the recording companies had sued her based on infringement of 1,000 copyrighted recordings instead of the twenty-four recordings that they selected, then an award of $9,250 per song would have resulted in a total award of $9,250,000. Because that hypothetical award would be obviously excessive and unreasonable, she reasons, an award of $222,000 based on the same amount per song must likewise be invalid. Whatever the constitutionality of the hypothetical award, we disagree that the validity of the lesser amount sought here depends on whether the Due Process Clause would permit the extrapolated award that she posits. The absolute amount of the award, not just the amount per violation, is relevant to whether the award is "so severe and oppressive as to be wholly disproportioned to the offense and obviously unreasonable." *Williams,* 251 U.S. at 67, 40 S.Ct. 71. The recording companies here opted to sue over twenty-four recordings. If they had sued over 1,000 recordings, then a finder of fact may well have considered the number of recordings and the proportionality of the total award as factors in determining where within the range to assess the statutory damages. If and when a jury returns a multi-million dollar award for noncommercial online copyright infringement, then there will be time enough to consider it.

* * *

For the foregoing reasons, we conclude that the recording companies are entitled to the remedies that they seek on appeal. The judgment of the district court is vacated, and the case is remanded with directions to enter a judgment for damages in the amount of $222,000, and to include an injunction that precludes Thomas–Rasset from making any of the plaintiffs' recordings available for distribution to the public through an online media distribution system.

QUESTIONS AND DISCUSSION

1. In A&M Records v. Napster, Inc., 293 F.3d 1004 (9th Cir. 2001), the court looked at the fair use defense of copyright infringement by the music downloader, Napster, which was in the business of the commercial recording, distribution, and sale of copyrighted musical compositions and sound recordings. Napster was found to be a contributory and vicarious copyright infringer. Is it not the goal of the Internet to provide complete access? Rightfully, copyright law does not allow it. What do you think? Is this more of a policing problem than a legal problem?

2. In MGM Studios, Inc. v. Grokster, Ltd., 518 F.Supp.2d 1197 (C.D. Cal. 2007), the court looked at music streamlining, and held that "streamCast will be required to use the most effective means available to reduce the infringing capabilities of the Morpheus Systems and Software, while preserving its noninfringing uses as feasible" (518 F.Supp.2d 1197, 1240). See also Digital Millenium Copyright Act (DMCA), 17 U.S.C. §1201 ("To amend title 17, United States Code, to implement the World Intellectual Propety Organization [WIPO] Copy Treaty and Performances and Phonograms Treaty...."]. See generally Sherri Burr, "The Piracy Gap: Protecting Intellectual Property in the Era of Artistic Creativity and Technological Change," 33 Williamette L. Rev. 745 (Winter 1997); and United States v. Am. Library Ass'n, 539 U.S. 194 (2003) (Children's Internet Protection Act (CIPA), 4 Stat. 2763A 335, permits a library receiving federal assistance to provide public Internet access to "disable" the filter to enable access for bona fide research (20 U.S.C. §9134(f)(3) & 47 U.S.C. §254 (h)(6)(D)).

CHAPTER 10
GLOBALIZATION

Intellectual property protection and piracy are new global propositions in a global market. The Agreement on Trade-related Aspects of Intellectual Property Rights (TRIPS), contains provisions relative to copyrights, patents, trademarks, designs, trade secrets, and semiconductor chips. There are also treaties under U.S. law and global patent, trademark, and copyright registration agreements (e.g., Berne Convention for the protection of literary Artistic Works). There is intentional domain name protection and litigation. (Domain names are unique addresses assigned to particular computers that are connected to the Internet.) It can definitely be said that the entertainment world is international in scope with global implications. Every Monday, Hollywood wants the foreign weekend movie sales. [Champion, Intellectual Property in the Sports and Entertainment Industries 203; reprinted with the permission of the authors for educational purposes].

In following case, P& D International v. Halsey Pub. Co., 672 F.Sup. 1429 (S.D. Fla. 1987), plaintiff alleges infringement of its AV materials by a British defendant, which were used in connection with selling advertising for use on cruise ships in the Caribbean Sea.

P & D INTERNATIONAL v. HALSEY PUB. CO.
United States District Court for the Southern District of Florida
November 4, 1987, Decided; November 4, 1987, Filed
No. 86-2420-CIV
672F.Supp.1429

AMENDED ORDER DENYING MOTION TO DISMISS AND DENYING MOTION TO STRIKE

EDWARD B. DAVIS, District Judge.

THIS CAUSE came before the Court on Defendant, CUNARD N.A.C. LINES, a/k/a Cunard Line Limited's (hereinafter "CUNARD") Motion to Dismiss the Complaint, and Defendant, HALSEY PUBLISHING COMPANY's (hereinafter "HALSEY") Joinder in said Motion, Plaintiff P & D INTERNATIONAL's (hereinafter "P & D") Memorandum in Opposition, and CUNARD's Reply thereto. Also pending before the Court is P & D's Motion to Strike Portions of CUNARD's Reply and Alternative Motion for Extension of Time to Conduct Discovery and Respond Thereto or to Strike Summary Judgment Motion, CUNARD's Opposition and P & D's Reply.

I. FACTUAL SUMMARY

P & D is a Cayman Islands corporation with its principal place of business in George Town, Grand Cayman, Cayman Islands. P & D publishes magazines, films and videotapes, and sells advertising principally for use on cruise ships in the Caribbean Sea.

Defendant CUNARD is a United Kingdom corporation with its principal place of business in New York. CUNARD's cruise ships sail in and of the Port of Miami and CUNARD otherwise conducts business in Florida. Defendant HALSEY is a Florida corporation and its principal place of business is this state.

On November 25, 1986, P & D filed a Complaint alleging that Defendants CUNARD and HALSEY committed acts of copyright infringement, unfair competition, and misappropriation. The Complaint alleges that prior to August 1980, P & D created, wrote, and filmed an original audio-visual work (hereinafter referred to as the "St. Thomas Film") about the Island of St. Thomas, B.V.I. The St. Thomas Film was allegedly shown on CUNARD cruise ships approximately 80 times a year during 1981, 1982, and 1983, pursuant to an agreement between P & D and an entity called Joint Marketing and Publishing Services Limited ("JMP"), CUNARD's advertising agency. Peter Savill Affidavit at 2. According to P & D President, Peter Savill, the agreement provided that P & D would pay CUNARD through JMP a fee of 200 British pounds per cruise for the showing of the St. Thomas Film. Savill Affidavit at 2.

CUNARD Vice–President, Michael Siavage, claims that the arrangement between JMP and CUNARD specified that CUNARD would have all ownership rights in the St. Thomas Film. Siavage Affidavit at 2. Siavage further states that JMP entered into a sub-contract agreement with P & D in connection with its production of the St. Thomas Film. Siavage Affidavit at 2. CUNARD severed all contractual relations with JMP in 1983 and subsequently entered into a Publisher's Agreement with HALSEY. Siavage Affidavit at 3. According to Siavage, it was in the course of HALSEY's work to produce a movie about St. Thomas that HALSEY received from CUNARD a copy of the St. Thomas Film. Count I of the Complaint alleges that HALSEY created, produced, and filmed two infringing audio-visual works in which, without P & D's prior knowledge or consent, substantial portions of the St. Thomas Film were copied.

P & D President Savill contends that after the relationship between CUNARD and P & D ended in or about 1983, P & D requested that CUNARD return all copies of the St. Thomas Film. Savill Affidavit at 3. Savill further states that CUNARD complied, but at the time of the filing of this suit, was still showing the St. Thomas Film or parts of it on its cruises, and that consequently CUNARD must have covertly kept one copy. Savill Affidavit at 3. P & D's Complaint alleges that CUNARD has been performing and displaying on its cruise ships, without P & D's consent, the work produced by HALSEY.

On June 11, 1986, P & D secured exclusive rights and privileges in and to the St. Thomas Film in compliance with United States copyright law.

II. DISCUSSION

In an earlier motion to dismiss, HALSEY successfully argued that the misappropriation and unfair competition claims could not be raised in this proceeding because they were preempted by federal copyright law. In this proceeding, Defendants seek to have the copyright infringement count dismissed on three grounds: (1) lack of subject matter jurisdiction; (2) *forum non conveniens;* and (3) failure to join an indispensable party. In its Reply Memorandum in Support of the Motion to Dismiss, CUNARD raises as an additional ground for dismissal that P & D is not the copyright owner in the Film, but rather, that CUNARD is by virtue of the "work for hire" doctrine. CUNARD asks the Court to treat this fourth argument as a motion for summary judgment. P & D has moved to strike this "motion" for summary judgment. All four arguments are addressed below.

A. *Subject Matter Jurisdiction*

P & D's Complaint alleges that this action arises under the United States Copyright Act, United States Code, Title 17, Sections 101, 102 and 104(a), and the Universal Copyright Convention, Paris Act of 1974, as ratified by the United Kingdom on July 10, 1974. CUNARD argues that this Court lacks subject matter jurisdiction because: (1) the claim against CUNARD does not "arise under" U.S. copyright law; (2) even if the claim arises under the United States Copyright Act, U.S. copyright law has no extraterritorial effect; and (3) the Universal Copyright Convention cannot expand the territorial reach of U.S. law.

1. *"Arising Under" the United States Copyright Act*

CUNARD asserts that because ownership of the copyright is the fundamental controversy here, the suit is not one "arising under" the Copyright Act within the meaning of 28 U.S.C. § 1338(a). CUNARD's Reply memorandum at 3. CUNARD provides the Court with a quotation from *Topolos v. Caldeway,* 698 F.2d 991 (9th Cir.1983), as controlling. A reading of the quoted passage appears to hold that where a court is asked to determine ownership or contractual rights, jurisdiction must be declined. The quotation reads as follows:

Generally, courts decide whether a case arises under the copyright laws by focusing on the nature of the principal claim asserted by the plaintiff.... Courts have directed inquiry to what they have variously described as the "primary and controlling purpose" of the suit, the "principal issue," the "fundamental controversy," and the "gist" or "essence" of the plaintiff's claim. *Wooster v. Crane & Co.,* 147 F. 515, 516 (8th Cir.1906); ....

In its Motion to Strike this Reply, P & D does not address this issue or the subject quote.

Although in *Topolos* the court did state that jurisdiction is declined where the "fundamental controversy" is ownership of the copyright,...

In infringement actions, ownership of a valid copyright and copying by the defendant are elements the plaintiff must prove. In the present case, a declaration of ownership in the St. Thomas Film is merely a threshold inquiry, and not the essence of P & D's claim. P & D owns a copyright to the St. Thomas Film; it only asks that the Court determine whether Defendants infringed its copyright. For this reason, the Court finds that this case does "arise under" U.S. copyright law.

2. *Extraterritorial Reach of U.S. Copyright Law*

As a general rule, U.S. copyright law has no extraterritorial effect and cannot be invoked to secure relief for acts of infringement occurring outside the

United States. However, to the extent that part of an "act" of infringement occurs within this country, although such act be completed in a foreign jurisdiction, those who contributed to the act within the United States may be liable under U.S. copyright law. 3 M. Nimmer, *Nimmer on Copyright,* Section 17.02 at 17–5.

P & D alleges and HALSEY admits that HALSEY copied the Film in Florida at the behest of CUNARD. Seymour Gerber Affidavit. If P & D's ownership interest is upheld, such an act would constitute an infringement under 17 U.S.C. § 106 (1976). As P & D maintains, the subsequent performances of the Film on the CUNARD cruise ships en route to the Island of St. Thomas would then simply be additional infringements of the Film.

The case of *Peter Starr Production Co. v. Twin Continental Films, Inc.,* 783 F.2d 1440 (9th Cir.1986) is factually apposite. In *Peter Starr,* the complaint alleged that defendant infringed plaintiff's copyright in a motion picture by authorizing a third party to exhibit the movie without plaintiff's consent. *Id.* at 1442. The complaint also suggested that the illegal authorization occurred in the United States, although the remaining infringing acts took place in Sweden or the United Kingdom, or both. *Id.* at 1442, 1443. The trial court in *Peter Starr* dismissed the complaint for lack of subject matter jurisdiction under 28 U.S.C. § 1338(a) (1982), finding that no infringement had occurred in the United States. *Id.* at 1441.

The Ninth Circuit reversed because the complaint alleged infringement inside the United States, and therefore, case law prohibiting jurisdiction over extraterritorial infringements was inapplicable. *Id. Cf. Ahbez v. Edwin H. Morris & Co., Inc.,* 548 F.Supp. 664, 667 (S.D.N.Y.1982) (court lacked subject matter jurisdiction where complaint failed to allege the occurrence of infringing acts in the United States).

Because an infringing act is alleged to have occurred in the United States, this Court has subject matter over P & D's claims.

3. *Universal Copyright Convention*

Defendants also maintain that this Court lacks subject matter jurisdiction over the infringing activity alleged to have occurred in the CUNARD vessels. CUNARD argues that the Universal Copyright Convention cannot expand the territorial reach of the Copyright Act for the exclusive benefit of foreign nationals. Given this Court's conclusion tht United States copyright law adequately confers subject matter jurisdiction, the Court need not address this last jurisdictional question. *Peter Starr,* 783 F.2d 1440, 1443, n. 3.

B. *Forum Non Conveniens*

"The doctrine of *forum non conveniens* authorizes a trial court to decline to exercise its jurisdiction, even though the court has venue, where it appears that the convenience of the parties and the court, and the interests of justice indicate that the action should be tried in another forum." *Sibaja v. Dow Chemical Co.,* 757 F.2d 1215, 1218 (11th Cir.1985), *cert. denied,* 474 U.S. 948, 106 S.Ct. 347, 88 L.Ed.2d 294 (1985)...

A prerequisite to dismissal of a case for *forum non conveniens* is the availability of an alternative forum. *Gulf Oil Corp. v. Gilbert,* 330 U.S. 501, 507, 67 S.Ct. 839, 842, 91 L.Ed. 1055 (1947). Here it is undisputed that the United Kingdom is a forum available to P & D to prosecute this case. CUNARD is a United Kingdom corporation and HALSEY has represented that it would submit to the jurisdiction of any forum to which this cause is transferred. *See* HALSEY's Joinder in CUNARD's Motion to Dismiss. CUNARD and HALSEY both maintain that trial of this action would be more convenient in the United Kingdom. P & D has not brought forth any evidence to indicate that it would be treated unfairly in the United Kingdom or that it would be deprived of all remedies. *See In Re Air Crash Disaster Near New Orleans, Louisiana,* 821 F.2d 1147, 1165 (5th Cir.1987) (*en banc*); *Reyno,* 454 U.S. at 255, 102 S.Ct. at 265. Thus, the United Kingdom would be an appropriate forum were this cause to be conditionally dismissed.

In weighing the relative advantages and obstacles to a fair trial in this forum and the United Kingdom, the Court is instructed to consider specific "private interest" and "public interest" factors in exercising its discretion. *Gilbert,* 330 U.S. at 507, 508, 67 S.Ct. at 843. Controlling weight cannot be given any one factor in the balancing process. *La Seguridad v. Transytur Line,* 707 F.2d 1304, 1307 (11th Cir.1983).

The private interest factors include the relative ease of access to sources of proof, the availability of compulsory process for attendance of unwilling witnesses, the cost of obtaining the attendance of witnesses, the possibility of a view of the premises, the enforceability of a judgment if one is obtained, and "all other practical problems that make trial of a case easy, expeditious and inexpensive." *Gilbert,* 330 U.S. at 508, 67 S.Ct. at 843; *Sigalas v. Lido Maritime, Inc.,* 776 F.2d 1512, 1519 (11th Cir.1985).

An analysis of the private interest factors requires that dismissal be denied. Initially, the Court notes that HALSEY did not raise the issue of *forum non conveniens* in a timely manner... Rather, HALSEY sought and obtained a dismissal of two counts in P & D's Complaint before ever raising inconvenience as a defense. Such dilatoriness "promotes and allows the very incurrence of costs and inconvenience the doctrine is meant to relieve." *Id.* at 1165.

CUNARD contends that all of the witnesses it would seek to produce in this action are in England or New York. CUNARD marketing and passenger service department documents are apparently located in the United Kingdom or in New York. Conversely, most, if not all of HALSEY's and P & D's witnesses and records are either in this district or presumably near, on the island of Grand Cayman. The cost of providing for the attendance of necessary witnesses in the United Kingdom appears then to exceed the cost of obtaining the attendance of these same witnesses in this country. Thus, on the factors bearing upon access to sources of proof, convenience dictates that this action remain where it is.

The remaining private interest factors also favor P & D. There is no accident site or view appropriate to this action. The enforceability of a judgment if one is obtained appears to be more readily available in this forum, as the Court has jurisdiction over HALSEY and CUNARD, whereas the United Kingdom only has jurisdiction over one party, CUNARD. In light of these variables, trial will be more expeditious in this district.

In addition to the above private interest factors, the Court must consider the *Gulf Oil* public interest factors. These public interest factors include the administrative difficulties flowing from court congestion, the unfairness of burdening citizens in an unrelated forum with jury duty, the local interest in having localized controversies decided at home, and the difficulties attendant in resolving conflicts-of-laws problems and applying foreign law. *Gulf Oil,* 330 U.S. at 508–09, 67 S.Ct. at 843; *Sigalas,* 776 F.2d at 1519.

It is well recognized that the Southern District of Florida is a heavily congested federal district. However, this forum has a direct interest in this litigation. The initial allegedly infringing act occurred in this forum, and continued to be repeated on a vessel sailing to and from the Port of Miami. It is the people of South Florida who, of any potential jurors, have the most relation to this litigation. Certainly no acts of infringement are alleged to have taken place in or near the United Kingdom.

Finally, although foreign law will in all likelihood have to be applied to part of this action, as the Court has previously stated, U.S. copyright law certainly applies to this action. This country has a strong interest in protecting valuable property interests especially where infringements within United States borders are alleged. The application of foreign law does not amount to such a problem warranting dismissal.

Although a foreign plaintiff's choice of forum is entitled to less deference than the choice of a local plaintiff, dismissal on *forum non conveniens* grounds is the exception rather than the rule. *In Re Air Crash,* 821 F.2d at 1164, n. 26, citing Wright, Miller & Cooper, *Federal Practice and Procedure: Jurisdiction* § 3828 at 291–92 (2d ed. 1986); *Piper Aircraft,* 454 U.S. at 256, 102 S.Ct. at 266. Because the majority of the significant contacts in this case are in Florida, retention of this case is warranted.

C. *Indispensable Party*

CUNARD maintains that its relationship to JMP, HALSEY's predecessor, was such that any copyright in any film produced pursuant to that relationship was a "work for hire" and sole property of CUNARD. Thus, CUNARD's position is that JMP is an "indispensable party" to this litigation.

The Court has the discretion whether or not to require joinder of a person having or claiming an interest in a copyright. 17 U.S.C. § 501(b); M. Nimmer, *Nimmer on Copyright,* § 12.03 at 12–32 (1987). "[J]oinder should occur if an issue is raised as to the validity of the copyright upon which the rights of the person to be joined, as well as those of the plaintiff, rest." M. Nimmer § 12.03 at 12–32.1. *Cf. Wales Indus. Inc. v. Hasbro Bradley, Inc.,* 612 F.Supp. 510, 517 (S.D.N.Y.1985) (joinder should not be required if the only issue is whether the defendant engaged in unlawful copying). Moreover, where the party to be joined is merely a member of the distribution chain, the victim of copyright infringement may sue as many or as few of the alleged wrongdoers as he chooses....

Under the foregoing standard, the Court finds that joinder of JMP is not necessary. At no time has CUNARD asserted that JMP has or claims an interest in the St. Thomas Film. Instead, CUNARD maintains that it owns the St. Thomas Film by virtue of its relationship to JMP. JMP is thus possibly an infringer or merely a witness for the defense, and any discovery sought from JMP or any other foreign parties may be effectuated through letters rogatory under Fed.R.Civ.P. 28(b).

Furthermore, CUNARD has not shown how or why it may be subjected to multiple suits if JMP is not joined as a party defendant. CUNARD's argument that any victory for P & D could give rise to the same claim of right on JMP's part respecting CUNARD's use of what would be the newly-unprotected work is unpersuasive. An adjudication by this Court that P & D is the rightful owner of the St. Thomas Film could hardly encourage JMP to attempt to establish ownership rights in that Film.

The preliminary issue of copyright ownership may be determined without the need of joinder of what is in truth merely a witness for CUNARD.

D. *Work For Hire*

The Siavage Affidavit states that the agreement between CUNARD and JMP provides that CUNARD will have all ownership rights in the St. Thomas Film and that therefore it is a "work for hire" within the meaning of the U.S. copyright laws. A "work made for hire" is

(1) a work prepared by an employee within the scope of his or her employment; or

(2) a work specially ordered or commissioned for use as a contribution to a collective work, as a translation, as a supplementary work, as a compilation ... if the parties expressly agree in a written instrument signed by them that the work shall be considered a work made for hire....

17 U.S.C. § 101.

In its Reply memorandum in support of its Motion to Dismiss, CUNARD presents the argument that summary judgment should be entered against P & D due to P & D's failure to proffer any facts concerning the alleged work for hire relationship between CUNARD and JMP. P & D moved to strike this "motion" for summary judgment, and quite properly so. It is highly improper to use a reply memorandum to convert a proceeding for dismissal on jurisdictional, venue, and indispensable party grounds to a motion for an adjudication on the merits. Summary judgment situations should not be created in reply memoranda, for under this Court's Local Rules, the nonmoving party has no further opportunity to respond. This work for hire argument is an affirmative defense and may be raised by CUNARD in that manner.

Nevertheless, in the interests of judicial economy, this Court has reviewed the summary judgment papers. Because the Savill Affidavit raises material issues of fact which are in dispute, summary judgment is not warranted.

In light of the foregoing, it is hereby ORDERED AND ADJUDGED that the Motion to Dismiss and the Motion to Strike are DENIED.

Dae Han Video Productions, Inc. v. Kuk Dong Oriental Food, Inc.
United States District Court for the District of Maryland
December 11, 1990; December 12, 1990, Filed
Civil No. H-87-436
1990 U.S. Dist. LEXIS 18329, 19 U.S.P.Q.2d (BNA) 1294,
Copy. L. Rep. (CCH) P26, 687

ALEXANDER, HARVEY, Chief Judge:

This civil action for copyright infringement was filed almost four years ago and has been the subject of continuing litigation since then. Numerous rulings have been made by the Court and various Orders have been entered, including the Order of December 15, 1988 permanently enjoining certain named defendants from infringing copyrights owned by plaintiff Korean Television Enterprises, Ltd. (hereinafter "KTE") and licensed to plaintiff Dae Han Video Productions, Inc. (hereinafter "Dae Han").

Plaintiff Dae Han is a New York Corporation, and plaintiff KTE is a California corporation. Dae Han is the exclusive licensee for home video distribution in the eastern United States of Korean language video tapes owned by KTE. KTE is a wholly owned subsidiary and the American agent of the Korean Broadcasting System (hereinafter "KBS") of Seoul, Korea. KBS produces Korean language television shows for television broadcast in Korea. Munwha Broadcasting Company (hereinafter "MBC"), like KBS, produces shows for television broadcast in Korea. KBS and MBC have assigned to KTE all rights owned by them with respect to the distribution of Korean video programs in the United States. Defendants are various corporations and individuals which rent or sell video tapes in Maryland. Plaintiffs filed their complaint on February 25, 1987, charging defendants with infringing their United States copyrights by renting or selling tapes of the Korean television shows.

In its Memorandum and Order of September 17, 1987, this Court denied defendants' motions to dismiss certain claims asserted by plaintiffs in their complaint. The Court there concluded that subject matter jurisdiction existed and that KTE was a proper party to this action.

Following a later hearing, this Court, in a Memorandum Opinion filed on March 14, 1988, granted plaintiffs' motion for a preliminary injunction. In that ruling, the Court concluded that the entry of a preliminary injunction was appropriate because plaintiffs had shown a very high probability of success in proving that they were the owners of valid copyrights which were being infringed by defendants. The Court further found that plaintiffs would suffer irreparable harm if a preliminary injunction were not issued and that the balance of hardships weighed in favor of the plaintiffs. An Order was entered on March 14, 1988 enjoining certain named defendants from copying plaintiffs' video during the pendency of further proceedings in the case.

Following the completion of discovery by the parties, plaintiffs moved for summary judgment. In a Memorandum Opinion dated December 15, 1988, this Court granted plaintiffs' motion for summary judgment. An Order was entered that same day permanently enjoining certain named defendants, including defendants Korean Korner, Inc. and Young Nam, d/b/a Korean Korner, from engaging in infringing activities and assessing statutory damages in the amount of $1,000 against each named defendant. In its Memorandum Opinion, the Court concluded that plaintiffs had established as a matter of law both their ownership of valid copyrights and the copying of the protected works by defendants.

The principal argument advanced by defendants in opposing plaintiffs' motion for summary judgment was that the Korean television shows in question were not "works made for hire" as defined in § 101 of the Copyright Act, 17 U.S.C. § 101. Defendants argued that the scripts were not works made for hire because the scriptwriters were not employees of the networks. Relying on the testimony of Yung Shik Shim, then the Chairman of the Korean Radio & TV Writers Association (hereinafter "the KRTWA"), at a trial in the Eastern District of New York involving similar issues, this Court found as matter of law that the scriptwriters were employees of the networks and that the scripts were works made for hire pursuant to § 101 of the Copyright Act. In the New York case, Chief Judge Weinstein, after conducting a bench trial, had permanently enjoined various corporations and individuals from infringing any of KTE's copyrighted works. *Korean Television Enterprises, Ltd. v. Duk Nam Lee, et al.,* Civil No. 85–3252 (slip op. E.D.N.Y. October 3, 1986).

In opposing plaintiff's motion for summary judgment, defendants had sought to discredit Shim's prior trial testimony and had relied on what they characterized as newly discovered evidence. This Court found no merit to this contention, and specifically concluded that the validity of plaintiffs' copyrights did not depend on the existence of any agreement between the Korean networks and the KRTWA. (Memorandum Opinion of December 15, 1988, slip op. at 11). This Court further found that Shim's testimony at the trial in the Eastern District of New York had been independently corroborated by the testimony of Kyo Sik Kim, a Korean scriptwriter.

In its Memorandum Opinion of December 15, 1988, this Court said the following (slip Op. at 11):

One of the findings of the Supreme Court of Korea even supports the conclusion reached herein. That Court found that the scriptwriters entered into contracts according to which they agreed to be paid to write scripts at the request of the broadcasting companies. Moreover, the evidence in this case demonstrates that the Korean networks at all times directed the activities of the scriptwriters and that KBS and MBC controlled the general outline of and paid for the scripts. The scriptwriters are consequently employees of the Korean networks, not simply independent contractors. The control exercised by KBS and MBC over the content, progress and production of scripts is clearly sufficient to render the scripts works made for hire under United States copyright law. *See Aldon Accessories, Ltd. v. Spiegel,* 738 F.2d 548, 552 (2d Cir.1984).

The proceedings in this case did not terminate with the entry of a permanent injunction on December 15, 1988. By Memorandum and Order dated January 31, 1989, plaintiffs' motion to alter or amend judgment was denied. On July 17, 1989, a Show Cause Order was entered by this Court directing certain named defendants to appear and show cause why they should not be found in contempt. Following a hearing on August 18, 1989, an Order was entered by the Court finding certain defendants to be in contempt, fining them the sum of $5,000 each and directing the United States Marshal to seize video tapes in the commercial establishment of those defendants.

One of the defendants permanently enjoined by the Court's Order of December 15, 1988 is Korean Korner, Inc., d/b/a Korean Korner. On September 25, 1990, defendant Korean Korner, represented by new counsel, filed a motion to dissolve the permanent injunction. In support of that motion, defendant Korean Korner has filed affidavits, excerpts from transcripts of depositions and exhibits. Plaintiffs have opposed the pending motion to dissolve and have submitted excerpts from deposition transcripts and exhibits. Memoranda in support of and in opposition to the pending motion have been reviewed by the Court. A hearing was recently held in open Court. For the reasons to be stated, the motion to dissolve of defendant Korean Korner will be denied.

I
Background Facts

Although the pending motion to dissolve has been filed on behalf of defendant Korean Korner, it appears that the moving party is in fact Washington Video, which purchased from Korean Korner a video business located in Rockville, Maryland. The name of this business has now been changed to Washington Video. Although it previously purchased Korean videos from Kuk–Dong Video, an authorized distributor of plaintiff KTS, commencing in March of 1990 Washington Video has been obtaining copies of Korean television shows from different sources and upon advice of counsel has placed certain royalty funds into an escrow account for an entity known as DuBon Corp. which now represents KRTWA in the United States. In its pending motion, Korean Korner contends that DuBon is the proper owner of United States copyrights in the video programs and that the escrow funds should be paid to DuBon.

In ruling on the pending motion, the Court is relying on all facts of record in this case. Many pertinent facts relating to the background of the dispute presently before the Court have been set forth in some detail in prior Opinions and Orders of the Court and will not be repeated herein. In particular, the Court would refer to its discussion of the facts in its Memorandum Opinion of March 14, 1988 and in its later Memorandum Opinion of December 15, 1988.

II
Discussion

American copyright law applies to this action for copyright infringement. *See* 3 M. Nimmer, *The Law of Copyright* § 17.05 at 17–39 (1990). The Copyright Act of 1976 vests copyright in works "made for hire" in the hiring, rather than the hired, party. *See* 17 U.S.C. § 201(b). A work is "made for hire" if (1) the hired party is an "employee" or (2) the hired party is an "independent contractor" and the parties expressly agree that the work shall be considered a work made for hire. 17 U.S.C. § 101. Because the Korean scriptwriters have never so agreed or transferred the copyrights of their scripts to the networks, the scripts are not works "made for hire" unless the scriptwriters are statutory "employees."

In granting the permanent injunction in this case on December 15, 1988, this Court found on the record before it that the Korean scriptwriters are "employees" of the networks. In seeking to dissolve the permanent injunction, defendant Korean Korner has challenged that finding, relying on purported new facts and a change in the law.

To prevail in its effort to dissolve the permanent injunction, defendant Korean Korner is faced with a double burden. First, defendant must clearly show that changes in the relevant law and/or the applicable facts require this Court to dissolve its long-standing permanent injunction. *See United States v. Swift & Co.,* 286 U.S. 106, 119 (1931); *Burkey v. Ellis,* 483 F.Supp. 897, 915 (N.D.Ala.1979). As the Supreme Court noted in *Swift & Co.,* "[n]othing less than a clear showing of grievous wrong evoked by new and unforeseen conditions should lead us to change what was decided after years of litigation ..." 286 U.S. at 119. This procedural burden is made even more onerous by a second burden imposed by copyright law. Defendant must rebut the presumption of ownership which arises from the issuance to plaintiff KTE by the United States Copyright Office of certificates of copyright registration. *See West Publishing Co. v. Mead Data Central, Inc.,* 616 F.Supp. 1571, 1575 (D.C.Minn.1985), *aff'g,* 799 F.2d 1219 (8th Cir.1986) *cert denied,* 479 U.S. 1070 (1987). On the record here, this Court finds and concludes that defendant has failed to satisfy these burdens.

Korean Korner urges that there has been a change in both the applicable law and the relevant facts. First, it is argued that this Court, in previously deciding that the scriptwriters were employees of the Korean networks, relied solely on *Aldon Accessories Ltd. v. Spiegel,* 738 F.2d 548, 552 (2d Cir.1984), a case recently overruled by the Supreme Court's opinion in *Community for Creative Non–Violence v. Reid,* — U.S. ——, 109 S.Ct. 2166, 2174 (1989). Second, it is contended that recent deposition testimony of Yung Shik Shim and others alter the record before the Court and require a finding under United States copyright law that the scriptwriters are not employees of the Korean networks.

The *Reid* case did indeed overrule *Aldon Accessories.* However, as indicated by its Memorandum Opinion of December 15, 1988, the Court did not rely exclusively on *Aldon Accessories.* Prior to its citation of *Aldon Accessories,* the Court had concluded that the evidence in the case demonstrated that the Korean networks directed the activities of the scriptwriters, that KBS and MBC controlled the general outline of the scripts and paid for them and that control exercised by KBS and MBC over the content, progress and production of the scripts was sufficient to render the scripts works made for hire under United States copyright law. The new facts of record do not essentially alter those findings. Accordingly, this Court has concluded that defendant Korean Korner has not met its burden of showing that the expanded record now before the Court requires that these findings be set aside.

Writing for the Court in *Reid,* Justice Marshall stated:

> To determine whether a work is for hire under the Act, a court first should ascertain, using principles of general common law of agency, whether the work was prepared by an employee or an independent contractor.... In determining whether a hired party is an employee under the general common law of agency, we consider the hiring party's right to control the manner and means by which the product is accomplished. Among the other factors relevant to this inquiry are the skill required; the source of the instrumentalities and tools; the location of the work; the duration of the relationship between the parties; whether the hiring party has the right to assign additional projects to the hired party; the extent of the hired party's direction over when and how to work; the method of payment; the hired party's role in hiring and paying assistants; whether the work is part of the regular business of the hiring party; the provision of employee benefits; and the tax treatment of the hired party. See Restatement [(Second) of Agency] § 220(2) (setting forth a non-exhaustive list of factors relevant to determining whether a hired party is an employee).

Id. at 2178–79 (footnotes omitted).

Defendant contends that *Reid,* when applied to the record here, requires dissolution of the permanent injunction. The parties initially dispute whether this Court, in ruling on the pending motion, should consider new evidence. However, in deciding to deny the motion, the Court has considered all affidavits, depositions, deposition excerpts and exhibits which have been filed by the parties in support of and in opposition to the pending motion.

Applying the agency test laid down by *Reid,* this Court is not persuaded that the scriptwriters are "independent contractors" rather than "employees." While the sculptor in *Reid* labored on a one time basis for less than two months, the Korean scriptwriters work for the network on a longtime basis. They are represented by KRTWA, which is essentially a union handling negotiations between the scriptwriters and the networks. The history of royalty agreements and negotiations between KRTWA and the networks provides evidence of a long term employment relationship between the parties. Rather than producing a single work, as did the sculptor in *Reid,* the scriptwriters produce scripts for numerous episodes of a particular show.

Other factors mentioned in *Reid* support the Court's previous finding that the scriptwriters are "employees." Production of shows is a regular, indeed integral, part of the networks' business. Network representatives including directors and producers participate in, and have control over, the scriptwriters' completion of scripts. The weekly or monthly pay received by a scriptwriter resembles a salary, inasmuch as withholding taxes are deducted from the amount paid.

As defendant has pointed out, there are also factors pointing the other way and suggesting that scriptwriters are not "employees" under the *Reid* test. Nevertheless, these countervailing factors are insufficient to convince this Court that Korean Korner has sustained the burden imposed on it of showing clearly that the permanent injunction should be dissolved. Even if all favorable inferences are given to the facts relied upon by Korean Korner, the very most that can be said is that the *Reid* factors are equally balanced. This Court must therefore decline to set aside the longstanding permanent injunction in this case on the basis of the showing made at this late date by the movant. Korean Korner has not made a clear showing that new and unforeseen conditions have created a grievous wrong and would require a change in a permanent decree entered after years of litigation. *Swift & Co., supra,* 286 U.S. at 119.

Defendant Korean Korner contends that, in the deposition testimony given by Yung Shik Shim by telephone in July of 1990, he "recanted" the testimony given by him at the trial before Judge Weinstein in 1986. Although, as might be expected, differences exist between Mr. Shim's 1990 telephone testimony and his 1986 trial testimony, the differences hardly amount to a complete "recanting." The Court has considered the testimony given at both times in concluding that defendant Korean Korner has not met the burdens imposed upon it by the applicable law. In its Memorandum Opinion of March 14, 1988, this Court rejected the contention of other defendants in this case that newly discovered evidence discredited the testimony of Mr. Shim given at the trial before Judge Weinstein in 1986. (Slip op. at 7). What is apparent is that Mr. Shim's motivations and perceptions are quite different in 1990 than they were when he testified in open court in 1986. At that time, he was Chairman of KRTWA, and his testimony was accepted by Judge Weinstein as that of the scriptwriters themselves. For the past several years, the Korean networks and KRTWA have been engaged in a dispute concerning a continuation of agreements between the scriptwriters and KTS.[4] When his deposition was taken in July, 1990, Mr. Shim was no longer associated with KRTWA, and his testimony was not that of a representative of the scriptwriters. Accordingly, this Court will give considerably more weight to the trial testimony of Mr. Shim in 1986 than to what he said in 1990 when his telephone deposition was taken. Moreover, Mr. Shim's 1986 trial testimony was corroborated by that of the witness Kyo Sik Kim, a Korean scriptwriter, who also testified at that trial.

Defendant continues to argue that under Korean law the scriptwriters and not plaintiff KTE own the copyrights at issue. But the Court in this case is dealing with copyright certificates issued by the United States Copyright Office. It is therefore the federal Copyright Act which is controlling and not any provision of Korean copyright law. As this Court ruled in its Memorandum Opinion of December 15, 1988, Korean law is not pertinent to the Court's determination that the scripts are works made for hire because the scriptwriters are employees of the networks. (Slip op. at 10).

The decision to deny defendant's motion is buttressed by consideration of circumstances other than the decision in *Reid.* Defendant Korean Korner (as did other defendants previously in this case) here contends that the scriptwriters rather than KTE own the copyrights at issue. If this be so, the Court is led to wonder why the scriptwriters have not sought at any time since the previous agreement expired in December of 1988 to assert in a federal court in the United States the valuable rights at issue. Significantly, the scriptwriters are not a party to this litigation, nor have they chosen to challenge the copyrights at issue in this or any other court. Their absence belies defendant's contention that the rights of these absent third parties shield defendant Korean Korner from the consequences of its infringing acts.

Even if the scriptwriters were not "employees" under § 101, KTE would still have a protectable copyright interest in the videotaped shows as "derivative works" under § 103. *See* 17 U.S.C. § 103; 3 M. Nimmer, *supra,* § 13.01 at 13–14; *Gilliam v. American Broadcasting Companies, Inc.,* 538 F.2d 14, 19–20 (2d Cir.1976) (finding television shows created from scripts to be "derivative works"). If the scripts themselves are viewed as separately owned by the scriptwriters and thus copyrightable, the KTE shows based on the scripts are derivative works also subject to copyright protection. In producing their shows, the networks bring the scripts to life by means of editing, lighting, directing, acting, and filming. *See Davis v. E.I. duPont de Nemours & Co.,* 240 F.Supp. 612 (S.D.N.Y.1965). Even if Korean Korner had been licensed to rent or sell videotapes of the scripts, its commercial use of taped shows would constitute infringement of the derivative works owned by KTE.

Finally, the Court would note that its finding that the scriptwriters are employees under applicable copyright law has been confirmed by every federal court which has considered the issue. United States District Courts in separate cases in New York, Pennsylvania, Virginia, Illinois and Texas have entered preliminary or permanent injunctions prohibiting the infringement of copyrights owned by KTE in programs produced in Korea. These injunctions were all based on findings by these courts that KTE was the owner of valid copyrights which were being infringed by corporations and individuals renting or selling Korean videotapes in each respective state. Each court rejected the argument made here that the scriptwriters and not the networks were the owners of the copyrights.

III
Conclusion

For the reasons stated, defendant's motion to dissolve the permanent injunction will be denied. Accordingly, it is this 11th day of December, 1990, by the United States District Court for the District of Maryland, ORDERED that the motion of defendant Korean Korner to dissolve the permanent injunction be and the same is hereby denied.

PEPE, LTD. v. GRUPO PEPE, LTDA.
United States District Court for the Southern District of Florida
June 3, 1992, Decided; June 3, 1992, Filed
CASE No. 91-1821-CIV-MOORE
1992 U.S. Dist. LEXIS 17144, 24 U.S.P.Q.2d (BNA) 1354

OMNIBUS ORDER

K. MICHAEL MOORE, District Judge.

THIS CAUSE came before the Court on the various motions of Defendants, Grupo Pepe, Ltda., ("Grupo Pepe"), Nader Chehade, Ltda., ("Chehade"), W. Nader Hnos, Ltda., ("Hnos"), and Wadith Nader, ("Nader"), as well as Plaintiffs' Motion for Leave to File their proposed Second Amended and Supplemental Complaint. After consideration of the various motions, and careful review of the pertinent portions of the record, the Court enters the following Omnibus Order.

MEMORANDUM

BACKGROUND

Plaintiffs in this action sought injunctive and monetary relief against Defendants for alleged copyright and trademark infringement with regard to the distribution of counterfeit Pepe jeans in South Florida. Defendants Chehade, Grupo Pepe, and Hnos are Colombian corporations under the ownership and control of Defendant Nader. Defendants filed several motions challenging the substantive, pleading, and jurisdictional allegations of Plaintiffs' First Amended Complaint, (the "Complaint"). The following discussion addresses the merits of the arguments raised before the Court.

I. Defendants' Motion to Compel

Defendants sought to require Plaintiffs to separate their claims asserted under theories of copyright and trademark, and the relief requested under each such legal theory. The Court has reviewed the Complaint and is satisfied that, as plead, the Complaint complies with the pleading requirements of the Federal Rules of Civil Procedure. Defendants should have little difficulty in formulating their response to the allegations and relief requested within the Complaint. Accordingly, Defendants' Motion to Compel is denied without further discussion.

II. Defendant's Notion to Strike the Word "Counterfeit" from the Pleadings

Rule 12(f) of the Federal Rules of Civil Procedure permits the Court upon motion, or on its own initiative, to strike "any insufficient defense or any redundant, immaterial, impertinent, or scandalous matter" from a pleading. Fed.R.Civ.P. 12(f). Defendants sought to strike the word "counterfeit" from the allegations of the Complaint. Defendants would have the Court determine, at this stage of the litigation, whether or not Plaintiffs can satisfy the requirements of the definition of "counterfeit" contained within the provisions of the Lanham Act. 15 U.S.C. §§ 1116(d)(1)(A) and (B). The Court declines Defendants' invitation at this time. In order to prevail on the merits, Plaintiffs must establish that the marks at issue were indeed counterfeit—Defendants will thus have opportunities to challenge Plaintiffs' allegations throughout the various stages of this litigation. Defendants' Motion to Strike is therefore denied.

III. Defendants' Motion to Dismiss for Failure to Join Indispensable and Necessary Parties

Defendants moved the Court under Rule 12(b)(7) of the Federal Rules of Civil Procedure to dismiss Count IV of the Complaint for copyright infringement for Plaintiffs' purported failure to join an indispensable party. Defendants argue that the allegations within the Complaint which state that Plaintiffs' employees authored the logo design mark at issue are insufficient to prevent possible duplicate litigation if those authors' rights are not represented in this action. Defendants assert that joinder of these alleged indispensable parties is necessary, "[i]n the absence of ... any other means of ascertaining the relationship between or among said authors (the employees) and the alleged claimant herein ...". Defendants' Motion to Dismiss at 3.

Plaintiffs have provided sworn evidence which is dispositive on this point. Plaintiffs attached the declaration of Mark Blenkinsop to their response memorandum. *See* Plaintiffs' Response Memorandum and Exhibit 1 thereto. Blenkinsop's declaration establishes that: (1) he personally developed the logo design mark at issue; (2) he developed the logo design mark while employed by Plaintiff, Pepe (UK) Ltd.; (3) he had no agreement with Pepe (UK) Ltd. reserving any copyright in the mark itself; and (4) he, as author of the subject mark, has no claim against Defendants regarding any alleged infringement of that mark. *Id.* Moreover, under the laws of the United Kingdom, works made by employees hired to design such marks are the property of the employer who is the first owner of the copyright therein. *See* Declaration of Richard Cooper, filed previously in opposition to Defendants' Motion to Set Aside Defaults at par. 7. United States copyright law is consistent therewith. *See Neva, Inc., v. Christian Duplications International, Inc.,* 743 F.Supp. 1533, 1544 (M.D.Fla.1990) (under work for hire doctrine, the hiring party who solicits the commissioned party to create a work for pay is presumed to be the author and copyright owner of the work). Blenkinsop has thus no right to sue, and can therefore not be considered as an indispensable party to this litigation. *See e.g. Moran v. London Records, Inc.,* 827 F.2d 180, 183 (7th Cir.1987) (employees in work made for hire arrangement have no right to sue under copyright laws).

IV. Defendants' Motions to Dismiss for Lack of Personal Jurisdiction

Defendants Grupo Pepe and Hnos challenge the assertion of personal jurisdiction over them as nonresident defendants by this Court. Hnos, through declaration of Eduardo Nader, attempted to establish that Hnos is merely a holding company for the premises utilized by Grupo Pepe in Colombia, and is not engaged in sales of any goods. Grupo Pepe, through declaration of Defendant Nader, admits that it manufactures garments which are the subject of this action, and that goods it sold to Defendant Chehade were in turn sold to Tradelink–Miami, Inc., a local South Florida distributor. Grupo Pepe, however, denies that it ever sold the alleged counterfeit garments directly for distribution into the United States, or that it ever conducted exporting activities directed towards distribution into the United States.

In addition to the allegations of the Complaint, Plaintiffs rely on numerous declarations filed with the Court to establish the activities necessary to justify the assertion of personal jurisdiction over Grupo Pepe and Hnos. The Court must first resolve the evidentiary effect of the conflicting declarations, and the corresponding burdens to be imposed in the determination of Defendants' motions challenging personal jurisdiction. When a district court does not conduct an evidentiary hearing on a motion to dismiss for lack of jurisdiction, the burden is on Plaintiffs to establish a prima facie case of personal jurisdiction over the non-resident defendants, Grupo Pepe and Hnos. *Madara v. Hall,* 916 F.2d 1510, 1514 (11th Cir.1990) (citing *Morris v. SSE, Inc.,* 843 F.2d 489, 492 (11th Cir.1988). Such a prima facie case is established if Plaintiffs present sufficient evidence to withstand a motion for directed verdict. *Id.* The Court must accept the facts alleged in the Complaint as true, and where the Plaintiffs' allegations and affidavits conflict with the affidavits of Defendants', the Court must construe all reasonable inferences in favor of Plaintiffs. *Id.*

The determination of personal jurisdiction over a non-resident defendant requires a two-part analysis: first, an inquiry into the jurisdictional question under the state, in this case, Florida, long-arm statute; and second, consideration of whether sufficient minimum contacts exist to satisfy the Due Process Clause of the Fourteenth Amendment. *Cable/Home Communication Corp. v. Network Productions, Inc.,* 902 F.2d 829, 855 (11th Cir.1990) (citations omitted). Only if both prongs of the analysis are satisfied may the Court exercise personal jurisdiction over the challenging Defendants. The Court's analysis begins with the Florida Long–Arm Statute.

A. *Florida Long–Arm Statute*

Florida Statutes § 48.193 governs the assertion of personal jurisdiction over a non-resident defendant. § 48.193, Fla. Stat. (1989). Subsections (l)(a) and (b) thereof state:

> (1) Any person, whether or not a citizen or resident of this state, who personally or through an agent does any of the acts enumerated in this subsection thereby submits himself, and if he is a natural person, his personal representative to the jurisdiction of the courts of this state for any cause of action arising from the doing of any of the following acts:
>
> (a) Operating, conducting, engaging in, or carrying on a business or business venture in this state or having an office or agency in this state.
>
> (b) Committing a tortious act within this state.
>
> §§ 48.193(1)(a), (b), Fla. Stat. (1989).

Plaintiffs argue that Grupo Pepe and Hnos' alleged involvement in sending and selling counterfeit garments in South Florida, subjects the Defendants to the jurisdiction of the Court under both subsections cited above. The Court agrees. Considering the allegations and declaration statements offered by Plaintiffs in support of the assertion of personal jurisdiction over the Defendants most favorably to the Plaintiffs, the alleged activities fall within the purview of the Florida Long–Arm Statue. Grupo Pepe and Hnos, based upon Plaintiffs' proffer, engaged in substantial business activities in allegedly selling a large volume of counterfeit garments in South Florida through a local distributor. § 48.193(1)(a), Fla. Stat. (1989). Further, the alleged conduct of the Defendants in selling such counterfeit products to the injury of Plaintiffs in Florida is sufficient to subject the Defendants to jurisdiction in this State. Accordingly, the Florida Long–Arm Statute subjects both Grupo Pepe and Hnos to the jurisdiction of the Court.

B. *Due Process Considerations*

The Court's determination of whether the assertion of personal jurisdiction over Defendants comports with due process is itself a two-prong inquiry. *Madara,* 916 F.2d 1515, 1516. First, it must be determined whether Defendants have established "minimum contacts" with Florida; and second, whether the exercise of personal jurisdiction over Defendants would offend " 'traditional notions of fair play and substantial justice.' " *Id.* at 1516 (citations omitted). In the assertion of personal jurisdiction over a non-resident defendant, "due process requires the defendant have 'fair warning' that a particular activity may subject him to the jurisdiction of a foreign sovereign. *Burger King v. Rudzewicz,* 471 U.S. 462, 472, 105 S.Ct. 2174, 2182, 85 L.Ed.2d 528 (1985). Defendants' conduct and connection with the forum must be of a character that he should reasonably anticipate being haled into court here in Florida. *Id.* at 474. "Jurisdiction is proper where the defendant's contacts with the forum proximately result from actions by the defendant *himself* that create a 'substantial connection' with the forum state." *Madara,* 916 F.2d at 1516 (citing *Burger King,* 471 U.S. at 475, 105 S.Ct. at 2183) (emphasis in original).

The Court is satisfied that Grupo Pepe purposefully established sufficient minimum contacts with Florida to reasonably anticipate being haled into court here. Among the allegations against Grupo Pepe are that Defendant Nader solicited business in Miami on behalf of Grupo Pepe, the manufacturer of the counterfeit garments, and took orders on Grupo Pepe order forms. Additionally, Plaintiffs allege that Grupo Pepe's name appears on labels of packages of counterfeit products sent to Florida for distribution. Accordingly, the "minimum contacts" necessary to justify personal jurisdiction over Grupo Pepe are established. *See e.g. International Harvester Company v. Mann,* 460 So.2d 580, 581 (Fla. 1st DCA 1984) (commission of a tort within Florida by a nonresident is sufficient "minimum contact" with Florida to justify personal jurisdiction in light of Constitutional due process requirements).

With regard to Hnos, Plaintiffs raised two bases for finding minimum contacts: first, that Defendant Nader, on behalf of Hnos, solicited business and represented Hnos in negotiations relating to the counterfeit garments; and second, that Hnos is an alter ego of Nader. The specific allegations regarding the initial assertion involve an incident in Los Angeles, California. This is insufficient contact to satisfy the Constitutional requirement for personal jurisdiction in Florida. The alter ego theory, however, supports a finding of minimum contacts in this case. Again considering Plaintiffs' allegations and declaration statements favorably, Hnos is the alter ego of Nader and is involved in the alleged activities conducted by Nader through his other alter ego corporations, Chehade and Grupo Pepe to bring the counterfeit garments into Florida. This is sufficient to meet the "minimum contacts" test and subject Hnos to the jurisdiction of the Court. *See Woods v. Jorgensen,* 522 So.2d 935, 937 (Fla. 1st DCA 1988) (jurisdiction proper over nonresident defendant under corporate alter ego theory).

"Once it has been determined that the nonresident defendant has purposefully established minimum contacts with the forum ... these contacts are considered in light of other factors to decide whether the assertion of personal jurisdiction would comport with "fair play and substantial justice.' " *Madara,* 916 F.2d at 1517 (citations omitted). Those factors include burden on the defendant in defending the lawsuit, the forum state's interest in adjudicating the dispute, the plaintiff's interest in obtaining convenient and effective relief, the interstate judicial system's interest in obtaining the most efficient resolution of controversies, and the shared interest of the states in furthering fundamental substantive social policies. *Id.* Defendants in this action would not be burdened in defending against Plaintiffs' allegations since Nader and Chehade submitted to the Court's jurisdiction and are obviously prepared to defend this case. Plaintiffs have a strong interest in obtaining relief to protect their licensing rights and proprietary interests therein. The State of Florida has an interest in adjudicating this claim as the alleged counterfeit goods landed on its shores and were distributed there. The policies sought to be furthered by both the judiciary and the states is also supported by resolution of this action before the Court. In light of the presence of minimum contacts for Grupo Pepe and Hnos, the factors discussed above, personal jurisdiction over the two moving defendants is reasonable.

V. DEFENDANTS' MOTION TO DISMISS COUNT IV FOR FAILURE TO STATE A CAUSE OF ACTION

Count IV of Plaintiffs' Complaint purports to state a cause of action for copyright infringement with regard to the Pepe logo design mark. Defendants contend that Count IV fails to state a cause of action because of its vague allegations and failure to establish a prima facie showing of validity of the copyright. The Court disagrees.

Rule 12(b)(6) of the Federal Rules of Civil Procedure authorizes the Court to dismiss a claim on the basis of a dispositive issue of law. *Neitzke v. Williams,* 109 S.Ct. 1827, 1832 (1989). However, the Court is confined to a review of the pleadings, must accept the pleaded facts as true, and must resolve any factual issues in a manner favorable to the nonmovant. *See Quinones v. Durkis,* 638 F.Supp. 856, 858 (S.D.Fla.1986). Thus, a claim is subject to dismissal under Rule 12(b)(6) only if it is clear that no relief could be granted under any set of facts that could be proved consistent with the allegations. *H.J., Inc., v. Northwestern Bell Telephone Co.,* 109 S.Ct. 2893, 2906 (1989) (quoting *Hishon v. King & Spaulding,* 104 S.Ct. 2229, 2232 (1984)); *Conley v. Gibson,* 355 U.S. 41, 45–46 (1957).

When taken as true, the allegations of Plaintiffs' Complaint affirmatively and clearly set out the elements of the claim which Defendants allege are deficient—i.e., ownership, originality, and pictorial-graphical quality of the work.[5] The Court cannot say that Plaintiffs would not be entitled to any relief under the facts alleged in the Complaint. *H.J., Inc.,* 109 S.Ct. at 2906. Defendants' Motion to Dismiss for Failure to State a Cause of Action is denied.

VI. Plaintiffs' Motion for Leave to File a Second Amended and Supplemental Complaint

During the pendency of Defendants' various motions, Plaintiffs sought leave of Court to file their proposed Second Amended and Supplemental Complaint. The Proposed Second Amended and Supplemental Complaint adds one new claim against Defendants alleging unfair competition under the Lanham Act; corrects factual matters contained within the First Amended Complaint; and adds a recently-obtained United States Trademark registration to the allegations of the First Amended Complaint.

Leave of Court to file an amended pleading shall be freely given when justice so requires. Fed.R.Civ.P. 15(a); *Foman v. Davis,* 371 U.S. 178 (1962). The policy behind Rule 15(a) is clear—amendments shall be liberally permitted absent a substantial reason to deny leave to amend. *Shipner v. Eastern Airlines,* 868 F.2d 401, 407 (11th Cir.1989). Although the granting of leave to amend is within the Court's discretion, that discretion is not broad enough to deny leave where there is no basis to do so. *Id.*

After consideration of the status of this action, and review of the proposed Second Amended and Supplemental Complaint, Plaintiffs shall be granted leave to file their amended pleading. This litigation is in its early stages, with no discovery yet taken. The record is devoid of any action or inaction which could warrant denial of leave. Defendants will not be prejudiced by having to respond to the amended pleading as it is substantially similar to the First Amended Complaint, and the added claim merely relies on the same factual allegations previously asserted by Plaintiffs in their former pleadings. Under these circumstances, it would be an abuse of discretion for the Court to deny Plaintiffs leave to file their amended pleading.

Accordingly, based upon the foregoing, it is hereby

ORDERED AND ADJUDGED that

1. Defendants' Motion to Compel Separation, Numbering and Paragraphing is **DENIED;**

2. Defendants' Motion to Strike the Word "Counterfeit" from the Pleadings is **DENIED;**

3. Defendants' Motion to Dismiss for Failure to Join Indispensable Parties is **DENIED;**

4. Defendant Grupo Pepe Ltda.'s Motion to Dismiss for Lack of Personal Jurisdiction is **DENIED;**

5. Defendant W. Nader Hnos. Ltda.'s Motion to Dismiss for Lack of Personal Jurisdiction is **DENIED;**

6. Defendants' Motion to Dismiss for Failure to State a Cause of Action is **DENIED;**

7. Plaintiffs' Motion for Leave to File Second Amended and Supplemental Complaint is **GRANTED.** The Second Amended and Supplemental

Complaint shall be deemed as served and filed as of the date of this Omnibus Order. Defendants shall have twenty (20) days from the date of this Omnibus Order to file their answers to the Second Amended and Supplemental Complaint.

DONE AND ORDERED.

In the following case, Sabafilms, Ltd. v. MGM-Pathe Communications Co., 24 F.3d 1088 (9th Cir. 1994), plaintiffs claim infringement of film's copyright and breach of contract, where defendants authorized its subsidiary to distribute worldwide the videocassette version of the film, *Yellow Submarine*.

SUBAFILMS, LTD. v. MGM-PATHE COMMUNICATIONS CO.
United States court of Appeals for the Ninth Circuit
February 24, 1994, Argued, Submitted; May 13, 1994, Filed
Nos. 91-56248, 91-56379, O. 91-56289

D.W. NELSON, Circuit Judge:

In this case, we consider the "vexing question" of whether a claim for infringement can be brought under the Copyright Act, 17 U.S.C. § 101 *et seq.* (1988), when the assertedly infringing conduct consists solely of the authorization within the territorial boundaries of the United States of acts that occur entirely abroad. We hold that such allegations do not state a claim for relief under the copyright laws of the United States.

Factual and Procedural Background

In 1966, the musical group The Beatles, through Subafilms, Ltd., entered into a joint venture with the Hearst Corporation to produce the animated motion picture entitled "Yellow Submarine" (the "Picture"). Over the next year, Hearst, acting on behalf of the joint venture (the "Producer"), negotiated an agreement with United Artists Corporation ("UA") to distribute and finance the film. Separate distribution and financing agreements were entered into in May, 1967. Pursuant to these agreements, UA distributed the Picture in theaters beginning in 1968 and later on television.

In the early 1980s, with the advent of the home video market, UA entered into several licensing agreements to distribute a number of its films on videocassette. Although one company expressed interest in the Picture, UA refused to license "Yellow Submarine" because of uncertainty over whether home video rights had been granted by the 1967 agreements. Subsequently, in 1987, UA's successor company, MGM/UA Communications Co. ("MGM/UA"), over the Producer's objections, authorized its subsidiary MGM/UA Home Video, Inc. to distribute the Picture for the domestic home video market, and, pursuant to an earlier licensing agreement, notified Warner Bros., Inc. ("Warner") that the Picture had been cleared for international videocassette distribution. Warner, through its wholly owned subsidiary, Warner Home Video, Inc., in turn entered into agreements with third parties for distribution of the Picture on videocassette around the world.

In 1988, Subafilms and Hearst ("Appellees") brought suit against MGM/UA, Warner, and their respective subsidiaries (collectively the "Distributors" or "Appellants"), contending that the videocassette distribution of the Picture, both foreign and domestic, constituted copyright infringement and a breach of the 1967 agreements. The case was tried before a retired California Superior Court Judge acting as a special master. The special master found for Appellees on both claims, and against the Distributors on their counterclaim for fraud and reformation. Except for the award of prejudgment interest, which it reversed, the district court adopted all of the special master's factual findings and legal conclusions. Appellees were awarded $2,228,000.00 in compensatory damages, split evenly between the foreign and domestic home video distributions. In addition, Appellees received attorneys' fees and a permanent injunction that prohibited the Distributors from engaging in, or authorizing, any home video use of the Picture.

A panel of this circuit, in an unpublished disposition, affirmed the district court's judgment on the ground that both the domestic and foreign distribution of the Picture constituted infringement under the Copyright Act. *See Subafilms, Ltd. v. MGM–Pathe Communications Co.,* Nos. 91–56248, 91–56379, 91–56289, 1993 WL 39269 (9th Cir. Feb. 17, 1993). With respect to the foreign distribution of the Picture, the panel concluded that it was bound by this court's prior decision in *Peter Starr Prod. Co. v. Twin Continental Films, Inc.,* 783 F.2d 1440 (9th Cir.1986), which it held to stand for the proposition that, although " 'infringing actions that take place entirely outside the United States are not actionable' [under the Copyright Act, an] 'act of infringement within the United States' [properly is] alleged where the illegal *authorization* of international exhibitions *t[akes] place in the United States," Subafilms,* slip op. at 4917–18 (quoting *Peter Starr,* 783 F.2d at 1442, 1443 (emphasis in original) (alterations added)). Because the Distributors had admitted that the initial authorization to distribute the Picture internationally occurred within the United States, the panel affirmed the district court's holding with respect to liability for extraterritorial home video distribution of the Picture.

We granted Appellants' petition for rehearing en banc to consider whether the panel's interpretation of *Peter Starr* conflicted with our subsequent decision in *Lewis Galoob Toys, Inc. v. Nintendo of Am., Inc.,* 964 F.2d 965 (9th Cir.1992), *cert. denied,* 507 U.S. 985, 113 S.Ct. 1582, 123 L.Ed.2d 149 (1993), which held that there could be no liability for authorizing a party to engage in an infringing act when the authorized "party's use of the work would not violate the Copyright Act," *id.* at 970; *see also Columbia Pictures Indus., Inc. v. Professional Real Estate Investors, Inc.,* 866 F.2d 278, 279–81 (9th Cir.1989) (holding that a hotel was not liable under the Copyright Act for making available videodisc players for in-room viewing), *rev'd on other grounds,* 508 U.S. 49, 113 S.Ct. 1920, 123 L.Ed.2d 611 (1993). Because we conclude that there can be no liability under the United States copyright laws for authorizing an act that *itself* could not constitute infringement of rights secured by those laws, and that wholly extraterritorial acts of infringement are not cognizable under the Copyright Act, we overrule *Peter Starr* insofar as it held that allegations of an authorization within the United States of infringing acts that take place entirely abroad state a claim for infringement under the Act. Accordingly, we vacate the panel's decision in part and return the case to the panel for further proceedings.

Discussion

I. The Mere Authorization of Extraterritorial Acts of Infringement does not State a Claim under the Copyright Act

As the panel in this case correctly concluded, *Peter Starr* held that the authorization within the United States of entirely extraterritorial acts stated a cause of action under the "plain language" of the Copyright Act. *Peter Starr,* 783 F.2d at 1442–43. Observing that the Copyright Act grants a copyright owner "the *exclusive rights* to do and *to authorize*" any of the activities listed in 17 U.S.C. § 106(1)–(5), *id.* at 1442 (emphasis in original), and that a violation of the "authorization" right constitutes infringement under section 501 of the Act, the *Peter Starr* court reasoned that allegations of an authorization within the United States of extraterritorial conduct that corresponded to the activities listed in section 106 "allege[d] an act of infringement within the United States," *id.* at 1442–43. Accordingly, the court determined that the district court erred "in concluding that 'Plaintiff allege[d] only infringing acts which took place outside of the United States,' " and reversed the district court's dismissal for lack of subject matter jurisdiction. *Id.* at 1443.

The *Peter Starr* court accepted, as does this court, that the acts *authorized* from within the United States themselves could not have constituted infringement under the Copyright Act because "[i]n general, United States copyright laws do not have extraterritorial effect," and therefore, "infringing actions that take place entirely outside the United States are not actionable." *Peter Starr,* 783 F.2d at 1442 (citing *Robert Stigwood Group, Ltd. v. O'Reilly,* 530 F.2d 1096, 1101 (2d Cir.), *cert. denied,* 429 U.S. 848, 97 S.Ct. 135, 50 L.Ed.2d 121 (1976)). The central premise of the *Peter Starr* court, then, was that a party could be held liable as an "infringer" under section 501 of the Act merely for authorizing a third party to engage in acts that, had they been committed *within* the United States, would have violated the exclusive rights granted to a copyright holder by section 106.

Since *Peter Starr,* however, we have recognized that, when a party authorizes an activity *not* proscribed by one of the five section 106 clauses, the authorizing party cannot be held liable as an infringer. In *Lewis Galoob,* we rejected the argument that "a party can unlawfully authorize another party to use a copyrighted work even if that party's use of the work would not violate the Copyright Act," *Lewis Galoob,* 964 F.2d at 970, and approved of Professor Nimmer's statement that " 'to the extent that an activity does not violate one of th[e] five enumerated rights [found in 17 U.S.C. § 106], authorizing such activity does not constitute copyright infringement,' " *id.* (quoting 3 David Nimmer & Melville B. Nimmer, Nimmer on Copyright § 12.04[A][3][a], at 12–80 n. 82 (1991)). Similarly, in *Columbia Pictures,* we held that no liability attached under the Copyright Act for providing videodisc players to hotel guests when the use of that equipment did not constitute a "public" performance within the meaning of section 106 of the Act, *see Columbia Pictures,* 866 F.2d at 279–81.

The apparent premise of *Lewis Galoob* was that the addition of the words "to authorize" in the Copyright Act was not meant to create a new form of liability for "authorization" that was divorced completely from the legal consequences of authorized conduct, but was intended to invoke the preexisting doctrine of contributory infringement... .

As the Supreme Court noted in *Sony,* and this circuit acknowledged in *Peter Starr,* under the 1909 Act courts differed over the *degree* of involvement required to render a party liable as a contributory infringer. *See Sony,* 464 U.S. at 437–38 & n. 18, 104 S.Ct. at 786–87 & n. 18; *Peter Starr,* 783 F.2d at 1443. Viewed with this background in mind, the addition of the words "to authorize" in the 1976 Act appears best understood as merely clarifying that the Act contemplates liability for contributory infringement, and that the bare act of "authorization" can suffice. This view is supported by the legislative history of the Act:

> The exclusive rights accorded to a copyright owner under section 106 are "to do and to authorize" any of the activities specified in the five numbered clauses. *Use of the phrase "to authorize" is intended to avoid any questions as to the liability of contributory infringers.* For example, a person who lawfully acquires an authorized copy of a motion picture would be an infringer if he or she engages in the business of renting it to others for purposes of unauthorized public performance.

H.R.Rep. No. 1476, 94th Cong., 2d Sess. 61, *reprinted in* 1976 U.S.C.C.A.N. 5659, 5674 (emphasis added).

Consequently, we believe that " 'to authorize' [wa]s simply a convenient peg on which Congress chose to hang the antecedent jurisprudence of third party liability." 3 Nimmer, *supra,* § 12.04[A][3][a], at 12–84 n. 81.

Although the *Peter Starr* court recognized that the addition of the authorization right in the 1976 Act "was intended to remove the confusion surrounding contributory ... infringement," *Peter Starr,* 783 F.2d at 1443, it did not consider the applicability of an essential attribute of the doctrine identified above: that contributory infringement, even when triggered solely by an "authorization," is a form of third party liability that requires the authorized acts to constitute infringing ones. We believe that the *Peter Starr* court erred in not applying this principle to the authorization of acts that cannot themselves be infringing because they take place entirely abroad. As Professor Nimmer has observed:

> Accepting the proposition that a direct infringement is a prerequisite to third party liability, the further question arises whether the direct infringement on which liability is premised must take place within the United States. Given the undisputed axiom that United States copyright law has no extraterritorial application, it would seem to follow necessarily that a primary activity outside the boundaries of the United States, not constituting an infringement cognizable under the Copyright Act, cannot serve as the basis for holding liable under the Copyright Act one who is merely related to that activity within the United States.

3 Nimmer, *supra,* § 12.04[A][3][b], at 12–86 (footnotes omitted).

Appellees resist the force of this logic, and argue that liability in this case is appropriate because, unlike in *Lewis Galoob* and *Columbia Pictures,* in which the alleged primary infringement consisted of acts that were entirely outside the purview of 17 U.S.C. § 106(1)–(5) (and presumably lawful), the conduct authorized in this case was precisely that prohibited by section 106, and is only uncognizable because it occurred outside the United States. Moreover, they contend that the conduct authorized in this case would have been prohibited under the copyright laws of virtually every nation....

Even assuming *arguendo* that the acts authorized in this case would have been illegal abroad, we do not believe the distinction offered by Appellees is a relevant one. Because the copyright laws do not apply extraterritorially, each of the rights conferred under the five section 106 categories must be read as extending "no farther than the [United States'] borders." 2 Goldstein, *supra,* § 16.0, at 675. *See, e.g., Robert Stigwood,* 530 F.2d at 1101 (holding that no damages could be obtained under the Copyright Act for public performances in Canada when preliminary steps were taken within the United States and stating that "[t]he Canadian performances, while they may have been torts in Canada, were not torts here"); *see also Filmvideo Releasing Corp. v. Hastings,* 668 F.2d 91, 93 (2d Cir.1981) (reversing an order of the district court that required the defendant to surrender prints of a film because the prints could be used to further conduct abroad that was not proscribed by United States copyright laws). In light of our above conclusion that the "authorization" right refers to the doctrine of contributory infringement, which requires that the authorized act *itself* could violate one of the exclusive rights listed in section 106(1)–(5), we believe that "[i]t is simply not possible to draw a principled distinction" between an act that does not violate a copyright because it is not the type of conduct proscribed by section 106, and one that does not violate section 106 because the illicit act occurs overseas. *Danjaq, S.A. v. MGM/UA Communications, Co.,* 773 F.Supp. 194, 203 (C.D.Cal.1991), *aff'd on other grounds,* 979 F.2d 772 (9th Cir.1992). In both cases, the authorized conduct could not violate the exclusive rights guaranteed by section 106. In both cases, therefore, there can be no liability for "authorizing" such conduct. *See also* 3 Nimmer, *supra,* § 12.04[A][3][b], at 12–87 to 12–88.

To hold otherwise would produce the untenable anomaly, inconsistent with the general principles of third party liability, that a party could be held liable as an infringer for violating the "authorization" right when the party that it authorized could not be considered an infringer under the Copyright Act. Put otherwise, we do not think Congress intended to hold a party liable for *merely* "authorizing" conduct that, had the *authorizing* party chosen to engage in itself, would have resulted in no liability under the Act. *Cf. Robert Stigwood,* 530 F.2d at 1101.

Appellees rely heavily on the Second Circuit's doctrine that extraterritorial application of the copyright laws is permissible "when the type of infringement permits further reproduction abroad." *Update Art, Inc. v. Modiin Publishing, Ltd.,* 843 F.2d 67, 73 (2d Cir.1988). Whatever the merits of the Second Circuit's rule, and we express no opinion on its validity in this circuit, it is premised on the theory that the copyright holder may recover damages that stem from a direct infringement of its exclusive rights that occurs *within* the United States. *See Robert Stigwood,* 530 F.2d at 1101; *Sheldon v. Metro–Goldwyn Pictures Corp.,* 106 F.2d 45, 52 (2d Cir.1939) (L. Hand, J.) ("The negatives were 'records' from which the work could be 'reproduced', and it was a tort to make them in this country. The plaintiffs acquired an equitable interest in them as soon as they were made, which attached to any profits from their exploitation...."), *aff'd,* 309 U.S. 390, 60 S.Ct. 681, 84 L.Ed. 825 (1940); *see also Ahbez v. Edwin H. Morris & Co., Inc.,* 548 F.Supp. 664, 667 (S.D.N.Y.1982); *Famous Music Corp. v. Seeco Records, Inc.,* 201 F.Supp. 560, 568–69 (S.D.N.Y.1961). In these cases, liability is not based on contributory infringement, but on the theory that the infringing use would have been actionable *even if* the subsequent foreign distribution that stemmed from that use never took place.

Accordingly, accepting that wholly extraterritorial acts of infringement cannot support a claim under the Copyright Act, we believe that the *Peter Starr* court, and thus the panel in this case, erred in concluding that the mere authorization of such acts supports a claim for infringement under the Act.

II. The Extraterritoriality of the Copyright Act

Appellees additionally contend that, if liability for "authorizing" acts of infringement depends on finding that the authorized acts themselves are cognizable under the Copyright Act, this court should find that the United States copyright laws *do extend* to extraterritorial acts of infringement when such acts "result in adverse effects within the United States." Appellees buttress this argument with the contention that failure to apply the copyright laws extraterritorially in this case will have a disastrous effect on the American film industry, and that other remedies, such as suits in foreign jurisdictions or the application of foreign copyright laws by American courts, are not realistic alternatives.

We are not persuaded by Appellees' parade of horribles. More fundamentally, however, we are unwilling to overturn over eighty years of consistent jurisprudence on the extraterritorial reach of the copyright laws without further guidance from Congress.

The Supreme Court recently reminded us that "[i]t is a long-standing principle of American law 'that legislation of Congress, unless a contrary intent appears, is meant to apply only within the territorial jurisdiction of the United States.' " *EEOC v. Arabian American Oil Co.* (*Aramco*), 499 U.S. 244, 248, 111 S.Ct. 1227, 1230, 113 L.Ed.2d 274 (1991) (quoting *Foley Bros., Inc. v. Filardo,* 336 U.S. 281, 285, 69 S.Ct. 575, 577, 93 L.Ed. 680 (1949)). Because courts must "assume that Congress legislates against the backdrop of the presumption against extraterritoriality," unless "there is 'the affirmative intention of the Congress clearly expressed' " congressional enactments must be presumed to be " 'primarily concerned with domestic conditions.' " *Id.* 499 U.S. at 248, 111 S.Ct. at 1230 (quoting *Foley Bros.,* 336 U.S. at 285, 69 S.Ct. at 577 and *Benz v. Compania Naviera Hidalgo, S.A.,* 353 U.S. 138, 147, 77 S.Ct. 699, 704, 1 L.Ed.2d 709 (1957)).

The "undisputed axiom," 3 Nimmer, *supra,* § 12.04[A][3][b], at 12–86, that the United States' copyright laws have no application to extraterritorial infringement predates the 1909 Act, *see, e.g., United Dictionary Co. v. G. & C. Merriam Co.,* 208 U.S. 260, 264–66, 28 S.Ct. 290, 290–91, 52 L.Ed. 478 (1908) (Holmes, J.), and, as discussed above, the principle of territoriality consistently has been reaffirmed, *see, e.g., Capitol Records, Inc. v. Mercury Records Corp.,* 221 F.2d 657, 662 (2d Cir.1955) (citing *American Code Co. v. Bensinger,* 282 F. 829, 833 (2d Cir.1922) ("The copyright laws of one country have no extraterritorial operation, unless otherwise provided." (citing *Ferris v. Frohman,* 223 U.S. 424, 32 S.Ct. 263, 56 L.Ed. 492 (1912))); *sources cited supra* pp. 1093–94. There is no clear expression of congressional intent in either the 1976 Act or other relevant enactments to alter the preexisting extraterritoriality doctrine. Indeed, the *Peter Starr* court itself recognized the continuing application of the principle that "infringing actions that take place entirely outside the United States are not actionable in United States federal courts." *Peter Starr,* 783 F.2d at 1442 (citing *Robert Stigwood,* 530 F.2d at 1101).

Furthermore, we note that Congress chose in 1976 to expand one specific "extraterritorial" application of the Act by declaring that the unauthorized importation of copyrighted works constitutes infringement even when the copies lawfully were made abroad. *See* 17 U.S.C.A. § 602(a) (West Supp.1992). Had Congress been inclined to overturn the preexisting doctrine that infringing acts that take place wholly outside the United States are not actionable under the Copyright Act, it knew how to do so. *See Argentine Republic v. Amerada Hess Shipping Corp.,* 488 U.S. 428, 440, 109 S.Ct. 683, 691, 102 L.Ed.2d 818 (1989) ("When it desires to do so, Congress knows how to place the high seas within the jurisdictional reach of a statute." (quoted in *Aramco,* 499 U.S. at 258, 111 S.Ct. at 1235)). Accordingly, the presumption against extraterritoriality, "far from being overcome here, is doubly fortified by the language of [the] statute," *Smith v. United States,* 507 U.S. 197, ——, 113 S.Ct. 1178, 1183, 122 L.Ed.2d 548 (1993) (quoting *United States v. Spelar,* 338 U.S. 217, 222, 70 S.Ct. 10, 13, 94 L.Ed. 3 (1949)), as set against its consistent historical interpretation.

Appellees, however, rely on dicta in a recent decision of the District of Columbia Circuit for the proposition that the presumption against extraterritorial application of U.S. laws may be "overcome" when denying such application would "result in adverse effects within the United States." *Environmental Defense Fund, Inc. v. Massey,* 986 F.2d 528, 531 (D.C.Cir.1993) (noting that the Sherman Act, Lanham Act, and securities laws have been applied to extraterritorial conduct). However, the *Massey* court did not state that extraterritoriality would be *demanded* in such circumstances, but that "the *presumption* is *generally* not *applied* where the failure to extend the scope of the statute to a foreign setting will result in adverse [domestic] effects." *Id.* at 531 (emphasis added). In each of the statutory schemes discussed by the *Massey* court, the ultimate touchstone of extraterritoriality consisted of an ascertainment of congressional intent; courts did not rest *solely* on the consequences of a failure to give a statutory scheme extraterritorial application. More importantly, as the *Massey* court conceded, *see id.* at 532–33, application of the presumption is particularly appropriate when "[i]t serves to protect against unintended clashes between our laws and those of other nations which could result in international discord," *Aramco,* 499 U.S. at 248, 111 S.Ct. at 1230 (citing *McCulloch v. Sociedad Nacional de Marineros de Honduras,* 372 U.S. 10, 20–22, 83 S.Ct. 671, 677–78, 9 L.Ed.2d 547 (1963)).[14]

We believe this latter factor is decisive in the case of the Copyright Act, and fully justifies application of the *Aramco* presumption even assuming *arguendo* that "adverse effects" within the United States "generally" would require a plenary inquiry into congressional intent. At the time that the international distribution of the videocassettes in this case took place, the United States was a member of the Universal Copyright Convention ("UCC"), and, in 1988, the United States acceded to the Berne Convention for the Protection of Literary and Artistic Works ("Berne Conv."). The central thrust of these multilateral treaties is the principle of "national treatment." A work of an American national first generated in America will receive the same protection in a foreign nation as that country accords to the works of its own nationals.

Indeed, a recognition of this principle appears implicit in Congress's statements in acceding to Berne that "[t]he primary mechanism for discouraging discriminatory treatment of foreign copyright claimants is the principle of national treatment," H.R.Rep. No. 609, 100th Cong., 2d Sess. 43 [hereinafter House Report], and that adherence to Berne will require "careful due regard for the[] values" of other member nations, *id.* at 20.

In light of the *Aramco* Court's concern with preventing international discord, we think it inappropriate for the courts to act in a manner that might disrupt Congress's efforts to secure a more stable international intellectual property regime unless Congress otherwise clearly has expressed its intent. The application of American copyright law to acts of infringement that occur entirely overseas clearly could have this effect. Extraterritorial application of American law would be contrary to the spirit of the Berne Convention, and might offend other member nations by effectively displacing their law in circumstances in which previously it was assumed to govern. Consequently, an extension of extraterritoriality might undermine Congress's objective of achieving " 'effective and harmonious' copyright laws among all nations." House Report, *supra,* at 20. Indeed, it might well send the signal that the United States does not believe that the protection accorded by the laws of other member nations is adequate, which would undermine two other objectives of Congress in joining the convention: "strengthen[ing] the credibility of the U.S. position in trade negotiations with countries where piracy is not uncommon" and "rais[ing] the like[li]hood that other nations will enter the Convention." S.Rep. 352, 100th Cong., 2d Sess. 4–5, *reprinted in* 1988 U.S.C.C.A.N., 3706, 3709–10.

Moreover, although Appellees contend otherwise, we note that their theory might permit the application of American law to the distribution of protected materials in a foreign country conducted exclusively by citizens of that nation. A similar possibility was deemed sufficient in *Aramco* to find a provision that, on its face, appeared to contemplate that Title VII would be applied overseas, insufficient to rebut the presumption against extraterritoriality. *See Aramco,* 499 U.S. at 254, 111 S.Ct. at 1234. Of course, under the Berne Convention, all states must guarantee minimum rights, *see* Berne Conv. Art. IV; Stewart, *supra,* at 39–40, and it is plausible that the application of American law would yield outcomes roughly equivalent to those called for by the application of foreign law in a number of instances. Nonetheless, extending the reach of American copyright law likely would produce difficult choice-of-law problems, *cf.* House Report, *supra,* at 43 ("[Berne] does not, however, require all countries to have identical legal systems and procedural norms."), dilemmas that the federal courts' general adherence to the territoriality principle largely has obviated. Even if courts, as a matter of comity, would assert extraterritorial jurisdiction only when the effects in the United States and the contacts of the offending party with this country are particularly strong, *cf. Timberlane Lumber Co. v. Bank of Am., N.T. & S.A.,* 549 F.2d 597, 615 (9th Cir.1976), *cert. denied,* 472 U.S. 1032, 105 S.Ct. 3514, 87 L.Ed.2d 643 (1985), that the assertion of such jurisdiction would engender new and troublesome choice-of-law questions provides a compelling reason for applying the *Aramco* presumption.

Accordingly, because an extension of the extraterritorial reach of the Copyright Act by the courts would in all likelihood disrupt the international regime for protecting intellectual property that Congress so recently described as essential to furthering the goal of protecting the works of American authors abroad, *see supra* note 10, we conclude that the *Aramco* presumption must be applied. *Cf. Benz,* 353 U.S. at 147, 77 S.Ct. at 704 ("For us to run interference in such a delicate field of international relations there must be present the affirmative intention of the Congress clearly expressed."). Because the presumption has not been overcome, we reaffirm that the United States copyright laws do not reach acts of infringement that take place entirely abroad. It is for Congress, and not the courts, to take the initiative in this field.

III. Other Arguments

Appellees raise a number of additional arguments for why the district court's judgment should be affirmed. Relying upon the Second Circuit's doctrine described above, *see supra* p. 1094, Appellees maintain that they may recover damages for international distribution of the Picture based on the theory that an act of direct infringement, in the form of a reproduction of the negatives for the Picture, took place in the United States. Appellees also suggest that they may recover, under United States law, damages stemming from the international distribution on the theory that the distribution was part of a larger conspiracy to violate their copyright that included actionable infringement within the United States. In addition, they maintain that Appellants are liable for the international distribution under foreign copyright laws. Finally, Appellees argue that the district court's damage award can be sustained under the breach of contract theory not reached by the panel.

We resolve none of these questions, but leave them for the panel, in its best judgment, to consider. A remand to the district court might well be necessary to permit further factual development in light of our decision to overrule aspects of *Peter Starr.* The panel, however, is free to take whatever action it views as appropriate that is consistent with our mandate. *See Haphey v. Linn County,* 953 F.2d 549, 552 (9th Cir.1992) (en banc).

Conclusion

We hold that the mere authorization of acts of infringement that are not cognizable under the United States copyright laws because they occur entirely outside of the United States does not state a claim for infringement under the Copyright Act. *Peter Starr* is overruled insofar as it held to the contrary. Accordingly, we vacate Part III of the panel's disposition, in which it concluded that the international distribution of the film constituted a violation of the United States copyright laws. We also vacate that portion of the disposition that affirmed the damage award based on foreign distribution of the film and the panel's affirmance of the award of attorneys' fees. Finally, we vacate the district court's grant of injunctive relief insofar as it was based on the premise that the Distributors had violated the United States copyright laws through authorization of the foreign distribution of the Picture on videocassettes. *Cf. Filmvideo,* 668 F.2d at 93–94.

The cause is remanded to the panel for further proceedings consistent with the mandate of this court.

Vacated in Part and **Remanded.**

FRINK AM., INC. v. CHAMPION RD. MACH. LTD.
United States District Court for the Nothern District of New York
April 8, 1997, Decided; April 9, 1997, Filed
Lead Case 96-CV-486, Member Case 96-CV-1576
961 F.Supp. 398

MEMORANDUM, DECISION & ORDER

McAVOY, Chief Judge.

I. BACKGROUND

A. Facts:

Corporate Evolution

The common corporate lineage of the parties involved in this action dates back to 1945, when Melvin O. Simpson founded Combined Enterprises Limited, a holding company later to become known as Compro Limited ("Compro"). Compro eventually acquired three companies relevant to the present discussion. In 1958, Compro acquired Hamilton Gear and Machine Company ("Hamilton"), a manufacturer of industrial gearing. (Aff. of S. Paul Battaglia ["Battaglia Aff."], Ex. A at 1). Also in 1958, Compro purchased Eastern Steel Products ("Eastern"), located in Cambridge, Ontario. (*Id.;* Aff. of Mark Turpin ["Turpin Aff."] ¶ 1). In 1961, Compro purchased **plaintiff Frink America ("Frink America"),** a company headquartered in Clayton, New York and engaged in the manufacture of highway and airport snow plows in the United States. (Battaglia Aff., Ex. A at 1; Turpin Aff. ¶ 2). At the time Compro acquired Eastern, Eastern was manufacturing Frink snow plows in Canada, (*id.*), and in fact later became known as "Frink Canada."

In 1973, the Simpson family founded Melson Incorporated ("Melson"), a private Arizona corporation, fifty-percent of the stock of which was held by Simpson's son, Melvin Jr., and fifty-percent by the Dorothy C. Simpson Family Trust of Scottsdale, Arizona. (Battaglia Aff., Ex. A at 1). During the 1970's, Melson became the common owner of the outstanding stock of both Compro and Frink America. (*Id.;* Aff. of Louis Montante ["Montante Aff."] ¶ 3).

The "Windrow" Plan

By the early 1990's, Melson and its subsidiaries apparently began suffering considerable losses. In an effort to make Frink and Compro more competitive in the snow plow business, Melvin Sr. and his son Scott developed a plan ("Operation Windrow") that called for the combining of Compro and Frink America's manufacturing operations at one location in the United States. (Battaglia Aff. ¶ 8 and Ex. A at 4). Before this consolidation occurred, however, the continuing financial losses forced Melson to cease Frink America's operations in Clayton and shift all production to the Eastern (Frink Canada) facility in Cambridge. (Battaglia Aff. ¶ 9, Ex. A at 4; Turpin Aff. ¶ 3). As part of this move, in August of 1991, certain of Frink America's product drawings, plans, jigs, machine tools and other items (the "intellectual property") were transferred to the Eastern facility so that Frink Canada could satisfy Frink America's outstanding obligations. The legal consequences of this transfer are the focus of this proceeding.

The Bankruptcy Proceedings

Compro's financial problems persisted, as did friction within the ranks of Melson and Compro's management. (Battaglia Aff. ¶ 11–12). As a result, defendant contends, Compro's chief financial backer, the Royal Bank of Canada (the "Royal Bank"), forced Compro into a Canadian bankruptcy proceeding sometime in late 1991. (*Id.,* ¶ 11). Frink America followed suit in the summer of 1992 by filling for Chapter 11 protection in the Northern District of New York.

Prior to filing Chapter 11, however, Frink America's manufacturing operations were recommenced at the Clayton facility. (*Id.;* Turpin Aff. ¶ 4). Thus, the intellectual property "loaned" to Frink Canada in connection with the failed Windrow operation was transferred from Cambridge back to the Clayton facility in June of 1992. (Battaglia Aff. ¶ 13, Ex. C; Turpin Aff. ¶ 5). This transfer additionally served a function in a larger scheme: since the Royal Bank actually was a creditor of both Compro and Frink America (Frink America having acted as guaranty on certain loans by the Royal Bank to Compro), the return of the intellectual property was part of an agreement[2] executed by the three parties which, plaintiff contends, was approved by the U.S. Bankruptcy Court in the Northern District. (Battaglia Aff. ¶ 15 and Ex. B).

In October of 1992, Peat Marwick Thorne Inc. ("Peat Marwick") was appointed Compro's receiver in the Canadian bankruptcy proceeding. (Battaglia Aff. Ex. D at 1). Peat Marwick sold Compro's assets to 1004704 Ontario Inc., a corporation controlled by David Lowry. (*Id.;* Compl. ¶ 25). While Frink America was emerging from bankruptcy, Lowry transferred Compro's assets to an entity called Frink Environmental, Inc. ("FEI"), which the Royal Bank subsequently forced into bankruptcy in Canada. Ernst & Young Ltd. ("Ernst & Young") was appointed receiver of FEI in September of 1994. (Affidavit of Brian William Gray ["Gray Aff."] Ex. 1). Finally, as receiver, Ernst & Young sold FEI's assets to **defendant Champion Road Machinery Limited ("Champion");** defendant allegedly came to possess the intellectual property of Frink America by way of this final transfer. (Gray Aff. Ex. 6).

The Prior Lawsuit

Plaintiff alleges that in 1995, Champion began manufacturing snow removal equipment with FEI's assets. Although Champion owns the rights to the Frink trademark in Canada, plaintiff contends that Champion began marketing snow removal equipment in the United States in direct competition with Frink America. (Pl. Mem. of Law at 8). These marketing efforts allegedly included distributing product catalogs and quotations to U.S. customers, and making unsupported claims to such customers that Frink America was in financial straits and would not be able to fill its warranty obligations. (*Id.*). In addition to the unlawful use of the Frink trademark, plaintiff alleges that equipment in the Champion product line was identical to the equipment previously manufactured exclusively by Frink America based upon the American designs and plans. (*Id.*).

On June 8, 1995, plaintiff filed suit in the Ontario Court of Justice (General Division) against the Royal Bank and Champion. (Gray Aff. Ex. 10). The lawsuit sought injunctive relief against Champion for the use of plaintiff's intellectual property, and damages against the Royal Bank for breach of contract, breach of confidentiality, conversion and breach of patent. (*Id.*). The parties subsequently consented to a dismissal of the action, (*id.* Ex. 14), but plaintiff contends that the dismissal was intended only against Royal Bank, and that Champion was dismissed as a defendant inadvertently. (*Id.* Ex. 15).

B. Procedural History:

Plaintiff filed its first action in this Court on March 22, 1996 alleging, *inter alia,* trademark infringement. Plaintiff filed the present action on September 25, 1996. This Complaint contains five claims: (1) misappropriation of trade secrets and conversion; (2) tortious interference with business relations; (3) trade dress infringement; (4) unfair competition; and (5) copyright infringement under Canadian law. While the present motion was pending, the two actions were consolidated by Order of Magistrate Judge Daniel Scanlon, Jr. dated March 21, 1997.

Defendant filed this motion on December 23, 1996, and moves for dismissal of the member case on three grounds: (1) *forum non conveniens;* (2) failure to state a claim upon which relief may be granted, based upon the doctrine of international comity; and (3) failure to join a party, pursuant to Fed.R.Civ.P. 12(b)(7) and 19.

The Court will address these arguments *seriatim.*

II. DISCUSSION
A. *Forum Non Conveniens*

While the venue-transferring aspect of *forum non conveniens* has been superseded by statute, *see* 28 U.S.C. § 1404(a), federal courts nonetheless retain the power to dismiss actions for damages under common-law application of the doctrine where the alternative forum is abroad.

Plaintiff, however, has chosen New York as its forum. Ordinarily, there is a strong presumption in favor of the plaintiff's selection of a forum which may be overcome only when the private and public factors clearly point toward trial in the alternative forum. *Piper,* 454 U.S. at 255, 102 S.Ct. at 265–66. This rule is based upon the logical assumption that the plaintiff's home forum is in fact the most convenient. *Id.* at 256, 102 S.Ct. at 266. We thus turn to the private/public interest balancing test of *Gilbert.*

Private Interests

The factors pertaining to the private interests of the litigants include: the "relative ease of access to sources of proof; availability of compulsory process for attendance of unwilling witnesses; possibility of view of premises, if view would be appropriate to the action; and all other practical problems that make trial of a case easy, expeditious and inexpensive." *Gilbert,* 330 U.S. at 508, 67 S.Ct. at 843; *see also Borden Inc. v. Meiji Milk Products Co.,* 919 F.2d 822, 827 (2d Cir.1990). "There may also be questions as to the enforcibility [sic] of a judgment if one is obtained ...". *Gilbert,* 330 U.S. at 508, 67 S.Ct. at 843.

Defendant argues generally that

> the dispute involves a Canadian bankruptcy proceeding. It involves assets located in Canada and the transfer of those assets from one Canadian company to another Canadian company, pursuant to a specific order of a Canadian Court. All the potential defendants reside in Canada: 1) Champion; 2) the bankruptcy petitioner, the Royal Bank; and 3) the bankruptcy trustee, Ernst & Young. Thus, the proper forum is clearly Canada.

(Def. Mem. of Law at 10). Defendant's emphasis on the Canadian bankruptcy proceeding, however, is steeped in misdirection. While the transfer of assets by Ernst & Young from FEI to defendant is a relevant transaction, a transaction of equal, if not greater significance is Frink America's transfer of intellectual property to Eastern in August of 1991, a transfer that originated in this very district. Moreover, as plaintiff points out, it will need to prove that certain of the drawings, plans, etc. were the products of Frink America employees, many of whom may still reside in the district. Such witnesses would not be subject to compulsory process in a Canadian action.

Other private interest factors weighing in plaintiff's favor are the relative proximity of the likely locations of much of the discovery material, and the situs of much of the conduct in question. While Upstate New York and Southern Ontario undoubtedly retain distinct provincial and national identities, this Court is uniquely aware that our neighbors to the North (and West) are, if not a stone's throw, at most a few hours' drive away. Indeed, there are points within the district as separated. Moreover, considerations of practical convenience must be evaluated "in light of the increased speed of travel and communication which makes ... no forum 'as inconvenient [today] as it was in 1947.' " *Manu Intern., S.A., v. Avon Products, Inc.,* 641 F.2d 62, 65 (2d Cir.1981) (quoting *Fitzgerald v. Texaco, Inc.,* 521 F.2d 448, 457 (2d Cir.1975)). Additionally, the very conduct upon which several of plaintiff's claims are premised, namely defendant's marketing, distribution and sales activities, occurred within the United States. Indeed, the *situs* of much of the conduct is a crucial issue, since plaintiff concedes that defendant owns the rights to the Frink trademark in Canada.

Defendant argues that since plaintiff seeks an injunction regarding acts of both defendant and non-parties taking place in Canada, this Court lacks the power to fashion a complete remedy in the event it finds in plaintiff's favor. Given that injunctive relief rests in the Court's discretion, however, such relief may be denied if this Court determines that an injunction would be unenforceable.

Public Interest

The public interest factors include: the administrative difficulties flowing from court congestion; the "local interest in having localized controversies decided at home;" the interest of having the trial of a case in a forum that is at home with the law that must govern the action; the avoidance of unnecessary problems in conflict of laws, or in the application of foreign law; and the unfairness of burdening citizens in an unrelated forum with jury duty. *Gilbert,* 330 U.S. at 509, 67 S.Ct. at 843.

Defendant makes no argument with respect to the first factor. As to the second, defendant posits that "copyright adjudications ... are matters of fundamentally local concern." (Def. Reply Mem. at 4). This argument ignores the fact that four of plaintiff's five claims are brought under American law.

This recognition brings us to the heart of the controversy embodied in the next two factors, namely whether trial of this action in this forum will require the Court to become enmeshed in matters of Canadian law. At the outset, we note that while the difficulties attendant in resolving questions of foreign law are a proper consideration, *see Scottish Air International, Inc. v. British Caledonian Group PLC,* 81 F.3d 1224, 1234 (2d Cir.1996), " 'it is well-established that the need to apply foreign law is not alone sufficient to dismiss under the doctrine of *forum non conveniens.'* " *Segal,* 89 F.3d at 47 (quoting *R. Maganlal & Co. v. M.G. Chemical Co., Inc.,* 942 F.2d 164, 169 (2d Cir.1991)). Ultimately, this Court cannot conclude, as does defendant, that plaintiff's claims under American copyright and common-law are simply "a smokescreen for its improper Canadian copyright claim." (Def. Reply Mem. at 4). Nor does defendant convincingly argue that the necessity of adjudicating the Canadian claim militates in favor of dismissal on *forum non conveniens* grounds.

Defendant does, however, raise serious questions as to this Court's *power* to hear such a claim, i.e., whether a federal district court has subject matter jurisdiction over a foreign copyright claim. In *Vanity Fair Mills, Inc. v. T. Eaton, Ltd.,* 234 F.2d 633 (2d Cir.1956), the Second Circuit upheld a district court's decision declining to exercise jurisdiction of claims of trademark infringement and unfair competition arising in Canada under Canadian law, noting:

> We do not think it the province of United States district courts to determine the validity of trademarks which officials of foreign countries have seen fit to grant. To do so would be to welcome conflicts with the administrative and judicial officers of the Dominion Canada.

Id. at 647. A copyright claim such as that presented here is distinguishable, however, as the Southern District noted in *London Film Productions v. Intercontinental Comm.,* 580 F.Supp. 47, 49 (S.D.N.Y.1984):

> '[i]n adjudicating an infringement action under a foreign copyright law there is ... no need to pass upon the validity of acts of foreign government officials,' since foreign copyright laws, by and large, do not incorporate administrative formalities which must be satisfied to create or perfect a copyright.

Id. at 49 (quoting 3 *Nimmer on Copyright,* § 1703 (1983)) (internal citations omitted).

In opposition, defendant cites *ITSI T.V. Productions, Inc. v. California Authority of Racing Fairs,* 785 F.Supp. 854 (E.D.Cal.1992), a case that declined the exercise of jurisdiction over copyright claims arising under Mexican law, noting that Professor Nimmer's general proposition regarding the lack of administrative formalities necessary to perfect a copyright "does not answer the question whether in any given case the particular foreign law does have administrative formalities which must be satisfied." *Id.* at 866 n. 19. As Professor Nimmer later noted, however, this objection need not detain us, since "administrative formalities are barred in all nations that adhere to the Berne Convention," 3 *Nimmer on Copyright,* § 17.03 (1996), a convention to which Canada has been a signatory since 1928. *Id.,* App. 22–2. Thus, defendant's objections to this Court's subject matter jurisdiction are without merit.

In summary, defendant has not shown that the relevant interests tilt so strongly in its favor as to overcome the strong presumption in favor of plaintiff's choice of forum. *See Peregrine,* 89 F.3d at 46; *Schertenleib,* 589 F.2d at 1160. Thus, defendant's motion to dismiss for *forum non conveniens* is denied.

B. Fed.R.Civ.P. 12(b)(6)/Comity

Defendant also argues that under the doctrine of comity, plaintiff fails to state a claim upon which relief may be granted. Specifically relying on *Clarkson Co., Ltd. v. Shaheen,* 544 F.2d 624 (2d Cir.1976), defendant argues that "[i]n this case, Frink America is collaterally attacking the Canadian bankruptcy proceeding, and the authority of the Canadian bankruptcy to transfer assets under a Canadian Court Order." (Def. Mem. of Law at 12). Once again, however, defendant mischaracterizes the theory behind plaintiff's claims. While considerations of comity certainly would militate against any collateral attack on the Canadian bankruptcy proceedings, see *Clarkson,* 544 F.2d at 629, the Court is unconvinced that plaintiff's case stands or falls on the validity of those proceedings. Rather, as plaintiff asserts, "the Complaint in this action emanates from Compro's failure to and breach of its Agreement to, return the intellectual property ... lent to it by Frink in 1991." (Battaglia Aff. ¶ 19).

The Ontario Court order approving the purchase by Champion from FEI of "certain of the assets" of FEI noted that the transfer was free and clear of claims by certain parties, but plaintiff was not among those listed. Moreover, the purchase agreement itself listed the intellectual property that was part of the transfer. (Gray Aff. Ex. 6 [Schedule "E"]). As plaintiff points out, the intellectual property transferred included only four Canadian patents, one lapsed U.S. patent and three Canadian trademarks; any intellectual property not included in Schedule "E" was specifically excluded. (*Id.*). Assuming that the items listed in Schedule "E" are not at issue in this lawsuit, the intellectual property in controversy here was not even *ostensibly* transferred by virtue of the Champion purchase. Thus, neither the validity of the Canadian Bankruptcy Order, nor the trustee's "authority" to transfer the assets listed in the agreement are implicated. For these reasons, defendants motion to dismiss under Fed. R.Civ. P. 12(b)(6) is denied.

C. Failure to Join a Necessary Party

Finally, defendant argues that because plaintiff alleges a conspiracy between the Royal Bank and defendant to deprive plaintiff of the intellectual property at issue, the Royal Bank (and possibly Ernst & Young, the trustee) should have been joined in this action.

Defendant's analysis, however, is incomplete. Rule 12(b)(7) lists, as a ground for dismissal, "failure to join a party under Rule 19." Rule 19 in turn provides a two-step process to determine whether an action may proceed in a party's absence. Rule 19(a) first provides that a person subject to service of process "whose joinder will not deprive the court of subject matter jurisdiction" must be joined (1) if full relief may not be granted among those already parties in the person's absence; or (2) if the person has an interest in the subject matter of the action, and disposition of the action in that person's absence would either impede the person's ability to protect that interest, or leave the original parties subject to multiple or inconsistent obligations. Fed.R.Civ.P. 19(a).

Second, if the person is determined to be a "necessary" party under Rule 19(a) but cannot be joined (either because they not amenable to service of process or would deprive the court of subject matter jurisdiction), the Court must determine whether the person is "indispensable," i.e., whether the action must be dismissed due to the person's absence. *Id.; see generally* 7 CHARLES A. WRIGHT, ARTHUR R. MILLER, AND MARY KAY KANE, FEDERAL PRACTICE AND PROCEDURE, § 1604 at 41 (1986) ("By proceeding in this orderly fashion the court will be able to avoid grappling with the difficult question of indispensability whenever it initially decides that the absentee's interest is not sufficient to warrant compelling his joinder."). In making this determination, the factors to be considered include:

> first, to what extent a judgment rendered in the person's absence might be prejudicial to the person or those already parties; second, the extent to which, by protective provisions in the judgment, by the shaping of relief, or other measures, the prejudice can be lessened or avoided; third, whether a judgment rendered in the person's absence will be adequate; fourth, whether the plaintiff will have an adequate remedy if the action is dismissed for nonjoinder.

Fed.R.Civ.P. 19(b).

Defendant has failed, as a threshold matter, to establish that either the Royal Bank or Ernst & Young is a necessary party under Rule 19(a). Defendant merely argues that since plaintiff may have settled with the Royal Bank, such a settlement may provide defendant with a defense. Defendant fails, however, to establish that the Royal Bank has any interest in the subject matter of this action, or that complete relief may not be accorded among the parties in the Royal Bank's absence. Furthermore, it is well-established that under federal law, neither joint tortfeasors nor co-conspirators are indispensable parties...

II. CONCLUSION:

For all of the foregoing reasons, then, it is hereby ORDERED, that defendant's motion to dismiss is denied on all grounds.

IT IS SO ORDERED.

In the next case, Yount v. Acuff-Rose-Opryland, plantiffs seek domestic and foreign royalties for their song, "Release me," during the renewal copyright period.

YOUNT v. ACUFF ROSE-OPRYLAND
United States Court of Appeals for the Ninth Circuit
November 4, 1996, Argued, Submitted; December 24, 1996, Filed
No. 95-56072, No.95-56151, No. 95-56563

FERNANDEZ, Circuit Judge:

Robert Gene Yount and his son, Robert Blue Yount, brought this action to recover both domestic and foreign royalties for the song "Release Me" during the renewal copyright period. James B. McCall, Geraldine McCall Silva, and Deborah McCall Aleto (the McCalls) asserted that they were entitled to those royalties because Yount had assigned all royalties from "Release Me" to their predecessor in interest, W.S. Stevenson. The district court determined that Yount was entitled to the domestic royalties because the assignment of them had not referred to the renewal copyright term, but that the McCalls were entitled to the foreign royalties. Both parties appealed. We reverse the judgment in favor of Yount and remand for further proceedings; we affirm the judgment in favor of the McCalls.

BACKGROUND

Between 1949 and 1954, Yount worked as a guitarist and songwriter with a now-deceased musician, Eddie Miller. In the course of this collaboration, Yount and Miller created the musical composition "Release Me." In 1949, Yount, Miller, and Dub Williams, another member of their band, entered into a single-song publishing agreement for "Release Me" with 4 Star Record Company, Inc. The agreement granted 4 Star the right to secure a copyright in "Release Me." The composers granted 4 Star: "[T]he right to secure copyright [in 'Release Me'] throughout the entire world, and to have and to hold the said copyright and all rights of whatsoever nature thereunder existing, including any and all renewals of copyright to which the writer(s) may be entitled hereafter." As consideration for the agreement, 4 Star agreed to pay royalties to the composers, who were to share them equally. In 1958, Yount assigned his royalty rights under the publishing agreement to Stevenson, in a document which read: "I, ROBERT YOUNT, do hereby sell, assign and transfer to W.S. STEVENSON, all of my rights, title and interest in and to the song entitled, 'RELEASE ME.' "

The parties agree that a copyright in "Release Me" was registered in the name of the 4 Star Sales Company, Inc. in 1954. The bankruptcy of 4 Star's successor in interest led to the sale of the "Release Me" copyright to Acuff–Rose Music, Inc. As the owner of the copyright, Acuff–Rose is obligated to pay royalties under the song publishing agreement for "Release Me." BMI has at various time collected—and now holds—royalties payable under the song publishing agreement.

The initial term of the copyright for "Release Me" ended in 1983, but it was renewed for a second term. Acuff–Rose paid royalties to Yount from 1983 to 1985. At that time, the McCalls wrote to Acuff–Rose, claiming that the 1958 assignment entitled them to the songwriters' royalties. Shortly thereafter, Acuff–Rose notified Yount and the McCalls that it would withhold payment of domestic royalties for "Release Me" until resolution of the dispute. This action eventually followed.

JURISDICTION AND STANDARD OF REVIEW

The district court had jurisdiction pursuant to 28 U.S.C. §§ 1331, 1338(a) and 1367(a). We have jurisdiction pursuant to 28 U.S.C. § 1291.

We review the district court's grant of summary judgment de novo. *See Warren v. City of Carlsbad,* 58 F.3d 439, 441 (9th Cir.1995), *cert. denied,* 516 U.S. 1171, 116 S.Ct. 1261, 134 L.Ed.2d 209 (1996); *Jesinger v. Nevada Fed. Credit Union,* 24 F.3d 1127, 1130 (9th Cir.1994). Our review "is governed by the same standard used by the trial courts under Federal Rule of Civil Procedure 56(c)." *Jesinger,* 24 F.3d at 1130. We "must determine whether the evidence, viewed in a light most favorable to the nonmoving party, presents any genuine issues of material fact and whether the district court correctly applied the law." *Warren,* 58 F.3d at 441; *see Jesinger,* 24 F.3d at 1130.

DISCUSSION

As we have already indicated, this case involves both a claim for domestic renewal term royalties and a claim for foreign royalties. The former involves both issues of domestic copyright law and issues of state contract law. The latter involves only issues of state contract law. We will discuss each in turn.

A. *The Right to Domestic Royalties.*

Yount correctly points out that the Copyright Act provisions which existed when he assigned his royalty interest to W.S. Stevenson declared that "the author of [a copyrighted work] if still living ... shall be entitled to a renewal and extension of the copyright in such work for a further term of twenty-eight years." Copyright Act of 1909, *as amended,* ch. 391, § 24, 61 Stat. 652, 659 (1947). It is equally true that an author can assign the right to the renewal term copyright long before it is scheduled to commence. However, there is a presumption that an assignment of the renewal term has not taken place. Thus, an assignment or transfer of the copyright in general terms, which makes no mention of the renewal rights, does not assign the renewal term. Nevertheless, "[b]y assigning the renewal copyright in the work without limitation, as in *Miller Music,* the author assigns all of [the rights of the copyright holder]." If the author survives to the commencement of the renewal period, the assignment is effective.

There can be little doubt that in 1949 Yount did assign the whole of the renewal term copyright and that he did survive to the commencement of that term. Thus, it cannot be gainsaid that he failed to retain any claim to the underlying legal interest in the copyright itself. Nevertheless, Yount asserts that the federal common law rule of construction that applies to the assignment of renewal terms of a copyright also governs assignment of contractual royalty interests alone. We do not agree.

Yount first argues that the copyright laws were designed to protect authors. No doubt they were. However, that assertion does not significantly advance analysis or indicate that contractual royalty interests have a protection separate from the protection afforded to renewal of the term of the copyright itself. Authors are not the only ones protected by the Copyright Act. Moreover, protection of authors may well come from laws that give them the freedom to contract at will rather than from laws which prevent them "from realizing on their assets when they are most in need of funds." *Fred Fisher Music,* 318 U.S. at 657, 63 S.Ct. at 779. Generally speaking, it is for Congress, not the courts, to decide just how much protection is needed and what form that protection should take. *Id.* at 656–58, 63 S.Ct. at 779–80. Congress has not declared a special rule regarding contractual royalties during the renewal term of copyright.

Yount, however, asserts that certain other statutory and common law provisions demonstrate that both Congress and the courts have sought to throw up special protections around authors' contractual royalty rights. He points to a provision which allows beneficial owners of a right under a copyright to sue for its infringement and says that the provision indicates that Congress intended to protect authors' royalty interests. *See* 17 U.S.C. § 501(b). However, that provision only indicates an intent to allow every beneficial owner to protect his interests, just in case the legal owner is not doing so. In other words, because an infringer may well injure those who have rights to royalties, standing has been conferred upon them. That, however, has no special reference to authors. It protects anyone who may own a right to royalties, but a determination of who those individuals may be in a given case is, again, a question of state law. Moreover, holding a royalty interest does not bespeak an interest in the underlying copyright itself—a royalty is simply an interest in receiving money when the owner of the copyright exploits it. *Cf. Fantasy, Inc. v. Fogerty,* 654 F.Supp. 1129, 1130–31 (N.D.Cal.1987).

Yount also points to a case which indicated that an egregious breach of the contract transferring a copyright may well give a royalty holder a right of rescission. *Fain v. Irving Trust Co. (In re Waterson, Berlin & Snyder Co.),* 48 F.2d 704, 709 (2d Cir.1931). But rescission itself is a creature of state law. *See Fantasy, Inc. v. Fogerty,* 984 F.2d 1524, 1529 (9th Cir.1993) (*Fantasy II*), *rev'd on other grounds,* 510 U.S. 517, 114 S.Ct. 1023, 127 L.Ed.2d 455 (1994). Nothing in *Waterson* suggests the contrary. Moreover, while the court did refer to "composers," nothing hinged on that designation. The case happened to involve composers. There is no reason to believe that a person to whom the composer had transferred all of his contractual rights would not have had the same right of rescission, if the legal owner had destroyed " 'the essential objects of the contract' " in a manner " 'so fundamental and pervasive as to result in substantial frustration.' " *Waterson,* 48 F.2d at 709 (citations omitted). Nothing in that case suggests that upon so egregious a breach all rights would revert to the composer, even though he had assigned his interest in the contract to someone else. Nothing suggests that the court would be less concerned about a person to whom the composer had transferred his interests.

We recognize that *Waterson* declared that the obligation to pay royalties cannot be severed from the ownership of the copyright itself and then destroyed in bankruptcy. *Id.* at 710. But that merely means that the copyright owner will always be burdened with the concomitant contractual obligation of paying royalties and cannot shrug it off through bankruptcy proceedings. To that extent ownership and obligation are inexorably intertwined, but that does not increase the royalty holder's rights or protections beyond those set forth in the contract.

Because the royalty does arise out of the contract itself, it is that contract which governs the rights of a holder of a royalty interest. Thus, the apposite cases are those which indicate that royalty rights reserved in a contract transferring a copyright are a concern of state contract law only and are not a concern of federal law at all. We have indicated that state law determines the rights and obligations arising under a publishing contract that assigns a copyright. *See Topolos v. Caldewey,* 698 F.2d 991, 993–95 (9th Cir.1983); *see also Vestron, Inc. v. Home Box Office, Inc.,* 839 F.2d 1380, 1382 (9th Cir.1988) (stating that an action for "contractual rights to ownership or royalties" is one that seeks "to vindicate rights created under state law"). We have also looked to state law in determining whether the withholding of royalties effected a material breach of a copyright assignment agreement. *See Fantasy II,* 984 F.2d at 1529–31.

Similarly, other cases have declared the principle that state law governs construction of royalty obligations.

When Yount transferred the underlying copyright, he obtained a contractual right to royalties. He no longer had a copyright; he had a mere contractual right-a promise by 4 Star that it would make royalty payments. At that point federal copyright law essentially ceased to be concerned with how that contractual royalty right or assignments of it would be enforced. Yount's right to royalties included both the original term and the renewal term. Therefore, in 1958 when Yount assigned "all of [his] rights, title and interest," construction of that assignment became a question of state law only, and the district court erred when it granted summary judgment to Yount based upon renewal term jurisprudence.

We express no opinion on the proper construction of the domestic renewal term royalty assignment from Yount to Stevenson as far as state contract law is concerned. That issue remains for the consideration of the district court.

B. *The Right to Foreign Royalties.*

It is axiomatic that United States copyright law does not apply extraterritorially. *See* 3 David Nimmer & Melville B. Nimmer, *Nimmer on Copyright,* § 17.02 (1996). Whether Yount is entitled to foreign royalties earned during the renewal term is, therefore, purely an issue of contract law. That requires interpretation of his 1958 assignment to Stevenson, as it relates to foreign royalties.

Under California law, "[a] contract must be so interpreted as to give effect to the mutual intention of the parties as it existed at the time of contracting, so far as the same is ascertainable and lawful." Cal.Civ.Code § 1636. However, when a contract has been reduced to writing, a court must ascertain the parties' intent from the writing alone, if possible. *Id.* § 1639. Contract interpretation is governed by the objective intent of the parties as embodied in the words of the contract. *Beck v. American Health Group Int'l, Inc.,* 211 Cal.App.3d 1555, 1562, 260 Cal.Rptr. 237, 242 (1989). And, "[t]he words of a written instrument are generally to be understood in their ordinary and popular sense." *Id.* A court will look beyond the terms of the writing where it appears that the parties intended to ascribe a "technical" or "special" meaning to the terms used. *Cooper Cos. v. Transcontinental Ins. Co.,* 31 Cal.App.4th 1094, 1101, 37 Cal.Rptr.2d 508, 511 (1995). However, evidence of the "subjective, uncommunicated intent of one of the parties" cannot be used to contradict the express terms of the contract. *Alex Robertson Co. v. Imperial Cas. & Indem. Co.,* 8 Cal.App.4th 338, 346, 10 Cal.Rptr.2d 165, 170 (1992).

Yount assigned "all" of his "rights, title, and interest" in the song to Stevenson. Those terms, if read in their "ordinary and popular sense," would encompass *all* of Yount's royalty rights from the song, including the right to foreign royalties earned during the whole term of the contract. To prevail at trial, Yount would have to demonstrate that he and Stevenson mutually intended to exclude foreign royalties despite their use of the term "all" in the 1958 assignment; to survive a motion for summary judgment, Yount had to show that the evidence at least presented a genuine issue of material fact on that question. Yount stated that he and Stevenson never discussed foreign royalties, prior to execution of the 1958 assignment. Moreover, he did not present evidence of some industry custom or some course of dealing which would show that a transfer of all foreign royalties was excluded. That indicates that as far as foreign royalties are concerned "all" meant just what it said-his whole interest under the 4 Star agreement. Even if Yount harbored a subjective intent to exclude foreign royalties from the assignment, it is clear that he never said so. To overcome the plain meaning of the written contract, however, Yount must introduce evidence that *both* he *and* Stevenson affirmatively intended to exclude foreign royalties from the assignment-that for them "all" meant "less than all." Yount has introduced no such evidence. Thus, the district court did not err when it granted summary judgment to the McCalls on the question of foreign royalties.

C. *The Failure to Award Attorneys Fees.*

Yount appeals the district court's denial of his request for attorney's fees. A district court's refusal to grant attorney's fees pursuant to 17 U.S.C. § 505 is reviewed for an abuse of discretion. *Fantasy, Inc. v. Fogerty,* 94 F.3d 553, 556 (9th Cir.1996); *Maljack Prods., Inc. v. GoodTimes Home Video Corp.,* 81 F.3d 881, 889 (9th Cir.1996); *Smith v. Jackson,* 84 F.3d 1213, 1221 (9th Cir.1996). We have reversed the district court's decision and remanded the case on the one issue that had been decided in Yount's favor—the claim to domestic royalties. We have affirmed the district court's decision on the issue decided in the McCalls' favor—the claim to foreign royalties. Because Yount has not prevailed on any of his claims at this time, he is not entitled to attorney's fees at this time.

CONCLUSION

There can be little doubt that Yount made an assignment of his royalty rights to Stevenson. He now seeks to cast himself in the mold of a put-upon author, who should have the special protection of the Copyright Act to save him from his own lack of discretion. But authors are not "wards under guardianship of the law." *Fred Fisher Music Co.,* 318 U.S. at 657, 63 S.Ct. at 779. Indeed, we, along with the Supreme Court, assume that they would resent being treated as if they were. *See id.*

Congress and the courts have provided some protection for authors as far as the twenty-eight-year copyright renewal term is concerned, but that form of protection ends once the term has been explicitly transferred. Authors are free to deal with any ensuing contract rights, such as royalties, as they will, subject only to the provisions of state law. In this case, we express no opinion on how those state law provisions may affect the right to royalties during the domestic copyright renewal term, although we agree with the district court that the foreign copyright royalties were validly transferred.

AFFIRMED in part, REVERSED in part, and REMANDED. Costs on appeal are awarded to McCall from appellants. BMI and Acuff–Rose shall bear their own costs on appeal.

In Itar-Tass Russian News Agency v. Russian Kurier, the court holds that under the Berne Convention, 17 U.S.C. §101 expressly provides that copyright ownership of films is a matter for registration in the country where the protection is claimed. However, with other works such as Russian newspaper articles, it could have any one of the three meanings: namely, negative implication, explicit assertion, and specific film provisions.

ITAR-TASS RUSSIAN NEWS AGENCY v. RUSSIAN KURIER
United States Court of Appeals for the Second Circuit
December 17, 1997, Argued; August 27, 1998, Decided
Docket No. 97-7498
153 F.3d 82

JON O. NEWMAN, Circuit Judge:

This appeal primarily presents issues concerning the choice of law in international copyright cases and the substantive meaning of Russian copyright law as to the respective rights of newspaper reporters and newspaper publishers. The conflicts issue is which country's law applies to issues of copyright ownership and to issues of infringement. The primary substantive issue under Russian copyright law is whether a newspaper publishing company has an interest sufficient to give it standing to sue for copying the text of individual articles appearing in its newspapers, or whether complaint about such copying may be made only by the reporters who authored the articles. Defendants-appellants Russian Kurier, Inc. ("Kurier") and Oleg Pogrebnoy (collectively "the Kurier defendants") appeal from the March 25, 1997, judgment of the District Court for the Southern District of New York (John G. Koeltl, Judge) enjoining them from copying articles that have appeared or will appear in publications of the plaintiffs-appellees, mainly Russian newspapers and a Russian news agency, and awarding the appellees substantial damages for copyright infringement.

On the conflicts issue, we conclude that, with respect to the Russian plaintiffs, Russian law determines the ownership and essential nature of the copyrights alleged to have been infringed and that United States law determines whether those copyrights have been infringed in the United States and, if so, what remedies are available. We also conclude that Russian law, which explicitly excludes newspapers from a work-for-hire doctrine, vests exclusive ownership interests in newspaper articles in the journalists who wrote the articles, not in the newspaper employers who compile their writings. We further conclude that to the extent that Russian law accords newspaper publishers an interest distinct from the copyright of the newspaper reporters, the publishers' interest, like the usual ownership interest in a compilation, extends to the publishers' original selection and arrangement of the articles, and does not entitle the publishers to damages for copying the texts of articles contained in a newspaper compilation. We therefore reverse the judgment to the extent that it granted the newspapers relief for copying the texts of the articles. However, because one non-newspaper plaintiff-appellee is entitled to some injunctive relief and damages and other plaintiffs-appellees may be entitled to some, perhaps considerable, relief, we also remand for further consideration of this lawsuit.

Background

The lawsuit concerns *Kurier,* a Russian language weekly newspaper with a circulation in the New York area of about 20,000. It is published in New York City by defendant Kurier. Defendant Pogrebnoy is president and sole shareholder of Kurier and editor-in-chief of *Kurier.* The plaintiffs include corporations that publish, daily or weekly, major Russian language newspapers in Russia and Russian language magazines in Russia or Israel; Itar–Tass Russian News Agency ("Itar–Tass"), formerly known as the Telegraph Agency of the Soviet Union (TASS), a wire service and news gathering company centered in Moscow, functioning similarly to the Associated Press; and the Union of Journalists of Russia ("UJR"), the professional writers union of accredited print and broadcast journalists of the Russian Federation.

The Kurier defendants do not dispute that *Kurier* has copied about 500 articles that first appeared in the plaintiffs' publications or were distributed by Itar–Tass. The copied material, though extensive, was a small percentage of the total number of articles published in *Kurier. See Itar–Tass Russian News Agency v. Russian Kurier, Inc.,* No. 95 Civ. 2144(JGK), 1997 WL 109481, at *13 (S.D.N.Y. Mar. 10, 1997) ("*Itar–Tass II*"). The Kurier defendants also do not dispute how the copying occurred: articles from the plaintiffs' publications, sometimes containing headlines, pictures, bylines, and graphics, in addition to text, were cut out, pasted on layout sheets, and sent to *Kurier*'s printer for photographic reproduction and printing in the pages of *Kurier.*

Most significantly, the Kurier defendants also do not dispute that, with one exception, they had not obtained permission from any of the plaintiffs to copy the articles that appeared in *Kurier.* Pogrebnoy claimed at trial to have received permission from the publisher of one newspaper, but his claim was rejected by the District Court at trial. *See id.* at *4. Pogrebnoy also claimed that he had obtained permission from the authors of six of the copied articles. The District Court made no finding as to whether this testimony was credible, since authors' permission was not pertinent to the District Court's view of the legal issues.

Preliminary injunction ruling. After a hearing in May 1995, the District Court issued a preliminary injunction, prohibiting the Kurier defendants from copying the "works" of four plaintiff news organizations. *See ITAR–TASS Russian News Agency v. Russion Kurier Inc.,* 886 F.Supp. 1120, 1131 (S.D.N.Y.1995) ("*Itar–Tass I*"). Since the Court's analysis framed the key issue that would be considered at trial and is raised on appeal, the Court's opinion and the Russian statutory provisions relied on need to be explained.

Preliminarily, the Court ruled that the request for a preliminary injunction concerned articles published after March 13, 1995, the date that Russia acceded to the Berne Convention. *See id.* at 1125. The Court then ruled that the copied works were "Berne Convention work[s]," 17 U.S.C. § 101, and that the plaintiffs' rights were to be determined according to Russian copyright law. *See Itar–Tass I,* 886 F.Supp. at 1125–26.

The Court noted that under Russian copyright law authors of newspaper articles retain the copyright in their articles unless there has been a contractual assignment to their employer or some specific provision of law provides that the author's rights vest in the employer. *See id.* at 1127. Since the defendants alleged no claim of a contractual assignment, the Court next considered the provision of the 1993 Russian Federation Law on Copyright and Neighboring Rights ("Russian Copyright Law") (World Intellectual Property Organization (WIPO) translation) concerning what the United States Copyrights Act calls "works made for hire," 17 U.S.C. § 201(b). *See* Russian Copyright Law, Art. 14(2). That provision gives employers the exclusive right to "exploit" the "service-related work" produced by employees in the scope of their employment, absent some contractual arrangement. However, the Court noted, Article 14(4) specifies that subsection 2 does not apply to various categories of works, including newspapers. *See Itar–Tass I,* 886 F.Supp. at 1127. Accepting the view of plaintiffs' expert, Professor Vratislav Pechota, Judge Koeltl therefore ruled that the Russian version of the work-for-hire doctrine in Article 14(2), though exempting newspapers, applies to press agencies, like Itar–Tass. *See id.*

Turning to the rights of the newspapers, Judge Koeltl relied on Article 11, captioned "Copyright of Compiler of Collections and Other Works." This Article contains two subsections. Article 11(1) specifies the rights of compilers generally:

> The author of a collection or any other composite work (compiler) shall enjoy copyright in the selection or arrangement of subject matter that he has made insofar as that selection or arrangement is the result of a creative effort of compilation.
>
> The compiler shall enjoy copyright subject to respect for the rights of the authors of each work included in the composite work.
>
> Each of the authors of the works included in the composite work shall have the right to exploit his own work independently of the composite work unless the author's contract provides otherwise.

....

Russian Copyright Law, Art. 11(1). Article 11(2), the interpretation of which is critical to this appeal, specifies the rights of compilers of those works that are excluded from the work-for-hire provision of Article 14(2):

> The exclusive right to exploit encyclopedias, encyclopedic dictionaries, collections of scientific works—published in either one or several

> installments—newspapers, reviews and other periodical publications shall belong to the editor thereof. The editor shall have the right to mention his name or to demand such mention whenever the said publications are exploited.
>
> The authors of the works included in the said publications shall retain the exclusive rights to exploit their works independently of the publication of the whole work.

Id., Art. 11(2). In another translation of the Russian Copyright Law, which was in evidence at the trial, the last phrase of Article 11(2) was rendered "independently from the publication as a whole." Russian Copyright Law, Art. 11(2) (Newton Davis translation). Because the parties' experts focused on the phrase "as a whole" in the Davis translation of Article 11(2), we will rely on the Davis translation for the rendering of this key phrase of Article 11(2), but all other references to the Russian Copyright Law will be to the WIPO translation.

The District Court acknowledged, as the plaintiffs' expert had stated, that considerable scholarly debate existed in Russia as to the nature of a publisher's right "in a work as a whole." *See Itar–Tass I,* 886 F.Supp. at 1128. Judge Koeltl accepted Professor Pechota's view that the newspaper could prevent infringing activity "sufficient to interfere with the publisher's interest in the integrity of the work." *Id.* Without endeavoring to determine what extent of copying would "interfere with" the "integrity of the work," Judge Koeltl concluded that a preliminary injunction was warranted because what *Kurier* had copied was "the creative effort of the newspapers in the compilation of articles including numerous articles for the same issues, together with headlines and photographs." *Id.* The Court's preliminary injunction opinion left it unclear whether at trial the plaintiffs could obtain damages only for copying the newspapers' creative efforts as a compiler, such as the selection and arrangement of articles, the creation of headlines, and the layout of text and graphics, or also for copying the text of individual articles.

Expert testimony at trial. At trial, this unresolved issue was the focus of conflicting expert testimony. The plaintiffs' expert witness at trial was Michael Newcity, coordinator for the Center for Slavic, Eurasian and East European Studies at Duke University and an adjunct member of the faculty at the Duke University Law School. He opined that Article 11(2) gave the newspapers rights to redress copying not only of the publication "as a whole," but also of individual articles. He acknowledged that the reporters retained copyrights in the articles that they authored, but stated that Article 11(2) created a regime of parallel exclusive rights in both the newspaper publisher and the reporter. He rejected the contention that exclusive rights could not exist in two parties, pointing out that co-authors share exclusive rights to their joint work.

Newcity offered two considerations in support of his position. First, he cited the predecessor of Article 11(2), Article 485 of the Russian Civil Code of

1964. That provision was similar to Article 11(2), with one change that became the subject of major disagreement among the expert witnesses. Article 485 had given compilers, including newspaper publishers, the right to exploit their works "as a whole." The 1993 revision deleted "as a whole" from the first paragraph of the predecessor of Article 11(2), where it had modified the scope of the compiler's right, and moved the phrase to the second paragraph of revised Article 11(2), where it modifies the reserved right of the authors of articles within a compilation to exploit their works "independently of the publication as a whole."

Though Newcity opined that even under Article 485, reprinting of "one or two or three, at most," articles from a newspaper would have constituted infringement of the copyright "as a whole," he rested his reading of Article 11(2) significantly on the fact that the 1993 revision dropped the phrase "as a whole" from the paragraph that specified the publisher's right. This deletion, he contended, eliminated whatever ambiguity might have existed in the first paragraph of Article 485.

Second, Newcity referred to an opinion of the Judicial Chamber for Informational Disputes of the President of the Russian Federation ("Informational Disputes Chamber"), issued on June 8, 1995. That opinion had been sought by the editor-in-chief of one of the plaintiffs in this litigation, *Moskovskie Novosti* (*Moscow News*), who specifically called the tribunal's attention to the pending litigation between Russian media organizations and the publisher of *Kurier*. The Informational Disputes Chamber stated, in response to one of the questions put to it, "In the event of a violation of its rights, including the improper printing of one or two articles, the publisher [of a newspaper] has the right to petition a court for defense of its rights."

Defendants' experts presented a very different view of the rights of newspapers. Professor Peter B. Maggs of the University of Illinois, Urbana–Champaign, College of Law, testifying by deposition, pointed out that Article 11(2) gives authors the exclusive rights to their articles and accords newspaper publishers only the "exclusive rights to the publication as a whole, because that's the only thing not reserved to the authors." He opined that a newspaper's right to use of the compiled work "as a whole" would be infringed by the copying of an entire issue of a newspaper and probably by copying a substantial part of one issue, but not by the copying of a few articles, since the copyright in the articles belongs to the reporters. He also disagreed with Newcity's contention that exclusive rights to individual articles belonged simultaneously to both the newspaper and the reporter. Exclusive rights, he maintained, cannot be held by two people, except in the case of co-authors, who have jointly held rights against the world.

The defendants' first expert witness at trial was Michael Solton, who has worked in Moscow and Washington as an associate of the Steptoe &

Johnson law firm. Under Article 11, he testified, authors retain exclusive rights to their articles in compilations, the compiler acquires a copyright in the selection and creative arrangement of materials in the compilation, and a newspaper publisher typically acquires the limited rights of the compiler by assignment from the compiler. The publisher, he said, does not acquire any rights to the individual articles. Solton declined to attach any significance to the decision issued by the Informational Disputes Chamber because, he explained, the bylaws of that body accord it authority only over limited matters concerning the mass media and explicitly preclude it from adjudicating matters that Russian law refers to courts of the Russian Federation, such as copyright law.

The defendants' second expert trial witness was Svetlana Rozina, a partner of the Lex International law firm, who has consulted for the Russian government. She wrote the first draft of what became the 1993 revision of the Russian Copyright Law. She also testified that authors of works in compilations retain the exclusive right to their works, and that publishers of compilations do not have any rights to individual articles. Turning to the change in the placement of the phrase "as a whole" from Article 11(1) to Article 11(2), she explained that no substantive change was intended; the shift was made "[f]or the purpose of Russian grammar." She also agreed with Solton that the Informational Disputes Chamber renders advice on matters concerning freedom of mass information and lacks the competence to adjudicate issues of copyright law.

Trial ruling. The District Court resolved the dispute among the experts by accepting Newcity's interpretation of Russian copyright law. *See Itar–Tass II,* 1997 WL 109481, at *9–*10. As he had previously ruled in granting the preliminary injunction, Judge Koeltl recognized that newspapers acquire no rights to individual articles by virtue of Article 14 since the Russian version of the work-for-hire doctrine is inapplicable to newspapers. Nevertheless, Judge Koeltl accepted Newcity's view of Article 11, relying on both the movement of the phrase "as a whole" from the first paragraph of Article 11(2) to the second paragraph of Article 11(2), and the opinion of the Informational Disputes Chamber. He also reasoned that publishers have "the real economic incentive to prevent wholesale unauthorized copying," and that, in the absence of assignments of rights to individual articles, widespread copying would occur if publishers could not prevent *Kurier* 's infringements. *Itar–Tass II,* 1997 WL 109481, at *10.

The District Court estimated *Kurier* 's profits during the relevant years at $2 million and found that 25 percent of these profits were attributable to the copied articles. The Court therefore awarded the plaintiffs $500,000 in actual damages against Kurier and Pogrebnoy. *See id.* at *14. The Court also ruled that the plaintiffs were entitled to statutory damages with respect to 28 articles for which the plaintiffs had obtained United States copyright registrations. *See id.* at *15. The Court found that the registered articles had originally appeared in 15 different publications and concluded that the plaintiffs were entitled to 15 awards of statutory damages. *See id.* at *16. The Court found the violations willful, *see* 17 U.S.C. § 504(c)(1), and set each statutory award at $2,700. *See Itar–Tass II,* 1997 WL 109481, at *16. However, to avoid duplicative recovery, the Court ruled that the actual and statutory damages could not be aggregated and afforded the plaintiffs their choice of whether to receive statutory damages (offsetting the statutory award from the actual damages award) or actual damages. The Court awarded $3,934 in total damages against defendant Linco Printing, which prints *Kurier;* this sum comprised actual damages of $1,017, reduced to $934 to avoid partial duplication with statutory damages, plus $3,000 in statutory damages. *See id.* at *17.

Discussion

I. Choice of Law

The threshold issue concerns the choice of law for resolution of this dispute. That issue was not initially considered by the parties, all of whom turned directly to Russian law for resolution of the case. Believing that the conflicts issue merited consideration, we requested supplemental briefs from the parties and appointed Professor William F. Patry as Amicus Curiae.[3] Prof. Patry has submitted an extremely helpful brief on the choice of law issue.

Choice of law issues in international copyright cases have been largely ignored in the reported decisions and dealt with rather cursorily by most commentators. Examples pertinent to the pending appeal are those decisions involving a work created by the employee of a foreign corporation. Several courts have applied the United States work-for-hire doctrine, *see* 17 U.S.C. § 201(b), without explicit consideration of the conflicts issue...

The Nimmer treatise briefly (and perhaps optimistically) suggests that conflicts issues "have rarely proved troublesome in the law of copyright." *Nimmer on Copyright* § 17.05 (1998) ("*Nimmer* ") (footnote omitted). Relying on the "national treatment" principle of the Berne Convention and the Universal Copyright Convention ("U.C.C."), *Nimmer* asserts, correctly in our view, that "an author who is a national of one of the member states of either Berne or the U.C.C., or one who first publishes his work in any such member state, is entitled to the same copyright protection in each other member state as such other state accords to its own nationals." *Id.* (footnotes omitted). *Nimmer* then somewhat overstates the national treatment principle: "The applicable law is the copyright law of the state in which the infringement occurred, not that of the state of which the author is a national, or in which the work is first published." *Id.* (footnote omitted). The difficulty with this broad statement is that it subsumes under the phrase "applicable law" the law concerning two distinct issues—ownership and substantive rights, *i.e.,* scope of protection.

Another commentator has also broadly stated the principle of national treatment, but described its application in a way that does not necessarily cover issues of ownership. "The principle of national treatment also means that both the question of whether the right exists and the question of the scope of the right are to be answered in accordance with the law of the country where the protection is claimed." S.M. Stewart, *International Copyright and Neighboring Rights* § 3.17 (2d ed. 1989). We agree with the view of the Amicus that the Convention's principle of national treatment simply assures that if the law of the country of infringement applies to the scope of substantive copyright protection, that law will be applied uniformly to foreign and domestic authors. *See Murray v. British Broadcasting Corp.,* 906 F.Supp. 858 (S.D.N.Y.1995), aff'd, 81 F.3d 287 (1996).

Source of conflicts rules. Our analysis of the conflicts issue begins with consideration of the source of law for selecting a conflicts rule. Though *Nimmer* turns directly to the Berne Convention and the U.C.C., we think that step moves too quickly past the Berne Convention Implementation Act of 1988, Pub. L. 100–568, 102 Stat. 2853, 17 U.S.C. § 101 note. Section 4(a)(3) of the Act amends Title 17 to provide: "No right or interest in a work eligible for protection under this title may be claimed by virtue of ... the provisions of the Berne Convention.... Any rights in a work eligible for protection under this title that derive from this title ... shall not be expanded or reduced by virtue of ... the provisions of the Berne Convention." 17 U.S.C. § 104(c).

We start our analysis with the Copyrights Act itself, which contains no provision relevant to the pending case concerning conflicts issues. We therefore fill the interstices of the Act by developing federal common law on the conflicts issue. *See D'Oench, Duhme & Co. v. FDIC,* 315 U.S. 447, 62 S.Ct. 676, 86 L.Ed. 956 (1942); *id.* at 472, 62 S.Ct. 676 (Jackson, J., concurring) ("The law which we apply to this case consists of principles of established credit in jurisprudence, selected by us because they are appropriate to effectuate the policy of the governing Act."). In doing so, we are entitled to consider and apply principles of private international law, which are " 'part of our law.' " *Maxwell Communication Corp. v. Societe Generale,* 93 F.3d 1036, 1047 (2d Cir.1996) (quoting *Hilton v. Guyot,* 159 U.S. 113, 143, 16 S.Ct. 139, 40 L.Ed. 95 (1895)).

The choice of law applicable to the pending case is not necessarily the same for all issues. *See* Restatement (Second) of Conflict of Laws § 222 ("The courts have long recognized that they are not bound to decide all issues under the local law of a single state."). We consider first the law applicable to the issue of copyright ownership.

Conflicts rule for issues of ownership. Copyright is a form of property, and the usual rule is that the interests of the parties in property are determined by the law of the state with "the most significant relationship" to the property and the parties. *See id.* The Restatement recognizes the applicability of this principle to intangibles such as "a literary idea." *Id.* Since the works at issue were created by Russian nationals and first published in Russia, Russian law is the appropriate source of law to determine issues of ownership of rights. That is the well-reasoned conclusion of the Amicus Curiae, Prof. Patry, and the parties in their supplemental briefs are in agreement on this point. In terms of the United States Copyrights Act and its reference to the Berne Convention, Russia is the "country of origin" of these works, *see* 17 U.S.C. § 101 (definition of "country of origin" of Berne Convention work); Berne Convention, Art. 5(4), although "country of origin" might not always be the appropriate country for purposes of choice of law concerning ownership.

To whatever extent we look to the Berne Convention itself as guidance in the development of federal common law on the conflicts issue, we find nothing to alter our conclusion. The Convention does not purport to settle issues of ownership, with one exception not relevant to this case....

Selection of Russian law to determine copyright ownership is, however, subject to one procedural qualification. Under United States law, an owner (including one determined according to foreign law) may sue for infringement in a United States court only if it meets the standing test of 17 U.S.C. § 501(b), which accords standing only to the legal or beneficial owner of an "exclusive right."

Conflicts rule for infringement issues. On infringement issues, the governing conflicts principle is usually *lex loci delicti,* the doctrine generally applicable to torts. *See Lauritzen v. Larsen,* 345 U.S. 571, 583, 73 S.Ct. 921, 97 L.Ed. 1254 (1953). We have implicitly adopted that approach to infringement claims, applying United States copyright law to a work that was unprotected in its country of origin. *See Hasbro Bradley, Inc. v. Sparkle Toys, Inc.,* 780 F.2d 189, 192–93 (2d Cir.1985). In the pending case, the place of the tort is plainly the United States. To whatever extent *lex loci delicti* is to be considered only one part of a broader "interest" approach, *see Carbotrade S.p.A. v. Bureau Veritas,* 99 F.3d 86, 89–90 (2d Cir.1996), United States law would still apply to infringement issues, since not only is this country the place of the tort, but also the defendant is a United States corporation.

The division of issues, for conflicts purposes, between ownership and infringement issues will not always be as easily made as the above discussion implies. If the issue is the relatively straightforward one of which of two contending parties owns a copyright, the issue is unquestionably an ownership issue, and the law of the country with the closest relationship to the work will apply to settle the ownership dispute. But in some cases, including the pending one, the issue is not simply who owns the copyright but also what is the nature of the ownership interest. Yet as a court considers the nature of an ownership interest, there is some risk that it will too readily shift the inquiry over to the issue of whether an alleged copy has infringed the asserted copyright. Whether a copy infringes depends in part on the scope of the interest of the copyright owner. Nevertheless, though the issues are related, the nature of a copyright interest is an issue distinct from the issue of whether the copyright has been infringed. *See, e.g., Kregos v. Associated Press,* 937 F.2d 700, 709–10 (2d Cir.1991) (pointing out that although work survives summary judgment on issue of copyrightability of compilation, scope of protection against claim of infringement might be limited). The pending case is one that requires consideration not simply of who owns an interest, but, as to the newspapers, the nature of the interest that is owned.

II. Determination of Ownership Rights Under Russian Law

Since United States law permits suit only by owners of "an exclusive right under a copyright," 17 U.S.C. § 501(b), we must first determine whether any of the plaintiffs own an exclusive right. That issue of ownership, as we have indicated, is to be determined by Russian law.

Determination of a foreign country's law is an issue of law. *See* Fed.R.Civ.P. 44.1; *Bassis v. Universal Line, S.A.,* 436 F.2d 64, 68 (2d Cir.1970). Even though the District Court heard live testimony from experts from both sides, that Court's opportunity to assess the witnesses' demeanor provides no basis for a reviewing court to defer to the trier's ruling on the content of foreign law. In cases of this sort, it is not the credibility of the experts that is at issue, it is the persuasive force of the opinions they expressed. *See Curley v. AMR Corp.,* 153 F.3d 5, 12 (2d Cir.1998) ("[A]ppellate courts, as well as trial courts, may find and apply foreign law.").

Under Article 14 of the Russian Copyright Law, Itar–Tass is the owner of the copyright interests in the articles written by its employees. However, Article 14(4) excludes newspapers from the Russian version of the work-for-hire doctrine. The newspaper plaintiffs, therefore, must locate their ownership rights, if any, in some other source of law. They rely on Article 11. The District Court upheld their position, apparently recognizing in the newspaper publishers "exclusive" rights *to the articles,* even though, by virtue of Article 11(2), the reporters also retained "exclusive" rights to these articles.

Having considered all of the views presented by the expert witnesses, we conclude that the defendants' experts are far more persuasive as to the meaning of Article 11. In the first place, once Article 14 of the Russian Copyright Law explicitly denies newspapers the benefit of a work-for-hire doctrine, which, if available, would accord them rights to individual articles written by their employees, it is highly unlikely that Article 11 would confer on newspapers the very right that Article 14 has denied them. Moreover, Article 11 has an entirely reasonable scope if confined, as its caption suggests, to defining the "Copyright of Compilers of Collections and Other Works." That article accords compilers copyright "in the selection and arrangement of subject matter that he has made insofar as that selection or arrangement is the result of a creative effort of compilation." Russian Copyright Law, Art. 11(1). Article 11(2) accords a publisher of compilations the right to exploit such works, including the right to insist on having their names mentioned, while expressly reserving to "authors of the works included" in compilations the "exclusive rights to exploit their works independently of the publication of the whole work." *Id.* Art. 11(2). As the defendants' experts testified, Article 11 lets *authors* of newspaper articles sue for infringement of their rights in the text of their articles, and lets *newspaper publishers* sue for wholesale copying of all of the newspaper or for copying any portions of the newspaper that embody their selection, arrangement, and presentation of articles (including headlines)—copying that infringes their ownership interest in the compilation.

Newcity's contrary interpretation, according publishers (and reporters) exclusive rights to the text of articles, draws entirely unwarranted significance from the shift of the phrase "as a whole" from the first to the second paragraph of Article 11(2). One would not expect drafters of the revised Article 11(2) to accomplish a major broadening of the rights of newspaper publishers simply by shifting the placement of this phrase. Moreover, the drafter of the revision testified that the shift was a matter of grammar, and not of any substance. Furthermore, Newcity's interpretation rests on the untenable premise that both the publisher of a newspaper and the author of an article have exclusive rights to the same article. Under his interpretation, as he acknowledged, the publisher could grant a license to a third party to publish an article, the "exclusive" rights to which are held by the author. That unlikely result cannot be accepted in the absence of clear statutory language authorizing it.

The opinion of the Informational Disputes Chamber is not a sufficient basis for upholding the plaintiffs' interpretation. As the defendants' experts pointed out, the bylaws of that body confine its authority to matters affecting free press issues, and explicitly preclude it from adjudicating issues arising under copyright law. Moreover, the opinion that the Chamber rendered does not necessarily support the plaintiffs' position. In asserting that a newspaper may petition for redress "in defense of its rights," the Chamber might have meant only that a newspaper can protect its limited compilation rights in the selection and arrangement of articles even when only a small number of articles are copied. The opinion of the Chamber does not state that the newspaper has a protectable copyright interest in the text of each article.

Nor can the District Court's conclusion be supported by its observation that extensive copying of newspapers will ensue unless newspapers are permitted to secure redress for the copying of individual articles. In the first place, copying of articles may always be prevented at the behest of the authors of the articles or their assignees. Second, the newspapers may well be entitled to prevent copying of the protectable elements of their compilations. Lastly, even if authors lack sufficient economic incentive to bring individual suits, as the District Court apprehended, Russian copyright law authorizes the creation of organizations "for the collective administration of the economic rights of authors ... in cases where the individual exercise thereof is hampered by difficulties of a practical nature." Russian Copyright Law, Art. 44(1). Indeed, UJR, the reporters' organization, may well be able in this litigation to protect the rights of the reporters whose articles were copied by *Kurier.*

Relief. Our disagreement with the District Court's interpretation of Article 11 does not mean, however, that the defendants may continue copying with impunity. In the first place, Itar–Tass, as a press agency, is within the scope of Article 14, and, unlike the excluded newspapers, enjoys the benefit of the Russian version of the work-for-hire doctrine. Itar–Tass is therefore entitled to injunctive relief to prevent unauthorized copying of its articles and to damages for such copying, and the judgment is affirmed as to this plaintiff.

Furthermore, the newspaper plaintiffs, though not entitled to relief for the copying of the text of the articles they published, may well be entitled to injunctive relief and damages if they can show that *Kurier* infringed the publishers' ownership interests in the newspaper compilations. Because the District Court upheld the newspapers' right to relief for copying the text of the articles, it had no occasion to consider what relief the newspapers might be entitled to by reason of *Kurier*'s copying of the newspapers' creative efforts in the selection, arrangement, or display of the articles. Since *Kurier*'s photocopying reproduced not only the text of articles but also headlines and graphic materials as they originally appeared in the plaintiffs' publication, it is likely that on remand the newspaper plaintiffs will be able to obtain some form of injunctive relief and some damages. On these infringement issues, as we have indicated, United States law will apply.

Finally, there remains for consideration what relief, if any, might be awarded to UJR, acting on behalf of any of its members whose articles have been copied. In its opinion granting the newspapers a preliminary injunction, the District Court noted that the plaintiffs had not "established the union's organizational standing to sue to enforce the rights of its members," an issue the Court expected would be considered later in the lawsuit. *See Itar–Tass I,* 886 F.Supp. at 1122 n. 2. In its ruling on the merits, the District Court ruled that the UJR had standing to sue on behalf of its members. *See Itar–Tass II,* 1997 WL 109481, at *11. However, the Court noted that UJR sought only injunctive relief and then ruled that since UJR declined to furnish a list of its members, the Court was unable to frame an injunction that would be narrowly tailored and sufficient to give the defendants notice of its scope. *See id.*

In view of our conclusion that the newspaper plaintiffs may not secure relief for the copying of the text of any articles as such, it will now become appropriate for the District Court on remand to revisit the issue of whether relief might be fashioned in favor of UJR on behalf of the authors. Despite UJR's unwillingness to disclose its entire membership list, it might be possible to frame some form of injunctive relief that affords protection for those author-members that UJR is willing to identify. And UJR should now be given an opportunity to amend its prayer for relief to state whatever claim it might have to collect damages for the benefit of its member-authors whose rights have been infringed. Finally, the District Court should consider the appropriateness and feasibility of giving some form of notice (perhaps at the defendants' expense) that is calculated to alert the authors of the infringed articles to their right to intervene in this lawsuit. Such notice might, for example, be addressed generally to the group of reporters currently employed at each of the plaintiff newspapers.

In view of the reckless conduct of the defendants in the flagrant copying that infringed the rights of Itar–Tass, the rights of the authors, and very likely some aspects of the limited protectable rights of the newspapers, we will leave the injunction in force until such time as the District Court has had an opportunity, on remand, to modify the injunction consistent with this opinion and with such further rulings as the District Court may make in light of this opinion.

Conclusion

Accordingly, we affirm the judgment to the extent that it granted relief to Itar–Tass, we reverse to the extent that the judgment granted relief to the other plaintiffs, and we remand for further proceedings. No costs.

L.A. NEWS SERV. v. REUTERS TEL. INT'L LTD.
United States Courts of Appeals for the Ninth Circuit
April 22, 2003, Submitted; August 21, 2003, Filed
No. 02-56956
340 F.3d 926

O'SCANNLAIN, Circuit Judge:

We must decide whether a news organization may recover actual damages under the Copyright Act for acts of infringement that mostly occurred outside the United States.

I

The copyrighted works at issue here ("the works") are two video recordings, "The Beating of Reginald Denny" and "Beating of Man in White Panel Truck," which depict the infamous events at Florence Ave. and Normandie Blvd. during the 1992 Los Angeles riots. Los Angeles News Service ("LANS"), an independent news organization which produces video and audio tape recordings of newsworthy events and licenses them for profit, produced the works (and two other videotapes not at issue here) while filming the riots from its helicopter. LANS copyrighted the works and sold a license to rebroadcast them to, among others, the National Broadcasting Company ("NBC") network, which used them on the *Today Show*.

Visnews International (USA), Ltd. ("Visnews") is a joint venture among NBC, Reuters Television Ltd., and the British Broadcasting Company ("BBC"). Pursuant to a news supply agreement between NBC and Visnews, NBC transmitted the *Today Show* broadcast by fiber link to Visnews in New York; Visnews made a videotape copy of the works, which it then transmitted via satellite to its subscribers in Europe and Africa and via fiber link to the New York office of the European Broadcast Union ("EBU"), a joint venture of Visnews and Reuters. The EBU subsequently made another videotape copy of the works, and transmitted it to Reuters in London, which in turn distributed the works via video "feed" to its own subscribers.

LANS sued Reuters Television International, Inc., Reuters America Holdings, Inc., Reuters America, Inc. (collectively, "Reuters"), and Visnews for copyright infringement and certain other claims not relevant here. The district court subsequently granted Reuters and Visnews partial summary judgment on the issue of extraterritorial infringement, holding that no liability could arise under the Copyright Act for acts of infringement that occurred outside the United States. *L.A. News Serv. v. Reuters Television Int'l, Ltd.* (*Reuters I*), 942

F.Supp. 1265, 1268–69 (C.D.Cal.1996). However, the district court held that Visnews's act of copying the works in New York was a domestic act of infringement[1] and rejected a claimed defense of fair use. *Id.* at 1269, 1271–74. The district court further concluded that LANS had failed to prove any actual damages arising domestically and that damages arising extraterritorially were unavailable under the Act, which meant that LANS was limited to statutory damages. *Id.* at 1274–75 & n. 7. After a bench trial on the issue of statutory damages, the district court awarded LANS a total of $60,000. *L.A. News Serv. v. Reuters Television Int'l, Ltd.* (*Reuters II*), 942 F.Supp. 1275, 1283–84 (C.D.Cal.1996).

LANS appealed the district court's ruling on actual damages, and Reuters and Visnews cross-appealed the fair use ruling and the statutory damages calculation. We subsequently reversed the district court's actual damages ruling, disagreeing with its interpretation of the Copyright Act's extraterritorial application. *L.A. News Serv. v. Reuters Television Int'l, Ltd.* (*Reuters III*), 149 F.3d 987, 992 (9th Cir.1998). We concluded that although the district court was correct to hold that the Copyright Act does not apply extraterritorially, an exception may apply where an act of infringement is completed entirely within the United States and that such infringing act enabled further exploitation abroad. *Id.* at 991–92. Relying on *Sheldon v. Metro–Goldwyn Pictures Corp.,* 106 F.2d 45 (2d Cir.1939), *aff'd,* 309 U.S. 390, 60 S.Ct. 681, 84 L.Ed. 825 (1940), which held that profits from overseas infringement can be recovered on the theory that the infringer holds them in a constructive trust for the copyright owner, we reversed the grant of summary judgment. *Reuters III* at 991–92. We held that "LANS [was] entitled to recover damages flowing from exploitation abroad of the domestic acts of infringement committed by defendants." *Id.* at 992.

Turning to the other issues, we affirmed the fair use ruling and the statutory damages calculation. *Id.* at 994–96. However, we vacated the award of statutory damages so that LANS could make a new election on remand. *Id.* at 995 & n. 8. After the Supreme Court denied certiorari, *Reuters Television Int'l, Ltd. v. L.A. News Serv.,* 525 U.S. 1141, 119 S.Ct. 1032, 143 L.Ed.2d 41 (1999), the case returned to the district court, where Reuters and Visnews moved for summary adjudication of the claim for actual damages. They asserted that the *Reuters III* decision permitted LANS to recover only Defendants' profits attributable to extraterritorial infringement—not actual damages for injuries the infringements caused LANS overseas. Reuters and Visnews further asserted that no factual dispute remained as to the amount of such profits.

After a hearing, the district court agreed with Reuters and Visnews on both points and granted the motion. The court concluded that *Reuters III* had held only that LANS could recover any profits or unjust enrichment from domestic infringers, on the theory that the infringers held such profits in a constructive trust for LANS. "To permit [LANS] to recover damages other than Defendants' profits or unjust enrichment," the court stated, "would ... effectively permit [LANS] to recover damages for extraterritorial acts of infringement."

Having determined that LANS could recover only Defendants' profits, if any, the district court concluded that Reuters and Visnews had reaped no such profits from their infringement. The court held that LANS's "speculative" testimony about the competitive advantage that exclusive footage gives a subscription broadcaster was insufficient to create a factual dispute. It accordingly granted the motion for summary adjudication. In its order, the district court stated that LANS could elect to take the $60,000 in statutory damages awarded in *Reuters II* and affirmed in *Reuters III.* In its haste, LANS timely appealed to this court, but failed to make the required election as to statutory damages. Because there was no "final decision," we dismissed for lack of jurisdiction. LANS subsequently cured the jurisdictional defect by making such election, and re-filed its appeal with this court.

II

LANS claims that the district court erred by disallowing recovery for actual damages. LANS, however, does not challenge the court's further conclusion that LANS had failed to show that Reuters and Visnews had earned any profits from the overseas infringement. Summary adjudication was therefore appropriate if the district court correctly concluded that LANS could not recover actual damages for overseas effects of Defendants' infringement.

A

Both parties engage in detailed exegesis of our opinion in *Reuters III.* On LANS's reading, the *Reuters III* court's use of the term "damages" is dispositive. The statute uses "actual damages" and "profits" separately and distinctly, and provides that an infringer may recover both (in the ordinary case). LANS asserts therefore that the *Reuters III* court should be read as having meant what it said: "damages" means actual damages.

But LANS's interpretation does not fit with the context in which the *Reuters III* court discussed the recoverability of "damages." There, we relied on Judge Learned Hand's opinion in *Sheldon* and discussed damages entirely in the context of that case, which dealt exclusively with the recovery of the defendants' profits.

The *Sheldon* court had previously affirmed the defendants' liability for infringing the plaintiffs' copyright by incorporating their play into a movie. *Sheldon v. Metro–Goldwyn Pictures Corp.,* 81 F.2d 49, 54–56 (2d Cir.1936). After a remand, the defendants appealed the district court's decision to award the plaintiffs all the defendants' profits from exhibiting the motion picture. *Sheldon,* 106 F.2d at 48. The Second Circuit, inter alia, determined that the profits traceable to overseas exhibition of the infringing movie should be included. Although "[a]t first blush it [seemed] that [the overseas profits] should be excluded" because the overseas exhibition of the infringing movie was not tortious under American copyright law, the court nonetheless concluded that the plaintiffs could recover the overseas profits under a different theory, based on one defendant's having made the negatives in the U.S. *Id.* at 52. The court elaborated:

> The negatives were "records" from which the work could be "reproduced," and it was a tort to make them in this country. The plaintiffs acquired an equitable interest in them as soon as they were made, which attached to any profits from their exploitation, whether in the form of money remitted to the United States, or of increase in the value of shares of foreign companies held by the defendants.... [A]s soon as any of the profits so realized took the form of property whose situs was in the United States, our law seized upon them and impressed them with a constructive trust, whatever their form.

Id. The *Sheldon* court relied exclusively on this rationale in holding that the plaintiffs could recover the defendants' profits from overseas exhibition.

As *Sheldon* considered only an award of profits, it is counterintuitive that a court applying Sheldon's rationale, but using the word "damages" as the *Reuters III* court did, was referring consciously to "actual damages" as opposed to "profits." Indeed our prior holding in *Reuters III,* based on the *Sheldon* constructive trust theory, demonstrates that we did not use the term "damages" in that formal sense. Rather, we used "damages" as a shorthand either for both the forms of relief that 17 U.S.C. § 504(b) makes available, *i.e.,* actual damages and defendants' profits, or only the recovery of defendants' profits. Understanding which applies requires closer analysis of *Sheldon* and its progeny.

B

Of course, *Sheldon* did not explicitly deal with the issue of actual damages. But as LANS points out, there is some support in the Second Circuit's post-*Sheldon* case law for the recovery of extraterritorial actual damages once an act of domestic infringement is proven.

The most direct support for such position comes from *Update Art, Inc. v. Modiin Publ'g, Ltd.,* 843 F.2d 67 (2d Cir.1988), in which the Second Circuit considered an Israeli newspaper's unauthorized reproduction of a poster copyrighted in the United States. *Id.* at 68–69. *Update Art* held, albeit without much discussion, that the defendants had failed to make any showing that the initial copying of the poster had occurred abroad; thus, in the case's procedural context, the court concluded that the "predicate act" of domestic infringement had occurred and that Update Art had stated a viable copyright claim. *Id.* at 73. The court also affirmed the award of "[d]amages accruing from the illegal infringement in the Israeli newspapers." *Id.*

Update Art, however, is distinguishable from LANS's claim in a couple of important respects. First, several issues of the newspaper in which the infringing reproduction appeared were circulated in the United States. *Id.* at 73 & n. 6. Second, and more importantly, the amount of damages awarded by the district court was based on defendants' profits. *Id.* at 70 & n. 4. Finally, the panel did not even discuss the distinction between damages and profits, much less cite *Sheldon.* Rather, it merely concluded that the damages award could stand despite the extraterritoriality issue, which the magistrate judge had not considered in calculating the amount. *Id.* at 70.

LANS also relies on a district court case, *Famous Music Corp. v. Seeco Records, Inc.,* 201 F.Supp. 560 (S.D.N.Y.1961). There, Famous Music sued Seeco for making infringing tape recordings of its copyrighted musical work, which Seeco then exported to foreign countries, where records were manufactured from the tapes. *Id.* at 564. Applying the Copyright Act of 1909, which was superseded in 1976 by the present Act, the *Famous Music* court held Seeco liable "by reason of its joint tort in manufacture of the tapes sent abroad," and awarded "such royalties as may be found in favor of plaintiffs by reason thereof." *Id.* at 570.

LANS is correct that the *Famous Music* court did award relief equivalent to what the current Act would term actual damages.[6] However, *Famous Music*'s only analysis of the issue of extraterritoriality came in a brief statement: "A holding ... that a copyright has no extra-territorial effect, does not solve this problem of manufacture since plaintiffs seek to hold defendant for what it did here rather than what it did abroad." *Id.* at 569. Moreover, it is incorrect to characterize this case as an application of the *Sheldon* rationale, as the court never mentioned *Sheldon.*

C

On the whole, we conclude that *Reuters III* adhered very closely to our decision in *Subafilms, Ltd. v. MGM–Pathe Communications Co.,* 24 F.3d 1088 (9th Cir.1994) (en banc). *Subafilms* reaffirmed that the copyright laws have no application beyond the U.S. border, *id.* at 1095–98, and expressly took no position on the merits of the *Update Art* court's apparent willingness to award damages, *id.* at 1094; *see id.* at 1099. LANS's appeal thus presents the precise question that *Subafilms* reserved, *Reuters III,* 149 F.3d at 991, and as the prior panel recognized, such question should be resolved in light of the principles the en banc court laid down.

The import of such principles counsel a narrow application of the adoption in *Reuters III* of the *Sheldon* exception to the general rule. In particular, the *Sheldon* constructive trust rationale includes a territorial connection, *see Sheldon,* 106 F.2d at 52, that preserves consistency with Congress's decision to keep the copyright laws—presumably including § 504, which prescribes remedies—territorially confined. Moreover, no rational deterrent function is served by making an infringer whose domestic act of infringement—from which he earns no profit—leads to widespread extraterritorial infringement, liable for the copyright owner's entire loss of value or profit from that overseas infringement, particularly if the overseas infringement is legal where it takes place. *See Subafilms,* 24 F.3d at 1097–98 (warning of the disruption to American foreign policy interests and to the policy of domestic enforcement expressed in the Berne Convention that extraterritorial enforcement would cause). Moreover, the resulting over-deterrence might chill the fair use of copyrighted works in close cases.

LANS counters that the assessment of damages based on a domestic act of infringement having had consequences in foreign territories is legitimate under "traditional tort principles." However, it offers no direct support for the proposition that those principles compel the extension of relief—legal or equitable—beyond the boundaries where Congress declared that liability stops Its policy arguments to the contrary seem largely a complaint about the failure of Congress to make the copyright laws—those creating both rights and remedies—applicable extraterritorially.

III

Accordingly we read *Reuters III* to allow only a narrow exception for the recovery of the infringer's profits to *Subafilms*'s general rule against extraterritorial application. We conclude therefore that the Copyright Act does not provide LANS recovery for actual damages resulting from Reuters's and Visnews's infringement.

AFFIRMED.

SILVERMAN, Circuit Judge, dissenting...

See also Films by Jove, Inc. v. Berov, 154 F.Supp.2d 432 (E.D. N.Y.2001) (American film studio and Russian joint stock company moved to hold defendant publishing group in contempt for violating an injunction issued in plaintiff's copyright infringement claim. However, third party intervenor/Russian State Enterprise sought declaration to secure its right to manage film copyrights.

After Perestroika reforms, the copyrights were owned by plaintiff joint stock company and legally assigned to plaintiff American studio.).

BYRNE v. BBC
United States District Court for the Southern District of New York
February 22, 2001, Decided; February 22, 2001, Filed
00 Civ. 3141 (SHS)
132 F.Supp.2d 229

STEIN, District Judge.

Christopher Byrne brought this action against the British Broadcasting Corporation alleging that the BBC infringed his copyright in a song entitled "Fenians" (the "Song") in both the United States and the United Kingdom. The BBC now moves for: (1) partial summary judgment declaring that it did not infringe Byrne's United States copyright; and (2) dismissal of the action on the grounds of *forum non conveniens.* The motion for a declaration of non-infringement is denied because disputed issues of material fact exist on the question of whether the BBC's use of "Fenians" was a "fair use" pursuant to the Copyright Act. Its motion to dismiss the action on the grounds of *forum non conveniens* is denied because the BBC has not shown that the public and private interest factors set forth in *Gulf Oil Corp. v. Gilbert,* 330 U.S. 501, 67 S.Ct. 839, 91 L.Ed. 1055 (1947), weigh "strongly in favor" of litigating in the United Kingdom.

I. BACKGROUND

The following facts are undisputed, unless otherwise noted.

Byrne is a musician and political activist outspoken in his opposition to British involvement in the affairs of Northern Ireland. He and a co-author wrote "Fenians" in 1997, and he subsequently recorded it with his group, Seanchai. Since its publication, Byrne and his coauthor have been the sole proprietors of all rights, title and interest to the copyrights in the Song.

In 1999, the BBC decided to investigate and produce a story on an FBI investigation and subsequent arrest of four individuals in Florida on charges of smuggling guns into Northern Ireland for its newsmagazine program "Spotlight." While planning the story, BBC producer Justin O'Brien decided to explore Irish–American media reaction to the investigation. To that end, O'Brien placed a call from his office in Belfast to John McDonagh, producer and host of a radio program called Radio Free Eireann, broadcast from the New York City studios of radio station WBAI. During that call, O'Brien obtained permission for a BBC crew to film a live broadcast of the radio show during which the Florida arrests would be discussed.

This telephone call was not O'Brien's first experience with Radio Free Eireann. O'Brien had been to the WBAI studio earlier in the summer during an airing of the program, and he periodically visits the program's Internet website at www.wbaifree.org/radiofreeeireann/.

WBAI uses, with permission, a portion of the Song as the musical introduction to Radio Free Eireann. O'Brien was aware from his experience as a television producer that WBAI used the Song; he was interested enough in the Song to ask McDonagh about it; McDonagh told him that "Fenians" was the theme music for Radio Free Eireann and had been so for some time.

The BBC crew, including O'Brien, traveled from Northern Ireland to the United States to obtain raw film footage for the story in early September 1999. After spending approximately two weeks in Florida, the crew traveled to New York, where they planned to attend and record the September 11, 1999 broadcast of Radio Free Eireann. During that broadcast, the BBC camera was plugged into the mixing desk of the radio station to record the broadcast audio while the BBC simultaneously filmed the interior of the studio. The BBC crew recorded "substantially all" of the September 11, 1999, broadcast, including the portion of the Song used to open the program.

After spending five days in New York obtaining footage, the BBC crew traveled to San Francisco and Miami to do further research. By the end of September, they had left the United States and returned to Belfast, where they transformed the raw footage into a story suitable for television broadcast.

The producers of the story used a technique called a "clean fade" three times in the story. A "clean fade" involves synchronizing visual images of a setting with sounds, in order to ease the viewer into a new segment of the story. The first clean fade consists of images of the Florida coast synchronized with the sound of portions of local weather reports. The second clean fade consists of images of the Miami skyline synchronized with a portion of Jimi Hendrix's "Sweet Angel." The third clean fade consists of images of the New York skyline synchronized with three seconds of drum beats and that portion of the Song that is used by WBAI as the opening music to Radio Free Eireann. This fade ends with a visual segue into the WBAI studio, where the broadcast audio portion of Radio Free Eireann is synchronized with the visual images captured by the BBC crew during the September 11, 2000, broadcast. The BBC never sought or obtained permission from Byrne or his co-author for the use of the Song in its broadcast.

The story was ultimately broadcast on television twice: once on BBC NI at 9:30 p.m. on October 5, 1999, and again on BBC Choice NI five days later. The story has never been sold or licensed for broadcast or use anywhere else in the world.

On April 25, 2000, Byrne brought this action alleging claims for copyright infringement pursuant to both United States and United Kingdom law. The BBC now moves for partial summary judgment of non-infringement under United States law and dismissal of the action on the grounds of *forum non conveniens.*

II. PARTIAL SUMMARY JUDGMENT OF NON–INFRINGEMENT

Summary judgment will be granted "only when the moving party demonstrates that 'there is no genuine issue as to any material fact and that the moving party is entitled to judgment as a matter of law.' " *Allen v. Coughlin,* 64 F.3d 77, 79 (2d Cir.1995) (quoting Fed. R. Civ. P. 56(c)). In determining whether a genuine dispute remains as to a material fact, the court must resolve all ambiguities, and draw all reasonable inferences, against the moving party. *See Matsushita Electrical Industrial Co. v. Zenith Radio Corp.,* 475 U.S. 574, 587–88, 106 S.Ct. 1348, 89 L.Ed.2d 538 (1986).

A. *The Recording of the Song is a Prima Facie Violation of the Copyright Act.*

To establish a claim of copyright infringement, a plaintiff must establish (1) ownership of a valid copyright and (2) unauthorized copying or a violation of one of the other exclusive rights afforded copyright owners pursuant to the Copyright Act. *Twin Peaks Productions v. Publications Int'l. Ltd.,* 996 F.2d 1366, 1372 (2d Cir.1993). Among these rights are the rights to reproduce and publicly perform the copyrighted work. *See* 17 U.S.C. § 106(1), (5). It is undisputed that Byrne owns a valid copyright in "Fenians" and that the BBC's recording of it in the United States and subsequent broadcast in Northern Ireland were unauthorized. The BBC contends, however, that the "act of filming" copyrighted material, even if unauthorized, does not constitute infringement when the film is to be used for "a program or movie," and that the only possible infringement was the broadcast in Northern Ireland, which is governed by U.K. law. Byrne agrees that U.K. law governs the broadcast.

The BBC's argument is belied by the words of the Copyright Act, which provide that among a copyright owner's "exclusive rights" is the right "to do and to authorize ... reproduc[tion of] the copyrighted work in copies." 17 U.S.C. § 106. Thus, unauthorized copying is a *prima facie* infringement of a copyright owner's rights. *See, e.g., UMG Recordings, Inc. v. MP3.Com,* 92 F.Supp.2d 349, 350 & n. 1 (S.D.N.Y.2000); *A & M Records, Inc. v. Napster, Inc.,* 114 F.Supp.2d 896, 912 (N.D.Cal.2000). Moreover, the fact that the BBC later broadcast the Song without authorization does not transform the recording and broadcast into a unitary act of infringement. An unauthorized copying of a copyrighted work constitutes a completed act of infringement, even when the copy is made for the purpose of transmission or broadcast abroad. *See Los Angeles News Serv. v. Reuters Television Int'l, Ltd.,* 149 F.3d 987, 991 (9th Cir.1998).

B. *Was the Recording of the Song a "Fair Use"?*

The BBC also contends that both the unauthorized recording and the unauthorized broadcast were "fair uses" of the Song within the intendment of 17 U.S.C. § 107. Because the parties agree that U.K. law applies to the BBC broadcast in the United Kingdom—as distinct from the recording of the Song in the United States—the "fair use" analysis pursuant to section 107 that follows is confined to the BBC's recording of the Song in the United States.

The doctrine of fair use has been used since "the infancy of copyright protection" to insure that copyright promotes, rather than hinders, "the Progress of Science and useful Arts." *Campbell v. Acuff–Rose Music, Inc.,* 510 U.S. 569, 575, 114 S.Ct. 1164, 127 L.Ed.2d 500 (1994) (quoting U.S. Const., art, I, § 8, cl. 8). The doctrine was codified in section 107 of the Copyright Act of 1976, which lists several examples of uses protected by the doctrine, including "news reporting," and mandates that courts consider four factors in determining whether a particular use is "fair": "(1) the purpose and character of the use, including whether such use is of a commercial nature ...; (2) the nature of the copyrighted work; (3) the amount and substantiality of the portion used in relation to the copyrighted work as a whole; and (4) the effect of the use upon the potential market for or value of the copyrighted work." 17 U.S.C. § 107. These four factors "guide but do not control [the] fair use analysis and 'are to be explored, and the results weighed together, in light of the purposes of copyright.' " *Castle Rock Entm't, Inc. v. Carol Publ'g Group, Inc.,* 150 F.3d 132, 141 (2d Cir.1998) (quoting *Campbell,* 510 U.S. at 577–78), 114 S.Ct. 1164. The burden of proving "fair use" rests squarely on the alleged infringer. *See Infinity Broadcast Corp. v. Kirkwood,* 150 F.3d 104, 107 (2nd Cir.1998).

In the summary judgment context, courts have often noted that as a mixed question of law and fact, the issue of whether an alleged infringement constitutes fair use is usually unsuited to summary disposition.

In this case, disputed issues of material fact exist, rendering summary judgment on the BBC's fair use defense inappropriate. Each of the statutory fair use factors will be examined in turn.

1. *Purpose and character of the use*

The first factor set forth in the statute to consider is "the purpose and character of the [allegedly infringing] use, including whether such use is of a commercial nature or is for nonprofit educational purposes." 17 U.S.C. § 107(1). The two most common inquiries in analyses of this factor are whether the use was for a commercial purpose and the extent to which the use was "transformative," *i.e.,* "whether the allegedly infringing work 'merely supersedes' the original work 'or instead adds something new, with a further purpose or different character, altering the first with new ... meaning [ ] or message.' " *Castle Rock Entm't,* 150 F.3d at 142 (quoting *Campbell,* 510 U.S. at 595, 114 S.Ct. 1164). The extent to which the use is transformative is "the more critical inquiry." *Id.*

The BBC contends that because it is a not-for-profit corporation, its use of the Song was necessarily "non-commercial," and was instead "for nonprofit educational purposes." However, "non-profit organizations enjoy no special immunity from determinations of copyright violation. The question under factor one is the purpose and character of the use, not of the alleged infringer." *Lish v. Harper's Magazine Found.,* 807 F.Supp. 1090, 1100–01 (S.D.N.Y.1992). The BBC also contends that because it recorded "Fenians" for use in a news program, its use constitutes "news reporting" within the meaning of 17 U.S.C. § 107—a "transformative" use—and, thus, it contends, the first fair use factor weighs in its favor.

Not all unlicensed uses of copyrighted material for inclusion in broadcasts that present material of interest to the public are protected by the fair use doctrine, even if they are labeled "news reporting" by defendants. If the purpose of the use was to entertain, rather than inform, *see Schumann v. Albuquerque Corp.,* 664 F.Supp. 473, 477 (D.N.M.1987), or if equally informative non-infringing alternatives were available, *see Roy Export Co. v. Columbia Broad. Sys., Inc.,* 503 F.Supp. 1137, 1144 (S.D.N.Y.1980), then the first fair use factor tips in favor of the plaintiff.

As discussed above, the overall topic of the television news story was the investigation and arrest of four Irish nationals on charges of gun running. The purpose of recording the WBAI radio program, according to O'Brien, was "to explore how the Irish–American media was reacting" to the criminal investigation. O'Brien Aff. ¶ 9. It is unclear, however, how recording the Song, as opposed to recording the on-air statements of the radio show's hosts and guests, served the BBC's stated purpose. Indeed, a reasonable jury could find, on the record as it exists so far, that recording the Song was wholly unnecessary to reporting on "how the Irish–American media was reacting" to the FBI investigation.

Moreover, there is ample evidence from which a reasonable jury could infer that the BBC's intent in recording the Song was not to gather facts on Irish–American media reaction, but to obtain music that would make the story more entertaining to viewers. As discussed above, the "clean fade" technique was used three times in the 20–minute story. These sequences involved both images and sounds that did not directly pertain to the topic of the story—the criminal investigation—but that were arguably used to make the story more appealing and entertaining to viewers. In each of the sequences, the sounds used were not the ambient sounds that accompanied the visual images as they were being filmed, but rather the work of third parties unrelated to the moment of filming, *i.e.,* the Song, Jimi Hendrix's "Sweet Angel," and weather reports from Florida broadcasters, obtained during the crew's stay in the United States. Accordingly, a reasonable jury could infer that the crew sought to record not only footage necessary to its news reporting, but also footage, including the Song, that would entertain, rather than inform, as its primary purpose.

The BBC's reliance on the decision in *Italian Book Corp. v. American Broadcasting Cos.,* 458 F.Supp. 65 (S.D.N.Y.1978), is misplaced. In *Italian Book Corp.,* a television news crew had recorded images of a New York street fair, the San Gennaro festival, including a portion of a parade consisting of a band on a float playing music—copyrighted by the plaintiff—for use in a news report about the festival. 458 F.Supp. at 67. That court found that the parade was "one of the most significant aspects of the festival," and that "ABC's employees had no advance knowledge that a band would come along on a float playing this particular song." *Id.* at 67–68. Thus, ABC's recording and subsequent broadcast of portions of the song was "wholly fortuitous." *Id.* at 68. In this case, in contrast, O'Brien had visited the WBAI studios before and "was ... aware ... that the music was closely associated with the station" before recording. Moreover, there is evidence to suggest that the BBC crew sought to record footage for entertainment, rather than news reporting, purposes. On this record, a reasonable jury could find that the BBC's recording of the Song was not "fortuitous," but a calculated attempt to obtain entertaining footage only tenuously related to its news reporting purpose.

In addition, a reasonable jury could find that even if the Song were recorded as part of an effort "to explore how the Irish–American media was reacting" to the reported investigation, there were equally informative non-infringing alternatives available. As discussed above, the on-air statements of the radio show's hosts and guests are an obvious alternative. The BBC crew presumably could also have interviewed other Irish–American media figures, or sought permission to use the work of other Irish–American artists.

In sum, the purpose and character of the use is a disputed issue of fact. At the summary judgment stage, therefore, this factor favors Byrne, the non-moving party.

2. *The nature of the copyrighted work*

The second factor set forth in section 107 of the Copyright Act to employ in determining whether an alleged infringement is a permissible fair use is "the nature of the copyrighted work." It is undisputed that "Fenians" is a creative work, and, thus, the type of work at "the core" of copyright law's protection. *See Campbell,* 510 U.S. at 586, 114 S.Ct. 1164. The BBC, relying on Judge John S. Martin's opinion in *Baraban v. Time Warner,* 54 U.S.P.Q.2d 1759

(S.D.N.Y.2000), contends, however that because the Song has been widely disseminated, the nature of the work favors it or is neutral.

Unpublished works are the "favorite sons" of the second fair use factor, and where a plaintiff proves unauthorized publication of an unpublished work, this factor weighs heavily against a finding of fair use. *See Wright v. Warner Books,* 953 F.2d 731, 737 (2d Cir.1991). Previously published works, on the other hand, qualify for "far less protection" against fair use, and, therefore, even where the work is "creative," the second factor may not weigh as "decisively" in the copyright holder's favor where the work has been previously distributed. *See Baraban,* 54 U.S.P.Q.2d at 1762–63.

Baraban does not hold, however, as the BBC contends, that the wide dissemination of a work tips this factor in the alleged infringer's favor. Rather, *Baraban* stands for the straightforward proposition that the second fair use factor may have little significance in the context of a transformative use. *See Baraban,* 54 U.S.P.Q.2d at 1763; *see also, e.g., Castle Rock Entm't,* 150 F.3d at 143–44. Where the allegedly infringing use is minimally transformative, however, the creative nature of a copyrighted work remains significant. *Castle Rock Entm't,* 150 F.3d at 144.

As noted above, whether the Song was recorded for a transformative purpose is a disputed issue of fact. Accordingly, the creative nature of work weighs in favor of Byrne on a motion for summary judgment.

3. *The amount and substantiality of the portion used*

Courts must examine the third fair use factor—"the amount and substantiality of the portion [of the copyrighted work] used in relation to the copyrighted work as a whole"—in context. *Castle Rock Entm't,* 150 F.3d at 144. "The inquiry must focus upon whether '[t]he extent of ... copying' is consistent with or more than necessary to further 'the purpose and character of the use.' " *Id.* (quoting *Campbell,* 510 U.S. at 587–87, 114 S.Ct. 1164).

The BBC recorded the entire 50–second portion of the Song used by WBAI. The BBC contends that because this was no more of the Song than was necessary to reproduce the radio program in its entirety, the third fair use factor weighs in its favor. This argument assumes, however, that reproduction of the radio program in its entirety was necessary to a transformative purpose, which, as discussed above, is in dispute.

At the summary judgment stage, the Court draws the inference that no part of the recording of the Song was necessary to the BBC's asserted news reporting purpose. The third fair use factor, therefore, favors Byrne.

4. *Effect of the use on the market for or value of the original*

The fourth factor to be employed in determining whether the use of the copyrighted work was a fair use is "the effect of the use on the potential market for or value of the copyrighted work." The BBC asserts that its "mere recordation ... cannot possibly have any effect on the actual or potential market" for the Song. When evaluating this fourth factor, however, the court must "consider not only the extent of market harm caused by the particular actions of the alleged infringer, but also whether unrestricted and widespread conduct of the sort engaged in by the defendant ... would result in a substantially adverse impact on the potential market" for the original or derivative works. *Campbell,* 510 U.S. at 590, 114 S.Ct. 1164.

As set forth above, a reasonable jury could infer that the BBC intentionally recorded the Song for the purpose of providing an audio component of a "clean fade." When a broadcaster makes an unauthorized copy of a song for such use, it has no need to purchase a copy from the copyright holder or his licensees, thus lessening the market for the song. *Cf. Los Angeles News Serv. v. Reuters Television Int'l Ltd.,* 149 F.3d 987, 994 (9th Cir.1998). Accordingly, this factor favors Byrne.

5. *Other factors*

Although the four statutory fair use factors are not exclusive, and courts may consider other factors, *see Castle Rock Entm't,* 150 F.3d at 146, the parties have not addressed any additional factors and the Court limits its analysis to the four statutory factors.

Considering the four statutory factors, the BBC's motion for summary judgment based on the fair use defense should be denied. The purpose and character of the BBC's use of the Song is a disputed issue of fact implicating each of the fair use factors and summary disposition is therefore inappropriate.

III. *FORUM NON CONVENIENS*

The doctrine of *forum non conveniens* was developed to thwart "a strategy of forcing the trial at a most inconvenient place for an adversary."

A. *An Adequate Alternative Forum Exists*

Dismissal of an action on the grounds of *forum non conveniens* is inappropriate in the absence of an adequate alternative forum "because application of the doctrine 'presupposes at least two forums in which the defendant is amenable to process.' " *Murray,* 81 F.3d at 292 (2d Cir.1996) (quoting *Gilbert,* 330 U.S. at 507, 67 S.Ct. 839); *see also Bybee v. Oper der Standt Bonn,* 899 F.Supp. 1217, 1222 (S.D.N.Y.1995). This requirement "is ordinarily satisfied if the defendant is amenable to process in another jurisdiction, except in 'rare circumstances' when 'the remedy offered by the other forum is clearly unsatisfactory.' " *Murray,* 81 F.3d at 292 (quoting *Piper Aircraft Co.,* 454 U.S. at 254 n. 22, 102 S.Ct. 252).

Byrne does not dispute that the BBC is amenable to suit in the United Kingdom, or that his remedies in the United Kingdom are both substantively and procedurally adequate. Rather, Byrne claims that the financial barriers he would face in bringing this action in either Northern Ireland or England, including the lack of a contingency-fee system in Northern Ireland, "effectively mean that the United Kingdom would be no forum at all."

The United States Court of Appeals for the Second Circuit, however, has explicitly held that a plaintiff's financial burdens, including hardships resulting from the absence of contingent fee arrangements, should be considered as one of the *Gilbert* factors only after a court determines that an alternative forum is available. *See Murray,* 81 F.3d at 292–93. Accordingly, this Court finds that the United Kingdom is an adequate alternative forum for this dispute.

B. *Application of the Gilbert Factors*

In applying the public and private interest factors of *Gilbert,* the plaintiff's choice of forum is ordinarily given great deference, especially where the plaintiff has chosen its "home forum." *Piper Aircraft Co.,* 454 U.S. at 255, 102 S.Ct. 252; *Murray,* 81 F.3d at 290; *see also Bybee,* 899 F.Supp. at 1222. A foreign plaintiff's choice of forum, however, is given less deference than that of a domestic plaintiff. *See Piper Aircraft Co.,* 454 U.S. at 256, 102 S.Ct. 252; *Murray,* 81 F.3d at 290. Byrne is a United States citizen living in the United States. The BBC contends, however, that the deference ordinarily given to Byrne's choice of forum should be diminished by his dual citizenship—he is also a citizen of the Republic of Ireland—and his regular travel to, and contacts with, Northern Ireland.

The Second Circuit, however, has recently held that courts should accord the choice of forum of foreign citizens who are legal residents of the United States the same deference as the choice of forum of United States citizens. *See Wiwa v. Royal Dutch Petroleum Co.,* 226 F.3d 88, 103. Certainly, then, Byrne's dual citizenship cannot diminish the deference his choice of forum will be given by this Court. Similarly, regular travel to the alternative forum does not diminish the deference given to plaintiff's choice, although it may be considered in the evaluation of the "private interests" of the parties. *See, e.g., Massaquoi v. Virgin Atlantic Airways,* 945 F.Supp. 58, 62–63 (S.D.N.Y.1996); *Sablic v. Armada Shipping Aps,* 973 F.Supp. 745, 748 (S.D.Tex.1997). Thus, in order to prevail on its motion to dismiss, the BBC must show that the balance of public and private interests is "strongly" in favor of litigating in the United Kingdom "in order to overcome the substantial weight accorded [Byrne's] choice of forum."...

The public interest factors include: (1) "the administrative difficulties flowing from court congestion"; (2) "the local interest in having controversies decided at home"; (3) "the interest in having the trial in a forum that is familiar with the law governing the action"; (4) "the avoidance of unnecessary problems in conflict of laws or in the application of foreign law"; and (5) "the unfairness of burdening citizens in an unrelated forum with jury duty." *Murray,* 81 F.3d at 293. None of these factors weighs heavily in favor of dismissal.

Each of the public interest factors are neutral. The parties have not demonstrated that the courts of the United Kingdom are any more or less congested than is the Southern District of New York. Moreover, both localities have an interest in having this dispute decided at home—the action involves alleged violations of the laws of both the United States and the United Kingdom based on acts that took place in each country. Courts in either country would have to apply the law of the other, and the application of the law of another English common law jurisdiction "does not impose a significant burden on this Court." *Gordon v. Long Bay (1980) Ltd.,* 94 Civ. 2141, 1995 WL 489474, at *4 (S.D.N.Y. Aug. 16, 1995). Finally, neither the United States nor the United Kingdom is an "unrelated forum," and, in addition, there is no right to a jury in this action in the United Kingdom.

The private interest factors include: (1) "the relative ease of access to sources of proof"; (2) "the availability of compulsory process for attendance of unwilling witnesses"; (3) "the cost of obtaining attendance of willing witnesses"; (4) "[i]ssues concerning the enforceability of a judgment"; and (5) "all other practical problems that make trial of a case easy, expeditious, and inexpensive—or the opposite." *Murray,* 81 F.3d at 294. As with the public interest factors, none of the public interest factors weigh heavily in favor of dismissal.

The first four factors are neutral. Documentary evidence and witnesses exist on both sides of the Atlantic. For example, while the BBC's raw footage is currently located in Northern Ireland, the records of Irish–American media outlets are in the United States. Similarly, while members of the BBC crew live or work in the United Kingdom and are presumably subject to compulsory process in United Kingdom courts, plaintiff, WBAI personnel, and plaintiff's experts all live or work within the subpoena power of this Court. There has been no showing that the cost of obtaining the attendance of willing witnesses would be significantly greater for either side in either forum, and the parties have not identified any issues relating to the enforceability of a judgment obtained in either the United Kingdom or the United States.

Although Byrne has submitted evidence that a trial in New York would be easier for him to finance because he has already obtained counsel on a contingency basis and he already maintains a home here, the BBC has submitted evidence that Byrne regularly visits the United Kingdom. Accordingly, the fifth factor is largely neutral, or, at most, weighs slightly in favor of denying the motion to dismiss.

Waxing creative, the BBC claims that "all roads lead to Britannia," Def.'s Mem. at 34, and Byrne asserts that "there's no place like home," Pl.'s Mem. at 33. Home is where Byrne is entitled to stay absent a showing that the *Gilbert* factors weigh "strongly in favor" of dismissal. *See Bybee,* 899 F.Supp. at 1222. The BBC has failed to make such a showing. Accordingly, the BBC's motion to dismiss the complaint on the grounds of *forum non conveniens* is denied.

IV. CONCLUSION

For the reasons set forth above, the BBC's motions for partial summary judgment of non-infringement under United States law and dismissal of the action on the grounds of *forum non conveniens* are denied.

SO ORDERED.

QUESTIONS AND DISCUSSION

1. See the Berne Convention for the Protection of Literary and Artistic Works (as amended 9/28/79), http://ww.wipo.int/treaties/en/test.jsp?file-id=283698#P374_68327; the Berne Convention Implementation Act of 1988, 17 U.S.C. § 101 note (see especially sections on copyright registration, registration and infringement actions, copyright infringement and remedies, copyright royalty tribunal, and works in the public domain); and the WIPO Copyright Treaty (WCT) (adopted in Geneva on December 20, 1996) (...Art 1 (1)). The WCT is a special agreement within the meaning of the Article 20 of the Berne Convention for the Protection of Literary and Artistic Works as regards to contracting parties that are countries of the union established by the Convention). (Source: International Bureau of WIPO...).

See also Graeme Austin, "Domestic Laws and Foreign Rights: Choice of Law in Transnational Copyright Infringement Litigation," 23 Colum.-VLA J.L. & Arts 1 (Wint. 1999): Daniel Gervais, "Transmissions of Music on the Internet: An Analysis of the Copyright Laws of Canada, France, Germany, Japan, the United Kingdom, and the United States," 34 Vand. J. Transnat' L. 1363 (Nov. 2001); and Howard Anawalt, "Internet Distribution of Intellectual Property Protected Works in the United States, in Japan and in the Future," 18 Santa Clara Comp. & High Tech. L. J. 207 (2002). Do all these international conventions and treaties work in the real world? Is it a losing battle?

2. Aldon Accessories v. Spiegel, Inc., 738 F.2d 548 (2d Cir. 1984), the question was whether the artist was plaintiff's employee for purposes of the work made for hire clause of the 1976 Copyright Act, 17 U.S.C. §101. The court held that the relationship between plaintiff and artist was an employee-employer relationship since the plaintiff controlled and supervised in the creation of figurines. These statuettes depicted mythological creatures, including a Unicorn and Pegasus. In September of 1977, plaintiff wrote a Japanese trading company concerning the design and production of the Unicorn and Pegasus, ultimately to be done in porcelain. In August 1979, plaintiff wrote to a company in Taiwan to initiate development of solid brass versions of the statuettes. Defendant Spiegel's catalog was selling identical unicorns! Spiegel argued that plaintiff's copyright was invalid since Spiegel had ordered its Unicorns from Taiwan before it had access to plaintiff's literature and statuettes. Confusing? Who should win and why? (Hint: It's not the Spiegel catalog.). This occurs rather frequently, as many of these entertainment-type merchandising objects (think Star Wars figurines and bobble-head dolls) are made overseas, not to mention knock-offs. Could this case apply to films and musical recordings?